Glencoe Literature

Internet resources are just a click away!

STEP 1 → Go to **glencoe.com**

STEP 2 → Connect to resources by entering  codes.

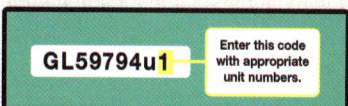 *Enter this code with appropriate unit numbers.*

STEP 3 → Access your **Online Student Edition**, handheld downloads, games, and more:

Literature and Reading Resources
- Author Search
- Literature Classics
- Big Idea Web Quests
- Literary Elements eFlashcards and Games
- Interactive Reading Practice

Selection Resources
- Audio Summaries
- Selection Quizzes
- Selection Vocabulary eFlashcards and Games
- Reading-Writing Connection Activities

Vocabulary Resources
- Academic and Selection eFlashcards and Games
- Multi-Language Glossaries

Writing, Grammar, and Research Resources
- Interactive Writing Models
- Writing and Research Handbook
- Graphic Organizers
- Sentence Combining Activities
- Publishing Options

Media Literacy, Speaking, Listening, and Viewing Resources
- Media Analysis Guides
- Project Ideas and Templates
- Presentation Tips and Strategies

Assessment Resources
- End of Unit Assessment
- ACT/SAT Vocabulary eFlashcards and games
- Test-Taking Tips and Strategies

On the Cover:

VanGogh, Vincent (1853-1890)
Mulberry Tree, 1889.
Oil on Canvas.

Program Consultants

Jeffrey D. Wilhelm, PhD

Douglas Fisher, PhD

Beverly Ann Chin, PhD

Jacqueline Jones Royster, DA

Acknowledgments

Grateful acknowledgment is given authors, publishers, photographers, museums, and agents for permission to reprint the following copyrighted material. Every effort has been made to determine copyright owners. In case of any omissions, the Publisher will be pleased to make suitable acknowledgements in future editions.

Acknowledgments continued on p. R98.

Copyright © 2009 by the McGraw-Hill Companies, Inc. All rights reserved. Except as permitted under the United States Copyright Act, no part of this publication may be reproduced or distributed in any form or by any means, or stored in a database or retrieval system, without prior permission of the publisher.

TIME © Time, Inc. TIME and the red border design are trademarks of Time, Inc. used under license.

Send all inquiries to:
Glencoe/McGraw-Hill
8787 Orion Place
Columbus, OH 43240-4027

ISBN: (student edition) 978-0-07-877979-4
MHID: (student edition) 0-07-877979-0
ISBN: (teacher edition) 978-0-07-877986-2
MHID: (teacher edition) 0-07-877986-3

Printed in the United States of America.

3 4 5 6 7 8 9 10 071/043 13 12 11 10 09

Consultants

Senior Program Consultants

Jeffrey D. Wilhelm, PhD, a former middle and secondary school English and reading teacher, is currently Professor of Education at Boise State University. He is the author or coauthor of numerous articles and several books on the teaching of reading and literacy, including award-winning titles such as *You Gotta BE the Book* and *Reading Don't Fix No Chevys*. He also works with local schools as part of the Adolescent Literacy Project and recently helped establish the National Writing Project site at Boise State University.

Douglas Fisher, PhD, is Professor of Language and Literacy Education and Director of Professional Development at San Diego State University, where he teaches English language development and literacy. He also serves as Director of City Heights Educational Pilot, which won the Christa McAuliffe Award from the American Association of State Colleges and Universities. He has published numerous articles on reading and literacy, differentiated instruction, and curriculum design. He is coauthor of the book *Improving Adolescent Literacies: Strategies That Work* and coeditor of the book *Inclusive Urban Schools*.

Program Consultants

Beverly Ann Chin, PhD, is Professor of English, Director of the English Teaching Program, former Director of the Montana Writing Project, and former Director of Composition at the University of Montana in Missoula. She currently serves as a Member at Large of the Conference of English Leadership. Dr. Chin is a nationally recognized leader in English language arts standards, curriculum, and assessment. Formerly a high school teacher and an adult education reading teacher, Dr. Chin has taught in English language arts education at several universities and has received awards for her teaching and service.

Jacqueline Jones Royster, DA, is Professor of English and Senior Vice Provost and Executive Dean of the Colleges of Arts and Sciences at The Ohio State University. She is currently on the Writing Advisory Committee of the National Commission on Writing and serves as chair for both the Columbus Literacy Council and the Ohioana Library Association. In addition to the teaching of writing, Dr. Royster's professional interests include the rhetorical history of African American women and the social and cultural implications of literate practices. She has contributed to and helped to edit numerous books, anthologies, and journals.

Advisory Board

Special Consultants

Donald R. Bear, PhD.
Professor, Department of Curriculum and Instruction Director, E. L. Cord Foundation Center for Learning and Literacy at the University of Nevada, Reno. Author of *Words Their Way* and *Words Their Way with English Learners*

Jana Echevarria, PhD.
Professor, Educational Psychology, California State University, Long Beach. Author of *Making Content Comprehensible for English Learners: the SIOP Model*

FOLDABLES Dinah Zike, MEd, was a classroom teacher and a consultant for many years before she began to develop Foldables™—a variety of easily created graphic organizers. Zike has written and developed more than 150 supplemental books and materials used in classrooms worldwide. Her *Big Book of Books and Activities* won the Teachers' Choice Award.

The Writers' Express
Immediate Impact. Lasting Transformation. wex.org

Glencoe National Reading and Language Arts Advisory Council

Mary A. Avalos, PhD
Assistant Department Chair, Department of Teaching and Learning
Research Assistant Professor, Department of Teaching and Learning
University of Miami
Coral Gables, Florida

Wanda J. Blanchett, PhD
Associate Dean for Academic Affairs and Associate Professor of Exceptional Education
School of Education
University of Wisconsin–Milwaukee
Milwaukee, Wisconsin

William G. Brozo, PhD
Professor of Literacy
Graduate School of Education
College of Education and Human Development
George Mason University
Fairfax, Virginia

Nancy Drew, EdD
LaPointe Educational Consultants
Corpus Christi, Texas

Susan Florio-Ruane, EdD
Professor
College of Education
Michigan State University
East Lansing, Michigan

Sharon Fontenot O'Neal, PhD
Associate Professor
Texas State University
San Marcos, Texas

Nancy Frey, PhD
Associate Professor of Literacy in Teacher Education
School of Teacher Education
San Diego State University
San Diego, California

Victoria Ridgeway Gillis, PhD
Associate Professor
Reading Education
Clemson University
Clemson, South Carolina

Kimberly Lawless, PhD
Associate Professor
Curriculum, Instruction and Evaluation
College of Education
University of Illinois at Chicago
Chicago, Illinois

William Ray, MA
Lincoln-Sudbury Regional High School
Sudbury, Massachusetts

Janet Saito-Furukawa, MEd
Literacy Coach
Washington Irving Middle School
Los Angeles, California

Bonnie Valdes, MEd
Independent Reading Consultant
CRISS Master Trainer
Largo, Florida

Teacher Reviewers

The following teachers contributed to the review of *Glencoe Literature*.

Bridget M. Agnew
St. Michael School
Chicago, Illinois

Monica Anzaldua Araiza
Dr. Juliet V. Garcia Middle School
Brownsville, Texas

Katherine R. Baer
Howard County Public Schools
Ellicott City, Maryland

Tanya Baxter
Roald Amundsen High School
Chicago, Illinois

Danielle R. Brain
Thomas R. Proctor Senior
 High School
Utica, New York

Yolanda Conder
Owasso Mid-High School
Owasso, Oklahoma

Gwenn de Mauriac
The Wiscasset Schools
Wiscasset, Maine

Courtney Doan
Bloomington High School
Bloomingon, Illinois

Susan M. Griffin
Edison Preparatory School
Tulsa, Oklahoma

Cindi Davis Harris
Helix Charter High School
La Mesa, California

Joseph F. Hutchinson
Toledo Public Schools
Toledo, Ohio

Ginger Jordan
Florien High School
Florien, Louisiana

Dianne Konkel
Cypress Lake Middle School
Fort Myers, Florida

Melanie A. LaFleur
Many High School
Many, Louisiana

Patricia Lee
Radnor Middle School
Wayne, Pennsylvania

Linda Copley Lemons
Cleveland High School
Cleveland, Tennessee

Heather S. Lewis
Waverly Middle School
Lansing, Michigan

Sandra C. Lott
Aiken Optional School
Alexandria, Louisiana

Connie M. Malacarne
O'Fallon Township High School
O'Fallon, Illinois

Lori Howton Means
Edward A. Fulton Junior
 High School
O'Fallon, Illinois

Claire C. Meitl
Howard County Public Schools
Ellicott City, Maryland

Patricia P. Mitcham
Mohawk High School
 (Retired)
New Castle, Pennsylvania

Lisa Morefield
South-Western Career Academy
Grove City, Ohio

Kevin M. Morrison
Hazelwood East High School
St. Louis, Missouri

Jenine M. Pokorak
School Without Walls Senior
 High School
Washington, DC

Susan Winslow Putnam
Butler High School
Matthews, North Carolina

Paul C. Putnoki
Torrington Middle School
Torrington, Connecticut

Jane Thompson Rae
Cab Calloway High School of
 the Arts
Wilmington, Delaware

Stephanie L. Robin
N. P. Moss Middle School
Lafayette, Louisiana

Ann C. Ryan
Lindenwold High School
Lindenwold, New Jersey

Pamela Schoen
Hopkins High School
Minnetonka, Minnesota

Megan Schumacher
Friends' Central School
Wynnewood, Pennsylvania

Fareeda J. Shabazz
Paul Revere Elementary School
Chicago, Illinois

Molly Steinlage
Brookpark Middle School
Grove City, Ohio

Barry Stevenson
Garnet Valley Middle School
Glen Mills, Pennsylvania

Paul Stevenson
Edison Preparatory School
Tulsa, Oklahoma

Kathy Thompson
Owasso Mid-High School
Owasso, Oklahoma

Book Overview

How to Use *Glencoe Literature* T35
Cyber Safety T39

UNIT ONE
The Short Story 1
Part 1: Encountering the Unexpected 7
Part 2: Making Choices 85
Part 3: Life Transitions 183

UNIT TWO
Nonfiction 277
Part 1: The Power of Memory 283
Part 2: Quests and Encounters 365
Part 3: Keeping Freedom Alive 391

UNIT THREE
Poetry 467
Part 1: The Energy of the Everyday 473
Part 2: Loves and Losses 531
Part 3: Issues of Identity 591

UNIT FOUR
Drama 651
Part 1: Loyalty and Betrayal 657
Part 2: Portraits of Real Life 817

Coming to America, 1985.
Malcah Zeldis.

Book Overview

Triumph of the Revolution, Distribution of Food (Trionfo de la revolucion, reparto de los alimentos), 1926–1927. Diego Rivera. Banco de Mexico Trust. Fresco, 3.54 x 3.67 m. Chapel. Universidad Autonoma, Chapingo, Mexico.

UNIT FIVE

Legends and Myths 893
Part 1: Acts of Courage 899
Part 2: Rescuing and Conquering 955

UNIT SIX

Genre Fiction 1015
The Extraordinary and Fantastic 1021

UNIT SEVEN

Consumer and Workplace Documents 1137

Reference Section
Literary Terms Handbook R1
Foldables® R20
Functional Documents R22
Writing Handbook R28
Reading Handbook R38
Language Handbook R40
Logic and Persuasion Handbook R60
Glossary/Glosario R64
Academic Word List R80
Index of Skills R83
Index of Authors and Titles R95
Acknowledgments R98

vii

Contents

Skills and Standards

UNIT ONE

The Short Story

Genre Focus: Short Story 2

Literary Analysis Model
ERNEST HEMINGWAY
Old Man at the Bridge .... Short Story 4

Wrap-Up 6

Part One — *Encountering the Unexpected* 7

Literary Focus Plot and Setting 8

*Flashback,
Identify Sequence*
SAKI **The Open Window** .... Short Story 10

*Foreshadowing, Analyze
Cause-and-Effect
Relationships*
MARK TWAIN **The Californian's Tale** ... Short Story 17

Literary Perspective
JOYCE CAROL OATES
Storytelling Is As Old As Mankind .... Essay 28

Vocabulary Workshop Denotation and Connotation 32

*Conflict,
Respond to Characters*
JACK FINNEY
Contents of the Dead Man's Pocket ... Short Story 33

Vocabulary Workshop Academic Vocabulary 52

*Mood,
Analyze Cultural Context*
R. K. NARAYAN **An Astrologer's Day** ... Short Story 54

Grammar Workshop Apostrophes in Possessives 63

*Dialect,
Analyze Historical Context*
CHINUA ACHEBE **Civil Peace** .... Short Story 64

Vocabulary Workshop Dictionary Use 72

*Allegory,
Interpret Imagery*
EDGAR ALLAN POE
The Masque of the Red Death .... Short Story 73

Contents

"Seize him and unmask him—that we may know whom we have to hang, at sunrise..."
—Edgar Allan Poe

Part Two

Making Choices 85

Literary Focus Theme and Character 86

Motivation, Connect to Personal Experience
AMY TAN **Two Kinds** .... Short Story 88

Dialogue, Make Generalizations About Characters
JAMES THURBER
The Car We Had to Push .... Short Story 103

Implied Theme, Make Inferences About Theme
GABRIEL GARCÍA MÁRQUEZ
Tuesday Siesta .... Short Story 112

Vocabulary Workshop Multiple-Meaning Words 122

Theme, Compare and Contrast Characters
JHUMPA LAHIRI
When Mr. Pirzada Came to Dine .... Short Story 123

Grammar Workshop Sentence Combining 142

Characterization, Make Inferences About Characters
PAULE MARSHALL
To Da-duh, in Memoriam .... Short Story 144

Irony, Analyze Plot
EDWIDGE DANTICAT
The Book of the Dead .... Short Story 157

LUISA VALENZUELA **The Censors** .... Short Story 172

Satire, Analyze Cause-and-Effect Relationships
CARL SAFINA
TIME Cry of the Ancient Mariner 178

Skills and Standards

Part Three

Life Transitions 183

Literary Focus Narrator and Voice 184

Reliable/Unreliable Narrator, Question

ALICE WALKER **Everyday Use** .... Short Story 186

Comparing Literature Across Genres

Point of View, Visualize

DORIS LESSING **Through the Tunnel** .. Short Story 199

LAME DEER **The Vision Quest** .... Legend 212

F. SCOTT FITZGERALD **Dear Pie** .... Letter 215

Point of View, Interpret Imagery

JUDITH ORTIZ COFER
Catch the Moon .... Short Story 218

Grammar Workshop Sentence Fragments 229

Persona, Analyze Sensory Details

ISABEL ALLENDE **And of Clay Are We Created** .... Short Story 230

Style, Evaluate Characters

LESLIE MARMON SILKO **Lullaby** .... Short Story 245

Writing Workshop Literary Criticism 258

Professional Model

PAULE MARSHALL
Real-Life Story Behind "To Da-Duh, In Memoriam" .... Essay 259

Speaking, Listening, and Viewing Workshop Literary Criticism 266

Independent Reading 268

Assessment 270

MARK TWAIN *from* **When the Buffalo Climbed a Tree** .... Short Story 270

JAMES THURBER
The Unicorn in the Garden .... Short Story 271

Skills and Standards

Contents

UNIT TWO

NONFICTION

Genre Focus: Nonfiction	278

Literary Analysis Model
ROBERT E. HEMENWAY
from **Zora Neale Hurston** .... Biography 280

Wrap-Up 282

PART ONE

THE POWER OF MEMORY 283

Literary Focus Narrative Nonfiction:
Autobiography and Biography 284

Historical Narrative, Summarize

JEANNE WAKATSUKI HOUSTON
AND JAMES D. HOUSTON
from **Farewell to Manzanar** .... Memoir 288

Grammar Workshop Subject-Verb Agreement 303

Theme, Analyze Cause-and-Effect Relationships

MARK MATHABANE *from* **Kaffir Boy** .... Memoir 304

Memoir, Draw Conclusions About Author's Beliefs

MAYA ANGELOU
Living Well. Living Good. .... Essay 321

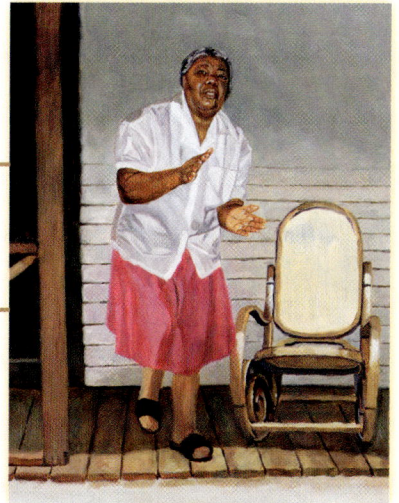

"Living life as art requires a readiness to forgive."
—Maya Angelou

When I Get that Feeling, 2000. Colin Bootman.
Oil on board. Private collection.

CONTENTS **xi**

Skills and Standards

Author's Purpose,
Make Generalizations About
Events

MARK STEVENS AND ANNALYN SWAN
First Impressions *from* **DeKooning:**
An American Master .... Biography 328

Vocabulary Workshop Jargon 340

Voice,
Analyze Style

FRANK McCOURT **Typhoid Fever**
from **Angela's Ashes** .... Memoir 341

Historical Perspective
CAROLYN T. HUGHES
from **Looking Forward to the Past** .... Profile 352

Anecdote,
Connect to Personal
Experience

ANNIE DILLARD **Terwilliger Bunts One**
from **An American Childhood** .... Memoir 356

PART TWO — QUESTS AND ENCOUNTERS ... 365

Literary Focus Expository and Personal Essays 366

Narrative Essay,
Connect to Personal
Experience

JEWELLE L. GOMEZ
A Swimming Lesson .... Narrative Essay 368

Structure,
Draw Conclusions About
Meaning

LEWIS THOMAS
The Tucson Zoo .... Expository Essay 375

Thesis,
Analyze Text Structure

SANDRA CISNEROS **Straw into Gold: The**
Metamorphosis of the Everyday .... Personal Essay 382

PART THREE — KEEPING FREEDOM ALIVE 391

Literary Focus Persuasive Essay and Speech 392

Rhetorical Devices,
Recognize Bias

SUSAN B. ANTHONY **On Women's Right**
to Vote .... Speech 394

Contents

Skills and Standards

Allusion, Identify Problem and Solution

MARTIN LUTHER KING JR. I've Been to the Mountaintop .... Speech 401

Comparing Literature Different Viewpoints

Rhetorical Devices, Identify Assumptions and Ambiguities

CHESTER BROWN
Not Just Comics .... Graphic Novel 419

TERESA MÉNDEZ "Hamlet" Too Hard?
Try a Comic Book .... Newspaper Article 422

ANDREW ARNOLD
The Graphic Novel
Silver Anniversary .... Web site Article 426

Quotation, Distinguish Fact and Opinion

CARL SANDBURG Address on the Anniversary of Lincoln's Birth .... Speech 431

BARACK OBAMA
TIME What I See in Lincoln's Eyes .... Personal Essay 439

Author's Purpose, Identify Problem and Solution

TONI MORRISON
Cinderella's Stepsisters .... Speech 442

Writing Workshop Biographical Narrative 448

Professional Model

ALICE JACKSON BAUGHN
from **Eudora Welty: 1909–2001** .... Biography 449

Speaking, Listening, and Viewing Workshop
Photo Essay 456

Independent Reading 458

Assessment 460

MAYA ANGELOU *from* **Wouldn't Take Nothing for My Journey Now** .... Personal Essay 460

CONTENTS **xiii**

Skills and Standards

UNIT THREE

Poetry

Genre Focus: Poetry 468

Literary Analysis Model
WALT WHITMAN
O Captain! My Captain! .... Poem 470
Wrap-Up 472

Part One — The Energy of the Everyday 473

Literary Focus Form and Structure 474

Line and Stanza, Analyze Tone

ROBERT HAYDEN **Those Winter Sundays** ..... Poem 476

Vocabulary Workshop Homonyms and Homophones 480

Enjambment, Analyze Poetic Structure

BILLY COLLINS **Creatures** .... Poem 481

Meter and Rhythm, Analyze Form

WILLIAM SHAKESPEARE **Shall I Compare Thee to a Summer's Day?** .... Sonnet 486

Rhyme and Rhyme Scheme, Analyze Meter and Rhythm

JEAN TOOMER **Reapers** .... Poem 492

Free Verse, Monitor Comprehension

PABLO NERUDA **Ode to My Socks** .... Ode 496

> "Violent socks, my feet were two fish made of wool"
>
> —Pablo Neruda

Personage Lancant Une Pierre a un Oiseau, 1926. Joan Miro.

Contents

Skills and Standards

*Prose Poetry,
Visualize*

ALEKSANDR SOLZHENITSYN
A Storm in the Mountains .... Prose Poem 504

Grammar Workshop:
Pronoun-Antecedent Agreement 509

*Speaker,
Apply Background Knowledge*

N. SCOTT MOMADAY
The Print of the Paw .... Prose Poem 510
To An Aged Bear .... Poem 513

*Haiku,
Interpret Imagery*

MATSUO BASHO Three Haiku .... Haiku 516

*Tanka,
Compare and Contrast
Imagery*

LADY ISE Two Tanka .... Tanka 521

*Verse Paragraph,
Make Inferences About the
Speaker*

CHITRA BANERJEE DIVAKARUNI
Woman with Kite .... Poem 525

Part Two

Loves and Losses 531

Literary Focus The Language of Poetry 532

*Personification,
Compare and Contrast Tone*

EMILY DICKINSON After Great Pain,
A Formal Feeling Comes .... Poem 534
Heart! We Will Forget Him! .... Poem 537

*Mood,
Analyze Diction*

THEODORE ROETHKE
The Meadow Mouse .... Poem 541

*Lyric Poetry,
Analyze Repetition and Rhyme*

WILLIAM BUTLER YEATS
Down by the Salley Gardens .... Poem 547
He Wishes for the Cloths of Heaven .... Poem 550

*Metaphor and Simile,
Preview and Review*

JIMMY SANTIAGO BACA
I Am Offering This Poem .... Poem 554

*Juxtaposition,
Paraphrase*

E.E. CUMMINGS since feeling is first .... Poem 559

*Repetition, Draw Conclusions
About Meaning*

GWENDOLYN BROOKS Horses Graze .... Poem 563

*Imagery,
Interpret Imagery*

RITA DOVE Parlor .... Poem 568

*Diction,
Visualize*

SHERMAN ALEXIE Secondhand Grief .... Poem 572

*Narrative Poetry,
Apply Background Knowledge*

DUDLEY RANDALL Ballad of Birmingham .. Ballad 576

CONTENTS **xv**

Skills and Standards

Media Workshop Compare Media Genres 582

Historical Perspective
ROGER EBERT
4 Little Girls .... Film Review 588

Part Three

Issues of Identity 591

Literary Focus Sound Devices 592

Alliteration,
Analyze Sensory Details
Assonance and Consonance,
Clarify Meaning

LUCILLE CLIFTON **miss rosie** .... Poem 594

ROBERT FROST **After Apple-Picking** .... Poem 599
Fire and Ice .... Poem 603

Symbol,
Analyze Rhythm

NAOMI SHIHAB NYE **Arabic Coffee** .... Poem 607

CHANG-RAE LEE
TIME We Are Family 612

Comparing Literature Across Genres

Rhyme and Rhyme Scheme,
Make Inferences About Theme

LANGSTON HUGHES **Dream Boogie** .... Poem 620
Motto .... Poem 621

STUDS TERKEL *from* **Giants of Jazz** .... Biography 623

WYNTON MARSALIS **Playing Jazz** .... Letter 627

Writing Workshop Reflective Essay 632

Professional Model

JOY HARJO
Suspended .... Essay 633

Speaking, Listening, and Viewing Workshop
Reflective Presentation 640

Skills and Standards

Contents

Independent Reading... 642

Assessment 644

LANGSTON HUGHES
Daybreak in Alabama .... Poem 644

NAOMI SHIHAB NYE
from **Red Velvet Dress** .... Short Story 644

UNIT FOUR

DRAMA

Genre Focus: Drama 652

Literary Analysis Model
AUGUST WILSON
The Janitor .... Modern Drama 654

Wrap-Up 656

Part One

LOYALTY AND BETRAYAL .. 657

Protagonist and Antagonist, Interpret Imagery

Literary Focus Tragedy 658

Literary History Classical Greek Drama 660

SOPHOCLES **Antigone** .... Tragedy 662

MARYANN BIRD
TIME Ever Alluring 709

Vocabulary Workshop Denotation and Connotation 713

Literary History Shakespearean Drama 714

CONTENTS **xvii**

Skills and Standards

*Blank Verse,
Make Inferences About
Characters*

WILLIAM SHAKESPEARE
The Tragedy of Julius Caesar .... Tragedy 716
Act I 720
Act II 739
Act III 760
Act IV 783
Act V 800

"We all stand up against the spirit of Caesar, and in the spirit of men there is no blood."

—William Shakespeare

Part Two

PORTRAITS OF REAL LIFE 817

Literary Focus Comedy and Modern Drama 818

*Farce,
Recognize Author's Purpose*

ANTON CHEKHOV
A Marriage Proposal .... Comedy 820

Grammar Workshop Commas with Interjections and
Parenthetical Expressions 836

*Conflict,
Analyze Mood*

HAROLD PINTER
That's Your Trouble .... Modern Drama 837

Literary Perspective
HAROLD PINTER
Writing for the Theater .... Speech 842

xviii

Skills and Standards   **Contents**

Comparing Literature Across Genres

Characterization, Analyze Plot and Setting

JOSEPHINA NIGGLI **The Ring of General Macías** .... Modern Drama 846

CARMEN TAFOLLA **Marked** .... Poem 866

ISAK DINESEN **The Ring** .... Short Story 867

Writing Workshop Persuasive Speech 874

Professional Model

EVERETT DIRKSEN **Why Marigolds Should Be the National Flower** .... Speech 875

Speaking, Listening, and Viewing Workshop
Persuasive Speech 882

Independent Reading 884

Assessment 886

SOPHOCLES *from* **Oedipus the King** .... Tragedy 886

UNIT FIVE

Legends and Myths

Genre Focus: Legends and Myths 894

Literary Analysis Model
JOAN C. VERNIERO AND ROBIN FITZSIMMONS
from **The Journey of Gilgamesh** .... Epic 896

Wrap-Up 898

Skills and Standards

Part One

Acts of Courage 899

Literary Focus The Legendary Hero 900

Dialogue,
Analyze Plot

SIR THOMAS MALORY
from **Le Morte d'Arthur** .... Legend 902

"Sir Launcelot, I know that Queen Gwynevere loves you, and you her."
—Sir Thomas Malory

Grammar Workshop Main and Subordinate Clauses 924

Parody,
Evaluate Characters

MIGUEL DE CERVANTES
from **Don Quixote** .... Novel 925

AMANDA RIPLEY
TIME What Makes a Hero? 937

Dialogue,
Identify Genre

D. T. NIANE *from* **Sundiata** .... Epic 942

Visual Perspective
WILL EISNER
The Lion of Mali, From **Sundiata:
A Legend of Africa** .... Graphic Novel 951

xx

Skills and Standards

Part Two

Rescuing and Conquering

Plot Pattern Archetypes, Make Inferences About Characters

Literary Focus Myth and the Oral Tradition 956

BRIAN BRANSTON **The Stealing of Thor's Hammer** .... Norse Myth 958

Vocabulary Workshop Word Origins 967

Image Archetype, Identify Sequence

EDITH HAMILTON *from* **Theseus** .... Greek Myth 968

Vocabulary Workshop Word Origins 979

Comparing Literature Across Time and Place

Suspense, Synthesize

JOSEPH BRUCHAC AND GAYLE ROSS **Where the Girl Rescued Her Brother** .... Native American Legend 981

ZORA NEALE HURSTON **John Henry** .... Tall Tale 988

ANONYMOUS **A Song of Greatness** .... Chippewa Song 990

Writing Workshop Research Report 992

Speaking, Listening, and Viewing Workshop
Multimedia Presentation 1002

Independent Reading 1006

Assessment 1008

DONNA ROSENBERG *from* **King Arthur** ...... Legend .. 1008

Skills and Standards

UNIT SIX

Genre Fiction

Genre Focus: Science Fiction, Modern Fables, and Mystery 1016

Literary Analysis Model
ITALO CALVINO
The Happy Man's Shirt .... Fable .. 1018

Wrap-Up 1020

The Extraordinary and Fantastic

Literary Focus Description and Style 1022

Foreshadowing, Identify Genre

RAY BRADBURY
A Sound of Thunder .... Science Fiction .. 1024

"Destroy this one man, and you destroy a race, a people, an entire history of life."
—Ray Bradbury

Moral, Visualize

STEPHEN VINCENT BENÉT
By the Waters of Babylon .... Science Fiction .. 1040

Grammar Workshop Dangling Participles 1057

xxii

Contents

Skills and Standards

Stream of Consciousness, Interpret Imagery

Comparing Literature Across Genres

JAMAICA KINCAID **What I Have Been Doing Lately** .... Short Story .. 1059

DENISE LEVERTOV **People at Night** .... Poem .. 1065

ANNA AKHMATOVA **A Dream** .... Poem .. 1068

Scientific Perspective

WILLIAM J. BROAD
One Legend Found, Many Still to Go .... Article .. 1070

Analogy, Activate Prior Knowledge

ISAAC ASIMOV **Robot Dreams** .... Science Fiction .. 1074

ADAM COHEN
TIME The Machine Nurturer 1083

Point of View, Recognize Author's Purpose

MARGARET ATWOOD **Bread** .... Fantasy .. 1088

Motivation, Make Inferences About Characters

AGATHA CHRISTIE **The Witness for the Prosecution** .... Mystery .. 1093

Grammar Workshop Semicolons as Connectors 1116

Vocabulary Workshop Thesaurus Use 1117

Writing Workshop Short Story 1118

Professional Model
ISAAC ASIMOV
from **Frustration** .... Short Story ... 1119

Speaking, Listening, and Viewing Workshop
Oral Interpretation of a Story 1126

Independent Reading 1128

Assessment 1130

FRANZ KAFKA
from **The Metamorphosis** .... Short Story .. 1130

UNIT SEVEN

CONSUMER AND WORKPLACE DOCUMENTS

Focus on Functional Documents 1138
E-mail 1141
Application 1142
Cover Letter 1143
Professional Article 1146
Warranty 1147
Software Product Information 1148
Installation Guide 1149
Announcement Memo 1152
Train Schedule and Itinerary 1153
Meeting Itinerary 1154
Written Directions 1155
Meeting Agenda 1156
Pamphlet 1159
Contract 1160
Web Site 1162

Contents

REFERENCE SECTION

Literary Terms Handbook	R1
Foldables®	R20
Functional Documents	R22
Writing Handbook	R28
Using the Traits of Strong Writing	R28
Research Paper Writing	R31
Reading Handbook	R38
Language Handbook	R40
Grammar Glossary	R40
Troubleshooter	R47
Mechanics	R53
Spelling	R57
Logic and Persuasion Handbook	R60
Glossary/Glosario	R64
Academic Word List	R80
Index of Skills	R83
Index of Authors and Titles	R95
Acknowledgments	R98

Selections by Genre

Fiction

Short Story

Old Man at the Bridge 4
   Ernest Hemingway

The Open Window 12
   Saki

The Californian's Tale 19
   Mark Twain

Contents of the Dead Man's Pocket 35
   Jack Finney

An Astrologer's Day 56
   R. K. Narayan

Civil Peace 66
   Chinua Achebe

The Masque of the Red Death 75
   Edgar Allan Poe

Two Kinds 90
   Amy Tan

The Car We Had to Push 105
   James Thurber

Tuesday Siesta 114
   Gabriel García Márquez

When Mr. Pirzada Came to Dine 125
   Jhumpa Lahiri

To Da-duh, in Memoriam 146
   Paule Marshall

The Book of the Dead 159
   Edwidge Danticat

The Censors 174
   Luisa Valenzuela

Everyday Use 188
   Alice Walker

Through the Tunnel 201
   Doris Lessing

Catch the Moon 220
   Judith Ortiz Cofer

And of Clay Are We Created 232
   Isabel Allende

Lullaby 247
   Leslie Marmon Silko

from **When the Buffalo Climbed a Tree** 270
   Mark Twain

The Unicorn in the Garden 271
   James Thurber

from **Red Velvet Dress** 644
   Naomi Shihab Nye

The Ring 867
   Isak Dinesen

A Sound of Thunder 1026
   Ray Bradbury

By the Waters of Babylon 1042
   Stephen Vincent Benét

What I Have Been Doing Lately 1061
   Jamaica Kincaid

Robot Dreams 1076
   Isaac Asimov

Bread 1090
   Margaret Atwood

The Witness for the Prosecution 1095
   Agatha Christie

from **Frustration** 1119
   Isaac Asimov

from **The Metamorphosis** 1130
   Franz Kafka

Myth, Folktale, and Fable

The Stealing of Thor's Hammer 960
   Brian Branston

from **Theseus** 970
   Edith Hamilton

John Henry 988
   Zora Neale Hurston

The Happy Man's Shirt 1018
   Italo Calvino

Selections by Genre

Epic

from **The Journey of Gilgamesh** 896
Joan C. Verniero and Robin Fitzsimmons

from **Sundiata** 944
D. T. Niane

Legend

The Vision Quest 212
Lame Deer

from **Le Morte d'Arthur** 904
Sir Thomas Malory

Where the Girl Rescued Her Brother 983
Joseph Bruchac and Gayle Ross

from **King Arthur** 1008
Donna Rosenberg

Novel

from **Don Quixote** 927
Miguel de Cervantes

Poetry

O Captain! My Captain! 470
Walt Whitman

Those Winter Sundays 478
Robert Hayden

Creatures 483
Billy Collins

Shall I Compare Thee to a Summer's Day? 488
William Shakespeare

Reapers 494
Jean Toomer

Ode to My Socks 498
Pablo Neruda

A Storm in the Mountains 506
Aleksandr Solzhenitsyn

The Print of the Paw 512
To An Aged Bear 513
N. Scott Momaday

Three Haiku 518
Matsuo Bashō

Two Tanka 523
Lady Ise

Woman with Kite 527
Chitra Banerjee Divakaruni

After Great Pain, A Formal Feeling Comes 536
Heart! We Will Forget Him! 537
Emily Dickinson

The Meadow Mouse 543
Theodore Roethke

Down by the Salley Gardens 549
He Wishes for the Cloths of Heaven 550
William Butler Yeats

I Am Offering This Poem 556
Jimmy Santiago Baca

since feeling is first 561
E. E. Cummings

Horses Graze 565
Gwendolyn Brooks

Parlor 570
Rita Dove

Secondhand Grief 574
Sherman Alexie

Ballad of Birmingham 578
Dudley Randall

miss rosie 596
Lucille Clifton

After Apple-Picking 601
Fire and Ice 603
Robert Frost

Woman Flying a Kite, 1750. Indian. Book illumination painting, miniature painting. Sangaram Singh.

Arabic Coffee 609
    Naomi Shihab Nye
Dream Boogie 620
Motto 621
    Langston Hughes
Daybreak in Alabama 644
    Langston Hughes
Marked 866
    Carmen Tafolla
People at Night 1065
    Denise Levertov
A Dream 1068
    Anna Akhmatova

Song

A Song of Greatness 990
    Chippewa

Drama

Tragedy

Antigone 664
    Sophocles
The Tragedy of Julius Caesar 718
    William Shakespeare
from **Oedipus the King** 886
    Sophocles

Comedy

A Marriage Proposal 822
    Anton Chekhov

Modern Drama

The Janitor 654
    August Wilson
That's Your Trouble 839
    Harold Pinter
The Ring of General Macías 848
    Josephina Niggli

Graphic Novel

Not Just Comics 419
    Chester Brown
The Lion of Mali, *from* **Sundiata: A Legend
    of Africa** 951
    Will Eisner

Nonfiction and Informational Text

Biography, Autobiography, or Memoir

from **Zora Neale Hurston** 280
    Robert E. Hemenway
from **Farewell to Manzanar** 288
    Jeanne Wakatsuki Houston and
    James D. Houston
from **Kaffir Boy** 306
    Mark Mathabane
Living Well. Living Good. 323
    Maya Angelou
First Impressions *from* **DeKooning:
    An American Master** 330
    Mark Stevens and Annalyn Swan
Typhoid Fever *from* **Angela's Ashes** 343
    Frank McCourt
Terwilliger Bunts One *from* **An American
    Childhood** 358
    Annie Dillard
from **Eudora Welty: 1909–2001** 449
    Alice Jackson Baughn
from **Giants of Jazz** 623
    Studs Terkel

Selections by Genre

Essay

Storytelling Is As Old As Mankind 28
Joyce Carol Oates

**Real-Life Story Behind "To Da-Duh,
In Memoriam"** 259
Paule Marshall

A Swimming Lesson 370
Jewelle L. Gomez

The Tucson Zoo 377
Lewis Thomas

**Straw into Gold: The Metamorphosis of
the Everyday** 384
Sandra Cisneros

What I See in Lincoln's Eyes 439
Barack Obama

from **Wouldn't Take Nothing for My
Journey Now** 460
Maya Angelou

We Are Family 612
Chang-rae Lee

Suspended 633
Joy Harjo

Profile

from **Looking Forward to the Past** 352
Carolyn T. Hughes

The Machine Nurturer 1083
Adam Cohen

Letter

Dear Pie 215
F. Scott Fitzgerald

Playing Jazz 627
Wynton Marsalis

Movie Review

4 Little Girls 588
Roger Ebert

Newspaper Article

"Hamlet" Too Hard? Try a Comic Book 422
Teresa Méndez

One Legend Found, Many Still to Go 1070
William J. Broad

Speech

On Women's Right to Vote 396
Susan B. Anthony

I've Been to the Mountaintop 403
Martin Luther King Jr.

**Address on the Anniversary of
Lincoln's Birth** 433
Carl Sandburg

Cinderella's Stepsisters 444
Toni Morrison

Writing for the Theater 842
Harold Pinter

**Why Marigolds Should Be the National
Flower** 875
Everett Dirksen

Web Site Article

The Graphic Novel Silver Anniversary 426
Andrew Arnold

Features

Perspectives

Award-winning nonfiction book excerpts and primary source documents

Literary Perspective Storytelling Is As Old As Mankind 28
  Joyce Carol Oates

Historical Perspective *from* Looking Forward to the Past 352
  Carolyn T. Hughes

Historical Perspective
4 Little Girls 588
  Roger Ebert

Literary Perspective
Writing for the Theater 842
  Harold Pinter

Visual Perspective
The Lion of Mali, from Sundiata: A Legend of Africa 951
  Will Eisner

Scientific Perspective One Legend Found, Many Still to Go 1070
  William J. Broad

TIME

High-interest, informative magazine articles

Cry of the Ancient Mariner 178
  Carl Safina
What I See in Lincoln's Eyes 439
  Barack Obama
We Are Family 612
  Chang-rae Lee
Ever Alluring 709
  Maryann Bird
What Makes a Hero? 937
  Amanda Ripley
The Machine Nurturer 1083
  Adam Cohen

Comparing Literature
Across Genres

UNIT ONE

Through the Tunnel
  Doris Lessing 201
The Vision Quest
  Lame Deer 212
Dear Pie
  F. Scott Fitzgerald 215

Comparing Literature
Different Viewpoints

UNIT TWO

Not Just Comics
  Chester Brown 419
"Hamlet" Too Hard? Try a Comic Book
  Teresa Méndez 422
The Graphic Novel Silver Anniversary
  Andrew Arnold 426

Comparing Literature
Across Genres

UNIT THREE

Dream Boogie 620
Motto
  Langston Hughes 620
from **Giants of Jazz**
  Studs Terkel 623

Playing Jazz
Wynton Marsalis 627

Comparing Literature
Themes Across Genres

UNIT FOUR

The Ring of General Macías
Josephina Niggli.................................848
Marked
Carmen Tafolla..................................866
The Ring
Isak Dinesen 867

Comparing Literature
Themes Across Genres

UNIT FIVE

Where the Girl Rescued Her Brother
Joseph Bruchac and Gayle Ross................983
John Henry
Zora Neale Hurston...............................988
A Song of Greatness
Chippewa 990

Comparing Literature
Themes Across Genres

UNIT SIX

What I Have Been Doing Lately
Jamaica Kincaid................................1061
People at Night
Denise Levertov 1065
A Dream
Anna Akhmatova 1068

Features

Independent Reading
Unit 1.................................268
Unit 2.................................458
Unit 3.................................642
Unit 4.................................884
Unit 5................................1006
Unit 6................................1128

Assessment
Unit 1.................................270
Unit 2.................................460
Unit 3.................................644
Unit 4.................................886
Unit 5................................1008
Unit 6................................1130

LITERARY FOCUS
Plot and Setting 8
Theme and Character 86
Narrator and Voice 184
Narrative Nonfiction: Autobiography
   and Biography................................284
Expository and Personal Essays 366
Persuasive Essay and Speech.................392
Form and Structure 474
The Language of Poetry........................532
Sound Devices 592
Tragedy..658
Comedy and Modern Drama 818
The Legendary Hero............................900
Myth and the Oral Tradition..................956
Description and Style.........................1022

Literary History
Classical Greek Drama..........................660
Shakespearean Drama..........................714

Skills Workshops

Writing Workshops

Literary Criticism 258
   PROFESSIONAL MODEL: **Real-Life Story Behind "To Da-Duh, In Memoriam"** by Paule Marshall

Biographical Narrative 448
   PROFESSIONAL MODEL: *from* **Eudora Welty: 1909–2001** by Alice Jackson Baughn

Reflective Essay 632
   PROFESSIONAL MODEL: **Suspended** by Joy Harjo

Persuasive Speech 874
   PROFESSIONAL MODEL: **Why Marigolds Should Be the National Flower** by Everett Dirksen

Research Report 992

Short Story 1118
   PROFESSIONAL MODEL: *from* **Frustration** by Isaac Asimov

Speaking, Listening, and Viewing Workshops

Literary Criticism 266
Photo Essay 456
Reflective Presentation 640
Persuasive Speech 882
Multimedia Presentation 1002
Oral Interpretation of a Story 1126

Media Workshops

Compare Media Genres 582

Grammar Workshops

Apostrophes in Possessives 63
Sentence Combining 142
Sentence Fragments 229
Subject-Verb Agreement 303
Pronoun-Antecedent Agreement 509
Commas with Interjections and Parenthetical Expressions 836
Main and Subordinate Clauses 924
Dangling Participles 1057
Semicolons as Connectors 1116

Vocabulary Workshops

Denotation and Connotation 32
Dictionary Use 72
Multiple-Meaning Words 122
Jargon 340
Homonyms and Homophones 480
Denotation and Connotation 713
Word Origins 967
Word Origins 979
Thesaurus Use 1117

How to Use *Glencoe Literature*

Organization

The literature you will read is organized by literary element and genre into six units: The Short Story, Nonfiction, Poetry, Drama, Legends and Myths, and Genre Fiction.

Each unit contains the following:

A **UNIT INTRODUCTION** provides you with the background information to help make your reading experience more meaningful.

- **GENRE FOCUS** defines the literary elements that make up a unit.

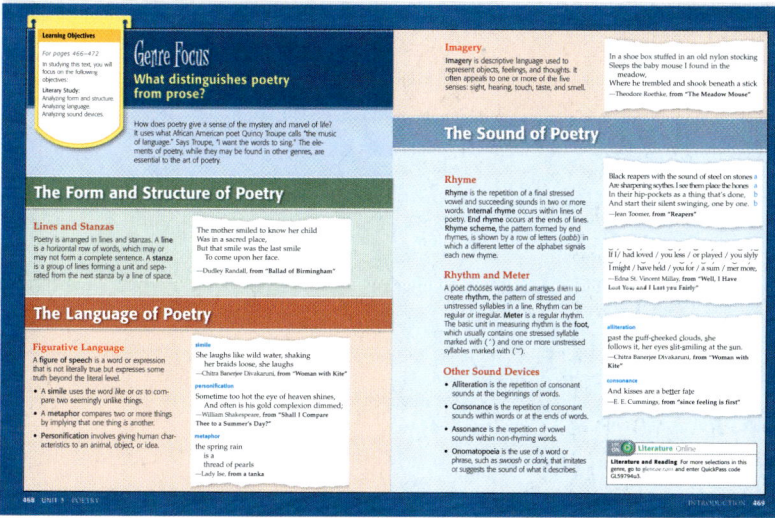

- The **LITERARY ANALYSIS MODEL** uses an example to help you identify different literary elements and analyze their use within the text.
- **BIG IDEAS** target three concepts that you can trace as you read the literature.

LITERARY SELECTIONS follow each Part Introduction. The selections are organized as follows.

Why do I need this book?

Glencoe Literature is more than just a collection of stories, poems, nonfiction articles, and other literary works. Every part is built around **Big Ideas,** concepts that you will want to think about, talk about, and maybe even argue about. Big Ideas help you become part of an important conversation. You can join in lively discussions about who we are, where we have been, and where we are going.

Reading and Thinking

The main literary works in your textbook are arranged in three parts.

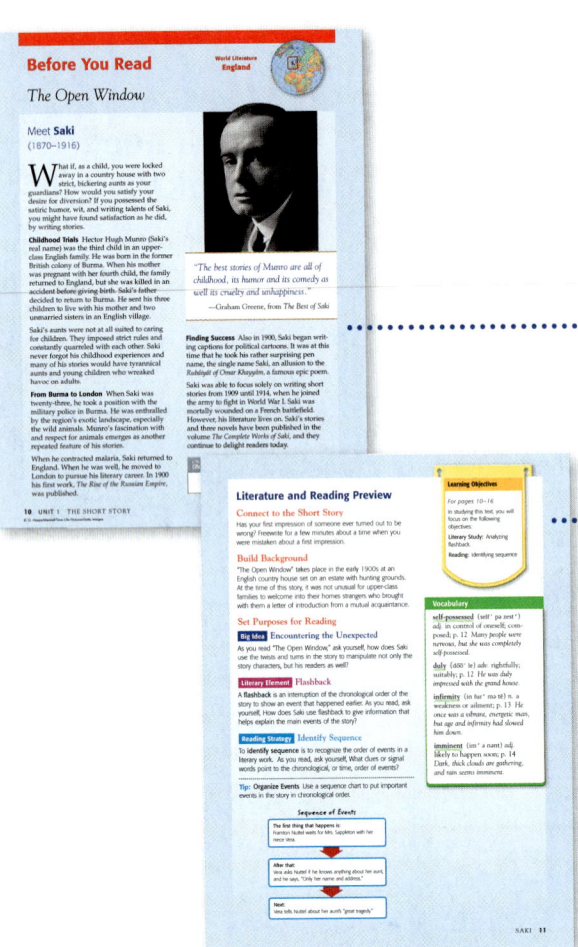

- Start with **BEFORE YOU READ**. Learn valuable background information about the literature and preview the skills and strategies that will guide your reading.

   MEET THE AUTHOR presents a detailed biography of the writer whose work you will read and analyze.

   LITERATURE AND READING PREVIEW lists the basic tools you will use to read and analyze the literary work.

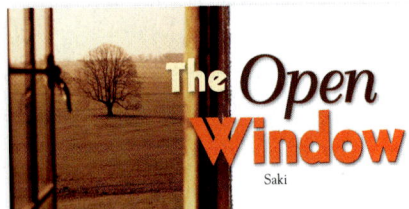

- Next, read the **LITERATURE SELECTION**. As you flip through the selections, you will notice that parts of the text are highlighted in different colors. At the bottom of the page are color-coded questions that relate to the highlighted text. Yellow represents a *Big Idea*, magenta represents a *Literary Element*, and blue represents a *Reading Strategy*. These questions will help you gain a better understanding of the text.

xxxiv

How to Use *Glencoe Literature*

- Wrap up the literature with **AFTER YOU READ**. Explore what you have learned through a wide range of reading, thinking, vocabulary, and writing activities.

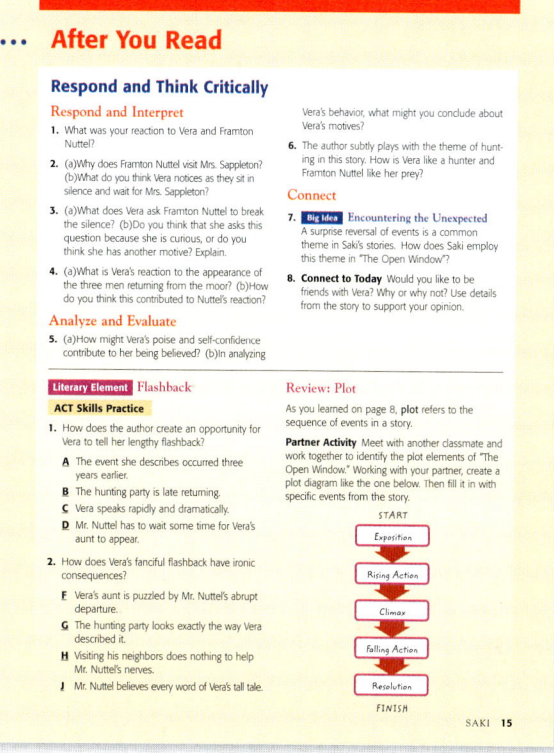

Vocabulary

VOCABULARY WORDS that may be new or difficult for you are chosen from most selections. They are introduced on the **BEFORE YOU READ** page. Each word is accompanied by its pronunciation, its part of speech, its definition, and the page number on which it appears. The vocabulary word is also used in a sample sentence. Vocabulary words are highlighted in the literary work.

VOCABULARY PRACTICE On the **AFTER YOU READ** pages, you will be able to practice using the vocabulary words in an exercise. This exercise will show you how to apply a vocabulary strategy to understand new or difficult words.

ACADEMIC VOCABULARY Many of the **AFTER YOU READ** pages will also introduce you to a word that is frequently used in academic work. You will be prompted to complete an activity based on that word.

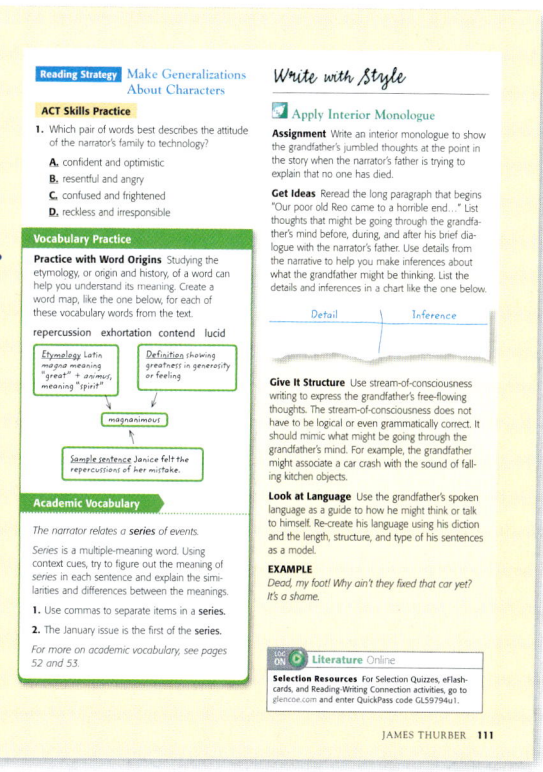

HOW TO USE GLENCOE LITERATURE   **xxxv**

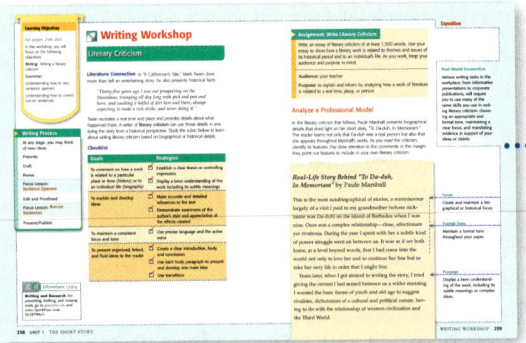

Writing Workshops

Each unit in *Glencoe Literature* includes a Writing Workshop. The workshop walks you through the writing process as you work on an extended piece of writing related to the unit.

- You will create writing goals and apply strategies to meet them.
- You will pick up tips and polish your critical skills as you analyze professional and workshop models.
- You will focus on mastering specific aspects of writing, including organization, grammar, and vocabulary.
- You will use a rubric to evaluate your own writing.

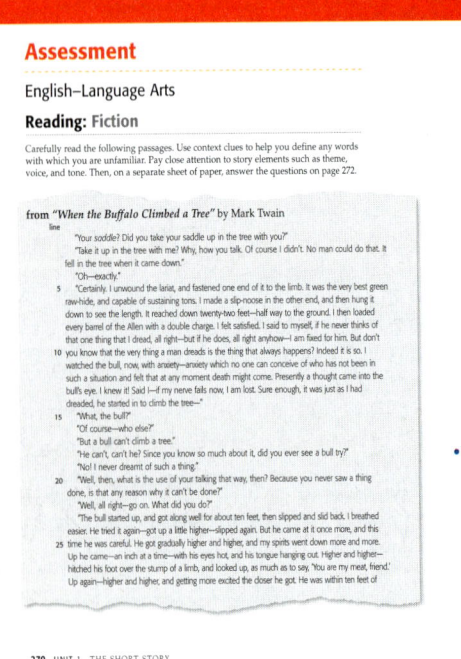

Assessment

At the end of each unit, you will be tested on the literature, reading, and vocabulary skills you have just learned. Designed to simulate standardized tests, this test will give you the practice you need to succeed while providing an assessment of how well you have met the unit objectives.

BOUND BOOK

Try using this organizer to explore your personal responses to the poetry, play and nonfiction.

Organizing Information

Graphic organizers—such as Foldables®, diagrams, and charts—help you keep your information and ideas organized.

Be Cyber Safe and Smart

Cyber Safety

As you explore the *Glencoe Literature* program, you will have many opportunities to go online. When you use the Internet at school or home, you enter a kind of community—the cyber world. In this online world, you need to follow safety rules and protect yourself. Here are some tips to keep in mind:

> **Words to Know**
>
> **cyber world** the world of computers and high-tech communications
> **cyber safety** actions that protect Internet users from harm
> **cyber ethics** responsible code of conduct for using the Internet
> **cyber bully** a person who uses technology to frighten, bother, or harm someone else
> **cyber citizen** a person who uses the Internet to communicate

- ☑ Be a responsible cyber citizen. Use the Internet to share knowledge that makes people's lives better. Respect other people's feelings and do not break any laws.
- ☑ Beware of cyber bullying. People can be hurt and embarrassed by comments that have been made public. You should immediately tell your teacher or counselor if you feel threatened by another student's computer postings.
- ☑ Do not give out personal information, such as your address and telephone number, without your parents' or guardians' permission.
- ☑ Tell your teacher, parent, or guardian right away if you find or read any information that makes you feel uneasy or afraid.
- ☑ Do not email your picture to anyone.
- ☑ Do not open email or text messages from strangers.
- ☑ Do not tell anyone your Internet password.
- ☑ Do not make illegal copies of computer games and programs, and software CDs.

Literature Online

For more about internet safety and responsibility, go to glencoe.com

Ta Matete (We Shall Not Go to Market Today), 1892. Paul Gauguin. Gouache on canvas, 73 x 92 cm. Kunstmuseum, Basel, Switzerland.

View the Art Many of Gauguin's paintings depict the people and lifestyle of the South Pacific. What story-like details can you infer from this painting?

UNIT ONE

The Short Story

Looking Ahead

There is no better place to begin a study of literature than with the short story. This concise, imaginative genre allows the reader to focus on a precisely crafted plot, often a single setting, and a limited number of characters. Whether creating a journey that is bizarre, realistic, or insightful, the writer will quickly and artfully make the point, often in a way the reader will never forget.

Each part in Unit One focuses on a Big Idea that can help you connect to the literary works.

PREVIEW	Big Ideas	Literary Focus
PART 1	Encountering the Unexpected	Plot and Setting
PART 2	Making Choices	Theme and Character
PART 3	Life Transitions	Narrator and Voice

Learning Objectives

For pages 1–6

In studying this text, you will focus on the following objectives:

Literary Study:

Analyzing plot and setting.

Analyzing theme and character.

Analyzing narrator and voice.

Genre Focus

What are the elements that shape a short story?

Katherine Anne Porter, one of the great American short story writers, said, "Human life itself may be almost pure chaos, but the work of the artist is to take these handfuls of confusion and disparate things, things that seem to be irreconcilable, and put them together in a frame to give them some kind of shape and meaning." Consciously or unconsciously, writers make choices. The writer chooses who will be the star of the story, who will tell the story, where the story will take place, and most importantly—what happens! In short story writing, authors make very precise and focused choices about these elements of fiction.

Plot and Setting in Short Stories

Where, When, and How

Setting is the time and place in which a story happens. The setting not only includes physical surroundings but can also include the ideas, customs, values, and beliefs of the period in which the story takes place.

Sequence of Events

Plot is the sequence of events in a story. Most plots begin with the **exposition,** which introduces the characters, setting, and conflicts. **Rising action** develops the conflict with complications and leads to the **climax,** when the story reaches its emotional high point. The **falling action** is the logical result of the climax, and the **resolution** presents the final outcome.

> Now, balanced easily and firmly, he stood on the ledge outside in the slight, chill breeze, eleven stories above the street, staring into his own lighted apartment, odd and different-seeming now.
>
> —Jack Finney, **from "Contents of the Dead Man's Pocket"**

> "You may wonder why we keep that window wide open on an October afternoon," said the niece, indicating a large French window that opened on to a lawn.
>
> —Saki (H. H. Munro), **from "The Open Window"**

Theme and Character in Short Stories

Protagonist and Antagonist

The main character in a story is the **protagonist.** The protagonist faces the main conflict of the story. In many stories, an **antagonist** works against the protagonist in overcoming the conflict. The antagonist is usually a character the reader does not like.

> Thirty-five years ago I was out prospecting on the Stanislaus, tramping all day long with pick and pan and horn, and washing a hatful of dirt here and there, always expecting to make a rich strike, and never doing it.
>
> —Mark Twain, **from "The Californian's Tale"**

Implied and Stated Themes

The central message of a story is its **theme.** For example, a theme might give an insight into human nature or a perception about life. Sometimes authors state their themes directly. More often, a theme is implied through elements in the story, such as what happens to the main character or what the character learns.

> Luis thought that maybe if they ate together once in a while things might get better between them, but he always had something to do around dinnertime and ended up at a hamburger joint.
>
> —Judith Ortiz Cofer, **from "Catch the Moon"**

Narrator and Voice in Short Stories

Point of View

The person telling a story is the **narrator.** The relationship of the narrator to the story is called **point of view.** Stories are usually told from a **first-** or **third-person point of view.** In a story with first-person point of view, the narrator is a character inside the story and uses "I" in telling the story. In a story with third-person point of view, the narrator is outside the story, using "she" or "he" to tell the story.

> The young man was daring and brave, eager to go up to the mountaintop. He had been brought up by good, honest people who were wise in the ancient ways.
>
> —Lame Deer, **from "The Vision Quest"**

Voice

Voice is the distinctive use of language that conveys the author's or narrator's personality to the reader. Every narrator, whether speaking from a first-person or third-person point of view, has a **voice.** Authors are careful to make the narrator's vocabulary and syntax consistent.

> No pestilence had ever been so fatal, or so hideous.
>
> —Edgar Allan Poe, **from "The Masque of the Red Death"**

Literature and Reading For more selections in this genre, go to glencoe.com and enter QuickPass code GL59794u1.

Literary Analysis Model
How do literary elements shape a short story?

Ernest Hemingway (1899–1961) influenced the fiction of his time and after. In "Old Man at the Bridge," he succinctly captures the effects of the Spanish Civil War on civilians.

**APPLYING
Literary Elements**

Narrator
The story is told from the first-person point of view.

Setting
The story takes place at a bridge in northeastern Spain during the Spanish Civil War (1936–1939).

Character
As you learn more about the old man, the story's protagonist, you may begin to care about him.

Voice
In the dialogue, the characters' speech is brief. This is characteristic of Hemingway's style.

Old Man at the Bridge
by Ernest Hemingway

An old man with steel rimmed spectacles and very dusty clothes sat by the side of the road. There was a pontoon bridge across the river and carts, trucks, and men, women and children were crossing it. The mule-drawn carts staggered up the steep bank from the
5 bridge with soldiers helping push against the spokes of the wheels. The trucks ground up and away heading out of it all and the peasants plodded along in the ankle deep dust. But the old man sat there without moving. He was too tired to go any further.

It was my business to cross the bridge, explore the bridgehead
10 beyond and find out to what point the enemy had advanced. I did this and returned over the bridge. There were not so many carts now and very few people on foot, but the old man was still there.

"Where do you come from?" I asked him.

"From San Carlos," he said, and smiled.

That was his native town and so it gave him pleasure to
15 mention it and he smiled.

"I was taking care of animals," he explained.

"Oh," I said, not quite understanding.

"Yes," he said, "I stayed, you see, taking care of animals. I was the last one to leave the town of San Carlos."
20 He did not look like a shepherd nor a herdsman and I looked at his black dusty clothes and his gray dusty face and his steel rimmed spectacles and said, "What animals were they?"

"Various animals," he said, and shook his head. "I had to leave them."

I was watching the bridge and the African looking country of
25 the Ebro Delta and wondering how long now it would be before we would see the enemy, and listening all the while for the first noises that would signal that ever mysterious event called contact, and the old man still sat there.

"What animals were they?" I asked.

"There were three animals altogether," he explained. "There were
30 two goats and a cat and then there were four pairs of pigeons."

"And you had to leave them?" I asked.

35 "Yes. Because of the artillery. The captain told me to go because of the artillery."

"And you have no family?" I asked, watching the far end of the bridge where a few last carts were hurrying down the slope of the bank.

40 "No," he said, "only the animals I stated. The cat, of course, will be all right. A cat can look out for itself, but I cannot think what will become of the others."

"What politics have you?" I asked.

"I am without politics," he said. "I am seventy-six years old. 45 I have come twelve kilometers now and I think now I can go no further."

"This is not a good place to stop," I said. "If you can make it, there are trucks up the road where it forks for Tortosa."

"I will wait a while," he said, "and then I will go. Where do the 50 trucks go?"

"Towards Barcelona," I told him.

"I know no one in that direction," he said, "but thank you very much. Thank you again very much."

He looked at me very blankly and tiredly, then said, having 55 to share his worry with some one, "The cat will be all right, I am sure. There is no need to be unquiet about the cat. But the others. Now what do you think about the others?"

"Why they'll probably come through it all right."

"You think so?"

60 "Why not," I said, watching the far bank where now there were no carts.

"But what will they do under the artillery when I was told to leave because of the artillery?"

"Did you leave the dove cage unlocked?" I asked.

65 "Yes."

"Then they'll fly."

"Yes, certainly they'll fly. But the others. It's better not to think about the others," he said.

"If you are rested I would go," I urged. "Get up and try to 70 walk now."

"Thank you," he said and got to his feet, swayed from side to side and then sat down backwards in the dust.

"I was taking care of animals," he said dully, but no longer to me. "I was only taking care of animals."

75 There was nothing to do about him. It was Easter Sunday and the Fascists were advancing toward the Ebro. It was a gray overcast day with a low ceiling so their planes were not up. That and the fact that cats know how to look after themselves was all the good luck that old man would ever have.

Plot
You may hope that the old man will be able to flee with the others, but, in the climax of the story, he is too tired to stand.

Theme
The implication is that war is unlucky for the civilians whose lives it touches.

Reading Check

Analyze How does the story reach its climax and how is it resolved?

Wrap-Up

Guide to Reading Short Stories

- Short stories often allow readers to focus on one setting and a small number of characters.
- Plot development in short stories tends to be very compact, especially the exposition, falling action, and resolution.
- Reading a short story well involves determining the theme, often by paying attention to what befalls the main character.
- Notice whether the narrator is inside the story (first-person point of view) or outside the story (third-person point of view).
- To help you stay engaged as you read a story, think of your own adjectives to describe the characters and the narrator.

Elements of Short Stories

- **Plot** is what happens in a story.
- **Setting** is where the story takes place.
- **Characters** are the actors in a story.
- The **narrator** tells the story.
- **Voice** refers to the kind of language the narrator uses to tell the story.
- The **theme** is the story's most meaningful message.

Unit Resources For additional skills practice, go to glencoe.com and enter QuickPass code GL59794u1.

Activities

Use what you have learned about reading and analyzing short stories to complete one of the following activities.

1. Literary Analysis Write about the relationship between the narrator and the old man in "Old Man at the Bridge." How did their interactions affect the plot?

2. Speaking and Listening In a small group, discuss the theme of "Old Man at the Bridge." Give each group member a chance to choose a line from the story that contributes to the theme and to explain how the line contributes to the story's meaning.

3. Take Notes Try using this study organizer to keep track of literary elements in the stories in Unit 1.

 **FOLDABLES STUDY ORGANIZER**

Plot
Setting
Theme
Character
Narrator
Voice

See page R20 for folding instructions.

PART 1

Encountering the Unexpected

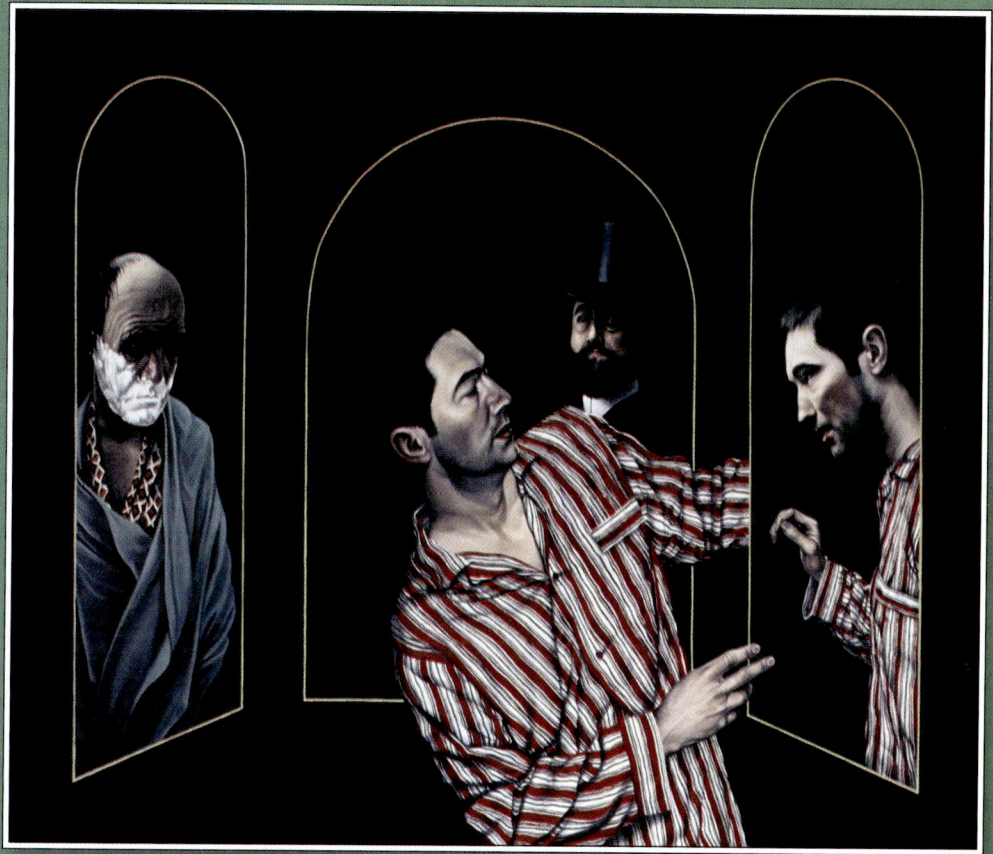

Accident in the Hall of Mirrors, 1999. Graeme Wilcox. Acrylic on canvas, 128 x 158 cm.

View the Art Wilcox has painted realistic figures which appear as if in a mirror. How are the reflections different from what you would expect? How does the center figure seem to react to his image?

BIG IDEA

People never know exactly what their futures will bring. Many people expect that tomorrow will be much like today. In the short stories in Part 1, you will encounter people and events that are not always what they initially seem to be. As you read these stories, ask yourself, How do people cope when they suddenly encounter the unexpected?

Learning Objectives

For pages 8–9

In studying this text, you will focus on the following objective:

Literary Study: Analyzing plot, setting, and conflict.

LITERARY FOCUS

Plot and Setting

How do short stories create events and places?

Think of a favorite story. Where does it take place? Can you imagine the same people, events, and themes happening somewhere else? Especially in a short story, where there is often only one setting, the setting can be an essential component of the tale being told. In Shirley Jackson's short stories, the bucolic, small-town settings she so often uses are an integral part of her stories' characteristic twists and turns.

The second chamber was purple in its ornaments and tapestries, and here the panes were purple. The third was green throughout, and so were the casements. The fourth was furnished and lighted with orange—the fifth with white—the sixth with violet. The seventh apartment was closely shrouded in black velvet tapestries that hung all over the ceiling and down the walls, falling in heavy folds upon a carpet of the same material and hue. But in this chamber only, the color of the windows failed to correspond with the decorations. The panes here were scarlet—a deep blood color.

—Edgar Allan Poe, **from "The Masque of the Red Death"**

Setting

Setting is the time and the place of a story. It also includes the customs, beliefs, and values of that time and place. An author can use the setting to create expectations in a reader. Then, the author can use those expectations to create a mood such as surprise, disappointment, or shock. Consider the setting of "The Masque of the Red Death":

Detail	Aspect of Setting
"panes were purple"	somber, dark place
"shrouded in black velvet"	reminder of death
"a deep blood color"	sense of foreboding

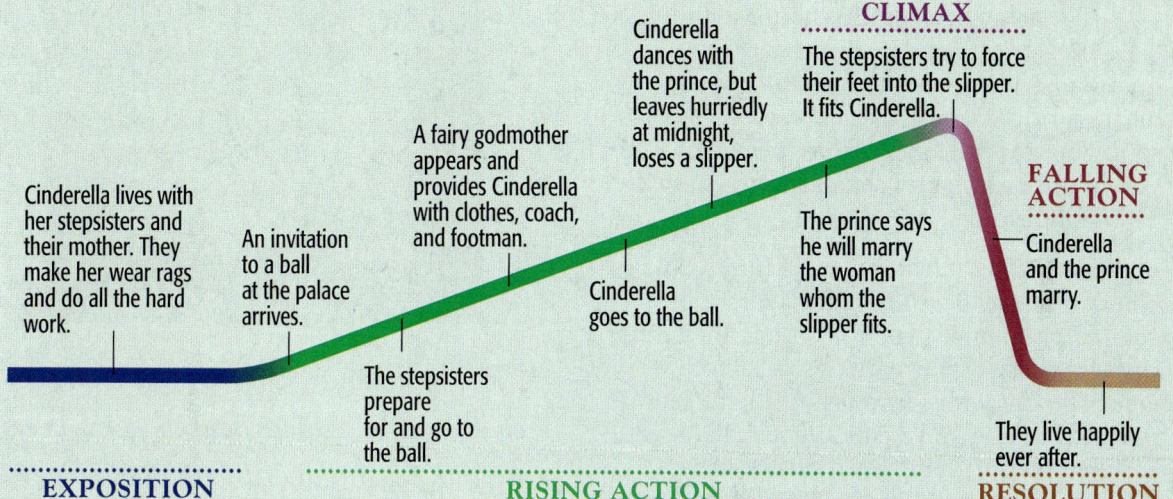

Plot

Plot is the sequence of events in a story—a series of related incidents. Plots usually involve a **conflict,** a struggle between opposing forces.

- An **external conflict** is a struggle between a character and an outside force, such as another character, nature, society, or fate.

- An **internal conflict** takes place within the mind of a character who struggles with opposing feelings or with indecision.

The events that make up the plot of "Cinderella" are shown in the diagram above.

Order of Events Authors vary the way they present plot events. They use **foreshadowing**—clues or hints to prepare readers for events that will happen later in the story. Authors use **flashback**—an interruption in the chronological order of a story to tell an event that happened earlier.

Quickwrite

Complete a Plot Diagram Choose a story that is familiar to you and diagram the plot. Give details about the exposition, the rising action, the climax, the falling action, and the resolution. If your story contains foreshadowing or flashback, show these elements on your diagram.

Literature and Reading For more about literary elements, go to glencoe.com and enter QuickPass code GL59794u1.

LITERARY FOCUS

Before You Read

World Literature
England

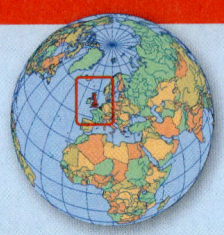

The Open Window

Meet Saki
(1870–1916)

What if, as a child, you were locked away in a country house with two strict, bickering aunts as your guardians? How would you satisfy your desire for diversion? If you possessed the satiric humor, wit, and writing talents of Saki, you might have found satisfaction as he did, by writing stories.

Childhood Trials Hector Hugh Munro (Saki's real name) was the third child in an upper-class English family. He was born in the former British colony of Burma. When his mother was pregnant with her fourth child, the family returned to England, but she was killed in an accident before giving birth. Saki's father decided to return to Burma. He sent his three children to live with his mother and two unmarried sisters in an English village.

Saki's aunts were not at all suited to caring for children. They imposed strict rules and constantly quarreled with each other. Saki never forgot his childhood experiences and many of his stories would have tyrannical aunts and young children who wreaked havoc on adults.

From Burma to London When Saki was twenty-three, he took a position with the military police in Burma. He was enthralled by the region's exotic landscape, especially the wild animals. Munro's fascination with and respect for animals emerges as another repeated feature of his stories.

When he contracted malaria, Saki returned to England. When he was well, he moved to London to pursue his literary career. In 1900 his first work, *The Rise of the Russian Empire*, was published.

> "The best stories of Munro are all of childhood, its humor and its comedy as well its cruelty and unhappiness."
>
> —Graham Greene, from *The Best of Saki*

Finding Success Also in 1900, Saki began writing captions for political cartoons. It was at this time that he took his rather surprising pen name, the single name Saki, an allusion to the *Rubáiyát of Omar Khayyám*, a famous epic poem.

Saki was able to focus solely on writing short stories from 1909 until 1914, when he joined the army to fight in World War I. Saki was mortally wounded on a French battlefield. However, his literature lives on. Saki's stories and three novels have been published in the volume *The Complete Works of Saki*, and they continue to delight readers today.

 **Literature** Online

Author Search For more about Saki, go to glencoe.com and enter QuickPass code GL59794u1.

10 UNIT 1 THE SHORT STORY

Literature and Reading Preview

Connect to the Short Story
Has your first impression of someone ever turned out to be wrong? Freewrite for a few minutes about a time when you were mistaken about a first impression.

Build Background
"The Open Window" takes place in the early 1900s at an English country house set on an estate with hunting grounds. At the time of this story, it was not unusual for upper-class families to welcome into their homes strangers who brought with them a letter of introduction from a mutual acquaintance.

Set Purposes for Reading

Big Idea **Encountering the Unexpected**

As you read "The Open Window," ask yourself, How does Saki use the twists and turns in the story to manipulate not only the story characters but his readers as well?

Literary Element **Flashback**

A **flashback** is an interruption of the chronological order of the story to show an event that happened earlier. As you read, ask yourself, How does Saki use flashback to give information that helps explain the main events of the story?

Reading Strategy **Identify Sequence**

To **identify sequence** is to recognize the order of events in a literary work. As you read, ask yourself, What clues or signal words point to the chronological, or time, order of events?

Tip: Organize Events Use a sequence chart to put important events in the story in chronological order.

Sequence of Events

> **The first thing that happens is:**
> Framton Nuttel waits for Mrs. Sappleton with her niece Vera.

> **After that:**
> Vera asks Nuttel if he knows anything about her aunt, and he says, "Only her name and address."

> **Next:**
> Vera tells Nuttel about her aunt's "great tragedy."

Learning Objectives

For pages 10–16

In studying this text, you will focus on the following objectives:

Literary Study: Analyzing flashback.

Reading: Identifying sequence

Vocabulary

self-possessed (self′ pə zest′) *adj.* in control of oneself; composed; p. 12 *Many people were nervous, but she was completely self-possessed.*

duly (dōō′ lē) *adv.* rightfully; suitably; p. 12 *He was duly impressed with the grand house.*

infirmity (in fur′ mə tē) *n.* a weakness or an ailment; p. 13 *He once was a vibrant, energetic man, but age and infirmity had slowed him down.*

imminent (im′ ə nənt) *adj.* likely to happen soon; p. 14 *Dark, thick clouds are gathering, and rain seems imminent.*

The Open Window
Saki

"My aunt will be down presently, Mr. Nuttel," said a very **self-possessed** young lady of fifteen; "in the meantime you must try and put up with me."

Framton Nuttel endeavored to say the correct something which should **duly** flatter the niece of the moment without unduly discounting the aunt that was to come. Privately he doubted more than ever whether these formal visits on a succession of total strangers would do much towards helping the nerve cure which he was supposed to be undergoing.

"I know how it will be," his sister had said when he was preparing to migrate to this rural retreat; "you will bury yourself down there and not speak to a living soul, and your nerves will be worse than ever from moping. I shall just give you letters of introduction to all the people I know there. Some of them, as far as I can remember, were quite nice."

Framton wondered whether Mrs. Sappleton, the lady to whom he was presenting one of the letters of introduction, came into the nice division.

"Do you know many of the people round here?" asked the niece, when she judged that they had had sufficient silent communion.

"Hardly a soul," said Framton. "My sister was staying here, at the rectory, you know, some four years ago, and she gave me letters of introduction to some of the people here."

He made the last statement in a tone of distinct regret.

"Then you know practically nothing about my aunt?" pursued the self-possessed young lady.

"Only her name and address," admitted the caller. He was wondering whether Mrs. Sappleton was in the married or widowed

---

Flashback *What background information does this flashback provide?*

Vocabulary

self-possessed (self′ pə zest′) *adj.* in control of oneself; composed

duly (dōō′ lē) *adv.* rightfully; suitably

Identify Sequence *Is this taking place before or after Framton Nuttel's arrival at the Sappletons' home? Explain how it relates to the flashback that precedes it.*

state. An undefinable something about the room seemed to suggest masculine habitation.

"Her great tragedy happened just three years ago," said the child; "that would be since your sister's time."

"Her tragedy?" asked Framton; somehow in this restful country spot tragedies seemed out of place.

"You may wonder why we keep that window wide open on an October afternoon," said the niece, indicating a large French window[1] that opened on to a lawn.

"It is quite warm for the time of the year," said Framton; "but has that window got anything to do with the tragedy?"

"Out through that window, three years ago to a day, her husband and her two young brothers went off for their day's shooting. They never came back. In crossing the moor to their favorite snipe-shooting ground they were all three engulfed in a treacherous piece of bog.[2] It had been that dreadful wet summer, you know, and places that were safe in other years gave way suddenly without warning. Their bodies were never recovered. That was the dreadful part of it." Here the child's voice lost its self-possessed note and became falteringly human. "Poor aunt always thinks that they will come back some day, they and the little brown spaniel that was lost with them, and walk in at that window just as they used to do. That is why the window is kept open every evening till it is quite dusk. Poor dear aunt, she has often told me how they went out, her husband with his white waterproof coat over his arm, and Ronnie, her youngest brother, singing, 'Bertie, why do you bound?' as he always did to tease her, because she said it got on her nerves. Do you know, sometimes on still, quiet evenings like this, I almost get a creepy feeling that they will all walk in through that window—"

She broke off with a little shudder. It was a relief to Framton when the aunt bustled into the room with a whirl of apologies for being late in making her appearance.

"I hope Vera has been amusing you?" she said.

"She has been very interesting," said Framton.

"I hope you don't mind the open window," said Mrs. Sappleton briskly; "my husband and brothers will be home directly from shooting, and they always come in this way. They've been out for snipe in the marshes today, so they'll make a fine mess over my poor carpets. So like you men-folk, isn't it?"

She rattled on cheerfully about the shooting and the scarcity of birds, and the prospects for duck in the winter. To Framton it was all purely horrible. He made a desperate but only partially successful effort to turn the talk on to a less ghastly topic; he was conscious that his hostess was giving him only a fragment of her attention, and her eyes were constantly straying past him to the open window and the lawn beyond. It was certainly an unfortunate coincidence that he should have paid his visit on this tragic anniversary.

"The doctors agree in ordering me complete rest, an absence of mental excitement, and avoidance of anything in the nature of violent physical exercise," announced Framton, who labored under the tolerably wide-spread delusion that total strangers and chance acquaintances are hungry for the least detail of one's ailments and **infirmities**, their

---

1. A *French window* is a pair of door-like windows hinged at opposite sides and opening in the middle.
2. A *moor* is a tract of open, rolling, wild land, often having marshes. *Snipe* are wetland game birds. The men here are hunting snipe.

Identify Sequence What is the sequence of events that leads up to Nuttel wanting to change the topic?

Vocabulary

infirmity (in fur′ mə tē) *n.* a weakness or an ailment

At the Window, 1894. William Merritt Chase. Pastel and paper, 18.5 x 11 in. Brooklyn Museum of Art, NY. Gift of Mrs. Henry Wolf, Austin M. Wolf, and Hamilton A. Wolf.

View the Art What qualities might the girl in this drawing share with the niece in the story?

cause and cure. "On the matter of diet they are not so much in agreement," he continued.

"No?" said Mrs. Sappleton, in a voice which only replaced a yawn at the last moment. Then she suddenly brightened into alert attention—but not to what Framton was saying.

"Here they are at last!" she cried. "Just in time for tea, and don't they look as if they were muddy up to the eyes!"

Framton shivered slightly and turned towards the niece with a look intended to convey sympathetic comprehension. The child was staring out through the open window with dazed horror in her eyes. In a chill shock of nameless fear Framton swung round in his seat and looked in the same direction.

In the deepening twilight three figures were walking across the lawn towards the window; they all carried guns under their arms, and one of them was additionally burdened with a white coat hung over his shoulders. A tired brown spaniel kept close at their heels. Noiselessly they neared the house, and then a hoarse young voice chanted out of the dusk: "I said, Bertie, why do you bound?"

Framton grabbed wildly at his stick and hat; the hall door, the gravel drive, and the front gate were dimly noted stages in his headlong retreat. A cyclist coming along the road had to run into the hedge to avoid **imminent** collision.

"Here we are, my dear," said the bearer of the white mackintosh,[3] coming in through the window; "fairly muddy, but most of it's dry. Who was that who bolted out as we came up?"

"A most extraordinary man, a Mr. Nuttel," said Mrs. Sappleton; "could only talk about his illnesses, and dashed off without a word of good-bye or apology when you arrived. One would think he had seen a ghost."

"I expect it was the spaniel," said the niece calmly; "he told me he had a horror of dogs. He was once hunted into a cemetery somewhere on the banks of the Ganges by a pack of pariah[4] dogs, and had to spend the night in a newly dug grave with the creatures snarling and grinning and foaming just above him. Enough to make any one lose their nerve." Romance[5] at short notice was her specialty.

---

3. A *mackintosh* is a heavy-duty raincoat.
4. The *Ganges* is a river in northern India. A *pariah* is one who is shunned or despised by others. In India, where dogs are not highly regarded, packs of wild dogs are considered pariahs.
5. Here, *romance* means "tales of extraordinary or mysterious events."

Encountering the Unexpected Why does Saki wait until the last line of the story to tell readers that telling tales was Vera's specialty?

Vocabulary

imminent (im′ ə nənt) *adj.* likely to happen soon

After You Read

Respond and Think Critically

Respond and Interpret

1. What was your reaction to Vera and Framton Nuttel?

2. (a) Why does Framton Nuttel visit Mrs. Sappleton? (b) What do you think Vera notices as they sit in silence and wait for Mrs. Sappleton?

3. (a) What does Vera ask Framton Nuttel to break the silence? (b) Do you think that she asks this question because she is curious, or do you think she has another motive? Explain.

4. (a) What is Vera's reaction to the appearance of the three men returning from the moor? (b) How do you think this contributed to Nuttel's reaction?

Analyze and Evaluate

5. (a) How might Vera's poise and self-confidence contribute to her being believed? (b) In analyzing Vera's behavior, what might you conclude about Vera's motives?

6. The author subtly plays with the theme of hunting in this story. How is Vera like a hunter and Framton Nuttel like her prey?

Connect

7. **Big Idea** Encountering the Unexpected A surprise reversal of events is a common theme in Saki's stories. How does Saki employ this theme in "The Open Window"?

8. **Connect to Today** Would you like to be friends with Vera? Why or why not? Use details from the story to support your opinion.

Literary Element Flashback

ACT Skills Practice

1. How does the author create an opportunity for Vera to tell her lengthy flashback?
   A. The event she describes occurred three years earlier.
   B. The hunting party is late returning.
   C. Vera speaks rapidly and dramatically.
   D. Mr. Nuttel has to wait some time for Vera's aunt to appear.

2. How does Vera's fanciful flashback have ironic consequences?
   F. Vera's aunt is puzzled by Mr. Nuttel's abrupt departure.
   G. The hunting party looks exactly the way Vera described it.
   H. Visiting his neighbors does nothing to help Mr. Nuttel's nerves.
   J. Mr. Nuttel believes every word of Vera's tall tale.

Review: Plot

As you learned on page 8, **plot** refers to the sequence of events in a story.

Partner Activity Meet with a classmate and work together to identify the plot elements of "The Open Window." Working with your partner, create a plot diagram like the one below. Then fill it in with specific events from the story.

| Reading Strategy | **Identify Sequence**

Within "The Open Window" is a second narrative. That is the story that Vera tells Nuttel about her uncle's death while hunting on the moors. Review the **sequence** chart you created for the main events in the story.

1. Use your sequence chart to summarize the story.
2. When the author used a flashback at the beginning of the story, what helped you recognize that as a flashback?

Vocabulary Practice

Practice with Context Clues Identify the context clues in the following sentences that help you determine the meaning of each boldfaced vocabulary word.

1. The older daughter was always confident and **self-possessed,** unlike her nervous younger sister.
2. He was **duly** polite as always and spoke and acted like a perfect gentleman.
3. Although the long illness had weakened him, the man never complained of his **infirmity.**
4. We knew the arrival of the train was **imminent** when we heard its whistle and then saw light flash on the walls of the tunnel.

Academic Vocabulary

Vera's words and actions allow the reader to **deduce** that she is creative, spontaneous, and, above all, mischievous.

Deduce is an academic word. More familiar words and phrases that are similar in meaning are *figure out, infer,* and *conclude.* Show the meaning of **deduce** by completing this sentence starter: I **deduce** that Lauren is not coming to the party _____.

For more on academic vocabulary, see pages 52 and 53.

Research and Report

 Literary Criticism

Assignment Evaluate literary criticism about Saki's work and write a short response in which you explain whether you agree or disagree that the criticism applies to "The Open Window" and to Vera. Present the response to the class.

Prepare Read the following quotation about Saki's work by critic Elizabeth Drew:

"The cruelty is certainly there, but it has nothing perverted or pathological about it…It is the genial heartlessness of the normal child, whose fantasies take no account of adult standards of human behavior."

Some literary criticism may include unfamiliar words or words with unfamiliar connotations. Use a dictionary to look up *perverted, pathological,* and *genial.* Determine your position. Craft a thesis statement about your position. Use a graphic organizer as below with story details to support your argument.

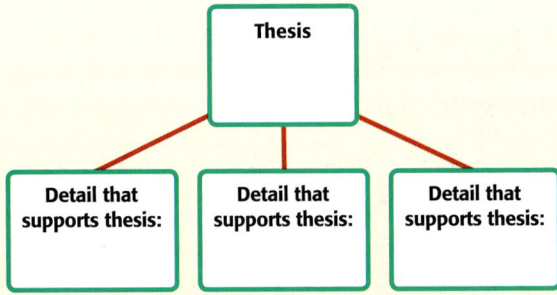

Report When you present your response, make eye contact, speak loudly and clearly, and maintain good posture to reflect confidence. Use an appropriate tone of voice to enhance appeals to logic and emotion.

Evaluate Write a paragraph evaluating your report. When your classmates present, offer oral feedback on their performances. Use the rubric on page 267 for help in your evaluation.

 **Literature** Online

Selection Resources For Selection Quizzes, eFlashcards, and Reading-Writing Connection activities, go to glencoe.com and enter QuickPass code GL59794u1.

Before You Read

The Californian's Tale

Meet Mark Twain
(1835–1910)

Mark Twain is the pen name of one of America's best-known and most beloved authors. Born Samuel Langhorne Clemens, he first used the name Mark Twain—a nautical term meaning "two fathoms deep"—when he wrote humorous pieces for a Nevada newspaper.

Twain lost his father when he was eleven. Within a few years he was helping to support his family. At age thirteen, he apprenticed to a local printer. Soon he was working at the local newspaper, which was established by his brother Orion. Twain's primary job was to set type, but he also wrote humorous articles.

During his late teens and early twenties, Twain moved from his home in Hannibal, Missouri, to St. Louis, then to several East Coast cities, and finally back to the Midwest. Eventually, he met a pilot who took him on as an apprentice. Twain loved being on the Mississippi. He gained his pilot's license and worked steering riverboats for several years until the Civil War interrupted the boat traffic.

> "The human race has one really effective weapon, and that is laughter."
> —Mark Twain

Western Adventures In 1861 Twain traveled west with Orion to Nevada. Twain tried to prospect for gold and silver and speculated in mines and timber, but he was unsuccessful. And so he returned to newspaper writing. Twain wrote a mix of biting political commentaries and humorous stories that earned him notice and respect. In 1866, on another travel-writing assignment, he took a steamboat trip from San Francisco, California, to Honolulu, Hawaii. The next year, Twain sailed from California to Central America, traveling by land across Panama, sailing to New York, and then across the Atlantic Ocean to Europe and Southwest Asia. He published accounts of his travels as his first book, *Innocents Abroad*.

Worldwide Popularity From that time forward, Twain gained both national and international acclaim as a writer and lecturer and wrote the books for which he is best known today: *The Adventures of Tom Sawyer* (1876), *The Prince and the Pauper* (1881), and *The Adventures of Huckleberry Finn* (1885). Twain's lectures were even more popular and lucrative than his books. Audiences all over the world loved his witty anecdotes, told in an exaggerated drawl with well-placed pauses that heightened dramatic tension and humor.

Author Search For more about Mark Twain, go to glencoe.com and enter QuickPass code GL59794u1.

Literature and Reading Preview

Connect to the Story
How important is it to have people that care about you? Write a journal entry about one person you care about in which you explain why that person is so important to you.

Build Background
Gold was first discovered in central California in 1848. Within the next year, almost 100,000 people, most of them young men, had moved to California, trying to strike it rich by prospecting for gold. They were called the "forty-niners," referring to the year in which they came to California. Only a few of the forty-niners made a fortune during the gold rush. Twain's story takes place in a deserted mining area in the late 1860s or early 1870s.

Set Purposes for Reading

Big Idea Encountering the Unexpected

As you read "The Californian's Tale," ask yourself, How does the unexpected affect the events of the story and the lives of the characters?

Literary Element Foreshadowing

Foreshadowing is a writer's use of clues to hint at events that will happen later in a story. As you read, ask yourself, What clues suggest that all is not necessarily as it seems?

Reading Strategy Analyze Cause-and-Effect Relationships

A **cause** is something that makes something else happen; an **effect** is what happens as a result of a cause. Fiction writers include **cause-and-effect relationships** to further the action of a plot. As you read, ask yourself, Where are the cause-and-effect relationships in this story?

Reading Tip: Take Notes Use diagrams like the one below to analyze some of the causes and effects in this short story.

Cause Narrator is prospecting for gold in a region where mining has been abandoned.

↓

Effect Narrator spends a lot of time by himself.

Learning Objectives
For pages 17–27

In studying this text, you will focus on the following objectives:

Literary Study: Analyzing foreshadowing.

Reading: Analyzing cause-and-effect relationships.

Vocabulary

predecessor (pred′ ə ses′ ər) *n.* one who comes, or has come before in another time; p. 19 *Groups of Native Americans were the predecessors of the miners who settled in central California.*

solace (sol′ is) *n.* relief from sorrow or disappointment; comfort; p. 20 *Homey touches in a hotel room may give solace to weary travelers.*

sedate (si dāt′) *adj.* quiet and restrained in style or manner; calm; p. 22 *Dominique felt so sedate while reading that she promptly fell asleep.*

imploring (im plôr′ ing) *adj.* asking earnestly; begging; p. 24 *He gave an imploring glance, as if to ask, "Did you bring me a gift for my birthday?"*

boding (bōd′ ing) *n.* a warning or an indication, especially of evil; p. 24 *Their boding about the theft was a result of the disorder.*

18   UNIT 1   THE SHORT STORY

Old House with Tree Shadows, 1916. Grant Wood. Oil on composition board, 13 x 15 inches. Cedar Rapids Museum of Art, Iowa.

The Californian's Tale

Mark Twain

Thirty-five years ago I was out prospecting on the Stanislaus, tramping all day long with pick and pan and horn, and washing a hatful of dirt here and there, always expecting to make a rich strike, and never doing it. It was a lovely region, woodsy, balmy, delicious, and had once been populous, long years before, but now the people had vanished and the charming paradise was a solitude.[1]

They went away when the surface diggings gave out. In one place, where a busy little city with banks and newspapers and fire companies and a mayor and aldermen had been, was nothing but a wide expanse of emerald turf, with not even the faintest sign that human life had ever been present there. This was down toward Tuttletown.[2] In the country neighborhood thereabouts, along the dusty roads, one found at intervals the prettiest little cottage homes, snug and cozy, and so cobwebbed with vines snowed thick with roses that the doors and windows were wholly hidden from sight—sign that these were deserted homes, forsaken years ago by defeated and disappointed families who could neither sell them nor give them away. Now and then, half an hour apart, one came across solitary log cabins of the earliest mining days, built by the first gold-miners, the **predecessors** of the cottage-builders. In some few cases these

---

1. The narrator was exploring for gold (*prospecting*) along the Stanislaus River in central California. Here, *solitude* refers to a lonely, isolated place.

Analyze Cause-and-Effect Relationships Why are there no longer many people living along the Stanislaus River in this part of California?

2. *Tuttletown* was a mining town near the Stanislaus.

Vocabulary

predecessor (pred´ə ses´ər) *n*. one who comes, or has come before in another time

cabins were still occupied; and when this was so, you could depend upon it that the occupant was the very pioneer who had built the cabin; and you could depend on another thing, too—that he was there because he had once had his opportunity to go home to the States rich, and had not done it; had rather lost his wealth, and had then in his humiliation resolved to sever[3] all communication with his home relatives and friends, and be to them thenceforth as one dead. Round about California in that day were scattered a host of these living dead men—pride-smitten[4] poor fellows, grizzled[5] and old at forty, whose secret thoughts were made all of regrets and longings—regrets for their wasted lives, and longings to be out of the struggle and done with it all.

It was a lonesome land! Not a sound in all those peaceful expanses of grass and woods but the drowsy hum of insects; no glimpse of man or beast; nothing to keep up your spirits and make you glad to be alive. And so, at last, in the early part of the afternoon, when I caught sight of a human creature, I felt a most grateful uplift. This person was a man about forty-five years old, and he was standing at the gate of one of those cozy little rose-clad cottages of the sort already referred to. However, this one hadn't a deserted look; it had the look of being lived in and petted and cared for and looked after; and so had its front yard, which was a garden of flowers, abundant, gay, and flourishing. I was invited in, of course, and required to make myself at home—it was the custom of the country.

It was delightful to be in such a place, after long weeks of daily and nightly familiarity with miners' cabins—with all which this implies of dirt floor, never-made beds, tin plates and cups, bacon and beans and black coffee, and nothing of ornament but war pictures from the Eastern illustrated papers tacked to the log walls. That was all hard, cheerless, materialistic[6] desolation, but here was a nest which had aspects to rest the tired eye and refresh that something in one's nature which, after long fasting, recognizes, when confronted by the belongings of art, howsoever cheap and modest they may be, that it has unconsciously been famishing and now has found nourishment. I could not have believed that a rag carpet could feast me so, and so content me; or that there could be such **solace** to the soul in wall-paper and framed lithographs,[7] and bright-colored tidies[8] and lamp-mats, and Windsor chairs, and varnished what-nots,[9] with sea-shells and books and china vases on them, and the score of little unclassifiable tricks and touches

Visual Vocabulary
A *Windsor chair* has a high, spoked back, slanting legs, and a slightly curving seat. It is named for the city in England where this style of chair was first designed and built.

---

3. To *sever* means to "break off."
4. Someone who is *smitten* is strongly affected by some powerful feeling.
5. *Grizzled* means "gray or mixed with gray."

Analyze Cause-and-Effect Relationships Summarize the circumstances that have caused these men to end up pride-smitten, poor, and alone.

Encountering the Unexpected How does the mood of the story here differ from the mood evoked in the first paragraph?

---

6. *Materialistic* means "having a strong focus on material wants and needs."
7. *Lithographs* are pictures printed by a process in which a flat surface is treated either to retain or to repel ink.
8. *Tidies* are small, decorative coverings placed over the back or arms of a chair or sofa to keep them from being soiled or worn.
9. *What-nots* are open shelves for displaying objects.

Vocabulary

solace (sol'is) *n.* relief from sorrow or disappointment; comfort

that a woman's hand distributes about a home, which one sees without knowing he sees them, yet would miss in a moment if they were taken away. The delight that was in my heart showed in my face, and the man saw it and was pleased; saw it so plainly that he answered it as if it had been spoken.

"All her work," he said, caressingly; "she did it all herself—every bit," and he took the room in with a glance which was full of affectionate worship. One of those soft Japanese fabrics with which women drape with careful negligence the upper part of a picture-frame was out of adjustment. He noticed it, and rearranged it with cautious pains, stepping back several times to gauge the effect before he got it to suit him. Then he gave it a light finishing pat or two with his hand, and said: "She always does that. You can't tell just what it lacks, but it does lack something until you've done that—you can see it yourself after it's done, but that is all you know; you can't find out the law of it. It's like the finishing pats a mother gives the child's hair after she's got it combed and brushed, I reckon. I've seen her fix all these things so much that I can do them all just her way, though I don't know the law of any of them. But she knows the law. She knows the why and the how both; but I don't know the why; I only know the how."

He took me into a bedroom so that I might wash my hands; such a bedroom as I had not seen for years: white counterpane, white pillows, carpeted floor, papered walls, pictures, dressing-table, with mirror and pin-cushion and dainty toilet things; and in the corner a washstand, with real china-ware bowl and pitcher, and with soap in a china dish, and on a rack more than a dozen towels—towels too clean and white for one out of practice to use without some vague sense of profanation.[10] So my face spoke again, and he answered with gratified words:

"All her work; she did it all herself—every bit. Nothing here that hasn't felt the touch of her hand. Now you would think— But I mustn't talk so much."

By this time I was wiping my hands and glancing from detail to detail of the room's belongings, as one is apt to do when he is in a new place, where everything he sees is a comfort to his eye and his spirit; and I became conscious, in one of those unaccountable ways, you know, that there was something there somewhere that the man wanted me to discover for myself. I knew it perfectly, and I knew he was trying to help me by furtive[11] indications with his eye, so I tried hard to get on the right track, being eager to gratify him. I failed several times, as I could see out of the corner of my eye without being told; but at last I knew I must be looking straight at the thing—knew it from the pleasure issuing in invisible waves from him. He broke into a happy laugh, and rubbed his hands together, and cried out:

"That's it! You've found it. I knew you would. It's her picture."

I went to the little black-walnut bracket on the farther wall, and did find there

Visual Vocabulary
A *counterpane* is a quilt or bedspread, often made by hand.

Visual Vocabulary
Here, *bracket* refers to a small shelf hung on the wall and supported by brackets.

---

10. *Profanation* is the act of making something impure through unworthy use.
11. Here, *furtive* means "stealthy."

Foreshadowing What idea or feeling does this detail give you about the home? About the woman?

what I had not yet noticed—a daguerreotype-case.[12] It contained the sweetest girlish face, and the most beautiful, as it seemed to me, that I had ever seen. The man drank the admiration from my face, and was fully satisfied.

"Nineteen her last birthday," he said, as he put the picture back; "and that was the day we were married. When you see her—ah, just wait till you see her!"

"Where is she? When will she be in?"

"Oh, she's away now. She's gone to see her people. They live forty or fifty miles from here. She's been gone two weeks today."

"When do you expect her back?"

"This is Wednesday. She'll be back Saturday, in the evening—about nine o'clock, likely."

I felt a sharp sense of disappointment.

"I'm sorry, because I'll be gone then," I said, regretfully.

"Gone? No—why should you go? Don't go. She'll be so disappointed."

She would be disappointed—that beautiful creature! If she had said the words herself they could hardly have blessed me more. I was feeling a deep, strong longing to see her—a longing so supplicating,[13] so insistent, that it made me afraid. I said to myself: "I will go straight away from this place, for my peace of mind's sake."

"You see, she likes to have people come and stop with us—people who know things, and can talk—people like you. She delights in it; for she knows—oh, she knows nearly everything herself, and can talk, oh, like a bird—and the books she reads, why, you would be astonished. Don't go; it's only a little while, you know, and she'll be so disappointed."

---

12. A *daguerreotype* (də gerʹə tīpʹ) is a photograph produced by exposing light to a silver-coated copper plate, a process invented by Louis Daguerre in France in the mid-1800s.
13. *Supplicating* means "asking for in a humble or earnest manner; beseeching."

I heard the words, but hardly noticed them, I was so deep in my thinkings and strugglings. He left me, but I didn't know. Presently he was back, with the picture-case in his hand, and he held it open before me and said:

"There, now, tell her to her face you could have stayed to see her, and you wouldn't."

That second glimpse broke down my good resolution. I would stay and take the risk. That night we smoked the tranquil pipe, and talked till late about various things, but mainly about her; and certainly I had had no such pleasant and restful time for many a day. The Thursday followed and slipped comfortably away. Toward twilight a big miner from three miles away came—one of the grizzled, stranded pioneers—and gave us warm salutation,[14] clothed in grave and sober speech. Then he said:

"I only just dropped over to ask about the little madam, and when is she coming home. Any news from her?"

"Oh yes, a letter. Would you like to hear it, Tom?"

"Well, I should think I would, if you don't mind, Henry!"

Henry got the letter out of his wallet, and said he would skip some of the private phrases, if we were willing; then he went on and read the bulk of it—a loving, **sedate,** and altogether charming and gracious piece of handiwork, with a postscript full of affectionate regards and messages to Tom, and Joe, and

---

14. A *salutation* is an expression of greeting.

Analyze Cause-and-Effect Relationships In staying, what risk does the narrator decide he will face?

Vocabulary

sedate (si dātʹ) *adj.* quiet and restrained in style or manner; calm

Charley, and other close friends and neighbors.

As the reader finished, he glanced at Tom, and cried out:

"Oho, you're at it again! Take your hands away, and let me see your eyes. You always do that when I read a letter from her. I will write and tell her."

"Oh no, you mustn't, Henry. I'm getting old, you know, and any little disappointment makes me want to cry. I thought she'd be here herself, and now you've got only a letter."

"Well, now, what put that in your head? I thought everybody knew she wasn't coming till Saturday."

"Saturday! Why, come to think, I did know it. I wonder what's the matter with me lately? Certainly I knew it. Ain't we all getting ready for her? Well, I must be going now. But I'll be on hand when she comes, old man!"

Late Friday afternoon another gray veteran tramped over from his cabin a mile or so away, and said the boys wanted to have a little gaiety and a good time Saturday night, if Henry thought she wouldn't be too tired after her journey to be kept up.

"Tired? She tired! Oh, hear the man! Joe, *you* know she'd sit up six weeks to please any one of you!"

When Joe heard that there was a letter, he asked to have it read, and the loving messages in it for him broke the old fellow all up; but he said he was such an old wreck that *that* would happen to him if she only just mentioned his name. "Lord, we miss her so!" he said.

Analyze Cause-and-Effect Relationships What does Tom do when he hears the woman's letter read aloud?

Encountering the Unexpected What questions do you have about this comment?

Young bride, c. 1885-1990. American photographer. Black and white photograph. Private collection.

View the Art A daguerreotype of Henry's wife like the one pictured was on display in his home. Which characteristics or qualities does the woman in the daguerreotype here share with Henry's wife? Explain.

Saturday afternoon I found I was taking out my watch pretty often. Henry noticed it, and said, with a startled look:

"You don't think she ought to be here so soon, do you?"

I felt caught, and a little embarrassed; but I laughed, and said it was a habit of mine when I was in a state of expectancy. But he didn't seem quite satisfied; and from that time on he began to show uneasiness. Four times he walked me up the road to a point whence we could see a long distance; and there he would stand, shading

Analyze Cause-and-Effect Relationships Why does Henry become uneasy in this situation?

MARK TWAIN 23

his eyes with his hand, and looking. Several times he said:

"I'm getting worried, I'm getting right down worried. I know she's not due till about nine o'clock, and yet something seems to be trying to warn me that something's happened. You don't think anything has happened, do you?"

I began to get pretty thoroughly ashamed of him for his childishness; and at last, when he repeated that **imploring** question still another time, I lost my patience for the moment, and spoke pretty brutally to him. It seemed to shrivel him up and cow[15] him; and he looked so wounded and so humble after that, that I detested myself for having done the cruel and unnecessary thing. And so I was glad when Charley, another veteran, arrived toward the edge of the evening, and nestled up to Henry to hear the letter read, and talked over the preparations for the welcome. Charley fetched out one hearty speech after another, and did his best to drive away his friend's **bodings** and apprehensions.[16]

"Anything *happened* to her? Henry, that's pure nonsense. There isn't anything going to happen to her; just make your mind easy as to that. What did the letter say? Said she was well, didn't it? And said she'd be here by nine o'clock, didn't it? Did you ever know her to fail of her word? Why, you know you never did. Well, then, don't you fret; she'll *be* here, and that's absolutely certain, and as sure as you are born. Come, now, let's get to decorating—not much time left."

Pretty soon Tom and Joe arrived, and then all hands set about adorning the house with flowers. Toward nine the three miners said that as they had brought their instruments they might as well tune up, for the boys and girls would soon be arriving now, and hungry for a good, old-fashioned breakdown.[17] A fiddle, a banjo, and a clarinet—these were the instruments. The trio took their places side by side, and began to play some rattling dance-music, and beat time with their big boots.

It was getting very close to nine. Henry was standing in the door with his eyes directed up the road, his body swaying to the torture of his mental distress. He had been made to drink his wife's health and safety several times, and now Tom shouted:

"All hands stand by! One more drink, and she's here!"

Joe brought the glasses on a waiter,[18] and served the party. I reached for one of the two remaining glasses, but Joe growled, under his breath:

"Drop that! Take the other."

Which I did. Henry was served last. He had hardly swallowed his drink when the clock began to strike. He listened till it finished, his face growing pale and paler; then he said:

"Boys, I'm sick with fear. Help me—I want to lie down!"

> **"Anything *happened* to her? Henry, that's pure nonsense."**

---

15. To *cow* is to frighten with threats.
16. *Apprehensions* are fears or anxieties about what might happen.

Vocabulary

imploring (im plôr′ ing) *adj.* asking earnestly; begging
boding (bōd′ ing) *n.* a warning or an indication, especially of evil

17. Here, *breakdown* refers to a fast, lively country dance.
18. The *waiter*, in this case, is a small tray.

Foreshadowing What hint does this image give you about what might happen?

Encountering the Unexpected Why do you think Joe says this to the narrator?

Prospector pans for gold in Northern California, c. 1890. Hand-tinted photograph.

View the Art How might the lonely pursuit of prospecting for gold have influenced Henry to react the way he did when his wife never returned home?

They helped him to the sofa. He began to nestle and drowse, but presently spoke like one talking in his sleep, and said: "Did I hear horses' feet? Have they come?"

One of the veterans answered, close to his ear: "It was Jimmy Parrish come to say the party got delayed, but they're right up the road a piece, and coming along. Her horse is lame, but she'll be here in half an hour."

"Oh, I'm *so* thankful nothing has happened!"

He was asleep almost before the words were out of his mouth. In a moment those handy men had his clothes off, and had tucked him into his bed in the chamber where I had washed my hands. They closed the door and came back. Then they seemed preparing to leave; but I said: "Please don't go, gentlemen. She won't know me; I am a stranger."

They glanced at each other. Then Joe said:

"She? Poor thing, she's been dead nineteen years!"

"Dead?"

"That or worse. She went to see her folks half a year after she was married, and on her way back, on a Saturday evening, the Indians captured her within five miles of this place, and she's never been heard of since."

"And he lost his mind in consequence?"

"Never has been sane an hour since. But he only gets bad when that time of the year comes round. Then we begin to drop in here, three days before she's due, to encourage him up, and ask if he's heard from her, and Saturday we all come and fix up the house with flowers, and get everything ready for a dance. We've done it every year for nineteen years. The first Saturday there was twenty-seven of us, without counting the girls; there's only three of us now, and the girls are all gone. We drug him to sleep, or he would go wild; then he's all right for another year—thinks she's with him till the last three or four days come round; then he begins to look for her, and gets out his poor old letter, and we come and ask him to read it to us. Lord, she was a darling!"

After You Read

Respond and Think Critically

Respond and Interpret

1. Did the ending of the story surprise you? Why or why not?

2. (a) Describe how the narrator comes upon Henry's cottage. How is his cottage different from the other dwellings that the narrator has seen in the area? (b) Why is this difference surprising?

3. (a) Explain what the narrator learns at the end of the story about the woman. (b) Why do Henry's friends wait so long to reveal the truth to the narrator?

Analyze and Evaluate

4. What is the narrator's attitude toward the men who live in the log cabins? Support your answer with evidence from the story.

5. (a) Identify three or more ways that Twain builds suspense. (b) Which do you think was most effective?

6. (a) Why do you think Twain decides not to reveal Henry's wife's name? (b) Do you think this makes the story more effective? Explain.

Connect

7. **Big Idea** Encountering the Unexpected
(a) In what ways does the final twist in the plot change the way you think about the characters? (b) Do you think Twain intended you to change your ideas about the characters? Why or why not?

8. **Connect to Today** If "The Californian's Tale" were set in today's society, how would you expect Henry's friends to react on the anniversary of his wife's death?

Literary Element Foreshadowing

Although the ending of the story "The Californian's Tale" proves to be a surprise for most readers, Twain uses **foreshadowing** to hint at the ending. Foreshadowing can be conveyed by mood or mood shifts, by details of the setting or the characters that are strange or jarring, or by plot events that serve as clues as to how the story will be resolved.

1. Which details related to the setting and the characters foreshadow the ending of the story? Explain how each detail you mention provides a hint about the ending.

2. Which plot events help foreshadow the ending of the story? Explain how each event hints at this ending.

Review: Plot

As you learned on pages 8–9, writers use exposition to introduce the setting, the characters, and the **plot** of a story. In "The Californian's Tale," the exposition helps readers picture the land along the Stanislaus River, the cottage, and Henry. The exposition also helps readers enter into the events witnessed by the narrator once he enters the cottage. Turn to the beginning of "The Californian's Tale" and reread Twain's exposition.

Partner Activity Work with a classmate to fill in a graphic organizer like the one shown. In the graphic organizer, record details of the story that help readers gain their first impressions of the setting, characters, and plot. Share your organizer with the class.

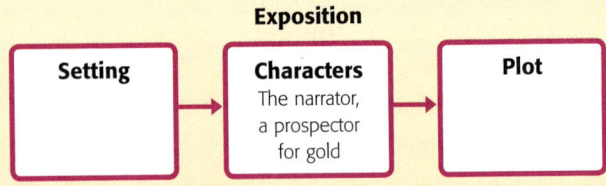

Reading Strategy Analyze Cause-and-Effect Relationships

ACT Skills Practice

1. What is a result of the trick Henry's friends play on him?

   A. Henry goes mad with grief.
   B. Henry's wife is captured by Indians.
   C. Henry enjoys a party with his neighbors once a year.
   D. Henry is all right for another year.

Vocabulary Practice

Practice with Word Parts For each boldfaced vocabulary word in the left column, identify the related word with a shared root in the right column. Write both words and underline the part they have in common. Use a printed or online dictionary to look up the meaning of the related word. Explain how it is related to the root of the vocabulary word.

1. **predecessor**   forebode
2. **solace**   deplorable
3. **sedate**   deceased
4. **imploring**   sedentary
5. **boding**   inconsolable

EXAMPLE
mal<u>ady</u>, mal<u>function</u>
A <u>mal</u>ady is a disease or disorder; it is something physically wrong with the body. To <u>mal</u>function is to function imperfectly or badly; it occurs when something goes wrong with a machine.

Connect to Science

Oral Research Report

Assignment Research the processes by which miners extracted gold from the land. Create a visual aid that helps to explain the process. Present the information in an oral report that includes a visual aid.

Investigate Generate four or five research questions, and derive your search terms from them. Use an Internet search engine and a library catalog. Decide which sources are most reliable by looking at the credentials of the author or sponsoring institution, as well as at the amount and kind of documentation given. Do not use unsigned sources or sources that do not come from reputable institutions or authorities. Take notes, and make an outline.

Create Create a visual to integrate into your word-processed document. Consider a flowchart showing steps in the process for different types of mining. Make your visual clear and precise. Provide a title, and number and/or label parts of the process. Place a source line (such as *Source:* Glencoe *The American Vision,* McPhearson, et al at the bottom of the graphic to give credit for information you used.

EXAMPLE:

	Mining for Gold	
Panning for Gold		
1.	2.	3.
Source:		

Report As you compile information in your report, cite your sources and evaluate their validity by using terms such as "well-researched" or "carefully documented." Use technical terms that are specific to your topic, but explain them for your audience.

Selection Resources For Selection Quizzes, eFlashcards, and Reading-Writing Connection activities, go to glencoe.com and enter QuickPass code GL59794u1.

Literary Perspective
on *Mark Twain*

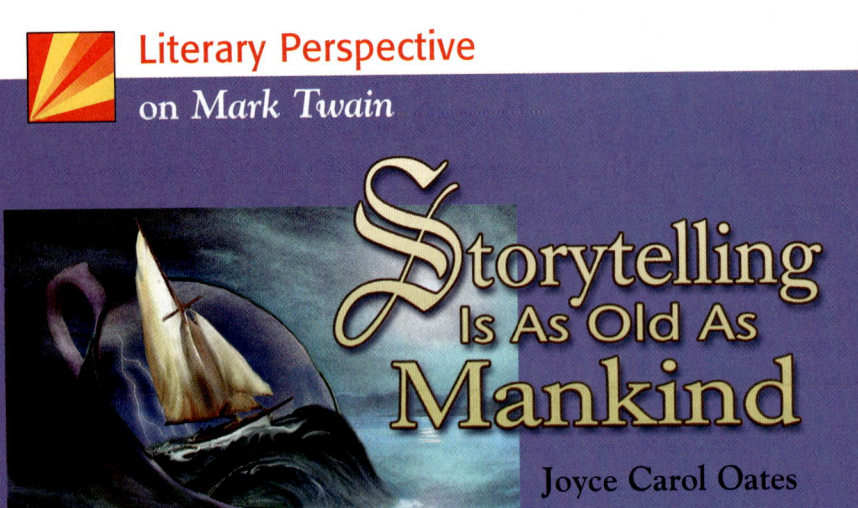

Storm In A Teacup. Cathy McKinty.

 **National Book Award Winner**

Learning Objectives

For pages 28–31

In studying this text, you will focus on the following objectives:

Reading:

Evaluating historical influences.

Analyzing informational text.

Set a Purpose for Reading
Read to discover the history of the short story and elements of fiction used by writers such as Mark Twain.

Build Background
A contemporary short story is a fictional narrative in prose containing the elements of plot, character, setting, theme, and point of view. In this excerpt from the introduction to the *Oxford Book of American Short Stories,* Joyce Carol Oates traces the history of the short story and how it has evolved with the voices of such writers as Mark Twain.

Reading Strategy
Evaluate Historical Influences
When you examine the social influences of a historical period on a literary work or genre you are **evaluating historical influences**. As you read, ask yourself, How has history influenced the short story? Take notes on a timeline like the one below.

| Egyptians write on papyri | Canterbury Tales | Mark Twain achieves popularity as an American writer |

The "literary" short story, the meticulously constructed short story, descends to us by way of the phenomenon of magazine publication, beginning in the nineteenth century, but has as its ancestor the oral tale.

We must assume that storytelling is as old as mankind, at least as old as spoken language. Reality is not enough for us—we crave the imagination's embellishments upon it. *In the beginning. Once upon a time. A long time ago there lived a princess who.* How the pulse quickens, hearing such beginnings! such promises of something new, strange, unexpected! . . .

Like a river fed by countless small streams, the modern short story derives from a multiplicity of sources. Historically, the earliest literary documents of which we have knowledge are Egyptian papyri[1] dating from 4000–3000 B.C., containing a work called, most intriguingly, *Tales of the Magicians*. The Middle Ages revered such secular works as fabliaux,[2]

---

1. *Papyri* are papers made from the stems or pith of the papyrus, which is a tall aquatic plant.
2. *Fabliaux* are medieval verse tales with comic themes about life.

Book of the Dead: Four Rudders of Heaven, Offerings to Osiris.
Egyptian Art. Papyrus. British Museum, London.

ballads,³ and verse romances; the Arabian *Thousand and One Nights*⁴ and the Latin tales and anecdotes of the *Gesta Romanorum*,⁵ collected before the end of the thirteenth century, as well as the one hundred tales of Boccaccio's *The Decameron*,⁶ and Chaucer's *Canterbury Tales*,⁷ were enormously popular for centuries. Storytelling as an oral art, like the folk ballad, was, or is, characteristic of non-literate cultures, for obvious reasons. Even the prolongation of light (by artificial means) had an effect upon the storytelling tradition of our ancestors. The rise in literacy marked the ebbing of interest in old fairy tales and ballads, as did the gradual stabilization of languages and the cessation⁸ of local dialects in which the tales and ballads had been told most effectively. (The Brothers Grimm⁹ noted this phenomenon: if, in High German, a fairy tale gained in superficial clarity, it "lost in flavor, and no longer had such a firm hold on the kernel of meaning.")

One of the signal accomplishments of American literature, most famously exemplified by the great commercial and critical success of Samuel Clemens, is the reclamation

---

3. *Ballads* are short narrative poems that are supposed to be sung. They have simple stanzas and a refrain and are often folk in origin.
4. *The Thousand and One Nights* is a collection of tales about Aladdin, Ali Baba, and Sinbad the Sailor. Their author and the date when they were written are unknown.
5. *Gesta Romanorum* is a collection of anecdotes and tales in Latin.
6. *Giovanni Boccacio* (1313–1375) was an Italian poet and scholar. He most likely wrote *The Decameron* from 1348 to 1353. *The Decameron*, which means "Ten Days' Work," contains one hundred stories.
7. *Geoffrey Chaucer* (1342/43–1400) was a famous English poet. *The Canterbury Tales*, his seminal work, tells the story of about thirty pilgrims who convene at a London Inn to travel to and from Thomas à Becket of Canterbury's shrine.
8. *Cessation* means "the act of coming to a stop."
9. *The Brothers Grimm* was the nickname for Jacob Ludwig Carl Grimm (1785–1863) and Wilhelm Carl Grimm (1786–1859), who wrote collections of folktales, including *Kinderund Hausmärchen,* which is commonly known as *Grimm's Fairy Tales.*

Informational Text

of that "lost" flavor—the use, as style, of dialect, regional, and strongly (often comically) vernacular[10] language. Of course, before Samuel Clemens cultivated the ingenuous-ironic persona of "Mark Twain," there were dialect writers and tale-tellers in America (for instance, Joel Chandler Harris, creator of the popular "Uncle Remus" stories[11]); but Mark Twain was a phenomenon of a kind previously unknown here—our first American writer to be avidly read, coast to coast, by all classes of Americans, from the most highborn to the least cultured and minimally literate. The development of mass-market newspapers and subscription book sales made this success possible, but it was the brilliant reclamation of the vernacular in Twain's work (the early "The Celebrated Jumping Frog of Calaveras County,"[12] for instance) that made him into so uniquely *American* a writer, our counterpart to Dickens.

Twain's rapid ascent was by way of popular newspapers, which syndicated features coast to coast, and his crowd-pleasing public performances, but the more typical outlet for a short story writer, particularly of self-consciously "literary" work, was the magazine. Virtually every writer, from Washington Irving[13] and Nathaniel Hawthorne[14] onward, began his or her career publishing short fiction in magazines before moving on to book publication; in the nineteenth century, such highly regarded, and, in some cases, high-paying magazines as *The North American Review, Harper's Monthly, Atlantic Monthly, Scribner's Monthly* (later *The Century*), *The Dial,* and *Graham's Magazine* (briefly edited by Edgar Allan Poe[15]) advanced the careers of writers who would otherwise have had financial difficulties in establishing themselves. In post-World War II America, the majority of short story writers publish in small-circulation "literary" magazines throughout their careers. It is all but unknown for a writer to publish a book of short stories without having published most of them in magazines beforehand.

Wooden Type Block. Marco Prozzo.

---

10. *Vernacular* means "the everyday speech of a country or region."
11. *Joel Chandler Harris* (1848–1908) was an American author of folktales. *Uncle Remus* was a character created by him in a series of adult and children's books.
12. *"The Celebrated Jumping Frog of Calaveras County"* is a tall tale that tells of a narrator who goes to the gold mining town of Angel's Camp and meets Simon Wheeler, who tells him the story of a pet frog that competed in jumping races.
13. *Washington Irving* (1783–1859) was an American novelist and short story writer.
14. *Nathaniel Hawthorne* (1804–1864) was a well-known American novelist and short story writer.
15. *Edgar Allan Poe* (1809–1849) was an American short story writer and poet.

Informational Text

The Printer, 1875. Adrien Ferdinand de Braekeleer. Oil on canvas, 78 x 68 cm. Koninklijk Museum voor Schone Kunsten, Antwerp, Belgium.

Respond and Think Critically

Respond and Interpret

1. Write a brief summary of the main ideas in this article before you answer the following questions. For help on writing a summary, see page 415.

2. (a) What is the earliest "ancestor" of the contemporary short story? (b) How is this heritage apparent in modern short stories you have read?

3. (a) What are some facets of Mark Twain's writing that recapture, as Oates writes, "that lost flavor" of American writing? (b) What do you think these elements of writing add to a literary work?

Analyze and Evaluate

4. (a) Why do you think short stories became popular selections for contemporary magazines? (b) Do you think that literature printed in magazines is any less significant than literature printed in books? Explain.

5. (a) Joyce Carol Oates is a prolific writer of fiction, including novels and short stories. What biases might she have about the craft of short story writing? (b) Do you think her biases affect her point of view in this excerpt? Why or why not?

Connect

6. (a) What did Oates claim made Mark Twain a "uniquely American writer"? (b) How is this trait represented in "The Californian's Tale"?

Vocabulary Workshop

Denotation and Connotation

Learning Objectives
In this workshop, you will focus on the following objective:

Vocabulary: Understanding denotation and connotation.

Literature Connection Mark Twain is a master at conveying suggestions both directly (through *denotation*, the literal meaning of words) and indirectly (through *connotation*, or implication).

> "Pretty soon Tom and Joe arrived, and then all hands set about adorning the house with flowers"
>
> —Mark Twain, from "The Californian's Tale"

In the quotation above, Twain uses the word *adorning*, instead of *decorating*, *ornamenting*, or *embellishing*. Although these words have a similar denotation, the connotations of *adorning* best fit the context. *Adorning* implies enhancing the appearance of something that is already beautiful in itself--namely, the "rose-clad" cottage that delighted the narrator.

A chart like the one below can help you analyze, or look more closely at, words—at their similarities, their differences, and their shades of meaning. Follow these instructions to create the chart:

- In the left-hand column of the chart, place the words you will analyze.
- Consult a dictionary to find definitions, or denotations, for them.
- In the second column of the chart, enter the definition for each term.
- In the third column of the chart, record ideas, images, or feelings that you associate with each word. Such associations are the word's connotations.

Vocabulary Terms
The **denotation** of a word is its literal meaning; the **connotation** of a word is its implied meaning, with the emotions it evokes.

Tip
If, during a test, you are asked about the denotation of a word, think about how you would define the word for someone else. To describe the word's connotation, think about the images and ideas the word brings to mind.

A Semantic Features Chart

Word	Denotation	Connotation
famishing	suffering from a lack of something necessary	starving, enduring terrible hunger

 **Literature** Online

Vocabulary For more vocabulary practice, go to glencoe.com and enter the QuickPass code GL59794u1.

Practice On a separate sheet of paper, copy and complete the chart. With your classmates, discuss the denotations and the connotations of the words you have chosen. Below the chart, explain briefly how words such as *bodings* contribute to the mood of the story and foreshadow its ending.

Before You Read
Contents of the Dead Man's Pocket

Meet Jack Finney
(1911–1995)

The author of novels, short stories, and television screenplays, Jack Finney is most famous as a science-fiction writer. Perhaps his best-known work is the novel *The Body Snatchers*, which he published in 1955. Renamed and reissued a year later as *Invasion of the Body Snatchers*, this science-fiction thriller was adapted into a film three times. Each version became a cult classic.

When the novel was first released in the mid-1950s, the age of McCarthyism, critics were quick to interpret it as an allegory based on the real fears of a Communist takeover in the United States. Finney scoffed at that interpretation, claiming that his novel was nothing more than popular entertainment. "It was just a story meant to entertain, and with no more meaning than that," Finney once stated, adding that "the idea of writing a whole book in order to say that it's not really a good thing for us all to be alike . . . makes me laugh."

> "One should never use the word 'fun' as an adjective except when referring to the writings of Jack Finney."
>
> —The San Francisco Examiner

Born in Milwaukee, Wisconsin, Finney grew up in suburban Chicago. After graduating from Knox College in Galesburg, Illinois, Finney moved to New York City, where he worked as a writer for an advertising agency.

In 1946 he published his first short story, "The Widow's Walk," which won a special prize in an *Ellery Queen's Mystery Magazine* contest. After that breakthrough, he continued to write and publish short stories in many popular magazines, including *The Saturday Evening Post*, *Collier's*, and *McCall's*.

In the early 1950s, Finney, his wife, and their two children moved from New York City to Marin County, California. In 1954, he published his first novel, *5 Against the House*. That novel, *Assault on a Queen* (1959), and *Good Neighbor Sam* (1963) were all adapted into popular films.

After the success of *Invasion of the Body Snatchers*, Finney continued to write science fiction, although he resisted classification as a science-fiction author, considering himself a fantasy writer who was most interested in ordinary people's responses to extraordinary situations. In 1957 he published a short-story collection entitled *The Third Level*, which contains the story you are about to read.

Author Search For more about Jack Finney, go to glencoe.com and enter QuickPass code GL59794u1.

Literature and Reading Preview

Connect to the Story
What are your priorities in life and how well do you divide your attention among them? List your priorities. After each priority write a comment about whether you should spend more time or less time or are spending the right amount of time on that priority.

Build Background
This story takes place in New York City, probably during the 1950s—a time before personal computers and widespread use of photocopying machines. Therefore, the main character types documents on a portable typewriter and uses carbon paper—thin, ink-coated sheets of paper placed between two pieces of writing paper—to make a copy of a typewritten document.

Set Purposes for Reading

Big Idea Encountering the Unexpected
As you read "Contents of the Dead Man's Pocket," ask yourself, How does the main character react when he encounters the unexpected?

Literary Element Conflict
Conflict is the struggle between opposing forces in a drama or story. An **external conflict** exists when a character struggles against an outside force, such as another person, nature, or society. An **internal conflict** is a struggle that takes place within the mind of a character who is torn between opposing feelings or goals. As you read, ask yourself, Which type of conflict does Tom experience in this story?

Reading Strategy Respond to Characters
When you respond to what you are reading, you interact with the text in an important way. To **respond to characters** in a literary work, ask yourself questions about what you like, what you do not like, what surprises you, and how you feel about the characters in a story. As you read "Contents of the Dead Man's Pocket," ask yourself, How does Tom make you feel?

Tip: Take Notes To better understand your responses to characters, take notes about your reactions to characters as you read.

Learning Objectives
For pages 33–51

In studying this text, you will focus on the following objectives:

Literary Study: Analyzing conflict.

Reading: Responding to characters.

Vocabulary

convoluted (kon′ və lōō′ tid) *adj.* turned in or wound up upon itself; coiled; twisted; p. 37 *Instead of a flat piece of wood, the ornate, antique railing was convoluted.*

improvised (im′ prə vīzd′) *adj.* invented, composed, or done without preparation; p. 38 *I was unprepared for John's strange question and had to give an improvised answer.*

taut (tôt) *adj.* tense; tight; p. 39 *The leash grew taut and straight when the dog leaped forward.*

pent-up (pent′ up) *adj.* not expressed or released; held in; p. 42 *I remained calm until I hung up the phone, but then my pent-up feelings made me burst into tears.*

reveling (rev′ əl ing) *adj.* taking great pleasure; p. 42 *Reveling in delight, the little boy ran up and down the aisle of toys.*

Tip: Analogies To solve an analogy, remember that the relationship might be a synonym, an antonym, a part to whole, or an object and a key quality of the object.

Contents of the Dead Man's Pocket

Jack Finney

Room in New York, 1932. Edward Hopper. Oil on canvas, 29 x 36 in. Sheldon Memorial Art Gallery, University of Nebraska–Lincoln, F. M. Hall Collection. 1936.H-166.

At the little living-room desk Tom Benecke rolled two sheets of flimsy and a heavier top sheet, carbon paper sandwiched between them, into his portable.[1] *Inter-office Memo,* the top sheet was headed, and he typed tomorrow's date just below this; then he glanced at a creased yellow sheet, covered with his own handwriting, beside the typewriter. "Hot in here," he muttered to himself. Then, from the short hallway at his back, he heard the muffled clang of wire coat hangers in the bedroom closet, and at this reminder of what his wife was doing he thought: Hot, hell—guilty conscience.

He got up, shoving his hands into the back pockets of his gray wash slacks,[2] stepped to the living-room window beside the desk and stood breathing on the glass, watching the expanding circlet of mist, staring down through the autumn night at Lexington Avenue, eleven stories below. He was a tall, lean, dark-haired young man in a pullover sweater, who looked as though he had played not football, probably, but basketball in college. Now he placed the heels of his hands against the top edge of the lower window frame and shoved upward. But as usual the window didn't budge, and he had to lower his hands and then shoot them hard upward to jolt the window open a few inches. He dusted his hands, muttering.

But still he didn't begin his work. He crossed the room to the hallway entrance and, leaning against the doorjamb, hands shoved into his back pockets again, he called, "Clare?" When his wife answered, he said, "Sure you don't mind going alone?"

"No." Her voice was muffled, and he knew her head and shoulders were in the bedroom closet. Then the tap of her high heels sounded on the wood floor and she appeared at the end of the little hallway,

---

1. Before the laptop computer, one might type on a compact, fairly lightweight typewriter called a *portable.*
2. *Wash slacks* are pants that, because they are cotton, can be washed instead of dry-cleaned.

Reference, 1991. Jeremy Annett. Oil on canvas. Private collection.

View the Art This painting shows a room filled with papers and books. What do these items tell you about the personality traits of the room's occupant? Are any of these traits shared by Tom?

wearing a slip, both hands raised to one ear, clipping on an earring. She smiled at him—a slender, very pretty girl with light brown, almost blonde, hair—her prettiness emphasized by the pleasant nature that showed in her face. "It's just that I hate you to miss this movie; you wanted to see it too." "Yeah, I know." He ran his fingers through his hair. "Got to get this done though."

She nodded, accepting this. Then, glancing at the desk across the living room, she said, "You work too much, though, Tom—and too hard."

He smiled. "You won't mind though, will you, when the money comes rolling in and I'm known as the Boy Wizard of Wholesale Groceries?"

"I guess not." She smiled and turned back toward the bedroom.

At his desk again, Tom lighted a cigarette; then a few moments later as Clare appeared, dressed and ready to leave, he set it on the rim of the ash tray. "Just after seven," she said. "I can make the beginning of the first feature."

He walked to the front-door closet to help her on with her coat. He kissed her then and, for an instant, holding her close, smelling the perfume she had used, he was tempted to go with her; it was not actually true that he had to work tonight, though he very much wanted to. This was his own project, unannounced as yet in his office, and it could be postponed. But then they won't see it till Monday, he thought once again, and if I give it to the boss tomorrow he might read it over the week-end . . . "Have a good time," he said aloud. He gave his wife a little swat and opened the door for her, feeling the air from the building hallway, smelling faintly of floor wax, stream gently past his face.

He watched her walk down the hall, flicked a hand in response as she waved, and then he started to close the door, but it resisted for a moment. As the door opening narrowed, the current of warm air from the

Respond to Characters How do you feel about Tom's decision to miss the movie? Would you have made the same choice?

Conflict What exterior conflict is implied by the dialogue between Tom and his wife, Clare?

hallway, channeled through this smaller opening now, suddenly rushed past him with accelerated force. Behind him he heard the slap of the window curtains against the wall and the sound of paper fluttering from his desk, and he had to push to close the door.

Turning, he saw a sheet of white paper drifting to the floor in a series of arcs, and another sheet, yellow, moving toward the window, caught in the dying current flowing through the narrow opening. As he watched, the paper struck the bottom edge of the window and hung there for an instant, plastered against the glass and wood. Then as the moving air stilled completely the curtains swinging back from the wall to hang free again, he saw the yellow sheet drop to the window ledge and slide over out of sight.

He ran across the room, grasped the bottom edge of the window and tugged, staring through the glass. He saw the yellow sheet, dimly now in the darkness outside, lying on the ornamental ledge a yard below the window. Even as he watched, it was moving, scraping slowly along the ledge, pushed by the breeze that pressed steadily against the building wall. He heaved on the window with all his strength and it shot open with a bang, the window weight rattling in the casing. But the paper was past his reach and, leaning out into the night, he watched it scud[3] steadily along the ledge to the south, half plastered against the building wall. Above the muffled sound of the street traffic far below, he could hear the dry scrape of its movement, like a leaf on the pavement.

The living room of the next apartment to the south projected a yard or more farther out toward the street than this one; because of this the Beneckes paid seven and a half dollars less rent than their neighbors. And now the yellow sheet, sliding along the stone ledge, nearly invisible in the night, was stopped by the projecting blank wall of the next apartment. It lay motionless, then, in the corner formed by the two walls—a good five yards away, pressed firmly against the ornate corner ornament of the ledge, by the breeze that moved past Tom Benecke's face.

He knelt at the window and stared at the yellow paper for a full minute or more, waiting for it to move, to slide off the ledge and fall, hoping he could follow its course to the street, and then hurry down in the elevator and retrieve it. But it didn't move, and then he saw that the paper was caught firmly between a projection of the **convoluted** corner ornament and the ledge. He thought about the poker from the fireplace, then the broom, then the mop—discarding each thought as it occurred to him. There was nothing in the apartment long enough to reach that paper.

It was hard for him to understand that he actually had to abandon it—it was ridiculous—and he began to curse. Of all the papers on his desk, why did it have to be this one in particular! On four long Saturday afternoons he had stood in supermarkets counting the people who passed certain displays, and the results were scribbled on that yellow sheet. From stacks of trade publications, gone over page by page in snatched half hours at work and during evenings at home, he had copied facts, quotations and figures onto that sheet. And he had carried it with him to the Public Library on Fifth Avenue, where he'd spent a dozen lunch hours and early evenings adding more. All were needed to support and lend authority to his idea for a new grocery-store display method; without them his idea was a mere opinion. And there they all lay, in his own

---

3. To *scud* is to run or move swiftly.

Vocabulary

convoluted (kon′ və loo′ tid) *adj.* turned in or wound up upon itself; coiled; twisted

improvised shorthand—countless hours of work—out there on the ledge.

For many seconds he believed he was going to abandon the yellow sheet, that there was nothing else to do. The work could be duplicated. But it would take two months, and the time to present this idea, was *now*, for use in the spring displays. He struck his fist on the window ledge. Then he shrugged. Even though his plan were adopted, he told himself, it wouldn't bring him a raise in pay—not immediately, anyway, or as a direct result. It won't bring me a promotion either, he argued—not of itself.

But just the same, and he couldn't escape the thought, this and other independent projects, some already done and others planned for the future, would gradually mark him out from the score of other young men in his company. They were the way to change from a name on the payroll to a name in the minds of the company officials. They were the beginning of the long, long climb to where he was determined to be, at the very top. And he knew he was going out there in the darkness, after the yellow sheet fifteen feet beyond his reach.

> The mental picture of himself sidling along the ledge outside was absurd—

By a kind of instinct, he instantly began making his intention acceptable to himself by laughing at it. The mental picture of himself sidling along the ledge outside was absurd—it was actually comical—and he smiled. He imagined himself describing it; it would make a good story at the office and, it occurred to him, would add a special interest and importance to his memorandum, which would do it no harm at all.

To simply go out and get his paper was an easy task—he could be back here with it in less than two minutes—and he knew he wasn't deceiving himself. The ledge, he saw, measuring it with his eye, was about as wide as the length of his shoe, and perfectly flat. And every fifth row of brick in the face of the building, he remembered—leaning out, he verified this—was indented half an inch, enough for the tips of his fingers, enough to maintain balance easily. It occurred to him that if this ledge and wall were only a yard aboveground—as he knelt at the window staring out, this thought was the final confirmation of his intention—he could move along the ledge indefinitely.

On a sudden impulse, he got to his feet, walked to the front closet and took out an old tweed jacket, it would be cold outside. He put it on and buttoned it as he crossed the room rapidly toward the open window. In the back of his mind he knew he'd better hurry and get this over with before he thought too much, and at the window he didn't allow himself to hesitate.

Encountering the Unexpected How has the unexpected experience of dropping the yellow paper affected Tom so far?

Respond to Characters What is Tom's highest priority? How do you feel about his priorities?

Vocabulary

improvised (im′ prə vīzd´) *adj.* invented, composed, or done without preparation

Encountering the Unexpected How does Tom try to combat his fear of falling?

He swung a leg over the sill, then felt for and found the ledge a yard below the window with his foot. Gripping the bottom of the window frame very tightly and carefully, he slowly ducked his head under it, feeling on his face the sudden change from the warm air of the room to the chill outside. With infinite care he brought out his other leg, his mind concentrating on what he was doing. Then he slowly stood erect. Most of the putty, dried out and brittle, had dropped off the bottom edging of the window frame, he found, and the flat wooden edging provided a good gripping surface, a half inch or more deep, for the tips of his fingers.

Now, balanced easily and firmly, he stood on the ledge outside in the slight, chill breeze, eleven stories above the street, staring into his own lighted apartment, odd and different-seeming now.

First his right hand, then his left, he carefully shifted his finger-tip grip from the puttyless window edging to an indented row of bricks directly to his right. It was hard to take the first shuffling sideways step then—to make himself move—and the fear stirred in his stomach, but he did it, again by not allowing himself time to think. And now—with his chest, stomach, and the left side of his face pressed against the rough cold brick—his lighted apartment was suddenly gone, and it was much darker out here than he had thought.

Without pause he continued—right foot, left foot, right foot, left—his shoe soles shuffling and scraping along the rough stone, never lifting from it, fingers sliding along the exposed edging of brick. He moved on the balls of his feet, heels lifted slightly; the ledge was not quite as wide as he'd expected. But leaning slightly inward toward the face of the building and pressed against it, he could feel his balance firm and secure, and moving along the ledge was quite as easy as he had thought it would be. He could hear the buttons of his jacket scraping steadily along the rough bricks and feel them catch momentarily, tugging a little, at each mortared crack. He simply did not permit himself to look down, though the compulsion to do so never left him; nor did he allow himself actually to think. Mechanically—right foot, left foot, over and again—he shuffled along crabwise, watching the projecting wall ahead loom steadily closer. . . .

Then he reached it and, at the corner—he'd decided how he was going to pick up the paper—he lifted his right foot and placed it carefully on the ledge that ran along the projecting wall at a right angle to the ledge on which his other foot rested. And now, facing the building, he stood in the corner formed by the two walls, one foot on the ledging of each, a hand on the shoulder-high indentation of each wall. His forehead was pressed directly into the corner against the cold bricks, and now he carefully lowered first one hand, then the other, perhaps a foot farther down, to the next indentation in the rows of bricks.

Very slowly, sliding his forehead down the trough of the brick corner and bending his knees, he lowered his body toward the paper lying between his outstretched feet. Again he lowered his fingerholds another foot and bent his knees still more, thigh muscles **taut**, his forehead sliding and bumping down the brick V. Half squatting now, he dropped his left hand to the next indentation and then slowly reached with his right hand toward the paper between his feet.

Respond to Characters *What is your reaction to Tom's current situation?*

Vocabulary
taut (tôt) *adj.* tense; tight

Conflict *What is Tom's internal conflict in this passage?*

Crystallized Abstraction (Day), 2001. Diana Ong. Computer graphics.

View the Art How does Diana Ong's use of color, lines, and shapes reflect the mood of the story and the crisis that Tom is facing?

He couldn't quite touch it, and his knees now were pressed against the wall; he could bend them no farther. But by ducking his head another inch lower, the top of his head now pressed against the bricks, he lowered his right shoulder and his fingers had the paper by a corner, pulling it loose. At the same instant he saw, between his legs and far below, Lexington Avenue stretched out for miles ahead.

He saw, in that instant, the Loew's theater sign, blocks ahead past Fiftieth Street; the miles of traffic signals, all green now; the lights of cars and street lamps; countless neon signs; and the moving black dots of people. And a violent instantaneous explosion of absolute terror roared through him. For a motionless instant he saw himself externally—bent practically double, balanced on this narrow ledge, nearly half his body projecting out above the street far below—and he began to tremble violently, panic flaring through his mind and muscles, and he felt the blood rush from the surface of his skin.

In the fractional moment before horror paralyzed him, as he stared between his legs

Respond to Characters Why does Tom feel a surge of terror when he actually grasps the yellow paper?

at that terrible length of street far beneath him, a fragment of his mind raised his body in a spasmodic jerk to an upright position again, but so violently that his head scraped hard against the wall, bouncing off it, and his body swayed outward to the knife edge of balance, and he very nearly plunged backward and fell. Then he was leaning far into the corner again, squeezing and pushing into it, not only his face but his chest and stomach, his back arching; and his fingertips clung with all the pressure of his pulling arms to the shoulder-high half-inch indentation in the bricks.

He was more than trembling now; his whole body was racked with a violent shuddering beyond control, his eyes squeezed so tightly shut it was painful, though he was past awareness of that. His teeth were exposed in a frozen grimace, the strength draining like water from his knees and calves. It was extremely likely, he knew, that he would faint, to slump down along the wall, his face scraping, and then drop backward, a limp weight, out into nothing. And to save his life he concentrated on holding onto consciousness, drawing deliberate deep breaths of cold air into his lungs, fighting to keep his senses aware.

Then he knew that he would not faint, but he could not stop shaking nor open his eyes. He stood where he was, breathing deeply, trying to hold back the terror of the glimpse he had of what lay below him; and he knew he had made a mistake in not making himself stare down at the street, getting used to it and accepting it, when he had first stepped out onto the ledge.

It was impossible to walk back. He simply could not do it. He couldn't bring himself to make the slightest movement. The strength was gone from his legs; his shivering hands—numb, cold and desperately rigid—had lost all deftness; his easy ability to move and balance was gone. Within a step or two, if he tried to move, he knew that he would stumble clumsily and fall.

Seconds passed, with the chill faint wind pressing the side of his face, and he could hear the toned-down volume of the street traffic far beneath him. Again and again he slowed and then stopped, almost to silence; then presently, even this high, he would hear the click of the traffic signals and the subdued roar of the cars starting up again. During a lull in the street sounds, he called out. Then he was shouting *"Help!"* so loudly it rasped his throat. But he felt the steady pressure of the wind, moving between his face and the blank wall, snatch up his cries as he uttered them, and he knew they must sound directionless and distant. And he remembered how habitually, here in New York, he himself heard and ignored shouts in the night. If anyone heard him, there was no sign of it, and presently Tom Benecke knew he had to try moving; there was nothing else he could do.

Eyes squeezed shut, he watched scenes in his mind like scraps of motion-picture film—he could not stop them. He saw himself stumbling suddenly sideways as he crept along the ledge and saw his upper body arc outward, arms flailing. He saw a dangling shoestring caught between the ledge and the sole of his other shoe, saw a foot start to move, to be stopped with a jerk, and felt his balance leaving him. He saw himself falling with a terrible speed as his body revolved in the air, knees clutched tight to his chest, eyes squeezed shut, moaning softly.

Out of utter necessity, knowing that any of these thoughts might be reality in the very next seconds, he was slowly able to shut his mind against every thought but what he now began to do. With fear-soaked slowness, he slid his left foot an inch or two toward his own impossibly

---

Encountering the Unexpected *What other unexpected experiences does Tom have once he is on the ledge?*

distant window. Then he slid the fingers of his shivering left hand a corresponding distance. For a moment he could not bring himself to lift his right foot from one ledge to the other; then he did it, and became aware of the harsh exhalation of air from his throat and realized that he was panting. As his right hand, then, began to slide along the brick edging, he was astonished to feel the yellow paper pressed to the bricks underneath his stiff fingers, and he uttered a terrible, abrupt bark that might have been a laugh or a moan. He opened his mouth and took the paper in his teeth, pulling it out from under his fingers.

By a kind of trick—by concentrating his entire mind on first his left foot, then his left hand, then the other foot, then the other hand—he was able to move, almost imperceptibly, trembling steadily, very nearly without thought. But he could feel the terrible strength of the **pent-up** horror on just the other side of the flimsy barrier he had erected in his mind; and he knew that if it broke through he would lose this thin artificial control of his body.

During one slow step he tried keeping his eyes closed; it made him feel safer, shutting him off a little from the fearful reality of where he was. Then a sudden rush of giddiness swept over him and he had to open his eyes wide, staring sideways at the cold rough brick and angled lines of mortar, his cheek tight against the building. He kept his eyes open then, knowing that if he once let them flick outward, to stare for an instant at the lighted windows across the street, he would be past help.

He didn't know how many dozens of tiny sidling steps he had taken, his chest, belly and face pressed to the wall; but he knew the slender hold he was keeping on his mind and body was going to break. He had a sudden mental picture of his apartment on just the other side of this wall—warm, cheerful, incredibly spacious. And he saw himself striding through it, lying down on the floor on his back, arms spread wide, **reveling** in its unbelievable security. The impossible remoteness of this utter safety, the contrast between it and where he now stood, was more than he could bear. And the barrier broke then, and the fear of the awful height he stood on coursed through his nerves and muscles.

A fraction of his mind knew he was going to fall, and he began taking rapid blind steps with no feeling of what he was doing, sidling with a clumsy desperate swiftness, fingers scrabbling along the brick, almost hopelessly resigned to the sudden backward pull and swift motion outward and down. Then his moving left hand slid onto not brick but sheer emptiness, an impossible gap in the face of the wall, and he stumbled.

His right foot smashed into his left anklebone; he staggered sideways, began falling, and the claw of his hand cracked against glass and wood, slid down it, and his finger tips were pressed hard on the puttyless edging of his window. His right hand smacked gropingly beside it as he fell to his knees; and, under the full weight and direct downward pull of his sagging body, the open window dropped

---

Respond to Characters How does Tom try to cope with his fear?

Vocabulary

pent-up (pent′ up) *adj.* not expressed or released; held in

Conflict What feeling is Tom attempting to overcome in this passage?

Vocabulary

reveling (rev′ əl ing) *adj.* taking great pleasure

shudderingly in its frame till it closed and his wrists struck the sill and were jarred off.

For a single moment he knelt, knee bones against stone on the very edge of the ledge, body swaying and touching nowhere else, fighting for balance. Then he lost it, his shoulders plunging backward, and he flung his arms forward, his hands smashing against the window casing on either side; and—his body moving backward—his fingers clutched the narrow wood stripping of the upper pane.

For an instant he hung suspended between balance and falling, his finger tips pressed onto the quarter-inch wood strips. Then, with utmost delicacy, with a focused concentration of all his senses, he increased even further the strain on his finger tips hooked to these slim edgings of wood. Elbows slowly bending, he began to draw the full weight of his upper body forward, knowing that the instant his fingers slipped off these quarter-inch strips he'd plunge backward and be falling. Elbows imperceptibly bending, body shaking with the strain, the sweat starting from his forehead in great sudden drops, he pulled, his entire being and thought concentrated in his finger tips. Then suddenly, the strain slackened and ended, his chest touching the window sill, and he was kneeling on the ledge, his forehead pressed to the glass of the closed window.

Dropping his palms to the sill, he stared into his living room—at the red-brown davenport across the room, and a magazine he had left there; at the pictures on the walls and the gray rug; the entrance to the hallway; and at his papers, typewriter and desk, not two feet from his nose. A movement from his desk caught his eye and he saw that it was a thin curl of blue smoke; his cigarette, the ash long, was still burning in the ash tray where he'd left it—this was past all belief—only a few minutes before.

His head moved, and in faint reflection from the glass before him he saw the yellow paper clenched in his front teeth. Lifting a hand from the sill he took it from his mouth; the moistened corner parted from the paper, and he spat it out.

> "he drew back his right hand, palm facing the glass, and then struck the glass with the heel of his hand."

For a moment, in the light from the living room, he stared wonderingly at the yellow sheet in his hand and then crushed it into the side pocket of his jacket.

He couldn't open the window. It had been pulled not completely closed, but its lower edge was below the level of the outside sill; there was no room to get his fingers underneath it. Between the upper sash and the lower was a gap not wide enough—reaching up, he tried—to get his fingers into; he couldn't push it open. The upper window panel, he knew from long experience, was impossible to move, frozen tight with dried paint.

Very carefully observing his balance, the finger tips of his left hand again hooked to the narrow stripping of the window casing, he drew back his right hand, palm facing the glass, and then struck the glass with the heel of his hand.

His arm rebounded from the pane, his body tottering, and he knew he didn't dare strike a harder blow.

But in the security and relief of his new position, he simply smiled; with only a sheet of glass between him and the room just before him, it was not possible that

JACK FINNEY

William Street at Night, 1981. Richard Haas. Watercolor, 33¼ x 23 in.

View the Art This painting depicts a grand city building. Is this the sort of building you imagine Tom living in? Why or why not?

there wasn't a way past it. Eyes narrowing, he thought for a few moments about what to do. Then his eyes widened, for nothing occurred to him. But still he felt calm: the trembling, he realized, had stopped. At the back of his mind there still lay the thought that once he was again in his home, he could give release to his feelings. He actually would lie on the floor, rolling, clenching tufts of the rug in his hands. He would literally run across the room, free to move as he liked, jumping on the floor, testing and reveling in its absolute security, letting the relief flood through him, draining the fear from his mind and body. His yearning for this was astonishingly intense, and somehow he understood that he had better keep this feeling at bay.

He took a half dollar from his pocket and struck it against the pane, but without any hope that the glass would break and with very little disappointment when it did not. After a few moments of thought he drew his leg up onto the ledge and picked loose the knot of his shoelace. He slipped off the shoe and, holding it across the instep, drew back his arm as far as he dared and struck the leather heel against the glass. The pane rattled, but he knew he'd been a long way from breaking it. His foot was cold and he slipped the shoe back on. He shouted again, experimentally, and then once more, but there was no answer.

The realization suddenly struck him that he might have to wait here till Clare came home, and for a moment the thought was funny. He could see Clare opening the front door, withdrawing her key from the lock, closing the door behind her and then glancing up to see him crouched on the other side of the window. He could see her rush across the room, face astounded and frightened, and hear himself shouting instructions: "Never mind how I got here! Just open the wind—" She couldn't open it, he remembered, she'd never been able to; she'd always had to call him. She'd have to get the building superintendent or a neighbor, and he pictured himself smiling and answering their questions as he climbed in. "I just wanted to get a breath of fresh air, so—"

He couldn't possibly wait here till Clare came home. It was the second feature she'd wanted to see, and she'd left in time to see the first. She'd be another three hours or—He glanced at his watch; Clare had been gone eight minutes. It wasn't possible, but only eight minutes ago he had kissed his wife good-by. She wasn't even at the theater yet!

It would be four hours before she could possibly be home, and he tried to picture himself kneeling out here, finger tips hooked to these narrow strippings, while first one movie, preceded by a slow listing of credits, began, developed, reached its climax and then finally ended. There'd be a newsreel next, maybe, and then an animated cartoon, and then interminable scenes from coming pictures. And then, once more, the beginning of a full-length picture—while all the time he hung out here in the night.

He might possibly get to his feet, but he was afraid to try. Already his legs were cramped, his thigh muscles tired; his knees hurt, his feet felt numb and his hands were stiff. He couldn't possibly stay out here for four hours, or anywhere near it. Long before that his legs and arms would give out; he would be forced to try changing his position often—stiffly, clumsily, his coordination and strength gone—and he would fall. Quite

---

Respond to Characters How have your feelings toward Tom changed? Explain.

Encountering the Unexpected What does Tom do on the ledge to try to regain his composure?

realistically, he knew that he would fall; no one could stay out here on this ledge for four hours.

A dozen windows in the apartment building across the street were lighted. Looking over his shoulder, he could see the top of a man's head behind the newspaper he was reading; in another window he saw the blue-gray flicker of a television screen. No more than twenty-odd yards from his back were scores of people, and if just one of them would walk idly to his window and glance out. . . . For some moments he stared over his shoulder at the lighted rectangles, waiting. But no one appeared. The man reading his paper turned a page and then continued his reading. A figure passed another of the windows and was immediately gone.

In the inside pocket of his jacket he found a little sheaf of papers, and he pulled one out and looked at it in the light from the living room. It was an old letter, an advertisement of some sort; his name and address, in purple ink, were on a label pasted to the envelope. Gripping one end of the envelope in his teeth, he twisted it into a tight curl. From his shirt pocket he brought out a book of matches. He didn't dare let go the casing with both hands but, with the twist of paper in his teeth, he opened the matchbook with his free hand; then he bent one of the matches in two without tearing it from the folder, its red-tipped end now touching the striking surface. With his thumb, he rubbed the red tip across the striking area.

He did it again, then again, and still again, pressing harder each time, and the match suddenly flared, burning his thumb. But he kept it alight, cupping the matchbook in his hand and shielding it with his body. He held the flame to the paper in his mouth till it caught. Then he snuffed out the match flame with his thumb and forefinger, careless of the burn, and replaced the book in his pocket. Taking the paper twist in his hand, he held it flame down, watching the flame crawl up the paper, till it flared bright. Then he held it behind him over the street, moving it from side to side, watching it over his shoulder, the flame flickering and guttering in the wind.

There were three letters in his pocket and he lighted each of them, holding each till the flame touched his hand and then dropping it to the street below. At one point, watching over his shoulder while the last of the letters burned, he saw the man across the street put down his paper and stand—even seeming, to Tom, to glance toward his window. But when he moved, it was only to walk across the room and disappear from sight.

There were a dozen coins in Tom Benecke's pocket and he dropped them, three or four at a time. But if they struck anyone, or if anyone noticed their falling, no one connected them with their source, and no one glanced upward.

His arms had begun to tremble from the steady strain of clinging to this narrow perch, and he did not know what to do now and was terribly frightened. Clinging to the window stripping with one hand, he again searched his pockets. But now—he had left his wallet on his dresser when he'd changed clothes—there was nothing left but the yellow sheet. It occurred to him irrelevantly that his death on the sidewalk below would be an eternal mystery; the window closed—why, how, and from where could he have fallen? No one would be able to identify his body for a time, either—the thought was somehow unbearable and increased his fear. All they'd find

---

Respond to Characters *What does this action suggest about Tom's state?*

in his pockets would be the yellow sheet. Contents of the dead man's pockets, he thought, *one sheet of paper bearing penciled notations—incomprehensible.*

He understood fully that he might actually be going to die; his arms, maintaining his balance on the ledge, were trembling steadily now. And it occurred to him then with all the force of a revelation that, if he fell, all he was ever going to have out of life he would then, abruptly, have had. Nothing, then, could ever be changed; and nothing more—no least experience or pleasure—could ever be added to his life. He wished, then, that he had not allowed his wife to go off by herself tonight—and on similar nights. He thought of all the evenings he had spent away from her, working; and he regretted them. He thought wonderingly of his fierce ambition and of the direction his life had taken; he thought of the hours he'd spent by himself, filling the yellow sheet that had brought him out here. *Contents of the dead man's pockets,* he thought with sudden fierce anger, *a wasted life.*

He was simply not going to cling here till he slipped and fell; he told himself that now. There was one last thing he could try; he had been aware of it for some moments, refusing to think about it, but now he faced it. Kneeling here on the ledge, the finger tips of one hand pressed to the narrow strip of wood, he could, he knew, draw his other hand back a yard perhaps, fist clenched tight, doing it very slowly till he sensed the outer limit of balance, then, as hard as he was able from the distance, he could drive his fist forward against the glass. If it broke, his fist smashing through, he was safe; he might cut himself badly, and probably would, but with his arm inside the room, he would be secure. But if the glass did not break, the rebound, flinging his arm back, would topple him off the ledge. He was certain of that.

He tested his plan. The fingers of his left hand clawlike on the little stripping, he drew back his other fist until his body began teetering backward. But he had no leverage now—he could feel that there would be no force to his swing—and he moved his fist slowly forward till he rocked forward on his knees again and could sense that his swing would carry its greatest force. Glancing down, however, measuring the distance from his fist to the glass, he saw that it was less than two feet.

It occurred to him that he could raise his arm over his head, to bring it down against the glass. But, experimenting in slow motion, he knew it would be an awkward girl-like blow without the force of a driving punch, and not nearly enough to break the glass.

Facing the window, he had to drive a blow from the shoulder, he knew now, at a distance of less than two feet; and he did not know whether it would break through the heavy glass. It might; he could picture it happening, he could feel it in the nerves of his arm. And it might not; he could feel that too—feel his fist striking this glass and being instantaneously flung back by the unbreaking pane, feel the fingers of his other hand breaking loose, nails scraping along the casing as he fell.

He waited, arm drawn back, fist balled, but in no hurry to strike; this pause, he knew, might be an extension of his life. And to live even a few seconds longer, he felt, even out here on this ledge in the night, was

---

Encountering the Unexpected *What other unexpected experiences do you think Tom will face in the future?*

Encountering the Unexpected *How might Tom be about to take a leap into the unknown?*

Conflict *How has Tom resolved an interior conflict?*

JACK FINNEY

He heard the sound, felt the blow, felt himself falling forward, and his hand closed on the living-room curtains, the shards and fragments of glass showering onto the floor. And then, kneeling there on the ledge, an arm thrust into the room up to the shoulder, he began picking away the protruding slivers and great wedges of glass from the window frame, tossing them in onto the rug. And, as he grasped the edges of the empty window frame and climbed into his home, he was grinning in triumph.

infinitely better than to die a moment earlier than he had to. His arm grew tired, and he brought it down and rested it.

Then he knew that it was time to make the attempt. He could not kneel here hesitating indefinitely till he lost all courage to act, waiting till he slipped off the ledge. Again he drew back his arm, knowing this time that he would not bring it down till he struck. His elbow protruding over Lexington Avenue far below, the fingers of his other hand pressed down bloodlessly tight against the narrow stripping, he waited, feeling the sick tenseness and terrible excitement building. It grew and swelled toward the moment of action, his nerves tautening. He thought of Clare—just a wordless, yearning thought—and then drew his arm back just a bit more, fist so tight his fingers pained him, and knowing he was going to do it. Then with full power, with every last scrap of strength he could bring to bear, he shot his arm forward toward the glass, and he said, *"Clare!"*

He did not lie down on the floor or run through the apartment, as he had promised himself; even in the first few moments it seemed to him natural and normal that he should be where he was. He simply turned to his desk, pulled the crumpled yellow sheet from his pocket and laid it down where it had been, smoothing it out; then he absently laid a pencil across it to weight it down. He shook his head wonderingly, and turned to walk toward the closet.

There he got out his topcoat and hat and, without waiting to put them on, opened the front door and stepped out, to go find his wife. He turned to pull the door closed and warm air from the hall rushed through the narrow opening again. As he saw the yellow paper, the pencil flying, scooped off the desk and, unimpeded by the glassless window, sail out into the night and out of his life, Tom Benecke burst into laughter and then closed the door behind him. ❧

Respond to Characters *What do you think is most important to Tom? How does this affect your opinion of him?*

Conflict *How has Tom resolved both an interior and an exterior conflict?*

After You Read

Respond and Think Critically

Respond and Interpret

1. Which part of the story did you react to most strongly? Explain.

2. (a)After Tom begins work, what happens to interrupt him, and what does he decide to do? (b)What rules does he make up for himself, and why?

3. (a)Briefly summarize Tom's risky adventure. (b)What lesson does this adventure teach him?

Analyze and Evaluate

4. (a)At the beginning of the story, what did Tom do that might lead someone to judge him as untruthful? b)What might he have done to be more honest and fair?

5. (a)Do you think his decision is realistic or does the author create an unbelievable situation? (b)What inferences can you draw about Tom, based on his decision to retrieve the paper? Explain.

Connect

6. **Big Idea** Encountering the Unexpected
What message is the author presenting about the unexpected situation that Tom finds himself in? Do you agree with the message? Explain.

7. **Connect to the Author** Finney was interested in writing suspenseful stories. Do you think he does a good job of using suspense and holding the reader's attention while Tom is out on the ledge? Give details from the story to support your response.

You're the Critic

Allegory or Fantasy?

People often disagree about Finney's purpose for writing. Read this summary of the opposing viewpoints.

> Many critics of Finney's novel The Body Snatchers interpreted the work as an allegory, a symbolic literary work in which the characters, settings, and events stand for things that are larger than themselves. The purpose of such an allegory is to teach a moral lesson. Some critics scoff at the idea of allegorical intent in Finney's work. They say that Finney's stories are just fun reading—suspenseful, thought-provoking fantasies. Finney was modest about his stories, saying that he just wanted to write about ordinary people's responses to extraordinary situations.

Group Activity Discuss the following questions. Cite evidence from the story and from the critical summary.

1. Do you think Finney's intent was to write an allegory or entertainment? Explain.

2. Do you think that "Contents of the Dead Man's Pocket" fits the description of Finney's writing as an ordinary person's reaction to an extraordinary situation?

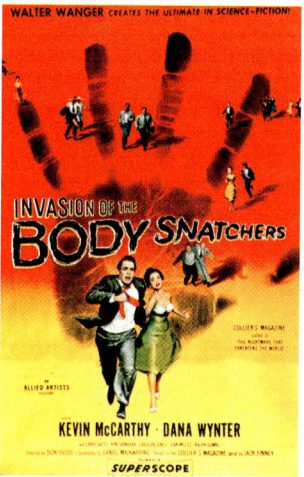

Literary Element Conflict

Sometimes a conflict can be both **internal** and **external.** For example, a character's conflict with another person or an outside force can trigger an inner struggle within the mind of the character.

1. Is Tom's conflict at the company where he works internal, external, or both? Cite evidence from the text to support your answer.

2. When Tom is on the window ledge struggling to survive, how are his conflicts both internal and external? Provide reasons and examples to support your answer.

Review: Foreshadowing

As you learned on page 18, **foreshadowing** is a writer's use of clues to hint at events that will happen later in the story.

Partner Activity Meet with a classmate to find hints in the story that foreshadow later events. Complete the following diagram.

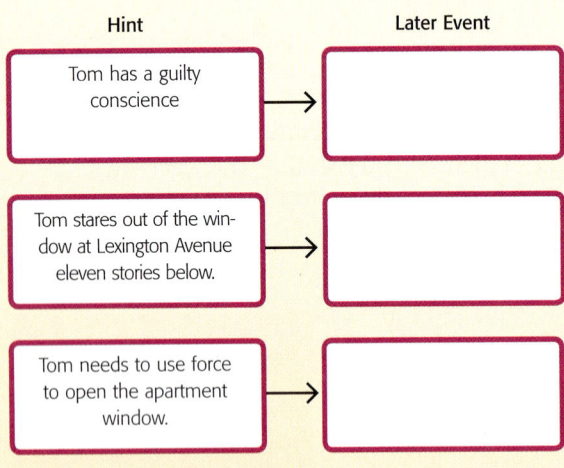

Reading Strategy Respond to Characters

When you **respond to characters** as you read, you are likely to get more from your reading. By paying attention to how characters make you feel, what questions they create for you, and how they might surprise you as you read, you become more engaged in your reading. Refer to the notes that you took about the characters as you read to answer the following questions.

1. How did you feel about Tom Benecke at the beginning of the story?

2. Were you surprised by Tom Benecke's decision to go after the yellow piece of paper? Explain.

3. How did you feel about Tom Benecke at the end of the story? Did your opinion of him change?

Vocabulary Practice

Practice with Analogies Choose the word that best completes each analogy.

1. knot : convoluted :: noose :
   a. tight   **b.** looped   **c.** stretched
2. tightrope : taut :: noodle :
   a. safe   **b.** delicate   **c.** slack
3. improvised : rehearsed :: temporary :
   a. voluntary   **b.** permanent   **c.** brief
4. pent-up : held in :: soldier :
   a. warrior   **b.** war   **c.** weapon
5. reveling : pleasure :: weeping :
   a. sadness   **b.** crying   **c.** tears

Academic Vocabulary

Tom's document represented so much effort—and so much expectation—that he risked his life for it.

Document is a multiple-meaning word. In everyday conversation, someone might refer to any file on a computer as a **document**. Using context clues, try to figure out the meaning of the word in the sentence above about the story. Check your guess in a dictionary.

For more on academic vocabulary, see pages 52 and 53.

 **Literature** Online

Selection Resources For Selection Quizzes, eFlashcards, and Reading-Writing Connection activities, go to glencoe.com and enter QuickPass code GL59794u1.

Respond Through Writing

Summary

Learning Objectives

In this assignment, you will focus on the following objectives:

Writing: Writing a summary.

Grammar: Using tenses correctly.

Report Story Events When you write a summary of a story, you tell a short version of the original and report the main events in sequence. A summary does not include personal opinions. In about 100 words, write a plot summary of "Contents of the Dead Man's Pocket." Write your plot summary in the present tense.

Understand the Task
- When you report events in **sequence,** you present them in the order they occur.
- In a **plot summary,** you report the main story events and also explain the main characters' problems and how they are resolved.

Prewrite List the main events. Pare down the story to its key events. For each event, add details about the characters, setting, or conflict that are crucial to understanding what happens. This organizer shows the key events and details needed to summarize "The Californian's Tale."

| 1. Narrator meets Henry
—miners
—CA gold rush | 2. Henry & others await wife
—play music
—toast | 3. Narrator learns truth
—Henry falls asleep before arrival
—wife dead 19 years |

Draft Use an objective tone throughout your summary. After naming the story and its author, introduce information that is at the core of the story, such as the main character, the conflict, or the setting; then retell the events in order. Use the following sentence frame to get started.

The story begins with _____.

Revise Ask a peer reader to identify the story, author, main character, conflict or problem, main events, and ending. Add or clarify anything your reader could not identify. Also ask your reader to identify any unnecessary details, and revise accordingly.

Edit and Proofread Proofread your paper, correcting any errors in grammar, spelling, and punctuation. Use the Grammar Tip in the side column for help with using tenses correctly.

Grammar Tip

Correct Verb Tenses

When summarizing a story, you should use the present tense:

*Henry **invites** him to his house.*

At the same time, you must make it clear that some story events occurred before others, which may require the use of the present perfect tense (formed with *has* or *have*) in the same sentence as the present tense. This tense shows an action that occurred in the past but continues or still affects the present.

*The narrator **learns** that Henry's **wife has been dead** for nineteen years.*

Learning Objectives

For pages 52–53

In this workshop, you will focus on the following objective:

Vocabulary: Understanding academic vocabulary.

For a complete list of academic vocabulary words, see pages R80–R82.

Test-Taking Tip

These key academic vocabulary words often appear on standardized tests.

Analyze: to systematically and critically examine all parts of an issue or event

Classify or categorize: to put people, things, or ideas into groups, based on a common set of characteristics

Compare: to show how things are alike

Contrast: to show how things are different

Describe: to present a sketch or an impression

Discuss: to systematically write about all sides of an issue or event

Evaluate: to make a judgment and support it with evidence

Explain: to clarify or make plain

Vocabulary For more vocabulary practice, go to glencoe.com and enter QuickPass code GL59794u1.

Vocabulary Workshop

Academic Vocabulary

What Is Academic Vocabulary? Words that are commonly used in academic texts, such as textbooks, directions, and tests, are called **academic vocabulary.** Learning academic vocabulary is important because these words will help you read, write, and research in many academic areas. These words will also help you succeed on standardized tests.

Different Kinds of Words Some words are specific to certain disciplines, or areas of study. For example, the words *alliteration, foreshadowing,* and *metaphor* pertain to literature. Other words, such as *concept, structure,* and *theory,* are used in many areas of study. The charts below show more examples of both kinds of words.

Discipline-Specific Words

Discipline	Words
Math	circumference, percentage, rectangle
Science	mitosis, chlorophyll, genus
Social Studies	confederation, federalism, antebellum

General Academic Vocabulary

process	perceive
survey	relevant
research	interpret
indicate	tradition

Academic Words in This Book You will learn about discipline-specific and general academic vocabulary words in this book. Words that are specific to literature and language arts will most often be introduced and explained in Literary Element and Reading Strategy features before and after you read literature texts. You will encounter more general academic vocabulary words in a feature called Academic Vocabulary. This feature appears in the After You Read pages following most literature texts.

Multiple-Meaning Words Many academic vocabulary words, such as *economy,* have more than one meaning. The first meaning is a literal, more common definition that you may be familiar with (*economy* means "the thrifty or efficient use of a material resource, such as money"). The second definition is more academic and may be unfamiliar to you (*economy* also means "the efficient use of a nonmaterial resource, such as language"). These two definitions are often related. In the case of *economy,* the two definitions are linked by the "efficient use of a resource." The chart below lists additional examples of academic words with more than one meaning.

Word	Definitions	Relationship
select	*v.* to choose *adj.* chosen because of excellence or preference	Both definitions involve choosing
range	*n.* the extent to which something varies *v.* to vary within specified limits	Both definitions involve variation within certain limits
conduct	*n.* a standard of personal behavior *v.* to lead from a position of power	Both definitions involve the correct way to do something

As you encounter academic vocabulary words in this book, you will master the words through various activities. You will have a chance to practice these activities in the exercise below.

Test-Taking Tip

These key academic vocabulary words often appear on standardized tests.

Illustrate: to provide examples or to show with a picture or another graphic

Infer: to read between the lines or to use knowledge or experience to draw conclusions, make generalizations, or form predictions

Justify: to prove or to support a position with specific facts and reasons

Predict: to tell what will happen in the future based on an understanding of prior events and behaviors

State: to briefly and concisely present information

Summarize: to give a brief overview of the main points of an event or issue

Trace: to present the steps or stages in a process or an event in sequential or chronological order

Exercise

1. **respond** (ri spond´) *v.* to act in response to

    In Saki's "The Open Window," how does Framton Nuttel **respond** when the men return from hunting?

    Use the word *respond* in a sentence of your own in which you explain how you reacted during a humorous encounter.

2. **establish** (es tab´lish) *v.* to bring into existence

    What details does Twain include to help **establish** the mood in "The Californian's Tale"?

    Use the word *establish* in a sentence of your own in which you describe how your ancestors came to live in your town, state, or country.

3. **construct** (kən strukt´) *v.* to make or form from disparate parts

    What techniques does Joyce Carol Oates use to **construct** her essay "Storytelling Is As Old As Mankind"?

    Another meaning of *construct* is "a theoretical entity" as in the sentence "Class is a social construct." This definition of *construct* is pronounced (kon´struct´). How is this definition related to the one given above?

Before You Read

An Astrologer's Day

World Literature
India

Meet R. K. Narayan
(1906–2001)

As a young boy, R. K. Narayan (nä rä´ yan) had absolutely no use for school. "Going to school seemed to be a never-ending nuisance each day," he once wrote. Narayan much preferred spending time with his pet monkey, who liked to hang by its tail from the roof, and his pet peacock, who acted as the family watchdog. Despite his aversion to school, Narayan's family placed a high value on education. But Narayan never changed his opinion that school was too serious. Today, Narayan's stories are regularly assigned to students in schools around the world. Considering his unenthusiastic view of formal education, Narayan might have enjoyed this irony.

> "I want a story to be entertaining, enjoyable, and illuminating in some way."
>
> —R. K. Narayan

The Decision to Be a Writer Rasipuram Krishnaswami Narayan was born in Madras, India, and brought up by his grandmother. After graduating from college, he turned to fiction writing as a career. He chose to write in English, a language that he was fond of and knew well. "English is a very adaptable language. And it's so transparent it can take on the tint of any country." Narayan did not find immediate success as a writer and once said that writing "was all frustration and struggle for more than fifteen years." His first novel, *Swami and Friends*, was finally published in 1935 with the help of British writer Graham Greene. Narayan went on to publish numerous other works.

A Literary Voice of India Narayan is probably best known as the creator of Malgudi, a fictional South Indian village that has been called a "zany, eccentric and, at the same time, true to life world." It is the setting for almost all of Narayan's novels and short stories, including "An Astrologer's Day." Of his invented village, Narayan remarked, "Malgudi was an earth-shaking discovery for me, because I had no mind for facts and things like that, which would be necessary in writing about . . . any real place." Narayan's stories about Malgudi are often comic considerations of individuals trying to find peace in a turbulent world.

Critic Judith Freeman writes that Narayan "takes a Western reader into the very heart of an Indian village. . . . The foreignness of the setting, rituals and traditions may seem to us exotic, but the underlying humanity of Narayan's dramas can't fail to strike a familiar chord."

Author Search For more about R. K. Narayan, go to glencoe.com and enter QuickPass code GL59794u1.

Literature and Reading Preview

Connect to the Short Story

In your opinion, how much of one's future is decided by the choices one makes, by fate, or by coincidence? Freewrite for a few minutes about an event, a coincidence, or a choice you made that changed the course of your life.

Build Background

Astrology is a form of fortune-telling. It originated in ancient Babylonia and has been practiced in many cultures, including those of ancient Rome, Greece, India, and China. Some astrologers claim the ability to foretell an individual's future by drawing and studying a chart called a *horoscope*. A horoscope shows the configuration of the planets and stars at the moment of an individual's birth.

Set Purposes for Reading

Big Idea Encountering the Unexpected

As you read "An Astrologer's Day," ask yourself, What is revealed when a man asks about his future?

Literary Element Mood

The **mood** is the overall emotional quality of a literary work. The writer's choice of language, subject matter, setting, diction, and tone all contribute to conveying a mood that helps draw the reader into the experience of the characters.

As you read, ask yourself, How does Narayan create a pervasive mood that helps me relate to a time and a culture different from my own?

Reading Strategy Analyze Cultural Context

When you **analyze cultural context,** you pay attention to details that reveal the setting, dress, speech, mannerisms, and behaviors characteristic of a particular culture at a particular time in history. As you read, ask yourself, What details does Narayan use to show the customs of 1940s India?

Tip: Take Notes As you read, take notes about cultural details that relate to the setting, characters, and main events in the plot.

Learning Objectives

For pages 54–62

In studying this text, you will focus on the following objectives:

Literary Study: Analyzing mood.

Reading: Analyzing cultural context.

Vocabulary

enhance (en hans′) *v.* to make greater, as in beauty or value; p. 56 *Wearing too much makeup may detract from your beauty, not enhance it.*

impetuous (im pech′ōō əs) *adj.* rushing headlong into things; rash; p. 57 *It was an impetuous decision, made without any thought.*

paraphernalia (par′ə fər nal′yə) *n.* things used in a particular activity; equipment; p. 58 *The traveling chef carried his own pots, pans, and other cooking paraphernalia.*

piqued (pēkt) *adj.* aroused in anger or resentment; offended; p. 58 *The director was piqued by the play's disastrous reviews.*

incantation (in′kan tā′shən) *n.* words spoken in casting a spell; p. 58 *In Shakespeare's* Macbeth, *witches utter an eerie incantation.*

Tip: Word Origins You can find a word's origin and history, or etymology, in a dictionary, usually near the beginning or end of an entry. If the origin does not appear there, look at the preceding word. If the two are closely related, your word most likely shares the same origin.

R. K. NARAYAN

An Astrologer's Day

R. K. Narayan

Indian Star Chart, ca. 1840. By permission of the British Library.

Punctually at midday he opened his bag and spread out his professional equipment, which consisted of a dozen cowrie[1] shells, a square piece of cloth with obscure mystic charts on it, a notebook and a bundle of palmyra writing. His forehead was resplendent with sacred ash and vermilion,[2] and his eyes sparkled with a sharp abnormal gleam which was really an outcome of a continual searching look for customers, but which his simple clients took to be a prophetic light and felt comforted. The power of his eyes was considerably enhanced by their position—placed as they were between the painted forehead and the dark whiskers which streamed down his cheeks: even a half-wit's eyes would sparkle in such a setting. To crown the effect he wound a saffron-colored[3] turban around his head. This color scheme never failed. People were attracted to him as bees are attracted to cosmos or dahlia stalks. He sat under the boughs of a spreading tamarind tree which flanked a path running through the Town Hall Park. It was a remarkable place in many ways: a surging crowd was always moving up and down this narrow road morning till night. A variety of trades and occupations was represented all along its

---

1. A *cowrie* (kour′ē) is a small snail commonly found in warm, shallow waters of the Pacific and Indian Oceans.
2. Here, *obscure* means "difficult to understand" and *mystic* means "having hidden or secret meanings." *Palmyra* (pal mī′rə) refers to paper made from the leaves of the palmyra tree. The man's forehead is full of splendor (*resplendent*) in that it is painted with dark ash and a red pigment called *vermilion*.

Encountering the Unexpected *What do customers misunderstand about the astrologer?*

3. *Saffron* is an orange-yellow color.

Analyze Cultural Context *How does the astrologer's manner of dress suit his character?*

Vocabulary

enhance (en hans′) *v.* to make greater, as in beauty or value

way: medicine-sellers, sellers of stolen hardware and junk, magicians and, above all, an auctioneer of cheap cloth, who created enough din all day to attract the whole town. Next to him in vociferousness[4] came a vendor of fried groundnuts,[5] who gave his ware a fancy name each day, calling it Bombay Ice-Cream one day, and on the next Delhi Almond, and on the third Raja's Delicacy, and so on and so forth, and people flocked to him. A considerable portion of this crowd dallied before the astrologer too. The astrologer transacted his business by the light of a flare which crackled and smoked up above the groundnut heap nearby. Half the enchantment of the place was due to the fact that it did not have the benefit of municipal lighting. The place was lit up by shop lights. One or two had hissing gaslights, some had naked flares stuck on poles, some were lit up by old cycle lamps and one or two, like the astrologer's, managed without lights of their own. It was a bewildering criss-cross of light rays and moving shadows. This suited the astrologer very well, for the simple reason that he had not in the least intended to be an astrologer when he began life; and he knew no more of what was going to happen to others than he knew what was going to happen to himself next minute. He was as much a stranger to the stars as were his innocent customers. Yet he said things which pleased and astonished everyone: that was more a matter of study, practice and shrewd guesswork. All the same, it was as much an honest man's labor as any other, and he deserved the wages he carried home at the end of a day.

He had left his village without any previous thought or plan. If he had continued there he would have carried on the work of his forefathers—namely, tilling the land, living, marrying and ripening in his cornfield and ancestral home. But that was not to be. He had to leave home without telling anyone, and he could not rest till he left it behind a couple of hundred miles. To a villager it is a great deal, as if an ocean flowed between.

He had a working analysis of mankind's troubles: marriage, money and the tangles of human ties. Long practice had sharpened his perception. Within five minutes he understood what was wrong. He charged three pice[6] per question and never opened his mouth till the other had spoken for at least ten minutes, which provided him enough stuff for a dozen answers and advices. When he told the person before him, gazing at his palm, "In many ways you are not getting the fullest results for your efforts," nine out of ten were disposed to agree with him. Or he questioned: "Is there any woman in your family, maybe even a distant relative, who is not well disposed[7] towards you?" Or he gave an analysis of character: "Most of your troubles are due to your nature. How can you be otherwise with Saturn where he is? You have an **impetuous** nature and a rough exterior." This endeared him to their hearts immediately, for even the mildest of us loves to think that he has a forbidding exterior.

The nuts-vendor blew out his flare and rose to go home. This was a signal for the astrologer to bundle up too, since it left him in darkness except for a little shaft of

---

4. *Vociferousness* (vō sif′ ər əs nəs) means "noisy outcrying."
5. *Groundnuts* are peanuts.

> **Mood** What does this description of lights add to the mood—the feeling—of the story?

6. A *pice* is a coin of India of very small value.
7. In this paragraph, *disposed* is used twice with slightly different meanings. The first time, you might substitute *likely* or *inclined*. The second time, substitute *favorable* for the phrase "well disposed."

Vocabulary

impetuous (im pech′ oo əs) *adj.* rushing headlong into things; rash

green light which strayed in from somewhere and touched the ground before him. He picked up his cowrie shells and **paraphernalia** and was putting them back into his bag when the green shaft of light was blotted out; he looked up and saw a man standing before him. He sensed a possible client and said: "You look so careworn. It will do you good to sit down for a while and chat with me." The other grumbled some vague reply. The astrologer pressed his invitation; whereupon the other thrust his palm under his nose, saying: "You call yourself an astrologer?" The astrologer felt challenged and said, tilting the other's palm towards the green shaft of light: "Yours is a nature . . ." "Oh, stop that," the other said. "Tell me something worthwhile. . . ."

Our friend felt **piqued.** "I charge only three pice per question, and what you get ought to be good enough for your money. . . ." At this the other withdrew his arm, took out an anna and flung it out to him, saying, "I have some questions to ask. If I prove you are bluffing, you must return that anna to me with interest."

"If you find my answers satisfactory, will you give me five rupees?"[8]

"No."

"Or will you give me eight annas?"

"All right, provided you give me twice as much if you are wrong," said the stranger. This pact was accepted after a little further argument. The astrologer sent up a prayer to heaven as the other lit a cheroot.[9] The astrologer caught a glimpse of his face by the matchlight. There was a pause as cars hooted on the road, jutka[10] drivers swore at their horses and the babble of the crowd agitated the semi-darkness of the park. The other sat down, sucking his cheroot, puffing out, sat there ruthlessly. The astrologer felt very uncomfortable. "Here, take your anna back. I am not used to such challenges. It is late for me today. . . ." He made preparations to bundle up. The other held his wrist and said, "You can't get out of it now. You dragged me in while I was passing." The astrologer shivered in his grip; and his voice shook and became faint. "Leave me today. I will speak to you tomorrow." The other thrust his palm in his face and said, "Challenge is challenge. Go on." The astrologer proceeded with his throat drying up. "There is a woman . . ."

"Stop," said the other. "I don't want all that. Shall I succeed in my present search or not? Answer this and go. Otherwise I will not let you go till you disgorge[11] all your coins." The astrologer muttered a few **incantations** and replied, "All right. I will speak. But will you give me a rupee if what I say is convincing? Otherwise I will not open my mouth, and you may do what you like." After a good deal of haggling the other agreed. The astrologer said, "You were left for dead. Am I right?"

---

8. The *anna* is a former coin of India that was equal to four pice. The *rupee* is a coin of India (and other countries) equal to sixteen annas.

> **Vocabulary**
> **paraphernalia** (par′ə fər nāl′yə) *n.* things used in a particular activity; equipment
> **piqued** (pēkt) *adj.* aroused in anger or resentment; offended

9. A *cheroot* (shə ro͞ot′) is a cigar cut square at both ends.
10. A *jutka* (jo͞ot′ kə) is a two-wheeled, horse-drawn vehicle.
11. Here, *disgorge* means "to give up or hand over."

> **Mood** Why is the din in this scene so unsuited to the atmosphere one would associate with astrological consultation?

> **Vocabulary**
> **incantation** (in′kan tā′shən) *n.* words spoken in casting a spell

58 UNIT 1 THE SHORT STORY

Untitled, 20th century. Image zoo.

View the Art This abstract painting shows a solitary figure suspended in what could be water or the night sky. How might the figure represent the astrologer? How might it represent Guru Nayak?

"Ah, tell me more."

"A knife has passed through you once?" said the astrologer.

"Good fellow!" He bared his chest to show the scar. "What else?"

"And then you were pushed into a well nearby in the field. You were left for dead."

"I should have been dead if some passerby had not chanced to peep into the well," exclaimed the other, overwhelmed by enthusiasm. "When shall I get at him?" he asked, clenching his fist.

"In the next world," answered the astrologer. "He died four months ago in a far-off town. You will never see any more of him." The other groaned on hearing it. The astrologer proceeded.

"Guru Nayak—"

"You know my name!" the other said, taken aback.[12]

"As I know all other things. Guru Nayak, listen carefully to what I have to say. Your village is two days' journey due north of this town. Take the next train and be gone. I see once again great danger to your life if you go from home." He took out a pinch of sacred ash and held it out to him. "Rub it on your forehead and go home. Never travel southward again, and you will live to be a hundred."

"Why should I leave home again?" the other said reflectively.[13] "I was only going away now and then to look for him and to choke out his life if I met him." He shook his head regretfully. "He has escaped my hands. I hope at least he died as he deserved." "Yes," said the astrologer. "He was crushed under a lorry."[14] The other looked gratified to hear it.

The place was deserted by the time the astrologer picked up his articles and put them into his bag. The green shaft was also gone, leaving the place in darkness and silence. The stranger had gone off into the night, after giving the astrologer a handful of coins.

It was nearly midnight when the astrologer reached home. His wife was waiting for him at the door and demanded an explanation. He flung the coins at her and said, "Count them. One man gave all that."

"Twelve and a half annas," she said, counting. She was overjoyed. "I can buy some *jaggery*[15] and coconut tomorrow. The child has been asking for sweets for so many days now. I will prepare some nice stuff for her."

"The swine has cheated me! He promised me a rupee," said the astrologer. She looked up at him. "You look worried. What is wrong?"

"Nothing."

After dinner, sitting on the *pyol*,[16] he told her, "Do you know a great load is gone from me today? I thought I had the blood of a man on my hands all these years. That was the reason why I ran away from home, settled here and married you. He is alive."

She gasped, "You tried to kill!"

"Yes, in our village, when I was a silly youngster. We drank, gambled and quarreled badly one day—why think of it now? Time to sleep," he said, yawning, and stretched himself on the *pyol*. ∾

---

12. The expression *taken aback* means "suddenly surprised or startled."
13. Here, *reflectively* (ri flek′ tiv lē) means "in a way that shows serious and careful consideration."

Encountering the Unexpected *Did it surprise you when the astrologer called his client by the correct name? Explain.*

14. Here, a *lorry* is a long, flat, horse-drawn wagon.
15. *Jaggery* is unrefined sugar made from palm tree sap.
16. A *pyol* (pī′ ôl) is a low bench.

Mood *How has the mood of the piece changed here?*

After You Read

Respond and Think Critically

Respond and Interpret

1. (a) What was your reaction to the conversation between the astrologer and his wife? (b) Does this new knowledge reinforce or change your opinion of the astrologer? Explain.

2. (a) According to the narrator, how does the astrologer's appearance help him attract customers? (b) In your opinion, how does the astrologer help the customers and satisfy their needs?

3. (a) Describe the astrologer's current life. (b) How does this differ from the life he expected to live?

4. (a) What details does the astrologer give the stranger about his past? (b) Why does he advise the stranger to go home immediately?

Analyze and Evaluate

5. (a) Why is it important that this story takes place in the evening? (b) How would the story have been different if it had taken place earlier in the day?

6. (a) How would you characterize the astrologer's attitude toward the stranger after their encounter? (b) What attitude did the astrologer seem to have about the incident from his past?

7. How do you think the astrologer would respond to these questions: What makes you such a successful astrologer? Why do most people want to know the future?

Connect

8. **Big Idea** Encountering the Unexpected Suspense is the feeling of anticipation you may have as you read. In this story, what details contributed to your feelings of suspense and surprise? Explain.

9. **Connect to Today** How might the astrologer's fate have been different if he had commited his crime in today's technologically advanced world instead of in a rural Indian village many years ago?

Literary Element Mood

Mood helps the reader imagine the feeling of being in the scene and experience the events as the characters do. Writers use diction, descriptive language, and sensory details to help create mood.

1. Which descriptive and sensory details help you experience the marketplace in which the astrologer conducts his business?

2. (a) Describe the mood of the scene in which Guru Nayak visits the astrologer in one or two sentences. (b) Which details in this scene did you draw on to write your description?

Review: Flashback

A **flashback** is an interruption in the chronological order of a narrative to describe an event that happened earlier.

Partner Activity Meet with a classmate and imagine that you are the writer and director of a film version of "An Astrologer's Day." Collaborate on a film script for the scene in which the astrologer realizes that Guru Nayak is his former victim but still has to act as his astrologer. Include a flashback sequence in your scene in which the astrologer remembers the attempted murder. Write a description of and dialogue for the flashback sequence and integrate it into your film script.

Reading Strategy **Analyze Cultural Context**

The cultural details that relate to setting, characters, and plot in "An Astrologer's Day" add authenticity to the story and make the characters and events believable. Review the notes you took as you read and answer the following items.

1. Compare the author's depiction of the astrologer's street to open markets you have seen.
2. How does the astrologer please his customers?

Vocabulary Practice

Practice with Word Origins Study the etymology, or origin and history, of a word to help you explore its meaning. Create a word map for each vocabulary word from the text.

enhance   **impetuous**   **paraphernalia**
piqued   **incantation**

EXAMPLE:

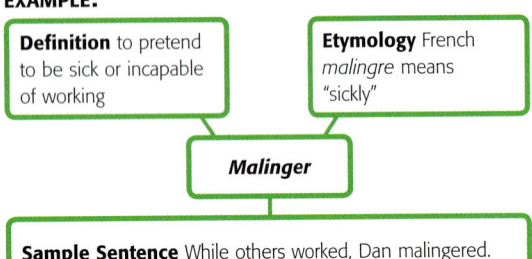

Academic Vocabulary

The reader must decide whether the astrologer's youth at the time of his crime against Guru Nayak can, in any way, **negate** *his guilt.*

Negate is an academic word. More familiar words that are similar in meaning are *deny* and *abolish. Create* and *affirm* are its antonyms. Answer this question in one or more complete sentences that use the word *negate:* Who or what could **negate** one of your accomplishments? Explain.

For more on academic vocabulary, see pages 52 and 53.

Write with Style

Apply Description

Assignment Describe a place you know well. Use details to create a recognizable mood.

Get Ideas Think of a place you know well. Then think back to how details help create mood in "An Astrologer's Day." For example, the green shaft of light and the ensuing darkness not only help to establish a time and place, they also create a mood of mystery.

EXAMPLE
"The nuts-vendor blew out his flare and rose to go home. This was a signal for the astrologer to bundle up too, since it left him in darkness except for a little shaft of green light which strayed in from somewhere and touched the ground before him."

Create a chart like the one below in which you list your place and some of the sensory details that create its atmosphere. Use your chart to help you write your description.

Give It Structure All the details in your description should come together to create the mood. The details should appear in a logical order. You may choose to organize the details of your description around a central character or event. If you are telling a story, consider using chronological order, problem/solution, or cause-and-effect relationships to organize your writing. If you are simply describing the place, consider moving from general to specific, or vice versa, as you write.

Look at Language Too many adjectives are like too much frosting on a piece of cake. Don't load them on. Focus on fewer, more precise words.

Selection Resources For Selection Quizzes, eFlashcards, and Reading-Writing Connection activities, go to glencoe.com and enter QuickPass code GL59794u1.

Grammar Workshop

Apostrophes in Possessives

Learning Objectives

In this workshop, you will focus on the following objective:

Grammar: Understanding how to use apostrophes in possessives.

Literature Connection In the following quotation, the possessive case of the singular noun *mankind* is *mankind's*.

> "He had a working analysis of mankind's troubles: marriage, money and the tangles of human ties."
>
> —R. K. Narayan, from "An Astrologer's Day"

An important use of the apostrophe is to form the possessive of nouns and indefinite pronouns. The possessive case is formed by adding either an apostrophe or an apostrophe and *s*.

Examples

To form the possessive of a singular noun that ends in *s*, add an apostrophe and *s*.

The <u>noise of the bus</u> agitated the semi-darkness of the park.

The <u>bus's noise</u> agitated the semi-darkness of the park.

To form the possessive of a plural noun that ends in *s*, add only an apostrophe.

The astrologer answered the <u>questions of the clients</u>.

The astrologer answered the <u>clients' questions</u>.

To form the possessive of a plural noun that does not end in *s*, add an apostrophe and *s*.

The <u>faces of the men</u> were revealed in the light.

The <u>men's faces</u> were revealed in the light.

To form the possessive of an indefinite pronoun (such as *somebody*), add an apostrophe and *s*.

The astrologer answered <u>the questions of everybody</u>.

The astrologer answered <u>everybody's questions</u>.

Vocabulary Terms

A **possessive** noun shows possession, ownership, or a relationship between two nouns that is similar to that of ownership.

Tip

To decide whether a noun needs an apostrophe alone or an apostrophe and *s*, consider the number of the noun. A plural noun that ends in *s* needs only an apostrophe to make it possessive.

Language Handbook

For more on using apostrophes to form possessives, see the Language Handbook p. R 51.

Revise If the sentence is correct, write C. If the sentence is incorrect, rewrite it correctly.

1. The fishermens catch was brought to market each morning.
2. Other vendors's stalls were clean and bright.
3. Each day the astrologer told everyone's fortune.

Grammar For more grammar practice, go to glencoe.com and enter QuickPass code GL59794u1.

Before You Read

Civil Peace

**World Literature
Nigeria**

Meet **Chinua Achebe**
(born 1930)

"The story is our escort; without it, we are blind." Chinua Achebe (ə chā´bā) wrote these words to stress the importance of keeping Africa's precolonial stories and culture alive.

Achebe was born in Ogidi, Nigeria. His family was Ibo and Christian. While growing up, Achebe experienced traditional village life. After graduating from University College in Ibadan, he worked for more than ten years for the Nigerian Broadcasting Company. Achebe left this job in 1966 partly because of political problems that led to civil war in Nigeria in 1967. The Ibo, one of Nigeria's largest ethnic groups, tried to separate from Nigeria to form the independent Republic of Biafra. Achebe worked for the Ibo cause and represented Biafra as a diplomat.

He has since taught in universities in Nigeria, Massachusetts, and Connecticut. Throughout his career, he has authored five novels, as well as many essays, poems, and children's stories. He was also the director of Heinemann Education Books Ltd. (now called the Heinemann African Writers Series) and helped develop series to foster publication of African and Caribbean writers.

However, his themes revolve around the people of Africa, their struggles under colonial rule, and their fight for independence. Achebe combines the rhythms and speech patterns of the Ibo with the English language so that English readers will gain a sense of the African people and culture. Achebe writes about his people honestly, detailing both the good and the bad. By communicating his messages about life, Achebe has preserved the African storytelling tradition.

Civil War and Civil Peace Achebe wrote radio programs that supported the Biafrans during the Civil War, but he could not bring himself to write novels during the war. He did, however, write three short stories about the war. "Civil Peace," which provides a true-to-life description of the region after the war, is one of those stories.

The title of Achebe's most popular novel, *Things Fall Apart,* is an allusion to the William Butler Yeats poem "The Second Coming." Achebe's novel, a powerful account of a "strong" man whose life is dominated by fear and anger, is recognized as a masterpiece of modern African literature.

> "It is the story that outlives the sound of war-drums and the exploits of brave fighters."
>
> —Chinua Achebe, from *Anthills of the Savannah*

The African Voice Achebe writes in English so that his stories will have a wider audience.

 **Literature** Online

Author Search For more about Chinua Achebe, go to glencoe.com and enter QuickPass code GL59794u1.

Literature and Reading Preview

Connect to the Story
If a disaster occurred today, what would you save to ensure your "happy survival"? Respond to this question in your journal.

Build Background
Nigeria, located on the western coast of Africa, is the most densely populated country on the continent. Once a British colony, it became an independent nation in 1960. The Nigerian civil war began in 1967 when the Ibo tried to separate from Nigeria to form the Republic of Biafra. After years of bloody battles, the Ibo were forced to surrender in 1970. This story takes place in Nigeria shortly after the end of the war.

Set Purposes for Reading

Big Idea **Encountering the Unexpected**

As you read "Civil Peace," ask yourself, How does Jonathan Iwegbu experience both joy and sorrow in encountering the unexpected?

Literary Element **Dialect**

A **dialect** is a variation of a language spoken by a region often within a particular group of people. Understanding a writer's use of dialect will give you a richer sense of a scene or character. As you read, ask yourself, How does Achebe use dialect to illustrate both British and African elements in Nigeria?

Reading Strategy **Analyze Historical Context**

When you **analyze a story's historical context**, you think of how the characters and events in the story are affected by what is taking place at the time the story is set. As you read, ask yourself, How does living through the Nigerian civil war affect Jonathan Iwegbu's life?

Tip: Analyze Effects Use a web diagram like the one below to list the effects of the Nigerian civil war on Jonathan Iwegbu's life.

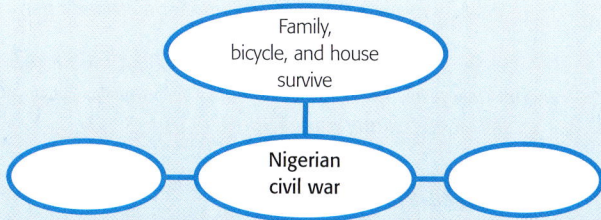

Learning Objectives

For pages 64–71

In studying this text, you will focus on the following objectives:

Literary Study: Analyzing dialect.

Reading: Analyzing historical context.

Vocabulary

commandeer (kom′ ən dēr′) *v.* to seize for use by the military or government; p. 66 *The general commandeered the commercial airplane for the battle.*

amenable (ə mē′ nə bəl) *adj.* responsive; able to be controlled; p. 66 *After being sedated, the animal was amenable to being treated by the veterinarian.*

retail (re′ tāl) *v.* to sell directly to consumers; p. 67 *The farmer retailed his produce door to door.*

fortnight (fôrt′ nīt) *n.* two weeks; p. 67 *The festival lasted for a fortnight, not just the usual week.*

edifice (ed′ ə fis) *n.* a building, especially a large, important-looking one; p. 67 *The castle was an impressive edifice.*

Tip: Connotation and Denotation As you read, it often helps to look beyond a word's dictionary meaning and consider the emotions and other suggestions that the word conveys.

CHINUA ACHEBE

Civil Peace

Chinua Achebe

Jonathan Iwegbu counted himself extraordinarily lucky. "Happy survival!" meant so much more to him than just a current fashion of greeting old friends in the first hazy days of peace. It went deep to his heart. He had come out of the war with five inestimable blessings—his head, his wife Maria's head and the heads of three out of their four children. As a bonus he also had his old bicycle—a miracle too but naturally not to be compared to the safety of five human heads.

The bicycle had a little history of its own. One day at the height of the war it was **commandeered** "for urgent military action." Hard as its loss would have been to him he would still have let it go without a thought had he not had some doubts about the genuineness of the officer. It wasn't his disreputable rags, nor the toes peeping out of one blue and one brown canvas shoes, nor yet the two stars of his rank done obviously in a hurry in biro,[1] that troubled Jonathan; many good and heroic soldiers looked the same or worse. It was rather a certain lack of grip and firmness in his manner. So Jonathan, suspecting he might be **amenable** to influence, rummaged in his raffia bag and produced the two pounds

---

1. The stars signifying the officer's rank had been hand-drawn in ink. *Biro* (bī´ rō) is a British term for a ballpoint pen.

Analyze Historical Context Why would Jonathan have let his bicycle go "without a thought"? Why did he think of himself as "extraordinarily lucky"?

Vocabulary

commandeer (kom´ ən dēr´) *v.* to seize for use by the military or government

Vocabulary

amenable (ə mē´ nə bəl) *adj.* responsive; able to be controlled

with which he had been going to buy firewood which his wife, Maria, **retailed** to camp officials for extra stock-fish and corn meal, and got his bicycle back. That night he buried it in the little clearing in the bush where the dead of the camp, including his own youngest son, were buried. When he dug it up again a year later after the surrender all it needed was a little palm-oil greasing. "Nothing puzzles God," he said in wonder.

Visual Vocabulary
A *raffia* bag is one woven from the fibers of the raffia palm tree.

He put it to immediate use as a taxi and accumulated a small pile of Biafran money ferrying camp officials and their families across the four-mile stretch to the nearest tarred road. His standard charge per trip was six pounds and those who had the money were only glad to be rid of some of it in this way. At the end of a **fortnight** he had made a small fortune of one hundred and fifteen pounds.

Then he made the journey to Enugu and found another miracle waiting for him. It was unbelievable. He rubbed his eyes and looked again and it was still standing there before him. But, needless to say, even that monumental blessing must be accounted also totally inferior to the five heads in the family. This newest miracle was his little house in Ogui Overside. Indeed nothing puzzles God! Only two houses away a huge concrete **edifice** some wealthy contractor had put up just before the war was a mountain of rubble. And here was Jonathan's little zinc house of no regrets built with mud blocks quite intact! Of course the doors and windows were missing and five sheets off the roof. But what was that? And anyhow he had returned to Enugu early enough to pick up bits of old zinc and wood and soggy sheets of cardboard lying around the neighborhood before thousands more came out of their forest holes looking for the same things. He got a destitute carpenter with one old hammer, a blunt plane and a few bent and rusty nails in his tool bag to turn this assortment of wood, paper and metal into door and window shutters for five Nigerian shillings or fifty Biafran pounds. He paid the pounds, and moved in with his overjoyed family carrying five heads on their shoulders.

His children picked mangoes near the military cemetery and sold them to soldiers' wives for a few pennies—real pennies this time—and his wife started making breakfast akara balls[2] for neighbors in a hurry to start life again. With his family earnings he took his bicycle to the villages around and bought fresh palm wine which he mixed generously in his rooms with the water which had recently started running again in the public tap down the road, and opened up a bar for soldiers and other lucky people with good money.

At first he went daily, then every other day and finally once a week, to the offices of the Coal Corporation where he used to be

---

Encountering the Unexpected Why was Jonathan surprised by the condition of his bicycle?

Vocabulary

retail (rē′ tāl) *v.* to sell directly to the consumer
fortnight (fôrt′ nīt) *n.* two weeks

---

2. *Akara balls* are ball-shaped bean cakes.

Analyze Historical Context What do the actions of Jonathan's family members show?

Vocabulary

edifice (ed′ ə fis) *n.* a building, especially a large, important-looking one

a miner, to find out what was what. The only thing he did find out in the end was that that little house of his was even a greater blessing than he had thought. Some of his fellow ex-miners who had nowhere to return at the end of the day's waiting just slept outside the doors of the offices and cooked what meal they could scrounge together in Bournvita tins. As the weeks lengthened and still nobody could say what was what Jonathan discontinued his weekly visits altogether and faced his palm wine bar.

Visual Vocabulary
Here a queue (kyū) means a line of people.

But nothing puzzles God. Came the day of the windfall when after five days of endless scuffles in queues and counter queues in the sun outside the Treasury he had twenty pounds counted into his palms as ex gratia[3] award for the rebel money he had turned in. It was like Christmas for him and for many others like him when the payments began. They called it (since few could manage its proper official name) *egg rasher.*

As soon as the pound notes were placed in his palm Jonathan simply closed it tight over them and buried fist and money inside his trouser pocket. He had to be extra careful because he had seen a man a couple of days earlier collapse into near madness in an instant before that oceanic crowd because no sooner had he got his twenty pounds than some heartless ruffian picked it off him. Though it was not right that a man in such an extremity of agony should be blamed yet many in the queues that day were able to remark quietly on the victim's carelessness, especially after he pulled out the innards of his pocket and revealed a hole in it big enough to pass a thief's head. But of course he had insisted that the money had been in the other pocket, pulling it out too to show its comparative wholeness. So one had to be careful.

Jonathan soon transferred the money to his left hand and pocket so as to leave his right free for shaking hands should the need arise, though by fixing his gaze at such an elevation as to miss all approaching human faces he made sure that the need did not arise, until he got home.

He was normally a heavy sleeper but that night he heard all the neighborhood noises die down one after another. Even the night watchman who knocked the hour on some metal somewhere in the distance had fallen silent after knocking one o'clock. That must have been the last thought in Jonathan's mind before he was finally carried away himself. He couldn't have been gone for long, though, when he was violently awakened again.

"Who is knocking?" whispered his wife lying beside him on the floor.

"I don't know," he whispered back breathlessly.

The second time the knocking came it was so loud and imperious that the rickety old door could have fallen down.

"Who is knocking?" he asked then, his voice parched and trembling.

"Na tief-man and him people," came the cool reply. "Make you hopen de door." This was followed by the heaviest knocking of all.

Maria was the first to raise the alarm, then he followed and all their children.

---

3. Something that is awarded *ex gratia* (eks grāsh′ ē ə) is given as a favor rather than as a legal right. The Latin word *gratia* means "kindness."

Encountering the Unexpected What visitors might be at the door? Are Jonathan and his wife completely surprised? Explain.

Children Dancing, c. 1948. Robert Gwathmey. Oil on canvas, 30 x 40 in. The Butler Institute of American Art, Youngstown, OH.

View the Art Inspired by African culture and Pablo Picasso, Gwathmey uses vibrant colors and symbolic abstraction to tell stories about his subjects. How might this painting reflect Jonathan and his family's outlook on life?

"Police-o! Thieves-o! Neighbors-o! Police-o! We are lost! We are dead! Neighbors, are you asleep? Wake up! Police-o!"

This went on for a long time and then stopped suddenly. Perhaps they had scared the thief away. There was total silence. But only for a short while.

"You done finish?" asked the voice outside. "Make we help you small. Oya, everybody!"

"Police-o! Tief-man-o! Neighbors-o! we done loss-o! Police-o! . . ."

There were at least five other voices besides the leader's.

Jonathan and his family were now completely paralyzed by terror. Maria and the children sobbed inaudibly like lost souls. Jonathan groaned continuously.

The silence that followed the thieves' alarm vibrated horribly. Jonathan all but begged their leader to speak again and be done with it.

"My frien," said he at long last, "we don try our best for call dem but I tink say dem all done sleep-o . . . So wetin we go do now? Sometaim you wan call soja? Or you wan make we call dem for you? Soja better pass police. No be so?"

"Na so!" replied his men. Jonathan thought he heard even more voices now

Analyze Historical Context Why does no one in the neighborhood respond when the thieves pound on Jonathan's door? Why do the thieves call for the police?

Dialect What does the term "soja" mean? Why are this and other words presented here with unusual spellings?

CHINUA ACHEBE

than before and groaned heavily. His legs were sagging under him and his throat felt like sandpaper.

"My frien, why you no de talk again. I de ask you say you wan make we call soja?"

"No."

"Awrighto. Now make we talk business. We no be bad tief. We no like for make trouble. Trouble done finish. War done finish and all the katakata[4] wey de for inside. No Civil War again. This time na Civil Peace. No be so?"

"Na so!" answered the horrible chorus.

"What do you want from me? I am a poor man. Everything I had went with this war. Why do you come to me? You know people who have money. We . . ."

"Awright! We know say you no get plenty money. But we sef no get even anini.[5] So derefore make you open dis window and give us one hundred pound and we go commot. Orderwise we de come for inside now to show you guitar-boy like dis . . ."

A volley of automatic fire rang through the sky. Maria and the children began to weep aloud again.

"Ah, missisi de cry again. No need for dat. We done talk say we na good tief. We just take our small money and go nwayorly. No molest. Abi we de molest?"

"At all!" sang the chorus.

"My friends," began Jonathan hoarsely. "I hear what you say and I thank you. If I had one hundred pounds . . ."

"Lookia my frien, no be play we come play for your house. If we make mistake and step for inside you no go like am-o. So derefore . . ."

---

4. The word *katakata* may be meant to imitate the sound of gunfire. The rest of the phrase is Nigerian dialect for "that went with it."
5. An *anini* (ä nē´ ē) is a small Nigerian coin worth less than one cent.

Dialect What does the author's use of dialect here add to the story?

"To God who made me; if you come inside and find one hundred pounds, take it and shoot me and shoot my wife and children. I swear to God. The only money I have in this life is this twenty-pounds *egg rasher* they gave me today . . ."

"OK. Time de go. Make you open dis window and bring the twenty pound. We go manage am like dat."

There were now loud murmurs of dissent among the chorus: "Na lie de man de lie; e get plenty money . . . Make we go inside and search properly well . . . Wetin be twenty pound? . . ."

"Shurrup!" rang the leader's voice like a lone shot in the sky and silenced the murmuring at once. "Are you dere? Bring the money quick!"

"I am coming," said Jonathan fumbling in the darkness with the key of the small wooden box he kept by his side on the mat.

At the first sign of light as neighbors and others assembled to commiserate with him he was already strapping his five-gallon demijohn to his bicycle carrier and his wife, sweating in the open fire, was turning over akara balls in a wide clay bowl of boiling oil. In the corner his eldest son was rinsing out dregs of yesterday's palm wine from old beer bottles.

"I count it as nothing," he told his sympathizers, his eyes on the rope he was tying. "What is *egg rasher*? Did I depend on it last week? Or is it greater than other things that went with the war? I say, let *egg rasher* perish in the flames! Let it go where everything else has gone. Nothing puzzles God." ∽

Visual Vocabulary
A *demijohn* is a large earthenware or glass bottle, encased in wicker.

After You Read

Respond and Think Critically

Respond and Interpret

1. What is Jonathan Iwegbu's attitude toward life?
2. Why did Jonathan mistrust the officer who wanted to take his bicycle?
3. In what ways does Jonathan begin to rebuild his life after the war?

Analyze and Evaluate

4. (a) What does Jonathan mean by his statement, "Nothing puzzles God"? (b) What does this statement reveal about Jonathan's character?
5. Do you think that the title of this story is appropriate, or would "Civil War" have been a better title? Explain.

Connect

6. **Big Idea** Encountering the Unexpected What message do you think emerges from Jonathan's unexpected, but repeated, good fortune?
7. **Connect to the Author** How might Achebe's personal history have influenced his portrayals of Jonathan and the other characters?

Literary Element Dialect

Dialect is regional variation in language. It identifies a group of people and tells about their history.

1. What words in the text show the British influence on the Ibo's language?
2. Why do you think the thieves who rob Jonathan speak English with a heavier African accent than Jonathan does?

Reading Strategy Analyze Historical Context

Through **historical context**, one can clearly picture the lawless setting of Nigeria. Review the web you made on page 65. Then answer the questions.

1. How would you describe the civil peace in Nigeria?
2. How does Jonathan feel about the changes that the war has inflicted on him and his family?

Vocabulary Practice

Practice with Denotation and Connotation Denotation is the literal, or dictionary, meaning of a word. **Connotation** is the implied, or cultural, meaning of a word. For example, the words *confused* and *flustered* have a similar denotation, but *flustered* suggests a nervous, flighty kind of confusion.

Each of these vocabulary words is listed with a word or term that has a similar denotation. Explain how the words vary in suggestions.

1. commandeer — take over
2. amenable — responsive
3. retail — sell
4. fortnight — two weeks
5. edifice — building

Literature Online

Selection Resources For Selection Quizzes, eFlashcards, and Reading-Writing Connection activities, go to glencoe.com and enter QuickPass code GL59794u1.

Writing

Write a List Imagine that a police officer has come to interview Jonathan about the robbery. List questions that the police officer might ask, and write what you imagine Jonathan's response might be.

CHINUA ACHEBE 71

Learning Objectives

In this workshop, you will focus on the following objective:

Vocabulary: Understanding dictionary use.

Vocabulary Workshop

Dictionary Use

"There were now loud murmurs of dissent among the chorus: 'Na lie de man de lie; e get plenty money...'"

—Chinua Achebe, from "Civil Peace"

Literature Connection In this scene from "Civil Peace," thieves surround Jonathan's house and demand payment. Their leader agrees to settle for twenty pounds. They are speaking in a Nigerian dialect. But there's a standard English word that is key to this passage. What does *dissent* mean? A dictionary can tell you.

Find a Word The main part of a dictionary consists of word entries and their definitions. Look for guide words at the top of each page. These tell you the first and last words listed on the page and can help you locate entries much more quickly than if you simply browse.

The Main Entry A main entry tells you far more about a word than its definition. Here is what one dictionary says about *dissent*:

Entry word is broken into syllables.

The pronunciation is indicated in simplified spelling.

The part or parts of speech of the word are indicated.

dis·sent (di sent´) *v.i.* **1.** to differ in opinion or feeling; withhold approval; disagree (often with *from*): *Many people dissented from the policy of the government. Of the ten board members, only one dissented.* **2.** to refuse to conform to the rules, doctrines, or beliefs of an established church. —*n.* **1.** difference of opinion or feeling; disagreement. **2.** refusal to conform to rules, doctrines, or beliefs of an established church. [Latin *dissentíre* to disagree.]

← Example sentences show how a word is used.

The etymology explains the history of a word.

Dictionary entries may also provide

- preferred spellings when alternate forms of words are acceptable
- inflected forms of the main entry word, such as plurals, adverbs, or adjectives
- cross references to synonyms and antonyms
- guidelines that show how a word is used in different contexts

Exercise

Use the dictionary entry in this lesson to answer the following questions.

1. Which syllable of *dissent* receives an accent?
2. Why might the dictionary have included two example sentences?
3. *Dissent* is often a verb. What other part of speech can it be?

Tip

Homographs are words that are spelled the same but have different meanings and histories. For example, *sole* can mean "the bottom of a foot"; it can also mean "a type of fish." Since these words are so distinct, they are listed separately. Each homograph is labeled with a small number.

Technology

Using an online dictionary, you simply enter a search word to find its definition. Online dictionaries also offer features such as illustrations, word games, language tips, and fun facts.

Vocabulary For more vocabulary practice, go to glencoe.com and enter QuickPass code GL59794u1.

Before You Read

The Masque of the Red Death

Meet Edgar Allan Poe
(1809–1849)

With his dark, deep-set eyes and intense gaze, Edgar Allan Poe looked the part of a Romantic poet. The rhythms of his poetry fascinated readers. His mystery and horror stories, with chilling plots and memorable characters, set a standard for subsequent writers.

> "All that we see or seem
> Is but a dream within a dream."
>
> —Edgar Allan Poe
> from "A Dream Within a Dream"

Early Struggles Poe was born in Boston, Massachusetts, to traveling actors. His father disappeared when Poe was an infant; his mother died when Poe was about two years old. John and Frances Allan of Richmond, Virginia, raised the boy but never legally adopted him. Poe took the Allans' surname as his middle name.

Poe attended the University of Virginia. He was an excellent student but also a gambler, accumulating debts he could not repay. A gifted writer, Poe published his first book of poems at age eighteen. However, he made no money from the book.

Poe served in the army for two years and then entered the military academy at West Point, which dismissed him for skipping classes and drills. Finally, he moved to New York City and turned to writing fulltime. His short story "MS. Found in a Bottle" won a writing prize, which led to a job at the *Southern Literary Messenger* in Richmond. The magazine published many of his reviews, poems, essays, and stories.

Terrifying Tales At twenty-six, Poe married Virginia Clemm, his teenage cousin, and lived with her and her mother. He continued to produce a steady stream of fiction, including the haunting horror tales "The Fall of the House of Usher" and "The Masque of the Red Death." "The Murders in the Rue Morgue" is considered to be the first detective story.

By 1844 Poe's melodic poem "The Raven" had become a great success. However, in 1847 his cherished young wife died of tuberculosis.

In 1849 Poe went to Richmond to give a lecture and was expected later in Philadelphia. But he was found unconscious on a street in Baltimore and died several days later. The cause of his death remains unknown.

Author Search For more about Edgar Allan Poe, go to glencoe.com and enter QuickPass code GL59794u1.

Literature and Reading Preview

Connect to the Story
What events do you perceive as beyond your control? Freewrite for a few minutes about these events.

Build Background
Plague is a contagious bacterial disease that spreads rapidly and is usually fatal. Throughout history it has caused major epidemics. The most widespread epidemic began in Constantinople in 1334 and quickly spread throughout Europe, causing an estimated twenty-five million deaths. At that time, the disease was known as the Black Death.

Set Purposes for Reading

Big Idea Encountering the Unexpected
As you read "The Masque of the Red Death," ask yourself, How does Poe use setting and plot twists to introduce unexpected events?

Literary Element Allegory
An **allegory** is a narrative work with two levels of meaning—the literal and the symbolic. All or most of the characters, settings, and events in an allegory are **symbols** that stand for ideas beyond themselves. The overall purpose of an allegory is to teach a moral lesson. As you read, ask yourself, What moral lesson does Poe teach the reader through his use of allegorical symbols in this story?

Reading Strategy Interpret Imagery
Writers often use **imagery,** which is language that appeals to one or more of the five senses. Imagery utilizes "word pictures" to evoke emotional responses and help readers understand a story's meaning and mood. As you read, ask yourself, Which of Poe's sensory details help generate suspense?

Tip: List Images Create a chart that lists images from the story and their emotional impact.

Imagery	Emotional Response
"Blood was its Avatar and its seal—the redness and the horror of blood."	The Red Death is a horrible disease.

Learning Objectives

For pages 73–84

In studying this text, you will focus on the following objectives:

Literary Study: Analyzing allegory.

Reading: Interpreting imagery.

Vocabulary

profuse (prə fūs′) *adj.* great in amount, plentiful; p. 75 *A profuse rain often leads to flooding.*

countenance (koun′ tə nəns) *n.* the face; p. 77 *Her smiling countenance revealed her happiness.*

wanton (wont′ ən) *adj.* shamelessly unrestrained, immoral; p. 78 *Sometimes, wild dancing makes dancers seem wanton.*

spectral (spek′ trəl) *adj.* ghostlike; p. 80 *The gleaming snow gave the scene a spectral quality.*

blasphemous (blas′ fə məs) *adj.* showing disrespect or scorn for God or anything sacred; p. 80 *As she grew angrier, her words became increasingly blasphemous.*

Tip: Analogies To solve an analogy, determine the relationship between the first pair of words. Then apply that relationship to the second pair of words.

The Masque of the Red Death

Bodiam Castle, 1906. Wilfred Ball.

Edgar Allan Poe

The "Red Death" had long devastated the country. No pestilence had ever been so fatal, or so hideous. Blood was its Avatar[1] and its seal—the redness and the horror of blood. There were sharp pains, and sudden dizziness, and then **profuse** bleeding at the pores, with dissolution.[2] The scarlet stains upon the body and especially upon the face of the victim, were the pest ban[3] which shut him out from the aid and from the sympathy of his fellowmen. And the whole seizure, progress, and termination of the disease, were the incidents of half an hour.

But the Prince Prospero was happy and dauntless[4] and sagacious.[5] When his dominions[6] were half depopulated, he summoned to his presence a thousand hale and light-hearted friends from

---

1. In Hinduism, an *Avatar* is a god that takes on human form. Here, the word means a visible form, or embodiment, of the disease.
2. Here, *dissolution* is death.
3. A *pest ban* is an official declaration that a person has been stricken with plague. Here, the blood stains on the victim's body became his or her own pest ban.

Vocabulary

profuse (prə fūs´) *adj.* great in amount, plentiful

---

4. *Dauntless* means "fearless" or "courageous."
5. *Sagacious* means "wise."
6. The prince's *dominions* are the territories he rules.

Encountering the Unexpected *From the grim description of the Red Death, why do you suppose Prince Prospero and his friends seem so light-hearted?*

EDGAR ALLAN POE **75**

among the knights and dames of his court, and with these retired to the deep seclusion of one of his castellated abbeys.[7] This was an extensive and magnificent structure, the creation of the prince's own eccentric yet august taste. A strong and lofty wall girdled it in. This wall had gates of iron. The courtiers, having entered, brought furnaces and massy hammers and welded the bolts. They resolved to leave means neither of ingress nor egress[8] to the sudden impulses of despair or of frenzy from within. The abbey was amply provisioned. With such precautions the courtiers might bid defiance to contagion. The external world could take care of itself. In the meantime it was folly to grieve, or to think. The prince had provided all the appliances of pleasure. There were buffoons, there were improvisatori,[9] there were ballet-dancers, there were musicians, there was Beauty, there was wine. All these and security were within. Without was the "Red Death."

It was toward the close of the fifth or sixth month of his seclusion, and while the pestilence raged most furiously abroad, that the Prince Prospero entertained his thousand friends at a masked ball of the most unusual magnificence.

It was a voluptuous[10] scene, that masquerade. But first let me tell of the rooms in which it was held. There were seven—an imperial suite. In many palaces, however, such suites form a long and straight vista, while the folding doors slide back nearly to the walls on either hand, so that the view of the whole extent is scarcely impeded. Here the case was very different; as might have been expected from the duke's love of the *bizarre*. The apartments were so irregularly disposed[11] that the vision embraced but little more than one at a time. There was a sharp turn at every twenty or thirty yards, and at each turn a novel effect. To the right and left, in the middle of each wall, a tall and narrow Gothic window looked out upon a closed corridor which pursued the windings of the suite. These windows were of stained glass whose color varied in accordance with the prevailing hue of the decorations of the chamber into which it opened. That at the eastern extremity was hung, for example, in blue—and vividly blue were its windows. The second chamber was purple in its ornaments and tapestries, and here the panes were purple. The third was green throughout, and so were the casements.[12] The fourth was furnished and lighted with orange—the fifth with

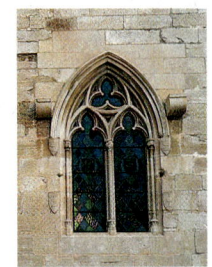

Visual Vocabulary
Gothic architecture developed in Europe between the twelfth and sixteenth centuries. A Gothic window has a pointed arch and many small panes of stained or clear glass.

---

7. A *castellated abbey* is a fortified structure originally built as a monastery or intended, as the prince's was, to resemble one.
8. With *means neither of ingress nor egress*, there is no way in and no way out.
9. *Buffoons* are clowns or comedians, and *improvisatori* (im prov′ ə zə tôr′ ē) are poets who improvise, or make up, verses as they perform.
10. Here, *voluptuous* (və lup′ cho͞o əs) means "giving great pleasure to the senses."

Allegory What does the secluded abbey symbolize?

11. *Bizarre* means "that which is extremely strange or odd." A bizarre feature of Prospero's abbey is the way the rooms (*apartments*) are arranged (*disposed*) so that only one is visible at a time.
12. *Casements* are windows.

Encountering the Unexpected How does the description of the layout of the rooms highlight the atmosphere in the story?

white—the sixth with violet. The seventh apartment was closely shrouded in black velvet tapestries that hung all over the ceiling and down the walls, falling in heavy folds upon a carpet of the same material and hue. But in this chamber only, the color of the windows failed to correspond with the decorations. The panes here were scarlet—a deep blood color. Now in no one of the seven apartments was there any lamp or candelabrum, amid the profusion of golden ornaments that lay scattered to and fro or depended from the roof. There was no light of any kind emanating from lamp or candle within the suite of chambers. But in the corridors that followed the suite, there stood, opposite to each window, a heavy tripod, bearing a brazier of fire, that projected its rays through the tinted glass and so glaringly illumined the room. And thus were produced a multitude of gaudy and fantastic appearances. But in the western or black chamber the effect of the fire-light that streamed upon the dark hangings through the blood-tinted panes was ghastly in the extreme, and produced so wild a look upon the <u>countenances</u> of those who entered, that there were few of the company bold enough to set foot within its precincts at all.

It was in this apartment, also, that there stood against the western wall, a gigantic clock of ebony. Its pendulum swung to and fro with a dull, heavy, monotonous clang; and when the minute-hand made the circuit of the face, and the hour was to be stricken, there came from the brazen[13] lungs of the clock a sound which was clear and loud and deep and exceedingly musical, but of so peculiar a note and emphasis that, at each lapse of an hour, the musicians of the orchestra were constrained to pause, momentarily, in their performance, to hearken to the sound; and thus the waltzers perforce ceased their evolutions; and there was a brief disconcert[14] of the whole gay company; and, while the chimes of the clock yet rang, it was observed that the giddiest grew pale, and the more aged and sedate passed their hands over their brows as if in confused revery or meditation. But when the echoes had fully ceased, a light laughter at once pervaded the assembly; the musicians looked at each other and smiled as if at their own nervousness and folly, and made whispering vows, each to the other, that the next chiming of the clock should produce in them no similar emotion; and then, after the lapse of sixty minutes (which embrace three thousand and six hundred seconds of the Time that flies), there came yet another chiming of the clock, and then were the same disconcert and tremulousness and meditation as before.

But, in spite of these things, it was a gay and magnificent revel. The tastes of the duke were peculiar. He had a fine eye for colors and effects. He disregarded the *decora* of mere fashion. His plans were bold and

Visual Vocabulary
A *brazier* is a metal pan used to hold burning coal or charcoal, as a source of heat and light.

Vocabulary
<u>countenance</u> (koun′ tə nəns) n. the face

---

13. The clock's outer parts are *ebony*, a black wood; its inner workings are brass *(brazen)*.
14. The musicians feel obliged *(constrained)* to stop playing, the waltzers halt their complex patterns of movement *(evolutions)*, and everyone experiences temporary confusion and disorder *(disconcert)*.

Interpret Imagery How do people react to the sound of the chimes? What do you think the chiming means?

Allegory What does the chiming of the clock symbolize?

Costume Ball in the Tuileries: Napoleon III and the Countess Castiglione, 1867. Jean Baptiste Carpeaux. Oil on canvas. Musée d'Orsay, Paris.

View the Art In this painting Jean Baptiste Carpeaux uses a thick application, visible brushstrokes, and a lack of definition between his subjects to show a party of revelers. In what ways does this painting and Carpeaux's techniques reflect the party in the story?

fiery, and his conceptions glowed with barbaric lustre. There are some who would have thought him mad. His followers felt that he was not. It was necessary to hear and see and touch him to be *sure* that he was not.

He had directed, in great part, the movable embellishments of the seven chambers, upon occasion of this great *fête*;[15] and it was his own guiding taste which had given character to the masqueraders. Be sure they were grotesque. There were much glare and glitter and piquancy and phantasm—much of what has been since seen in "Hernani."[16] There were arabesque figures with unsuited limbs and appointments. There were delirious fancies such as the madman fashions. There were much of the beautiful, much of the **wanton**, much of the *bizarre*, something of the terrible, and not a little of that which might have excited disgust. To and fro in the seven chambers there stalked, in fact, a multitude of dreams. And these—the dreams—writhed in and about, taking hue from the rooms, and causing the wild music of the orchestra to seem as the echo of their steps. And, anon, there strikes the ebony clock which stands in the hall of the velvet. And then, for a moment, all is still, and all is silent save the voice of the clock. The dreams are stiff-frozen as they stand. But the echoes of the chime die away—they have endured but an instant—and a light, half-subdued laughter floats after them as they depart. And now again the music

---

15. A *fête* (fet) is a large, elaborate party.

16. Here, *piquancy* (pē′ kən sē) refers to what is charming, and *phantasm* to what is fantastic and unreal. *Hernani*, an 1830 drama and, especially, an opera based on the drama, is notable for its use of colorful, imaginative spectacle.

Vocabulary

wanton (wont′ ən) *adj.* shamelessly unrestrained, immoral

swells, and the dreams live, and writhe to and fro more merrily than ever, taking hue from the many-tinted windows through which stream the rays from the tripods. But to the chamber which lies most westwardly of the seven there are now none of the maskers who venture; for the night is waning away; and there flows a ruddier light through the blood-colored panes; and the blackness of the sable drapery appals[17]; and to him whose foot falls upon the sable carpet, there comes from the near clock of ebony a muffled peal more solemnly emphatic than any which reaches *their* ears who indulge in the more remote gaieties of the other apartments.

But these other apartments were densely crowded, and in them beat feverishly the heart of life. And the revel went whirlingly on, until at length there commenced the sounding of midnight upon the clock. And then the music ceased, as I have told; and the evolutions of the waltzers were quieted; and there was an uneasy cessation of all things as before. But now there were twelve strokes to be sounded by the bell of the clock; and thus it happened, perhaps that more of thought crept, with more of time, into the meditations of the thoughtful among those who revelled. And thus too, it happened, perhaps, that before the last echoes of the last chime had utterly sunk into silence, there were many individuals in the crowd who had found leisure to become aware of the presence of a masked figure which had arrested the attention of no single individual before. And the rumor of this new presence having spread itself whisperingly around, there arose at length from the whole company a buzz, or murmur, expressive of disapprobation[18] and surprise—then, finally, of terror, of horror, and of disgust.

In an assembly of phantasms such as I have painted, it may well be supposed that no ordinary appearance could have excited such sensation. In truth the masquerade license of the night was nearly unlimited; but the figure in question had out-Heroded Herod,[19] and gone beyond the bounds of even the prince's indefinite decorum. There are chords in the hearts of the most reckless which cannot be touched without emotion. Even with the utterly lost, to whom life and death are equally jests, there are matters of which no jest can be made. The whole company, indeed, seemed now deeply to feel that in the costume and bearing of the stranger neither wit nor propriety existed. The figure was tall and gaunt, and shrouded from head to foot in the habiliments[20] of the grave. The mask which concealed the visage was made so nearly to resemble the countenance of a stiffened corpse that the closest scrutiny must have had difficulty in detecting the cheat. And yet all this might have been endured, if not approved, by the mad revellers around. But the mummer had gone so far as to assume the type of the Red Death. His vesture[21] was dabbled in *blood*—and his broad brow, with all the features of the face, was besprinkled with the scarlet horror.

---

17. To *appal* means "to horrify, dismay, or shock."

Encountering the Unexpected What clues does the author give that something is about to happen?

18. *Disapprobation* means "disapproval."
19. To have *out-Heroded Herod,* the mysterious figure has done something even more outrageous than Herod the Great, the tyrant who, in an effort to kill the baby Jesus, ordered the murder of all male infants in Bethlehem.
20. *Habiliments* are clothes.
21. A *mummer* is a person dressed in a mask and costume for a party or play, and *vesture* is clothing.

Interpret Imagery In a room full of bizarrely costumed people, why does this new figure cause such a stir?

EDGAR ALLAN POE

Eyes in Darkness. Artist Unknown.

View the Art In *Eyes in Darkness*, the artist creates a shadowy figure who gazes directly at the viewer in an almost confrontational manner. How does the directness that this figure exhibits compare with the demeanor of the intruder who brings the Red Death?

When the eyes of Prince Prospero fell upon this **spectral** image (which, with a slow and solemn movement, as if more fully to sustain its *rôle*, stalked to and fro among the waltzers) he was seen to be convulsed, in the first moment with a strong shudder either of terror or distaste; but, in the next, his brow reddened with rage.

"Who dares"—he demanded hoarsely of the courtiers who stood near him—"who dares insult us with this **blasphemous**

> **Vocabulary**
> **spectral** (spekʹ trəl) *adj.* ghostlike

> **Vocabulary**
> **blasphemous** (blasʹ fə məs) *adj.* showing disrespect or scorn for God or anything sacred

mockery? Seize him and unmask him—that we may know whom we have to hang, at sunrise, from the battlements!"

It was in the eastern or blue chamber in which stood the Prince Prospero as he uttered these words. They rang throughout the seven rooms loudly and clearly, for the prince was a bold and robust man, and the music had become hushed at the waving of his hand.

It was in the blue room where stood the prince, with a group of pale courtiers by his side. At first, as he spoke, there was a slight rushing movement of this group in the direction of the intruder, who, at the moment was also near at hand, and now, with deliberate and stately step, made closer approach to the speaker. But from a certain nameless awe with which the mad assumptions of the mummer had inspired the whole party, there were found none who put forth hand to seize him; so that, unimpeded, he passed within a yard of the prince's person; and, while the vast assembly, as if with one impulse, shrank from the centres of the rooms to the walls, he made his way uninterruptedly, but with the same solemn and measured step which had distinguished him from the first, through the blue chamber to the purple—through the purple to the green—through the green to the orange—through this again to the white—and even thence to the violet, ere a decided movement had been made to arrest him. It was then, however, that the Prince Prospero, maddening with rage and the shame of his own momentary cowardice, rushed hurriedly through the six chambers, while none followed him on account of a deadly terror that had seized upon all. He bore aloft a drawn dagger, and had approached, in rapid impetuosity, to within three or four feet of the retreating figure, when the latter, having attained the extremity of the velvet apartment, turned suddenly and confronted his pursuer. There was a sharp cry—and the dagger dropped gleaming upon the sable carpet, upon which, instantly afterward, fell prostrate in death the Prince Prospero. Then, summoning the wild courage of despair, a throng of the revellers at once threw themselves into the black apartment, and, seizing the mummer, whose tall figure stood erect and motionless within the shadow of the ebony clock, gasped in unutterable horror at finding the grave cerements and corpse-like mask, which they handled with so violent a rudeness, untenanted[22] by any tangible form.

Visual Vocabulary
Cerements are strips of cloth used to wrap a dead body.

And now was acknowledged the presence of the Red Death. He had come like a thief in the night. And one by one dropped the revellers in the blood-bedewed halls of their revel, and died each in the despairing posture of his fall. And the life of the ebony clock went out with that of the last of the gay. And the flames of the tripods expired. And Darkness and Decay and the Red Death held illimitable[23] dominion over all.

Encountering the Unexpected Why do you think the figure is able to walk from room to room without anyone stopping him?

22. *Untenanted* means "unoccupied" or "uninhabited."
23. *Illimitable* means "limitless" or "incapable of being bounded."

Allegory What is the significance of the dropped dagger?

After You Read

Respond and Think Critically

Respond and Interpret

1. Describe your feelings about the masked ball at the beginning and as the story progressed.

2. (a) Why is the "Red Death" such a terrible and feared disease? (b) What aspect of the "Red Death" is portrayed as sinister? Explain.

3. (a) How does Prince Prospero respond to the costume and behavior of the uninvited guest? (b) What details does his response reveal about his attitude toward death in general?

Analyze and Evaluate

4. (a) How is the seventh room different from the other rooms? (b) Why is the clock in this room?

5. (a) Why do you think the prince is determined to kill the intruder? (b) How does Poe weave images from the story together to build the sense of hopelessness in the scene leading up to the prince's death?

Connect

6. **Big Idea** Encountering the Unexpected Does Poe prepare you for the ending, or is it unexpected? Explain.

7. **Connect to Today** (a) How would you expect people in today's world to react to an epidemic? (b) How might a person's economic situation influence his or her decision?

Primary Visual Artifact

Plague Doctors

Protective uniforms such as these were worn by doctors during the Great Plague, which killed 75,000 people in London from 1664 to 1666. Doctors at the time did not know how diseases spread. Many people thought that the plague was punishment from God. Doctors did realize that contact with an infected person often led to the spread of disease. As a result, they tried to keep the plague at bay by wearing protective uniforms: a long tunic of linen or waxed cloth, a mask, full-length boots, leather gloves, a leather hat, eyeglasses, and a beak. The beak was filled with aromatic herbs thought to filter the air that the doctor breathed. The herbs also helped to mitigate the stench of death.

Group Activity Discuss the following questions with your classmates.

1. What types of modern protective clothing do these protective uniforms remind you of?

2. How effective do you think these uniforms would have been at protecting doctors from the plague? Explain.

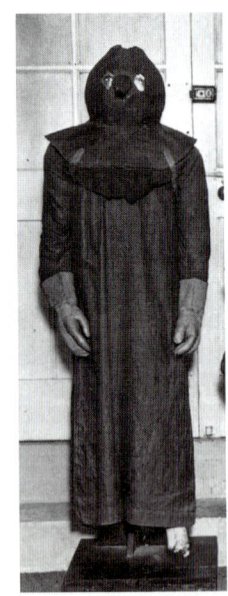

Protective clothing on display at the Welcome Museum worn by doctors treating patients during the Great Plague of 1665.

Literary Element: Allegory

The underlying symbolic meaning of an **allegory** has philosophical, social, religious, or political significance. Characters or material objects stand for something beyond themselves and are often personifications of abstract ideas, such as justice, evil, or truth. The purpose of an allegory is to teach a moral lesson.

1. (a) What is the symbolic significance of Prince Prospero's name? (b) In his representation of Prince Prospero and the revelers, what lesson does Poe teach about class divisions in society?
2. What does the abbey's seventh chamber represent?
3. What philosophical truth about human life does Poe teach in his allegory?

Review: Setting

As you learned on page 2, **setting** is the time and place in which the events of a story occur. Setting can also include the ideas, customs, values, and beliefs of a particular time and place. Setting often helps create an atmosphere or mood that is appropriate to the story.

Partner Activity Poe uses the setting mainly to evoke moods ranging from the ominous to the grotesque. With a partner, create a chart similar to the one below. In the left column, cite examples of descriptive language about the abbey. In the right column, label each example with an adjective that designates the mood.

Example	Mood
p. 76 "A strong and lofty wall girdled it in"	intimidating
p. 77 "the profusion of golden ornaments that lay scattered to and fro"	
p. 77 "fire-light that streamed upon the dark hangings through the blood-tinted panes"	

Reading Strategy: Interpret Imagery

SAT Skills Practice

1. The description of Prince Prospero's seventh room (pages 76–77) is calculated to remind the reader of death because

   (A) it has two tall gothic windows
   (B) all the light originates from two corridors outside the room
   (C) alone among the rooms, its window glass is of a different color from the furnishings
   (D) an enormous ebony clock stands against its western wall
   (E) it is the last in the series of rooms and is furnished entirely in black

Vocabulary Practice

Practice with Analogies Choose the word that best completes each analogy.

1. nose : countenance :: finger :
   a. thumb   **b.** knuckle   **c.** hand
2. generous : stingy :: profuse :
   a. sufficient   **b.** meager   **c.** abundant
3. blasphemous : reverent :: healthy :
   a. robust   **b.** sickly   **c.** hale
4. jealous : possessive :: spectral :
   a. grisly   **b.** gruesome   **c.** ghostly
5. bizarre : ordinary :: wanton :
   a. restrained   **b.** immoral   **c.** cruel

Literature Online

Selection Resources For Selection Quizzes, eFlashcards, and Reading-Writing Connection activities, go to glencoe.com and enter QuickPass code GL59794u1.

Respond Through Writing

Expository Essay

Analyze Symbolism "The Masque of the Red Death" is an allegory: a story in which the character, settings, and events stand for figures beyond themselves. In an essay, analyze how Poe uses the clock as a symbol in the allegory. Support your ideas with evidence from the story.

Understand the Task A **symbol** is something that exists on a literal level but also represents something on a figurative level.

Prewrite Locate references to the clock in the story and think about how the clock functions as a symbol by creating a question-and-answer chart like this one.

Question	Answer
What does the clock do?	
How do the chimes affect people?	
What is unique or unusual about the clock?	

Use your ideas to come up with the thesis, or controlling idea, for your essay. Then list the main ideas you will use to support your thesis.

Draft As you draft the body of your essay, incorporate evidence from the story. That is, quote details about the clock and its effects and then explain them. For example, explain why the size of the clock contributes to its symbolic significance.

Revise Exchange papers with a classmate and evaluate each other's essays according to the strategies on page 258. Does each body paragraph contain at least one piece of quoted evidence? Is each piece of quoted evidence followed by an explanation of what it means?

Edit and Proofread Proofread your paper, correcting any errors in grammar, spelling, and punctuation. Use the Grammar Tip in the side column to help you with the use of the colon.

Learning Objectives

For page 84

In this assignment, you will focus on the following objectives:

Writing: Analyzing symbolism in a short story.
Grammar: Using colons with long quotations.

Grammar Tip

Colon

Use a colon when you introduce a long quotation.

In the following sentence, words such as clang, stricken, brazen, *and* peculiar *emphasize the clock's eerie power:* "Its pendulum swung to and fro with a dull, heavy, monotonous clang; and when the minute-hand made the circuit of the face, and the hour was to be stricken, there came from the brazen lungs of the clock a sound which was clear and loud and deep and exceedingly musical, but of so peculiar a note. . .".

PART 2

Making Choices

Girl with Red Gloves, 2001. Lizzie Riches. Oil on canvas, 29.92 x 22.83 in. Private collection.

View the Art The artist titled this painting *Girl with Red Gloves,* but the girl also has black gloves before her. What messages about choice does this painting demonstrate?

BIG IDEA

Morning to night, people are faced with choices. Some of those choices have the power to change who we are. In the short stories in Part 2, you will read about difficult choices and surprising consequences. As you read these stories, ask yourself, How do the choices you make affect your life?

LITERARY FOCUS

Theme and Character

Learning Objectives

For pages 86–87

In studying this text, you will focus on the following objective:

Literary Study: Analyzing theme and character.

How do short stories develop themes and create characters?

Have you ever been so angry that you said something you later regretted? Perhaps, like many teenagers, you have argued with a parent or guardian and later regretted the fight. How is it sometimes hard for people who are feeling strong emotions to make choices about what they say? How do your feelings affect the choices you make?

Distributed By Universal Press Syndicate. Reprinted with permission. All rights reserved.

"Only two kinds of daughters," she shouted in Chinese. "Those who are obedient and those who follow their own mind! Only one kind of daughter can live in this house. Obedient daughter!"

"Then I wish I weren't your daughter. I wish you weren't my mother," I shouted. As I said these things I got scared. It felt like worms and toads and slimy things crawling out of my chest, but it also felt good, that this awful side of me had surfaced, at last.

"Too late to change this," my mother said shrilly.

And I could sense her anger rising to its breaking point. I wanted to see it spill over.

—Amy Tan, *from "Two Kinds"*

Theme

The **theme** of a story is its message about life. Sometimes a theme is expressed directly. This is called a **stated theme**. More commonly, a reader must look closely at the experiences of the main character and the lessons he or she learns to discover the theme. This is called an **implied theme**. The theme of "Two Kinds" is implied. What lessons might the narrator of "Two Kinds" learn? How might those lessons relate to the theme?

Author's Purpose The **author's purpose** will affect the delivery and impact of a story's theme. An author writing to entertain or tell a story usually implies the theme through lessons the important characters learn.

Characterization The way in which an author lets the reader know about a character is called **characterization.** Methods of characterization fall into two basic categories: direct and indirect. In **direct characterization,** a writer makes clear and direct statements about a character's personality. For example, in the excerpt here from "The Car We Had to Push," Thurber describes the grandfather as having "unexpected, and extremely lucid moments." In **indirect characterization,** the writer uses a character's words and actions as well as other characters' thoughts and statements to reveal a character's personality. In the excerpt from "An Astrologer's Day," Narayan uses the character's thoughts to tell the reader that the man does not see the future but does possess insight into his customers.

> He thought of all the evenings he had spent away from her, working; and he regretted them. He thought wonderingly of his fierce ambition and of the direction his life had taken; he thought of the hours he'd spent by himself, filling the yellow sheet that had brought him out here.
>
> —Jack Finney, *from "Contents of the Dead Man's Pocket"*

Character

A person in a literary work is called a **character.** Main characters are the most important. Secondary characters are less important and are also called minor characters. There are other ways to describe characters. A **round character** reveals more than one personality trait. A **flat character** reveals only one personality trait throughout the story. A **static character** does not change in the course of a story, whereas a **dynamic character** does.

> He was as much a stranger to the stars as were his innocent customers. Yet he said things which pleased and astonished everyone: that was more a matter of study, practice and shrewd guesswork.
>
> —R. K. Narayan, *from "An Astrologer's Day"*

> Grandfather was given to these sudden, unexpected, and extremely lucid moments; they were generally more embarassing than his other moments.
>
> —James Thurber, *from "The Car We Had to Push"*

Quickwrite

Create a Character Create your own fictional character using a graphic organizer like the one below. In the center oval, write your character's name. In each of the eight circles, write an adjective that describes your character. Then use each adjective in a sentence that could appear in your story. Use the examples from authors on this page to guide you. You may write sentences of dialogue, direct characterization, or indirect characterization. Try to suggest whether your character is flat or round, as well as static or dynamic, through the sentences you write. Finally, write a theme that a story about that character might convey.

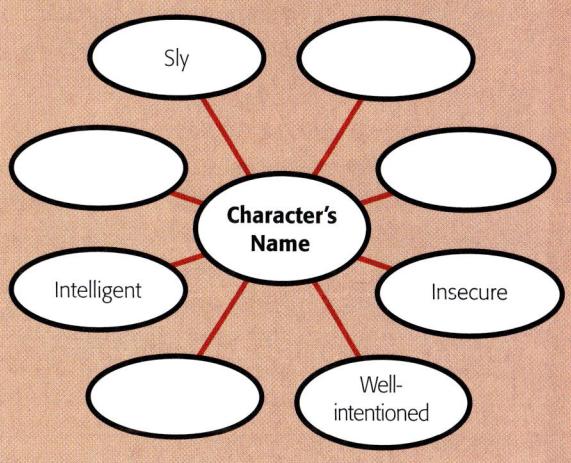

LITERARY FOCUS **87**

Before You Read

Two Kinds

Meet Amy Tan
(born 1952)

"I have a life that inspires me with a lot of stories."

—Amy Tan

Writing has always been Amy Tan's passion. In fact, she published her first essay, "What the Library Means to Me," when she was just eight years old. Though Tan went on to become an award-winning author, her fame did not come easily.

Troubled Years Amy Tan was born in Oakland, California. Her parents had immigrated to the United States from China. When Tan was a teenager, her father and her older brother both died of brain tumors within the space of a few months. Tan's mother, who began to worry that toxic chemicals in the environment were responsible, moved the family first to Holland, then to Germany, and later to Switzerland. These were difficult years for Tan. She escaped by diving into the world of books. "Reading for me was a refuge," she says.

Tan describes herself at that time as "a horrible child. I was angry. I was numb. Teenagers are already cynical at that age. But I also had this layer of grief that came out in anger." Conflicts arose between mother and daughter, which lasted for years. Some of the issues were cultural, some were generational, and others were purely personal.

Fact and Fiction Later, Tan incorporated this tension into several novels, the first of which was *The Joy Luck Club*, published in 1989. This novel detailed the many differences between a young Chinese woman and her late mother's Chinese friends. The novel earned a great deal of praise for Tan and has since been turned into an audiotape, a play, and a successful film. The story "Two Kinds" comes from that book.

Tan eventually resolved her differences with her mother, who encouraged her to tell the truth about painful details of their family's past. Many of these details found their way into Tan's next novel, *The Kitchen God's Wife*, as well as later works. Tan has now written five novels, a screenplay of *The Joy Luck Club*, and a book of essays titled *The Opposite of Fate: A Book of Musings*.

In these essays, Tan explores her own cultural heritage. As a young person, Tan has said, she tried to distance herself from her Chinese origins. However, her writing helped her discover how much her Chinese mother had influenced her. "My books have amounted to taking her stories—a gift to me—and giving them back to her."

Author Search For more about Amy Tan, go to glencoe.com and enter QuickPass code GL59794u1.

88 UNIT 1 THE SHORT STORY

Literature and Reading Preview

Connect to the Story
What experiences truly motivate people to achieve? List several of these experiences and then elaborate on one that motivated you to achieve something significant.

Build Background
The story is set in San Francisco's Chinatown, which is one of the largest Chinese communities outside of Asia. The neighborhood—with its fascinating mix of restaurants, shops, businesses, and religious and cultural institutions—is a crowded and bustling place. The area was settled by Chinese immigrants who arrived during the Gold Rush of 1849.

Big Idea Making Choices

As you read "Two Kinds," ask yourself, How are the narrator's choices different from her mother's?

Literary Element Motivation

Motivation is the reason or cause for a character's actions. Knowing a character's motivation for acting a certain way can help you understand his or her behavior more fully. Sometimes an author will state a character's motivation directly, while other times the motivation will be implied. As you read "Two Kinds," ask yourself, How does the author communicate the motivations that drive the characters' behavior?

Reading Strategy Connect to Personal Experience

Connecting is linking what you read to events and situations in your life or in other selections that you have read. When you **connect to personal experience,** you identify more closely with the characters' experiences as well as with the story's central theme. As you read, ask yourself, How can I link the experiences of the characters to my own life?

Tip: Connect Look for connections between story details and your life. Use a simple chart to note the connections.

Story Detail	Personal Connection
narrator is child of immigrants	my grandparents were immigrants

---

Learning Objectives

For pages 88–102

In studying this text, you will focus on the following objectives:

Literary Study: Analyzing motivation.

Reading: Connecting to personal experience.

Vocabulary

prodigy (prod′ə jē) *n.* an extraordinarily gifted or talented person, especially a child; p. 90 *The child prodigy played the difficult piece well.*

reproach (ri prōch′) *n.* blame; disgrace; discredit; p. 91 *My aunt did not criticize me aloud, but her look was filled with reproach.*

reverie (rev′ər ē) *n.* fanciful thinking, daydream; p. 94 *The teacher's abrupt question snapped me out of my reverie.*

discordant (dis kôrd′ənt) *adj.* not in agreement or harmony; p. 94 *While some violinists make beautiful music, I produce only discordant sounds.*

fiasco (fē as′kō) *n.* a complete or humiliating failure; p. 97 *None of the actors knew their lines, so the play was a fiasco.*

Tip: Word Usage Different contexts call for different levels of formality in word choice. You might use the word *daydream* to tell your thoughts to friends but in a formal composition, you would likely use the word *reverie* instead.

AMY TAN 89

Two Kinds

Amy Tan

Sign in Chinatown Section of San Francisco.

My mother believed you could be anything you wanted to be in America. You could open a restaurant. You could work for the government and get good retirement. You could buy a house with almost no money down. You could become rich. You could become instantly famous.

"Of course, you can be **prodigy**, too," my mother told me when I was nine. "You can be best anything. What does Auntie Lindo know? Her daughter, she is only best tricky."

America was where all my mother's hopes lay. She had come to San Francisco in 1949 after losing everything in China: her mother and father, her family home, her first husband, and two daughters, twin baby girls. But she never looked back with regret. Things could get better in so many ways.

We didn't immediately pick the right kind of prodigy. At first my mother thought I could be a Chinese Shirley Temple. We'd watch Shirley's old movies on TV as though they were training films. My mother would poke my arm and say, "*Ni kan.* You watch." And I would see Shirley tapping her feet, or singing a sailor song, or pursing her lips into a very round O while saying "Oh, my goodness."

Visual Vocabulary
Shirley Temple was a popular child movie star of the 1930s.

Vocabulary

prodigy (prod′ə jē) *n.* an extraordinarily gifted or talented person, especially a child

Motivation What reasons might the mother have for her optimism about the United States?

Visual Vocabulary
The Mission District is a residential neighborhood in San Francisco.

"*Ni kan,*" my mother said, as Shirley's eyes flooded with tears. "You already know how. Don't need talent for crying!"

Soon after my mother got this idea about Shirley Temple, she took me to the beauty training school in the Mission District and put me in the hands of a student who could barely hold the scissors without shaking. Instead of getting big fat curls, I emerged with an uneven mass of crinkly black fuzz. My mother dragged me off to the bathroom and tried to wet down my hair.

"You look like Negro Chinese," she lamented, as if I had done this on purpose.

The instructor of the beauty training school had to lop off these soggy clumps to make my hair even again. "Peter Pan is very popular these days," the instructor assured my mother. I now had hair the length of a boy's, with curly bangs that hung at a slant two inches above my eyebrows. I liked the haircut, and it made me actually look forward to my future fame.

In fact, in the beginning I was just as excited as my mother, maybe even more so. I pictured this prodigy part of me as many different images, and I tried each one on for size. I was a dainty ballerina girl standing by the curtain, waiting to hear the music that would send me floating on my tiptoes. I was like the Christ child lifted out of the straw manger, crying with holy indignity. I was Cinderella stepping from her pumpkin carriage with sparkly cartoon music filling the air.

In all of my imaginings I was filled with a sense that I would soon become perfect. My mother and father would adore me. I would be beyond **reproach.** I would never feel the need to sulk, or to clamor for anything.

But sometimes the prodigy in me became impatient. "If you don't hurry up and get me out of here, I'm disappearing for good," it warned. "And then you'll always be nothing."

Every night after dinner my mother and I would sit at the Formica-topped[1] kitchen table. She would present new tests, taking her examples from stories of amazing children that she had read in Ripley's Believe It or Not or Good Housekeeping, Reader's Digest, or any of a dozen other magazines she kept in a pile in our bathroom. My mother got these magazines from people whose houses she cleaned. And since she cleaned many houses each week, we had a great assortment. She would look through them all, searching for stories about remarkable children.

The first night she brought out a story about a three-year-old boy who knew the capitals of all the states and even of most of the European countries. A teacher was quoted as saying that the little boy could also pronounce the names of the foreign cities correctly. "What's the capital of Finland?" my mother asked me, looking at the story.

---

1. *Formica* (fôr mī′kə) is a plastic substance used to cover kitchen and bathroom surfaces because it is resistant to heat and water.

Motivation *What motivates the mother to ask her daughter this question?*

Connect to Personal Experience *What kinds of daydreams about success are common today?*

Vocabulary
reproach (ri prōch′) *n.* blame; disgrace; discredit

All I knew was the capital of California, because Sacramento was the name of the street we lived on in Chinatown. "Nairobi!"[2] I guessed, saying the most foreign word I could think of. She checked to see if that might be one way to pronounce *Helsinki* before showing me the answer.

The tests got harder—multiplying numbers in my head, finding the queen of hearts in a deck of cards, trying to stand on my head without using my hands, predicting the daily temperatures in Los Angeles, New York, and London. One night I had to look at a page from the Bible for three minutes and then report everything I could remember. "Now Jehoshaphat[3] had riches and honor in abundance and . . . that's all I remember, Ma," I said.

And after seeing, once again, my mother's disappointed face, something inside me began to die. I hated the tests, the raised hopes and failed expectations. Before going to bed that night I looked in the mirror above the bathroom sink, and when I saw only my face staring back—and understood that it would always be this ordinary face—I began to cry. Such a sad, ugly girl! I made high-pitched noises like a crazed animal, trying to scratch out the face in the mirror.

And then I saw what seemed to be the prodigy side of me—a face I had never seen before. I looked at my reflection, blinking so that I could see more clearly. The girl staring back at me was angry, powerful. She and I were the same. I had new thoughts, willful thoughts—or, rather, thoughts filled with lots of won'ts. I won't let her change me, I promised myself. I won't be what I'm not. So now when my mother presented her tests, I performed listlessly, my head propped on one arm. I pretended to be bored. And I was. I got so bored that I started counting the bellows of the foghorns out on the bay while my mother drilled me in other areas. The sound was comforting and reminded me of the cow jumping over the moon. And the next day I played a game with myself, seeing if my mother would give up on me before eight bellows. After a while I usually counted only one bellow, maybe two at most. At last she was beginning to give up hope.

Two or three months went by without any mention of my being a prodigy. And then one day my mother was watching the *Ed Sullivan Show*[4] on TV. The TV was old and the sound kept shorting out. Every time my mother got halfway up from the sofa to adjust the set, the sound would come back on and Sullivan would be talking. As soon as she sat down, Sullivan would go silent again. She got up—the TV broke into loud piano music. She sat down—silence. Up and down, back and forth, quiet and loud. It was like a stiff, embraceless dance between her and the TV set. Finally, she stood by the set with her hand on the sound dial.

She seemed entranced by the music, a frenzied little piano piece with a mesmerizing quality, which alternated between quick, playful passages and teasing, lilting[5] ones.

"*Ni kan*," my mother said, calling me over with hurried hand gestures. "Look here."

I could see why my mother was fascinated by the music. It was being pounded out by a little Chinese girl, about nine years old, with a Peter Pan haircut. The girl had the sauciness[6] of a Shirley Temple. She

---

2. *Nairobi* (nī rō′ bē) is the capital of Kenya in east central Africa.
3. *Jehoshaphat* (ji hosh′ ə fat′) was a king of Judah in the ninth century B.C.
4. The *Ed Sullivan Show* was a popular weekly TV variety show that aired from 1955 to 1971.
5. *Lilting* means "light and lively."
6. *Sauciness* means "boldness that is playful and lighthearted."

was proudly modest, like a proper Chinese child. And she also did a fancy sweep of a curtsy, so that the fluffy skirt of her white dress cascaded to the floor like the petals of a large carnation.

In spite of these warning signs, I wasn't worried. Our family had no piano and we couldn't afford to buy one, let alone reams of sheet music and piano lessons. So I could be generous in my comments when my mother bad-mouthed the little girl on TV.

"Play note right, but doesn't sound good!" my mother complained. "No singing sound." "What are you picking on her for?" I said carelessly. "She's pretty good. Maybe she's not the best, but she's trying hard." I knew almost immediately that I would be sorry I had said that.

"Just like you," she said. "Not the best. Because you not trying." She gave a little huff as she let go of the sound dial and sat down on the sofa.

The little Chinese girl sat down also, to play an encore of "Anitra's Tanz," by Grieg. I remember the song, because later on I had to learn how to play it.

Visual Vocabulary
Edvard *Grieg* (grēg), 1843–1907, was a Norwegian composer.

Three days after watching the *Ed Sullivan Show* my mother told me what my schedule would be for piano lessons and piano practice. She had talked to Mr. Chong, who lived on the first floor of our apartment building. Mr. Chong was a retired piano teacher, and my mother had traded housecleaning services for weekly lessons and a piano for me to practice on every day, two hours a day, from four until six.

When my mother told me this, I felt as though I had been sent to hell. I whined, and then kicked my foot a little when I couldn't stand it anymore.

"Why don't you like me the way I am?" I cried, "I'm *not* a genius! I can't play the piano. And even if I could, I wouldn't go on TV if you paid me a million dollars!"

My mother slapped me. "Who ask you to be genius?" she shouted. "Only ask you be your best. For you sake. You think I want you to be genius! Hnnh! What for! Who ask you!"

"So ungrateful," I heard her mutter in Chinese. "If she had as much talent as she has temper, she'd be famous now."

Mr. Chong, whom I secretly nicknamed Old Chong, was very strange, always tapping his fingers to the silent music of an invisible orchestra. He looked ancient in my eyes. He had lost most of the hair on the top of his head, and he wore thick glasses and had eyes that always looked tired. But he must have been younger than I thought, since he lived with his mother and was not yet married.

I met Old Lady Chong once, and that was enough. She had a peculiar smell, like a baby that had done something in its pants, and her fingers felt like a dead person's, like an old peach I once found in the back of the refrigerator; its skin just slid off the flesh when I picked it up.

I soon found out why Old Chong had retired from teaching piano. He was deaf. "Like Beethoven!" he shouted to me. "We're both listening only in our head!"

Making Choices What might the narrator's choice to ignore the "warning signs" reveal about her?

Connect to Personal Experience Can you recall a situation in which you felt similarly about a decision you did not like?

Visual Vocabulary
Ludwig van *Beethoven* (bāʹ tō vən), 1770–1827, was a German composer.

And he would start to conduct his frantic silent sonatas.[7]

Our lessons went like this. He would open the book and point to different things, explaining their purpose: "Key! Treble! Bass! No sharps or flats! So this is C major! Listen now and play after me!"

And then he would play the C scale a few times, a simple chord, and then, as if inspired by an old unreachable itch, he would gradually add more notes and running trills and a pounding bass until the music was really something quite grand.

I would play after him, the simple scale, the simple chord, and then just play some nonsense that sounded like a cat running up and down on top of garbage cans. Old Chong would smile and applaud and say, "Very good! But now you must learn to keep time!"

So that's how I discovered that Old Chong's eyes were too slow to keep up with the wrong notes I was playing. He went through the motions in half time. To help me keep rhythm, he stood behind me and pushed down on my right shoulder for every beat. He balanced pennies on top of my wrists so that I would keep them still as I slowly played scales and arpeggios.[8] He had me curve my hand around an apple and keep that shape when playing chords. He marched stiffly to show me how to make each finger dance up and down, staccato,[9] like an obedient little soldier.

He taught me all these things, and that was how I also learned I could be lazy and get away with mistakes, lots of mistakes. If I hit the wrong notes because I hadn't practiced enough, I never corrected myself. I just kept playing in rhythm. And Old Chong kept conducting his own private **reverie.**

So maybe I never really gave myself a fair chance. I did pick up the basics pretty quickly, and I might have become a good pianist at that young age. But I was so determined not to try, not to be anybody different, that I learned to play only the most ear-splitting preludes, the most **discordant** hymns.

Over the next year I practiced like this, dutifully in my own way. And then one day I heard my mother and her friend Lindo Jong both talking in a loud, bragging tone of voice so that others could hear. It was after church, and I was leaning against a brick wall, wearing a dress with stiff white petticoats. Auntie Lindo's daughter, Waverly, who was my age, was standing farther down the wall, about five feet away. We had grown up together and shared all the closeness of two sisters, squabbling over crayons and dolls. In other words, for the most part, we hated each other. I thought she was snotty. Waverly Jong had gained a certain amount of fame as "Chinatown's Littlest Chinese Chess Champion."

Making Choices What choice has the narrator made about her piano playing?

Connect to Personal Experience In what situations have you experienced the type of relationship described here?

Vocabulary

reverie (revʹ ər ē) *n.* fanciful thinking, daydream
discordant (dis kôrdʹ ənt) *adj.* not in agreement or harmony

---

7. *Sonatas* are instrumental compositions, commonly written for piano.
8. *Arpeggios* (är pejʹ ē ōz) are chords in which the notes are played in succession instead of all at the same time.
9. To play music *staccato* (stə käʹ tō) is to produce sharp, distinct breaks between successive tones.

"She bring home too many trophy," Auntie Lindo lamented that Sunday. "All day she play chess. All day I have no time do nothing but dust off her winnings." She threw a scolding look at Waverly, who pretended not to see her.

"You lucky you don't have this problem," Auntie Lindo said with a sigh to my mother.

And my mother squared her shoulders and bragged: "Our problem worser than yours. If we ask Jing-mei[10] wash dish, she hear nothing but music. It's like you can't stop this natural talent."

==And right then I was determined to put a stop to her foolish pride.==

A few weeks later Old Chong and my mother conspired to have me play in a talent show that was to be held in the church hall. By then my parents had saved up enough to buy me a secondhand piano, a black Wurlitzer spinet with a scarred bench. It was the showpiece of our living room.

Visual Vocabulary
A *spinet* (spin′it) is a small, upright piano.

For the talent show I was to play a piece called "Pleading Child," from Schumann's[11] *Scenes From Childhood*. It was a simple, moody piece that sounded more difficult than it was. I was supposed to memorize the whole thing. But I dawdled over it, playing a few bars and then cheating, looking up to see what notes followed. I never really listened to what I was playing. I daydreamed about being somewhere else, about being someone else.

The part I liked to practice best was the fancy curtsy: right foot out, touch the rose on the carpet with a pointed foot, sweep to the side, bend left leg, look up, and smile.

My parents invited all the couples from their social club to witness my debut. Auntie Lindo and Uncle Tin were there. Waverly and her two older brothers had also come. The first two rows were filled with children either younger or older than I was. The littlest ones got to go first. They recited simple nursery rhymes, squawked out tunes on miniature violins, and twirled hula hoops in pink ballet tutus, and when they bowed or curtsied, the audience would sigh in unison, "*Awww*," and then clap enthusiastically.

When my turn came, I was very confident. I remember my childish excitement. It was as if I knew, without a doubt, that the prodigy side of me really did exist. I had no fear whatsoever, no nervousness. I remember thinking, This is it! This is it! I looked out over the audience, at my mother's blank face, my father's yawn, Auntie Lindo's stiff-lipped smile, Waverly's sulky expression. I had on a white dress, layered with sheets of lace, and a pink bow in my Peter Pan haircut. ==As I sat down, I envisioned people jumping to their feet and Ed Sullivan rushing up to introduce me to everyone on TV.==

And I started to play. Everything was so beautiful. I was so caught up in how lovely I looked that I wasn't worried about how I would sound. So I was surprised when I hit the first wrong note. And then I hit another, and another. A chill started at the top of my head and began to trickle down. Yet I couldn't stop playing, as though my hands were bewitched. I kept

---

10. *Jing-mei* (jing′mā)
11. Robert *Schumann* (shōō′ män), 1810–1856, was a German composer.

Motivation *What do you think motivated the narrator's decision here?*

Motivation *What desire motivates the narrator here?*

AMY TAN 95

Little Dancer of Fourteen Years, 1880–1881. Edgar Degas. Philadelphia Museum of Art.

View the Art The model for Degas's sculpture, Marie Van Goethem, was a poor girl from Belgium who dreamed of becoming the most famous dancer in the world. What similarities and differences can you find between Jing-mei and the girl in this sculpture?

---

her stricken face. The audience clapped weakly, and as I walked back to my chair, with my whole face quivering as I tried not to cry, I heard a little boy whisper loudly to his mother, "That was awful," and the mother whispered back, "Well, she certainly tried."

And now I realized how many people were in the audience—the whole world, it seemed. I was aware of eyes burning into my back. I felt the shame of my mother and father as they sat stiffly through the rest of the show.

We could have escaped during intermission. Pride and some strange sense of honor must have anchored my parents to their chairs. And so we watched it all: The eighteen-year-old boy with a fake moustache who did a magic show and juggled flaming hoops while riding a unicycle. The breasted girl with white makeup who sang an aria[12] from *Madame Butterfly* and got an honorable mention. And the eleven-year-old boy who won first prize playing a tricky violin song that sounded like a busy bee.

After the show the Hsus, the Jongs, and the St. Clairs, from the Joy Luck Club, came up to my mother and father.

"Lots of talented kids," Auntie Lindo said vaguely, smiling broadly.

"That was somethin' else," my father said, and I wondered if he was referring to me in a humorous way, or whether he even remembered what I had done.

Visual Vocabulary
Madame Butterfly is a famous opera by Italian composer Giacomo Puccini.

thinking my fingers would adjust themselves back, like a train switching to the right track. I played this strange jumble through to the end, the sour notes staying with me all the way.

When I stood up, I discovered my legs were shaking. Maybe I had just been nervous, and the audience, like Old Chong, had seen me go through the right motions and had not heard anything wrong at all. I swept my right foot out, went down on my knee, looked up, and smiled. The room was quiet, except for Old Chong, who was beaming and shouting, "Bravo! Bravo! Well done!" But then I saw my mother's face,

---

12. An *aria* (är′ē ə) is an elaborate composition for solo voice.

Storefront Window, Chinatown, NY, 1993. Don Jacot.

View the Art Look closely—this isn't a photograph, it's a *photorealistic* painting. Artist Don Jacot said he wanted his paintings to "reflect the culture around [him]." What do you think this painting reflects about the culture of Chinatown?

Waverly looked at me and shrugged her shoulders. "You aren't a genius like me," she said matter-of-factly. And if I hadn't felt so bad, I would have pulled her braids and punched her stomach.

But my mother's expression was what devastated me: a quiet, blank look that said she had lost everything. I felt the same way, and everybody seemed now to be coming up, like gawkers at the scene of an accident, to see what parts were actually missing.

When we got on the bus to go home, my father was humming the busy-bee tune and my mother was silent. I kept thinking she wanted to wait until we got home before shouting at me. But when my father unlocked the door to our apartment, my mother walked in and went straight to the back, into the bedroom. No accusations. No blame. And in a way, I felt disappointed. I had been waiting for her to start shouting, so that I could shout back and cry and blame her for all my misery.

I had assumed that my talent-show **fiasco** meant that I would never have to play the

---

Motivation *Why do you think the mother reacted this way?*

Vocabulary

fiasco (fē as′kō) *n.* a complete or humiliating failure

piano again. But two days later, after school, my mother came out of the kitchen and saw me watching TV.

"Four clock," she reminded me, as if it were any other day. I was stunned, as though she were asking me to go through the talent-show torture again. I planted myself more squarely in front of the TV.

"Turn off TV," she called from the kitchen five minutes later.

I didn't budge. And then I decided. I didn't have to do what my mother said anymore. I wasn't her slave. This wasn't China. I had listened to her before, and look what happened. She was the stupid one.

She came out from the kitchen and stood in the arched entryway of the living room. "Four clock," she said once again, louder.

"I'm not going to play anymore," I said nonchalantly. "Why should I? I'm not a genius."

She stood in front of the TV. I saw that her chest was heaving up and down in an angry way.

"No!" I said, and I now felt stronger, as if my true self had finally emerged. So this was what had been inside me all along. "No! I won't!" I screamed.

She snapped off the TV, yanked me by the arm and pulled me off the floor. She was frighteningly strong, half pulling, half carrying me toward the piano as I kicked the throw rugs under my feet. She lifted me up and onto the hard bench. I was sobbing by now, looking at her bitterly. Her chest was heaving even more and her mouth was open, smiling crazily as if she were pleased that I was crying.

"You want me to be someone that I'm not!" I sobbed. "I'll never be the kind of daughter you want me to be!"

"Only two kinds of daughters," she shouted in Chinese. "Those who are obedient and those who follow their own mind! Only one kind of daughter can live in this house. Obedient daughter!"

"Then I wish I weren't your daughter. I wish you weren't my mother," I shouted. As I said these things I got scared. It felt like worms and toads and slimy things crawling out of my chest, but it also felt good, that this awful side of me had surfaced, at last.

"Too late change this," my mother said shrilly.

And I could sense her anger rising to its breaking point. I wanted to see it spill over. And that's when I remembered the babies she had lost in China, the ones we never talked about. "Then I wish I'd never been born!" I shouted. "I wish I were dead! Like them."

It was as if I had said magic words. Alakazam!—her face went blank, her mouth closed, her arms went slack, and she backed out of the room, stunned, as if she were blowing away like a small brown leaf, thin, brittle, lifeless.

It was not the only disappointment my mother felt in me. In the years that followed, I failed her many times, each time asserting my will, my right to fall short of expectations. I didn't get straight *A*s. I didn't become class president. I didn't get into Stanford. I dropped out of college.

Unlike my mother, I did not believe I could be anything I wanted to be. I could only be me.

Connect to Personal Experience Think of a time when you said something you regretted. How did your reaction compare to the narrator's?

Making Choices Why is this a serious choice?

Motivation Why do you think the narrator had this desire?

Young Girl at a Grand Piano, 1904. Carl Larsson.

View the Art Carl Larsson was a Swedish Realist painter who often used his own children as models in his art. Compare and contrast the attitude of the girl in this painting with that of Jing-mei.

And for all those years we never talked about the disaster at the recital or my terrible declarations afterward at the piano bench. Neither of us talked about it again, as if it were a betrayal that was now unspeakable. So I never found a way to ask her why she had hoped for something so large that failure was inevitable.

And even worse, I never asked her about what frightened me the most: Why had she given up hope? For after our struggle at the piano, she never mentioned my playing again. The lessons stopped. The lid to the piano was closed, shutting out the dust, my misery, and her dreams.

So she surprised me. A few years ago she offered to give me the piano, for my thirtieth birthday. I had not played in all those years. I saw the offer as a sign of forgiveness, a tremendous burden removed.

"Are you sure?" I asked shyly. "I mean, won't you and Dad miss it?"

"No, this your piano," she said firmly. "Always your piano. You only one can play."

"Well, I probably can't play anymore," I said. "It's been years."

"You pick up fast," my mother said, as if she knew this was certain. "You have natural talent. You could be genius if you want to."

"No, I couldn't."

"You just not trying," my mother said. And she was neither angry nor sad. She said it as if announcing a fact that could never be disproved. "Take it," she said.

But I didn't, at first. It was enough that she had offered it to me. And after that, every time I saw it in my parents' living room, standing in front of the bay window, it made me feel proud, as if it were a shiny trophy that I had won back.

Last week I sent a tuner over to my parents' apartment and had the piano reconditioned, for purely sentimental reasons. My mother had died a few months before, and I had been getting things in order for my father, a little bit at a time. I put the jewelry in special silk pouches. The sweaters she had knitted in yellow, pink, bright orange—all the colors I hated—I put in mothproof boxes. I found some old Chinese silk dresses, the kind with little slits up the sides. I rubbed the old silk against my skin, and then wrapped them in tissue and decided to take them home with me.

After I had the piano tuned, I opened the lid and touched the keys. It sounded even richer than I remembered. Really, it was a very good piano. Inside the bench were the same exercise notes with handwritten scales, the same secondhand music books with their covers held together with yellow tape.

I opened up the Schumann book to the dark little piece I had played at the recital. It was on the left-hand page, "Pleading Child." It looked more difficult than I remembered. I played a few bars, surprised at how easily the notes came back to me. And for the first time, or so it seemed, I noticed the piece on the right-hand side. It was called "Perfectly Contented." I tried to play this one as well. It had a lighter melody but with the same flowing rhythm and turned out to be quite easy. "Pleading Child" was shorter but slower; "Perfectly Contented" was longer but faster. And after I had played them both a few times, I realized they were two halves of the same song.

Making Choices *Do you think the mother's choice here is consistent with how she has been portrayed thus far? Explain.*

Motivation *Do you think the narrator is correct about the motivation behind her mother's offer?*

After You Read

Respond and Think Critically

Respond and Interpret

1. (a) What was your reaction to the conflict between Jing-mei and her mother? (b) Do you think that one person was more at fault than the other?

2. (a) What two faces does Jing-mei see when she looks in the mirror after another failed prodigy training session? (b) Why does Jing-mei decide to stop trying to become a prodigy?

3. (a) How does Jing-mei feel when it is her turn to perform at the recital? (b) Why do she and her parents feel so humiliated by her performance?

4. (a) What hurtful remark does Jing-mei say to her mother after their big argument? (b) In your opinion, what makes her comments so brutal?

5. (a) What reasons does Jing-mei's mother give for offering Jing-mei the piano for her thirtieth birthday? (b) Do you think Jing-mei's mother finally forgives her daughter for her hurtful comment?

Analyze and Evaluate

6. (a) What do you think is the underlying issue of Jing-mei and her mother's final argument? (b) How does the author illustrate the mounting tension between them?

7. (a) Why do you think Jing-mei's mother set unrealistic goals for her daughter? (b) What do Jing-mei's responses tell you about her?

8. (a) In what ways had Jing-mei changed by the end of the story? (b) How had Jing-mei's mother changed by the end of the story?

Connect

9. **Big Idea** **Making Choices** Which choice do you think is most central to the outcome of this story? Explain.

10. **Connect to the Author** Like Jing-mei, Tan also dealt with deaths in her family and conflicts with her mother. Why do you think Tan chose to include painful autobiographical elements in her story?

Literary Element Motivation

In literature, a character's **motivation** is not always perfectly clear. At times, a character's motivation may be weak or mixed, making it difficult to discern or understand. Think about the characters in "Two Kinds." Was it easy or difficult to determine the motivation for their actions?

1. Although the mother says that she only wants Jing-mei to "be [her] best. For [her] sake," what else might motivate her? Use details from the text to support your answer.

2. Jing-mei decides to thwart her mother's "foolish pride," but she does prepare for the talent show, including practicing her fancy curtsy. Why do you think she does this?

Review: Theme

As you learned on page 3, the **theme** is the central message of a story that readers can apply to life.

Partner Activity Meet with another classmate and review the title and main events in the story. Then determine how they contribute to the story's theme. You might note the main events and other important details on a web like the one shown here.

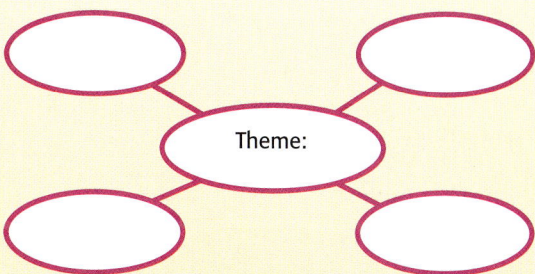

Reading Strategy Connect to Personal Experience

When you **connect** to characters, you focus on the emotions, situations, or concepts. Review your chart from page 89 to help you with the following items.

1. List feelings, situations, or concepts from this story that are familiar to you from other literary works, films, or television shows.

2. With your classmates, identify entries that appeared on a majority of your lists. Discuss why certain concepts or situations are common in literature, film, and television.

Vocabulary Practice

Practice with Usage Respond to these statements to help you explore the meanings of vocabulary words from the text.

1. Tell what a musical **prodigy** might do.
2. Give an example of a **reproach**.
3. Name two qualities of a **reverie**.
4. Give an example of something **discordant**.
5. Describe what happens in a **fiasco**.

Academic Vocabulary

*The mother's desire for a prodigy was out of **proportion** with her daughter's average talent.*

In the quotation above, *proportion* means "balance." The word *proportion* has additional meanings in specific subject areas, such as mathematics and architecture. Using context clues, try to figure out the meaning of *proportion* in each sentence. Check a dictionary to confirm your deductions.

1. James expressed the **proportion** as 8/2 = 20/5.
2. The critic praised the columns for their size and **proportion**.

For more on academic vocabulary, see pages 52 and 53.

Speaking and Listening

Literature Groups

Assignment With a small group, discuss whether it is advantageous to require children to participate in music, sports, academic contests, and similar activities. Try to reach a consensus—a general agreement within a group on an issue.

Prepare Before your group meets, look back at "Two Kinds" to review the mother's requirements of Jing-mei and evaluate the advantages and disadvantages of the requirements. Write your evaluations in a chart like the one below. Add details from your own experiences or from the experiences of others you may know or have heard about.

Requirement	Advantage	Disadvantage
take many tests to see if Jing-mei is a genius	raises hopes for mother and Jing-mei	exposes Jing-mei and mother to many failures by Jing-mei

Discuss Respect others' viewpoints by listening attentively. Deliver your opinions in a normal tone of voice, providing clear, specific examples from your chart to support your judgments.

Report Have one group member orally state your consensus to the class or state that no consensus was reached, being sure to address the class clearly and loudly enough for all to hear.

Evaluate Write a paragraph in which you assess the effectiveness of your discussion. Use the rubric on page 267 to help in your evaluation.

 **Literature** Online

Selection Resources For Selection Quizzes, eFlashcards, and Reading-Writing Connection activities, go to glencoe.com and enter QuickPass code GL59794u1.

Before You Read

The Car We Had to Push

Meet James Thurber
(1894–1961)

Although known as a humorist and a lover of pranks, James Thurber has also been called a "complicated and tormented man." He enjoyed vast success as a writer for much of his life, but his later years were marred by unhappiness and ill health.

Thurber was born at the end of the nineteenth century, and he died at the dawn of the Space Age. He saw many social changes, yet his most widely read stories are set in the years of his youth. Thurber was born in Columbus, Ohio, where he lived with his parents and brothers until he left for college. His family and home appear in modified form in many of his best works.

The *New Yorker* Years Thurber lost an eye in a childhood accident, and this injury kept him out of the service during World War I. He spent a year in Paris working for the State Department and later worked as a reporter. In 1927 he joined the staff of the newly formed *New Yorker*. The magazine and its staff changed his life.

> "If I couldn't write, I couldn't breathe."
> —James Thurber

The magazine became famous, and Thurber was one of its best-known writers. He was also a constant doodler and sketcher, sometimes even drawing on office walls. His office-mate E. B. White, also a respected author, urged Thurber to submit drawings to the magazine's art department. Thurber refused, so one day the frustrated White snatched drawings from the trash and submitted them.

Soon Thurber's cartoons as well as his stories graced the pages of the *New Yorker*.

Later Works From 1929 to 1967, Thurber wrote one new book every year or two. In 1942 he published a collection of stories that included "The Secret Life of Walter Mitty." The title character was a timid man who daydreamed about taking part in heroic adventures. The story became a classic that was turned into several movies and has inspired many television plots.

In the 1940s, Thurber began writing fables, plays, and children's books as well as essays. These were difficult years for Thurber; he had numerous health problems and lost sight in his remaining eye. He continued to work, however, by dictating his books.

In 1959 he published *The Years with Ross*, a biography of editor Harold Ross and an account of Thurber's years at the *New Yorker*. Thurber published only one major work after that, *A Thurber Carnival*, which was a series of skits.

People today read Thurber's works for their humor and vitality. His humor, wrote one critic, "has a timeless quality that should guarantee him a readership far into the future."

Author Search For more about James Thurber, go to glencoe.com and enter QuickPass code GL59794u1.

JAMES THURBER 103

Literature and Reading Preview

Connect to the Story
What technologies have been introduced in your lifetime? List several significant new technologies and write about how they have affected your life.

Build Background
In the early twentieth century, cars were viewed as exotic and unpredictable machines. Early cars ran on steam and inspired fears about explosions. Later cars had to be started manually, using a crank that the motorist inserted into the front of the engine and turned forcefully until the engine started.

Set Purposes for Reading

Big Idea Making Choices

As you read "The Car We Had to Push," ask yourself, Why do some of the characters choose to try to trick another character?

Literary Element Dialogue

Dialogue is conversation between characters in a literary work. Besides adding interest, dialogue can contribute to characterization by revealing aspects of a character's personality. As you read "The Car We Had to Push," ask yourself, How does each character's dialogue reveal aspects of his or her personality?

Reading Strategy Make Generalizations About Characters

When you **make generalizations about a character,** you draw upon various details to make a general statement about that character. Such conclusions can enhance the richness and meaning of a story. As you read, ask yourself, What details lead you to make generalizations about characters?

Tip: Chart Clues Use a graphic organizer to record details that provide clues to make a generalization about the character.

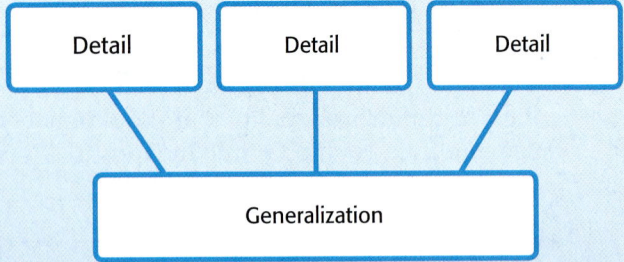

Learning Objectives

For pages 103–111

In studying this text, you will focus on the following objectives:

Literary Study: Analyzing dialogue.

Reading: Making generalizations about characters.

Vocabulary

repercussion (rē′pər kush′ən) *n.* an effect or a result of some action; p. 105 *The repercussions of cheating can be very serious.*

exhortation (eg′zôr tā′shən) *n.* a strong appeal or warning; p. 106 *The exhortations of the crowd spurred on the runners.*

contend (kən tend′) *v.* to declare or maintain as a fact; to argue; p. 108 *My mother contends that I ate raw turnips as a child.*

lucid (lōō′sid) *adj.* clear-headed, mentally alert; p. 109 *My father is lucid even when half-asleep.*

Tip: Word Origins Use your knowledge of word origins when you encounter an unfamiliar word with a familiar root.

104 UNIT 1 THE SHORT STORY

The Car We Had to Push

James Thurber

It took sometimes as many as five or six. James Thurber. Illustration from *My Life and Hard Times*, 1933.

Many autobiographers, among them Lincoln Steffens and Gertrude Atherton,[1] describe earthquakes their families have been in. I am unable to do this because my family was never in an earthquake, but we went through a number of things in Columbus that were a great deal like earthquakes. I remember in particular some of the **repercussions** of an old Reo we had that wouldn't go unless you pushed it for quite a way and suddenly let your clutch out. Once, we had been able to start the engine easily by cranking it, but we had had the car for so many years that finally it wouldn't go unless you pushed it and let your clutch out. Of course, it took more than one person to do this; it took sometimes as many as five or six, depending on the grade of the roadway and conditions underfoot. The car was unusual in that the clutch and brake were on the same pedal, making it quite easy to stall the engine after it got started, so that the car would have to be pushed again.

My father used to get sick at his stomach pushing the car, and very often was unable to go to work. He had never liked the machine, even when it was good, sharing my ignorance and suspicion of all automobiles of twenty years ago and longer. The boys I went to school with used to be able to identify every car as it passed by: Thomas Flyer, Firestone-Columbus, Stevens Duryea, Rambler, Winton, White Steamer, etc. I never could. The only car I was really interested in

---

1. Besides their autobiographies, *Steffens* wrote nonfiction books and articles and *Atherton* wrote novels. Their major works were published between 1898 and 1936.

Vocabulary

repercussion (rē′pər kush′ ən) *n.* an effect or a result of some action

Make Generalizations About Characters *From this statement, what sort of generalization could be made about the narrator's father?*

was one that the Get-Ready Man, as we called him, rode around town in: a big Red Devil with a door in the back. The Get-Ready Man was a lank unkempt elderly gentleman with wild eyes and a deep voice who used to go about shouting at people through a megaphone to prepare for the end of the world. "get ready! get read-y!" he would bellow. "the worllld is coming to an end!" His startling <u>exhortations</u> would come up, like summer thunder, at the most unexpected times and in the most surprising places. I remember once during Mantell's production of "King Lear" at the Colonial Theatre, that the Get-Ready Man added his bawlings to the squealing of Edgar and the ranting of the King and the mouthing of the Fool, rising from somewhere in the balcony to join in. The theatre was in absolute darkness and there were rumblings of thunder and flashes of lightning offstage. Neither father nor I, who were there, ever completely got over the scene, which went something like this:

EDGAR: Tom's a-cold.—O, do de, do de, do de!—Bless thee from whirlwinds, star-blasting, and taking . . . the foul fiend vexes!

[*Thunder off.*]

LEAR: What! Have his daughters brought him to this pass?—

GET-READY MAN: Get ready! Get ready!

EDGAR: Pillicock sat on Pillicock-hill:—
      Halloo, halloo, loo, loo!

[*Lightning flashes.*]

GET-READY MAN: The Worllld is com-ing to an End!

FOOL: This cold night will turn us all to fools and madmen!

EDGAR: Take heed o' the foul fiend: obey thy paren—

GET READY MAN: Get *Rea*-dy!

EDGAR: Tom's *a-cold!*

> **Vocabulary**
> **exhortation** (eg´zôr tā´shən) *n.* a strong appeal or warning

> **Dialogue** What do the Get-Ready Man's interjected warnings reveal about his personality?

The Get-Ready Man. James Thurber. Illustration from *My Life and Hard Times,* 1933.

View the Art Thurber's drawings were so beloved that when the *New Yorker* changed locations, they carved his cartoons off his office walls to bring along. How effective is this drawing in capturing the story's details and mood? Explain.

GET-READY MAN: The *Worr*-uld is coming to an end! . . .

They found him finally, and ejected him, still shouting. The Theatre, in our time, has known few such moments.

But to get back to the automobile. One of my happiest memories of it was when, in its eighth year, my brother Roy got together a great many articles from the kitchen, placed them in a square of canvas, and swung this under the car with a string attached to it so that, at a twitch, the canvas would give way and the steel and tin things would clatter to the street. This was a little scheme of Roy's to frighten father, who had always expected the car might explode. It worked perfectly. That was twenty-five years ago, but it is one of the few things in my life I would like to live over again if I could. I don't suppose that I can, now. Roy twitched the string in the middle of a lovely afternoon, on Bryden Road, near Eighteenth Street. Father had closed his eyes and, with his hat off, was enjoying a cool breeze. The clatter on the asphalt was tremendously effective: knives, forks, can-openers, pie pans, pot lids, biscuit-cutters, ladles, eggbeaters fell, beautifully together, in a lingering, clamant[2] crash. "Stop the *car*!" shouted father. "I can't," Roy said. "The engine fell out." "God Almighty!" said father, who knew what *that* meant, or knew what it sounded as if it might mean.

It ended unhappily, of course, because we finally had to drive back and pick up the stuff and even father knew the difference between the works of an automobile and the equipment of a pantry. My mother wouldn't have known, however, nor *her* mother. My mother, for instance, thought—or, rather, knew—that it was dangerous to drive an automobile without gasoline: it fried the valves, or something. "Now don't you dare drive all over town without gasoline!" she would say to us when we started off. Gasoline, oil, and water were much the same to her, a fact that made her life both confusing and perilous. Her greatest dread, however, was the Victrola—we had a very early one, back in the "Come Josephine in My Flying Machine" days. She had an idea that the Victrola might blow up. It alarmed her, rather than reassured her, to explain that the phonograph was run neither by gasoline nor by electricity. She could only suppose that it was propelled by some newfangled and untested apparatus which was likely to

Visual Vocabulary
Victrola is the trademark name of a record player; early models were hand-cranked, just as wind-up toys are. Electric phonographs were first produced in the 1920s.

let go at any minute, making us all the victims and martyrs of the wild-eyed Edison's dangerous experiments.[3] The telephone she was comparatively at peace with, except, of course, during storms, when for some reason or other she always took the receiver off the hook and let it hang. She came naturally by her confused and groundless fears, for her own mother lived the latter years of her life in the horrible suspicion that electricity was dripping invisibly all over the house. It

---

2. Anything *clamant* (klā′ mənt) is noisy and demanding of attention.

Make Generalizations About Characters *What does this incident suggest about Roy's personality?*

3. *Martyrs* are those who suffer or die for a cause. The *dangerous experiments* of Thomas A. *Edison* produced inventions that changed the world, including the light bulb, the first practical phonograph (1877), and important improvements to the telephone.

Making Choices *Why does the narrator's mother choose to remove the telephone from the hook during storms? What does this action tell you about the mother?*

Electricity was leaking all over the house. James Thurber. Illustration from *My Life and Hard Times,* 1933.

View the Art Thurber was famous for his line drawings. What are some distinguishing characteristics of this style of drawing?

leaked, she **contended**, out of empty sockets if the wall switch had been left on. She would go around screwing in bulbs, and if they lighted up she would hastily and fearfully turn off the wall switch and go back to her *Pearson's* or *Everybody's*,[4] happy in the satisfaction that she had stopped not only a costly but a dangerous leakage. Nothing could ever clear this up for her.

Our poor old Reo came to a horrible end, finally. We had parked it too far from the curb on a street with a car line. It was late at night and the street was dark. The first streetcar[5] that came along couldn't get by. It picked up the tired old automobile as a terrier might seize a rabbit and drubbed it unmercifully, losing its hold now and then but catching a new grip a second later. Tires booped and whooshed, the fenders queeled and graked, the steering wheel rose up like a spectre and disappeared in the direction of Franklin Avenue with a melancholy whistling sound, bolts and gadgets flew like sparks from a Catherine wheel.[6] It was a splendid spectacle but, of course, saddening to everybody (except the motorman of the streetcar, who was sore). I think some of us broke down and wept. It must have been the weeping that caused grandfather to take on so terribly. Time was all mixed up in his mind; automobiles and the like he never remembered having seen. He apparently gathered, from the talk and excitement and

---

4. These were popular magazines of the early 1900s.

Vocabulary

contend (kən tend´) *v.* to declare or maintain as a fact; to argue

5. Since a *streetcar* runs on rails, it cannot avoid things in its path.
6. A *spectre* is a ghost or ghostly vision. The *Catherine wheel* is a firework that, when lighted, spins like a pinwheel and spouts colorful sparks and flames.

Make Generalizations About Characters What generalization about the grandmother could you logically make from this passage?

weeping, that somebody had died. Nor did he let go of this delusion. He insisted, in fact, after almost a week in which we strove mightily to divert him, that it was a sin and a shame and a disgrace on the family to put the funeral off any longer. "Nobody is dead! The automobile is smashed!" shouted my father, trying for the thirtieth time to explain the situation to the old man. "Was he drunk?" demanded grandfather, sternly. "Was who drunk?" asked father. "Zenas," said grandfather. He had a name for the corpse now: it was his brother Zenas, who, as it happened, *was* dead, but not from driving an automobile while intoxicated. Zenas had died in 1866. A sensitive, rather poetical boy of twenty-one when the Civil War broke out, Zenas had gone to South America—"just," as he wrote back, "until it blows over." Returning after the war had blown over, he caught the same disease that was killing off the chestnut trees in those years, and passed away. It was the only case in history where a tree doctor had to be called in to spray a person, and our family had felt it very keenly; nobody else in the United States caught the blight. Some of us have looked upon Zenas' fate as a kind of poetic justice.

Now that grandfather knew, so to speak, who was dead, it became increasingly awkward to go on living in the same house with him as if nothing had happened. He would go into towering rages in which he threatened to write to the Board of Health unless the funeral were held at once. We realized that something had to be done. Eventually, we persuaded a friend of father's, named George Martin, to dress up in the manner and costume of the eighteen-sixties and pretend to be Uncle Zenas, in order to set grandfather's mind at rest. The impostor looked fine and impressive in sideburns and a high beaver hat, and not unlike the daguerreotypes of Zenas in our album. I shall never forget the night, just after dinner, when this Zenas walked into the living room. Grandfather was stomping up and down, tall, hawk-nosed, round-oathed. The newcomer held out both his hands. "Clem!" he cried to grandfather. Grandfather turned slowly, looked at the intruder, and snorted. "Who air *you*?" he demanded in his deep, resonant voice. "I'm Zenas!" cried Martin. "Your brother Zenas, fit as a fiddle and sound as a dollar!" "Zenas, my foot!" said grandfather. "Zenas died of the chestnut blight in '66!"

Visual Vocabulary
Daguerreotypes (də ger′ə tīps′) are photographs made by exposing light to silver-coated copper plates; Louis Daguerre invented the process in France in the mid-1800s.

Grandfather was given to these sudden, unexpected, and extremely **lucid** moments; they were generally more embarrassing than his other moments. He comprehended before he went to bed that night that the old automobile had been destroyed and that its destruction had caused all the turmoil in the house. "It flew all to pieces, Pa," my mother told him, in graphically describing the accident. "I knew 'twould," growled grandfather. "I allus told ye to git a Pope-Toledo."

Making Choices Why do you think the narrator's family chooses to stage an impersonation as a way of setting "grandfather's mind at rest"?

Dialogue How does this exclamation contrast with the grandfather's earlier dialogue?

Vocabulary
lucid (lōō′sid) *adj.* clear-headed; mentally alert

After You Read

Respond and Think Critically

Respond and Interpret

1. Which character or situation did you find funniest? Explain.

2. (a) Who owned the car, and why did it have to be pushed? (b) What does the car symbolize in this story? Support your answer with details from the story.

3. (a) What confusion does grandfather have about his brother Zenas? (b) Why might the narrator consider the grandfather's lucid moments to be "more embarrassing than his other moments"?

Analyze and Evaluate

4. Why do you think Thurber includes the Get-Ready Man in the story? What effect does this part of the story create?

5. How does the car's demise match the overall mood, or atmosphere, of the story?

6. What qualities of this story do you think helped lead to Thurber's enormous popular success during his lifetime? Cite examples from the story to support your opinion.

Connect

7. **Big Idea** Making Choices Why do you think Thurber chose to remember the episodes in this story as humorous? How else might he have portrayed them?

8. **Connect to Today** People in the narrator's childhood were often suspicious of technology, in particular the narrator's parents and grandparents. What sorts of technology do you use today that would make people of your parents' or grandparents' generation suspicious? Why might they have that reaction?

Literary Element Dialogue

Dialogue is one technique of introducing a character to the reader. Good dialogue sounds natural, so it often contains sentence fragments or pauses. Used effectively, dialogue not only helps to reveal a character's personality but also contains details that help readers understand the events of the story and predict what might happen next. Dialogue can also add drama or humor to a story.

1. Thurber weaves together dialogue from Shakespeare's *King Lear*, with the Get-Ready Man's warnings. Note the interplay between the dialogue in the play, the scenic elements, and the Get-Ready Man's warnings. Why is this more humorous than merely describing what happened during the play?

2. Reread the dialogue between the narrator's grandfather and father when the father tries to explain that no one has died. List two details that you learn from that dialogue.

Review: Dialect

As you learned on page 65, **dialect** is a variation of a language that is spoken in a particular region or by a certain group of people. Dialects often differ from the standard form of a language in vocabulary, pronunciation, or grammatical form. In "The Car We Had to Push," the grandfather uses dialect when he says, "I knew 'twould . . . . I allus told ye to git a Pope-Toledo."

Partner Activity Meet with a classmate and find another example of dialect in the story. Rewrite the dialect using Standard English. Afterwards, compare the two versions and draw conclusions about why Thurber chose to use dialect rather than Standard English.

Reading Strategy **Make Generalizations About Characters**

ACT Skills Practice

1. Which pair of words best describes the attitude of the narrator's family to technology?

   A. confident and optimistic
   B. resentful and angry
   C. confused and frightened
   D. reckless and irresponsible

Vocabulary Practice

Practice with Word Origins Studying the etymology, or origin and history, of a word can help you understand its meaning. Create a word map, like the one below, for each of these vocabulary words from the text.

repercussion   exhortation   contend   lucid

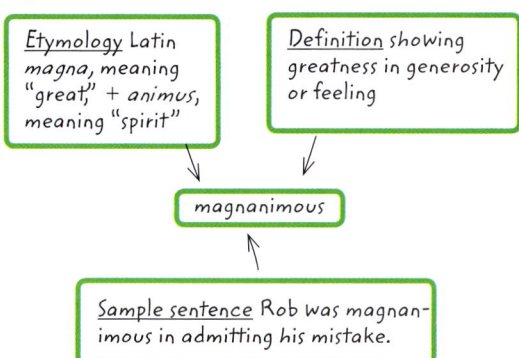

Academic Vocabulary

The narrator relates a **series** of events.

Series is a multiple-meaning word. Using context clues, try to figure out the meaning of *series* in each sentence and explain the similarities and differences between the meanings.

1. Use commas to separate items in a **series**.

2. The January issue is the first of the **series**.

For more on academic vocabulary, see pages 52 and 53.

Write with Style

 Apply Interior Monologue

Assignment Write an interior monologue to show the grandfather's jumbled thoughts at the point in the story when the narrator's father is trying to explain that no one has died.

Get Ideas Reread the long paragraph that begins "Our poor old Reo came to a horrible end…" List thoughts that might be going through the grandfather's mind before, during, and after his brief dialogue with the narrator's father. Use details from the narrative to help you make inferences about what the grandfather might be thinking. List the details and inferences in a chart like the one below.

Give It Structure Use stream-of-consciousness writing to express the grandfather's free-flowing thoughts. The stream-of-consciousness does not have to be logical or even grammatically correct. It should mimic what might be going through the grandfather's mind. For example, the grandfather might associate a car crash with the sound of falling kitchen objects.

Look at Language Use the grandfather's spoken language as a guide to how he might think or talk to himself. Re-create his language using his diction and the length, structure, and type of his sentences as a model.

EXAMPLE
Dead, my foot! Why ain't they fixed that car yet? It's a shame.

 **Literature** Online

Selection Resources For Selection Quizzes, eFlashcards, and Reading-Writing Connection activities, go to glencoe.com and enter QuickPass code GL59794u1.

Before You Read

**World Literature
Colombia**

Tuesday Siesta

Meet **Gabriel García Márquez**
(born 1928)

Born in Aracataca, Colombia, Gabriel García Márquez lived with his grandparents in "an enormous house, full of ghosts." His grandparents loved telling imaginative folktales, filled with omens, premonitions, and spirits. His grandfather also told stories about his war experiences, the triumphs of the South American revolutionary hero Simón Bolívar, and the plight of impoverished local farmers under an oppressive government. It is only natural then that García Márquez's literature is often built of realistic themes and plots related to the culture and people of his childhood village, fantastic elements from his grandparents' tales, and new magical details from his imagination. He once said that the goal of all his writing is to conjure "the magic in commonplace events." This style of writing has come to be known as magical realism.

> "There's not a single line in all my work that does not have a basis in reality. The problem is that Caribbean reality resembles the wildest imagination."
>
> —Gabriel García Márquez

Education and Early Writing When García Márquez was eight years old, he was sent to a boarding school in the port city of Barranquilla, where his classmates nicknamed him "the Old Man" because he seemed so shy and serious. At twelve, he won a scholarship to a Jesuit school for gifted students, where he became an avid reader and writer. Although he focused on writing nonfiction in college, he wrote fiction as well. In 1946, when he was nineteen, he published his first short story, "The Third Resignation," in the Bogotá newspaper, *El Espectador.*

García Márquez worked for the newspaper for the next ten years. In 1955, after he wrote an exposé on government corruption in Colombia, Gustavo Rojas Pinilla, the Colombian dictator, shut down the newspaper. García Márquez then returned to fiction writing.

International Fame In 1960 García Márquez moved to Mexico City, where he gained fame as a screenwriter, journalist, novelist, and publicist. In 1967 he published his most famous work, the novel *One Hundred Years of Solitude,* which has been translated into many different languages and has sold millions of copies. In 1982 García Márquez received the highest international award for writing—the Nobel Prize in Literature.

Author Search For more about Gabriel Gardía Márquez, go to glencoe.com and enter QuickPass code GL59794u1.

112 UNIT 1 THE SHORT STORY

Literature and Reading Preview

Connect to the Story

What advice have you gleaned from people or books that has helped you make better choices? Discuss this question with a partner. Consider the best advice you have been given.

Build Background

In tropical climates, many people avoid heatstroke and sunstroke by taking *siestas,* or naps. Siesta time usually begins around noon. Schools, shops, and even post offices often close so that people can go home, have a meal, and then rest for several hours. Later in the day, when the heat of the sun has diminished, activities resume.

Set Purposes for Reading

Big Idea Making Choices

As you read "Tuesday Siesta," ask yourself, What are the circumstances that lead a young man to make a tragic choice?

Literary Element Implied Theme

The theme of a piece of literature is its main idea or message. Most often, authors do not state the theme directly. Instead, they offer an **implied theme,** which they reveal gradually through details in the setting, plot events, dialogue, and action. As you read, ask yourself, How does García Márquez use the setting and characters' actions to imply the theme of this story?

Reading Strategy Make Inferences About Theme

To **infer** is to make a reasonable guess about the meaning of a literary work based on what the author implies. As you read, ask yourself, How do details in the setting, plot, and dialogue give hints about the implied theme?

Tip: Take Notes Use a diagram like the one below to record your inferences about the theme.

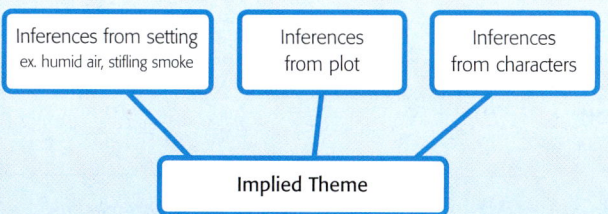

Learning Objectives

For pages 112–121

In studying this text, you will focus on the following objectives:

Library Study: Analyzing implied theme.

Reading: Making inferences about theme.

Vocabulary

interminable (in turʹmi nə bəl) *adj.* lasting, or seeming to last, forever; endless; p. 114 *We tried to be patient, but the rainstorm seemed interminable.*

serenity (sə renʹə tē) *n.* calmness; peacefulness; p. 115 *The serenity of the deep, silent forest calmed my jittery nerves.*

scrutinize (skrootʹən īzʹ) *v.* to look at closely; to inspect carefully; p. 117 *I'm not sure I will recognize Sally, so I'll scrutinize the face of each woman who gets off the train.*

inscrutable (in skrooʹtə bəl) *adj.* mysterious; p. 118 *His face was inscrutable as he scanned the group—it was impossible to figure out what he was thinking.*

skeptical (skepʹti kəl) *adj.* having or showing doubt or suspicion; questioning; disbelieving; p. 118 *Roger is extremely forgetful, so I'm skeptical that he will remember to call.*

GABRIEL GARCÍA MÁRQUEZ

Tuesday Siesta

Gabriel García Márquez
Translated by J. S. Bernstein

The train emerged from the quivering tunnel of sandy rocks, began to cross the symmetrical, **interminable** banana plantations, and the air became humid and they couldn't feel the sea breeze any more. A stifling blast of smoke came in the car window. On the narrow road parallel to the railway there were oxcarts loaded with green bunches of bananas. Beyond the road, in uncultivated spaces set at odd intervals there were offices with electric fans, red-brick buildings, and residences with chairs and little white tables on the terraces among dusty palm trees and rosebushes. It was eleven in the morning, and the heat had not yet begun.

"You'd better close the window," the woman said. "Your hair will get full of soot."

The girl tried to, but the shade wouldn't move because of the rust.

They were the only passengers in the lone third-class car. Since the smoke of the locomotive kept coming through the window, the girl left her seat and put down the only things they had with them: a plastic sack with some things to eat and a bouquet of flowers wrapped in newspaper. She sat on the opposite seat, away from the window, facing her mother. They were both in severe and poor mourning clothes.

Vocabulary
interminable (in tur′mi nə bəl) *adj.* lasting, or seeming to last, forever; endless

Make Inferences About Theme *What does this passage suggest about the characters' economic and emotional situation? How might these details reveal the author's implied theme?*

Visual Vocabulary
A *cassock* is a full-length garment worn by the clergy.

The girl was twelve years old, and it was the first time she'd ever been on a train. The woman seemed too old to be her mother, because of the blue veins on her eyelids and her small, soft, and shapeless body, in a dress cut like a cassock. She was riding with her spinal column braced firmly against the back of the seat, and held a peeling patent-leather handbag in her lap with both hands. She bore the conscientious **serenity** of someone accustomed to poverty.

By twelve the heat had begun. The train stopped for ten minutes to take on water at a station where there was no town. Outside, in the mysterious silence of the plantations, the shadows seemed clean. But the still air inside the car smelled like untanned leather. The train did not pick up speed. It stopped at two identical towns with wooden houses painted bright colors. The woman's head nodded and she sank into sleep. The girl took off her shoes. Then she went to the washroom to put the bouquet of flowers in some water.

When she came back to her seat, her mother was waiting to eat. She gave her a piece of cheese, half a corn-meal pancake, and a cookie, and took an equal portion out of the plastic sack for herself. While they ate, the train crossed an iron bridge very slowly and passed a town just like the ones before, except that in this one there was a crowd in the plaza. A band was playing a lively tune under the oppressive sun. At the other side of town the plantations ended in a plain which was cracked from the drought.

The woman stopped eating.

"Put on your shoes," she said.

The girl looked outside. She saw nothing but the deserted plain, where the train began to pick up speed again, but she put the last piece of cookie into the sack and quickly put on her shoes. The woman gave her a comb.

"Comb your hair," she said.

The train whistle began to blow while the girl was combing her hair. The woman dried the sweat from her neck and wiped the oil from her face with her fingers. When the girl stopped combing, the train was passing the outlying houses of a town larger but sadder than the earlier ones.

"If you feel like doing anything, do it now," said the woman. "Later, don't take a drink anywhere even if you're dying of thirst. Above all, no crying."

The girl nodded her head. A dry, burning wind came in the window, together with the locomotive's whistle and the clatter of the old cars. The woman folded the plastic bag with the rest of the food and put it in the handbag. For a moment a complete picture of the town, on that bright August Tuesday, shone in the window. The girl wrapped the flowers in the soaking-wet newspapers, moved a little farther away from the window, and stared at her mother. She received a pleasant expression in return. The train began to whistle and slowed down. A moment later it stopped.

There was no one at the station. On the other side of the street, on the sidewalk shaded by the almond trees, only the pool hall was open. The town was floating in the heat. The woman and the girl got off the train and

> "The town was floating in the heat."

Vocabulary
serenity (sə ren′ ə tē) *n.* calmness; peacefulness

Implied Theme What do the mother's words and tone to her daughter suggest about their situation?

Campanario, c. 1947. Joaquín Torres-García. Oil on board laid down on panel, 13¼ x 16½ in. Private collection.

View the Art Joaquín Torres-García was a Uruguayan painter who used geometric shapes and symbols to create a uniquely South American style of painting. How does this scene help you envision the town during siesta?

Keeping to the protective shade of the almond trees, the woman and the girl entered the town without disturbing the siesta. They went directly to the parish house.[1] The woman scratched the metal grating on the door with her fingernail, waited a moment, and scratched again. An electric fan was humming inside. They did not hear the steps. They hardly heard the slight creaking of a door, and immediately a cautious voice, right next to the metal grating: "Who is it?" The woman tried to see through the grating.

"I need the priest," she said.

"He's sleeping now."

"It's an emergency," the woman insisted. Her voice showed a calm determination.

The door was opened a little way, noiselessly, and a plump, older woman appeared, with very pale skin and hair the color of iron. Her eyes seemed too small behind her thick eyeglasses.

"Come in," she said, and opened the door all the way.

They entered a room permeated with an old smell of flowers. The woman of the house

crossed the abandoned station—the tiles split apart by the grass growing up between—and over to the shady side of the street.

It was almost two. At that hour, weighted down by drowsiness, the town was taking a siesta. The stores, the town offices, the public school were closed at eleven, and didn't reopen until a little before four, when the train went back. Only the hotel across from the station, with its bar and pool hall, and the telegraph office at one side of the plaza stayed open. The houses, most of them built on the banana company's model, had their doors locked from inside and their blinds drawn. In some of them it was so hot that the residents ate lunch in the patio. Others leaned a chair against the wall, in the shade of the almond trees, and took their siesta right out in the street.

---

1. A *parish house* is the home of the priest of a local church district.

Making Choices *Do you think the mother chooses to arrive when most people are inside? Explain.*

Making Choices *Why does the woman use that tone of voice? Why does the woman say that it is an emergency?*

led them to a wooden bench and signaled them to sit down. The girl did so, but her mother remained standing, absent-mindedly, with both hands clutching the handbag. No noise could be heard above the electric fan.

The woman of the house reappeared at the door at the far end of the room. "He says you should come back after three," she said in a very low voice. "He just lay down five minutes ago."

"The train leaves at three-thirty," said the woman.

It was a brief and self-assured reply, but her voice remained pleasant, full of undertones.² The woman of the house smiled for the first time.

"All right," she said.

When the far door closed again, the woman sat down next to her daughter. The narrow waiting room was poor, neat, and clean. On the other side of the wooden railing which divided the room, there was a worktable, a plain one with an oilcloth cover, and on top of the table a primitive typewriter next to a vase of flowers. The parish records were beyond. You could see that it was an office kept in order by a spinster.³

The far door opened and this time the priest appeared, cleaning his glasses with a handkerchief. Only when he put them on was it evident that he was the brother of the woman who had opened the door.

"How can I help you?" he asked.

"The keys to the cemetery," said the woman.

The girl was seated with the flowers in her lap and her feet crossed under the bench. The priest looked at her, then looked at the woman, and then through the wire mesh of the window at the bright, cloudless sky.

"In this heat," he said. "You could have waited until the sun went down."

The woman moved her head silently. The priest crossed to the other side of the railing, took out of the cabinet a notebook covered in oilcloth, a wooden penholder, and an inkwell, and sat down at the table. There was more than enough hair on his hands to account for what was missing on his head.

"Which grave are you going to visit?" he asked.

"Carlos Centeno's," said the woman.

"Who?"

"Carlos Centeno," the woman repeated.

The priest still did not understand.

"He's the thief who was killed here last week," said the woman in the same tone of voice. "I am his mother."

The priest **scrutinized** her. She stared at him with quiet self-control, and the Father blushed. He lowered his head and began to write. As he filled the page, he asked the woman to identify herself, and she replied unhesitatingly, with precise details, as if she were reading them. The Father began to sweat. The girl unhooked the buckle of her left shoe, slipped her heel out of it, and rested it on the bench rail. She did the same with the right one.

It had all started the Monday of the previous week, at three in the morning, a few blocks from there. Rebecca, a lonely widow who lived in a house full of odds and ends, heard above the sound of the drizzling rain someone trying to force the front door from outside. She got up, rummaged around in her closet for an ancient revolver that no one had fired since the days of Colonel Aureliano Buendía,⁴ and went into the living room without turning on the

---

2. *Undertones* are underlying or implied meanings.
3. *Spinster* usually refers to an older woman who has never been married.
4. *Aureliano Buendía* (ou′ rä lyä′ nō bwän dē′ ä) is a character in García Márquez's famous novel, *One Hundred Years of Solitude*.

Make Inferences About Theme *Why does the priest blush after finding out that he is talking with the thief's mother?*

Vocabulary

scrutinize (skrōōt′ ən īz′) *v.* to look at closely; to inspect carefully

lights. Orienting herself not so much by the noise at the lock as by a terror developed in her by twenty-eight years of loneliness, she fixed in her imagination not only the spot where the door was but also the exact height of the lock. She clutched the weapon with both hands, closed her eyes, and squeezed the trigger. It was the first time in her life that she had fired a gun. Immediately after the explosion, she could hear nothing except the murmur of the drizzle on the galvanized roof. Then she heard a little metallic bump on the cement porch, and a very low voice, pleasant but terribly exhausted: "Ah, Mother." The man they found dead in front of the house in the morning, his nose blown to bits, wore a flannel shirt with colored stripes, everyday pants with a rope for a belt, and was barefoot. No one in town knew him.

"So his name was Carlos Centeno," murmured the Father when he finished writing.

"Centeno Ayala,"[5] said the woman. "He was my only boy."

The priest went back to the cabinet. Two big rusty keys hung on the inside of the door; the girl imagined, as her mother had when she was a girl and as the priest himself must have imagined at some time, that they were Saint Peter's keys.[6] He took them down, put them on the open notebook on the railing, and pointed with his forefinger to a place on the page he had just written, looking at the woman.

"Sign here."

The woman scribbled her name, holding the handbag under her arm. The girl picked up the flowers, came to the railing shuffling her feet, and watched her mother attentively.

The priest sighed.

"Didn't you ever try to get him on the right track?"

The woman answered when she finished signing.

"He was a very good man."

The priest looked first at the woman and then at the girl, and realized with a kind of pious[7] amazement that they were not about to cry. The woman continued in the same tone:

"I told him never to steal anything that anyone needed to eat, and he minded me. On the other hand, before, when he used to box, he used to spend three days in bed, exhausted from being punched."

"All his teeth had to be pulled out," interrupted the girl.

"That's right," the woman agreed. "Every mouthful I ate those days tasted of the beatings my son got on Saturday nights."

"God's will is **inscrutable**," said the Father.

But he said it without much conviction, partly because experience had made him a little **skeptical** and partly because of the heat. He suggested that they cover their heads to guard against sunstroke. Yawning, and now almost completely asleep, he gave them instructions about how to find Carlos Centeno's grave. When they came back, they didn't have to knock. They should put

---

5. *[Ayala]* The young man's full name was Carlos *Centeno Ayala* (sen tā′ nō ä yä′ lə). In Spanish-speaking countries, one's first name and surname are, by custom, followed by the mother's maiden name.
6. *Saint Peter's keys* refers to the traditional belief of some Christians that Saint Peter is in charge of the keys to the gates of heaven.

Implied Theme What might these details say about the thief's motive? What might his motive say about the theme?

7. The word *pious* (pī′ əs) may mean either having genuine reverence for God or having a false *or* hypocritical religious devotion.

Make Inferences About Theme Why does the mother share this memory?

Vocabulary

inscrutable (in skroō′ tə bəl) *adj.* mysterious
skeptical (skep′ ti kəl) *adj.* having or showing doubt or suspicion; questioning; disbelieving

Landscape with Figures (Paisaje con Figura). Arturo Gordon Vargas (1853–1933). Oil on canvas, 43 x 54 cm.

View the Art Arturo Gordon Vargas uses bright colors and colored shadows in his works, which include landscapes and depictions of everyday life. In your opinion, how are the characters in the painting similar to the woman and the girl in the story?

the key under the door; and in the same place, if they could, they should put an offering for the Church. The woman listened to his directions with great attention, but thanked him without smiling.

The Father had noticed that there was someone looking inside, his nose pressed against the metal grating, even before he opened the door to the street. Outside was a group of children. When the door was opened wide, the children scattered. Ordinarily, at that hour there was no one in the street. Now there were not only children. There were groups of people under the almond trees. The Father scanned the street swimming in the heat and then he understood. Softly, he closed the door again.

"Wait a moment," he said without looking at the woman.

His sister appeared at the far door with a black jacket over her nightshirt and her hair down over her shoulders. She looked silently at the Father.

"What was it?" he asked.

"The people have noticed," murmured his sister.

"You'd better go out by the door to the patio," said the Father.

"It's the same there," said his sister. "Everybody is at the windows."

The woman seemed not to have understood until then. She tried to look into the street through the metal grating. Then she took the bouquet of flowers from the girl and began to move toward the door. The girl followed her.

"Wait until the sun goes down," said the Father.

"You'll melt," said his sister, motionless at the back of the room. "Wait and I'll lend you a parasol."

"Thank you," replied the woman. "We're all right this way."

She took the girl by the hand and went into the street.

Making Choices Why might the mother have chosen not to accept the woman's parasol?

After You Read

Respond and Think Critically

Respond and Interpret

1. For which character in this story do you feel the most sympathy? Explain.

2. (a) What do the mother and daughter see as they walk from the train station to the parish house? (b) Why might the mother have decided to arrive in town during the afternoon siesta?

3. Carlos's mother refers to him as a thief but also tells the priest that he was "a very good man." What might she mean by this? Use details from the story to support your opinion.

Analyze and Evaluate

4. (a) Why might the author have chosen such an oppressively hot day for the setting of the story? (b) Do you feel that the heat of the day adds to the drama and theme of the story? Explain.

5. (a) How would you describe the relationship between the mother and the daughter? (b) Do you think the story would have been more interesting if the daughter had played a larger role? Explain.

6. (a) What feelings might the mother have chosen to hide from others? (b) Do you think that hiding her feelings was an effective defense?

Connect

7. **Big Idea** Making Choices In your opinion, who is at fault for Carlos's death: Carlos, his mother, the widow who shot him, society, or some combination?

8. **Connect to Today** If this story took place today, what do you think would have happened once Carlos Centeno was murdered?

Literary Element Implied Theme

The **theme** of a piece of literature is its main idea or message. Some themes are universal, meaning that they are widely held ideas about life. An **implied theme** is not stated directly. Think back to details that provide hints about the theme that Gabriel García Márquez implies in this story.

1. (a) From the details of the story, what kind of a life do you think the Centeno Ayala family leads before the robbery? (b) What does the story imply about Carlos Centeno's motives for trying to rob the widow?

2. (a) Why do the townspeople gather around the priest's house? (b) What does the mother's response to their presence tell you about her?

3. What theme, or insight into life or human nature, does the story express? Explain how the story details help to imply the theme.

Review: Characters

As you learned on pages 86–87, a **flat** character reveals only one personality trait. By contrast, a **round** character shows varied and, sometimes, contradictory traits, like the "main characters" in your own life.

Partner Activity With a partner, use a chart like the one below to classify the characters in this story as flat or round. Then meet with the class to discuss the characters' traits that led to your classifications.

Flat Characters	Round Characters

Reading Strategy: Make Inferences About Theme

ACT Skills Practice

1. Which sentence best expresses the implied theme of "Tuesday Siesta"?

    A. Any crime is justified when the criminal is needy.

    B. Religious leaders do not always reach out to the poor and oppressed.

    C. Climate has a powerful effect on the way people behave.

    D. Even the very poor have the right to mourn their dead with dignity.

Vocabulary Practice

Practice with Word Parts Use a dictionary to find the meaning of each vocabulary word's root, prefix, and suffix. Then use a dictionary to find three words that contain the same root, prefix, or suffix. Circle the word part that would best help a person guess each word's meaning.

> interminable serenity scrutinize
> inscrutable skeptical

EXAMPLE:
reflexive

Prefix
(re-), "back"

Root
(flex), "to bend"

Suffix
(-ive), "performing an action"

Related words: retract, inflection, definitive

Academic Vocabulary

Gabriel García Márquez **locates** *his story in a fantastic version of reality.*

Locate is a multiple-meaning word. In a more casual conversation, someone might ask where a person's home is located. Using context clues, try to figure out the meaning of the word in the sentence above about Gabriel García Márquez.

For more on academic vocabulary, see pages 52 and 53.

Research and Report

Internet Connection

Assignment Use the Internet to research a Latin American country and compile information on its culture. Create a travel brochure that includes visuals.

Get Ideas Develop a search plan with research questions, such as questions about religion and customs, and with search terms, such as *Panama culture customs.* As you study the results, refine your terms and develop a specific focus. Search library databases for multicultural reference works.

Research Evaluate sources for authorship, documentation, and objectivity. For each source, including sources of visuals, record the following:

✔ author or Web site sponsor, if given

✔ name of Web site

✔ complete URL

✔ the date posted or last updated

✔ the date you viewed the information

✔ complete bibliographic information (if there is a print version)

Take notes that summarize and paraphrase. Use quotation marks for words or phrases that you quote verbatim. Then put your notes in a logical order, organized by main idea or topic. Before you draft, develop an outline from your notes. Remember to cite information you add from your sources.

Report Synthesize information from several sources to create a travel brochure for your country in print, online, or slideshow form. Use formatting and images to make the most important information stand out. Use text to discuss the culture, noting customs or perspectives that vary according to region, class, or other distinctions. Cite your sources at the end, as well as in parenthetical references and image source lines throughout your brochure.

 Literature Online

Selection Resources For Selection Quizzes, eFlashcards, and Reading-Writing Connection activities, go to glencoe.com and enter QuickPass code GL59794u1.

Learning Objectives

In this workshop, you will focus on the following objective:

Vocabulary: Understanding multiple-meaning words.

Vocabulary Workshop

Multiple-Meaning Words

Literature Connection The second sentence in this quotation includes two **multiple-meaning words**.

> "She sat on the opposite seat, away from the window, facing her mother. They were both in severe and poor mourning clothes."
>
> —Gabriel García Márquez, from "Tuesday Siesta"

Severe can mean either "plain" or "harshly judgmental"; and *poor* can mean "pitiable," "humble," or "poverty-stricken." From the context, the surrounding text, readers conclude that the women's clothes were plain and humble.

Examples

Word	Meaning	Example
plain	*n.* flat, treeless land	The **plain** stretched, unbroken, into the distance.
	adj. simple and unadorned	They were **plain** and simple people.
	adj. evident	The priest's embarrassment was **plain** to them.
still	*adv.* yet	They **still** had not reached the station.
	adj. quiet and unmoving	During the siesta, the whole town was **still**.
	v. to calm	The rabbi **stilled** the woman's fears.
train	*n.* connected line of railroad cars	The women took a **train** to visit her aunt.
	n. trailing part of a dress	The bride's gown had a long, intricate **train**.
	v. to teach or instruct	She **trained** her puppy to be obedient.

Vocabulary Term

A **multiple-meaning word** is a word that has two or more meanings.

Tip

To determine the intended meaning of a multiple-meaning word, use context clues. Remember that the right meaning will be the correct part of speech.

Practice Choose the correct definition for the multiple-meaning word in each sentence. Consult a dictionary if you need help.

1. After softball practice, the girl went shopping for a new *bat*.
   a. a winged mammal   **b.** a wooden sports implement
2. He used *tape* to close the box.
   a. a sticky fastening strip   **b.** record
3. To land, the plane must *bank* steeply.
   a. follow a curve   **b.** a ridge
4. He waited to start work until the sun *rose*.
   a. moved upward   **b.** an aromatic flower
5. *Nail* the sides of the box securely.
   a. a metal fastener   **b.** secure

Vocabulary For more vocabulary practice, go to glencoe.com and enter the QuickPass code GL59794u1.

Before You Read

When Mr. Pirzada Came to Dine

Meet Jhumpa Lahiri
(born 1967)

Jhumpa (joom′ pa) Lahiri began her writing career when she was a child. In elementary school, she and her best friend composed stories during recess, thinking them aloud "sentence by sentence." Many sentences later, in 2000, Lahiri won the Pulitzer Prize for fiction for *Interpreter of Maladies*, her collection of short stories about people in India and Indian immigrants in the United States. "It's been the happiest possible ending," she says.

> "The question of identity is always a difficult one, but especially so for those who are culturally displaced."
>
> —Jhumpa Lahiri

The Interpreter of Maladies Jhumpa Lahiri was born in London, but her Bengali parents, a librarian and a teacher, emigrated to Rhode Island, where she grew up. As a child, Lahiri often spent time with her extended family in Calcutta, India, as well. She received her bachelor's degree from Barnard College and then three master's degrees and a doctorate in Renaissance Studies from Boston University. Within a year of completing her dissertation, Lahiri had hired a literary agent, sold a book, and published a story in *The New Yorker*.

Lahiri's work often deals with the difficulties that Indian immigrants face in trying to cope with a new culture. Lahiri notes that her work reflects the sense of displacement she experienced as a child of immigrants. As she says, "For immigrants, the challenges of exile, the loneliness, the constant sense of alienation, the knowledge of and longing for a lost world, are more explicit and distressing than for their children. On the other hand, the problem for the children of immigrants, those with strong ties to their country of origin, is that they feel neither one thing nor the other. The feeling that there was no single place to which I fully belonged bothered me growing up."

Her First Novel In 2003 Lahiri published *The Namesake*. The novel deals with a rebellious son who is learning how to come to terms with Indian and American identities and to understand the significance of his first name, "Gogol." Lahiri says, "I had always been aware of having an unusual name and the difficulties one faces living with a name in a place where it doesn't make sense." The novel, allows Lahiri to develop her characters at a slower pace. In her review, Michiko Kakutani called it "a debut novel that is as assured and eloquent as the work of a long-time master of the craft."

Author Search For more about Jhumpa Lahiri, go to glencoe.com and enter QuickPass code GL59794u1.

Literature and Reading Preview

Connect to the Story
How would you interact with friends who know how worried you are about your family's safety? Write a journal entry about how much of your anxiety you would reveal.

Build Background
In 1971, when this story takes place, West Pakistan and East Pakistan were engaged in conflict as a result of East Pakistan's demand for independence from West Pakistan.

Set a Purpose for Reading

Big Idea **Making Choices**

As you read, ask yourself, How do the circumstances lead Mr. Pirzada to make the difficult choice to stay in the United States?

Literary Element **Theme**

A **theme** is a central message of a written work that readers can apply to life. Some works have a **stated theme** that is expressed directly. More commonly, works have an **implied theme** that is revealed gradually. As you read, ask yourself, What are the major themes in Lahiri's story?

Reading Strategy **Compare and Contrast Characters**

To **compare and contrast characters** is to determine similarities and differences between them. Comparing and contrasting characters can help you better understand the characters and why they act in certain ways. As you read, ask yourself, How are the characters like and unlike one another?

Tip: Take Notes Use a chart to record various similarities and differences between characters.

Mr. Pirzada	from Dacca, is Muslim, speaks Bengali and English
Lilia's father	from Calcutta, is Hindu, speaks Bengali and English
Lilia's mother	
Lilia	

Learning Objectives

For pages 123–141

In studying this text, you will focus on the following objectives:

Literary Study: Analyzing theme.

Reading: Comparing and contrasting characters.

Vocabulary

ascertaining (as′ ər tān′ ing) *v.* finding out definitely; p. 125 *The police were ascertaining who had robbed the bank.*

austere (ôs tēr′) *adj.* without ornament, very simple; p. 127 *Her dress was austere, lacking any embroidery or decoration.*

impeccably (im pek′ ə blē) *adv.* without error or flaw; p. 128 *His manners were impeccably polite.*

imperceptible (im′ pər sep′ tə bəl) *adj.* slight, barely capable of being seen or sensed; p. 129 *The movement in the grass was so imperceptible that we did not see the snake.*

intimidation (in tim′ ə dā shən) *n.* act of making one feel afraid or discouraged; p. 134 *The opposing team used intimidation to threaten the soccer players.*

When Mr. Pirzada Came to Dine

Jhumpa Lahiri

Avenue of the Elysian Fields, 1888. Vincent van Gogh. Oil on canvas.

In the autumn of 1971 a man used to come to our house, bearing confections[1] in his pocket and hopes of **ascertaining** the life or death of his family. His name was Mr. Pirzada, and he came from Dacca, now the capital of Bangladesh, but then a part of Pakistan. That year Pakistan was engaged in civil war. The eastern frontier, where Dacca was located, was fighting for autonomy[2] from the ruling regime[3] in the west. In March, Dacca had been invaded, torched, and shelled by the Pakistani army. Teachers were dragged onto streets and shot, women dragged into barracks and raped. By the end of the summer, three hundred thousand people were said to have died. In Dacca Mr. Pirzada had a three-story home, a lectureship in botany at the university, a wife of twenty years, and seven daughters between the ages of six and sixteen whose names all began with the letter A. "Their mother's idea," he explained one day, producing from his wallet a black-and-white picture of seven girls at a picnic, their braids tied with ribbons, sitting cross-legged in a row, eating chicken curry[4] off of banana leaves. "How am I to distinguish? Ayesha, Amira, Amina, Aziza, you see the difficulty."

---

1. *Confections* are sweets, such as candy or preserves.
2. To have *autonomy* is to have the right to self-rule.
3. A *regime* (rə zhēm´) is a system of government.

Vocabulary

ascertaining (as ər tān´ ing) *v.* finding out definitely

---

4. *Chicken curry* is chicken cooked with various spices including curry powder, ginger, and turmeric.

Theme A theme of a story can often develop out of contrasts in setting. How would you describe life in Dacca?

Each week Mr. Pirzada wrote letters to his wife, and sent comic books to each of his seven daughters, but the postal system, along with most everything else in Dacca, had collapsed, and he had not heard word of them in over six months. Mr. Pirzada, meanwhile, was in America for the year, for he had been awarded a grant from the government of Pakistan to study the foliage[5] of New England. In spring and summer he had gathered data in Vermont and Maine, and in autumn he moved to a university north of Boston, where we lived, to write a short book about his discoveries. The grant was a great honor, but when converted into dollars it was not generous. As a result, Mr. Pirzada lived in a room in a graduate dormitory,[6] and did not own a proper stove or a television set of his own. And so he came to our house to eat dinner and watch the evening news.

At first I knew nothing of the reason for his visits. I was ten years old, and was not surprised that my parents, who were from India, and had a number of Indian acquaintances at the university, should ask Mr. Pirzada to share our meals. It was a small campus, with narrow brick walkways and white pillared buildings, located on the fringes of what seemed to be an even smaller town. The supermarket did not carry mustard oil,[7] doctors did not make house calls, neighbors never dropped by without an invitation, and of these things, every so often, my parents complained. In search of compatriots,[8] they used to trail their fingers, at the start of each new semester, through the columns of the university directory, circling surnames[9] familiar to their part of the world. It was in this manner that they discovered Mr. Pirzada, and phoned him, and invited him to our home.

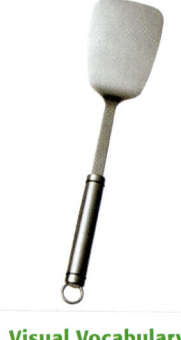

Visual Vocabulary
A *spatula* is a cooking utensil with a broad flexible blade used to spread or mix food.

I have no memory of his first visit, or of his second or his third, but by the end of September I had grown so accustomed to Mr. Pirzada's presence in our living room that one evening, as I was dropping ice cubes into the water pitcher, I asked my mother to hand me a fourth glass from a cupboard still out of my reach. She was busy at the stove, presiding over a skillet of fried spinach with radishes, and could not hear me because of the drone of the exhaust fan and the fierce scrapes of her spatula. I turned to my father, who was leaning against the refrigerator, eating spiced cashews from a cupped fist.

"What is it, Lilia?"

"A glass for the Indian man."

"Mr. Pirzada won't be coming today. More importantly, Mr. Pirzada is no longer considered Indian," my father announced, brushing salt from the cashews out of his trim black beard. "Not since Partition.[10] Our country was divided. 1947."

When I said I thought that was the date of India's independence from Britain, my father said, "That too. One moment we were free and then we were sliced up," he explained, drawing an X with his finger on

---

5. *Foliage* (fō′ lē ij) is clusters of leaves or branches.
6. A *dormitory* is a residence building with private rooms, typically for college students.
7. *Mustard oil* is made from mustard seeds and is used in cooking Indian foods.
8. *Compatriots* are people from one's home country.

Making Choices Why do you think Mr. Pirzada decides to stay in the United States instead of going home?

---

9. A *surname* is a person's family name.
10. *Partition* refers to the creation of independent countries out of parts of the British Empire. Partition created India and Pakistan.

the countertop, "like a pie. Hindus here, Muslims there. Dacca no longer belongs to us." He told me that during Partition Hindus and Muslims had set fire to each other's homes. For many, the idea of eating in the other's company was still unthinkable.

It made no sense to me. Mr. Pirzada and my parents spoke the same language, laughed at the same jokes, looked more or less the same. They ate pickled mangoes[11] with their meals, ate rice every night for supper with their hands. Like my parents, Mr. Pirzada took off his shoes before entering a room, chewed fennel[12] seeds after meals as a digestive, drank no alcohol, for dessert dipped austere biscuits into successive cups of tea. Nevertheless my father insisted that I understand the difference, and he led me to a map of the world taped to the wall over his desk. He seemed concerned that Mr. Pirzada might take offense if I accidentally referred to him as an Indian, though I could not really imagine Mr. Pirzada being offended by much of anything. "Mr. Pirzada is Bengali, but he is a Muslim," my father informed me. "Therefore he lives in East Pakistan, not India." His finger trailed across the Atlantic, through Europe, the Mediterranean, the Middle East, and finally to the sprawling orange diamond that my mother once told me resembled a woman wearing a sari with her left arm extended. Various cities had been circled with lines drawn between them to indicate my parents' travels, and the place of their birth, Calcutta, was signified by a small silver star. I had been there only once and had no memory of the trip. "As you see, Lilia, it is a different country, a different color," my father said. Pakistan was yellow, not orange. I noticed that there were two distinct parts to it, one much larger than the other, separated by an expanse of Indian territory; it was as if California and Connecticut constituted a nation apart from the U.S.

Visual Vocabulary
A *sari* is a garment consisting of a long piece of cloth worn by Hindu women.

My father rapped his knuckles on top of my head. "You are, of course, aware of the current situation? Aware of East Pakistan's fight for sovereignty?"

I nodded, unaware of the situation.

We returned to the kitchen, where my mother was draining a pot of boiled rice into a colander. My father opened up the can on the counter and eyed me sharply over the frames of his glasses as he ate some more cashews. "What exactly do they teach you at school? Do you study history? Geography?"

"Lilia has plenty to learn at school," my mother said. "We live here now, she was born here." She seemed genuinely proud of the fact, as if it were a reflection of my character. In her estimation, I knew, I was assured a safe life, an easy life, a fine education, every opportunity. I would never have to eat rationed food, or obey curfews, or watch riots from my rooftop, or hide neighbors in water tanks to prevent them from being shot, as she and my father had. "Imagine having to place her in a

---

11. *Mangoes* are the sweet fruit from the tropical mango tree.
12. *Fennel* is a plant with aromatic seeds used to flavor foods.

Compare and Contrast Characters Why does Lilia think that Mr. Pirzada is Indian?

Vocabulary
austere (ôs tēr′) *adj.* without ornament, very simple

Making Choices Why do you think Lilia's mother seems proud of this fact?

decent school. Imagine her having to read during power failures by the light of kerosene lamps. Imagine the pressures, the tutors, the constant exams." She ran a hand through her hair, bobbed[13] to a suitable length for her part-time job as a bank teller. "How can you possibly expect her to know about Partition? Put those nuts away."

"But what does she learn about the world?" My father rattled the cashew can in his hand. "What is she learning?"

We learned American history, of course, and American geography. That year, and every year, it seemed, we began by studying the Revolutionary War. We were taken in school buses on field trips to visit Plymouth Rock, and to walk the Freedom Trail, and to climb to the top of the Bunker Hill Monument. We made dioramas[14] out of colored construction paper depicting George Washington crossing the choppy waters of the Delaware River, and we made puppets of King George wearing white tights and a black bow in his hair. During tests we were given blank maps of the thirteen colonies, and asked to fill in names, dates, capitals. I could do it with my eyes closed.

The next evening Mr. Pirzada arrived, as usual, at six o'clock. Though they were no longer strangers, upon first greeting each other, he and my father maintained the habit of shaking hands.

"Come in, sir. Lilia, Mr. Pirzada's coat, please."

He stepped into the foyer,[15] **impeccably** suited and scarved, with a silk tie knotted

---

13. *Bobbed* means "cut short."
14. *Dioramas* are three-dimensional miniature scenes.
15. A *foyer* (foi′ ər) is an entrance hall.

Theme Why do you think Lahiri includes this detail?

Vocabulary

impeccably (im pek′ ə blē) *adv.* without error or flaw

Woman's head cover (detail), 19th century. Gujarat. c. 1860–1870. Silk, printed in imitation of tie-dye. Victoria and Albert Museum, London.

View the Art Some Muslim women in India, Pakistan, and Bangladesh wear head covers, or head scarves, as a sign of modesty. This head scarf comes from the Indian state of Gujarat, which is located in the extreme west of the country adjacent to Pakistan. Do you think Lilia's and Mr. Pirzada's reactions to seeing a woman in a head scarf would differ?

at his collar. Each evening he appeared in ensembles[16] of plums, olives, and chocolate browns. He was a compact man, and though his feet were perpetually splayed,[17] and his belly slightly wide, he nevertheless maintained an efficient posture, as if balancing in either hand two suitcases of equal weight. His ears were insulated by tufts of graying hair that seemed to block out the unpleasant traffic

---

16. Here, *ensembles* (än säm′ bəls) are clothes of matching colors.
17. *Splayed* feet are spread out awkwardly.

of life. He had thickly lashed eyes shaded with a trace of camphor, a generous mustache that turned up playfully at the ends, and a mole shaped like a flattened raisin in the very center of his left cheek. On his head he wore a black fez made from the wool of Persian lambs, secured by bobby pins, without which I was never to see him. Though my father always offered to fetch him in our car, Mr. Pirzada preferred to walk from his dormitory to our neighborhood, a distance of about twenty minutes on foot, studying trees and shrubs on his way, and when he entered our house his knuckles were pink with the effects of crisp autumn air.

Visual Vocabulary
A *fez* is a tall felt hat, usually red, with a black tassel hanging from the crown.

"Another refugee, I am afraid, on Indian territory."

"They are estimating nine million at the last count," my father said.

Mr. Pirzada handed me his coat, for it was my job to hang it on the rack at the bottom of the stairs. It was made of finely checkered gray-and-blue wool, with a striped lining and horn buttons, and carried in its weave the faint smell of limes. There were no recognizable tags inside, only a hand-stitched label with the phrase "Z. Sayeed, Suitors" embroidered on it in cursive with glossy black thread. On certain days a birch or maple leaf was tucked into a pocket. He unlaced his shoes and lined them against the baseboard; a golden paste clung to the toes and heels, the result of walking through our damp, unraked lawn. Relieved of his trappings, he grazed my throat with his short, restless fingers, the way a person feels for solidity behind a wall before driving in a nail. Then he followed my father to the living room, where the television was tuned to the local news. As soon as they were seated my mother appeared from the kitchen with a plate of mincemeat kebabs with coriander chutney.[18] Mr. Pirzada popped one into his mouth.

"One can only hope," he said, reaching for another, "that Dacca's refugees are as heartily fed. Which reminds me." He reached into his suit pocket and gave me a small plastic egg filled with cinnamon hearts. "For the lady of the house," he said with an almost **imperceptible** splay-footed bow.

"Really, Mr. Pirzada," my mother protested. "Night after night. You spoil her."

"I only spoil children who are incapable of spoiling."

It was an awkward moment for me, one which I awaited in part with dread, in part with delight. I was charmed by the presence of Mr. Pirzada's rotund[19] elegance, and flattered by the faint theatricality of his attentions, yet unsettled by the superb ease of his gestures, which made me feel, for an instant, like a stranger in my own home. It had become our ritual, and for several weeks, before we grew more comfortable with one another, it was the only time he spoke to me directly. I had no response, offered no comment, betrayed no visible reaction to the steady stream of honey-filled lozenges, the raspberry truffles, the

---

18. *Mincemeat . . . chutney* is a mixture of chopped apples, raisins, and meat skewered and broiled, served with a relish made with the aromatic herb coriander.
19. *Rotund* means "plump."

Vocabulary

imperceptible (im´ pər sep´ tə bəl) *adj.* slight, barely capable of being seen or sensed

---

Compare and Contrast Characters Why does Mr. Pirzada call himself a "refugee . . . on Indian territory"?

slender rolls of sour pastilles. I could not even thank him, for once, when I did, for an especially spectacular peppermint lollipop wrapped in a spray[20] of purple cellophane, he had demanded, "What is this thank-you? The lady at the bank thanks me, the cashier at the shop thanks me, the librarian thanks me when I return an overdue book, the overseas operator thanks me as she tries to connect me to Dacca and fails. If I am buried in this country I will be thanked, no doubt, at my funeral."

It was inappropriate, in my opinion, to consume the candy Mr. Pirzada gave me in a casual manner. I coveted each evening's treasure as I would a jewel, or a coin from a buried kingdom, and I would place it in a small keepsake box made of carved sandalwood beside my bed, in which, long ago in India, my father's mother used to store the ground areca[21] nuts she ate after her morning bath. It was my only memento of a grandmother I had never known, and until Mr. Pirzada came to our lives I could find nothing to put inside it. Every so often before brushing my teeth and laying out my clothes for school the next day, I opened the lid of the box and ate one of his treats.

That night, like every night, we did not eat at the dining table, because it did not provide an unobstructed view of the television set. Instead we huddled around the coffee table, without conversing, our plates perched on the edges of our knees. From the kitchen my mother brought forth the succession of dishes: lentils with fried onions, green beans with coconut, fish cooked with raisins in a yogurt sauce. I followed with the water glasses, and the plate of lemon wedges, and the chili peppers, purchased on monthly trips to Chinatown and stored by the pound in the freezer, which they liked to snap open and crush into their food.

Before eating Mr. Pirzada always did a curious thing. He took out a plain silver watch without a band, which he kept in his breast pocket, held it briefly to one of his tufted ears, and wound it with three swift flicks of his thumb and forefinger. Unlike the watch on his wrist, the pocket watch, he had explained to me, was set to the local time in Dacca, eleven hours ahead. For the duration of the meal the watch rested on his folded paper napkin on the coffee table. He never seemed to consult it.

Now that I had learned Mr. Pirzada was not an Indian, I began to study him with extra care, to try to figure out what made him different. I decided that the pocket watch was one of those things. When I saw it that night, as he wound it and arranged it on the coffee table, an uneasiness possessed me; life, I realized, was being lived in Dacca first. I imagined Mr. Pirzada's daughters rising from sleep, tying ribbons in their hair, anticipating breakfast, preparing for school. Our meals, our actions, were only a shadow of what had already happened there, a lagging ghost of where Mr. Pirzada really belonged.

At six-thirty, which was when the national news began, my father raised the volume and adjusted the antennas. Usually I occupied myself with a book, but that night my father insisted that I pay attention. On the screen I saw tanks rolling through dusty streets, and fallen buildings, and forests of

---

20. Here, *spray* means that the cellophane has been shaped or twisted to look like a flower.
21. *Areca* nuts come from the betel palm, a type of tall palm tree.

Theme Why do you think Mr. Pirzada makes such an outburst when Lilia thanks him for the candy?

Compare and Contrast Characters How does winding the pocket watch make Mr. Pirzada different from Lilia's family?

Romantic India I, 2000. Gerry Charm. Collage.

View the Art Gerry Charm is a contemporary American artist who explores the cultures of ancient and modern civilizations through collage. How do you think Lilia would react if an American from her town were to suddenly express an interest in learning about India and Indian culture?

unfamiliar trees into which East Pakistani refugees had fled, seeking safety over the Indian border. I saw boats with fan-shaped sails floating on wide coffee-colored rivers, a barricaded university, newspaper offices burnt to the ground. I turned to look at Mr. Pirzada; the images flashed in miniature across his eyes. As he watched he had an immovable expression on his face, composed but alert, as if someone were giving him directions to an unknown destination.

During the commercial my mother went to the kitchen to get more rice, and my father and Mr. Pirzada deplored the policies of a general named Yahyah Khan.[22]

---

22. *Yahyah Khan,* or Agha Mohammad Yahya Khan, was a West Pakistan general who led troops into East Pakistan.

They discussed intrigues I did not know, a catastrophe I could not comprehend. "See, children your age, what they do to survive," my father said as he served me another piece of fish. But I could no longer eat. I could only steal glances at Mr. Pirzada, sitting beside me in his olive green jacket, calmly creating a well in his rice to make room for a second helping of lentils. He was not my notion of a man burdened by such grave concerns. I wondered if the reason he was always so smartly dressed was in preparation to endure with dignity whatever news assailed[23] him, perhaps even to attend a funeral at a moment's notice. I wondered, too, what would happen if suddenly his seven daughters were to appear on television, smiling and waving and blowing kisses to Mr. Pirzada from a balcony. I imagined how relieved he would be. But this never happened.

That night when I placed the plastic egg filled with cinnamon hearts in the box beside my bed, I did not feel the ceremonious satisfaction I normally did. I tried not to think about Mr. Pirzada, in his lime-scented overcoat, connected to the unruly, sweltering world we had viewed a few hours ago in our bright, carpeted living room. And yet for several moments that was all I could think about. My stomach tightened as I worried whether his wife and seven daughters were now members of the drifting, clamoring crowd that had flashed at intervals on the screen. In an effort to banish[24] the image I looked around my room, at the yellow canopied[25] bed with matching flounced[26] curtains, at framed class pictures

---

23. *Assailed* means "attacked" or "assaulted."
24. *Banish* means "to drive away" or "force to leave."
25. A *canopy* is a cloth covering fastened above a bed.
26. *Flounced* means "gathered" or "pleated."

Compare and Contrast Characters Why do you think Lilia cannot comprehend the scope and complexities of the war?

mounted on white and violet papered walls, at the penciled inscriptions by the closet door where my father recorded my height on each of my birthdays. But the more I tried to distract myself, the more I began to convince myself that Mr. Pirzada's family was in all likelihood dead. Eventually I took a square of white chocolate out of the box, and unwrapped it, and then I did something I had never done before. I put the chocolate in my mouth, letting it soften until the last possible moment, and then as I chewed it slowly, I prayed that Mr. Pirzada's family was safe and sound. I had never prayed for anything before, had never been taught or told to, but ==I decided, given the circumstances, that it was something I should do.== That night, when I went to the bathroom I only pretended to brush my teeth, for I feared that I would somehow rinse the prayer out as well. I wet the brush and rearranged the tube of paste to prevent my parents from asking any questions, and fell asleep with sugar on my tongue.

No one at school talked about the war followed so faithfully in my living room. We continued to study the American Revolution, and learned about the injustices of taxation without representation, and memorized passages from the Declaration of Independence. During recess the boys would divide in two groups, chasing each other wildly around the swings and seesaws, Redcoats against the colonies. In the classroom our teacher, Mrs. Kenyon, pointed frequently to a map that emerged like a movie screen from the top of the chalkboard, charting the route of the *Mayflower,* or showing us the location of the Liberty Bell. Each week two members of the class gave a report on a particular aspect of the Revolution, and so one day I was sent to the school library with my friend Dora to learn about the surrender at Yorktown. Mrs. Kenyon handed us a slip of paper with the names of three books to look up in the card catalogue. We found them right away, and sat down at a low round table to read and take notes. But I could not concentrate. I returned to the blond-wood shelves, to a section I had noticed labeled "Asia." I saw books about China, India, Indonesia, Korea. Eventually I found a book titled *Pakistan: A Land and Its People.* I sat on a footstool and opened the book. The laminated jacket crackled in my grip. I began turning the pages, filled with photos of rivers and rice fields and men in military uniforms. There was a chapter about Dacca, and I began to read about its rainfall, and its jute[27] production. I was studying a population chart when Dora appeared in the aisle.

"What are you doing back here? Mrs. Kenyon's in the library. She came to check up on us."

I slammed the book shut, too loudly. Mrs. Kenyon emerged, the aroma of her perfume filling up the tiny aisle, and lifted the book by the tip of its spine as if it were a hair clinging to my sweater. She glanced at the cover, then at me.

"Is this book a part of your report, Lilia?"

"No, Mrs. Kenyon."

=="Then I see no reason to consult[28] it,"== she said, replacing it in the slim gap on the shelf. "Do you?"

As weeks passed it grew more and more rare to see any footage[29] from Dacca on the

---

27. *Jute* is a fiber from the jute plant that is used to make rope, burlap, or sacks.
28. Here, *consult* means "to get information from."
29. *Footage* refers to a segment of newsreel film.

Making Choices Why do you think Lilia decides to pray for Mr. Pirzada's family?

Theme Why do you think Lahiri chose to include this scene?

news. The report came after the first set of commercials, sometimes the second. The press had been censored, removed, restricted, rerouted. Some days, many days, only a death toll was announced, prefaced by a reiteration[30] of the general situation. More poets were executed, more villages set ablaze. In spite of it all, night after night, my parents and Mr. Pirzada enjoyed long, leisurely meals. After the television was shut off, and the dishes washed and dried, they joked, and told stories, and dipped biscuits in their tea. When they tired of discussing political matters they discussed, instead, the progress of Mr. Pirzada's book about the deciduous[31] trees of New England, and my father's nomination for tenure, and the peculiar eating habits of my mother's American coworkers at the bank. Eventually I was sent upstairs to do my homework, but through the carpet I heard them as they drank more tea, and listened to cassettes of Kishore Kumar,[32] and played Scrabble on the coffee table, laughing and arguing long into the night about the spellings of English words. I wanted to join them, wanted, above all, to console Mr. Pirzada somehow. But apart from eating a piece of candy for the sake of his family and praying for their safety, there was nothing I could do. They played Scrabble until the eleven o'clock news, and then, sometime around midnight, Mr. Pirzada walked back to his dormitory. For this reason I never saw him leave, but each night as I drifted off to sleep I would hear them, anticipating the birth of a nation on the other side of the world.

One day in October Mr. Pirzada asked upon arrival, "What are these large orange vegetables on people's doorsteps? A type of squash?"

"Pumpkins," my mother replied. "Lilia, remind me to pick one up at the supermarket."

"And the purpose? It indicates what?"

"You make a jack-o'-lantern," I said, grinning ferociously. "Like this. To scare people away."

"I see," Mr. Pirzada said, grinning back. "Very useful."

The next day my mother bought a ten-pound pumpkin, fat and round, and placed it on the dining table. Before supper, while my father and Mr. Pirzada were watching the local news, she told me to decorate it with markers, but I wanted to carve it properly like others I had noticed in the neighborhood.

"Yes, let's carve it," Mr. Pirzada agreed, and rose from the sofa. "Hang the news tonight." Asking no questions, he walked into the kitchen, opened a drawer, and returned, bearing a long serrated[33] knife. He glanced at me for approval. "Shall I?"

I nodded. For the first time we all gathered around the dining table, my mother,

> "... each night as I drifted off to sleep I would hear them, anticipating the birth of a nation on the other side of the world."

---

30. *Reiteration* is repeating or saying over again.
31. *Deciduous* trees lose their leaves each year.
32. *Kishore Kumar* was a famous actor and singer in Indian films.

Compare and Contrast Characters What draws Mr. Pirzada and Lilia's parents together?

33. *Serrated* means having a sawlike edge.

Theme Why does Mr. Pirzada decide not to watch the news?

my father, Mr. Pirzada, and I. While the television aired unattended we covered the tabletop with newspapers. Mr. Pirzada draped his jacket over the chair behind him, removed a pair of opal[34] cuff links, and rolled up the starched sleeves of his shirt.

"First go around the top, like this," I instructed, demonstrating with my index finger.

He made an initial incision[35] and drew the knife around. When he had come full circle he lifted the cap by the stem; it loosened effortlessly, and Mr. Pirzada leaned over the pumpkin for a moment to inspect and inhale its contents. My mother gave him a long metal spoon with which he gutted the interior until the last bits of string and seeds were gone. My father, meanwhile, separated the seeds from the pulp and set them out to dry on a cookie sheet, so that we could roast them later on. I drew two triangles against the ridged surface for the eyes, which Mr. Pirzada dutifully carved, and crescents for eyebrows, and another triangle for the nose. The mouth was all that remained, and the teeth posed a challenge. I hesitated.

"Smile or frown?" I asked.

"You choose," Mr. Pirzada said.

As a compromise I drew a kind of grimace,[36] straight across, neither mournful nor friendly. Mr. Pirzada began carving, without the least bit of **intimidation**, as if he had been carving jack-o'-lanterns his whole life. He had nearly finished when the national news began. The reporter

Home Coming—After a Long Absence, 1998. Shanti Panchal. Watercolor on paper, 98 x 79 cm. Private collection.

View the Art In explaining his creative process, artist Shanti Panchal said that "escape and shifting of focus is the essence of survival." How might this statement apply to the situation that Mr. Pirzada finds himself in?

mentioned Dacca, and we all turned to listen: An Indian official announced that unless the world helped to relieve the burden of East Pakistani refugees, India would have to go to war against Pakistan. The reporter's face dripped with sweat as he relayed the information. He did not wear a tie or a jacket, dressed instead as if he himself were about to take part in the battle. He shielded his scorched face as he hollered things to the cameraman. The knife slipped from Mr. Pirzada's hand and made a gash dipping toward the base of the pumpkin.

---

34. *Opal* is a type of mineral used as a gemstone.
35. *Initial incision* means the "first cut."
36. A *grimace* (grim′ is) is a twisting of the face into an ugly or painful smile.

Vocabulary

intimidation (in tim′ ə dā shən) *n.* act of making one feel afraid or discouraged

"Please forgive me." He raised a hand to one side of his face, as if someone had slapped him there. "I am—it is terrible. I will buy another. We will try again."

"Not at all, not at all," my father said. He took the knife from Mr. Pirzada, and carved around the gash, evening it out, dispensing altogether with[37] the teeth I had drawn. What resulted was a disproportionately large hole the size of a lemon, so that our jack-o'-lantern wore an expression of placid[38] astonishment, the eyebrows no longer fierce, floating in frozen surprise above a vacant, geometric gaze.

For Halloween I was a witch. Dora, my trick-or-treating partner, was a witch too. We wore black capes fashioned from dyed pillowcases and conical hats with wide cardboard brims. We shaded our faces green with a broken eye shadow that belonged to Dora's mother, and my mother gave us two burlap sacks that had once contained basmati rice,[39] for collecting candy. That year our parents decided that we were old enough to roam the neighborhood unattended. Our plan was to walk from my house to Dora's, from where I was to call to say I had arrived safely, and then Dora's mother would drive me home. My father equipped us with flashlights, and I had to wear my watch and synchronize it with his. We were to return no later than nine o'clock.

When Mr. Pirzada arrived that evening he presented me with a box of chocolate-covered mints.

---

37. *Dispensing. . .with* means "getting rid of."
38. *Placid* means "calm, undisturbed."
39. *Basmati rice* is a kind of long-grain rice grown in India.

Theme Is there more than one reason for which Mr. Pirzada feels he needs to be forgiven? Explain.

Compare and Contrast Characters How does this detail emphasize the differences between children's lives in Boston and in East Pakistan?

"In here," I told him, and opened up the burlap sack. "Trick or treat!"

"I understand that you don't really need my contribution this evening," he said, depositing the box. He gazed at my green face, and the hat secured by a string under my chin. Gingerly he lifted the hem of the cape, under which I was wearing a sweater and a zipped fleece jacket. "Will you be warm enough?"

I nodded, causing the hat to tip to one side.

He set it right. "Perhaps it is best to stand still."

The bottom of our staircase was lined with baskets of miniature candy, and when Mr. Pirzada removed his shoes he did not place them there as he normally did, but inside the closet instead. He began to unbutton his coat, and I waited to take it from him, but Dora called me from the bathroom to say that she needed my help drawing a mole on her chin. When we were finally ready my mother took a picture of us in front of the fireplace, and then I opened the front door to leave. Mr. Pirzada and my father, who had not gone into the living room yet, hovered in the foyer. Outside it was already dark. The air smelled of wet leaves, and our carved jack-o'-lantern flickered impressively against the shrubbery by the door. In the distance came the sounds of scampering feet, and the howls of the older boys who wore no costume at all other than a rubber mask, and the rustling apparel of the youngest children, some so young that they were carried from door to door in the arms of their parents.

"Don't go into any of the houses you don't know," my father warned.

Making Choices How does Mr. Pirzada's comment reflect his own actions?

JHUMPA LAHIRI

Mr. Pirzada knit his brows together. "Is there any danger?'

"No, no," my mother assured him. "All the children will be out. It's a tradition."

"Perhaps I should accompany them?" Mr. Pirzada suggested. He looked suddenly tired and small, standing there in his splayed, stockinged feet, and his eyes contained a panic I had never seen before. In spite of the cold I began to sweat inside my pillowcase.

"Really, Mr. Pirzada," my mother said, "Lilia will be perfectly safe with her friend."

"But if it rains? If they lose their way?"

"Don't worry," I said. It was the first time I had uttered those words to Mr. Pirzada, two simple words I had tried but failed to tell him for weeks, had said only in my prayers. It shamed me now that I had said them for my own sake.

He placed one of his stocky fingers on my cheek, then pressed it to the back of his own hand, leaving a faint green smear. "If the lady insists," he conceded, and offered a small bow.

We left, stumbling slightly in our black pointy thrift-store shoes, and when we turned at the end of the driveway to wave good-bye, Mr. Pirzada was standing in the frame of the doorway, a short figure between my parents, waving back.

"Why did that man want to come with us?" Dora asked.

"His daughters are missing." As soon as I said it, I wished I had not. I felt that my saying it made it true, that Mr. Pirzada's daughters really were missing, and that he would never see them again.

"You mean they were kidnapped?" Dora continued. "From a park or something?"

"I didn't mean they were missing. I meant, he misses them. They live in a different country, and he hasn't seen them in a while, that's all."

We went from house to house, walking along pathways and pressing doorbells. Some people had switched off all their lights for effect, or strung rubber bats in their windows. At the McIntyres' a coffin was placed in front of the door, and Mr. McIntyre rose from it in silence, his face covered with chalk, and deposited a fistful of candy corns into our sacks. Several people told me that they had never seen an Indian witch before. Others performed the transaction without comment. As we paved our way with the parallel beams of our flashlights we saw eggs cracked in the middle of the road, and cars covered with shaving cream, and toilet paper garlanding[40] the branches of trees. By the time we reached Dora's house our hands were chapped from carrying our bulging burlap bags, and our feet were sore and swollen. Her mother gave us bandages for our blisters and served us warm cider and caramel popcorn. She reminded me to call my parents to tell them I had arrived safely, and when I did I could hear the television in the background. My mother did not seem particularly relieved to hear from me. When I replaced the phone on the receiver it occurred to me that the television wasn't on at Dora's house at all. Her father was lying on the couch, reading a magazine, with a glass of wine on the coffee

---

Compare and Contrast Characters Why is Mr. Pirzada so worried about the girls, while Lilia's mother does not seem concerned about their safety?

Making Choices Why does Lilia choose to tell Mr. Pirzada not to worry at this point, instead of earlier in the story?

---

40. A *garland* is a wreath, usually of flowers or leaves. Here, the garland is toilet paper strewn through the branches.

Compare and Contrast Characters Why are Dora's parents not watching the news?

table, and there was saxophone music playing on the stereo.

After Dora and I had sorted through our plunder, and counted and sampled and traded until we were satisfied, her mother drove me back to my house. I thanked her for the ride, and she waited in the driveway until I made it to the door. In the glare of her headlights I saw that our pumpkin had been shattered, its thick shell strewn in chunks across the grass. I felt the sting of tears in my eyes, and a sudden pain in my throat, as if it had been stuffed with the sharp tiny pebbles that crunched with each step under my aching feet. I opened the door, expecting the three of them to be standing in the foyer, waiting to receive me, and to grieve for our ruined pumpkin, but there was no one. In the living room Mr. Pirzada, my father, and mother were sitting side by side on the sofa. The television was turned off, and Mr. Pirzada had his head in his hands.

What they heard that evening, and for many evenings after that, was that India and Pakistan were drawing closer and closer to war. Troops from both sides lined the border, and Dacca was insisting on nothing short of independence. The war was to be waged on East Pakistani soil. The United States was siding with West Pakistan, the Soviet Union with India and what was soon to be Bangladesh. War was declared officially on December 4, and twelve days later, the Pakistani army, weakened by having to fight three thousand miles from their source of supplies, surrendered in Dacca. All of these facts I know only now, for they are available to me in any history book, in any library. But then it

Girls in a Wood. Indian Art.

View the Art In this painting, three Indian girls spend their leisure time in a beautiful wood. How does this scene compare to the situation of Mr. Pirzada's daughters in East Pakistan and Shillong?

remained, for the most part, a remote mystery with haphazard[41] clues. What I remember during those twelve days of the war was that my father no longer asked me to watch the news with them, and that Mr. Pirzada stopped bringing me candy, and that my mother refused to serve anything other than boiled eggs with rice for dinner. I remember some nights helping my mother spread a sheet and blankets on the couch so that Mr.

---

41. *Haphazard* means "random, occurring by chance."

JHUMPA LAHIRI

Pirzada could sleep there, and high-pitched voices hollering in the middle of the night when my parents called our relatives in Calcutta to learn more details about the situation. Most of all I remember the three of them operating during that time as if they were a single person, sharing a single meal, a single body, a single silence, and a single fear.

In January, Mr. Pirzada flew back to his three-story home in Dacca, to discover what was left of it. We did not see much of him in those final weeks of the year; he was busy finishing his manuscript, and we went to Philadelphia to spend Christmas with friends of my parents. Just as I have no memory of his first visit, I have no memory of his last. My father drove him to the airport one afternoon while I was at school. For a long time we did not hear from him. Our evenings went on as usual, with dinners in front of the news. The only difference was that Mr. Pirzada and his extra watch were not there to accompany us. According to reports Dacca was repairing itself slowly, with a newly formed parliamentary government. The new leader, Sheikh Mujib Rahman, recently released from prison, asked countries for building materials to replace more than one million houses that had been destroyed in the war. Countless refugees returned from India, greeted, we learned, by unemployment and the threat of famine.[42] Every now and then I studied the map above my father's desk and pictured Mr. Pirzada on that small patch of yellow, perspiring heavily, I imagined, in one of his suits, searching for his family. Of course, the map was outdated by then.

Finally, several months later, we received a card from Mr. Pirzada commemorating[43] the Muslim New Year, along with a short letter. He was reunited, he wrote, with his wife and children. All were well, having survived the events of the past year at an estate belonging to his wife's grandparents in the mountains of Shillong.[44] His seven daughters were a bit taller, he wrote, but otherwise they were the same, and he still could not keep their names in order. At the end of the letter he thanked us for our hospitality, adding that although he now understood the meaning of the words "thank you" they still were not adequate to express his gratitude. To celebrate the good news my mother prepared a special dinner that evening, and when we sat down to eat at the coffee table we toasted our water glasses, but I did not feel like celebrating. Though I had not seen him for months, it was only then that I felt Mr. Pirzada's absence. It was only then, raising my water glass in his name, that I knew what it meant to miss someone who was so many miles and hours away, just as he had missed his wife and daughters for so many months. He had no reason to return to us, and my parents predicted, correctly, that we would never see him again. Since January, each night before bed, I had continued to eat, for the sake of Mr. Pirzada's family, a piece of candy I had saved from Halloween. That night there was no need to. Eventually, I threw them away. ∞

---

42. **Famine** is an extreme lack of food, leading to starvation.

Compare and Contrast Characters What has finally given all the adults the same single-minded sense of fear?

43. *Commemorating* means "honoring the memory of."
44. *Shillong* is a part of India north of East Pakistan.

Theme Why do you think that this is the first time Lilia feels Mr. Pirzada's absence?

Making Choices Why has Lilia decided to throw the candy away?

After You Read

Respond and Think Critically

Respond and Interpret

1. What was your reaction when you realized that Mr. Pirzada decided to stay in the United States instead of returning to Dacca and to his family?

2. (a) Why does Mr. Pirzada come to dinner at Lilia's house? (b) Why does he give Lilia candy?

3. (a) What does Mr. Pirzada discover about his family when he gets back to Dacca? (b) Why do you think Lilia's parents predict that they will never see Mr. Pirzada again?

Analyze and Evaluate

4. Lahiri vividly describes the war and political situation in East Pakistan. How accurate do you think a writer should be in a fictional story? Explain.

5. Analyze Lahiri's use of food in the story. Consider the food Lilia's mother serves and the candy Mr. Pirzada brings Lilia.

Connect

6. **Big Idea** **Making Choices** Who do you think has made the most difficult choice in the story? Explain.

7. **Connect to Author** (a) How might Lahiri's own childhood have influenced her description of Lilia's experiences? (b) Where in the story does Lahiri's focus on how it must have felt for Lilia to be one of the only Indian children in the town?

Daily Life & Culture

The Aftermath of Partition

In 1947, the partition of British India along religious lines created two independent nations, Muslim-dominated East and West Pakistan and Hindu India. On the Indian subcontinent, culture and regional differences are stronger identification markers than religion. This became clear when, in 1971, the largely Muslim West Pakistan army waged war on the inhabitants of East Pakistan, most of whom were Muslims themselves.

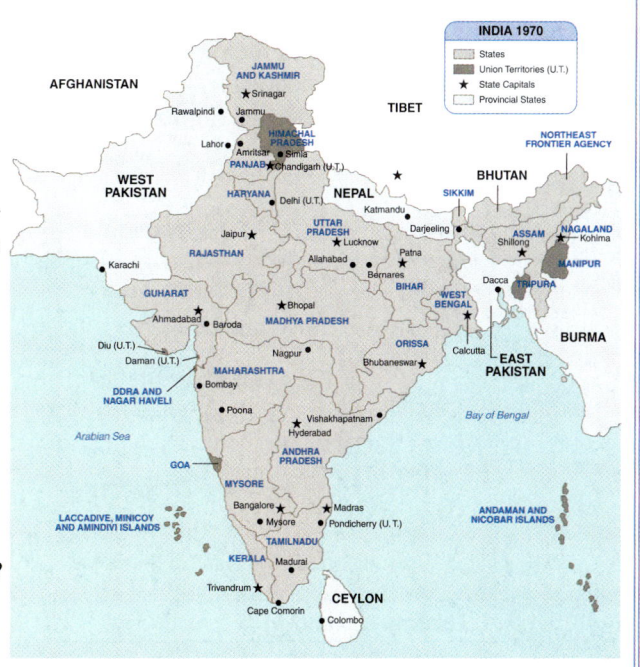

1. Find East and West Pakistan and Calcutta on the map shown here. What might have been the consequences of East Pakistan's separation from Calcutta, its economic hub?

2. What can you infer about the reasons the people of East Pakistan wanted self-rule?

Literary Element Theme

In some stories a **theme** is stated directly, but more often it is implied, as in "When Mr. Pirzada Came to Dine." To discover an implied theme, you might look at the experiences of the main characters and ask what message about life the story communicates.

1. Cultural belonging is an important element in the story. How attached is Lilia to American culture? How attached is Mr. Pirzada to American culture? Explain.

2. What message, or theme, does Lahiri portray through the experiences of Lilia and Mr. Pirzada?

Review: Motivation

As you learned on page 89, **motivation** is the stated or implied reason that a character acts, thinks, or feels a certain way. Motivation may be an external circumstance, an internal moral, or an emotional impulse.

Partner Activity Meet with a classmate and discuss the different motivations that the two main characters, Lilia and Mr. Pirzada, experience during the story. Create a two-column chart like the one below in which you list the character's name in the left column and his or her motivations in the right column. Remember that characters can have several motivations.

Character	Motivation
Mr. Pirzada	wants to see his wife and daughters
	is motivated to dote on Lilia

Reading Strategy Compare and Contrast Characters

ACT Skills Practice

1. Which detail about Mrs. Kenyon best underscores the contrast between her cultural background and that of Lilia's family?

   A. She teaches elementary school.
   B. She assigns Lilia and Dora a report on the surrender of Yorktown.
   C. She frequently uses a map to show her students geography of colonial America.
   D. She takes *Pakistan: A Land and Its People* away from Lilia.

Vocabulary Practice

Practice with Context Clues Identify the context clues that help you determine the meaning of each boldfaced vocabulary word.

1. Maria consulted several sources when **ascertaining** the value of the used car.

2. The princess, who was used to elaborate meals, did not enjoy the **austere** meal of bread and carrots.

3. The runner navigated the obstacle course **impeccably**, never even touching, let alone knocking over, a single pin.

4. Some could not see the nearly **imperceptible** shift from green to bluish-green.

5. The bully rarely lifted a hand, relying instead on **intimidation**.

Literature Online

Selection Resources For Selection Quizzes, eFlashcards, and Reading-Writing Connection activities, go to glencoe.com and enter QuickPass code GL59794u1.

Respond Through Writing

Short Story

Learning Objectives

In this assignment, you will focus on the following objectives:

Writing: Writing a short story.

Grammar: Using quotation marks.

Apply Characterization Lahiri creates complex, nuanced characters by providing sensory details about how they look, speak, think, and act. That is, she *shows*, rather than *tells*, what her characters are like. Write a short story in which you use sensory details to *show* characters.

Prewrite First, make a story map to be sure you have a setting, characters, and a conflict or problem, as well as a series of events that leads to a resolution of that conflict. Next, make two-column character charts for each of the main characters. Model them on the following chart, which Lahiri might have made for Mr. Pirzada:

Trait	Sensory Details That Show Trait
family-oriented	winds his watch to time in Dacca, where family is
private	never talks about this ritual

Draft As you draft, provide sensory details (sights, sounds, smells, tastes, and textures) to *show* (not tell) characters and reveal the significance of their actions, gestures, movements, appearances, and feelings. At the same time, pace the events to reflect the mood of your story. For example, while a story like Lahiri's requires a slow pace, a story with a more cheerful mood might move along far more rapidly.

Revise Check that you have used sensory details to help evoke the sights, sounds, smells, and other characteristics of the place and time. Also revise to be specific about where and when the story takes place. Then exchange your stories with a classmate. Make and incorporate suggestions for additional ways to show the characters.

Edit and Proofread Proofread your paper, correcting any errors in grammar, spelling, and punctuation. Use the Grammar Tip in the side column to help you with the use of quotation marks.

Grammar Tip

Quotation Marks

When you write dialogue, place commas and periods inside the quotation marks.

"Really, Mr. Pirzada," my mother protested. "Night after night. You spoil her."

If a question mark or an exclamation point is part of the quotation, place it inside the closing quotation marks. If it is not, place it outside. Place the question mark or exclamation point outside the closing quotation marks when it is part of the entire sentence.

Mr. Pirzada asked, "Is there any danger?"

Did they hear Mr. Pirzada say, "Trick or treat"?

Learning Objectives

For pages 142–143

In this workshop, you will focus on the following objective:

Grammar: Understanding how to combine sentences.

Grammar Workshop

Sentence Combining

Literature Connection In this story opener, Jhumpa Lahiri combines several ideas into one sentence.

> "In the autumn of 1971 a man used to come to our house, bearing confections in his pocket and hopes of ascertaining the life or death of his family"
>
> —Jhumpa Lahiri, "When Mr. Pirzada Came to Dine"

Lahiri might have chosen to open her story by not combining ideas and by using short sentences like these: *This happened in the autumn of 1971. A man used to come to our house. He had confections in his pocket. He also had hopes of ascertaining the life or death of his family.*

To write effectively, you must make similar choices about sentence length and structure. Combining short sentences into longer ones helps you develop your own writing style.

Examples

Solution 1 Use a **prepositional phrase,** a group of words that begins with a preposition and ends with a noun or a pronoun.

> Original: Mr. Pirzada arrived every evening. He always brought a bag of sweets.
>
> Combined with a prepositional phrase: Mr. Pirzada arrived every evening with a bag of sweets.

Solution 2 Use an **appositive,** a noun or pronoun placed next to another noun or pronoun to give additional information about it. An **appositive phrase** is an appositive plus any words that modify it.

> Original: East Pakistan was Mr. Pirzada's home. It is now Bangladesh.
>
> Combined with an appositive phrase: East Pakistan, now Bangladesh, was Mr. Pirzada's home.

Solution 3 Use a **participial phrase.** A **participle** is a verb form, often ending in *–ing* or *–ed,* that functions as an adjective. A participial phrase—which includes a participle and other words that add to it—also functions as an adjective. In the sentence *Worried about his family, Mr. Pirzada*

Drafting Tip

Vary the length and structure of your sentences. Work for a rhythmic, interesting balance of long and short sentences, remembering that brevity often has dramatic force. By using different kinds of sentence openers—and by sometimes placing information in the middle of a sentence—you can create stylistic interest.

Revising Tip

Read your draft aloud, stopping now and then to experiment with clusters of sentences. Whisper them to yourself in various combinations. As you read, listen to which version sounds most effective. This process is faster than rewriting and helps you decide on a "best sentence" to write down.

buried his face in his hands, for example, *worried* is the participle and *worried about his family* is the phrase. They both describe Mr. Pirzada.

> Separate: The reporter described the war. He was dripping with sweat.
>
> Combined with a participial phrase: Dripping with sweat, the reporter described the war.

Solution 4 Use a coordinating conjunction to join words or groups of words with equal grammatical weight in a sentence. Coordinating conjunctions include words such as *and, but, or, so, nor, for,* and *yet.*

> Separate: Mr. Pirzada returned home. He wrote to say his family was safe. Lilia did not feel like celebrating.
>
> Combined with coordinating conjunctions: Mr. Pirzada returned home and wrote to say his family was safe, but Lilia did not feel like celebrating.

Solution 5 Use a subordinating conjunction to join two clauses, or ideas, in such a way as to make one dependent upon the other. Subordinating conjunctions include words such as *after, although, as, because, if, since,* and *when.*

> Separate: Mr. Pirzada couldn't use the knife. His hands were shaking.
>
> Combined with a subordinating conjunction: Mr. Pirzada couldn't use the knife because his hands were shaking.

Solution 6 Use an adjective clause, a group of words with a subject and a predicate that modify a noun or a pronoun. Adjective clauses often begin with *who, whom, whose, that,* and *which.*

> Separate: Mr. Pirzada visited most nights. He worked at the university.
>
> Combined with an adjective clause: Mr. Pirzada, who worked at the university, visited most nights.

Test-Taking Tip

Remember that there are many ways of combining sentences. When deciding which solution works best, ask yourself the following questions:

Is my solution free of excess words?

Does my solution emphasize the important idea of the sentence?

Does my solution flow naturally when I read it aloud?

Is my solution a complete sentence with a subject and predicate and not just a long fragment?

Revise

1. Use a prepositional phrase to combine the following sentences: *Mr. Pirzada was a short, dapper man. He had a curly moustache.*

2. Use a subordinating conjunction and an appositive phrase or an adjective clause to combine these sentences: *The adults finished eating. They played Scrabble. Scrabble is a spelling game.*

3. Use a participial phrase and a coordinating conjunction to combine the following sentences: *Lilia prayed for peace. She was worried about Mr. Pirzada's family. The war dragged on for months.*

Grammar For more grammar practice, go to glencoe.com and enter QuickPass code GL59794u1.

Before You Read

To Da-duh, in Memoriam

Meet Paule Marshall
(born 1929)

A basement kitchen may sound like an unlikely place for a writer to find her inspiration, but that is where the award-winning African American writer Paule Marshall found hers.

Homegrown Inspiration "I grew up among poets," Marshall wrote in her autobiographical essay, "From the Poets in the Kitchen." Each afternoon, these "poets," who, in reality, were ordinary housewives, gathered around the kitchen table of the brownstone home in the close-knit, West-Indian community of 1930s Brooklyn, New York, where Marshall was born and raised. Marshall sat in the corner and listened as the women, including her mother, talked "endlessly, passionately, poetically, and with impressive range."

The Rhythm of Language During these late afternoon conversations, Marshall learned about the "old country," the small Caribbean island of Barbados, the homeland of Marshall's parents. Her ear became attuned to their idiomatic, rhythmic language that was a combination of English words, Barbadian syntax, and African sounds. These women were to become Marshall's primary writing teachers. "They taught me my first lessons in the narrative art. They trained my ear. They set a standard of excellence." While Marshall also credits both white and African American "literary giants" with helping her find her literary voice, she attributes the best of her work to these women. It is a "testimony to the rich legacy of language and culture they so freely passed on to me in the wordshop of the kitchen."

> "My work asks that you become involved, that you think."
>
> —Paule Marshall

Finding the Writer's Path Marshall was around eight or nine years old when she "graduated" from the corner of her kitchen to the neighborhood library. She was a voracious reader, consuming volumes by Austen, Thackeray, Fielding, and Dickens. One day she picked up a book by Paul Laurence Dunbar. Until then, she had been unaware that there was an African American voice in literature.

In 1953 Marshall graduated with honors from Brooklyn College with a degree in English Literature. In 1954 she published her first short story, "The Valley Between." Today, Marshall is widely read and recognized as, according to critic Carol Field, a "highly gifted writer." Her first book, *Brown Girl, Brownstones*, is now considered a classic coming-of-age novel.

Author Search For more about Paule Marshall, go to glencoe.com and enter QuickPass code GL59794u1.

Literature and Reading Preview

Connect to the Story
Is it ever acceptable to argue with a grandparent or another older person? Discuss this question with a partner. Talk about whether such an argument would ever be acceptable in your family.

Build Background
"To Da-duh, in Memoriam" takes place in Barbados in the 1930s. Barbados is a tiny Caribbean island with mostly flat terrain. The stalks of sugar cane referred to in the story can grow from seven to thirty feet high. Although the people of Barbados speak English, the folk culture is of African origin.

Set Purposes for Reading

Big Idea Making Choices

As you read "To Da-duh, in Memoriam," ask yourself, How does the narrator's relationship with her grandmother affect her later in life?

Literary Element Characterization

Characterization is the method a writer uses to reveal a character's personality. A writer may use direct statements, or **direct characterization,** to describe a character. The writer may also reveal the character's personality through **indirect characterization,** or through his or her words, thoughts, and actions or through what other characters think and say about the character. As you read the story, ask yourself, How does Marshall use characterization to reveal the personalities of the narrator and her grandmother?

Reading Strategy Make Inferences About Characters

To **infer** is to make a reasonable guess about some element of a story from what a writer implies. As you read "To Da-duh, in Memoriam," ask yourself, How can I observe details to make inferences about the characters?

Tip: Take Notes Use a chart to record the inferences you draw about the narrator and Da-duh.

Detail	Inference
"intense, unrelenting struggle between her back ... and the rest of her"	Da-duh is proud, strong, and determined.

Learning Objectives

For pages 144–156

In studying this text, you will focus on the following objectives:

Literary Study: Analyzing characterization.

Reading: Making inferences about characters.

Vocabulary

formidable (fôr′ mi də bəl) *adj.* causing fear, dread, or awe by reason of size, strength, or power; p. 148 *Defeat was almost guaranteed against such a formidable opponent.*

decrepit (di krep′ it) *adj.* broken down by long use or old age; p. 149 *A strong wind would surely blow down the decrepit wooden shack.*

hurtle (hurt′ əl) *v.* to move rapidly, especially with much force or noise; p. 150 *They hurtle toward the finish line on their homemade scooters.*

arrogant (ar′ ə gənt) *adj.* full of self-importance; haughty; p. 150 *She spoke in an arrogant tone, as if the rest of us were inferior to her.*

malicious (mə lish′ əs) *adj.* having or showing a desire to harm another; p. 154 *His malicious actions resulted in injuries to several bystanders.*

PAULE MARSHALL

To Da-duh, in Memoriam

Paule Marshall

Wash Day. Victor Collector. Oil on canvas. Private collection.

"... Oh Nana! all of you
is not involved in this
evil business Death,
Nor all of us in life."
—*from* "At My
Grandmother's Grave,"
by Lebert Bethune

I did not see her at first I remember. For not only was it dark inside the crowded disembarkation[1] shed in spite of the daylight flooding in from outside, but standing there waiting for her with my mother and sister I was still somewhat blinded from the sheen of tropical sunlight on the water of the bay which we had just crossed in the landing boat, leaving behind us the ship that had brought us from New York lying in the offing.[2] Besides, being only nine years of age at the time and knowing nothing of islands I was busy attending to the alien sights and sounds of Barbados, the unfamiliar smells.

I did not see her, but I was alerted to her approach by my mother's hand which suddenly tightened around mine, and looking up I traced her gaze through the gloom in the shed until I finally made out the small, purposeful, painfully erect figure of the old woman headed our way.

Her face was drowned in the shadow of an ugly rolled-brim brown felt hat, but the details of her slight body and of the struggle taking place within it were clear enough—an intense, unrelenting[3] struggle between her back which was beginning to bend ever so slightly under the weight of her eighty-odd years and the rest of her which sought to deny those years and hold that back straight, keep it in line. Moving swiftly toward us (so swiftly it seemed she did not intend stopping when she reached us but would sweep past us out the doorway which opened onto the sea and like Christ walk upon the water!), she was caught between the sunlight at her end of the building and the darkness inside—and for a moment she appeared to contain them both: the light in the long severe old-fashioned white dress she wore which brought the sense of a past that was still alive into our bustling present and in the snatch of white at her eye; the darkness in her black high-top shoes and in her face which was visible now that she was closer.

It was as stark and fleshless as a death mask, that face. The maggots might have already done their work, leaving only the framework of bone beneath the ruined skin and deep wells at the temple and jaw. But her eyes were alive, unnervingly so for one so old, with a sharp light that flicked out of the dim clouded depths like a lizard's tongue to snap up all in her view. Those eyes betrayed a child's curiosity about the world, and I wondered vaguely seeing them, and seeing the way the bodice of her ancient dress had collapsed in on her flat chest (what had happened to her breasts?), whether she might not be some kind of child at the same time that she was a woman, with fourteen children, my mother included, to prove it. Perhaps she was both, both child and woman, darkness and light, past and present, life and death—all the opposites contained and reconciled in her.

"My Da-duh," my mother said formally and stepped forward. The name sounded like thunder fading softly in the distance.

"Child," Da-duh said, and her tone, her quick scrutiny of my mother, the brief embrace in which they appeared to shy from each other rather than touch, wiped out the fifteen years my mother had been away and restored the old relationship.

---

1. To *disembark* is to get off a ship or plane.
2. In this context, *in the offing* means "just in view from the shore."
3. An *unrelenting* (un′ ri len′ ting) struggle is one that does not ease or lessen in intensity.

Characterization What does the description reveal here about this old woman?

Make Inferences About Characters What can you infer about Da-duh from how she is dressed?

PAULE MARSHALL

Central Park Skyline, 1999. Mary Iverson.

View the Art In this painting, a towering cityscape is juxtaposed against the dense green foliage of Central Park. How does this image reflect the conflict between the narrator and Da-duh?

My mother, who was such a **formidable** figure in my eyes, had suddenly with a word been reduced to my status.

"Yes, God is good," Da-duh said with a nod that was like a tic.[4] "He has spared me to see my child again."

We were led forward then, apologetically because not only did Da-duh prefer boys but she also liked her grandchildren to be "white," that is, fair-skinned; and we had, I was to discover, a number of cousins, the outside children of white estate managers and the like, who qualified. We, though, were as black as she.

---

4. Here, a *tic* is an involuntary twitch.

Vocabulary

formidable (fôr´ mi də bəl) *adj.* causing fear, dread, or awe by reason of size, strength, or power

My sister being the oldest was presented first. "This one takes after the father," my mother said and waited to be reproved.

Frowning, Da-duh tilted my sister's face toward the light. But her frown soon gave way to a grudging smile, for my sister with her large mild eyes and little broad winged nose, with our father's high-cheeked Barbadian cast to her face, was pretty.

"She's goin' be lucky," Da-duh said and patted her once on the cheek. "Any girl child that takes after the father does be lucky."

She turned then to me. But oddly enough she did not touch me. Instead leaning close, she peered hard at me, and then quickly drew back. I thought I saw her hand start up as though to shield her eyes. It was almost as if she saw not only me,

148   UNIT 1   THE SHORT STORY

a thin truculent[5] child who it was said took after no one but myself, but something in me which for some reason she found disturbing, even threatening. We looked silently at each other for a long time there in the noisy shed, our gaze locked. She was the first to look away.

"But Adry," she said to my mother and her laugh was cracked, thin, apprehensive. "Where did you get this one here with this fierce look?"

"We don't know where she came out of, my Da-duh," my mother said, laughing also. Even I smiled to myself. After all I had won the encounter. Da-duh had recognized my small strength—and this was all I ever asked of the adults in my life then.

Visual Vocabulary
Lorry is what the British call a truck.

"Come, soul," Da-duh said and took my hand. "You must be one of those New York terrors you hear so much about."

She led us, me at her side and my sister and mother behind, out of the shed into the sunlight that was like a bright driving summer rain and over to a group of people clustered beside a **decrepit** lorry. They were our relatives, most of them from St. Andrews although Da-duh herself lived in St. Thomas, the women wearing bright print dresses, the colors vivid against their darkness, the men rusty black suits that encased them like straitjackets. Da-duh, holding fast to my hand, became my anchor as they circled round us like a nervous sea, exclaiming, touching us with their calloused hands, embracing us shyly. They laughed in awed bursts: "But look Adry got big-big children!" / "And see the nice things they wearing, wristwatch and all!" / "I tell you, Adry has done all right for sheself in New York. . . ."

Da-duh, ashamed at their wonder, embarrassed for them, admonished them the while. . . . "Why you all got to get on like you never saw people from 'Away' before? You would think New York is the only place in the world to hear wunna.[6] That's why I don't like to go anyplace with you St. Andrews people, you know. You all ain't been colonized."

We were in the back of the lorry finally, packed in among the barrels of ham, flour, cornmeal and rice and the trunks of clothes that my mother had brought as gifts. We made our way slowly through Bridgetown's clogged streets, part of a funereal[7] procession of cars and open-sided buses, bicycles and donkey carts. The dim little limestone shops and offices along the way marched with us, at the same mournful pace, toward the same grave ceremony—as did the people, the women balancing huge baskets on top their heads as if they were no more than hats they wore to shade them from the sun. Looking over the edge of the lorry I watched as their feet slurred the dust. I listened, and their voices, raw and loud and dissonant in the heat, seemed to be grappling with each other high overhead.

Da-duh sat on a trunk in our midst, a monarch amid her court. She still held

---

5. To be *truculent* is to be fierce and ready to fight.

Characterization Why do you think Marshall has the narrator describe herself in this way?

Vocabulary

decrepit (di krep′ it) *adj.* broken down by long use or old age

6. *To hear wunna* may be Da-duh's way of saying "to have wonders."
7. *Funereal* means "like, or suitable to, a funeral."

Characterization What does this detail tell you about Da-duh?

my hand, but it was different now. I had suddenly become her anchor, for I felt her fear of the lorry with its asthmatic motor (a fear and distrust, I later learned, she held of all machines) beating like a pulse in her rough palm.

As soon as we left Bridgetown behind though, she relaxed, and while the others around us talked she gazed at the canes standing tall on either side of the winding marl[8] road. "C'dear," she said softly to herself after a time. "The canes this side are pretty enough."

They were too much for me. I thought of them as giant weeds that had overrun the island, leaving scarcely any room for the small tottering houses of sunbleached pine we passed or the people, dark streaks as our lorry **hurtled** by. I suddenly feared that we were journeying, unaware that we were, toward some dangerous place where the canes, grown as high and thick as a forest, would close in on us and run us through with their stiletto blades. I longed then for the familiar: for the street in Brooklyn[9] where I lived, for my father who had refused to accompany us ("Blowing out good money on foolishness," he had said of the trip), for a game of tag with my friends under the chestnut tree outside our aging brownstone house.

"Yes, but wait till you see St. Thomas canes," Da-duh was saying to me. "They's canes father, bo," she gave a proud **arrogant** nod. "Tomorrow, God willing, I goin' take you out in the ground and show them to you."

True to her word Da-duh took me with her the following day out into the ground. It was a fairly large plot adjoining her weathered board and shingle house and consisting of a small orchard, a good-sized canepiece and behind the canes, where the land sloped abruptly down, a gully. She had purchased it with Panama money sent her by her eldest son, my uncle Joseph, who had died working on the canal. We entered the ground along a trail no wider than her body and as devious and complex as her reasons for showing me her land. Da-duh strode briskly ahead, her slight form filled out this morning by the layers of sacking petticoats she wore under her working dress to protect her against the damp. A fresh white cloth, elaborately arranged around her head, added to her height, and lent her a vain, almost roguish air.

Her pace slowed once we reached the orchard, and glancing back at me occasionally over her shoulder, she pointed out the various trees.

"This here is a breadfruit," she said. "That one yonder is a papaw. Here's a guava. This is a mango. I know you don't have anything like these in New York. Here's a sugar apple." (The fruit looked more like artichokes than apples to me.) "This one bears limes. . . ." She went on for some time, intoning the names of the trees as though they were those of her gods. Finally, turning to me, she said, "I know

---

8. A *marl* road is paved with crumbly clay of the sort used to make cement.
9. *Brooklyn* is one of New York City's five boroughs, or districts.

Make Inferences About Characters What kind of inference could you make about the narrator from this detail?

Vocabulary

hurtle (hurt′ əl) *v.* to move rapidly, especially with much force or noise

Making Choices Based on what you already know about Da-duh, why do you think she wants to show her land to her granddaughter?

Vocabulary

arrogant (ar′ ə gənt) *adj.* full of self-importance; haughty

you don't have anything this nice where you come from." Then, as I hesitated: "I said I know you don't have anything this nice where you come from. . . ."

"No," I said and my world did seem suddenly lacking.

Da-duh nodded and passed on. The orchard ended and we were on the narrow cart road that led through the canepiece, the canes clashing like swords above my cowering head. Again she turned and her thin muscular arms spread wide, her dim gaze embracing the small field of canes, she said—and her voice almost broke under the weight of her pride, "Tell me, have you got anything like these in that place where you were born?"

"No."

"I din' think so. I bet you don't even know that these canes here and the sugar you eat is one and the same thing. That they does throw the canes into some damn machine at the factory and squeeze out all the little life in them to make sugar for you all so in New York to eat. I bet you don't know that."

"I've got two cavities and I'm not allowed to eat a lot of sugar."

But Da-duh didn't hear me. She had turned with an inexplicably angry motion and was making her way rapidly out of the canes and down the slope at the edge of the field which led to the gully below. Following her apprehensively down the incline amid a stand of banana plants whose leaves flapped like elephants' ears

"It was a violent place, the tangled foliage fighting each other for a chance at the sunlight. . . ."

in the wind, I found myself in the middle of a small tropical wood—a place dense and damp and gloomy and tremulous with the fitful play of light and shadow as the leaves high above moved against the sun that was almost hidden from view. It was a violent place, the tangled foliage fighting each other for a chance at the sunlight, the branches of the trees locked in what seemed an immemorial[10] struggle, one both necessary and inevitable. But despite the violence, it was pleasant, almost peaceful in the gully, and beneath the thick undergrowth the earth smelled like spring.

This time Da-duh didn't even bother to ask her usual question, but simply turned and waited for me to speak.

"No," I said, my head bowed. "We don't have anything like this in New York."

"Ah," she cried, her triumph complete. "I din' think so. Why, I've heard that's a place where you can walk till you near drop and never see a tree."

"We've got a chestnut tree in front of our house," I said.

"Does it bear?" She waited. "I ask you, does it bear?"

"Not anymore," I muttered. "It used to, but not anymore."

She gave the nod that was like a nervous twitch. "You see," she said. "Nothing can bear there." Then, secure behind her scorn,

---

10. An *immemorial* struggle would be one that extended back beyond memory or record.

Make Inferences About Characters *Why does the child make a negative comment about sugar?*

Make Inferences About Characters *Why does the grandmother show the child all of these wonderful places?*

PAULE MARSHALL

she added, "But tell me, what's this snow like that you hear so much about?"

Looking up, I studied her closely, sensing my chance, and then I told her, describing at length and with as much drama as I could summon not only what snow in the city was like, but what it would be like here, in her perennial summer kingdom.

"... And you see all these trees you got here," I said. "Well, they'd be bare. No leaves, no fruit, nothing. They'd be covered in snow. You see your canes. They'd be buried under tons of snow. The snow would be higher than your head, higher than your house, and you wouldn't be able to come down into this here gully because it would be snowed under...."

She searched my face for the lie, still scornful but intrigued. "What a thing, huh?" she said finally, whispering it softly to herself.

"And when it snows you couldn't dress like you are now," I said. "Oh no, you'd freeze to death. You'd have to wear a hat and gloves and galoshes and ear muffs so your ears wouldn't freeze and drop off, and a heavy coat. I've got a Shirley Temple[11] coat with fur on the collar. I can dance. You wanna see?"

Before she could answer I began, with a dance called the Truck which was popular back then in the 1930s. My right forefinger waving, I trucked around the nearby trees and around Da-duh's awed and rigid form. After the Truck I did the Suzy-Q, my lean hips swishing, my sneakers sidling zigzag over the ground. "I can sing," I said and did so, starting with "I'm Gonna Sit Right Down and Write Myself a Letter," then without pausing, "Tea For Two," and ending with "I Found a Million Dollar Baby in a Five and Ten Cent Store."

For long moments afterwards Da-duh stared at me as if I were a creature from Mars, an emissary from some world she did not know but which intrigued her and whose power she both felt and feared. Yet something about my performance must have pleased her, because bending down she slowly lifted her long skirt and then, one by one, the layers of petticoats until she came to a drawstring purse dangling at the end of a long strip of cloth tied round her waist. Opening the purse she handed me a penny. "Here," she said half-smiling against her will. "Take this to buy yourself a sweet at the shop up the road. There's nothing to be done with you, soul."

From then on, whenever I wasn't taken to visit relatives, I accompanied Da-duh out into the ground, and alone with her amid the canes or down in the gully I told her about New York. It always began with some slighting remark on her part: "I know they don't have anything this nice where you come from," or "Tell me, I hear those foolish people in New York does do such and such. ..." But as I answered, recreating my towering world of steel and concrete and machines for her, building the city out of words, I would feel her give way. I came to know the signs of her surrender: the total stillness that would come over the little hard dry form, the probing gaze that like a surgeon's knife sought to cut through my skull to get at the images there, to see if I were lying; above all, her fear, a fear nameless and profound, the same one I had felt beating in the palm of her hand that day in the lorry.

---

11. Shirley Temple was a popular child movie star of the 1930s.

Making Choices *Why does the child choose to respond to her grandmother's question in this way?*

Making Choices *Why do you think Da-duh chooses to take the child with her, instead of someone else?*

Make Inferences About Characters *Why does Da-duh have this reaction when the child talks about New York City?*

Over the weeks I told her about refrigerators, radios, gas stoves, elevators, trolley cars, wringer washing machines, movies, airplanes, the cyclone at Coney Island, subways, toasters, electric lights: "At night, see, all you have to do is flip this little switch on the wall and all the lights in the house go on. Just like that. Like magic. It's like turning on the sun at night."

Visual Vocabulary
Coney Island is an amusement park and beach in Brooklyn, and the *Cyclone* was a popular thrill ride.

"But tell me," she said to me once with a faint mocking smile, "do the white people have all these things too or it's only the people looking like us?"

I laughed. "What d'ya mean," I said. "The white people have even better." Then: "I beat up a white girl in my class last term."

"Beating up white people!" Her tone was incredulous.

"How you mean!" I said, using an expression of hers. "She called me a name."

For some reason Da-duh could not quite get over this and repeated in the same hushed, shocked voice, "Beating up white people now! Oh, the lord, the world's changing up so I can scarce recognize it anymore."

One morning toward the end of our stay, Da-duh led me into a part of the gully that we had never visited before, an area darker and more thickly overgrown than the rest, almost impenetrable. There in a small clearing amid the dense bush, she stopped before an incredibly tall royal palm which rose cleanly out of the ground, and drawing the eye up with it, soared high above the trees around it into the sky. It appeared to be touching the blue dome of sky, to be flaunting its dark crown of fronds right in the blinding white face of the late morning sun.

Da-duh watched me a long time before she spoke, and then she said, very quietly, "All right, now, tell me if you've got anything this tall in that place you're from."

I almost wished, seeing her face, that I could have said no. "Yes," I said. "We've got buildings hundreds of times this tall in New York. There's one called the Empire State Building that's the tallest in the world. My class visited it last year and I went all the way to the top. It's got over a hundred floors. I can't describe how tall it is. Wait a minute. What's the name of that hill I went to visit the other day, where they have the police station?"

"You mean Bissex?"

"Yes, Bissex. Well, the Empire State Building is way taller than that."

"You're lying now!" she shouted, trembling with rage. Her hand lifted to strike me.

"No, I'm not," I said. "It really is, if you don't believe me I'll send you a picture postcard of it soon as I get back home so you can see for yourself. But it's way taller than Bissex."

All the fight went out of her at that. The hand poised to strike me fell limp to her side, and as she stared at me, seeing not me but the building that was taller than the highest hill she knew, the small stubborn light in her eyes (it was the same amber as the flame in the kerosene lamp she lit at dusk) began to fail. Finally, with a vague gesture that even in the midst of her defeat still tried

Make Inferences About Characters *What does this comment tell you about the relationship between the child and Da-duh?*

Making Choices *Why does the girl choose to answer as she does?*

Characterization *How does the light in Da-duh's eyes help to characterize her in this scene?*

to dismiss me and my world, she turned and started back through the gully, walking slowly, her steps groping and uncertain, as if she were suddenly no longer sure of the way, while I followed triumphant yet strangely saddened behind.

The next morning I found her dressed for our morning walk but stretched out on the Berbice chair in the tiny drawing room where she sometimes napped during the afternoon heat, her face turned to the window beside her. She appeared thinner and suddenly indescribably old.

"My Da-duh," I said.

"Yes, nuh," she said. Her voice was listless and the face she slowly turned my way was, now that I think back on it, like a Benin mask, the features drawn and almost distorted by an ancient abstract sorrow.

"Don't you feel well?" I asked.

"Girl, I don't know."

"My Da-duh, I goin' boil you some bush tea," my aunt, Da-duh's youngest child, who lived with her, called from the shed roof kitchen.

"Who tell you I need bush tea?" she cried, her voice assuming for a moment its old authority. "You can't even rest nowadays without some **malicious** person looking for you to be dead. Come girl," she motioned me to a place beside her on the old-fashioned lounge chair, "give us a tune."

I sang for her until breakfast at eleven, all my brash irreverent Tin Pan Alley[12] songs, and then just before noon we went out into the ground. But it was a short, dispirited walk. Da-duh didn't even notice that the mangoes were beginning to ripen and would have to be picked before the village boys got to them. And when she paused occasionally and looked out across the canes or up at her trees it wasn't as if she were seeing them but something else. Some huge, monolithic[13] shape had imposed itself, it seemed, between her and the land, obstructing her vision. Returning to the house she slept the entire afternoon on the Berbice chair.

She remained like this until we left, languishing away the mornings on the chair at the window gazing out at the land as if it were already doomed; then, at noon, taking the brief stroll with me through the ground during which she seldom spoke, and afterwards returning home to sleep till almost dusk sometimes.

On the day of our departure she put on the austere, ankle length white dress, the black shoes and brown felt hat (her town clothes she called them), but she did not go with us to town. She saw us off on the road outside her house and in the midst of my mother's tearful protracted[14] farewell, she leaned down and whispered in my ear, "Girl, you're not to forget now to send me the picture of that building, you hear."

By the time I mailed her the large colored picture postcard of the Empire State Building she was dead. She died during the famous '37 strike which began shortly after we left. On the day of her death England sent planes flying low over the island in a show of force—so low, according to my aunt's letter, that the downdraft from them shook the ripened mangoes

---

12. *Tin Pan Alley* was a district in New York City associated with composers and publishers of popular music. These pop songs were bright and lively, often treating their subjects with rude and disrespectful *(brash, irreverent)* mockery.

Vocabulary

malicious (mə lish′ əs) *adj.* having or showing a desire to harm another

13. A *monolithic* shape would resemble a monument or another structure formed from a single, giant block of stone.
14. A *protracted* (prō trak′ təd) farewell would be one that takes a lot of time.

Tropical Scene. Albert Bierstadt (1830–1902). Oil on paper laid on board. Private collection.

View the Art Bierstadt was an American painter whose vibrant landscapes were intended to awe and impress the viewer. What qualities does the tropical scene in this painting share with the settings described in the story?

from the trees in Da-duh's orchard. Frightened, everyone in the village fled into the canes. Except Da-duh. She remained in the house at the window so my aunt said, watching as the planes came swooping and screaming like monstrous birds down over the village, over her house, rattling her trees and flattening the young canes in her field. It must have seemed to her lying there that they did not intend pulling out of their dive, but like the hardback beetles which hurled themselves with suicidal force against the walls of the house at night, those menacing silver shapes would hurl themselves in an ecstasy of self-immolation[15] onto the land, destroying it utterly.

When the planes finally left and the villagers returned they found her dead on the Berbice chair at the window.

She died and I lived, but always, to this day even, within the shadow of her death. For a brief period after I was grown I went to live alone, like one doing penance,[16] in a loft above a noisy factory in downtown New York and there painted seas of sugarcane and huge swirling Van Gogh suns and palm trees striding like brightly-plumed Tutsi[17] warriors across a tropical landscape, while the thunderous tread of the machines downstairs jarred the floor beneath my easel, mocking my efforts.

---

15. *Self-immolation* is the act of setting oneself on fire.
16. *Penance* (pen′ əns) is a punishment one undergoes, usually voluntarily, to show sorrow for having committed a sin or offense.
17. The *Tutsi* are a people in central Africa.

Make Inferences About Characters
What does the narrator mean when she says she lives within the shadow of her grandmother's death?

Characterization *How does the author reveal that the narrator remains troubled by the conflict with her grandmother?*

PAULE MARSHALL

After You Read

Respond and Think Critically

Respond and Interpret

1. Do you think that either Da-duh or the child "won" their battle of wills? Explain.

2. (a) Describe the narrator's initial impression of Da-duh. (b) Why do you think the narrator tries to "win" in her initial encounter with Da-duh?

3. In your opinion, why does Da-duh compare Barbados with New York City?

Analyze and Evaluate

4. (a) At what point in the story do Da-duh's appearance and behavior abruptly change? Describe this change. (b) What do you think causes this change, and what does it signify?

5. Which of these aphorisms best describes the relationship between the narrator and Da-duh: "Birds of a feather flock together" or "Opposites attract"? Explain.

Connect

6. **Big Idea** **Making Choices** How did the narrator choose to treat Da-duh? Do you approve of this decision? Explain.

7. **Connect to the Author** Paule Marshall's writing frequently deals with themes of racial identity and relationships to African or African Caribbean heritage. What purpose do these references serve in the story?

Literary Element Characterization

Marshall uses both **direct characterization** and **indirect characterization** in her descriptions of Da-duh and her granddaughter.

1. Give an example of each characterization type.
2. What method of characterization does the author use to show how Da-duh has changed?

Reading Strategy Make Inferences About Characters

Paule Marshall provides specific and vivid details to help you **make inferences** about the characters' personalities. Review the inference chart you created to help you answer the following questions.

1. How are the personalities of the narrator and Da-duh alike? How are they different?
2. List at least two important details that helped you form each opinion.

Literature Online

Selection Resources For Selection Quizzes, eFlashcards, and Reading-Writing Connection activities, go to glencoe.com and enter QuickPass code GL59794u1.

Vocabulary Practice

Practice with Synonyms A synonym is a word that has the same or nearly the same meaning as another word. With a partner, match each boldfaced vocabulary word below with its synonym. You will not use all the answer choices. Use a thesaurus or dictionary to check your answers.

1. formidable
2. decrepit
3. hurtle
4. arrogant
5. malicious

a. fearsome
b. evil
c. rampant
d. haughty
e. dilapidated
f. resonant
g. propel

Writing

Write a Dialogue In this story, the narrator tells her grandmother about "refrigerators, radios, gas stoves, elevators…" Write a present-day dialogue in which the girl explains, and Da-duh comments on, computers, the Internet, and other technological breakthroughs. How might your dialogue best reveal aspects of each of the characters' personalities?

Before You Read

World Literature: Haiti

The Book of the Dead

Meet Edwidge Danticat
(born 1969)

The Haitian storyteller calls out "Krik?" This means, roughly, "Want to hear a story?" "Krak," the listeners answer, "We do." The scene takes place in Haiti, and the words are spoken in Haitian Creole, a language that evolved from French. This is the storytelling culture into which Edwidge Danticat (ed wēdj´ dän tə kah´) was born.

> "One of [my] most important themes is migration, the separation of families, and how much that affects the parents and children who live through that experience."
>
> —Edwidge Danticat

Living in Two Worlds Edwidge Danticat grew up in Port-au-Prince, a large port city that is the capital of Haiti. When she was very young, her parents left their home for the United States. Danticat remained behind, in the care of an aunt and uncle. She joined her parents in Brooklyn, New York, when she was twelve. Fitting in was not easy for Danticat; she spoke only Haitian Creole and reflected Haitian culture in her dress and hairstyle. One way she coped with the experience of being an outsider was by keeping journals in Haitian Creole, French, and English. When she began to write for an audience, one of her goals was to explain the experience of leaving one land for another.

Always a Writer Although Danticat always had an interest in writing—she had begun by the age of nine—her parents wanted her to prepare for a practical occupation, preferably in medicine. Danticat attempted to follow this route in high school, but she also never stopped writing.

Danticat's first novel, *Breath, Eyes, Memory*, written when she was a graduate student, was a selection for Oprah Winfrey's book club. Danticat continued with a rapid outpouring of books, which has included several more novels, a work of fiction for young adults, and a collection of short stories called *Krik? Krak!* Danticat has also edited a collection of writing about Haitian immigration and written a travel book.

A finalist for the National Book Award, Danticat won the prestigious PEN/Faulkner Award for fiction in 2005 for her novel *The Dew Breaker*. Although originally written as a short story, "The Book of the Dead" became the first chapter of this novel. Her latest book, *Brother, I'm Dying*, a memoir centering around her father and uncle, tells of exile, loss, and family love.

Author Search For more about Edwidge Danticat, go to glencoe.com and enter QuickPass code GL59794u1.

EDWIDGE DANTICAT

Literature and Reading Preview

Connect to the Story
What kinds of facts about a parent's past are important for a child to know? List facts about a parent's past that you think a child should know.

Build Background
This selection takes place in contemporary times but also refers to dark days in the history of Haiti. From 1957 to 1971, the country was ruled by the brutal dictator François "Papa Doc" Duvalier. During this time, thugs employed by his government terrorized citizens, arresting, torturing, and beating Duvalier's opponents. Illiterate, poor, and desperate, many of these torturers and murderers did their jobs just to feed their families.

Set Purposes for Reading
As you read "The Book of the Dead," ask yourself, What are the effects of the choices that the narrator and her father make?

Literary Element Irony
Irony is a contrast between what is expected and what actually happens. In **situational irony**, the outcome of a situation is the opposite of a character's expectations. In **dramatic irony**, the reader has information that characters do not have. As you read, ask yourself, How and why does Danticat use irony in this story?

Reading Strategy Analyze Plot
The **plot** is the sequence of events in a narrative. It includes the *exposition*, in which the characters, the setting, and the conflict are introduced; the *rising action*, in which suspense is built and complications are added; the *climax*, or turning point; the *falling action*; and the *resolution*, or *dénouement*, in which the results of the climax are revealed. As you read, ask yourself, How far has the plot progressed to this point?

Tip: **Make a Diagram** Use a Venn diagram to compare information about the narrator's family with information about the Fonteneau family.

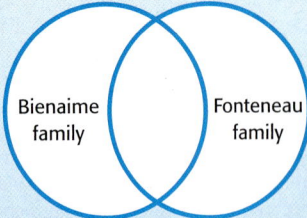

Learning Objectives
For pages 157–171

In studying this text, you will focus on the following objectives:

Literary Study: Analyzing irony.

Reading: Analyzing plot.

Vocabulary

interject (in´tər jekt´) *v.* to cut into with a comment; p. 160 *Lily likes to interject her own comments into other people's conversations.*

mesmerize (mez´mə rīz´) *v.* to hypnotize; p. 163 *Diego was so mesmerized by the waterfall that he could not leave.*

vulnerability (vul´nər ə bil´ə tē) *n.* a state of being open to harm, damage, or illness; p. 164 *The buyers understood the vulnerability of the small cottage by the sea, but they bought it anyway.*

eradicate (i rad´ə kāt´) *v.* to do away with completely; p. 164 *The thief tried to eradicate all traces of his presence from the crime scene.*

testament (tes´tə mənt) *n.* proof of or tribute to; p. 165 *Winning the race after her injury was a testament to Rosa's determination.*

Tip: **Word Usage** Each word has a special meaning and will not fit every context. Even though *eradicate* means "do away with completely," its usage is limited. For example, you can eradicate a disease but not a stomachache.

158 UNIT 1 THE SHORT STORY

The Book of the Dead

Edwidge Danticat

My father is gone. I am slouched in a cast-aluminum chair across from two men, one the manager of the hotel where we're staying and the other a policeman. They are waiting for me to explain what has become of him, my father.

The manager—"Mr. Flavio Salinas," the plaque on his office door reads—has the most striking pair of chartreuse[1] eyes I have ever seen on a man with an island-Spanish lilt[2] to his voice.

The officer is a baby-faced, short white Floridian with a pot belly.

"Where are you and your daddy from, Ms. Bienaime?" he asks.

I answer "Haiti" even though I was born and raised in East Flatbush, Brooklyn, and have never visited my parents' birthplace. I do this because it is one more thing I have longed to have in common with my parents.

The officer plows forward. "You down here in Lakeland from Haiti?"

"We live in New York. We were on our way to Tampa."

I find Manager Salinas's office gaudy. The walls are covered with orange-and-green wallpaper, briefly interrupted by a giant gold-leaf-bordered print of a Victorian cottage that somehow resembles the building we're in. Patting his light-green tie, he whispers reassuringly, "Officer Bo and I will do

---

1. *Chartreuse* (shär trōōz′) is a brilliant yellow-green.
2. A *lilt* is a rhythmic flow of speech.

Analyze Plot Which of these characters do you predict will be the main ones in this story? Why do you think so?

Making Choices What details in the narrator's life are out of her control?

the best we can to help you find your father."

We start out with a brief description: "Sixty-four, five feet eight inches, two hundred and twenty pounds, moon-faced, with thinning salt-and-pepper hair. Velvet-brown eyes—"

"Velvet-brown?" says Officer Bo.

"Deep brown—same color as his complexion."

My father has had partial frontal dentures for ten years, since he fell off his and my mother's bed when his prison nightmares began. I mention that, too. Just the dentures, not the nightmares. I also bring up the claw-shaped marks that run from his left ear down along his cheek to the corner of his mouth—the only visible reminder of the year he spent at Fort Dimanche, the Port-au-Prince prison ironically named after the Lord's Day.[3]

"Does your daddy have any kind of mental illness, senility?" asks Officer Bo.

"No."

"Do you have any pictures of your daddy?"

I feel like less of a daughter because I'm not carrying a photograph in my wallet. I had hoped to take some pictures of him on our trip. At one of the rest stops I bought a disposable camera and pointed it at my father. No, no, he had protested, covering his face with both hands like a little boy protecting his cheeks from a slap. He did not want any more pictures taken of him for the rest of his life. He was feeling too ugly.

"That's too bad," says Officer Bo. "Does he speak English, your daddy? He can ask for directions, et cetera?"

"Yes."

"Is there anything that might make your father run away from you—particularly here in Lakeland?" Manager Salinas **interjects.** "Did you two have a fight?"

I had never tried to tell my father's story in words before now, but my first sculpture of him was the reason for our trip: a two-foot-high mahogany figure of my father, naked, crouching on the floor, his back arched like the curve of a crescent moon, his down-cast eyes fixed on his short stubby fingers and the wide palms of his hands. It was hardly revolutionary, minimalist[4] at best, but it was my favorite of all my attempted representations of him. It was the way I had imagined him in prison.

The last time I had seen my father? The previous night, before falling asleep. When we pulled into the pebbled driveway, densely lined with palm and banana trees, it was almost midnight. All the restaurants in the area were closed. There was nothing to do but shower and go to bed.

"It is like a paradise here," my father said when he saw the room. It had the same orange-and-green wallpaper as Salinas's office, and the plush green carpet matched the walls. "Look, Annie," he said, "it is like grass under our feet." He was always searching for a glimpse of paradise, my father.

He picked the bed closest to the bathroom, removed the top of his gray jogging suit, and unpacked his toiletries. Soon after, I heard him humming, as he always did, in the shower.

After he got into bed, I took a bath, pulled my hair back in a ponytail, and checked on the sculpture—just felt it a little bit through

---

3. In French, *dimanche* means "Sunday."

Irony What is ironic about the prison's name?

4. A *minimalist* work of art is simple and spare.

Vocabulary

interject (in´tər jekt´) *v.* to cut into with a comment

the bubble padding and carton wrapping to make sure it wasn't broken. Then I slipped under the covers, closed my eyes, and tried to sleep.

I pictured the client to whom I was delivering the sculpture: Gabrielle Fonteneau, a young woman about my age, an actress on a nationally syndicated[5] television series. My friend Jonas, the principal at the East Flatbush elementary school where I teach drawing to fifth graders, had shown her a picture of my "Father" sculpture, and, the way Jonas told it, Gabrielle Fonteneau had fallen in love with it and wished to offer it as a gift to her father on his birthday.

Since this was my first big sale, I wanted to make sure that the piece got there safely. Besides, I needed a weekend away, and both my mother and I figured that my father, who watched a lot of television, both in his barbershop and at home, would enjoy meeting Gabrielle, too. But when I woke up the next morning my father was gone.

I showered, put on my driving jeans and a T-shirt, and waited. I watched a half hour of midmorning local news, smoked three mentholated cigarettes even though we were in a nonsmoking room, and waited some more. By noon, four hours had gone by. And it was only then that I noticed that the car was still there but the sculpture was gone.

I decided to start looking for my father: in the east garden, the west garden, the dining room, the exercise room, and in the few guest rooms cracked open while the maid changed the sheets; in the little convenience store at the Amoco gas station nearby; even in the Salvation Army thrift shop that from a distance seemed to blend into the interstate. All that waiting and looking actually took six hours, and I felt guilty for having held back so long before going to the front desk to ask, "Have you seen my father?"

I feel Officer Bo's fingers gently stroking my wrist. Up close he smells like fried eggs and gasoline, like breakfast at the Amoco. "I'll put the word out with the other boys," he says. "Salinas here will be in his office. Why don't you go back to your room in case he shows up there?"

I return to the room and lie in the unmade bed, jumping up when I hear the

Room with a View, 1999. Pam Ingalls.

View the Art This painting uses both dark and light colors to capture light streaming into a room. Does this color palette reflect the mood in "The Book of the Dead"? Why or why not?

---

5. A *nationally syndicated* television show is one that is shown nationwide.

Making Choices *Have the father's actions restricted or expanded the choices the narrator can make?*

click from the electronic key in the door. It's only the housekeeper. I turn down the late-afternoon cleaning and call my mother at the beauty salon where she perms, presses, and braids hair, next door to my father's barbershop. But she isn't there. So I call my parents' house and leave the hotel number on their machine. "Please call me as soon as you can, Manman. It's about Papi."[6]

Once, when I was twelve, I overheard my mother telling a young woman who was about to get married how she and my father had first met on the sidewalk in front of Fort Dimanche the evening that my father was released from jail. (At a dance, my father had fought with a soldier out of uniform who had him arrested and thrown in prison for a year.) That night, my mother was returning home from a sewing class when he stumbled out of the prison gates and <mark>collapsed into her arms, his face still bleeding from his last beating. They married and left for New York a year later.</mark> "We were like two seeds planted in a rock," my mother had told the young woman, "but somehow when our daughter, Annie, came we took root."

My mother soon calls me back, her voice staccato[7] with worry:

"Where is Papi?"

"I lost him."

"How you lost him?"

"He got up before I did and disappeared."

"How long he been gone?"

"Eight hours," I say, almost not believing myself that it's been that long. My mother is clicking her tongue and humming. I can see her sitting at the kitchen table, her eyes closed, her fingers sliding up and down her flesh-colored stockinged legs.

"You call police?"

"Yes."

"What they say?"

"To wait, that he'll come back."

My mother is thumping her fingers against the phone's mouthpiece, which is giving me a slight ache in my right ear.

"Tell me where you are," she says. "Two more hours and he's not there, call me, I come."

I dial Gabrielle Fonteneau's cellular-phone number. When she answers, her voice sounds just as it does on television, but more silken and seductive without the sitcom laugh track.

"To think," my father once said while watching her show, "Haitian-born actresses on American television."

"And one of them wants to buy my stuff," I'd added.

When she speaks, Gabrielle Fonteneau sounds as if she's in a place with cicadas, waterfalls, palm trees, and citronella candles to keep the mosquitoes away. I realize that I, too, am in such a place, but I can't appreciate it.

"So nice of you to come all this way to deliver the sculpture," she says. "Jonas tell you why I like it so much? My papa was a journalist in Port-au-Prince. In 1975,[8] he wrote a story criticizing the dictatorship, and he was arrested and put in jail."

Visual Vocabulary
Cicadas are large-winged insects that make loud buzzing sounds.

---

6. *Manman* and *Papi* are Haitian Creole words for "Mom" and "Dad."
7. *Staccato* means "short and clipped."

Irony What is ironic about this situation?

8. The year *1975* reveals a difference between the two fathers: although both lived during horrible political times, the narrator's father experienced the more brutal regime of "Papa Doc" Duvalier while Fonteneau's father was imprisoned under the regime of his son, "Baby Doc."

"Fort Dimanche?"

"No, another one," she says. "Caserne. Papa kept track of days there by scraping lines with his fingernails on the walls of his cell. One of the guards didn't like this, so he pulled out all his fingernails with pliers."

I think of the photo spread I saw in the *Haitian Times* of Gabrielle Fonteneau and her parents in their living room in Tampa. Her father was described as a lawyer, his daughter's manager; her mother a court stenographer.[9] There was no hint in that photograph of what had once happened to the father. Perhaps people don't see anything in my father's face, either, in spite of his scars.

"We celebrate his birthday on the day he was released from prison," she says. "It's the hands I love so much in your sculpture. They're so strong."

I am drifting away from Gabrielle Fonteneau when I hear her say, "So when will you get here? You have instruction from Jonas, right? Maybe we can make you lunch. My mother makes great *lanbi.*"[10]

"I'll be there at twelve tomorrow," I say. "My father is with me. We are making a little weekend vacation of this."

My father loves museums. When he isn't working in his barbershop, he's often at the Brooklyn Museum. The ancient Egyptian rooms are his favorites.

"The Egyptians, they was like us," he likes to say. The Egyptians worshipped their gods in many forms and were often ruled by foreigners. The pharaohs were like the dictators he had fled. But what he admires most about the Egyptians is the way they mourned.

"Yes, they grieve," he'll say. He marvels at the mummification that went on for weeks, resulting in bodies that survived thousands of years.

My whole adult life, I have struggled to find the proper manner of sculpting my father, a man who learned about art by standing with me most of the Saturday mornings of my childhood, **mesmerized** by the golden masks, the shawabtis,[11] and Osiris, ruler of the underworld.

When my father finally appears in the hotel-room doorway, I am awed by him. Smiling, he looks like a much younger man, further bronzed after a long day at the beach.

"Annie, let your father talk to you." He walks over to my bed, bends down to unlace his sneakers. "*On ti koze*, a little chat."

"Where were you? Where is the sculpture, Papi?" I feel my eyes twitching, a nervous reaction I inherited from my mother.

"That's why we need to chat," he says. "I have objections with your statue."

He pulls off his sneakers and rubs his feet with both hands.

"I don't want you to sell that statue," he says. Then he picks up the phone and calls my mother.

---

9. A *court stenographer* is a person who writes or types legal proceedings word for word.
10. *Lanbi* is a Creole dish made from conch, a mollusk that lives in a shell. (The shell is also called a conch.)

Analyze Plot How does Gabrielle's revelation contribute to the rising action?

Making Choices Why does the narrator choose to withhold information here?

11. In ancient Egyptian belief, *shawabtis* are guardian spirits—miniature figures that would be placed in a coffin with the deceased and perform work for the person through the afterlife.

Vocabulary

mesmerize (mez′ mə rīz′) *v.* to hypnotize

EDWIDGE DANTICAT **163**

"I know she called you," he says to her in Creole. "Her head is so hot. She panics so easily: I was just out walking, thinking."

I hear my mother lovingly scolding him and telling him not to leave me again. When he hangs up the phone, he picks up his sneakers and puts them back on.

"Where is the sculpture?" My eyes are twitching so hard now that I can barely see.

"Let us go," he says. "I will take you to it."

As my father maneuvers the car out of the parking lot, I tell myself he might be ill, mentally ill, even though I have never detected anything wrong beyond his prison nightmares. I am trying to piece it together, this sudden yet familiar picture of a parent's **vulnerability.** When I was ten years old and my father had the chicken pox, I overheard him say to a friend on the phone, "The doctor tells me that at my age chicken pox can kill a man." This was the first time I realized that my father could die. I looked up the word "kill" in every dictionary and encyclopedia at school, trying to comprehend what it meant, that my father could be **eradicated** from my life.

My father stops the car on the side of the highway near a man-made lake, one of those artificial creations of the modern tropical city, with curved stone benches surrounding stagnant water. There is little light to see by except a half-moon. He heads toward one of the benches, and I sit down next to him, letting my hands dangle between my legs.

Making Choices Why did the narrator look up the word "kill" in the dictionary and the encyclopedia?

Vocabulary

vulnerability (vul′ nər ə bil′ ə tē) *n.* state of being open to harm, damage, or illness

eradicate (i rad′ ə kāt′) *v.* to do away with completely

"Is this where the sculpture is?" I ask.

"In the water," he says.

"O.K.," I say. "But please know this about yourself. You are an especially harsh critic."

My father tries to smother a smile.

"Why?" I ask.

He scratches his chin. Anger is a wasted emotion, I've always thought. My parents got angry at unfair politics in New York or Port-au-Prince, but they never got angry at my grades—at all the B's I got in everything but art classes—or at my not eating vegetables or occasionally vomiting my daily spoonful of cod-liver oil. Ordinary anger, I thought, was a weakness. But now I am angry. I want to hit my father, beat the craziness out of his head.

"Annie," he says. "When I first saw your statue, I wanted to be buried with it, to take it with me into the other world."

"Like the ancient Egyptians," I say.

He smiles, grateful, I think, that I still recall his passions.

"Annie," he asks, "do you remember when I read to you from *The Book of the Dead?*"

"Are you dying?" I say to my father. "Because I can only forgive you for this if you are. You can't take this back."

He is silent for a moment too long.

I think I hear crickets, though I cannot imagine where they might be. There is the highway, the cars racing by, the half-moon, the lake dug up from the depths of the ground, the allee[12] of royal palms beyond. And there is me and my father.

"You remember the judgment of the dead," my father says, "when the heart of a person is put on a scale. If it is heavy,

---

[12] An *allee* is a tree-lined walkway.

Irony Relate the narrator's anger to situational irony. Remember that her father has information that she does not.

then this person cannot enter the other world."

It is a **testament** to my upbringing that I am not yelling at him.

"I don't deserve a statue," he says, even while looking like one: the Madonna of Humility,[13] for example, contemplating[14] her losses in the dust.

"Annie, your father was the hunter," he says. "He was not the prey."

"What are you saying?" I ask.

"We have a proverb," he says. "'One day for the hunter, one day for the prey.' Your father was the hunter. He was not the prey." Each word is hard won as it leaves my father's mouth, balanced like those hearts on the Egyptian scale.

"Annie, when I saw your mother the first time, I was not just out of prison. I was a guard in the prison. One of the prisoners I was questioning had scratched me with a piece of tin. I went out to the street in a rage, blood all over my face. I was about to go back and do something bad, very bad. But instead comes your mother. I smash into her, and she asks me what I am doing there. I told her I was just let go from prison and she held my face and cried in my hair."

"And the nightmares, what are they?"

"Of what I, your father, did to others."

"Does Manman know?"

"I told her, Annie, before we married."

---

13. The *Madonna of Humility* refers to a particular representation of the Virgin Mary, the mother of Christ, in a humble attitude.
14. Here *contemplating* means "thoughtfully considering."

Analyze Plot What makes you think that this may be the climax of the story?

Making Choices Why do you think the father decides to reveal the truth of his past to his daughter?

Vocabulary

testament (tes´ tə mənt) *n.* proof of or tribute to

Palm Trees, 1997. Patti Mollica. Oil on canvas. Collection of the artist.

View the Art Palm trees line the coast of both Florida and Haiti but not, of course, New York. What do you think palm trees represent to Annie and her father?

I am the one who drives back to the hotel. In the car, he says, "Annie, I am still your father, still your mother's husband. I would not do these things now."

When we get back to the hotel room, I leave a message for Officer Bo, and another for Manager Salinas, telling them that I have found my father. He has slipped into the bathroom, and now he runs the shower at

EDWIDGE DANTICAT

full force. When it seems that he is never coming out, I call my mother at home in Brooklyn.

"How do you love him?" I whisper into the phone.

My mother is tapping her fingers against the mouthpiece.

"I don't know, Annie," she whispers back, as though there is a chance that she might also be overheard by him. "I feel only that you and me, we saved him. When I met him, it made him stop hurting the people. This is how I see it. He was a seed thrown into a rock, and you and me, Annie, we helped push a flower out of a rock."

Visual Vocabulary
A *praying mantis* is a large green insect that feeds on other insects. It carries its forelegs in a position that resembles hands in prayer.

When I get up the next morning, my father is already dressed. He is sitting on the edge of his bed with his back to me, his head bowed, his face buried in his hands. If I were sculpting him, I would make him a praying mantis, crouching motionless, seeming to pray while waiting to strike.

With his back still turned, my father says, "Will you call those people and tell them you have it no more, the statue?"

"We were invited to lunch there. I believe we should go."

He raises his shoulders and shrugs. It is up to me.

The drive to Gabrielle Fonteneau's house seems longer than the twenty-four hours it took to drive from New York: the ocean, the palms along the road, the highway so imposingly neat. My father fills in the silence in the car by saying, "So now you know, Annie, why your mother and me, we have never returned home."

The Fonteneaus' house is made of bricks of white coral, on a cul-de-sac with a row of banyans separating the two sides of the street.

Silently, we get out of the car and follow a concrete path to the front door. Before we can knock, an older woman walks out.

Visual Vocabulary
Banyans are fig trees.

Like Gabrielle, she has stunning midnight-black eyes and skin the color of sorrel,[15] with spiralling curls brushing the sides of her face. When Gabrielle's father joins her, I realize where Gabrielle Fonteneau gets her height. He is more than six feet tall.

Mr. Fonteneau extends his hands, first to my father and then to me. They're large, twice the size of my father's. The fingernails have grown black, thick, densely dark, as though the past had nestled itself there in black ink.

We move slowly through the living room, which has a cathedral ceiling and walls covered with Haitian paintings—Obin, Hyppolite, Tiga, Duval-Carrié.[16] Out on the back terrace, which towers over a nursery of orchids and red dracaenas,[17] a table is set for lunch.

Mr. Fonteneau asks my father where his family is from in Haiti, and my father lies. In the past, I thought he always said a different province because he had lived in all

---

15. *Sorrel* is brown-orange.
16. *Obin, Hyppolite, Tiga,* and *Duval-Carrié* are Haitian artists.
17. *Dracaenas* are tropical shrubs, trees, or houseplants.

Analyze Plot How may this point suggest the beginning of the falling action?

The Garden, Giverny, 1902. Claude Monet. Oil on canvas, 89.5 x 92.3 cm. Oesterreichische Galerie im Belvedere, Vienna.

View the Art Claude Monet created extensive gardens at his home in Giverny, a hamlet in the Normandy region of France. How does the place shown here suit the description of the Fonteneaus' home?

those places, but I realize now that he says this to keep anyone from tracing him, even though twenty-six years and eighty more pounds shield him from the threat of immediate recognition.

When Gabrielle Fonteneau makes her entrance, in an off-the-shoulder ruby dress, my father and I stand up.

"Gabrielle," she says, when she shakes hands with my father, who blurts out spontaneously, "You are one of the flowers of Haiti."

Gabrielle Fonteneau tilts her head coyly.

"We eat now," Mrs. Fonteneau announces, leading me and my father to a bathroom to wash up before the meal. Standing before a pink seashell-shaped sink, my father and I dip our hands under the faucet flow.

"Annie," my father says, "we always thought, your mother and me, that children could raise their parents higher. Look at what this girl has done for her parents."

During the meal of conch, plantains,[18] and mushroom rice, Mr. Fonteneau tried to draw my father into conversation. He asks when my father was last in Haiti.

"Twenty-six years," my father replies.

"No going back for you?" asks Mrs. Fonteneau.

"I have not had the opportunity," my father says.

"We go back every year to a beautiful place overlooking the ocean in the mountains in Jacmel," says Mrs. Fonteneau.

"Have you ever been to Jacmel?"[19] Gabrielle Fonteneau asks me.

I shake my head no.

---

18. *Plantains*, a type of banana, are a staple food of the tropics.
19. *Jacmel* is a small, picturesque beach town on Haiti's southern peninsula.

Irony What is ironic about this statement?

EDWIDGE DANTICAT

"We are fortunate," Mrs. Fonteneau says, "that we have another place to go where we can say our rain is sweeter, our dust is lighter, our beach is prettier."

"So now we are tasting rain and weighing dust," Mr. Fonteneau says, and laughs.

"There is nothing like drinking the sweet juice from a green coconut you fetched yourself from your own tree, or sinking your hand in sand from the beach in your own country," Mrs. Fonteneau says.

"When did you ever climb a coconut tree?" Mr. Fonteneau says, teasing his wife.

I am imagining what my father's nightmares might be. Maybe he dreams of dipping his hands in the sand on a beach in his own country and finds that what he comes up with is a fist full of blood.

After lunch, my father asks if he can have a closer look at the Fonteneaus' back-yard garden. While he's taking the tour, I confess to Gabrielle Fonteneau that I don't have the sculpture.

"My father threw it away," I say.

Gabrielle Fonteneau frowns.

"I don't know," she says. "Was there even a sculpture at all? I trust Jonas, but maybe you fooled him, too. Is this some scam, to get into our home?"

"There was a sculpture," I say. "Jonas will tell you that. My father just didn't like it, so he threw it away."

She raises her perfectly arched eyebrows, perhaps out of concern for my father's sanity or my own.

"I'm really disappointed," she says. "I wanted it for a reason. My father goes home when he looks at a piece of art.

He goes home deep inside himself. For a long time he used to hide his fingers from people. It's like he was making a fist all the time. I wanted to give him this thing so that he knows we understand what happened to him."

"I am truly sorry," I say.

Over her shoulders, I see her parents guiding my father through rows of lemongrass. I want to promise her that I will make her another sculpture, one especially modeled on her father. But I don't know when I will be able to work on anything again. I have lost my subject, the father I loved as well as pitied.

In the garden, I watch my father snap a white orchid from its stem and hold it out toward Mrs. Fonteneau, who accepts it with a nod of thanks.

"I don't understand," Gabrielle Fonteneau says. "You did all this for nothing."

I wave to my father to signal that we should perhaps leave now, and he comes toward me, the Fonteneaus trailing slowly behind him.

With each step he rubs the scars on the side of his face.

Perhaps the last person my father harmed had dreamed this moment into my father's future—his daughter seeing those marks, like chunks of warm plaster still clinging to a cast, and questioning him about them, giving him a chance to either lie or tell the truth. After all, we have the proverb, as my father would say: "Those who give the blows may try to forget, but those who carry the scars must remember."

> "You did this all for nothing."

Analyze Plot *In what way does this proverb represent the resolution in the plot?*

After You Read

Respond and Think Critically

Respond and Interpret

1. Do you feel more sympathy for the narrator or her father? Explain.

2. (a) Why are the narrator and her father going to Florida? (b) Name two or more reasons why this is such an important trip for the narrator.

3. (a) What happens to the narrator's father after they reach the hotel? (b) What are the father's motives for his actions?

Analyze and Evaluate

4. (a) Why do you think the father never told his daughter the truth before? (b) What is the effect of telling the truth now?

5. Once the sculpture is gone, there is no reason to go to the Fonteneau home. Why do you think the author includes this scene?

6. How do the references to the ancient Egyptians and the Book of the Dead enrich the story?

Connect

7. **Big Idea** Making Choices How does the father's decision to dispose of the sculpture affect the narrator? Explain.

8. **Connect to the Author** Danticat found it difficult to adapt to the American way of life. How is her bond with her Haitian heritage reflected in those of the characters?

You're the Critic

Style and Substance

Read the two excerpts of literary criticism below. The first quotation is about Danticat's style. The second quotation is about her style as well as her underlying themes.

> *The slow accumulation of details pinpointing the past's effects on the present make for powerful reading . . . and Danticat is a crafter of subtle, gorgeous sentences and scenes*
> —Publishers Weekly

> *Danticat allows her characters (and readers) no answers, no resolutions. She's a master at capturing the inarticulate sorrow and bafflement that evil inspires.*
> —Ron Charles, The Christian Science Monitor

Group Activity Work with classmates to discuss and answer the following questions.

1. (a) Restate the quotation from *Publishers Weekly* in your own words. (b) Find two or more sentences or scenes from the story that support or rebut the critic's comment. Explain the reasons for your choices.

2. Discuss the quotation from Ron Charles. Then talk about the ending of "The Book of the Dead" to determine whether there are any answers or resolutions. Reach a group consensus of agreement or disagreement with the critic. Give reasons for your opinion.

EDWIDGE DANTICAT

Literary Element Irony

Writers sometimes use **irony** to express an idea without having to spell it out for readers or add a moral to the story. For example, Danticat sets up a situation in which both her narrator and the readers are in the dark about the father's past. The **situational irony** is that a trip to sell a sculpture that honors the father's past leads to a revelation that the father's past is not at all honorable.

1. What do the ironies in the story suggest about relationships between individuals?
2. Would you describe the fate of the sculpture as ironic? Explain your answer.

Review: Conflict

As you learned on page 34, there are two basic types of **conflict**—internal and external. An **internal conflict** takes place within the mind of a character who is torn between opposing feelings, desires, or goals. An **external conflict** exists when a character struggles against some outside force, such as another person, nature, society, or fate.

Partner Activity Meet with a partner to discuss the conflict in the story. Make a chart like the one below to list two or more conflicts that the narrator faces in the story. Then list two or more conflicts that the father faces.

Conflict	Internal	External
Not reporting her father's disappearance right away	X	

Literature Online

Selection Resources For Selection Quizzes, eFlashcards, and Reading-Writing Connection activities, go to glencoe.com and enter QuickPass code GL59794u1.

Reading Strategy Analyze Plot

Refer to the diagram below and your chart from page 158 as you answer the questions.

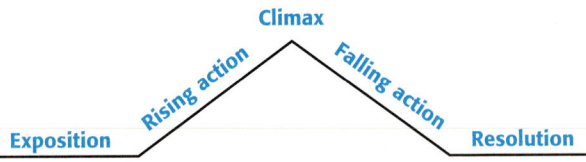

1. The principal characters are introduced slowly in a lengthy exposition. Why is this device effective?
2. What complications build suspense in the story?

Vocabulary Practice

Practice with Usage Respond to these statements to help you explore the meanings of vocabulary words from the text.

1. Name a comment that might be **interjected** in a conversation between two of your friends.
2. Describe what a **mesmerized** person looks like or does.
3. Identify a **vulnerability** of an earlier civilization.
4. Tell why legislators do not **eradicate** taxation.
5. Name something that is a **testament** to your intelligence, your talent, your physical ability, your faith, or your compassion.

Academic Vocabulary

Danticat's **vision** of the storyteller was shaped by the culture into which she was born.

Vision is a multiple-meaning word. In a different context, someone might say they had a **vision** of the future in a dream. Using context clues, try to figure out the meaning of the word in the sentence above about Danticat. Check your guess in a dictionary.

For more on academic vocabulary, see pages 52 and 53.

Respond Through Writing

Autobiographical Narrative

Apply Irony Danticat uses irony to examine a situation between a father and daughter. Think of a situation in your own life where some ironic twist forced you to take a second look at someone or something. Write an autobiographical narrative of at least 1,500 words.

Understand the Task An **autobiographical narrative** is a story in which an author tells a sequence of events from his or her life and reveals the personal significance of the experience. **Mood** is the emotional quality of a literary work. A writer's choice of language, subject matter, setting, and tone contribute to creating mood.

Prewrite Brainstorm, look over journal entries, and flip through photo albums to stimulate your memory. When you have identified the situation you want to write about, freewrite (write without stopping) for 10 minutes to get the basic events of that situation down on paper.

Draft Effective irony depends on how you suggest to the reader one result—and then contrast it with an unexpected result. Keep this in mind as you structure your narrative and organize the sequence of events. The chart below shows one example of the contrast between expectations and reality in Danticat's story. You can create a similar chart to help you while you draft.

Expectation	Reality
The narrator's father was imprisoned for beating a guard	The narrator's father was a guard—not a prisoner

As you write, use concrete details (who, what, when, and where) and sensory details (sights, sounds, smells, tastes, and textures) to describe actions, events, thoughts, and feelings.

Revise Check that you have used concrete and sensory details to describe the story setting as well. Also check to see whether the mood and pacing of your story are appropriate for the irony. For example, if the ironic situation changes your happiness into rage, the mood and pacing should reflect that change. Use the Writing Workshop checklist for Autobiographical Narratives on page 448 as you revise.

Edit and Proofread Proofread your paper, correcting any errors in grammar, spelling, and punctuation. Use the Grammar Tip in the side column to help you with sentence fragments.

Learning Objectives

For page 171

In this assignment, you will focus on the following objectives:

Writing: Writing an autobiographical narrative.

Grammer: Understanding sentence fragments.

Grammar Tip

Sentence Fragments

In formal writing, avoid using sentence fragments—incomplete sentences that lack a subject or a verb. In creative writing, you can use sentence fragments to create certain effects. Here is an example from Danticat's story:

"And the nightmares, what are they?"

"Of what I, your father, did to others."

The father's reply is a sentence fragment that represents realistic dialogue and also emphasizes the irony of the nightmares. As you write your essay, incorporate sentence fragments for emphasis or dialogue. Use them sparingly so you do not dilute their effect.

Before You Read

The Censors

World Literature
Argentina

Meet **Luisa Valenzuela**
(born 1938)

As the political situation in her homeland grew increasingly violent, Luisa Valenzuela turned to writing to cope. One of the most recognized Latin American writers in the United States, Valenzuela writes novels and short stories that expose the injustices of society through satire and wit.

> "[Luisa Valenzuela] wears an opulent, baroque crown, but her feet are naked."
>
> —Carlos Fuentes

Luisa Valenzuela was born in Argentina to a well-respected physician and a writer. She began her career as a journalist working for magazines and newspapers in Buenos Aires. When she was just seventeen, Valenzuela wrote and published her first story. In 1966 her first novel, *Hay que sonreír* (translated as *Clara*), was published. During the 1970s, Argentina's economy deteriorated and the political situation in the country became very volatile. According to Valenzuela, the political atmosphere in Argentina pushed her to leave her home: "I decided to leave in order not to fall into self-censorship. Exile may be devastating, but perspective and separation sharpen the aim."

A Unique Style Known for her experimental style, Valenzuela blends the ordinary with the fantastical. Critics often note her ability to play with words and language. Many critics also classify her work as "magical realism," a type of fiction that inserts fantastic events into a very believable, ordinary reality. However, Valenzuela seeks to push the boundaries of the genre. She says that "Magical realism was a beautiful resting place, but the thing is to go forward."

Politics and Society Valenzuela's most popular novel, *The Lizard's Tail*, details a sorcerer's rise, fall, and return to power. The book gives voice to the political upheaval and social change that took place in Argentina during the 1970s. Using dark humor, Valenzuela offers a powerful satire of government censorship and the difficult circumstances of war. Her stories identify the absurdities of society and expose the shameful operations of totalitarian regimes. As she says, "If the country is to heal, each and every shadow of the dark times has to come out into the open."

Achievements and Endeavors Valenzuela has published numerous novels and collections of short stories, and many of her works have been translated into other languages. Currently, she teaches creative writing in New York. She frequently returns home to Buenos Aires.

Author Search For more about Luisa Valenzuela, go to glencoe.com and enter QuickPass code GL59794u1.

Literature and Reading Preview

Connect to the Story
How might your life be altered if you lost your freedom of speech? Discuss this question with a small group.

Build Background
"The Censors" was first published in 1976, the year that a military faction overthrew Argentina's government. The new government severely restricted constitutional liberties and systematically began to eliminate any opposition to their regime. Innocent citizens as well as dissidents were tortured and killed. Thirteen to fifteen thousand citizens were killed in the *Guerra Sucia*—the "Dirty War," as it came to be called.

Set Purposes for Reading

Big Idea Making Choices

As you read "The Censors," ask yourself, What choices does Juan make to "protect" himself and Mariana from the censors?

Literary Element Satire

Satire is the use of humor or wit to ridicule institutions or humanity with the goal of entertaining or causing change. Recognizing satire can help you discern a persuasive argument presented as a witty portrayal. As you read, ask yourself, What is Valenzuela satirizing and what might she like to change?

Reading Strategy Analyze Cause-and-Effect Relationships

One event often impacts another event. Knowing how to **analyze cause and effect** can help you understand both the relationships between those events and the literary work as a whole. As you read, ask yourself, How is each event influenced by the events that have preceded it?

Tip: Identify Sequence Use a graphic organizer to help you determine the order of events.

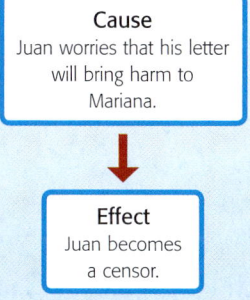

Learning Objectives

For pages 172–177

In studying this text, you will focus on the following objectives:

Literary Study: Analyzing satire.

Reading: Analyzing cause-and-effect relationships.

Vocabulary

irreproachable (ir´ i prō´ chə bəl) *adj.* free from blame or criticism; faultless; p. 174 *The boy's kind behavior was irreproachable.*

albeit (ôl bē´ it) *conj.* although; even if; p. 175 *I like the fall, albeit I am always eager for spring.*

ulterior (ul tēr´ ē ər) *adj.* intentionally withheld or concealed; p. 175 *Sam had an ulterior motive for not wanting to tell the truth.*

subversive (səb vur´ siv) *adj.* seeking to weaken, destroy, or overthrow; p. 176 *Subversive people wished to overthrow the government.*

LUISA VALENZUELA 173

THE CENSORS

Luisa Valenzuela

Postal Montage. Natalie Racioppa.

Poor Juan! One day they caught him with his guard down before he could even realize that what he had taken as a stroke of luck was really one of fate's dirty tricks. These things happen the minute you're careless, as one often is. Juancito[1] let happiness—a feeling you can't trust—get the better of him when he received from a confidential source Mariana's new address in Paris and knew that she hadn't forgotten him. Without thinking twice, he sat down at his table and wrote her a letter. *The* letter that now keeps his mind off his job during the day and won't let him sleep at night (what had he scrawled, what had he put on that sheet of paper he sent to Mariana?).

Juan knows there won't be a problem with the letter's contents, that it's **irreproachable**, harmless. But what about the rest? He knows that they examine, sniff, feel, and read between the lines of each and every letter, and check its tiniest comma and most accidental stain. He knows that all letters pass from hand to hand and go through all sorts of tests in the huge censorship offices and that, in the end, very few continue on their way. Usually it takes months, even years, if there aren't any snags; all this time the freedom, maybe even the life, of both sender and receiver is in jeopardy. And that's why Juan's so troubled: thinking that something might happen to Mariana because of his letters. Of all people, Mariana, who must finally feel safe there where she always dreamt she'd live. But he knows that the *Censor's Secret Command*

---

1. *Juancito* (wän sē′ tō)

Vocabulary

irreproachable (ir′ i prō′ chə bəl) *adj.* free from blame or criticism; faultless

Businessmen Reading the Fine Print.
Bruno Budrovic.

View the Art In this illustration, the artist presents a satirical view of businessmen. How does this image complement the tone of the story?

operates all over the world and cashes in on the discount in air fares; there's nothing to stop them from going as far as that hidden Paris neighborhood, kidnapping Mariana, and returning to their cozy homes, certain of having fulfilled their noble mission.

Well, you've got to beat them to the punch, do what everyone tries to do: sabotage the machinery, throw sand in its gears, get to the bottom of the problem so as to stop it.

This was Juan's sound plan when he, like many others, applied for a censor's job—not because he had a calling or needed a job: no, he applied simply to intercept his own letter, a consoling **albeit** unoriginal idea. He was hired immediately, for each day more and more censors are needed and no one would bother to check on his references.

Ulterior motives couldn't be overlooked by the *Censorship Division*, but they needn't be too strict with those who applied. They knew how hard it would be for the poor guys to find the letter they wanted and even if they did, what's a letter or two when the new censor would snap up so many others? That's how Juan managed to join the *Post Office's Censorship Division*, with a certain goal in mind.

The building had a festive air on the outside that contrasted with its inner staidness.[2] Little by little, Juan was absorbed by his job, and he felt at peace since he was doing everything he could to get his letter for Mariana. He didn't even worry when, in his first month, he was sent to *Section K*

---

2. *Staidness* (stād′ nəs) is the state or quality of being serious, steady, or conservative in character.

Vocabulary

albeit (ôl bē′ it) *conj.* although; even if
ulterior (ul tēr′ ē ər) *adj.* intentionally withheld or concealed

where envelopes are very carefully screened for explosives.

It's true that on the third day, a fellow worker had his right hand blown off by a letter, but the division chief claimed it was sheer negligence on the victim's part. Juan and the other employees were allowed to go back to their work, though feeling less secure. After work, one of them tried to organize a strike to demand higher wages for unhealthy work, but Juan didn't join in; after thinking it over, he reported the man to his superiors and thus got promoted.

You don't form a habit by doing something once, he told himself as he left his boss's office. And when he was transferred to *Section J*, where letters are carefully checked for poison dust, he felt he had climbed a rung in the ladder.

By working hard, he quickly reached *Section E* where the job became more interesting, for he could now read and analyze the letters' contents. Here he could even hope to get hold of his letter, which, judging by the time that had elapsed, had gone through the other sections and was probably floating around in this one.

Soon his work became so absorbing that his noble mission blurred in his mind. Day after day he crossed out whole paragraphs in red ink, pitilessly chucking many letters into the censored basket. These were horrible days when he was shocked by the subtle and conniving ways employed by people to pass on **subversive** messages; his instincts were so sharp that he found behind a simple "the weather's unsettled" or "prices continue to soar" the wavering hand of someone secretly scheming to overthrow the Government.

His zeal brought him swift promotion. We don't know if this made him happy. Very few letters reached him in *Section B*—only a handful passed the other hurdles—so he read them over and over again, passed them under a magnifying glass, searched for microprint with an electronic microscope, and tuned his sense of smell so that he was beat by the time he made it home. He'd barely manage to warm up his soup, eat some fruit, and fall into bed, satisfied with having done his duty. Only his darling mother worried, but she couldn't get him back on the right track. She'd say, though it wasn't always true: Lola called, she's at the bar with the girls, they miss you, they're waiting for you. Or else she'd leave a bottle of red wine on the table. But Juan wouldn't overdo it: any distraction could make him lose his edge and the perfect censor had to be alert, keen, attentive, and sharp to nab cheats. He had a truly patriotic task, both self-denying and uplifting.

His basket for censored letters became the best fed as well as the most cunning basket in the whole *Censorship Division*. He was about to congratulate himself for having finally discovered his true mission, when his letter to Mariana reached his hands. Naturally, he censored it without regret. And just as naturally, he couldn't stop them from executing him the following morning, another victim of his devotion to his work.

Vocabulary

subversive (səb vur′ siv) *adj.* seeking to weaken, destroy, or overthrow

---

Analyze Cause-and-Effect Relationships What do the cause and effect in this sentence reveal about Juan's superiors?

Satire Explain what is satirical in this passage.

Making Choices How does Juan's choice affect his final outcome?

After You Read

Respond and Think Critically

Respond and Interpret

1. Did your feelings about Juan change during the course of the story? Explain.

2. (a) What does Juan fear will happen to Mariana as a result of his letter? (b) What does this tell you about the kind of government Juan lives under?

3. Why are "more and more censors" needed, making it easy for Juan to get hired?

Analyze and Evaluate

4. (a) What parts of this story seem logical and believable to you? (b) Are there any parts that are unbelievable? Use details from the story to support your answer.

Connect

5. **Big Idea** Making Choices Do you think Juan's choices or the government's had a greater impact on the outcome of the story? Explain.

6. **Connect to the Author** How might Valenzuela's perspective as both an insider and an exile have influenced her writing in this story?

Literary Element Satire

Humor—an element of **satire**—can often be persuasive as well as entertaining because it is less likely to alienate people who might initially disagree.

1. How does Juan's transformation into the perfect censor become the "punch line" for this satire?

2. Is the author's satire aimed more at the government or at individuals like Juan?

Reading Strategy Analyze Cause-and-Effect Relationships

When authors do not tell their stories chronologically, the reader must pay close attention in order to determine the actual sequence of events and the **cause-and-effect relationships** of those events to one another. Review the chart you made on page 173 and respond to the following items.

1. Describe how the story is organized.

2. How would the impact of the story change if events were ordered differently?

 Literature Online

Selection Resources For Selection Quizzes, eFlashcards, and Reading-Writing Connection activities, go to glencoe.com and enter QuickPass code GL59794u1.

Vocabulary Practice

Practice with Word Parts For each boldfaced vocabulary word in the left column, identify the related word with a shared root in the right column. Write both words and underline the part they have in common. Use a dictionary to look up the meaning of the related word. Explain its relation to the root word of the vocabulary word.

1. **irreproachable**   convert
2. **albeit**   interior
3. **ulterior**   although
4. **subversive**   biodegradable

Writing

Write a Journal Entry Put yourself in Juan's place. Write a journal entry in which he responds to his mother's efforts to get him "back on the right track." Use satire in the entry by having Juan unwittingly reveal some of the negative aspects of his job as a censor—aspects to which he is now blind.

Learning Objectives

For pages 178–182

In studying this text, you will focus on the following objectives:

Reading: Analyzing informational text.

Reading: Determining the main idea and supporting details.

Set a Purpose for Reading

As you read, ask yourself, What environmental concern is being raised and what is the writer's viewpoint on saving ocean life?

Preview the Article

1. From the title, what words would you use to describe what the tone of the article might be?
2. Skim the article. What do you think it will be about?

Reading Strategy

Determine the Main Idea and Supporting Details

In order to determine the main idea, ask yourself, What is the most important thought the writer is trying to convey about his or her subject? The main idea is not always obvious, so use the **supporting details** in the text to guide you. As you read, create and complete a graphic organizer like the one shown below.

Main Idea:

Supporting Detail 1: Fishing destroys over eighty million sea creatures each year.

Supporting Detail 2:

TIME

Cry of the Ancient Mariner

"Even in the middle of the deep blue sea, the albatross feels the hard hand of humanity"

By CARL SAFINA

AT THE LONELY CENTER OF THE NORTH PACIFIC Ocean, farther from just about everything than just about anywhere, lies Midway Atoll, a coral reef enclosed by a lagoon. I've come with Canadian writer and zoologist Nancy Baron to the world's largest Laysan albatross colony—400,000 exquisite masters of the air—a feathered nation gathered to breed, cramming an isle a mile by two.

Ravenous, goose-size chicks so jam the landscape that it resembles a poultry farm. Many have waited more than a week for a meal, while both parents forage the ocean's vast expanse. An adult glides in on 7-ft. wings. After flying perhaps 2,000 miles nonstop to return here, in 10 minutes she will be gone again, searching for more food. She surveys the scene through lovely dark pastel-shadowed eyes, then calls, "Eh-eh-eh." Every nearby chick answers, but she recognizes her own chick's voice and weaves toward it.

Aggressive with hunger, the whining chick bites its parent's bill to stimulate her into throwing up her payload. The adult hunches, vomiting, pumping out fish eggs and several squid. The chick swallows in seconds what its parent logged 4,000 miles to get. The chick begs for more. The adult arches her neck and vomits again. Nothing comes. We whisper, "What's wrong?"

Slowly comes the surreal sight of a green plastic toothbrush emerging from the bird's gullet. With her neck

178 UNIT 1 THE SHORT STORY

arched, the mother cannot fully pass the straight brush. She tries several times to disgorge it, but can't. Nancy and I can hardly bear this. The albatross reswallows and, with the brush stuck inside, wanders away.

Message from the Albatross

In the world in which albatrosses came from, the birds swallowed pieces of floating pumice, or lightweight, volcanic glass, for the fish eggs stuck to them. Albatrosses transferred this survival strategy to toothbrushes, bottle caps, nylon netting, toys, and other floating junk. Where chicks die, a pile of colorful plastic particles that used to be in their stomachs often marks their graves.

Through the intimate bond between parent and offspring flows the continuity of life itself. That our human trash stream crosses even this sacred bond is evidence of a wounded world, its relationships disfigured. The albatross's message: Consumer culture has reached every watery point on the compass. From sun-bleached coral reefs to icy polar waters, no place, no creature, remains apart.

Set the Record Straight

If albatrosses' eating plastic seems surprising, so do many of the oceans' problems. The facts often defy common perceptions. Examples:

- Most people think oil spills cause the most harm to ocean life. They don't. Fishing does. When a tanker wrecks, news crews flock to film gooey beaches and dying animals. Journalists rush right past the picturesque fishing boats whose huge nets and 1,000-hook longlines cause far more havoc on the marine world than spilled oil.

Fishing annually extracts more than 80 million tons of sea creatures worldwide. An additional 20 million tons of unwanted fish, seabirds, marine mammals, and turtles get thrown overboard, dead. Overfishing has seriously reduced major populations of cod, swordfish, tuna, snapper, grouper, and sharks. Instead of sensibly living off nature's interest, many fisheries have mined the wild capital, and famous fishing banks lie bankrupt, including the revered cod grounds of New England and Atlantic Canada.

Enforcing fishing limits—to give the most devastated fish populations a chance to rebuild—could ultimately enable us to catch at least 10 million more tons of sea life than we do now. Government-subsidized shipbuilders and fleets drive much of the overfishing. Ending those subsidies—as New Zealand has already done—would mean paying less to get more in the long run.

CATCH OF THE DAY
These Alaskan salmon are still abundant, but many other species are not so fortunate.

Informational Text

- Most ocean pollution doesn't come from ships. It comes from land. Gravity is the sea's enemy. Silt running off dirt roads and clear-cut forest land ruins coral reefs and U.S. salmon rivers. Pesticides and other poisons sprayed into the air and washed into rivers find the ocean. (Midway's albatrosses have in their tissues as much of the industrial chemicals called PCBs as do Great Lakes bald eagles.) The biggest sources of coastal pollution are waste from farm animals, fertilizers, and human sewage. They can spawn red tides and other harmful algae blooms that rob oxygen from the water, killing sea life. The Mississippi River, whose fine heartland silt once built fertile delta wetlands, now builds in the Gulf of Mexico a spreading dead zone—almost empty of marine life—the size of New Jersey. Improving sewage treatment and cleaning up the runoff from farms will be increasingly vital to preserving coastal water quality.

VIOLATING A SACRED BOND
Because of humankind's endless trash stream, the seabirds feed plastic to their young.

- Fish farming—aquaculture—doesn't take pressure off wild fish. Many farms use large numbers of cheap, wild-caught fish as feed to raise fewer shrimp and fish of more profitable varieties. And industrial-scale fish- and shrimp-aquaculture operations sometimes damage the coastlines where the facilities are located. The farms can foul the water, destroy mangroves and marshes, drive local fishers out of business, and serve as breeding grounds for fish diseases. In places such as Bangladesh, Thailand, and India, which grow shrimp mainly for export to richer countries, diseases and pollution usually limit a farm's life to 10 years. The companies then move and start again.

To avoid becoming just another environmental headache, aquaculture needs standards. Raising fish species foreign to the local habitat should be discouraged, since escapees can drive out native fish or infect them with disease. Penning fish in open waterways is also problematic. Even when the impact on the environment is minimized—as it is with well-run Maine salmon farms—rows of large fish corrals in natural waterways can be eyesores. Fish farming is best done in indoor, onshore facilities. The

> **"Heartland silt from the Mississippi River is creating a spreading dead zone in the Gulf of Mexico."**

fish rarely escape, and the wastewater can be treated before being released. Growing vegetarian species such as tilapia is ideal, since they don't have to be fed wild fish.

- The biologically richest stretches of ocean are more disrupted than the richest places on land. Continents still have roadless wilderness areas where motorized vehicles have never gone. But on the world's continental shelves, it is hard to find places where boats dragging nets haven't etched tracks into sea-floor habitats. In Europe's North Sea and along New England's Georges Bank and Australia's Queensland coast, trawlers, boats used for catching fish in large nets, may scour the bottom four to eight times every year. And the U.S. National Marine Sanctuaries hardly deserve the name. Commercial and recreational fishing with lines, traps, or nets is allowed almost everywhere in these "sanctuaries."

New Zealand and the Philippines are among the countries that have set up reserves in which fish are actually left alone. Marine life tends to recover in these areas, then spread beyond them, providing cheap insurance against overfishing outside the reserves.

Though the oceans' problems can seem overwhelming, solutions are emerging and attitudes are changing. Most people have shed the fantasy that the sea can provide

WHAT YOU CAN DO

AVOID EATING SEAFOOD FROM ENDANGERED POPULATIONS

Like fish but don't want to help wipe out a species? The Monterey Bay Aquarium in California has published a menu of dos and don'ts. Some excerpts:

BEST CHOICES

Dungeness crab
Halibut (Alaska)
Mahi-mahi
Salmon (Alaska, wild caught)
Tilapia
Striped bass

BAD CHOICES

Atlantic cod
Orange roughy
Chilean sea bass
Shark
Shrimp
Swordfish

food forever, lessen endless pollution, and accept unlimited trash. In 1996, the U.S. passed the Sustainable Fisheries Act, which set up rules against overfishing—a recognition that protecting sea life is good business. Some fish, such as striped bass and redfish, are recovering because of catch limits. Alaskan, Falkland, Australian, and New Zealand longline boats are taking care not to kill albatrosses. Turtles are being saved by trapdoors in shrimp nets so they can escape.

Joining Together to Help the Seas

The oceans' future depends most of all on international cooperation. Working through the U.N., the world's nations have outlawed giant drift nets. Other treaties to protect the seas and the fish in them are in the works, though not all nations are enthusiastic about signing them. Among top fishing nations, Japan relies heavily on seafood and yet is exceptionally disrespectful toward the ocean. It has disagreed with international limits on catches of southern bluefin tuna and used "scientific research" as a phony justification for hunting whales in the International Whaling Commission's Antarctic Sanctuary. A world leader in so many ways, Japan would greatly improve its moral position by helping to heal the seas.

A good place to start that healing would be to give albatrosses a future with more food and less plastic trash to swallow. A U.N. marine-pollution treaty makes dumping plastics illegal, but policing at sea is impractical. Nonetheless, ships could be required to carry up-to-date equipment for handling garbage and storing liquid waste that might otherwise be dumped into the water.

Informational Text

Routine discharges put more oil into the sea than major spills.

We should expand our idea of zoning from land to sea. Instead of an ocean free-for-all, we should mark some areas for fishing only with traps and hooks and lines, and others as wildlife sanctuaries. As we've seen with once rich cod grounds, if we don't declare some areas closed by foresight, they will declare themselves closed by collapse. The map of the land has many colors, while in most minds the sea is still the blank space between continents. Let's start coloring in that blue expanse and map a more sensible future for the sea.

Four centuries ago, poet John Donne wrote that no man is an island entire to himself. On Midway an albatross gagging on a toothbrush taught me that no island is an island. In the oceans, less is truly more: less trash, less habitat destruction, and catching fewer fish now will mean more food later on for both people and wildlife. The oceans make our planet habitable, and the wealth of oceans spans nutritional, climatological, biological, aesthetic, spiritual, emotional, and ethical areas. Like the albatross, we need the seas more than the seas need us. Will we understand this well enough to reap all the riches that a little restraint, cooperation, and compassion could bring?

— Updated 2005,
from TIME, Special Earth Day
Issue, Spring 2000

Carl Safina, founder of the National Audubon Society's Living Oceans Program, is the author of Song for the Blue Ocean.

Respond and Think Critically

Respond and Interpret

1. Write a brief summary of the main ideas in this article before you answer the following questions. For help on writing a summary, see page 415.

2. How did you feel about the importance of preventing the destruction of marine life before and after you read the article?

3. (a) What is one solution to the problem of overfishing that the writer provided? (b) Did he provide evidence as to why this would work?

4. (a) On what, in the writer's opinion, does the ocean's future depend? (b) How did the writer support his opinion on this concern?

Analyze and Evaluate

5. (a) Choose the sentence that best describes the main idea of the reading selection.

    i Saving the environment is a necessity for humankind.

    ii Marine life can only continue to survive if immediate action is taken.

    iii Overfishing, fish farming, and pollution must be curbed and/or prevented in order to save the oceans and marine life.

6. (a) How can you tell which of the writer's claims are facts and which are opinions? (b) How do you think this affects the validity of his claims?

Connect

7. **Connect to the Author** The writer is the founder of the National Audubon Society's Living Oceans Program. The National Audubon Society is a network of community-based centers as well as scientific and educational programs geared toward sustaining the life of birds and promoting conservation. How do you think the writer's background influenced his opinions and writing style?

PART 3

Life Transitions

All the Days of My Life No. 2, 1999. Evelyn Williams. Oil on canvas, 48.03 x 59.84 in. Private collection.

View the Art The figures in this painting appear to be sharing a moment in daily life. Describe the mood of this painting. What can you infer from the figures and their expressions and gestures?

BIG IDEA

Life transitions are universal, prevalent in all cultures. Some cultures mark transitions with ceremony, while others simply observe a gradual shift in perspective and worldview. In the short stories in Part 3, you will encounter various rites of passage. As you read these stories, ask yourself, How do you, your family, and your friends mark transitions in your lives?

Learning Objectives

For pages 184–185

In studying this text, you will focus on the following objectives:

Literary Study: Analyze narrator and voice.

Writing: Writing descriptive sentences.

LITERARY FOCUS

Narrator and Voice

How are stories told?

Who will tell the story? This is an important question for anyone who is writing a short story. Choosing a narrator is a decision that shapes the style of a story. A narrator can speak from within the story, providing first-person narration, or from outside the story. There, it is possible to view the thoughts and feelings of all the characters. Based on who is telling it, a story can be told in vastly different ways.

In real life I am a large, big-boned woman with rough, man-working hands. In the winter I wear flannel nightgowns to bed and overalls during the day. I can kill and clean a hog as mercilessly as a man. My fat keeps me hot in zero weather. I can work outside all day, breaking ice to get water for washing; I can eat pork liver cooked over the open fire minutes after it comes steaming from the hog. One winter I knocked a bull calf straight in the brain between the eyes with a sledge hammer and had the meat hung up to chill before nightfall.

—Alice Walker, *from "Everyday Use"*

Cows, 1890. Vincent van Gogh. Oil on canvas. Musee des Beaux-Arts, Lille, France.

Point of View

A story with a **first-person point of view** is told by a character, referred to as "I." The reader sees people and events through the eyes of one character, and the reader cannot know more than this character knows. For example, the reader cannot know what another character thinks. **Limited third-person point of view** is similar. The narrator is outside the story, but only reveals the thoughts of one character, referred to as "he" or "she." A **third-person omniscient point of view** differs greatly from the first two: The narrator is outside the story but knows everything about the characters and events.

Voice

Voice is the distinctive use of language that conveys the author's personality to the reader. Sentence structure, word choice, and tone are elements that contribute to an author's voice. When reading other works by the same author, a reader can recognize the author's voice by his or her unique use of language.

A narrator has a voice too, because the author gives the narrator a particular way of speaking and using language, which contributes to the overall emotional quality of the story. The tone of the narrator's voice also contributes to the setting, plot, and theme.

> When at last he started on his quest, it was a beautiful morning in late spring. The grass was up, the leaves were out, nature was at its best. Two medicine men accompanied him.
>
> —Lame Deer, **from "The Vision Quest"**

Diction Good writers choose words carefully. **Diction** refers to an author's choice of words. Authors choose their words to give the reader a specific feeling or to convey a particular meaning. Consider the difference in diction between these two examples:

> Constance hates lap swimming.
> Constance loathes repetitive lap swimming.

Tone Diction also helps communicate the **tone** of a story. Tone is the author's attitude toward the subject. An author's tone might be sympathetic, objective, serious, ironic, sad, bitter, or humorous.

For example, even the title of Isabel Allende's story "And of Clay Are We Created" incorporates the story's tone. Notice that she did not call her story "We Are Created of Clay." The title she wrote immediately communicates the story's solemn tone to the reader. On the other hand, James Thurber uses an amused, affectionate tone in "The Car We Had to Push."

Style

The sum total of language choices an author makes is his or her **style.** How sophisticated is the narrator's vocabulary? Does he or she speak in long, flowing sentences or short, choppy ones? Is the language formal or informal? It makes a difference whether the author writes about an *automobile* or a *car*. Like tone, style can tell a reader about the author's purpose in writing and his or her attitude toward the subject and audience.

> Luis heard a car drive up and someone honk their horn. His father emerged from inside a new red Mustang that had been totaled. He usually dismantled every small feature by hand before sending the vehicle into the *cementerio,* as he called the lot. Luis watched as the most beautiful girl he had ever seen climbed out of a vintage white Volkswagen Bug. She stood in the sunlight in her white sundress waiting for his father, while Luis stared. She was like a smooth wood carving. Her skin was mahogany, almost black, and her arms and legs were long and thin, but curved in places so that she did not look bony and hard—more like a ballerina.
>
> —Judith Ortiz Cofer, **from "Catch the Moon"**

Quickwrite

Analyze Style Write a few sentences describing your classroom, or some other room, in your own style. Do not worry about trying to sound like a writer; write the way you talk. After you write your sentences, use the checklist below to analyze your style. Think about your choices, then rewrite your description for a different purpose. Write as if you were trying to sell the room. Then analyze your style in the second description.

☐ Words: long or short?
☐ Sentences: long or short?
☐ Language: formal or informal?
☐ How would you describe the tone?
☐ How would you describe the voice?

LITERARY FOCUS

Before You Read

Everyday Use

Meet Alice Walker
(born 1944)

If Alice Walker's brother had not accidentally shot her in the eye with a BB gun when she was eight, she might not have become a writer. After children at school made fun of her, she "retreated into solitude, and read stories and began to write poems." Her great love for the written word had begun.

Early Years Walker grew up in Eatonton, Georgia, a small town where her parents farmed. They were sharecroppers—people who rented other people's land to grow crops. Sharecroppers made just enough money to survive and viewed education as the means to a better life for their children. Walker received a scholarship to Spelman College in Atlanta, the nation's oldest college for African American women. At Spelman during some of the most important years of the Civil Rights Movement, Walker was lured into political activism.

> *"We will be ourselves and free, or die in the attempt. Harriet Tubman was not our great-grandmother for nothing."*
>
> —Alice Walker

A Child of the Civil Rights Movement Walker was ten years old when the Supreme Court ruled that "separate but equal" was unconstitutional in schools. Her parents in the rural South knew only the days of segregation and racism, but Walker came to know a different way of life. Walker saw people beaten and battered for protesting for their rights, yet she also experienced what it was like to live in a world that was not completely segregated. Walker knew that the changes she went through were difficult for the previous generation. She wrote, "In the Sixties many of us scared our parents profoundly when we showed up dressed in our 'African' . . . clothes. We shocked them. . . ." In "Everyday Use," Walker portrays the clash between generations that sometimes resulted from this rapid change.

An African American Woman's Voice Walker has published many volumes of fiction, nonfiction, and poetry. Her most famous book, *The Color Purple,* won the Pulitzer Prize and the American Book Award. Steven Spielberg's movie version garnered numerous Academy Award nominations.

One of Walker's greatest influences was Zora Neale Hurston, whom Walker praised for portraying African American people as "complete, complex, *undiminished* human beings." Walker's own work reflects a similar commitment to portraying the beauty and complexity of the African American experience.

Author Search For more about Alice Walker, go to glencoe.com and enter QuickPass code GL59794u1.

Literature and Reading Preview

Connect to the Story
Why might adult family members disapprove of how other members of their family live? Write a journal entry about a time when you saw this happen in real life or in movies or television, and explain how the family members dealt with the situation.

Build Background
"Everyday Use" takes place in the rural South in the 1970s. At that time, there was often a great contrast between African Americans living in cities, especially in the North, and African Americans living in the rural South.

Set Purposes for Reading

Big Idea Life Transitions

As you read "Everyday Use," ask yourself, How does the selection address change: who changes, who does not change, and why?

Literary Element Reliable/Unreliable Narrator

The **narrator** is the person who tells the story. The narrator may be a **reliable,** or trustworthy, source of information and interpretation. A narrator might also be **unreliable,** or unable to be trusted. Determining if the narrator of a story is reliable or unreliable will help you assess whether aspects of the story are true and unbiased. As you read "Everyday Use," ask yourself, Who is the narrator and is her version of events likely to be true or objective? Why or why not?

Reading Strategy Question

When you **question,** you ask yourself whether specific information in a selection is important, as well as whether you understand what you have read. As you read, ask yourself, What do the details in this story say about Mama and her daughters?

Tip: Make a Chart Use a chart like the one shown to record details and your questions.

Detail	My Question
"When the hard clay is swept clean"	Why is this detail here?

Learning Objectives

For pages 186–197

In studying this text, you will focus on the following objectives:

Literary Study: Analyzing reliable/unreliable narrator.

Reading: Questioning.

Vocabulary

sidle (sīd´əl) *v.* to move sideways; p. 189 *The shy child quietly sidled up to me.*

furtive (fur´tiv) *adj.* secret; shifty; sly; p. 190 *The guilty man wore a furtive smile while maintaining his innocence.*

oppress (ə pres´) *v.* to control or govern by the cruel or unjust use of force or authority; p. 192 *Some governments further oppress people living in poverty.*

doctrine (dok´trin) *n.* particular principle or position that is taught or supported, as of a religion; p. 193 *They believe in the doctrine of original sin.*

Tip: Word Usage Select words not only for their meaning but for the context in which you will place them. For example, you might use *sneaky* when talking with your friends about an action but *furtive* when presenting an analysis of a character.

Fog over Rural Road in Great Smoky Mountains. William Manning.

EVERYDAY USE

Alice Walker

I will wait for her in the yard that Maggie and I made so clean and wavy yesterday afternoon. A yard like this is more comfortable than most people know. It is not just a yard. It is like an extended living room. When the hard clay is swept clean as a floor and the fine sand around the edges lined with tiny, irregular grooves, anyone can come and sit and look up into the elm tree and wait for the breezes that never come inside the house.

Maggie will be nervous until after her sister goes: she will stand hopelessly in corners, homely and ashamed of the burn scars down her arms and legs, eying her sister with a mixture of envy and awe. She thinks her sister has held life always in the palm of one hand, that "no" is a word the world never learned to say to her.

You've no doubt seen those TV shows where the child who has "made it" is confronted, as a surprise, by her own mother and father, tottering in weakly from backstage. (A pleasant surprise, of course: What would they do if parent and child came on the show only to curse out and insult each other?) On TV mother and child embrace and smile into each other's faces. Sometimes the mother and father weep, the child wraps them in her arms

---

Reliable/Unreliable Narrator What have you learned about the narrator so far?

and leans across the table to tell how she would not have made it without their help. I have seen these programs.

Sometimes I dream a dream in which Dee and I are suddenly brought together on a TV program of this sort. Out of a dark and soft-seated limousine I am ushered into a bright room filled with many people. There I meet a smiling, gray, sporty man like Johnny Carson who shakes my hand and tells me what a fine girl I have. Then we are on the stage and Dee is embracing me with tears in her eyes. She pins on my dress a large orchid, even though she has told me once that she thinks orchids are tacky flowers.

Visual Vocabulary
Johnny Carson hosted *The Tonight Show*, the popular late-night TV talk show, from 1962 to 1992.

In real life I am a large, big-boned woman with rough, man-working hands. In the winter I wear flannel nightgowns to bed and overalls during the day. I can kill and clean a hog as mercilessly as a man. My fat keeps me hot in zero weather. I can work outside all day, breaking ice to get water for washing; I can eat pork liver cooked over the open fire minutes after it comes steaming from the hog. One winter I knocked a bull calf straight in the brain between the eyes with a sledge hammer and had the meat hung up to chill before nightfall. But of course all this does not show on television. I am the way my daughter would want me to be: a hundred pounds lighter, my skin like an uncooked barley pancake. My hair glistens in the hot bright lights. Johnny Carson has much to do to keep up with my quick and witty tongue.

But that is a mistake. I know even before I wake up. Who ever knew a Johnson with a quick tongue? Who can even imagine me looking a strange white man in the eye? It seems to me I have talked to them always with one foot raised in flight, with my head turned in whichever way is farthest from them. Dee, though. She would always look anyone in the eye. Hesitation was no part of her nature.

"How do I look, Mama?" Maggie says, showing just enough of her thin body enveloped in pink skirt and red blouse for me to know she's there, almost hidden by the door.

"Come out into the yard," I say.

Have you ever seen a lame animal, perhaps a dog run over by some careless person rich enough to own a car, **sidle** up to someone who is ignorant enough to be kind to him? That is the way my Maggie walks. She has been like this, chin on chest, eyes on ground, feet in shuffle, ever since the fire that burned the other house to the ground.

Dee is lighter than Maggie, with nicer hair and a fuller figure. She's a woman now, though sometimes I forget. How long ago was it that the other house burned? Ten, twelve years? Sometimes I can still hear the flames and feel Maggie's arms sticking to me, her hair smoking and her dress falling off her in little black papery flakes. Her eyes seemed stretched open, blazed open by the flames reflected in them. And Dee. I see her standing off under the sweet gum tree she used to dig gum out of; a look of concentration on her face as she watched the last dingy gray

---

Question Why might the narrator have this dream?

Reliable/Unreliable Narrator What conflict does the narrator reveal between her and her daughter? Do you think this conflict affects the narrator's ability to be objective about her daughter? Explain.

Vocabulary
sidle (sīd′əl) *v.* to move sideways

board of the house fall in toward the red-hot brick chimney. Why don't you do a dance around the ashes? I'd wanted to ask her. She had hated the house that much.

I used to think she hated Maggie, too. But that was before we raised the money, the church and me, to send her to Augusta[1] to school. She used to read to us without pity; forcing words, lies, other folks' habits, whole lives upon us two, sitting trapped and ignorant underneath her voice. She washed us in a river of make-believe, burned us with a lot of knowledge we didn't necessarily need to know. Pressed us to her with the serious way she read, to shove us away at just the moment, like dimwits, we seemed about to understand.

Dee wanted nice things. A yellow organdy[2] dress to wear to her graduation from high school; black pumps to match a green suit she'd made from an old suit somebody gave me. She was determined to stare down any disaster in her efforts. Her eyelids would not flicker for minutes at a time. Often I fought off the temptation to shake her. At sixteen she had a style of her own: and knew what style was.

I never had an education myself. After second grade the school was closed down. Don't ask me why: in 1927 colored asked fewer questions than they do now. Sometimes Maggie reads to me. She stumbles along good-naturedly but can't see well. She knows she is not bright. Like good looks and money, quickness passed her by. She will marry John Thomas (who has mossy teeth in an earnest face) and then I'll be free to sit here and I guess just sing church songs to myself. Although I never was a good singer. Never could carry a tune. I was always better at a man's job. I used to love to milk till I was hooked in the side in '49. Cows are soothing and slow and don't bother you, unless you try to milk them the wrong way.

I have deliberately turned my back on the house. It is three rooms, just like the one that burned, except the roof is tin; they don't make shingle roofs any more. There are no real windows, just some holes cut in the sides, like the portholes in a ship, but not round and not square, with rawhide holding the shutters up on the outside. This house is in a pasture, too, like the other one. No doubt when Dee sees it she will want to tear it down. She wrote me once that no matter where we "choose" to live, she will manage to come see us. But she will never bring her friends. Maggie and I thought about this and Maggie asked me, "Mama, when did Dee ever *have* any friends?"

She had a few. **Furtive** boys in pink shirts hanging about on washday after school. Nervous girls who never laughed. Impressed with her they worshiped the well-turned phrase, the cute shape, the scalding humor that erupted like bubbles in lye. She read to them.

When she was courting Jimmy T she didn't have much time to pay to us, but turned all her faultfinding power

---

1. *Augusta* is a city in Georgia.
2. *Organdy* is a lightweight fabric, usually made of cotton.

Question What questions do you have about the fire or about Dee's relationship to it?

Reliable/Unreliable Narrator How does Mama feel about her daughter's education and new ideas?

Life Transitions How have things changed since Mama was young?

Reliable/Unreliable Narrator How do you think it makes the narrator feel that Dee hates her house? Do you think this affects how she tells her story? Explain.

Vocabulary

furtive (fur´tiv) *adj.* secret; shifty; sly

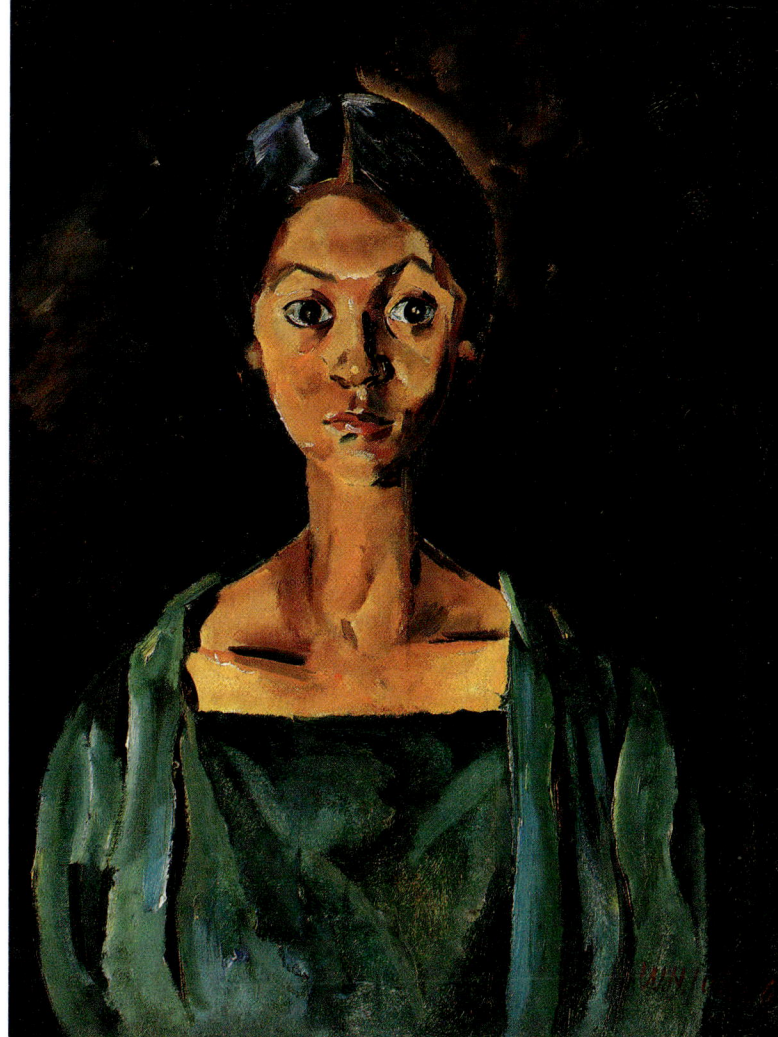

Girl in a Green Dress, 1930. William H. Johnson. Oil on canvas, 24¼ x 19 ½ in. National Museum of American Art, Washington, DC.

William H. Johnson's art focuses on the African American experience. His earlier works—like this one—are influenced by the Expressionist Style, a form that emphasizes intense emotions.

View the Art Which of the two sisters in the story might be more like the girl in this portrait? Explain.

It is hard to see them clearly through the strong sun. But even the first glimpse of leg out of the car tells me it is Dee. Her feet were always neat-looking, as if God himself had shaped them with a certain style. From the other side of the car comes a short, stocky man. Hair is all over his head a foot long and hanging from his chin like a kinky mule tail. I hear Maggie suck in her breath. "Uhnnnh," is what it sounds like. Like when you see the wriggling end of a snake just in front of your foot on the road. "Uhnnnh."

Dee next. A dress down to the ground, in this hot weather. A dress so loud it hurts my eyes. There are yellows and oranges enough to throw back the light of the sun. I feel my whole face warming from the heat waves it throws out. Earrings gold, too, and hanging down to her shoulders. Bracelets dangling and making noises when she moves her arm up to shake the folds of the dress out of her armpits. The dress is loose and flows, and as she walks closer, I like it. I hear Maggie go "Uhnnnh" again. It is her sister's hair. It stands straight up like the wool on a sheep. It is black as night and around the edges are two long pigtails

on him. He *flew* to marry a cheap city girl from a family of ignorant flashy people. She hardly had time to recompose herself.

When she comes I will meet—but there they are!

Maggie attempts to make a dash for the house, in her shuffling way, but I stay her with my hand. "Come back here," I say. And she stops and tries to dig a well in the sand with her toe.

Life Transitions Why do the man's hair and beard signify change to Mama?

ALICE WALKER

that rope about like small lizards disappearing behind her ears.

"Wa-su-zo-Tean-o!" she says, coming on in that gliding way the dress makes her move. The short stocky fellow with the hair to his navel is all grinning and follows up with "Asalamalakim,³ my mother and sister!" He moves to hug Maggie but she falls back, right up against the back of my chair. I feel her trembling there and when I look up I see the perspiration falling off her chin.

"Don't get up," says Dee. Since I am stout it takes something of a push. You can see me trying to move a second or two before I make it. She turns, showing white heels through her sandals, and goes back to the car. Out she peeks next with a Polaroid. She stoops down quickly and lines up picture after picture of me sitting there in front of the house with Maggie cowering behind me. She never takes a shot without making sure the house is included. When a cow comes nibbling around the edge of the yard she snaps it and me and Maggie *and* the house. Then she puts the Polaroid in the back seat of the car, and comes up and kisses me on the forehead.

Meanwhile Asalamalakim is going through motions with Maggie's hand. Maggie's hand is as limp as a fish, and probably as cold, despite the sweat, and she keeps trying to pull it back. It looks like Asalamalakim wants to shake hands but wants to do it fancy. Or maybe he don't know how people shake hands. Anyhow, he soon gives up on Maggie.

"Well," I say. "Dee."

"No, Mama," she says. "Not 'Dee,' Wangero Leewanika Kemanjo!"⁴

---

3. *Wa-su-zo-Tean-o!* (wä sōō´ zō tēn´o) and *Asalamalakim* (ä säl ä mä´ lä kēm) are greetings.
4. *Wangero Leewanika Kemanjo* (wän gär´ ō lē wä´ nē kə ke män´ jō)

"What happened to 'Dee'?" I wanted to know.

"She's dead," Wangero said. "I couldn't bear it any longer, being named after the people who **oppress** me."

"You know as well as me you was named after your aunt Dicie," I said. Dicie is my sister. She named Dee. We called her "Big Dee" after Dee was born.

"But who was *she* named after?" asked Wangero.

"I guess after Grandma Dee," I said.

"And who was she named after?" asked Wangero.

"Her mother," I said, and saw Wangero was getting tired. "That's about as far back as I can trace it," I said. Though, in fact, I probably could have carried it back beyond the Civil War through the branches.

"Well," said Asalamalakim, "there you are."

"Uhnnnh," I heard Maggie say.

"There I was not," I said, "before 'Dicie' cropped up in our family, so why should I try to trace it that far back?"

He just stood there grinning, looking down on me like somebody inspecting a Model A car. Every once in a while he and Wangero sent eye signals over my head.

Visual Vocabulary
The *Model A* was manufactured by the Ford Motor Company from 1927 to 1931.

Question How do you think Asalamalakim's comment makes Mama feel?

Reliable/Unreliable Narrator What is Mama's view of this conversation? What do you think Asalamalakim's view might be?

Vocabulary

oppress (ə pres´) *v.* to control or govern by the cruel or unjust use of force or authority

Giving Thanks, 1942. Horace Pippin.
The Barnes Foundation, Merion Station, PA.

View the Art Horace Pippin uses a primitive style with bold colors and flat forms to depict the everyday lives of African Americans, their history, and their struggle for equality. What elements from the story can you locate in this image?

"How do you pronounce this name?" I asked.

"You don't have to call me by it if you don't want to," said Wangero.

"Why shouldn't I?" I asked. "If that's what you want us to call you, we'll call you."

"I know it might sound awkward at first," said Wangero.

"I'll get used to it," I said. "Ream it out again."

Well, soon we got the name out of the way. Asalamalakim had a name twice as long and three times as hard. After I tripped over it two or three times he told me to just call him Hakim-a-barber.[5] I wanted to ask him was he a barber, but I didn't really think he was, so I didn't ask.

"You must belong to those beef cattle peoples down the road," I said. They said "Asalamalakim" when they met you, too, but they didn't shake hands. Always too busy: feeding the cattle, fixing the fences, putting up salt-lick shelters, throwing down hay. When the white folks poisoned some of the herd the men stayed up all night with rifles in their hands. I walked a mile and a half just to see the sight.

Hakim-a-barber said, "I accept some of their **doctrines,** but farming and raising cattle is not my style." (They didn't tell me, and I didn't ask, whether Wangero (Dee) had really gone and married him.)

We sat down to eat and right away he said he didn't eat collards and pork was unclean. Wangero, though, went on through the chitlins and corn bread, the greens and everything else. She talked a blue streak over the sweet potatoes. Everything delighted her. Even the fact

---

Reliable/Unreliable Narrator *From this narration of events, what impressions are you gaining of Asalamalakim? Explain.*

---

5. *Hakim-a-barber* (hä kēm′ ä bär′ bər)

Question *Do you think that Mama knew all along that Asalamalakim was a greeting, not a name? Explain.*

Vocabulary

doctrine (dok′ trin) *n.* a particular principle or position that is taught or supported, as of a religion

ALICE WALKER 193

that we still used the benches her daddy made for the table when we couldn't afford to buy chairs.

"Oh, Mama!" she cried. Then turned to Hakim-a-barber. "I never knew how lovely these benches are. You can feel the rump prints," she said, running her hands underneath her and along the bench. Then she gave a sigh and her hand closed over Grandma Dee's butter dish. "That's it!" she said. "I knew there was something I wanted to ask you if I could have." She jumped up from the table and went over in the corner where the churn stood, the milk in it clabber[6] by now. <mark>She looked at the churn and looked at it.</mark>

"This churn top is what I need," she said. "Didn't Uncle Buddy whittle it out of a tree you all used to have?"

"Yes," I said.

"Uh huh," she said happily. "And I want the dasher, too."

"Uncle Buddy whittle that, too?" <mark>asked the barber.</mark>

Dee (Wangero) looked up at me.

"Aunt Dee's first husband whittled the dash," said Maggie so low you almost couldn't hear her. "His name was Henry, but they called him Stash."

"Maggie's brain is like an elephant's," Wangero said, laughing. "I can use the churn top as a centerpiece for the alcove[7] table," she said, sliding a plate over the churn, "and I'll think of something artistic to do with the dasher."

---

6. *Clabber* is the thick, clotted part of sour milk.
7. An *alcove* (al´ kōv) is a small room or recessed opening off of a larger room.

<mark>**Life Transitions** Why is Dee so interested in these everyday objects?</mark>

<mark>**Reliable/Unreliable Narrator** Mama calls Hakim-a-barber "the barber." What does this reveal about her attitude toward him?</mark>

When she finished wrapping the dasher the handle stuck out. I took it for a moment in my hands. You didn't even have to look close to see where hands pushing the dasher up and down to make butter had left a kind of sink in the wood. In fact, there were a lot of small sinks; you could see where thumbs and fingers had sunk into the wood. It was beautiful light yellow wood, from a tree that grew in the yard where Big Dee and Stash had lived.

Visual Vocabulary
A *dasher* is part of a churn, an old-fashioned device for making butter.

After dinner Dee (Wangero) went to the trunk at the foot of my bed and started rifling through it. Maggie hung back in the kitchen over the dishpan. Out came Wangero with two quilts. They had been pieced by Grandma Dee and then Big Dee and me had hung them on the quilt frames on the front porch and quilted them. One was in the Lone Star pattern. The other was Walk Around the Mountain. In both of them were scraps of dresses Grandma Dee had worn fifty and more years ago. Bits and pieces of Grandpa Jarrell's Paisley shirts. And one teeny faded blue piece, about the size of a penny matchbox, that was from Great Grandpa Ezra's uniform that he wore in the Civil War.

"Mama," Wangero said sweet as a bird. "Can I have these old quilts?"

<mark>I heard something fall in the kitchen, and a minute later the kitchen door slammed.</mark>

Question Why might Maggie have slammed the kitchen door?

Quilts on the Line, 1994. Anna Belle Lee Washington. Oil on canvas, 20 x 30 in. National Museum of American Art, Washington, DC.
A former social worker, Anna Belle Lee Washington paints images that focus on connections between people. Quilts are a prominent feature in many of her paintings.

View the Art Compare and contrast the family and the setting of this painting with those in the story. What are the most striking differences? Similarities?

"Why don't you take one or two of the others?" I asked. "These old things was just done by me and Big Dee from some tops your grandma pieced before she died."

"No," said Wangero. "I don't want those. They are stitched around the borders by machine."

"That'll make them last better," I said.

"That's not the point," said Wangero. "These are all pieces of dresses Grandma used to wear. She did all this stitching by hand. Imagine!" She held the quilts securely in her arms, stroking them.

"Some of the pieces, like those lavender ones, come from old clothes her mother handed down to her," I said, moving up to touch the quilts. Dee (Wangero) moved back just enough so that I couldn't reach the quilts. They already belonged to her.

"Imagine!" she breathed again, clutching them closely to her bosom.

"The truth is," I said, "I promised to give them quilts to Maggie, for when she marries John Thomas."

She gasped like a bee had stung her.

"Maggie can't appreciate these quilts!" she said. "She'd probably be backward enough to put them to everyday use."

Reliable/Unreliable Narrator Would Dee explain her action the same way that Mama does? Do you judge Mama to be a reliable narrator at this point? Explain.

Life Transitions How does this passage suggest a fundamental difference in values between Dee, Mama, and Maggie?

ALICE WALKER

"I reckon she would," I said. "God knows I been saving 'em for long enough with nobody using 'em. I hope she will!" I didn't want to bring up how I had offered Dee (Wangero) a quilt when she went away to college. Then she had told me they were old-fashioned, out of style.

"But they're *priceless!*" she was saying now, furiously; for she has a temper. "Maggie would put them on the bed and in five years they'd be in rags. Less than that!"

"She can always make some more," I said. "Maggie knows how to quilt."

Dee (Wangero) looked at me with hatred. "You just will not understand. The point is these quilts, *these* quilts!"

"Well," I said, stumped. "What would *you* do with them?"

"Hang them," she said. As if that was the only thing you *could* do with quilts.

Maggie by now was standing in the door. I could almost hear the sound her feet made as they scraped over each other.

"She can have them, Mama," she said, like somebody used to never winning anything, or having anything reserved for her. "I can 'member Grandma Dee without the quilts."

I looked at her hard. She had filled her bottom lip with checkerberry snuff[8] and it gave her face a kind of dopey, hangdog look. It was Grandma Dee and Big Dee who taught her how to quilt herself. She stood there with her scarred hands hidden in the folds of her skirt. She looked at her sister with something like fear but she wasn't mad at her. This was Maggie's portion. This was the way she knew God to work.

When I looked at her like that something hit me in the top of my head and ran down to the soles of my feet. Just like when I'm in church and the spirit of God touches me and I get happy and shout. I did something I never had done before: hugged Maggie to me, then dragged her on into the room, snatched the quilts out of Miss Wangero's hands and dumped them into Maggie's lap. Maggie just sat there on my bed with her mouth open.

"Take one or two of the others," I said to Dee.

But she turned without a word and went out to Hakim-a-barber.

"You just don't understand," she said, as Maggie and I came out to the car.

"What don't I understand?" I wanted to know.

"Your heritage," she said. And then she turned to Maggie, kissed her, and said, "You ought to try to make something of yourself, too, Maggie. It's really a new day for us. But from the way you and Mama still live you'd never know it."

She put on some sunglasses that hid everything above the tip of her nose and her chin.

Maggie smiled; maybe at the sunglasses. But a real smile, not scared. After we watched the car dust settle I asked Maggie to bring me a dip of snuff. And then the two of us sat there just enjoying, until it was time to go in the house and go to bed. ∞

---

8. *Snuff* ('snəf) is finely ground tobacco that can be sniffed, snorted, placed against the gums or chewed. Checkerberry ('che-kər-ˌber-ē) is the fruit of the wintergreen plant.

Question Why does Dee want the quilts now, when she did not want to take one to college?

Life Transitions Why do you think Mama reacts this way?

Reliable/Unreliable Narrator How does Mama feel about the way Dee's visit ended? If Dee had been the narrator, how might the story have ended differently?

After You Read

Respond and Think Critically

Respond and Interpret

1. To whom would you have given the quilts? Explain.

2. (a) How does Mama describe each daughter before Dee's arrival? (b) How do you think Mama feels about Maggie and Dee based on these descriptions?

3. How does the origin of the quilts affect Maggie's and Dee's feelings about them?

Analyze and Evaluate

4. How might the story be different if the characters lived in another time and place?

5. How does the character of Hakim-a-barber make the story richer and more interesting?

Connect

6. **Big Idea** **Life Transitions** Mama does not like many of the ways that Dee has changed since leaving home. What is your opinion of the changes that Dee has undergone? Explain.

7. **Connect to Today** In the story, Dee's (Wangero's) bright African clothes, "Afro" hairstyle, and new name are linked to a social movement and certain political beliefs. Give examples of movements today that have certain styles of dress or behavior associated with them.

Literary Element Reliable/Unreliable Narrator

In "Everyday Use," Mama is the **narrator,** and everything the reader learns is from her point of view.

1. Why do you think the author chose Mama as the narrator?

2. In what ways is Mama a reliable narrator? In what ways might she be unreliable?

Reading Strategy Question

Review the chart you filled in as you read the text.

1. What are Walker's ideas about change and the clash between old and new ways?

2. Do you think Walker's goal was to give us a story with predictable answers? Explain.

LOG ON ▶ **Literature** Online

Selection Resources For Selection Quizzes, eFlashcards, and Reading-Writing Connection activities, go to glencoe.com and enter QuickPass code GL59794u1.

Vocabulary Practice

Practice with Usage Respond to these statements to help you explore the meanings of vocabulary words from the selection.

1. Describe what people do when they **sidle**.

2. Describe what a **furtive** person looks like or does.

3. Name two ways in which a government might **oppress** its citizens.

4. Identify a **doctrine** in which you believe.

Writing

Write a Character Sketch Write a description of Maggie's personality, using details from the story to support the points you make. Keep in mind that you need not accept Mama's interpretations of Maggie's actions.

ALICE WALKER   197

Comparing Literature
Across Genres

Learning Objectives

For pages 198–217

In studying these texts, you will focus on the following objectives:

Literary Study: Comparing across genres. Analyzing point of view.

Reading: Visualizing.

Compare Literature About Life's Lessons

How do writers and storytellers pass along lessons they have learned about life? The three literary works compared here—a short story, a legend, and a personal letter—each share wisdom.

Through the Tunnel by Doris Lessing............short story.................199

The Vision Quest by Lame Deer..............................legend................212

"Dear Pie" from *Rules to Live By*
by F. Scott Fitzgerald...letter.................215

COMPARE THE Big Idea Life Transitions

Young people setting off on their own, even for a short time, face challenges. The three selections you are about to read treat this theme in different ways. As you read, ask yourself, How do the young people in these selections find strength in their families, their cultures, and their own inner resources?

COMPARE Narrators

The relationship between the narrator and the literary work is the **narrative point of view.** In a letter or personal essay, the narrator always speaks in the first-person point of view. In fiction, the narrator can be inside or outside the story. A first-person narrator is a character who has access only to his or her own thoughts and feelings. A third-person narrator speaks to the reader from outside the story. As you read, ask yourself, How is the narrative point of view of each selection suited to the author's purpose?

COMPARE Authors' Cultures

The writers featured here share rites of passage within their cultures—rituals associated with a change in status for an individual. The rite of passage takes different forms in each of these selections: the first involves an individual, internal conflict; the second involves the relationship between an individual and his community; and the third involves fatherly advice to a teenage girl. As you read, ask yourself, What do these rites of passage have in common, and how are they different?

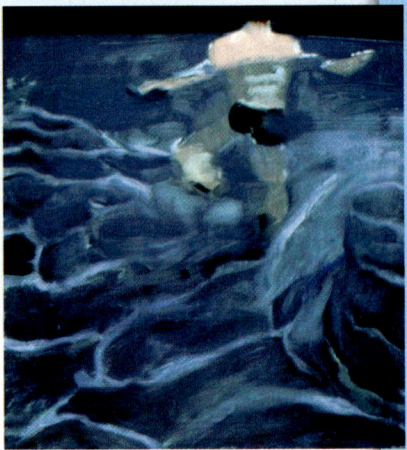

Figure In Water. Kari Van Tine.

LOG ON **Literature** Online

Author Search For more about the authors, go to glencoe.com and enter QuickPass code GL59794u1.

198 COMPARING LITERATURE

Before You Read

Through the Tunnel

World Literature: Zimbabwe

Meet Doris Lessing
(born 1919)

A theme of Lessing's life, starting fresh, took roots early. At the age of four, Lessing traveled with her parents on a transcontinental journey by train, leaving their home in Persia (now Iran) and traversing Russia, Europe, and England. From there, her family began their quest for a new life in Southern Rhodesia (now Zimbabwe).

Adjusting to Africa Doris's world as an energetic child was the African bush. She reveled in the land's wildlife, spaciousness, and smells. As was customary at the time for expatriates, Lessing was sent to boarding schools—first a convent and then to a British girls' school. There, the young teenager developed pinkeye. Even after she had fully recovered, Lessing insisted that her eyesight was ruined: her mother came and got her, and "that was the end of [her] life at school." Educating herself at home, Lessing developed her writing skills. Soon after, she sold her first story to a magazine. Her first novel, *The Grass Is Singing*, was published in 1950. Her early work draws heavily on her years in Africa.

Unaffected by Criticism Lessing's books have received mixed reviews. Critics have characterized her style as being "blunt," having "analytical purity," and possessing "frankness and clarity." The range of literary forms Lessing has tackled is impressive: short stories, fiction, nonfiction, "space fiction," essays, and plays. In 1962 Lessing published the controversial feminist novel *The Golden Notebook*. It quickly became a best seller. Her nonfiction books include *The Wind Blows away Our Words*, concerning the wars in Afghanistan during the 1980s, and *African Laughter: Four Visits to Zimbabwe*, an account of the new nation. Lessing was awarded the Nobel Prize in Literature in 2007.

> "That is what learning is. You suddenly understand something you've understood all your life, but in a new way."
>
> —Doris Lessing

Critic William Peden summed up Lessing's strengths: "She tells a story which can be read with delight and wonder . . . a meaningful commentary on one or another phase of the endlessly varied human experience."

Literature Online
Author Search For more about Doris Lessing, go to glencoe.com and enter QuickPass code GL59794u1.

DORIS LESSING 199

Comparing Literature

Literature and Reading Preview

Connect to the Story
Why do you think people challenge themselves to accomplish dangerous goals? List several difficult or challenging tasks or endeavors you have undertaken and explain their significance.

Build Background
The story takes place on the Mediterranean coast during the 1940s or 1950s. Here, boys dove off rocks and practiced breath-hold diving. This type of diving uses no equipment other than goggles or a facemask. Most breath-hold divers can remain submerged for less than one minute, although with training, some divers can stay underwater for several minutes.

Set Purposes for Reading

Big Idea Life Transitions

As you read, ask yourself, What is Jerry's personal challenge and why is this transition so important to him at this time in his life?

Literary Element Point of View

Point of view is the relationship of the narrator to the story. When a narrator in the third-person who is all-knowing tells a story, it is called **third-person omniscient point of view.** As you read, ask yourself, What does the point of view in this story reveal about the characters and events?

Reading Strategy Visualize

To **visualize** is to form a mental image of events and places in a story through the descriptive words that the writer uses to appeal to senses of sight, hearing, touch, taste, and smell. As you read, ask yourself, How is visualizing a scene a useful and effective way to remember and understand what I read?

Tip: Identify Sensory Descriptions Use a chart like the one below to record Jerry's description of his tunnel experience and the corresponding senses.

Descriptive Phrases	Sense
"hot roughness"	touch
"fanged and angry boulders"	sight

Vocabulary

conscientiously (kon′shē en′shəs lē) *adv.* thoughtfully and carefully; p. 201 *Slowly and conscientiously, the jury examined the evidence.*

contrition (kən trish′ən) *n.* sorrow for one's sin or wrongdoing; repentance; p. 201 *A thief who shows contrition is on his way to being reformed.*

supplication (sup′lə kā′shən) *n.* an earnest and humble request; p. 203 *After numerous supplications, the downtrodden man was finally given a job.*

beseeching (bi sēch′ing) *adj.* begging; asking earnestly; p. 206 *The homeless woman raised beseeching hands to all who passed by.*

incredulous (in krej′ə ləs) *adj.* unwilling or unable to believe; p. 208 *We were incredulous at the child's story of the candy-stealing ghost.*

Tip: Antonyms You can find Internet sites that list antonyms by entering *antonyms* and other search terms such as *reference* and *thesaurus* into a search box.

Comparing Literature

Through the Tunnel

Doris Lessing

Beach. Bobbi Tull.

Going to the shore on the first morning of the vacation, the young English boy stopped at a turning of the path and looked down at a wild and rocky bay, and then over to the crowded beach he knew so well from other years. His mother walked on in front of him, carrying a bright striped bag in one hand. Her other arm, swinging loose, was very white in the sun. The boy watched that white, naked arm, and turned his eyes, which had a frown behind them, toward the bay and back again to his mother. When she felt he was not with her, she swung around. "Oh, there you are, Jerry!" she said. She looked impatient, then smiled. "Why, darling, would you rather not come with me? Would you rather—"

She frowned, **conscientiously** worrying over what amusements he might secretly be longing for, which she had been too busy or too careless to imagine. He was very familiar with that anxious, apologetic smile. **Contrition** sent him running after her. And yet, as he ran, he looked back over his shoulder at the wild bay; and all

Point of View By expressing Jerry's and his mother's perspectives here, how does the narrator help you understand the mother's character?

Vocabulary

conscientiously (kon′ shē en′ shəs lē) *adv.* thoughtfully and carefully

contrition (kən trish′ ən) *n.* sorrow for one's sin or wrongdoing; repentance

DORIS LESSING 201

Comparing Literature

morning, as he played on the safe beach, he was thinking of it.

Next morning, when it was time for the routine of swimming and sunbathing, his mother said, "Are you tired of the usual beach, Jerry? Would you like to go somewhere else?"

"Oh, no!" he said quickly, smiling at her out of that unfailing impulse of contrition—a sort of chivalry.[1] Yet, walking down the path with her, he blurted out, "I'd like to go and have a look at those rocks down there."

She gave the idea her attention. It was a wild looking place, and there was no one there; but she said, "Of course, Jerry. When you've had enough, come to the big beach. Or just go straight back to the villa,[2] if you like." She walked away, that bare arm, now slightly reddened from yesterday's sun, swinging. And he almost ran after her again, feeling it unbearable that she should go by herself, but he did not.

She was thinking, Of course he's old enough to be safe without me. Have I been keeping him too close? He mustn't feel he ought to be with me. I must be careful.

He was an only child, eleven years old. She was a widow. She was determined to be neither possessive nor lacking in devotion. She went worrying off to her beach.

As for Jerry, once he saw that his mother had gained her beach, he began the steep descent to the bay. From where he was, high up among red-brown rocks, it was a scoop of moving bluish green fringed with white. As he went lower, he saw that it spread among small promontories and inlets of rough, sharp rock, and the crisping, lapping surface showed stains of purple and darker blue. Finally, as he ran sliding and scraping down the last few yards, he saw an edge of white surf and the shallow, luminous movement of water over white sand, and, beyond that, a solid, heavy blue.

He ran straight into the water and began swimming. He was a good swimmer. He went out fast over the gleaming sand, over a middle region where rocks lay like discolored monsters under the surface, and then he was in the real sea—a warm sea where irregular cold currents from the deep water shocked his limbs.

When he was so far out that he could look back not only on the little bay but past the promontory that was between it and the big beach, he floated on the buoyant surface and looked for his mother. There she was, a speck of yellow under an umbrella that looked like a slice of orange peel. He swam back to shore, relieved at being sure she was there, but all at once very lonely.

On the edge of a small cape that marked the side of the bay away from the promontory was a loose scatter of rocks. Above them, some boys were stripping off their clothes. They came running, naked, down to the rocks. The English boy swam

Visual Vocabulary
Promontories are high points of land or rock overlooking the water.

---

1. Here, *chivalry* (shiv′ əl rē) means "an act of courtesy or politeness."
2. *Villa*, from the Italian word, means "house," usually one in the country or at the seashore.

Visualize What mental picture does the word "wild" provoke? How does it contrast with the beach where the characters swim and sunbathe?

Point of View Here, the omniscient narrator reveals the mother's concerns. What internal conflict might she be experiencing?

Figure In Water. Kari Van Tine.

View the Art The dark atmosphere of this painting contrasts with the sunny days when Jerry attempts his feat. How might this dark mood relate to Jerry's obsessive and potentially self-destructive desire to emulate the older boys?

toward them, but kept his distance at a stone's throw. They were of that coast; all of them were burned smooth dark brown and speaking a language he did not understand. To be with them, of them, was a craving that filled his whole body. He swam a little closer; they turned and watched him with narrowed, alert dark eyes. Then one smiled and waved. It was enough. In a minute, he had swum in and was on the rocks beside them, smiling with a desperate, nervous **supplication**. They shouted cheerful greetings at him; and then, as he preserved his nervous, uncomprehending smile, they understood that he was a foreigner strayed from his own beach, and they proceeded to forget him. But he was happy. He was with them.

They began diving again and again from a high point into a well of blue sea between rough, pointed rocks. After they had dived and come up, they swam around, hauled themselves up, and waited their turn to dive again. They were big boys—men, to Jerry. He dived, and they watched him; and when he swam around to take his place, they made way for him. He felt he was accepted, and he dived again, carefully, proud of himself.

Soon the biggest of the boys poised himself, shot down into the water, and did not come up. The others stood about, watching. Jerry, after waiting for the sleek brown head to appear, let out a yell of warning;

Life Transitions Why might Jerry value the boys' acceptance so much?

Vocabulary

supplication (sup′ lə kā′ shən) *n.* an earnest and humble request

Comparing Literature

School of Fish, 1991. John Bunker. Mixed media.

they looked at him idly and turned their eyes back toward the water. After a long time, the boy came up on the other side of a big dark rock, letting the air out of his lungs in a sputtering gasp and a shout of triumph. Immediately the rest of them dived in. One moment, the morning seemed full of chattering boys; the next, the air and the surface of the water were empty. But through the heavy blue, dark shapes could be seen moving and groping.

Jerry dived, shot past the school of underwater swimmers, saw a black wall of rock looming at him, touched it, and bobbed up at once to the surface, where the wall was a low barrier he could see across. There was no one visible; under him, in the water, the dim shapes of the swimmers had disappeared. Then one, and then another of the boys came up on the far side of the barrier of rock, and he understood that they had swum through some gap or hole in it. He plunged down again. He could see nothing through the stinging salt water but the blank rock. When he came up the boys were all on the diving rock, preparing to attempt the feat again. And now, in a panic of failure, he yelled up, in English, "Look at me! Look!" and he began splashing and kicking in the water like a foolish dog.

They looked down gravely, frowning. He knew the frown. At moments of failure, when he clowned to claim his mother's attention, it was with just this grave, embarrassed inspection that she rewarded him. Through his hot shame, feeling the pleading grin on his face like a scar that he could never remove, he looked up at the group of big brown boys on the rock and

Point of View *The narrator explains Jerry's response to failure with a simile. What does this figure of speech imply about Jerry?*

shouted, *"Bonjour! Merci! Au revoir! Monsieur, monsieur!"*[3] while he hooked his fingers round his ears and waggled them.

Water surged into his mouth; he choked, sank, came up. The rock, lately weighted with boys, seemed to rear up out of the water as their weight was removed. They were flying down past him, now, into the water; the air was full of falling bodies. Then the rock was empty in the hot sunlight. He counted one, two, three. . . .

At fifty, he was terrified. They must all be drowning beneath him, in the watery caves of the rock! At a hundred, he stared around him at the empty hillside, wondering if he should yell for help. He counted faster, faster, to hurry them up, to bring them to the surface quickly, to drown them quickly—anything rather than the terror of counting on and on into the blue emptiness of the morning. And then, at a hundred and sixty, the water beyond the rock was full of boys blowing like brown whales. They swam back to the shore without a look at him.

He climbed back to the diving rock and sat down, feeling the hot roughness of it under his thighs. The boys were gathering up their bits of clothing and running off along the shore to another promontory. They were leaving to get away from him. He cried openly, fists in his eyes. There was no one to see him, and he cried himself out.

It seemed to him that a long time had passed, and he swam out to where he could see his mother. Yes, she was still

---

3. *"Bonjour! . . . monsieur!"* These words are French for "Hello! Thanks! Good-bye! Sir, sir!"

Visualize What mental image do you have of "boys blowing like brown whales"?

Comparing Literature

there, a yellow spot under an orange umbrella. He swam back to the big rock, climbed up, and dived into the blue pool among the fanged and angry boulders. Down he went, until he touched the wall of rock again. But the salt was so painful in his eyes that he could not see.

He came to the surface, swam to shore, and went back to the villa to wait for his mother. Soon she walked slowly up the path, swinging her striped bag, the flushed, naked arm dangling beside her. "I want some swimming goggles," he panted, defiant and **beseeching**.

She gave him a patient, inquisitive look as she said casually, "Well, of course, darling."

But now, now, now! He must have them this minute, and no other time. He nagged and pestered until she went with him to a shop. As soon as she had bought the goggles, he grabbed them from her hand as if she were going to claim them for herself, and was off, running down the steep path to the bay.

Jerry swam out to the big barrier rock, adjusted the goggles, and dived. The impact of the water broke the rubber-enclosed vacuum, and the goggles came loose. He understood that he must swim down to the base of the rock from the surface of the water. He fixed the goggles tight and firm, filled his lungs, and floated, face down, on the water. Now, he could see. It was as if he had eyes of a different kind—fish eyes that showed everything clear and delicate and wavering in the bright water.

Under him, six or seven feet down, was a floor of perfectly clean, shining white sand, rippled firm and hard by the tides. Two grayish shapes steered there, like long, rounded pieces of wood or slate. They were fish. He saw them nose toward each other, poise motionless, make a dart forward, swerve off, and come around again. It was like a water dance. A few inches above them the water sparkled as if sequins were dropping through it. Fish again—myriads of minute fish, the length of his fingernail, were drifting through the water, and in a moment he could feel the innumerable tiny touches of them against his limbs. It was like swimming in flaked silver. The great rock the big boys had swum through rose sheer out of the white sand—black, tufted lightly with greenish weed. He could see no gap in it. He swam down to its base.

Again and again he rose, took a big chestful of air, and went down. Again and again he groped over the surface of the rock, feeling it, almost hugging it in the desperate need to find the entrance. And then, once, while he was clinging to the black wall, his knees came up, and he shot his feet out forward and they met no obstacle. He had found the hole.

He gained the surface, clambered about the stones that littered the barrier rock until he found a big one, and, with this in his arms, let himself down over the side of the rock. He dropped, with the weight, straight to the sandy floor.

Clinging tight to the anchor of stone, he lay on his side and looked in under the dark shelf at the place where his feet had gone. He could see the hole. It was an irregular, dark gap; but he could not see deep into it. He let go of his anchor, clung

---

Visualize What mental image does "fanged and angry" help you create?

Vocabulary

beseeching (bi sēch′ ing) *adj.* begging; asking earnestly

with his hands to the edges of the hole, and tried to push himself in.

He got his head in, found his shoulders jammed, moved them in sidewise, and was inside as far as his waist. He could see nothing ahead. Something soft and clammy touched his mouth; he saw a dark frond[4] moving against the grayish rock, and panic filled him. He thought of octopuses, of clinging weed. He pushed himself out backward and caught a glimpse, as he retreated, of a harmless tentacle of seaweed drifting in the mouth of the tunnel. But it was enough. He reached the sunlight, swam to shore, and lay on the diving rock. He looked down into the blue well of water. He knew he must find his way through that cave, or hole, or tunnel, and out the other side.

Visual Vocabulary
A *tentacle* is a long, flexible limb that could belong to a plant or to a creature such as an octopus.

First, he thought, he must learn to control his breathing. He let himself down into the water with another big stone in his arms, so that he could lie effortlessly on the bottom of the sea. He counted. One, two, three. He counted steadily. He could hear the movement of blood in his chest. Fifty-one, fifty-two. . . . His chest was hurting. He let go of the rock and went up into the air. He saw that the sun was low. He rushed to the villa and found his mother at her supper. She said only, "Did you enjoy yourself?" and he said, "Yes."

All night the boy dreamed of the water-filled cave in the rock, and as soon as breakfast was over he went to the bay.

That night, his nose bled badly. For hours he had been underwater, learning to hold his breath, and now he felt weak and dizzy. His mother said, "I shouldn't overdo things, darling, if I were you."

That day and the next, Jerry exercised his lungs as if everything, the whole of his life, all that he would become, depended upon it. Again his nose bled at night, and his mother insisted on his coming with her the next day. It was a torment to him to waste a day of his careful self training, but he stayed with her on that other beach, which now seemed a place for small children, a place where his mother might lie safe in the sun. It was not his beach.

He did not ask for permission, on the following day, to go to his beach. He went, before his mother could consider the complicated rights and wrongs of the matter. A day's rest, he discovered, had improved his count by ten. The big boys had made the passage while he counted a hundred and sixty. He had been counting fast, in his fright. Probably now, if he tried, he could get through that long tunnel, but he was not going to try yet. A curious, most unchildlike persistence, a controlled impatience, made him wait. In the meantime, he lay underwater on the white sand, littered now by stones he had brought down from the upper air, and studied the entrance to the tunnel. He knew every jut and corner of it, as far as it was possible to see. It was as if he already felt its sharpness about his shoulders.

He sat by the clock in the villa, when his mother was not near, and checked his time.

---

4. A *frond* is a large leaf with many divisions, or a leaf-like part of a plant such as seaweed.

Life Transitions In what ways will this feat be a transition for Jerry?

Point of View What sort of change in Jerry's character is the narrator describing here?

Comparing Literature

He was **incredulous** and then proud to find he could hold his breath without strain for two minutes. The words "two minutes," authorized by the clock, brought close the adventure that was so necessary to him.

In another four days, his mother said casually one morning, they must go home. On the day before they left, he would do it. He would do it if it killed him, he said defiantly to himself. But two days before they were to leave—a day of triumph when he increased his count by fifteen—his nose bled so badly that he turned dizzy and had to lie limply over the big rock like a bit of seaweed, watching the thick red blood flow on to the rock and trickle slowly down to the sea. He was frightened. Supposing he turned dizzy in the tunnel? Supposing he died there, trapped? Supposing—his head went around, in the hot sun, and he almost gave up. He thought he would return to the house and lie down, and next summer, perhaps, when he had another year's growth in him—*then* he would go through the hole.

But even after he had made the decision, or thought he had, he found himself sitting up on the rock and looking down into the water; and he knew that now, this moment, when his nose had only just stopped bleeding, when his head was still sore and throbbing—this was the moment when he would try. If he did not do it now, he never would. He was trembling with fear that he would not go; and he was trembling with horror at that long, long tunnel under the rock, under the sea. Even in the open sunlight, the barrier rock seemed very wide and very heavy; tons of rock pressed down on where he would go. If he died there, he would lie until one day—perhaps not before next year—those big boys would swim into it and find it blocked.

He put on his goggles, fitted them tight, tested the vacuum. His hands were shaking. Then he chose the biggest stone he could carry and slipped over the edge of the rock until half of him was in the cool, enclosing water and half in the hot sun. He looked up once at the empty sky, filled his lungs once, twice, and then sank fast to the bottom with the stone. He let it go and began to count. He took the edges of the hole in his hands and drew himself into it, wriggling his shoulders in sidewise as he remembered he must, kicking himself along with his feet.

Soon he was clear inside. He was in a small rock-bound hole filled with yellowish-gray water. The water was pushing him up against the roof. The roof was sharp and pained his back. He pulled himself along with his hands—fast, fast—and used his legs as levers. His head knocked against something; a sharp pain dizzied him. Fifty, fifty-one, fifty-two. . . . He was without light, and the water seemed to press upon him with the weight of rock. Seventy-one, seventy-two. . . . There was no strain on his lungs. He felt like an inflated balloon, his lungs were so light and easy, but his head was pulsing.

He was being continually pressed against the sharp roof, which felt slimy as well as sharp. Again he thought of octopuses, and wondered if the tunnel might be filled with weed that could tangle him. He gave himself a panicky, convulsive kick forward, ducked his head, and swam.

Point of View How realistic and convincing is Jerry's internal conflict?

Vocabulary

incredulous (in krej′ ə ləs) *adj.* unwilling or unable to believe

Visualize To what senses do the words and images in this sentence appeal?

Rocky Sea Shore, 1916–1919. Edward Hopper. Oil on canvas panel, 9½ x 12¹⁵⁄₁₆ in. Collection of Whitney Museum of American Art, New York. Josephine N. Hopper Bequest. 70.166.

View the Art This panoramic view appears as if seen from a promontory or cliff. How do the scale and point of view in this painting compare with the point of view in the story? How would the story be different if it were told from the point of view that Hopper adopts for this painting?

His feet and hands moved freely, as if in open water. The hole must have widened out. He thought he must be swimming fast, and he was frightened of banging his head if the tunnel narrowed.

A hundred, a hundred and one. . . . The water paled. Victory filled him. His lungs were beginning to hurt. A few more strokes and he would be out. He was counting wildly; he said a hundred and fifteen, and then, a long time later, a hundred and fifteen again. The water was a clear jewel-green all around him. Then he saw, above his head, a crack running up through the rock. Sunlight was falling through it, showing the clean, dark rock of the tunnel, a single mussel shell, and darkness ahead.

He was at the end of what he could do. He looked up at the crack as if it were filled with air and not water, as if he could put his mouth to it to draw in air. A hundred and fifteen, he

Visual Vocabulary
A *mussel* is a kind of shellfish. Mussels are in the same scientific classification as clams, oysters, and scallops.

Comparing Literature

heard himself say inside his head—but he had said that long ago. He must go on into the blackness ahead, or he would drown. His head was swelling, his lungs cracking. A hundred and fifteen, a hundred and fifteen pounded through his head, and he feebly clutched at rocks in the dark, pulling himself forward, leaving the brief space of sunlit water behind. He felt he was dying. He was no longer quite conscious. He struggled on in the darkness between lapses into unconsciousness. An immense, swelling pain filled his head, and then the darkness cracked with an explosion of green light. His hands, groping forward, met nothing; and his feet, kicking back, propelled him out into the open sea.

He drifted to the surface, his face turned up to the air. He was gasping like a fish. He felt he would sink now and drown; he could not swim the few feet back to the rock. Then he was clutching it and pulling himself up on to it. He lay face down, gasping. He could see nothing but a red-veined, clotted dark. His eyes must have burst, he thought; they were full of blood. He tore off his goggles and a gout[5] of blood went into the sea. His nose was bleeding, and the blood had filled the goggles.

He scooped up handfuls of water from the cool, salty sea, to splash on his face, and did not know whether it was blood or salt water he tasted. After a time, his heart quieted, his eyes cleared, and he sat up. He could see the local boys diving and playing half a mile away. He did not want them. He wanted nothing but to get back home and lie down.

In a short while, Jerry swam to shore and climbed slowly up the path to the villa. He flung himself on his bed and slept, waking at the sound of feet on the path outside. His mother was coming back. He rushed to the bathroom, thinking she must not see his face with bloodstains, or tearstains, on it. He came out of the bathroom and met her as she walked into the villa, smiling, her eyes lighting up.

"Have a nice morning?" she asked, laying her hand on his warm brown shoulder a moment.

"Oh, yes, thank you," he said.

"You look a bit pale." And then, sharp and anxious, "How did you bang your head?"

"Oh, just banged it," he told her.

She looked at him closely. He was strained; his eyes were glazed-looking. She was worried. And then she said to herself, Oh, don't fuss! Nothing can happen. He can swim like a fish.

They sat down to lunch together.

"Mummy," he said, "I can stay under water for two minutes—three minutes, at least." It came bursting out of him.

"Can you, darling?" she said. "Well, I shouldn't overdo it. I don't think you ought to swim any more today."

She was ready for a battle of wills, but he gave in at once. It was no longer of the least importance to go to the bay.

---

5. Here, *gout* refers to a mass of fluid that gushes or bursts forth.

Life Transitions Why is Jerry no longer interested in the local boys?

Life Transitions Why do you think Jerry kept his triumph of swimming through the tunnel to himself?

After You Read

Respond and Think Critically

Respond and Interpret

1. (a) How would you have challenged yourself if you had been in Jerry's place? (b) With whom would you have shared your experience?

2. (a) Summarize what Jerry does when he goes to the beach the second time. (b) Why do you think Jerry decides that he must go through the tunnel?

3. (a) How is Jerry's preparation unlike the real test? (b) In your opinion, what is the most dramatic moment of Jerry's actual test? Explain.

Analyze and Evaluate

4. (a) How would you describe the mother's feelings toward Jerry? (b) Do you think Lessing makes the mother a realistic character? Why or why not?

5. (a) How has Lessing made Jerry's decision to go through the tunnel seem credible or genuine? (b) Does it seem believable that Jerry does not tell his mother what he has accomplished?

Connect

6. **Big Idea** Life Transitions Both Jerry and his mother go through a major transition in this story. How is each character's response to the other helpful to these transitions?

7. **Connect to the Author** Doris Lessing spent many years living in Persia and Southern Rhodesia before settling in England in 1949. How might her experiences as an expatriate have informed "Through the Tunnel"?

Literary Element Point of View

A **third-person omniscient narrator** can give us insight into all characters by revealing and interpreting their deepest thoughts and feelings.

1. In the story's first paragraph, how does Lessing use the third-person omniscient point of view?

2. How did Lessing's point of view in this story make its telling more effective?

Reading Strategy Visualize

Visualizing the scenes and events in the story can help increase your understanding of their meaning.

1. What does Jerry experience as he swims through the tunnel?

2. The narrator never describes Jerry's physical appearance. How do you visualize Jerry?

LOG ON **Literature** Online

Selection Resources For Selection Quizzes, eFlashcards, and Reading-Writing Connection activities, go to glencoe.com and enter QuickPass code GL59794u1.

Vocabulary

Practice with Antonyms An antonym is a word that has a meaning opposite to that of another word. With a partner, match each boldfaced vocabulary word below with its antonym. You will not use all the answer choices. Then use a thesaurus or dictionary to check your answers.

1. conscientiously
2. contrition
3. supplication
4. beseeching
5. incredulous

a. demanding
b. consistency
c. revelation
d. certain
e. edict
f. remorselessness
g. carelessly

Writing

Write a Letter Was Jerry brave or foolish in swimming through the tunnel? Write a letter to Jerry in which you express your opinion of his venture.

Comparing Literature

Build Background

Lame Deer is a spiritual name that has been handed down from father to son in one Sioux family. Richard Erdoes met John Fire Lame Deer in 1967 and recorded this story.

THE VISION QUEST

Told by Lame Deer
Recorded by Richard Erdoes

Mountain Spirit. Stephan Daige.

A young man wanted to go on a *hanbleceya,* or vision seeking, to try for a dream that would give him the power to be a great medicine man. Having a high opinion of himself, he felt sure that he had been created to become great among his people and that the only thing lacking was a vision.

The young man was daring and brave, eager to go up to the mountaintop. He had been brought up by good, honest people who were wise in the ancient ways and who prayed for him. All through the winter they were busy getting him ready, feeding him wasna,[1] corn, and plenty of good meat to make him strong. At every

---

1. *Wasna* is a high-energy food made of meat, fat, and berries pounded together.

212 UNIT 1 THE SHORT STORY

Visual Vocabulary
A *travois* (trə voi′) is a V-shaped sled made of hide or netting supported by two long poles that are harnessed to a horse or dog.

meal they set aside something for the spirits so that they would help him to get a great vision. His relatives thought he had the power even before he went up, but that was putting the cart before the horse, or rather the travois before the horse, as this is an Indian legend.

When at last he started on his quest, it was a beautiful morning in late spring. The grass was up, the leaves were out, nature was at its best. Two medicine men accompanied him.

Visual Vocabulary
A *sweat lodge* is a hut in which steam is produced by pouring or sprinkling water over red-hot rocks contained in a central pit.

They put up a sweat lodge to purify him in the hot, white breath of the sacred steam. They sanctified him with the incense of sweet grass, rubbing his body with sage, fanning it with an eagle's wing. They went to the hilltop with him to prepare the vision pit and make an offering of tobacco bundles. Then they told the young man to cry, to humble himself, to ask for holiness, to cry for power, for a sign from the Great Spirit, for a gift which would make him into a medicine man. After they had done all they could, they left him there.

He spent the first night in the hole the medicine men had dug for him, trembling and crying out loudly. Fear kept him awake, yet he was cocky, ready to wrestle with the spirits for the vision, the power he wanted. But no dreams came to ease his mind. Toward morning before the sun came up, he heard a voice in the swirling white mists of dawn. Speaking from no particular direction, as if it came from different places, it said: "See here, young man, there are other spots you could have picked; there are other hills around here. Why don't you go there to cry for a dream? You disturbed us all night, all us creatures and birds; you even kept the trees awake. We couldn't sleep. Why should you cry here? You're a brash young man, not yet ready or worthy to receive a vision."

But the young man clenched his teeth, determined to stick it out, resolved to force that vision to come. He spent another day in the pit, begging for enlightenment which would not come, and then another night of fear and cold and hunger.

When dawn arrived once more, he heard the voice again: "Stop disturbing us; go away!" The same thing happened the third morning. By this time he was faint with hunger, thirst, and anxiety. Even the air seemed to oppress him, to fight him. He was panting. His stomach felt shriveled up, shrunk tight against his backbone. But he was determined to endure one more night, the fourth and last. Surely the vision would come. But again he cried for it out of the dark and loneliness until he was hoarse, and still he had no dream.

Just before daybreak he heard the same voice again, very angry: "Why are you still here?" He knew then that he had suffered in vain; now he would have to go back to his people and confess that he had gained no knowledge and no power. The only thing he could tell them was that he got bawled out every morning. Sad and cross, he replied, "I can't help myself; this is my last day, and

Comparing Literature

I'm crying my eyes out. I know you told me to go home, but who are you to give me orders? I don't know you. I'm going to stay until my uncles come to fetch me, whether you like it or not."

All at once there was a rumble from a larger mountain that stood behind the hill. It became a mighty roar, and the whole hill trembled. The wind started to blow. The young man looked up and saw a boulder poised on the mountain's summit. He saw lightning hit it, saw it sway. Slowly the boulder moved. Slowly at first, then faster and faster, it came tumbling down the mountainside, churning up earth, snapping huge trees as if they were little twigs. And the boulder was coming right down on him!

The young man cried out in terror. He was paralyzed with fear, unable to move. The boulder dwarfed everything in view; it towered over the vision pit. But just as it was an arm's length away and about to crush him, it stopped. Then, as the young man stared open-mouthed, his hair standing up, his eyes starting out of his head, the boulder *rolled up the mountain,* all the way to the top. He could hardly believe what he saw. He was still cowering motionless when he heard the roar and rumble again and saw that immense boulder coming down at him once more. This time he managed to jump out of his vision pit at the last moment. The boulder crushed it, obliterated it, grinding the young man's pipe and gourd rattle into dust.

Again the boulder rolled up the mountain, and again it came down. "I'm leaving, I'm leaving!" hollered the young man. Regaining his power of motion, he scrambled down the hill as fast as he could. This time the boulder actually leap-frogged over him, bouncing down the slope, crushing and pulverizing everything in its way. He ran unseeingly, stumbling, falling, getting up again. He did not even notice the boulder rolling up once more and coming down for the fourth time. On this last and most fearful descent, it flew through the air in a giant leap, landing right in front of him and embedding itself so deeply in the earth that only its top was visible. The ground shook itself like a wet dog coming out of a stream and flung the young man this way and that.

Gaunt, bruised, and shaken, he stumbled back to his village. To the medicine men he said: "I have received no vision and gained no knowledge. I have made the spirits angry. It was all for nothing."

"Well, you did find out one thing," said the older of the two, who was his uncle. "You went after your vision like a hunter after buffalo, or a warrior after scalps. You were fighting the spirits. You thought they owed you a vision. Suffering alone brings no vision nor does courage, nor does sheer will power. A vision comes as a gift born of humility, of wisdom, and of patience. If from your vision quest you have learned nothing but this, then you have already learned much. Think about it." ∽

Discussion Starter

Can an experience be useful even if you fail to reach your goal? Discuss this question in a small group. List some benefits a person might get from an experience even if the original goal is not reached. Use specific details from the legend to support your opinions. Then share your conclusions with the rest of the class.

Build Background

In the summer of 1933, F. Scott Fitzgerald was in Maryland working on his novel *Tender Is the Night*. His wife was being treated for the mental illness that would last the rest of her life. During that time he wrote the following letter to their beloved daughter, Scottie, who was twelve years old and away at summer camp.

Dear Pie

F. Scott Fitzgerald to
Frances Scott "Scottie" Fitzgerald

La Paix, Rodgers' Forge,
Towson, Maryland,
August 8, 1933.

Dear Pie:

I feel very strongly about you doing duty. Would you give me a little more documentation about your reading in French? I am glad you are happy—but I never believe much in happiness. I never believe in misery either. Those are things you see on the stage or the screen or the printed page, they never really happen to you in life.

All I believe in in life is the rewards for virtue (according to your talents) and the *punishments* for not fulfilling your duties, which are doubly costly. If there is such a volume in the camp library, will you ask Mrs. Tyson to let you look up a sonnet of Shakespeare's in which the line occurs *"Lilies that fester smell far worse than weeds."*

Have had no thoughts today, life seems composed of getting up a *Saturday Evening Post* story. I think of you, and always pleasantly; but if you call me "Pappy" again I am going to take the

Comparing Literature

American novelist F. Scott Fitzgerald, his wife Zelda, and daughter, Scottie, go for a motor jaunt in Italy.

White Cat out and beat his bottom *hard, six times for every time you are impertinent.* Do you react to that?

> I will arrange the camp bill. Halfwit, I will conclude. Things to worry about:

Worry about courage
Worry about cleanliness
Worry about efficiency
Worry about horsemanship
Worry about . . .

Things not to worry about:

Don't worry about popular opinion
Don't worry about dolls
Don't worry about the past
Don't worry about the future
Don't worry about growing up
Don't worry about anybody getting ahead of you
Don't worry about triumph
Don't worry about failures unless it comes through your own fault
Don't worry about mosquitoes
Don't worry about flies
Don't worry about insects in general
Don't worry about parents

Don't worry about boys
Don't worry about disappointments
Don't worry about pleasures
Don't worry about satisfactions

Things to think about:

What am I really aiming at?
How good am I really in comparison to my contemporaries in regard to:
(a) Scholarship
(b) Do I really understand about people and am I able to get along with them?
(c) Am I trying to make my body a useful instrument or am I neglecting it?

With dearest love,

   P.S. My come-back to your calling me Pappy is christening you by the word Egg, which implies that you belong to a very rudimentary state of life and that I could break you up and crack you open at my will and I think it would be a word that would hang on if I ever told it to your contemporaries. "Egg Fitzgerald." How would you like that to go through life with "Eggie Fitzgerald" or "Bad Egg Fitzgerald" or any form that might occur to fertile minds? Try it once more and I swear to God I will hang it on you and it will be up to you to shake it off. Why borrow trouble?

   Love anyhow.

> **Quickwrite**
>
> Fitzgerald writes that he does not believe much in happiness or misery, only in rewards and punishments. Do you agree or disagree with his opinion? Reread the first two paragraphs of the letter and write a paragraph explaining your views.

Wrap-Up: Comparing Literature
Across Genres

- *Through the Tunnel* by Doris Lessing
- *The Vision Quest* by Lame Deer
- *Dear Pie* by F. Scott Fitzgerald

COMPARE THE **Big Idea** Life Transitions

Write Make two three-column charts with the following headings: Things to Worry About, Things Not to Worry About, Things to Think About. Then fill in one chart to give to the boy in "Through the Tunnel" and the other to give to the young man in "The Vision Quest." What wisdom can you share with each to help them through their life transitions?

COMPARE Narrator

Group Activity "Through the Tunnel" is told from a **third-person omniscient**, or all-knowing, **point of view**. "The Vision Quest," in which the narrator reveals the thoughts and feelings of only one character, has a **third-person limited point of view**. "Dear Pie," a personal letter, has a **first-person point of view**. In a group, discuss the following questions.

1. How would "Through the Tunnel" be different if it had a first-person point of view?
2. Even though the narrator of "Dear Pie" is writing about his daughter, what do you learn about him? Do you think he is a good parent?
3. Suppose that someone else had accompanied the young man on his vision quest and had written about it. From what point of view would the account be written? How would the story be different?

COMPARE Authors' Cultures

Write an Analysis The characters in "Through the Tunnel" and "The Vision Quest" experienced rites of passage. Investigate initiation customs of a society or a group. Write an analysis comparing the customs you studied with those of the culture in one of the stories. Plan by charting your main points.

Initiation Customs of (society or group)	Initiation Customs in ("The Tunnel" or "The Vision Quest")	Comparison of Initiation Customs

Before You Read

Catch the Moon

Meet Judith Ortiz Cofer
(born 1952)

"Latina wherever I am," is the way Judith Ortiz Cofer sees herself. When she was a child, her family moved from her birthplace of Puerto Rico to Paterson, New Jersey. However, they made frequent trips back to Puerto Rico, so she always felt close to her cultural roots. She has a childhood memory of sitting in her grandmother's living room, which was furnished with mahogany rocking chairs. "It was on these rockers that my mother, her sisters and my grandmother sat on these afternoons of my childhood to tell their stories, teaching each other and my cousin and me what it was like to be a woman, more specifically, a Puerto Rican woman."

> "I write in English, yet I write obsessively about my Puerto Rican experience."
> —Judith Ortiz Cofer

Bilingual Advantage Early on, Cofer experienced a disadvantage of the family's frequent moving. Cofer was teased for having "a Spanish accent when [she] spoke English; and, when [she] spoke Spanish, [she] was told that [she] sounded like a 'Gringa.'" Cofer transformed this into an advantage when she began writing fiction and poetry. Writer Marian C. Gonsior says that Cofer deals with "the effect on Puerto Rican Americans of living in a world split between the island culture of their homeland and the teeming tenement life of the United States." After receiving her bachelor's degree from Augusta College in Georgia, Cofer began her long teaching career, first as a bilingual teacher in Florida public schools and then as an English and Spanish teacher at colleges and universities. She is currently the Franklin Professor of English and Creative Writing at the University of Georgia, Athens.

Writer of Poetry and Fiction In graduate school Cofer began writing poetry in order to express the concerns of Latina women. Cofer believes that "poetry has made me more disciplined. . . . Poetry taught me about economizing in language and about the power of language." Ten years later, Cofer began writing fiction, and her first novel, *The Line of the Sun*, was nominated for a Pulitzer Prize in 1989. Cofer has also written *An Island Like You: Stories of the Barrio*, a book of short stories for young adults. The stories are set in Paterson, New Jersey, and deal with the problems facing Puerto Rican teenagers. Chicana author Sandra Cisneros says, "In these stories, both hilarious and tragic, [Cofer] has captured the isolated lives of those wobbling between two clashing cultures—childhood and adulthood." "Catch the Moon" is one of the stories in *An Island Like You*.

Author Search For more about Judith Ortiz Cofer, go to glencoe.com and enter QuickPass code GL59794u1.

218 UNIT 1 THE SHORT STORY

Literature and Reading Preview

Connect to the Story
Why does gift giving make the giver feel good? Freewrite for a few minutes about a gift you have given someone and how it made you feel to give it.

Build Background
A *barrio* is an urban neighborhood where most of the people are of Hispanic heritage. People in a *barrio* may have been born in the United States or have come from Spanish-speaking countries. Hubcaps, or wheel covers, come in thousands of different styles. While they are mostly for show, hubcaps do keep dirt and moisture away from the wheel nuts and bearings in a car's wheel assembly.

Set Purposes for Reading

Big Idea | Life Transitions
As you read "Catch the Moon," ask yourself, How does a self-centered young man learn the value of giving selflessly?

Literary Element | Point of View
Point of view is the standpoint from which a story is told. In a **third-person limited point of view**, the narrator describes events as one character perceives them. This enables readers to learn a lot about this particular character's thoughts and feelings, though the information about other characters is much more limited. As you read, ask yourself, Why did Cofer choose to tell the story from the third-person limited point of view?

Reading Strategy | Interpret Imagery
Writers use **imagery**, details that appeal to the senses, to help readers see, hear, smell, taste, or feel what the writer is describing. As you read, ask yourself, What are examples of imagery in this story? What do they signify?

Tip: Take Notes Use a chart like the one below to record instances of imagery and your interpretation of them.

Imagery	Interpretation
p. 220 "steel jungle of his car junkyard"	Here "steel jungle" is used figuratively to suggest a place that is hard and dense with debris.

Learning Objectives
For pages 218–228

In studying this text, you will focus on the following objectives:

Literary Study: Analyzing point of view.

Reading: Interpreting imagery.

Vocabulary

harass (hə ras′) *v.* to bother or annoy repeatedly; p. 221 *Several times a day the bully would harass the children.*

makeshift (māk′shift′) *adj.* suitable as a temporary substitute for the proper or desired thing; p. 222 *He used a tent as his makeshift home.*

vintage (vin′tij) *adj.* characterized by enduring appeal; classic; p. 222 *He drove a vintage Model T car.*

decapitate (di kap′ə tāt′) *v.* to cut off the head of; p. 223 *We watched the hunter decapitate the elk he had shot.*

relic (rel′ik) *n.* an object that has survived decay, destruction, or the passage of time and is valued for its historic interest; p. 225 *We saw a knight's armor and other relics at the museum.*

Catch the Moon

Judith Ortiz Cofer

Luis Cintrón sits on top of a six-foot pile of hubcaps and watches his father walk away into the steel jungle of his car junkyard. Released into his old man's custody after six months in juvenile hall—for breaking and entering—and he didn't even take anything. He did it on a dare.

But the old lady with the million cats was a light sleeper, and good with her aluminum cane. He has a scar on his head to prove it.

Now Luis is wondering whether he should have stayed in and done his full time. Jorge Cintrón of Jorge Cintrón & Son, Auto Parts and Salvage, has decided that Luis should wash and polish every hubcap in the yard. The hill he is sitting on is only the latest couple of hundred wheel covers that have come in. Luis grunts and stands up on top of his silver mountain. He yells at no one, "Someday, son, all this will be yours," and sweeps his arms like the Pope blessing a crowd over the piles of car sandwiches and mounds of metal parts that cover this acre of land outside the city. He is the "Son" of Jorge Cintrón & Son, and so far his father has had more than one reason to wish it was plain Jorge Cintrón on the sign.

Luis has been getting in trouble since he started high school two years ago,

---

Interpret Imagery *What does this image tell you about Luis?*

mainly because of the "social group" he organized—a bunch of guys who were into **harassing** the local authorities. Their thing was taking something to the limit on a dare or, better still, doing something dangerous, like breaking into a house, not to steal, just to prove that they could do it. That was Luis's specialty, coming up with very complicated plans, like military strategies, and assigning the "jobs" to guys who wanted to join the Tiburones.[1]

Tiburón means "shark," and Luis had gotten the name from watching an old movie[2] about a Puerto Rican gang called the Sharks with his father. Luis thought it was one of the dumbest films he had ever seen. Everybody sang their lines, and the guys all pointed their toes and leaped in the air when they were supposed to be slaughtering each other. But he liked their name, the Sharks, so he made it Spanish and had it air-painted on his black T-shirt with a killer shark under it, jaws opened wide and dripping with blood. It didn't take long for other guys in the barrio to ask about it.

Man, had they had a good time. The girls were interested too. Luis outsmarted everybody by calling his organization a social club and registering it at Central High. That meant they were legal, even let out of last-period class on Fridays for their "club" meetings. It was just this year, after a couple of botched[3] jobs, that the teachers had started getting suspicious. The first one to go wrong was when he sent Kenny Matoa to *borrow* some "souvenirs" out of Anita Robles's locker. He got caught. It seems that Matoa had been reading Anita's diary and didn't hear her coming down the hall. Anita was supposed to be in the gym at that time but had copped out with the usual female excuse of cramps. You could hear her screams all the way to Market Street.

She told the principal all she knew about the Tiburones, and Luis had to talk fast to convince old Mr. Williams that the club did put on cultural activities such as the Save the Animals talent show. What Mr. Williams didn't know was that the animal that was being "saved" with the ticket sales was Luis's pet boa, which needed quite a few live mice to stay healthy and happy. They kept E.S. (which stood for "Endangered Species") in Luis's room, but she belonged to the club and it was the members' responsibility to raise the money to feed their mascot. So last year they had sponsored their first annual Save the Animals talent show, and it had been a great success. The Tiburones had come dressed as Latino Elvises and did a grand finale to "All Shook Up" that made the audience go wild. Mr. Williams had smiled while Luis talked, maybe remembering how the math teacher, Mrs. Laguna, had dragged him out in the aisle to rock-and-roll with her. Luis had gotten out of that one, but barely.

His father was a problem too. He objected to the T-shirt logo, calling it disgusting and vulgar. Mr. Cintrón prided himself on his own neat, elegant style of dressing after work, and on his manners and large vocabulary, which he picked up by taking correspondence courses in just about everything.

---

1. *Tiburones* (tē′ boo rō′ nās)
2. [old movie...] The narrator is describing the feature film *West Side Story,* a 1961 musical based on Shakespeare's play *Romeo and Juliet,* set in the youth gang atmosphere of New York City in the late 1950s.
3. *Botched* means "badly or clumsily done."

Vocabulary

harass (hə ras′) *v.* to bother or annoy repeatedly

Life Transitions Do you think that Luis feels any remorse for the actions of the Tiburones at this point? Explain.

Luis thought that it was just his way of staying busy since Luis's mother had died, almost three years ago, of cancer. He had never gotten over it.

All this was going through Luis's head as he slid down the hill of hubcaps. The tub full of soapy water, the can of polish, and the bag of rags had been neatly placed in front of a **makeshift** table made from two car seats and a piece of plywood. Luis heard a car drive up and someone honk their horn. His father emerged from inside a new red Mustang that had been totaled. He usually dismantled every small feature by hand before sending the vehicle into the *cementerio*,[4] as he called the lot. Luis watched as the most beautiful girl he had ever seen climbed out of a **vintage** white Volkswagen Bug. She stood in the sunlight in her white sundress waiting for his father, while Luis stared. She was like a smooth wood carving. Her skin was mahogany, almost black, and her arms and legs were long and thin, but curved in places so that she did not look bony and hard—more like a ballerina. And her ebony hair was braided close to her head. Luis let his breath out, feeling a little dizzy. He had forgotten to breathe. Both the girl and his father heard him. Mr. Cintrón waved him over.

"Luis, the señorita here has lost a wheel cover. Her car is twenty-five years old, so it will not be an easy match. Come look on this side."

Luis tossed a wrench he'd been holding into a toolbox like he was annoyed, just to make a point about slave labor. Then he followed his father, who knelt on the gravel and began to point out every detail of the hubcap. Luis was hardly listening. He watched the girl take a piece of paper from her handbag.

"Señor Cintrón, I have drawn the hubcap for you, since I will have to leave soon. My home address and telephone number are here, and also my parents' office number." She handed the paper to Mr. Cintrón, who nodded.

"Sí, señorita, very good. This will help my son look for it. Perhaps there is one in that stack there." He pointed to the pile of caps that Luis was supposed to wash and polish. "Yes, I'm almost certain that there is a match there. Of course, I do not know if it's near the top or the bottom. You will give us a few days, yes?"

Luis just stared at his father like he was crazy. But he didn't say anything because the girl was smiling at him with a funny expression on her face. Maybe she thought he had X-ray eyes like Superman, or maybe she was mocking him.

"Please call me Naomi, Señor Cintrón. You know my mother. She is the director of the funeral home. . . ." Mr. Cintrón seemed surprised at first; he prided himself on having a great memory. Then his friendly expression changed to one of sadness as he recalled the day of his wife's burial. Naomi did not finish her sentence. She reached over and placed her hand on Mr. Cintrón's arm for a moment. Then she said "Adiós" softly, and got in her shiny white car. She waved to them as she left, and her gold bracelets flashing in the sun nearly blinded Luis.

---

4. *Cementerio* (se men tā´ rē ō) is Spanish for "cemetery."

Point of View *What does this sentence tell you about Luis?*

Interpret Imagery *How would you interpret the description of the beautiful girl in the midst of the junkyard?*

Vocabulary

makeshift (māk´shift´) *adj.* suitable as a temporary substitute for the proper or desired thing

vintage (vin´tij) *adj.* characterized by enduring appeal; classic

Point of View *Why do you think Luis reacts this way?*

September 16, c. 1955. René Magritte. Oil on canvas, 14 x 10⅞ in. The Minneapolis Institute of Arts. ©ARS, NY.

View the Art René Magritte, a Belgian Surrealist painter, often includes elements of mystery, comedy, and danger in his art. In what ways does this painting express the title and mood of the story?

Mr. Cintrón shook his head. "How about that," he said as if to himself. "They are the Dominican owners of Ramirez Funeral Home." And, with a sigh, "She seems like such a nice young woman. Reminds me of your mother when she was her age."

Hearing the funeral parlor's name, Luis remembered too. The day his mother died, he had been in her room at the hospital while his father had gone for coffee. The alarm had gone off on her monitor and nurses had come running in, pushing him outside. After that, all he recalled was the anger that had made him punch a hole in his bedroom wall. And afterward he had refused to talk to anyone at the funeral. Strange, he did see a black girl there who didn't try like the others to talk to him, but actually ignored him as she escorted family members to the viewing room and brought flowers in. Could it be that the skinny girl in a frilly white dress had been Naomi? She didn't act like she had recognized him today, though. Or maybe she thought that he was a jerk.

Luis grabbed the drawing from his father. The old man looked like he wanted to walk down memory lane. But Luis was in no mood to listen to the old stories about his falling in love on a tropical island. The world they'd lived in before he was born wasn't his world. No beaches and palm trees here. Only junk as far as he could see. He climbed back up his hill and studied Naomi's sketch. It had obviously been done very carefully. It was signed "Naomi Ramirez" in the lower right-hand corner. He memorized the telephone number.

Luis washed hubcaps all day until his hands were red and raw, but he did not come across the small silver bowl that would fit the VW. After work he took a few practice Frisbee shots across the yard before showing his rows and rows of shiny rings drying in the sun. His father nodded and showed him the bump on his temple where one of Luis's flying saucers had gotten him. "Practice makes perfect, you know. Next time you'll probably **decapitate** me." Luis heard him struggle with the word *decapitate*, which Mr. Cintrón pronounced in syllables. Showing off his big vocabulary again, Luis thought. He looked closely at the bump, though. He felt bad about it.

"They look good, hijo."[5] Mr. Cintrón made a sweeping gesture with his arms over the yard. "You know, all this will have to be

---

5. *Hijo* (ē′hō) is Spanish for "son."

Life Transitions Does this passage show a change in Luis's attitude? Explain.

Vocabulary

decapitate (di kap′ə tāt′) *v.* to cut off the head of

JUDITH ORTIZ COFER **223**

Scrap Merchant, 1983. Reg Cartwright. Oil on canvas, 91.4 x 76.2 cm. Private collection.

View the Art Reg Cartwright is a British painter and illustrator whose work is influenced by Cubism. What might this painting suggest about how Luis might feel while working in his father's junkyard?

classified. My dream is to have all the parts divided by year, make of car, and condition. Maybe now that you are here to help me, this will happen."

"Pop . . ." Luis put his hand on his father's shoulder. They were the same height and build, about five foot six and muscular. "The judge said six months of free labor for you, not life, okay?" Mr. Cintrón nodded, looking distracted. It was then that Luis suddenly noticed how gray his hair had turned—it used to be shiny black like his own—and that there were deep lines in his face. His father had turned into an old man and he hadn't even noticed.

"Son, you must follow the judge's instructions. Like she said, next time you get in trouble, she's going to treat you like an adult, and I think you know what that means. Hard time, no breaks."

"Yeah, yeah. That's what I'm doing, right? Working my hands to the bone instead of enjoying my summer. But listen, she didn't put me under house arrest, right? I'm going out tonight."

"Home by ten. She did say something about a curfew, Luis." Mr. Cintrón had stopped smiling and was looking upset. It had always been hard for them to talk more than a minute or two before his father got offended at something Luis said, or at his sarcastic tone. He was always doing something wrong.

Luis threw the rag down on the table and went to sit in his father's ancient Buick, which was in mint condition. They drove home in silence.

After sitting down at the kitchen table with his father to eat a pizza they had picked up on the way home, Luis asked to borrow the car. He didn't get an answer then, just a look that meant "Don't bother me right now."

Before bringing up the subject again, Luis put some ice cubes in a Baggie and handed it to Mr. Cintrón, who had made the little bump on his head worse by rubbing it. It had GUILTY written on it, Luis thought.

"Gracias, hijo." His father placed the bag on the bump and made a face as the ice touched his skin.

They ate in silence for a few minutes more; then Luis decided to ask about the car again.

"I really need some fresh air, Pop. Can I borrow the car for a couple of hours?"

"You don't get enough fresh air at the yard? We're lucky that we don't have to sit in a smelly old factory all day. You know that?"

"Yeah, Pop. We're real lucky." Luis always felt irritated that his father was so grateful to own a junkyard, but he held his anger back and just waited to see if he'd get the keys without having to get in an argument.

"Where are you going?"

"For a ride. Not going anywhere. Just out for a while. Is that okay?"

Point of View Do you think Mr. Cintrón would agree with Luis's perception?

His father didn't answer, just handed him a set of keys, as shiny as the day they were manufactured. His father polished everything that could be polished: doorknobs, coins, keys, spoons, knives, and forks, like he was King Midas counting his silver and gold. Luis thought his father must be really lonely to polish utensils only he used anymore. They had been picked out by his wife, though, so they were like **relics**. Nothing she had ever owned could be thrown away. Only now the dishes, forks, and spoons were not used to eat the yellow rice and red beans, the fried chicken, or the mouth-watering sweet plantains that his mother had cooked for them. They were just kept in the cabinets that his father had turned into a museum for her. Mr. Cintrón could cook as well as his wife, but he didn't have the heart to do it anymore. Luis thought that maybe if they ate together once in a while things might get better between them, but he always had something to do around dinnertime and ended up at a hamburger joint. Tonight was the first time in months they had sat down at the table together.

Luis took the keys. "Thanks," he said, walking out to take his shower. His father kept looking at him with those sad, patient eyes. "Okay. I'll be back by ten, and keep the ice on that egg," Luis said without looking back.

Visual Vocabulary
A *plantain* (plant′ən) is a tropical fruit similar to a banana that must be cooked before eating.

Interpret Imagery Why do you think Mr. Cintrón takes such good care of his wife's belongings?

Vocabulary
relic (rel′ik) *n.* an object that has survived decay, destruction, or the passage of time and is valued for its historic interest

He had just meant to ride around his old barrio, see if any of the Tiburones were hanging out at El Building, where most of them lived. It wasn't far from the single-family home his father had bought when the business started paying off: a house that his mother lived in for three months before she took up residence at St. Joseph's Hospital. She never came home again. These days Luis wished he still lived in that tiny apartment where there was always something to do, somebody to talk to.

Instead Luis found himself parked in front of the last place his mother had gone to: Ramirez Funeral Home. In the front yard was a huge oak tree that Luis remembered having climbed during the funeral to get away from people. The tree looked different now, not like a skeleton, as it had then, but green with leaves. The branches reached to the second floor of the house, where the family lived.

For a while Luis sat in the car allowing the memories to flood back into his brain. He remembered his mother before the illness changed her. She had not been beautiful, as his father told everyone; she had been a sweet lady, not pretty but not ugly. To him, she had been the person who always told him that she was proud of him and loved him. She did that every night when she came to his bedroom door to say good-night. As a joke he would sometimes ask her, "Proud of what? I haven't done anything." And she'd always say, "I'm just proud that you are my son." She wasn't perfect or anything. She had bad days when nothing he did could make her smile, especially after she got sick. But he never heard her say anything negative about anyone. She always blamed *el destino,* fate, for what went wrong. He missed her. He missed her so much.

JUDITH ORTIZ COFER **225**

Suddenly a flood of tears that had been building up for almost three years started pouring from his eyes. Luis sat in his father's car, with his head on the steering wheel, and cried, "Mami, I miss you."

When he finally looked up, he saw that he was being watched. Sitting at a large window with a pad and a pencil on her lap was Naomi. At first Luis felt angry and embarrassed, but she wasn't laughing at him. Then she told him with her dark eyes that it was okay to come closer. He walked to the window, and she held up the sketch pad on which she had drawn him, not crying like a baby, but sitting on top of a mountain of silver disks, holding one up over his head. He had to smile.

The plate-glass window was locked. It had a security bolt on it. An alarm system, he figured, so nobody would steal the princess. He asked her if he could come in. It was soundproof too. He mouthed the words slowly for her to read his lips. She wrote on the pad, "I can't let you in. My mother is not home tonight." So they looked at each other and talked through the window for a little while. Then Luis got an idea. He signed to her that he'd be back, and drove to the junkyard.

Luis climbed up on his mountain of hubcaps. For hours he sorted the wheel covers by make, size, and condition, stopping only to call his father and tell him where he was and what he was doing. The old man did not ask him for explanations, and Luis was grateful for that. By lamppost light, Luis worked and worked, beginning to understand a little why his father kept busy all the time. Doing something that had a beginning, a middle, and an end did something to your head. It was like the satisfaction Luis got out of planning "adventures" for his Tiburones, but there was another element involved here that had nothing to do with showing off for others. This was a treasure hunt. And he knew what he was looking for.

Finally, when it seemed that it was a hopeless search, when it was almost midnight and Luis's hands were cut and bruised from his work, he found it. It was the perfect match for Naomi's drawing, the moon-shaped wheel cover for her car, Cinderella's shoe. Luis jumped off the small mound of disks left under him and shouted, "Yes!" He looked around and saw neat stacks of hubcaps that he would wash the next day. He would build a display wall for his father. People would be able to come into the yard and point to whatever they wanted.

Luis washed the VW hubcap and polished it until he could see himself in it. He used it as a mirror as he washed his face and combed his hair. Then he drove to the Ramirez Funeral Home. It was almost pitch-black, since it was a moonless night. As quietly as possible, Luis put some gravel in his pocket and climbed the oak tree to the second floor. He knew he was in front of Naomi's window—he could see her shadow through the curtains. She was at a table, apparently writing or drawing, maybe waiting for him. Luis hung the silver disk carefully on a branch near the window, then threw the gravel at the glass. Naomi ran to the window and drew the curtains aside while Luis held on to the thick branch and waited to give her the first good thing he had given anyone in a long time.

Interpret Imagery *What does the imagery of a flood suggest about Luis's emotional response?*

Point of View *How does this passage demonstrate the third-person limited point of view?*

Life Transitions *What do you think the last sentence of the story means?*

After You Read

Respond and Think Critically

Respond and Interpret

1. (a) Were you surprised by Luis's actions at the end of the story? Explain. (b) How did your feelings about Luis change as you read the story?

2. Why does Luis work at his father's junkyard?

3. (a) Describe the relationship between Luis and his father. (b) Do you think there is a chance for Luis and his father to build a better relationship? Use details from the story to support your answer.

4. (a) What does Luis leave in the tree for Naomi? (b) What do you think Luis discovers about himself as he searches for his gift to Naomi?

Analyze and Evaluate

5. In what ways can Naomi be compared with Luis's mother?

6. Explain how Luis also gives a gift to his father as he searches for the hubcap.

Connect

7. **Big Idea** Life Transitions The story begins with Luis sitting on a pile of hubcaps and ends with him hanging a hubcap in a tree. What kind of character transition has Luis made by the end of the story?

8. **Connect to the Author** As a child, Judith Ortiz Cofer spoke both English and Spanish but struggled with each. In the story, Luis's father is enrolled in a correspondence class to improve his vocabulary. Why is it important to the father to have a good vocabulary? Do you think the author has the same beliefs? Explain.

Literary Element Point of View

The third-person limited narrator of "Catch the Moon" describes events as only Luis perceives them. Readers hear Luis's thoughts as he describes his gang activities and comments on his father and Naomi. Readers have to judge whether Luis's comments are fair and infer what his thoughts reveal about his character. Readers also should be alert to dramatic irony in the story: a contrast between what Luis thinks and what the reader knows is true.

1. The narrator does not reveal Naomi's opinion of Luis. After she leaves the junkyard, Luis worries if "maybe she thought that he was a jerk." How accurate is Luis's concern?

2. The narrator reveals Luis's pride in his gang activities. Contrast Luis's feelings about his gang activities with your own perspective on gangs. What dramatic irony do you notice?

Plot and Setting

Plot is the series of events that make up a story. **Setting** is the time and place in which the story takes place. As you learned on pages 8–9, a key feature of the plot is exposition, which introduces the story's characters, setting, and situation.

Partner Activity Meet with a classmate to discuss what the exposition of the story reveals about Luis, specifically regarding the setting he is in and why he is there. Working with your partner, create a chart similar to the one below and fill it with details about Luis, the setting, and his situation.

Details About Luis	Setting Details	Situation Details
gang leader	junkyard	released into custody of his father

Reading Strategy: Interpret Imagery

SAT Skills Practice

1. The contrast between the way Luis and his father eat in the story and the food that Mrs. Cintrón used to cook (page 225) highlights

   (A) Luis's anger with his father
   (B) a loss of intimacy in the family
   (C) that neither Luis nor his father can cook
   (D) Luis's love for his mother
   (E) that the junkyard is at last making a profit

Vocabulary Practice

Practice with Denotation and Connotation

Denotation is the literal, or dictionary, meaning of a word. **Connotation** is the implied, or cultural, meaning of a word. For example, the words *fib* and *lie* have a similar denotation, a "mistruth," but they have different connotations:

Weaker	Stronger
fib	lie

Each of the vocabulary words is listed with a word that has a similar denotation. Choose the word that has a stronger connotation.

1. harass — bother
2. makeshift — temporary
3. vintage — classic
4. relic — artifact

Academic Vocabulary

Naomi helps Luis realize that there is an **alternative** to the life he is living.

Alternative is an academic word. In casual conversation, someone might refer to an alternative school or alternative medicine. These adjectives suggest the meaning of the noun *alternative*. What alternative might you consider to the way you usually spend your after-school time? Why?

For more on academic vocabulary, see pages 52 and 53.

Write with Style

Apply Point of View

Assignment Use the first person and Luis's diction to retell the last two paragraphs of the story from Luis's point of view.

Get Ideas Make a sequence chain to list the events that take place in the last two paragraphs, and for each event, write a comment that Luis himself might make. Base your word choices on the words and phrasing that Luis uses elsewhere in the story.

Event	Luis's comment
Luis finally finds the matching hubcap.	Just when I figured I was never gonna find it, I saw this hubcap shaped like the moon and I knew it was the matching one. It was perfect.

Luis washes and polishes the hubcap.	

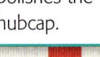

Luis drives to the funeral home.	

Give It Structure Narrate the events in the order in which they occur. Use transitions that signal chronological order where they are needed.

Look at Language Remember to use the pronoun *I* only as a subject and the pronoun *me* only as an object. For example, Luis might say, "I am into cars" or "My friends and I are into cars." He could also say "Cars are cool to me" or "Cars are cool to me and my friends." In the first pair of sentences, *I* is the subject. In the second pair of sentences, *Cars* is the subject and *me* is the object. Be sure each word that Luis speaks in the narrative reflects not only his perspective but also his characteristic speech patterns.

Literature Online

Selection Resources For Selection Quizzes, eFlashcards, and Reading-Writing Connection activities, go to glencoe.com and enter QuickPass code GL59794u1.

Grammar Workshop

Sentence Fragments

Learning Objectives

In this workshop, you will focus on the following objective:

Grammar: Understanding how to avoid sentence fragments.

Literature Connection A fragment is an incomplete part of something. A **sentence fragment** is a word or group of words that is only part of a sentence. People often use sentence fragments in conversation, as in the quotation from "Catch the Moon."

> "'Home by ten. She did say something about a curfew, Luis.'
> Mr. Cintrón had stopped smiling and was looking upset."
>
> —Judith Ortiz Cofer, from "Catch the Moon"

Although the fragment *Home by ten* lacks both a verb and a subject, Luis understands that Mr. Cintrón is reminding him of his curfew. Sometimes, however, a fragment that leaves out important information can be confusing.

Problem 1 Word group missing a subject, a verb, or both

Needs a new hubcap. [lacks a subject]
Only three hubcaps on the car. [lacks a verb]

Solution Add the missing subject and/or verb.

The car needs a new hubcap.
The car only has three hubcaps.

Problem 2 Subordinate clause that does not express a complete thought

Because the judge sentenced him to work in the junkyard.

Solution A Join the subordinate clause to a main clause.

Luis was helping his father because the judge sentenced him to work in the junkyard.

Solution B Remove the subordinating conjunction at the beginning of the clause.

The judge sentenced him to work in the junkyard.

Proofread Use the strategies shown above to correct the sentence fragments in this paragraph.

Luis and his father had not gotten along. Since his mother's death. Often got into trouble and was punished. Luis saw Naomi at the junkyard. The most beautiful girl in the world. Worked hard to find a match for her missing hubcap. He memorized her telephone number. Had written on the paper with her drawing of the hubcap.

Vocabulary Terms

A sentence is a group of words that expresses a complete thought. A **sentence fragment** does not express a complete thought and often lacks a subject, a verb, or both.

Tip

When writing for a test, check carefully to make sure that each sentence has a subject and a verb and conveys a complete thought.

Language Handbook

For more on sentence fragments, see the Language Handbook p. R47.

Sentence Fragments for Effect

At times a sentence fragment can be used to create a dramatic effect. In such an instance, what is left unsaid can be as effective as what is said—in a wry observation, for example, or an exclamation. Consider the following: *An impossible situation.* or *Under no circumstances!*

Grammar For more grammar practice, go to glencoe.com and enter QuickPass code GL59794u1.

Before You Read

**World Literature
Chile**

And of Clay Are We Created

Meet Isabel Allende
(born 1942)

For most of her life, Isabel Allende (ēs´ äbel ä yen´dā) has felt like a wanderer. Although she is Chilean, she was born in Lima, Peru, where her father held a diplomatic post. Her parents divorced when she was young, and she lived with her grandparents for several years in Santiago, Chile. When her mother remarried, Allende moved with her mother and stepfather, also a diplomat, to La Paz, Bolivia.

Life in Chile From Bolivia, the family was next stationed in Beirut, Lebanon, and then moved on to Europe. The threat of war in the Middle East returned Allende back to her grandfather's house in Chile. She was fifteen years old and wanted to put down roots. Her grandfather provided Allende with an intensive education in Chilean history and geography, which deepened her love for her country. Trips that she and her grandfather took to different parts of Chile fueled this love, as did her reading of great Chilean poets, including Pablo Neruda and Gabriela Mistral.

> *"I write to preserve memory. I write what should not be forgotten."*
>
> —Isabel Allende

Allende's grandfather also gave her gifts that she would later call upon as a writer. He entertained her with folk tales and admonished her with proverbs. He told her fascinating accounts of strange characters in their family and recited lengthy poems from memory.

In 1959 Allende started working for the United Nations Food and Agricultural Organization in Santiago, first as a secretary, then as an editor and a press officer. She later became a broadcast journalist and wrote for and edited a feminist magazine.

Exile Isabel Allende's life changed forever on September 11, 1973, when the president of Chile, Salvador Allende, was killed and a brutal military dictatorship took over. The murdered president had been Isabel's beloved uncle. Within a few years, it was no longer safe for Allende and her family to stay in Chile, so they went into exile in Venezuela.

Allende could not find a job in journalism in Venezuela and worked as a teacher for several years. In 1981 she began writing a letter to her grandfather, who was almost 100 years old and in poor health, and continued working on it for an entire year. The letter became the manuscript for her first novel, *The House of the Spirits*.

Since 1982 Allende has written nearly a dozen books, most of them novels.

Author Search For more about Isabel Allende, go to glencoe.com and enter QuickPass code GL59794u1.

Literature and Reading Preview

Connect to the Story
What are some different factors that might influence how you would respond during a natural disaster? List some internal and external factors that might influence how you respond in a crisis situation.

Build Background
This story is based on an event that occurred in the South American country of Colombia. In November 1985, an active, snow-covered volcano erupted. Heat from the eruption melted snow and ice and sent a monstrous mudslide crashing into the valley. 25,000 people and 15,000 animals perished in the disaster, and thousands of people were injured or left homeless.

Set Purposes for Reading

Big Idea Life Transitions
As you read, ask yourself, How does Allende use the mud as a device to hold the lives of the three main characters in suspension?

Literary Element Persona
The **persona** is the voice an author creates to tell a story. Even if the story is told from a first-person point of view, as is "And of Clay Are We Created," the narrator is not the author. As you read, ask yourself, What are the characteristics of the first-person narrator in the story?

Reading Strategy Analyze Sensory Details
Sensory details are highly descriptive words and phrases that appeal to one or more of the senses: hearing, sight, smell, taste, and touch. As you read, ask yourself, Where does Allende appeal to each of these five senses?

Tip: Take Notes Use a chart to record sensory details in this story.

Sense	Detail from the story
touch	p. 239 "her silk hair against his cheek"

Learning Objectives

For pages 230–243

In studying this text, you will focus on the following objectives:

Literary Study: Analyzing persona.

Reading: Analyzing sensory details.

Vocabulary

presentiment (pri zen′ tə mənt) *n.* a feeling that something is about to happen; p. 233 *Although the scientists had no monitoring equipment, they had a presentiment that the volcano would soon erupt.*

equanimity (ēk′ wə nim′ ə tē) *n.* the ability to remain calm and assured; p. 233 *The equanimity of the mayor helped calm the hurricane survivors.*

fortitude (fôr′ tə tōōd′) *n.* firm courage or strength of mind in the face of pain or danger; p. 233 *Relief workers often show fortitude when they aid people during a disaster.*

pandemonium (pan′ də mō′ nē əm) *n.* wild disorder and uproar; p. 235 *Pandemonium broke out as looters smashed grocery store windows.*

tribulation (trib′ yə lā′ shən) *n.* great misery or distress; suffering; p. 239 *A natural disaster nearly always brings tribulation, but it sometimes brings people together as well.*

ISABEL ALLENDE

And of Clay Are We Created

Isabel Allende
Translated by
Margaret Sayers Peden

Volcano, 1999. Sally Elliott. Watercolor on paper, 27.9 x 38.1 cm. Private collection.

They discovered the girl's head protruding from the mudpit, eyes wide open, calling soundlessly. She had a First Communion name, Azucena.[1] Lily. In that vast cemetery where the odor of death was already attracting vultures from far away, and where the weeping of orphans and wails of the injured filled the air, the little girl obstinately clinging to life became the symbol of the tragedy.

The television cameras transmitted so often the unbearable image of the head budding like a black squash from the clay that there was no one who did not recognize her and know her name. And every time we saw her on the screen, right behind her was Rolf Carlé,[2] who had gone there on assignment, never suspecting that he would find a fragment of his past, lost thirty years before.

---

1. *Azucena* (ä zōō kē′nä)

Analyze Sensory Details *Which senses do these details appeal to?*

2. *Rolf Carlé* (rälf cär lā′)

Life Transitions *What questions does this passage prompt for you?*

First a subterranean[3] sob rocked the cotton fields, curling them like waves of foam. Geologists had set up their seismographs[4] weeks before and knew that the mountain had awakened again. For some time they had predicted that the heat of the eruption could detach the eternal ice from the slopes of the volcano, but no one heeded their warnings; they sounded like the tales of frightened old women. The towns in the valley went about their daily life, deaf to the moaning of the earth, until that fateful Wednesday night in November when a prolonged roar announced the end of the world, and walls of snow broke loose, rolling in an avalanche of clay, stones, and water that descended on the villages and buried them beneath unfathomable[5] meters of telluric[6] vomit. As soon as the survivors emerged from the paralysis of that first awful terror, they could see that houses, plazas, churches, white cotton plantations, dark coffee forests, cattle pastures—all had disappeared. Much later, after soldiers and volunteers had arrived to rescue the living and try to assess the magnitude of the cataclysm, it was calculated that beneath the mud lay more than twenty thousand human beings and an indefinite number of animals putrefying in a viscous soup. Forests and rivers had also been swept away, and there was nothing to be seen but an immense desert of mire.[7]

When the station called before dawn, Rolf Carlé and I were together. I crawled out of bed, dazed with sleep, and went to prepare coffee while he hurriedly dressed. He stuffed his gear in the green canvas backpack he always carried, and we said goodbye, as we had so many times before. I had no **presentiments.** I sat in the kitchen, sipping my coffee and planning the long hours without him, sure that he would be back the next day.

He was one of the first to reach the scene, because while other reporters were fighting their way to the edges of that morass[8] in jeeps, bicycles, or on foot, each getting there however he could, Rolf Carlé had the advantage of the television helicopter, which flew him over the avalanche. We watched on our screens the footage captured by his assistant's camera, in which he was up to his knees in muck, a microphone in his hand, in the midst of a bedlam[9] of lost children, wounded survivors, corpses, and devastation. The story came to us in his calm voice. For years he had been a familiar figure in newscasts, reporting live at the scene of battles and catastrophes with awesome tenacity. Nothing could stop him, and I was always amazed at his **equanimity** in the face of danger and suffering; it seemed as if nothing could shake his **fortitude** or deter his curiosity. Fear

---

8. A *morass* (mə ras′) is any difficult, confused, or entangling condition or situation.
9. Here, *bedlam* refers to the noisy uproar and confusion of the situation.

Persona Summarize what you learn about the narrator from this excerpt.

Vocabulary

presentiment (pri zen′tə mənt) *n.* a feeling that something is about to happen

equanimity (ēk′wə nim′ə tē) *n.* the ability to remain calm and assured

fortitude (fôr′tə to͞od′) *n.* firm courage or strength of mind in the face of pain or danger

---

3. Something *subterranean* is beneath the earth's surface.
4. *Seismographs* are scientific instruments that record the intensity and duration of earthquakes.
5. Here, *unfathomable* (un fath′əm ə bəl) means "immeasurable."
6. *Telluric* (te loor′ik) means "coming or rising from the earth."
7. The decaying *(putrefying)* corpses are buried in the muddy slime, a thick, syrupy *(viscous)* soup; the landscape has become a wasteland of mud *(mire)*.

Landscape (Camaldoli), 1928. Arthur Bowen Davies. Albright-Knox Art Gallery, Buffalo, NY.

View the Art In this painting, the sleepy countryside of Camaldoli, Italy, sits in the shadow of an active volcano. How must the people in the town, such as Azucena, have felt the moment they realized that the slumbering volcano nearby had suddenly erupted? Explain.

seemed never to touch him, although he had confessed to me that he was not a courageous man, far from it. I believe that the lens of the camera had a strange effect on him; it was as if it transported him to a different time from which he could watch events without actually participating in them. When I knew him better, I came to realize that this fictive distance seemed to protect him from his own emotions.

Rolf Carlé was in on the story of Azucena from the beginning. He filmed the volunteers who discovered her, and the first persons who tried to reach her; his camera zoomed in on the girl, her dark face, her large desolate eyes, the plastered-down tangle of her hair. The mud was like quicksand around her, and anyone attempting to reach her was in danger of sinking. They threw a rope to her that she made no effort to grasp until they shouted to her to catch it; then she pulled a hand from the mire and tried to move, but immediately sank a little deeper. Rolf threw down his knapsack and the rest of his equipment and waded into the quagmire, commenting for his assistant's microphone that it was cold and that one could begin to smell the stench of corpses.

Persona *From what you already know about the narrator, why is she qualified to give this information?*

Analyze Sensory Details *At this point in the story, what is Rolf Carlé's attitude about the mudslide? What is his attitude about the young girl he is approaching?*

"What's your name?" he asked the girl, and she told him her flower name. "Don't move, Azucena," Rolf Carlé directed, and kept talking to her, without a thought for what he was saying, just to distract her, while slowly he worked his way forward in mud up to his waist. The air around him seemed as murky as the mud.

It was impossible to reach her from the approach he was attempting, so he retreated and circled around where there seemed to be firmer footing. When finally he was close enough, he took the rope and tied it beneath her arms, so they could pull her out. He smiled at her with that smile that crinkles his eyes and makes him look like a little boy; he told her that everything was fine, that he was here with her now, that soon they would have her out. He signaled the others to pull, but as soon as the cord tensed, the girl screamed. They tried again, and her shoulders and arms appeared, but they could move her no farther; she was trapped. Someone suggested that her legs might be caught in the collapsed walls of her house, but she said it was not just rubble, that she was also held by the bodies of her brothers and sisters clinging to her legs.

"Don't worry, we'll get you out of here," Rolf promised. Despite the quality of the transmission, I could hear his voice break, and I loved him more than ever. Azucena looked at him, but said nothing.

> *The girl could not move, she barely could breathe, but she did not seem desperate...*

During those first hours Rolf Carlé exhausted all the resources of his ingenuity to rescue her. He struggled with poles and ropes, but every tug was an intolerable torture for the imprisoned girl. It occurred to him to use one of the poles as a lever but got no result and had to abandon the idea. He talked a couple of soldiers into working with him for a while, but they had to leave because so many other victims were calling for help. The girl could not move, she barely could breathe, but she did not seem desperate, as if an ancestral resignation allowed her to accept her fate. The reporter, on the other hand, was determined to snatch her from death. Someone brought him a tire, which he placed beneath her arms like a life buoy, and then laid a plank near the hole to hold his weight and allow him to stay closer to her. As it was impossible to remove the rubble blindly, he tried once or twice to dive toward her feet, but emerged frustrated, covered with mud, and spitting gravel. He concluded that he would have to have a pump to drain the water, and radioed a request for one, but received in return a message that there was no available transport and it could not be sent until the next morning.

"We can't wait that long!" Rolf Carlé shouted, but in the **pandemonium** no one stopped to commiserate.[10] Many more

---

10. No one stopped to show or express sympathy—to *commiserate* (kə miz´ ə rāt´).

Vocabulary

pandemonium (pan´ də mō´ nē əm) *n.* wild disorder and uproar

---

Life Transitions What does Azucena's idea about why she cannot move tell you about her feelings concerning the situation?

ISABEL ALLENDE 235

hours would go by before he accepted that time had stagnated and reality had been irreparably distorted.

A military doctor came to examine the girl, and observed that her heart was functioning well and that if she did not get too cold she could survive the night.

"Hang on, Azucena, we'll have the pump tomorrow," Rolf Carlé tried to console her.

"Don't leave me alone," she begged.

"No, of course I won't leave you."

Someone brought him coffee, and he helped the girl drink it, sip by sip. The warm liquid revived her and she began telling him about her small life, about her family and her school, about how things were in that little bit of world before the volcano had erupted. She was thirteen, and she had never been outside her village. ==Rolf Carlé, buoyed by a premature optimism, was convinced that everything would end well:== the pump would arrive, they would drain the water, move the rubble, and Azucena would be transported by helicopter to a hospital where she would recover rapidly and where he could visit her and bring her gifts. He thought, She's already too old for dolls, and I don't know what would please her; maybe a dress. I don't know much about women, he concluded, amused, reflecting that although he had known many women in his lifetime, none had taught him these details. To pass the hours he began to tell Azucena about his travels and adventures as a newshound, and when he exhausted his memory, he called upon imagination, inventing things he thought might entertain her. From time to time she dozed, but he kept talking in the darkness, to assure her that he was still there and to overcome the menace of uncertainty.

That was a long night.

> **Life Transitions** What is the mood at this point in the story? What hint does the author give that things are likely to change?

Many miles away, I watched Rolf Carlé and the girl on a television screen. I could not bear the wait at home, so I went to National Television, where I often spent entire nights with Rolf editing programs. There, I was near his world, and I could at least get a feeling of what he lived through during those three decisive days. I called all the important people in the city, senators, commanders of the armed forces, the North American ambassador, and the president of National Petroleum, begging them for a pump to remove the silt, but obtained only vague promises. I began to ask for urgent help on radio and television, to see if there wasn't *someone* who could help us. Between calls I would run to the newsroom to monitor the satellite transmissions that periodically brought new details of the catastrophe. While reporters selected scenes with most impact for the news report, I searched for footage that featured Azucena's mudpit. The screen reduced the disaster to a single plane and accentuated the tremendous distance that separated me from Rolf Carlé; nonetheless, I was there with him. The child's every suffering hurt me as it did him; I felt his frustration, his impotence. Faced with the impossibility of communicating with him, the fantastic idea came to me that if I tried, I could reach him by force of mind and in that way give him encouragement. I concentrated until I was dizzy—a frenzied and futile activity. At times I would be overcome with compassion and burst out crying; at other times, I was so drained I felt as if I were staring through a telescope at the light of a star dead for a million years.

I watched that hell on the first morning broadcast, cadavers of people and animals awash in the current of new rivers formed overnight from the melted snow. Above the mud rose the tops of trees and the bell towers of a church where several people had taken refuge and were patiently awaiting rescue teams. Hundreds of soldiers and volunteers from the Civil Defense were clawing through rubble searching for survivors, while long rows of ragged specters awaited their turn for a cup of hot broth. Radio networks announced that their phones were jammed with calls from families offering shelter to orphaned children. Drinking water was in scarce supply, along with gasoline and food. Doctors, resigned to amputating arms and legs without anesthesia, pled that at least they be sent serum and painkillers and antibiotics; most of the roads, however, were impassable, and worse were the bureaucratic obstacles that stood in the way. To top it all, the clay contaminated by decomposing bodies threatened the living with an outbreak of epidemics.

Azucena was shivering inside the tire that held her above the surface. Immobility and tension had greatly weakened her, but she was conscious and could still be heard when a microphone was held out to her. Her tone was humble, as if apologizing for all the fuss. Rolf Carlé had a growth of beard, and dark circles beneath his eyes; he looked near exhaustion. Even from that enormous distance I could sense the quality of his weariness, so different from the fatigue of other adventures. He had completely forgotten the camera; he could not look at the girl through a lens any longer. The pictures we were receiving were not his assistant's but those of other reporters who had appropriated Azucena, bestowing on her the pathetic responsibility of embodying the horror[11] of what had happened in that place. With the first light Rolf tried again to dislodge the obstacles that held the girl in her tomb, but he had only his hands to work with; he did not dare use a tool for fear of injuring her. He fed Azucena a cup of the cornmeal mush and bananas the Army was distributing, but she immediately vomited it up. A doctor stated that she had a fever, but added that there was little he could do: antibiotics were being reserved for cases of gangrene. A priest also passed by and blessed her, hanging a medal of the Virgin around her neck. By evening a gentle, persistent drizzle began to fall.

"The sky is weeping," Azucena murmured . . .

"The sky is weeping," Azucena murmured, and she, too, began to cry.

"Don't be afraid," Rolf begged. "You have to keep your strength up and be calm. Everything will be fine. I'm with you, and I'll get you out somehow."

Reporters returned to photograph Azucena and ask her the same questions, which she no longer tried to answer. In the meanwhile, more television and movie teams arrived with spools of cable, tapes, film, videos, precision lenses, recorders, sound consoles, lights, reflecting screens, auxiliary motors, cartons of supplies, electricians, sound technicians, and cameramen: Azucena's face was beamed to millions of screens around the world. And all the while Rolf Carlé kept pleading for a pump.

Analyze Sensory Details *How do these sensory details enliven the activities of the disaster area?*

Persona *Based on what you know about Rolf, why would his decision not to use the camera be significant?*

---

11. [appropriated . . . horror] In other words, the reporters are using televised images of Azucena's situation, making her a living symbol of the tragedy.

The improved technical facilities bore results, and National Television began receiving sharper pictures and clearer sound; the distance seemed suddenly compressed, and I had the horrible sensation that Azucena and Rolf were by my side, separated from me by impenetrable glass. I was able to follow events hour by hour; I knew everything my love did to wrest the girl from her prison and help her endure her suffering; I overheard fragments of what they said to one another and could guess the rest; I was present when she taught Rolf to pray, and when he distracted her with the stories I had told him in a thousand and one nights beneath the white mosquito netting of our bed.

When darkness came on the second day, Rolf tried to sing Azucena to sleep with old Austrian folk songs he had learned from his mother, but she was far beyond sleep. They spent most of the night talking, each in a stupor of exhaustion and hunger, and shaking with cold. That night, imperceptibly, the unyielding floodgates that had contained Rolf Carlé's past for so many years began to open, and the torrent of all that had lain hidden in the deepest and most secret layers of memory poured out, leveling before it the obstacles that had blocked his consciousness for so long. He could not tell it all to Azucena; she perhaps did not know there was a world beyond the sea or time previous to her own; she was not capable of imagining Europe in the years of the war. So he could not tell her of defeat, nor of the afternoon the Russians had led them to the concentration camp to bury prisoners dead from starvation. Why should he describe to her how the naked bodies piled like a mountain of firewood resembled fragile china? How could he tell this dying child about ovens and gallows? Nor did he mention the night that he had seen his mother naked, shod in stiletto-heeled red boots, sobbing with humiliation. There was much he did not tell, but in those hours he relived for the first time all the things his mind had tried to erase. Azucena had surrendered her fear to him and so, without wishing it, had obliged Rolf to confront his own. There, beside that hellhole of mud, it was impossible for Rolf to flee from himself any longer, and the visceral[12] terror he had lived as a boy suddenly invaded him. He reverted to the years when he was the age of Azucena, and younger, and, like her, found himself trapped in a pit without escape, buried in life, his head barely above ground; he saw before his eyes the boots and legs of his father, who had removed his belt and was whipping it in the air with the never-forgotten hiss of a viper coiled to strike. Sorrow flooded through him, intact and precise, as if it had lain always in his mind, waiting. He was once again in the armoire where his father locked him to punish him for imagined misbehavior, there where for eternal hours he had crouched with his eyes closed, not to see the darkness, with his hands over his ears, to shut out the beating of his heart, trembling, huddled like a cornered animal. Wandering in the mist of his memories he found his sister Katherina, a sweet, retarded child who spent her life hiding, with the hope that her father would forget the disgrace of her having been born. With Katherina, Rolf crawled beneath the dining room table, and with her hid there under the long

---

12. Here, *visceral* means "emotional or instinctive rather than intellectual."

Persona What do you infer the narrator might be feeling as she witnesses these interactions? Explain.

Life Transitions How are Rolf and Azucena now in a similar situation?

white tablecloth, two children forever embraced, alert to footsteps and voices. Katherina's scent melded with his own sweat, with aromas of cooking, garlic, soup, freshly baked bread, and the unexpected odor of putrescent clay. His sister's hand in his, her frightened breathing, her silk hair against his cheek, the candid gaze of her eyes. Katherina . . . Katherina materialized before him, floating on the air like a flag, clothed in the white tablecloth, now a winding sheet, and at last he could weep for her death and for the guilt of having abandoned her. He understood then that all his exploits as a reporter, the feats that had won him such recognition and fame, were merely an attempt to keep his most ancient fears at bay, a stratagem[13] for taking refuge behind a lens to test whether reality was more tolerable from that perspective. He took excessive risks as an exercise of courage, training by day to conquer the monsters that tormented him by night. But he had come face to face with the moment of truth; he could not continue to escape his past. He was Azucena; he was buried in the clayey mud; his terror was not the distant emotion of an almost forgotten childhood, it was a claw sunk in his throat. In the flush of his tears he saw his mother, dressed in black and clutching her imitation-crocodile pocketbook to her bosom, just as he had last seen her on the dock when she had come to put him on the boat to South America. She had not come to dry his tears, but to tell him to pick up a shovel: the war was over and now they must bury the dead.

"Don't cry. I don't hurt anymore. I'm fine," Azucena said when dawn came.

"I'm not crying for you," Rolf Carlé smiled. "I'm crying for myself. I hurt all over."

The third day in the valley of the cataclysm began with a pale light filtering through storm clouds. The President of the Republic visited the area in his tailored safari jacket to confirm that this was the worst catastrophe of the century; the country was in mourning; sister nations had offered aid; he had ordered a state of siege; the Armed Forces would be merciless, anyone caught stealing or committing other offenses would be shot on sight. He added that it was impossible to remove all the corpses or count the thousands who had disappeared; the entire valley would be declared holy ground, and bishops would come to celebrate a solemn mass for the souls of the victims. He went to the Army field tents to offer relief in the form of vague promises to crowds of the rescued, then to the improvised hospital to offer a word of encouragement to doctors and nurses worn down from so many hours of **tribulations.** Then he asked to be taken to see Azucena, the little girl the whole world had seen. He waved to her with a limp statesman's hand, and microphones recorded his emotional voice and paternal[14] tone as he told her that her courage had served as an example to the nation. Rolf Carlé interrupted to ask for a pump, and the President assured him that he personally would attend to the matter. I caught a glimpse of Rolf for a few seconds kneeling beside the mudpit. On the evening news broadcast, he was still in the same position;

---

14. Here, *paternal* means "fatherly."

Analyze Sensory Details What point is the writer making by including this detail about how the president was dressed?

Vocabulary

tribulation (trib′yə lā′shən) *n.* great misery or distress; suffering

---

13. A *stratagem* is a trick or scheme for achieving some purpose.

Country Road, 1813. Alexei Savrasov.
The State Tretyakov Gallery, Moscow, Russia.

View the Art Alexei Savrasov's landscapes, like this one that shows the aftermath of a storm, have been praised for their lyrical yet realistic depiction of the awakening of the natural world. Do you think the natural disaster in Allende's story represents total destruction, a new beginning, or some combination of the two? Explain.

and I, glued to the screen like a fortune-teller to her crystal ball, could tell that something fundamental had changed in him. I knew somehow that during the night his defenses had crumbled and he had given in to grief; finally he was vulnerable. The girl had touched a part of him that he himself had no access to, a part he had never shared with me. Rolf had wanted to console her, but it was Azucena who had given him consolation.

I recognized the precise moment at which Rolf gave up the fight and surrendered to the torture of watching the girl die. I was with them, three days and two nights, spying on them from the other side of life. I was there when she told him that in all her thirteen years no boy had ever loved her and that it was a pity to leave this world without knowing love. Rolf assured her that he loved her more than he could ever love anyone, more than he loved his mother, more than his sister, more than all the women who had slept in his arms, more than he loved me, his life companion, who would have given anything to be trapped in that well in her place, who would have exchanged her life for Azucena's, and I watched as he leaned down to kiss her poor forehead, consumed by a sweet, sad emotion he could not name. I felt how in that instant both were saved from despair, how they were freed from the clay, how they rose above the vultures and helicopters, how together they flew above the vast swamp of corruption and laments. How, finally, they were able to accept death. Rolf Carlé prayed in silence that she would die quickly, because such pain cannot be borne.

By then I had obtained a pump and was in touch with a general who had agreed to ship it the next morning on a military cargo plane. But on the night of that third day, beneath the unblinking focus of quartz lamps and the lens of a hundred cameras, Azucena gave up, her eyes locked with those of the friend who had sustained her to the end. Rolf Carlé removed the life buoy, closed her eyelids, held her to his chest for a few moments, and then let her go. She sank slowly, a flower in the mud.

You are back with me, but you are not the same man. I often accompany you to the station and we watch the videos of Azucena again; you study them intently, looking for something you could have done to save her, something you did not think of in time. Or maybe you study them to see yourself as if in a mirror, naked. Your cameras lie forgotten in a closet; you do not write or sing; you sit long hours before the window, staring at the mountains. Beside you, I wait for you to complete the voyage into yourself, for the old wounds to heal. I know that when you return from your nightmares, we shall again walk hand in hand, as before.

Life Transitions *From what you have learned about Azucena, how might she have helped Rolf make this transition?*

Persona *What do you learn about the narrator here? Does this detail surprise you? Why or why not?*

Analyze Sensory Details *In what ways were Azucena and Rolf stuck in, then freed from, the clay? Explain.*

ISABEL ALLENDE 241

After You Read

Respond and Think Critically

Respond and Interpret

1. Which character in the story do you admire the most? Why?

2. (a) What are Azucena's circumstances at the beginning of the story? (b) What did she come to symbolize as the story progressed?

3. (a) What attitude did you notice among the people who survived the disaster? (b) What does this indicate about their culture?

Analyze and Evaluate

4. Irony is a contrast between appearance and reality. (a) What ironic situations did you notice in this story? (b) How do you think these ironies furthered the main message of the story? Explain.

5. What do you think the title of this story means? In your opinion, is it an appropriate title? Why or why not?

6. One critic wrote that Allende is capable of moving "between the personal and the political, between reality and fantasy." Do these observations apply to this story? Why or why not?

Connect

7. **Big Idea** **Life Transitions** In what ways do Rolf and Azucena exchange roles in this story?

8. **Connect to the Author** Allende worked as a broadcast journalist and as an editor of a feminist magazine. Where in the story does Allende use the knowledge she gained in these two endeavors to create a more believable story?

Visual Literacy

Put Events in Time Order

Make a timeline like the one below. Reread "And of Clay Are We Created," filling in the timeline as you read. Above the timeline, include external events relating to the mudslide and the rescue operation. Below the timeline, include what is happening to Rolf Carlé internally as he participates in the disaster.

External Events

●———|———————|———————|———→
    Day 1   Day 2   Day 3

Internal Events (for Rolf)

Group Activity Share your timeline with your classmates. Then discuss the following questions, referring to your timelines. Look back at the story to resolve any disagreements about the sequence of events.

1. Summarize the different efforts Rolf makes to save Azucena.

2. How does Rolf's attitude toward Azucena change as the story progresses? Find specific evidence from the story to support your answer.

3. Why do you think Rolf tries so hard to save Azucena? Support your answer with two or more reasons.

Literary Element Persona

A **persona** is the person created by the author to tell a story. Adopting a persona allows an author to distance himself or herself from the reader. It is like slipping on a mask, or a different personality. The attitudes and beliefs expressed by the narrator may not be the same as those of the author.

1. Reread the information about Isabel Allende on page 230. What do the unnamed narrator and Allende have in common? How might Allende have drawn on her own life to create both the narrator and Rolf?

2. Why do you think Allende chose the persona of someone not at the scene of the action? How would the story have been different if Rolf Carlé had been the narrator?

3. Even though Allende distances herself from the reader through a persona, her narrator is nevertheless affected by the action of the story. What consequences does the narrator face as a result of Rolf's attempt to save Azucena?

Review: Voice

As you learned on page 185, **voice** is the distinctive use of language that conveys the author's or the narrator's personality in a literary work. Voice is determined by elements of style, such as word choice, imagery, figurative language, and tone.

Partner Activity In this story, the narrator's tone is grimly realistic when describing the details of the mudslide's devastation. Work with a classmate to analyze the language the narrator uses to achieve this dark tone. Create a web diagram similar to the one below, in which you list examples of imagery and figurative language that contribute to the narrator's tone.

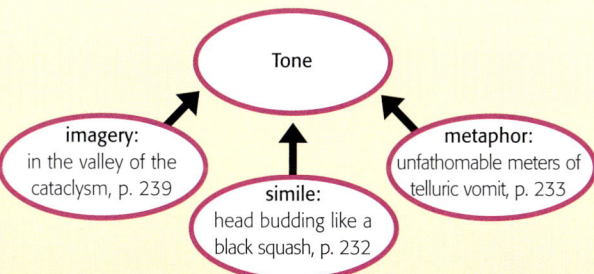

Reading Strategy Analyze Sensory Details

Allende uses **sensory details** to make the setting and characters more vivid and to evoke a strong emotional reaction in the reader. Refer to the chart of sensory details that you began on page 231.

1. Which details do you think are the strongest? Do some appeal to more than one sense?

2. Skim the story for more sensory details to add to your chart. Try to add at least one more to each row. Explain why you think each one evokes an emotional reaction.

Vocabulary Practice

Practice with Analogies Choose the word that best completes each analogy.

1. ecstasy : celebrant :: tribulation :
   a. surveyor   b. victim   c. participant

2. hostility : unfriendliness :: pandemonium :
   a. simplicity   b. insecurity   c. confusion

3. fortitude : weakness :: bedlam :
   a. peace   b. cruelty   c. uproar

4. dream : pleasure :: presentiment :
   a. danger   b. discomfort   c. change

5. equanimity : serenity :: obscurity :
   a. insensitivity   b. uneasiness   c. vagueness

Academic Vocabulary

*Allende makes a **link** between the mud or clay in which Azucena is mired and a metaphorical mud or clay out of which life is created.*

Link is an academic word. More familiar words with similar meanings are *connection*, *bond*, and *relationship*. To study this word further, fill out the graphic organizer below.

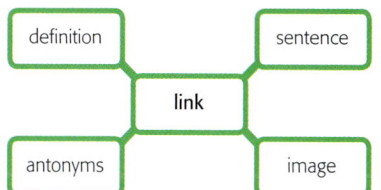

For more on academic vocabulary, see pages 52 and 53.

Respond Through Writing

Expository Essay

Analyze Imagery "And of Clay Are We Created" relies heavily on sensory details to create both the narrative present and the past. In an essay, analyze how Allende uses sensory details to create powerful imagery in this story and how that imagery results in nuances or ambiguity. Support your ideas with evidence from the story.

Understand the Task
- To **analyze** is to examine how parts of the work, such as the setting or symbols, help create the work as a whole.
- A **nuance** is a subtle distinction or a shade of meaning.
- **Ambiguity** is lack of certainty. It results from details that suggest unclear or contradictory interpretations.

Prewrite As you read, look back at the chart you made in which you recorded sensory details. Expand the chart to help you analyze imagery.

Sense	Story Detail	Effect of the Image	Nuances/Ambiguity
touch	"her silk hair against his cheek"	creates feelings of softness, closeness, intimacy	Two strangers become like father and daughter

Draft State your thesis in the opening paragraph. Structure the body of your essay by creating a separate paragraph for each supporting point. Begin each body paragraph with a topic sentence that relates to, supports, or explains your thesis. Follow the topic sentence with quoted evidence from the story, which you might introduce in this way:

> For example, the image of _____ is ambiguous.

Follow each example with your analysis of the shades of meaning, multiple meanings, or contradictions that the quoted evidence suggests. Conclude your essay by restating your thesis in a fresh way.

Revise Exchange essays with a classmate. Identify each other's thesis statement and supporting ideas. Offer suggestions for increased, more detailed, or more specific references to the text. Discuss your suggestions and revise as needed.

Edit and Proofread Proofread your paper, correcting any errors in grammar, spelling, and punctuation. Use the Grammar Tip in the side column to help you with relating your topic sentences to your thesis.

Learning Objectives

In this assignment, you will focus on the following objectives:

Writing: Writing an expository essay.

Grammar: Paragraphing.

Grammar Tip

Paragraphing
Begin each body paragraph with a topic sentence that presents the main idea. Be sure the main idea relates directly to your thesis.

Example:

Thesis: Allende uses (clay) as a (metaphor) for (life) itself.

Topic Sentence 1: The (clay) is a (metaphor) for something that can change, shape, or mold (life) experience.

Topic Sentence 2: The (clay) is a (metaphor) for how two lives are molded together.

Topic Sentence 3: The (clay) is a (metaphor) for how (life) can appear or disappear, as if out of mud.

Before You Read

Lullaby

Meet **Leslie Marmon Silko**
(born 1948)

"I suppose at the core of my writing is the attempt to identify what it is . . . to grow up neither white nor fully traditional Indian," Leslie Marmon Silko has written. Silko, who is of Laguna Pueblo, Mexican, and white descent, grew up on the Laguna Pueblo Reservation. Although her writing focuses on Native American identity, Silko does not claim to represent Native Americans in general. Silko has written, "I am only one human being, one Laguna woman."

> "I was never afraid or lonely though I was high in the hills, many miles from home—because I carried with me the feeling I'd acquired from listening to the old stories."
>
> —Leslie Marmon Silko

Steeped in Tradition Leslie Marmon Silko was born in Albuquerque, New Mexico. Her father was a professional photographer and manager of the Marmon Trading Post in Old Laguna, the small village where Leslie and her two sisters grew up. Silko's extended family contributed to the rich culture and historical legacy of Old Laguna. Silko credits her family's love of books and storytelling as instrumental to the development of her own creativity and interest in literature. She also notes that the physical and social landscape surrounding her hometown provide the setting and background for much of her writing.

Silko attended the University of New Mexico, where she studied English and creative writing. While there, her first short story, "The Man to Send Rain Clouds," was published. In 1974 she went on to publish several additional short stories in a Native American anthology, as well as *Laguna Woman,* a collection of poetry. After moving to Ketchikan, Alaska, Silko began writing the novel *Ceremony,* which was published in 1977. She returned to the Southwest and has since published novels, poetry, and short stories.

Other Artistic Pursuits Silko has also been involved in the visual arts of filmmaking and photography and has published photographs in acclaimed arts magazines as well as in her own literary works. Her fiction and poetry collection *Storyteller,* published in 1981, features photos of her family and childhood environment. Silko founded the Laguna Film Project and filmed *Arrowboy and the Witches*, an hour-long version of her story "Estoy-eh-moot and the Kunideeyahs."

Author Search For more about Leslie Marmon Silko, go to glencoe.com and enter QuickPass code GL59794u1.

Literature and Reading Preview

Connect to the Story
Why do you think memories are so powerful? Freewrite for a few minutes about one of your fondest or strongest memories.

Build Background
"Lullaby" takes place in west central New Mexico, near the Cañoncito (Navajo) Reservation. In the 1950s, U.S. government health agencies began testing Navajos for pulmonary tuberculosis, also known as TB. Infected people were sent away—sometimes against their will—to special hospitals, called sanatoriums, for long-term care.

Set Purposes for Reading

Big Idea Life Transitions

As you read, ask yourself, How does Silko use the experiences of death, loss, and change to portray life in transition?

Literary Element Style

The author's choice and arrangement of words make up the **style** of a literary work. Style can reveal the author's purpose and attitude toward his or her subject, characters, and audience. As you read, ask yourself, How does Silko's choice and arrangement of words help her to create her particular style?

Reading Strategy Evaluate Characters

Characters are the people portrayed in a literary work. When you **evaluate characters**, you make judgments or form opinions about them. Such evaluations help the reader develop a framework for explaining a character's actions, statements, thoughts, and feelings. As you read, ask yourself, Where does Silko provide opportunities for the reader to evaluate different characters?

Tip: Ask Questions Use a chart like the one shown to record details from the story that help you form opinions about Ayah.

Detail	Opinion About Ayah
"She smiled at the snow which was trying to cover her little by little."	She is at home in nature.

Learning Objectives

For pages 245–257

In studying this text, you will focus on the following objectives:

Literary Study: Analyzing style.

Reading: Evaluating character.

Vocabulary

arroyo (ə roi′ō) *n.* a dry gully or stream bed; p. 248 *The thirsty horse did not find water as it cantered along the arroyo.*

crevice (krev′is) *n.* a narrow crack into or through something; p. 251 *Mark watched his father fill in the crevice in the wall.*

sparse (spärs) *adj.* thinly spread or distributed; p. 254 *The berries were so sparse that we could not gather enough to make a pie.*

distortion (dis tôr′shən) *n.* an appearance of being twisted or bent out of shape; p. 255 *The crack in the mirror caused a distortion in my reflection.*

Lullaby
Leslie Marmon Silko

Owl Watching Over Wildlife. Stephan Daigle.

The sun had gone down but the snow in the wind gave off its own light. It came in thick tufts like new wool—washed before the weaver spins it. Ayah[1] reached out for it like her own babies had, and she smiled when she remembered how she had laughed at them. She was an old woman now, and her life had become memories. She sat down with her back against the wide cottonwood tree, feeling the rough bark on her back bones; she faced east and listened to the wind and snow sing a high-pitched Yeibechei[2] song. Out of the wind she felt warmer, and she could watch the wide fluffy snow fill in her tracks, steadily, until the direction she had come from was gone. By the light of the snow she could see the dark outline of the big arroyo a few feet away. She was sitting on the edge of Cebolleta[3] Creek, where in the springtime the thin cows would graze on grass already chewed flat to the ground. In the wide deep creek bed where only a trickle of water flowed in the summer, the skinny cows would wander, looking for new grass along winding paths splashed with manure.

Ayah pulled the old Army blanket over her head like a shawl. Jimmie's blanket—the one he had sent to her. That was a long time ago and the green wool was faded, and it was unraveling on the edges. She did not want to think about Jimmie. So she thought about the weaving and the way her mother had done it. On the tall wooden loom set into the sand under a tamarack[4] tree for shade. She could see it clearly. She had been only a little girl when her grandma gave her the wooden combs to pull the twigs and burrs from the raw, freshly washed wool. And while she combed the wool, her grandma sat beside her, spinning a silvery strand of yarn around the smooth cedar spindle. Her mother worked at the loom with yarns dyed bright yellow and red and gold. She watched them dye the yarn in boiling black pots full of beeweed petals, juniper berries, and sage. The blankets her mother made were soft and woven so tight that rain rolled off them like birds' feathers. Ayah remembered sleeping warm on cold windy nights, wrapped in her mother's blankets on the hogan's[5] sandy floor.

Visual Vocabulary
In yarn-making, the *spindle* is a round, tapered stick that is turned by hand to twist wool fibers into a thread of yarn.

The snow drifted now, with the northwest wind hurling it in gusts. It drifted up around her black overshoes—old ones with little metal buckles. She smiled at the snow which was trying to cover her little by little. She could remember when they had no black rubber overshoes; only the high buckskin leggings that they wrapped over their elkhide moccasins. If the snow was dry or frozen, a person could walk all day and not get wet; and in the evenings the beams of the ceiling would hang with lengths of pale buckskin leggings, drying out slowly.

---

1. *Ayah* (ä′yə)
2. The *Yeibechei* (yä′bə chā) are masked Navajo dancers who sing in high-pitched voices.
3. *Cebolleta* (se′bō yä′tä) is also the name of a town in the story.

Evaluate Characters What does this sentence reveal about Ayah?

Vocabulary

arroyo (ə roi′ō) *n.* a dry gully or stream bed

4. *Tamarack* is another name for larch, a tree in the pine family.
5. A *hogan* is a traditional Navajo dwelling made of wood and covered with earth.

She felt peaceful remembering. She didn't feel cold any more. Jimmie's blanket seemed warmer than it had ever been. And she could remember the morning he was born. She could remember whispering to her mother, who was sleeping on the other side of the hogan, to tell her it was time now. She did not want to wake the others. The second time she called to her, her mother stood up and pulled on her shoes; she knew. They walked to the old stone hogan together, Ayah walking a step behind her mother. She waited alone, learning the rhythms of the pains while her mother went to call the old woman to help them. The morning was already warm even before dawn and Ayah smelled the bee flowers blooming and the young willow growing at the springs. She could remember that so clearly, but his birth merged into the births of the other children and to her it became all the same birth. They named him for the summer morning and in English they called him Jimmie.

It wasn't like Jimmie died. He just never came back, and one day a dark blue sedan with white writing on its doors pulled up in front of the boxcar shack where the rancher let the Indians live. A man in a khaki uniform trimmed in gold gave them a yellow piece of paper and told them that Jimmie was dead. He said the Army would try to get the body back and then it would be shipped to them; but it wasn't likely because the helicopter had burned after it crashed. All of this was told to Chato[6] because he could understand English. She stood inside the doorway holding the baby while Chato listened. Chato spoke English like a white man and he spoke Spanish too. He was taller than the white man and he stood straighter too. Chato didn't explain why; he just told the military man they could keep the body if they found it. The white man looked bewildered; he nodded his head and he left. Then Chato looked at her and shook his head, and then he told her, "Jimmie isn't coming home anymore," and when he spoke, he used the words to speak of the dead. She didn't cry then, but she hurt inside with anger. And she mourned him as the years passed, when a horse fell with Chato and broke his leg, and the white rancher told them he wouldn't pay Chato until he could work again. She mourned Jimmie because he would have worked for his father then; he would have saddled the big bay[7] horse and ridden the fence lines each day, with wire cutters and heavy gloves, fixing the breaks in the barbed wire and putting the stray cattle back inside again.

She mourned him after the white doctors came to take Danny and Ella away. She was at the shack alone that day they came. It was back in the days before they hired Navajo women to go with them as interpreters. She recognized one of the doctors. She had seen him at the children's clinic at Cañoncito[8] about a month ago. They were wearing khaki uniforms and they waved papers at her and a black ball-point pen, trying to make her understand their English words. She was frightened by the way they looked at the children, like the lizard watches the fly. Danny was swinging on the tire swing on the elm tree behind the rancher's house, and Ella was toddling around the front door, dragging the broomstick horse Chato made for her. Ayah could see they wanted her to sign the papers, and Chato had taught her to sign her name. It

---

6. *Chato* (chä′ tō)

Evaluate Characters *What does this detail tell you about Chato?*

7. Here, *bay* is the horse's color—a reddish brown.
8. *Cañoncito* (kan′ yən sē′ tō) is the name of the Navajo reservation located in west central New Mexico.

Style *What does this simile mean?*

was something she was proud of. She only wanted them to go, and to take their eyes away from her children.

She took the pen from the man without looking at his face and she signed the papers in three different places he pointed to. She stared at the ground by their feet and waited for them to leave. But they stood there and began to point and gesture at the children. Danny stopped swinging. Ayah could see his fear. She moved suddenly and grabbed Ella into her arms; the child squirmed, trying to get back to her toys. Ayah ran with the baby toward Danny; she screamed for him to run and then she grabbed him around his chest and carried him too. She ran south into the foothills of juniper trees and black lava rock. Behind her she heard the doctors running, but they had been taken by surprise, and as the hills became steeper and the cholla cactus were thicker, they stopped. When she reached the top of the hill, she stopped to listen in case they were circling around her. But in a few minutes she heard a car engine start and they drove away. The children had been too surprised to cry while she ran with them. Danny was shaking and Ella's little fingers were gripping Ayah's blouse.

Visual Vocabulary
A *cholla* (choi′ə) is a spiny, shrubby, or treelike cactus.

She stayed up in the hills for the rest of the day, sitting on a black lava boulder in the sunshine where she could see for miles all around her. The sky was light blue and cloudless, and it was warm for late April. The sun warmth relaxed her and took the fear and anger away. She lay back on the rock and watched the sky. It seemed to her that she could walk into the sky, stepping through clouds endlessly. Danny played with little pebbles and stones, pretending they were birds' eggs and then little rabbits. Ella sat at her feet and dropped fistfuls of dirt into the breeze, watching the dust and particles of sand intently. ==Ayah watched a hawk soar high above them, dark wings gliding; hunting or only watching, she did not know.== The hawk was patient and he circled all afternoon before he disappeared around the high volcanic peak the Mexicans called Guadalupe.[9]

Late in the afternoon, Ayah looked down at the gray boxcar shack with the paint all peeled from the wood; the stove pipe on the roof was rusted and crooked. The fire she had built that morning in the oil drum stove had burned out. Ella was asleep in her lap now and Danny sat close to her, complaining that he was hungry; he asked when they would go to the house. "We will stay up here until your father comes," she told him, "because those white men were chasing us." The boy remembered then and he nodded at her silently.

If Jimmie had been there he could have read those papers and explained to her what they said. Ayah would have known then, never to sign them. The doctors came back the next day and they brought a BIA[10] policeman with them. They told Chato they had her signature and that was all they needed. Except for the kids. She listened to Chato sullenly; she hated him when he told her it was the old woman who died in the winter, spitting blood; it was her old grandma who had given the children this disease. "They don't spit blood," she said coldly. "The whites lie."

---

9. *Guadalupe* (gwä′ də lōō′pä)
10. The Bureau of Indian Affairs, or *BIA,* is the federal agency in charge of administering government policies toward Native Americans.

Life Transitions Why do you think Ayah remembers even the smallest details of this day?

Monument Valley at Sunset. Robert McIntosh.

View the Art Monument Valley is located on the Navajo reservation on the border of southern Utah and northern Arizona. Where in the story does Silko describe a setting or time that corresponds with the image in the painting?

She held Ella and Danny close to her, ready to run to the hills again. "I want a medicine man first," she said to Chato, not looking at him. He shook his head. "It's too late now. The policeman is with them. You signed the paper." His voice was gentle.

It was worse than if they had died: to lose the children and to know that somewhere, in a place called Colorado, in a place full of sick and dying strangers, her children were without her. There had been babies that died soon after they were born, and one that died before he could walk. She had carried them herself, up to the boulders and great pieces of the cliff that long ago crashed down from Long Mesa; she laid them in the **crevices** of sandstone and buried them in fine brown sand with round quartz pebbles that washed down the hills in the rain. She had endured it because they had been with her. But she could not bear this pain. She did not sleep for a long time after they took her children. She stayed on the hill where they had fled the first time, and she slept rolled up in the blanket Jimmie had sent her. She carried the pain in her belly and it was fed by everything she saw: the blue sky of their last day together and the dust and pebbles they played with; the swing in the elm tree and broomstick horse choked life from her. The pain filled her stomach and there was no room for food or for her lungs to fill with air. The air and the food would have been theirs.

Evaluate Characters What does this detail tell you about Chato's personality?

Vocabulary

crevice (krev′is) *n.* a narrow crack into or through something

Life Transitions Why is the absence of Danny and Ella more upsetting to Ayah than the deaths of her other children?

Style How does the author describe Ayah's feelings after losing her children?

LESLIE MARMON SILKO

She hated Chato, not because he let the policeman and doctors put the screaming children in the government car, but because he had taught her to sign her name. Because it was like the old ones always told her about learning their language or any of their ways: it endangered you. She slept alone on the hill until the middle of November when the first snows came. Then she made a bed for herself where the children had slept. She did not lie down beside Chato again until many years later, when he was sick and shivering and only her body could keep him warm. The illness came after the white rancher told Chato he was too old to work for him anymore, and Chato and his old woman should be out of the shack by the next afternoon because the rancher had hired new people to work there. That had satisfied her. To see how the white man repaid Chato's years of loyalty and work. All of Chato's fine-sounding English talk didn't change things.

It snowed steadily and the luminous light from the snow gradually diminished into the darkness. Somewhere in Cebolleta a dog barked and other village dogs joined with it. Ayah looked in the direction she had come, from the bar where Chato was buying the wine. Sometimes he told her to go on ahead and wait; and then he never came. And when she finally went back looking for him, she would find him passed out at the bottom of the wooden steps to Azzie's Bar. All the wine would be gone and most of the money too, from the pale blue check that came to them once a month in a government envelope. It was then that she would look at his face and his hands, scarred by ropes and the barbed wire of all those years, and she would think, this man is a stranger; for forty years she had smiled at him and cooked his food, but he remained a stranger. She stood up again, with the snow almost to her knees, and she walked back to find Chato.

It was hard to walk in the deep snow and she felt the air burn in her lungs. She stopped a short distance from the bar to rest and readjust the blanket. But this time he wasn't waiting for her on the bottom step with his old Stetson hat pulled down and his shoulders hunched up in his long wool overcoat.

She was careful not to slip on the wooden steps. When she pushed the door open, warm air and cigarette smoke hit her face. She looked around slowly and deliberately, in every corner, in every dark place that the old man might find to sleep. The bar owner didn't like Indians in there, especially Navajos, but he let Chato come in because he could talk Spanish like he was one of them. The men at the bar stared at her, and the bartender saw that she left the door open wide. Snowflakes were flying inside like moths and melting into a puddle on the oiled wood floor. He motioned to her to close the door, but she did not see him. She held herself straight and walked across the room slowly, searching the room with every step. The snow in her hair melted and she could feel it on her forehead. At the far corner of the room, she saw red flames at the mica window of the old stove door; she looked behind the stove just to make sure. The bar got quiet except for the Spanish polka music playing on the jukebox. She stood by the stove and shook the snow from her blanket and held it near the stove to dry. The wet wool smell reminded her of newborn goats in early March, brought inside to warm near the fire. She felt calm.

Visual Vocabulary
Mica is a mineral (abundant in New Mexico) that can be split into thin, strong, flexible sheets. A sheet of colorless mica makes a decent, inexpensive substitute for glass.

Vision Quest, 1999. John Newcomb.
Acrylic on canvas. Private collection.

View the Art A vision quest is a Native American ritual in which the participant, usually an adolescent boy, seeks spiritual power and knowledge by communing with a guardian spirit animal through prayer, fasting, isolation, or other means. How might Ayah's story be a sort of vision quest?

In past years they would have told her to get out. But her hair was white now and her face was wrinkled. They looked at her like she was a spider crawling slowly across the room. They were afraid; she could feel the fear. She looked at their faces steadily. They reminded her of the first time the white people brought her children back to her that winter. Danny had been shy and hid behind the thin white woman who brought them. And the baby had not known her until Ayah took her into her arms, and then Ella had nuzzled close to her as she had when she was nursing. The blonde woman was nervous and kept looking at a dainty gold watch on her wrist. She sat on the bench near the small window and watched the dark snow clouds gather around the mountains; she was worrying about the unpaved road. She was frightened by what she saw inside too: the strips of venison drying on a rope across the ceiling and the children jabbering excitedly in a language she did not know. So they stayed for only a few hours. Ayah watched the government car disappear down the road and she knew they were already being weaned from these lava hills and from this sky. The last time they came was in early June, and Ella stared at her the way the men in the bar were now staring. Ayah did not try to pick her up; she smiled at her instead and spoke cheer-

---

Life Transitions What does the author mean by this statement?

fully to Danny. When he tried to answer her, he could not seem to remember and he spoke English words with the Navajo. But he gave her a scrap of paper that he had found somewhere and carried in his pocket; it was folded in half, and he shyly looked up at her and said it was a bird. She asked Chato if they were home for good this time. He spoke to the white woman and she shook her head. "How much longer?" he asked, and she said she didn't know; but Chato saw how she stared at the boxcar shack. Ayah turned away then. She did not say good-bye.

She felt satisfied that the men in the bar feared her. Maybe it was her face and the way she held her mouth with teeth clenched tight, like there was nothing anyone could do to her now. She walked north down the road, searching for the old man. She did this because she had the blanket, and there would be no place for him except with her and the blanket in the old adobe barn near the arroyo. They always slept there when they came to Cebolleta. If the money and the wine were gone, she would be relieved because then they could go home again: back to the old hogan with a dirt roof and rock walls where she herself had been born. And the next day the old man could go back to the few sheep they still had, to follow along behind them, guiding them, into dry sandy arroyos where **sparse** grass grew. She knew he did not like walking behind old ewes when for so many years he rode big quarter horses and worked with cattle. But she wasn't sorry for him; he should have known all along what would happen.

There had not been enough rain for their garden in five years; and that was when Chato finally hitched a ride into the town and brought back brown boxes of rice and sugar and big tin cans of welfare[11] peaches. After that, at the first of the month they went to Cebolleta to ask the postmaster for the check; and then Chato would go to the bar and cash it. They did this as they planted the garden every May, not because anything would survive the summer dust, but because it was time to do this. The journey passed the days that smelled silent and dry like the caves above the canyon with yellow painted buffaloes on their walls.

He was walking along the pavement when she found him. He did not stop or turn around when he heard her behind him. She walked beside him and she noticed how slowly he moved now. He smelled strong of woodsmoke and urine. Lately he had been forgetting. Sometimes he called her by his sister's name and she had been gone for a long time. Once she had found him wandering on the road to the white man's ranch, and she asked him why he was going that way; he laughed at her and said, "You know they can't run that ranch without me," and he walked on determined, limping on the leg that had been crushed many years before. Now he looked at her curiously, as if for the first time, but he kept shuffling along, moving slowly along the side of the highway. His gray hair had grown long and spread out on the shoulders of the long overcoat. He wore the old felt hat pulled down over his ears. His boots were worn out at the toes and he had stuffed pieces of an old red shirt in the holes. The rags made his feet

---

11. The canned peaches came from a government *welfare* program to help needy people.

Style *How does this description echo the mood of the story at this point?*

Vocabulary

sparse (spärs) *adj.* thinly spread or distributed

look like little animals up to their ears in snow. She laughed at his feet; the snow muffled the sound of her laugh. He stopped and looked at her again. The wind had quit blowing and the snow was falling straight down; the southeast sky was beginning to clear and Ayah could see a star.

"Let's rest awhile," she said to him. They walked away from the road and up the slope to the giant boulders that had tumbled down from the red sandrock mesa throughout the centuries of rainstorms and earth tremors. In a place where the boulders shut out the wind, they sat down with their backs against the rock. She offered half of the blanket to him and they sat wrapped together.

The storm passed swiftly. The clouds moved east. They were massive and full, crowding together across the sky. She watched them with the feeling of horses—steely blue-gray horses startled across the sky. The powerful haunches pushed into the distances and the tail hairs streamed white mist behind them. The sky cleared. Ayah saw that there was nothing between her and the stars. The light was crystalline.[12] There was no shimmer, no **distortion** through earth haze. She breathed the clarity of the night sky; she smelled the purity of the half moon and the stars. He was lying on his side with his knees pulled up near his belly for warmth. His eyes were closed now, and in the light from the stars and the moon, he looked young again.

---

12. Here, *crystalline* means "clear and pure as a crystal."

Evaluate Characters Do Ayah's actions indicate that she has forgiven Chato? Explain.

Vocabulary

distortion (dis tôr′shən) *n.* an appearance of being twisted or bent out of shape

She could see it descend out of the night sky: an icy stillness from the edge of the thin moon. She recognized the freezing. It came gradually, sinking snowflake by snowflake until the crust was heavy and deep. It had the strength of the stars in Orion, and its journey was endless. Ayah knew that with the wine he would sleep. He would not feel it. She tucked the blanket around him, remembering how it was when Ella had been with her; and she felt the rush so big inside her heart for the babies. And she sang the only song she knew to sing for babies. She could not remember if she had ever sung it to her children, but she knew that her grandmother had sung it and her mother had sung it:

Visual Vocabulary
The constellation *Orion* contains two of the brightest stars in the sky. In Greek mythology, Orion is traditionally depicted as a hunter wearing a belt with a sword at his side.

> The earth is your mother,
>   she holds you.
> The sky is your father,
>   he protects you.
> Sleep,
> sleep.
> Rainbow is your sister,
>   she loves you.
> The winds are your brothers,
>   they sing to you.
> Sleep,
> sleep.
> We are together always
> We are together always
> There never was a time
> when this
> was not so. ∾

Life Transitions Why do you think Ayah finds the lullaby comforting?

After You Read

Respond and Think Critically

Respond and Interpret

1. For which character did you have more sympathy, Ayah or Chato? Explain.

2. (a) In the first three paragraphs of the story, what reminds Ayah of events in the past? (b) Why might Ayah's thoughts turn so often to the past?

3. (a) When Ayah finally finds Chato near the end of the story, how does he look and act? (b) What do Chato's appearance and actions reveal about him?

Analyze and Evaluate

4. Why do you think the author chose to title this story "Lullaby"?

5. (a) Why does Chato react as he does when the white doctors come to take Danny and Ella? (b) Could Chato and Ayah have done anything to prevent the doctors from taking their children? Explain.

6. (a) How have Ayah and Chato learned to cope with the hardships they have experienced? (b) How have their ways of coping affected their relationship?

Connect

7. **Big Idea** **Life Transitions** Think about the many obstacles and tragedies that have shaped Ayah and Chato's lives. In your opinion, have they triumphed over adversity, or has it defeated them? Explain.

8. **Connect to the Author** Silko founded the Laguna Film Project and filmed an hour-long version of one of her stories. If you were the casting director of a film version of "Lullaby", which actors or people you know would you cast as Ayah and Chato? Explain.

Literary Element Style

SAT Skills Practice

1. What idea does Silko introduce in the opening three sentences (page 248) that she continues to use as a motif throughout the story?

   (A) sunlight and darkness
   (B) laughter and play
   (C) snow and rain
   (D) sheep and wool
   (E) weaving and blankets

2. In the last prose paragraph of the story (page 255) Silko speaks of "the freezing," by which she means

   (A) extreme cold
   (B) the pain of old memories
   (C) a deep sleep
   (D) death
   (E) Ayah's lost children

Review: Narrator

As you learned on pages 184–185, the narrator is the person who tells a story.

Partner Activity With a classmate, discuss the narrator's role in this story. Draw a chart as below to help you think about the narrator's relationship to the main characters. Then answer the questions.

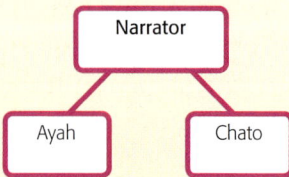

1. What is the narrator's relationship to the characters in the story? Give reasons for your answer.

2. How would the story be different if Ayah were the narrator? If Chato were the narrator? Do you think Silko made the best choice of narrator for this story? Explain.

Reading Strategy Evaluate Characters

When you **evaluate characters,** you form opinions and make judgments about them. Review your chart from page 246 to help you answer the following questions.

1. What is your opinion of Ayah? Give three details from the story to provide support for your answer.

2. How does your opinion of Ayah affect your enjoyment of the story? Explain.

Vocabulary Practice

Practice with Word Origins Studying the etymology, or origin and history, of a word can help you better understand and explore its meaning. Create a word map, like the one below, for each of these vocabulary words from the selection.

arroyo   crevice   sparse   distortion

EXAMPLE:

Definition	Etymology
moving from place to place	Latin *migrare* means "to move"

migratory

Sample sentence
Each year, flocks of migratory birds pass over our home on their way to their winter home.

Academic Vocabulary

The Bureau of Indian Affairs is an agency of the **federal** government.

Federal is an academic word. It applies specifically to a government in which states have individual powers but are governed collectively by a central authority. *Federal* is also often used to refer to anything related to or organized by the national, rather than state, government. Complete this sentence starter. Mr. Michaelson voted for federal _____ because _____.

For more on academic vocabulary, see pages 52 and 53.

Speaking and Listening

 Performance

Assignment With a partner, write a dialogue that might take place between Ayah and a dear friend. Perform it for the class.

Prepare Write a dialogue that reflects one or more parts of Ayah's life and involves a sympathetic listener. Rehearse it until you are sure your dialogue and performance accurately and sympathetically convey Ayah's personality and perspective.

Perform As you perform, strive to re-create the tone you hear as you read. Vary your volume and pitch according to the meaning you want to convey, use gestures and body language that complement your dialogue, and adopt the postures of two friends who are earnestly engaged in each other's thoughts. Monitor the effect of your dialogue on your audience, and adjust as needed:

If the audience is—	then—
looking away	make eye contact with them
doodling or fidgeting	bring up the volume, or make a dramatic change in posture or gestures
straining to follow or understand	slow down the pace, or speak more clearly

Evaluate After the performance, decide with your partner how successful your performance was and how it might have been better. Use the tips on page 1127 as a guide to writing your evaluation.

 Literature Online

Selection Resources For Selection Quizzes, eFlashcards, and Reading-Writing Connection activities, go to glencoe.com and enter QuickPass code GL59794u1.

Learning Objectives

For pages 258–265

In this workshop, you will focus on the following objectives:

Writing: Writing a literary criticism.

Grammar:
Understanding how to vary sentence openers.
Understanding how to correct run-on sentences.

Writing Process

At any stage, you may think of new ideas.

Prewrite

Draft

Revise

Focus Lesson:
Sentence Openers

Edit and Proofread

Focus Lesson: Run-on Sentences

Present/Publish

Writing and Research For prewriting, drafting, and revising tools, go to glencoe.com and enter QuickPass code GL59794u1.

Writing Workshop

Literary Criticism

Literature Connection In "A Californian's Tale," Mark Twain does more than tell an entertaining story—he also presents historical facts.

> "Thirty-five years ago I was out prospecting on the Stanislaus, tramping all day long with pick and pan and horn, and washing a hatful of dirt here and there, always expecting to make a rich strike, and never doing it."

Twain re-creates a real time and place and provides details about what happened there. A writer of **literary criticism** can use those details in analyzing the story from a historical perspective. Study the rubric below to learn about writing literary criticism based on biographical or historical details.

Checklist

Goals	Strategies
To comment on how a work is related to a particular place or time (history) or to an individual life (biography)	☑ Establish a clear thesis or controlling impression ☑ Display a keen understanding of the work including its subtle meanings
To explain and develop ideas	☑ Make accurate and detailed references to the text ☑ Demonstrate awareness of the author's style and appreciation of the effects created
To maintain a consistent focus and tone	☑ Use precise language and the active voice
To present organized, linked, and fluid ideas to the reader	☑ Create a clear introduction, body, and conclusion ☑ Use each body paragraph to present and develop one main idea ☑ Use transitions

258 UNIT 1 THE SHORT STORY

Exposition

Assignment: Write Literary Criticism

Write an essay of literary criticism of at least 1,500 words. Use your essay to show how a literary work is related to themes and issues of its historical period and to an individual's life. As you work, keep your audience and purpose in mind.

Audience: your teacher

Purpose: to explain and inform by analyzing how a work of literature is related to a real time, place, or person

Real-World Connection

Various writing tasks in the workplace, from informative presentations to corporate publications, will require you to use many of the same skills you use in writing literary criticism: choosing an appropriate and formal tone, maintaining a clear focus, and marshaling evidence in support of your ideas or claims.

Analyze a Professional Model

In the literary criticism that follows, Paule Marshall presents biographical details that shed light on her short story "To Da-duh, in Memoriam." The reader learns not only that Da-duh was a real person but also that she appears throughout Marshall's works. As you read the criticism, identify its features. Pay close attention to the comments in the margin: they point out features to include in your own literary criticism.

Real-Life Story Behind "To Da-duh, in Memoriam" by Paule Marshall

This is the most autobiographical of stories, a reminiscence largely of a visit I paid to my grandmother (whose nickname was Da-duh) on the island of Barbados when I was nine. Ours was a complex relationship—close, affectionate yet rivalrous. During the year I spent with her a subtle kind of power struggle went on between us. It was as if we both knew, at a level beyond words, that I had come into the world not only to love her and to continue her line but to take her very life in order that I might live.

   Years later, when I got around to writing the story, I tried giving the contest I had sensed between us a wider meaning. I wanted the basic theme of youth and old age to suggest rivalries, dichotomies of a cultural and political nature, having to do with the relationship of western civilization and the Third World.

Focus
Create and maintain a biographical or historical focus.

Formal Tone
Maintain a formal tone throughout your paper.

Purpose
Display a keen understanding of the work, including its subtle meanings or complex ideas.

Organization
Present your main ideas in topic sentences and support them in the body of each paragraph.

Support
Use examples as evidence and to support the points you make.

Consistent Focus
Relate all details and explanations to the thesis or controlling impression.

  Apart from this story, Da-duh also appears in one form or another in my other work as well. She's the old hairdresser, Mrs. Thompson, in *Brown Girl, Brownstones,* who offers Selina total, unquestioning love. She's Leesy Walkes and the silent cook, Carrington, in *The Chosen Place, the Timeless People.* She's Aunt Vi in "Reena" and Medford, the old family retainer in "British Guiana" from *Soul Clap Hands and Sing.* And she's Avey Johnson's Great-aunt Cuney in *Praisesong for the Widow.* Da-duh turns up everywhere.

  She's an ancestor figure, symbolic for me of the long line of black women and men—African and New World—who made my being possible, and whose spirit I believe continues to animate my life and work. I wish to acknowledge and celebrate them. I am, in a word, an unabashed ancestor worshipper.

Reading-Writing Connection Think about the writing techniques that you have just encountered and try them out in the literary criticism you write.

Forsaken Treasures. Victor Collector. Oil on canvas. Private collection.

Prewrite

Find the Work and Decide Your Approach The work of literature you choose must contain enough biographical or historical details for a successful essay. Always "test" the work before you begin writing to see whether it will work for a biographical or historical approach.

▶ To write a **biographical criticism,** first identify the life you will focus on. Organize details that illustrate the life in a list or cluster diagram.

▶ To take a **historical approach to literary criticism,** begin by identifying the time, the place, and the culture. Then find details in the story that show this historical world. Use a cluster diagram or make a list.

Develop a Thesis Review your list of ideas or your cluster. Decide on a focus. That is, write a sentence or two that provides an overview of what the details seem to say. This is your working thesis, which you can revise as you go along.

Working Thesis: Details in "Lullaby" show Navajo culture.

Develop an Organizational Plan Your next step is to decide on the main points to make in your essay. Either you can revise your thesis to show those main points and base your paragraph plan on it, or you can begin mapping out your body paragraphs and then revise your thesis. Either way, follow these steps to create a plan for each body paragraph.

▶ Think of a main idea for the body paragraph.
▶ List details, quotations, or examples from the story that illustrate or support that main idea.
▶ Add thoughts of your own about the main idea, as this plan shows.

Body Paragraph Plan

Main Idea: Because she is Navajo and speaks a different language, Ayah is suspicious of the English-speaking doctors.

Details from the Story: The doctors looked at the children "like the lizard watches the fly."

My Thoughts: This simile shows Ayah's fear. It shows how alien the doctors are to her. After, Ayah goes to the foothills to find comfort.

Talk About Your Ideas Meet with a partner. Refer to your working theses and paragraph plans as you discuss the focus of your papers so far and the main ideas you will present to support them. Ask your partner for suggestions on how to revise your thesis and make sure that your main ideas relate to it. Then talk about your writing voice. For this assignment, you want to sound objective, not personal. Ask your partner to comment on how objective, formal, and impersonal your plan is so far.

Exposition

A Working Thesis

You need not worry if you cannot come up with a perfect thesis during the prewriting stage. As you develop your draft, the focus of your paper will become clearer to you. You can improve your thesis at any time during your writing process.

Avoid Plagiarism

Avoid the dishonest use of others' ideas during this task by relying on your own careful reading and insights alone. If a task does not require the use of outside sources, avoid using them to shape your thinking or your writing.

Draft

Integrate Questions Introduce quoted evidence with transitional phrases, such as, "The [main character] reflects/thinks…" Transition to your own explanation with phrases such as "These words show…"

Analyze a Workshop Model

Here is a final draft of an essay that takes a historical approach to literary criticism. Read the essay and answer the questions in the margin. Use the answers to these questions to guide you as you write.

Lullaby

The short story "Lullaby" by Leslie Marmon Silko is about Ayah, an aging Navajo woman who waits for, looks for, and finally takes care of her husband, Chato. While she waits for and then searches for Chato, Ayah reflects on her memories, both happy and painful. She remembers her childhood and her children. She recalls how one child died and two were taken from her because they had tuberculosis. She thinks about the difficulties and indignities that her husband, Chato, endured while working for the white men. In "Lullaby" Silko conveys aspects of Navajo culture—a deep connection with nature, strong ties to family, reliance on tradition—and demonstrates how these cultural elements affect Ayah. Silko reflects Navajo culture in her story through unusual similes and through beautifully crafted descriptions.

For example, in the story's first paragraph, Silko uses a simile to show how Ayah sees the world symbolically through the tradition of weaving: "the snow in the wind gave off its own light. It came in thick tufts like new wool—washed before the weaver spins it."

Silko then uses description to show how the tradition of weaving is handed down from one generation to the next. Ayah thinks "about the weaving and the way her mother

Tone
What is the author's tone? Give examples of choices the writer makes to create the tone.

Thesis
What is the thesis? How is it related to history?

Support
What main idea does this evidence support? How does the evidence relate to the thesis of the paper?

[did] it. . . . She could see it clearly. She had been only a little girl. . . . And while she combed the wool, her grandma sat beside her, spinning, . . . Her mother worked at the loom. . . ." These lines show that strong family ties are important to Ayah. She comforts herself with pleasant family memories such as this when she does not want to think about more painful memories, such as those of her dead son, Jimmie.

    Details about the natural world provide insights into Ayah's life. For example, the yarn for weaving is dyed in "boiling black pots full of beeweed petals, juniper berries, and sage." This detail is followed by a beautiful, haunting simile: "The blankets her mother made were soft and woven so tight that rain rolled off them like birds' feathers."

    The vivid details that Silko uses to describe Ayah's memories reflect Ayah's connection to nature and tradition. Ayah remembers the "high buckskin leggings that they wrapped over their elkhide moccasins" when she was young. She recalls how she walked "a step behind her mother" when they "walked to the old stone hogan together" when Ayah was ready to give birth. In her house, strips of venison are hung up to dry.

    Through description, the author also shows the reader how Ayah and her family face the challenges and consequences of generations of poverty. Their cows are "skinny." Their house is a "boxcar shack." Ayah grew up in an "old hogan with a dirt roof and rock walls." They live in an area of "dry sandy arroyos where sparse grass grew."

    At the end of the story, Ayah sings Chato a traditional lullaby that likens earth, sky, rainbow, and wind to mother, father, sister, and brother. Thus, Silko's ending reinforces her use of beautiful descriptive and figurative language to reflect the deep connection with nature, family, and tradition that characterizes Navajo culture. Despite the many deep troubles that Ayah has endured, she—like many Navajo—is able to take comfort in her cultural heritage and to derive strength from it.

Exposition

Historical Focus
How does this analysis shed light on a time or place?

Organization
What is the main idea of this paragraph? How do the details explain and support it?

Consistent Focus
How are these ideas consistent with the ideas presented earlier?

Purpose
How does the writer demonstrate a thorough understanding of the work, including complex and subtle ideas?

Traits of Strong Writing

Include these traits of strong writing to express your ideas effectively.

Ideas message or theme and the details that develop it
Organization arrangement of main ideas and supporting details
Voice writer's unique way of using tone and style
Word Choice vocabulary a writer uses to convey meaning
Sentence Fluency rhythm and flow of sentences
Conventions correct spelling, grammar, usage, and mechanics
Presentation the way words and design elements look on a page

See also pages R28–R30

Word Choice

This academic vocabulary word appears in the student model:

element (el´ə mənt) *n.*
1. a part; 2. a factor determining the outcome of a process; 3. *Chemistry:* a substance consisting of a single type of atom; a substance that cannot be separated into smaller substances. Silko demonstrates how these cultural *elements* affect Ayah. Try to use academic vocabulary when it will strengthen your writing. See the complete list on pages R80–R82.

Revise

Peer Review Ask a classmate to read your draft to identify your thesis and the main ideas that support it. Ask your reviewer to review the traits of strong writing too; then think about how they apply to your work. Use any comments to guide you as you revise. Use the checklist below to help you evaluate and strengthen each other's writing.

Checklist
- ✓ Do you show how a work relates to a time, place, culture, or life?
- ✓ Do you present a clear thesis or controlling impression?
- ✓ Do you maintain a consistent focus and tone?
- ✓ Do you make accurate and detailed references to the work?
- ✓ Do you use precise language and the active voice?
- ✓ Do you demonstrate a thorough understanding of the work, including its most complex or subtle ideas?

Focus Lesson

Vary Sentence Openers

Avoid beginning consecutive sentences with *it, the,* or a noun or pronoun. Instead, vary your openers. You can begin with a descriptive word (such as *suddenly* or *inside*); a phrase (such as *in the shadows* or *having seen enough*); or a clause (such as *when the man spoke* or *because it was Saturday*).

Draft:

Silko uses a graphic simile to illustrate Ayah's past fears of what the English-speaking doctors would do to her children: "She was frightened by the way they looked at the children, like the lizard watches the fly." Ayah fled with her children in to the comfort of nature, into the "foothills of juniper trees and black lava rock" where "the sun warmth relaxed her and took the fear and anger away."

Revision:

<u>Later,</u>[1] Silko uses a graphic simile to illustrate Ayah's past fears of what the English-speaking doctors would do to her children: "She was frightened by the way they looked at the children, like the lizard watches the fly." <u>Seeking comfort</u>,[2] Ayah fled with her children into nature, into the "foothills of juniper trees and black lava rock" where "the sun warmth relaxed her and took the fear and anger away."

1: **Opens with a Descriptive Word**   2: **Opens with a Phrase**

Edit and Proofread

Get It Right When you have completed the final draft of your literary criticism, proofread it for errors in grammar, usage, mechanics, and spelling. Refer to the Language Handbook, pages R40–R59, as a guide.

> **Focus Lesson**
>
> ## Correct Run-on Sentences
>
> Be sure that all the sentences in your essay are complete. Avoid run-on sentences, which present two or more independent clauses (groups of words that could stand alone as sentences) without the correct punctuation. Below is an example of a problem with run-on sentences and possible solutions from the Workshop Model.
>
> **Problem: The following is a run-on sentence.**
>
> *Their cows are "skinny," their house is a "boxcar shack."*
>
> **Solution A:** Create two sentences.
>
> *Their cows are "skinny." Their house is a "boxcar shack."*
>
> **Solution B:** Use a semicolon to separate the two independent clauses.
>
> *Their cows are "skinny"; their house is a "boxcar shack."*
>
> **Solution C:** Use a comma and a coordinating conjunction to join the independent clauses.
>
> *Their cows are "skinny," and their house is a "boxcar shack."*

Present/Publish

Follow Conventional Style Do not strive to give your essay an original or creative look. Instead, be sure to follow the guidelines your teacher sets for page formats, fonts, and spacing. Also eliminate underlining and exclamation marks used only for emphasis. Your words, not your formatting, should create all the emphasis you need.

Exposition

Peer Review Tips

When reviewing a classmate's literary criticism, read slowly, writing notes as you read for constructive feedback. Use the following questions to get started:

Does the criticism deepen your own understanding of the work?

Does the writer maintain the flow of ideas when providing quoted evidence?

Does the writer's tone match the content and purpose of the essay?

Word-Processing

Select a readable, conservative font like one you might see in a major newspaper. Reserve cursive and other ornamental fonts for less formal purposes, such as personal letters. 12-point is an ideal size for most essays.

Writer's Portfolio

Place a copy of your literary criticism in your portfolio to review later.

Writing and Research For editing and publishing tools, go to glencoe.com and enter QuickPass code GL59794u1.

Learning Objectives

For pages 266–267

In this workshop, you will focus on the following objective:

Speaking and Listening: Delivering a literary criticism.

Speaking, Listening, and Viewing Workshop

Literary Criticism

Literature Connection Leslie Marmon Silko, the author of "Lullaby," was raised in a culture in which all knowledge was once passed along orally. In this culture, she says, "All information, scientific, technological, historical, religious, is put into narrative form. It is easier to remember that way." In this workshop, you will deliver your literary criticism orally.

> **Assignment** Adapt your literary criticism to create an oral report and present it to the class.

Plan Your Presentation

Your goal is to present your literary criticism in an interesting and informative way. Follow these guidelines to plan your presentation.

- Focus on your thesis. This is the most important idea in your presentation: be sure that you make it clear. Plan to state it and to restate it.
- Create a clear and engaging introduction that includes your thesis, a body that presents your main ideas, and a conclusion that restates or summarizes your most important points.
- Support each main idea you present with details from the literature. Add your own explanations to link those details to your thesis.
- Show how well you understand the work. Identify aspects of the author's style and tell how you respond to them. Note subtle shifts in meaning, apparent contradictions, and other aspects of the work that make it rich and complex. Tell how they affect you as a reader.

Get Started

- Work with a classmate to identify main ideas in your literary criticism. Discuss which details belong in your presentation and which, if any, to omit.
- Discuss ways to make the introduction and the conclusion more interesting or lively for listeners. Consider adding a quotation or anecdote.
- Work alone to create an outline or another plan for your presentation.

Create Slides or Posters

To help your listeners follow your presentation, create slides on the computer, overhead transparencies, or posters that present your thesis and main points. Your visuals should be easy to view, presented in the same font or handwriting, and spaced for maximum legibility.

The tradition of weaving is handed down.	Ayah is connected to nature and tradition.
Descriptive details and story evidence - "she combed the wool" - "her grandma sat beside her spinning"	Descriptive details and story evidence - "their elk hide moccasins" - hanging up strips of venison to dry

Rehearse

Rehearse your presentation several times by yourself, making sure that your words and your graphic aids are working together. Then present in front of a family member or a classmate. Ask for comments, as well as for any questions your listener might have. This will help you anticipate questions your audience might ask later. Finally, keep these verbal and nonverbal techniques in mind.

Techniques for Delivering an Oral Presentation of Literary Criticism

Verbal Techniques	Nonverbal Techniques
☑ **Volume** Speak loudly enough that everyone can hear you.	☑ **Display** Be sure that your audience can see your slides or posters. Consider using an easel for posters.
☑ **Repetition** Some repetition is good. For example, you could restate your thesis as you state each main point.	☑ **Eye Contact** As you point out your posters or slides, look at them. As you make other points, look at your audience.
☑ **Tone** This is a formal presentation. Your tone should be formal throughout.	☑ **Gestures** Use natural hand gestures as you speak. Do your best to avoid nervous fidgeting.
☑ **Pronunciation** Speak each word clearly.	☑ **Posture** Stand up straight and hold your head up.

Make Visual Connections
Be sure that your visuals and your oral presentation work together. As you deliver your thesis and your main points, point to them on your visuals.

Speaking Frames
Consider using the following frames in your oral presentation of your literary criticism:

One detail from the story that supports this idea is _____.

Let's return for a moment to my thesis, which is _____.

Presentation Tips
Use the following checklist to evaluate your oral presentation.

☑ Did you create interest at the beginning, state and restate your thesis, and conclude effectively?

☑ Did you support your ideas with accurate and detailed references to the work?

☑ How well did you use volume, tone, gestures, posture, and other techniques to create interest and convey your meaning?

Speaking, Listening, Viewing For project ideas, templates, and presentation tips, go to glencoe.com and enter QuickPass code GL59794u1.

Independent Reading

Short Stories and Novels

In only a few pages, short stories do it all: they introduce characters, setting, and the first events of the plot; they build up tension or suspense and rise to a climax; they develop characters; they present a theme; and they deliver a satisfying ending. For more short stories with a variety of themes, try the two suggestions below. For novels that incorporate the Big Ideas of Encountering the Unexpected, Making Choices, and Life Transitions, try the titles from the Glencoe Literature Library on the next page.

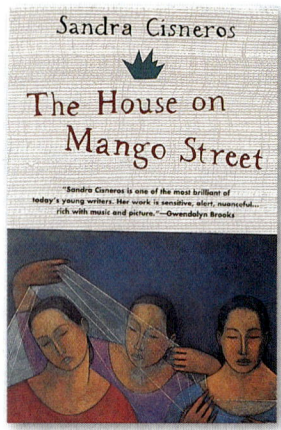

The House on Mango Street

Sandra Cisneros

This collection of related short stories details the life of Esperanza, a Mexican American girl. Like Sandra Cisneros, who often uses her life experiences as subjects in both her fiction and nonfiction, Esperanza Cordero lives in a Spanish-speaking community in Chicago. Esperanza's hopes, joys, and fears are explored in a series of short vignettes, each of which focuses on a seemingly minor incident, such as an interaction with a mean boy or a troubling episode at school. The stories in *The House on Mango Street* can stand individually, or the book can be read as a novel.

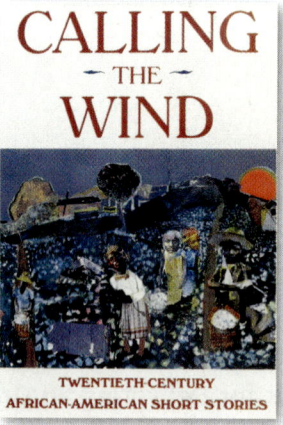

Calling the Wind: Twentieth Century African-American Short Stories

edited by Clarence Major

This collection of fifty-nine short stories begins with a tale written by Charles Chestnutt in 1899 and ends with Terry McMillan's short story "Quilting on the Rebound," written in 1991. In between are stories by some of the greatest authors of the twentieth century, including Richard Wright, Ralph Ellison, Langston Hughes, James Baldwin, Ernest Gaines, Toni Morrison, and Jamaica Kincaid. In his introduction, Major explains that the collection sets out, among other things, to deny readers the chance for racial stereotyping.

GLENCOE LITERATURE LIBRARY

The Friends
by Rosa Guy

Encountering the Unexpected, the main character tries to understand the problems that develop between her and her best friend.

Nectar in a Sieve
by Kamala Markandaya

The process of *Making Choices* to adapt to life's ordeals is recorded through the eyes of a woman from a small village in India.

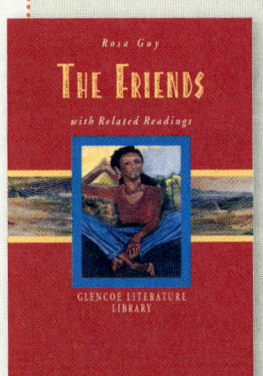

My Ántonia
by Willa Cather

A novel about the struggles and rewards and *Life Transitions* of pioneer life on the Great Plains in the nineteenth century.

CRITICS' CORNER

"Poe assumed in his tales one crucial condition: every mind is either half-mad or capable of slipping easily into madness. He was not so much concerned with precisely what madness was but with the conditions and stages whereby madness came to exist and evidenced itself in otherwise average, commonplace human beings."

—Edward H. Davidson, *Selected Writings of Edgar Allan Poe*

Complete Stories and Poems of Edgar Allan Poe
by Edgar Allan Poe

For more thrilling tales from one of the earliest and greatest masters of horror and suspense, try this collection of his complete works. Popular tales include "The Tell-Tale Heart," the story of a heart that goes on beating after death, as well as "The Murders in the Rue Morgue," a forerunner of the detective story genre. For a trip through an underground cemetery and the horrors of being buried alive, read "The Cask of Amontillado." For a journey into the world's most famous haunted house, open to "The Fall of the House of Usher."

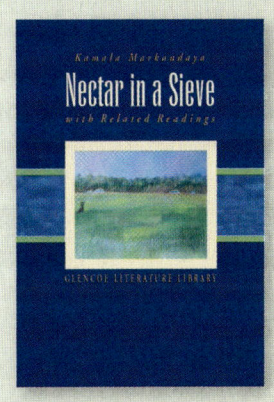

 Write a Review

Read one of the books shown and write a review of it for your classmates. Be sure to explain why other students might enjoy the book, or offer suggestions on how they might overcome difficulties in reading the book. Present your review to the class.

Assessment

English–Language Arts

Reading: Fiction

Carefully read the following passages. Use context clues to help you define any words with which you are unfamiliar. Pay close attention to story elements such as theme, voice, and tone. Then, on a separate sheet of paper, answer the questions on page 272.

from *"When the Buffalo Climbed a Tree"* by Mark Twain

"Your *saddle*? Did you take your saddle up in the tree with you?"

"Take it up in the tree with me? Why, how you talk. Of course I didn't. No man could do that. It fell in the tree when it came down."

"Oh—exactly."

5   "Certainly. I unwound the lariat, and fastened one end of it to the limb. It was the very best green raw-hide, and capable of sustaining tons. I made a slip-noose in the other end, and then hung it down to see the length. It reached down twenty-two feet—half way to the ground. I then loaded every barrel of the Allen with a double charge. I felt satisfied. I said to myself, if he never thinks of that one thing that I dread, all right—but if he does, all right anyhow—I am fixed for him. But don't
10   you know that the very thing a man dreads is the thing that always happens? Indeed it is so. I watched the bull, now, with anxiety—anxiety which no one can conceive of who has not been in such a situation and felt that at any moment death might come. Presently a thought came into the bull's eye. I knew it! Said I—if my nerve fails now, I am lost. Sure enough, it was just as I had dreaded, he started in to climb the tree—"

15   "What, the bull?"

"Of course—who else?"

"But a bull can't climb a tree."

"He can't, can't he? Since you know so much about it, did you ever see a bull try?"

"No! I never dreamt of such a thing."

20   "Well, then, what is the use of your talking that way, then? Because you never saw a thing done, is that any reason why it can't be done?"

"Well, all right—go on. What did you do?"

"The bull started up, and got along well for about ten feet, then slipped and slid back. I breathed easier. He tried it again—got up a little higher—slipped again. But he came at it once more, and this
25   time he was careful. He got gradually higher and higher, and my spirits went down more and more. Up he came—an inch at a time—with his eyes hot, and his tongue hanging out. Higher and higher—hitched his foot over the stump of a limb, and looked up, as much as to say, 'You are my meat, friend.' Up again—higher and higher, and getting more excited the closer he got. He was within ten feet of

me! I took a long breath,—and then said I, 'It is now or never.' I had the coil of the lariat all ready; I paid it out slowly, till it hung right over his head; all of a sudden I let go of the slack, and the slip-noose fell fairly round his neck! Quicker than lightning I out with the Allen and let him have it in the face. It was an awful roar, and must have scared the bull out of his senses. When the smoke cleared away, there he was dangling in the air, twenty foot from the ground, and going out of one convulsion into another faster than you could count! I didn't stop to count, anyhow I shinned down the tree and shot for home."

"Bemis, is all that true, just as you have stated it?"

"I wish I may rot in my tracks and die the death of a dog if it isn't."

"The Unicorn in the Garden" by James Thurber

line

Once upon a sunny morning a man who sat in a breakfast nook looked up from his scrambled eggs to see a white unicorn with a golden horn quietly cropping the roses in the garden. The man went up to the bedroom where his wife was still asleep and woke her. "There's a unicorn in the garden," he said. "Eating roses." She opened one unfriendly eye and looked at him. "The unicorn is a mythical beast," she said, and turned her back on him. The man walked slowly downstairs and out into the garden. The unicorn was still there; he was now browsing among the tulips. "Here, unicorn," said the man, and pulled up a lily and gave it to him. The unicorn ate it gravely. With a high heart, because there was a unicorn in his garden, the man went upstairs and roused his wife again. "The unicorn," he said, "ate a lily." His wife sat up in bed and looked at him, coldly. "You are a booby," she said, "and I am going to have you put in the booby-hatch." The man, who had never liked the words "booby" and "booby-hatch," and who liked them even less on a shining morning when there was a unicorn in the garden, thought for a moment. "We'll see about that," he said. He walked over to the door. "He has a golden horn in the middle of his forehead," he told her. Then he went back to the garden to watch the unicorn; but the unicorn had gone away. The man sat among the roses and went to sleep.

And as soon as the husband had gone out of the house, the wife got up and dressed as fast as she could. She was very excited and there was a gloat in her eye. She telephoned the police and she telephoned the psychiatrist; she told them to hurry to her house and bring a strait-jacket. When the police and the psychiatrist arrived, they sat down in chairs and looked at her, with great interest. "My husband," she said, "saw a unicorn this morning." The police looked at the psychiatrist and the psychiatrist looked at the police. "He told me it ate a lily," she said. The psychiatrist looked at the police and the police looked at the psychiatrist. "He told me it had a golden horn in the middle of its forehead," she said. At a solemn signal from the psychiatrist, the police leaped from their chairs and seized the wife. They had a hard time subduing her, for she put up a terrific struggle, but they finally subdued her. Just as they got her into the strait-jacket, the husband came into the house.

"Did you tell your wife you saw a unicorn?" asked the police. "Of course not," said the husband. "The unicorn is a mythical beast." "That's all I wanted to know," said the psychiatrist. "Take her away. I'm sorry sir, but your wife is as crazy as a jay bird." So they took her away, cursing and screaming, and shut her up in an institution. The husband lived happily ever after.

Moral: don't count your boobies until they are hatched.

Items 1–7 apply to "When the Buffalo Climbed a Tree."

1. Which best describes the setting of Twain's story?
   A. Bemis is sitting in a tree.
   B. Bemis is relating a recent event.
   C. Bemis is telling a joke.
   D. Bemis is lying to his friend.

2. How far down did the lariat hang?
   A. twenty feet
   B. thirty feet
   C. to the ground
   D. halfway to the ground

3. Which of the following best describes the mood of the listener in Twain's story?
   A. jealous
   B. deceived
   C. doubtful
   D. sincere

4. In what manner does Bemis tell his story?
   A. with assurance
   B. with humor
   C. with hesitancy
   D. with calmness

5. How many voices appear in Twain's story?
   A. three—Bemis's, his listener's, the bull's
   B. one—Bemis's
   C. two—Bemis's and his listener's
   D. one—the narrator's

6. How would you best describe the character of Bemis in the selection by Twain?
   A. He is untrustworthy.
   B. He is prone to exaggeration.
   C. He is believable.
   D. He is truthful.

7. Which best describes the selection by Twain?
   A. narration
   B. fiction
   C. drama
   D. a tall tale

Items 8–12 apply to "The Unicorn in the Garden."

8. Which best describes the tone of Thurber's story?
   A. tragic
   B. comic
   C. mythical
   D. fictional

9. How many voices appear in Thurber's story?
   A. one—the husband's
   B. one—the wife's
   C. four—the husband's, the wife's, the unicorn's, and the psychiatrist's
   D. four—the husband's, the wife's, the police officer's, and the psychiatrist's

10. How many times does the husband go upstairs to tell his wife about the unicorn?
    A. twice
    B. once
    C. three times
    D. none

11. What does the word *gloat*, in line 17, suggest about the wife's character?
    A. Locking her husband up would please her.
    B. Unicorns excite her.
    C. She cannot understand her husband.
    D. Confrontations between the two are common.

12. From the ending, what do you conclude that the husband, in line 12, is thinking about?
    A. He decides to return to watch the unicorn.
    B. He becomes intent on proving his sanity.
    C. He plans to turn the tables on his wife.
    D. He is determined to ignore his wife.

272 UNIT 1   THE SHORT STORY

Vocabulary Skills: Sentence Completion

For each item, choose the word that best completes the sentence.

1. The courtroom anxiously awaited the jury's _____ verdict after hours of deliberation.
   A. imminent
   B. dire
   C. cautious
   D. self-possessed

2. The mayor, as a(n) _____ elected official, worked comfortably with the support of the entire community.
   A. impeccably
   B. vaguely
   C. duly
   D. amiably

3. Rosa Parks, a famous civil rights figure, carried herself with strength and determination; her _____ served as a model for others.
   A. infirmity
   B. equanimity
   C. vulnerability
   D. fortitude

4. Unlike those who followed him, George Washington had no _____ when he was elected the first president.
   A. doctrine
   B. predecessor
   C. obscurity
   D. prodigy

5. Hiking alongside the _____ ensured that the traveler would always have water in this desert area.
   A. solace
   B. derision
   C. arroyo
   D. moor

6. The steep mountains presented a _____ barrier to an inexperienced climber.
   A. convoluted
   B. decrepit
   C. imperceptible
   D. formidable

7. The couple believed that counseling could only _____ their already-close relationship.
   A. eradicate
   B. assuage
   C. contend
   D. enhance

8. The principal had a _____ demeanor that conveyed dignity and calm.
   A. sedate
   B. furtive
   C. droll
   D. wanton

9. The crisis demanded swift attention, so the bystander _____ passersby for help.
   A. ascertained
   B. implored
   C. harassed
   D. oppressed

10. Investors who watch the stock market with _____ fear that their investments will not do well.
    A. credulity
    B. infirmity
    C. pandemonium
    D. presentiments

Literature Online

Assessment For additional test practice, go to glencoe.com and enter QuickPass code GL59794u1.

Grammar and Writing Skills: Paragraph Improvement

Read carefully through the following draft of a student's essay. Pay close attention to word choice, content, and grammar, especially run-on and comma-splice errors. Also watch verb tense and punctuation. Then, on a separate sheet of paper, answer the questions on pages 274–275.

(1) *Mark Twain, a great humorist of the American nineteenth century, is widely recognized as one of the greatest American writers.* (2) *His stories are often humorous, the serious side of them makes them more interesting.* (3) *He sometimes used darker humor, relying on satire and irony to make his points.* (4) *Often critical about human nature.*

(5) *His most famous novel* The Adventures of Huckleberry Finn *condemn the ethical practices, such as slavery, in the South.* (6) *It is about a boy named Huck and his friend Jim a slave.* (7) *The two are friends during their adventures.*

(8) *When Huck rejects society an important event for the story.* (9) *He is confused between what he's been taught and what he feels for Jim.* (10) *His friend Jim is a slave according to the rules of society.* (11) *As a friend Huck has a problem with that.* (12) *He sees the human side of Jim.*

(13) *Twain tried to make people to look at themselves and change for the better.* (14) *It is ironic that the people he made fun of were among his most devoted readers.* (15) *Twains cynical view of human nature more seen in his later writing.* (16) *He influenced many other writers, like James Thurber, who also went on to become a popular humorist.*

1. Which is the best way to revise sentence 1?
   A. Insert a colon after *is*.
   B. Delete the comma after *Twain*.
   C. Insert a comma after *recognized*.
   D. Make no change.

2. Which of the following grammatical errors appears in sentence 2?
   A. sentence fragment
   B. comma splice
   C. misplaced modifier
   D. incorrect verb tense

3. Which of the following is the best revision of sentence 2?
   A. His stories, which are often humorous, the serious side of them makes them more interesting.
   B. Although his stories are often humorous, there is a serious side to them that makes them more interesting.
   C. Although his stories, which are often humorous, the serious side of them makes them more interesting.
   D. His stories are often humorous, but they have a serious side, which makes them more interesting.

4. Which of the following revisions is the best way to combine sentences 3 and 4?
   A. His humor sometimes used satire and irony to make his points, often critical about human nature.
   B. He sometimes used a darker humor, using satire and irony to make his points critical about human nature.
   C. His humor was sometimes dark, relying on satire and irony to make points often critical of human nature.
   D. His humor was sometimes dark relying on satire and irony to make points often critical of human nature.

5. Which of the following is the best revision of sentence 5?
   A. His most famous novel, *The Adventures of Huckleberry Finn*, condemns unethical practices, such as slavery, in the South.
   B. His most famous novel *The Adventures of Huckleberry Finn* condemns unethical practices, such as slavery, in the South.
   C. His most famous *The Adventures of Huckleberry Finn* condemns the ethical practices, such as slavery, in the South.
   D. His most famous book, *The Adventures of Huckleberry Finn*, condemns the ethical practices, such as slavery, in the South.

6. Which of the following revisions is the best way to combine sentences 6 and 7?
   A. It is about a boy named Huck and his friend Jim, a slave, and about how the two are friends during their adventures.
   B. It is about a boy named Huck and his friend Jim a slave, the two become friends during their adventures.
   C. It is a story about a boy named Huck and a slave named Jim, who become friends through their adventures.
   D. It is a story about a boy named Huck and his friend, a slave, Jim, who become friends through their adventures.

7. Which of the following grammatical errors appears in sentence 8?
   A. incorrect verb tense
   B. run-on sentence
   C. comma splice (fused sentence)
   D. sentence fragment

8. Which of the following is the best revision for sentence 15?
   A. Twain's view of human nature increased in his later writing.
   B. Twain's cynical view of human nature is saw more and more in his later writing.
   C. Twain's cynical view of human nature seen more in his later writing.
   D. Twain's cynical view of human nature increased in his later writing.

Essay

Compare and contrast the two stories by Twain and Thurber. Discuss how the use of humor, irony, or satire contributes to the meaning of each story. What effect do these have on the reader? As you write, keep in mind that your essay will be checked for **ideas, organization, voice, word choice, sentence fluency, conventions,** and **presentation.**

Coming to America, 1985. Malcah Zeldis.

View the Art Malcah Zeldis's painting shows the epic scale of the journey from the old world to the new. If you were to write nonfiction about the journey to America, what would you focus on?

UNIT TWO

NONFICTION

Looking Ahead

Nonfiction—writing about real people, events, and ideas—includes autobiographies, memoirs, biographies, diaries, letters, essays, news articles, and speeches. Through reading nonfiction, we find others who share our experiences, feelings, passions, and values. Our ideas, ideals, and causes are articulated and defended by the nonfiction writer.

Each part in Unit Two focuses on a Big Idea that can help you connect to the literary works.

PREVIEW	Big Ideas	Literary Focus
PART 1	The Power of Memory	Narrative Nonfiction: Autobiography and Biography
PART 2	Quests and Encounters	Expository and Personal Essay
PART 3	Keeping Freedom Alive	Persuasive Essay and Speeches

Learning Objectives

For pages 276–282

In studying this text, you will focus on the following objectives:

Literary Analysis:
Analyzing narrative nonfiction: autobiography and biography.

Analyzing expository and personal essay.

Analyzing persuasive essay and speeches.

Genre Focus

What forms make up the nonfiction genre?

The motivations for writing and reading nonfiction are as diverse as the writers and readers of nonfiction. Some writers seek to share the lives of others with readers to illustrate a lesson or to provide insight into a particular time and place. Others look within and share their own experiences.

Narrative Nonfiction: Autobiography and Biography

Writing About Oneself

A literary work that tells the story of an author's own experiences can be an autobiography or a memoir. **Autobiography** usually refers to a work that attempts to tell a person's entire life. **Memoir** usually refers to a work that focuses on the author's personal experiences during a particular event or period.

Our father kept in his breast pocket a little black notebook. There he noted jokes he wanted to remember. Remembering jokes was a moral obligation. People who said, "I can never remember jokes," were like people who said, obliviously, "I can never remember names," or "I don't bathe."

—Annie Dillard, **from "An American Childhood"**

Distributed By Universal Press Syndicate. Reprinted with permission. All rights reserved.

Writing About Another

An account of another person's life is called a **biography** whether it is long or short. People are curious about the lives of famous, successful, or inspiring people, from royalty, such as Queen Elizabeth, to media stars, such as Oprah Winfrey.

De Kooning brought over a portfolio of drawings and began leafing through them. At last, he seemed to settle on one. He looked at it. But then he slipped the drawing back into the portfolio. "No," he said, "I want to give one that I'll miss."

—Mark Stevens and Annalyn Swan,
from *De Kooning: An American Master*

Expository and Personal Essay

Formal and Informal Essays

Essays are written to communicate ideas or opinions. They are short works of nonfiction that focus on a single topic.

Formal essays are serious in tone, meaning the author expresses a serious attitude toward his or her subject matter. This type of essay comprises most of the papers, essays, and assignments that high school and college students write. Formal essays can be expository (explanatory) or persuasive. In an expository essay—an essay examining a work of literature for example—the writer should take an objective tone and use quotations and reasoned analysis to support a thesis statement. In a persuasive essay, the writer can use a more subjective tone. In certain circumstances, the writer may want to use the first-person in a persuasive essay to strengthen his or her appeals to emotion and logic with personal testimony. Newspaper editorials—jointly authored articles that give the opinion of the editors or publishers on a topic—are often persuasive essays.

Informal essays, also called **personal essays,** are conversational in tone, use the first-person, and are written on any topic that the writer wishes to share with the reader. Many blogs, zines, and magazines include informal essays. The content of an informal essay usually relates to an experience in the writer's life.

Persuasive Essay and Speech

Writing for Change

One type of formal essay is the **persuasive essay.** Letters may be written by organizations to encourage readers to donate money. Advertisements are written by corporations to encourage readers to purchase products. Essays and articles are sometimes written to change the way readers think on subjects from letter writing to space travel. Speeches are usually written to encourage a certain behavior or to win over the listener to a cause.

One type of persuasion is **argument,** which relies on logic, reason, and evidence to convince the reader. Notice that the excerpt from King's speech contains both argument and sarcasm, which is a type of emotional appeal.

Secondly, let us keep the issues where they are. The issue is injustice. The issue is the refusal of Memphis to be fair and honest in its dealings with its public servants, who happen to be sanitation workers. Now, we've got to keep attention on that. That's always the problem with a little violence. You know what happened the other day, and the press dealt only with the window-breaking. I read the articles. They very seldom got around to mentioning the fact that one thousand, three hundred sanitation workers were on strike, and that Memphis is not being fair to them, and that Mayor Loeb is in dire need of a doctor. They didn't get around to that.

—Martin Luther King Jr., **from "I've Been to the Mountaintop"**

 **Literature** Online

Literature and Reading For more selections in this genre, go to glencoe.com and enter QuickPass code GL59794u2.

LITERARY ANALYSIS MODEL

How will literary elements help readers analyze nonfiction?

Robert E. Hemenway (born 1941) has been a professor of English and American Studies and a University Dean and Chancellor. His literary biography *Zora Neale Hurston* was a "Best Books" pick by the *New York Times* in 1978.

**APPLY
Literary Elements**

Nonfiction
Nonfiction is writing about real people and events.

Nonfiction
In trying to determine which category of nonfiction the excerpt belongs to, you can rule out the **essay** because the author is narrating events in the life of a person, not expressing ideas and opinions. You can also rule out **speech**.

from *Zora Neale Hurston*
by Robert E. Hemenway

In the first week of January, 1925, Zora Neale Hurston arrived in New York City with one dollar and fifty cents in her purse, no job, no friends, but filled with "a lot of hope." She came from Washington, leaving a steady job as a manicurist in a
5 Seventh Avenue barbershop to explore the opportunities for a career as a writer. As a part-time student at Howard University for the previous five years, she had been an aspiring English major, much praised for her short stories and poems, and she had a vague idea of studying writing in one of Manhattan's
10 many colleges. She carried most of her belongings in her bag, including a number of manuscripts that she hoped would impress. Even if they did not, she was confident of her ability to survive in the big city; she had been on her own since the age of fourteen. Brown skinned, big boned, with freckles and
15 high cheekbones, she was a striking woman; her dark brown eyes were both impish and intelligent, her voice was rich and black—with the map of Florida on her tongue.

    She went first to the offices of the National Urban League on East Twenty-third Street, where she asked to be introduced to
20 Charles S. Johnson, editor of the Urban League's magazine, *Opportunity: A Journal of Negro Life.* A month earlier he had published one of her short stories, and since September he had been encouraging her to submit material to the literary contest his magazine currently sponsored. Johnson, director of research
25 for the league, had single-handedly turned *Opportunity* into an expression of "New Negro" thought. "New Negroes" were black people who made clear that they would not accept a subordinate role in American society, and Johnson believed that young writers like Zora Neale Hurston would help prove the

cultural parity of the races. He urged her to stay in New York, and as she settled in, he helped her find a series of odd jobs. Mrs. Johnson often gave Zora carfare to make sure she could accept the frequent dinner invitations at the Johnson house.

For a young girl from rural Florida and provincial Washington who had been working for ten years to secure an education, this interest and help must have made all the sacrifice seem worthwhile. She had arrived at a hard-won sense of self built around the knowledge that because she was black her life had been graced in unusual ways, and she had confidence that she could express that grace in fiction. The story Johnson had printed a month earlier, "Drenched in Light," embodied this personal vision she brought to New York; it was her initial contribution to the cultural uprising that Johnson and others were calling a "Harlem Renaissance."

"Drenched in Light" was Hurston's calling card on literary New York, the tangible evidence she could point to that she was indeed a serious writer. It is also a statement of personal identity. It tells of a day in the life of Isie Watts, a "little brown figure perched upon the gate-post" in front of her Eatonville, Florida, home. Isie likes to race up and down the road to Orlando, "hailing gleefully all travelers." As a result, "everybody in the country" knows "Isie Watts, the joyful," and how she likes to laugh and play, beg rides in cars, and live to the fullest every minute of her young life. Isie gets into various scrapes, including an impish attempt to shave her sleeping grandmother, and eventually is given a ride by a passing white motorist, despite her grandmother's disapproval. There is no building toward a dramatic climax, and very little plot. The structure of the story is thematic. The point is that Isie, poor and black, is far from tragic; rather, she is "drenched in light," a condition which endears her to everyone, although it presents her grandmother with a discipline problem. Isie is persistently happy, and the implication is that whites suffer from an absence of such joy. Isie's white benefactor ends the story, "I want a little of her sunshine to soak into my soul. I need it."

Hurston may have been manipulating white stereotypes of black people here, but it is not a matter of satire. She remembered Eatonville as a place of great peace and happiness, identifying that happiness as a function of her family and communal existence.

Writer Zora Neale Hurston

Biography
Hurston is referred to as "she" rather than "I," so you can rule out **autobiography** and **memoir** and determine that the kind of nonfiction you have just read is **biography**.

Biography
Biographies can be short or long. This excerpt is from a book-length biography.

Reading Check
Interpret What would you expect the rest of this book to be about?

Wrap-Up

Guide to Reading Nonfiction

- When reading nonfiction, first determine what type of work you are reading.
- Try to identify the author's purpose. Is he or she writing to explain, to entertain, or to persuade you?
- If the author's purpose is to inform or explain, look for a thesis statement and support for the thesis.
- If the author's purpose is to entertain, look for literary elements, such as figurative language, dialogue, and suspense.
- If the author's purpose is to persuade, determine whether the author is presenting an argument, emotional appeals, or a combination of both.

 Literature Online

Unit Resources For additional skills practice, go to glencoe.com and enter QuickPass code GL59794u2.

Types of Nonfiction

- **Nonfiction** is writing about real people and real events.
- An **autobiography** tells the story of the writer's own life.
- A **memoir** tells about an event in the writer's own life.
- A **biography** tells the story of another person's life.
- An **essay** is a short work of nonfiction on a single topic. An essay can be **formal** or **informal**.
- Informal, or **personal**, essays are meant primarily to entertain. Formal essays may be intended to explain or persuade.
- **Persuasive** essays and speeches are intended to change the way people act and think. Persuasive writing contains argument that persuades through logic, reason, and evidence.

Activities

Use what you have learned about reading and analyzing nonfiction to complete one of these activities.

1. Generate Questions In small groups, discuss the excerpt from *Zora Neale Hurston* and list three questions you could research that are suggested by the text.

2. Research/Inquire Analyze the author's motivation for writing about Zora Neale Hurston. Use your analysis as the first entry in a chart that shows your ideas about the kinds of motivations writers might have for writing autobiographies, memoirs, essays, or speeches.

3. Take Notes Try using this study organizer to practice identifying forms of nonfiction. For each selection, write clues you used to determine the form.

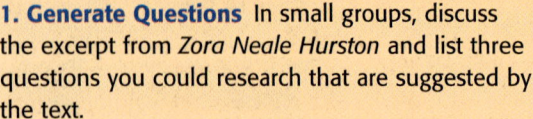 **THREE-TAB BOOK**

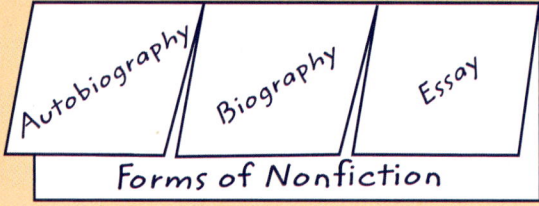

See page R20 for folding instructions

PART 1

THE POWER OF MEMORY

Souvenir, 1891. Émile Friant. Oil on canvas. Musée de la Ville de Paris, Musée du Petit-Palais, France.

View the Art This painting depicts an elderly woman lost in thought while children play by the waterside. How might memories and the power of memory become more important as one grows old?

BIG IDEA

Shared personal memories have the power to create a bond between the writer and reader. Historical memories have the power to shape national identities. In the nonfiction works in Part 1, you will read excerpts from life stories that could change the way you view the world. As you read these texts, ask yourself, When someone shares a personal memory with me, do I feel closer to them or understand them better? Why or why not?

Learning Objectives

For pages 284–285

In studying this text, you will focus on the following objective:

Literary Study: Analyzing narrative nonfiction: autobiography and biography.

LITERARY FOCUS

Narrative Nonfiction: Autobiography and Biography

How do you write about yourself or another person?

Nonfiction writing should be factual, and a biography should tell the facts of the life of its subject. But which facts should be told? To write down all the facts of any life, or even of one day, is inconceivable. The art of biography is in choosing interesting and telling facts and in explaining them in an engaging way.

from *Living Well. Living Good.*
by Maya Angelou

Aunt Tee said that what occurred during every Saturday party startled her and her friends the first time it happened. They had been playing cards, and Aunt Tee, who had just won the bid, held a handful of trumps. She felt a cool breeze on her back and sat upright and turned around. Her employers had cracked her door open and beckoned to her. Aunt Tee, a little peeved, laid down her cards and went to the door. The couple backed away and asked her to come into the hall, and there they both spoke and won Aunt Tee's sympathy forever.

Interior at Ciboure, 1912. Henri Matisse. Canvas. Musee Toulouse-Lautrec, Albi, France. ©ARS, NY.

284 UNIT 2 NONFICTION

Biography

The word *biography* comes from the Greek *bio-*, meaning "life," and *-graphy*, meaning "writing." In **biography** the author gives the reader an account of another person's life. The author will use the pronouns "he" or "she" to refer to the subject. Biographies can be book-length, but they can also be short pieces.

Biography does not need to limit itself to discussing a single person. Poet Langston Hughes refused to differentiate between his personal experience and the common experience of African Americans in the United States. For him, one man's experience was the experience of everyone. In this way, a writer may explore a group's experience through that of an individual or several individuals.

Autobiography

When a person writes about his or her own life, it is called **autobiography.** *Auto-* is from the Greek word meaning "self." In an autobiography, the pronoun "I" refers to the subject, who is the author. Authors have many purposes for sharing the stories of their lives. Some, like Martin Luther King Jr., write to help others live satisfying and meaningful lives. Others, like Jeanne Wakatsuki Houston and James D. Houston, write to give readers a personal glimpse of an event in U.S. history.

> None of these kids ever actually attacked. It was the threat that frightened us, their fearful looks, and the noises they would make, like miniature Samurai, in a language we couldn't understand.
>
> —Jeanne Wakatsuki Houston and James D. Houston, **from** *Farewell to Manzanar*

Memoir The term **memoir** is sometimes used as a synonym for **autobiography.** The label can also be applied to a particular kind of autobiography—autobiographical writing that focuses on a specific period or event in the writer's life. It can also refer to an autobiographical style that is more story-like. Annie Dillard's memoir captures her mother's unusual personality.

> "Spell 'poinsettia,'" Mother would throw out at me, smiling with pleasure. "Spell 'sherbet.'" The idea was not to make us whizzes, but, quite the contrary, to remind us—and I, especially, needed reminding—that we didn't know it all just yet.
>
> —Annie Dillard, **from** *An American Childhood*

Woman in Calico, 1944. William H. Johnson. Oil on paperboard, 67.4 x 52.0 cm. Smithsonian American Art Museum, Washington, DC.

Quickwrite

Write a Journal Entry Write a private journal entry about an event in your life that you would like to remember. Write it just for yourself without worrying about spelling, grammar, or punctuation. You do not have to show it to anyone. Later, you can rewrite it using the "five Ws" (who, what, where, when, why) and share it with a partner.

Literature Online

Literature and Reading For more about literary elements, go to glencoe.com and enter QuickPass code GL59794u2.

Before You Read

from Farewell to Manzanar

Meet Jeanne Wakatsuki Houston (born 1934)
Meet James D. Houston (1933–2009)

Jeanne Wakatsuki Houston was only seven years old when her family, just for being Japanese, was relocated to an internment camp during World War II. It took her nearly twenty-five years to talk about her life in the Manzanar internment camp, but when she did, she broached the subject in the form of an award-winning book, *Farewell to Manzanar,* co-authored by her husband, James D. Houston.

> "[Writing was] a way of coming to terms with the impact these years have had on my life."
>
> —Jeanne Wakatsuki Houston

The United States at War When Japan attacked a United States fleet at Pearl Harbor in 1941, the U.S. was drawn into World War II. Many people unfairly blamed Japanese Americans. Despite the fact that many of them had U.S. citizenship, they were distrusted and systematically discriminated against. For example, Japanese American people in the fishing industry were seen as threats to national security because in theory, they could smuggle oil to the Japanese navy. Wakatsuki Houston's father was arrested because he was a fisherman.

Memories of Internment Wakatsuki Houston was born in Inglewood, California. When the war began, Wakatsuki Houston's family was sent to the Manzanar internment camp, where the conditions were very harsh. Manzanar was built very quickly, so no modern conveniences existed. Approximately eleven-thousand people of Japanese ancestry lived there in a one-square-mile block of wooden barracks, surrounded by barbed wire and posted guards. The people there worked hard to build a community by planting gardens, painting, and forming schools and churches. Many were full-fledged U.S. citizens and many did not even speak Japanese. Despite their loyalty to the United States, however, they were treated as if they were the enemy. For Wakatsuki Houston, the memory of Manzanar changed her life.

After her family's release in 1945, Wakatsuki Houston continued to struggle to overcome prejudice and the shame of being punished simply for being Japanese. During her college years, she met and married James D. Houston. She went back to visit Manzanar in 1972, a visit she says helped her come to terms with the experience. According to Wakatsuki Houston, "Papa's life ended at Manzanar, though he lived for twelve more years after getting out. Until this trip I had not been able to admit that my own life really began there."

Author Search For more about Jeanne Wakatsuki Houston and James D. Houston, go to glencoe.com and enter QuickPass code GL59794u2.

Literature and Reading Preview

Connect to the Historical Narrative
How would you feel if you were given forty-eight hours to pack a few of your belongings and leave your home? Freewrite for a few minutes about what you might take with you, and why.

Build Background
In February 1942, President Franklin D. Roosevelt issued Executive Order 9066, which gave the U.S. War Department the authority to confine Japanese Americans to special camps for the duration of the war. Some 110,000 Japanese Americans, two-thirds of them U.S. citizens, were relocated to ten remote, prison-like camps.

Set Purposes for Reading

Big Idea The Power of Memory
As you read the story, ask yourself, How does sharing memories help people learn more about themselves and make connections to other people?

Literary Element Historical Narrative
A **historical narrative** is a nonfiction account that tells about important historical events. As you read, ask yourself, What real-life details does Wakatsuki Houston use to tell the story of Japanese Americans in an internment camp?

Reading Strategy Summarize
When you **summarize**, you determine the most important ideas in a selection and then restate them concisely in your own words. As you read, ask yourself, Do I remember and understand the text better when I summarize?

Tip: Summarize Details As you read, use a graphic organizer to help you list details from a paragraph. Then write one or two sentences to sum up the main idea of the paragraph.

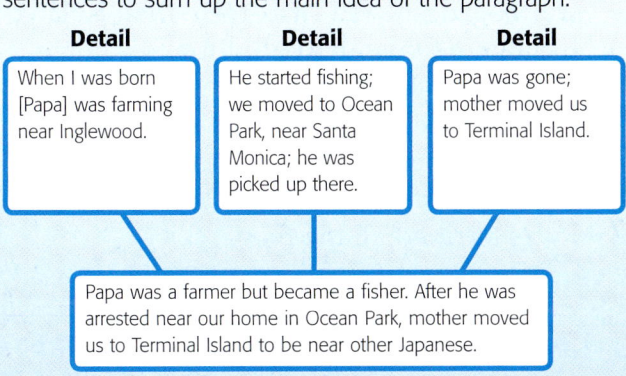

Learning Objectives
For pages 286–302

In studying this text, you will focus on the following objectives:

Reading:
Analyzing historical narrative.
Summarizing.

Vocabulary

patriarch (pā′trē ärk′) n. the male head of a family or group; p. 291 *My brother became the patriarch of our family after my father died.*

designation (dez′ig nā′shən) n. a distinguishing name or mark; p. 292 *The scientist gave the seeds that were not watered the designation "test group."*

alleviate (ə lē′vē āt′) v. to make easier to bear; relieve; lessen; p. 294 *The medicine promised to alleviate his suffering.*

subordinate (sə bôr′də nāt′) v. to cause to be, or treat as, secondary, inferior, or less important; p. 300 *A mother subordinates her own needs to care for the needs of her children.*

Tip: Word Parts You can find the meanings of common prefixes, such as *a-, ad-, ante-, bi, de-, per-, pre-, pro-,* and *sub-,* by looking them up in a dictionary.

School Children Say Pledge of Allegiance in San Francisco, April 16, 1942. Dorothea Lange. Silver Gelatin Photograph.

Farewell to Manzanar

Jeanne Wakatsuki Houston and James D. Houston

In December of 1941 Papa's disappearance didn't bother me nearly so much as the world I soon found myself in.

He had been a jack-of-all-trades. When I was born he was farming near Inglewood. Later, when he started fishing, we moved to Ocean Park, near Santa Monica, and until they picked him up, that's where we lived, in a big frame house with a brick fireplace, a block back from the beach. We were the only Japanese family in the neighborhood. Papa liked it that way. He didn't want to be labeled or grouped by anyone. But with him gone and no way of knowing what to expect, my mother moved all of us down to Terminal Island.[1]

Woody already lived there, and one of my older sisters had married a Terminal Island boy. Mama's first concern now was to keep the family together; and once the war began, she felt safer there than isolated racially in Ocean Park. But for me, at age seven, the island was a country as foreign as India or Arabia would have been. It was the first time I had lived among other Japanese, or gone to school with them, and I was terrified all the time.

---

1. *Terminal Island,* part of the Port of Los Angeles, is at the city's southern tip.

Historical Narrative Why does Mama feel safer in Terminal Island?

This was partly Papa's fault. One of his threats to keep us younger kids in line was "I'm going to sell you to the Chinaman." When I had entered kindergarten two years earlier, I was the only Oriental in the class. They sat me next to a Caucasian girl who happened to have very slanted eyes. I looked at her and began to scream, certain Papa had sold me out at last. My fear of her ran so deep I could not speak of it, even to Mama, couldn't explain why I was screaming. For two weeks I had nightmares about this girl, until the teachers finally moved me to the other side of the room. And it was still with me, this fear of Oriental faces, when we moved to Terminal Island.

In those days it was a company town, a ghetto owned and controlled by the canneries. The men went after fish, and whenever the boats came back—day or night—the women would be called to process the catch while it was fresh. One in the afternoon or four in the morning, it made no difference. My mother had to go to work right after we moved there. I can still hear the whistle—two toots for French's, three for Van Camp's—and she and Chizu would be out of bed in the middle of the night, heading for the cannery.

The house we lived in was nothing more than a shack, a barracks with single plank walls and rough wooden floors, like the cheapest kind of migrant workers' housing. The people around us were hardworking, boisterous, a little proud of their nickname, *yo-go-re*, which meant literally *uncouth one*, or roughneck, or dead-end kid. They not only spoke Japanese exclusively, they spoke a dialect peculiar to Kyushu,[2] where their families had come from in Japan, a rough, fisherman's language, full of oaths and insults. Instead of saying *ba-ka-ta-re*, a common insult meaning *stupid*, Terminal Islanders would say *ba-ka-ya-ro*, a coarser and exclusively masculine use of the word, which implies gross stupidity. They would swagger and pick on outsiders and persecute anyone who didn't speak as they did. That was what made my own time there so hateful. I had never spoken anything but English, and the other kids in the second grade despised me for it. They were tough and mean, like ghetto kids anywhere. Each day after school I dreaded their ambush. My brother Kiyo, three years older, would wait for me at the door, where we would decide whether to run straight home together, or split up, or try a new and unexpected route.

None of these kids ever actually attacked. It was the threat that frightened us, their fearful looks, and the noises they would make, like miniature Samurai, in a language we couldn't understand.

Visual Vocabulary
For centuries, the *Samurai* (sam′ oo rī′) were a class of fearsome warriors. Japan abolished its class system in the 1860s.

At the time it seemed we had been living under this reign of fear for years. In fact, we lived there about two months. Late in February the navy decided to clear Terminal Island completely. Even though most of us were American-born, it was dangerous having that many Orientals so close to the Long Beach Naval Station, on the opposite end

---

2. *Kyushu* is the southernmost of Japan's four main islands.

Summarize How does Wakatsuki Houston describe the other Japanese at Terminal Island?

Historical Narrative Why did the navy think it was dangerous to have Asian Americans close to the Long Beach Naval Station?

of the island. We had known something like this was coming. But, like Papa's arrest, not much could be done ahead of time. There were four of us kids still young enough to be living with Mama, plus Granny, her mother, sixty-five then, speaking no English, and nearly blind. Mama didn't know where else she could get work, and we had nowhere else to move *to*. On February 25 the choice was made for us. We were given forty-eight hours to clear out.

The secondhand dealers had been prowling around for weeks, like wolves, offering humiliating prices for goods and furniture they knew many of us would have to sell sooner or later. Mama had left all but her most valuable possessions in Ocean Park, simply because she had nowhere to put them. She had brought along her pottery, her silver, heirlooms like the kimonos Granny had brought from Japan, tea sets, lacquered tables, and one fine old set of china, blue and white porcelain, almost translucent. On the day we were leaving, Woody's car was so crammed with boxes and luggage and kids we had just run out of room. Mama had to sell this china.

Visual Vocabulary
A *kimono* (ki mō′nō) is a loose robe or gown tied with a sash, traditionally worn as an outer garment by Japanese men and women.

One of the dealers offered her fifteen dollars for it. She said it was a full setting for twelve and worth at least two hundred. He said fifteen was his top price. Mama started to quiver. Her eyes blazed up at him. She had been packing all night and trying to calm down Granny, who didn't understand why we were moving again and what all the rush was about. Mama's nerves were shot, and now navy jeeps were patrolling the streets. She didn't say another word. She just glared at this man, all the rage and frustration channeled at him through her eyes.

He watched her for a moment and said he was sure he couldn't pay more than seventeen fifty for that china. She reached into the red velvet case, took out a dinner plate and hurled it at the floor right in front of his feet.

The man leaped back shouting, "Hey! Hey, don't do that! Those are valuable dishes!"

Mama took out another dinner plate and hurled it at the floor, then another and another, never moving, never opening her mouth, just quivering and glaring at the retreating dealer, with tears streaming down her cheeks. He finally turned and scuttled out the door, heading for the next house. When he was gone she stood there smashing cups and bowls and platters until the whole set lay in scattered blue and white fragments across the wooden floor.

The American Friends Service[3] helped us find a small house in Boyle Heights, another minority ghetto, in downtown Los Angeles, now inhabited briefly by a few hundred Terminal Island refugees. Executive Order 9066 had been signed by President Roosevelt, giving the War Department authority to define military areas in the western states and to exclude from them anyone who might threaten the war effort. There was a lot of talk about internment, or moving inland, or something like that in store for all Japanese Americans. I remember my brothers sitting around the table talking very intently about what we were

---

3. The *American Friends Service* is a Quaker charity that provides assistance to political and religious refugees and other displaced persons.

Summarize Summarize the information Wakatsuki Houston provides about the factors that affected Japanese Americans as the war progressed.

Dust Storm at Manzanar (California), July 3, 1942. Dorothea Lange. Silver Gelatin Photograph.

View the Art Manzanar, located in the Owens Valley in California, is a high altitude desert with brutally hot summers, freezing cold winters, and constant dust storms. How might the harsh climate have impacted the lives of the prisoners at Manzanar?

going to do, how we would keep the family together. They had seen how quickly Papa was removed, and they knew now that he would not be back for quite a while. Just before leaving Terminal Island Mama had received her first letter, from Bismarck, North Dakota. He had been imprisoned at Fort Lincoln, in an all-male camp for enemy aliens.

Papa had been the **patriarch**. He had always decided everything in the family. With him gone, my brothers, like councilors in the absence of a chief, worried about what should be done. The ironic thing is, there wasn't much left to decide. These were mainly days of quiet, desperate waiting for what seemed at the time to be inevitable. There is a phrase the Japanese use in such situations, when something difficult must be endured. You would hear the older heads, the Issei,[4] telling others very quietly, "Shikata ga nai" (It cannot be helped). "Shikata ga nai" (It must be done).

Mama and Woody went to work packing celery for a Japanese produce dealer. Kiyo and my sister May and I enrolled in the local school, and what sticks in my

Vocabulary

patriarch (pā′trē ärk′) *n.* the male head of a family or group

4. *Issei* (ēs′sā′) literally means "first generation" and refers to Japanese natives who immigrated to the United States.

memory from those few weeks is the teacher—not her looks, her remoteness. In Ocean Park my teacher had been a kind, grandmotherly woman who used to sail with us in Papa's boat from time to time and who wept the day we had to leave. In Boyle Heights the teacher felt cold and distant. I was confused by all the moving and was having trouble with the classwork, but she would never help me out. She would have nothing to do with me.

This was the first time I had felt outright hostility from a Caucasian. Looking back, it is easy enough to explain. Public attitudes toward the Japanese in California were shifting rapidly. In the first few months of the Pacific war, America was on the run. Tolerance had turned to distrust and irrational fear. The hundred-year-old tradition of anti-Orientalism on the west coast soon resurfaced, more vicious than ever. Its result became clear about a month later, when we were told to make our third and final move.

The name Manzanar meant nothing to us when we left Boyle Heights. We didn't know where it was or what it was. We went because the government ordered us to. And, in the case of my older brothers and sisters, we went with a certain amount of relief. They had all heard stories of Japanese homes being attacked, of beatings in the streets of California towns. They were as frightened of the Caucasians as Caucasians were of us. Moving, under what appeared to be government protection, to an area less directly threatened by the war seemed not such a bad idea at all. For some it actually sounded like a fine adventure.

Summarize *How does the author summarize the prejudice against the Japanese in America at this time?*

Historical Narrative *What do these details suggest about the dangers of scapegoating a group of people?*

Our pickup point was a Buddhist church in Los Angeles. It was very early, and misty, when we got there with our luggage. Mama had bought heavy coats for all of us. She grew up in eastern Washington and knew that anywhere inland in early April would be cold. I was proud of my new coat, and I remember sitting on a duffel bag trying to be friendly with the Greyhound driver. I smiled at him. He didn't smile back. He was befriending no one. Someone tied a numbered tag to my collar and to the duffel bag (each family was given a number, and that became our official **designation** until the camps were closed), someone else passed out box lunches for the trip, and we climbed aboard.

I had never been outside Los Angeles County, never traveled more than ten miles from the coast, had never even ridden on a bus. I was full of excitement, the way any kid would be, and wanted to look out the window. But for the first few hours the shades were drawn. Around me other people played cards, read magazines, dozed, waiting. I settled back, waiting too, and finally fell asleep. The bus felt very secure to me. Almost half its passengers were immediate relatives. Mama and my older brothers had succeeded in keeping most of us together, on the same bus, headed for the same camp. I didn't realize until much later what a job that was. The strategy had been, first, to have everyone living in the same district when the evacuation began, and then to get all of us included under the same family number, even though names had been changed by marriage. Many families weren't as lucky as ours and suffered months of anguish while trying to arrange transfers from one camp to another.

Vocabulary

designation (dez´ ig nā´ shən) *n.* a distinguishing name or mark

We rode all day. By the time we reached our destination, the shades were up. It was late afternoon. The first thing I saw was a yellow swirl across a blurred, reddish setting sun. The bus was being pelted by what sounded like splattering rain. It wasn't rain. This was my first look at something I would soon know very well, a billowing flurry of dust and sand churned up by the wind through Owens Valley.[5]

We drove past a barbed-wire fence, through a gate, and into an open space where trunks and sacks and packages had been dumped from the baggage trucks that drove out ahead of us. I could see a few tents set up, the first rows of black barracks, and beyond them, blurred by sand, rows of barracks that seemed to spread for miles across this plain. People were sitting on cartons or milling around, with their backs to the wind, waiting to see which friends or relatives might be on this bus. As we approached, they turned or stood up, and some moved toward us expectantly. But inside the bus no one stirred. No one waved or spoke. They just stared out the windows, ominously silent. I didn't understand this. Hadn't we finally arrived, our whole family intact? I opened a window, leaned out, and yelled happily. "Hey! This whole bus is full of Wakatsukis!"

Outside, the greeters smiled. Inside there was an explosion of laughter, hysterical, tension-breaking laughter that left my brothers choking and whacking each other across the shoulders.

We had pulled up just in time for dinner. The mess halls[6] weren't completed yet. An outdoor chow line snaked around a half-finished building that broke a good part of the wind. They issued us army mess kits, the round metal kind that fold over, and plopped in scoops of canned Vienna sausage, canned string beans, steamed rice that had been cooked too long, and on top of the rice a serving of canned apricots. The Caucasian servers were thinking that the fruit poured over rice would make a good dessert. Among the Japanese, of course, rice is never eaten with sweet foods, only with salty or savory foods. Few of us could eat such a mixture. But at this point no one dared protest. It would have been impolite. I was horrified when I saw the apricot syrup seeping through my little mound of rice. I opened my mouth to complain. My mother jabbed me in the back to keep quiet. We moved on through the line and joined the others squatting in the lee[7] of half-raised walls, dabbing courteously at what was, for almost everyone there, an inedible concoction.

After dinner we were taken to Block 16, a cluster of fifteen barracks that had just been finished a day or so earlier—although finished was hardly the word for it. The shacks were built of one thickness of pine planking covered with tarpaper. They sat on concrete footings, with about

Visual Vocabulary
A soldier in the field eats from a *mess kit*, which is a metal container that holds eating utensils and opens into a plate with two compartments.

---

5. Manzanar was built in *Owens Valley*, near Death Valley, about two hundred miles north of Los Angeles.
6. In the army, a *mess hall* is the place where meals are eaten.

The Power of Memory Why does the author remember the people in the bus and the greeters laughing?

7. *Lee* is shelter or protection, especially on the side of something facing away from the wind.

Summarize Summarize the information given in this passage about the food at Manzanar. What point is the author making here?

two feet of open space between the floorboards and the ground. Gaps showed between the planks, and as the weeks passed and the green wood dried out, the gaps widened. Knotholes gaped in the uncovered floor.

Each barracks was divided into six units, sixteen by twenty feet, about the size of a living room, with one bare bulb hanging from the ceiling and an oil stove for heat. We were assigned two of these for the twelve people in our family group; and our official family "number" was enlarged by three digits—16 plus the number of this barracks. We were issued steel army cots, two brown army blankets each, and some mattress covers, which my brothers stuffed with straw.

The first task was to divide up what space we had for sleeping. Bill and Woody contributed a blanket each and partitioned off the first room: one side for Bill and Tomi, one side for Woody and Chizu and their baby girl. Woody also got the stove, for heating formulas.

The people who had it hardest during the first few months were young couples like these, many of whom had married just before the evacuation began, in order not to be separated and sent to different camps. Our two rooms were crowded, but at least it was all in the family. My oldest sister and her husband were shoved into one of those sixteen-by-twenty-foot compartments with six people they had never seen before—two other couples, one recently married like themselves, the other with two teenage boys. Partitioning off a room like that wasn't easy. It was bitter cold when we arrived, and the wind did not abate.[8] All they had to use for room dividers were those army blankets, two of which were barely enough to keep one person warm.

They argued over whose blanket should be sacrificed and later argued about noise at night—the parents wanted their boys asleep by 9:00 P.M.—and they continued arguing over matters like that for six months, until my sister and her husband left to harvest sugar beets in Idaho. It was grueling[9] work up there, and wages were pitiful, but when the call came through camp for workers to **alleviate** the wartime labor shortage, it sounded better than their life at Manzanar. They knew they'd have, if nothing else, a room, perhaps a cabin of their own.

That first night in Block 16, the rest of us squeezed into the second room—Granny, Lillian, age fourteen, Ray, thirteen, May, eleven, Kiyo, ten, Mama, and me. I didn't mind this at all at the time. Being youngest meant I got to sleep with Mama. And before we went to bed I had a great time jumping up and down on the mattress. The boys had stuffed so much straw into hers, we had to flatten it some so we wouldn't slide off. I slept with her every night after that until Papa came back.

We woke early, shivering and coated with dust that had blown up through the knotholes and in through the slits around the doorway. During the night Mama had unpacked all our clothes and heaped them on our beds for warmth. Now our cubicle looked as if a great laundry bag had exploded and then been sprayed with fine dust. A skin of sand covered the floor. I looked over Mama's shoulder at Kiyo, on top of his fat mattress, buried under jeans and overcoats and sweaters. His eyebrows

---

8. The fact that the wind did not *abate* means that it did not lessen in force or intensity.

9. *Grueling* work is very difficult, exhausting work.

Summarize Summarize what happened to the author's sister and brother-in-law.

Vocabulary

alleviate (ə lē′ vē āt′) *v.* to make easier to bear; relieve; lessen

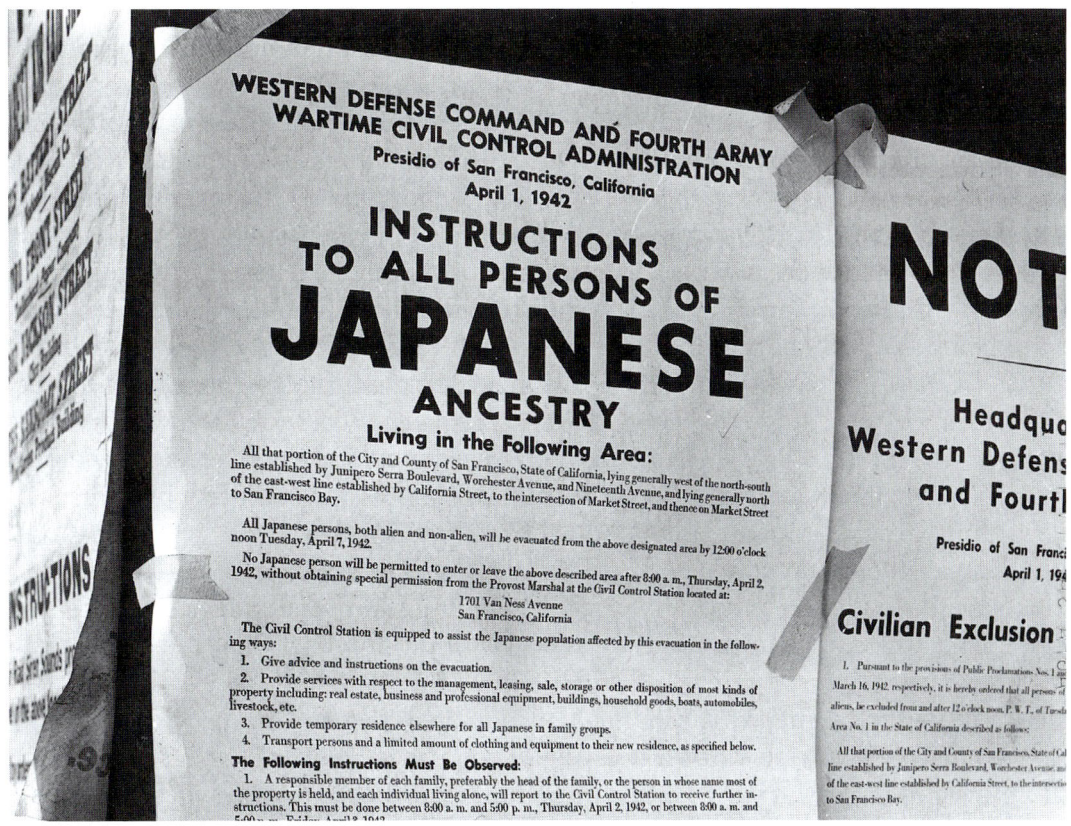

Posted notice informing people of Japanese ancestry of imminent relocation rules due to fears of treason and spying during early years of WWII, April 1, 1942. Dorothea Lange. Silver Gelatin Photograph.

View the Art If you saw a sign like this posted today, how would it make you feel? Explain.

were gray, and he was starting to giggle. He was looking at me, at my gray eyebrows and coated hair, and pretty soon we were both giggling. I looked at Mama's face to see if she thought Kiyo was funny. She lay very still next to me on our mattress, her eyes scanning everything—bare rafters, walls, dusty kids—scanning slowly, and I think the mask of her face would have cracked had not Woody's voice just then come at us through the wall. He was rapping on the planks as if testing to see if they were hollow.

"Hey!" he yelled. "You guys fall into the same flour barrel as us?"

The Power of Memory Why does the author remember moments of humor during her stay at Manzanar?

"No," Kiyo yelled back. "Ours is full of Japs."

All of us laughed at this.

"Well, tell 'em it's time to get up," Woody said. "If we're gonna live in this place, we better get to work."

He gave us ten minutes to dress, then he came in carrying a broom, a hammer, and a sack full of tin can lids he had scrounged somewhere. Woody would be our leader for a while now, short, stocky, grinning behind his mustache. He had just turned twenty-four. In later years he would tour the country with Mr. Moto, the Japanese tag-team wrestler, as his sinister assistant Suki—karate chops through the ropes from outside the ring, a chunky leg reaching from under his kimono to trip up Mr. Moto's foe. In the ring Woody's smile looked sly and crafty; he hammed it up. Offstage it was whimsical, as if some joke were bursting to be told.

"Hey, brother Ray, Kiyo," he said. "You see these tin can lids?"

"Yeah, yeah," the boys said drowsily, as if going back to sleep. They were both young versions of Woody.

"You see all them knotholes in the floor and in the walls?"

They looked around. You could see about a dozen.

Woody said, "You get those covered up before breakfast time. Any more sand comes in here through one of them knotholes, you have to eat it off the floor with ketchup."

"What about sand that comes in through the cracks?" Kiyo said.

Woody stood up very straight, which in itself was funny, since he was only about five-foot-six.

"Don't worry about the cracks," he said. "Different kind of sand comes in through the cracks."

He put his hands on his hips and gave Kiyo a sternly comic look, squinting at him through one eye the way Papa would when he was asserting his authority. Woody mimicked Papa's voice: "And I can tell the difference. So be careful."

The boys laughed and went to work nailing down lids. May started sweeping out the sand. I was helping Mama fold the clothes we'd used for cover, when Woody came over and put his arm around her shoulder. He was short; she was even shorter, under five feet.

He said softly, "You okay, Mama?"

She didn't look at him, she just kept folding clothes and said, "Can we get the cracks covered too, Woody?"

Outside the sky was clear, but icy gusts of wind were buffeting our barracks every few minutes, sending fresh dust puffs up through the floorboards. May's broom could barely keep up with it, and our oil heater could scarcely hold its own against the drafts.

"We'll get this whole place as tight as a barrel, Mama. I already met a guy who told me where they pile all the scrap lumber."

"Scrap?"

"That's all they got. I mean, they're still building the camp, you know. Sixteen blocks left to go. After that, they say maybe we'll get some stuff to fix the insides a little bit."

Her eyes blazed then, her voice quietly furious. "Woody, we can't live like this. Animals live like this."

It was hard to get Woody down. He'd keep smiling when everybody else was ready to explode. Grief flickered in his eyes. He blinked it away and hugged her tighter. "We'll make it better, Mama. You watch."

We could hear voices in other cubicles now. Beyond the wall Woody's baby girl started to cry.

"I have to go over to the kitchen," he said, "see if those guys got a pot for heating bottles. That oil stove takes too long—something wrong with the fuel line. I'll find out what they're giving us for breakfast."

"Probably hotcakes with soy sauce," Kiyo said, on his hands and knees between the bunks.

"No." Woody grinned, heading out the door. "Rice. With Log Cabin Syrup and melted butter."

I don't remember what we ate that first morning. I know we stood for half an hour in cutting wind waiting to get our food. Then we took it back to the cubicle and ate huddled around the stove. Inside, it was warmer than when we left, because Woody was already making good his promise to

---

Historical Narrative *How does Kiyo's comment reflect the misperceptions many people in the United States had about Japanese Americans?*

Children Awaiting Relocation (Assembly Center, Turlock, California), May 2, 1942. Dorothea Lange. Silver Gelatin Photograph.

View the Art Acclaimed photographer Dorothea Lange was hired by the War Relocation Authority (WRA) to document the evacuation and internment of thousands of Californians of Japanese ancestry. What does this photograph suggest about life in the internment camp?

Mama, tacking up some ends of lath[10] he'd found, stuffing rolled paper around the door frame.

Trouble was, he had almost nothing to work with. Beyond this temporary weather stripping, there was little else he could do. Months went by, in fact, before our "home" changed much at all from what it was the day we moved in—bare floors, blanket partitions, one bulb in each compartment dangling from a roof beam, and open ceilings overhead so that mischievous boys like Ray and Kiyo could climb up into the rafters and peek into anyone's life.

The simple truth is the camp was no more ready for us when we got there than we were ready for it. We had only the dimmest ideas of what to expect. Most of the families, like us, had moved out from southern California with as much luggage as each person could carry. Some old men left Los Angeles wearing Hawaiian shirts and Panama hats and stepped off the bus at an altitude of 4000 feet, with nothing available but sagebrush and tarpaper to stop the April winds pouring down off the back side of the Sierras.[11]

---

10. In construction, *lath* is any of the thin, narrow strips of wood used as a foundation for plaster or tiles.

11. The *Sierras,* or Sierra Nevada Mountains, run through eastern California. Manzanar was between these mountains and Death Valley.

Group of evacuees of Japanese ancestry lined up outside train after arriving at Santa Anita Assembly Center from San Pedro as row of US soldiers face them, March 31, 1942. Dorothea Lange. Silver Gelatin Photograph.

View the Art What is the mood of this photograph? What are some of the thoughts or feelings that the people in the evacuee line might be experiencing in this scene?

Visual Vocabulary
A *peacoat* is a double-breasted jacket of thick woolen cloth, often worn by sailors.

The War Department was in charge of all the camps at this point. They began to issue military surplus from the First World War—olive-drab knit caps, earmuffs, peacoats, canvas leggings. Later on, sewing machines were shipped in, and one barracks was turned into a clothing factory. An old seamstress took a peacoat of mine, tore the lining out, opened and flattened the sleeves, added a collar, put arm holes in and handed me back a beautiful cape. By fall dozens of seamstresses were working full-time transforming thousands of these old army clothes into capes, slacks and stylish coats. But until that factory got going and packages from friends outside began to fill out our wardrobes, warmth was more important than style. I couldn't help laughing at Mama walking around in army earmuffs and a pair of wide-cuffed, khaki-colored wool trousers several sizes

The Power of Memory What was significant about the author's memory of the seamstresses?

Visual Vocabulary
The great actor and director *Charlie Chaplin* gained fame for his role as a tramp in baggy pants in a series of movies in the 1920s.

too big for her. Japanese are generally smaller than Caucasians, and almost all these clothes were oversize. They flopped, they dangled, they hung.

It seems comical, looking back; we were a band of Charlie Chaplins marooned in the California desert. But at the time, it was pure chaos. That's the only way to describe it. The evacuation had been so hurriedly planned, the camps so hastily thrown together, nothing was completed when we got there, and almost nothing worked.

I was sick continually, with stomach cramps and diarrhea. At first it was from the shots they gave us for typhoid, in very heavy doses and in assembly-line fashion: swab, jab, swab, *Move along now,* swab, jab, swab, *Keep it moving.* That knocked all of us younger kids down at once, with fevers and vomiting. Later, it was the food that made us sick, young and old alike. The kitchens were too small and badly ventilated. Food would spoil from being left out too long. That summer, when the heat got fierce, it would spoil faster. The refrigeration kept breaking down. The cooks, in many cases, had never cooked before. Each block had to provide its own volunteers. Some were lucky and had a professional or two in their midst. But the first chef in our block had been a gardener all his life and suddenly found himself preparing three meals a day for 250 people.

Historical Narrative What does this information tell you about living conditions at Manzanar?

"The Manzanar runs" became a condition of life, and you only hoped that when you rushed to the latrine, one would be in working order.

That first morning, on our way to the chow line, Mama and I tried to use the women's latrine in our block. The smell of it spoiled what little appetite we had. Outside, men were working in an open trench, up to their knees in muck—a common sight in the months to come. Inside, the floor was covered with excrement, and all twelve bowls were erupting like a row of tiny volcanoes.

Mama stopped a kimono-wrapped woman stepping past us with her sleeve pushed up against her nose and asked, "What do you do?"

"Try Block Twelve," the woman said, grimacing. "They have just finished repairing the pipes."

It was about two city blocks away. We followed her over there and found a line of women waiting in the wind outside the latrine. We had no choice but to join the line and wait with them.

Inside it was like all the other latrines. Each block was built to the same design, just as each of the ten camps, from California to Arkansas, was built to a common master plan. It was an open room, over a concrete slab. The sink was a long metal trough against one wall, with a row of spigots for hot and cold water. Down the center of the room twelve toilet bowls were arranged in six pairs, back to back, with no partitions. My mother was a very modest person, and this was going to be agony for her, sitting down in public, among strangers.

One old woman had already solved the problem for herself by dragging in a large cardboard carton. She set it up around one of the bowls, like a three-sided screen. OXYDOL was printed in large black letters down the front. I remember this well, because that was the soap we were issued for laundry; later on, the smell of it would permeate these rooms. The upended carton was about four feet high. The old woman behind it wasn't much taller. When she stood, only her head showed over the top.

She was about Granny's age. With great effort she was trying to fold the sides of the screen together. Mama happened to be at the head of the line now. As she approached the vacant bowl, she and the old woman bowed to each other from the waist. Mama then moved to help her with the carton, and the old woman said very graciously, in Japanese, "Would you like to use it?"

Happily, gratefully, Mama bowed again and said, *"Arigato"* (Thank you). *"Arigato gozaimas"* (Thank you very much). "I will return it to your barracks."

"Oh, no. It is not necessary. I will be glad to wait."

The old woman unfolded one side of the cardboard, while Mama opened the other; then she bowed again and scurried out the door.

Those big cartons were a common sight in the spring of 1942. Eventually sturdier partitions appeared, one or two at a time. The first were built of scrap lumber. Word would get around that Block such and such had partitions now, and Mama and my older sisters would walk halfway across the camp to use them. Even after every latrine in camp was screened, this quest for privacy continued. Many would wait until late at night. Ironically, because of this, midnight was often the most crowded time of all. ==Like so many of the women there, Mama never did get used to the latrines.== It was a humiliation she just learned to endure: *shikata ga nai*, this cannot be helped. She would quickly **subordinate** her own desires to those of the family or the community, because she knew cooperation was the only way to survive. At the same time she placed a high premium on personal privacy, respected it in others and insisted upon it for herself. Almost everyone at Manzanar had inherited this pair of traits from the generations before them who had learned to live in a small, crowded country like Japan. Because of the first they were able to take a desolate stretch of wasteland and gradually make it livable. ==But the entire situation there, especially in the beginning—the packed sleeping quarters, the communal mess halls, the open toilets—all this was an open insult to that other, private self, a slap in the face you were powerless to challenge.==

shikata ga nai, this cannot be helped

The Power of Memory *How would it affect you to see friends or family members endure humiliations such as the ones Mama endured?*

Summarize *What does this summary of conditions at Manzanar show the reader? What might have been the author's purpose in including it here?*

Vocabulary

subordinate (sə bôr′ də nāt′) *v.* to cause to be, or treat as, secondary, inferior, or less important

After You Read

Respond and Think Critically

Respond and Interpret

1. What detail of Manzanar affected you the most? Explain.

2. (a)How did the author feel about moving to Terminal Island? (b)Why do you think the author felt this way?

3. What did Mama do when the secondhand dealer offered her a low price for her valuable dishes?

4. (a)How did the teacher at Boyle Heights treat the author? (b)Compare and contrast that teacher to the teacher from Ocean Park.

Analyze and Evaluate

5. (a)Why does the author mention various events in U.S. history throughout the selection? (b)Do you think this makes her story more effective?

6. (a)Why does the author offer descriptions of her houses throughout this time period? (b)Do the comparisons of the houses achieve an important purpose within the selection? Explain.

Connect

7. **Big Idea** The Power of Memory Jeanne Wakatsuki Houston said that going back to visit Manzanar made her realize that her life began there. Discuss the lessons you learned about U.S. internment of Japanese Americans from reading about Wakatsuki Houston's memories

8. **Connect to Today** Executive Order 9066 came as a shock to Japanese Americans, many of whom had been United States citizens for many years or had been born in the United States. Do you think an event like the Japanese Internment could happen in the United States today? Why or why not?

Literary Element Historical Narrative

A **historical narrative** can blend elements of objectivity and subjectivity. For instance, some facts mentioned by Wakatsuki Houston are verifiable and recounted in numerous other sources. Other details described by Wakatsuki Houston are anecdotal, deal with feelings and perceptions, and come from her personal memories. Both kinds of details—the objective and the subjective—have much to teach the reader about what happened to many Japanese Americans during World War II.

1. How would this story be different if someone who had no personal experiences related to Manzanar had written it? Do you think it would be as effective?

2. Does Wakatsuki Houston give enough objective details about the historical period to help the reader understand the context of the narrative?

Review: Autobiography

As you learned on pages 284–285, an **autobiography** is a person's account of his or her own life. In most autobiographies, the writer tells the story from the first-person point of view, using the pronoun *I*. The use of this point of view makes most autobiographies very personal and subjective.

Partner Activity Meet with another student and list some details from the selection that you would not find in a more objective source, such as an encyclopedia. How do these details help you better understand this episode in U.S. history?

Details	Evaluation
Mama breaks her valuable china.	gives a personal account; offers a perspective that a strictly factual account wouldn't

Reading Strategy Summarize

SAT Skills Practice

1. Which sentence best summarizes the main idea of this excerpt from *Farewell to Manzanar?*

    A. For the families involved, internment was bewildering, unjust, and humiliating.
    B. Japanese Americans had done nothing to threaten national security.
    C. Many families of Japanese origin were not involved in mainstream American culture.
    D. Internment camps for Japanese Americans were poorly planned and constructed.
    E. The old and the young adapted differently to the restrictions of internment camps.

Vocabulary Practice

Practice with Word Parts Use a dictionary to find the meaning of each vocabulary word's root. Organize the meanings in a diagram as shown. Use the word correctly in a sentence.

patriarch   designation   alleviate   subordinate

EXAMPLE:

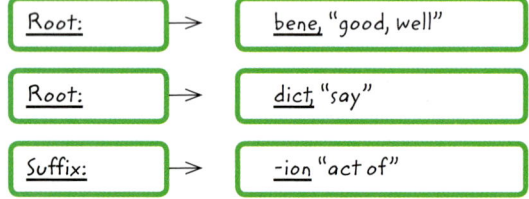

The holy man said a benediction.

Academic Vocabulary

*Wakatsuki cannot **modify** events of the past but can hope they will not occur again.*

Modify is an academic word. Use context clues to figure out the meaning of *modify* in each sentence. Explain the difference in meaning.

1. This idea will **modify** the plan to our benefit.
2. Choose a precise adjective to **modify** that noun.

For more on academic vocabulary, see pages 52 and 53.

Research and Report

 Internet Connection

Assignment Use the Internet to research the internment of Japanese Americans during World War II. Write an informational report.

Get Ideas List five questions to focus your research on narrow topics, such as living quarters, or broader topics, such as psychological effects. Develop a search plan that includes primary sources from archived news accounts, which you might access through a library database.

Research Take notes, creating separate electronic files or notecards for each bit of information you record. Include notes about the reliability of each source. Paraphrase and summarize most information; directly quote only memorable or incisive ideas. For all information you record—quoted, paraphrased, or summarized—integrate citations.

Information from Site	Example of Parenthetical Citation
Author given;	(Hashimori)
if no author, cite sponsor;	(University of Utah Historic Collections)
if no author or sponsor, cite Web site title;	("Children of the Camps")

Also integrate attributions such as these:

*According to _____, author of _____,
the _____ Web site reports _____.*

Organize your notes by main ideas.

Report As you synthesize ideas from at least three sources, use topic sentences for main ideas and supporting sentences for specific data, facts, and ideas. Use transitions such as *On the other hand* and *nevertheless* to introduce varying or contradictory ideas or opinions. Cite all sources at the end, as well as in parenthetical references.

Selection Resources For Selection Quizzes, eFlashcards, and Reading-Writing Connection activities, go to glencoe.com and enter QuickPass code GL59794u2.

Grammar Workshop

Subject-Verb Agreement

Literature Connection In every sentence, the **verb** (or action word) must agree with the **subject** (or actor) in both person and number. In the sentence below, although the subject, *barracks,* looks plural, it functions as a unit and takes the singular auxiliary verb *was.*

> "Each barracks was divided into six units, sixteen by twenty feet, about the size of a living room. . . ."
>
> —Jeanne Wakatsuki Houston and James D. Houston, from "Farewell to Manzanar"

Examples:

With a compound subject that is joined by *and* . . .

Use a singular verb if the parts of the subject make up a single unit.

Rice and fruit is an unheard-of combination to the Japanese.

Use a plural verb if the parts of the subject are not considered a unit.

The neighborhood bully and his friend were frightening.

With a compound subject that is joined by *or* or *nor* . . .

Use a verb that agrees with the subject closest to it.

Either their homework or their chores keep the children inside. Neither below-zero temperatures nor a blizzard prevents him from sledding.

With a subject that is a collective noun . . .

Use a singular verb if the noun refers to a group as a whole.

The committee has to come to a decision by noon.

Learning Objectives

In this workshop, you will focus on the following objective:

Grammar: Understanding how to correct subject-verb agreement.

Subjects and Verbs

A **verb** is the action word in a sentence, and the **subject** is who or what performs the action. **Subject-verb** agreement occurs when the subject and verb match in person and number.

Tip

To help ensure subject-verb agreement, identify each subject as singular or plural and use an appropriate verb.

Language Handbook

For more on subject-verb agreement, see the Language Handbook, pp. R48–R49.

Practice Write out the correct form of the verb in each sentence below.

1. The family (tries, try) to stick together and support each other.
2. The children (doesn't, don't) learn to speak Japanese.
3. Neither Mother nor the other parents (stops, stop) worrying.
4. Manzanar and another camp (is, are) located on the west coast.
5. Harvesting beets in Idaho (were, was) hard work.

Grammar For more grammar practice, go to glencoe.com and enter QuickPass code GL59794u2.

Before You Read

from *Kaffir Boy*

World Literature
South Africa

Meet **Mark Mathabane**
(born 1960)

What was it like to grow up in South Africa under the system of apartheid? For Mark Mathabane (mä tä bä′ne) "it meant hate, bitterness, hunger, pain, terror, violence, fear, dashed hopes and dreams."

Dark Childhood Mathabane spent his early years living in poverty and fear under the apartheid government, which relegated black South Africans to ghettos and treated them as inferior people. Constant police raids and relocation to worthless parcels of land where work and education were scarce made life unbearable for black South Africans.

Mathabane's family lived in Alexandra township, in a square-mile ghetto packed with 200,000 black South Africans. Barely subsisting on the ten dollars that Mathabane's father made each week, the family already found life in the Alexandra township to be brutal and harsh. But when Mathabane's father was arrested for being unemployed, the family fell into even deeper poverty.

> "Books aren't written with the comfort of readers in mind. I know I didn't write Kaffir Boy that way."
>
> —Mark Mathabane

Escape from Oppression Although illiterate, Mathabane's mother understood the importance of education and insisted that her son attend school. Mathabane decided to master English, which black South Africans were forbidden to learn. At the age of thirteen, he took up tennis and five years later won a tennis scholarship to an American college; he called the scholarship "my passport to freedom."

In 1986 Mathabane published his first book, *Kaffir Boy,* an honest portrayal of the horrors of growing up under apartheid. Despite being banned by the South African government for its powerful anti-apartheid sentiment, this autobiography was hugely successful.

A New Life *Kaffir Boy in America,* an account of Mathabane's arrival and first years in the United States, followed in 1989. This sequel relates Mathabane's difficulties in adapting to a new culture and lifestyle in a land that was wonderfully different from, but possessed unfortunate similarities to, the apartheid system. His most recent book is the memoir *Miriam's Song* (2001), about his sister's experience of the last days of apartheid.

Literature Online

Author Search For more about Mark Mathabane, go to glencoe.com and enter QuickPass code GL59794u2.

Literature and Reading Preview

Connect to the Autobiography
How does education change the way you see the world? Freewrite for a few minutes about the ways your education has affected your perception of the world.

Build Background
Under apartheid, black South Africans, who made up more than seventy-five percent of the population, and other non-white people were forced to live and work under a system of strict racial segregation. Apartheid sparked strong opposition in South Africa and in many other parts of the world and came to a definitive end in 1994 with the electoral victory of Nelson Mandela's African National Congress.

Set Purposes for Reading

Big Idea The Power of Memory

As you read this excerpt from *Kaffir Boy,* ask yourself, How does Mathabane show the power of memory to change one's life for the better?

Literary Element Theme

Theme is the central message of a work of literature that readers can apply to life. Finding the theme of a story helps you connect with the author's purpose in writing. As you read, ask yourself, What is the central theme of this literary text?

Reading Strategy Analyze Cause-and-Effect Relationships

A **cause-and-effect relationship** is a connection between the reason for an occurrence and the occurrence itself. Analyzing these relationships helps to explain why things happen and why a character or person makes the decisions he or she makes. As you read, ask yourself, What influences the characters in *Kaffir Boy* to make the decisions they do?

Tip: Make Connections Use a chart like the one below to make connections between causes and effects in the selection.

Cause	Effect
His gang refuses to go to school.	Narrator decides not to go to school.

Learning Objectives

For pages 304–320

In studying this text, you will focus on the following objectives:

Literary Analysis: Analyzing theme.

Reading: Analyzing cause-and-effect relationships.

Vocabulary

coterie (kō′tə rē) *n.* a small group of people who share a particular interest and often meet socially; p. 309 *Janelle and her airplane-loving coterie crafted model airplanes.*

admonish (ad mon′ish) *v.* to warn, as against a specific action; p. 309 *José's parents admonished him to stay out of the canyon.*

peruse (pə rōōz′) *v.* to read through or examine carefully; p. 311 *The doctor perused the medical journals for detailed information.*

credence (krēd′əns) *n.* trustworthiness, especially in the reports or statements of others; p. 313 *The lawyer's argument had more credence than the accounts of bystanders.*

vehemently (vē′ə mənt lē) *adv.* strongly; intensely; passionately; p. 315 *The peace activists argued vehemently against the war.*

MARK MATHABANE

from
Kaffir Boy

Mark Mathabane

South African boys play soccer with an undersized ball in Soweto, 1990. South Africa. David Turnley.

"Education will open doors where none seem to exist."

When my mother began dropping hints that I would soon be going to school, I vowed never to go because school was a waste of time. She laughed and said, "We'll see. You don't know what you're talking about." My philosophy on school was that of a gang of ten-, eleven-, and twelve-year-olds whom I so revered that their every word seemed that of an oracle.[1]

These boys had long left their homes and were now living in various neighborhood junkyards, making it on their own. They slept in abandoned cars, smoked glue and benzene,[2] ate pilchards[3] and brown bread, sneaked into the white world to caddy and, if unsuccessful, came back to the township to steal beer and soda bottles from shebeens,[4] or goods from the Indian traders on First Avenue. Their life style was exciting, adventurous, and full of surprises; and I was attracted to it. My mother told me that they were no-gooders, that they would amount to nothing, that I should not associate with them, but I paid no heed. What does she know? I used to tell myself. One thing she did not know was that the gang's way of life had captivated me wholly, particularly their philosophy on school: they hated it and considered an education a waste of time.

They, like myself, had grown up in an environment where the value of an education

---

1. In Greek mythology, the gods sometimes spoke through an *oracle*, or a person such as a priestess.
2. The boys are taking a risk with *benzene,* a poisonous liquid obtained from coal.
3. *Pilchard*s are small fish of the herring family.
4. *Shebeens* are taverns operating without government license or approval.

Analyze Cause-and-Effect Relationships *Why do you think the gang has such appeal for Mathabane compared to the life his mother wants for him?*

was never emphasized, where the first thing a child learned was not how to read and write and spell, but how to fight and steal and rebel; where the money to send children to school was grossly[5] lacking, for survival was first priority. I kept my membership in the gang, knowing that for as long as I was under its influence, I would never go to school.

One day my mother woke me up at four in the morning.

"Are they here? I didn't hear any noises," I asked in the usual way.

"No," my mother said. "I want you to get into that washtub over there."

"What!" I balked, upon hearing the word washtub. I feared taking baths like one feared the plague. Throughout seven years of hectic living the number of baths I had taken could be counted on one hand with several fingers missing. I simply had no natural inclination for water; cleanliness was a trait I still had to acquire. Besides, we had only one bathtub in the house, and it constantly sprung a leak.

"I said get into that tub!" My mother shook a finger in my face.

Reluctantly, I obeyed, yet wondered why all of a sudden I had to take a bath. My mother, armed with a scropbrush and a piece of Lifebuoy soap, purged[6] me of years and years of grime till I ached and bled. As I howled, feeling pain shoot through my limbs as the thistles of the brush encountered stubborn calluses, there was a loud knock at the door.

---

5. Here, *grossly* means "totally; entirely."
6. To *purge* is to cleanse or get rid of whatever is unclean or undesirable.

Theme *Do you think the author has strong convictions of his own at this point? Explain.*

Theme *What do you think is the connection between cleanliness and Mathabane's life in the gang?*

Instantly my mother leaped away from the tub and headed, on tiptoe, toward the bedroom. Fear seized me as I, too, thought of the police. I sat frozen in the bathtub, not knowing what to do.

"Open up, Mujaji [my mother's maiden name]," Granny's voice came shrilling through the door. "It's me."

My mother heaved a sigh of relief; her tense limbs relaxed. She turned and headed to the kitchen door, unlatched it, and in came Granny and Aunt Bushy.

"You scared me half to death," my mother said to Granny. "I had forgotten all about your coming."

"Are you ready?" Granny asked my mother.

"Yes—just about," my mother said, beckoning me to get out of the washtub.

She handed me a piece of cloth to dry myself. As I dried myself, questions raced through my mind: What's going on? What's Granny doing at our house this ungodly[7] hour of the morning? And why did she ask my mother, "Are you ready?" While I stood debating, my mother went into the bedroom and came out with a stained white shirt and a pair of faded black shorts.

"Here," she said, handing me the togs, "put these on."

"Why?" I asked.

"Put them on I said!"

I put the shirt on; it was grossly loose-fitting. It reached all the way down to my ankles. Then I saw the reason why: it was my father's shirt!

"But this is Papa's shirt," I complained. "It don't fit me."

"Put it on," my mother insisted. "I'll make it fit."

"The pants don't fit me either," I said. "Whose are they anyway?"

---

7. In this context, *ungodly* means "outrageous; shocking."

Children in Alexandra Township. Louise Gubb. Alexandra continues to be one of the poorest areas in the Gauteng region of South Africa, suffering from overcrowding, crime, and a lack of infrastructure. Half of all young people in the area do not receive education.

View the Art What does the background in this photograph tell you about daily life for these children? How might the older three react to being enrolled in school like the author was?

"Put them on," my mother said. "I'll make them fit."

Moments later I had the garments on; I looked ridiculous. My mother started working on the pants and shirt to make them fit. She folded the shirt in so many intricate ways and stashed it inside the pants, they too having been folded several times at the waist. She then choked the pants at the waist with a piece of sisal rope to hold them up. She then lavishly smeared my face, arms, and legs with a mixture of pig's fat and vaseline.

Visual Vocabulary
Sisal is a coarse, strong fiber obtained from the leaves of a tropical plant.

"This will insulate you from the cold," she said. My skin gleamed like the morning star, and I felt as hot as the center of the sun, and I smelled God knows like what. After embalming me, she headed to the bedroom.

"Where are we going, Gran'ma?" I said, hoping that she would tell me what my mother refused to tell me. I still had no idea I was about to be taken to school.

"Didn't your mother tell you?" Granny said with a smile. "You're going to start school."

"What!" I gasped, leaping from the chair where I was sitting as if it were made of hot lead. "I am not going to school!" I blurted out and raced toward the kitchen door.

My mother had just reappeared from the bedroom and guessing what I was up to, she yelled, "Someone get the door!"

Aunt Bushy immediately barred the door. I turned and headed for the window. As I leaped for the windowsill, my mother lunged at me and brought me down. I tussled, "Let go of me! I don't want to go to school! Let me go!" but my mother held fast onto me.

"It's no use now," she said, grinning triumphantly as she pinned me down.

Turning her head in Granny's direction, she shouted, "Granny! Get a rope quickly!"

Granny grabbed a piece of rope nearby and came to my mother's aid. I bit and clawed every hand that grabbed me, and howled protestations against going to school; however, I was no match for the two determined matriarchs.[8] In a jiffy they had me bound, hands and feet.

"What's the matter with him?" Granny, bewildered, asked my mother. "Why did he suddenly turn into an imp[9] when I told him you're taking him to school?"

"You shouldn't have told him that he's being taken to school," my mother said. "He doesn't want to go there. That's why I requested you come today, to help me take him there. Those boys in the streets have been a bad influence on him."

As the two matriarchs hauled me through the door, they told Aunt Bushy not to go to school but stay behind and mind the house and the children.

==The sun was beginning to rise from beyond the veld[10] when Granny and my mother dragged me to school.== The streets were beginning to fill with their everyday traffic: old men and women, wizened,[11] bent, and ragged, were beginning their rambling; workless men and women were beginning to assemble in their usual **coteries** and head for shebeens in the backyards where they discussed how they escaped the morning pass raids[12] and contemplated the conditions of life amidst intense beer drinking and vacant, uneasy laughter; young boys and girls, some as young as myself, were beginning their aimless wanderings along the narrow, dusty streets in search of food, carrying bawling infants piggyback.

As we went along some of the streets, boys and girls who shared the same fears about school as I were making their feelings known in a variety of ways. They were howling their protests and trying to escape. A few managed to break loose and make a mad dash for freedom, only to be recaptured in no time, **admonished** or whipped, or both, and ordered to march again.

As we made a turn into Sixteenth Avenue, the street leading to the tribal school I was being taken to, a short, chubby black woman came along from the opposite direction. She had a scuttle[13] overflowing with coal on her *doek*-covered (cloth-covered) head. An infant, bawling deafeningly, was loosely swathed with a piece of sheepskin onto her back. Following closely behind the woman, and picking up pieces of coal as they fell from the scuttle and placing them in a small plastic bag, was a half-naked, potbellied, and thumb-sucking boy of about four. The woman stopped abreast.[14] For some reason we stopped too.

"I wish I had done the same to my oldest son," the strange woman said in a regretful

---

8. *Matriarchs* (mā′trē ärks′) are women who head families or who have great authority in other groups.
9. Here, *imp* means "a mischievous child."
10. In South Africa, the *veld* (velt) is a rolling grassland with scattered trees or bushes.
11. When the elderly become wizened (wiz′ ənd), they are shriveled or withered due to age.

The Power of Memory *Why might Mathabane remember so vividly the details of that day later in life?*

Vocabulary

coterie (kō′tə rē) *n.* a small group of people who share a particular interest and often meet socially

12. *Pass raids* refers to the practice whereby police periodically stopped black South Africans to see that they had the proper papers authorizing them to be in specific areas.
13. Here, a *scuttle* is a coal container.
14. *Abreast* means "alongside the others."

Vocabulary

admonish (ad mon′ish) *v.* to warn, as against a specific action

A schoolboy does homework at his desk, Mali. 1960, Paul Almasy Mali. Resources for education are scarce throughout Africa, but many old organizations have targeted education as a key component for fighting poverty and hunger.

View the Art How do this child's attitude and activities reflect the theme of Mathabane's tale?

voice, gazing at me. I was confounded[15] by her stopping and offering her unsolicited opinion.

"I wish I had done that to my oldest son," she repeated, and suddenly burst into tears; amidst sobs, she continued, "before . . . the street claimed him . . . and . . . turned him into a *tsotsi*."[16]

Granny and my mother offered consolatory remarks to the strange woman.

"But it's too late now," the strange woman continued, tears now streaming freely down her puffy cheeks. She made no attempt to dry them. "It's too late now," she said for the second time, "he's beyond any help. I can't help him even if I wanted to. *Uswile*[17] [He is dead]."

"How did he die?" my mother asked in a sympathetic voice.

"He shunned school and, instead, grew up to live by the knife. And the same knife he lived by ended his life. That's why whenever I see a boy-child refuse to go to school, I stop and tell the story of my dear little *mbitsini*[18] [heartbreak]."

Having said that, the strange woman left as mysteriously as she had arrived.

"Did you hear what that woman said!" my mother screamed into my ears. "Do you want the same to happen to you?"

I dropped my eyes. I was confused.

"Poor woman," Granny said ruefully. "She must have truly loved her son."

Finally, we reached the school and I was ushered into the principal's office, a tiny cubicle facing a row of privies[19] and a patch of yellowed grass.

"So this is the rascal we'd been talking about," the principal, a tall, wiry man,

---

15. To be *confounded* is to be confused or bewildered.
16. A *tsotsi* (tsot′sē) is an armed street hoodlum or gangster.
17. *Uswile* (o͞o swēl′ā)

18. *mbitsini* (əm bit sē′nē)
19. *Privies* (priv′ēz) are outhouses, or toilets.

Analyze Cause-and-Effect Relationships What does the woman think caused her son to become a tsotsi?

Theme Why is it significant that Mathabane encounters this woman?

foppishly[20] dressed in a black pin-striped suit, said to my mother as we entered. His austere,[21] shiny face, inscrutable and imposing, reminded me of my father. He was sitting behind a brown table upon which stood piles of dust and cobweb-covered books and papers. In one upper pocket of his jacket was arrayed a variety of pens and pencils; in the other nestled a lily-white handkerchief whose presence was more decorative than utilitarian.[22] Alongside him stood a disproportionately portly[23] black woman, fashionably dressed in a black skirt and a white blouse. She had but one pen, and this she held in her hand. The room was hot and stuffy and buzzing with flies.

"Yes, Principal," my mother answered, "this is he."

"I see he's living up to his notoriety," remarked the principal, noticing that I had been bound. "Did he give you too much trouble?"

"Principal," my mother sighed. "He was like an imp."

"He's just like the rest of them, Principal," Granny sighed. "Once they get out into the streets, they become wild. They take to the many vices of the streets like an infant takes to its mother's milk. They begin to think that there's no other life but the one shown them by the *tsotsis*. They come to hate school and forget about the future."

"Well," the principal said. "We'll soon remedy all that. Untie him."

"He'll run away," my mother cried.

"I don't think he's that foolish to attempt that with all of us here."

"He *is* that foolish, Principal," my mother said as she and Granny began untying me. "He's tried it before. Getting him here was an ordeal in itself."

The principal rose from his seat, took two steps to the door and closed it. As the door swung closed, I spotted a row of canes of different lengths and thicknesses hanging behind it. The principal, seeing me staring at the canes, grinned and said, in a manner suggesting that he had wanted me to see them, "As long as you behave, I won't have to use any of those on you."

Use those canes on me? I gasped. I stared at my mother—she smiled; at Granny—she smiled too. That made me abandon any inkling of escaping.

"So they finally gave you the birth certificate and the papers," the principal addressed my mother as he returned to his chair.

"Yes, Principal," my mother said, "they finally did. But what a battle it was. It took me nearly a year to get all them papers together." She took out of her handbag a neatly wrapped package and handed it to the principal. "They've been running us around for so long that there were times when I thought he would never attend school, Principal," she said.

"That's pretty much standard procedure, Mrs. Mathabane," the principal said, unwrapping the package. "But you now have the papers and that's what's important.

"As long as we have the papers," he continued, minutely **perusing** the contents

---

20. The man surely would not think that he dressed *foppishly*—in the style of one who pays too much attention to his or her clothes.
21. *Austere* means "serious, strict, or severe."
22. Something that is *utilitarian* is functional or practical.
23. A *portly* person has a heavy or stout but dignified appearance.

Analyze Cause-and-Effect Relationships What effect do you think the principal's statement will have on Mathabane's commitment to attending school?

Vocabulary

peruse (pə rōoz′) v. to read through or examine carefully

of the package, "we won't be breaking the law in admitting your son to this school, for we'll be in full compliance with the requirements set by the authorities in Pretoria."[24]

"Sometimes I don't understand the laws from Pitori,"[25] Granny said. "They did the same to me with my Piet and Bushy. Why, Principal, should our children not be allowed to learn because of some piece of paper?"

"The piece of paper you're referring to, Mrs. Mabaso [Granny's maiden name]," the principal said to Granny, "is as important to our children as a pass is to us adults. We all hate passes; therefore, it's only natural we should hate the regulations our children are subjected to. But as we have to live with passes, so our children have to live with the regulations, Mrs. Mabaso. I hope you understand, that is the law of the country. We would have admitted your grandson a long time ago, as you well know, had it not been for the papers. I hope you understand."

"I understand, Principal," Granny said, "but I don't understand," she added paradoxically.

One of the papers caught the principal's eye and he turned to my mother and asked, "Is your husband a Shangaan, Mrs. Mathabane?"

"No, he's not Principal," my mother said. "Is there anything wrong? He's Venda and I'm Shangaan."[26]

The principal reflected for a moment or so and then said, concernedly, "No, there's nothing seriously wrong. Nothing that we can't take care of. You see, Mrs. Mathabane, technically, the fact that your child's father is a Venda makes him ineligible to attend this tribal school because it is only for children whose parents are of the Shangaan tribe. May I ask what language the children speak at home?"

"Both languages," my mother said worriedly, "Venda and Shangaan. Is there anything wrong?"

The principal coughed, clearing his throat, then said, "I mean which language do they speak more?"

"It depends, Principal," my mother said, swallowing hard. "When their father is around, he wants them to speak only Venda. And when he's not, they speak Shangaan. And when they are out at play, they speak Zulu and Sisotho."[27]

"Well," the principal said, heaving a sigh of relief. "In that case, I think an exception can be made. The reason for such an exception is that there's currently no school for Vendas in Alexandra. And should the authorities come asking why we took in your son, we can tell them that. Anyway, your child is half-half."

Everyone broke into a nervous laugh, except me. I was bewildered by the whole thing. I looked at my mother, and she seemed greatly relieved as she watched the principal register me; a broad smile broke across her face. It was as if some enormously heavy burden had finally been lifted from her shoulders and her conscience.

"Bring him back two weeks from today," the principal said as he saw us to the door. "There're so many children registering

---

24. The rules come from South Africa's capital, *Pretoria*.
25. *Pitori* is Granny's pronunciation of "Pretoria."
26. The people of South Africa belong to many different ethnic groups, including *Venda* and *Shangaan*, each with its own language.

---

27. *Zulu* and *Sisotho* are ethnic groups as well as languages.

Theme How does this passage contribute to a recurring theme in the story?

The Power of Memory What detail of her own life might Mathabane's mother be remembering or thinking about at this moment?

today that classes won't begin until two weeks hence. Also, the school needs repair and cleaning up after the holidays. If he refuses to come, simply notify us, and we'll send a couple of big boys to come fetch him, and he'll be very sorry if it ever comes to that."

As we left the principal's office and headed home, my mind was still against going to school. I was thinking of running away from home and joining my friends in the junkyard.

I didn't want to go to school for three reasons: I was reluctant to surrender my freedom and independence over to what I heard every school-going child call "tyrannous discipline." I had heard many bad things about life in tribal school—from daily beatings by teachers and mistresses who worked you like a mule to long school hours—and the sight of those canes in the principal's office gave ample **credence** to rumors that school was nothing but a torture chamber. And there was my allegiance to the gang.

But the thought of the strange woman's lamentations over her dead son presented a somewhat strong case for going to school: I didn't want to end up dead in the streets. A more compelling argument for going to school, however, was the vivid recollection of all that humiliation and pain my mother had gone through to get me the papers and the birth certificate so I could enroll in school. What should I do? I was torn between two worlds.

But later that evening something happened to force me to go to school.

I was returning home from playing soccer when a neighbor accosted[28] me by the gate and told me that there had been a bloody fight at my home.

"Your mother and father have been at it again," the neighbor, a woman, said.

South African man with passbook. Juda Ngwenya.

View the Art During apartheid, Black South Africans were required to carry a passbook with them that stated where they were allowed to work and live. If their passbooks were not in order, they could be arrested and jailed. As the principal in *Kaffir Boy* explains it, how are the student regulations similar to the passbooks?

---

28. In this case, to *accost* is to approach and speak to, often in a pushy way.

Theme What does the contrast between these two different worlds have to do with the themes of the story?

Vocabulary

credence (krēd′əns) *n.* trustworthiness, especially in the reports or statements of others

"And your mother left."

I was stunned.

"Was she hurt badly?"

"A little bit," the woman said. "But she'll be all right. We took her to your grandma's place."

I became hot with anger.

"Is anyone in the house?" I stammered, trying to control my rage.

"Yes, your father is. But I don't think you should go near the house. He's raving mad. He's armed with a meat cleaver. He's chased out your brother and sisters, also. And some of the neighbors who tried to intervene he's threatened to carve them to pieces. I have never seen him this mad before."

I brushed aside the woman's warnings and went. Shattered windows convinced me that there had indeed been a skirmish of some sort. Several pieces of broken bricks, evidently broken after being thrown at the door, were lying about the door. I tried opening the door; it was locked from the inside. I knocked. No one answered. I knocked again. Still no one answered, until, as I turned to leave:

"Who's out there?" my father's voice came growling from inside.

"It's me, Johannes,"[29] I said.

"Go away, . . . !" he bellowed. "I don't want you or that . . . mother of yours setting foot in this house. Go away before I come out there and kill you!"

"Let me in!" I cried. "Dammit, let me in! I want my things!"

"What things? Go away, you black swine!"

I went to the broken window and screamed obscenities at my father, daring him to come out, hoping that if he as much as ever stuck his black face out, I would pelt him with the half-a-loaf brick in my hand. He didn't come out. He continued launching a tirade[30] of obscenities at my mother and her mother. . . . He was drunk, but I wondered where he had gotten the money to buy beer because it was still the middle of the week and he was dead broke. He had lost his entire wage for the past week in dice and had had to borrow bus fare.

"What happened, Mama?" I asked, fighting to hold back the tears at the sight of her disfigured face.

"Nothing, child, nothing," she mumbled, almost apologetically, between swollen lips. "Your papa simply lost his temper, that's all."

"But why did he beat you up like this, Mama?" Tears came down my face. "He's never beaten you like this before."

My mother appeared reluctant to answer me. She looked searchingly at Granny, who was pounding millet with pestle and mortar and mixing it with sorghum[31] and nuts for an African delicacy. Granny said, "Tell him, child, tell him. He's got a right to know. Anyway, he's the cause of it all."

Visual Vocabulary
The *pestle* is a blunt tool used to pound or grind substances in a *mortar*, a thick, hard bowl, often made of wood or stone.

"Your father and I fought because I took you to school this morning," my mother began. "He had told me not to, and when I told him that I had, he became very upset. He was drunk. We started arguing, and one thing led to another."

---

29. The author's name was *Johannes* (yō hä´nis) before he changed it to Mark.
30. A *tirade* (tī rād´) is a long, angry, or scolding speech.
31. *Millet* is a grain similar to wheat, and *sorghum* is a syrup made from a tropical grass.

Analyze Cause-and-Effect Relationships *How might Mathabane respond to discovering that he is the "cause of it all"?*

"Why doesn't he want me to go to school?"

"He says he doesn't have money to waste paying for you to get what he calls a useless white man's education," my mother replied. "But I told him that if he won't pay for your schooling, I would try and look for a job and pay, but he didn't want to hear that, also. 'There are better things for you to work for,' he said. 'Besides, I don't want you to work. How would I look to other men if you, a woman I owned, were to start working?' When I asked him why shouldn't I take you to school, seeing that you were now of age, he replied that he doesn't believe in schools. I told him that school would keep you off the streets and out of trouble, but still he was belligerent."

"Is that why he beat you up?"

"Yes, he said I disobeyed his orders."

"He's right, child," Granny interjected. "He paid *lobola* [bride price] for you. And your father ate it all up before he left me."

To which my mother replied, "But I desperately want to leave this beast of a man. But with his *lobola* gone I can't do it. That worthless thing you call your husband shouldn't have sold Jackson's scrawny cattle and left you penniless."

"Don't talk like that about your father, child," Granny said. "Despite all, he's still your father, you know. Anyway, he asked for *lobola* only because he had to get back what he spent raising you. And you know it would have been taboo for him to let you or any of your sisters go without asking for *lobola*."

"You and Papa seemed to forget that my sisters and I have minds of our own," my mother said. "We didn't need you to tell us whom to marry, and why, and how. If it hadn't been for your interference, I could have married that schoolteacher."

Granny did not reply; she knew well not to. When it came to the act of "selling" women as marriage partners, my mother was **vehemently** opposed to it. Not only was she opposed to this one aspect of tribal culture, but to others as well, particularly those involving relations between men and women and the upbringing of children. But my mother's sharply differing opinion was an exception rather than the rule among tribal women. Most times, many tribal women questioned her sanity in daring to question well-established mores.[32] But my mother did not seem to care; she would always scoff at her opponents and call them fools in letting their husbands enslave them completely.

Though I disliked school, largely because I knew nothing about what actually went on there, and the little I knew had painted a dreadful picture, the fact that a father would not want his son to go to school, especially a father who didn't go to school, seemed hard to understand.

"Why do you want me to go to school, Mama?" I asked, hoping that she might, somehow, clear up some of the confusion that was building in my mind.

"I want you to have a future, child," my mother said. "And, contrary to what your father says, school is the only means to a future. I don't want you growing up to be like your father."

---

32. The customs and moral standards followed by most people in a given society are called *mores* (môr´āz).

The Power of Memory How is Mathabane's mother trying to pass along her strong convictions to her son?

The Power of Memory What aspects of the life of Mathabane's father might explain his attitudes toward education and a working wife?

Vocabulary

vehemently (ve′ə mənt lē) *adv.* strongly; intensely; passionately

Alexandra Township, South Africa. Louise Gubb. A recent estimate suggests that more than half of Alexandra's population lives in shacks and informal dwellings like these.

View the Art What does this photograph tell you about life under apartheid?

The latter statement hit me like a bolt of lightning. It just about shattered every defense mechanism and every pretext[33] I had against going to school.

"Your father didn't go to school," she continued, dabbing her puffed eyes to reduce the swelling with a piece of cloth dipped in warm water, "that's why he's doing some of the bad things he's doing. Things like drinking, gambling, and neglecting his family. He didn't learn how to read and write; therefore, he can't find a decent job. Lack of any education has narrowly focused his life. He sees nothing beyond himself. He still thinks in the old, tribal way, and still believes that things should be as they were back in the old days when he was growing up as a tribal boy in Louis Trichardt. Though he's my husband, and your father, he doesn't see any of that."

"Why didn't he go to school, Mama?"

"He refused to go to school because his father led him to believe that an education was a tool through which white people were going to take things away from him, like they did black people in the old days. And that a white man's education was worthless insofar as black people were concerned because it prepared them for jobs they can't have. But I know it isn't totally so, child, because times have changed somewhat. Though our lot isn't any better today, an education will get you a decent job. If you can read or write

---

33. A *pretext* is a false reason or excuse one gives to hide a true reason or motive.

Analyze Cause-and-Effect Relationships Why do you think the statement had such a strong effect on Mathabane?

you'll be better off than those of us who can't. Take my situation: I can't find a job because I don't have papers, and I can't get papers because white people mainly want to register people who can read and write. But I want things to be different for you, child. For you and your brother and sisters. I want you to go to school, because I believe that an education is the key you need to open up a new world and a new life for yourself, a world and life different from that of either your father's or mine. It is the only key that can do that, and only those who seek it earnestly and perseveringly will get anywhere in the white man's world. Education will open doors where none seem to exist. It'll make people talk to you, listen to you, and help you; people who otherwise wouldn't bother. It will make you soar, like a bird lifting up into the endless blue sky, and leave poverty, hunger, and suffering behind. It'll teach you to learn to embrace what's good and shun what's bad and evil. Above all, it'll make you a somebody in this world. It'll make you grow up to be a good and proud person. That's why I want you to go to school, child, so that education can do all that, and more, for you."

A long, awkward silence followed, during which I reflected upon the significance of my mother's lengthy speech. I looked at my mother; she looked at me.

Finally, I asked, "How come you know so much about school, Mama? You didn't go to school, did you?"

"No, child," my mother replied. "Just like your father, I never went to school." For the second time that evening, a mere statement of fact had a thunderous impact on me. All the confusion I had about school seemed to leave my mind, like darkness giving way to light. And what had previously been a dark, yawning void in my mind was suddenly transformed into a beacon of light that began to grow larger and larger, until it had swallowed up, blotted out, all the blackness. That beacon of light seemed to reveal things and facts, which, though they must have always existed in me, I hadn't been aware of up until now.

"But unlike your father," my mother went on, "I've always wanted to go to school, but couldn't because my father, under the sway of tribal traditions, thought it unnecessary to educate females. That's why I so much want you to go, child, for if you do, I know that someday I too would come to go, old as I would be then. Promise me, therefore, that no matter what, you'll go back to school. And I, in turn, promise that I'll do everything in my power to keep you there."

With tears streaming down my cheeks and falling upon my mother's bosom, I promised her that I would go to school "forever." That night, at seven and a half years of my life, the battlelines in the family were drawn. My mother on the one side, illiterate but determined to have me drink, for better or for worse, from the well of knowledge. On the other side, my father, he too illiterate, yet determined to have me drink from the well of ignorance. Scarcely aware of the magnitude of the decision I was making or, rather, the decision which was being emotionally thrust upon me, I chose to fight on my mother's side, and thus my destiny was forever altered.

The Power of Memory *How do you think his mother's statements might change Mathabane's feelings now and later in his life?*

After You Read

Respond and Think Critically

Respond and Interpret

1. (a) What scene from this selection lingers in your mind? (b) What about the scene is memorable?

2. As this excerpt begins, what is Mathabane's attitude toward school and where did this attitude come from?

3. (a) How does Mathabane's father react to the day's events? (b) How does the conflict between Mathabane's parents reflect their different outlooks on his life?

Analyze and Evaluate

4. Mathabane uses South African words throughout the text. In your opinion, do these words enhance or detract from the reading experience? Explain.

5. How important is the setting—the time and place—of this autobiographical story? How does it influence the events that occur?

6. Consider Mathabane's use of cultural details such as the treatment of women. How do these details illuminate Mathabane's purpose in this selection?

Connect

7. **Big Idea** The Power of Memory Mathabane tells this story with the benefit of hindsight. How can he now see that his mother's past altered her son's life?

8. **Connect to the Author** Mathabane writes that by choosing "to fight on [his] mother's side," his "destiny was forever altered." What might his life have been like if he had chosen to fight on his father's side instead?

Daily Life & Culture

A Life Apart

Apartheid classified South Africans into one of three categories: the Bantu, or black citizens, the "Coloured," or biracial citizens, and white citizens. The Bantu group was separated and divided into powerless tribal "homelands" called Bantustans. These areas had few jobs and limited opportunities for education. Once they had been ousted from urban areas, Bantu access to cities was strictly regulated. Nonwhite South Africans were required to carry a "pass," or documents that allowed their presence in otherwise restricted areas. Social interaction between the races was also strictly limited.

Group Activity Discuss the following questions with your classmates.

1. What are some ways that people can try to change oppressive policies like apartheid?

2. What similarities and differences do you see between apartheid and the slavery and segregation laws that once existed in the United States?

Literary Element Theme

Some works of literature have a **stated theme,** which is expressed directly. More works have an **implied theme,** which is revealed gradually through events, dialogue, or description. A literary work may have more than one theme.

1. What is the central theme in this selection from *Kaffir Boy*? Is this theme stated or implied? Explain.
2. What other themes can you identify from this selection? Are they connected to the central theme? Explain.

Review: Voice

As you learned on pages 184–185, **voice** is the distinctive use of language that conveys the author's or narrator's personality to the reader. Voice is determined by elements of style such as word choice and tone.

Partner Activity With a classmate, offer three examples of writing from *Kaffir Boy* that demonstrate Mathabane's voice. For each example, provide an explanation of what makes its language so effective. Make a chart like the one below.

Example	Why Voice Is Distinctive
"The streets were beginning to fill with their everyday traffic: old men and women, wizened, bent, and ragged, were beginning their rambling..."	The author uses vivid, creative language and alliteration, such as "women, wizened" and "ragged... rambling"...

Literature Online

Selection Resources For Selection Quizzes, eFlashcards, and Reading-Writing Connection activities, go to glencoe.com and enter QuickPass code GL59794u2.

Reading Strategy Analyze Cause-and-Effect Relationships

ACT Skills Practice

1. The main reason the narrator agrees to go to school is:

    A. a chance encounter with a stranger who tells of her dead son.
    B. his mother's determination that he not end up like his father.
    C. the sight of the canes hanging on the principal's door.
    D. the thought of his mother's humiliating efforts to get the correct papers.

Vocabulary Practice

Practice with Context Clues Identify the context clues in the following sentences that help you determine the meaning of each boldfaced vocabulary word.

1. The **coterie** of go players met every week at the Yakamuras' house.
2. My parents **admonish** me often on the subject of not falling behind in my studies.
3. We will **peruse** the information for several hours before we make a decision.
4. Lily did not know whether to distrust the story or to give it **credence**.
5. Will **vehemently** urged his listeners to support plans for the new park.

Academic Vocabulary

Mathabane's mother believed passionately in education, **whereas** his father did not.

Whereas is an academic word. It is often found in formal and legal documents. More casual ways of saying *whereas* include *although*, "while on the contrary," and "in view of the fact that." Show the meaning of **whereas** by completing this sentence starter: The students at __ **whereas** the students at my school __.

For more on academic vocabulary, see pages 53 and 54.

 Respond Through Writing

Research Report

Investigate Apartheid Research the apartheid system in South Africa during the 1900s. Using primary and secondary sources, prepare a research report of 1,500 words or more on some aspect of the policy that denied rights to the Bantu and other African groups. Incorporate information and examples from Mathabane's memoir into your report.

Learning Objectives
In this assignment, you will focus on the following objectives:

Research: Investigating apartheid.

Grammar: Understanding how to use hyphens.

Understand the Task
- **Primary sources** are firsthand accounts of an event, such as diaries or eyewitness accounts written or recorded at the time an event took place.
- **Secondary sources** are sources written by people who did not experience or observe the event.

Prewrite Write four or five questions to guide your research. Use a variety of reliable sources to find the answers, and take notes. Develop a thesis that reveals your focus, such as the specific rights that were denied, the different ways that men and women felt the effects of apartheid, or the effects of this political and social system on children. Then outline the main ideas you will use to develop and support your thesis.

Draft Use your introduction to define *apartheid* and to present your thesis. Use your body paragraphs to present evidence from your notecards, choosing only those details that strengthen your thesis. As you weave in sources, use introductory phrases such as "As __ writes in __, …" Add a chart, a graph, or another visual display both to communicate information and to add interest to your report.

Grammar Tip
Hyphens
When you use two words as a single adjective before a noun, join the words with a hyphen.

half-awake, thumb-sucking boy of about four

a *lily-white* handkerchief

black-owned businesses

"As __ writes in __, …"

Revise Ask yourself:
- ☑ What information does my reader still need to understand my thesis?
- ☑ Where do I need to give more background information?
- ☑ Where should I add an introduction or an explanation to make the meaning of a quotation clearer or more relevant to my thesis?
- ☑ Which terms in my paper might be unfamiliar to my readers? How can I better explain them?

Revise for clarity by rewriting any potentially misleading information.

Edit and Proofread Proofread your paper, correcting any errors in spelling, grammar, and punctuation. Use the Grammar Tip in the side column to help you use hyphens correctly.

Before You Read

Living Well. Living Good.

Meet Maya Angelou
(born 1928)

Maya Angelou had a difficult early life, but she overcame her obstacles to become a successful performer and writer. She is considered one of the most influential African American women of her time.

Angelou was born Marguerite Johnson in St. Louis, Missouri. She spent most of her childhood in Stamps, Arkansas, with her paternal grandmother. As a young girl, she spent a lot of time reading books. She developed a love of literature, including the works of Langston Hughes and William Shakespeare.

> "In all my work, what I try to say is that as human beings we are more alike than we are unalike."
>
> —Maya Angelou

In 1940 Angelou and her brother were taken to San Francisco, California. Five years later, at the age of seventeen, Angelou graduated from high school and gave birth to a son. To support herself and her son, she held odd jobs, working as a waitress, cook, and dancer. During the 1950s, she performed professionally using the stage name of Maya Angelou.

Her Literary Career Begins After touring twenty-two countries performing in a production of *Porgy and Bess,* Angelou left the United States. For a few years she lived in Cairo, Egypt, where she worked as an associate editor for the *Arab Observer.* In 1962 she moved to Ghana. There she wrote for the *African Review* and worked at the University of Ghana's School of Music and Drama.

When Angelou returned to the United States, James Baldwin, whom she had met through the Harlem Writers Guild several years earlier, encouraged her to write an autobiography. At first she rejected the idea, but later she reconsidered and decided to write *I Know Why the Caged Bird Sings.* This autobiography details her life from her childhood in Stamps to the birth of her son.

Continued Success After the success of her first autobiography, Angelou published four more. In addition to her autobiographies, Angelou wrote several collections of poetry, including *Just Give Me a Cool Drink of Water 'fore I Diiie,* which was nominated for a Pulitzer Prize in 1972. Angelou also wrote and presented a poem called "On the Pulse of Morning" for the 1993 inauguration of President Bill Clinton.

Author Search For more about Maya Angelou, go to glencoe.com and enter QuickPass code GL59794u2.

Literature and Reading Preview

Connect to the Essay
If you had all the money you wanted, what would you still need to live a good life? Discuss this question with a partner.

Build Background
This selection includes a reference to meals consisting of pigs' feet, greens, and fried chicken. These and similar foods are sometimes called "soul food." This culinary tradition began when Africans became enslaved people in the American South. They combined African and European cooking methods into a new style of cooking. Today there are soul food restaurants throughout the United States.

Set Purposes for Reading

Big Idea The Power of Memory

As you read, ask yourself, Why has Angelou's memory of this anecdote stayed with her?

Literary Element Memoir

A **memoir** is a nonfiction narrative illustrating some event or memory from the author's life. As you read, ask yourself, Why did Angelou choose to tell this story in her essay?

Reading Strategy Draw Conclusions About Author's Beliefs

Authors often include clues to their own beliefs in their writing. By looking for these clues, you can **draw conclusions about the author's beliefs** and gain a deeper appreciation for the work itself. As you read, ask yourself, What does this essay say about Angelou's beliefs?

Tip: Look at Details When you are trying to draw conclusions, look at the details the author has included in the essay. They can provide you with the information you need to make your conclusions.

Details	Conclusion
Sofas and chairs were tautly upholstered.	Angelou respects Aunt Tee's neatness.

Learning Objectives

For pages 321–327

In studying this text, you will focus on the following objectives:

Literary Study: Analyzing memoir.

Reading: Drawing conclusions about author's beliefs.

Vocabulary

meticulous (mi tik′yə ləs) *adj.* characterized by great or excessive concern about details; p. 323 *Editors have to be meticulous when they are proofreading.*

commodious (kə mō′dē əs) *adj.* having or containing ample room; spacious; p. 324 *The house was commodious for a family of four.*

convivial (kən viv′ē əl) *adj.* fond of merriment and parties with good company; sociable; p. 325 *Everyone agreed she was a convivial person.*

scenario (si när′ē ō′) *n.* an outline or model of an expected or imagined series of events; p. 325 *The worst-case scenario is that it will rain.*

inhibit (in hib′it) *v.* to hold back one's natural impulses; to restrain; p. 325 *A lack of encouragement can inhibit a child's talents.*

Living Well. Living Good.

Maya Angelou

Interior at Ciboure, 1912. Henri Matisse. Canvas. Musee Toulouse-Lautrec, Albi, France © ARS, NY.

Aunt Tee was a Los Angeles member of our extended family.[1] She was seventy-nine when I met her, sinewy,[2] strong, and the color of old lemons. She wore her coarse, straight hair, which was slightly streaked with gray, in a long braided rope across the top of her head. With her high cheekbones, old gold skin, and almond eyes, she looked more like an Indian chief than an old black woman. (Aunt Tee described herself and any favored member of her race as Negroes. *Black* was saved for those who had incurred her disapproval.)

She had retired and lived alone in a dead, neat ground-floor apartment. Wax flowers and china figurines sat on elaborately embroidered and heavily starched doilies. Sofas and chairs were tautly upholstered. The only thing at ease in Aunt Tee's apartment was Aunt Tee.

I used to visit her often and perch on her uncomfortable sofa just to hear her stories. She was proud that after working thirty years as a maid, she spent the next thirty years as a live-in housekeeper, carrying the keys to rich houses and keeping **meticulous** accounts.

"Living in lets the white folks know Negroes are as neat and clean as they are, sometimes more so. And it gives the Negro maid a chance to see white folks ain't no

---

1. Parents and their children make up what is called the nuclear family. One's *extended family* includes other relatives who are related by blood or marriage.
2. Here, *sinewy* (sin′ ū ē) could mean "physically powerful" or "vigorously healthy."

Memoir *How does this passage suggest that the essay is an example of a memoir and not an autobiography?*

Vocabulary

meticulous (mi tik′ yə ləs) *adj.* characterized by great or excessive concern about details

smarter than Negroes. Just luckier. Sometimes."

Aunt Tee told me that once she was housekeeper for a couple in Bel Air,[3] California, lived with them in a fourteen-room ranch house. There was a day maid who cleaned, and a gardener who daily tended the lush gardens. Aunt Tee oversaw the workers. When she had begun the job, she had cooked and served a light breakfast, a good lunch, and a full three- or four-course dinner to her employers and their guests. Aunt Tee said she watched them grow older and leaner. After a few years they stopped entertaining and ate dinner hardly seeing each other at the table. Finally, they sat in a dry silence as they ate evening meals of soft scrambled eggs, melba toast, and weak tea. Aunt Tee said she saw them growing old but didn't see herself aging at all.

She became the social maven.[4] She started "keeping company" (her phrase) with a chauffeur down the street. Her best friend and her friend's husband worked in service[5] only a few blocks away.

On Saturdays Aunt Tee would cook a pot of pigs' feet, a pot of greens, fry chicken, make potato salad, and bake a banana pudding. Then, that evening, her friends—the chauffeur, the other housekeeper, and her husband—would come to Aunt Tee's **commodious** live-in quarters. There the four would eat and drink, play records and dance. As the evening wore on, they would settle down to a serious game of bid whist.[6]

Naturally, during this revelry jokes were told, fingers snapped, feet were patted, and there was a great deal of laughter.

Aunt Tee said that what occurred during every Saturday party startled her and her friends the first time it happened. They had been playing cards, and Aunt Tee, who had just won the bid, held a handful of trumps. She felt a cool breeze on her back and sat upright and turned around. Her employers had cracked her door open and beckoned to her. Aunt Tee, a little peeved, laid down her cards and went to the door. The couple backed away and asked her to come into the hall, and there they both spoke and won Aunt Tee's sympathy forever.

"Theresa, we don't mean to disturb you . . ." the man whispered, "but you all seem to be having such a good time . . ."

The woman added, "We hear you and your friends laughing every Saturday night, and we'd just like to watch you. We don't want to bother you. We'll be quiet and just watch."

The man said, "If you'll just leave your door ajar, your friends don't need to know. We'll never make a sound." Aunt Tee said she saw no harm in agreeing, and she talked it over with her company. They said it was OK with them, but it was sad that the employers ==owned the gracious house, the swimming pool, three cars, and numberless palm trees, but had no joy==. Aunt Tee told me that laughter and relaxation had left the house; she agreed it was sad.

---

3. *Bel Air* is one of the wealthiest, most fashionable communities in Los Angeles.
4. A *maven* is one who has special knowledge or experience and is an expert in a given field.
5. Aunt Tee's two friends *in service* are servants in another household.

Vocabulary

commodious (kə mō′ dē əs) *adj.* having or containing ample room; spacious

---

6. *Bid whist* is a card game, somewhat like bridge, for two players or two teams of two players.

The Power of Memory *Why would Aunt Tee feel that it was especially meaningful to share this memory with Angelou?*

When I Get that Feeling, 2000. Colin Bootman. Oil on board. Private collection.

be founts of fun, and if you are lucky, they can become even **convivial** comrades.

Living life as art requires a readiness to forgive. I do not mean that you should suffer fools gladly, but rather remember your own shortcomings, and when you encounter another with flaws, don't be eager to righteously seal yourself away from the offender forever. Take a few breaths and imagine yourself having just committed the action which has set you at odds.

Because of the routines we follow, we often forget that life is an ongoing adventure. We leave our homes for work, acting and even believing that we will reach our destinations with no unusual event startling us out of our set expectations. The truth is we know nothing, not where our cars will fail or when our buses will stall, whether our places of employment will be there when we arrive, or whether, in fact, we ourselves will arrive whole and alive at the end of our journeys. Life is pure adventure, and the sooner we realize that, the quicker we will be able to treat life as art: to bring all our energies to each encounter, to remain flexible enough to notice and admit when what we expected to happen did not happen. We need to remember that we are created creative and can invent new **scenarios** as frequently as they are needed.

Life seems to love the liver of it. Money and power can liberate only if they are used to do so. They can imprison and **inhibit** more finally than barred windows and iron chains.

That story has stayed with me for nearly thirty years, and when a tale remains fresh in my mind, it almost always contains a lesson which will benefit me.

My dears, I draw the picture of the wealthy couple standing in a darkened hallway, peering into a lighted room where black servants were lifting their voices in merriment and comradery, and I realize that living well is an art which can be developed. Of course, you will need the basic talents to build upon: They are a love of life and ability to take great pleasure from small offerings, an assurance that the world owes you nothing and that every gift is exactly that, a gift. That people who may differ from you in political stance, sexual persuasion, and racial inheritance can

The Power of Memory What does Angelou seem to imply that one should do with personal memories?

Draw Conclusions About Author's Beliefs What does this statement reveal about Angelou's beliefs about life?

Vocabulary

convivial (kən viv′ē əl) *adj.* fond of merriment and parties with good company; sociable

scenario (si nār′ē ō′) *n.* an outline or model of an expected or imagined series of events

inhibit (in hib′it) *v.* to hold back one's natural impulses; to restrain

After You Read

Respond and Think Critically

Respond and Interpret

1. (a) Why do Aunt Tee's employers want to watch her parties? (b) What does Aunt Tee's cooperation with her employers reveal about her attitude toward them?

2. (a) How would you describe Aunt Tee's personality? (b) How do these traits reflect her life?

3. (a) Describe the parties of Aunt Tee and the routines of the employers. (b) How happy are Aunt Tee and her employers?

4. (a) Why does Angelou say that "life is pure adventure"? (b) Do you agree with this definition of life? Explain.

Analyze and Evaluate

5. Why do you think Angelou chose to include the story of her Aunt Tee in this essay, instead of only explaining her idea of "living well"?

6. At the end of the essay, Angelou comments about the effects of money and power. How does Angelou value them?

7. Assess Angelou's suggestions about "living well." Is it possible to live the way she suggests? Explain.

Connect

8. **Big Idea** The Power of Memory Memory can influence our lives in many ways. (a) Did memories influence Aunt Tee? Explain. (b) How might the memory of Aunt Tee have influenced Angelou's life? Explain.

9. **Connect to the Author** Angelou says that people are "more alike than we are unalike." How does she illustrate this idea in her memoir?

Literary Element Memoir

A **memoir** is a personal account of events from the author's past. It is usually written from the first-person point of view, using the pronoun *I*. While an autobiography usually tells the story of a person's entire life, a memoir typically focuses on a single incident or a particular period in a person's life.

1. Why is "Living Well. Living Good." classified as a memoir?

2. What role does Angelou play in the essay?

3. Could Angelou have converted this essay into an autobiography? Explain.

Review: Theme

As you learned on page 124, **theme** is the central idea of a piece of literature. The theme can be stated directly, meaning that the author points out the main idea of the work for the reader. The theme can also be implied, meaning that the reader must use context clues to determine the central idea.

Partner Activity Discuss the theme of "Living Well. Living Good." with a classmate. First, write down the theme. Next, decide if the theme is stated directly or implied in the content. Support your decision by listing specific examples from the selection. Use a web like the one below to organize your ideas.

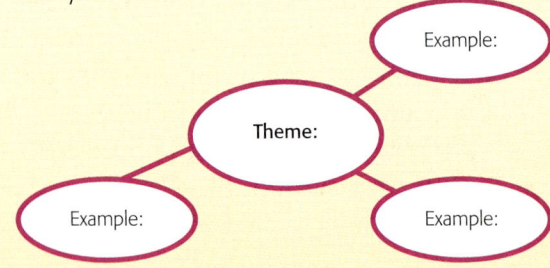

Reading Strategy Draw Conclusions About Author's Beliefs

SAT Skills Practice

1. The description of the evening meal that her employers eat (page 324) serves to
   - (A) emphasize their lack of interest in wealth
   - (B) point out their dull, colorless lives
   - (C) suggest that they are in failing health
   - (D) underscore the idea that the poor enjoy life more than the rich
   - (E) reveal that Aunt Tee had lost interest in her job

Vocabulary Practice

Practice with Analogies Choose the word pair that best completes each analogy.

1. meticulous : perfectionist ::
   a. tiny : housekeeper   b. irritable : grouch

2. commodious : space ::
   a. large : gigantic   b. luxurious : comfort

3. convivial : socialite ::
   a. victorious : winner   b. careless : child

4. outline : scenario ::
   a. describe : description   b. deceive : truth

5. inhibit : restraint ::
   a. distinct : conception
   b. imagine : visualization

Academic Vocabulary

Details in this memoir combine to **promote** *the idea that life should be lived well every day.*

Promote is a multiple-meaning word. A teacher might **promote** a student to the next grade, while an ad campaign might **promote** a product. Using context clues, try to figure out the meaning of *promote* in the sentence above about the memoir.

For more on academic vocabulary, see pages 52 and 53.

Write with Style

 Apply Tone

Assignment Write a character sketch focused on someone who reflects your own beliefs about how to live life. Use a tone that is consistent with your feelings about the person and with your beliefs.

Get Ideas Tone is an author's attitude toward his or her subject matter. A tone can be inspirational or critical, happy or sad, humorous or serious. Look back at the chart you made about Angelou's beliefs (p. 322). List details you could use to show your own beliefs and attitude toward your subject.

	Steven Gomez
Tone: Respect/ Admiration	• president of conservation committee; library volunteer; scout leader • says more with the light in his eyes than some people say with a hundred words

Give It Structure Do not state your beliefs or attitude directly. Instead, let the details of your character sketch convey your attitude. Then decide on a logical order for your details.

Look at Language Word choice contributes to your style. As you write, pay close attention to your choice of words and their connotation. "Light in one's eye" is not the same as a *twinkle*; *volunteer* does not carry the same connotations as *helper* or *servant*.

Proofread Proofread your paper, correcting any errors in grammar, spelling, and punctuation. As a guide, refer to the Traits of Strong Writing on pages R28–R29.

 Literature Online

Selection Resources For Selection Quizzes, eFlashcards, and Reading-Writing Connection activities, go to glencoe.com and enter QuickPass code GL59794u2.

Before You Read

First Impressions from *De Kooning: An American Master*

Meet **Mark Stevens and Annalyn Swan**

Mark Stevens and Annalyn Swan live in New York.

Mark Stevens, an art critic for *New York* magazine, has written about a wide variety of artists. His subjects range from masters like Vincent van Gogh and Willem de Kooning to folk and outsider artists. Stevens's wife and coauthor, Annalyn Swan, is an award-winning music critic who has written for magazines including *Time*, *The New Republic*, *The Atlantic Monthly*, and *New York*. She has also been a senior arts editor at *Newsweek*.

A Long Time Coming Swan and Stevens dedicated ten years of their lives to researching and writing their biography of Willem de Kooning. While one conducted research and interviews exploring the first half of de Kooning's life, the other did research about the second half. Then the couple worked together to shape their material into a coherent whole.

> "We were lucky. We had a subject that never bored us. . . . we really liked de Kooning."
> —Annalyn Swan

Writing About a Life The art of biography writing has developed as times and literary traditions have changed. Many authors today see biography as the creation of art from fact; to be successful, a biographer can fail neither art nor truth.

Over the many years of their research and writing, Stevens and Swan found that their respect and admiration for de Kooning deepened. They were keen to do justice to this original and complex man. Swan said, "That de Kooning was an immigrant colored everything in his life. He was forever caught between Europe and the New World, suffused with private longings, regret, loneliness and joy. . . . For a biographer, exploring such a complicated subject is fascinating."

Stevens and Swan's years of labor were validated when they were awarded a Pulitzer Prize in 2005. One reviewer had this to say about their work: "When we get the chance to look at the whole life and work of Willem de Kooning, the upheaval in American art in the middle of the 20th century comes into clearer focus. That alone makes *De Kooning: An American Master* . . . an important book."

LOG ON  **Literature** Online

Author Search For more about Mark Stevens and Annalyn Swan, go to glencoe.com and enter QuickPass code GL59794u2.

Literature and Reading Preview

Connect to the Biography
How would you feel and how would you handle the challenges of everyday life if no one around you spoke your language? Write a journal entry that explores this question.

Build Background
Willem de Kooning was born in the Netherlands in 1904. He eventually became a leader in an artistic movement called Abstract Expressionism. Abstract artists make no attempt to re-create the world as it really exists.

Set Purposes for Reading

Big Idea The Power of Memory
As you read, ask yourself, How do Stevens and Swan emphasize de Kooning's recollections of his arrival in the United States?

Literary Element Author's Purpose
The **author's purpose** is the author's reason for writing a literary work. Understanding the author's purpose enables you to grasp why the author presents certain events and characters as he or she does. As you read, ask yourself, What do Stevens and Swan hope to accomplish by sharing de Kooning's first impressions of America with the reader?

Reading Strategy Make Generalizations About Events
When you base conclusions about a text on specific examples, ideas, or anecdotes, you are **making generalizations**, observations that may relate universal themes and ideas to a text. As you read, ask yourself, Why are these events occurring?

Tip: Take Notes As you read, record specific examples in the text and then generalize.

Passage	Generalization
De Kooning first lived with other Dutch immigrants in the United States.	This made him feel comfortable, since his surroundings were new.

Learning Objectives

For pages 328–339

In studying this text, you will focus on the following objectives:

Literary Study: Analyzing author's purpose.

Reading: Making generalizations about events.

Vocabulary

obligatory (ə blig′ə tôr′ē) *adj.* required or necessary; p. 331 *The student went to class regularly because the teacher said attendance was obligatory.*

artisan (är′tə zən) *n.* a skilled craftsman; p. 332 *Fine details reveal the cabinetmaker as an artisan.*

belie (bi lī′) *v.* to misrepresent; to give a false impression of; p. 334 *The warm loving light in the small child's eyes belied her refusal to hug her mother.*

torrential (tô ren′chəl) *adj.* flowing rapidly and abundantly; p. 334 *Walking in the torrential rain left us completely soaked.*

Tip: Connotation and Denotation Remember that words often carry positive or negative suggestions. Reacting to these connotations is part of active reading.

The Statue of Liberty. Francis Hopkinson Smith (1851–1915).

First Impressions

from *De Kooning: An American Master*

Mark Stevens and Annalyn Swan

I didn't think there were any artists in America.

"Look Bill, America!" With that shout from the sailors, de Kooning looked out over the water—and looked again. He saw "a sort of Holland, lowlands, just like back home," as he remembered it. No skyscrapers with glittering lights. No beckoning Statue of Liberty. Not only was he disappointed at his first glimpse of America, he was also apprehensive as the ship steamed into the Virginia port of Newport News on July 30. The voyage itself had been stressful. He found the English ship filthy and, for much of the trip, was forced to hide in the hot, dark engine room where the sailors—while never officially acknowledging his presence—gave him lots of work. . . .

What sort of country, de Kooning wondered, was this America? He felt particularly uneasy because he knew no English, which forced him to rely completely upon friends. Cohan, as cheerful and optimistic as ever, proved a resourceful companion who helped

---

The Power of Memory Why was de Kooning disappointed when he first saw America?

steer de Kooning to New York without passing through the usual entry point for immigrants on Ellis Island—the **obligatory** first step for legal entrance into the United States by way of Manhattan. The passage of the Immigration Act of 1924 had sharply curtailed the flow of immigrants into America, and, while the new quotas were less restrictive for northern Europeans than for others, illegal immigrants like Cohan and de Kooning faced certain deportation from Ellis Island. Calling upon his network of Dutch friends, Cohan arranged to board a coast vessel carrying goods from Newport News to Boston.

Throughout the next week, as they steamed up the eastern seaboard, de Kooning and Cohan stoked the engines and worked as firemen. Disembarking in Boston, they proceeded by train to Rhode Island, where, with a group of Dutch sailors, they boarded another coast vessel bound for the old South Street port at the tip of Manhattan. Although South Street had been the center of the city's harbor life from the colonial era through the nineteenth century, the shipping business had mostly moved by the 1920s to docks along the Hudson River on the West Side of Manhattan. South Street was a quiet back door into the city for those who wanted to avoid scrutiny.

"We had enough money to buy a ticket on a passenger boat," de Kooning remembered of the trip from Rhode Island, "with music and dancing, and early one morning I just walked off the ship and I couldn't believe it—I was free on the streets of New York." As at Newport News, he was not overwhelmed by his first impressions. De Kooning, who always relished the debunking[1] observation, said about his first view of New York: "This I remember: no skyscrapers. They had disappeared in the fog." Their few possessions in hand, the group of Dutchmen headed purposefully uptown to Barclay Street, where they boarded one of the ferries connecting Manhattan to Hoboken, New Jersey, the town across the river where they planned to stay. This is probably when de Kooning saw the counterman recklessly pouring coffee into the row of cups and was suddenly seized by the difference between Holland and America—the first slow and deliberate, the other driven, haphazard, profligate.[2]

Like most immigrants, de Kooning spent his early months in America swaddled among his own countrymen. Hoboken was the logical place for a Dutch stowaway to live during the first unsettling days, as Cohan, the impresario of their emigration, recognized. Once a sleepy river town and leafy retreat for New Yorkers eager to escape the summer heat, Hoboken had become by the 1920s an important shipping town with a population of about seventy thousand. Four ferries connected it with its huge neighbor. The ships of nine big oceangoing lines docked at its piers, including the Netherlands-American Steam Navigation Company, which attracted a number of Dutch settlers. By the time de Kooning arrived, the traditionally German flavor of Hoboken had almost disappeared, owing in part to a huge wave of Italian immigrants around the turn of the century. There remained a northern European overlay to

---

Make Generalizations About Events *Why do de Kooning and his friend avoid the more traditional points of entry into the United States?*

Vocabulary

obligatory (ə blig′ ə tôr′ ē) *adj.* required or necessary

---

1. *Debunking* means "exposing a myth."
2. *Profligate* means "reckless or extravagant."

Author's Purpose *What does this observation reveal about the place de Kooning has come from? What does it help you understand about de Kooning?*

the city, however, along with a liberal sprinkling of Dutch inhabitants. The first Dutch Reformed Church had been founded in 1850 and maintained a high profile in the local community, and the Holland Seaman's Home provided a welcoming refuge for Dutch, German, and Scandinavian sailors and immigrants. "My sailor friends knew the Dutch settlement there, and they brought me to the Dutch Seaman's Home, a sort of boarding house," de Kooning said. "Thanks to them the landlady gave me three weeks' credit. It was a nice, very clean little house. I liked it quite well."

Located at 332 River Street, the Holland Seaman's Home was across the road from the docks lining the river and near the Lutheran Seaman's Mission. Just down River Street were the Holland bakery, the Holland Hotel, and a restaurant called Holland. Despite his desire to leave the Old World, de Kooning—who instantly dropped his Dutch name, Willem, in favor of the all-American "Bill"— found the traces of home comforting. Plenty of work was available. More than thirty painters and decorators worked in Hoboken in 1926, a number of them either German or Dutch immigrants. Their establishments bore such names as Braue and Schermerhorn, Otto Burckhardt and Son, and Fred Schlegel. "Three days later I was a housepainter," de Kooning said, "and got nine dollars a day, a nice salary for that time."

For someone who with a few notable exceptions paid little attention to how he dressed, de Kooning showed a particular preoccupation with clothes during his early days in America: they represented both a badge of success and a symbol of a new identity. After only one week of work, de Kooning proudly remembered, "I could buy a new suit, black for Sundays, low-belt trousers, nice workmen's clothes, for I didn't want to be different. . . . I do like a fine suit and a nice tie." If in one week he could afford a suit, "In three weeks I could pay off my rent and had new underwear and socks." Like many immigrants, de Kooning also wanted to demonstrate his success to his family and maintain the legend of a land of riches. A photograph taken in 1926, and no doubt sent home to Holland, shows de Kooning and a Dutch friend on the ferry between New York and Hoboken. De Kooning is lolling back against the railing, clearly at ease with the camera, the world, and his relative prosperity. In contrast to his Dutch companion, who is dressed in a poorly fitting jacket and workingman's cap, de Kooning is handsomely turned out. His three-piece suit is elegant, his shirt collar starchily correct. On his head is a fedora, raked jauntily over his forehead and all but hiding his eyes.

De Kooning could get by without much English, though it was not always easy. In the beginning, he knew how to order only one thing in restaurants—a hamburger. (When he finally tried to order something else at the local restaurant, the waiter said, "Hamburger, right?" de Kooning meekly nodded.) On the job, he found he had much to learn about the way his new country operated, which often differed from the careful, **artisanal** manners of Holland. "I was impressed by the workers' efficiency and their tools," he said. "We worked without stopping for eight hours and used much larger and better brushes than those we had in Holland. I learned a great deal on how to

---

Author's Purpose Why do the authors describe Hoboken, New Jersey, at length and in such detail?

The Power of Memory In what ways did clothing become meaningful to de Kooning as he began his life in America?

Vocabulary

artisan (är′tə zən) *n.* a skilled craftsman

mix pigment with water and oil." He was struck by the American willingness simply to slap new paint over old; in Holland, housepainters would strip a window down to the wood before repainting. He also tried his hand at sign painting, and came away with a high regard for the veterans with whom he worked. "Sign painting was difficult for me because they used other letters here," he said. "How those old guys smoking their pipes did it, I don't know."

De Kooning soon found helpful and congenial Dutch friends. Leo Cohan, who worked as a cook in a restaurant in Hoboken, sometimes arranged for de Kooning to get free meals; between lodgings, de Kooning occasionally stayed in Cohan's rented room. A man named Wimpy Deruyter—a ship's mechanic who befriended de Kooning on the voyage to America—visited whenever he was back in town. De Kooning's keenest friendship, however, was with a Dutch singer named Bart van der Schelling. Well known for never keeping a job or having any money, Bart was big, charming, and exceedingly attractive. (He would later fight in the Spanish Civil War and eventually became a naïve,[3] or "primitive," painter.) Like Leo Cohan, he remained close to de Kooning for years: in the early thirties Bill and Bart spent so much time together they seemed like brothers.

On Sundays, de Kooning would go sightseeing with friends. Little remained of the rustic charm that had once brought New Yorkers across the river to Hoboken. Its main allure in the Prohibition[4] era was its great number of speakeasies;[5] a local poll taken in 1930 named Hoboken the "wettest"[6] city in New Jersey. But there was some greenery in the area. Only steps

Willem de Kooning, 1953. Tony Vaccaro.

---

3. *Naïve painters* usually have no formal artistic training and are known for painting directly on a canvas without preliminary drawings.

Make Generalizations About Events *What insights into Holland and America did de Kooning gain from working as a house painter in Hoboken?*

4. The *Prohibition era* officially began in 1919 with the 18th Amendment to the Constitution, which prohibited the sale or consumption of alcoholic beverages anywhere in the U.S. The 18th Amendment was repealed in 1933 with the 21st Amendment.
5. *Speakeasies* were places that existed during the Prohibition era where people could go to purchase illegal alcohol.
6. *Wet* means that alcohol was available for purchase, so the reference to Hoboken being the *"wettest"* city in New Jersey means that one could find a lot of places to obtain alcohol.

from the Holland Seaman's Home was Hudson Square, which looked over the river. Just beyond lay the Stevens Institute of Technology, which was housed in a mansion on a promontory known as Castle Point. De Kooning went there often to look across the water at the city. With friends like Bart, Wimpy, and Leo—who sounded like a troupe of comics—de Kooning also began to explore New York. He felt comfortable with its kaleidoscopic jumble of ethnic groups, which recalled the mixing of Dutch and foreigners around the Rotterdam[7] docks. He saw the poverty, too, which **belied** the myth of easy riches: the slums on the Lower East Side;[8] the tenements with windowless inner rooms and public toilets on every other floor; the two-bit flophouses on the Bowery.[9] (One day, he would come to love the photographs of Weegee[10]—the great chronicler of the city's meaner streets.) But that was not the New York that caught his eye. The Roaring Twenties were one of the city's great decades. It thrived on too much money, not enough sleep, and worried cries from the rest of the country about "decadence."[11] The WPA[12] guide to the city, compiled as part of the 1930s Federal Writers' Project, perfectly captured the proudly self-conscious, rhetorical flair of the period:

> All through the 1920s New York had been not only the symbol of America but the symbol of the modern—the fortunate giant in his youth, the world city whose past weighed least heavily upon its future. . . . It was a city infallible in finance, **torrential** in pace, unlimited in resource, hard as infrangible diamonds, forever leaping upon the moment beyond. "You can get away with anything," said Ellen Thatcher in John Dos Passos' *Manhattan Transfer*, "if you do it quick enough." Speed—with its dividend, sensation—became the master formula in every human activity and technique: Wall Street, dancing, crime, the theater, construction, even death.

What de Kooning thrilled to was the pop energy of the city, which was exotic to a Dutchman who grew up in the subdued culture of northern Europe. Here was freedom from the constraints of class, taste, and disapproving looks; here was a new kind of openness, an invitation to wonder. One of the first places he visited was Coney Island, a masterpiece of rhinestone splendor that provided entertainment for New York's lower and middle classes. Cecil Beaton described it this way during the 1930s:

---

7. *Rotterdam* is a city in the southwestern portion of the Netherlands.
8. The *Lower East Side* of New York City's Manhattan borough attracted many immigrants because of the availability of cheap housing.
9. *Flophouses* were cheap hotels or rooming houses that could be found in a section of New York City called *the Bowery*.
10. *Weegee* is the professional name of photographer Arthur Fellig, who became famous for his crime-scene photos.
11. *Decadence* is the process of falling into decay or decline.
12. The *WPA* is the Works Progress Administration Federal Arts Project. The program started in the 1930s and was known for hiring artists who ranged in experience and style.

Vocabulary

belie (bi līʹ) *v.* to misrepresent; to give a false impression of

---

Author's Purpose What insights into de Kooning's artistic sensibilities do the authors suggest by including these observations?

Vocabulary

torrential (tô renʹchəl) *adj.* flowing rapidly and abundantly

Coney Island, 1931. John Wenger. Watercolor and tempera over pencil on paperboard, 55.1 x 71.1 cm. Brooklyn Museum of Art, New York.

View the Art How does this painting help viewers understand Coney Island's appeal? Coney Island has featured amusement parks, thrill rides, and a colorful boardwalk of attractions since the 1800s.

Every Saturday and Sunday a million people go to bathe at Coney Island, reached by subway in half an hour. They stay until the electric bulbs silhouette the minarets, domes and turrets, illumine the skeletons of roller-coasters and the magnificent pleasure-palace of George C. Tilyou (the Barnum of Coney Island), which with its many columns and electrical splendour, resembles something from the Pan-American exposition of 1900. The passengers on the Cyclone rend the air with their concerted screams.

"I liked the sentimental side of the people," de Kooning said, "the girls, the houses on the avenues, and the skyscrapers." Not surprisingly, he relished Times Square. Perhaps it reminded him of the square at the foot of the Coolsingel[13] in Rotterdam, where he had whiled away time with the Randolfis. Except it was bigger, more extravagant, crazier. Like the harbor of Rotterdam, Times Square was a crossroads populated by . . . just about everyone. Times Square in 1926 was lined with movie houses, shooting galleries, and amusement arcades. At night, it shimmered with thousands of brightly colored

---

13. *Coolsingel* is a main street in the old part of Rotterdam.

electric lights. De Kooning had himself photographed amid the bustle of Times Square. He looked like a man at home. Once de Kooning found his footing in America, Hoboken seemed too much like North Rotterdam. Crowded tenements, cold-water walk-ups, and communal backyard toilets or privies were the realities of working-class life in Hoboken; he had not left Rotterdam to move to a similarly depressed city across the ocean. More important, he missed living in a bohemian milieu. It was one thing to be a workingman living among artists or people like the Randolfis who flourished on the margins of society. It was quite another to be a workingman among workers. On Sundays, a friend with an old car sometimes drove him to Storm King, a high promontory of land up the Hudson with sweeping views down the river. "We would stand by the parapet and look at the view of the city," de Kooning said. "It used to scare me to death. I would say to myself, 'There's no art here. You came to the wrong place.'" Although he visited the galleries on Fifty-seventh Street, they mostly showed plummy European paintings intended for conservative apartments on the Upper East Side. He saw nothing like Mondrian.[14]

Leo Cohan urged de Kooning to move across the river. "I said to him, 'Bill, you mustn't hang around in Hoboken. You must go to Manhattan. There you'll find other artists.'" In Hoboken, de Kooning began to hear about a community in the city called Greenwich Village, where poets and painters were said to live. He determined its location—south of Fourteenth Street and north of Canal Street—and one day found himself amid the oddly angled streets and old brownstones. But he could not find "the Village" he had heard about. "There were just lots of Italians standing around on corners. Inside, you know, the Village was nice, but from the outside, you couldn't tell it was there—it was so quiet." Then, while still living in Hoboken, de Kooning met a Sicilian artist named Mirabaggo, who lived in the Village. When a barber

Door to the River, 1960. Willem de Kooning. The Willem de Kooning Foundation.

View the Art De Kooning is associated with a form known as *action painting,* characterized by rapid, forceful brushstrokes, abstraction, and emotional expression. In your opinion, what elements of this painting most vividly demonstrate de Kooning's originality?

---

14. Piet *Mondrian* was a Dutch abstract painter.

Author's Purpose Why do you think de Kooning is ready for a change?

whom Mirabaggo knew retired, he bought the empty barbershop and opened a coffeehouse decorated with plaster copies of Greek and Roman sculpture. De Kooning began to spend time there on weekends. Soon he was also going to Café Rienzi, another coffeehouse that opened shortly after Mirabaggo's. He began to discover old Village hangouts, such as the Pepper Pot, the MacDougal Tavern, and the Jumble Shop. All of them had been in varying degrees haunts of writers and artists since the 1890s. Of greatest importance to de Kooning, however, was the living presence of painters. "Here in Greenwich Village there was a strong tradition of painting and poetry," he said. "I had not known this, and it brought back memories of my interests when I was 14, 15 or 16 years old."

Now that he had located an American art world, de Kooning naturally wanted to join it. He made some drawings and illustrations to replace the portfolio that he had left behind in Belgium, and began to read the Help Wanted ads for commercial artists in the Manhattan newspapers, just as he had in Brussels. When one ran in the *New York World* he dropped off his portfolio at the stated address. To his dismay, the place was mobbed with applicants for the job. He had all but given up hope when a man appeared holding aloft a portfolio and shouting, "Where's de Kooning?" The American's pronunciation was jarring. In Dutch, de Kooning was pronounced with a hard "o"—as in Koning. In American, he was de K*oo*ning.

The job was his. De Kooning was so pleased—his first triumph in America!—that he signed up immediately, no questions asked. "I didn't even ask them the salary because I thought if I made twelve dollars a day as a house painter [de Kooning variously described his Hoboken wages as nine or twelve dollars a day] I would make at least twenty dollars a day being an artist." The elation abruptly ended after a week when he was handed twenty-five dollars. "I was so astonished I asked him if that was a day's pay," said de Kooning. "He said, 'No, that's for the whole week.'" De Kooning had learned the hard way that less skilled labor could pay more than an arts-related job and that life in America was not going to be easy. "It turned out to be quite different from what I thought," de Kooning said of America. "Nowhere near as luxurious as I imagined it."

Disgruntled, de Kooning spent the weekend wondering whether or not to return to housepainting in Hoboken. Cohan and other Dutch friends urged him to keep the new job. As Cohan sensed, art and the company of artists would finally prove far more important to his friend than a fatter paycheck. Although de Kooning by no means considered himself a serious painter—that would only come years later—he made an essential decision that weekend: he must at least live in the neighborhood of art. His hopes of making a fortune waned, but his interest in an American art world strengthened. A little more than a year after his arrival in Hoboken, de Kooning packed his few possessions, said good-bye to his sailor friends, and took the ferry into Manhattan.

Make Generalizations About Events *What does this story illustrate about the experiences of many immigrants to America?*

The Power of Memory *Why do you think this recollection is significant for de Kooning?*

The Power of Memory *What do you think changed for de Kooning?*

After You Read

Respond and Think Critically

Respond and Interpret

1. What did you consider most interesting or surprising about de Kooning's experiences? Explain.

2. (a) What was missing from de Kooning's first glimpse of the United States? (b) How did his first impressions affect him?

3. (a) What reasons do Stevens and Swan cite for de Kooning's departure from Hoboken? (b) Why might the move have helped his career as an artist? Explain.

Analyze and Evaluate

4. De Kooning eventually becomes an influential and innovative abstract painter. Do you believe that the biographers' description of de Kooning's arrival in the United States helps you understand his eventual success? Explain.

5. To be successful, a biographer must provide facts about a person's life and must also capture the essence of that person. Do you believe that Stevens and Swan accomplish this goal? Explain why or why not.

6. At first, de Kooning viewed success in the United States in terms of income. Later, his views of success shifted. Analyze de Kooning's transition and determine what brought about the change in his attitude.

Connect

7. **Big Idea** The Power of Memory From the comparisons between Holland and the United States, do you believe that de Kooning would have achieved the same artistic success had he remained in Holland? Explain.

8. **Connect to Today** De Kooning is considered one of the most important and influential contributions to modern American art. Does knowledge of de Kooning as a person help you to gain appreciation for him as an artist? Why or why not?

Literary Element Author's Purpose

Authors often write to achieve one or more of the following **purposes:** to persuade, to inform, to explain, to entertain, or to describe. One might attribute several of these purposes to Stevens and Swan's biography of Willem de Kooning.

1. Which purpose do you think most applies to this selection? Explain.

2. Cite several passages that support your claim.

Review: Biography

As you learned on pages 284–285, a **biography** is an account of someone's life written by someone else. In addition to describing a person's life, a biography provides insight into the time and place in which the person lived.

Partner Activity Pair up with a classmate and examine the selection you just read. Determine how the authors' use of quotations helps provide a historical and cultural context. Working with your partner, create a two-column chart similar to the one below.

Examples of Quotations from Other Sources	Explanation of Historical or Cultural Context
p. 335 "Every Saturday and Sunday a million people go to bathe at Coney Island,..."	It was an inexpensive and appealing form of entertainment, so it attracted a lot of people from the lower and middle classes.

| Reading Strategy | Make Generalizations About Events |

Making generalizations helps readers understand the main points and implications of a work.

For example, considering de Kooning's experiences enables us to generalize about other immigrants' lives at the time.

1. (a) What generalizations can you make about de Kooning's reasons for coming to the United States? (b) What does the selection suggest about how the United States could both confound and reward the expectations of immigrants?
2. Find three examples from the text that support your ideas. Explain.

Vocabulary

Practice with Denotation and Connotation

Denotation is the literal, or dictionary, meaning of a word. **Connotation** is the implied, or cultural, meaning of a word. For example, the words *embarrassing* and *humiliating* have a similar denotation, but *humiliating* suggests a more profound embarrassment and has a more negative connotation.

Each of these vocabulary words is listed with a word or term that has a similar denotation. Decide whether the second word or term is more negative, more positive, or about the same, and explain why.

1. obligatory — required
2. artisan — skilled worker
3. belie — misrepresent
4. torrential — heavy

Connect to *Art*

 Research Report

Assignment Research de Kooning and his fellow New York "rebel artists" who helped create Abstract Expressionism. Create a multimedia presentation about the artists and their art.

Investigate Generate four or five research questions about who the artists were, how they became friends, what made their art groundbreaking, and so on. Answer your questions by using reliable primary and secondary sources. As you take notes, compile a list of art terms and their definitions. Develop a table like this one to organize your research.

Source	Assessment
Sylvester, David. *Modern Art.* NY: Franklin Watts, 1965. Primary source.	author—respected British art critic and curator; book—documented primary source

Create Use appropriate software to create a multimedia slideshow or other presentation of your findings. Include reproductions or videos of the work of the Abstract Expressionists, and integrate music of the time period. Include a final slide that documents your sources. See pages R35–R37 for help with bibliographic style.

Report As you compile information in your report, use your visuals to help explain terms that are specific to Abstract Expressionism. Make links between the artists and the movement and what the artwork shows. Focus on what defines Abstract Expressionism, explaining varying perspectives on the era and art while maintaining a focus on the central concerns and accomplishments of the artists.

Selection Resources For Selection Quizzes, eFlashcards, and Reading-Writing Connection, go to glencoe.com and enter QuickPass code GL59794u2.

Learning Objectives

In this workshop, you will focus on the following objective:

Vocabulary: Understanding jargon.

Vocabulary Workshop

Jargon

Literature Connection You may not be familiar with the word *artisanal* in the quotation below.

> "On the job, he found he had much to learn about the way his new country operated, which often differed from the careful, artisanal manners of Holland."
>
> —Mark Stevens and Annalyn Swan, from "First Impressions" from *De Kooning, An American Master*

You may, however, have read or heard the word *artisan*, meaning "a skilled worker," and know many words with the suffix *–al*, which means "like" or "characterized by." The context, or setting in which the word appears, also gives you a clue that *artisanal* means "skillfully crafted."

Words like *artisanal*, which are related to a specific field or occupation, are called **jargon**. This specialized language also includes specific meanings for common words. For example, in "First Impressions," a painter is described as *naïve*, which generally means "lacking experience and understanding." As jargon, though, it refers to a painting style characterized by a lack of formal training. A *brush* in this selection probably is a paintbrush, not a hairbrush. The chart below shows some examples of jargon.

Vocabulary Terms

Jargon is the specialized or technical language of a trade, a profession such as law or medicine, art, and sports.

Test-Taking Tip

When you encounter unfamiliar jargon in a reading selection, look for word parts you already know. Then consider the subject of the selection and the context of the sentence to determine the meaning of the word.

Jargon	Specific field or occupation	Meaning when used as jargon
anomaly	medicine	defect
bug	computers and technology	error, especially in a program
czar	politics	person who is in charge of a policy or an agenda

Practice Identify the jargon in each of the following sentences related to "First Impressions." Then use the context to help you write a definition for the jargon. Check your answers, using a dictionary.

1. De Kooning learned about how to mix pigments with oil and water while painting houses.
2. In Holland, housepainters always stripped windows down to the wood before repainting them.
3. De Kooning created new paintings and illustrations for his portfolio to show employers.
4. Hoboken was very much like North Rotterdam, not the bohemian setting he had expected.

Literature Online

Vocabulary For more vocabulary practice, go to glencoe.com and enter the QuickPass code GL59794u2.

Before You Read

Typhoid Fever
from *Angela's Ashes*

Meet **Frank McCourt**
(born 1930)

"When I look back on my childhood I wonder how I survived at all. It was, of course, a miserable childhood: the happy childhood is hardly worth your while." Thus begins Frank McCourt's powerful memoir, *Angela's Ashes*.

Frank McCourt was born in Brooklyn, New York, to recently immigrated Irish parents. His father, Malachy McCourt, struggled with alcoholism and unemployment. His mother, Angela Sheehan, bore the grim task of raising young children in the face of unrelenting poverty. In the mid-1930s, the McCourts moved back to Limerick, Ireland, to better their lives.

An Irish Childhood In Ireland, however, the McCourts fared no better, given the country's economic depression, unstable employment, and wretched living conditions. Angela tried to sustain the family by scrimping and saving and by soliciting help from Catholic charities and the government. She also endured the deaths of three of her children.

Breaking Free When he was nineteen, McCourt decided to return to the United States to begin a new life. After working a series of jobs, McCourt served in the Korean War, which entitled him to benefits under the GI Bill and funded his education at New York University. He became a teacher and taught in New York City public schools for twenty-seven years.

A Story to Tell McCourt knew he had a story to tell and struggled for years trying to tell it. "All along I wanted to do this book badly. I would have to do it or I would have died howling." In 1996, at the age of sixty-six, he finally published *Angela's Ashes*.

> "I learned the significance of my own insignificant life."
>
> —Frank McCourt

McCourt's gritty story gripped readers almost immediately. When he wrote *Angela's Ashes*, McCourt did not want to write something "charming or lyrical." Instead, he wanted to offer a description of his poverty-stricken Irish childhood that was real and honest. He won several prestigious awards for the book, including the Pulitzer Prize.

Two years later, McCourt followed *Angela's Ashes* with *'Tis*, the second work in his memoir series. *'Tis* chronicles his adventures in the United States, including his first job, his time in the military, his college education, and his profession as a teacher. McCourt published another book, in 2005, *Teacher Man*. It is based on his own unique experience of teaching in the U.S. public school system.

Author Search For more about Frank McCourt, go to glencoe.com and enter QuickPass code GL59794u2.

Literature and Reading Preview

Connect to the Memoir
When you are sick, what do you do to keep your mind occupied? Write a journal entry about the last time you were sick and what you did or thought about to pass the time.

Build Background
Typhoid fever is an infection spread via food, water, and milk contaminated with the *Salmonella typhi* bacteria. Diphtheria is a disease caused by bacteria that have been infected by certain viruses. If left untreated, both diseases can be fatal.

Set Purposes for Reading

Big Idea The Power of Memory
As you read, ask yourself, How does McCourt portray his childhood decades after he lived it?

Literary Element Voice
Voice is the distinctive use of language that conveys the author's or narrator's personality. Voice is determined by elements of style such as word choice and tone. As you read, ask yourself, What does the author's voice reveal about his personality and credibility?

Reading Strategy Analyze Style
Style consists of the expressive qualities that distinguish an author's work, including word choice and the length and arrangement of sentences, as well as the use of figurative language and imagery. As you read, ask yourself, How can **analyzing style** reveal an author's attitude and purpose?

Tip: Ask Questions Ask yourself questions about style as you read and record them in a chart like the one shown below.

Question	Answer	Example
What kinds of imagery does McCourt use?	He uses fantastical and nonsensical imagery to create an air of innocence.	"an owl and a pussycat that went to sea in a green boat with honey and money"

Learning Objectives
For pages 341–351

In studying this text, you will focus on the following objectives:

Literary Study: Analyzing voice.

Reading: Analyzing style.

Vocabulary

induce (in doos′) *v.* to lead or move by persuasion; to bring about; p. 345 *The physicians decided to induce labor.*

potent (pōt′ ənt) *adj.* having strength or authority; powerful; p. 345 *The black widow spider injects a potent poison into its victims.*

rapier (rā′ pē ər) *n.* a narrow, long-bladed, two-edged sword; p. 347 *The pirates drew their rapiers and dueled on deck.*

Tip: Word Origins Remember that knowledge of a word's origins supplies you with clues to, rather than a full account of, a word's current meaning.

A Sick Ward at the Salpetriere. Mabel Henrietta May. Oil on canvas. Musée de l'Assistance Publique, Hopitaux de Paris, France.

Typhoid Fever

from *Angela's Ashes* Frank McCourt

The other two beds in my room are empty. The nurse says I'm the only typhoid patient and I'm a miracle for getting over the crisis.

The room next to me is empty till one morning a girl's voice says, Yoo hoo, who's there?

I'm not sure if she's talking to me or someone in the room beyond.

Yoo hoo, boy with the typhoid, are you awake?

I am.

Are you better?

I am.

Well, why are you here?

I don't know. I'm still in the bed. They stick needles in me and give me medicine.

What do you look like?

I wonder. What kind of a question is that? I don't know what to tell her.

Yoo hoo, are you there, typhoid boy?

I am.

What's your name?

Frank.

That's a good name. My name is Patricia Madigan. How old are you?

Ten.

Oh. She sounds disappointed.

But I'll be eleven in August, next month.

Well, that's better than ten. I'll be fourteen in September. Do you want to know why I'm in the Fever Hospital?

I do.

Analyze Style McCourt does not use quotation marks to set off dialogue. What effect does this style have?

I have diphtheria and something else.

What's something else?

They don't know. They think I have a disease from foreign parts because my father used to be in Africa. I nearly died. Are you going to tell me what you look like?

I have black hair.

You and millions.

I have brown eyes with bits of green that's called hazel.

You and thousands.

I have stitches on the back of my right hand and my two feet where they put in the soldier's blood.

Oh, God, did they?

They did.

You won't be able to stop marching and saluting.

There's a swish of habit and click of beads and then Sister Rita's voice. Now, now, what's this? There's to be no talking between two rooms especially when it's a boy and a girl. Do you hear me, Patricia?

I do, Sister.

Do you hear me, Francis?

I do, Sister.

You could be giving thanks for your two remarkable recoveries. You could be saying the rosary. You could be reading *The Little Messenger of the Sacred Heart* that's beside your beds. Don't let me come back and find you talking.

She comes into my room and wags her finger at me. Especially you, Francis, after thousands of boys prayed for you at the Confraternity.[1] Give thanks, Francis, give thanks.

She leaves and there's silence for awhile. Then Patricia whispers, Give thanks, Francis, give thanks, and say your rosary, Francis, and I laugh so hard a nurse runs in to see if I'm all right. She's a very stern nurse from the County Kerry and she frightens me. What's this, Francis? Laughing? What is there to laugh about? Are you and that Madigan girl talking? I'll report you to Sister Rita. There's to be no laughing for you could be doing serious damage to your internal apparatus.

She plods out and Patricia whispers again in a heavy Kerry accent, No laughing, Francis, you could be doin' serious damage to your internal apparatus. Say your rosary, Francis, and pray for your internal apparatus.

Mam visits me on Thursdays. I'd like to see my father, too, but I'm out of danger, crisis time is over, and I'm allowed only one visitor. Besides, she says, he's back at work at Rank's Flour Mills and please God this job will last a while with the war on and the English desperate for flour. She brings me a chocolate bar and that proves Dad is working. She could never afford it on the dole. He sends me notes. He tells me my brothers are all praying for me, that I should be a good boy, obey the doctors, the nuns, the nurses, and don't forget to say my prayers. He's sure St. Jude pulled me through the crisis because he's the patron saint[2] of desperate cases and I was indeed a desperate case.

Patricia says she has two books by her bed. One is a poetry book and that's the one she loves. The other is a short history of England and do I want it? She gives it to Seamus,[3] the man who mops the floors every day, and he brings it to me. He says, I'm not supposed to be bringing anything from a dipteria room to a typhoid room

---

1. A *confraternity* is a group of people dedicated to a religious cause.

Voice What does McCourt's use of voice convey about Patricia's personality?

2. A *patron saint* is a saint to whom a craft, an activity, or the protection of a person or place is dedicated.
3. Seamus (shā′mus)

Analyze Style McCourt blends narration and dialogue here. What is the effect of this stylistic technique?

with all the germs flying around and hiding between the pages and if you ever catch dipteria on top of the typhoid they'll know and I'll lose my good job and be out on the street singing patriotic songs with a tin cup in my hand, which I could easily do because there isn't a song ever written about Ireland's sufferings I don't know.

Oh, yes, he knows Roddy McCorley. He'll sing it for me right enough but he's barely into the first verse when the Kerry nurse rushes in. What's this, Seamus? Singing? Of all the people in this hospital you should know the rules against singing. I have a good mind to report you to Sister Rita.

Ah, God, don't do that, nurse.

Very well, Seamus. I'll let it go this one time. You know the singing could lead to a relapse in these patients.

When she leaves he whispers he'll teach me a few songs because singing is good for passing the time when you're by yourself in a typhoid room. He says Patricia is a lovely girl the way she often gives him sweets from the parcel her mother sends every fortnight. He stops mopping the floor and calls to Patricia in the next room, I was telling Frankie you're a lovely girl, Patricia, and she says, You're a lovely man, Seamus. He smiles because he's an old man of forty and he never had children but the ones he can talk to here in the Fever Hospital. He says, Here's the book, Frankie. Isn't it a great pity you have to be reading all about England after all they did to us, that there isn't a history of Ireland to be had in this hospital.

The book tells me all about King Alfred and William the Conqueror and all the kings and queens down to Edward, who had to wait forever for his mother, Victoria, to die before he could be king. The book has the first bit of Shakespeare I ever read.

The Power of Memory Why might McCourt remember this so many years later?

Bernadette Soubirous, Visionary of Lourdes, 1844–1879. Artist unknown.

View the Art Notice how the artist uses light and shades of color to highlight elements in the painting. Does the image capture the personality of Sister Rita? Support your opinion.

I do believe, **induced** *by* **potent** *circumstances*
That thou art mine enemy.

The history writer says this is what Catherine, who is a wife of Henry the Eighth, says to Cardinal Wolsey, who is trying to have her head cut off. I don't know what it means and I don't care

Vocabulary

induce (in dōōs′) v. to lead or move by persuasion; to bring about

potent (pōt′ənt) adj. having strength or authority; powerful

Stained glass window of Saint Elizabeth Healing the Sick, 13th Century. Gothic. St. Elizabeth, Marburg, Germany.

View the Art Thirteenth Century Germanic stained glass features detailed backgrounds, figures with expressive faces, and ornate geometric frames around the scenes depicted. Do the figures in this scene reflect the characters in "Typhoid Fever"? Why or why not?

makes no sense and when I say that Patricia gets huffy and says that's the last poem she'll ever read to me. She says I'm always reciting the lines from Shakespeare and they make no sense either. Seamus stops mopping again and tells us we shouldn't be fighting over poetry because we'll have enough to fight about when we grow up and get married. Patricia says she's sorry and I'm sorry too so she reads me part of another poem which I have to remember so I can say it back to her early in the morning or late at night when there are no nuns or nurses about,

because it's Shakespeare and it's like having jewels in my mouth when I say the words. If I had a whole book of Shakespeare they could keep me in the hospital for a year.

Patricia says she doesn't know what induced means or potent circumstances and she doesn't care about Shakespeare, she has her poetry book and she reads to me from beyond the wall a poem about an owl and a pussycat that went to sea in a green boat with honey and money and it

The wind was a torrent of darkness among the gusty trees,
The moon was a ghostly galleon tossed upon cloudy seas,
The road was a ribbon of moonlight over the purple moor,[4]
And the highwayman came riding
Riding riding
The highwayman came riding, up to the old inn-door.
He'd a French cocked-hat on his forehead, a bunch of lace at his chin,

Voice What does McCourt's use of voice in this sentence tell you about his personality as a child?

4. A *moor* is a wide, boggy expanse of land.

A coat of the claret[5] velvet, and breeches[6] of brown doe-skin,

They fitted with never a wrinkle, his boots were up to the thigh.

And he rode with a jewelled twinkle,

His pistol butts a-twinkle,

His rapier hilt a-twinkle, under the jewelled sky.

Visual Vocabulary
A French cocked-hat is a triangular hat with its brim turned upward in three places.

Every day I can't wait for the doctors and nurses to leave me alone so I can learn a new verse from Patricia and find out what's happening to the highwayman and the landlord's red-lipped daughter. I love the poem because it's exciting and almost as good as my two lines of Shakespeare. The redcoats are after the highwayman because they know he told her, I'll come to thee by moonlight, though hell should bar the way.

I'd love to do that myself, come by moonlight for Patricia in the next room, though hell should bar the way. She's ready to read the last few verses when in comes the nurse from Kerry shouting at her, shouting at me, I told ye there was to be no talking between rooms. Diphtheria is never allowed to talk to typhoid and visa versa. I warned ye. And she calls out,

---

5. *Claret,* also the name of a red wine, is a dark, purplish red color.
6. *Breeches* is an old term for pants.

Voice What does this statement tell you about the narrator's personality?

Vocabulary
rapier (rā′ pē ər) *n.* a narrow, long-bladed, two-edged sword

Seamus, take this one. Take the by. Sister Rita said one more word out of him and upstairs with him. We gave ye a warning to stop the blathering but ye wouldn't. Take the by, Seamus, take him.

Ah, now, nurse, sure isn't he harmless. 'Tis only a bit o' poetry.

Take that by, Seamus, take him at once.

He bends over me and whispers, Ah, God, I'm sorry, Frankie. Here's your English history book. He slips the book under my shirt and lifts me from the bed. He whispers that I'm a feather. I try to see Patricia when we pass through her room but all I can make out is a blur of dark head on a pillow.

Sister Rita stops us in the hall to tell me I'm a great disappointment to her, that she expected me to be a good boy after what God had done for me, after all the prayers said by hundreds of boys at the Confraternity, after all the care from the nuns and nurses of the Fever Hospital, after the way they let my mother and father in to see me, a thing rarely allowed, and this is how I repaid them lying in the bed reciting silly poetry back and forth with Patricia Madigan knowing very well there was a ban on all talk between typhoid and diphtheria. She says I'll have plenty of time to reflect on my sins in the big ward upstairs and I should beg God's forgiveness for my disobedience reciting a pagan English poem about a thief on a horse and a maiden with red lips who commits a terrible sin when I could have been praying or reading the life of a saint. She made it her business to read that poem so she did and I'd be well advised to tell the priest in confession.

The Kerry nurse follows us upstairs gasping and holding on to the banister. She tells me I better not get the notion she'll be

---

The Power of Memory Why do you think McCourt remembers and is able to re-create details like this?

running up to this part of the world every time I have a little pain or a twinge.

There are twenty beds in the ward, all white, all empty. The nurse tells Seamus put me at the far end of the ward against the wall to make sure I don't talk to anyone who might be passing the door, which is very unlikely since there isn't another soul on this whole floor. She tells Seamus this was the fever ward during the Great Famine[7] long ago and only God knows how many died here brought in too late for anything but a wash before they were buried and there are stories of cries and moans in the far reaches of the night. She says 'twould break your heart to think of what the English did to us, that if they didn't put the blight on the potato they didn't do much to take it off. No pity. No feeling at all for the people that died in this very ward, children suffering and dying here while the English feasted on roast beef and guzzled the best of wine in their big houses, little children with their mouths all green from trying to eat the grass in the fields beyond, God bless us and save us and guard us from future famines.

Seamus says 'twas a terrible thing indeed and he wouldn't want to be walking these halls in the dark with all the little green mouths gaping at him. The nurse takes my temperature, 'Tis up a bit, have a good sleep for yourself now that you're away from the chatter with Patricia Madigan below who will never know a gray hair.

She shakes her head at Seamus and he gives her a sad shake back.

Nurses and nuns never think you know what they're talking about. If you're ten going on eleven you're supposed to be simple like my uncle Pat Sheehan who was dropped on his head. You can't ask questions. You can't show you understand what the nurse said about Patricia Madigan, that she's going to die, and you can't show you want to cry over this girl who taught you a lovely poem which the nun says is bad.

The nurse tells Seamus she has to go and he's to sweep the lint from under my bed and mop up a bit around the ward. Seamus tells me she's a right oul' witch for running to Sister Rita and complaining about the poem going between the two rooms, that you can't catch a disease from a poem . . . . He never heard the likes of it, a little fella shifted upstairs for saying a poem and he has a good mind to go to the *Limerick Leader*[8] and tell them print the whole thing except he has this job and he'd lose it if ever Sister Rita found out. Anyway, Frankie, you'll be outa here one of these fine days and you can read all the poetry you want though I don't know about Patricia below, I don't know about Patricia, God help us.

He knows about Patricia in two days because she got out of the bed to go to the lavatory when she was supposed to use a bedpan and collapsed and died in the lavatory. Seamus is mopping the floor and there are tears on his cheeks and he's saying, 'Tis a dirty rotten thing to die in a lavatory when you're lovely in yourself. She told me she was sorry she had you reciting that poem and getting you shifted from the room, Frankie. She said 'twas all her fault.

It wasn't, Seamus.

I know and didn't I tell her that.

---

7. The *Great Famine* refers to the Irish potato famine of the 1840s, during which many Irish citizens died from starvation and disease.

8. *Limerick* is the town in Ireland in which the story takes place. The *Limerick Leader* is a local publication, probably a newspaper.

Voice What does this tell you about the narrator's level of maturity?

The Power of Memory How do you think Patricia's death and her sorrow over McCourt's departure affected McCourt?

After You Read

Respond and Think Critically

Respond and Interpret

1. (a) How did you feel after reading the selection? (b) What specifically about the selection made you feel this way? Explain.

2. (a) What is the first reason Sister Rita gives for telling Frank and Patricia not to talk to each other? (b) What does this tell you about the time period and setting in which this selection takes place?

3. (a) What are the subjects of McCourt's and Patricia's poetry? (b) What does their love for these written passages tell you about their different tastes in literature?

4. (a) Which patients had Frankie's new ward previously housed? (b) How does this knowledge affect the mood of the selection?

Analyze and Evaluate

5. Does Frank and Patricia's dialogue sound like the dialogue of a ten-year-old and a fourteen-year-old? Illustrate your answer with examples from the text.

6. What kind of effect do you think the portrayal of the adults has on the excerpt as a whole?

Connect

7. **Big Idea** The Power of Memory Do you think this selection reads more like fiction or nonfiction? Explain.

8. **Connect to Today** In "Typhoid Fever", the sick children entertain themselves and each other by reciting poetry. What might sick children look to for entertainment in a hospital today?

Primary Source Quotation

A Child's Perspective

McCourt waited many years to write *Angela's Ashes* because he needed time to understand his painful childhood. As he says, "I couldn't have written this book fifteen years ago because I was carrying a lot of baggage around. . . . and I had attitudes and these attitudes had to be softened. I had to get rid of them, I had to become, as it says in the Bible, as a child. . . . The child started to speak in this book. And that was the only way to do it, without judging."

Group Activity Discuss the following questions with classmates. Refer back to the quotation and cite evidence from the selecion for support.

1. Why do you think it was important for McCourt to become "as a child" in *Angela's Ashes*?

2. What are some ways in which the excerpt reflects the perspective of a child? Support your answer with specific examples.

Literary Element Voice

An author uses **voice** to communicate his personality or opinions to the reader. The voice in an autobiographical work such as *Angela's Ashes* is the voice of the author's younger self as perceived by his adult self. When analyzing a writer's voice, look at how the writer uses elements such as sentence structure, word choice, and tone.

1. Is the voice in this selection credible as that of a young boy or that of an adult? Explain.
2. What stylistic devices does McCourt use to create his narrator's voice?

Review: Memoir

As you learned on pages 284–285, **memoir** is a type of narrative nonfiction that presents the story of a period in the writer's life. It is usually written from the first-person point of view and emphasizes the narrator's own experience of this period. It may also reveal the impact of significant historical events on his or her life.

Partner Activity With a classmate, discuss "Typhoid Fever" as a memoir. Working with your partner, create a two-column chart similar to the one below. Fill in the left-hand column with examples of historical details or events referenced in the text. In the right-hand column, describe each example's effect on the author's life.

Historical Detail or Event	Effect on Author
old-fashioned medicine	had to stay isolated in the Fever Hospital

Literature Online

Selection Resources For Selection Quizzes, eFlashcards, and Reading-Writing Connection activities, go to glencoe.com and enter QuickPass code GL59794u2.

Reading Strategy Analyze Style

SAT Skills Practice

1. The opening dialogue between the narrator and Patricia (pages 343–344) serves to
   (A) inform the reader about health care in Ireland
   (B) prepare the reader for tragedy
   (C) reveal the average child's mature thinking skills
   (D) show children to be open and honest with each other
   (E) point out differences in the way boys and girls view the same situation

Vocabulary Practice

Practice with Word Origins Studying the etymology, or origin and history, of a word can help you understand and explore its meaning. Create a word map like the one below for each of these vocabulary words from the text.

induce   **potent**   **rapier**

EXAMPLE:

Definition	Etymology
an historical account told in time order	Greek *chronos* means "time"

chronicle

Sample Sentence
The novel was a chronicle of three generations.

Academic Vocabulary

*The Sisters did not want to **expose** the children to other diseases.*

Expose is a multiple-meaning word. A hiker might be **exposed** to the elements, or a reporter might **expose** the illegal actions of a government official. Use context clues to try to figure out the meaning of *expose* in the sentence above about the memoir. Check your guess in a dictionary.

For more on academic vocabulary, see pages 52 and 53.

Respond Through Writing

Persuasive Essay

Offer a Solution McCourt's essay reflects the biases of a certain place, time, and group of people regarding the behavior of children in a hospital. Imagine you are a reporter for the *Limerick Leader*. Write an editorial suggesting a more or less strict approach to the behavior of Patricia and Francis. Explain why your solution is reasonable, and refute the counterclaims and biases that you see as part of the problem.

Understand the Task
- An **editorial** is a short article written to express an opinion.
- **Counterclaims**, or counterarguments, are opposing arguments.
- **Biases** are values or ways of thinking that prevent people from considering facts in an objective way.

Prewrite Begin by identifying your audience, purpose, and controlling idea or thesis, which is your opinion. Then list points you will make to support your thesis, or the reasons for your opinion. Also list counterclaims and biases you will address, such as the Sisters' belief that reciting or listening to poetry will harm the children.

Draft As you draft, put your arguments in a logical order. For example, you could begin with your least important idea and build to your most important or convincing one. For each reason you discuss, present evidence, such as commonly accepted beliefs, facts, expert opinions, or logical reasoning. Incorporate persuasive techniques and rhetorical devices by using these frames or others like them:

Appeal to Authority As ____, the author states, ____ .
Appeal to Ethical Belief It is only right that ____ .
Appeal to Logic The most logical thing to do is ____ .
Rhetorical Question What good would it do to ____ ?

Revise Exchange papers with a partner. Be sure you can identify each other's thesis or opinion and at least two logical, well-supported reasons that directly support the thesis. Also, identify at least one counterclaim and one bias that your partner has addressed. Revise your essay to improve your thesis, your reasons, your evidence, or your responses to possible arguments or ways of thinking that oppose your own.

Edit and Proofread Proofread your paper, correcting any errors in spelling, grammar, and punctuation. Use the Grammar Tip in the side column to help you with absolutes and absolute phrases.

Learning Objectives
In this assignment, you will focus on the following objectives:

Writing: Writing an editorial.

Grammar: Understanding how to use absolutes and absolute phrases.

Grammar Tip

Absolutes and Absolute Phrases

Absolutes and absolute phrases are unrelated. An absolute is a modifier that cannot be compared.

Examples of absolutes are *dead*, *perfect*, and *empty*; for example, something cannot be any more or any less dead than something else.

An absolute phrase is a phrase that modifies the entire remainder of the sentence in which it is found. Many absolute phrases are verbal phrases: they consist of a noun or pronoun and a participle:
The work finished, Seamus left the room.
That said, they went on reading anyway.

Prepositional phrases can also function as absolutes:
In fact, Seamus breaks the rules.

Historical Perspective
on *Angela's Ashes*

from

Looking Forward to the Past
A Profile of Frank McCourt

Carolyn T. Hughes

Frank McCourt, 1998, New York.

Learning Objectives

For pages 352–355
In studying this text, you will focus on the following objective:

Reading: Recognizing author's purpose.

National Book Award Winner

Set a Purpose for Reading
Read to learn about McCourt's personal journey in writing *Angela's Ashes*.

Build Background
Author Frank McCourt, who spent his childhood in Limerick, Ireland, revisits his early years in *Angela's Ashes*. In this selection, Hughes discusses why McCourt was inspired to write a memoir of his childhood in Limerick.

Reading Strategy
Recognize Author's Purpose
Recognizing the author's purpose involves identifying the author's intent for writing a literary work. Authors may write for any or all of the following purposes: to persuade, inform, explain, entertain, or describe. As you read, use a web diagram like the one below to take notes on the details of the interview.

Angela's Ashes is McCourt's attempt to come to terms with his childhood—one so beset by tragedy and misfortune that he has called his work simply an "epic of woe." In 1930 McCourt was born in Brooklyn, to Irish immigrants Malachy and Angela. His parents, crushed by the recent death of their daughter and by the alcoholic Malachy's inability to hold a job, moved the family back to Ireland—but bad luck followed them. McCourt's twin brothers died shortly after the family returned to Limerick, and he himself almost perished from typhoid fever. But the greatest challenge for McCourt to contend with was his father's continued drinking and eventual abandonment of the family. In 1941 Malachy McCourt, Sr., left for England, ostensibly to get a factory job. He was supposed to send home money. It never happened. He disappeared, leaving his family to fend for themselves.

At times, the landscape of *Angela's Ashes* is so bleak it's downright depressing. But McCourt's use of a child narrator (an idea that came to him "in a dream") works to soften the tragedy of the story. Instead of being delivered through an adult's jaded vision, the events are relayed from an innocent, even lighthearted perspective, without judgment, which makes room for the poignancy and humor so celebrated by readers and critics.

Much of *Angela's Ashes* is devoted to the depiction of McCourt's educational experience at Leamy National School in Limerick, where, he says, his teachers had about as light a touch as the Marquis de Sade.[1] When McCourt became a teacher himself, he was determined to provide a creative, productive environment for his students. He began his career in 1959 at McKee Vocational and Technical High School on Staten Island, and after 13 years went on to Stuyvesant High, where he became the kind of teacher students dream of. Claire Costello, a Stuyvesant alumna who now works as a Manhattan attorney, says that McCourt was so popular that students who were not assigned to his classes would audit them (now not many teachers can claim *that* kind of approbation).[2] In class McCourt was known to play Irish records, and even to break out his harmonica and play a tune or two himself. While his approachability endeared him to his students, McCourt insists he learned more from his students than they did from him.

"I found that in the beginning of my teaching career, just like everybody else, I would put on an act and try to be what I wasn't: the teacher who knows *everything*. Sometimes I felt I was saying things that I really didn't mean. 'Oh, yeah, I understand *The Waste Land*,[3] I understand Shakespeare,' when I might not. But one of the things I discovered in the classroom was honesty. I don't mean it from any moral or ethical sense. It's a powerful tool to tell the truth."

The practice of telling the truth was an exercise that would prove important for McCourt. And in having to articulate to his students lessons on how to write, he was formulating the strategies that he would eventually put to use himself. "I told them, 'If you write, it's like having a Geiger counter[4] you can run over your life. There will be hot spots—when you had your first fight with your brother, when you fell in love, your first kiss, and all that—then you look for conflict.' The ol' conflict dilemma. I also told them to get the stories of their fathers and mothers and grandparents. There are grandparents sitting at home now who are mines of information and stories. They want to tell them, but most people cast them aside. I told my students, 'There's your material; get out the tape recorder, take notes.'"

McCourt acknowledges being an avid note taker himself and says it helped him with the writing of his book. "I've been keeping journals for forty years, and there were things I discovered in my notebooks that I had forgotten about—like how my mother was attracted to my father and his hangdog look. Well, one of the reasons why he had a hangdog look then was because he had just been released from three months in prison for hijacking a truck. He thought it was full of cans of pork and beans, but it turned out to be buttons." McCourt laughs. "I had forgotten about that completely."

Although McCourt has spent much of his life teaching writing, he admits he's suspicious of today's writing programs. "It depends on the person, but I think you'd be better off falling in love, you'd be better off getting rejected by someone. These are valuable experiences!" McCourt says. "My point is, anything is worth writing about. I gave my students an assignment. I said, 'Look, pick somebody in this class, don't look at

---

1. The *Marquis de Sade* (1740–1814) was a French nobleman and writer condemned for his abusive behavior.
2. *Approbation* means "praise."
3. *The Waste Land* is a famous poem by American writer T. S. Eliot.
4. A *Geiger counter*, an instrument with a tube and electronic equipment, is used to detect particles of radiation.

Informational Text

Frank McCourt in New York. January 4, 2000. Tore Bergsake.

them right now, but you are going to write about this person. You are going to observe them for a month and then write.' It forced them, encouraged them, to observe another human being and perhaps realize the significance of insignificance."

One of the major reasons it took McCourt so long to write *Angela's Ashes* was that he didn't understand the truth of his own lesson. He marginalized the significance of his early life, believing that his family's crushing poverty rendered their story inconsequential. His background, in fact, was a source of embarrassment: "In my twenties and thirties, I didn't want to write about being poor. I had to overcome a lot of fear—overcome the shame. I guess you could say I was suffering from low self-esteem."

In 1969, McCourt did attempt to write a book about his life. "I think I called it *If You Were in the Lane*. It was completely derivative. I was imitating everybody, even Evelyn Waugh.[5] Imagine me writing like Evelyn Waugh!"

Although he didn't give up writing completely, it was 25 years before McCourt would try to tackle his own story again. In the meantime he wrote the occasional article—he published a piece about a Jewish cemetery in Limerick in the *Village Voice* and a series of articles about New York for the *Manhattan Spirit*. McCourt even tried his hand as an entertainer. In 1984, he starred with brother Malachy, an actor, Manhattan bar owner, and renowned bon vivant,[6] in a cabaret show called *A Couple of Blaguards*. The show premiered in New York and went on to Chicago, San Francisco, and Ireland. The brothers McCourt sang Irish songs and told stories about their family. (The play, directed by Howard Platt, is now enjoying a successful run at New York's Triad Theater.)

When McCourt retired from teaching and finally turned to the writing of *Angela's Ashes*, it didn't take long for him to finish it. He wrote most of the book at his home in Pennsylvania. "I started it in October 1994. The actual writing took a year—actually, less than a year because I was distracted by various events and people visiting, so maybe it took ten months of straight writing. I just got up every morning and I wrote. What was it Red Smith[7] said? 'You sit at the desk and you open a vein.' That was my routine. I wrote on the right-hand page of my notebook, and on the left-hand

---

5. *Evelyn Waugh* (1903–1966) was a British writer, known for his satiric portrayals of the British upper classes.
6. *Bon vivant* means "a person with sophisticated tastes, especially of food and drink."
7. *Red Smith* (1905–1982) was an American sports columnist.

side I jotted down notes about what I needed to dig deeper into." McCourt didn't have any set schedule for how many hours a day he would work: "I didn't push. . . . When it came, it came." Having his wife as a sounding board helped. "I would read passages to Ellen—and she thought it was fine."

McCourt showed the first 159 pages to Molly Friedrich, a New York City neighbor who also happens to be a literary agent. She agreed to work with McCourt, and passed the manuscript on to Nan Graham, editor in chief at Scribner. Graham, no easy sell, loved it: "I edited *The Liar's Club*,"[8] Graham says. "I've seen a lot of memoirs, but from the beginning I thought the work and voice in *Angela's Ashes* was extraordinary. I bought the book within a week. There really was so little to do as far as editing. This man is a stunning writer."

McCourt handed in his final draft to Graham on November 30, 1995, the 328th anniversary of the birth of Jonathan Swift,[9] one of McCourt's favorite writers (he has a thing for significant dates). Although working on the book was emotionally draining, McCourt felt an overwhelming sense of accomplishment when he finished it. "I would have been very unhappy if I had died without writing it. I would have begged for another year. 'Jesus, give me another year!' I would have died howling. So I did it, and I'm glad it's out of the way. You see, it's a great thing to know why you were put on this earth. I was a teacher, but teaching was my second occupation. All the time I was a writer not writing, just jotting things down in notebooks and so on. But all the time the book was developing in my head as I taught the kids at Stuyvesant. It was forming and waiting to be born."

---

8. *Liar's Club* was author Mary Karr's popular 1995 memoir.

9. *Jonathan Swift* (1667–1745) was an Irish author celebrated for his satiric prose in such works as *Gulliver's Travels*.

Respond and Think Critically

Respond and Interpret

1. Write a brief summary of the main ideas in this article before you answer the following questions. For help on writing a summary, see page 415.

2. What is your opinion of McCourt's claim that "anything is worth writing about"?

3. (a) For what reason(s) did McCourt decide to use a child's point of view to narrate *Angela's Ashes*? (b) What might this say about his perspective on childhood?

4. (a) What was the most important quality that McCourt realized he must have in order to be a good teacher? (b) How did he apply what he learned as a teacher to his work as a writer?

Analyze and Evaluate

5. (a) Hughes delves into McCourt's upbringing, his off-beat methods of teaching, and his brief stint as an actor. Why do you think she includes these details of McCourt's life? (b) Do these details support McCourt's message about writing? Why or why not?

6. (a) Hughes says that "one of the major reasons it took McCourt so long to write *Angela's Ashes* was that he didn't understand the truth of his own lesson." What do you think Hughes means by this comment? (b) What do you think Hughes believes the act of writing can teach a person?

Connect

7. McCourt attempted to write a book about his life in 1969. It took another twenty-five years before he wrote *Angela's Ashes*. Do you think the passing of time distanced him from or made him more aware of his memories of the past? How do you think the passage of time colors your memories?

Before You Read

Terwilliger Bunts One
from *An American Childhood*

Meet **Annie Dillard**
(born 1945)

As a child, Annie Dillard was encouraged by her parents to investigate the world around her. That keen attention to detail and fascination for living things is reflected in Dillard's writing, whether she is describing a grasshopper on her window or discussing her family's idiosyncrasies.

> *"The dedicated life is worth living. You must give with your whole heart."*
>
> —Annie Dillard

An American Childhood Annie Dillard, the oldest of three daughters, had an unusual childhood. Her parents, the Doaks, were creative thinkers who encouraged and inspired creativity in Dillard and her sisters. The world was open to the Doak sisters to explore, question, and discover. During adolescence, Dillard began experimenting with writing poetry. She read poets of all kinds and particularly admired the works of Ralph Waldo Emerson. Dillard wrote poetry in her own style as well as in the style of her favorite poets. She was also a voracious reader; she notes that, at the age of thirteen, "I was reading books on drawing, painting, rocks, criminology, birds, moths, beetles, stamps, ponds and streams, medicine." In fact, Dillard reread her favorite book—*The Field Book of Ponds and Streams*—every year.

Tinker Creek and Beyond In college Dillard wrote a 40-page paper about Henry David Thoreau, and her book *Pilgrim at Tinker Creek* is often compared to Thoreau's *Walden; or Life in the Woods*. Dillard spent time living in nature next to Tinker Creek in Virginia's Roanoke Valley. Just as Thoreau described life in the woods in *Walden*, in *Pilgrim at Tinker Creek*, Dillard examines the beautiful and sometimes brutal natural world. *Pilgrim at Tinker Creek* won the Pulitzer Prize for Nonfiction in 1975, when Dillard was only thirty years old.

Dillard was inspired by the birth of her first daughter to complete a memoir, entitled *An American Childhood*. Dillard describes growing up with eccentric parents: a father who quit his lucrative job to mimic Mark Twain's journey down the Mississippi River and a mother who encouraged her daughters to explore the world outside the family home as soon as they could remember their phone number. According to Michael J. Farrell, "Dillard urges us not to turn away, coaxes us instead to look Life in the eye." Whether writing about the natural world or the human one, Dillard observes with an unflinching gaze.

Author Search For more about Annie Dillard, go to glencoe.com and enter QuickPass code GL59794u2.

Literature and Reading Preview

Connect to the Memoir
How do you use humor in your daily life? List moments throughout your day that you treat with humor.

Build Background
An American Childhood is set in Pittsburgh, Pennsylvania, in the 1950s. At that time, most middle-class married women did not work outside the home or pursue their own careers. It was often assumed that women fortunate or wealthy enough to attend college were looking for husbands.

Set Purposes for Reading

Big Idea The Power of Memory

As you read, ask yourself, How does Dillard link her humorous memories of her mother to her development as a writer?

Literary Element Anecdote

An **anecdote** is a brief account of an interesting occurrence. Anecdotes add depth and variety to the text and help the reader to visualize the characters and events. As you read the story, ask yourself, How does Dillard use anecdotes to deepen our understanding of her mother's approach to life?

Reading Strategy Connect to Personal Experience

Authors often write about situations, settings, or characters to which or to whom the reader can relate. **Connecting to personal experience** can help you better understand the author's message. As you read, ask yourself, What situations in the text remind me of instances in my own life?

Tip: Make a Chart Choose events, characters, or situations from the excerpt that seem familiar to compare to your personal experiences. Record your thoughts in a chart like the one below.

Situations in the text	Reminds me of...
Mother rolled down the hill at the beach.	I have an aunt who was like that when she was younger.

Learning Objectives

For pages 356–364

In studying this text, you will focus on the following objectives:

Literary Study: Analyzing anecdote.

Reading: Connecting to personal experience.

Vocabulary

tremulously (trem′yə ləs lē) *adv.* in a trembling or vibrating way; p. 359 *After he heard the knock at the door, he tremulously asked, "Who's there?"*

eschew (es chōō′) *v.* to keep apart from something disliked or harmful; avoid; p. 359 *Because I dislike music with violent lyrics, I eschew it.*

advocate (ad′və kāt′) *v.* to publicly support; p. 360 *I advocate the passing of that law, and I will be sure to vote for it.*

stolid (stol′id) *adj.* showing little or no emotion; p. 361 *Her face was stolid after hearing the bad news; we never knew how sad she was.*

Tip: Word Parts Word parts are prefixes, suffixes, and base words or roots. Words that have the suffix -ly are often adverbs.

Terwilliger Bunts One
from An American Childhood

S&H Green Stamps, 1965. Andy Warhol.
The Andy Warhol Foundation for the Visual Arts.

Annie Dillard

One Sunday afternoon Mother wandered through our kitchen, where Father was making a sandwich and listening to the ball game. The Pirates were playing the New York Giants at Forbes Field. In those days, the Giants had a utility infielder[1] named Wayne Terwilliger. Just as Mother passed through, the radio announcer cried—with undue drama—"Terwilliger bunts one!"

"Terwilliger bunts one?" Mother cried back, stopped short. She turned. "Is that English?"

"The player's name is Terwilliger," Father said. "He bunted."

"That's marvelous," Mother said. "'Terwilliger bunts one.' No wonder you listen to baseball. 'Terwilliger bunts one.'"

For the next seven or eight years, Mother made this surprising string of syllables her own. Testing a microphone, she repeated, "Terwilliger bunts one"; testing a pen or a typewriter, she wrote it. If, as happened surprisingly often in the course of various improvised gags, she pretended to whisper something else in my ear, she actually whispered, "Terwilliger bunts one." Whenever someone used a French phrase, or a Latin one, she answered solemnly, "Terwilliger bunts one." If Mother had had, like Andrew Carnegie,[2] the opportunity to cook up a motto for a coat of arms, hers would have read simply and tellingly, "Terwilliger bunts one." (Carnegie's was "Death to Privilege.")

She served us with other words and phrases. On a Florida trip, she repeated

---

1. In this context, *utility* means "useful generally rather than in a specialized function." So, a *utility infielder* is capable of playing shortstop or first, second, or third base.

Anecdote How does this opening anecdote draw the reader in?

2. Based in Pittsburgh, *Andrew Carnegie* (1835–1919) made a fortune in the steel industry and donated $350 million to social and educational institutions.

Visual Vocabulary
A *coat of arms* is an arrangement of symbols on a shield that, along with a motto, represents one's ancestry.

tremulously, "That . . . is a royal poinciana." I don't remember the tree; I remember the thrill in her voice. She pronounced it carefully, and spelled it. She also liked to say "portulaca."³

The drama of the words "Tamiami Trail" stirred her, we learned on the same Florida trip. People built Tampa on one coast, and they built Miami on another. Then—the height of visionary⁴ ambition and folly—they piled a slow, tremendous road through the terrible Everglades to connect them. To build the road, men stood sunk in muck to their armpits. They fought off cottonmouth moccasins and six-foot alligators. They slept in boats, wet. They blasted muck with dynamite, cut jungle with machetes; they laid logs, dragged drilling machines, hauled dredges, heaped limestone. The road took fourteen years to build up by the shovelful, a Panama Canal in reverse, and cost hundreds of lives from tropical, mosquito-carried diseases. Then, capping it all, some genius thought of the word Tamiami: they called the road from Tampa to Miami, this very road under our spinning wheels, the Tamiami Trail. Some called it Alligator Alley. Anyone could drive over this road without a thought.

---

3. The *royal poinciana* and the *portulaca* (pôr′ chə lakə) are native to the tropics and bear bright flowers.
4. Here, *visionary* refers to imagining something in perfect but unrealistic form. People had foreseen the benefits of connecting the two cities but overlooked practical considerations involved in constructing the road.

Connect to Personal Experience What does the author reveal here about her mother's personality?

Vocabulary

tremulously (trem′ yə ləs lē) *adv.* in a trembling or vibrating way

Hearing this, moved, I thought all the suffering of road building was worth it (it wasn't my suffering), now that we had this new thing to hang these new words on— Alligator Alley for those who like things cute, and, for connoisseurs like Mother, for lovers of the human drama in all its boldness and terror, the Tamiami Trail.

Back home, Mother cut clips from reels of talk, as it were, and played them back at leisure. She noticed that many Pittsburghers confuse "leave" and "let." One kind relative brightened our morning by mentioning why she'd brought her son to visit: "He wanted to come with me, so I left him." Mother filled in Amy and me on locutions we missed. "I can't do it on Friday," her pretty sister told a crowded dinner party, "because Friday's the day I lay in the stores."⁵

(All unconsciously, though, we ourselves used some pure Pittsburghisms. We said "tele pole," pronounced "telly pole," for that splintery sidewalk post I loved to climb. We said "slippy"—the sidewalks are "slippy." We said, "That's all the farther I could go." And we said, as Pittsburghers do say, "This glass needs washed," or "The dog needs walked"—a usage our father **eschewed**; he knew it was not standard English, nor even comprehensible English, but he never let on.)

"Spell 'poinsettia,'" Mother would throw out at me, smiling with pleasure. "Spell 'sherbet.'" The idea was not to make us whizzes, but, quite the contrary, to remind us—and I, especially, needed reminding—

---

5. *Locutions* are forms or styles of verbal expression. Where this woman said she had to *lay in the stores,* Mother might have said she had to go grocery shopping.

The Power of Memory Why do you think her mother is trying to remind the author that she does not "know it all just yet"?

Vocabulary

eschew (es chōō′) *v.* to keep apart from something disliked or harmful; avoid

that we didn't know it all just yet. "There's a deer standing in the front hall," she told me one quiet evening in the country.

"Really?"

"No. I just wanted to tell you something once without your saying, 'I know.'"

Supermarkets in the middle 1950s began luring, or bothering, customers by giving out Top Value Stamps or Green Stamps.[6] When, shopping with Mother, we got to the head of the checkout line, the checker, always a young man, asked, "Save stamps?"

"No," Mother replied genially, week after week, "I build model airplanes." I believe she originated this line. It took me years to determine where the joke lay.

Anyone who met her verbal challenges she adored. She had surgery on one of her eyes. On the operating table, just before she conked out, she appealed feelingly to the surgeon, saying, as she had been planning to say for weeks, "Will I be able to play the piano?" "Not on me," the surgeon said. "You won't pull that old one on me."

It was, indeed, an old one. The surgeon was supposed to answer, "Yes, my dear, brave woman, you will be able to play the piano after this operation," to which Mother intended to reply, "Oh, good, I've always wanted to play the piano." This pat scenario bored her; she loved having it interrupted. It must have galled[7] her that usually her acquaintances were so predictably unalert; it must have galled her that, for the length of her life, she could surprise everyone so continually, so easily, when she had been the same all along. At any rate, she loved anyone who, as she put it, saw it coming, and called her on it.

She regarded the instructions on bureaucratic forms as straight lines.[8] "Do you **advocate** the overthrow of the United States government by force or violence?" After some thought she wrote, "Force." She regarded children, even babies, as straight men.[9] When Molly learned to crawl, Mother delighted in buying her gowns with drawstrings at the bottom, like Swee'pea's, because, as she explained energetically, you could easily step on the drawstring without the baby's noticing, so that she crawled and crawled and crawled and never got anywhere except into a small ball at the gown's top.

Visual Vocabulary
Swee'pea is the baby in "Popeye" cartoons.

When we children were young, she mothered us tenderly and dependably; as we got older, she resumed her career of anarchism.[10] She collared us into her gags. If she answered the phone on a wrong number, she told the caller, "Just a minute," and dragged the receiver to Amy or me, saying, "Here, take this, your name is Cecile," or, worse, just, "It's for you." You had to think on your feet. But did you want to perform well as Cecile, or did

---

6. *[Top Value . . . Stamps]* Stores gave customers a certain number of stamps per dollar spent. These stamps were saved up and later exchanged for merchandise.
7. Here, *galled* means "irritated."

Anecdote What does the exchange with the surgeon reveal about what Dillard's mother values in life?

8. *Bureaucratic* refers to the rigidly formal paperwork and procedures involved in dealing with government officials and agencies. For Mother, these things were setups for jokes—the *straight lines* that led to punch lines.
9. *Straight men* are people who assist comedians by feeding them straight lines or serving as objects of fun.
10. Here, *anarchism* refers to active resistance against what is oppressive and undesirable.

Connect to Personal Experience Which option do you think the author might have chosen in this situation? Why?

Vocabulary

advocate (ad′ və kāt′) *v.* to publicly support

you want to take pity on the wretched caller?

During a family trip to the Highland Park Zoo, Mother and I were alone for a minute. She approached a young couple holding hands on a bench by the seals, and addressed the young man in dripping[11] tones: "Where have you been? Still got those baby-blue eyes; always did slay me. And this"—a swift nod at the dumbstruck young woman, who had removed her hand from the man's—"must be the one you were telling me about. She's not so bad, really, as you used to make out. But listen, you know how I miss you, you know where to reach me, same old place. And there's Ann over there—see how she's grown? See the blue eyes?"

And off she sashayed,[12] taking me firmly by the hand, and leading us around briskly past the monkey house and away. She cocked an ear back, and both of us heard the desperate man begin, in a high-pitched wail, "I swear, I never saw her before in my life. . . ."

On a long, sloping beach by the ocean, she lay stretched out sunning with Father and friends, until the conversation gradually grew tedious, when without forethought she gave a little push with her heel and rolled away. People were stunned. She rolled deadpan and apparently effortlessly, arms and legs extended and tidy, down the beach to the distant water's edge, where she lay at ease just as she had been, but half in the surf, and well out of earshot.

She dearly loved to fluster people by throwing out a game's rules at whim[13]— when she was getting bored, losing in a dull sort of way, and when everybody else was taking it too seriously. If you turned your back, she moved the checkers around on the board. When you got them all straightened out, she denied she'd touched them; the next time you turned your back, she lined them up on the rug or hid them under your chair. In a betting rummy game called *Michigan,* she routinely played out of turn, or called out a card she didn't hold, or counted backward, simply to amuse herself by causing an uproar and watching the rest of us do double takes and have fits. (Much later, when serious suitors came to call, Mother subjected them to this fast card game as a trial by ordeal; she used it as an intelligence test and a measure of spirit. If the poor man could stay a round without breaking down or running out, he got to marry one of us, if he still wanted to.)

She excelled at bridge, playing fast and boldly, but when the stakes were low and the hands dull, she bid slams[14] for the devilment of it, or raised her opponents' suit to bug them, or showed her hand, or tossed her cards in a handful behind her back in a characteristic swift motion accompanied by a vibrantly innocent look. It drove our **stolid** father crazy. The hand was over before it began, and the guests were appalled. How do you score it, who deals now, what do you do with a crazy person who is having so much fun? Or they were down seven, and the guests were appalled. "Pam!" "Dammit, Pam!" He groaned. What ails such people? What on earth possesses them? He rubbed his face.

She was an unstoppable force; she never let go. When we moved across town, she persuaded the U.S. Post Office to let her keep her old address—forever—because

---

11. *Dripping* here refers to using excessive charm or appeal.
12. She *sashayed* or walked in a way that showed a seeming lack of interest.
13. The phrase *at whim* means "suddenly and unexpectedly."
14. When she *bid slams,* Mother "went for broke," betting that she would win every or all but one of the tricks in a round of play.

Vocabulary

stolid (stol′id) *adj.* showing little or no emotion

she'd had stationery printed. I don't know how she did it. Every new post office worker, over decades, needed to learn that although the Doaks' mail is addressed to here, it is delivered to there.

Mother's energy and intelligence suited her for a greater role in a larger arena—mayor of New York, say—than the one she had. She followed American politics closely; she had been known to vote for Democrats. She saw how things should be run, but she had nothing to run but our household. Even there, small minds bugged her; she was smarter than the people who designed the things she had to use all day for the length of her life.

Anecdote What does this sentence reveal about how some women of that generation may have felt?

"Look," she said. "Whoever designed this corkscrew never used one. Why would anyone sell it without trying it out?" So she invented a better one. She showed me a drawing of it. The spirit of American enterprise never faded in Mother. If capitalizing and tooling up[15] had been as interesting as theorizing and thinking up, she would have fired up a new factory every week, and chaired several hundred corporations.

"It grieves me," she would say, "it grieves my heart," that the company that

---

15. *Capitalizing* and *tooling up* has to do with providing the finances and equipment necessary to start up a new business or factory.

Connect to Personal Experience Why do you think people like Dillard's mother may prefer theorizing and inventing to running a business?

Ringling Brothers and Barnum & Bailey—Trains. Artist unknown.

View the Art Travelling circuses used posters that featured exaggeration and excitement to attract audiences. What idea in the selection does this advertisement help illustrate?

made one superior product packaged it poorly, or took the wrong tack[16] in its advertising. She knew, as she held the thing mournfully in her two hands, that she'd never find another. She was right. We children wholly sympathized, and so did Father; what could she do, what could anyone do, about it? She was Samson[17] in chains. She paced.

She didn't like the taste of stamps so she didn't lick stamps; she licked the corner of the envelope instead. She glued sandpaper to the sides of kitchen drawers, and under kitchen cabinets, so she always had a handy place to strike a match. She designed, and hounded workmen to build against all norms,[18] doubly wide kitchen counters and elevated bathroom sinks. . . . She drew plans for an over-the-finger toothbrush for babies, an oven rack that slid up and down, and—the family favorite—Lendalarm. Lendalarm was a beeper you attached to books (or tools) you loaned friends. After ten days, the beeper sounded. Only the rightful owner could silence it.

She repeatedly reminded us of P. T. Barnum's dictum:[19] You could sell anything to anybody if you marketed it right. The adman who thought of making Americans believe they needed underarm deodorant was a visionary. So, too, was the hero who made a success of a new product, Ivory soap. The executives were horrified, Mother told me, that a cake of this stuff floated. Soap wasn't supposed to float. Anyone would be able to tell it was mostly whipped-up air. Then some inspired adman made a leap: Advertise that it floats. Flaunt it. The rest is history.

She respected the rare few who broke through to new ways. "Look," she'd say, "here's an intelligent apron." She called upon us to admire intelligent control knobs and intelligent pan handles, intelligent andirons and picture frames and knife sharpeners. She questioned everything, every pair of scissors, every knitting needle, gardening glove, tape dispenser. Hers was a restless mental vigor that just about ignited the dumb household objects with its force.

Torpid[20] conformity was a kind of sin; it was stupidity itself, the mighty stream against which Mother would never cease to struggle. If you held no minority opinions, or if you failed to risk total ostracism for them daily, the world would be a better place without you. . . .

She simply tried to keep us all awake. And in fact it was always clear to Amy and me, and to Molly when she grew old enough to listen, that if our classmates came to cruelty, just as much as if the neighborhood or the nation came to madness, ==we were expected to take, and would be each separately capable of taking, a stand.==

---

16. The company took the wrong course of action or *tack*.
17. In the Bible, *Samson* is powerful and mighty until an enemy tricks him. Soon Samson is chained up in prison.
18. Here, the *norms* are rules, standards, and accepted practices.
19. In the 1800s, *Barnum* presented many popular entertainments, including what is now the Ringling Brothers and Barnum & Bailey Circus. The actual words of his famous saying *(dictum)* were "There's a sucker born every minute."
20. Something that's *torpid* is dull and lifeless.

The Power of Memory *Why do you think the author used the words "and would be each separately capable of taking" here?*

After You Read

Respond and Think Critically

Respond and Interpret

1. What questions would you like to ask the author about her mother?

2. (a) Why does Dillard's mother enjoy the phrase "Terwilliger bunts one"? (b) What does her mother's reaction to and use of this phrase suggest about her personality?

3. (a) Describe two incidents that illustrate how her mother's unexpected behavior flusters people. (b) Do you think the author's mother cares about the consequences of her actions?

Analyze and Evaluate

4. What does Dillard mean when she says the "spirit of American enterprise never faded in Mother"?

5. (a) Identify places in the selection that illustrate the author's attention to detail. (b) How do these details enhance your appreciation of the selection?

Connect

6. **Big Idea** **The Power of Memory** How does the author's mother compare with your idea of an ideal mother? Explain

7. **Connect to Today** Which of Dillard's mother's opinions or actions would be appropriate or relevant today?

Literary Element Anecdote

Essayists often use **anecdotes** to support their opinions, clarify their ideas, and get a reader's attention.

1. What main point do you think Dillard wanted to make through the anecdotes about her mother?

2. Dillard's mother tested suitors. What insight does this give you into Dillard's relationship with her mother?

Reading Strategy Connect to Personal Experience

Personal experiences guide readers toward insightful analysis of the text. Use your chart from p. 357 to answer the following questions.

1. Which of your personal experiences most helped you relate to Dillard's stories about her mother?

2. Do you think most readers would be able to connect to these stories? Why or why not?

Literature Online

Selection Resources For Selection Quizzes, eFlashcards, and Reading-Writing Connection activities, go to glencoe.com and enter QuickPass code GL59794u2.

Vocabulary Practice

Practice with Synonyms A **synonym** is a word that has the same or nearly the same meaning as another word. With a partner, match each boldfaced vocabulary word below with its synonym. Use a thesaurus or dictionary to check your answers.

1. **tremulously**   a. avoid
2. **eschew**   b. tremblingly
3. **advocate**   c. listlessly
4. **stolid**   d. haughty
                       e. unemotional
                       f. recommend

Writing

Write an Anecdote In one or two paragraphs, write an anecdote about a person you know, in which the person reveals an amusing quirk or some other notable personality trait. Make it clear that the anecdote is not a description of an isolated event but an illustration of the person's habitual behavior.

PART 2

QUESTS AND ENCOUNTERS

Le Château des Pyrénées, 1959. René Magritte. Oil on canvas, 100 x 140 cm. Israel Museum, Jerusalem.

View the Art René Magritte, a Belgian Surrealist painter, used symbols to express the mystery and absurdity of perception and reality. How might this image represent a quest to be undertaken or a thought-provoking encounter?

BIG IDEA

Sometimes what seems like an ordinary day is transformed into something extraordinary. Unexpectedly, your routine is turned into a quest or a meeting is elevated to an encounter. In the nonfiction works in Part 2, you will read essays about ordinary and extraordinary quests and encounters. As you read these texts, ask yourself, When in my life have I been asked to take on the role of the hero?

Learning Objectives

For pages 366–367

In studying this text, you will focus on the following objective:

Literary Study: Analyzing expository and personal essays.

LITERARY FOCUS

Expository and Personal Essay

Why write an essay?

Essayists write for many reasons. They may wish to make their readers think about a new idea or to share an experience with them. Others are motivated by a passion for truth or by a political purpose. In "The Tucson Zoo," Lewis Thomas seeks to share an experience with his readers.

from *The Tucson Zoo*

by Lewis Thomas

I was transfixed. As I now recall it, there was only one sensation in my head: pure elation mixed with amazement at such perfection. Swept off my feet, I floated from one side to the other, swiveling my brain, staring astounded at the beavers, then at the otters. I could hear shouts across my corpus callosum, from one hemisphere to the other. I remember thinking, with what was left in charge of my consciousness, that I wanted no part of the science of beavers and otters; I wanted never to know how they performed their marvels; I wished for no news about the physiology of their breathing, the coordination of their muscles, their vision, their endocrine systems, their digestive tracts. I hoped never to have to think of them as collections of cells. All I asked for was the full hairy complexity, then in front of my eyes, of whole, intact beavers and otters in motion.

366 UNIT 2 NONFICTION

The Essay

An **essay** is a short work of nonfiction that focuses on a single topic. The essays in this part were written to inform or to share experiences with the reader. The excerpt on the previous page by Lewis Thomas is an example of a **personal** essay because he shares his feelings about beavers and otters. Essays are generally categorized as **expository, personal,** and **persuasive.**

The Expository Essay

The word *expository* is derived from of the verb *expose,* which means "to make known or to explain." Whenever you write to inform, to give directions, to explain an idea, or to make something clear, you are writing **exposition.**

> When I was living in an artists' colony in the south of France, some fellow Latin-Americans who taught at the university in Aix-en-Provence invited me to share a home-cooked meal with them. I had been living abroad almost a year then on an NEA grant, subsisting mainly on French bread and lentils so that my money could last longer.
>
> —Sandra Cisneros, **from "The Metamorphosis of the Everyday"**

The Personal Essay

Personal essays are usually informal in their language and tone, and they often contain passages of expository writing. A personal essay often reflects on an incident in the writer's life. The writer may share a life lesson with the reader or perhaps shed light on a time or place long gone. Other personal essays can be written to please oneself or an audience of like-minded readers.

But a personal essay can also be a kind of writing that is common on applications, such as those for college admissions. These essays should be more formal in language and tone. When you write a personal essay for a college application, your audience will be a selection committee.

> None of the social issues of 1957 had a chance of catching my attention that year. All that existed for me was my grandmother, rising from the surf like a Dahomean queen, shaking her head free of her torturous rubber cap, beaming down at me when I finally took the first strokes on my own.
>
> —Jewelle L. Gomez, **from "A Swimming Lesson"**

The Persuasive Essay

In **persuasive** writing, the writer attempts to influence the reader to accept an idea, adopt a point of view, or perform an action. Persuasive writing may appeal to the reader's emotions. However, a type of persuasive writing called **argument** relies solely on reason, logic, and evidence. Many persuasive essays and speeches use a combination of argument and appeal to the emotions. You will encounter persuasive writing and speaking in Part 3.

Quickwrite

Describe a Quest Think of quests and encounters from your own life. Remember times when you were afraid or discouraged but still persevered. Think of encounters that changed you, even if they were with a creature as small as a mouse. Choose one of the prompts from the list below and then write about your quest or encounter for ten minutes without stopping. As you write, tell the sequence of an event in your life and explain its significance to you.

Prompts

Listen...I remember...

I want to tell you...

LITERARY FOCUS

Before You Read

A Swimming Lesson

Meet Jewelle L. Gomez
(born 1948)

"What do I hope to achieve by writing? Changing the world!" Award-winning writer and social activist Jewelle L. Gomez attributes much of her success to her great-grandmother. "My great-grandmother . . . was born on an Indian reservation in Iowa and had been a widow for fifty years. She maintained an intellectual curiosity and graciousness that no amount of education could have created. She formed the basis of much of my intellectual yearnings."

> "My writing flows directly out of the great storytelling that runs in my family."
>
> —Jewelle L. Gomez

In Her Blood Gomez was born in Boston to parents of African American, Native American, and Portuguese ancestry. She lived with her great-grandmother until she was twenty-two years old. Although she lived in poverty as a child and young adult, Gomez was able to attend college. She earned a bachelor's degree from Northeastern University and a master's degree from Columbia University School of Journalism. Before becoming a published writer, Gomez worked as a television production assistant in Boston and as a stage manager for plays in New York City.

Growing up in a family of storytellers, Gomez always knew she wanted to be a writer. But she struggled for many years before discovering a subject that inspired her. A play written by African American poet Ntozake Shange changed her life. The play celebrated ordinary African American women, portraying them as strong and beautiful. Until that point, Gomez had never seen or read anything that described African American women as heroes. Watching Shange's play, she found herself thinking of her grandmother and great-grandmother. What if she wrote about them and other women like them? At that moment, she discovered a subject she wanted to write about for the rest of her life.

Fact and Imagination Growing up during the Civil Rights Movement and the Black Power Movement of the 1960s taught Gomez about social activism. It seemed everyone she knew was trying to make U.S. society a better place for people of color. Since then, Gomez's strong belief in equality—for minorities, women, and other groups—has been the guiding force in her writing and her life. "All oppressions are interconnected," she once said. Themes of equality, power, and responsibility are evident in her essays, plays, poetry, novels, and short stories.

Literature Online

Author Search For more about Jewelle L. Gomez, go to glencoe.com and enter QuickPass code GL59794u2.

Literature and Reading Preview

Connect to the Narrative Essay

What skill do you possess that you learned from a family member or another adult? Discuss this question with a partner. Consider the methods that person used to teach you the skill.

Build Background

This story takes place in the summer of 1957 at Revere Beach in Revere, Massachusetts, five miles north of Boston. Established in 1896, it was the first public beach in the United States. People from the entire Boston metropolitan area were able to reach Revere Beach by public transportation, and they flocked there during the summer months.

Set Purposes for Reading

Big Idea Quests and Encounters

As you read, ask yourself, How does Gomez's encounter with the beach and the ocean teach her more than just swimming?

Literary Element Narrative Essay

A **narrative essay** is a short nonfiction story. Written in the first person, narrative essays usually relate events drawn from the writer's own life, allowing the reader to directly experience the author's perspective. Compared with a formal essay, a narrative essay differs in its use of a light, conversational tone. As you read, ask yourself, Why did Gomez choose the narrative essay form for this essay?

Reading Strategy Connect to Personal Experience

When you **connect to personal experience,** you connect what you read to events or experiences in your own life. This type of connection can help you better understand a story and its characters. As you read "A Swimming Lesson," ask yourself, What aspects of this essay can I connect to my own life?

Tip: Make a Diagram As you read "A Swimming Lesson," write down details about the author's experiences that are similar to yours where the two circles of the Venn diagram intersect.

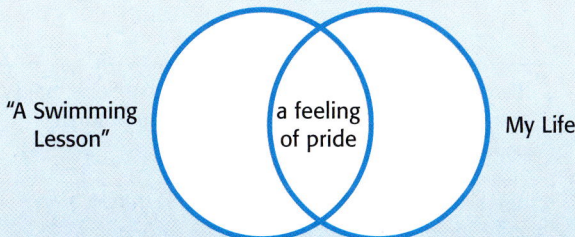

Learning Objectives

For pages 368–374

In studying this text, you will focus on the following objectives:

Literary Study: Analyzing narrative essay.

Reading: Connecting to personal experience.

Vocabulary

benevolence (bə nev′ə ləns) *n.* kindness; generosity; p. 371 *Gabriel's benevolence was apparent in his tireless work for the poor.*

vulnerable (vul′nər ə bəl) *adj.* easily damaged or hurt; p. 371 *Children are vulnerable to injuries.*

mainstream (mān′strēm′) *adj.* representing the most widespread attitudes and values of a society or group; p. 371 *The play was very popular because it appealed to mainstream audiences.*

superfluous (soo pur′floo əs) *adj.* not needed; unnecessary; p. 371 *The student's research paper contained a great deal of superfluous information.*

invaluable (in val′ū ə bəl) *adj.* very great in value; p. 371 *I probably would not have found the building without my father's invaluable directions.*

Tip: Context Clues Use context clues to figure out the meaning, or part of the meaning, of an unfamiliar word.

JEWELLE L. GOMEZ 369

A Swimming Lesson

Jewelle L. Gomez

At nine years old I didn't realize my grandmother, Lydia, and I were doing an extraordinary thing by packing a picnic lunch and riding the elevated train from Roxbury[1] to Revere Beach. It seemed part of the natural rhythm of summer to me. I didn't notice how the subway cars slowly emptied of most of their Black passengers as the train left Boston's urban center and made its way into the Italian and Irish suburban neighborhoods to the north. It didn't seem odd that all of the Black families stayed in one section of the beach and never ventured onto the boardwalk to the concession stands or the rides except in groups.

I do remember Black women perched cautiously on their blankets, tugging desperately at bathing suits rising too high in the rear and complaining about their hair "going back." Not my grandmother, though. She glowed with unashamed athleticism as she waded out, just inside the reach of the waves, and moved along the riptide[2] parallel to the shore. Once submerged, she would load me onto her back and begin her long, tireless strokes. With the waves partially covering us, I followed her rhythm with my short, chubby arms, taking my cues from the powerful movement of her back muscles. We did this again and again until I'd fall off, and she'd catch me and set me upright in the strong New England surf. I was thrilled by the wildness of the ocean and my grandmother's fearless relationship to it. I loved the way she never consulted her mirror after her swim, but always looked as if she had been born to the sea, a kind of aquatic heiress.

---

1. Boston's *Roxbury* neighborhood is southwest of downtown.

2. The *riptide* is the strong surface current that flows rapidly away from shore, returning to sea the water carried landward by waves.

Narrative Essay From this sentence, what do you learn about the relationship between white and African American people at Revere Beach?

Quests and Encounters How does the author's grandmother seem to feel about the ocean?

None of the social issues of 1957 had a chance of catching my attention that year. All that existed for me was my grandmother, rising from the surf like a Dahomean[3] queen, shaking her head free of her torturous rubber cap, beaming down at me when I finally took the first strokes on my own. She towered above me in the sun with a **benevolence** that made simply dwelling in her presence a reward in itself. Under her gaze I felt part of a long line of royalty. I was certain that everyone around us—Black and white—saw and respected her magnificence.

Although I sensed her power, I didn't know the real significance of our summers together as Black females in a white part of town. Unlike winter, when we were protected by the cover of coats, boots and hats, summer left us **vulnerable** and at odds with the expectations for women's bodies—the narrow hips, straight hair, flat stomachs, small feet—handed down from the **mainstream** culture and media. But Lydia never noticed. Her long chorus-girl legs ended in size-nine shoes, and she dared to make herself even bigger as she stretched her broad back and became a woman with a purpose: teaching her granddaughter to swim.

My swimming may have seemed a **superfluous** skill to those who watched our lessons. After all, it was obvious that I wouldn't be doing the backstroke on the Riviera[4] or in the pool of a penthouse spa. Certainly nothing in the popular media at that time made the "great outdoors" seem a hospitable place for Black people. It was a place in which we were meant to feel comfortable at best and hunted at worst. But my prospects for utilizing my skill were irrelevant to me, and when I finally got it right I felt as if I had learned some **invaluable** life secret.

When I reached college and learned the specifics of slavery and the Middle Passage,[5] the magnitude of that "peculiar institution"[6] was almost beyond my comprehension; it was like nothing I'd learned before about the history of my people. It was difficult making a connection with those Africans who had been set adrift from their own land. My initial reaction was "Why didn't the slaves simply jump from the ships while they were still close to shore, and swim home?" The child in me who had learned to survive in water was crushed to find that my ancestors had not necessarily shared this skill. Years later when I visited West Africa and learned of the poisonous, spiny fish that inhabit most of the coastal waters, I understood why

---

3. *Dahomean* (də hō′mā ən) refers to Dahomey, a country in western Africa now called Benin (ben in′). Several kingdoms flourished in this region from the 1300s to the 1600s.

Connect to Personal Experience Think about an adult whom you admire. How do you identify with the author's feelings here?

Vocabulary

benevolence (bə nev′ə ləns) *n.* kindness; generosity

vulnerable (vul′nər ə bəl) *adj.* easily damaged or hurt

mainstream (mān′strēm′) *adj.* representing the most widespread attitudes and values of a society or group

---

4. A popular resort area, the *Riviera* lies along the Mediterranean coasts of Italy and France.
5. The *Middle Passage* was the route followed by slave traders from Africa to the Americas. Through the months-long voyage, slaves suffered filth, disease, abuse, and death.
6. Prior to the Civil War, Southerners referred to slavery as their *peculiar institution*, meaning that they considered it to be vital to their economy and way of life.

Vocabulary

superfluous (soo pur′floo əs) *adj.* not needed; unnecessary

invaluable (in val′ū ə bəl) *adj.* very great in value

Southwold, July Morning. Hugo Grenville (b. 1958). Oil on canvas, 71.1 x 91.4 cm. Private collection.

View the Art In this painting, British artist Hugo Grenville depicts a summer morning at the small English beach town of Southwold. What elements from the essay does this painting bring to mind?

swimming was not the local sport there that it was in New England. And now when I take to the surf, I think of those ancestors and of Lydia.

The sea has been a fearful place for us. It swallowed us whole when there was no escape from the holds of slave ships. For me, to whom the dark fathoms of a tenement hallway were the most unknowable thing so far encountered in my nine years, the ocean was a mystery of terrifying proportions. In teaching me to swim, my grandmother took away my fear. I began to understand something outside myself—the sea—and consequently something about myself as well. I was no longer simply a fat little girl: My body had become a sea vessel—sturdy, enduring, graceful. I had the means to be safe.

Before she died last summer I learned that Lydia herself couldn't really swim that well. As I was splashing, desperately trying to learn the right rhythm—face down, eyes closed, air out, reach, face up, eyes open, air in, reach—Lydia was brushing the ocean's floor with her feet, keeping us both afloat. When she told me, I was stunned. I reached into my memory trying to combine this new information with the Olympic vision I'd always kept of her. At first I'd felt disappointed, tricked, the way I used to feel when I'd learn that a favorite movie star was only five feet tall. But then I quickly realized what an incredible act of bravery it was for her to pass on to me a skill she herself had not quite mastered—a skill that she knew would always bring me a sense of accomplishment. And it was more than just the swimming. It was the ability to stand on any beach anywhere and be proud of my large body, my African hair. It was not fearing the strong muscles in my own back; it was gaining control over my own life.

After You Read

Respond and Think Critically

Respond and Interpret

1. (a) Why do you think Lydia hid the fact that she was walking on the ocean floor from her granddaughter? (b) What is your reaction to Lydia's deception?

2. (a) What is Lydia's attitude toward the sea and toward her own body? (b) How does this attitude seem to affect the author's feelings for her grandmother?

3. (a) According to Gomez, why might observers have considered her swimming lessons a waste of time? (b) Why do you think Gomez views the lessons differently than what she speculates the observers think?

4. (a) What historical information has helped Gomez understand her ancestors' attitude toward the sea? (b) Compare Gomez's own attitude with that of her ancestors.

Analyze and Evaluate

5. (a) What are the "social issues of 1957" to which Gomez refers in this essay? (b) How does her adult view of these issues differ from her childhood view of them?

6. What is the theme, or main idea, of this essay? Explain.

Connect

7. **Big Idea** Quests and Encounters Have you ever conquered a fear, as Gomez did with Lydia's help? Describe your experience.

8. **Connect to the Author** Growing up, Gomez was greatly influenced by the Civil Rights Movement, and her commitment to equal rights for all people is frequently reflected in her work. How does Gomez address issues of inequality in this essay?

Literary Element Narrative Essay

A good narrative essay, or nonfiction story, contains all the elements of any good narrative: characters, setting, and plot. Like short stories, most narrative essays include a central conflict or problem and have a climax and resolution. Many narrative essays are autobiographical, and the author's purpose is to tell about life experiences and life lessons.

1. Compare and contrast Gomez's essay with a short story. Use details from the essay to support your answer.

2. Authors typically write for one or more of the following purposes: to inform, to persuade, to describe, to explain, to entertain. What do you think Gomez's purpose was in writing her essay? Explain.

Review: Anecdote

As you learned on page 357, an **anecdote** is a brief, personal account of a remarkable incident or event. Essayists often use anecdotes to support their opinions, to clarify their ideas, to entertain, or to get the reader's attention.

Group Activity With two other students, share anecdotes from your own lives. After each student has shared an anecdote, discuss how the anecdotes could be used to support opinions or ideas in a narrative essay. Use the chart from "A Swimming Lesson" as a model for your personal examples.

Anecdote	Ideas and Opinions
I loved the way she never consulted her mirror after her swim.	Lydia was comfortable with her appearance.

JEWELLE L. GOMEZ

| **Reading Strategy** | **Connect to Personal Experience** |

Even when a piece of narrative writing describes unfamiliar places and events, it is easy to connect with the universal emotions an author evokes.

1. Find a passage that evokes a particular emotion. How does the narrator feel at that moment?
2. Which parts of the sentence or passage helped to create your emotional reaction?

Vocabulary Practice

Practice with Context Clues Identify the context clues in the following sentences that help you determine the meaning of each bold-faced vocabulary word.

1. One theme of the book was the **benevolence** of the generous king.
2. Homes built on the seashore or on cliffs are **vulnerable** to damage during storms.
3. The teacher made a list of **mainstream** newspapers that included the widely read *Los Angeles Times* and *New York Times*.
4. The director decided to do away with the **superfluous** fourth camera and used three cameras instead.
5. We could not tell the difference between the **invaluable** statue and the trinket from the souvenir stand.

Academic Vocabulary

Lydia's confidence more than **compensated** for her lack of skill.

Compensate is a multiple-meaning word. Among its meanings are *balance, counterbalance, offset, repay,* and *pay.*

For more on academic vocabulary, see pages 52 and 53.

Speaking and Listening

 Literature Groups

Assignment With a small group, discuss whether children can ever become productive members of society without good role models and mentors. Set a discussion goal, and, when you have met it, present your ideas to the class.

Prepare Set a purpose. If your purpose is to reach consensus, agree on what you mean by consensus. If your purpose is to explore different points of view fully, set criteria, such as the following, for meeting that goal.

- compile and consider each group member's personal experience
- compile and consider evidence from "A Swimming Lesson"
- compile and consider evidence from public and historical experience, such as the lives of famous people who were orphans

Discuss Listen respectfully, and ask questions when you do not follow a point or the support for it. Actively evaluate as you listen to each group member's ideas, deciding how well each person's ideas answer questions about the need for role models or mentors. Support your judgment of ideas with specific examples.

Report Have one group member present the consensus, or have several group members explain varying points of view. Each speaker should make eye contact, use gestures effectively, and employ language that will engage the audience.

Evaluate Evaluate your work for these qualities: clarity of content; use of evidence; verbal presentation skills, including word choice and syntax; and nonverbal skills, including gestures.

LOG ON ▶ **Literature** Online

Selection Resources For Selection Quizzes, eFlashcards, and Reading-Writing Connection activities, go to glencoe.com and enter QuickPass code GL59794u2.

Before You Read

The Tucson Zoo

Meet Lewis Thomas
(1913–1993)

Award-winning author Lewis Thomas was a renowned physician and research biologist. He taught at some of the top medical schools in the United States. As a writer, he established a reputation as a master of the short essay. In his inquisitive musings on nature, science, technology, and other subjects, he celebrated the mystery and marvel of life.

> "We are built to make mistakes, coded for error."
>
> —Lewis Thomas

Medical Background The son of a doctor and a nurse, Thomas had an early interest in the medical profession. He enrolled at Princeton University at fifteen and graduated when he was only nineteen years old. He entered Harvard Medical School at an exciting and dynamic time for the field of medicine—clinical science and antibiotics were both in the early stages of development. He graduated from medical school at the age of twenty-three.

During the course of his medical career, he worked at many U.S. universities, including New York University, Yale, Johns Hopkins, Tulane, and the University of Minnesota. His roles at these institutions varied. Over the years, he worked as a researcher, a teacher, an administrator, and a pediatrician, among other specialties. He also served in the U.S. Navy Medical Corps.

Writer and Researcher Thomas's interest in writing began almost as early as his interest in science and medicine. He developed an interest in poetry while at Princeton, and after medical school, during his internship at Boston City Hospital, he supported himself in part by publishing poems in various magazines, including *Harper's Bazaar* and the *Saturday Evening Post*. Before becoming a respected prose writer, he began writing his essays simply "for fun."

Popular Appeal The interest and wonder that Thomas brought to both science and life was at the heart of his appeal to a wide audience. He combined common sense, daily observations, and detailed scientific knowledge in his writing. Thomas's philosophy of life and science could be symbolized by the concept of symbiosis, a relationship between organisms that benefits both. As one writer explained, "Thomas's scientific training enabled him to show how human biology is . . . linked to the biology of the planet as a whole."

Thomas's first book, *The Lives of a Cell: Notes of a Biology Watcher*, is a collection of essays originally published in his column in the *New England Journal of Medicine*. In 1975 *The Lives of a Cell: Notes of a Biology Watcher* won a National Book Award. Thomas's other works include *The Medusa and the Snail* (1979), *The Youngest Science* (1983), *Late Night Thoughts on Listening to Mahler's Ninth Symphony* (1983), and *The Fragile Species* (1992).

Author Search For more about Lewis Thomas, go to glencoe.com and enter QuickPass code GL59794u2.

Literature and Reading Preview

Connect to the Essay
Do you act on instinct, or do you analyze your reactions and emotions? Discuss this question with a partner.

Build Background
The cortex of the brain has two hemispheres, or sides. The left side is analytical; it allows one to recognize the parts, or details, of a whole. It cannot, however, combine the parts to let one see the whole. The right hemisphere is creative. It allows one to see the whole of something from its parts. The *corpus callosum*, which Thomas refers to in his essay, is an arch of nervous tissue that bridges the two hemispheres and allows them to communicate with each other.

Set Purposes for Reading

Big Idea Quests and Encounters

As you read, ask yourself, How does Thomas explore his encounter and interpret it as a journey of human discovery?

Literary Element Structure

Structure refers to the particular order or pattern a writer uses to present ideas. Narratives commonly follow a chronological order, while the structure of persuasive or expository writing may vary. As you read, ask yourself, How does Thomas structure his essay?

Reading Strategy Draw Conclusions About Meaning

When readers **draw conclusions about meaning,** they are actively thinking about and interpreting content while they are reading. As you read, ask yourself, What conclusions can I draw from this story?

Tip: Ask and Answer Questions Asking and then answering questions while you read can help you draw conclusions.

Question	Answer
Why does Thomas say that he "wanted no part of the science of beavers and otters"?	He is so enthralled by their antics that he does not want to analyze their behaviors.

Learning Objectives
For pages 375–381

In studying this text, you will focus on the following objectives:

Literary Study: Analyzing structure.

Reading: Drawing conclusions about meaning.

Vocabulary

elation (i lā′shən) *n.* a feeling of great joy; ecstasy; p. 377 *The whole team experienced elation when Mara scored the winning goal.*

intact (in takt′) *adj.* entire; untouched, uninjured, and having all parts; p. 378 *She dropped the egg, but somehow it remained intact.*

exultation (eg′zul tā′shən) *n.* joy; jubilation; p. 378 *The woman experienced exultation when her lost child was found.*

debasement (di bās′mənt) *n.* the state of being lowered in quality, value, or character; degradation; p. 379 *Those collectibles have suffered a debasement in their value recently.*

attribute (at′rə būt′) *n.* a quality or characteristic of a person or thing; p. 379 *Honesty is a good attribute to possess.*

The Tucson Zoo

Lewis Thomas

Science gets most of its information by the process of reductionism,[1] exploring the details, then the details of the details, until all the smallest bits of the structure, or the smallest parts of the mechanism, are laid out for counting and scrutiny. Only when this is done can the investigation be extended to encompass the whole organism or the entire system. So we say.

Sometimes it seems that we take a loss, working this way. Much of today's public anxiety about science is the apprehension that we may forever be overlooking the whole by an endless, obsessive preoccupation with the parts. I had a brief, personal experience of this misgiving one afternoon in Tucson, where I had time on my hands and visited the zoo, just outside the city. The designers there have cut a deep pathway between two small artificial ponds, walled by clear glass, so when you stand in the center of the path you can look into the depths of each pool, and at the same time you can regard the surface. In one pool, on the right side of the path, is a family of otters; on the other side, a family of beavers. Within just a few feet from your face, on either side, beavers and otters are at play, underwater and on the surface, swimming toward your face and then away, more filled with life than any creatures I have ever seen before, in all my days. Except for the glass, you could reach across and touch them.

I was transfixed. As I now recall it, there was only one sensation in my head: pure **elation** mixed with amazement at such perfection. Swept off my feet, I floated from one side to the other, swiveling my brain, staring astounded at the beavers, then at the otters. I could hear shouts across my corpus

---

1. *Reductionism* is a method of explaining complex processes or structures by reducing them to more basic principles or units.

Structure *How does this sentence change the essay's structure?*

Vocabulary

elation (i lā′shən) *n.* a feeling of great joy; ecstasy

callosum, from one hemisphere to the other. I remember thinking, with what was left in charge of my consciousness, that I wanted no part of the science of beavers and otters; I wanted never to know how they performed their marvels; I wished for no news about the physiology[2] of their breathing, the coordination of their muscles, their vision, their endocrine systems,[3] their digestive tracts. I hoped never to have to think of them as collections of cells. All I asked for was the full hairy complexity, then in front of my eyes, of whole, **intact** beavers and otters in motion.

It lasted, I regret to say, for only a few minutes, and then I was back in the late twentieth century, reductionist as ever, wondering about the details by force of habit, but not, this time, the details of otters and beavers. Instead, me. Something worth remembering had happened in my mind, I was certain of that; I would have put it somewhere in the brain stem; maybe this was my limbic system[4] at work. I became a behavioral scientist, an experimental psychologist, an ethologist,[5] and in the instant I lost all the wonder and the sense of being overwhelmed. I was flattened.

But I came away from the zoo with something, a piece of news about myself: I am coded, somehow, for otters and beavers. I exhibit instinctive behavior in their presence, when they are displayed close at hand behind glass, simultaneously below water and at the surface. I have receptors[6] for this display. Beavers and otters possess a "releaser" for me, in the terminology of ethology, and the releasing was my experience. What was released? Behavior. What behavior? Standing, swiveling flabbergasted, feeling **exultation** and a rush of friendship. I could not, as the result of the transaction, tell you anything more about beavers and otters than you already know. I learned nothing new about them. Only about me, and I suspect also about you, maybe about human beings at large: we are endowed with genes which code out our reaction to beavers and otters, maybe our reaction to each other as well. We are stamped with stereotyped, unalterable patterns of response, ready to be released. And the behavior released in us, by such

---

2. *Physiology* is the branch of biology that studies the functions of living organisms and their parts.
3. The *endocrine system* consists of glands that secrete hormones into the bloodstream, affecting such bodily processes as growth and sexual development.

Draw Conclusions About Meaning What does Thomas come to realize by this statement?

Vocabulary

intact (in takt′) *adj.* entire; untouched, uninjured, and having all parts

---

4. The *limbic system* is a region of the brain involved in the control of emotions and some types of behavior.
5. *Ethology* (eth ol′ ə jē) is the study of animal behavior, including instinctive, or inherited, behavior.
6. *Receptor* refers to a sensory nerve cell that responds to a stimulus in the environment and sends a message to the brain.

Draw Conclusions About Meaning Why does Thomas feel flattened at this moment?

Vocabulary

exultation (eg′zul tā′shən) *n.* joy; jubilation

confrontations, is, essentially, a surprised affection. It is compulsory behavior and we can avoid it only by straining with the full power of our conscious minds, making up conscious excuses all the way. Left to ourselves, mechanistic and autonomic,[7] we hanker for friends.

Everyone says, stay away from ants. They have no lessons for us; they are crazy little instruments, inhuman, incapable of controlling themselves, lacking manners, lacking souls. When they are massed together, all touching, exchanging bits of information held in their jaws like memoranda, they become a single animal. Look out for that. It is a **debasement**, a loss of individuality, a violation of human nature, an unnatural act.

Sometimes people argue this point of view seriously and with deep thought. Be individuals, solitary and selfish, is the message. Altruism,[8] a jargon word for what used to be called love, is worse than weakness, it is sin, a violation of nature. Be separate. Do not be a social animal. But this is a hard argument to make convincingly when you have to depend on language to make it. You have to print up leaflets or publish books and get them bought and sent around, you have to turn up on television and catch the attention of millions of other human beings all at once, and then you have to say to all of them, all at once, all collected and paying attention: be solitary; do not depend on each other. You can't do this and keep a straight face.

Maybe altruism is our most primitive **attribute,** out of reach, beyond our control. Or perhaps it is immediately at hand, waiting to be released, disguised now, in our kind of civilization, as affection or friendship or attachment. I don't see why it should be unreasonable for all human beings to have strands of DNA coiled up in chromosomes, coding out instincts for usefulness and helpfulness. Usefulness may turn out to be the hardest test of fitness for survival, more important than aggression, more effective, in the long run, than grabbiness. If this is the sort of information biological science holds for the future, applying to us as well as to ants, then I am all for science.

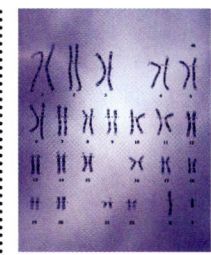

Visual Vocabulary
Chromosomes are strands of DNA and proteins in the nucleus of cells. DNA carries the genes that pass on hereditary information from parent to child.

One thing I'd like to know most of all: when those ants have made the Hill, and are all there, touching and exchanging, and the whole mass begins to behave like a single huge creature, and *thinks,* what on earth is that thought? And while you're at it, I'd like to know a second thing: when it happens, does any single ant know about it? Does his hair stand on end?

---

7. In psychology, *compulsory* means "arising from an irresistible, illogical urge." Here, *mechanistic* means physically or biologically determined, and *autonomic* means involuntary and spontaneous.
8. In ethology, *altruism* is an animal's self-sacrificing behavior that benefits another animal or group of animals. Similarly, in humans, the term means "unselfish concern for others."

Quests and Encounters *How does the encounter with beavers and otters lead Thomas to this conclusion?*

Vocabulary
debasement (di bās′mənt) *n.* the state of being lowered in quality, value, or character; degradation

Draw Conclusions About Meaning *Explain what you think the author means in this sentence.*

Vocabulary
attribute (at′rə būt′) *n.* a quality or characteristic of a person or thing

After You Read

Respond and Think Critically

Respond and Interpret

1. Were you surprised by Thomas's conclusions about people? Why or why not?

2. (a) According to the process of reductionism, when can an entire organism be investigated? (b) How does this process contrast with the author's experience with the beavers and otters?

3. (a) According to Thomas, why does everyone say to "stay away from ants"? (b) What message do some people learn from ants?

4. (a) What ideas does Thomas present about altruism? (b) What do you think Thomas means in his final reference to ants?

Analyze and Evaluate

5. In your opinion, what was Thomas's purpose?

6. Do you agree with the conclusions that Thomas draws about instinctive behavior in people? Explain.

7. In your opinion, is Thomas a reductionist? Explain your answer and cite passages from the text.

Connect

8. **Big Idea** Quests and Encounters (a) What does this essay suggest that new encounters can do for a person? (b) Would you say that Thomas is on a quest? If so, what is his quest?

9. **Connect to the Author** Thomas had a background in both science and poetry. Can you find places in this essay where scientific ideas overlap with more poetic ideas? How might the two fields complement each other?

Literary Element Structure

All expository texts have a **structure,** or organizational pattern. Writers can organize or order their ideas in expository writing in a variety of ways. Here are three examples. A writer can use a structure following a pattern of **cause and effect** to present an event or occurrence and explain why it happened. With a **problem/solution** structure, the writer describes a problem and offers a solution. The writer using a **comparison/contrast** structure explains the differences and similarities of something to allow the reader to compare.

1. How would you describe the essay's structure? Cite evidence from the selection to support your choice.

2. Can you think of an alternative structure for this essay? Do you think your proposed alternative would be more or less effective? Explain.

Review: Voice

As you learned on pages 184–185, **voice** in a literary work is the distinctive use of language that conveys the personality of the writer or narrator to the reader. Voice is determined by elements of style, such as word choice and tone. A unique aspect of Thomas's voice is that he writes as both a learned scientist and an animal lover.

Partner Activity With a classmate, analyze this dual aspect of Thomas's voice by focusing on his word choice. Use a two-column chart like the one below. In the first column, list a word or phrase that conveys Thomas's voice. In the next column, show the aspect of Thomas's voice the words reveal.

Word Choice	Voice
p. 377 elation	joy of an animal lover
p. 378 full hairy complexity	
p. 378 I was flattened.	

Reading Strategy Draw Conclusions About Meaning

SAT Skills Practice

1. In the paragraph beginning "Everyone says, stay away from ants" (page 379) Thomas is

   (A) making the point that human being are not comparable to ants
   (B) summarizing an argument that he will later refute
   (C) pointing out the importance of social activity in all creatures
   (D) establishing the similarity between ants and otters
   (E) arguing that ants are superior to people

Vocabulary Practice

Practice with Antonyms An antonym is a word that has a meaning opposite to that of another word. With a partner, brainstorm three antonyms for each boldfaced vocabulary word below. Be prepared to explain why you chose your words.

elation   intact   exultation   debasement

EXAMPLE:
ambiguous
Antonyms: *clear, certain, transparent*
Sample explanation: An explanation that is clear is easy to understand or interpret, but one that is ambiguous has different possible interpretations.

Academic Vocabulary

Thomas uses his experience at the Tucson Zoo to reflect on **mental** *processes.*

Mental is an academic word. A person refers to a friend as more **mental** than emotional or to a word problem or math puzzle as a **mental** challenge. Answer this question: In what area is your **mental** capacity greatest? Give examples to support your answer.

For more on academic vocabulary, see pages 52 and 53.

Speaking and Listening

 Debate

Assignment Thomas argues against reductionism in our responses to life. Instead, he favors "big picture" thinking. With a partner, debate which represents a preferable way to learn—an emphasis on the whole or an emphasis on parts.

Prepare Each person should begin by taking a side, formulating a thesis or position, and marshaling evidence to support that position. Support might consist of examples, statistics, testimony, or other facts. All support should be credible and relevant.

Debate A debate requires you to inform and persuade at the same time. You may need to use technical language to inform; on the other hand, you should also incorporate informal language where it is persuasive. Present your thesis first; then present each reason with ample facts that inform and persuade. Consider saving your most persuasive reason or clincher evidence for last. Include the following appeals:

Appeal	Example in Support of My Thesis
Logical—uses facts, statistics, and other solid evidence to make or support claims	
Emotional—presents information and ideas that target emotions	
Ethical—addresses the listener's values and morals	

Evaluate Write one paragraph evaluating your own participation and skills in the debate. Use the checklist on page 883 to help in your evaluation.

 Literature Online

Selection Resources For Selection Quizzes, eFlashcards, and Reading-Writing Connection activities, go to glencoe.com and enter QuickPass code GL59794u2.

Before You Read
Straw into Gold: The Metamorphosis of the Everyday

Meet **Sandra Cisneros**
(born 1954)

Sandra Cisneros is one of the most distinctive voices in American literature today. Born in Chicago to a Mexican American mother and a Mexican father, Cisneros spent her childhood living uncomfortably between two worlds. The family frequently traveled to Mexico for extended periods of time. Each time they returned to the United States, the family would settle in a new location and at a new school in Chicago's *barrios*. The frequent moves made it difficult for Cisneros to make friends. Being the only girl in a family of brothers did not help either, as she was often left out and overlooked.

> "You can't erase what you know. You can't forget who you are."
>
> —Sandra Cisneros

Because she was shy, she was often lonely. But, Cisneros writes, "that loneliness . . . was good for a would-be writer—it allowed me time to think and think, to imagine, to read and prepare myself." In high school, a teacher helped Cisneros nurture her love of writing. After high school, Cisneros received a scholarship to Loyola University in Chicago. She graduated in 1976 with a bachelor's degree in English and went on to the prestigious University of Iowa Writers' Workshop. At the Writers' Workshop, Cisneros felt keenly aware of her status as an outsider.

Finding Her Voice Yet, it was at the Iowa Writers' Workshop that Cisneros found her voice. She realized that the very thing she had tried to escape—the shame and separation of being different—made her unique. She knew then that her role as a writer was to depict the loneliness, isolation, tragedies, and triumphs of the outsider.

Mango Street In 1982 Cisneros received her first National Endowment for the Arts grant, which allowed her to write full-time. Two years later, she published her breakthrough work, *The House on Mango Street*, a series of vignettes about a young girl, Esperanza, growing up in a Chicago *barrio*. The stories, a blend of fiction and poetry, echo Cisneros's own youth and her yearning to make sense of her life in relation to her surroundings.

After the success of her first work, Cisneros went on to publish other works of fiction: *Woman Hollering Creek and Other Stories* (1991) and *Caramelo* (2002). She has also published two collections of poetry, including *My Wicked Wicked Ways* (1987).

In 1995 Cisneros received a MacArthur Fellowship—a prestigious monetary award known as the "genius grant." The award is an official acknowledgement of her permanent status in the American literary world.

Author Search For more about Sandra Cisneros, go to glencoe.com and enter QuickPass code GL59794u2.

Literature and Reading Preview

Connect to the Essay
Does thinking about the past help you understand the person you are today? Freewrite for a few minutes about an event from the past that has shaped you as a person.

Build Background
The National Endowment for the Arts (NEA) was created by Congress in 1965 and is an independent agency of the federal government. Artists of every medium, from dance to literature, apply to the NEA for grant money they can use to support themselves while pursuing artistic endeavors.

Set Purposes for Reading

Big Idea Quests and Encounters

As you read this essay, ask yourself, How does Cisneros connect everyday life to the idea of the heroic quest?

Literary Element Thesis

The **thesis** is the main idea in a work of nonfiction. The thesis may be stated directly or implied by the details and examples in the work. Recognizing a writer's thesis is vital to an understanding of his or her purpose in writing the selection. As you read, ask yourself, What is Cisneros's main idea, or thesis, in this essay?

Reading Strategy Analyze Text Structure

Text structure is the particular order or pattern a writer uses to present ideas. A reflective essay is an example of narrative writing. Narratives commonly follow a chronological order, while the structure of persuasive or expository writing may vary. As you read, ask yourself, How does Cisneros structure her essay?

Tip: Ask Questions To analyze text structure, ask yourself questions as you read. Use a chart to record your questions and the answers you uncover as you read.

Question	Answer
Are the ideas presented in chronological order?	No, they are not in time order.

Learning Objectives

For pages 382–390
In studying this text, you will focus on the following objectives:

Literary Study: Analyzing thesis.

Reading: Analyzing text structure.

Vocabulary

intuitively (in tōō′ə tiv lē) *adv.* knowing, sensing, or understanding instinctively; p. 385 *The stand-up comedian intuitively knew what not to joke about.*

taboo (ta bōō′) *n.* a cultural or social rule forbidding something; p. 385 *Speaking disrespectfully to one's elders is a social taboo.*

Tip: Analogies Remember that writers sometimes extend analogies. That is, they create a comparison and then elaborate or develop it by exploring qualities and characteristics that work within the same comparison.

SANDRA CISNEROS 383

STRAW INTO GOLD

The Metamorphosis of the Everyday

Sandra Cisneros

Women Making Tortilla Dough. Diego Rivera. Fresco. Court of Labour. Ministry of Public Information, Mexico.

When I was living in an artists' colony in the south of France, some fellow Latin-Americans who taught at the university in Aix-en-Provence invited me to share a home-cooked meal with them. I had been living abroad almost a year then on an NEA grant, subsisting mainly on French bread and lentils so that my money could last longer. So when the invitation to dinner arrived, I accepted without hesitation. Especially since they had promised Mexican food.

What I didn't realize when they made this invitation was that I was supposed to be involved in preparing the meal. I guess they assumed I knew how to cook Mexican food because I am Mexican. They wanted specifically tortillas, though I'd never made a tortilla in my life.

It's true I had witnessed my mother rolling the little armies of dough into perfect circles, but my mother's family is from Guanajuato; they are *provincianos*, country folk. They only know how to make flour tortillas. My father's family, on the other hand, is *chilango*[1] from Mexico City. We ate corn tortillas but we didn't make them. Someone was sent to the corner tortilleria to buy some. I'd never seen anybody make corn tortillas. Ever.

---

1. *Chilango* (chē län′ gō) is a Mexican slang term that means "native to Mexico City."

Somehow my Latino hosts had gotten a hold of a packet of corn flour, and this is what they tossed my way with orders to produce tortillas. *Así como sea.* Any ol' way, they said and went back to their cooking.

Why did I feel like the woman in the fairy tale who was locked in a room and ordered to spin straw into gold? I had the same sick feeling when I was required to write my critical essay for the MFA[2] exam—the only piece of noncreative writing necessary in order to get my graduate degree. How was I to start? There were rules involved here, unlike writing a poem or story, which I did **intuitively**. There was a step by step process needed and I had better know it. I felt as if making tortillas—or writing a critical paper, for that matter—were tasks so impossible I wanted to break down into tears.

Somehow though, I managed to make tortillas—crooked and burnt, but edible nonetheless. My hosts were absolutely ignorant when it came to Mexican food; they thought my tortillas were delicious. (I'm glad my mama wasn't there.) Thinking back and looking at an old photograph documenting the three of us consuming those lopsided circles I am amazed. Just as I am amazed I could finish my MFA exam.

I've managed to do a lot of things in my life I didn't think I was capable of and which many others didn't think I was capable of either. Especially because I am a woman, a Latina, an only daughter in a family of six men. My father would've liked to have seen me married long ago. In our culture men and women don't leave their father's house except by way of marriage. I crossed my father's threshold with nothing carrying me but my own two feet. A woman whom no one came for and no one chased away.

To make matters worse, I left before any of my six brothers had ventured away from home. I broke a terrible **taboo**. Somehow, looking back at photos of myself as a child, I wonder if I was aware of having begun already my own quiet war.

I like to think that somehow my family, my Mexicanness, my poverty, all had something to do with shaping me into a writer. I like to think my parents were preparing me all along for my life as an artist even though they didn't know it. From my father I inherited a love of wandering. He was born in Mexico City but as a young man he traveled into the U.S. vagabonding. He eventually was drafted and thus became a citizen. Some of the stories he has told about his first months in the U.S. with little or no English surface in my stories in *The House on Mango Street* as well as others I have in mind to write in the future. From him I inherited a sappy heart. (He still cries when he watches Mexican soaps—especially if they deal with children who have forsaken their parents.)

---

2. **MFA** stands for Master of Fine Arts—an academic degree.

Quests and Encounters Why does Cisneros use this particular analogy?

Analyze Text Structure Explain how the essay has been structured so far.

Vocabulary

intuitively (in tōō′ ə tiv lē) *adv.* knowing, sensing, or understanding instinctively

Thesis At this point in the essay, how do you think that this statement might relate to Cisneros's main idea?

Vocabulary

taboo (ta bōō′) *n.* a cultural or social rule forbidding something

South Side Street, Franklin McMahon.

View the Art McMahon depicts a streetscape with vacant buildings on Chicago's South Side. How does the economic situation in the painting relate to Cisneros's situation in this essay?

My mother was born like me—in Chicago but of Mexican descent. It would be her tough streetwise voice that would haunt all my stories and poems. An amazing woman who loves to draw and read books and can sing an opera. A smart cookie.

When I was a little girl we traveled to Mexico City so much I thought my grandparents' house on La Fortuna, number 12, was home. It was the only constant in our nomadic ramblings from one Chicago flat to another. The house on Destiny Street, number 12, in the colonia Tepeyac would be perhaps the only home I knew, and that nostalgia for a home would be a theme that would obsess me.

My brothers also figured greatly in my art. Especially the older two; I grew up in their shadows. Henry, the second oldest and my favorite, appears often in poems I have written and in stories which at times only borrow his nickname, Kiki. He played a major role in my childhood. We were bunk-bed mates. We were co-conspirators. We were pals. Until my oldest brother came back from studying in Mexico and left me odd woman out for always.

What would my teachers say if they knew I was a writer now? Who would've guessed it? I wasn't a very bright student. I didn't much like school because we moved so much and I was always new and funny looking. In my fifth-grade report card I have nothing but an avalanche of C's and D's, but I don't remember being that stupid. I was good at art and I read plenty of library books and Kiki laughed at all my jokes. At home I was fine, but at school I never opened my mouth except when the teacher called on me.

When I think of how I see myself it would have to be at age eleven. I know I'm thirty-two on the outside, but inside I'm eleven. I'm the girl in the picture with skinny arms and a crumpled skirt and crooked hair. I didn't like school because all they saw was the outside me. School was lots of rules and sitting with your hands folded and being very afraid all the time. I liked looking out the window and thinking. I liked staring at the girl across the way writing her name over and over again in red ink. I wondered why the boy with the dirty collar in front of me didn't have a mama who took better care of him.

Analyze Text Structure How does the essay's middle section differ from the beginning?

I think my mama and papa did the best they could to keep us warm and clean and never hungry. We had birthday and graduation parties and things like that, but there was another hunger that had to be fed. There was a hunger I didn't even have a name for. Was this when I began writing?

In 1966 we moved into a house, a real one, our first real home. This meant we didn't have to change schools and be the new kids on the block every couple of years. We could make friends and not be afraid we'd have to say goodbye to them and start all over. My brothers and the flock of boys they brought home would become important characters eventually for my stories—Louie and his cousins, Meme Ortiz and his dog with two names, one in English and one in Spanish.

My mother flourished in her own home. She took books out of the library and taught herself to garden—to grow flowers so envied we had to put a lock on the gate to keep out the midnight flower thieves. My mother has never quit gardening.

This was the period in my life, that slippery age when you are both child and woman and neither, I was to record in *The House on Mango Street.* I was still shy. I was a girl who couldn't come out of her shell.

How was I to know I would be recording and documenting the women who sat their sadness on an elbow and stared out a window? It would be the city streets of Chicago I would later record, as seen through a child's eyes.

I've done all kinds of things I didn't think I could do since then. I've gone to a prestigious university, studied with famous writers, and taken an MFA degree. I've taught poetry in schools in Illinois and Texas. I've gotten an NEA grant and run away with it as far as my courage would take me. I've seen the bleached and bitter mountains of the Peloponnesus.[3] I've lived on an island. I've been to Venice twice. I've lived in Yugoslavia. I've been to the famous Nice[4] flower market behind the opera house. I've lived in a village in the pre-Alps and witnessed the daily parade of promenaders.

I've moved since Europe to the strange and wonderful country of Texas, land of Polaroid-blue skies and big bugs. I met a mayor with my last name. I met famous Chicana and Chicano artists and writers and *políticos.*[5]

Texas is another chapter in my life. It brought with it the Dobie-Paisano Fellowship, a six-month residency on a 265-acre ranch. But most important, Texas brought Mexico back to me.

In the days when I would sit at my favorite people-watching spot, the snakey Woolworth's counter across the street from the Alamo[6] (the Woolworth's which has since been torn down to make way for progress), I couldn't think of anything else I'd rather be than a writer. I've traveled and lectured from Cape Cod to San Francisco, to Spain, Yugoslavia, Greece, Mexico, France, Italy, and now today to Texas. Along the way there has been straw for the taking. With a little imagination, it can be spun into gold.

---

3. *Peloponnesus* (pĕl′ə pə nē′səs) is the peninsula forming the southern part of mainland Greece.
4. *Nice* (nēs) is a port city in southern France.
5. *Políticos* (pô lē′ tē kôs) means "politicians."
6. The *Alamo* is a mission chapel in San Antonio, Texas. It was the site of a famous battle in Texas's war for independence from Mexico.

Quests and Encounters In what ways does Texas bring Mexico back to Cisneros?

Thesis What do straw and gold represent for Cisneros?

After You Read

Respond and Think Critically

Respond and Interpret

1. (a) How does Cisneros show that her childhood relates to her experiences as a writer? (b) What things in Cisneros's experience of life are similar to your own?

2. (a) How was Cisneros's departure from her family home atypical of her culture? (b) What does this suggest about Cisneros as a person?

3. (a) How does Cisneros describe her mother? (b) What does this description suggest about how Cisneros feels about her mother?

4. (a) Why did Cisneros not enjoy school? (b) What do her memories of school reveal about the kind of child Cisneros was?

Analyze and Evaluate

5. How is Cisneros's difficult experience trying to make corn tortillas an effective analogy for her life?

6. (a) How would you describe Cisneros's narrative style? (b) Did her style capture your attention? Why?

7. Explain how Cisneros succeeds in creating a nostalgic atmosphere in her essay.

Connect

8. **Big Idea** Quests and Encounters Cisneros goes on a quest to trace her own origins as a writer. In what ways does her essay help her succeed on this quest?

9. **Connect to the Author** Cisneros spent much of her childhood and her life as an outsider. Where in this narrative does Cisneros feel like an outsider? Where does she appear to be an insider?

You're the Critic

Style and Craft

Critics and fellow writers have praised Sandra Cisneros for her evocative and detailed language. In her fiction, Cisneros weaves Spanish phrases, poetry, interior monologue, images, and engaging sensory details into the story to enliven her narrative structure. Read the two excerpts of literary criticism about Cisneros's writing style below.

> *"Cisneros' finest skill is her descriptive language. It conjures up gorgeous visions of colors and forms."*
> —Carol Memmott, USA Today

> *"Sandra Cisneros is one of the most brilliant of today's young writers. Her work is sensitive, alert, nuanceful…rich with music and picture."*
> —Gwendolyn Brooks

Partner Activity Discuss and answer the following questions with a partner.

1. Could either of the excerpts apply to "Straw Into Gold: The Metamorphosis of the Everyday"? Why or why not?

2. Describe Cisneros's writing style and language in "Straw Into Gold: The Metamorphosis of the Everyday." Use the excerpts above as models.

Literary Element: Thesis

SAT Skills Practice

1. Which statement best expresses the thesis of Cisneros's essay?

   (A) Lonely people often have a special insight into the lives of others.
   (B) Latina women are as capable of succeeding as the men in their families.
   (C) Difficult childhoods are the source of most great writing.
   (D) Obstacles can be surmounted through hard work and determination.
   (E) Strong families help create strong individuals.

2. How does the essay's title relate to the author's anecdote of how she made tortillas?

   (A) Life is very like a fairy tale.
   (B) We are sometimes asked to accomplish impossible tasks.
   (C) To the hungry person, tortillas are as valuable as gold.
   (D) Foolish people cannot tell straw from gold or a good tortilla from a bad one.
   (E) We can often achieve what at first seems impossible.

Review: Author's Purpose

As you learned on page 87, the **author's purpose** is the author's reason for writing a literary work. Authors often write to achieve one or more of the following purposes: to persuade, to inform, to explain, to entertain, or to describe.

Group Activity With a small group of classmates, discuss this essay, focusing on Cisneros's purpose or purposes for writing. Does she have one main purpose? If so, what is it? Also, identify any other purposes you may find in the essay. Be sure to cite examples from the text to support your ideas.

Literature Online

Selection Resources For Selection Quizzes, eFlashcards, and Reading-Writing Connection activities, go to glencoe.com and enter QuickPass code GL59794u2.

Reading Strategy: Analyze Text Structure

Text structure is a crucial component of a piece of writing because it helps the author guide readers through a story or essay. The text structure can help writers convey their messages. Think about what Cisneros's message is in this essay, and how the text structure she created helps convey her message. Refer to the chart that you created on page 383 and that you completed as you read. Use the chart to help you answer the following questions.

1. How does Cisneros organize "Straw into Gold: The Metamorphosis of the Everyday"?

2. One could describe the essay the following way: "The words are the straw, the essay is the gold, and the text structure is the loom." Do you agree or disagree with this analysis of the essay?

Vocabulary Practice

Practice with Analogies Choose the word that best completes each analogy.

1. exit : departure :: intuitively :
   a. instinctively   b. intelligently   c. inaccurately

2. requirement : demands :: taboo :
   a. describes   b. recommends   c. forbids

Academic Vocabulary

Cisneros was faced with seemingly impossible tasks; **nevertheless,** she executed them.

Nevertheless is an academic word. More familiar words that are similar in meaning are *however, still,* and *yet.* Complete this sentence: The weather looks good for our picnic on Saturday; **nevertheless,** _____.

For more on academic vocabulary, see pages 52 and 53.

Respond Through Writing

Reflective Essay: Explore Theme

Writing Task In this essay, Cisneros reflects on how her past has shaped who she is today. She discovers a pattern of turning straw into gold and presents a theme of overcoming obstacles. Write a reflective essay in which you explore your own past and how it has made you who you are today. Like Cisneros, use your essay to present a theme about how you have chosen to live your life.

Understand the Task A **theme** is the central message about life in an essay or a work of literature. Like a thesis, a theme is a controlling idea in a work. Unlike a thesis, a theme is almost always unstated. Instead, the reader infers the theme by thinking about the overall meaning conveyed by the work.

Prewrite First, list people, events, and personal experiences that have helped shape you. Next, write down ideas about how each has helped to make you who you are today. Then look for themes in your notes. Do you see a pattern of beating the odds, fighting back, letting things go, or taking chances? That pattern may be the theme of your life story.

Draft As you describe your past, connect your experiences to an abstract idea, or an analogy, such as spinning straw into gold. You might also, like Cisneros, compare your story with a fairy tale, myth, or fable. Structure each paragraph to reveal the theme of your life by means of analogy. You might use this order of information or Cisneros's example to guide you:

Elements of a Reflective Paragraph
    Event/Experience: I was called upon to make tortillas.
    Details: Impossible task; I had never done it before; I made the tortillas, though they were nothing to be proud of.
    Reflections/Connections/Analogy: It was like being asked to spin straw into gold.
    Theme, stated or implied by details: I overcame the obstacle; I did it somehow.

Revise Exchange essays with a partner. Determine whether your partner's essay clearly shows how the past has influenced his or her life. Also, identify the essay's theme. Weigh the feedback you receive to determine how best to revise your essay.

Edit and Proofread Proofread your paper, correcting any errors in grammar, spelling, and punctuation. Use the Grammar Tip in the side column to help you with using dashes.

Learning Objectives

For page 390
In this assignment, you will focus on the following objectives:

Writing: Writing a reflective essay.

Grammar: Using dashes.

Grammar Tip

Dashes

Dashes are often used in personal or informal writing. They can set off and emphasize extra information.

My mother was born like me—in Chicago but of Mexican descent.

Dashes can also be used like parentheses to add comments.

I felt as if making tortillas—or writing a critical paper, for that matter—were tasks so impossible I wanted to break down into tears.

Note that dashes can be used in pairs or singly. In both cases, there are no spaces on either side of a dash.

PART 3

KEEPING FREEDOM ALIVE

Lift Up Thy Voice and Sing, ca. 1942–44. William H. Johnson, Oil on paperboard, 25.55 x 21.26 in. Smithsonian American Art Museum, Washington, DC.

View the Art William H. Johnson's bright colors and flattened perspective were inspired by art he saw in North Africa. How do these artistic choices help convey his message of hope in this painting?

BIG IDEA

Freedom can mean many things. There is freedom to express yourself. There is also the freedom to pursue your dreams, even if that means making sacrifices along the way. In the nonfiction works in Part 3, you will read speeches, articles, and essays from people who have reached for freedom. As you read these selections, ask yourself, What does freedom mean to me, and what would I give up to keep it?

Learning Objectives

For pages 392–393

In studying this text, you will focus on the following objective:

Literary Study: Analyzing persuasive essay and speech.

LITERARY FOCUS

Persuasive Essay and Speech

What makes writing convincing?

There are various methods for convincing a person to change his or her ideas or actions. You can use emotional appeals, which encourage a person to respond to his or her desire for pleasure, happiness, security, or satisfaction. Or you can appeal to a listener's reason. If you can use logic to prove that your idea is correct, then you can often persuade someone to think and act accordingly.

from *On Women's Right to Vote*
by Susan B. Anthony

Webster, Worcester, and Bouvier all define a citizen to be a person in the United States, entitled to vote and hold office. The only question left to be settled now is: Are women persons? And I hardly believe any of our opponents will have the hardihood to say they are not. Being persons, then, women are citizens; and no state has a right to make any law, or to enforce any old law, that shall abridge their privileges or immunities. Hence, every discrimination against women in the constitutions and laws of the several states is today null and void, precisely as is every one against Negroes.

Portrait of American woman suffrage leader Susan B. Anthony (1820–1906). She is shown in profile, seated at her desk. Photograph, 1900.

Persuasion

Persuasion is writing that attempts to convince readers to think or act in a particular way. Writers of persuasive essays may appeal to logic, as in argument, but they might also appeal to emotion. Consider the combination of logic and emotion in this argument in favor of comic books and graphic novels.

> For the reluctant reader, they are absorbing. For the struggling reader or the reader still learning English, they offer accessibility: pictures for context, and possibly an alternate path into classroom discussions of higher-level texts. They expand vocabulary and introduce the ideas of plot, pacing, and sequence.
>
> —*Teresa Méndez*, **from "'Hamlet' too hard? Try a comic book"**

One of the important skills persuasive writers must develop is that of anticipating the opposition and confronting their arguments. Below, Toni Morrison anticipates the argument that to be successful, people must be concerned only with their own best interests.

> In your rainbow journey toward the realization of personal goals, don't make choices based only on your security and your safety. Nothing is safe. That is not to say that anything ever was, or that anything worth achieving ever should be. . . . But in pursuing your highest ambitions, don't let your personal safety diminish the safety of your stepsister. In wielding the power that is deservedly yours, don't permit it to enslave your stepsisters.
>
> —*Toni Morrison*, **from "Cinderella's Stepsisters"**

Argument

Argument is a specific type of persuasive writing or speaking in which logic and evidence are used to appeal to the reader's or listener's reason. Notice in the excerpt on the previous page how Anthony ignores emotional appeals and tries to persuade the reader through reason and logic. This may be the more difficult path to changing people's thoughts and actions, but it also may lead to permanent change. Anthony died before women won the right to vote, but her argument prodded a nation toward a change in its constitution. Martin Luther King Jr. also used logical argument in his many speeches. King wished to convince people that African Americans deserved to enjoy the same rights and privileges that other people in the United States enjoyed.

> We aren't engaged in any negative protest and in any negative arguments with anybody. We are saying that we are determined to be men. We are determined to be people. We are saying that we are God's children. And that we don't have to live like we are forced to live.
>
> —*Martin Luther King Jr.*, **from "I've Been to the Mountaintop"**

Quickwrite

Anticipate Arguments Think of a local issue and choose a position. Practice anticipating the argument of your opposition by listing three arguments you are likely to encounter from their side. Follow the example below.

Issue: Build a new municipal pool
Position: The city should build the pool

The Opposing Side:

1. Municipal pools are too expensive to maintain.

2.

3.

LITERARY FOCUS **393**

Before You Read

On Women's Right to Vote

Meet Susan B. Anthony
(1820–1906)

"The fight must not cease; you must see that it does not stop. . . .Failure is impossible."

—Susan B. Anthony

It seems unbelievable today, but picture an adult woman (and U.S. citizen) going to a local polling place to vote—and getting arrested. That is what happened to Susan B. Anthony when she attempted to cast her ballot for a presidential candidate in 1872. Unjustly convicted of the "crime" (the judge had decided that she was guilty before the trial began) and fined $100, she refused to pay the fee. Anthony's choice to act on her belief that women should have the same voting rights as men was a risky one at that time. Yet Anthony was a bold and determined woman, and such brave actions characterized her life, work, and writing.

An Early Achiever Anthony was born into a Massachusetts Quaker family whose religious values encouraged her independent spirit and ensured that she could express herself freely. Anthony was three when she began to read and write, and she received an excellent education, unlike many women of her time. She began teaching in 1840 and eventually became the respected headmistress at a school in upstate New York.

A Lasting Partnership A decisive career and life change for Anthony came in 1851 when she met Elizabeth Cady Stanton. Stanton was already active in the women's rights movement when Anthony joined the cause. The two women became lifelong friends and colleagues. Although Stanton was the principal speechwriter, both women lectured and published articles and books, including the first volumes of *History of Woman Suffrage*. Many recognized Anthony's determined spirit and organizational skills as the human engine that propelled the women's rights movement forward.

Women's Rights Leader Anthony had always been involved in social causes. She had begun her activist career as a temperance reformer, helping those who suffered from the effects of alcoholism. Later she had joined leading abolitionists in the struggle to end slavery. However, she spent the majority of her time in bringing about the passage of the Nineteenth Amendment—the addition to the Constitution that gave women the right to vote. Unfortunately, Anthony did not live to see this crucial legal victory, one that suffragists had worked for five decades to enact. The Nineteenth Amendment became law on August 26, 1920, fourteen years after Anthony's death. In 1979 Anthony's contributions were recognized when her image became the first female historical figure to be put on a U.S. coin—the Susan B. Anthony dollar. It is a fitting tribute to a woman who devoted much of her life to protecting the rights of all women in the United States.

 Literature Online

Author Search For more about Susan B. Anthony, go to glencoe.com and enter QuickPass code GL59794u2.

Literature and Reading Preview

Connect to the Speech
What actions would you take if you felt that your rights were being violated? Freewrite for a few minutes about what you would do in order to protect and secure your rights.

Build Background
In 1873, when Anthony delivered this speech, many people in the United States were fighting for woman suffrage. *Suffrage* means "the right to vote." In 1920, the Nineteenth Amendment was added to the Constitution, and all American women were finally able to vote.

Set Purposes for Reading

Big Idea **Keeping Freedom Alive**

As you read Anthony's speech, ask yourself, How does she define freedom?

Literary Element **Rhetorical Devices**

Rhetorical devices are tools of persuasion, such as appeals to logic, emotion, ethics, or authority, used by an author or a speaker. Noting an author's rhetorical devices may provide clues about his or her objective. As you read, ask yourself, What rhetorical devices does Anthony use?

Reading Strategy **Recognize Bias**

Bias is an author's inclination toward a particular opinion or position. As you read, ask yourself, What are examples of bias in Anthony's reasons for why women should get the right to vote?

Tip: Identify Bias Identifying bias can help you understand an author's motivation and identify when bias may affect his or her credibility or logic. Use a chart to keep track of any examples of bias.

Example	Why It Shows Bias
"I not only committed no crime..."	The judge found Anthony guilty before the trial started.

Learning Objectives

For pages 394–400

In studying this text, you will focus on the following objectives:

Literary Study: Analyzing rhetorical devices.

Reading: Recognizing bias.

Vocabulary

domestic (də mes′tik) *adj.* relating to a country, especially one's own; p. 396 *We must mind our domestic policy, while not ignoring global strategy.*

ordain (ôr dān′) *v.* to order or establish; to appoint; p. 396 *The king ordained that food would not be taxed.*

odious (ō′dē əs) *adj.* disgusting or offensive; p. 397 *An odious smell was coming from the garbage.*

aristocracy (ar′is tok′rə sē) *n.* type of government in which a minority of upper-class individuals rule; p. 397 *The country was governed by a wealthy aristocracy.*

dissension (di sen′shən) *n.* disagreement within a group; p. 397 *Decisions were hindered by the dissension in the group.*

SUSAN B. ANTHONY

On Women's Right to Vote

Susan B. Anthony

Friends and fellow citizens: I stand before you tonight under indictment[1] for the alleged crime of having voted at the last presidential election, without having a lawful right to vote. It shall be my work this evening to prove to you that in thus voting, I not only committed no crime, but, instead, simply exercised[2] my citizen's rights, guaranteed to me and all United States citizens by the National Constitution, beyond the power of any state to deny.

The preamble of the Federal Constitution says: "We, the people of the United States, in order to form a more perfect union, establish justice, insure **domestic** tranquility, provide for the common defense, promote the general welfare,[3] and secure the blessings of liberty to ourselves and our posterity,[4] do **ordain** and establish this Constitution for the United States of America."

It was we, the people; not we, the white male citizens; nor yet we, the male citizens; but we, the whole people, who formed the Union. And we formed it, not to give the blessings of liberty, but to secure them; not to the half of ourselves and the half of our posterity, but to the whole people—women as well as men. And it is a downright mockery to talk to women of their enjoyment of the blessings of liberty while they are denied the use of the only means of securing them provided by this democratic republican government—the ballot.

For any state to make sex a qualification that must ever result in the disfranchise-

---

1. An *indictment* is a statement that charges someone with committing a crime.
2. Here, *exercised* means "used or practiced."
3. Here, *welfare* refers to well-being.
4. *Posterity* means "future generations."

Rhetorical Devices What type of reaction is Anthony trying to evoke in listeners with this statement?

Keeping Freedom Alive Why does Anthony believe that women need the right to vote in order to secure their liberties?

Vocabulary
domestic (də mes' tik) *adj.* relating to one's own country

Vocabulary
ordain (ôr dān') *v.* to order or establish; to appoint

ment[5] of one entire half of the people is to pass a bill of attainder,[6] or an *ex post facto* law,[7] and is therefore a violation of the supreme law of the land. By it the blessings of liberty are forever withheld from women and their female posterity.

To them this government has no just powers derived from the consent of the governed. To them this government is not a democracy. It is not a republic. It is an **odious aristocracy**; a hateful oligarchy[8] of sex; the most hateful aristocracy ever established on the face of the globe; an oligarchy of wealth, where the rich govern the poor. An oligarchy of learning, where the educated govern the ignorant, or even an oligarchy of race, where the Saxon rules the African, might be endured; but this oligarchy of sex, which makes father, brother, husband, sons, the oligarchs over the mother and sisters, the wife and daughters, of every household—which ordains all men sovereigns,[9] all women subjects, carries **dissension**, discord, and rebellion into every home of the nation.

---

5. *Disfranchisement* means the taking away of someone's rights as a citizen.
6. A *bill of attainder* is an act of the legislature in which someone is declared guilty of a serious crime without a trial.
7. An *ex post facto law* is a law that punishes an individual for committing a crime even though the act was not considered criminal when the person committed it.
8. An *oligarchy* is a government in which a small group has authority.
9. *Sovereigns* are individuals invested with supreme authority.

Recognize Bias *Explain how Anthony's bias is present in this statement.*

Vocabulary

odious (ō′dē əs) *adj.* disgusting or offensive
aristocracy (ar′is tok′rə sē) *n.* a type of government in which a minority of upper-class individuals rule
dissension (di sen′shən) *n.* disagreement within a group

Women marching for woman suffrage in New York City. c. 1910.

View the Art Women across the country used various tactics to draw attention and build support for the suffrage movement, from lobbying and petitions to marches and protests. How do the women in this photograph reflect the argument of Anthony's speech?

Webster, Worcester, and Bouvier[10] all define a citizen to be a person in the United States, entitled to vote and hold office. The only question left to be settled now is: Are women persons? And I hardly believe any of our opponents will have the hardihood to say they are not. Being persons, then, women are citizens; and no state has a right to make any law, or to enforce any old law, that shall abridge their privileges or immunities.[11] Hence, every discrimination against women in the constitutions and laws of the several states is today null and void, precisely as is every one against Negroes.

---

10. *Webster, Worcester, and Bouvier* refers to Noah Webster, Joseph Emerson Worcester, and John Bouvier, all of whom published dictionaries.
11. Here, *immunities* means "protection from penalties or prosecution."

Rhetorical Devices *How does Anthony attempt to persuade her audience of the legitimacy of her view here? Is she successful? Explain.*

After You Read

Respond and Think Critically

Respond and Interpret

1. Do you agree with Anthony's argument? Explain.

2. (a) What are two reasons Anthony gives for why women should be allowed to vote? (b) Why do you think it took so long for the laws to finally change? Explain.

3. (a) To what does Anthony compare laws forbidding women to vote? (b) Is her comparison a valid one? Explain.

4. (a) Why does Anthony ask "Are women persons?" (b) Do you agree with her logic? Explain.

Analyze and Evaluate

5. Why does Anthony close her speech with a reference to "Negroes"?

6. In this speech, Anthony is trying to persuade her listeners. If you were listening to her speech in 1873, would you have been persuaded to support her cause? Explain.

Connect

7. **Big Idea** Keeping Freedom Alive (a) Why does Anthony believe that freedom requires giving all citizens the right to vote? (b) Do you agree with Anthony's opinion? Explain.

8. **Connect to Today** Do you think Anthony would be satisfied with the social status of American women today? Defend your answer.

Primary Visual Artifact

Propaganda Postcard

While some men were passionate supporters of women's suffrage, others saw the movement as a threat to their masculinity. This propaganda poster is meant to sway people to think that the suffrage movement would destroy traditional gender roles and family structure. These views were sometimes expressed through images such as this postcard from 1910.

Group Activity

Discuss the following questions with your classmates.

1. What is unfair or untruthful about the message conveyed in this postcard? Who is the intended audience?

2. What changes would you make to this image and to the caption to present a more balanced and accurate portrayal of the suffrage movement?

Literary Element | Rhetorical Devices

SAT Skills Practice

1. In the paragraph beginning "For any state to make sex a qualification . . ." (page 396) Anthony

   (A) uses analogy
   (B) appeals to logic
   (C) uses repetition
   (D) appeals to ethics
   (E) appeals to emotion

2. What does Anthony compare to a "hateful oligarchy of sex" (page 397)?

   (A) the English aristocracy
   (B) an oligarchy
   (C) Saxon rule over the African
   (D) the Constitution of the United States
   (E) the United States government

Review: Argument

As you learned on page 393, **argument** refers to statements, reasons, and facts that support or oppose a point. Many persuasive techniques and rhetorical devices can be used to bolster an argument.

Partner Activity With a classmate, discuss Anthony's argument for allowing women to vote. Create a two-column chart similar to the one below. In one column, list one of the logical points Anthony makes to support her argument. In the second column, brainstorm about some of the possible responses that people arguing against Anthony may have had.

Anthony's Argument	Critics' Responses
Women played a role in establishing the United States.	Women had not played any role in the government previously.

Reading Strategy | Recognize Bias

To detect **bias** in a written work, use strategies such as looking for oversimplification, analyzing the writer's reasoning, and identifying emotionally charged language.

1. Identify two examples of bias in Anthony's speech. Which strategies helped you identify them?

2. In your opinion, did the bias in Anthony's speech affect her credibility? Explain.

Vocabulary Practice

Practice with Word Parts Use a printed or online dictionary to find the meaning of each vocabulary word's root and to find the meanings of any prefixes or suffixes in the word. List the meanings in a diagram like the one shown. Then use a dictionary to help you find words that contain the same prefix, suffix, or root as the vocabulary word. Circle the word part that could help a person guess each word's meaning.

domestic   ordain   odious
aristocracy   dissension

EXAMPLE:
archaic

Root
archaeo, "early, old"

Suffix
-ic, "having, being, or related to"

Related words: archaeology, energetic

Literature Online

Selection Resources For Selection Quizzes, eFlashcards, and Reading-Writing Connection activities, go to glencoe.com and enter QuickPass code GL59794u2.

Respond Through Writing

Persuasive Essay

Learning Objectives
In this assignment, you will focus on the following objectives:

Writing: Writing a persuasive essay.

Grammar: Understanding voice.

Argue a Position Susan B. Anthony argued for women's right to vote. Find out your school's policy on freedom of speech for students. Write an essay in which you argue for or against this policy, making use of appeals to logic, appeals to emotion, and appeals to authority.

Understand the Task
- An **appeal to logic** is any reference to reason, facts, or statistics to support a claim or an opinion.
- An **appeal to emotion** is any use of words or information to arouse the reader's emotions in order to persuade.
- An **appeal to authority** is a reference to any learned or respected figure or institution to support a claim or an opinion.

Prewrite Brainstorm about ways in which free speech could be used and abused by students. Then enter terms such as "free speech" and "high school" into a search engine to discover issues that might help you arrive at your own opinion. Create an outline to state your thesis or opinion and to list, in order, the reasons you will use to support it.

Draft As you draft, strengthen your arguments by using persuasive techniques such as appeals to logic, emotion, and authority. Consider quoting reliable, credible sources you found on the Internet or school authorities. Use frames like these for introducing and countering arguments:
Of course, some might disagree with my claim and say that _____.
Some might object that _____, but my answer to that is _____.
While it is true that _____, that does not necessarily mean that _____.

Decide whether the most effective placement for your opinion statement or claim is at the beginning or end of your essay.

Revise Exchange papers with a partner. Identify and evaluate each other's appeals to logic, emotion, and authority. Identify at least one way in which your partner refuted a counterclaim or opposing view and comment on its effectiveness. Use your feedback and revise; introduce sources to support information. For example, include names of authorities or institutions whose ideas form the basis of your appeals or evidence.

Edit and Proofread Proofread your paper, correcting any errors in spelling, grammar, and punctuation. Use the Grammar Tip in the side column to help you with active and passive voice.

Grammar Tip

Voice

You should almost always use the active voice. There are times, however, when the passive voice is necessary or preferred.

Use the passive voice when the doer of the action is not known.
The graffiti was written on the bathroom wall.

Use the passive voice when the doer of the action is not important—or not as important as the action, or when the passive voice shifts emphasis to a more worthy subject.
Freedom of speech was added to the Constitution with the Bill of Rights.

Before You Read

I've Been to the Mountaintop

Meet **Martin Luther King Jr.**
(1929–1968)

During the historic March on Washington in 1963, Martin Luther King Jr. set the moral tone for the Civil Rights Movement with his famous "I Have a Dream" speech. In 1964 he was awarded the Nobel Peace Prize for leading nonviolent demonstrations to help African Americans gain civil rights. With great courage and insight, King inspired Americans of all backgrounds to come together to work for a more just and compassionate society.

> *"I have a dream my four little children will one day live in a nation where they will not be judged by the color of their skin but by the content of their character."*
>
> —Martin Luther King Jr.

Launching the Civil Rights Movement Born the son of a minister in Atlanta, Georgia, King began his rise to leadership by entering Morehouse College at the age of fifteen. After receiving a PhD in theology from Boston University, King became a minister in a Montgomery, Alabama, church. Shortly after moving there, King became a leader of the first major nonviolent protest of the Civil Rights Movement. Inspired by the life and teachings of Mohandas Gandhi, whose doctrine of passive resistance was to become his own guiding principle, King began the Montgomery bus boycott. The African American citizens of Montgomery, who had been required to give up their seats for whites, stayed off the buses for more than a year to force an end to segregation. Their peaceful protest was successful, and King's leadership skills drew national attention.

Expanding the Struggle After the boycott, King served as president of the Southern Christian Leadership Conference and helped spread the civil rights struggle throughout the South and the nation. In 1963, when the center of the struggle shifted to Birmingham, Alabama, King and other demonstrators were jailed, and violence exploded in the streets. However, King's stance on nonviolent resistance remained firm. While behind bars, King wrote his famous document *Letter from a Birmingham Jail*, in which he answered his critics and galvanized support for his program of civil disobedience.

In the mid to late 1960s, King expanded his agenda to include protests against the rapidly escalating war in Vietnam. In 1968, at the age of thirty-nine, King fell victim to an assassin's bullet. At his funeral, over a thousand people, including political leaders and foreign dignitaries, crowded into King's church, Ebenezer Baptist Church in Atlanta, Georgia. Outside, almost one hundred thousand more paid tribute. King's message of respect, for democracy and for the dignity of all people, still lives.

Author Search For more about Martin Luther King Jr., go to glencoe.com and enter QuickPass code GL59794u2.

Literature and Reading Preview

Connect to the Speech
Would you be willing to stand up for the rights of other people even if you might be harmed in the process? Discuss this question with a partner.

Build Background
In April 1968, Martin Luther King Jr. traveled to Memphis, Tennessee, to support African American sanitation workers who were on strike against the city. Memphis Mayor Henry Loeb had refused to recognize and negotiate with the nearly all-African American union organization that had called the strike.

Set Purposes for Reading

Big Idea Keeping Freedom Alive

In this speech, King argues that freedom and equality belong to everyone. As you read, ask yourself, What arguments does King give to support his ideas?

Literary Element Allusion

An **allusion** is a reference to a character, a place, or a situation from history, music, art, or literature. In his speeches, King uses allusions to make his points clear. As you read, ask yourself, Where and why does King include well-known quotations and examples from history?

Reading Strategy Identify Problem and Solution

One purpose of persuasive speeches is to **identify** a **problem** and suggest a **solution** or solutions for that problem. As you read this speech, ask yourself, Which problems does King discuss and which solutions does he propose?

....

Tip: Ask Questions Ask yourself questions as you read, such as: What are the problems? What details about the problems does King provide? What solutions does King suggest? What support does he give for his solutions? As you read, fill in a chart like the one shown below.

Problems	Solutions

Learning Objectives

For pages 401–415

In studying this text, you will focus on the following objectives:

Literary Study: Analyzing allusion.

Reading: Identifying problem and solution.

Vocabulary

grapple (grap′əl) *v.* to struggle, as though wrestling; to come to terms with; p. 404 *The city council is meeting tonight to discuss how best to grapple with town budget issues.*

relevant (rel′ə vənt) *adj.* related to the issue at hand; p. 407 *Though pollution is an important issue, it is not relevant to our discussion of the need for a new library.*

agenda (ə jen′də) *n.* an outline of tasks to be accomplished; p. 408 *The agenda lists what we need to discuss during this meeting.*

compassionate (kəm pash′ə nit) *adj.* having or showing sympathy for another's misfortune, combined with a desire to help; p. 409 *A variety of compassionate organizations work to help victims of disasters.*

I've Been to the Mountaintop

Martin Luther King Jr.

Segregation Protest March. Birmingham, AL.

Thank you very kindly, my friends. As I listened to Ralph Abernathy[1] in his eloquent and generous introduction and then thought about myself, I wondered who he was talking about. It's always good to have your closest friend and associate say something good about you. And Ralph is the best friend that I have in the world.

I'm delighted to see each of you here tonight in spite of a storm warning. You reveal that you are determined to go on anyhow. Something is happening in Memphis, something is happening in our world.

As you know, if I were standing at the beginning of time, with the possibility of general and panoramic view of the whole human history up to now, and the Almighty said to me, "Martin Luther King, which age would you like to live in?"—I would take my mental flight by Egypt through, or rather across the Red Sea, through the wilderness on toward the promised land. And in spite of its magnificence, I wouldn't stop there. I would move on by Greece, and take my mind to Mount Olympus. And I would see Plato, Aristotle, Socrates, Euripides and Aristophanes[2] assembled around the Parthenon as they

Visual Vocabulary
The *Parthenon*, a temple built in the fifth century B.C., still stands in Athens, Greece.

---

1. With King and other African American ministers, *Ralph Abernathy* founded the Southern Christian Leadership Conference (SCLC), an organization devoted to the nonviolent struggle against racism and discrimination.

2. The lives of these five Greek teachers and writers spanned a 160-year period ending with Aristotle's death in 322 B.C. Their ideas greatly influenced modern Western civilization.

Visual Vocabulary
Martin Luther (1483–1546) was a German theologian whose arguments challenging certain teachings of the Roman Catholic Church led to the Protestant Reformation.

discussed the great and eternal issues of reality.

But I wouldn't stop there. I would go on, even to the great heyday of the Roman Empire. And I would see developments around there, through various emperors and leaders. But I wouldn't stop there. I would even come up to the day of the Renaissance, and get a quick picture of all that the Renaissance did for the cultural and esthetic life of man. But I wouldn't stop there. I would even go by the way that the man for whom I'm named had his habitat. And I would watch Martin Luther as he tacked his ninety-five theses[3] on the door at the church in Wittenberg.

But I wouldn't stop there. I would come on up even to 1863, and watch a vacillating president by the name of Abraham Lincoln finally come to the conclusion that he had to sign the Emancipation Proclamation. But I wouldn't stop there. I would even come up to the early thirties, and see a man grappling with the problems of the bankruptcy of his nation. And come with an eloquent cry that we have nothing to fear but fear itself.[4]

But I wouldn't stop there. Strangely enough, I would turn to the Almighty, and say, "If you allow me to live just a few years in the second half of the twentieth century, I will be happy." Now that's a strange statement to make, because the world is all messed up. The nation is sick. Trouble is in the land. Confusion all around. That's a strange statement. But I know, somehow, that only when it is dark enough, can you see the stars. And I see God working in this period of the twentieth century in a way that men, in some strange way, are responding—something is happening in our world. The masses of people are rising up. And wherever they are assembled today, whether they are in Johannesburg, South Africa; Nairobi, Kenya; Accra, Ghana; New York City; Atlanta, Georgia; Jackson, Mississippi; or Memphis, Tennessee—the cry is always the same—"We want to be free."

And another reason that I'm happy to live in this period is that we have been forced to a point where we're going to have to **grapple** with the problems that men have been trying to grapple with through history, but the demands didn't force them to do it. Survival demands that we grapple with them. Men, for years now, have been talking about war and peace. But now, no longer can they just talk about it. It is no longer a choice between violence and nonviolence in this world; it's nonviolence or nonexistence.

That is where we are today. And also in the human rights revolution, if something isn't done, and in a hurry, to bring the colored peoples of the world out of their long years of poverty, their long years of

---

3. Here, *theses* means "arguments."
4. In these two sentences, King is referring to President Franklin D. Roosevelt, who led the United States during the Great Depression of the 1930s.

Allusion *How would you characterize the kinds of people and events that King is alluding to?*

Keeping Freedom Alive *What issues do you think the people in these places have in common?*

Identify Problem and Solution *What problems has King identified?*

Vocabulary
grapple (grap′əl) *v.* to struggle, as though wrestling; to come to terms with

Portrait of Martin Luther King Jr. Flip Schulke.

View the Art Schulke traveled with and documented Martin Luther King Jr. and other civil rights leaders during the 1960s. What do you think King's body language here reveals about his speaking style?

hurt and neglect, the whole world is doomed. Now, I'm just happy that God has allowed me to live in this period, to see what is unfolding. And I'm happy that he's allowed me to be in Memphis.

I can remember, I can remember when Negroes were just going around as Ralph has said, so often, scratching where they didn't itch, and laughing when they were not tickled. But that day is all over. We mean business now, and we are determined to gain our rightful place in God's world.

And that's all this whole thing is about. We aren't engaged in any negative protest and in any negative arguments with anybody. We are saying that we are determined to be men. We are determined to be people. We are saying that we are God's children. And that we don't have to live like we are forced to live.

Now, what does all of this mean in this great period of history? It means that we've got to stay together. We've got to stay together and maintain unity. You know, whenever Pharaoh[5] wanted to prolong the period of slavery in Egypt, he had a favorite, favorite formula for doing it. What was that? He kept the slaves fighting among themselves. But whenever the slaves get together, something happens in Pharaoh's court, and he cannot hold the slaves in slavery. When the slaves get together, that's the beginning of getting out of slavery. Now let us maintain unity.

Secondly, let us keep the issues where they are. The issue is injustice. The issue is the refusal of Memphis to be fair and honest in its dealings with its public servants, who happen to be sanitation workers. Now, we've got to keep attention on that. That's always the problem with a little violence. You know what happened the other day, and the press dealt only with the window-breaking. I read the articles. They very seldom got around to mentioning the fact that one thousand, three hundred sanitation workers were on strike, and that Memphis is not being fair to them, and that Mayor Loeb is in dire[6] need of a doctor. They didn't get around to that.

---

5. In the Bible, the *Pharaoh* (ruler) of ancient Egypt enslaved the Israelites until Moses led them out of Egypt and into Canaan, which they called the "promised land."
6. *Dire* means "dreadful" or "terrible."

Allusion What point does the allusion to Pharaoh's court help bring home to King's listeners?

Now we're going to march again, and we've got to march again, in order to put the issue where it is supposed to be. And force everybody to see that there are thirteen hundred of God's children here suffering, sometimes going hungry, going through dark and dreary nights wondering how this thing is going to come out. That's the issue. And we've got to say to the nation: we know it's coming out. For when people get caught up with that which is right and they are willing to sacrifice for it, there is no stopping point short of victory.

We aren't going to let any mace stop us. We are masters in our nonviolent movement in disarming police forces; they don't know what to do. I've seen them so often. I remember in Birmingham, Alabama, when we were in that majestic struggle there we would move out of the 16th Street Baptist Church day after day; by the hundreds we would move out. And Bull Connor[7] would tell them to send the dogs forth and they did come; but we just went before the dogs singing, "Ain't gonna let nobody turn me round." Bull Connor next would say, "Turn the fire hoses on." And as I said to you the other night, Bull Connor didn't know history. He knew a kind of physics that somehow didn't relate to the transphysics[8] that we knew about. And that was the fact that there was a certain kind of fire that no water could put out. And we went before the fire hoses; we had known water. If we were Baptist or some other denomination, we had been immersed. If we were Methodist, and some others, we had been sprinkled, but we knew water.[9]

That couldn't stop us. And we just went on before the dogs and we would look at them; and we'd go on before the water hoses and we would look at it, and we'd just go on singing "Over my head I see freedom in the air." And then we would be thrown in the paddy wagons, and sometimes we were stacked in there like sardines in a can. And they would throw us in, and old Bull would say, "Take them off," and they did; and we would just go in the paddy wagon singing, "We Shall Overcome." And every now and then we'd get in the jail, and we'd see the jailers looking through the windows being moved by our prayers, and being moved by our words and our songs. And there was a power there which Bull Connor couldn't adjust to; and so we ended up transforming Bull into a steer, and we won our struggle in Birmingham.

Now we've got to go on to Memphis just like that. I call upon you to be with us Monday. Now about injunctions: We have an injunction[10] and we're going into court tomorrow morning to fight this illegal, unconstitutional injunction. All we say to America is, "Be true to what you said on paper." If I lived in China or even Russia, or any totalitarian country, maybe I could understand the denial of certain basic First Amendment privileges, because they hadn't

---

7. *Bull Connor*, whose given name was Eugene, was Birmingham's Commissioner of Public Safety and a candidate for mayor in the 1964 election.
8. *Physics* is the study of the physical properties of light, heat, electricity, magnetism, and so on. With the invented word *transphysics*, King refers to things that transcend, or go beyond, the physical, such as morality and philosophy.

Identify Problem and Solution *What problem does King explain in this sentence? What does he encourage people to do to address this problem?*

9. King is referring to the Christian ritual of baptism, which may involve immersion in water or the sprinkling or pouring of water over a person's head.
10. An *injunction* is a court order barring a specific action, such as a march, demonstration, or strike.

Allusion *Why does King make these allusions in these two sentences?*

committed themselves to that over there. But somewhere I read of the freedom of assembly. Somewhere I read of the freedom of speech. Somewhere I read of the freedom of the press. Somewhere I read that the greatness of America is the right to protest for right. And so just as I say, we aren't going to let any injunction turn us around. We are going on.

We need all of you. And you know what's beautiful to me, is to see all of these ministers of the Gospel. It's a marvelous picture. Who is it that is supposed to articulate the longings and aspirations of the people more than the preacher? Somehow the preacher must be an Amos,[11] and say, "Let justice roll down like waters and righteousness like a mighty stream." Somehow, the preacher must say with Jesus, "The spirit of the Lord is upon me, because he hath anointed me to deal with the problems of the poor."[12]

And I want to commend the preachers, under the leadership of these noble men: James Lawson, one who has been in this struggle for many years; he's been to jail for struggling; but he's still going on, fighting for the rights of his people. Rev. Ralph Jackson, Billy Kiles; I could just go right on down the list, but time will not permit. But I want to thank them all. And I want you to thank them, because so often, preachers aren't concerned about anything but themselves. And I'm always happy to see a **relevant** ministry.

It's alright to talk about "long white robes over yonder," in all of its symbolism. But ultimately people want some suits and dresses and shoes to wear down here. It's alright to talk about "streets flowing with milk and honey," but God has commanded us to be concerned about the slums down here, and his children who can't eat three square meals a day. It's alright to talk about the new Jerusalem, but one day, God's preacher must talk about the New York, the new Atlanta, the new Philadelphia, the new Los Angeles, the new Memphis, Tennessee. This is what we have to do.

Now the other thing we'll have to do is this: Always anchor our external direct action with the power of economic withdrawal. Now, we are poor people, individually, we are poor when you compare us with white society in America. We are poor. Never stop and forget that collectively, that means all of us together, collectively we are richer than all the nations in the world, with the exception of nine. Did you ever think about that? After you leave[13] the United States, Soviet Russia, Great Britain, West Germany, France, and I could name the others, the Negro collectively is richer than most nations of the world. We have an annual income of more than thirty billion dollars a year, which is more than all of the exports of the United States, and more than the national budget of Canada. Did you know that? That's power right there, if we know how to pool it.

We don't have to argue with anybody. We don't have to curse and go around acting bad with our words. We don't need any bricks and bottles, we don't need any Molotov cocktails, we just need to go around to these stores, and to these massive industries in our country, and say, "God sent us by

---

11. The Hebrew prophet *Amos* lived in the eighth century B.C.
12. Here, King has freely paraphrased the words that Jesus was reading from the prophet Isaiah.

Keeping Freedom Alive What arguments does King make against the court injunction?

Vocabulary

relevant (rel′ ə vənt) *adj.* related to the issue at hand

---

13. Here, the expression *after you leave* means "not counting" or "apart from."

Allusion In this paragraph, King alludes to common ideas of heaven and the afterlife. What point does he make about these ideas?

here, to say to you that you're not treating his children right. And we've come by here to ask you to make the first item on your **agenda**—fair treatment, where God's children are concerned. Now, if you are not prepared to do that, we do have an agenda that we must follow. And our agenda calls for withdrawing economic support from you . . ."

But not only that, we've got to strengthen black institutions. I call upon you to take your money out of the banks downtown and deposit your money in Tri-State Bank—we want a "bank-in" movement in Memphis. So go by the savings and loan association. I'm not asking you something that we don't do ourselves at SCLC. Judge Hooks and others will tell you that we have an account here in the savings and loan association from the Southern Christian Leadership Conference. We're just telling you to follow what we're doing. Put your money there. You have six or seven black insurance companies in Memphis. Take out your insurance there. We want to have an "insurance-in."

Civil rights marchers in Washington, D.C. Marching for equality.

View the Art This photograph of a civil rights demonstration focuses on two exuberant young women in a crowd of marchers. What is King's attitude toward women in this speech?

Now these are some practical things we can do. We begin the process of building a greater economic base. And at the same time, we are putting pressure where it really hurts. I ask you to follow through here.

Now, let me say as I move to my conclusion that we've got to give ourselves to this struggle until the end. Nothing would be more tragic than to stop at this point, in Memphis. We've got to see it through. And when we have our march, you need to be

---

Identify Problem and Solution *What good outcomes could be obtained by pooling economic resources, according to King?*

Vocabulary

agenda (ə jen′də) *n.* an outline of tasks to be accomplished

there. Be concerned about your brother. You may not be on strike. But either we go up together, or we go down together.

Let us develop a kind of dangerous unselfishness. One day a man came to Jesus; and he wanted to raise some questions about some vital matters in life. At points, he wanted to trick Jesus, and show him that he knew a little more than Jesus knew, and through this, throw him off base. Now that question could have easily ended up in a philosophical and theological debate. But Jesus immediately pulled that question from mid-air, and placed it on a dangerous curve between Jerusalem and Jericho. And he talked about a certain man, who fell among thieves. You remember that a Levite and a priest passed by on the other side. They didn't stop to help him. And finally a man of another race came by. He got down from his beast, decided not to be **compassionate** by proxy.[14] But with him, administered first aid, and helped the man in need. Jesus ended up saying, this was the good man, this was the great man, because he had the capacity to project the "I" into the "thou," and to be concerned about his brother. Now you know, we use our imagination a great deal to try to determine why the priest and the Levite didn't stop. At times we say they were busy going to church meetings—an ecclesiastical gathering—and they had to get on down to Jerusalem so they wouldn't be late for their meeting. At other times we would speculate that there was a religious law that "One who was engaged in religious ceremonials was not to touch a human body twenty-four hours before the ceremony." And every now and then we begin to wonder whether maybe they were not going down to Jerusalem, or down to Jericho, rather to organize a "Jericho Road Improvement Association." That's a possibility. Maybe they felt that it was better to deal with the problem from the causal root, rather than to get bogged down with an individual effort.

> "And let us move on in these powerful days, these days of challenge to make America what it ought to be."

But I'm going to tell you what my imagination tells me. It's possible that these men were afraid. You see, the Jericho road is a dangerous road. I remember when Mrs. King and I were first in Jerusalem. We rented a car and drove from Jerusalem down to Jericho. And as soon as we got on that road, I said to my wife, "I can see why Jesus used this as a setting for his parable."[15] It's a winding, meandering road. It's really conducive for ambushing. You start out in Jerusalem, which is about 1200 miles, or rather 1200 feet above sea level. And by the time you get down to Jericho, fifteen or twenty minutes later, you're about 2200 feet below sea level. That's a dangerous road. In the days of Jesus it came to be known as the "Bloody Pass."

---

14. In ancient Israel, men of the *Levite* tribe were temple priests or assistants. One might expect the two religious men to help, especially since the victim is also Jewish. Instead, it is *a man of another race* who decides not to leave it to someone else—a *proxy,* or substitute—to help.

Identify Problem and Solution What argument does King make for attending the march?

Vocabulary

compassionate (kəm pash′ə nit) *adj.* having or showing sympathy for another's misfortune, combined with a desire to help

15. A *parable* is a brief story intended to illustrate some truth or moral lesson.

Allusion According to King, what kinds of excuses do people make for not stopping to help one another?

And you know, it's possible that the priest and the Levite looked over that man on the ground and wondered if the robbers were still around. Or it's possible that they felt that the man on the ground was merely faking. And he was acting like he had been robbed and hurt, in order to seize them over there, lure them there for quick and easy seizure. And so the first question that the Levite asked was, "If I stop to help this man, what will happen to me?" But then the Good Samaritan came by. And he reversed the question: "If I do not stop to help this man, what will happen to him?"

That's the question before you tonight. Not, "If I stop to help the sanitation workers, what will happen to all of the hours that I usually spend in my office every day and every week as a pastor?" The question is not, "If I stop to help this man in need, what will happen to me?" ==If I do not stop to help the sanitation workers, what will happen to them?" That's the question.==

Let us rise up tonight with a greater readiness. Let us stand with a greater determination. And let us move on in these powerful days, these days of challenge to make America what it ought to be. We have an opportunity to make America a better nation. And I want to thank God, once more, for allowing me to be here with you.

You know, several years ago, I was in New York City autographing the first book that I had written. And while sitting there autographing books, a demented[16] black woman came up. The only question I heard from her was, "Are you Martin Luther King?"

And I was looking down writing, and I said yes. And the next minute I felt something beating on my chest. Before I knew it I had been stabbed by this demented

---

16. *Demented* means "insane."

Keeping Freedom Alive *What attitude or spirit does King encourage his listeners to adopt?*

woman. I was rushed to Harlem Hospital. It was a dark Saturday afternoon. And that blade had gone through, and the X rays revealed that the tip of the blade was on the edge of my aorta, the main artery. And once that's punctured, you drown in your own blood—that's the end of you.

It came out in the *New York Times* the next morning, that if I had sneezed, I would have died. Well, about four days later, they allowed me, after the operation, after my chest had been opened, and the blade had been taken out, to move around in the wheel chair in the hospital. They allowed me to read some of the mail that came in, and from all over the states, and the world, kind letters came in. I read a few, but one of them I will never forget. I had received one from the President and the Vice-President. I've forgotten what those telegrams said. I'd received a visit and a letter from the Governor of New York, but I've forgotten what the letter said. But there was another letter that came from a little girl, a young girl who was a student at the White Plains High School. And I looked at that letter, and I'll never forget it. It said simply, "Dear Dr. King: I am a ninth-grade student at the White Plains High School." She said, "While it should not matter, I would like to mention that I am a white girl. I read in the paper of your misfortune, and of your suffering. And I read that if you had sneezed, you would have died. And I'm simply writing you to say that I'm so happy that you didn't sneeze."

And I want to say tonight, I want to say that I am happy that I didn't sneeze. Because if I had sneezed, I wouldn't have been around here in 1960, when students all over the South started sitting in at lunch counters. And I knew that as they were sitting in, they were really standing up for the best in the American dream. And taking the whole nation back to those great

Dr. Martin Luther King Jr. hugs his wife, Coretta, after learning he had been awarded the Nobel Prize for Peace.

because a man can't ride your back unless it is bent. If I had sneezed, I wouldn't have been here in 1963, when the black people of Birmingham, Alabama, aroused the conscience of this nation, and brought into being the Civil Rights Bill. If I had sneezed, I wouldn't have had a chance later that year, in August, to try to tell America about a dream that I had had. If I had sneezed, I wouldn't have been down in Selma, Alabama,[18] to see the great movement there. If I had sneezed, I wouldn't have been in Memphis to see a community rally around those brothers and sisters who are suffering. I'm so happy that I didn't sneeze.

And they were telling me, now it doesn't matter now. It really doesn't matter what happens now. I left Atlanta this morning, and as we got started on the plane, there were six of us, the pilot said over the public address system, "We are sorry for the delay, but we have Dr. Martin Luther King on the plane. And to be sure that all of the bags were checked, and to be sure that nothing would be wrong with the plane, we had to check out everything carefully. And we've had the plane protected and guarded all night."

walls of democracy which were dug deep by the Founding Fathers in the Declaration of Independence and the Constitution. If I had sneezed, I wouldn't have been around in 1962, when Negroes in Albany, Georgia,[17] decided to straighten their backs up. And whenever men and women straighten their backs up, they are going somewhere,

17. In 1962 King took part in demonstrations in *Albany, Georgia,* protesting the segregation of public facilities.

18. In *Selma, Alabama,* in 1965, King led a march to protest restrictions on African American voting rights. Soon afterward, the Voting Rights Act of 1965 was passed.

Keeping Freedom Alive *What does King hope to illustrate by mentioning these events?*

An African American student sits at a lunch counter reserved for white customers during a sit-in to protest segregation. Packages of napkins have been placed on nearby stools to discourage other protesters from joining the sit-in.

And then I got into Memphis. And some began to say the threats, or talk about the threats that were out. What would happen to me from some of our sick white brothers?

Well, I don't know what will happen now. We've got some difficult days ahead. But it doesn't matter with me now. Because I've been to the mountaintop. And I don't mind. Like anybody, I would like to live a long life. Longevity has its place. But I'm not concerned about that now. I just want to do God's will. And He's allowed me to go up to the mountain. And I've looked over. And I've seen the promised land. I may not get there with you. But I want you to know tonight, that we, as a people will get to the promised land. And I'm happy, tonight. I'm not worried about anything. I'm not fearing any man. Mine eyes have seen the glory of the coming of the Lord.

Allusion In this final passage, King alludes to the "promised land" and ends by quoting the patriotic American song "The Battle Hymn of the Republic." What is the meaning of the passage?

After You Read

Respond and Think Critically

Respond and Interpret

1. Which sentence or passage made the greatest impression on you? Why?

2. (a) Summarize King's mental journey through history. In which age does he want to live? (b) What might you infer about King's character and beliefs on the basis of the age he chooses?

3. (a) What plan of action does King outline for African American people in Memphis? (b) What is the purpose of King's plan of action?

4. What feelings does King express about the dangers he faces? What reasons does he give for his feelings?

Analyze and Evaluate

5. What is your opinion of King's nonviolent approach to political and social change?

6. How did the prophetic aspects of this speech affect your reaction to it? Explain.

Connect

7. **Big Idea** Keeping Freedom Alive If King were alive today, what issues do you think he might be addressing? Why?

8. **Connect to the Author** How is Martin Luther King Jr.'s experience as a preacher and minister evident in his speech "I've Been to the Mountaintop"?

Visual Literacy

Image of a Leader

In this photograph, Reverend Martin Luther King, Jr. leads a march from Selma to Montgomery, Alabama, to protest the lack of suffrage for African Americans. The date is March 1965. The photographer chooses not to show those who were opposed to racial desegregation. Instead, he focuses on the pride and promise of those leading the march for freedom by showing them with arms linked, flags emblazoned behind them.

Group Activity Discuss the following questions in a small group. Refer back to the photograph and cite specific details to use as support.

1. How might a person who was against desegregation have viewed this photograph?

2. What choices did the photographer make in the framing and subject matter of the picture that show his bias?

Literary Element Allusion

In this speech, King uses both historical and biblical **allusions**. For example, King says, "I would take my mental flight by Egypt through, or rather across the Red Sea, through the wilderness toward the promised land." He is alluding to the biblical story in which Moses leads the Israelites out of slavery in Egypt to the promised land of Canaan.

1. Why do you think King alludes to the Israelites' flight from Egypt?
2. Locate two more examples of historical allusions in the speech, and explain why they are included.

Review: Tone

As you learned on page 185, **tone** is the writer's attitude toward his or her subject. Tone is conveyed through elements such as word choice, sentence structure, and figurative language. In this speech, King's tone conveys a variety of attitudes, such as seriousness, sadness, sarcasm, optimism, humor, and sympathy.

Partner Activity With a classmate, analyze King's shifting tone in this speech. Create a web diagram similar to the one below. Fill in the ovals with appropriate examples.

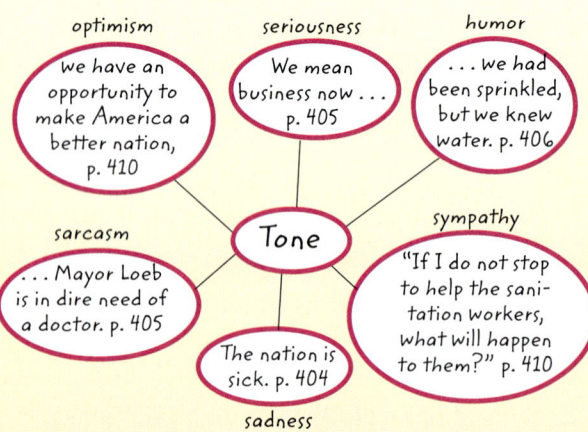

 **Literature** Online

Selection Resources For Selection Quizzes, eFlashcards, and Reading-Writing Connection activities, go to glencoe.com and enter QuickPass code GL59794u2.

Reading Strategy Identify Problem and Solution

SAT Skills Practice

1. What solution to the problem of inequality does King propose in the paragraph beginning "Now we're going to march again . . ." (page 406)?

   (A) economic boycotts
   (B) force
   (C) reason
   (D) persistence
   (E) suffering

Vocabulary Practice

Practice with Synonyms A synonym is a word that has the same or a similar meaning as another word. Match each boldfaced vocabulary word below with its synonym. Use a thesaurus or dictionary to check your answers.

1. compassionate
2. grapple
3. relevant
4. agenda

   a. plan
   b. applicable
   c. accepting
   d. decline
   e. struggle
   f. kindhearted

Academic Vocabulary

*King's words are so powerful that no amount of time can **diminish** their significance.*

Diminish is an academic word. The word might be used to refer to how enthusiasm can be **diminished** by bad weather or someone's negative attitude. Study this word further. Write its definition and give a synonym and an antonym.

For more on academic vocabulary, see pages 52 and 53.

Respond Through Writing

Summary

Learning Objectives

For page 415

In this assignment, you will focus on the following objective:

Writing: Writing a summary.

Report Main Ideas or Events When you write a summary of nonfiction, you restate the main ideas or events in a short version of the original. A summary does not include personal opinions. In about 100 words, summarize Martin Luther King Jr.'s speech.

Understand the Task When you **restate,** you retell written or spoken text in your own words.

Prewrite Skim the text to find the main ideas or events. Look for answers to the following six questions: *who? what? when? where? why?* and *how?* You may find it helpful to make notes in a chart like the one below, which was created for "On Women's Right to Vote" on page 396.

Who	Susan B. Anthony
What	the speech "On Women's Right to Vote"
When	1873
Where	the United States
Why	to argue for woman suffrage
How	by citing passages from the U.S. Constitution

Draft Draw on the answers to the six questions as you draft your summary. Follow a logical order.

Revise Have a partner read your summary and ask him or her to circle the answers to the six questions listed above. In the margin of your paper, your partner should write the question that the circled text answers. If your partner cannot find the answers to all the questions, you may have to revise your summary.

Edit and Proofread Proofread your paper, correcting any errors in grammar, spelling, and punctuation. Use the Grammar Tip in the side column for help with sentence fragments.

Grammar Tip

Sentence Fragments

A sentence fragment lacks a subject, a verb, or a complete thought. Because you can easily miss a sentence fragment in the flow of related sentences, read your summary backwards, starting with the last sentence. Often a fragment begins with *which, because,* or *that,* so be on the lookout for these words.

INCORRECT
Because it denies half of its citizens the rights that it prides itself on granting all of its citizens.

CORRECT
She claims that the United States is hypocritical because it denies half of its citizens the rights that it prides itself on granting all of its citizens.

Comparing Literature
Different Viewpoints

Learning Objectives

For pages 416–430

In studying these texts, you will focus on the following objectives:

Literary Study:
Comparing different viewpoints.
Analyzing rhetorical devices.

Reading: Identifying assumptions and ambiguities.

Compare Literature About the Graphic Novel

Who should read comic books? When should they be read? Where should they be read? Should they be read at all? Answers to these questions depend on the perspective of the person who is answering them. The three works compared here—by Chester Brown, Teresa Méndez, and Andrew Arnold—each explore the development of the comic book and the related graphic novel from a different perspective.

Not Just Comics by Chester Brown.............graphic novel.................419

"Hamlet" too hard? Try a comic book
by Teresa Méndez...newspaper article.................422

The Graphic Novel Silver Anniversary
by Andrew Arnold...Web site article.................426

COMPARE THE Big Idea Keeping Freedom Alive

Freedom of expression remains one of the cornerstones of the United States. Without the ability to speak, create, and think freely, freedom itself would cease to exist. As you read these works by Brown, Méndez, and Arnold, ask yourself, Should the graphic novel eventually earn a place of respect in the literary world?

COMPARE Persuasive Appeals

Persuasive appeals are attempts on the part of authors to influence their readers. As you read, ask yourself, How do these writers use persuasion to express their thoughts about the graphic novel's place in modern culture?

COMPARE Author's Viewpoint

Each of these authors explores the graphic novel from a slightly different perspective and for a different purpose. Popular culture plays an important role in determining what people read, and a generation raised on the graphic images found on television and in video games seems to be drawn naturally to an art form that combines words and images to tell a story. As you read, ask yourself, What is each author's viewpoint, or set of beliefs, about the value and effectiveness of the graphic novel when used in an educational context?

Young Woman Doing a Martial Arts Kick in Front of a Robot. Steve and Ghy Sampson.

Author Search For more about Brown, Méndez, and Arnold, go to glencoe.com and enter QuickPass code GL59794u2.

Before You Read

Persuasive Text

Read and Analyze Persuasive Text

An **argument** is a reason given to prove or support a point. It is often used in persuasive speaking or writing. In order to recognize when a writer or speaker is attempting to persuade, it is important for the audience to understand the structure of an argument and the appeals that are likely to be made.

The Structure of an Argument An argument consists of a position and supporting evidence. The strongest argument is a logical argument. An argument can be structured logically by using either inductive or deductive reasoning. **Inductive reasoning** involves drawing a general conclusion from specific facts. The chart below shows how inductive reasoning led the Health Department of ABCville to test fifteen people to determine what caused an illness for one hundred people. If the sample is selected randomly from the entire hundred, it will be fairly representative of the population.

> **Sample:** Fifteen of one hundred people
>
> ↓
>
> **Facts:** All fifteen of the sample suffer nausea and dizziness Thursday evening. All one hundred ate lunch at Ye Olde XYZ Shoppe on Thursday.
>
> ↓
>
> **Generalization:** One hundred got food poisoning at Ye Olde XYZ Shoppe.

Deductive reasoning involves drawing a specific conclusion from general facts. In deductive reasoning, you make a generalization, state a related fact, and draw a conclusion based on the generalization and the fact.

> **Generalization:** Food poisoning is caused by bacteria that grow in cooked food left at room temperature for six hours.
>
> ↓
>
> **Fact:** At Ye Olde XYZ Shoppe, Juanita ate food that had been left out all day.
>
> ↓
>
> **Conclusion:** It is likely that Juanita will get food poisoning.

Persuasive Appeals and Problems with Arguments A **persuasive appeal** is an attempt to convince someone of something by creating a sympathetic response. Writers appeal to logical, emotional, and ethical appeals. Logical appeals contain solid evidence, such as facts, examples, statistics, or testimony, that appeals to the intellect. Emotional appeals contain information or ideas that target emotions. Ethical appeals address the reader's morals and values.

Fallacies, or errors in reasoning, can weaken an argument. A **deductive fallacy** is an invalid deductive argument. For example, all European countries have U.N. ambassadors, and Sierra Leone has a U.N. ambassador. However, you cannot then conclude that Sierra Leone is in Europe. An **inductive fallacy** is when an argument appears to be inductive but does not provide adequate support for a generalization. For example, water in a certain lake is toxic. Factory runoff causes toxicity. However, assuming that the toxic chemicals in the lake are due to factory runoff is an inductive fallacy.

Comparing Literature

Literature and Reading Preview

Connect to the Selections
Do you think the graphic novel format has educational value? List ways in which you think it can contribute to education.

Build Background
Graphic novels not only are popular but are also considered a literary form and have become a part of school curriculums and libraries. Examples of graphic novels include Art Spiegelman's *Maus*, a memoir on the Holocaust, for which he won the Pulitzer Prize in 1992, and the Japanese comic form called "manga."

Set Purposes for Reading

Big Idea Keeping Freedom Alive

As you read, ask yourself, How does the use of the graphic novel play a role in preserving freedom of expression?

Literary Element Rhetorical Devices

Rhetoric is the effective use of language in order to persuade, so **rhetorical devices** are techniques of persuasive writing. These techniques include repetition, parallelism, analogy, and logic. As you read, ask yourself, How do the authors use these devices?

Reading Strategy Identify Assumptions and Ambiguities

A writer may assume that a point is true, rather than prove it. Or the writer may be ambiguous, using other meanings. When you **identify assumptions and ambiguities,** you develop your own conclusions by distinguishing fact from opinion. As you read, ask yourself, What are the author's assumptions and ambiguities?

Tip: Make Inferences Using logic to evaluate the evidence in the texts will allow you to arrive at a conclusion or to infer the meaning of passages that contain assumptions or ambiguities. Use a chart like the one below to help you organize your thoughts.

Assumption/Ambiguity	Inference
"Once kids know how to read, there is no good reason to continue to use dumbed-down materials."	The speaker of the quote has assumed that all writing in a graphic novel format is dumbed down.

Vocabulary

dilution (di lōō′ shən) *n.* the state of being diminished or lessened; p. 422 *The dilution of public education in the county was a popular topic during the political campaign.*

aficionado (ə fi′ shē ə nä′ dō) *n.* people who like, know about, and appreciate an interest or activity; p. 425 *During the convention, the exhibition hall filled with science fiction aficionados dressed as their favorite characters.*

renaissance (ren′ ə säns) *n.* rebirth or comeback; p. 428 *Once shuttered and silent, the opera house is now in the midst of a renaissance and a revival of its long-lost glory.*

Tip: Word Usage Remember that a word's usage depends on its context. For example, "uh" fits perfectly in a comic book or dialogue. In an analysis of that dialogue, however, the same meaning may be best described as hesitation.

Build Background

Cartoons with word balloons were popular as far back as the eighteenth century, especially in political caricatures. Chester Brown, one of Canada's best known cartoonists, spoke of the future of comics in an interview with *TIME*. Brown said, "I certainly think that this is the most exciting time in terms of the work coming out. There has never been better work being published."

Not Just Comics
Chester Brown

Comparing Literature

Comparing Literature

"Hamlet" Too Hard?
Try a Comic Book
Teresa Méndez

Build Background

The following article discusses the value of the graphic novel in the classroom, especially when used as a tool to connect with students.

Teresa Méndez is a staff writer for the *Christian Science Monitor*. Many of her articles focus on the status of education in the United States.

It may be a shocking *dilution* of academics —or an ingenious way to hook reluctant readers.

At Oneida High School in upstate New York, Diane Roy teaches the students who failed ninth-grade English the first time around. Last year, on the heels of "Hamlet," she presented her class with a graphic novel—essentially a variety of comic book.

Comic books have long been deemed inappropriate classroom reading material. If they appeared at all, they were smuggled in, disguised within the pages of a physics textbook or a volume of Shakespeare.

It's this image—of comic book as contraband[1]—that has endured in the popular imagination at least since the 1950s, when the Senate Judiciary Committee investigated the comic book's sinister influence and potential to inspire juvenile delinquency.

---
1. *Contraband* items are illegal or prohibited. Here, the term refers to reading material not considered appropriate for the classroom.

Vocabulary

dilution (di lōō´shən) *n.* something weakened by the presence of another element

Spider-Man Reading Daily Bugle Newspaper, 2005. Mike Mayhew Marvel Comics.

Comparing Literature

But now the books are turning up on some classroom bookshelves—especially in classes where teachers are desperate to engage struggling and reluctant adolescent readers. For a certain type of student—particularly those who are visually oriented and bright but may lack the motivation or maturity to succeed in freshman English—the graphic novel can become a "bridge to other things," explains Ms. Roy.

Today, the comic book—and its lengthier sibling, the graphic novel—are growing in scope and popularity. In 2002, the theme of the annual Teen Read Week sponsored by YALSA, the youth branch of the American Library Association, was "Get Graphic." Graphic novels can be found in public and school libraries, as well as bookstores, where entire shelves are often devoted to the genre. Manga, the Japanese graphic novels, have swept up teen readers.

And in July, the *New York Times Magazine* ran a cover story positing that the comic book could become the next "new literary form."

Roy's experiment with the graphic novel as text struck gold when she assigned Art Spiegelman's "Maus," the story of his parents' experience in the Holocaust told as a cat and mouse allegory—a highly regarded work that won the Pulitzer Prize. From there, some students moved to graphic novels about Hitler, and finally made their way to traditional books about the Holocaust.

Each student was required to read five graphic novels. But "there wasn't a single student in this class of kids—nonreaders who don't enjoy reading—who didn't read double that number," Roy says. "They would read them overnight . . . they were reading them at lunch, in the hallway."

Roy adapted her curriculum on graphic novels from a series developed for teachers by the New York City Comic Book Museum.

Literacy efforts have traditionally focused not on adolescents, but on younger students.

And some reading experts are worried that with most reform efforts being directed at students in the third grade or lower, another crisis is being ignored.

Even as elementary student scores on federal tests are increasing slightly, high school scores are declining. Only about one third of 12th-graders were reading at a proficient level in 2002, down from 40 percent in 1992.

Adolescent readers face a host of complicated problems, ranging from general reluctance to pick up a book to aliteracy, an inability to fully grasp the meaning of words. Proponents suggest that comic books and graphic novels can help.

For the reluctant reader, they are absorbing. For the struggling reader or the reader still learning English, they offer accessibility: pictures for context, and possibly an alternate path into classroom discussions of higher-level texts. They expand vocabulary, and introduce the ideas of plot, pacing, and sequence.

But such arguments remain unconvincing to many other educators who firmly believe this form of pop culture has no place in the classroom.

"Once kids know how to read, there is no good reason to continue to use dumbed-down materials," writes Diane

---

Identify Assumptions and Ambiguities *What assumption is made here about the value of graphic novels in the classroom?*

Keeping Freedom Alive *How do you think graphic novels might help struggling readers feel freer to join in class discussions?*

TERESA MÉNDEZ

Comparing Literature

Dream Book, 1195. Christian Pierre. Acrylic. Private Collection.

View the Art The theme of this painting is the power of imagination. How does this theme relate to your ideas about the graphic novel as a literary form?

Ravitch, a professor of education at New York University, in an e-mail. "They should be able to read poems, novels, essays, books that inform them, enlighten them, broaden their horizons."

And there is always a concern about the appropriateness of content.

But just getting reluctant adolescents to read—anything—can be a boon to their discovery of the joy of reading, says Marilyn Reynolds, author of "I Won't Read and You Can't Make Me: Reaching Reluctant Teen Readers."

Ms. Reynolds, who worked for decades at an alternative high school for struggling students in a Los Angeles suburb, tells the story of a girl "steeped" in graphic novels whom she met at a library.

"That's probably all she will read in high school," says Reynolds. "She's a rebel. She's probably failing English . . . because she doesn't conform, but she's got this fervor for that kind of expression. How much better that than not having any fervor at all."

Reynolds may be extreme in her belief that reading a comic book or graphic novel is a worthy end in itself. Most educators hold that the genre is best used as a bridge to more complex material.

For example, Wonder Woman comics could interest students in Greek mythology, says Philip Charles Crawford, the library director at Essex High School, in Essex Junction, VT.

Rhetorical Devices *Do you think that readers of comics about mythical heroes will indeed be interested in literary mythology? Is this a valid argument for letting young people read comic books?*

Pilot Giving Thumbs Up Signal. Steve and Ghy Sampson.

View the Art This image represents a style often used in graphic novels. What does this style of drawing readily portray? Why is it suitable for graphic novels?

"The subject matter leads you other places and I think the majority of readers are going to read other things," says Mr. Crawford, who has written "Graphic Novels 101: Selecting and Using Graphic Novels to Promote Literacy for Children and Young Adults."

And graphic novels like Marjane Satrapi's memoirs, "Persepolis" and "Persepolis 2," have exposed readers to life in Iran in the wake of the Islamic Revolution. Ms. Satrapi recently spoke at Edwin G. Foreman High School in Chicago, where students read "Persepolis" for class.

But others worry that the comics versions of classics like "Frankenstein" or "The Odyssey" may come to replace the originals. Carol Jago, an English teacher at Santa Monica High School in California, believes this raises questions of equity in the classroom. "If we end up giving the real thing to our honors students and the comic books to everyone else, we're actually demeaning the nature of public education," she says.

Yet defenders of the comic book point out that many adolescent *aficionados* of the genre have gone on to excel at the written word.

For his book "Give Our Regards to the Atomsmashers!" editor Sean Howe collected essays in which established writers like Jonathan Lethem and Aimee Bender divulge their longtime love of comics.

Even Edward P. Jones, who won this year's Pulitzer Prize for his novel "The Known World," recently admitted that he was weaned on comic books. Until he was 13, he says, he'd never read a book without a picture.

Identify Assumptions and Ambiguities What is ambiguous about the phrase "the nature of public education"?

Vocabulary

aficionado (ə fi shē ə nä′dō) *n.* people who like, know about, and appreciate an interest or activity

Discussion Starter

Méndez presents arguments both for and against using graphic novels as teaching tools. With a small group, discuss your opinion about the place of the graphic novel in a school setting. Do you think that graphic novels should be used in the classroom? If so, what uses are appropriate? Should graphic novels be used as a bridge to other material? Should they be used to teach all students or only certain students? Summarize your discussion for the rest of your class.

Comparing Literature

Build Background

The superheroes and super-villains of comic books have given way to a new type of content. Graphic novels cover anything from current and historical events to biographical and autobiographical accounts. In the following article, Andrew Arnold assesses the state of the graphic novel on its twenty-fifth anniversary.

The GRAPHIC NOVEL
Silver Anniversary

Andrew Arnold

Young Woman Doing a Martial Arts Kick in Front of a Robot. Steve and Ghy Sampson.

Japanese manga, superhero collections, non-fiction, autobiography—all of these are "graphic novels," a term that now applies to any square-bound book with a story told in comics format. "The problem with the word 'graphic novel' is that it is an arguably misguided bid for respectability where graphics are respectable and novels are respectable so you get double respectability," Spiegelman[1] says. Eisner[2] himself dislikes the phrase, calling it a "limited term," and prefers "graphic literature or graphic story."

Either of those terms seems preferable to the striving, mostly-inaccurate "graphic novel." But some would argue against any such terminology. Chip Kidd, book designer and "graphic novel" editor at Pantheon, an imprint of the giant trade publisher Random House, loathes the ghettoizing of such books, starting with their name. "What I don't like is when we have to categorize everything in

---

1. Art Spiegelman is the author of *Maus* (1986), a Holocaust memoir in graphic novel form.
2. Will Eisner's *A Contract with God, and Other Tenement Stories*, published in 1978, is an admired, early graphic novel.

Rhetorical Devices A *ghetto* is a section of a city where a minority group lives due to economic pressure. How does this analogy describe the perception of graphic novels by many publishers?

Comparing Literature

order to appreciate or understand it," he wrote in an email. "At Pantheon, we do not see these books as part of a 'line,' or a 'program' any more than we would books by Ha Jin or Stanley Crouch.[3] They are simply books we want to publish that happen to use the form of visual narrative."

As a critic, though, I would argue that these types of books are fundamentally different from prose. Blurring the line between them would be charmingly quixotic[4] at best and harmful at worst. That which distinguishes drawn books from prose is what we love about them. The Artistry is different—way beyond mere genre—and must be celebrated. In order to talk about the unique pleasures of drawn books we necessarily distinguish them from their text-only relatives.

But categorizing graphic novels goes beyond artistic semantics[5] to the real bottom line—dollars and cents. Most big bookstores put all the graphic novels together in one place. Trade bookstores have become an increasingly important outlet for comic publishers so the strategy for selling them on the floor has become critical. Should Superman, manga and "Maus," sit side by side? Chip Kidd, among many others, can't stand this. "I truly believe that Spiegelman's 'Maus' should be shelved next to Elie Wiesel and Primo Levi,[6] not next to the X-Men. Maus is a Holocaust memoir first and a comic book second." Micha Hershman, the graphic novel buyer for a bookstore chain has no such doubts. "The graphic novel is a format," he says. "We would not segment the category by splitting up the graphic novel section." According to Hershman, research shows the "demographics for 'Maus' overlap with the ones for Spider-Man," so that it is theoretically easier to lure the reader of one to the other than it is to lure a reader of Elie Wiesel to "Maus."

Something seems to be working because graphic novels have finally reached a point of critical mass in both popular consciousness and sales.

Could graphic novels eventually make the traditional comic book disappear? Frank Miller, author of "The Dark Knight Returns," recently shocked a comics industry crowd at the annual Eisner awards by pronouncing the format to be a goner, declaring, "Our future is not in pamphlets." Nick Purpura disputes this, saying, "the serialized versions pay for the trades. That way publishers get to sell it twice—once to comics fans and again to people who only buy collections." Even so, he says, "books that sold marginally as comics sell better as graphic novels." Additionally, there have been an increasing number of "original graphic novels," as Purpura calls them, which never appeared in serialized form. The most impressive example of these is DC comics' October release of "Sandman: Endless Nights," by Neil Gaiman, which reached number 20 on the New York Times bestseller list.

---

3. *Ha Jin* is an award-winning Chinese American author. *Stanley Crouch* is an American journalist and critic.
4. *Quixotic* means "foolishly impractical."
5. *Semantics* is the branch of linguistics that deals with the meanings of words, as well as their historical development.
6. *Elie Wiesel* and *Primo Levi* are both Jewish writers who survived Nazi concentration camps.

Identify Assumptions and Ambiguities *Is this statement an assumption, an ambiguity, or neither? Explain.*

Keeping Freedom Alive *Why do individual bookstores in a chain usually not have the freedom to organize books as they wish?*

ANDREW ARNOLD

Comparing Literature

Superman from the Myths Series, 1981. Andy Warhol. The Andy Warhol Foundation for the Visual Arts.

lic awareness of these books has vastly increased, creating a kind of **renaissance era of intense creativity and quality.** Says Spiegelman, "Ultimately the future of the graphic novel is dependent on how much great work gets produced against all odds. I'm much more optimistic than I was that there's room for something and I know that right now there's more genuinely interesting comic art than there's been for decades and decades."

Keeping Freedom Alive In what ways have graphic novels spurred artistic freedom among writers and artists?

Vocabulary

renaissance (ren′ ə säns′) *n.* rebirth or comeback

The future of the graphic novel seems both sunny and dim. As a term for a kind of book, "graphic novel" has become increasingly dissatisfying. "Maybe for a short window it was enough to say 'graphic novel' but soon it won't be," says Art Spiegelman, "because if you talk about [Chris Ware's] 'Jimmy Corrigan' as a graphic novel you'll have to explain that it's not manga or Marvel. Then you are left saying, 'well it's got a seriousness of purpose' that the phrase 'graphic novel' alone won't offer." On the positive side, the pub-

Rhetorical Devices Here the writer uses sensory words to create a mental image. If this article were part of a graphic novel, how might this imagery be shown?

Quickwrite

In this selection, Andrew Arnold says of the graphic novel: "That which distinguishes drawn books from prose is what we love about them. The Artistry is different—way beyond mere genre—and must be celebrated." Write two to three paragraphs addressing this comment. Consider the following in your response: How does Arnold define the graphic novel as opposed to regular literature? How might he define "Artistry" and why did he capitalize that word? What does he mean when he refers to "mere genre" and asserts that the artistry "must be celebrated"?

428 UNIT 2 NONFICTION

After You Read

Respond and Think Critically

Respond and Interpret

1. (a) With which of these authors do you agree most? (b) With which do you disagree? Explain.

2. What reasons does Méndez give that support using graphic novels in the classroom? Do you believe that her evidence is valid? Explain.

3. (a) What does Arnold say about the term "graphic novel"? (b) Why do you think he believes that the topic is important enough to be discussed in his column?

Analyze and Evaluate

4. Evaluate Méndez's use of rhetorical devices. Consider whether her argument is valid and whether she incorporates any fallacies into her argument.

5. Arnold describes the marketing approach used by many bookstores to sell graphic novels. Decide whether he uses similar techniques in his column to promote the graphic novel as a literary form.

Connect

6. **Big Idea** Keeping Freedom Alive Méndez writes that graphic novels reach all students. In what ways does educational opportunity relate to keeping freedom alive? Explain.

7. **Connect to Today** What current events do you think might belong in a graphic novel? Explain.

Literary Element Rhetorical Devices

Writers use **rhetorical devices**, such as appeals to logic, emotion, morality, or authority, to persuade their readers. A common rhetorical device is the **analogy**, a comparison that shows similarities between two dissimilar things.

1. What analogy does Brown make in his comic? Explain.

2. Does Méndez appeal to logic, emotion, morality, or authority? Explain.

Reading Strategy Identify Assumptions and Ambiguities

Sometimes authors try to influence readers by presenting their personal assumptions as facts, or by making statements that are ambiguous. **Identifying assumptions and ambiguities** will help you determine whether you agree with the author's opinions.

1. What assumption is Brown's comic based upon?

2. See Brown's graphic-novel defender as he protests: "I don't have to put up with this sort of juvenile nonsense." How is this statement ambiguous?

Vocabulary Practice

Practice with Usage Respond to these statements to help you explore the meanings of vocabulary words from the selection.

1. Give an example of a **dilution**.

2. Describe the behavior of a sports **aficionado**.

3. Name two characteristics of a **renaissance** era.

Writing

Write a Letter Imagine you are a graphic novelist who wants to convince a publisher to publish your graphic version of a well-known story. Write the publisher a letter. Use rhetorical devices to persuade the publisher that your version will appeal to readers. See page R22 for the format you should use in a business letter.

Wrap-Up: Comparing Literature
Different Viewpoints

- *Not Just Comics* by Chester Brown
- *"Hamlet" too hard? Try a comic book* by Teresa Méndez
- *The Graphic Novel Silver Anniversary* by Andrew Arnold

COMPARE THE Big Idea Keeping Freedom Alive

Partner Activity The authors of "Not Just Comic Books" and "The Graphic Novel Silver Anniversary" both present the graphic novel as a new form of expression worthy of literary and artistic merit. Consider what literary and artistic thought mean in terms of freedom of expression. With a partner, write a brief essay in which you consider the contributions by graphic novelists to a free society. Also consider how negative public opinion toward the genre might affect it.

COMPARE Persuasive Appeals

Group Activity Although each of the selections compared here has a different purpose, they all contain persuasive appeals that communicate the authors' positions. With a small group, discuss the following questions:

1. What is each author trying to communicate about the graphic novel format?
2. What persuasive appeals does each author use to influence the reader?
3. Which of the selections, in your opinion, presents the strongest argument about the role of the graphic novel in modern culture? Support your answer with passages from the selections.

COMPARE Authors' Viewpoints

Speaking and Listening Chester Brown, Teresa Méndez, and Andrew Arnold each have a different viewpoint on the format of the graphic novel. Make inferences about each author's viewpoint on the following topics:

- the role of the graphic novel in modern or pop culture
- the influence of pop culture on the reading habits of young people
- the effectiveness of the graphic novel when used in an educational setting

Support your inferences with details from the selections. Use a graphic organizer like the one below to organize your ideas. Then present your insights in an oral report to the class.

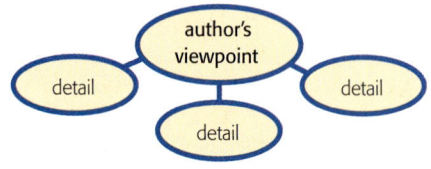

Selection Resources For Selection Quizzes, eFlashcards, and Reading-Writing Connection activities, go to glencoe.com and enter QuickPass code GL59794u2.

Before You Read

Address on the Anniversary of Lincoln's Birth

Meet Carl Sandburg
(1878–1967)

Few people would have predicted that Carl Sandburg would grow up and become a noteworthy writer of his generation. The son of working-class Swedish immigrants, Sandburg was born in Galesburg, Illinois. He left school after eighth grade in order to work at a variety of jobs that included washing dishes, shining shoes, selling newspapers, and driving a milk truck.

Early Books Sandburg enlisted in the army during the Spanish-American war and later returned to Galesburg, where he enrolled at Lombard College. Sandburg worked for a while as a journalist in Milwaukee and Chicago but then began writing poetry and published *Chicago Poems*. This work was controversial because Sandburg wrote about the working class and used colloquial, as opposed to literary, language. To some critics, using "the language of factory and sidewalk" was almost an insult; to others, it was a bold and distinguishing characteristic.

> *"Slang is a language that rolls up its sleeves, spits on its hands and goes to work."*
>
> —Carl Sandburg

Sandburg began to travel around the country, collecting poems, folk stories, and songs. He made a series of public appearances, at which he recited his own poems and sang some of the folk songs that he had collected. Later, Sandburg published a book of several hundred songs that he had collected over time, called *American Songbag*.

The Lincoln Books From an early age, Sandburg had an interest in Abraham Lincoln. In the mid-1920s, Sandburg began collecting information about Abraham Lincoln for a biography. Originally, he envisioned it to be a children's book, but it gradually grew into a large, two-volume work called *Abraham Lincoln: The Prairie Years*. The book covered the period of time between Lincoln's birth and his move to Washington, D.C., when he became president.

The book was a popular success that presented a portrait of Lincoln that few had seen before; Sandburg's Lincoln was a complex individual, not a legend. Sandburg later produced a four-volume biography about Lincoln's later life called *Abraham Lincoln: The War Years*. This book earned him a Pulitzer Prize in 1939.

Author Search For more about Carl Sandburg, go to glencoe.com and enter QuickPass code GL59794u2.

CARL SANDBURG **431**

Literature and Reading Preview

Connect to the Address
What would cause you to admire a national leader? List several qualities that you would expect to find in a leader you admire. Why are those qualities important?

Build Background
The Confederate States of America had formed by the time Abraham Lincoln was sworn in as the nation's sixteenth president in 1861. Lincoln accepted the fact that only a vigorous war effort would restore the Union. The history of Lincoln's administration followed the course of the Civil War.

Set Purposes for Reading

Big Idea Keeping Freedom Alive

As you read "Address on the Anniversary of Lincoln's Birth," ask yourself, How does Sandburg relate his impressions of Lincoln to the preservation of freedom and national unity?

Literary Element Quotation

A **quotation** is a passage taken from another author's text and inserted word for word into a speech or work of literature. The use of quotations can provide insights about a writer's character or message. As you read, ask yourself, How does Sandburg incorporate Lincoln's words into his own, original text?

Reading Strategy Distinguish Fact and Opinion

A **fact** is a statement that can be proven beyond a reasonable doubt. An **opinion** is a personal interpretation or belief. As you read, ask yourself, Is what I am reading fact or opinion? How can this help me evaluate the author's message and purpose?

Tip: Identify Facts and Opinions Use a chart to list facts and opinions as you read.

Fact	Opinion
"He enforced conscription of soldiers for the first time in American history." p. 434	Lincoln is described as a man "who is both steel and velvet." p. 433

Learning Objectives
For pages 431–438

In studying this text, you will focus on the following objectives:

Literary Analysis: Analyzing quotation.

Reading: Distinguishing fact and opinion.

Vocabulary

paradox (par′ə doks′) *n.* a statement that seems contradictory and yet may be true; p. 433 *They were puzzled by the paradox in the song lyrics.*

imperative (im per′ə tiv) *adj.* expressing a command or an order; p. 434 *Their mother said it was imperative that they come straight home after school.*

turbulent (tur′byə lənt) *adj.* causing unrest, violent action, or disturbance; p. 434 *Turbulent seas caused the captain to seek calmer waters.*

emancipation (i man′sə pā′shən) *n.* the process of becoming free from control or the power of another; p. 434 *After their emancipation, the former slaves were no longer considered property.*

valor (val′ər) *n.* courageous spirit; personal bravery; p. 435 *The soldiers showed valor when they did not flee from the enemy's gunfire.*

Address on the Anniversary of Lincoln's Birth

CARL SANDBURG

President Lincoln's Address at Gettysburg.
Artist unknown. Hand colored halftone.

Not often in the story of mankind does a man arrive on earth who is both steel and velvet, who is as hard as rock and soft as drifting fog, who holds in his heart and mind the **paradox** of terrible storm and peace unspeakable and perfect. Here and there across centuries come reports of men alleged to have these contrasts. And the incomparable Abraham Lincoln, born 150 years ago this day, is an approach if not a perfect realization of this character.

In the time of the April lilacs in the year 1865, on his death, the casket with his body was carried north and west a thousand miles, and the American people wept as never before. Bells sobbed, cities wore crepe, people stood in tears and with hats off as the railroad burial car paused in the leading cities of seven states, ending its journey at Springfield, Illinois, the home town.

During the four years he was president, he at times, especially in the first three

> **Vocabulary**
> **paradox** (par′ə doks′) *n.* a statement that seems contradictory and yet may be true

months, took to himself the powers of a dictator. He commanded the most powerful armies till then assembled in modern warfare. He enforced conscription of soldiers for the first time in American history. Under **imperative** necessity he abolished the right of habeas corpus. He directed politically and spiritually the wild, massive, **turbulent** forces let loose in civil war.

He argued and pleaded for compensated **emancipation** of the slaves. The slaves were property, they were on the tax books along with horses and cattle, the valuation of each slave next to his name on the tax assessor's books. Failing to get action on compensated emancipation, as a chief executive having war powers, he issued the paper by which he declared the slaves to be free under "military necessity." In the end nearly $4 million worth of property was taken away from those who were legal owners of it, property confiscated, wiped out as by fire and turned to ashes, at his instigation and executive direction. Chattel[1] property recognized and lawful for 300 years was expropriated, seized without payment.

In the month the war began he told his secretary, John Hay,[2] "My policy is to have no policy." Three years later in a letter to a Kentucky friend made public, he confessed plainly, "I have been controlled by events." His words at Gettysburg were sacred, yet strange with a color of the familiar: "We cannot consecrate—we cannot hallow—this ground. The brave men, living and dead, who struggled here, have consecrated it, far beyond our poor power to add or detract."

He could have said "the brave Union men." Did he have a purpose in omitting the word *Union?* Was he keeping himself and his utterance clear of the passion that would not be good to look at when the time came for peace and reconciliation? Did he mean to leave an implication that there were brave Union men, and brave Confederate men, living and dead, who had struggled there? We do not know of a certainty. Was he thinking of the Kentucky father whose two sons died in battle, one in Union blue, the other in Confederate gray, the father inscribing on the stone over their double grave, "God knows which was right"? We do not know. . . .

While the war winds howled, he insisted that the Mississippi was one river meant to belong to one country, that railroad connection from coast to coast must be pushed through and the Union Pacific Railroad[3] made a reality. While the luck of war wavered and broke and came again, as generals failed and campaigns were lost, he held enough forces of the North together to raise new armies and supply them, until generals were found who made war as victorious war has always been

---

1. *Chattel*, in this context, means "slave."
2. *John Milton Hay*, President Lincoln's secretary, became Secretary of State in 1898.

Keeping Freedom Alive What does this statement reveal about Lincoln's character and values?

Vocabulary

imperative (im per´ə tiv) *adj.* expressing a command or an order

turbulent (tur´byə lənt) *adj.* causing unrest, violent action, or disturbance

emancipation (i man´sə pā´shən) *n.* the process of becoming free from control or the power of another

---

3. The *Union Pacific Railroad* came into being when President Lincoln signed the Pacific Railway Act, which directed the Union Pacific and the Central Pacific companies to construct a transcontinental railroad.

Quotation How do the quotations in this paragraph help the reader understand Lincoln?

The Death of Lincoln (1809–1865), 1868. Alonzo Chappel. Oil on canvas. Chicago Historical Society.

View the Art In 1865, Abraham Lincoln was assassinated. What might this image suggest about the way Lincoln was regarded by his peers? How does it reflect Sandburg's thoughts on Lincoln?

made—with terror, frightfulness, destruction, and on both sides, North and South, **valor** and sacrifice past words of man to tell.

In the mixed shame and blame of the immense wrongs of two crashing civilizations, often with nothing to say, he said nothing, slept not at all, and on occasions he was seen to weep in a way that made weeping appropriate, decent, majestic. . . .

The people of many other countries take Lincoln now for their own. He belongs to them. He stands for decency, honest dealing, plain talk, and funny stories. "Look where he came from. Don't he know all us strugglers, and wasn't he a kind of tough struggler all his life right up to the finish?" Something like that you can hear in any nearby neighborhood and across the seas.

Millions there are who take him as a personal treasure. He had something they would like to see spread everywhere over the world. Democracy? We can't find words to say exactly what it is, but he had it. In his blood and bones he carried it. In the breath of his speeches and writings it is there. Popular government? Republican institution? Government where the people have the say-so, one way or another telling their elected leaders what they want? He had the idea. It's there in the lights and shadows of his personality, a mystery that can be lived but never fully spoken in words.

Distinguish Fact and Opinion What in this statement is factual? What cannot be proved?

Vocabulary

valor (val′ər) *n.* courageous spirit; personal bravery

Funeral of Abraham Lincoln, at Springfield, Illinois, 1868. S.M. Fassett.

Our good friend the poet and playwright Mark Van Doren[4] tells us, "To me, Lincoln seems, in some ways, the most interesting man who ever lived. He was gentle, but his gentleness was combined with a terrific toughness, an iron strength."

How did Lincoln say he would like to be remembered? His beloved friend, Representative Owen Lovejoy[5] of Illinois, had died in May of 1864 and friends wrote to Lincoln and he replied that the pressure of duties kept him from joining them in efforts for a marble monument to Lovejoy, the last sentence of his letter saying, "Let him have the marble monument along with the well-assured and more enduring one in the hearts of those who love liberty, unselfishly, for all men."

So perhaps we may say that the well-assured and most enduring memorial to Lincoln is invisibly there, today, tomorrow, and for a long time yet to come in the hearts of lovers of liberty, men and women who understand that wherever there is freedom there have been those who fought, toiled, and sacrificed for it.

---

4. **Mark Van Doren** (1894-1973) was an American poet and teacher who is known for his verse *The Last Days of Lincoln* (1959).
5. **Owen Lovejoy** was elected to the House of Representatives from the state of Illinois in 1856 and served five terms.

Quotation *What does Sandburg hope to accomplish by quoting Mark Van Doren here?*

After You Read

Respond and Think Critically

Respond and Interpret

1. How did you react to Sandburg's claim that the "most enduring memorial to Lincoln is invisibly there, today, tomorrow, and for a long time yet to come in the hearts of lovers of liberty"?

2. (a) According to Sandburg, what makes people everywhere feel that Lincoln is "their own"? (b) What does this comment suggest about how Sandburg viewed the lives of people everywhere?

3. (a) From the quotations, what was Lincoln's opinion about the way in which he conducted the Civil War? (b) What might these comments reveal about his state of mind and his personal ability?

Analyze and Evaluate

4. In the first paragraph, Sandburg portrays Lincoln in terms of metaphorical contrasts, such as "steel and velvet." Is this an effective introduction? Explain.

5. Sandburg twice claims that "we do not know" when he speculates about Lincoln's thoughts. By doing this, does he help or hinder his reader's understanding of Lincoln? Explain.

6. The speech ends with the phrase "wherever there is freedom there have been those who fought, toiled, and sacrificed for it." How does this conclusion fit into Sandburg's discussion of Lincoln?

Connect

7. **Big Idea** **Keeping Freedom Alive** Lincoln is often referred to as "the great emancipator." How does this speech support this view?

8. **Connect to Today** How have modern understandings of liberty been shaped by Lincoln's legacy?

Literary Element Quotation

Authors use **quotations** for various purposes. For example, a quotation may provide the reader with greater insight into an author's or another person's life or philosophy. Quotations can also make nonfiction texts, which generally do not contain much dialogue, "come alive."

1. Why does Sandburg include quotations in his speech?

2. Explain how the following Lincoln quotation contributes to Sandburg's purpose: "Let him have the marble monument along with the well-assured and more enduring one in the hearts of those who love liberty, unselfishly, for all men."

Review: Persuasion

As you learned on pages 392–393, **persuasion** is writing that attempts to convince readers to think or act in a particular way. Among other techniques, writers of persuasive works appeal to reason or emotion to sway readers.

Partner Activity With a classmate, discuss Sandburg's use of persuasion in his speech. Create a two-column chart similar to the one below to help you identify the types of appeals used to persuade.

Examples of Persuasion	Type of Appeal
"Bells sobbed, cities wore crepe, people stood in tears."	emotional appeal

Literature Online

Selection Resources For Selection Quizzes, eFlashcards, and Reading-Writing Connection activities, go to glencoe.com and enter QuickPass code GL59794u2.

Reading Strategy: Distinguish Fact and Opinion

SAT Skills Practice

1. In the second paragraph of the address, Sandburg is making an unprovable assertion when he states that

   (A) Lincoln died in April when lilacs were in flower
   (B) the casket was carried north and west a thousand miles
   (C) Americans wept as never before
   (D) bells rang and people removed their hats as the train paused in major cities
   (E) the journey ended in Springfield, Illinois

Vocabulary Practice

Practice with Denotation and Connotation

Denotation is the literal, or dictionary, meaning of a word. **Connotation** is the implied, or cultural, meaning of a word. For example, the words *awful* and *unspeakable* have a similar denotation, but they have different connotations:

Weaker awful *Stronger* unspeakable

Work with a partner to complete a graphic organizer like the one below for each vocabulary word.

paradox   imperative
turbulent   emancipation   valor

EXAMPLE:

Vocabulary word: → awful

Similar word: → unspeakable

Explanation: → Unspeakable has the stronger connotation because awful can apply to a range of things, from not so bad (a headache), to very bad (a car crash). Unspeakable, however, suggests only extraordinarily bad things.

Research and Report

 Literary Criticism

Assignment Write five blurbs, or excerpts from complete reviews, that might appear on the cover of a magazine containing Sandburg's speech about Lincoln.

Prepare Read the following quotation from the *New York Times* about Sandburg's biography of Lincoln:

"A new experience awaits the reader of Carl Sandburg's book on Lincoln. There has never been a biography quite like this before.... There is no question here of a new school of biographical writing. The thing Mr. Sandburg has done cannot well be repeated; his achievement is an intensely individual one, suffused by the qualities which are peculiarly his own as a poet. As those who have read him know, they are not qualities of conventional poetry, nor is this new book of his merely an emotional rendering of the Lincoln story. It is as full of facts as Jack Horner's pie was full of plums."

Just as this reviewer praised, and, perhaps, sold the book, decide how you want to praise or sell Sandburg's speech to your audience. Then find brief bits of evidence from the speech, such as poetic phrases, clever puns, or insightful facts, to support your praise.

Meet with classmates to collaborate on creating the blurbs. Use the quotation from the *New York Times* as a model.

Report Read each blurb aloud to the class. Make eye contact, speak clearly, and show enthusiasm and conviction through your gestures and stance. Use an enthusiastic tone of voice to engage your audience.

Evaluate Decide how effective each of the following was in praising or "selling" the speech: your tone, clarity, and body language, as well as the main idea of and support for each blurb. Write a suggestion for self-improvement in one or more areas. Use the checklist on page 457 for ideas.

TIME

What I See in Lincoln's Eyes

He never won Illinois' Senate seat. But in many ways, he paved the way for me.

By BARACK OBAMA

MY FAVORITE PORTRAIT OF ABRAHAM LINCOLN comes from the end of his life. In it, Lincoln's face is as finely lined as a pressed flower. He appears frail, almost broken; his eyes, averted from the camera's lens, seem to contain a heartbreaking melancholy, as if he sees before him what the nation had so recently endured.

It would be a sorrowful picture except for the fact that Lincoln's mouth is turned ever so slightly into a smile. The smile doesn't negate the sorrow. But it alters tragedy into grace. It's as if this rough-faced, aging man has cast his gaze toward eternity and yet still cherishes his memories—of an imperfect world and its fleeting, sometimes terrible beauty. On trying days, the portrait, a reproduction of which hangs in my office, soothes me; it always asks me questions.

What is it about this man that can move us so profoundly? Some of it has to do with Lincoln's humble beginnings, which often speak to our own. When I moved to Illinois 20 years ago to work as a community organizer, I had no money in my pockets and didn't know a single soul. During my first six years in the state legislature, Democrats were in the minority, and I couldn't get a bill heard, much less passed. In my first race for Congress, I had my head handed to me. So when I, an African American man with a funny name, born in Hawaii of a father from Kenya and a mother from Kansas, announced my candidacy for the United States Senate, it was hard to imagine a less likely scenario than that I would win—except, perhaps, for the one that allowed a child born in the backwoods of Kentucky

---

Learning Objectives

For pages 439–441

In studying this text, you will focus on the following objectives:

Reading:
Analyzing a visual image.
Analyzing informational text.

Set a Purpose for Reading

Read to learn about Barack Obama's opinion of President Lincoln and how it shapes his view of people in the United States.

Preview the Article

1. From what you have already learned about him, what is your perspective on President Lincoln?
2. Skim the first two paragraphs. What can you assume about Obama's use of language in the article?

Reading Strategy — Analyze a Visual Image

Analyzing a visual image involves looking at a part of the selection in order to understand the entire selection. When you analyze a visual image, you consider the word pictures a writer uses to evoke an emotional response. Ask yourself, "How does this visual image further the writer's purpose?" As you read, take notes using a graphic organizer like the one below.

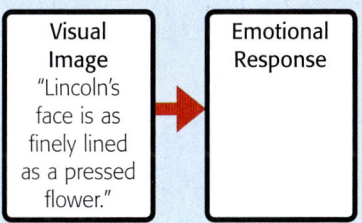

Visual Image: "Lincoln's face is as finely lined as a pressed flower." → Emotional Response

Informational Text

with less than a year of formal education to end up as Illinois' greatest citizen and our nation's greatest President.

In Lincoln's rise from poverty, his ultimate mastery of language and law, his capacity to overcome personal loss and remain determined in the face of repeated defeat—in all this, he reminded me not just of my own struggles. He also reminded me of a larger, fundamental element of American life—the enduring belief that we can constantly remake ourselves to fit our larger dreams.

A connected idea attracts us to Lincoln: As we remake ourselves, we remake our surroundings. He didn't just talk or write or theorize. He split rail, fired rifles, tried cases, and pushed for new bridges and roads and waterways. In his sheer energy, Lincoln captures a hunger in us to build and to innovate. It's a quality that can get us in trouble; we may be blind at times to the costs of progress. And yet, when I travel to other parts of the world, I remember that it is precisely such energy that sets us apart, a sense that there are no limits to the heights our nation might reach.

Still, as I look at his picture, it is the man and not the icon that speaks to me. I cannot swallow whole the view of Lincoln as the Great Emancipator. As a law professor and civil rights lawyer and as an African American, I am fully aware of his limited views on race. Anyone who actually reads the Emancipation Proclamation knows it was more a military document than a clarion call for justice. Scholars tell us too that Lincoln wasn't immune from political considerations and that his temperament could be indecisive and morose.

But it is precisely those imperfections—and the painful self-awareness of those failings etched in every crease of his face and reflected in those haunted eyes—that make him so compelling. For when the time came to confront the greatest moral challenge this nation has ever faced, this all too human man did not pass the challenge on to future generations. He neither demonized the fathers and sons who did battle on the other side nor sought to diminish the terrible costs of his war. In the midst of slavery's dark storm and the complexities of governing a house divided, he somehow kept his moral compass pointed firm and true.

April 10, 1865

CHARACTER STUDY
The Senator looks to Lincoln for guidance.

What I marvel at, what gives me such hope, is that this man could overcome depression, self-doubt, and the constraints of biography and not only act decisively but retain his humanity. Like a figure from the Old Testament, he wandered the earth, making mistakes, loving his family but causing them pain, despairing over the course of events, trying to divine God's will. He did not know how things would turn out, but he did his best.

A few weeks ago, I spoke at the commencement at Knox College in Galesburg, Illinois. I stood in view of the spot where Lincoln and Stephen Douglas held one of their famous debates during their race in 1858 for the U.S. Senate. The only way for Lincoln to get onto the podium was to squeeze his lanky frame through a window, whereupon he reportedly remarked, "At last I have finally gone through college." Waiting for the soon-to-be graduates to assemble, I thought that even as Lincoln lost that Senate race, his arguments that day would result, centuries later, in my occupying the same seat that he coveted. He may not have dreamed of that exact outcome. But I like to believe he would have appreciated the irony. Humor, ambiguity, complexity, compassion—all were part of his character. And as Lincoln called once upon the better angels of our nature, I believe that he is calling still, across the ages, to summon some measure of that character, the American character, in each of us today.

—From TIME

Respond and Think Critically

Respond and Interpret

1. Write a brief summary of the main ideas in this article before you answer the following questions. For help on writing a summary, see page 415.

2. How did you react to Obama opening the article by describing the portrait of Lincoln?

3. Why does Obama say that he "cannot swallow whole the view of Lincoln as the Great Emancipator"?

4. What qualities does Obama say defined "the American character"?

Analyze and Evaluate

5. Choose the sentence that best describes the main idea of the reading selection:

   i   Lincoln could be "indecisive and morose," contrary to most people's perceptions of him.

   ii Barack Obama gives Lincoln direct credit for his political success.

   iii Lincoln remains a profound source of inspiration to many people in the United States, largely due to the story of his success and his actions as president.

6. Obama says that Lincoln's portrait "always asks me questions." From the topics covered in this article, what might those questions be?

7. Good persuasive writing presents and refutes counterarguments to its thesis. Do you think that Obama's article is an example of good persuasive writing? Why or why not?

Connect

8. Obama draws a comparison between his own journey to the U.S. Senate and Lincoln's path from being "a child born in the backwoods of Kentucky with less than a year of formal education . . . [to] our nation's greatest President." In what ways do both of their lives and accomplishments represent the U.S. ideals of freedom and liberty and the achievement of the "American dream"?

Before You Read

Cinderella's Stepsisters

Meet **Toni Morrison**
(born 1931)

In 1993 Toni Morrison became the first African American woman to be awarded the Nobel Prize in Literature. This prestigious prize, given to one outstanding writer every year, recognizes a variety of literature and authors. This recognition of Morrison solidified her standing as an internationally renowned and respected author.

> *"At some point in life the world's beauty becomes enough."*
>
> —Toni Morrison

Beginnings Toni Morrison was born Chloe Anthony Wofford in Lorain, Ohio. She later changed her first name to "Toni" because she grew tired of people mispronouncing "Chloe." As a child, Morrison read constantly. She also enjoyed listening to her community's folktales, which her father related to her. She began her studies at Howard University, where she received a bachelor's degree in English. She went on to earn a master's degree from Cornell University. After graduating, she taught English at Texas Southern University and Howard University. She became a textbook editor and later a senior editor at a major publishing house in New York City. Morrison published her first novel, *The Bluest Eye,* in 1970. *The Bluest Eye* is set in 1941 in Ohio and tells the story of a young African American girl who is consumed with wanting to achieve a white ideal of beauty: blonde hair and blue eyes.

Style Morrison's work is praised for its examination of the experience of being an African American woman in the United States at various historical times. Morrison does not necessarily use straightforward narrative to tell her stories and sometimes abruptly changes scenes or point of view. Morrison also incorporates elements such as myth and superstition.

Continued Success Morrison's successes include the novels *Sula* (1973), *Song of Solomon* (1977), *Tar Baby* (1981), *Jazz* (1992), *Paradise* (1998), and *Love* (2003). *Beloved* (1987), won a Pulitzer Prize for fiction. In addition to her novels, Morrison has written short stories, plays, speeches, essays, and nonfiction, including *Playing in the Dark: Whiteness and Literary Imagination* (1992) and *Remember: The Journey to School Integration* (2004).

Morrison writes to communicate the female African American experience. She claims that one of her goals in writing is to encourage other African American women to "repossess, re-name [and] re-own." Yet ultimately her books are popular with a wide variety of readers and, as a result, Morrison has been called one of the best American writers of her time.

Author Search For more about Toni Morrison, go to glencoe.com and enter QuickPass code GL59794u2.

Literature and Reading Preview

Connect to the Speech
When were you responsible for others? Freewrite for a few minutes about such a time and explain how you remained concerned about and compassionate towards others.

Build Background
Toni Morrison was asked to speak at graduation at Barnard College, a women's college affiliated with Columbia University in New York City. In her speech, Morrison uses the fairy tale of Cinderella to make the point that women in positions of power should still look out for their fellow females.

Set Purposes for Reading

Big Idea Keeping Freedom Alive

As you read Morrison's speech, ask yourself, How does she take a stand against selfish behavior and for freedom for women?

Literary Element Author's Purpose

An **author's purpose** is his or her intent in writing a literary work. An author's purpose depends in part on the audience. For example, the author may intend to inform, persuade, entertain, tell a story, or express an opinion. As you read, ask yourself, What particular characteristics of Morrison's audience may have influenced her purpose in the speech?

Reading Strategy Identify Problem and Solution

Persuasive essays and speeches are often built on a **problem-solution** pattern. The author tries to convince the reader that an undesirable belief, situation, or practice needs to be changed in a certain way. As you read this speech, ask yourself, What problem does Morrison call to the reader's attention, and what solution does she suggest?

Tip: Chart the Problem and Solution Create a two-column chart similar to the one below. In the left column, list aspects of the problem. In the right column, list aspects of the solution.

Problem	Solution
Women stop the promotion of other women's careers.	Women must come to the aid of the victims.

Learning Objectives

For pages 442–447

In studying this text, you will focus on the following objectives:

Literary Study: Analyzing author's purpose.

Reading: Analyzing text structure.

Vocabulary

fetish (fet′ish) *n.* abnormally obsessive preoccupation or attachment; a fixation; p. 444 *She has a fetish for books; she buys them constantly.*

dominion (də min′yən) *n.* control or the exercise of control; p. 444 *The king's dominion spans the entire country.*

deflect (di flekt′) *v.* to cause to turn aside; to bend or deviate; p. 445 *The wind deflected the ball from its straight path.*

emanate (em′ə nāt′) *v.* to come or set forth, as from a source; p. 445 *The campfire emanated heat throughout the night.*

abstraction (ab strak′shən) *n.* theoretical concept isolated from real application; p. 445 *An idea is an abstraction, while an action is not.*

Tip: Context Clues Remember that some context clues restate while others provide synonyms, antonyms, or examples.

TONI MORRISON

Two Young Girls from Finland, 1907. Sonia Delaunay Coll. Henri Nannen, Emden, Germany.

Cinderella's Stepsisters
Toni Morrison

Let me begin by taking you back a little. Back before the days at college. To nursery school, probably, to a once-upon-a-time time when you first heard, or read, or, I suspect, even saw "Cinderella." Because it is Cinderella that I want to talk about; because it is Cinderella who causes me a feeling of urgency. What is unsettling about that fairy tale is that it is essentially the story of household—a world, if you please—of women gathered together and held together in order to abuse another woman. There is, of course, a rather vague absent father and a nick-of-time prince with a foot **fetish**. But neither has much personality. And there are the surrogate "mothers," of course (god- and step-), who contribute both to Cinderella's grief and to her release and happiness. But it is her stepsisters who interest me. How crippling it must have been for those young girls to grow up with a mother, to watch and imitate that mother, enslaving another girl.

I am curious about their fortunes after the story ends. For contrary to recent adaptations,[1] the stepsisters were not ugly, clumsy, stupid girls with outsize feet. The Grimm collection describes them as "beautiful and fair in appearance." When we are introduced to them they are beautiful, elegant, women of status, and clearly women of power. Having watched and participated in the violent **dominion** of another woman, will they be any less cruel when it comes their turn to enslave other children, or even when they are required to take care of their own mother?

It is not a wholly medieval problem. It is quite a contemporary[2] one: feminine power when directed at other women has histori-

---

1. *Adaptations* are compositions that are written in a new form.
2. *Contemporary* means "current" or "modern."

Author's Purpose How does this statement help Morrison engage her audience's attention?

Vocabulary
fetish (fet′ish) *n*. abnormally obsessive preoccupation or attachment; a fixation

Identify Problem and Solution How does Morrison's allusion to the Cinderella story foreshadow the main problem posed in her speech?

Vocabulary
dominion (də min′yən) *n*. control or the exercise of control

cally been wielded in what has been described as a "masculine" manner. Soon you will be in a position to do the very same thing. Whatever your background—rich or poor—whatever the history of education in your family—five generations or one—you have taken advantage of what has been available to you at Barnard and you will therefore have both the economic and social status of the stepsisters *and* you will have their power.

I want not to *ask* you but to *tell* you not to participate in the oppression of your sisters. . . . Women who stop the promotion of other women in careers are women, and another woman must come to the victim's aid. Social and welfare workers who humiliate their clients may be women, and other women colleagues have to **deflect** their anger.

I am alarmed by the violence that women do to each other: professional violence, competitive violence, emotional violence. I am alarmed by the willingness of women to enslave other women. I am alarmed by a growing absence of decency on the killing floor of professional women's worlds. You are the women who will take your place in the world where *you* can decide who shall flourish and who shall wither; you will make distinctions between the deserving poor and the undeserving poor; where you can yourself determine which life is expendable[3] and which is indispensable. Since you will have the power to do it, you may also be persuaded that you have the right to do it. As educated women the distinction between the two is first-order business.

I am suggesting that we pay as much attention to our nurturing sensibilities as to our ambition. You are moving in the direction of freedom and the function of freedom is to free somebody else. You are moving toward self-fulfillment, and the consequences of that fulfillment should be to discover that there is something just as important as you are and that just-as-important thing may be Cinderella—or your stepsister.

In your rainbow journey toward the realization of personal goals, don't make choices based only on your security and your safety. Nothing is safe. That is not to say that anything ever was, or that anything worth achieving ever should be. Things of value seldom are. It is not safe to have a child. It is not safe to challenge the status quo.[4] It is not safe to choose work that has not been done before. Or to do old work in a new way. There will always be someone there to stop you. But in pursuing your highest ambitions, don't let your personal safety diminish the safety of your stepsister. In wielding the power that is deservedly yours, don't permit it to enslave your stepsisters. Let your might and your power **emanate** from that place in you that is nurturing and caring.

Women's rights is not only an **abstraction**, a cause; it is also a personal affair. It is not only about "us"; it is also about me and you. Just the two of us.

---

3. *Expendable* means "easily replaced."

Author's Purpose How does Morrison make this plea to her audience effective?

Identify Problem and Solution What aspect of the problem does Morrison identify in this paragraph?

Vocabulary

deflect (di flekt´) *v.* to cause to turn aside; to bend or deviate

---

4. *Status quo* means "the existing condition."

Keeping Freedom Alive What is Morrison asking the audience to do to protect freedom for themselves and for women in general?

Vocabulary

emanate (em´ə nāt´) *v.* to come or set forth, as from a source

abstraction (ab strak´shən) *n.* theoretical concept isolated from real application

After You Read

Respond and Think Critically

Respond and Interpret

1. (a) What are the main points Morrison made in her speech? (b) If you were a Barnard graduate, what comments might you have offered in response to her speech?

2. (a) According to Morrison, how do women in power often treat one another? (b) How might this affect the graduates to whom she is speaking?

3. (a) From Morrison's view, how should those in power treat one another? (b) How should the students' education distinguish them from others in power?

Analyze and Evaluate

4. (a) How does Morrison persuade her listeners to take action? (b) How does Morrison's alignment with Cinderella's stepsisters strengthen or weaken her argument?

5. Is this speech appropriate for men as well as women? Explain your position.

6. Morrison claims that women often oppress other women. What evidence does she use to support this statement?

Connect

7. **Big Idea** Keeping Freedom Alive Morrison takes a stand against women oppressing women in this speech. In what ways do you find her argument to be valid?

8. **Connect to Today** Think of women who are in positions of power in the world today. In your opinion, do those women try to help other women, or do they "participate in the oppression of [their] sisters"? Give reasons to support your belief.

Literary Element Author's Purpose

SAT Skills Practice

1. Morrison's purpose in making this speech was to

   (A) explain that women can be as competitive and cutthroat as men
   (B) persuade her listeners to be encouraging and nurturing to other women
   (C) point out that fairy tales do not always teach sound lessons for life
   (D) demonstrate how to be successful without being cruel
   (E) provide examples of how women have participated in their own oppression

Review: Analogy

An **analogy** is a comparison that shows the relationship between two things that are otherwise dissimilar. Writers often use an analogy to explain something unfamiliar by comparing it to a familiar concept.

Partner Activity With a classmate, discuss how Morrison uses the familiar Cinderella story to make a point. Make a web like the one below to organize your thoughts about the analogy. Then, evaluate whether you think that this analogy is successful and why.

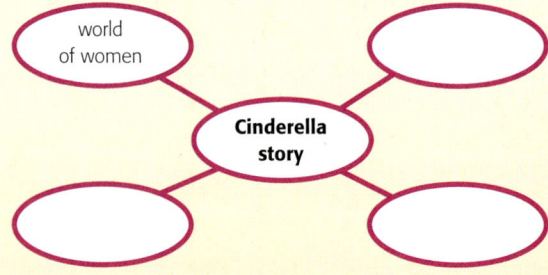

446 UNIT 2 NONFICTION

Reading Strategy: Identify Problem and Solution

Some persuasive essays or speeches present multiple problems and solutions. In her brief commencement address, Morrison chooses to focus on one significant problem and solution. Refer to the chart you made as you read the selection to help you answer the following questions.

1. In your own words, state the problem that Morrison poses in her speech.

2. What solution does Morrison propose to remedy the problem? Do you think this solution is adequate? Explain.

Vocabulary Practice

Practice with Context Clues Identify the context clues in the following sentences that help you determine the meaning of each boldfaced vocabulary word.

1. Because Kara did not want to answer the questions, she tried to **deflect** them.

2. The powerful speaker held **dominion** over the mesmerized audience.

3. A stench **emanates** from the garbage cans and rises into the apartment building.

4. Mr. Chang had a **fetish** for model airplanes, which filled every shelf in his house.

5. Although world peace seems like an **abstraction,** there are concrete ways to make it a reality.

Write with Style

Apply Repetition

Assignment Write a letter to the editor that uses repetition or other rhetorical devices to help persuade the reader.

Get Ideas As part of her personal style, Morrison uses repetition to make appeals and lend rhetorical force to her writing. Review Morrison's use of repetition. Then find an editorial with which you strongly agree or disagree. List two or three points you can make to support or rebut the argument presented in the editorial.

Give It Structure Make an outline like the one below that states your thesis and orders your points from most important to least important or vice versa. For each point, list rhetorical devices, such as repetition, analogies, or anecdotes, that you can weave in as you support your points. Begin your letter with a thesis statement that refers to the editorial.

> I. Thesis Statement
>   A. Most Important Point
>   1. Rhetorical Device
>   2. Rhetorical Device
>   B. Another Important Point
>   1.
>   2.

Look at Language Make sure you make strong points; then give them rhetorical force by means of repetition or another device.

Point Example: A dog park is a necessity in a city with 2,348 licensed dogs.

Repetition conveys and emphasizes point Example: The dogs aren't going away. The dog owners aren't going away. The need for open space for exercise isn't going away, either.

Edit and Proofread Proofread your letter, correcting any errors in spelling, grammar, and punctuation.

Literature Online

Selection Resources For Selection Quizzes, eFlashcards, and Reading-Writing Connection activities, go to glencoe.com and enter QuickPass code GL59794u2.

Learning Objectives

For pages 448–455

In this workshop, you will focus on the following objectives:

Writing: Writing a biographical narrative.

Grammar: Understanding how to use action verbs. Understanding how to correct verb tense.

Writing Workshop

Biographical Narrative

Literature Connection Mark Stevens and Annalyn Swan present Willem de Kooning through his words, his actions, and other methods of characterization.

> "De Kooning had learned the hard way . . . that life in America was not going to be easy. 'It turned out to be quite different from what I thought,' de Kooning said of America. 'Nowhere near as luxurious as I imagined it.'"
>
> —Mark Stevens and Annalyn Swan, from "First Impressions"

In a biographical narrative, specific and descriptive details create interest and establish a controlling impression. The rubric below highlights the goals and strategies for writing a successful creative nonfiction narrative of a life.

Writing Process

At any stage of a writing process, you may think of new ideas. Feel free to return to earlier stages as you write.

- Prewrite
- Draft
- Revise
- Focus Lesson: **Use Action Verbs**
- Edit and Proofread
- Focus Lesson: **Verb Tense**
- Present

Checklist

Goals	Strategies
To present an engaging life story	✓ Relate a clear, focused sequence of events
To use effective narrative techniques	✓ Show character through words, gestures, or emotions ✓ Use precise nouns, action verbs, sensory and concrete details, and the active voice
To narrate events or describe qualities in a logical order	✓ Locate scenes and incidents in specific places ✓ Use chronological order for events
To establish a controlling impression of the subject	✓ Communicate the significance of details and events ✓ Use descriptions of appearance, images, and shifting perspectives ✓ Pace the narrative effectively

Writing and Research For prewriting, drafting, and revising tools, go to glencoe.com and enter QuickPass code GL59794u2

Narration / Exposition

> **Assignment**
>
> ## Tell a Life Story
>
> Write a creative nonfiction narrative of 1,500 words. As you work, keep your audience and purpose in mind.
>
> **Audience:** classmates and peers
>
> **Purpose:** to create a controlling impression of a person by narrating selected events and presenting selected main ideas

Real-World Connection

You may be required to use nonfiction narrative skills to tell facts about your own life when you apply to college or for a job. The main points you present about your experiences and your character, along with the details that support them, may be used to judge your merits as a future student or employee.

Analyze a Professional Model

In the nonfiction life story that follows, Alice Jackson Baughn presents a brief look at the author Eudora Welty. As you read, notice how Baughn selects just a few important main ideas to tell her audience about Welty, presenting each in a well-developed paragraph. Pay close attention to the comments in the margin. They point out features to include in your biographical narrative.

From *Eudora Welty: 1909–2001* by Alice Jackson Baughn

In Mississippi, to hear Eudora Welty read from her works was as prized as a pair of tickets to the state's Egg Bowl, the annual gridiron classic between the University of Mississippi and Mississippi State University. That strong Southern accent delivered with her unique inflections drew her audience to a special place. The grande dame of American literature died Monday in a Jackson, Miss., hospital near the family home where she had lived for almost all of her 92 years. She was hospitalized with pneumonia on Saturday.

Considered by many literary critics to be America's greatest living writer, Welty's many honors included the Pulitzer Prize in 1973 for *The Optimist's Daughter.* The recipient of numerous honorary degrees, including ones from Harvard and Yale, Welty was also recognized internationally. In 1987, France knighted her. Welty's autobiography, *One Writer's*

Narrative Techniques

Create interest through figurative language, action verbs, and precise nouns.

Controlling Impression

Create a single dominant impression of your subject through effective supporting details.

WRITING WORKSHOP **449**

Engaging Life Story
Present interesting details from your research.

Scenes and Incidents
Present specific details about a place to help establish a controlling impression.

Narrative Techniques
Use descriptive details, images, and shifting perspectives to reveal your subject.

Beginnings, became the longest-running book on *The New York Times'* best-seller list in 1984. It described how the daughter of a Mississippi insurance salesman grew into an astute observer of human nature with a keen sense of place in story-telling. Welty translated that knowledge into essays, short stories, novels and photography over eight decades....

Welty's love of photography began during the 1930s. She was working for the Works Progress Administration, a job that took her across Mississippi, and she took her camera along. Besides photographing people, Welty snapped images of a Mississippi that no longer exists, except in her stories. Some of Welty's photos were exhibited in small New York galleries in 1936 and 1937. Today, they are highly valued collector's items.

Welty never married and lived alone—until several years ago when failing health demanded that she hire nurses and a caretaker—in the house she had occupied with her parents and siblings in the historic Belhaven section of Jackson, the state's capital. Nothing about the Tudor-styled house on the oak-canopied street alerted passersby to the status of Welty's literary existence....

Welty shopped almost daily at the old Jitney-Jungle grocery store only a few blocks from her home. Fans too timid to knock on her front door often went to the store and waited for her to appear. But Welty was always gracious to her adoring fans, particularly young writers. As her health declined, her doctors ordered her to post a sign at the entrance of her home forbidding visitors without an appointment. But Welty, always the gracious southern lady, thought the message was too curt. Beneath the warning, in a spidery script, she had scrawled a penciled note of apology.

Reading-Writing Connection Think about the writing techniques that you have just encountered and try them out in the biographical narrative you write.

Prewrite

Choose Your Subject Make a list of people who interest you. For each one, jot down facts you already know about the person or reasons to choose that person as a subject. Study your list and choose your best idea.

Research and Read Find out more about your subject by using the Internet, library databases, or books. Take notes.

Identify Your Focus To bring your character to life, you will need to establish a dominant impression of the person and narrate events to support it. In a two-column chart, list important events (in the first column) and main ideas about the person (in the second column). Circle an idea that could serve as a controlling impression.

Make a Plan There are several ways to make a plan for writing.

- ▶ **Make a formal outline.** A formal outline might show your main points in order as well as the details or subtopics that support or develop the main points.

- ▶ **Make an informal outline.** An informal outline might show events in chronological order, as well as prewriting notes related to each event.

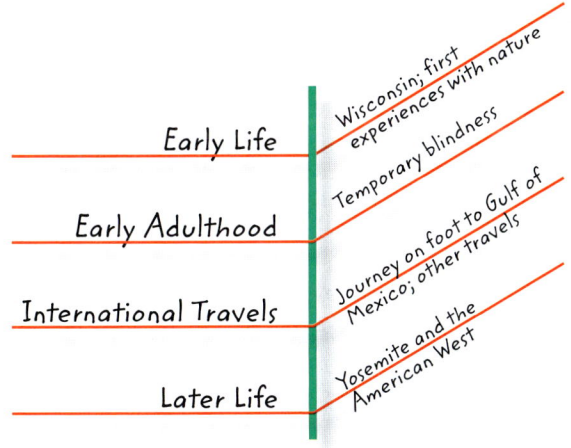

Discuss Your Ideas Consult your writing plan as you tell a partner about your ideas so far. To develop your writing voice, listen to your own speaking voice as you talk about your subject. Ask your partner to identify words and phrases that convey your enthusiasm, wonder, or other emotions and attitudes toward your subject. Jot down those words and phrases.

Narration/Exposition

Audience and Purpose

Did you notice how the model does *not* begin with *She was born* and end with *She died?* The author engages the audience and keeps her purpose—lauding a remarkable woman—in mind.

Avoid Plagiarism

Avoid plagiarism at this stage by paraphrasing and summarizing what you read—and then putting your sources away.

Draft

Create a Focused Sequence of Events You may want to begin by creating interest or establishing your controlling impression of your subject in your body paragraphs. Be sure to arrange your details in chronological order. Use transitions such as *first, next,* and *then* to connect ideas.

Analyze a Workshop Model

Here is a final draft of a biographical narrative. Read the narrative and answer the questions in the margin. Use the answers to these questions to guide you as you write.

Writing Frames

As you read the workshop model, think about the writer's use of the following frames:

Over the next several years, _____ . . .

Soon afterward _____ .

Throughout his life, ... _____ .

This _____ changed _____ . . .

Consider using frames like these in your own biological narrative.

Controlling Impression
What do you expect the following paragraphs to convey?

Narrative Techniques
How does the narrative create interest as it retells events?

John Muir, Nature Observer

When I go hiking in Muir Woods near San Francisco, I think about John Muir, a famous person in U.S. history. Like me, John Muir loved the outdoors and had fun exploring wild places. He inspired many people, including students my age, to learn more about nature and to protect the environment. Last year my friend and I worked on a project titled "Speaking Out for Nature: John Muir's Legacy." Here are a few significant events from his life that I studied.

John Muir was born in Scotland sometime in the 1830s. When Muir was a young boy, he and his family left their homeland and came to the United States. They settled in Wisconsin, an area filled with spectacular scenery and wildlife. At an early age, Muir became very curious about the world of

Meadow of Daisies and Wildflowers. Walter Geiersperger.

The early morning moon sets above a Sierra Nevada mountain at Mono Lake. Phil Schermeister.

Narration / Exposition

nature and enjoyed observing plants and animals. For example, the sight of fireflies filled him with wonder. He found the songs of robins during springtime enchanting. The beautiful Wisconsin flowers that grew in the meadows fascinated him. Throughout his life, Muir continued this habit of closely watching nature.

In the late 1860s, after the Civil War had ended, another experience had a major influence on Muir's view of nature and the course of his life. While working in a carriage shop, he injured his eyes and, as a result, became blind for a month. This unfortunate accident changed Muir's outlook forever, making him appreciate the value of his eyesight. When he regained his ability to see, he resolved to devote himself to observing nature. Soon afterward he began an extended journey on foot from the Midwest to the Gulf of Mexico. Next he sailed to Cuba, crossed over to Panama, and then sailed up the West Coast to San Francisco, the city where I live today. Then Muir began to explore the Sierra Nevada and the Yosemite regions of California.

Scenes and Incidents

How do specific details about place help create the controlling impression?

Engaging Life Story

How do precise words make the writing more interesting? Consider nouns, action verbs, and sensory details.

WRITING WORKSHOP 453

Revise

Traits of Strong Writing

Include these traits of strong writing to express your ideas effectively.

Ideas

Organization

Voice

Word Choice

Sentence Fluency

Conventions

Presentation

For more information on using the Traits of Strong Writing, see pages R28–R30.

Word Choice

This academic vocabulary word appears in the student model:

resolve (ri zolv´) *v.* to make a firm decision about something; to determine; *He resolved to devote himself to observing nature.* Using academic vocabulary may help strengthen your writing. Try to use one or two academic vocabulary words in your biographical narrative. See the complete list on pages R80–R82.

 **Literature** Online

Writing and Research For editing and publishing tools, go to glencoe.com and enter QuickPass code GL59794u2.

Peer Review Ask a classmate to read your draft and to identify the controlling impression, the sequence of events, and the narrative techniques you used. As you revise, refer to the traits of strong writing. Use the checklist below to help you evaluate and stengthen each other's narrative.

Checklist

☑ Do you establish a controlling impression of your subject?

☑ Do you narrate a clear sequence of events?

☑ Do you locate scenes and events in specific places?

☑ Do you vividly describe the details of your experience?

☑ Do you use sensory details and other precise language to bring your subject to life?

☑ Do you show character through words, gestures, and emotions?

☑ Do you include descriptions of appearance, images, and shifting perspectives?

Focus Lesson

Use Action Verbs

Action verbs, such as *thought*, *begged*, and *climbed*, are preferable to state-of-being verbs, such as *were*, *is*, and *would be*. Action verbs show what is happening; they also often make a sentence clearer and more concise. Notice how action verbs improve the passage from the Workshop Model below.

Draft:

While working in a carriage shop, he was not careful and was, as a result, blind for a month. This unfortunate accident is what changed Muir forever and is what made him value his eyesight. When he was able to see again, he was sure that he was a "nature" person.

Revision:

While working in a carriage shop, he <u>injured his eyes</u>[1] and, as a result, became blind for a month. This unfortunate accident <u>changed Muir's outlook forever, making him appreciate the value</u>[2] of his eyesight. When <u>he regained his ability to see, he resolved to devote himself to observing nature.</u>[3]

1: Reasons   **2: Descriptions**   **3: Dialogue**

Edit and Proofread

Get It Right When you have completed the final draft of your narrative, proofread it for errors in grammar, usage, mechanics, and spelling. Refer to the Language Handbook, pages R40–R57, as a guide.

> **Focus Lesson**
>
> ## Correct Verb Tense
>
> The tense of a verb shows whether the action takes place in the present, the past, or the future. When you edit, check to see that you have used the correct form of each verb. Also be sure that you have maintained or changed verb tenses to reflect the time of the action.
>
> **Problem:** The verb ending is missing or incorrect.
>
> *He <u>resolve</u> to devote himself to observing nature.*
>
> **Solution:** Use the *-ed* form of a regular verb for the past tense.
>
> *He <u>resolved</u> to devote himself to observing nature.*
>
> **Problem:** The tense of the sentence does not shift to show that events occurred at different times.
>
> *Here <u>are</u> a few significant events from his life that I <u>study</u>.*
>
> **Solution:** Shift from the present to the past to show an event that occurred before the present action.
>
> *Here <u>are</u> a few significant events from his life that I <u>studied</u>.*

Present/Publish

Maximum Readability Be sure that you present your work in the most readable way. That means using neat handwriting or a font that can be read easily. It also means double-spacing word-processed copy, creating one-inch margins, and indenting paragraphs five spaces.

Narration/Exposition

Peer Review Tips

A classmate may ask you to read his or her biographical narrative. Take your time and jot down notes as you read so you can give constructive feedback. Use the following questions to get started:

- Has the writer created interest in the events that make up the life story?

- Do details about place help create the controlling impression about the person's life?

- Is the word choice powerful, precise, and descriptive?

Word Processing

To number your pages, select the header or footer from your edit menu. If you are placing the page number in the header, the upper right hand corner is the conventional placement. If you want to put the page number on the bottom of each page, center it. Do not include a page number on the first page.

Writer's Portfolio

Place a copy of your biographical narrative in your portfolio to review later.

Learning Objectives

For pages 456–457

In this workshop, you will focus on the following objective:

Speaking and Listening: Delivering a narrative presentation.

Speaking, Listening, and Viewing Workshop

Photo Essay

Literature Connection When authors present life stories, they convey not only facts and observations about lives but also images that help the reader locate the time and place. For example, in "First Impressions," the reader can visualize de Kooning's first glimpse of New York City—skyscrapers hidden by thick fog. Throughout the excerpt, images help show the reader de Kooning's life and world.

> **Assignment** Present a narrated visual re-creation of the life and world of the subject you wrote about in your nonfiction narrative.

Plan Your Presentation

Consider which visual form best lends itself to the events of your creative narrative and your audience's interests:

- An illustrated **time line** is a good choice for representing a narrative essay with a clear sequence of events.
- A **biopic**, a series of images that tell a life story, is a great choice if you are using technology such as slides or a video.
- A **montage**, a series of images presented as a single group, is a good choice for representing main ideas as well as events.

This illustration shows part of a montage of the life of John Muir. Note how the accompanying narrative uses concrete sensory details to convey sights and sounds.

Keep Your Options Open

After you have gathered images, reevaluate your choice for presenting. For example, certain groups of images may lend themselves better to a montage than to a time line.

Muir began observing plants and animals at an early age. Distant horizons, sun-drenched fields of wildflowers, the warbles and trills of birds, and the habitats of animals all drew his attention.

Create Your Visual Media

First, do research to find your images. Consider these options:

- Concentrate on the general category of images you need, such as nature, construction, a particular sport or hobby, or government. Look for general-interest books on these topics for possible images.
- Search the Internet for free downloadable images of your subject or your subject's world.

Next, prepare and assemble the images. You may want to mount them on the same color poster board or digitize them for a slide presentation. Consider ways to group, label, and organize the images that will show the main ideas or events most effectively. Be sure to credit the source of each image. Use a standard method of citation (see R35–R37).

Coordinate Your Words and Images

Photographs do not speak for themselves. It is up to you to create the narrative that links the images and tells the story.

In part, you can tell the story through labels you attach to your images. Go beyond that, however, to introduce your subject and provide important background information. Pace your narrative to reflect the images and the mood they create. Add interest by using figurative language.

Techniques for Presenting a Narrative

Verbal Techniques	Nonverbal Techniques
☑ **Tone** Convey your interest in your subject through your tone of voice.	☑ **Facial Expression** Convey your interest in your subject through your facial expressions.
☑ **Enunciation** Avoid rushing through your points and running your words together. Be sure that everyone can hear and understand you.	☑ **Focus** When you are talking about your images, look at and point them out. The rest of the time, make eye contact with your audience.
☑ **Volume** Be sure to speak loudly enough that everyone can hear you.	☑ **Posture** Stand up straight and hold your head up but try not to look stiff.

Remind Listeners of the Main Ideas and Events
Be sure that you link your images to the events or main ideas. Don't assume that your listeners and viewers will make these connections themselves.

Speaking Frames
Consider using the following frames in your photo essay presentation:

Over the next several days/weeks/years, _____.

Throughout his/her life, _____.

One important influence _____.

LOG ON **Literature** Online
Speaking, Listening, and Viewing For project ideas, templates, and presentation tips, go to glencoe.com and enter QuickPass code GL59794u2.

Independent Reading

Nonfiction and Novels

PEOPLE HAVE BEEN WRITING nonfiction ever since they scratched into stone the first records of loans and trades, births and deaths, and suns and moons. Nonfiction writing encompasses everything from history to data analyses. For more nonfiction with a variety of themes, try the first three suggestions below. For novels that incorporate the Big Ideas of *The Power of Memory, Quests and Encounters,* and *Keeping Freedom Alive,* try the titles from the Glencoe Literature Library on the next page.

What Are You? Voices of Mixed-Race Young People
Pearl Fuyo Gaskins

Gaskins, whose mother was Japanese and whose father was American, spent years gathering reflections from mixed-race students. They reflect on the issues of appearing not to belong to any one group, of being categorized inaccurately, and of never being able to check the correct "box" about race because more than one box applies. Many affirm their own identities with statements such as "I know who I am," while some focus on the assumptions others make about them.

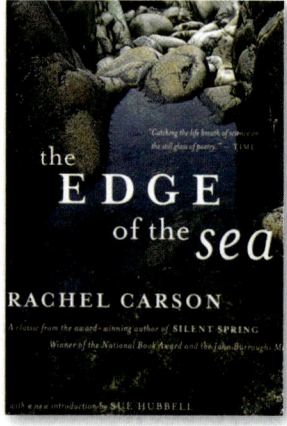

The Edge of the Sea
Rachel Carson

How do small sea creatures hold on to rocks while strong waves wash over them? How does the arctic jellyfish survive "being solidly frozen for hours"? Carson, a keen observer of nature and an early environmentalist, reveals the dramatic and varied communities of plant and animal life along the rocky shores, sandy beaches, and coral reefs of the Atlantic Ocean. Delicate drawings depict the rich variety of life forms.

GLENCOE LITERATURE LIBRARY

Night
Elie Wiesel

This autobiographical novel shows the *Power of Memory* and brings the brutal reality of the Holocaust to life.

Adventures of Huckleberry Finn
Mark Twain

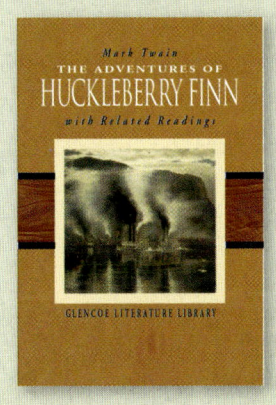

Embarking on a series of *Quests and Encounters*, Huck sails down the Mississippi River with Jim, who has escaped from slavery.

The Autobiography of Miss Jane Pittman
Ernest J. Gaines

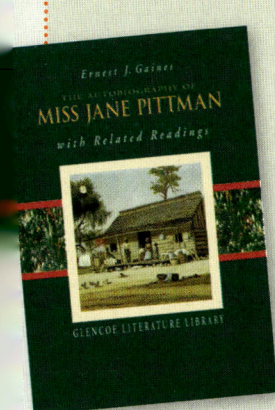

The strength and courage of Jane Pittman, a formerly enslaved woman, are an inspiration and a testament to the concept of *Keeping Freedom Alive*.

CRITICS' CORNER

"*Mountains Beyond Mountains* is inspiring, disturbing, and completely absorbing. It will rattle our complacency; it will prick our conscience. One senses that Farmer's life and work has affected Kidder, and it is a measure of Kidder's honesty that he is willing to reveal this to the reader. . . . I had the . . . feeling after reading *Mountains Beyond Mountains* that . . . something had changed in me and it was impossible not to become involved."

—Abraham Verghese, the *New York Times Book Review*

Mountains Beyond Mountains
Tracy Kidder

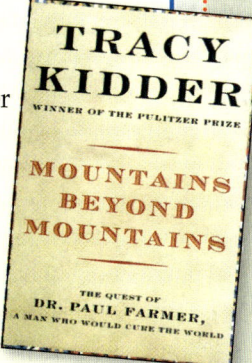

This Pulitzer-Prize-winning biography chronicles the career of Dr. Paul Farmer, an American doctor who has spent much of his life solving health care problems for the people of Haiti and other nations. Committed to the ideal of equality in health care, Farmer and many other dedicated volunteers devote their considerable talents and energy to controlling diseases and saving lives by taking measures that others have found too difficult or expensive.

Write a Journal

Keep a reader-response journal in which you record your thoughts as you read one of the books listed on this page. Include your feelings about the characters and events you discover, or connect this book to other pieces you have read. Publish your journal for your class.

Assessment

English–Language Arts

Reading: Nonfiction

Carefully read the following passages. Use context clues to help you define any words with which you are unfamiliar. Pay close attention to story elements such as theme, voice, and tone. Then, on a separate sheet of paper, answer the questions on pages 461–462.

from *Wouldn't Take Nothing for My Journey Now* by Maya Angelou

When my son was six and I twenty-two, he told me quite solemnly that he had to talk to me. We both sat down at the kitchen table, and he asked with an old man's eyes and a young boy's voice, "Mother, do you have any sweaters that match?" I was puzzled at first. I said, "No," and then I understood he was talking about the pullover and cardigan sets which were popular with white women. And I said, "No, I don't," maybe a little huffily. And he said, "Oh, I wish you did. So that you could wear them to school when you come to see me."

I was tickled but I am glad I didn't laugh because he continued, "Mother, could you please only come to school when they call you?" Then I realized that my attire, which delighted my heart and certainly activated my creativity, was an embarrassment to him.

When people are young, they desperately need to conform, and no one can embarrass a young person in public so much as an adult to whom he or she is related. Any outré action or wearing of "getups" can make a young person burn with self-consciousness.

I learned to be a little more discreet to avoid causing him displeasure. As he grew older and more confident, I gradually returned to what friends thought of as my eccentric way of dressing. I was happier when I chose and created my own fashion.

I have lived in this body all my life and know it much better than any fashion designer. I think I know what looks good on me, and I certainly know what feels good on me.

I appreciate the creativity which is employed in the design of fabric and the design of clothes, and when something does fit my body and personality, I rush to it, buy it quickly, and wear it frequently. But I must not lie to myself for fashion's sake. I am only willing to purchase the item which becomes me and to wear that which enhances my image of myself to myself.

If I am comfortable inside my skin, I have the ability to make other people comfortable inside their skins although their feelings are not my primary reason for making my fashion choice. If I feel good inside my skin and clothes, I am thus free to allow my body its sway, its natural grace, its natural gesture. Then I am so comfortable that whatever I wear looks good on me even to the external fashion arbiters.

1. What does the son find embarrassing about his mother?
   A. She has very little money.
   B. She feels comfortable in her skin.
   C. She comes to school in unusual outfits.
   D. She never wears clothes that match.

2. From what point of view is the selection written?
   A. first person
   B. second person
   C. third person omniscient
   D. third person limited

3. In line 10, the mother states that young people "desperately need to conform." Which of the following best explains what she means by this statement?
   A. They do not want to grow up.
   B. They do not like independence.
   C. They are needy and insecure.
   D. They face pressure to fit in with the crowd.

4. From the context in line 11, what do you conclude that the word *outré* means?
   A. immodest
   B. unconventional
   C. feverish
   D. shameful

5. Which of the following best defines the phrase *burn with self-consciousness*, as it is used in line 12?
   A. be aware of one's self
   B. be aware of others
   C. be ill at ease socially
   D. be angry at others

6. How does Angelou reveal the personality of her son?
   A. through direct characterization
   B. through indirect characterization
   C. through both direct and indirect characterization
   D. through implied characterization

7. From the context, what do you conclude that the word *arbiters,* in the last line, means?
   A. enforcers
   B. contemporaries
   C. critics
   D. onlookers

8. Which of the following best describes the mother's personality?
   A. controversial
   B. self-confident
   C. passive
   D. conformist

9. What is the overall tone of the reading selection?
   A. sarcastic
   B. tense
   C. ironic
   D. encouraging

10. From the context, which of the following do you think is the best synonym for the word *eccentric,* in line 14?
    A. unusual
    B. absurd
    C. energetic
    D. casual

ASSESSMENT   461

11. The selection is from an autobiography. Which of the following best defines this genre, or style of writing?
    A. personal experience told in the author's words
    B. personal experience told through the words of an outside observer
    C. fictional account of a personal experience
    D. narration that is largely unreliable because of its limited perspective

12. From the selection, which of the following do you conclude is a characteristic of a published autobiography?
    F. personal experience meant to be private
    G. personal experience meant to impress others
    H. personal experience meant to be shared
    I. personal experience meant to enhance the truth

13. Which of the following best describes the author's purpose in writing the selection?
    A. to explain a process
    B. to describe her taste in fashion
    C. to entertain the reader
    D. to express her individuality

14. Which of the following best states the main idea of this selection from Angelou's continuing autobiography?
    F. Clothes make the woman.
    G. Security comes from within.
    H. Life is full of prejudice.
    I. If you've got it, flaunt it.

Vocabulary Skills: Sentence Completion

For each item, choose the word that best completes the sentence.

1. The student set an hour aside to _____ his notes before tomorrow's test.
   A. peruse
   B. ordain
   C. induce
   D. advocate

2. The warrior used his shield to _____ a storm of arrows.
   A. inhibit
   B. deflect
   C. ordain
   D. debase

3. The scientist, a _____ man, attended to every detail of his work himself.
   A. meticulous
   B. nomadic
   C. abstract
   D. vague

4. Before the championship game, the coach tried to imagine all possible _____ in which his team could win.
   A. advocates
   B. scenarios
   C. agenda
   D. dominions

5. Her unwillingness to help _____ her expressions of concern.
   A. emanated
   B. belied
   C. admonished
   D. eschewed

6. As he thought over the problem, the old chief wore a/an _____ expression that betrayed no emotion.
   A. stolid
   B. potent
   C. indelible
   D. infallible

7. Because the safety report contained too much _____ information, it was difficult to determine what was essential.
   A. obligatory
   B. superfluous
   C. tremulous
   D. indelible

8. The directions contained _____ information that was essential for completing the project.
   A. commodious
   B. intermittent
   C. invaluable
   D. mainstream

9. The most _____ people are usually good listeners.
   A. superfluous
   B. renaissance
   C. convivial
   D. compassionate

Literature Online

Assessment For additional test practice, go to glencoe.com and enter QuickPass code GL59794u2.

Grammar and Writing Skills: Paragraph Improvement

Read carefully through the following first draft of a student's essay. Pay close attention to the content and organization. Watch for grammatical errors (such as sentence fragments, run-on sentences, and lack of subject-verb agreement) and punctuation errors, such as misplaced or missing commas. Then, on a separate sheet of paper, answer the questions on pages 464–465.

(1) *Native American writers of autobiographical literature continue to reach a wide audience.* (2) *These writers oral traditions with modern literary forms.* (3) *There are; however, differences between this literature and traditional Western autobiographies.* (4) *Are the most notable.*

(5) *Autobiography in Western tradition commonly tells the story of an individual's rise.* (6) *Through personal achievements.* (7) *Western culture praises the individual he or she overcomes adversity.* (8) *Benjamin Franklin's autobiography is well known for this approach.* (9) *When he outlines his accomplishments, he instructs us in how to be better people.*

(10) *Conversely American Indian cultures tends to downplay the individual's importance.* (11) *In their worldview—the people, land, universe, are all of equal importance.* (12) *The individual are just a small part of something larger not the center of everything.* (13) *Black Elk and Lame Deer are two of the best known Native American authors of autobiographies.*

1. What grammatical error occurs in sentence 2?
   A. comma splice
   B. fused sentence
   C. sentence fragment
   D. misplaced modifier

2. Which of the following is the best revision for sentence 2?
   A. These writers combine oral tradition with modern literary forms.
   B. These writers combine oral tradition; with modern literary forms.
   C. These writers combine oral traditions with, modern literary forms.
   D. These writers combine oral traditions. With modern literary forms.

3. Which of the following is the best revision for sentence 3?
   A. There are; however, differences between this literature, and traditional Western autobiographies.
   B. There are however; differences between this literature and traditional Western autobiographies.
   C. There are, however, differences between this literature; and traditional Western autobiographies.
   D. There are, however, differences between this literature and traditional Western autobiographies.

4. What part of speech is necessary to transform sentence 4 from a sentence fragment to a complete sentence?
   A. verb
   B. subject
   C. adjective
   D. adverb

5. What would be the best way to revise sentence 6?
   A. Make no change.
   B. Delete the sentence.
   C. Combine it with sentence 7.
   D. Combine it with sentence 5.

6. Which of the following errors occurs in sentence 7?
   A. run-on sentence
   B. fragment
   C. lack of subject-verb agreement
   D. misplaced modifier

7. Sentence 9 contains two clauses separated by a comma. Which of the following choices represents the sentence structure?
   A. independent clause, independent clause
   B. independent clause, dependent clause
   C. dependent clause, independent clause
   D. dependent clause, complete sentence

8. Which of the following is the best revision for sentence 10?
   A. Conversely: American Indian cultures tend to downplay the individual's importance.
   B. Conversely, American Indian cultures tends to downplay the individual's importance.
   C. American Indian cultures tend to conversely downplay the individual's importance.
   D. Conversely, American Indian cultures tend to downplay the individual's importance.

9. Which of the following is the best revision for sentence 11?
   A. In their worldview: the people, land, universe, are all of equal importance.
   B. In their worldview, the people, the land, and everything else in the universe are of equal importance.
   C. In their worldview, all—the people, the land, and the universe—are of equal importance.
   D. In their worldview; the people, the land, and the universe, are all of equal importance.

10. Which of the following would be the best addition to the essay?
    A. an introduction about several tribal nations
    B. a bibliography
    C. background about the student writer
    D. elaboration on the authors mentioned in the closing sentence

Essay

Discuss a few characteristics of the autobiographical genre. Consider the following points: How does this literary form differ from fiction? Why might a writer choose to write about his or her life? Can the writer be as creative in writing autobiography as in writing fiction? As you write, keep in mind that your essay will be checked for **ideas, organization, voice, word choice, sentence fluency, conventions,** and **presentation.**

Orpheus, 1969. Marc Chagall. Oil on canvas, 97 x 130 cm. Private collection.

View the Art Marc Chagall's paintings and other works have been called musical, poetic, and dream-like. Do you think *Orpheus* fits this description? Why or why not?

UNIT THREE

Poetry

Looking Ahead

Like other forms of literature, poetry concerns real life, but it distills that life to its essence. Poetry is the most concentrated form of literature: It makes every word and even every syllable count. All good poems allow the reader to experience the power and magic of words in a way that no other form of literature can.

Each part in Unit Three focuses on a Big Idea that can help you connect to the literary works.

PREVIEW	Big Ideas	Literary Focus
PART 1	The Energy of the Everyday	Form and Structure
PART 2	Loves and Losses	Language
PART 3	Issues of Identity	Sound Devices

Learning Objectives

For pages 466–472

In studying this text, you will focus on the following objectives:

Literary Study:
Analyzing form and structure.
Analyzing language.
Analyzing sound devices.

Genre Focus
What distinguishes poetry from prose?

How does poetry give a sense of the mystery and marvel of life? It uses what African American poet Quincy Troupe calls "the music of language." Says Troupe, "I want the words to sing." The elements of poetry, while they may be found in other genres, are essential to the art of poetry.

The Form and Structure of Poetry

Lines and Stanzas

Poetry is arranged in lines and stanzas. A **line** is a horizontal row of words, which may or may not form a complete sentence. A **stanza** is a group of lines forming a unit and separated from the next stanza by a line of space.

> The mother smiled to know her child
> was in a sacred place,
> but that smile was the last smile
> to come upon her face.
>
> —Dudley Randall, **from "Ballad of Birmingham"**

The Language of Poetry

Figurative Language

A **figure of speech** is a word or an expression that is not literally true but expresses some truth beyond the literal level.

- A **simile** uses the word *like* or *as* to compare two seemingly unlike things.
- A **metaphor** compares two or more things by implying that one thing *is* another.
- **Personification** involves giving human characteristics to an animal, object, or idea.

simile

> She laughs like wild water, shaking
>   her braids loose, she laughs
> —Chitra Banerjee Divakaruni, **from "Woman with Kite"**

personification

> Sometime too hot the eye of heaven shines,
> And often is his gold complexion dimmed;
> —William Shakespeare, **from "Shall I Compare Thee to a Summer's Day?"**

metaphor

> the spring rain
>   is a
>   thread of pearls
> —Lady Ise, **from a tanka**

Imagery

Imagery is descriptive language used to represent objects, feelings, and thoughts. It often appeals to one or more of the five senses: sight, hearing, touch, taste, and smell.

> In a shoe box stuffed in an old nylon stocking
> Sleeps the baby mouse I found in the meadow,
> Where he trembled and shook beneath a stick
> —Theodore Roethke, **from "The Meadow Mouse"**

The Sound of Poetry

Rhyme

Rhyme is the repetition of a final stressed vowel and succeeding sounds in two or more words. **Internal rhyme** occurs within lines of poetry. **End rhyme** occurs at the ends of lines. **Rhyme scheme,** the pattern formed by end rhymes, is shown by a row of letters (*aabb*) in which a different letter of the alphabet signals each new rhyme.

> Black reapers with the sound of steel on stones a
> Are sharpening scythes. I see them place the hones a
> In their hip-pockets as a thing that's done, b
> And start their silent swinging, one by one. b
> —Jean Toomer, **from "Reapers"**

Rhythm and Meter

A poet chooses words and arranges them to create **rhythm,** the pattern of stressed and unstressed syllables in a line. Rhythm can be regular or irregular. **Meter** is a regular rhythm. The basic unit in measuring rhythm is the **foot,** which usually contains one stressed syllable marked with (´) and one or more unstressed syllables marked with (˘).

> If I / had loved / you less / or played / you slyly
> I might / have held / you for / a sum / mer more,
> —Edna St. Vincent Millay, **from "Well, I Have Lost You; and I Lost You Fairly"**

Other Sound Devices

- **Alliteration** is the repetition of consonant sounds at the beginnings of words.
- **Consonance** is the repetition of consonant sounds within words or at the ends of words.
- **Assonance** is the repetition of vowel sounds within non-rhyming words.
- **Onomatopoeia** is the use of a word or phrase, such as *swoosh* or *clank,* that imitates or suggests the sound of what it describes.

alliteration

> past the puff-cheeked clouds, she
> follows it, her eyes slit-smiling at the sun.
> —Chitra Banerjee Divakaruni, **from "Woman with Kite"**

consonance

> and kisses are a better fate
> —E. E. Cummings, **from "since feeling is first"**

Literature and Reading For more selections in this genre, go to glencoe.com and enter QuickPass code GL59794u3.

Literary Analysis Model
How do literary elements create meaning in a poem?

Abraham Lincoln is the subject of "O Captain! My Captain!" In the poem, Walt Whitman captures his emotions after the assassination of President Lincoln. Walt Whitman (1819–1892) is one of the pioneers of modern poetry.

APPLYING Literary Elements

Stanza (lines 1–4)
The first half of each stanza, or major division, focuses on the crowd.

Speaker (lines 5–8)
The second half of each stanza focuses on the speaker's sadness.

Imagery (lines 3 and 6)
The sound of bells and the sight of blood are vivid sensory details.

Repetition (lines 1 and 9; 8, 16, and 24)
The repeated use of words such as *Captain* and phrases such as "fallen cold and dead" helps create a musical and emotional effect.

Alliteration (lines 10–11)
The repeated initial consonant sounds in phrases such as *"Flag is Flung"* and *"ribbon'd wreaths"* produce musical effects as well.

O Captain! My Captain!
by Walt Whitman

O Captain! my Captain! our fearful trip is done;
The ship has weather'd every rack, the prize we sought is won;
The port is near, the bells I hear, the people all exulting,
While follow eyes the steady keel, the vessel grim and daring:
5   But O heart! heart! heart!
           O the bleeding drops of red,
                 Where on the deck my Captain lies,
                       Fallen cold and dead.

O Captain! my Captain! rise up and hear the bells;
10 Rise up—for you the flag is flung—for you the bugle trills,
    For you bouquets and ribbon'd wreaths—for you the shores
         a-crowding,
    For you they call, the swaying mass, their eager faces turning;
         Here Captain! dear father!
              This arm beneath your head;
15   It is some dream that on the deck,
                       You've fallen cold and dead.

My Captain does not answer, his lips are pale and still;
My father does not feel my arm, he has no pulse nor will;
The ship is anchor'd safe and sound, its voyage closed and done;
20 From fearful trip, the victor ship, comes in with object won;
     Exult, O shores, and ring, O bells!
        But I, with mournful tread,
           Walk the deck my Captain lies,
              Fallen cold and dead.

Figurative Language (lines 17–18)

The speaker uses metaphor in comparing Lincoln to a captain and a father.

Rhythm (lines 21–24)

The pattern of stressed and unstressed syllables produces a regular rhythm.

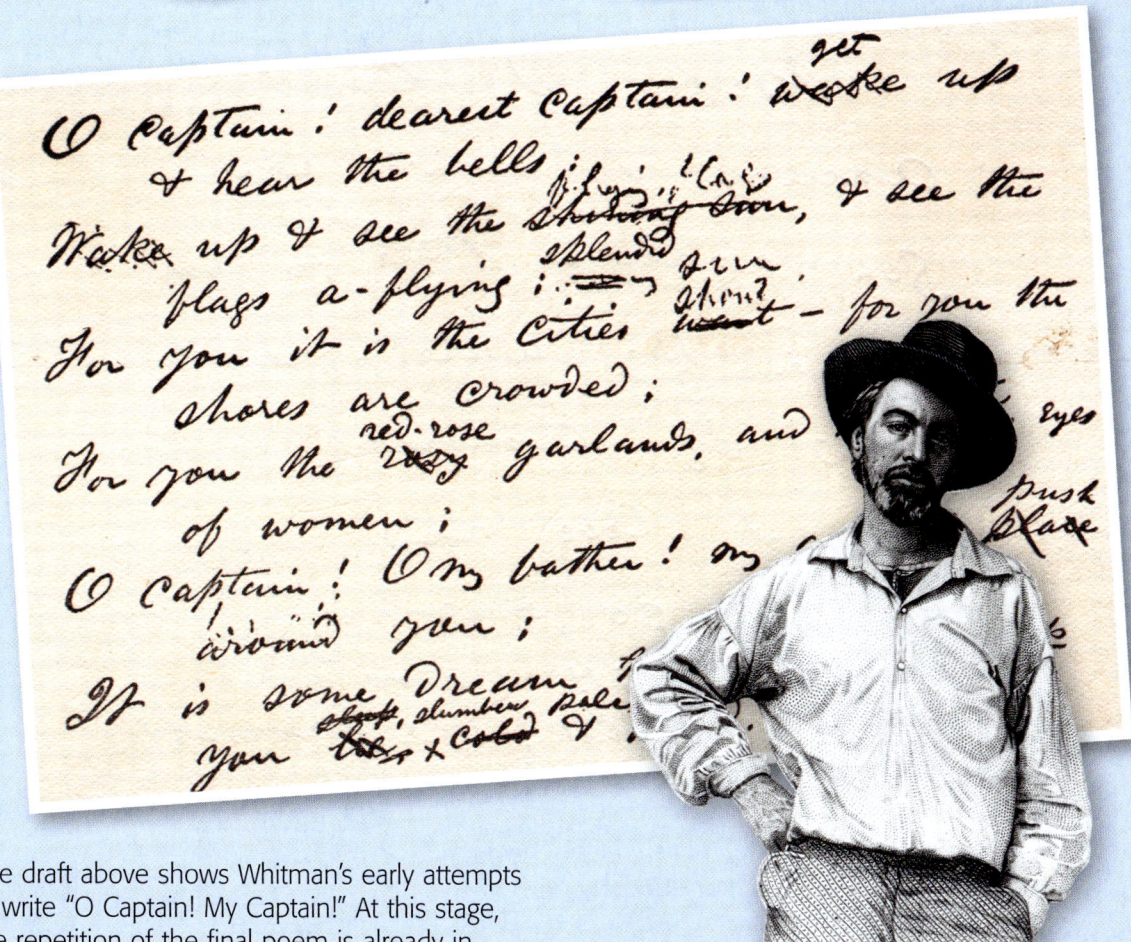

The draft above shows Whitman's early attempts to write "O Captain! My Captain!" At this stage, the repetition of the final poem is already in place, as well as the metaphor of Lincoln as the captain and father to the country. Whitman uses specific words to create imagery that is powerful and packed with meaning. What emotions do these stanzas capture?

Reading Check

Evaluate In your opinion, which of the literary elements did Whitman use most successfully in "O Captain! My Captain!"? Explain your choice.

INTRODUCTION **471**

Wrap-Up

Guide to Reading Poetry

- Poets use words differently than do writers of prose.
- Reading poetry well involves using your emotions, experiences, and imagination as well as your intelligence.
- Read a poem from beginning to end several times.
- Focus on what the words of the poem are actually saying.
- Respond to the poem as a whole before analyzing it.

Elements of Poetry

- **Imagery** is descriptive language that appeals to the five senses.
- **Figurative language** compares unlike things in imaginative ways.
- The pattern of stressed and unstressed syllables in a line of poetry creates **rhythm**.
- **Rhyme** and other sound devices repeat certain sounds to create musical effects.
- The **speaker** is the voice in the poem that talks to the reader.
- A **line** is a row of words; a **stanza** is a group of lines that form a unit.

Literature Online

Unit Resources For additional skills practice, go to glencoe.com and enter QuickPass code GL59794u3.

Activities

Use what you have learned about reading and analyzing poetry to do one of these activities.

1. Speaking and Listening How would you present the poem "O Captain! My Captain!" to convey the speaker's intense emotions? Record a dramatic reading of Whitman's poem to play for the class.

2. Visual Literacy Create a concept web illustrating the elements that work together to create meaning in a poem.

3. Take Notes You might try using this graphic organizer to keep track of the main kinds of literary elements in this unit.

 **THREE-POCKET BOOK**

See page R20 for folding instructions.

PART 1
The Energy of the Everyday

The Girl with Paddleboat, 1865. Gustave Courbet.

View the Art Gustave Courbet, a French painter whose work shunned Romanticism and embraced Realism, often portrayed average citizens at everyday tasks. Does this painting capture the energy of the everyday? Why or why not?

BIG IDEA

We sometimes hear people say, "If I had it to do over again, I would take time to stop and smell the roses." We are constantly surrounded with opportunities to take in the wonder of life. The poems in Part 1 find wonder in everyday experiences. As you read the poems, ask yourself, What are some of my favorite memories of everyday experiences? What made those times special?

Learning Objectives

For pages 474–475

In studying this text, you will focus on the following objective:

Literary Study: Analyzing form and structure.

LITERARY FOCUS

Form and Structure

How does a poem fit together?

What is a poem? What are its parts? While many poems at first appear to be simple collections of rhymed lines, their structure can be far more complex. The structure of prose is a relatively simple matter of proper sentences grouped into paragraphs. The structure of poetry offers many more possibilities to explore. In the following cartoon, Calvin presents his father with an ode.

Distributed By Universal Press Syndicate. Reprinted with permission. All rights reserved.

Form and Structure

Line A **line** of poetry is a row consisting of a word or words that may or may not form a complete sentence. All writers use **structure,** or the organization of images, ideas, and words, to present a unified impression or idea to the reader. Poets often organize the ideas and images in their poems into **stanzas**—the "paragraphs" of poetry. Poems can have stanzas of varying lengths or have no stanza divisions at all. **Form** refers to the external pattern of a poem, including the way lines and stanzas are organized.

Stanza A **stanza** is a group of lines followed by a line of space. A stanza of two lines that rhyme is a **couplet.** The rhyme scheme is *aa.* Stanzas of four, six, and eight lines are respectively called **quatrains, sestets,** and **octaves.** In English poetry, quatrains with an *abab* rhyme scheme are common.

Rhyme scheme The term **rhyme scheme** refers to the rhyming pattern of a poem. Lowercase letters are used to show rhyme schemes. Each end sound is assigned its own letter. Study the *abab* rhyme scheme in this stanza.

If I had loved you less or played you slyly	a
I might have held you for a summer more,	b
But at the cost of words I value highly,	a
And no such summer as the one before.	b

—Edna St. Vincent Millay, *from "Well, I Have Lost You; and I Lost You Fairly"*

Rhythm Stressed and unstressed syllables create a pattern in poetry, called **rhythm.** When the pattern is predictable it is called **meter,** but it does not have to be predictable. Rhythm can create a musical quality, but it can also draw attention to certain words or ideas. Langston Hughes uses rhythm in this way in "A Dream Deferred," when in the last line he asks, "Or does it explode?"

Meter Predictable rhythms are called **meter.** Different meters are named for how many feet are in each line. **Trimeter** has three feet, **tetrameter** has four feet, **pentameter** has five feet, and **hexameter** has six feet. Iambic pentameter appears in many English poems. An **iamb** is a foot that has an unstressed syllable followed by a stressed syllable, and pentameter means there are five of them in a line.

> Shall I compare thee to a summer's day?
>
> Thou art more lovely and more temperate.
>
> —William Shakespeare, *from "Shall I Compare Thee to a Summer's Day?"*

Foot The **foot** is the basic unit of stressed and unstressed syllables used to describe rhythm in poetry. A foot usually has two or three syllables.

Scansion In addition to paying close attention to the sounds of letters and words in poems, poets pay attention to each syllable and whether it is stressed or unstressed. Stressed and unstressed syllables create **rhythms.** Each rhythmical unit is called a **foot,** and a regular pattern of stressed and unstressed syllables is called **meter.** Stressed syllables are marked with (´) and unstressed syllables are marked with (˘).

> Rough winds do shake the darling buds of May,
>
> And summer's lease hath all too short a date.
>
> —William Shakespeare, *from "Shall I Compare Thee to a Summer's Day?"*

Lyric Poem Lyric poems are short poems by one speaker who expresses thoughts and feelings to create a single, unified impression. Jimmy Santiago Baca's poem "I Am Offering This Poem" is an example of a lyric poem.

> It's all I have to give,
> and all anyone needs to live,
> and to go on living inside,
> when the world outside
> no longer cares if you live or die;
> remember,
>   I love you
>
> —Jimmy Santiago Baca, *from "I Am Offering This Poem"*

Free Verse Poetry without a fixed pattern of meter and rhyme is called **free verse.** Some free verse uses sound devices and a rhythm similar to speaking patterns.

> Speaking indifferently to him,
> who had driven out the cold
> and polished my good shoes as well.
> What did I know, what did I know
> of love's austere and lonely offices?
>
> —Robert Hayden, *from "Those Winter Sundays"*

Quickwrite

Write a Poem Choose a form from the examples above and write a poem, paying special attention to the form, stanzas, lines, and rhyme scheme.

 **Literature** Online

Literature and Reading For more about literary elements, go to glencoe.com and enter QuickPass code GL59794u3.

Before You Read

Those Winter Sundays

Meet Robert Hayden
(1913–1980)

Ever wonder what will happen to your classmates, those burrowing bookworms, who enjoy reading for reading's sake? Well, they just might grow up to be famous authors and poets. Robert Hayden was one of those bookish students, and he went on to become a poet and professor, earning a living through the written word.

> "I loved those books, partly because they took me completely out of the environment I lived in, and they appealed to my imagination. . . ."
> —Robert Hayden

A Life with Books Hayden was born in Detroit, Michigan. Growing up, he was too nearsighted to play sports with his friends, so he found companionship in books. After high school, he read many contemporary poets including those of the Harlem Renaissance—which he discovered by accident, stumbling upon the famous anthology *The New Negro* at a time when he could not afford to go to college. Later he won a scholarship to Detroit City College (now called Wayne State University), where he majored in foreign languages and minored in English.

After receiving a master's degree in 1944, Hayden began his academic career. He spent twenty-three years at Fisk University, where he eventually became a professor of English. He ended his academic career at the University of Michigan, teaching there for eleven years. Hayden once said that he considered himself to be "a poet who teaches in order to earn a living so that he can write a poem or two now and then."

Politics, Poetry, and Faith Hayden's poetry was deeply influenced by the poetry of his mentor and graduate school professor, W. H. Auden. Hayden creates stanza structures that are creative and original, even when they appear in traditional forms. In this way, his poetry balances free verse and traditional forms. Hayden's poetry is usually arranged into even stanzas with lines in regular patterns. Another main feature of Hayden's verse is that he avoids full rhyme; in some cases, he substitutes assonance or consonance.

The subject matter of Hayden's poetry tends to focus on historical themes and events, and he was influenced by the politics of the times. He experienced discrimination and segregation while he lived in Nashville. However, he refrained from writing aggressively about the injustices he witnessed. Instead, he strove to approach subjects such as civil rights as "an artist and not a propagandist."

Author Search For more about Robert Hayden, go to glencoe.com and enter QuickPass code GL59794u3.

Literature and Reading Preview

Connect to the Poem
How often do you reflect on what your family members do to show their love for you? Freewrite for a few minutes about your family's love for you and how you have responded.

Build Background
Hayden's poems often balance painful experiences with hope, possibility, and a celebration of humanity. Hayden says, "I believe in the essential oneness of all people." His poems often portray the universal human concerns of loss and love.

Set Purposes for Reading

Big Idea The Energy of the Everyday

As you read, ask yourself, How does Hayden capture the different moods and actions of his characters through vivid imagery?

Literary Element Line and Stanza

A **line** in a poem usually consists of a single word or row of words. A **stanza** is a group of lines forming a unit in a poem or song and is similar to the paragraph in prose. Typically, stanzas are separated by a line of space. As you read, ask yourself, What is the author's focus and thematic intent for each stanza?

Reading Strategy Analyze Tone

Tone refers to an author's attitude toward the subject matter. A writer's tone might project a variety of attitudes such as sympathy or humor. As you read, ask yourself, What is the speaker's tone, and what does it suggest about the author's message?

Tip: Ask Questions Use a diagram to identify how the speaker uses description to achieve a certain tone. Fill in the circles with descriptions from the poem and note the tone conveyed.

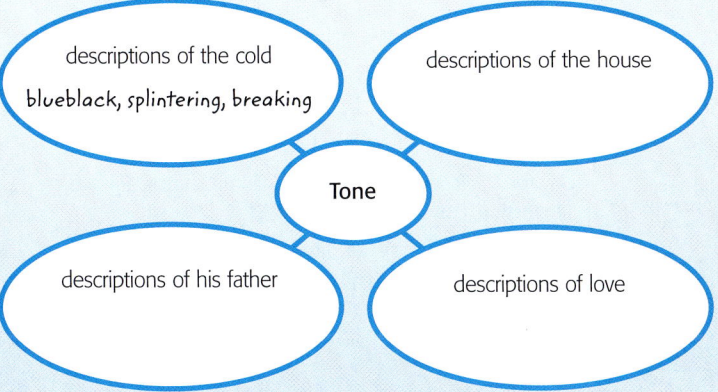

Learning Objectives

For pages 476–479

In studying this text, you will focus on the following objectives:

Literary Study: Analyzing line and stanza.

Reading: Analyzing tone.

Vocabulary

chronic (kron′ik) *adj.* persistent; ongoing, especially of sickness or pain; p. 478 *Chronic backaches made it difficult for my mom to garden.*

indifferently (in dif′ər ənt lē) *adv.* not concerned about someone or something; without a preference; p. 478 *When Mr. Tate spoke, his children listened indifferently, as they were not interested.*

austere (ôs tēr′) *adj.* stern; severe in appearance; p. 478 *Micky's austere expression let us know that he was disappointed.*

ROBERT HAYDEN **477**

Those Winter Sundays

Robert Hayden

Sundays too my father got up early
and put his clothes on in the blueblack cold,
then with cracked hands that ached
from labor in the weekday weather made
5   banked fires[1] blaze. No one ever thanked him.

I'd wake and hear the cold splintering, breaking.
When the rooms were warm, he'd call,
and slowly I would rise and dress,
fearing the **chronic** angers of that house,

10 Speaking **indifferently** to him,
who had driven out the cold
and polished my good shoes as well.
What did I know, what did I know
of love's **austere** and lonely offices?[2]

1. *Banked fires* are ones that have been covered with ashes to keep them burning at a very low level.
2. *Offices* can mean both "duties and responsibilities" or "favors and kindness."

Analyze Tone *How do these five words from the speaker contribute to the tone of the poem?*

Vocabulary

chronic (kron′ ik) *adj.* persistent; ongoing, especially of sickness or pain
indifferently (in dif′ ər ənt lē) *adv.* not concerned about someone or something; without a preference
austere (ôs tēr′) *adj.* stern; severe in appearance

Lynford, 1969. Karen Armitage. Oil on canvas. Private collection.

View the Art Armitage often paints solitary figures who appear deep in thought. How would you describe this man's expression and mood? Compare and contrast them with the personal qualities conveyed by the speaker of the poem.

After You Read

Respond and Think Critically

Respond and Interpret

1. Which one line or image from "Those Winter Sundays" resonated most with you? Explain.

2. As a child, did the speaker appreciate his father's efforts? How do you know?

3. (a) Why do you think the speaker spoke indifferently to his father? (b) In the third stanza, how has the father "driven out the cold"?

4. What does the speaker now understand that he did not understand before?

Analyze and Evaluate

5. (a) How does the speaker personify the cold? (b) How does this reflect the son's feelings?

Connect

6. **Big Idea** The Energy of the Everyday In what ways does Hayden bring greater significance to the daily responsibilities a parent performs? Explain.

7. **Connect to the Author** What was Robert Hayden's motive in writing this poem?

Literary Element — Line and Stanza

Examining the contribution each **line** and **stanza** makes to the overall movement and thematic development of the poem can help you better understand the poet's purpose and intention.

1. What is the specific focus of each separate stanza?

2. How does each line in the poem trace the speaker's development as a person?

Reading Strategy — Analyze Tone

SAT Skills Practice

1. The speaker's description of the cold house

   (A) creates an affectionate, nostalgic tone
   (B) contrasts with the warmth of feeling he had for his father
   (C) mirrors the lack of sympathy he felt for his father
   (D) reveals that his feelings toward his father remain unchanged
   (E) suggests that he is incapable of expressing love

Literature Online

Selection Resources For Selection Quizzes, eFlashcards, and Reading-Writing Connection activities, go to glencoe.com and enter QuickPass code GL59794u3.

Vocabulary Practice

Practice with Context Clues Identify the context clues in the following sentences that help you determine the meaning of each boldfaced vocabulary word.

1. Every time Jane fidgeted, Grandmother gave her an **austere**, disapproving look.

2. Over the years, Duncan suffered from **chronic** allergies and could not find relief no matter what he did.

3. Shipra did not care which movie we saw, so she reacted **indifferently** when I chose one.

Writing

Write a Character Sketch Use the information presented in "Those Winter Sundays" to write a character sketch of the speaker's father—a description of his personality and character traits. As you write, be sure to consider not only what the speaker directly states but also what can be inferred from the speaker's tone.

Learning Objectives

For page 480

In this workshop, you will focus on the following objective:

Vocabulary: Understanding context clues.

Vocabulary Workshop

Homonyms and Homophones

Literature Connection In this excerpt from his poem "Those Winter Sundays," Hayden uses the word *banked,* meaning not "stored for safekeeping" or "steeply inclined," but rather "covered with ashes to burn slowly."

> ". . . with cracked hands that ached / from labor in the weekday weather made / banked fires blaze."
>
> —Robert Hayden, from "Those Winter Sundays"

Words like *banked* that sound and are spelled alike but have different meanings are called **homonyms.** Words such as *there* and *their,* which sound alike but are spelled differently, are called **homophones.** Homonyms and homophones can be confusing, but the context, or setting, in which a word appears usually provides clues to the word's meaning. From Hayden's use of *banked* to describe fires and our own knowledge of them, we can determine the appropriate definition.

Part of the reason why English is difficult for many non-native speakers to learn is its many homophones.

Examples

ate/eight	none/nun	some/sum
for/fore/four	one/won	their/there/they're
here/hear	right/rite/write	to/too/two
higher/hire	row/roe	wholly/holy/holey
its/it's	scent/sent/cent	
morning/mourning	site/sight/cite	

Homonyms and Homophones

Homonyms are words that sound alike and are spelled alike but have different meanings. **Homophones** are words that sound alike but are spelled differently and have different meanings.

Tip

Homographs are words that look alike in writing but have different word origins and sometimes different pronunciations. Context clues help distinguish homographs from homonyms.

Practice Use context clues to decide which homonym or homophone belongs in each sentence below. Use a dictionary if you need help.

1. Father (passed/past) him a pair of freshly shined shoes.
2. The boy was the sole (heir/air) to the family fortune.
3. The warmth helped (heel/heal) their chilled bodies.
4. The stars counteracted the loneliness of the (night/knight).
5. He did not (know, no) how to express his feelings to his father.

 **Literature** Online

Vocabulary For more vocabulary practice, go to glencoe.com and enter the QuickPass code GL59794u3.

Before You Read

Creatures

Meet **Billy Collins**
(born 1941)

Billy Collins has managed a most unusual feat for a contemporary poet: popular and critical acclaim. Whether musing about the three blind mice or a museum painting, Collins writes with a wry humor that gently ushers the reader into his poem and reveals truths about the human experience using twists of language and thought. Collins says that he envisions the beginning of a poem as "a kind of welcome mat where I invite the reader inside."

Beginnings Collins is a native of New York City, the son of a nurse and an electrician. After high school, he attended the College of the Holy Cross in Worchester, Massachusetts. Collins then earned a doctorate in Romantic Poetry from the University of California at Riverside in 1971. He returned to New York to teach at the City University of New York.

> "I believe poetry belongs in unexpected places—in elevators and on buses and subways."
>
> —Billy Collins

During the 1970s, Collins's poetry began to appear in many literary publications, including the *American Poetry Review*, the *Paris Review*, and the *New Yorker*. In 1977 Collins published his first book of poetry, *Pokerface*, followed by his second collection, *Video Poems*, in 1980. Eight years later, Collins published *The Apple that Astonished Paris*. His next book, *Questions about Angels*, was included in the 1990 National Poetry Series.

A National Reputation With the publication of *Questions about Angels*, Collins's popularity reached the national level. The New York Public Library named him a "Literary Lion" in 1992, and the following year he was awarded the Bess Hokin Prize by the prestigious *Poetry* magazine. His poems appeared in the *Best American Poetry* anthologies in 1992, 1993, and 1997. He continued to publish and also edited two anthologies of poetry and released *The Best Cigarette*, a CD of Collins reading thirty-three of his poems. His other accolades include various literary prizes and fellowships from the Guggenheim Foundation and the National Endowment for the Arts.

Collins was named Poet Laureate of the United States in 2001, a position he held for two years. During that time, he developed *Poetry 180: A Poem a Day for High Schools*. Collins selected 180 poems, one to be read aloud each morning along with the school announcements. He described the project as a "jukebox of poems" and emphasized that the students were not to analyze the poetry—they were to simply experience the language.

 **Literature** Online

Author Search For more about Billy Collins, go to glencoe.com and enter QuickPass code GL59794u3.

Literature and Reading Preview

Connect to the Poem
Do you ever see creatures in clouds or ordinary objects? Discuss this question with a partner. Consider whether these observations change based on a person's age or experience.

Build Background
Appearances sometimes defy reality, and it is possible for people to view the same object or occurrence in different ways. When something can be perceived or interpreted differently, each person brings his or her own background knowledge and imagination into the process.

Set Purposes for Reading

Big Idea | The Energy of the Everyday
As you read this poem, ask yourself, What creatures are seen in everyday objects and how does the speaker react to them?

Literary Element | Enjambment
Enjambment is the continuation of the sense of a sentence or phrase from one line of a poem to the next without a pause:
> Many times I would be daydreaming
> on the carpet and one would appear next to me,

Enjambment can occur in both metered and free-verse poetry. As you read, ask yourself, Where does enjambment occur in this poem?

Reading Strategy | Analyze Poetic Structure
When you **analyze poetic structure**, you identify the order or pattern the poet uses to organize his or her materials. As you read, ask yourself, How does Collins structure "Creatures"?

Tip: Note Descriptive Words As you read, note the adjectives that Collins uses in a web similar to the one below.

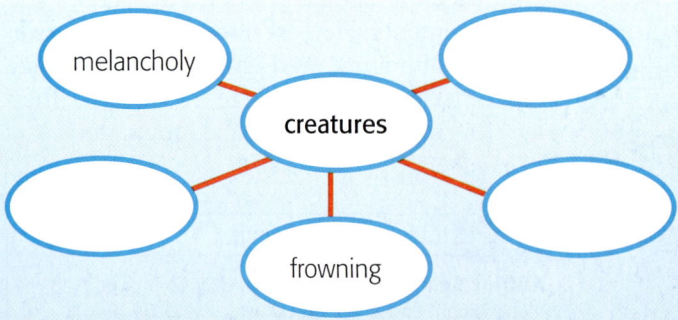

Learning Objectives
For pages 481–485

In studying this text, you will focus on the following objectives:

Literary Study: Analyzing enjambment.

Reading: Analyzing structure.

Vocabulary

submerged (səb murjd´) *adj.* hard to see; sunken; p. 483 *The real plan was submerged in a mass of detail.*

bureau (byoor´ō) *n.* a chest of drawers for the bedroom; p. 483 *Please put the clothes back in the bureau.*

melancholy (mel´ən kol´ē) *adj.* depressed; dejected; p. 484 *The dark and rainy day created a melancholy mood in the school.*

grimace (gri mās´) *v.* to make a face expressing disgust, disapproval, or pain; p. 484 *The boy grimaced at his mother when she scolded.*

fissure (fish´ər) *n.* a narrow crack; p. 484 *The earthquake caused a fissure in the earth.*

Tip: Word Usage A dictionary definition provides limited guidance when it comes to using words. You can gather additional clues from reading and listening to words used in context.

482 UNIT 3 POETRY

Invisible Afghan with Apparition on Beach of Face of Garcia in Form of Fruit Dish with 3 Figs, 1938. Salvador Dali. Private collection.

Creatures

Billy Collins

Hamlet[1] noticed them in the shapes of clouds,
but I saw them in the furniture of childhood,
creatures trapped under surfaces of wood,

one **submerged** in a polished sideboard,
5   one frowning from a chair-back,
another howling from my mother's silent **bureau,**
locked in the grain of maple, frozen in oak.

1. *Hamlet.* In Shakespeare's *Hamlet,* Act III, Scene II, Hamlet compares the shape of a cloud to a camel, a weasel, and a whale.

Vocabulary

submerged (səb murjd′) *adj.* hard to see; sunken
bureau (byoor′ō) *n.* a chest of drawers for the bedroom

I would see these presences, too,
in a swirling pattern of wallpaper
10　or in the various greens of a porcelain lamp,
each looking so **melancholy**, so damned,
some peering out at me as if they knew
all the secrets of a secretive boy.

Many times I would be daydreaming
15　on the carpet and one would appear next to me,
the oversize nose, the hollow look.

So you will understand my reaction
this morning at the beach
when you opened your hand to show me
20　a stone you had picked up from the shoreline.

"Do you see the face?" you asked
as the cold surf circled our bare ankles.
"There's the eye and the line of the mouth,
like it's **grimacing**, like it's in pain."

25　"Well, maybe that's because it has a **fissure**
running down the length of its forehead
not to mention a kind of twisted beak," I said,

taking the thing from you and flinging it out
over the sparkle of blue waves
30　so it could live out its freakish existence
on the dark bottom of the sea

and stop bothering innocent beachgoers like us,
stop ruining everyone's summer.

Analyze Poetic Structure *What is the function of these lines in the poem's structure?*

Enjambment *How do these lines exemplify enjambment? Explain.*

> **Vocabulary**
> **melancholy** (mel´ən kol´ē) *adj.* depressed; dejected
> **grimace** (gri mās´) *v.* to make a face expressing disgust, disapproval, or pain
> **fissure** (fish´ər) *n.* a narrow crack

After You Read

Respond and Think Critically

Respond and Interpret

1. Describe your feelings about the creatures after reading the poem.

2. (a) How does the speaker describe the "creatures" in the furniture? (b) Why do you think the speaker sees creatures in the furniture?

3. (a) How does the speaker react to the stone his companion finds on the beach? (b) Why do you think the speaker reacts in this way?

Analyze and Evaluate

4. Does the speaker's reaction to the stone seem rational? Explain and support your answer.

5. How does Collins help you to identify with the experience described in the poem?

6. (a) Why do you think the speaker directly addresses his companion in the fifth stanza? (b) Is this technique effective? Explain.

Connect

7. **Big Idea** The Energy of the Everyday The everyday is usually considered non-threatening. In what ways has Collins made the everyday threatening? Explain.

8. **Connect to the Author** Collins's poems are known for their playful, conversational style. Where can you identify that style in "Creatures"?

Literary Element Enjambment

Poets use **enjambment** to create a conversational tone and flow in their poems.

1. Where does the poet use enjambment in the poem?

2. How effective is the author's use of enjambment? Explain and support your response.

Reading Strategy Analyze Structure

Poets may structure the ideas in a poem by cause and effect, chronological order, and problem and solution. Refer to the web you made while reading.

1. How do the adjectives the speaker uses support his reaction in the final two lines of the poem?

2. What structure does Collins use to organize the ideas in the poem? Support your response.

Vocabulary Practice

Practice with Usage Respond to these statements to help you explore the meanings of vocabulary words from the selection.

1. Name something that is likely to be **submerged**.

2. Tell what a **bureau** is likely to contain.

3. Describe your face, posture, or body language when you are **melancholy**.

4. Identify two things that might make you **grimace**.

5. Explain what you would do if you came across a **fissure** while hiking.

Writing

Write an Interior Monologue What might the speaker's companion be thinking during the events described in the last five stanzas of "Creatures"? Write an interior monologue (a verbalization of the thoughts running through a character's mind) that expresses the companion's reactions.

LOG ON **Literature** Online

Selection Resources For Selection Quizzes, eFlashcards, and Reading-Writing Connection activities, go to glencoe.com and enter QuickPass code GL59794u3.

Before You Read

World Literature
England

Shall I Compare Thee to a Summer's Day?

Meet **William Shakespeare**
(1564–1616)

Over the years he has had many names. Some have called him "Gentle Will." Many are familiar with his most common nickname, "The Bard." And though the name Shakespeare brings to mind images of great onstage romance, horrific tragedy, and uproarious comedy, he was, before all else, "The Poet."

The Early Years Born to Mary Arden and John Shakespeare, William lived his early years in Stratford-upon-Avon, England, where he most likely received an extensive education in Latin literature and grammar, history, and mythology. This immersion in the classics fuels much of the imagery in Shakespeare's works.

Little else is known about his early life, but literary historians do know that in 1582 he married Anne Hathaway, with whom he had three children, Susanna, Hamnet, and Judith. By 1592, Shakespeare began showing up in the world of London theater, though there are conflicting stories as to how he arrived there.

> "[Shakespeare] was not of an age, but for all time!"
>
> —Ben Jonson

The Poet Shakespeare's first poems, *Venus and Adonis* and *The Rape of Lucrece*, were published in 1593 and 1594. Both were narrative works that demonstrated Shakespeare's education in ancient Roman history and mythology, specifically the mythical romance of the goddess Aphrodite and the mortal Adonis and the tale of the rape of Lucrece—the daughter of an important ancient Roman family that supposedly incited a rebellion in Rome.

Shakespeare the Poet is best-known and regarded for his sonnets. Although probably written in the 1590s, Shakespeare's 154 sonnets were not published until 1609. These poems express a universal theme of the power of love and beauty over nature and time.

Ghosts of Rhyme and Rhythm Several mysteries surround this collection of sonnets. Someone dedicated the first 126 of the sonnets to a set of initials, a person who has been known to history only as W. H. Another oddity is that sonnets 127–152 are dedicated to a mysterious "dark lady." Theories abound as to whom this person might be and to whom those initials might belong, but the world may never know the true answer.

Shakespeare lived to the age of fifty-two, not an unusual age for the seventeenth century. Both his poetic drama and dramatic poetry live on today as some of the most quoted and esteemed literature of all time.

Author Search For more about William Shakespeare, go to glencoe.com and enter QuickPass code GL59794u3.

Literature and Reading Preview

Connect to the Sonnet
To what would you compare someone you love or the emotion of love itself? Respond to this question in your journal.

Build Background
Throughout history, people in love have expressed their feelings by giving tokens of their affection, such as flowers, poems, jewelry, and locks of hair. In this sonnet, the speaker expresses his love by making his beloved the subject of the poem.

Set Purposes for Reading

Big Idea The Energy of the Everyday

As you read this poem, ask yourself, How does Shakespeare use everyday occurrences?

Literary Element Meter and Rhythm

Meter is the regular pattern of stressed and unstressed syllables that give a line of poetry a predictable rhythm, or pattern of beats. **Rhythm** gives poetry a musical quality, adds emphasis to certain words, and helps reinforce meaning. The basic unit of meter is the **foot**, consisting of one or two stressed syllables (marked ´) and/or one or more unstressed syllables (marked ˘). As you read, ask yourself, What is the pattern of stressed and unstressed syllables in each line?

Reading Strategy Analyze Form

Form is the structure of a literary work. The form of a poem is determined by several factors: the number and length of lines, the number of **stanzas**, the rhyme scheme, and the meter. This is an English, or Shakespearean, sonnet. As you read, ask yourself, What are the elements of this form?

Tip: Scan the lines Choose two lines from the poem and mark the meter with the appropriate stress symbols. Use the chart below as a guide.

Scansion	˘ / ˘ / ˘ / ˘ / ˘ /
Line	And often is his gold complexion dimmed

Learning Objectives

For pages 486–491

In studying this text, you will focus on the following objectives:

Literary Study: Determining meter and rhyme.

Reading: Analyzing form.

Vocabulary

temperate (tem´pər it) *adj.* calm and free from extremes of temperature; p. 488 *Most areas in the state of Virginia, which experiences few extreme temperatures, are considered temperate in climate.*

Tip: Analogies To complete an analogy, decide on the relationship represented by the first pair of words. Then apply that relationship to the second pair of words. For example, consider the following analogy:

temperate : extreme :: quiet : loud

The words *temperate* and *extreme* are antonyms as are the words *quiet* and *loud*.

WILLIAM SHAKESPEARE

Shall I Compare Thee to a Summer's Day?

William Shakespeare

The Great Oak, Moat Lawn with Rhododendrons & Azaleas—Morning, June, 2004. Charles Neal. Oil on canvas.

    Shall I compare thee to a summer's day?
    Thou art more lovely and more **temperate**.
    Rough winds do shake the darling buds of May,
    And summer's lease hath all too short a date.
5 Sometime too hot the eye of heaven shines,
    And often is his gold complexion dimmed;
    And every fair[1] from fair sometime declines,
    By chance, or nature's changing course untrimmed:[2]
    But thy eternal summer shall not fade
10 Nor lose possession of that fair thou ow'st,[3]
    Nor shall Death brag thou wand'rest in his shade,
    When in eternal lines to time thou grow'st.
       So long as men can breathe or eyes can see,
       So long lives this, and this gives life to thee.

---

1. *Fair,* in this context, is a synonym for *beauty.*
2. Here, *untrimmed* means "stripped of beauty."
3. *[thou ow'st]* Read this poetic phrase as "you own" or "you possess."

Analyze Form How would you describe the meter in the first four lines of the poem?

Vocabulary

temperate (tem′pər it) *adj.* calm and free from extremes of temperature

After You Read

Respond and Think Critically

Respond and Interpret

1. (a) Does this poem reflect your personal views on love? Explain. (b) Do you think that a poem would make a good token of affection? Why or why not?

2. (a) Who might the speaker of this poem be? (b) In your opinion, who is the speaker addressing? Use details from the poem to support your answers.

3. (a) What two things is the speaker comparing? (b) Which one does the speaker consider to be superior? How do you know this?

4. (a) According to the speaker, why will the subject of the poem have a summer that is eternal? (b) What might this tell you about the poet's reason for writing the poem?

Analyze and Evaluate

5. (a) In your opinion, will the speaker's love ever fade? Explain. (b) If the speaker's love fades, will the subject's beauty fade along with the speaker's love? Explain your reasoning.

Connect

6. **Big Idea** The Energy of the Everyday This poem is generally considered a powerful and fervently romantic love poem. How does this poem also connect to nature and everyday occurrences?

7. **Connect to Today** The speaker asserts that his sonnet will make his lover immortal. What art forms today can make their subjects immortal?

The Betrothed Couple, 16th century AD. Lucas van Leyden. Musee des Beaux-Arts, Palais Rohan.

Primary Visual Artifact

The Betrothed Couple

Lucas van Leyden (1489/94–1533) was a sixteenth century Dutch engraver and painter known for his ability to capture narrative in his painting. A precocious student, he completed many works while still in his teens. In his early paintings, he often did not fully articulate, or give clear definition to, all shapes and objects, in the composition. As he matured, Leyden began to merge narrative and composition, as in his masterpiece, the triptych *The Last Judgment*. Here, in *The Betrothed Couple*, Leyden shows a simpler scene, that of a man offering his beloved a ring as a symbol of his love.

Group Activity Discuss the following questions with your classmates.

1. How realistic is the scene? Cite details that show whether or not the composition is fully articulated.

2. How does this expression of love compare with the speaker's expression of love in "Shall I Compare Thee to a Summer's Day?"?

Literary Element Meter and Rhythm

The basic unit of **meter** is the foot. The length of a metrical line can be expressed in terms of the number of feet it contains. The meter in "Shall I Compare Thee to a Summer's Day?" is **iambic pentameter**, the most common meter in English poetry. In iambic pentameter, the predominant foot, or unit of rhythm, is the iamb. An iamb consists of an unstressed syllable followed by a stressed one. There are five feet in each line of iambic pentameter. Sometimes poets vary the rhythm to create certain effects. For instance, if the reader has come to expect a certain rhythm, a slight variation in the metrical pattern may heighten the meaning of a line.

1. What is unusual about the rhythm in line 11?
2. What effect does Shakespeare create by varying the rhythm of this line?

Review: Personification

Personification is a figure of speech in which an animal, an object, a force of nature, or an idea is given human characteristics.

Partner Activity With a classmate, discuss the use of personification in "Shall I Compare Thee to a Summer's Day?" Work together to find three examples of personification. Why might Shakespeare have chosen to use personification? Use a chart, like the one below, to organize your discussion.

Example of Personification	Possible Reason
"Nor shall Death brag thou wand'rest in his shade"	Giving death human characteristics is a common, traditional device

Selection Resources For Selection Quizzes, eFlashcards, and Reading-Writing Connection activities, go to glencoe.com and enter QuickPass code GL59794u3.

Reading Strategy Analyze Form

A Shakespearean sonnet is a lyric poem of fourteen lines, following strict patterns of meter and rhyme. Review the chart you made on page 487 and answer these questions.

1. How might the meter and rhythm be important to the meaning of the poem?
2. What is the rhyme scheme of this sonnet? How is this sonnet structured?
3. The rhymed couplet of a sonnet often presents a conclusion to the issues or questions discussed in the three quatrains, or four-line stanzas, preceding it. What is the effect of the couplet in the Shakespearean sonnet you have just read?

Vocabulary Practice

Practice with Analogies Choose the word that best completes each analogy. Use a dictionary if you need help.

1. temperate : moderate :: loyal :
   a. faithful   b. treacherous   c. respectful
2. rough : tree bark :: waxy :
   a. candle   b. glass   c. steel
3. possessions : purse :: textbooks :
   a. backpack   b. wallet   c. cylinder
4. decline : improve :: console :
   a. cheer   b. merge   c. distress

Academic Vocabulary

In writing sonnets, poets can't make **arbitrary** decisions; they must follow rules of the form.

Arbitrary is an academic word. More familiar words that are similar in meaning include *personal, chance, inconsistent,* and *random*. To study this word further, answer these questions: What **arbitrary** choices have you made lately? What made your choices arbitrary?

For more on academic vocabulary, see pages 52 and 53.

Respond Through Writing

Reflective Essay

Develop a Comparison Write a reflective essay about a beloved friend or family member in which you compare him or her to something else. To develop the comparison, relate events from the subject's life, explain their significance, and connect them to broader themes or ideas. Use narration, exposition, and description.

Understand the Task In a **reflective essay**, you describe experiences to better understand what they mean and what they might teach others. **Narration** is writing that tells a story. **Exposition** is writing that informs or explains. **Description** is writing that re-creates experiences primarily through the use of sensory details.

Prewrite Brainstorm, flip through photo albums, and review videos to help you identify a subject for your essay and generate ideas. You might start your prewriting by listing some of the person's qualities and then identifying things that have similar qualities as this person. For example, if your beloved is moody, you might compare him or her to unpredictable spring weather. Then list events that illustrate the subject's key quality. Use a chart like the one below.

Subject	Key Quality	Possible Comparison
My aunt Beth	Wise; observant	An owl

Draft Once you have finished listing events, begin drafting your essay. Develop an engaging introduction, body, and conclusion. Your body paragraphs should provide specific details and events. Your writing should reflect the significance of your subject's experience. Use smooth transitions, and pay attention to word choice, sentence structure, and tone.

Revise Exchange papers with a classmate and evaluate each other's essays. Does the writing fully develop a comparison? Is the pattern of organization clear and logical? Are there enough specific details for your reader to understand the comparison and the significance of your subject's experience? Provide comments for your partner and revise your essay according to the comments you receive.

Edit and Proofread Proofread your paper, correcting any errors in grammar, spelling, and punctuation. Use the Grammar Tip in the side column to help you with using the comparative and superlative degrees.

Learning Objectives

In this assignment, you will focus on the following objectives:

Writing: Writing a reflective essay.

Grammar: Understanding how to use comparative and superlative adjectives.

Grammar Tip

Comparative and Superlative Adjectives

Use the comparative form of adjectives to compare two things. Use the superlative form of adjectives to compare three or more things. In general, for one-syllable and most two-syllable adjectives, add -*er* to form the comparative and -*est* to form the superlative.

*Does summer seem **shorter** than winter? Does spring feel like the **shortest** season of all?*

For adjectives of three or more syllables, always use *more* and *most* to form the comparative and superlative degrees, respectively.

*The subject of the sonnet is **more beautiful** than a summer's day and perhaps the **most beautiful** person the speaker knows.*

Before You Read

Reapers

Meet Jean Toomer
(1894–1967)

Jean Toomer envisioned a new American identity, forged from many races. "Here in America we are in the process of forming a new race," Toomer once said. "I had seen the divisions, the separatisms and antagonisms . . . [yet] a new type of man was arising in this country—not European, not African, not Asiatic—but American. And in this American I saw the divisions mended, the differences reconciled."

A Divided Identity Born in Washington, D.C., Toomer spent most of his childhood living in white neighborhoods while attending African American schools. As a child, he lived with his mother and his grandfather, who was the first governor of African American descent in U.S. history. Even as a child, Toomer was deeply aware of racial divisions in his society. Toomer had both European and African ancestry, and strangers often misidentified him as belonging to one race or another. By the time he graduated from high school, Toomer began to deny any racial identity, instead preferring to classify himself as an American.

> "We learn the rope of life by untying its knots."
> —Jean Toomer

After high school, Toomer completed courses in a variety of subjects at several universities, but he never received a degree. Instead, he pursued his literary studies on his own. He attended lectures and read the works of William Shakespeare and Leo Tolstoy. Between 1918 and 1923, Toomer wrote a number of short stories, poems, and plays. He drew his inspiration from the poetry of Walt Whitman and Charles Baudelaire.

Finding His Heritage In 1921 Toomer took a teaching job in Georgia, which turned out to be a life-changing experience. Toomer viewed his time in Georgia as a return to his African American roots. As a result, Toomer wrote *Cane*, an experimental novel combining short stories, poems, and a play. The book, published in 1923, inspired authors of the Harlem Renaissance, a great flourishing of African American arts from the 1920s through the 1940s.

Toomer's Legacy Despite his early literary success, Toomer's writing was nearly forgotten after his death. Gradually, the significance of his work gained recognition. In 1969 critic Robert Bone wrote: "It was Jean Toomer's genius to discover and to celebrate the qualities of 'soul,' and thereby to inaugurate the Negro Renaissance. For this alone he will be enshrined as a major figure in the canon of American Negro letters."

 **Literature** Online

Author Search For more about Jean Toomer, go to glencoe.com and enter QuickPass code GL59794u3.

Literature and Reading Preview

Connect to the Poem
Do you think machines and technology have diminished the need for human contact? In a journal entry, write your views.

Build Background
Reapers are workers who cut and harvest grain by hand using special cutting tools. The work of reaping by hand is exhausting: the same motion is repeated hundreds and thousands of times, and the work is performed in a stooped-over position.

Set Purposes for Reading

Big Idea The Energy of the Everyday

As you read "Reapers," ask yourself, How does Toomer endow a seemingly ordinary event with new energy and emotion?

Literary Element Rhyme and Rhyme Scheme

Rhyme is the repetition of the same stressed vowel sounds and any succeeding sounds in two or more words. **Rhyme scheme** is the pattern that end rhymes form in a stanza or in a poem. As you read, ask yourself, What is the effect of the rhyme and the rhyme scheme found in Toomer's poem?

Reading Strategy Analyze Rhythm and Meter

Poets utilize **rhythm and meter** to enhance the musical quality and meaning of their work. **Analyze** the meter, the regular pattern of stressed and unstressed syllables, and rhythm, which can be either regular or irregular. As you read, ask yourself, How does Toomer's use of rhythm and meter create a meaningful and evocative poem?

Tip: Visualize Listen to the "beat" of the poem. Visualize the images that the author is trying to portray through the rhythm. Use a graphic organizer like the one below to list images you visualize and how they affect your understanding of the poem.

> Line: "And start their silent swinging, one by one."
>
> ⬇
>
> Images from meter and rhyme: regular motion of people working in the fields; people working in a synchronized way
>
> ⬇
>
> Effect on mood: somber, tedious, repetitive—makes me think of tiring and dull work

Learning Objectives
For pages 492–495

In studying this text, you will focus on the following objectives:

Literary Study: Analyzing rhyme and rhyme scheme.

Reading: Analyzing meter and rhythm.

Vocabulary

reaper (rē´pər) *n.* machine or person that cuts grain for harvesting; p. 494 *The reapers worked in the fields all day.*

scythe (sīth) *n.* cutting implement made of a long, curved single-edged blade; p. 494 *The men used scythes to cut through the long wheat in the fields.*

hone (hōn) *n.* whetstone or similar tool used to sharpen knives and other types of blades; p. 494 *They used hones to make the knives razor-sharp.*

JEAN TOOMER

Harvesting, 19th Century. Adolphe Joseph Thomas Monticelli. Oil on canvas, 121 x 92.5 cm. Ciurlionis State Art Museum. Kaunas, Lithuania.

Reapers

Jean Toomer

Black **reapers** with the sound of steel on stones
Are sharpening **scythes**. I see them place the **hones**
In their hip-pockets as a thing that's done,
And start their silent swinging, one by one.
5   Black horses drive a mower through the weeds,
And there, a field rat, startled, squealing bleeds.
His belly close to ground. I see the blade,
Blood-stained, continue cutting weeds and shade.

The Energy of the Everyday *How do these lines add meaning to an otherwise ordinary object?*

Vocabulary

reaper (rē´pər) *n.* machine or person that cuts grain for harvesting
scythe (sīth) *n.* cutting implement made of a long, curved single-edged blade
hone (hōn) *n.* whetstone or similar tool used to sharpen knives and other types of blades

After You Read

Respond and Think Critically

Respond and Interpret

1. What image or description in the poem did you find most striking?

2. (a) Describe in your own words what the reapers do. (b) What attitude do the reapers seem to have toward their work?

3. (a) What happens to the field rat in the poem? (b) Why does Toomer include this incident?

Analyze and Evaluate

4. (a) What connections do you see between the reapers and the horses? (b) Why do you think Toomer links the reapers and the horses?

5. (a) How does the rhythm of this poem reflect its content? (b) If the poem did not have this kind of rhythm, would it have the same impact? Explain.

Connect

6. **Big Idea** **The Energy of the Everyday** How does the meter of "Reapers" add to the reader's sensory experience of "the everyday"?

7. **Connect to the Author** Toomer was aware of racial identities but chose to classify himself as simply American. What does his depiction of the reapers suggest about his attitudes toward race?

Literary Element Rhyme and Rhyme Scheme

Toomer uses a particular **rhyme** and **rhyme scheme** to achieve a certain purpose.

1. What kind of rhyme does "Reapers" have? Explain.

2. What is the rhyme scheme of "Reapers"? How is it important to the poem?

Reading Strategy Analyze Meter and Rhythm

Poets often try to convey meaning through meter and rhythm. Refer back to the graphic organizer you made on page 493 to help you answer the following questions.

1. How do you think the rhythm is important to the meaning of the poem?

2. Try reading the poem with a different rhythm. Does this change the poem's effect? Explain.

Literature Online

Selection Resources For Selection Quizzes, eFlashcards, and Reading-Writing Connection activities, go to glencoe.com and enter QuickPass code GL59794u3.

Vocabulary Practice

Practice with Word Origins Studying the etymology, or origin and history, of a word can help you better understand and explore its meaning. Create a word map, like the one below, for each of these vocabulary words from the selection.

reaper   scythe   hone

EXAMPLE:
dictum

<u>Definition</u> *an important statement, announcement, or judgment*
<u>Etymology</u> *Latin* dicere *means "say"*
<u>Sample sentence</u> *The king issued a dictum applied to all his subjects.*

Writing

Write a Movie Scene Write directions for filming the events presented in "Reapers." First, decide how to divide the events into a series of individual camera shots. You may choose to divide the events by line or by couplet. Then, for each shot, describe what the camera should show, how close the camera should be to the activity, how the camera should move, and what sounds viewers should hear.

Before You Read

Ode to My Socks

World Literature
Chile

Meet Pablo Neruda
(1904–1973)

Equally enchanted with a pair of socks, an artichoke, or olive oil, the poet Pablo Neruda (pä´blō nā roo´dä) could transform an ordinary object into a rich treasure. He was a master of the ode, a poem that praises its subject matter, and collected these poems in a book called *Elemental Odes*. These odes are full of celebration for the objects and circumstances of everyday life, a reflection of Neruda's desire to write for the common person rather than for an elite audience.

Neruda was born Neftalí Ricardo Reyes Basoalto in rural Chile. His father was a railway worker, and his mother was a teacher. Neruda began writing poetry at the age of ten and published his first book of poems at age nineteen, under the pen name Pablo Neruda. He later legally changed his name.

> *"I could not live separated from nature."*
>
> —Pablo Neruda

A Life of Poetry and Passion His second book, *Twenty Love Poems and a Song of Despair*, was an instant success, and Neruda was well on his way to becoming a world-renowned poet. However, despite his early success with poetry, he did not neglect his other passions, namely his interest in politics and social causes. Shortly after the publication of his first two books, he went to Asia as Chile's honorary consul. This was the first of many positions in his consular career, which would take him to Spain, France, and Mexico.

Love, Nature, and Social Concerns Neruda is widely known for his passionate and poignant expressions of love. However, his works cover a broad range of subjects. Neruda wanted his poetry to be accessible; he did not believe in poetry as an elitist art form. His major work, *Canto General*, was a book of 340 poems that celebrated the history of Latin America from ancient times. He was equally passionate about social justice for the people of his native Chile and was involved in political causes there throughout his life. Neruda's controversial communist beliefs led to his exile from his native country for a number of years.

Chile awarded him the National Literature Prize in 1945. In 1971 he received the Nobel Prize in Literature "for poetry that with the action of an elemental force brings alive a continent's destiny and dreams."

Author Search For more about Pablo Neruda, go to glencoe.com and enter QuickPass code GL59794u3.

Literature and Reading Preview

Connect to the Poem
Of your prized possessions, which is most valuable to you? Why? Freewrite for a few minutes about how a particular item came to be your prized possession.

Build Background
Neruda's odes celebrate their subjects, but they do not use the lofty style characterized by traditional odes. Rather, they sing the praises of the ordinary, the fundamental, and the essential.

Set Purposes for Reading

Big Idea **The Energy of the Everyday**

As you read, ask yourself, How does Neruda's reverence for his socks capture the magic and energy of the everyday?

Literary Element **Free Verse**

Free verse is poetry without a fixed pattern of rhyme, meter, line length, or stanza arrangement. As you read, ask yourself, How does the unrestrained feel of the free verse form affect the way in which Neruda communicates his ideas?

Reading Strategy **Monitor Comprehension**

Monitoring comprehension by paraphrasing and questioning can help you better understand the poem's figurative language, symbolism, and overall meaning. As you read, ask yourself, Am I doing all I can to understand the poem?

Tip: Track Your Understanding After reading the poem once, revisit each stanza individually. As you complete a stanza, paraphrase it and ask yourself questions about its meaning. Use a chart to record your use of paraphrasing and questioning.

Stanza	Maru Mori brought me / a pair / of socks / which she knitted herself / with her sheepherder's hands, / two socks as soft / as rabbits.
Paraphrase	A loved one or friend knitted, with her own hands, a delicate pair of socks.
Question	Why has the author described Maru Mori's hands as "sheepherder's hands"?
Answer	Sheepherders, by trade, protect and care for flocks of sheep. This image is a metaphor for his friend's loving ways.

Learning Objectives

For pages 496–502

In studying this text, you will focus on the following objectives:

Literary Study: Analyzing free verse.

Reading: Monitoring comprehension.

Vocabulary

immense (i mens´) *adj.* immeasurable; vast; huge; p. 499 *I felt immense pleasure in presenting the student with the scholarship.*

decrepit (di krep´it) *adj.* ruined with age; depleted; p. 499 *The decrepit bus did not look safe.*

sacred (sā´krid) *adj.* worthy of reverence; p. 500 *The archaeologist eagerly uncovered the sacred texts.*

remorse (ri môrs´) *n.* distress stemming from the guilt of past wrongs; p. 500 *The sobbing prisoner showed remorse in court.*

Tip: Synonyms Even though two words are synonyms, they may still have slightly different meanings and connotations.

Personage Lancant Une Pierre a un Oiseau, 1926. Joan Miro.

Ode to My Socks

Pablo Neruda
Translated by Robert Bly

    Maru Mori brought me
    a pair
    of socks
    which she knitted herself
5   with her sheepherder's hands,
    two socks as soft
    as rabbits.
    I slipped my feet
    into them

10   as though into
     two
     cases
     knitted
     with threads of
15   twilight
     and sheepskin.

     Violent socks,
     my feet were
     two fish made
20   of wool,
     two long sharks
     sea-blue, shot
     through
     by one golden thread,
25   two **immense** blackbirds,
     two cannons:
     my feet
     were honored
     in this way
30   by
     these
     heavenly
     socks.
     They were
35   so handsome
     for the first time
     my feet seemed to me
     unacceptable
     like two **decrepit**
40   firemen, firemen
     unworthy
     of that woven
     fire,
     of those glowing
45   socks.

     Nevertheless
     I resisted
     the sharp temptation
     to save them somewhere

Monitor Comprehension *How might you paraphrase this line?*

Vocabulary

immense (i mens´) *adj.* immeasurable; vast; huge
decrepit (di krep´it) *adj.* ruined with age; depleted

50 as schoolboys
    keep
    fireflies,
    as learned men
    collect
55 sacred texts,
    I resisted
    the mad impulse
    to put them
    into a golden
60 cage
    and each day give them
    birdseed
    and pieces of pink melon.
    Like explorers
65 in the jungle who hand
    over the very rare
    green deer
    to the spit[1]
    and eat it
70 with remorse,
    I stretched out
    my feet
    and pulled on
    the magnificent
75 socks
    and then my shoes.

    The moral
    of my ode is this:
    beauty is twice
80 beauty
    and what is good is doubly
    good
    when it is a matter of two socks
    made of wool
85 in winter.

---

1. A *spit* is a rod on which meat is roasted.

The Energy of the Everyday *What kind of schoolboy impulse is the author trying to convey here?*

Free Verse *What elements of free verse does the writer use here?*

Vocabulary

sacred (sā′krid) *adj.* worthy of reverence
remorse (ri môrs′) *n.* distress stemming from the guilt of past wrongs

After You Read

Respond and Think Critically

Respond and Interpret

1. How has Neruda's tribute to socks affected your feelings about material possessions?

2. (a) What does the speaker call his feet? (b) Why might the speaker choose to represent feet in so many ways?

3. According to the speaker, which two types of people hoard things?

Analyze and Evaluate

4. (a) Using specific examples, explain how Neruda has veered from the traditional form of an ode. (b) Why do you think Neruda chose to break with tradition in writing this ode?

5. How might Neruda's decision to summarize his ode in the last stanza affect the reader's interpretation of its ideas?

Connect

6. **Big Idea** The Energy of the Everyday
Neruda is known for his praise of the ordinary. What examples best illustrate this characteristic in "Ode to My Socks"? Explain.

7. **Connect to the Author** Many of Neruda's odes focus on simple subjects found in nature, such as tomatoes, salt, or a chestnut on the ground. Although socks are not "found in nature," how does Neruda connect them to the natural world in the poem?

You're the Critic

Ode to the Elementary

Pablo Neruda's odes differ greatly from the traditional form. Although some traditionalists might prefer the conventional form, most readers and critics respond favorably to Neruda's innovative approach. Read the following excerpt of literary criticism and answer the questions that follow.

> "The 'Elemental Odes'. . . were like nothing else people had seen. With them, Neruda hoped to reach a wider audience than he already had, and his hope was realized. The 'Odes' gained immediate and universal praise. They are about the things of everyday life: a lemon, a dead carob tree, a boy with a hare, a stamp album. And they were read by people who had never before paid attention to poetry. Written in very short lines, some as short as a single word, the 'Odes' tumble effortlessly down the page in chainlike sentences. Everything is seen in its best light, everything has value, everything deserves to be the subject of a poem."
>
> —Mark Strand, the *New Yorker*

1. How do you think someone who prefers traditional odes, which have an elevated style, would respond to Strand's comments?

2. Which opinion do you agree with more: that Neruda created a valuable and accessible new kind of ode, or that his modifications degraded the form? Support your opinion.

The Magician, 1992. Maria Angelica Ruiz-Tagle. Oil on canvas, 130 x 97 cm.

Literary Element Free Verse

Free verse allows the poet to arrange lines and stanzas according to sound, importance of ideas, appearances, or any other criteria. The free verse Neruda uses in his odes has been praised for creating "a river of print flowing down the page."

1. Which lines in "Ode to My Socks" would you say are the most unconventional? Explain.
2. How do the varied line lengths affect the recitation of the poem?

Review: Structure

As you learned on page 376, **structure** is the distinct order or arrangement used to present a writer's ideas. Ideas may be presented in chronological order, according to relevancy, in order of importance, or in some other organized manner.

Group Activity With a group of two or three classmates, analyze the structure of "Ode to My Socks." Each student should evaluate one stanza. Once all have examined a stanza, record your group's findings in a chart like the one below. Use the left column to indicate the stanza number. Use the right column to describe the stanza's structure.

Stanza	Structure
Stanza 1	This stanza is ordered sequentially. The events in order are that first Maru Mori brings the socks, then the speaker puts them on.

Literature Online

Selection Resources For Selection Quizzes, eFlashcards, and Reading-Writing Connection activities, go to glencoe.com and enter QuickPass code GL59794u3.

Reading Strategy Monitor Comprehension

When you **monitor comprehension**, you gain a deeper understanding of the poem and its meaning, especially in an unconventional poem like this Neruda ode. Refer to the chart you made on page 497 as you answer the following questions.

1. Paraphrase "Ode to My Socks."
2. What, do you think, is the most important aspect of this poem?

Vocabulary Practice

Practice with Synonyms A synonym is a word that has the same or nearly the same meaning as another word. With a partner, match each boldfaced vocabulary word below with its synonym. Use a thesaurus or dictionary to check your answers.

1. **immense**
2. **decrepit**
3. **sacred**
4. **remorse**

a. dismayed
b. holy
c. regret
d. despair
e. dilapidated
f. vast

Academic Vocabulary

An everyday object like a sock is not **compatible** with some people's idea of beauty.

Compatible is an academic word. In more casual conversation, a person might say that a certain couple is **compatible**. To study this word further, fill out the graphic organizer below.

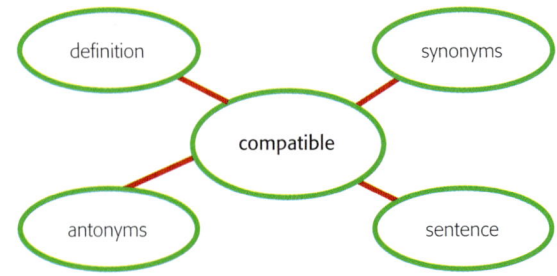

For more on academic vocabulary, see pages 52 and 53.

Respond Through Writing

Research Report

Investigate Poetry Poetry is a form of personal expression, but it can also express social, political, and cultural ideas. This type of commentary is achieved through the poem's content and its tone. Research how tone in poetry can express social, political, or cultural attitudes or dissent and present your findings in a research report of at least 1,500 words.

Understand the Task Tone is an author's attitude toward his or her subject. A tone might be sympathetic, serious, ironic, sad, or funny.

Prewrite Reread Neruda's biography on page 496. Consider what you learn about his political attitudes. Think about who and what is honored in "Ode to My Socks." Then find additional poems by Neruda and other poets whose tone expresses social, political, or cultural attitudes or dissent. Develop a thesis based on the tone you hear in Neruda's work as well as the work of two other poets. Plan paragraphs supporting your thesis.

Draft As you draft, include evidence from the poems to support your thesis. Explain how quotations from the poems express cultural, social, or political attitudes or dissent. One way to explain quoted material is by commenting on its relative value or significance. For example, does the quotation clearly state a political point, or does it make the point more subtly? Integrate and comment on literary criticism from other writers.

Revise Decide if your draft meets the criteria from the rubric below. Then revise to improve your essay.

Sources: Uses a variety of sources and uses only reliable sources	**Evidence:** Body paragraphs accurately convey and evaluate information from a variety of sources
Thesis/Controlling Idea: Thesis makes a clear, interesting, focused claim about tone in specified poems	**Audience:** Anticipates and addresses any potential misunderstandings; provides all necessary background

Revise for clarity by rewriting any potentially misleading information.

Edit and Proofread Proofread your paper, correcting any errors in spelling, grammar, and punctuation. Use the Grammar Tip in the side column to help you use ellipses correctly.

Learning Objectives

In this assignment, you will focus on the following objectives:

Writing: Investigating poetry.

Grammar: Understanding how to use ellipses.

Grammar Tip

Ellipses

Use an ellipsis (three periods) to show that you are omitting words from a quotation. When you are omitting the end of a line of poetry, use four ellipsis points if a complete grammatical sentence precedes what you leave out.

I stretched out / my feet / and pulled on / the magnificent / socks....

If you are omitting words that follow a comma, include the comma before the ellipsis points.

Violent socks,...

Before You Read

World Literature: Russia

A Storm in the Mountains

Meet Aleksandr Solzhenitsyn
(1918–2008)

In a life rendered chaotic—personally, professionally, and politically—Aleksandr Isayevich Solzhenitsyn created order through his writing.

Solzhenitsyn served in the Russian army during World War II. However, in 1945 he was arrested and charged with treason for writing a personal letter in which he criticized Soviet ruler Joseph Stalin. The government sentenced Solzhenitsyn, without a fair trial, to eight years in a camp for political prisoners.

> *"Own only what you can carry with you; know language, know countries, know people. Let your memory be your travel bag."*
>
> —Aleksandr Solzhenitsyn

During his imprisonment, Solzhenitsyn worked as a mathematician and physicist. He was later transferred to a forced-labor camp, where he was diagnosed with intestinal cancer. It was not treated until he was near death. Eventually, he was sent to Khazakhstan for treatment and survived. Finally, in 1956, he was freed from exile.

Memory as Inspiration Throughout his entire ordeal, Solzhenitsyn wrote in secret. The experiences of his forced imprisonment and illness served as the basis for his writing. Eventually, Solzhenitsyn decided to take his secret writing public. He published his first work, *One Day in the Life of Ivan Denisovich*, a widely read tale of an "everyman" dealing with the horrors of a single day in a forced labor camp. The book sparked political attention and activity in both the Soviet Union and abroad.

The Line That Shifts Awarded the Nobel Prize for Literature in 1970, Solzhenitsyn did not accept his prize in person, fearing that the Soviet government would not allow him to reenter the country.

The Gulag Archipelago (1973)—a catalogue of Soviet abuses detailing the harsh labor camps called the "Gulag"—established Solzhenitsyn as a chronicler of modern Russian history. The controversial publication, however, led to another exile in 1974. Solzhenitsyn lived and wrote in the United States until the *glasnost*—a political openness that allowed for criticism of the government—brought Russians a renewed interest in and wider accessibility to his writing, prompting a return to his homeland in 1994.

Author Search For more about Aleksandr Solzhenitsyn, go to glencoe.com and enter QuickPass code GL59794u3.

Literature and Reading Preview

Connect to the Poem
Recall a time when you witnessed severe weather. How did it make you feel? Describe the experience to a partner.

Build Background
The former Soviet Union, also known as the Union of Soviet Socialist Republics, or U.S.S.R., was vast in size, and its climate varied greatly. Extreme weather was common; only winter and summer existed as distinct seasons. The milder temperatures of spring and fall were typically short-lived points during periods of rapid weather change.

Set Purposes for Reading

Big Idea **The Energy of the Everyday**

As you read, ask yourself, What descriptive language does Solzhenitsyn use to describe an event as common as a storm?

Literary Element **Prose Poetry**

An alternative to verse form, **prose poetry** avoids line breaks and uses sentence and paragraph form instead. Even though prose poetry is printed as a short prose compostition, it uses elements of poetry, such as rhythm, internal rhyme, figures of speech, assonance and consonance, symbolism, and imagery. As you read, ask yourself, How does this prose poem use imagery to convey ideas and emotions?

Reading Strategy **Visualize**

When you **visualize,** you use words to create a mental picture. Authors often use imagery to help readers experience the environment or mood of a poem or story. Visualizing is not limited to visual images; it encompasses perceptions from all five senses. As you read the poem, ask yourself, How can I create a mental representation of the sensations described?

Tip: Create a List Use a chart like the one below to list words or phrases from the poem that appeal to your senses.

Words/Expressions	Sense
"Everything was black—no peaks, no valleys, no horizon to be seen."	Sight

---

Learning Objectives

For pages 504–508

In studying this text, you will focus on the following objectives:

Literary Study: Analyzing prose poetry.

Reading: Visualizing.

Vocabulary

searing (sēr′ing) *adj.* extremely hot or bright; p. 507 *The searing sunlight woke me up before my alarm clock went off.*

chaos (kā′os) *n.* a state of disorder and confusion; p. 507 *After the tornado hit, the town was filled with chaos.*

gorge (gôrj) *n.* the passageway between two higher land areas, such as a narrow valley; p. 507 *The Grand Canyon is one of the United States' most famous gorges.*

serpentine (sur′pən tēn′) *adj.* snake-like, twisting, winding; p. 507 *He had to pay attention as he drove on the serpentine mountain road.*

primal (prī′məl) *adj.* a basic, original state of being; p. 507 *One primal instinct is survival.*

Tip: Analogies Check your answer to an analogy by reading it backward: start with your answer, and find its relationship to the last term in the item. Then see whether that is the same relationship that the first two terms convey.

ALEKSANDR SOLZHENITSYN 505

Before the Separation, 1999. Brenda Chrystie.

A Storm in the Mountains

Aleksandr Isayevich Solzhenitsyn
Translated by Michael Glenny

It caught us one pitch-black night at the foot of the pass. We crawled out of our tents and ran for shelter as it came towards us over the ridge.

Everything was black—no peaks, no valleys, no horizon to be seen, only the **searing** flashes of lightning separating darkness from light, and the gigantic peaks of Belaya-Kaya and Djuguturlyuchat[1] looming up out of the night. The huge black pine trees around us seemed as high as the mountains themselves. For a split second we felt ourselves on terra firma;[2] then once more everything would be plunged into darkness and **chaos**.

The lightning moved on, brilliant light alternating with pitch blackness, flashing white, then pink, then violet, the mountains and pines always springing back in the same place, the hugeness filling us with awe;[3] yet when they disappeared, we could not believe that they had ever existed.

The voice of the thunder filled the **gorge**, drowning the ceaseless roar of the rivers. Like the arrows of Sabaoth,[4] the lightning flashes rained down on the peaks, then split up into **serpentine** streams as though bursting into spray against the rock face, or striking and then shattering like a living thing.

As for us, we forgot to be afraid of the lightning, the thunder, and the downpour, just as a droplet in the ocean has no fear of a hurricane. Insignificant yet grateful, we became part of this world—a **primal** world in creation before our eyes.

---

1. *Belaya-Kaya* and *Djuguturlyuchat* are mountains in the western Caucasus mountain range in Russia.
2. *Terra firma* means "solid ground."
3. *Awe* is a feeling of wonderment or amazement.
4. *Sabaoth*, a Biblical reference, means "armies."

Visualize How does Solzhenitsyn's imagery help you imagine the setting of the poem?

Vocabulary

searing (sēr´ing) *adj.* extremely hot or bright
chaos (kā´os) *n.* a state of disorder and confusion
gorge (gôrj) *n.* the passageway between two higher land areas, such as a narrow valley
serpentine (sur´pən tēn´) *adj.* snake-like, twisting, winding
primal (prī´məl) *adj.* a basic, original state of being

After You Read

Respond and Think Critically

Respond and Interpret

1. What example of imagery in the poem did you find most striking? Explain.

2. (a) How does the speaker describe the lightning in the fourth paragraph? (b) What does this comparison suggest about his view of nature?

3. (a) What does the speaker compare himself and his group to at the end of the poem? (b) What do the speaker's changing feelings about the storm indicate about people's place in nature?

Analyze and Evaluate

4. Why, in your opinion, does the speaker think he can report on others' feelings and thoughts?

5. How can the storm make the speaker feel that one moment he is firmly on the ground, yet the very next he is plunged into chaos? Explain.

Connect

6. **Big Idea** The Energy of the Everyday How would you explain the author's view of the relationship between people and nature?

7. **Connect to the Author** Solzhenitsyn suffered great injustice under the repressive dictatorship that controlled his native Russia, yet he always felt deeply connected to his country. How might this poem reflect Solzhenitsyn's conflicting feelings for his life in Russia?

Literary Element Prose Poetry

Unlike poetry that use verses and stanzas, **prose poetry** follows the narrative style with sentences and paragraphs but also maintains rhythm.

1. Read aloud the following phrase, "Everything was black—no peaks, no valleys, no horizon to be seen. . . ." Explain how this line blends poetic elements with prose format.

2. Where in the prose poem does the writing most resemble poetry? Explain.

Reading Strategy Visualize

Visualizing allows the reader to connect to the poem and understand its tone and meaning.

1. Which sensory details help you understand or connect to the poem? Explain.

2. Which sensory details do you think best communicate the tone and meaning of the poem?

LOG ON Literature Online

Selection Resources For Selection Quizzes, eFlashcards, and Reading-Writing Connection activities, go to glencoe.com and enter QuickPass code GL59794u3.

Vocabulary Practice

Practice with Analogies Choose the word that best completes each analogy.

1. searing : hot :: freezing :
   a. cold   b. temperature

2. chaotic : disorder :: boisterous :
   a. male   b. noise

3. gorge : land :: channel :
   a. television   b. sea

4. serpentine : twisting :: circuitous :
   a. circus-like   b. circular

5. primal : civilized :: puerile :
   a. infant   b. adult

Writing

Write a Prose Poem Think about encounters you have had with the natural world. Choose one and write a prose poem about it, using "A Storm in the Mountains" as a model. Be sure to include sensory details to convey the mood of the experience and help readers clearly visualize the images you create.

Grammar Workshop

Pronoun-Antecedent Agreement

Learning Objectives

In this workshop, you will focus on the following objectives:

Grammar: Understanding how to use correct pronoun-antecedent agreement.

Literature Connection In this line from "A Storm in the Mountains," Aleksandr Solzhenitsyn describes the speaker's experience in the first person plural.

> "We crawled out of our tents and ran for shelter as it came towards us over the ridge."
>
> —Aleksandr Solzhenitsyn, from "A Storm in the Mountains"

The quotation is an example of correct **pronoun reference** because the pronouns *our* and *us* are the same person (first, second, and third), number, and gender (masculine, feminine, neuter) as the subject of the sentence, *we*. Incorrect pronoun reference is the use of a pronoun that has an unclear antecedent or does not agree with its antecedent.

Examples

Problem A pronoun has an unclear antecedent in a sentence.

The prisoner gave his cellmate his book.
They sent Solzhenitsyn to a prison camp.

Solution Replace the pronoun with an appropriate noun.

The prisoner gave his cellmate the cellmate's book.
The government sent Solzhenitsyn to a prison camp.

Problem A pronoun does not agree with its antecedent.

A writer must choose what they include in their work.

Solution Replace the pronoun with one that agrees with its antecedent or reword the sentence.

A writer must choose what to include in his or her work.
Writers must choose what they include in their work.

Pronoun Reference

Correct **pronoun reference** is agreement of a pronoun with its antecedent in person, number, and gender.

Tip

To identify incorrect pronoun reference on a test, find the antecedent for each pronoun. If there is not one, replace the pronoun with an appropriate noun. If the antecedent differs in person, gender, and/or number from the pronoun, change the pronoun to agree with the antecedent.

Language Handbook

For more on pronoun reference, see the Language Handbook, pp. R49–R50.

Practice Rewrite the following sentences to correct any incorrect pronoun references.

1. Aleksandr Solzhenitsyn had to work as a mathematician because one had little money.
2. Solzhenitsyn was born in Russia during a time when you had to censor their ideas.
3. I think that they should be able to write about any topic.
4. When one reads Solzhenitsyn's poetry, you find striking imagery.

Grammer For more grammer practice, go to glencoe.com and enter QuickPass code GL59794u3.

Before You Read

The Print of the Paw, To An Aged Bear

Meet N. Scott Momaday
(born 1934)

Poet and novelist Navarre Scott Momaday absorbed the storytelling culture of American Indians throughout his youth. His father, a Kiowa, was a talented painter. His mother, of mixed English and Cherokee heritage, wrote children's books. Both of his parents taught literature and art on reservations throughout the southwestern United States.

A Teaching Heritage As they moved among the Apache, the Navajo, and the Pueblo, Momaday developed his creative writing skills. His parents encouraged his love of classic literature as much as they cultivated his love of traditional Native American storytelling. After earning a degree from the University of New Mexico, Momaday followed in his parents' footsteps by teaching on the Jicarilla Apache Reservation in New Mexico.

> *"If you are really compelled to write, that's where happiness is."*
> —N. Scott Momaday

Stanford University offered Momaday a poetry fellowship to its creative writing program. He spent the next five years studying under poet and critic Yvor Winters. In 1963 Momaday left Stanford with a Ph.D. in English literature.

Next, he moved to Santa Barbara to take a teaching position at the University of California. Over the next five years, he channeled his ideas of conflict between nature and the modern world into his first novel, *House Made of Dawn*.

Lifestyles in Conflict Still his best-known work, the book tells the story of a conflicted Army veteran, Abel, who returns to his Kiowa pueblo. Having seen the world and all of its technological wonders, Abel struggles with his people's traditions and lifestyle.

House Made of Dawn earned Momaday a Pulitzer Prize in Fiction in 1969. Few authors have earned this major recognition; fewer still have earned it for their debut work. The book revitalized interest in the plight and the heritage of American Indians. Soon after, Momaday moved to Berkeley, California. He used the prestige of his award to help launch a course in American Indian oral tradition.

Rekindling Tradition Momaday spent the next three decades of his career teaching that course at several prestigious universities. Meanwhile, he published books that showcase the American Indian style of storytelling.

Author Search For more about N. Scott Momaday, go to glencoe.com and enter QuickPass code GL59794u3.

Literature and Reading Preview

Connect to the Poems
How would you react if you came across the paw print of a bear? Freewrite for a few minutes about what you might think, feel, or do in this situation.

Build Background
Momaday challenges us to disconnect ourselves from the bustle of modern living. In these selections, Momaday reminds us that American Indians hold bears in high regard. His language evokes the strength, wisdom, and nobility of these creatures that American Indians have honored for centuries.

Set Purposes for Reading

Big Idea The Energy of the Everyday

As you read these poems, ask yourself, How does the poet link animals, humans, and the natural world?

Literary Element Speaker

The **speaker** is the person whose "voice" we "hear" in a poem, much like the narrator who tells the story in a work of prose. The speaker may be the poet or a character created to represent a specific point of view. As you read, ask yourself, Who is the speaker in each of the poems?

Reading Strategy Apply Background Knowledge

Applying background knowledge can help you recognize different perspectives. Sometimes a poet will deliberately have the speaker reflect an attitude different from that of the poet, to exaggerate an opposing view. As you read, ask yourself, What perspectives are represented in the selections?

Tip: Understand Perspective In a chart like the one below, list words that the author uses to describe the bear and briefly explain how the word helps to reveal the speaker's perspective.

Author's Description of Bear	How Word Reveals Perspective
mythic	Connects bear to concept of ancient legends

Learning Objectives

For pages 510–515

In studying this text, you will focus on the following objectives:

Literary Study: Analyzing speaker.

Reading: Applying background knowledge.

Vocabulary

meticulous (mi tik′ yə ləs) *adj.* precise; careful; worried about details; p. 512 *Sondra, meticulous about her stamp collection, kept it in cabinets.*

cipher (sī′ fər) *n.* a signifying figure; a number or symbol; p. 512 *A zero is a cipher representing a numberless quantity.*

glyph (glif) *n.* an engraved, symbolic figure; p. 512 *Scientists study ancient glyphs to learn secrets from, and clues about, the past.*

infirmity (in fur′ mə tē) *n.* weakness; frailty; failing; p. 513 *Mrs. Palltuck's infirmity prevented her from doing errands by herself.*

conflagration (kon′ flə grā′ shən) *n.* a huge fire; p. 513 *Even veteran firefighters rarely witnessed this kind of conflagration.*

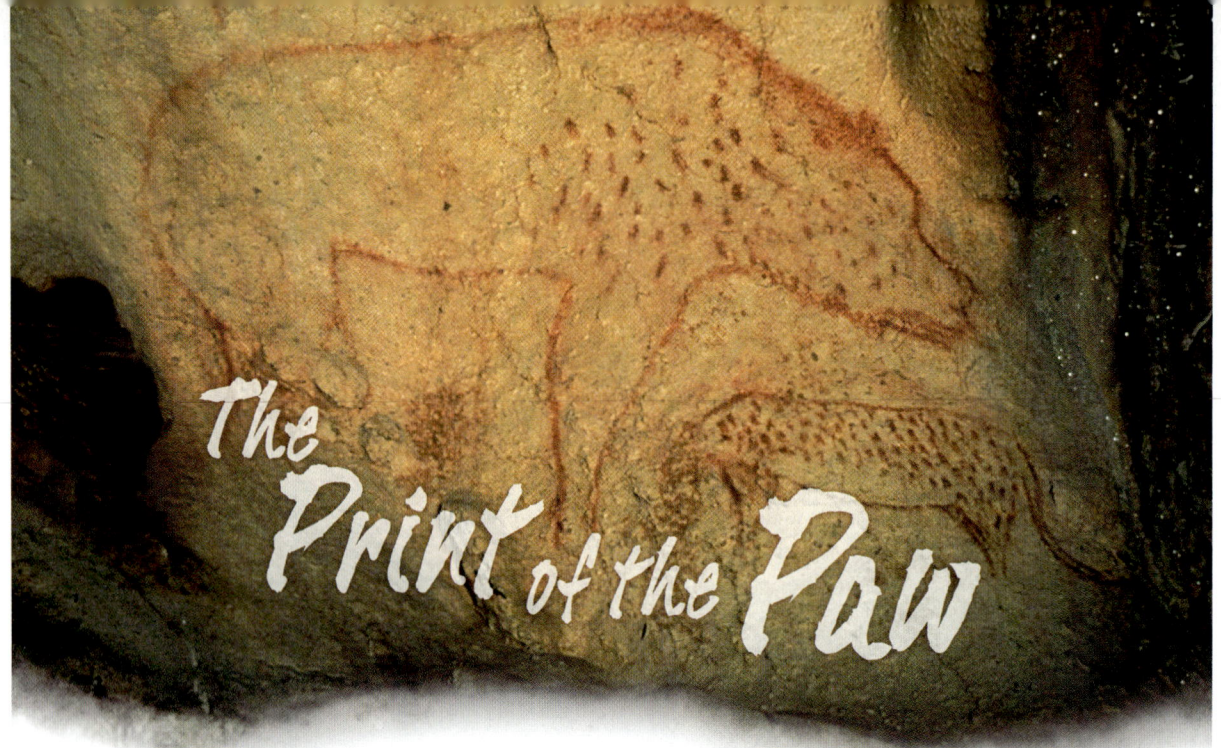

The Print of the Paw

N. Scott Momaday

It lies among leaves. Indeed, a leaf, fast and broken, is impressed in the heel's deep hollow. The leaf is yellow and brown, and brittle at the edges. The edges have been crushed; there is a fine dust of color, like pollen, in the mold. Deeper than the heel's hollow are the claw's piercings. They are precisely placed in the earth as if the great beast moved with **meticulous** grace. The toes turn inward, perhaps to describe like a keel[1] the center of gravity upon which a great weight is balanced. Were I to construct a model of this bear, based upon this single print, it would turn out to be a mythic and wondrous thing. It would be a **cipher**, a **glyph**, a huge shape emergent on the wall of a cave, a full figure in polychrome[2]—splotches of red and yellow in black outline. And I would be an artist of the first rank on this occasion, if on no other, for I should proceed directly, in the disinterested manner of a child, from this nearly perfect print of the paw. And all who should lay eyes upon my work would know, beyond any shadow of a doubt, how much I love the bear whose print this is.

Jemez Springs, 1997

---

1. A *keel* is the long piece of wood or steel along the bottom of a boat or ship that helps keep it stable.

2. *Polychrome* means "decorated in many colors."

The Energy of the Everyday What effect does the "nearly perfect" paw print have on the speaker?

Vocabulary

meticulous (mi tik′yə ləs) *adj.* precise; careful; worried about details

cipher (si′fər) *n.* a signifying figure; a number or symbol
glyph (glif) *n.* an engraved, symbolic figure

Weapons and Physiognomy of the Grizzly Bear, 1846. George Catlin. Oil on canvas. Smithsonian American Art Museum, Washington, DC.

To An Aged Bear

N. Scott Momaday

Hold hard this **infirmity**.
It defines you. You are old.

Now fix yourself in summer,
In thickets of ripe berries,

5   And venture toward the ridge
Where you were born. Await there

The setting sun. Be alive
To that old **conflagration**

One more time. Mortality
10 Is your shadow and your shade.

Translate yourself to spirit;
Be present on your journey.

Keep to the trees and waters.
Be the singing of the soil.

Santa Fe, 1995

Speaker *What are your impressions of this poem's speaker?*

Vocabulary

infirmity (in fur′mə tē) *n.* weakness; frailty; failing
conflagration (kon′flə grā′shən) *n.* a huge fire

After You Read

Respond and Think Critically

Respond and Interpret

1. Did these poems alter the way you feel or think about bears in the wild? If so, how?

2. (a)To what type of vessel does the speaker compare the bear's claws in "The Print of the Paw"? (b)What impression does this analogy evoke?

3. (a)In "To An Aged Bear," what does the speaker tell the bear to "await"? (b)In the context of the poem, to what else might this phrase refer?

4. (a)In "To An Aged Bear," what two words does the speaker use to describe mortality? (b)By using these words, what is the speaker saying about the bear's relationship to mortality?

Analyze and Evaluate

5. (a)How would you classify the tone of the first half of "The Print of the Paw"? (b)How is this tone an effective choice in relation to the rest of the poem? Explain.

6. (a)In "To An Aged Bear," what natural images are used? (b)Are these images effective in creating a setting for the poem? Why or why not?

Connect

7. **Big Idea** The Energy of the Everyday From the ideas expressed in these two poems, how does the energy of a creature like a bear resonate throughout our world? Explain.

8. **Connect to Today** What lessons can you take from these poems that apply to the way you live in the world today?

Literary Element Speaker

The **speaker** in each of Momaday's poems expresses poignant feelings for nature and for animals. Yet each speaker expresses his or her feelings and ideas in a different style and form. How did you respond to each speaker? Review these poems, paying careful attention to each speaker. Then answer the following questions:

1. What clues are given to help you identify each speaker?

2. Is it your impression that you are hearing from the same speaker in both poems? Support your answer with details from the texts.

Review: Prose Poetry

As you learned on page 505, **prose poetry** uses imagery, rhythm, and other poetic devices to express ideas and emotions. Instead of using line breaks, the author of a prose poem writes in sentences and paragraphs.

Partner Activity With a classmate, discuss the advantages and disadvantages of writing a prose poem, compared to writing a poem in a more traditional form. Working with your partner, create a two-column chart similar to the one below. Fill in the left-hand column with advantages of prose poems and the right-hand column with disadvantages.

Pro	Con
Uses imagery and sensory details to create vivid descriptions	Often, there is not a rhyme scheme or regular meter

Literature Online

Selection Resources For Selection Quizzes, eFlashcards, and Reading-Writing Connection activities, go to glencoe.com and enter QuickPass code GL59794u3.

Reading Strategy **Apply Background Knowledge**

You read about Momaday's American Indian heritage on page 510. When you **apply background knowledge** to your reading of the poems, you can better understand their context.

1. Do you think that the speaker in each poem represents Momaday's own point of view? Explain.

2. How does knowing about the author's American Indian heritage help you understand the poems?

Vocabulary Practice

Practice with Word Origins Studying the etymology, or origin and history, of a word can help you understand its meaning. Create a word map, like the one below, for each of these vocabulary words from the poems.

meticulous   cipher   glyph
   infirmity   conflagration

EXAMPLE:

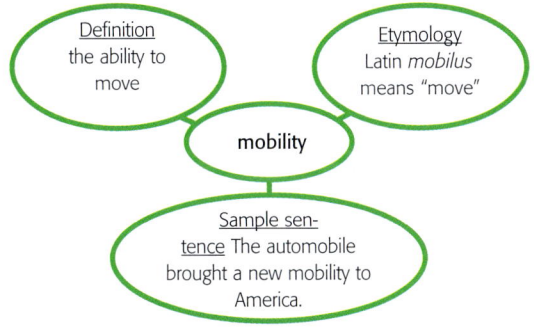

Academic Vocabulary

*The speaker **inspects** a leaf that the bear crushed underfoot.*

Inspect is an academic word. A detective might **inspect** a crime scene for clues. A mechanic might **inspect** a car to be sure it is in safe working order. What object or place might you inspect? Why?

For more on academic vocabulary, see pages 52 and 53.

Speaking and Listening

 Oral Interpretation

Assignment Recite and present oral interpretations of "The Print of the Paw" and "To an Aged Bear" to your class.

Prepare Decide whether and how well the prose poetry format of "The Print of the Paw" and the traditional poetic form of "To an Aged Bear" influence and fit each poem's meaning. As you rehearse your recital of each poem—first by yourself, and then for a partner—choose and practice recitation techniques that you think are right for both your audience and these poems.

Perform Make notes in a chart like this one to show how you will demonstrate understanding of the poems and engage your audience:

	Verbal Techniques	Nonverbal Techniques
"Print of the Paw"	Pace—faster than "Aged Bear," like reading a paragraph Tone—admiration, wonder	Body language—relaxed stance Gestures—mime picking up and examining a leaf
"To an Aged Bear"	Pace—[ ] Tone—[ ]	Body language—[ ] Gestures [ ]

As you recite each poem, use techniques that suit your audience and the poem. Make choices about tone of voice, appropriate body language and gestures, and the best times for direct eye contact.

Evaluate Decide how clearly and effectively you recited the poems. Then write a paragraph rating the delivery and content of your recitations and interpretations. Use the Techniques and presentation tips on page 1127 to help.

Before You Read

World Literature
Japan

Three Haiku

Meet **Matsuo Bashō**
(1644–1694)

Japanese poet Matsuo Bashō devoted his life to perfecting the haiku. The shortest poetic form in the world, the haiku contains just seventeen syllables, in three lines of five, seven, and five syllables. Inspired by the teachings of Zen Buddhism, which emphasized surpassing logical, everyday thought, seventeenth-century Japanese poets turned their attention to capturing the small details of life, especially focusing on nature.

Rarely did Bashō and his contemporaries think of themselves as poets, but rather as guides. The early writers of haiku strove to place the reader within an experience in nature—such as observing a misty rain or listening closely to a bird's call. Writing as specifically and simply as they could about the details of such an experience, they hoped the poem might lead their reader to enlightenment. "What is important," Bashō wrote, "is . . . returning to daily experience, seek therein the true and the beautiful."

> "Every day is a journey, and the journey itself is home."
> —Matsuo Bashō

From Samurai Son to Master Poet Born in 1644 to a family of samurai warriors in the province of Iga, Bashō spent most of his youth in service to a feudal lord. During the first half of his life, a new era of Japanese culture unfolded, when a drastic policy caused the country to close itself to foreigners. This resulted in a new interest in Japanese art, ethics, history, and poetry. Bashō and the young lord he served, Todo Yoshitada, became close companions, sharing a passion for poetry. When Yoshitada died in his early twenties, it is believed Bashō's grief inspired him to leave Iga and set out for a life committed to poetry, traveling, and following a Zen ideology.

Travel The details of Bashō's life after his departure from Iga are obscure, though it is certain that he became a master of haiku by his early thirties and gained many disciples. One such disciple built him a cottage near Edo (now Tokyo), where another student planted him a banana plant.

During the remainder of his life, Bashō continued to produce elegant haiku that explored themes of beauty, loneliness, and suffering. He eventually became a Zen priest, giving up all possessions and wandering on pilgrimages with fellow priests and poets. He spent the last ten years of his life traveling through Japan; one such journey to the northern interior of Japan is captured in his most famous work, *Narrow Road to the Deep North*, a kind of travel diary in *haiban* form, or prose alternating with haiku.

Author Search For more about Matsuo Bashō, go to glencoe.com and enter QuickPass code GL59794u3.

Literature and Reading Preview

Connect to the Haiku
Can you identify any images related to rebirth? Freewrite for a few minutes about beautiful images related to rebirth.

Build Background
Matsuo Bashō's sentiments—"Don't follow in the footsteps of the old poets, seek what they sought"—urge poets to honor writers who came before them and to learn from them.

Set Purposes for Reading

Big Idea **The Energy of the Everyday**

As you read the three haiku, ask yourself, How is Bashō attentive to the intricate details of a changing season?

Literary Element **Haiku**

Haiku is an unrhymed Japanese verse form consisting of seventeen syllables that are arranged in three lines. The first and third lines have five syllables each; the second line has seven syllables. While some translations of haiku lose the poet's original syllable count when translated into English, the traditional goal of haiku—to suggest large ideas using simple, few words—remains. As you read, ask yourself, How closely do these translations conform to haiku line and stanza requirements?

Reading Strategy **Interpret Imagery**

Imagery refers to descriptions and sensory details that evoke emotional responses in the reader. When you **interpret imagery,** you use your own knowledge of the world and your understanding of the text to create meaning from the images. As you read, ask yourself, What do the images signify?

Tip: Visualize A reader can understand imagery by picturing what the writer describes. As you read, picture the author's accounts of nature. Record your imagined pictures in a graphic organizer. Expand your recordings to describe a full scene.

Line	Visualization	Expansion
It would melt in my hand.	A hand cupped and holding a lump of frost.	A man, warmly dressed, leans down to gather a chunk of frost between his fingers.

Learning Objectives

For pages 516–520

In studying this text, you will focus on the following objectives:

Literary Study: Analyzing haiku.

Reading: Interpreting imagery.

Pine and Bamboo and Cranes, 17th century. Japanese school. Watercolour on panel. American Museum of Natural History, NY.

Autumn Tree. Japanese School 17th century. Silk painting. Private collection.

Three Haiku

Matsuo Bashō
Translated by Robert Hass

It would melt
in my hand—
the autumn frost.

First day of spring—
I keep thinking about
the end of autumn.

Spring!
a nameless hill
in the haze.

Haiku How does the number of syllables in each line of this stanza differ from the number of syllables in a traditional Japanese haiku?

After You Read

Respond and Think Critically

Respond and Interpret

1. Are the images in the three haiku familiar to you? Describe your feelings about the changing seasons.

2. (a) What substance melts in the speaker's hand? (b) Why might the author have chosen to include this kind of sensory detail here?

3. (a) What is the speaker reminded of on spring's first day? (b) Draw inferences about the speaker's life from his feelings about the end of autumn.

4. (a) How does the speaker describe spring in the third haiku? (b) Analyze the author's decision to identify spring using this image.

Analyze and Evaluate

5. How does the author appeal to the reader's senses? Cite specific examples from the text.

6. How well has Bashō disclosed the wonder of changing seasons in these short poems? Could he have done a better job with longer poems?

Connect

7. **Big Idea** The Energy of the Everyday Nature is often described as both a powerful and gentle force. What powerful elements do you see in the three haiku? What gentle elements do you see?

8. **Connect to Today** Through his writing, Bashō sought to connect readers to the truth and beauty of everyday life. What elements of truth and beauty can you identify in *your* everyday life?

Literary Element   Haiku

Haiku generally address some subject in nature and simultaneously deal with grand ideas in a very limited amount of space. The strict format makes haiku a challenge to create, but Bashō's work is a demonstration of how beauty can be both encompassing and concise.

1. (a) What conflicting elements are present in the haiku? (b) How do these elements help the author communicate the haiku's message in only three lines?

2. What striking idea about the relationship between birth and death in nature is addressed by the author?

prose. The lines in haiku consist of only one word or very few words because the goal of the haiku poet is to convey an idea or impression within a strict poetic form using as few words as possible. The one-stanza, seventeen-syllable form demands that the poet express his or her ideas concisely, without unnecessary elaboration.

Partner Activity With a partner, discuss the following questions.

1. Could any words be deleted from these three haiku without detracting from their meaning? Explain.

2. How does the brevity of these three haiku make a strong impression on the reader?

Review: Line and Stanza

As you learned on page 477, a **line** in a poem usually consists of a single word or a row of words. A **stanza** is a group of lines forming a unit in a poem or song, similar to the paragraph in

Reading Strategy: Interpret Imagery

ACT Practice

1. The first haiku includes

    A. a visual image of autumn's beauty
    B. no specific appeal to the senses
    C. an olefactory image conjuring up the musty odors of autumn
    D. a tactile detail suggesting the chill delicacy of autumn

Academic Vocabulary

*Haiku, which relies on a **minimal** number of words, can express volumes of meaning and sentiment.*

Minimal is an academic word. In more casual conversation, a person might refer to the **minimal** effort someone made to be helpful or friendly. To study this word further, fill out the graphic organizer below.

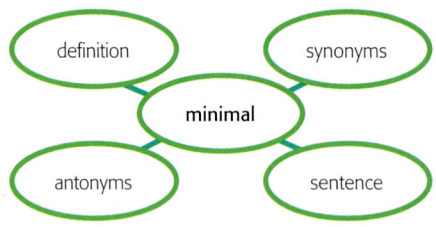

For more on academic vocabulary, see pages 52 and 53.

Write with Style

 Apply Imagery

Assignment Choose one image from Bashō's haiku. Describe a scene based on that image.

Get Ideas Look at the chart you made on page 517 to help you visualize and interpret imagery. Choose one expanded image. Create a cluster diagram around the image to generate more details that appeal to the senses.

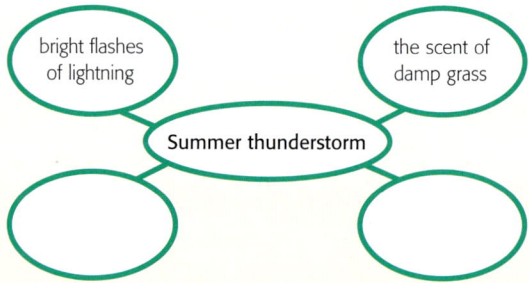

Give It Structure Use spatial order to structure your writing. For example, you may begin with observations from afar and then zoom in; describe from top to bottom or left to right; or start in the center and move toward the perimeter. Unify your writing by creating a controlling impression and editing out any details that do not support that impression.

Look at Language All the details you select will come together to create a mood, such as loss, peacefulness, or mystery. Carefully choose words to best evoke that mood.

Selection Resources For Selection Quizzes, eFlashcards, and Reading-Writing Connection activities, go to glencoe.com and enter QuickPass code GL59794u3.

Before You Read

Two Tanka

World Literature
Japan

Meet Lady Ise
(c. 875–c. 938)

Considered one of the Thirty-six Poetic Geniuses of Japan, Lady Ise enjoyed the celebrity status and fame that accompanied literary accomplishment in ancient Japan. Her achievement is especially impressive considering that official poetry during that era was written primarily by men.

A Woman of the Court Lady Ise served in Emperor Uda's Kyoto court and was known there for her literary works. Ise was part of a court "salon," a place where women developed and enjoyed their own culture. In addition to her writing, Ise was also a talented musician.

Murasaki Shikibu, c. 978–1014. Japanese court lady and author, who wrote *Genji Monogatari* (Tale of the *Genji*).

"... Why then do rumors /
Like swirling pillars of dust /
Rise as high as the heavens?"
—Lady Ise

Ise's poetry is formal in style, the rigidity of its structure reflecting the formality of the court. It subtly critiques the political scene and the role of women, allowing her an opportunity for political and social maneuvering. Much of her work is found in a collection of Japanese poetry known as the *Kokin Wakashū*, or *Kokinshū*, published around the year 905. The first in a series of imperially commissioned collections of Japanese poetry, the *Kokinshū* is also the first major work in *kana*, a Japanese writing system using syllable-based characters. In addition, Ise assembled the *Ise Shū*, a separate collection of her own work. The first thirty-two or thirty-three poems of this collection, usually referred to as her "diary," and their prose introductions are assumed to be autobiographical, but scholars question how much fiction they contain.

Ise was well represented in official Japanese collections. She also participated in poetry contests, in which she often triumphed over leading male poets.

Lady Ise's Life Many of the facts of Lady Ise's life are uncertain. Scholars believe that she was the daughter of Fujiwara no Tsugukage, a provincial governor of Ise. Ise entered the service of the consort of Emperor Uda at about the age of fifteen. After the emperor's death, Ise continued in service to the household until her death. Evidence suggests that her two children were of royal heritage. Her son died in infancy; however, her daughter, Nakatsukasa, lived to become an accomplished poet.

Author Search For more about Lady Ise, go to glencoe.com and enter QuickPass code GL59794u3.

LADY ISE **521**

Literature and Reading Preview

Connect to the Tanka
What types of moments are worth capturing? List several of these moments and explain why they should be remembered.

Build Background
Rhyme is typically not a feature of Japanese poetry because all Japanese words end in one of five vowels. Japanese words do not have stressed syllables, so rhythm is not a device used in Japanese poetry. Japanese poetry can be distinguished from Japanese prose by its traditional syllabic pattern.

Set Purposes for Reading

Big Idea The Energy of the Everyday

As you read, ask yourself, How does Ise paint a picture of the everyday using words that capture the reader's emotion?

Literary Element Tanka

Tanka is an unrhymed Japanese verse form. Most tanka focus on a single thought or idea related to love or to an appreciation of nature, common themes in Japanese poetry. Tanka adhere to a strict form that consists of five lines. The first and third lines have five syllables each; the other lines have seven syllables each. Keep in mind that the two tanka presented here are translated from Japanese to English. Therefore, the syllables per line may not always fit the prescribed structure. As you read, ask yourself, How does the tanka form contribute to the meaning of the poems?

Reading Strategy Compare and Contrast Imagery

When reading poetry, it helps to **compare and contrast images** created by different poems. As you read, ask yourself, How does the speaker portray images from nature?

....

Tip: Visualize the Images Use a Venn diagram like the one below to record similarities and differences between the images in the two tanka.

Learning Objectives

For pages 521–524

In studying this text, you will focus on the following objectives:

Literary Study: Analyzing tanka.

Reading: Comparing and contrasting imagery.

Deer Under a Maple Tree. Mori Sushin Tessan. Hand painted, ink and colour on paper. British Library, London.

First Tanka — There are bright shiny droplets of water.

Second Tanka — The geese spread wings as they prepare to take flight.

(Overlap) These images suggest spring.

Two Tanka

Lady Ise

Print of a River Under Cherry Blossoms, 1833–1834.
Ando Hiroshige.

Translated by Willis Barnstone

Hanging from the branches of a green
willow tree,
the spring rain
is a
thread of pearls.

Translated by Etsuko Terasaki
with Irma Brandeis

Lightly forsaking[1]
the Spring mist as it rises,
the wild geese are setting off.
Have they learned to live
in a flowerless country?

---

1 *Forsaking* means "turning away from" or "abandoning."

The Energy of the Everyday How does this line evoke the energy of the everyday?

After You Read

Respond and Think Critically

Respond and Interpret

1. (a) What about these images seems familiar to you? (b) Describe the images in your own words.
2. (a) What two things are compared in the first tanka? (b) What insights about these things does the comparison bring to mind?
3. (a) What question does the speaker ask in the second tanka? (b) What might be its meaning?

Analyze and Evaluate

4. How do the images of spring in the two tanka reflect your own observations of spring? Explain.
5. In your opinion, which tanka offers more for you to think about? Why?

Connect

6. **Big Idea** **The Energy of the Everyday** Do you agree or disagree that the language and imagery used in these two poems captures the reader's emotion rather than intellect? Support your answer with evidence from the poems.
7. **Connect to the Author** What aspects of living a privileged life might have contributed to the author's outlook?

Literary Element Tanka

Because **tanka** are so short and simple, the tanka writer, like the haiku poet, must rely on precise, direct language to suggest ideas.

1. How does the length of the poem affect the impression it leaves upon the reader? Explain.
2. Rewrite one of the tanka in your own words.

Reading Strategy Compare and Contrast Imagery

Comparing and contrasting imagery in poems helps readers draw conclusions about themes.

1. Compare and contrast the images in the two tanka and determine the themes of each.
2. In support of your opinion, list details from each of the poems.

> **LOG ON** **Literature** Online
> **Selection Resources** For Selection Quizzes, eFlashcards, and Reading-Writing Connection activities, go to glencoe.com and enter QuickPass code GL59794u3.

Academic Vocabulary

At the **core** *of both tanka is a theme of how precious and fleeting beauty is.*

Core can have different meanings in different subject areas. Using context clues, try to figure out the meaning of *core* in each sentence and explain the difference between the two meanings.

1. Earth's inner **core** is solid iron.
2. Those courses are part of the required **core**.

For more on academic vocabulary, see pages 52 and 53.

Writing

Write a Poem Write a tanka of your own, using the traditional form of five lines containing five, seven, five, seven, and seven syllables. Remember, a tanka should focus on a single thought or idea and is usually but not necessarily related to love or the appreciation of nature.

Before You Read

Woman with Kite

World Literature
India

Meet **Chitra Banerjee Divakaruni** (born 1956)

When Chitra Divakaruni arrived in the United States from India in 1976, the nineteen-year-old from Calcutta received a shock. As she walked with her family in Chicago, she was taunted by white teens who shouted racial slurs. At first, she kept quiet about the episode. Later she wrote, "I never talked to anyone about it; I felt ashamed. Writing was a way to go beyond the silence." When Divakaruni found her voice, she used it to speak for the marginalized and the silenced, namely women and immigrants.

> "Women in particular respond to my work because I'm writing about them, women in love, in difficulties, women in relationships."
> —Chitra Banerjee Divakaruni

A New Awareness In the United States, Divakaruni found many new opportunities. She earned a Ph.D. from the University of California at Berkeley. She also began to reevaluate the circumstances of women in India. She saw how women's options were limited by lack of education and oppressive marriages and that these experiences continued even after they came to the United States. "At Berkeley, I volunteered at the women's center," she says. "As I got more involved, I became interested in helping battered women." In 1991 she and her friends created Maitri, an organization that provides services to Indian American women. Her experiences working for Maitri deepened her understanding of the plight of immigrant women. "I saw that a lot of problems stemmed from issues of domestic violence," Divakaruni said.

Speaking for Women Divakaruni says that the women at Maitri "made me think a lot more about the issues I was seeing and how it related to the lives of immigrants, and I wanted to write about it." She began to write poems about immigrant women forging a new identity while retaining ties to tradition. She also wrote short stories about these women, which she collected in *Arranged Marriages*. Divakaruni has won awards for her poetry, short stories, and novels.

Divakaruni still pursues her goal of speaking for women. In addition to teaching at the University of Houston, she serves on the board of Maitri and the advisory board of Houston-based Asians Against Domestic Abuse.

Author Search For more about Chitra Banerjee Divakaruni, go to glencoe.com and enter QuickPass code GL59794u3.

Literature and Reading Preview

Connect to the Poem
Do you ever set aside your inhibitions and act on impulse regardless of the opinions of others? Write a journal entry about a time when you acted on impulse or wished that you would have.

Build Background
Many contemporary authors of Indian descent write about the conflict of their social traditions with those of Western society. Immigrants face broad challenges involving not only language barriers, but also religious concerns and marked differences in the roles that women play in society.

Set Purposes for Reading

Big Idea **The Energy of the Everyday**

As you read this poem, ask yourself, How does the poet infuse everyday objects and experiences with passion and energy?

Literary Element **Verse Paragraph**

A **verse paragraph** is a group of lines that forms a unit. Unlike a stanza, a verse paragraph does not have a fixed number of lines. As you read, ask yourself, How does Divakaruni use verse paragraphs to emphasize key thoughts in the poem?

Reading Strategy **Make Inferences About the Speaker**

Some poems feature speakers who are presenting a particular point or perspective. So readers must **make inferences about the speaker.** By being aware of the language and images a speaker uses, readers can make inferences about the speaker and the speaker's message. As you read, ask yourself, What can I infer about the speaker's personality and purpose?

Tip: Look for Word Clues When reading poetry, watch for clues about the speaker's opinion or perspective. List the most powerful words, noting the speaker's feelings toward the subject.

Words	Opinions
sure-footed (line 16)	shows her strength and confidence

Learning Objectives

For pages 525–530

In studying this text, you will focus on the following objectives:

Literary Study: Analyzing verse paragraph.

Reading: Making inferences about the speaker.

Vocabulary

querulous (kwer′ə ləs) *adj.* argumentative; uncooperative; p. 527 *Because of the actor's querulous nature, he is very difficult to work with.*

disgruntled (dis grun′tld) *adj.* in a state of sulky dissatisfaction; p. 527 *The disgruntled children spent the rainy day complaining about being stuck in the house.*

translucent (trans lōō′sənt) *adj.* allowing light to pass through; almost clear, see-through; p. 528 *She could make out the shapes of the performers through the translucent curtain.*

fleck (flek′) *v.* to leave spots or streaks; p. 528 *Mud from the road flecked the windshield, making it difficult for the driver to see.*

Tip: Word Parts Some suffixes tell you a word's part of speech. For example, *-ous* and *-ent/-ant* are suffixes that indicate adjectives.

Woman Flying a Kite, 1750. Indian. Book illumination painting, miniature painting. Sangaram Singh.

Woman with Kite

Chitra Banerjee Divakaruni

Meadow of crabgrass, faded dandelions,
querulous child-voices. She takes
from her son's **disgruntled** hands the spool
of a kite that will not fly.

> **Vocabulary**
>
> **querulous** (kwer´ə ləs) *adj.* argumentative; uncooperative
> **disgruntled** (dis grun´tld) *adj.* in a state of sulky dissatisfaction

5 Pulls on the heavy string, ground-glass rough
   between her thumb and finger. Feels the kite,
   translucent purple square, rise in a resistant arc,
   flapping against the wind. Kicks off her *chappals*,[1]
   tucks up her *kurta*[2] so she can run with it,
10 light **flecking** off her hair as when she was
   sexless-young. Up, up

   past the puff-cheeked clouds, she
   follows it, her eyes slit-smiling at the sun.
   She has forgotten her tugging children, their
15 *give me, give me* wails. She sprints
   backwards, sure-footed, she cannot
   fall, connected to the air, she
   is flying, the wind blows through her, takes
   her red *dupatta*,[3] mark of marriage.
20 And she laughs like a woman should never laugh

   so the two widows on the park bench
   stare and huddle their white-veiled heads
   to gossip-whisper. The children have fallen,
   breathless, in the grass behind.
25 She laughs like wild water, shaking
   her braids loose, she laughs
   like a fire, the spool a blur
   between her hands,
   the string unraveling all the way
30 to release it into space, her life,
   into its bright, weightless orbit.

1. *Chappals* are traditional Indian sandals, resembling flip-flops.
2. A *kurta* is a loose shirt, often worn by both men and women in India and Pakistan.
3. A *dupatta* is a long scarf traditionally worn by Indian women across both shoulders and sometimes used to cover the head. A *dupatta* has long been regarded as a symbol of modesty.

Verse Paragraph *What effect does the poet create by breaking after these words?*

The Energy of the Everyday *What do the similes, or comparisons, in lines 25–27 tell you about the woman?*

Vocabulary

translucent (trans lōō′sənt) *adj.* allowing light to pass through; almost clear, see-through

fleck (flek′) *v.* to leave spots or streaks

After You Read

Respond and Think Critically

Respond and Interpret

1. What is your opinion of the woman's behavior? Explain.

2. (a) What three items of traditional Indian clothing does the poet mention? (b) Why does Divakaruni mention these items in the poem?

3. (a) What garment does the wind blow off the woman? (b) What significance does this incident have for her?

4. (a) What happens to the kite? (b) What conclusion about the character's future can you make from the poet's description?

Analyze and Evaluate

5. (a) What do "crabgrass" and "dandelions" contribute to the setting of "Woman with Kite"? (b) Explain how the poet uses them as metaphors for the main character's life.

6. (a) In line 12, how does Divakaruni personify nature? (b) What effect does this personification have on the character?

7. (a) Explain one of the similes the poet uses in the final verse paragraph to describe the main character. (b) What is the significance of these similes?

Connect

8. **Big Idea** The Energy of the Everyday
Describe how Divakaruni uses images of everyday elements and combines them to transform the main character.

9. **Connect to the Author** Divakaruni created an organization that provides services to Indian American women. Where in the poem does her sensitivity toward women's issues shine through?

Literary Element Verse Paragraph

Contemporary poets often use **verse paragraphs** to organize their ideas. Divakaruni uses three verse paragraphs in "Woman with Kite" to raise dramatic tension and to highlight conflict.

1. Explain how the author uses a transition between the first and second verse paragraphs to underscore a change in her character's attitude.

2. How does the transition between the second and third paragraphs mimic the first transition?

Review: Enjambment

As you learned on page 482, **enjambment**, also known as a run-on line, is the continuation of the sense of a sentence or phrase from one line of a poem to the next without a pause between the lines. Enjambment offers poets the opportunity to underscore the dramatic elements of their work.

Partner Activity With a classmate, look for six examples of enjambment in "Woman with Kite." Working with your partner, create a two-column chart similar to the one below. Fill in the left column with examples of enjambment. In the right column, describe how this device gives the words at the beginning or at the end of the line a deeper meaning or more dramatic effect.

Key words	Deeper meaning
"Kicks off her chappals, / tucks up her kurta"	Emphasizes abandoning traditional behavior

CHITRA BANERJEE DIVAKARUNI 529

Reading Strategy **Make Inferences About the Speaker**

Many contemporary poets, like Divakaruni, use their work to comment on events or situations in society. You can **make inferences about the speaker** to help reveal the poet's agenda.

1. What does the speaker think of the woman's actions?
2. List three details from the poem that support your opinion.

Vocabulary Practice

Practice with Word Parts For each boldfaced vocabulary word, find the meaning of the word's root and the meanings of any prefixes or suffixes in the word. Use a printed or online dictionary to help you. List the meanings in a diagram like the one shown. Then find three words that contain the same prefix, suffix, or root as the vocabulary word. Circle the word part that could help a person guess each word's meaning.

querulous   disgruntled   translucent   fleck

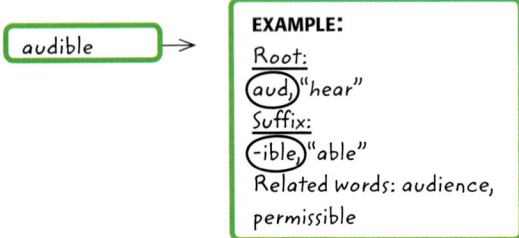

Academic Vocabulary

The woman breaks cultural stereotypes about how a **mature** woman should act.

Mature is an academic word. A parent might suggest that a child will have certain privileges when he or she is more **mature**. Use context clues to figure out the meaning of **mature** in the sentence above.

For more on academic vocabulary, see pages 52 and 53.

Connect to Social Studies

Research a Hobby or Sport

Assignment Research a popular hobby, sport, or game in India. Create a report with a bibliography, and present your report orally to your classmates.

Investigate Follow these steps:

- ☑ Ask research questions.
- ☑ Locate multiple primary and secondary sources.
- ☑ Assess sources, ruling out those whose authorship or authority is unknown or questionable.
- ☑ Focus your topic; avoid topics that are too broad or too narrow.
- ☑ Use notecards, a table, or e-files to take and organize notes on your specific focus.
- ☑ As you take notes, look up and define unfamiliar terms.
- ☑ Note discrepancies and different perspectives among sources.
- ☑ Paraphrase or summarize most information, but quote when the words are just right and will create interest in your oral report.

Create Draft your report, making sure it has an introduction, a body, and a conclusion. Follow the guidelines on pages R31–R32 to create your bibliography, entitled "Works Cited," on a separate page.

Report Be sure your report correctly integrates and cites information from your sources. Refer to information about parenthetical documentation on page R34. Maintain the flow of ideas by introducing your sources and linking them with transitional words and phrases that help to show where sources agree, disagree, or leave questions unanswered. Share your oral presentation with your classmates.

LOG ON **Literature** Online

Selection Resources For Selection Quizzes, eFlashcards, and Reading-Writing Connection activities, go to glencoe.com and enter QuickPass code GL59794u3.

PART 2
Loves and Losses

River Diego, 1996, Daniel Nevins, Oil, acrylic, and collage on wood. Private collection.

View the Art Nevins is known for his narrative paintings. How might this painting tell a narrative about Loves and Losses?

BIG IDEA

The poems in Part 2 express the joys and insights love can bring as well as the emptiness and ache of its loss. As you read the following poems, ask yourself, What elements of poetry work to express love and loss? What is the author's purpose in using these elements?

Learning Objectives

For pages 532–533

In studying this text, you will focus on the following objective:

Literary Study: Analyzing language.

LITERARY FOCUS

The Language of Poetry

How does poetry appeal to the senses?

In his autobiography, William Carlos Williams described writing "The Great Figure": "I heard a great clatter of bells and the roar of a fire engine passing the end of the street down Ninth Avenue. I turned just in time to see the golden figure 5 on a red background flash by. The impression was so sudden and forceful that I took a piece of paper out of my pocket and wrote a short poem." That poem inspired Williams's friend Charles Demuth to paint *The Figure 5 in Gold*. The artist used colors to create visual images; the poet used words to create images that appeal to a variety of senses.

Among the rain
and lights
I saw the figure 5
in gold
on a red
fire truck
moving
tense
unheeded
to gong clangs
siren howls
and wheels rumbling
through the dark city

—William Carlos Williams, *"The Great Figure"*

The Figure 5 in Gold, 1928. Charles Demuth. Oil on composition board, 91.4 x 75.6 cm. Metropolitan Museum of Art, New York.

Imagery

Imagery refers to the "word pictures" that writers create to represent a feeling, trigger a memory or an idea, or evoke a sensory experience. To create effective images, writers use sensory details. Consider some of the images in "The Great Figure":

Images	Sensory Appeal
"Among the rain"	sight and touch
"the figure 5 / in gold"	sight
"gong clangs"	hearing

> No one lived there
> but silence, a pale china gleam
>
> —Rita Dove, *from* "Parlor"

In this metaphor, the speaker is comparing silence to a soft glimmer of light.

Personification This figure of speech gives human qualities to nonhuman things. William Shakespeare **personifies** death in this line from "Shall I Compare Thee to a Summer's Day?":

> Nor shall Death brag thou wand'rest in his shade

Shakespeare compares death to a human who boasts that he has won a sought-after prize.

Hyperbole This figure of speech uses an obvious overstatement or exaggeration for either serious or comic effect. For example, when the speaker in "He Wishes for the Cloths of Heaven" says, "I have spread my dreams under your feet," the exaggeration conveys the passion and desire with which he loves.

Figurative Language

Figurative language conveys meaning beyond the literal meaning of the words. Poets often make use of figurative language to convey fresh and original comparisons. Figures of speech are types of figurative language. Among the most common are simile, metaphor, personification, and hyperbole.

Simile Poets often make imaginative comparisons to convey ideas, feelings, and insights. One kind of comparison is called a **simile**. In this figure of speech, the writer uses words such as *like* or *as* or the phrase "as if" to make the comparison. For example, in the line "her eyes sparkled like diamonds," the comparison suggests the subject's eyes are radiant and luminous.

Metaphor In contrast to a simile, a **metaphor** implies a comparison instead of stating it directly. Metaphors do not use *like* or *as*. An **extended metaphor** continues the comparison throughout a paragraph, a stanza, or an entire work.

Quickwrite

Analyze Imagery Find three or four more examples of imagery in William Carlos Williams's poem. Then write a paragraph in which you explain the appeal of each as a literary device.

 **Literature** Online

Literature and Reading For more about literary elements, go to glencoe.com and enter QuickPass code GL59794u3.

LITERARY FOCUS **533**

Before You Read

After Great Pain, A Formal Feeling Comes and Heart! We Will Forget Him!

Meet Emily Dickinson
(1830–1886)

Now considered one of the most important poets in American literature, Emily Dickinson saw her name in print only once: as second-place finisher for her entry in a bread contest. In fact, during her lifetime, her work remained largely private.

Emily Dickinson was born in Amherst, Massachusetts, to a prominent New England family. Her education included one year at Mount Holyoke Female Seminary, where she was greatly influenced by the Puritan religious tradition. Dickinson never married, and for nearly her entire life, she lived with her parents and her younger sister, Lavinia.

> *"The brain is wider than the sky."*
> —Emily Dickinson

A Private Life Dickinson began writing poems early in her life. However, as her life was private, so was her poetry. Of the nearly 1,800 poems she penned, Dickinson published only ten during her lifetime, and even then, she published them anonymously.

After Dickinson's death in 1886, her sister Lavinia discovered Dickinson's work in her bedroom. Lavinia decided to reveal her sister's talent to the world. In 1890 and 1891, two collections of Dickinson's poetry were published, followed in later years by subsequent editions.

Throughout her life, Dickinson preferred solitude over socializing—a fact that has led to much speculation about her personal life.

Despite many popular theories of loneliness or lovesickness, her self-imposed isolation may be viewed in another way. In the mid-nineteenth century, after completing their education, young women of Dickinson's social and economic standing were expected to marry and have children. Perhaps Dickinson desired something different for herself.

A Room of Her Own By not marrying, Dickinson carved out a space for herself to be able to write her poetry. She did however have family around her. Dickinson cared for her ailing mother and was much involved in the lives of her brother's children. The domestic sphere is one of Dickinson's major themes.

A Daring New Voice Dickinson's poetic style was daring and unique. In her choice of topics, she departed from her female contemporaries by veering away from sentimentality and toward questioning life, death, God, and nature.

Author Search For more about Emily Dickinson, go to glencoe.com and enter QuickPass code GL59794u3.

Literature and Reading Preview

Connect to the Poems
How do people typically respond to emotionally painful events? Discuss this question with a small group.

Build Background
Dickinson wrote "Heart! We Will Forget Him!" in the late 1850s. Her letters from the time describe the joy and frustration she experienced as a result of her love for an unnamed man. She wrote "After Great Pain, A Formal Feeling Comes" in 1862, a year when the danger of the Civil War threatened many of Dickinson's friends.

Set Purposes for Reading

Big Idea **Loves and Losses**

As you read the poems, ask yourself, How does Dickinson describe the themes of love and loss?

Literary Element **Personification**

Personification is a figure of speech in which inanimate objects are given human characteristics. Recognizing personification can help you understand the poet's intentions. As you read, ask yourself, Which objects does Dickinson personify?

Reading Strategy **Compare and Contrast Tone**

A poet's **tone** is his or her attitude toward the subject matter. Dickinson often uses a playful tone in her poems. As you read, ask yourself, How does the speaker's tone contribute to the poem's meaning?

Tip: Ask Questions Use a chart like the one below to help you formulate questions about Dickinson's tone in the poems.

Questions	"After Great Pain, A Formal Feeling Comes"	"Heart! We Will Forget Him!"
Who is the speaker?	Someone who has suffered a painful loss	
Who does the speaker address?		The speaker's heart
What is the subject?		
What is the overall tone of the poem?		

Learning Objectives

For pages 534–539

In studying these texts, you will focus on the following objectives:

Literary Study: Analyzing personification.

Reading: Comparing and contrasting tone.

Vocabulary

ceremonious (ser´ə mō´nē əs) *adj.* carefully observant of the formal acts required by ritual, custom, or etiquette; p. 536 *Sam's graduation was a ceremonious occasion.*

recollect (rek´ə lekt´) *v.* to remember; p. 536 *We used pictures to help Grandma recollect her childhood.*

stupor (stoo´pər) *n.* a state of extreme lethargy; p. 536 *After twenty hours of traveling, Dan arrived in a stupor.*

lag (lag) *v.* to fall behind; p. 537 *If you continue to lag, we will be late for practice.*

EMILY DICKINSON   535

Cotswold Park, Winter Woodland (Morning, December). Charles Neal. Oil on canvas.

After Great Pain, A Formal Feeling Comes

Emily Dickinson

After great pain, a formal feeling comes —
The Nerves sit **ceremonious**, like Tombs —
The stiff Heart questions was it He, that bore,
And Yesterday, or Centuries before?

5 The Feet, mechanical, go round —
Of Ground, or Air, or Ought[1]—
A Wooden way
Regardless grown,
A Quartz contentment, like a stone —

10 This is the Hour of Lead —
Remembered, if outlived,
As Freezing persons, **recollect** the Snow —
First — Chill — then **Stupor** — then the letting go —

---

1. Here, *Ought* means "anything" and is an archaic variant of *aught*.

Compare and Contrast Tone *How does this stanza's extra line help convey the tone of the poem?*

Vocabulary

ceremonious (ser´ ə mō´ nē əs) *adj.* carefully observant of the formal acts required by ritual, custom, or etiquette

recollect (rek´ ə lekt´) *v.* to remember

stupor (stoo´ pər) *n.* a state of extreme lethargy

Heart! We Will Forget Him!

Emily Dickinson

Ricordo di un dolore o Ritratto di Santina Negri (Memory of a Sorrow/Portrait of Santina Negri), 1889. Giuseppe Pellizza da Volpedo. Oil on canvas, 107 x 79 cm. Bergamo, Italy.

Heart! We will forget him!
You and I — tonight!
You may forget the warmth he gave —
I will forget the light!

When you have done, pray tell me
That I may straight begin!
Haste! lest[1] while you're **lagging**
I remember him!

---

1. Here, *lest* means "in order to prevent any possibility that."

Loves and Losses Why do you think that Dickinson directly addresses the Heart?

Vocabulary

lag (lag) *v.* to fall behind

After You Read

Respond and Think Critically

Respond and Interpret

1. Do you think "After Great Pain, A Formal Feeling Comes" and "Heart! We Will Forget Him!" express positive ideas about love and loss? Explain.

2. (a) In "After Great Pain, A Formal Feeling Comes," to what are nerves compared? (b) What does this image suggest about the sufferer's physical feelings?

3. (a) What does the speaker in "Heart! We Will Forget Him!" want to be told? (b) Why does the speaker need this information?

Analyze and Evaluate

4. A **simile** is a figure of speech, using *like* or *as,* that is used to compare two things. (a) Identify two similes in "After Great Pain, A Formal Feeling Comes." (b) Discuss how Dickinson uses them to convey her grief in the poem.

5. Analyze Dickinson's use of exclamation marks in "Heart! We Will Forget Him!" Do you find them effective? Explain.

Connect

6. **Big Idea** **Loves and Losses** Dickinson is praised for the conciseness and intensity of her poems. How well do these qualities serve her ideas of love and loss?

7. **Connect to Today** Are Dickinson's themes still relevant to readers today? Explain.

Daily Life & Culture

Living Single

Before 1800, it was extremely uncommon and difficult to live as a single woman. This idea began to change during the nineteenth century, when the proportion of never-married women rose steadily. Emily Dickinson lived as a single, middle-class woman during a period marked by the emergence of the women's rights movement and vigorous debate over the proper roles for women.

Women in general did not have many options or much real power. Single women, however, did retain certain civil rights that women who married did not have. Single women could, for example, make contracts and open bank accounts, and they often served as treasurers for the increasing number of women's organizations that developed during the pre-war era. Many feminists debated the opportunities available to women and pushed for women's rights.

1. How do the lives of single, middle-class women of the 1800s compare to the lives of single, middle-class women of today?

2. Why do you think Emily Dickinson chose to live in relative seclusion? Explain.

Literary Element Personification

Writers personify animals, objects, forces of nature, and ideas. Many human qualities, including emotions, physical gestures, and powers of speech, are attributed to personified items. **Personification** is used in both prose and poetry.

1. List the things personified in "After Great Pain, A Formal Feeling Comes" and "Heart! We Will Forget Him!"

2. Explain how the absence of personification would affect the poems.

Review: Rhythm and Rhyme

As you learned on pages 474–475, **rhythm** is the pattern of beats created by the order of stressed and unstressed syllables and **rhyme** is the repetition of the same stressed vowel sounds and any succeeding sounds in two or more words.

Partner Activity With a classmate, analyze the rhythm and rhyme of Dickinson's two poems. In most of Dickinson's early poems, the rhythm, or meter, models that of Puritan hymns. Common forms include quatrains (four lines) with steady six, eight, or ten iambs—unstressed and then stressed syllables, such as *da-DUM*. With your partner, count syllables in each line. Use letters to label the basic rhyme scheme. Chart your information as below.

"After Great Pain, A Formal Feeling Comes"		
Line Number	Number of Syllables	Rhyme Scheme
Stanza 1	1	
	2	
	3	
	4	
Stanza 2		

Literature Online

Selection Resources For Selection Quizzes, eFlashcards, and Reading-Writing Connection activities, go to glencoe.com and enter QuickPass code GL59794u3.

Reading Strategy Compare and Contrast Tone

ACT Skills Practice

1. By personifying her own body in both poems, the speaker creates:

   A. a relieved tone, permitting her to overcome her sadness.

   B. a solemn tone, distancing her slightly from her pain.

   C. an angry tone, giving her something to rage at.

   D. an objective tone, allowing her to forget her grief.

Vocabulary Practice

Practice with Antonyms An **antonym** is a word that has a meaning opposite to that of another word. With a partner, match each bold-faced vocabulary word below with its antonym. Use a thesaurus or dictionary to check your answers.

1. ceremonious   a. informal
2. recollect   b. consistency
3. stupor   c. overlook
4. lag   d. keep up
                 e. dignified
                 f. awareness

Academic Vocabulary

Do the dashes in this poem restrain the emotion, or do they help to emphasize it?

Restrain is an academic word. A person might **restrain** a dog or an impulse. To study this word further, fill out the graphic organizer below.

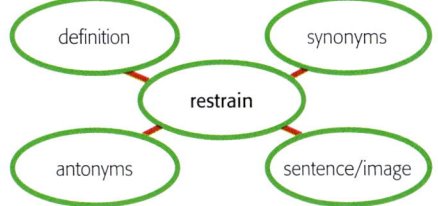

For more on academic vocabulary, see pages 52 and 53.

EMILY DICKINSON   539

Respond Through Writing

Expository Essay

Analyze Style Dickinson uses dashes, capitalization, diction, other punctuation, personification, and rhyme scheme in unique ways. Choose two or three of these aspects of her style and explain how they create or reinforce meaning in the poems.

Understand the Task Style is the expressive qualities that distinguish a writer's work. Diction is a writer's choice of words.

Prewrite To help you organize your essay, make a three-column chart like the one shown below.

Aspect of Style	Example from Poem	Contribution to Meaning
dashes		
unexpected capitalization		
slant (almost) rhymes		

List other examples and for all examples tell how they contribute to the meaning of the poem. Use your chart to determine the aspects of style you will include in your thesis. Then make an outline that includes the quotations you will use as examples.

Draft As you draft, remember to discuss style and to demonstrate your understanding of both works. State your thesis clearly in your introductory paragraph. Then structure your body paragraphs by beginning with a topic sentence that supports your thesis, providing one or more examples, and fully explaining how the examples support your thesis.

Revise Exchange essays with a classmate. Identify each other's thesis and supporting ideas. Give suggestions for additional references to the text and/or better explanation of quoted evidence. Revise accordingly.

Edit and Proofread Proofread your paper, correcting any errors in grammar, spelling, and punctuation. Use the Grammar Tip in the side column to help you with the use of semicolons as connectors.

Learning Objectives

In this assignment, you will focus on the following objectives:

Writing: Writing an expository essay.

Grammar: Understanding how to use semicolons.

Grammar Tip

Semicolons

Semicolons are often used before transitional words and phrases in compound and complex sentences.

EXAMPLES:

Capitalization calls attention to the word Lead*;* **as a result,** *capitalization emphasizes heaviness.*

The exclamation point after light *helps emphasize the command to forget;* **moreover,** *it creates a feeling of finality.*

Before You Read

The Meadow Mouse

Meet Theodore Roethke
(1908–1963)

In his book *Teacher Man,* author Frank McCourt recounts searching for poems that his restless high school students would enjoy. No other poem touched his students as deeply as "My Papa's Waltz" by Theodore Roethke. Students from a variety of backgrounds saw their lives and complicated feelings about their families captured perfectly by Roethke's words.

Roethke was a much loved and honored poet during his lifetime, winning the Pulitzer Prize and the National Book Award. His poems are closely observed lyrics that detail the processes of the natural world.

> "Any serious writer uses the imagery he saw and heard and felt about him as a youth. This is the imagery most vivid to him. It becomes symbolic."
>
> —Theodore Roethke

Memory and Poetry Roethke fashioned many of his poems from strong memories about his childhood in Saginaw, Michigan. Roethke's father and grandfather were florists, and Roethke grew up in a world of flowers, plants, and large commercial greenhouses. Like Emerson and Whitman, Roethke almost mystically identified with nature: "In my veins, in my bones I feel it."

During Roethke's sophomore year of high school, his father died from lung cancer. Roethke was devastated by the loss. At seventeen, he entered the University of Michigan, the first in his family to attend college. Later, in graduate school at Harvard University, he gave three of his poems to poet and professor Robert Hillyer. Hillyer said, "Any editor who wouldn't buy these is a fool!" Encouraged, Roethke turned to poetry as a career.

Teacher and Writer Roethke also began to teach, eventually serving as professor at Michigan State College, Pennsylvania State University, Bennington College, and the University of Washington. Over the years, Roethke mentored many important poets, including Richard Hugo, James Wright, and David Wagoner. According to Hugo, Roethke was "an outrageous man who would take outrageous stances and create something beautiful out of them. . . . That gave me a faith that you could be a pretty ridiculous person and still do something worthwhile or beautiful."

Roethke died of a heart attack when he was only fifty-five. He left behind grateful students and many classic poems.

Author Search For more about Theodore Roethke, go to glencoe.com and enter QuickPass code GL59794u3.

Literature and Reading Preview

Connect to the Poem
How does your impression of wild animals differ from your impression of domestic ones? Respond in a journal entry.

Build Background
The most common rodents in North America are meadow voles, also called meadow mice. Similar to mice, they have short tails, blunt snouts, small eyes and ears, and short limbs. They are somewhat larger than house mice, and they have shaggier fur. Because voles have enormous appetites, they sometimes cause great damage to crops and trees. Their natural predators include cats, foxes, coyotes, weasels, hawks, owls, snakes, and skunks.

Set Purposes for Reading

Big Idea Loves and Losses

As you read the poem, ask yourself, How does Roethke convey the themes of love and loss?

Literary Element Mood

The **mood** is the emotional quality of a literary work. A writer's diction, subject matter, setting, and tone—as well as sound devices such as rhyme and rhythm—contribute to creating mood. As you read, ask yourself, How would I describe the mood of each section of this poem?

Reading Strategy Analyze Diction

Diction includes the writer's choice of words, an important element in the writer's voice or style. Skilled writers choose their words carefully to convey a particular tone and meaning. As you read, ask yourself, What words and phrases in the poem seem particularly effective?

Tip: Note Words In a chart like the one below, list words and phrases that you find interesting or intriguing. Then write down other words that the poet might have chosen instead.

Words and Phrases	Possible Alternate Words and Phrases
Trembling (line 6)	shaking

Learning Objectives

For pages 541–546

In studying this text, you will focus on the following objectives:

Literary Study: Determining mood.

Reading: Analyzing diction.

Vocabulary

minuscule (min′əs kūl′) *adj.* very, very small; p. 543 *Sarah's miniscule cookie was one tenth the size of Lisa's.*

hapless (hap′ lis) *adj.* unlucky or unfortunate; p. 544 *The hapless student had to walk ten miles after missing the last bus.*

Tip: Denotation and Connotation
A word's **denotation** is its dictionary meaning; its **connotations** are the emotional associations it evokes. To identify a word's connotations, think about the images and ideas the word brings to mind. For example, in the sentence *The hapless student had to walk ten miles after missing the last bus,* the word *hapless* has negative connotations, suggesting great misfortune.

542 UNIT 3 POETRY

The Meadow Mouse

Theodore Roethke

1

In a shoe box stuffed in an old nylon stocking
Sleeps the baby mouse I found in the meadow,
Where he trembled and shook beneath a stick
Till I caught him up by the tail and brought him in,
5   Cradled in my hand
A little quaker, the whole body of him trembling,
His absurd whiskers sticking out like a cartoon-mouse,
His feet like small leaves,
Little lizard-feet,
10 Whitish and spread wide when he tried to struggle away,
Wriggling like a **minuscule** puppy

Now he's eaten his three kinds of cheese and drunk from his bottle-cap watering-trough—
So much he just lies in one corner,
His tail curled under him, his belly big
15 As his head; his bat-like ears
Twitching, tilting toward the least sound.

Do I imagine he no longer trembles
When I come close to him?
He seems no longer to tremble.

The Raspberry-Mouse. Ditz. Private collection.

View the Art Does this mouse capture your sympathies the way the meadow mouse captured the sympathies of the speaker? Explain why or why not.

Analyze Diction Why do you think the poet chose the word *cradled* rather than *carried*?

Vocabulary

minuscule (min′ əs kūl′) *adj.* very, very small

2

20 But this morning the shoe-box house on the back porch
     is empty.
Where has he gone, my meadow mouse,
My thumb of a child that nuzzled in my palm?—
To run under the hawk's wing,
Under the eye of the great owl watching from the elm-tree,
25 To live by courtesy of the shrike,[1] the snake, the tom-cat.

I think of the nestling[2] fallen into the deep grass,
The turtle gasping in the dusty rubble of the highway,
The paralytic stunned in the tub, and the water rising,—
All things innocent, **hapless**, forsaken.

---

1. A *shrike* is a bird that feeds on small animals. It is sometimes called a butcherbird.
2. A *nestling* is a young bird that has not yet left the nest.

Mood *What emotions do these lines convey?*

Vocabulary

hapless (hap′ lis) *adj.* unlucky or unfortunate

After You Read

Respond and Think Critically

Respond and Interpret

1. What went through your mind as you finished reading this poem?

2. (a) What does the speaker do after finding the meadow mouse? (b) What does the speaker's action suggest about his personality and values?

3. (a) How does the mouse behave at the beginning of the poem? (b) How does the speaker interpret the mouse's behavior after it has been fed?

4. (a) What is the speaker afraid of in the last two stanzas of the poem? (b) Why is he so affected by what has happened?

Analyze and Evaluate

5. In lines 21–22, the speaker calls the mouse "my meadow mouse, / My thumb of a child." Is the speaker reasonable or misguided to think of the mouse as his own? Explain.

6. What is the **theme**, or perception about life or human nature, of this poem? Consider what happens in section 2 and what this event causes the speaker to think about.

7. A **simile** is a figure of speech using a word such as *like* or *as* to compare seemingly unlike things. What effect do the similes in lines 7 and 8 create?

Connect

8. **Big Idea** Loves and Losses (a) Which phrases in section 1 convey the endearing qualities of the mouse? (b) Which phrases in section 2 convey the speaker's sense of loss?

9. **Connect to the Author** Roethke once wrote, "I have a genuine love of nature." Where in the poem does he reveal his love for nature?

Literary Element · Mood

ACT Skills Practice

1. How do lines 5–6 help establish a tender mood?
   - **A** The imagery suggests the vulnerability of the mouse.
   - **B** The speaker uses contradictions.
   - **C** The speaker describes his love of nature.
   - **D** The speaker laments his loss of the mouse.

2. The mood of section 2 can best be described as:
   - **E** bitter and cynical.
   - **F** playful and lighthearted.
   - **G** calm and accepting.
   - **H** threatening and fearful.

Review: Verse Paragraph

As you learned on page 526, a **verse paragraph** is a group of lines that forms a unit. Unlike a stanza, a verse paragraph does not have a fixed number of lines. Contemporary poets often use verse paragraphs to organize their ideas.

Partner Activity With a partner, examine the five verse paragraphs in "The Meadow Mouse" and identify the ideas that each one conveys. Complete a chart like the one below.

Verse paragraph	Idea
Lines 1–11	delight in observing the mouse's features and actions

Reading Strategy **Analyze Diction**

Roethke carefully chooses words and phrases to convey his feelings. Review the chart you made on page 542 and then answer these questions.

1. Roethke describes the mouse as "my thumb of a child that nuzzled in my palm." What images does this phrase bring to mind?
2. What effect do the three adjectives in the last line create?

Vocabulary Practice

Practice with Denotation and Connotation Although the words *politician* and *legislator* have similar denotations, the word *politician* has negative connotations, but *legislator* generally does not. In the sentences below decide whether the connotations of each vocabulary word are positive, negative, or neutral.

1. The huge bass gobbled up the **minuscule** minnow.

   a. positive   **b.** negative   **c.** neutral

2. Tripping over his shoelaces, the **hapless** boy toppled headlong down the stairs.

   a. positive   **b.** negative   **c.** neutral

Academic Vocabulary

*In Roethke's poem, the speaker creates an environment that **simulates** some of the conditions found in the mouse's natural habitat.*

Simulate (sim′yə lāt′) is an academic word that means "to imitate the look and/or feel of something." The word is also used in more casual settings—for example, an actor might **simulate** tears during a performance. To further explore the meaning of this word, list some features of a standardized test that a practice test might **simulate**.

For more on academic vocabulary, see pages 52 and 53.

Speaking and Listening

 Oral Interpretation

Assignment Organize and present an oral interpretation of Roethke's poem "The Meadow Mouse" to convey its literal and implied meanings.

Prepare Rehearse the poem several times, and, if possible, memorize it. Refer to the chart you made on page 542 to identify words and phrases to emphasize in your presentation. As you rehearse, choose and practice techniques that support meaning and mood. Rehearse the poem until you can perform it smoothly, focusing on volume, pacing, enunciation, eye contact, and gestures. Consider using props, visual aids, and music to enhance your performance.

Use a chart like the one below to identify key lines in the poem and your techniques for conveying mood.

Key Lines	Mood	Tone of Voice and/or Gestures
"Cradled in my hand" (line 5)	tenderness	warm and gentle tone

Perform Present your dramatic reading to the class. Read slowly and clearly, pausing briefly from time to time to reinforce meaning. Convey the changes in mood as the poem moves from the speaker's affection for the mouse to his sense of bewilderment and loss and finally to his feelings of compassion for other endangered living things.

Evaluate Decide how clearly and effectively you interpreted the poem. Consider asking members of your audience to identify what went well in your performance and what needed improvement. Then write a paragraph to critique and evaluate your skills in oral interpretation. Use the rubric on page 1127 to help in your evaluation.

 **Literature** Online

Selection Resources For Selection Quizzes, eFlashcards, and Reading-Writing Connection activities, go to glencoe.com and enter QuickPass code GL59794u3.

Before You Read

World Literature: Ireland

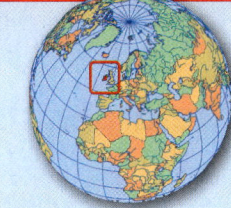

Down by the Salley Gardens and *He Wishes for the Cloths of Heaven*

Meet William Butler Yeats
(1865–1939)

When William Butler Yeats was fourteen years old, he could not spell and struggled with grammar. Today, however, Yeats is considered one of the most influential poets of the twentieth century.

A Voice of Ireland The oldest child of John Butler Yeats, a lawyer who later became a portrait painter, Yeats was born in Dublin, Ireland. His family moved to London when he was two, but he returned to Ireland often, spending holidays with his grandparents in the Irish countryside. He did not receive any formal schooling until he was twelve. A few years later, in 1880, his family returned to Dublin.

Yeats's mother helped him develop a love of Ireland and an interest in Irish folklore and legend that remained with him all his life. When he was in his early twenties, Yeats began to write poetry. Soon afterward, he met the Irish nationalist John O'Leary, who helped channel the young man's love of Irish literature and myths into the cause of preserving Irish identity. At the time, the British were trying to eliminate Gaelic, the traditional language of Ireland. Yeats and others feared that Ireland's cultural heritage—especially its literature and folklore—would vanish with the outlawed language.

One way Yeats worked to preserve Irish literature and culture was through drama. In the late 1880s, he began writing plays, which were often based on Irish legends. In 1896 he met Lady Gregory, an aristocrat and fellow playwright. Yeats, Lady Gregory, and others helped found the Irish Literary Theatre in 1899, which in time grew into the renowned Abbey Theatre.

Love and Loss Yeats met Maud Gonne, an actress and a fiery political activist, when he was a young man in Dublin. They shared an interest in freeing Ireland from English domination. Yeats fell in love, but Gonne refused two of his marriage proposals. When Yeats wrote about love and loss, he seared the pain of his own unrequited love onto the page.

> "Think like a wise man but express yourself like the common people."
>
> —William Butler Yeats

Ironically, when Yeats won the Nobel Prize in Literature in 1923, it was awarded for his drama, which has not endured to the extent that his poetry has.

Literature Online

Author Search For more about William Butler Yeats, go to glencoe.com and enter QuickPass code GL59794u3.

WILLIAM BUTLER YEATS 547

Literature and Reading Preview

Connect to the Poems
How does love feel when it is not returned? Respond to this question in your journal.

Build Background
Both "Down by the Salley Gardens" and "He Wishes for the Cloths of Heaven" deal with love. In the first poem, the speaker berates himself for getting love wrong. The second poem is a tribute to a love who has power over the speaker.

Set Purposes for Reading

Big Idea Loves and Losses

As you read these poems, ask yourself, How does Yeats express feelings of love, longing, and loss?

Literary Element Lyric Poetry

Lyric poetry expresses a speaker's personal thoughts and feelings and is typically short and musical. The subject of a lyric poem can be an object, a person, or an event, but the emphasis of the poem is an emotional experience. As you read, ask yourself, What elements of lyric poetry do these poems reflect?

Reading Strategy Analyze Repetition and Rhyme

Repetition and rhyme are techniques used to enhance a poem's sense of rhythm, to emphasize particular sounds, and to add to the musical quality of poetry. As you read, ask yourself, What examples of repetition and rhyme can you identify in these poems?

Tip: Take Notes Use a graphic organizer to record examples of each device and your thoughts about why the author might have used them.

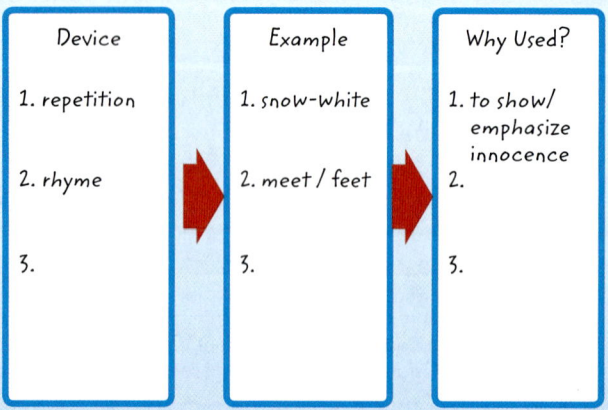

Learning Objectives

For pages 547–552

In studying these texts, you will focus on the following objectives:

Literary Study: Analyzing lyric poetry.

Reading: Analyzing repetition and rhyme.

Vocabulary

embroidered (em broi′dərd) *adj.* decorated with needlework; p. 550 *The Guatemalan women wore colorful embroidered dresses to the fiesta.*

tread (tred) *v.* to step or walk on; p. 550 *We encourage our guests to tread lightly on the antique carpet.*

Tip: Context Clues When you come across an unfamiliar term, pay close attention to the surrounding words and try to determine a possible meaning. For example, in the sentence *The Guatemalan women wore colorful embroidered dresses to the fiesta,* the words *colorful, dresses,* and *fiesta* provide clues that suggest that *embroidered* means "sewn with decorative designs."

The Artist's Garden at Giverny, 1900. Claude Monet. Oil on canvas. Musée d'Orsay, Paris.

Down by the Salley Gardens

William Butler Yeats

Down by the salley[1] gardens my love and I did meet;
She passed the salley gardens with little snow-white feet.
She bid me take love easy, as the leaves grow on the tree;
But I, being young and foolish, with her would not agree.
In a field by the river my love and I did stand,
And on my leaning shoulder she laid her snow-white hand.
She bid me take life easy, as the grass grows on the weirs;[2]
But I was young and foolish, and now am full of tears.

---

1. *Salley* is a variation of *sallow,* which is a type of willow tree.
2. Here, *weirs* are dams.

Analyze Repetition and Rhyme What does the repetition of the word "grow(s)" in lines 3 and 7 suggest about the meaning of the poem?

Loves and Losses What cause and effect are suggested in this line?

He Wishes for the Cloths of Heaven

William Butler Yeats

Lotto Tapestry from Ushak, Anatolia. Turkish. Museo Nazionale del Bargello, Florence.

Had I the heavens' **embroidered** cloths,
Enwrought[1] with golden and silver light,
The blue and the dim and the dark cloths
Of night and light and the half light,
I would spread the cloths under your feet:
But I, being poor, have only my dreams;
I have spread my dreams under your feet;
Tread softly because you tread on my dreams.

---

1. *Enwrought* means "made with"; here, it means "embroidered with."

Lyric Poetry How do the repeated words at the ends of the lines tie in with the definition of lyric poetry?

Vocabulary

embroidered (em broi′ dərd) *adj.* decorated with needlework

tread (tred) *v.* to step or walk on

After You Read

Respond and Think Critically

Respond and Interpret

1. With which of the emotions in these poems do you identify most or least? Explain.

2. (a) What advice did the speaker's love give him in "Down by the Salley Gardens"? (b) Why do you think she referred to the leaves and grass as examples?

3. (a) Why didn't the speaker agree with his love? (b) At the end of the poem, why is the speaker "full of tears"?

4. (a) What does the speaker in "He wishes for the Cloths of Heaven" say he has spread under his love's feet? (b) What can you infer about the treatment he hopes to receive from his love?

Analyze and Evaluate

5. The sadness in "Down by the Salley Gardens" is not suggested until the last line. Describe the **mood** of the poem's first seven lines.

6. How well does the speaker express intense emotion in "He Wishes for the Cloths of Heaven"? Cite words and phrases from the poem to support your answer.

Connect

7. **Big Idea** Loves and Losses In which poem do you think the speaker conveys his sense of loss more effectively? Explain.

8. **Connect to Today** (a) Why do you think people today, like the speakers in Yeats's poems, sometimes reach for unrealistic goals? (b) What might be gained or lost by reaching?

You're the Critic

Beautifully Simple or Simply Silly?

Read the two excerpts of literary criticism below. Both critics agree that Yeats was a man of genius. As you read the excerpts, notice the difference in tone between the two critics.

> "[Yeats] has made for himself a poetical style which is much more simple, as it is much more concise, than any prose style; and, in the final perfecting of his form, he has made for himself a rhythm which is more natural, more precise in its slow and wandering cadence, than any prose rhythm. . . . Poetry, if it is to be of the finest quality, is bound to be simple, a mere breathing, in which individual words almost disappear into music."
> —Arthur Symons

> "[Yeats] hangs in the balance between genius and (to speak rudely) fool."
> —Edward Dowden

Group Activity Discuss the following questions with your classmates.

1. Do you think that Yeats's poetry style is more simple than "any prose style"?

2. What do you think Edward Dowden means by his statement?

Literary Element: Lyric Poetry

Often short and highly musical, **lyric poetry** expresses personal thoughts and emotions, rather than telling a story as narrative poetry does. Yeats is considered an outstanding lyric poet. What makes the poems you just read good examples of his art? What makes them good examples of lyric poetry in particular?

1. What qualities in "He Wishes for the Cloths of Heaven" identify it as a lyric poem? Cite evidence from the poem in your answer.
2. What elements of "Down by the Salley Gardens" make it possible to imagine the poem set to music?

Review: Speaker

As you learned on page 468, the speaker is the voice that communicates with the reader of a poem, similar to a narrator in a work of prose. The speaker's words convey a particular tone, or attitude, toward the subject of the poem.

Partner Activity Meet with a classmate and discuss the speaker in each poem. Create a chart like the one below to record information about the speakers. Decide whether the speakers are individuals in a specific time and place or whether each represents people who undergo a universal experience.

	Speaker in "Down by the Salley Gardens"	Speaker in "He Wishes for the Cloths of Heaven"
Clues to Identity	"I"	"I"
Facts About Speaker's Actions/Life	The speaker was once "young and foolish"; now, the speaker feels regret.	
Speaker's Attitude		

 **Literature** Online

Selection Resources For Selection Quizzes, eFlashcards, and Reading-Writing Connection activities, go to glencoe.com and enter QuickPass code GL59794u3.

Reading Strategy: Analyze Repetition and Rhyme

Repetition is the recurrence of sounds, words, phrases, lines, or stanzas in a piece of writing. Writers use repetition to emphasize important ideas, to create rhythm, and to increase a feeling of unity in a work. **Rhyme** is the repetition of the same stressed vowel sounds and any succeeding sounds in two or more words. Rhyme is another device used by writers to emphasize ideas, to create rhythm, and to increase a work's unity. Review your chart on page 548 and answer the following.

1. Choose one of the poems and list three examples of repetition within it. How did these examples help to strengthen the work?
2. What was one example of rhyme in the poems that struck you as particularly effective? Explain.

Vocabulary Practice

Practice with Context Clues Identify the context clues in the following sentences that help you determine the meaning of each bold-faced vocabulary word.

1. Colorful threads form an intricate pattern on the **embroidered** blouse.
2. The stairs are worn from the footsteps of many people who **tread** on them each day.

Academic Vocabulary

In "Down by the Salley Gardens," the speaker *reverses* his youthful ideas about love.

Reverse is a word that has many different meanings. Using context clues, figure out the meaning of *reverse* in each sentence and then explain the difference between the two meanings.

1. She signed her name on the **reverse** side of the contract.
2. If you will **reverse** the image, you'll see what I mean.

For more on academic vocabulary, see pages 52–53.

Respond Through Writing

Expository Essay

Analyze Theme Both poems deal with the topics of love and loss. What does each poem say specifically about these topics? In an essay, analyze the theme of each poem. Build your essay around a thesis that contrasts the themes. Support your ideas with examples from the text.

Understand the Task The **theme** is the central message of a literary work, often expressed as a general statement about life. The **thesis** states your paper's controlling idea or what you're trying to prove or support.

Prewrite For each poem, list specific words and phrases that help you infer the theme. Complete the following to formulate a thesis statement:

Both (Poem 1) and (Poem 2) are about _____, but (Poem 1) says _____, while (Poem 2) says _____.

Draft After you have formulated a clear thesis, provide credible, valid, and relevant evidence to support it. Consider this pattern of organization:

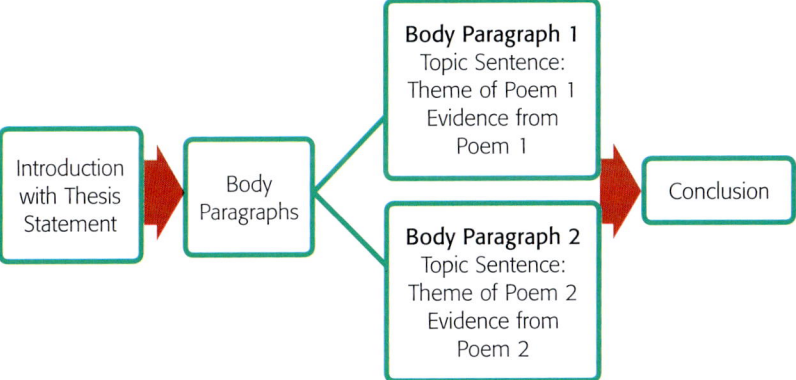

Develop an introduction, a body, and a conclusion. Use transitional words and phrases to achieve coherence. As you draft, support your important ideas with detailed references to the text. Remember to assess the effects created by words or lines that suggest multiple or complex meanings. Base your analysis on Yeats's diction and stylistic choices.

Revise Exchange essays with a classmate and evaluate each other's essays. Provide comments for your classmate and revise your own paper according to the comments you receive.

Edit and Proofread Proofread your paper. Correct errors in grammar, spelling, and punctuation. Use the Grammar Tip for help with commas.

Learning Objectives

In this assignment, you will focus on the following objectives:

Writing: Writing an expository essay.

Grammar: Understanding how to use introductory transitions and words and phrases.

Grammar Tip

Commas and Introductory Transitional Words and Phrases

Look at the commas in these two sentences.

Like "Down by the Salley Gardens," "He Wishes for the Cloths of Heaven" features a sorrowful speaker.

In contrast to the happy mood of the first line, the final line expresses grief.

In each sentence, a comma is used to set off introductory transitional words or phrases. *"Like 'Down by the Salley Gardens'"* is a single long introductory prepositional phrase; *"In contrast to the happy mood of the first line"* consists of two introductory prepositional phrases.

Before You Read

I Am Offering This Poem

Meet Jimmy Santiago Baca
(born 1952)

Jimmy Santiago Baca, a self-descibed "child of the earth" and "Chicano," is today a famous poet. Yet his path to literary success was neither conventional nor easy. Formerly illiterate, Baca did not learn to read and write until he reached adulthood. Baca was twenty-one and serving a prison term before he struggled to pull some meaning from a bilingual book given to him as a gift. Eventually, the words before him ceased to resemble a confusing mix of letters and transformed into decipherable, meaningful syllables and sentences. Asked to describe this experience of self-teaching, Baca explained the process as revolutionary.

> "I came upon poetry in much the same way that an infant first gasps for breath."
>
> —Jimmy Santiago Baca

A Deserted Poet Born in Santa Fe, New Mexico, Jimmy Santiago Baca has both Apache and Chicano heritage. He was deserted by his parents when he was only two years old; he then spent several years with his grandmother before being sent to an orphanage. Baca lived on the streets until he was faced with incarceration. Baca spent six years in prison, including four years in isolation, during which he taught himself to read and write.

Captive and nearly hopeless, Baca found a passion for poetry—"I was writing things that I remember doing as a kid and as an adult and so forth. And what happened was that, in a place like prison where all sensory enjoyment was deprived, language became more real, more tangible than bars or concrete, than the structure of buildings in the landscape." Encouraged by a fellow prisoner, Baca submitted some of his poetry to *Mother Jones* magazine. Editor Denise Levertov printed Baca's poems and ultimately published his first major collection: *Immigrants in Our Own Land*.

Poet of the People Since the publication of his first book, Baca has produced many compositions, including novels and screenplays. In 2001, he published an award-winning memoir titled *A Place To Stand*, and in 2004 a collection of short stories, *The Importance of a Piece of Paper*, was released. Currently, he continues to write in several genres and travels across the United States facilitating writing workshops for adults and children. Wherever he goes, he carries a powerful message: "Poetry is what we speak to each other."

Baca is a recipient of the National Poetry Award, the American Book Award, the International Hispanic Heritage Award, and the Pushcart Prize.

Author Search For more about Jimmy Santiago Baca, go to glencoe.com and enter QuickPass code GL59794u3.

Literature and Reading Preview

Connect to the Poem
The speaker in this poem compensates for a lack of material wealth with love. What value do you place on love? Write a journal entry in which you respond to the question.

Build Background
The traditional homes of Navajo Indians, called hogans, are most often built from logs and mud. Occasionally constructed from stone, the humble dwellings have no windows and frame a single entrance facing east.

Set Purposes for Reading

Big Idea Loves and Losses

As you read "I Am Offering This Poem," ask yourself, How does the speaker show love?

Literary Element Metaphor and Simile

Simile is a figure of speech that makes a direct comparison between two otherwise dissimilar objects or ideas by connecting them with the words *like* or *as.* **Metaphor** is a figure of speech that compares two seemingly unlike things. Metaphor implies the comparison rather than stating it directly and does not use the connectives *like* or *as.* As you read, ask yourself, How does the speaker use simile and metaphor?

Reading Strategy Preview and Review

Previewing is looking over a selection before you read it to see what you already know and what you will need to know. **Reviewing** is going back over what you have read to remember what is important and to organize your ideas. As you read, ask yourself, How much of the poem am I understanding?

....

Tip: Scan Use a chart like the one below to jot down lines that interest you. List why they interest you. Then note the stylistic patterns of the author.

Line of Interest	Why I Like It	Author's Stylistic Choice
to warm your belly in winter	This is an interesting way to describe a full belly. Usually, fullness is illustrated through a sense of heaviness and not temperature.	The author's descriptions are unusual without using unfamiliar words.

Learning Objectives

For pages 554–558

In studying this text, you will focus on the following objectives:

Literary Study: Analyzing metaphor and simile.

Reading: Previewing and reviewing.

Vocabulary

mature (mə choor´) *adj.* having reached a desired state; p. 556
The seed has grown into a vast and mature tree.

dense (dens) *adj.* thick; p. 556
The girl's hair was dense with waves and curls.

Tip: Connotation and Denotation
As you read, think about which words arouse your emotions, which words don't, and why.

JIMMY SANTIAGO BACA

I Am Offering This Poem

Jimmy Santiago Baca

I am offering this poem to you,
since I have nothing else to give.
Keep it like a warm coat
when winter comes to cover you,
5 or like a pair of thick socks
the cold cannot bite through,

        I love you,

I have nothing else to give you,
so it is a pot full of yellow corn
10 to warm your belly in winter,
it is a scarf for your head, to wear
over your hair, to tie up around your face,

        I love you,

Keep it, treasure this as you would
15 if you were lost, needing direction,
in the wilderness life becomes when
    mature;
and in the corner of your drawer,
tucked away like a cabin or hogan
in **dense** trees, come knocking,
20 and I will answer, give you directions,
and let you warm yourself by this fire,
rest by this fire, and make you feel safe,

        I love you,

It's all I have to give,
25 and all anyone needs to live,
and to go on living inside,
when the world outside
no longer cares if you live or die;
remember,

30   I love you.

Angola's Dreams Grasp Finger Tips, 1973. Emilio Cruz. Smithsonian American Art Museum, Washington, DC.

Metaphor and Simile What device has the poet employed here?

Preview and Review Besides expressing feelings for one person, what else is the speaker expressing in this poem?

Vocabulary

mature (mə choor´) *adj.* having reached a desired state
dense (dens) *adj.* thick

After You Read

Respond and Think Critically

Respond and Interpret

1. (a) Who do you think this poem is intended for? Explain. (b) How would you expect the recipient to feel after reading the poem?

2. (a) What reason does the speaker give for offering this poem? (b) What does this suggest about the speaker?

3. (a) What does the speaker propose is the one thing people require for existence? (b) What can you infer about the poet from this proposal?

Analyze and Evaluate

4. (a) How does the poem's structure help convey its message? (b) How else might the poem be structured and still communicate this message?

5. (a) How does Baca divide the poem's stanzas? (b) How does the first stanza compare with the second? With the third and fourth stanzas?

Connect

6. **Big Idea** **Loves and Losses** Baca has experienced great loss in his life, including the loss of loved ones and his own freedom. How might these losses have inspired "I Am Offering This Poem"?

7. **Connect to the Author** Baca has had little formal training in poetry. How do you think this has affected his writing style?

Literary Element Metaphor and Simile

SAT Skills Practice

1. In lines 3-6 the speaker uses

    (A) a pair of similes comparing his poem to a coat and socks.
    (B) personification giving winter and cold human characteristics.
    (C) a metaphor comparing the cold to a dog.
    (D) a metaphor comparing winter to a coat.
    (E) a simile comparing his poem to the winter cold.

2. In inviting his loved one to "warm yourself by this fire" (line 21), the speaker employs

    (A) a metaphor comparing himself to a fire.
    (B) a simile comparing the loved one to a poem.
    (C) a metaphor comparing the poem to a fire.
    (D) a simile comparing himself to his own poem.
    (E) a literal invitation to stand by a real fire.

Review: Lyric Poetry

As you learned on page 533, **lyric poetry** articulates the private thoughts and feelings of its speaker. Generally, lyric poetry is brief and melodic, yet packed with emotional intensity.

Partner Activity With a partner, read "I Am Offering This Poem" one stanza at a time. After completing a stanza, discuss the thoughts, feelings, and level of emotional intensity conveyed through its lines. Use a chart like the one below to track your discussion. Record the ideas and emotions you imagine the author experienced when writing the poem or record the ideas and emotions you experienced while reading it.

Stanza	Sentiment
1	Because the speaker has nothing but the poem to offer his or her loved one, he or she is sad. Modest means are replaced with creativity, though, and by offering a symbolic coat and scarf, he or she reveals a deep affection.

Reading Strategy **Preview and Review**

By **previewing,** you can often find clues about the content of a selection before you begin reading. Similarly, **reviewing** the material will help you to remember important details. Refer to the chart you made on page 555 and answer the following questions.

1. The speaker compares his or her love to things that provide warmth. What does this tell you about the speaker?
2. Restate the speaker's message in your own words.

Vocabulary Practice

Practice with Denotation and Connotation
Denotation is the literal, or dictionary, meaning of a word. **Connotation** is the implied, or cultural, meaning of a word. For example, the words *disobedient* and *bad* have a similar denotation in the context of a child's behavior, but they have different connotations.

Weaker	*Stronger*
disobedient	bad

Work with a partner to complete a graphic organizer like the one below for each vocabulary word. Include the vocabulary word in one box and a word that has a similar denotation in another. Then explain which word has the stronger connotation.

mature   dense

EXAMPLE:

> Vocabulary word:
> disobedient

> Similar word:
> bad

> Explanation: Bad has the stronger connotation. Both words refer to undesirable behavior, but disobedient suggests only minor transgressions, while bad can suggest major transgressions.

Write with Style

 Apply Figurative Language

Assignment Write two sentences that each contain a simile. Then rewrite each sentence so that it contains a metaphor instead of a simile.

Get Ideas Review the similes and metaphors you identified in "I Am Offering This Poem." Determine what makes them fresh, interesting, and convincing. Think of scenes and images from everyday life to help you write comparisons of your own. You may want to consult magazines, newspapers, the Internet, or your journal or diary to generate ideas. Jot down a few notes.

Give It Structure Write your two best comparisons as complete sentences that contain similes. Then rewrite the sentences to express each comparison as a metaphor.

Look at Language Use precise, original words to bring life to your language. When you rewrite your similes as metaphors, do not simply remove the word *like* or *as*. Instead, restructure or extend the idea.

Simile: The dark clouds were like a "no trespassing" sign.

Not: The dark clouds were a "no trespassing" sign.

Restructured as Metaphor: The gathering storm clouds formed themselves into an ominous "no trespassing" sign.

Extended: The gathering storm clouds were a "no trespassing" sign; when we saw them we decided to stay indoors.

 **Literature** Online

Selection Resources For Selection Quizzes, eFlashcards, and Reading-Writing Connection activities, go to glencoe.com and enter QuickPass code GL59794u3.

Before You Read

since feeling is first

Meet E. E. Cummings
(1894–1962)

In his later poetry, E. E. Cummings experimented with poetic form and language to create a distinctive style. He also wrote essays, short stories, a novel, plays, children's fiction, and a travel diary. But Cummings was not only a writer. He was a painter who had many solo exhibitions and a professor of poetry at Harvard University.

Starting Out Edward Estlin Cummings was born in Cambridge, Massachusetts, home of Harvard University. His father was a professor at the school, which Cummings later attended. While at Harvard, Cummings was influenced by the works of experimental writers such as Gertrude Stein and Ezra Pound. He graduated with a master's degree in English and Classical Studies in 1916.

> *"It takes courage to grow up and become who you really are."*
>
> —E. E. Cummings

By April of 1917, World War I was raging in Europe, but the United States had not yet entered the war. Cummings volunteered to serve as an ambulance driver in France. Due to a misunderstanding, he was imprisoned on suspicion of treason for three months in a French detention camp.

A Champion of the Individual After the war, Cummings returned to Paris to study art. He turned his experiences in the French detention camp into his first book, *The Enormous Room*, published in 1922. This fictionalized account of his captivity depicted it as a time of personal growth. In 1923 he published a book of poetry, *Tulips and Chimneys*. While many of the poems are conventional in style, some show the playful form and punctuation that are hallmarks of Cummings's later work.

Cummings moved to New York City in 1924 and found himself regarded as a celebrity. *Vanity Fair* magazine gave him a long-term assignment as an essayist and a portrait artist. This allowed him to set up his lifelong routine of painting after lunch and writing after dinner. Over the ensuing years, Cummings wrote twelve volumes of poems and won numerous awards.

Cummings wrote some of his poems in free verse, with no fixed meter or rhyme, but many have a rhyming sonnet structure. Despite the unusual form of many of Cummings's poems, his themes are often traditional: love, nature, childhood. Yet he was critical of conventional thinking and of society's restrictions on freedom of expression. In one of his lectures at Harvard, Cummings said, "So far as I am concerned, poetry and every other art was, is, and forever will be strictly and distinctly a question of individuality."

Author Search For more about E. E. Cummings, go to glencoe.com and enter QuickPass code GL59794u3.

Literature and Reading Preview

Connect to the Poem
Do you ever make a decision based on the way you feel? Freewrite for a few minutes about times when you have let your feelings dictate your decisions.

Build Background
E. E. Cummings is known for manipulating syntax, or word order, in his poetry. Cummings uses familiar words in unexpected places to surprise his readers and call their attention to the flexibility of language.

Set Purposes for Reading

Big Idea Loves and Losses

As you read "since feeling is first," ask yourself, What does Cummings consider to be of lesser value than feeling?

Literary Element Juxtaposition

Juxtaposition is placing two or more distinct items or ideas side by side in order to compare or contrast them. As you read the poem, ask yourself, How does Cummings use juxtaposition to increase his reader's understanding of the power of feeling?

Reading Strategy Paraphrase

Paraphrasing is taking the author's exact meaning and putting it into your own words. Paraphrasing a poem can help you get past unusual phrasing and punctuation. As you read, ask yourself, How can I paraphrase Cummings's main ideas?

Tip: List Important Words Use a chart like the one below to list important words as you read. Note which part of speech each word represents—is the word a noun, a verb, an adjective, or an adverb? Be sure you understand the meaning of each word. Make the chart any length you need. Then try rewriting lines of the poem in your own words.

Word	Part of Speech	Meaning
feeling	noun	emotion

Learning Objectives

For pages 559–562

In studying this text, you will focus on the following objectives:

Literary Study: Analyzing juxtaposition.

Reading: Paraphrasing.

Vocabulary

syntax (sin´taks) *n.* ordered structure or systematic arrangement; the rules of language; p. 561 *Standard English* syntax *places the subject before the verb in a sentence.*

parenthesis (pə ren´thə sis) *n.* digression or afterthought; disruption in continuity; p. 561 *No* parenthesis *marred the flow of main ideas in his argument.*

since feeling is first

E. E. Cummings

Composition, 1933. Joan Miro. Oil on canvas, 1.66 x 1.33 m. Prague, Czech Republic.

since feeling is first
who pays any attention[1]
to the **syntax** of things
will never wholly kiss you;
5   wholly to be a fool
while Spring is in the world

my blood approves,
and kisses are a better fate
than wisdom
10   lady i swear by all flowers. Don't cry
—the best gesture of my brain is less than
your eyelids' flutter which says

we are for each other: then
laugh, leaning back in my arms
15   for life's not a paragraph

And death i think is no **parenthesis**

---

1. Here, *who pays any attention* is the subject of the statement rather than a question.

Juxtaposition Why does Cummings choose to compare kisses and wisdom?

Vocabulary

syntax (sin´taks) *n.* ordered structure or systematic arrangement; the rules of language

parenthesis (pə ren´thə sis) *n.* digression or afterthought; disruption in continuity

After You Read

Respond and Think Critically

Respond and Interpret

1. When you read "since feeling is first," does it seem like a love poem? Explain.

2. (a) What kind of person does the poem's speaker say "will never wholly kiss you"? (b) What do you think Cummings means by this?

3. (a) In the poem, when is it acceptable to be a fool? (b) Why do you think the speaker limits being foolish to a particular time period?

Analyze and Evaluate

4. Does the poem suggest that "feeling is first" only in a relationship of love? Explain.

5. Cummings ends the poem with "life's not a paragraph" and death "is no parenthesis." Does this ending fit the rest of the poem? Why or why not?

6. Does Cummings's disregard for rules of capitalization strengthen or weaken the poem? Explain.

Connect

7. **Big Idea** Loves and Losses What does the poem suggest to you about where feelings should rank in your own life? How much importance do you place on your emotions?

8. **Connect to Today** In the modern world, do you think more decisions are made based on feelings or logic? Explain.

Literary Element Juxtaposition

In "since feeling is first," Cummings juxtaposes intellectual activity with emotional response.

1. Identify examples of juxtaposition in "since feeling is first." Explain how they support the theme.

2. How effective are these juxtapositions in conveying the speaker's meaning?

Reading Strategy Paraphrase

When you **paraphrase**, you completely restate the original text in your own words. Refer to the chart you made on page 560 and answer these questions.

1. What main idea does Cummings try to communicate in "since feeling is first"?

2. Support your opinion by paraphrasing at least two quotations from the poem.

Vocabulary Practice

Practice with Analogies Choose the word that best completes each analogy.

1. syntax : language :: etiquette :
   a. eating   b. grammar   c. behavior

2. parenthesis : continuation :: acceptance :
   a. rejection   b. welcoming   c. punctuation

Writing

Write an Essay Poets often juxtapose seemingly unlike things and use metaphors to compare them. Write a short essay in which you identify and explain the juxtapositions and metaphors for emotion and reason that Cummings uses in "since feeling is first."

LOG ON **Literature** Online

Selection Resources For Selection Quizzes, eFlashcards, and Reading-Writing Connection activities, go to glencoe.com and enter QuickPass code GL59794u3.

Before You Read

Horses Graze

Meet Gwendolyn Brooks
(1917–2000)

"I want to write poems," said Gwendolyn Brooks, "that I could take . . . into the street, into the halls of a housing project." Witty, original, and sometimes outspoken, Brooks was one of the most respected American poets of the twentieth century. Brooks captured the hopes of urban African Americans, as well as their feelings of rage and despair in the face of racism and poverty.

An Early Love of Poetry Many characters in Brooks's poems are based on people who lived in her neighborhood on Chicago's South Side. Brooks knew the South Side intimately, having spent most of her life there. She was born to parents who had little money but who did have a deep love of literature and high expectations for their children. When Brooks, at age seven, brought her mother her first poems, her mother said, "You are going to be the lady Paul Laurence Dunbar," referring to a prominent African American poet.

> "If you love songs and rap, you love poetry."
>
> —Gwendolyn Brooks

By the time she was sixteen, Brooks had written more than seventy-five poems, and she had met two of the leading African American writers of her day, Langston Hughes and James Weldon Johnson. Both writers encouraged her to continue writing. Hughes became her friend and mentor. With the publication of her second book, *Annie Allen*, Brooks became the first African American writer to win the Pulitzer Prize for poetry. Brooks later became Poet Laureate of Illinois, poetry consultant to the Library of Congress, and a member of the National Women's Hall of Fame.

In her early books, Brooks chronicled the dreams and disappointments of everyday African Americans using traditional verse forms such as the ballad and the sonnet. In the 1960s, Brooks's poetry underwent an immense change in tone and content. Inspired by African American activism, Brooks began to write more overtly political poems. "This is not time for sonnets," she once said, "but a time for raw, ragged free verse."

As Blyden Jackson notes, Brooks's poems brim with "insights and revelations of universal application." They speak to the human condition and to all citizens of the world.

Author Search For more about Gwendolyn Brooks, go to glencoe.com and enter QuickPass code GL59794u3.

Literature and Reading Preview

Connect to the Poem
How do the concerns of animals compare with those of humans? Make lists of concerns for animals and for humans.

Build Background
Horses are hoofed, plant-eating mammals. They have wide, flat teeth for grinding grasses and other plants and long foot bones that enable swift running. For centuries, horses were used extensively in warfare, agriculture, and transportation.

Set Purposes for Reading

Big Idea Loves and Losses

As you read, ask yourself, What might the poem be saying about human flaws and foibles?

Literary Element Repetition

Repetition is a literary device in which sounds, words, phrases, lines, or stanzas are repeated for emphasis. Writers use repetition to emphasize an important point, to expand an idea, or to help create rhythm. Repetition increases the unity of a work. As you read the poem, ask yourself, What are examples of repetition and what ideas do they reinforce?

Reading Strategy Draw Conclusions About Meaning

When you draw conclusions, you use pieces of information to make a general statement about people, places, events, and ideas. When you **draw conclusions about** a poem's **meaning**, you look at details throughout the poem and decide what the author wanted to say through these details.

Tip: **Record Details** As you read, record details and use them to draw conclusions. Use a diagram similar to the one below.

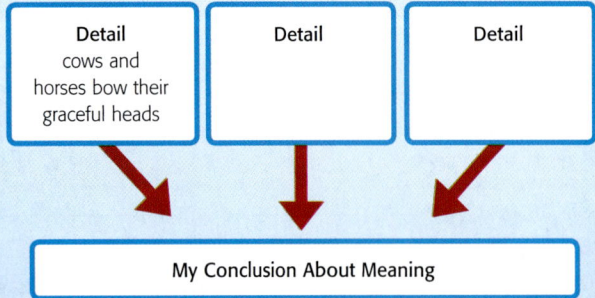

Learning Objectives

For pages 563–567

In studying this text, you will focus on the following objectives:

Literary Study: Analyzing repetition.

Reading: Drawing conclusions about meaning.

Writing: Writing a summary.

Vocabulary

oblivion (ə bliv′ē ən) *n.* a lack of awareness or memory; p. 565 *After the song's popularity passed, the group was consigned to oblivion.*

crest (krest) *n.* a peak, high point, or climax; p. 566 *Leah's joy was at its crest; she had never been happier.*

affirmation (af′ər mā′shən) *n.* positive agreement or judgment; p. 566 *As she bent down towards the child, the mother's face shone with affirmation.*

Tip: **Word Usage** Select words carefully, always keeping their specific usage in mind. For example, even though *grazing* means "eating" you would not thank your hosts for grazing at their dinner table.

Horses Graze

Gwendolyn Brooks

Indo-Aryan Pottery Horses, ca. 2000 BC.

Cows graze.
Horses graze.
They
eat
5   eat
eat.
Their graceful heads
are bowed
bowed
10 bowed
in majestic[1] **oblivion**.
They are nobly oblivious
to your follies,
your inflation,[2]

1. Here, *majestic* means "a quality of dignified greatness."
2. *Inflation* is an economic condition that occurs when consumer prices continuously rise or the purchasing power of money continuously declines; it can also mean "pomposity" or "empty pretentiousness."

Repetition *What does the repetition of* eat *and* bowed *help the author to stress?*

Draw Conclusions About Meaning *What does this detail contribute to the meaning of the poem?*

Vocabulary

oblivion (ə blivˊē ən) *n.* a lack of awareness or memory

15 the knocks and nettles³ of administration.
They
eat
eat
eat.
20 And at the **crest** of their brute satisfaction,
with wonderful gentleness, in **affirmation**,
they lift their clean calm eyes and they lie down
and love the world.
They speak with their companions.
25 They do not wish that they were
    otherwise.
Perhaps they know that creature
    feet may press
only a few earth inches at a time,
that earth is anywhere earth,
that an eye may see,
30 wherever it may be,
the Immediate arc, alone, of life,
    of love.
In Sweden,
China,
Afrika,
35 in India or Maine
the animals are sane;
they know and know and know
there's ground below
and sky
40 up high.

3. A *knock* is a sharp blow or hit. A *nettle* is a weedy plant that releases a substance irritating to the skin; metaphorically, nettle can be anything that irritates.

Landscape with Horses, 18th–19th century. Yi Myong-Gi. Ink and coloured paper. Musée Guimet Paris.

Vocabulary

crest (krest) *n.* a peak, high point, or climax
affirmation (af′ ər mā′shən) *n.* positive agreement or judgment

After You Read

Respond and Think Critically

Respond and Interpret

1. What image or description in the poem did you find most striking? Explain.

2. (a) How does the speaker describe the animals in lines 7–11? (b) Explain what you think the speaker means by "bowed / in majestic oblivion."

3. (a) According to the speaker, what do the animals "know," and in what way are they "sane"? (b) What might the poet be implying here?

Analyze and Evaluate

4. Brooks uses only a few words to describe people. Why might she have chosen the word *inflation*? Explain its meaning in the poem's context.

5. (a) What does the speaker think people could learn from animals? (b) Do you agree? Explain.

Connect

6. **Big Idea** **Loves and Losses** (a) What does this poem suggest to you about what is truly important in life? (b) What does it suggest about the things that all people, and all creatures, have in common? Explain your answer.

7. **Connect to the Author** How does this poem reveal Brooks's commitment to activism and social change?

Literary Element Repetition

In poetry, **repetition** can emphasize words or ideas and can add a musical quality to the work.

1. Identify three examples of repetition in the poem.

2. For each example, answer these questions. What rhythmic or musical quality does the repetition have? How is it distributed throughout the poem? What ideas or meanings are reinforced?

Reading Strategy Draw Conclusions About Meaning

When the main idea of a poem is not directly stated, the poem's meaning must be drawn from the details. Refer to the diagram you made while reading the poem to help you answer the following.

1. What conclusion can you draw from the details in lines 24–31?

2. What conclusion can you draw from the details in lines 32–40?

Vocabulary Practice

Practice with Usage Respond to these statements to help you explore the meanings of vocabulary words from the selection.

1. Name two characteristics of a state of **oblivion**.

2. Describe what you might feel at the **crest** of a successful pursuit.

3. Identify two things you might say in **affirmation**.

LOG ON **Literature** Online

Selection Resources For Selection Quizzes, eFlashcards, and Reading-Writing Connection activities, go to glencoe.com and enter QuickPass code GL59794u3.

 Writing

Write a Summary Write a summary of "Horses Graze," making sure that you convey the poem's essential meaning. For help with summarizing, see page 51.

Before You Read

Parlor

Meet Rita Dove
(born 1952)

"One can be a poet, but you have to have a life," poet Rita Dove says. "If you don't have a life, then I don't see where you're going to write your poems from." In order to inspire her own poetry, Dove devotes her time to many pursuits, including music, singing, and dancing.

> "All the moments that make up a human being have to be written about, talked about, painted, danced, in order to really talk about life."
>
> —Rita Dove

Finding Her Voice Dove was born in the industrial city of Akron, Ohio, to a middle-class family. Her father was the first African American research chemist at a nationally prominent tire manufacturer. Dove's parents encouraged her to read, and as she says, "Going to the library was the one place we got to go without asking really for permission." Dove began writing at an early age, but she did not think she could have a career writing poetry. As she explains, "I didn't know writers could be real live people, because I never knew any writers." Fortunately, Dove had a high school English teacher who noticed her talent and invited her to a writer's conference. There her deep interest in literary endeavors took hold, and Dove went on to study poetry in college and in Germany on a prestigious Fulbright scholarship. She attended the highly esteemed University of Iowa Writers' Workshop, where she met her husband, the German writer Fred Viebahn.

A Champion for Poetry Many of Dove's poems revolve around trying to understand history, family, and a sense of one's place. Her most famous work, *Thomas and Beulah,* is a re-creation of her grandparents' lives from the 1920s to the 1960s. The book earned Dove a Pulitzer Prize.

Dove has enjoyed much success as a poet. She served as Poet Laureate of the United States from 1993 to 1995, the youngest person and the first African American to do so. For Dove, the position "offers someone as a spokesperson for literature and poetry in this country. It means that one becomes an automatic role model." Dove's works have proven to appeal to a wide audience. She has read her poetry at a White House State dinner and also on the popular children's television show *Sesame Street.* In 2004 she published the poetry collection *American Smooth.* She currently works as the Commonwealth Professor of English at the University of Virginia in Charlottesville.

Author Search For more about Rita Dove, go to glencoe.com and enter QuickPass code GL59794u3.

Literature and Reading Preview

Connect to the Poem
Have you ever disagreed with someone about an important topic? Freewrite for a few minutes about your experience.

Build Background
Transistor radios were popular in the 1950s and 1960s. These lightweight radios ran on batteries and were small enough to hold in the hand or fit in a pocket.

Set Purposes for Reading

Big Idea **Loves and Losses**

As you read, ask yourself, What lessons does the speaker learn from his or her grandmother's life and death?

Literary Element **Imagery**

Imagery is descriptive language that appeals to one or more of the five senses: sight, hearing, touch, taste, and smell. This use of sensory detail helps create an emotional response in the reader. As you read "Parlor," ask yourself, How does Dove's imagery contribute to the meaning of the poem?

Reading Strategy **Interpret Imagery**

Writers use imagery to help the reader respond emotionally to their work. When you **interpret imagery,** you form a picture in your mind's eye of the images the writer has painted with words. As you read, ask yourself, How does the imagery that Dove uses help you understand the speaker's ideas?

Tip: Summarize Try visualizing the setting that Dove has created in the poem by summarizing each stanza using your own words and by drawing on the images created in your mind's eye. To help develop your thoughts use a graphic organizer like the one below for each stanza.

> **Stanza 1**
> We passed through
> on the way to anywhere else.
> No one lived there
> but silence, a pale china gleam,

- Summarize stanza's meaning: _____
- Summarize images within the stanza: _____

Learning Objectives

For pages 568–571

In studying this text, you will focus on the following objectives:

Literary Study: Analyzing imagery.

Reading: Interpreting imagery.

Vocabulary

china (chī′nə) *n.* fine, glossy pottery used for tableware; p. 570 *I washed and dried the china after we ate dinner.*

aglow (ə glō′) *adj.* glowing; p. 570 *The house was so aglow with lights, she could see into every room.*

Tip: Context Clues Some context clues may become clear only after you read an entire paragraph, stanza, or poem. Especially in a short poem, use the overall meaning or theme with context clues to help you understand unfamiliar words.

RITA DOVE **569**

Two Tea Cups. Kari Van Tine.

Parlor
Rita Dove

We passed through
on the way to anywhere else.
No one lived there
but silence, a pale **china** gleam,

5   and the tired eyes of saints
aglow on velvet.

Mom says things are made
to be used. But Grandma insisted
peace was in what wasn't there,
10 strength in what was unsaid.

It would be nice to have a room
you couldn't enter, except in your mind.
I like to sit on my bed
plugged into my transistor radio,
15 "Moon River" pouring through my
      head.

How do you *use* life?
How do you *feel* it? Mom says

things harden with age; she says
Grandma is happier now. After the
      funeral,
20 I slipped off while they stood around
remembering—away from all
the talking and eating and weeping

to sneak a peek. She wasn't there.
Then I understood why
25 she had kept them just so:

so quiet and distant,
the things that she loved.

Vocabulary
china (chī′nə) *n.* fine, glossy pottery used for tableware
aglow (ə glō′) *adj.* glowing

Loves and Losses *What does this statement tell you about the beliefs of the speaker's grandmother with regard to love and loss?*

After You Read

Respond and Think Critically

Respond and Interpret

1. The speaker seems to think that it's best to keep the things you love at a distance. Do you agree? Why or why not?

2. (a) What do the speaker's mother and grandmother disagree about? (b) How would you characterize the speaker's grandmother?

3. (a) How do you interpret the speaker's mother saying "things harden with age"? (b) What does the mother's view say about her?

Analyze and Evaluate

4. (a) How does Dove establish setting in this poem? (b) Do you think that her establishment of setting is effective?

5. Where does the ending of the poem take place? What clues lead you to think that this is the setting?

Connect

6. **Big Idea** Loves and Losses What does the speaker come to realize about loves and losses at the end of the poem? How does he or she come to realize this?

7. **Connect to Today** How do people today use their houses? Are there still formal rooms that are rarely used, or do people live in all of the rooms of a house? Explain.

Literary Element   Imagery

Many writers use **imagery** to evoke an emotional response from their readers. Imagery often appeals to one or more of the five senses.

1. How does the imagery in the poem appeal to your senses?

2. Is Dove's use of imagery effective in "Parlor"? Explain.

Reading Strategy   Interpret Imagery

When you **interpret imagery,** you determine the deeper meaning of images. Review the chart you made on page 569 and answer the following questions.

1. What main message do you think the poet is trying to convey in "Parlor"?

2. How does the imagery support the meaning of the poem?

LOG ON   Literature Online

Selection Resources For Selection Quizzes, eFlashcards, and Reading-Writing Connection activities, go to glencoe.com and enter QuickPass code GL59794u3.

Vocabulary Practice

Practice with Context Clues Identify the context clues in the following sentences that help you determine the meaning of each boldfaced vocabulary word.

1. They received a set of **china** for their wedding, and they used it every night for dinner.

2. The lights on the computer were **aglow**, so she knew it was on.

Writing

Write a Description Do you, or does someone you know, have a room filled with beloved things? Write a description of the room and its contents. Use sensory details and imagery to create an emotional response in the reader. Order your description spatially, telling about the objects in the order one would encounter them while walking through the room.

Before You Read

Secondhand Grief

Meet Sherman Alexie
(born 1966)

Sherman Alexie has overcome medical issues and the poverty of a reservation to become one of the preeminent Native American authors of our time.

An Early Love of Literature Alexie learned to read by the age of three. When he was only five years old, he was reading tomes such as John Steinbeck's *Grapes of Wrath*. However, Alexie's love of literature isolated him from other children on the Spokane, Washington, reservation where his family lived.

Alexie decided to attend high school away from the reservation, where he hoped to obtain a better education than his parents had received. While at Reardan High, he excelled in academics and became a basketball star. Additionally, he was the only American Indian to attend the school during his time there.

> "If I were a doctor, nobody would be inviting me to talk to reservations... Writers can influence more people."
> —Sherman Alexie

Alexie attended Gonzaga University in Spokane on a scholarship. In his junior year, he transferred to Washington State University in Pullman. Alexie planned to become a doctor until he fainted several times in a human anatomy class and decided to switch majors. Alexie enrolled in a poetry workshop, and he excelled at writing. With his teacher's encouragement, he decided to make a career of it.

Same Passion, Different Forms Alexie has published twenty books—most recently, a collection of poems titled *Dangerous Astronomy*. Alexie draws on his experience and perspective to tell stories about modern American Indian life. He addresses themes of displacement, loss, and love, while challenging audiences to look past clichéd portrayals of American Indians in mass media. His characters strive for meaningful lives in the face of racism and economic disadvantage.

Alexie reaches out to audiences in a variety of media. He co-authored a screenplay based on one of his short stories, which became an award-winning, independent motion picture, *Smoke Signals*. The film is the first feature film entirely written, directed, produced, and acted by American Indians. Alexie also mentors young film writers through the Sundance Institute and judges a variety of writing contests.

Author Search For more about Sherman Alexie, go to glencoe.com and enter QuickPass code GL59794u3.

Literature and Reading Preview

Connect to the Poem
How connected do you feel to other people in your community? Write a journal entry about friendships or connections you have with people in your community.

Build Background
Alexie frequently writes about the conflicting desires and emotions felt by characters who leave their homes or societies to live elsewhere. In these new places, they may feel alienated and alone yet may also have opportunities.

Set Purposes for Reading

Big Idea Loves and Losses

As you read, ask yourself, How does Alexie highlight the character's loneliness among a sea of people?

Literary Element Diction

Diction is a writer's choice of words. Diction is an important element in the writer's voice or style. Understanding why authors choose some words over others will help you understand the tone and meaning of a poem. As you read, ask yourself, How does Alexie's careful choice of words affect how I interpret the poem and its speaker?

Reading Strategy Visualize

When you **visualize**, you picture a writer's ideas or descriptions in your mind's eye. Poets often show action without using cause-and-effect descriptions. As you read, ask yourself, What are five actions that the main character takes in the present?

Tip: Create a Flow Chart Use a chart like the one below to capture the poet's images as a sequence of events.

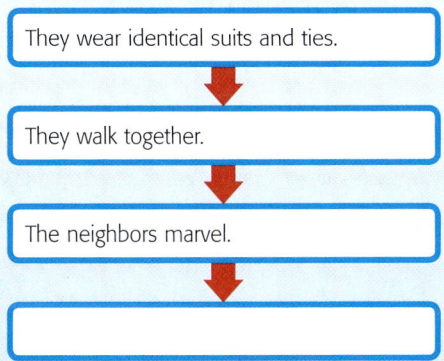

Learning Objectives

For pages 572–575

In studying this text, you will focus on the following objectives:

Literary Study: Analyzing diction.

Reading: Visualizing.

Vocabulary

nostalgic (nos tal′jik) *adj.* longing for persons, things, or situations from the past; p. 574 *The old man was nostalgic for the music of his youth.*

marvel (mär′vəl) *v.* to become filled with wonder or astonishment; p. 574 *The young girl marveled at the dolls in the toy store.*

Tip: Word Origins In the dictionary, a word's origins usually appear in square brackets. Root words appear in italics.

Décalcomanie, 1966. René Magritte. Oil on canvas, 81 x 100 cm. Private collection. © ARS, NY

Secondhand Grief

Sherman Alexie

After his father dies
The son wears his clothes.

First, the black shoes
then the wool pants

5   and finally the blazer
with **nostalgic** lapels.

When he was a child
walking with his father

both of them wearing
10 identical suits and ties

the neighbors **marveled**
at how much they looked alike.

A thousand miles away
from his father's grave

15 He steps into his favorite overcoat
and then steps outside

to walk among fathers
and sons, strangers

strangers, strangers
20 strangers, strangers

strangers, strangers
strangers, all of them.

Diction What does the author's choice of "blazer" say about the father?

Loves and Losses Besides invoking the loss of a father, what other loss might the poet be referring to here?

Vocabulary

nostalgic (nos tal′ jik) *adj.* longing for persons, things, or situations from the past

marvel (mär′ vəl) *v.* to become filled with wonder or astonishment

After You Read

Respond and Think Critically

Respond and Interpret

1. How do you feel about the idea of following in the footsteps of someone in your family?
2. (a) Who does the son walk among? (b) How does the son feel about walking among these people?
3. (a) How far away from his family has the son moved? (b) What kind of environment does Alexie suggest the main character now lives in?

Analyze and Evaluate

4. How does Alexie use descriptions of clothing worn by the characters to suggest loss?
5. How does the author use images of clothing to suggest a change within the son?

Connect

6. **Big Idea** Loves and Losses Alexie suggests that the main character has lost not just his father, but also his connection to his heritage. Explain.
7. **Connect to Today** In the modern world, young people are increasingly likely to move far away from their families and the places where they were raised. Do you think these people are likely to identify with the sentiments expressed in "Secondhand Grief"? Why or why not?

Literary Element Diction

Especially in poetry, where authors must convey much meaning in fewer words, **diction** can provide clues to attitude and meaning.

1. Without using verbs, Alexie paints a picture of a man getting dressed. What three transitions does he use to keep those images moving?
2. What shift in words does Alexie use to describe his character's increasing dislocation?

Reading Strategy Visualize

When you **visualize,** you can better understand the action in a text. Visualizing can also help you remember information. Review the chart you made on page 573 and answer the following questions.

1. What kind of scene do you visualize when reading the last eight lines of the poem?
2. Does the repetition of "strangers" help you visualize them? Explain.

Literature Online

Selection Resources For Selection Quizzes, eFlashcards, and Reading-Writing Connection activities, go to glencoe.com and enter QuickPass code GL59794u3.

Vocabulary Practice

Practice with Word Origins Studying the etymology, or origin and history, of a word can help you better understand and explore its meaning. Create a word map, like the one below, for each of these vocabulary words from the selection.

nostalgic   marvel

EXAMPLE:

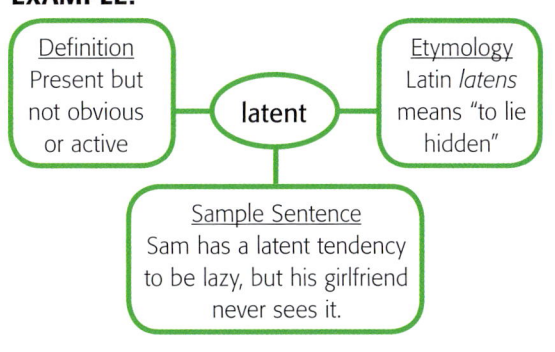

Writing

Write a Dialogue Write a dialogue between the child and his father as they are out walking, "both of them wearing identical suits and ties." Instead of identifying each speaker when reporting his words, use differences in diction and sentence structure that will allow readers to know who is talking.

Before You Read

Ballad of Birmingham

Meet Dudley Randall
(1914–2000)

A man whose first poem was published when he was only thirteen, Dudley Randall later started a publishing company with just twelve dollars. His tireless work and dedication brought recognition to a generation of African American writers.

The Broadside Dudley Randall is widely renowned for founding Broadside Press in 1965. This successful firm got its name from Randall's printing of his poem "Ballad of Birmingham" on a single sheet of paper, known in publishing lingo as a "broadside." Randall followed up that poem with another of his, "Dressed All in Pink," then continued the series with broadside printings of previously published work by Margaret Walker and Robert Hayden.

> "A poet writes about what he feels, what agitates his heart and sets his pen in motion."
>
> —Dudley Randall

Broadside Press then began to publish poetry collections, like Randall's *Poem Counterpoem,* co-written with Margaret Esse Danner, *Cities Burning, Love You,* and *More to Remember.* By bringing into the literary spotlight such prominent writers as Alice Walker, Amiri Baraka, and Sonia Sanchez, Broadside Press proved itself to be an important and immensely valuable resource for a number of minority writers.

Before Birmingham Born in Washington, D.C., Randall grew up in Detroit after a series of family migrations. Over the years, he was a foundry worker, a soldier in the South Pacific during World War II, a postal worker, and a librarian.

The Mind of a Poet "The Ballad of Birmingham" is the most famous of Randall's poems, many of which were written during the tumultuous period of the Civil Rights Movement in the United States. The collection *Cities Burning* is a response to the Detroit race riot of 1967. Brought about in part by police brutality toward African Americans, the chaos lasted for five days. Forty-three people died and more than seven thousand people were arrested.

His Legacy Randall's success as a poet grew while he was a poet in residence at the University of Detroit and during his later appointment as poet laureate of Detroit in 1981. The National Endowment for the Arts awarded Randall a Lifetime Achievement Award in 1996.

Author Search For more about Dudley Randall, go to glencoe.com and enter QuickPass code GL59794u3.

Literature and Reading Preview

Connect to the Poem
Have you ever read or heard about a tragic event? Write a list of ways you could respond creatively to a tragic event.

Build Background
Birmingham was the site of much racial turbulence during the U.S. Civil Rights Movement. "Ballad of Birmingham" is a response to the September 15, 1963, dynamite bombing of the Sixteenth Street Baptist Church, which killed four African American girls.

Set Purposes for Reading

Big Idea **Loves and Losses**

As you read, ask yourself, How does Randall put a human face on historical facts, particularly the loss of loved ones throughout the Civil Rights Movement?

Literary Element **Narrative Poetry**

Narrative poetry is verse that tells a story. A literary ballad, such as "Ballad of Birmingham," usually recounts an exciting or a dramatic episode. As you read, ask yourself, How does Randall's choice of the ballad form help him effectively tell this story?

Reading Strategy **Apply Background Knowledge**

What you learn when you read is connected in part to what you already know. **Applying background knowledge** to your reading of a text can help you better understand and interpret it. As you read "Ballad of Birmingham," ask yourself, What do I already know about this event?

Tip: Take Notes It might be useful to create a chart like the one below to keep track of what you know about the subject.

Detail	Background Knowledge
Birmingham	a city in Alabama; the site of activity during the Civil Rights Movement

Learning Objectives

For pages 576–581

In studying this text, you will focus on the following objectives:

Literary Study: Analyzing poetry.

Reading: Applying background knowledge.

Landscape, 2006. Julian Cifuentes. Oil on canvas.

DUDLEY RANDALL

Ballad of Birmingham

Dudley Randall

"Mother dear, may I go downtown
instead of out to play,
and march the streets of Birmingham
in a freedom march today?"

5 "No, baby, no, you may not go,
for the dogs are fierce and wild,
and clubs and hoses, guns[1] and jails
ain't good for a little child."

"But, mother, I won't be alone.
10 Other children will go with me,
and march the streets of Birmingham
to make our country free."

"No, baby, no, you may not go,
for I fear those guns will fire.
15 But you may go to church instead,
and sing in the children's choir."

1. *Clubs, hoses,* and *guns* were common weapons used by police and military troops to frighten and suppress demonstrators during peace and civil rights marches.

Apply Background Knowledge *What information do you know about churches in Birmingham?*

Sunday Best, 20th century. Ben Watson III. Watercolor. Private collection.

She has combed and brushed her nightdark hair,
and bathed rose petal sweet,
and drawn white gloves on her small brown hands,
20   and white shoes on her feet.

The mother smiled to know her child
was in the sacred place,
but that smile was the last smile
to come upon her face.

25   For when she heard the explosion,
her eyes grew wet and wild.
She raced through the streets of Birmingham
calling for her child.

She clawed through bits of glass and brick,
30   then lifted out a shoe.
"O, here's the shoe my baby wore,
but, baby, where are you?"

Narrative Poetry *How does this stanza contribute to Randall's storytelling?*

After You Read

Respond and Think Critically

Respond and Interpret

1. (a) How did you feel at the end of the poem? (b) What about the poem made you feel this way?

2. (a) What does the child want to do at the beginning of the poem? (b) Why is this a significant detail?

3. (a) Why does the mother smile? (b) How is this an ironic moment?

Analyze and Evaluate

4. In what way does the fifth stanza paint an effective picture of youth and innocence? Explain.

5. (a) How does the structure of the dialogue in the final stanza differ from the structure of the dialogue earlier in the poem? (b) How does this affect the emotional impact of the poem?

Connect

6. **Big Idea** Loves and Losses "Ballad of Birmingham" depicts a family tragedy against the backdrop of an important historical period. What might Randall be trying to say about the Civil Rights Movement?

7. **Connect to Today** How do artists today respond to tragic events?

Literary Element Narrative Poetry

Narrative poetry comes in many forms, including ballads, epics, and shorter works that focus on a specific event. "Ballad of Birmingham" takes the ballad form, which is usually made up of several ballad stanzas, a common four-line structure that is part of a long tradition in English poetry.

1. Read about ballad in the Literary Terms Handbook on page R3. How does "Ballad of Birmingham" demonstrate characteristics of a ballad?

2. Does "Ballad of Birmingham" have a traditional narrative structure? Explain and cite examples from the poem to support your opinion.

Review: Rhyme and Rhyme Scheme

As you learned on page 469, **rhyme** is the repetition of the same stressed vowel sounds and any succeeding sounds in two or more words. End rhyme occurs at the ends of lines of poetry. **Rhyme scheme** is the pattern that end rhymes form in a stanza or poem. The rhyme scheme of a poem can be determined by designating a different letter of the alphabet to each new rhyme. In a ballad stanza, only the second and fourth lines rhyme.

Partner Activity With a partner, take turns reading Randall's poem aloud. Listen for the rhyme scheme. Then determine the rhyme scheme by assigning letters to the end of each line. Does the rhyme scheme follow the pattern of the ballad stanza throughout the poem? Create a chart like the one shown below. Use it to help you and your partner as you discuss the question and determine the rhyme scheme of the poem stanza by stanza.

Stanza	End Words	Rhyme Pattern
1	downtown	a
	play	b
	Birmingham	c
	today	d

Reading Strategy **Apply Background Knowledge**

"Ballad of Birmingham" blends historical fact and fiction. To understanding the full meaning of the poem, it is essential to **apply background knowledge**. Refer to the chart you made on page 577 and answer the following questions.

1. If you did not already know about the Birmingham church bombing, would you have interpreted the poem differently? Explain.

2. How did your background knowledge of the church bombing and the Civil Rights Movement affect your response to this poem.

Academic Vocabulary

A literary critic might say Randall's poem is meant to **convince** *the reader that there was no safe place for the child to be.*

Convince is an academic word. Familiar words that are similar in meaning are *persuade* and *prove to*. To study this word further, fill out the graphic organizer below.

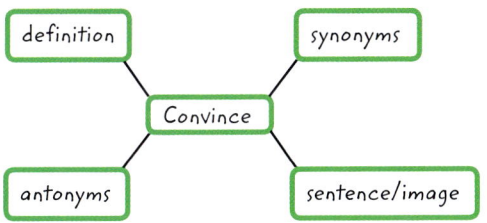

For more on academic vocabulary, see pages 52 and 53.

Speaking and Listening

 Speech

Assignment "Ballad of Birmingham" presents a grim event in our nation's history. What is the poem's message or theme? Deliver a speech in which you explain the lessons that can be learned from the poem.

Prepare Develop a thesis that states the theme of the poem. Select exact words and phrases from the poem to support your thesis. Outline your speech, beginning with a hook to engage your audience and a statement of your thesis. Follow with reasons and evidence that explain and support your thesis while persuading your reader to interpret the theme as you do.

Deliver Make eye contact with your audience. Speak loudly and clearly so they can understand you. Maintain good posture to reflect your confidence. Use gestures as appropriate, and be sure your stance and movements show your engagement with your audience.

Evaluate Evaluate your speech with the following criteria. Provide examples of how well you met each of the criteria below.

Criterion	Example	My Rating
Nonverbal Techniques	• Made eye contact after stating my thesis and each main reason; • Used gestures to show first, second, and third most important reasons	Good to Excellent
Verbal Techniques		
Content and Clarity		

Literature Online

Selection Resources For Selection Quizzes, eFlashcards, and Reading-Writing Connection activities, go to glencoe.com and enter QuickPass code GL59794u3.

Media Workshop

Compare Media Genres

Learning Objectives

Pages 582–587

In this workshop, you will focus on the following objectives:

Media Literacy:
Comparing forms of media. Distinguishing between propaganda and ethical reasoning strategies. Explaining how text features, such as subheads, captions, and illustrations, aid the reader's understanding.

Literature Connection A 1963 news event—the bombing of the Sixteenth Street Baptist Church in Birmingham, Alabama—inspired Dudley Randall to write the poem "Ballad of Birmingham." Nearly three decades later, filmmaker Spike Lee cast a fresh perspective on this national tragedy in his film *4 Little Girls*. Both forms of media—the poem and the film—pay tribute to a historic moment in the Civil Rights Movement of the 1960s.

Forms of Media

Every day you are exposed to different kinds of media messages in a variety of **genres,** or forms. **Print media** convey messages through images and texts, such as newspapers, magazines, books, and billboards. **Electronic media** use sound and moving images to reach audiences. Radio, television, CDs, DVDs, movies, videotapes, documentary films, and the Internet are all forms of electronic media.

Each media genre has its own unique characteristics that determine the message and the way it affects you as a reader, listener, or viewer. Consider the difference between watching a short news report about a scientific discovery and reading a lengthy magazine article about the same discovery. Which media genre teaches you more? All media genres have strengths and weaknesses, and all are intended to stir a wide range of reactions among their audiences.

Strategies for Comparing Media Genres

All media messages are intended to shape the audience's attitudes. How the information is presented reflects the viewpoints, beliefs, or even biases of people who create the messages. The limitations of the media genre determine which of the many techniques can be used to craft a powerful and effective message. When comparing how different media genres cover or present information on the same topic or news event, look at what elements the genres have in common. Sources, language, images—these are elements you'll find in most print and electronic media. Also consider the genres' strengths: TV is a visual medium, radio is all about sounds, and newspapers are primarily text-based. Refer to the chart on the next page to help you analyze, or deconstruct, and compare media strategies and genres.

Media Literacy For project ideas, templates, and media analysis guides, go to glencoe.com and enter QuickPass code GL59794u3.

Strategy		Questions to Ask Yourself
source	✓	Who created this media message? Do the creators' viewpoints and biases affect the message? How believable is the evidence that the source presents to support the message?
purpose	✓	Why was this message created? To persuade? To entertain? To inform? Does the media genre help or hinder the purpose of the message?
language	✓	How is language used to deliver the message? Is the language formal? Informal? Technical? Does the language convey political or cultural ideas, trends, or beliefs?
target audience	✓	Is the message designed for a specific audience? Are stereotypes of people—such as children or teenagers—used to sway the reader, listener, or viewer? Does the media genre exclude certain audiences?
design elements and/or film techniques	✓	How do the creators visually compose the message? How is color, line, shape, or texture used? Do the creators use visual symbols that represent popular ideas or values? Are film techniques or special effects used to manipulate the audience's reaction?

> **Focus Lesson**

Persuasive Techniques: Logical Fallacies

The messages in many media genres are intended to get the viewer, listener, or reader to agree with a viewpoint or take a specific action. Some creators of messages use the persuasive technique of logical fallacy, or purposeful error in reasoning, to try to sway the audience. Logical fallacies can sometimes be used for humor (as in a funny ad campaign), but they are too often used for more serious purposes like propaganda—the use of ideas, information, or rumors to spread information or beliefs. Try to spot the following types of logical fallacies in all media genres:

- **overgeneralization** using sweeping statements with no reasonable supporting evidence as proof
- **either-or fallacy** presenting only two possible sides or solutions to an issue when there are more options
- **bandwagon** urging people to do something because everyone else is doing it
- **false cause** drawing a cause-and-effect relationship between two events that follow one after another but are completely unrelated
- *ad hominem* attacking someone personally to shift attention away from the person's views or ideas
- **red herring** purposely changing the subject in order to avoid the issue at hand

Activity
Create a Comparison Chart

Use the Media Strategies chart on this page as a guide to examine a news story from two different media genres—for example, a TV broadcast and a newsmagazine article. Create an expanded version of the chart in which you add a third and fourth column, one for each media genre you examine. Use the new columns to analyze the questions in the second column. Remember to choose an event that is appropriate to discuss in your classroom.

Media Genre: Radio Transcript

Build Background Since 1963, news coverage of the search for suspects involved in the bombing of the Sixteenth Street Baptist Church continued for decades. Over the years, radio, television, newsmagazines, and other media have all tracked the progress of this criminal investigation. The National Public Radio (NPR) transcript below from 2003 reflects on the impact of the bombing and reports on the men who were finally brought to justice.

16th Street Baptist Church Bombing

Forty Years Later, Birmingham Still Struggles with Violent Past

The bells of the 16th Street Baptist Church in Birmingham, Alabama, tolled Monday in remembrance of the four girls who were killed when a bomb exploded at the church on this day 40 years ago.

The church is still grappling with its place in history, Melanie Peeples reports. Just last year, the last living man believed responsible for the attack, Bobby Frank Cherry, was convicted of the crime.

The bomb exploded mid-morning, during Sunday services. Carolyn McKinstry, who was 14 years old at the time, was secretary of her Sunday school class. She was taking attendance records into the sanctuary when the bomb went off.

Source → The reporter uses an eyewitness as a source for the story. Notice that the reporter allows the source to describe what happened in her own words.

"I heard something that sounded, at first, a little like thunder and then just this terrific noise and the windows came crashing in," McKinstry told NPR in 2001. "And then a lot of screaming, just a lot of screaming and I heard someone say, 'Hit the floor.' And I remember being on the floor ... and it was real quiet."

Source → The reporter provides the key facts about the victims of the bombing.

The bomber had hidden under a set of cinder block steps on the side of the church, tunneled under the basement and placed a bundle of dynamite under what turned out to be the girls' rest room. The blast killed four girls: Cynthia Wesler, Carole Robertson and Addie Mae Collins—all 14—and 11-year-old Denise McNair. More than 20 others were injured, including Addie Mae's sister Sarah, who lost an eye in the attack.

Opinion → McKinstry uses reasons to support her opinion about why the bombers chose the 16th Street Baptist Church.

McKinstry says it was no accident that the Ku Klux Klan targeted the 16th Street Baptist Church. "It was the largest black church in Birmingham, but because of its central location it was used for a lot of other things, all kinds of meetings, national, local and so forth," she recalls.

584 UNIT 3 POETRY

The Byzantine-style structure, with two domed towers and a roomy basement auditorium, served as the hub for the mass meetings of the civil rights movement, drawing leaders like Martin Luther King Jr. Marchers would assemble at the church and then cross the street to demonstrate at Kelly Ingram Park, the site of violent clashes between Birmingham police and civil rights activists.

The brutal attack and the death of four girls rocked the nation and drew international attention to the violent struggle for civil rights in Birmingham. But despite the outrage and an intense FBI investigation, no one was charged in the crime. That was the real horror of it, according to McKinstry.

"These are friends of mine," she said. "And we come to Sunday school one day and they're gone. They're dead. They're just blown away and Birmingham goes on with business as usual."

It was more than a decade before state authorities took action. Then Attorney General Bill Baxley charged Klan leader Robert "Dynamite Bob" Chambliss with murder. In 1977, he was convicted.

Chambliss died in jail, never publicly admitting to the bombing. Baxley left office before he could pursue charges against Chambliss' suspected accomplices. One of them has since died.

Thirty-eight years after the bombing, Thomas Blanton Jr. was finally convicted of murder and sentenced to life in prison. A year later, in May 2002, Bobby Frank Cherry was also found guilty for the deaths of the four girls, and given a mandatory sentence of life in prison.

The 16th Street Baptist Church in Birmingham

Description
The reporter's vivid words help radio listeners visualize the church and its location.

Language
Notice the difference in word choices in this paragraph. The first two sentences are the reporter's retelling of the facts of the FBI investigation. The third sentence expresses McKinstry's personal reaction.

Objective Account
The reporter closes the news story with facts that inform listeners about the outcome of the criminal investigation.

Activity
Listening and Speaking

Meet in small groups to discuss the following questions:

1. What is the intended purpose of this news report?
2. Who is the target audience for the report?
3. How reliable is the one source quoted for this story? What other sources could the reporter have used?
4. If you were going to present this report on television, what kind of visuals would you include?

Media Genre: **Documentary**

Build Background When asked in an interview about why he made *4 Little Girls,* Spike Lee said, "African Americans are far too quick to want to forget. Consequently, we have a generation of black kids who think this is the way it always was—that we could always live where we wanted, eat where we wanted, have church where we wanted. We need to remember." His documentary mixes live footage filmed at the site of the bombing and its aftermath, as well as still photography from newspaper photographers and Birmingham citizens. A still photograph is a static image, like a picture you would take with a regular camera. Stills can also be taken from individual frames of a motion picture.

Composition

Notice how the wooden doorframe serves as a kind of frame within the photo: the rubble and damage are inside the church, but outside life continues on.

The destruction of the 16th Street Baptist Church was caused by a bomb that exploded in a basement room.

Cultural Symbol

By September 1963, Dr. Martin Luther King Jr. had become the face of the Civil Rights Movement. Notice how almost everyone in the crowd is watching him.

Dr. Martin Luther King Jr. spoke at the 1963 funeral service for the four girls killed in the Birmingham church bombing.

Film Technique

This photo is taken from a low angle, meaning the photographer was filming from below the subjects. This effect makes the subjects look bigger or more impressive. Notice the effect this angle has on the way you view the men holding hands and the large columns behind them.

Civil rights leaders clasp hands and sing at the 1963 memorial service held in New York City for the victims of the Birmingham bombing.

Film Technique

The photographer has taken this picture as if he is standing in line with the churchgoers. From this perspective, you see the rebuilt church from the point of view of the people returning to it. Notice what the people are wearing and how they are walking in an orderly line into the church.

In June 1964, members of the 16th Street Baptist Church return to the newly rebuilt church for the first time.

Activity

Listening and Speaking

Meet in small groups to discuss the following questions:

1. What was your reaction to the images from this documentary?
2. Do you get a sense of the creators' viewpoint or biases in either the radio broadcast or the documentary?
3. Which genre—the radio broadcast or the documentary—gives you more information about the church bombing?
4. Do you think visual images can tell a story better than a spoken or written version? Explain.

MEDIA WORKSHOP **587**

Historical Perspective
on "Ballad of Birmingham"

4 Little Girls

Roger Ebert, *Chicago Sun-Times*, October 24, 1997

Learning Objectives

For pages 588–590
In studying this text, you will focus on the following objectives:

Reading:
Evaluating evidence.
Analyzing informational text.

National Book Award Winner

Set a Purpose for Reading
Read to discover the plot of *4 Little Girls* and the history of the Birmingham, Alabama, church bombing.

Build Background
Roger Ebert is a renowned film critic and recipient of the Pulitzer Prize for criticism in 1975. He has reviewed films in print for the *Chicago Sun-Times* since 1967 and on television for the former program *Siskel and Ebert* and currently for *At the Movies with Ebert and Roeper*. In this review, Ebert praises Spike Lee's documentary film *4 Little Girls*.

Reading Strategy — Evaluate Evidence

Evaluating evidence is making a judgment or forming an opinion about the evidence an author uses to make a point or support an argument. Evaluating evidence also involves distinguishing between fact and opinion. As you read, use a chart like the one below to track facts and opinions.

Fact	Opinion
Four girls were killed in the bombing.	Denise McNair was "filled with charisma."

Spike Lee's *4 Little Girls* tells the story of the infamous Birmingham, Ala., church bombing of September 15, 1963, when the lives of an 11-year-old and three 14-year-olds, members of the choir, were ended by an explosion. More than any other event, that was the catalyst for the civil rights movement, the moment when all of America could look away no longer from the face of racism. "It was the awakening," says Walter Cronkite[1] in the film.

The little girls had gone to church early for choir practice, and we can imagine them, dressed in their Sunday best, meeting their friends in the room destroyed by the bomb. We can fashion the picture in our minds because Lee has, in a way, brought them back to life, through photographs, through old home movies and especially through the memories of their families and friends.

By coincidence, I was listening to the radio not long after seeing *4 Little Girls*, and I heard a report from Charlayne

---

1. *Walter Cronkite* (born 1916) was a *CBS Evening News* anchor from 1962 to 1981.

Hunter-Gault. In 1961, when she was 19, she was the first black woman to desegregate the University of Georgia. Today she is an NPR[2] correspondent. That is what happened to her. In 1963, Carole Robertson was 14, and her Girl Scout sash was covered with merit badges. Because she was killed that day, we will never know what would have happened in her life.

That thought keeps returning: The four little girls never got to grow up. Not only were their lives stolen, but so were their contributions to ours. I have a hunch that Denise McNair, who was 11 when she died, would have made her mark. In home movies, she comes across as poised and observant, filled with charisma. Among the many participants in the film, two of the most striking are her parents, Chris and Maxine McNair, who remember a special child.

Chris McNair talks of a day when he took Denise to downtown Birmingham, and the smell of onions frying at a store's lunch counter made her hungry. "That night I knew I had to tell her she couldn't have that sandwich because she was black," he recalls. "That couldn't have been any less painful than seeing her with a rock smashed into her head." Lee's film re-creates the day of the bombing through newsreel footage, photographs and eyewitness reports. He places it within a larger context of the Southern civil rights movement, and sit-ins and the arrests, the marches, the songs and the killings.

Birmingham was a tough case. Police commissioner Bull Connor is seen directing the resistance to marchers and traveling in an armored vehicle—painted white, of course. Gov. George Wallace makes his famous vow to stand in the schoolhouse door and personally bar any black students from entering. Though they could

Film producer and director Spike Lee talks about his film, *4 Little Girls*, during a reception on Capitol Hill in Washington, DC, February 11, 1998.

not know it, their resistance was futile after September 15, 1963, because the hatred exposed by the bomb pulled all of their rhetoric[3] and rationalizations out from under them.

Spike Lee[4] says he has wanted to make this film since 1983, when he read a *New York Times Magazine* article by Howell Raines about the bombing. "He wrote me asking permission back then," Chris McNair told me in an interview. "That was before he had made any of his films." It is perhaps good that Lee waited, because he is more of a filmmaker now, and events have supplied him a dénouement[5] in the conviction of a man named Robert Chambliss ("Dynamite Bob") as the bomber. He was, said Raines, who met quite a few, "the most pathological[6] racist I've ever encountered."

---

2. NPR, or *National Public Radio*, is a public radio network.
3. Here, *rhetoric* means "persuasive use of language."
4. *Spike Lee* (born 1957) is a filmmaker known for his provocative films, including *Do the Right Thing, Malcolm X*, and *Summer of Sam*.
5. *Dénouement* means "the outcome of a series of events."
6. Here, *pathological* means "diseased."

Birmingham Race Riot, 1964. Andy Warhol.

The other victims were Addie Mae Collins and Cynthia Wesley, both 14. In shots that are almost unbearable, we see the victims' bodies in the morgue. Why does Lee show them? To look full into the face of what was done, I think. To show racism its handiwork. There is a memory in the film of a burly white Birmingham policeman who after the bombing tells a black minister, "I really didn't believe they would go this far." The man was a Klansman,[7] the movie says, but in using the word "they" he unconsciously separates himself from his fellows. He wants to disassociate himself from the crime. So did others. Before long even Wallace was apologizing for his behavior and trying to define himself in a different light. There is a scene in the film where the former governor, now old and infirm,[8] describes his black personal assistant, Eddie Holcey, as his best friend. "I couldn't live without him," Wallace says, dragging Holcey in front of the camera, insensitive to the feelings of the man he is tugging over for display.

Why is that scene there? It's sort of associated with the morgue photos, I think. There is mostly sadness and regret at the surface in *4 Little Girls,* but there is anger in the depths, as there should be.

---

7. A *Klansman* is a member of the white supremacist organization the Ku Klux Klan.
8. Here, *infirm* means "feeble."

Respond and Think Critically

Respond and Interpret

1. Write a brief summary of the main ideas in this article before you answer the following questions. For help on writing a summary, see page 415.

2. Would you be interested in seeing the film *4 Little Girls*? Why or why not?

3. (a) What is the film *4 Little Girls* about? (b) What is different about documenting history on film versus other mediums?

4. (a) How does Spike Lee re-create the day of the Birmingham church bombing? (b) How does a documentary film director influence the message an audience receives from a film?

Analyze and Evaluate

5. Do you think Ebert supports his position that the Birmingham church bombing "was the catalyst for the civil rights movement"? What evidence does he present for his position?

6. (a) What images or moments in *4 Little Girls* does Ebert identify as ironic? (b) What does Ebert interpret Lee's message to be?

Connect

7. Both Dudley Randall's poem, "The Ballad of Birmingham," and Roger Ebert's film review of *4 Little Girls* make statements about the outcome of the Birmingham church bombing of 1963. What is similar about their messages? How are their messages different? In your opinion, which message is stronger? Explain.

8. **Connect to the Author** What special skills do you think Ebert—a professional film critic—brings to his review of a historically based film?

PART 3

Issues of Identity

Real Truth. Jerzy Kolacz.

View the Art Jerzy Kolacz believes that art plays a key role in self discovery. Consider the title and multiple images in this painting. How does this painting relate to the theme of identity and change?

BIG IDEA

Your identity is more than the clothes you wear, your interests, or your thoughts and emotions. Through all the changes of life, part of you does not change—that something by which you recognize yourself, no matter what. The poems in Part 3 deal with changing identity. As you read them, ask yourself, How have I changed in the last several years? What about me has not changed?

Learning Objectives

For pages 592–593

In studying this text, you will focus on the following objective:

Literary Study: Analyzing sound devices.

LITERARY FOCUS

Sound Devices

What makes poetry musical?

Most poems are written to be heard, like music, or to be imagined aloud in the reader's mind. The actor Ossie Davis said of Langston Hughes's work, "Langston Hughes belongs to whoever is listening. A possession in common, like the sights and sounds of a street corner hangout, or the barbershop debate over pretty girls, and baseball players: Open your ears and your heart if you've got one; Langston will walk right in and do the rest." As you read poetry, can you hear music in the words?

Distributed By Universal Press Syndicate. Reprinted with permission. All rights reserved.

Onomatopoeia

Onomatopoeia is the use of a word or phrase that imitates or suggests the sound of what it describes, like the words *moan* and *thump*. Which word in the poem below is an example of onomatopoeia?

I heard a fly buzz—when I died—
The Stillness in the Room
Was like the Stillness in the Air—
Between the Heaves of Storm—

—Emily Dickinson, *from "I Heard a Fly Buzz When I Died"*

Rhyme

Rhyme is the repetition of stressed vowel sounds and all the sounds that follow in two or more words. For example, *cat* and *hat* rhyme, as do *willowier* and *billowier*. Rhymes at the ends of lines of poetry are called **end rhymes.**

From what I've tasted of desire
I hold with those who favor fire.

—Robert Frost, *from "Fire and Ice"*

Rhyming words within one line are called **internal rhyme:**

> The mother *smiled* to know her *child*
>
> —Dudley Randall, *from "Ballad of Birmingham"*

Both end and internal rhymes can be **slant rhymes,** or rhymes that are close, but not exact.

Alliteration

Poets pay special attention to all the sounds in their lines. The term **alliteration** refers to consonant sounds that repeat at the beginnings of words. Notice the use of alliteration, the repetition of *w*, *s*, and *p* sounds, in these lines:

> when i watch you
> wrapped up like garbage
> sitting, surrounded by the smell
> of too old potato peels
>
> —Lucille Clifton, *from "Miss Rosie"*

Assonance

When the repeated sound is a vowel sound rather than a consonant sound, the sound device is called **assonance.** Listen for the ē sounds in this line:

> She bid *me* take love *easy*, as the *leaves* grow on the *tree;*
>
> —W. B. Yeats, *from "Down by the Salley Gardens"*

Literature and Reading For more about literary elements, go to glencoe.com and enter QuickPass code GL59794u3.

Consonance

Alliteration, described above, is actually a special kind of **consonance,** the repetition of consonant sounds before and after different vowel sounds. Note the repetition of the *s* and *l* sounds in the following line:

> She passed the salley gardens with little
>   snow-white feet.
>
> —W. B. Yeats, *from "Down by the Salley Gardens"*

In the following two lines, note the repetition of *f*, *wh*, and *th* sounds:

> From what I've tasted of desire
> I hold with those who favor fire.
>
> —Robert Frost, *from "Fire and Ice"*

Quickwrite

Using Onomatopoeia Describe your morning in sounds. Think about all of the sounds you hear when you wake up and get ready for school. Create a graphic organizer like the one shown and write words that you associate with your morning sounds. Then use your graphic organizer to guide you as you write a paragraph describing your morning. Include your examples of onomatopoeia.

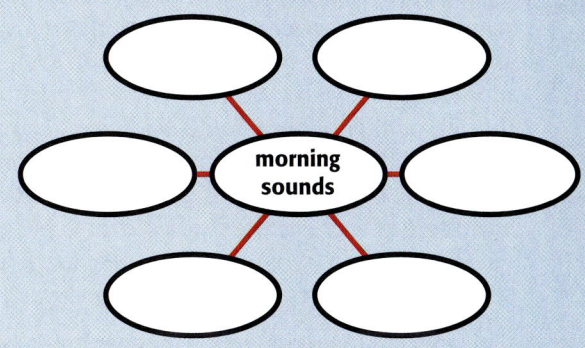

Before You Read

miss rosie

Meet **Lucille Clifton**
(born 1936)

Lucille Clifton has been compared to great poets such as Walt Whitman and Emily Dickinson. Her poems celebrate the everyday and the ordinary while revealing the complexities of life.

In her poems, Clifton often focuses on the struggles of people in the inner city. Despite gritty portrayals, Clifton's poems maintain a sense of hope and spiritual strength. Clifton's family history plays a large part in her ability to write about the pain of living while also offering a message about the ability to overcome: One of her female ancestors was kidnapped and brought to America against her will and another was the first African American female to be lynched in Virginia.

> "All of our stories become The Story. If mine is left out, something's missing."
> —Lucille Clifton

Humble Beginnings Clifton was born in New York during the Great Depression. Her father was a steel mill worker, and her mother worked as a laundress and homemaker. Clifton's mother also enjoyed writing poetry. Even though neither of her parents had been formally educated, they passed on an appreciation for learning. Clifton was prepared to enter college at the age of sixteen. She studied drama at Howard University and became an actor before seriously cultivating her interest in poetry.

Clifton's first book, a poetry collection titled *Good Times*, was published in 1969. It was hailed by the *New York Times* as one of the year's ten best books. Since then, Clifton has published several volumes of poetry. She has also written more than twenty children's books, including an award-winning fiction series about the life of a young African American boy named Everett Anderson.

Taking Her Place Clifton's many poems and stories have garnered her a rightful place among America's best writers. She has won many honors, including an Emmy Award, for her work. She was nominated for a Pulitzer Prize, becoming the first author to have two poetry books (*Next* and *Good Woman*) selected as finalists in the same year (1988).

Some of Clifton's major works of poetry include *Good News About the Earth, An Ordinary Woman, Quilting: Poems 1987–1990,* and *The Terrible Stories*. She also penned *Generations: A Memoir,* a work of prose focusing on her family's origins.

Author Search For more about Lucille Clifton, go to glencoe.com and enter QuickPass code GL59794u3.

Literature and Reading Preview

Connect to the Poem
What makes you like or dislike a person when you first meet him or her? With a partner, discuss how someone's first impression can affect you.

Build Background
Many of Clifton's poems examine roles and identities of women in society. Our roles in life change over time. Our identities are often related to our roles. For example, you might have roles as child, friend, sibling, and student.

Set Purposes for Reading

Big Idea Issues of Identity
As you read, ask yourself, How has the identity of Miss Rosie changed over time?

Literary Element Alliteration
Alliteration is the repetition of consonant sounds at the beginnings of words. The opening line of "miss rosie" is a good example of alliteration because it contains repeated *w* sounds.

"when i watch you"

Alliteration can help you picture what an author is trying to portray. As you read, ask yourself, How does Clifton's use of alliteration affect the text?

Reading Strategy Analyze Sensory Details
Sensory details are words that evoke one of the five senses for the reader. Recognizing these details can foster a deeper connection to a literary work. As you read, ask yourself, Which sensory details does Clifton use and which senses do they evoke?

Tip: Find Details Use a chart like the one below to record the sensory details in the poem and the senses they evoke.

Sensory Detail	Sense
"wrapped up like garbage"	sight, smell
"you wet brown bag of a woman"	touch, sight

> **Learning Objectives**
>
> *For pages 594–598*
>
> In studying this text, you will focus on the following objectives:
>
> **Literary Study:** Analyzing alliteration.
>
> **Reading:** Analyzing sensory details.

LUCILLE CLIFTON 595

Yellow Hat, 1936. Norman Lewis. Oil on burlap, 36½ x 26 in. Collection of Loide Lewis and the late Reginald Lewis.

View the Art How does the woman in the painting compare with your image of the speaker in the poem or with the young Miss Rosie?

miss rosie

Lucille Clifton

when i watch you
wrapped up like garbage
sitting, surrounded by the smell
of too old potato peels
5   or
when i watch you
in your old man's shoes
with the little toe cut out
sitting, waiting for your mind
10 like next week's grocery
i say
when i watch you
you wet brown bag of a woman
who used to be the best looking
    gal in georgia
15 used to be called the Georgia Rose
i stand up
through your destruction
i stand up

Alliteration How is this line a good example of alliteration?

Issues of Identity How does this description of Miss Rosie change her identity?

After You Read

Respond and Think Critically

Respond and Interpret

1. (a) How do you feel about Miss Rosie? (b) Did you feel differently about her at the end of the poem than you did at the beginning? Explain.

2. (a) How does Clifton describe Miss Rosie in lines 9–10? (b) What does this description imply about Miss Rosie?

3. (a) How does the speaker respond to Miss Rosie by the end of the poem? (b) In your opinion, what does the speaker think about Miss Rosie?

Analyze and Evaluate

4. (a) Write a short physical description of Miss Rosie, based on the details in the poem. (b) Do you think Clifton has given you enough details to go on?

5. In your opinion, does this poem present a stronger picture of Miss Rosie or of the speaker? Support your response with details from the poem.

Connect

6. **Big Idea** **Issues of Identity** In what ways does this poem relate to issues of identity? Explain and support your answer with evidence from the poem.

7. **Connect to the Author** Lucille Clifton's work is concerned with the history of violence against women, as well as the ability for people to overcome difficult times. How does "miss rosie" reflect those concerns?

Literary Element Alliteration

Alliteration is often used by poets who like working with the sounds of words. Although we often think of poems as only being read silently, poetry is also an oral art. Many poems are read aloud, and poets often enjoy reading their own poems aloud. In these cases, the sounds of the words become very important to the overall reception of the poem by the audience.

1. Where does Clifton use alliteration in this poem? Give two examples.

2. How does Clifton's use of alliteration enhance the use of sensory details in the poem? Explain your response.

Review: Metaphor

As you learned on page 468, a **metaphor** is a type of figurative language in which two seemingly unlike things are compared to reveal their underlying similarities. Unlike a simile, which states the comparison directly with the words *like* or *as,* the comparison in a metaphor is implied. Identifying and understanding the poet's metaphors is often vital to understanding the poem's meaning.

Partner Activity Work with a partner to identify the metaphor in Clifton's poem. Explain what is being compared in the metaphor. How does the metaphor function in the poem? Discuss this question with your partner.

Reading Strategy **Analyze Sensory Details**

Often an author will use **sensory details** to help the reader envision what the author is describing. The selection of sensory words gives the reader a positive, negative, or neutral view of the person, object, or event being described.

1. What do you think Clifton's purpose is when she chooses certain words to create sensory details?
2. In support of your opinion, list three sensory details from the poem.

Academic Vocabulary

Rosie's current condition arouses **intense** *feelings in the speaker, which are conveyed most forcefully in the poem's final lines.*

Intense is an academic word. In a more casual conversation, a speaker might describe a situation as **intense,** suggesting that it was fraught with tension or challenge or that it was extreme in some way. Using context clues and your knowledge of the poem, try to figure out the meaning of the word *intense* in the sentence above about Rosie. Check your guess in a dictionary.

Speaking and Listening

Oral Report

Assignment Present an oral report in response to the following: Ronald Baugham writes that "the poem . . . functions both as a lament for the woman destroyed and as a tribute to the new black woman who rises from the ashes of her predecessor's destruction."

Prepare Make a judgment about the quotation. Is the poem a lament? Is it a judgment? Identify exact words in the poem to support one or both claims. To get started, make a chart listing evidence.

Judgment	Evidence
lament for the woman destroyed	• "wrapped up like garbage" • "surrounded by the smell of too old potato peels"
tribute to the new black woman	

Use your chart to determine your thesis. Based on your evidence, formulate a statement in response to Baugham's claim. Write your report, and rehearse it several times by yourself and at least once with someone who can give you feedback. Incorporate the feedback, and rehearse again.

Report Analyze your audience and choose the best verbal and nonverbal techniques for both the audience and the occasion. Make eye contact as you state your thesis loudly and clearly. Use gestures to emphasize evidence that supports your thesis.

Evaluate Write a paragraph evaluating your presentation for its content (including the clarity and quality of your thesis, your organization, and your evidence) and delivery (including diction, eye contact, and gestures). Use the rubric on page 267 to help in your evaluation.

Literature Online

Selection Resources For Selection Quizzes, eFlashcards, and Reading-Writing Connection activities, go to glencoe.com and enter QuickPass code GL59794u3.

Before You Read

After Apple-Picking and Fire and Ice

Meet Robert Frost
(1874–1963)

Robert Frost won the highest admiration and respect throughout the twentieth century and was asked by President John F. Kennedy to read a poem, "The Gift Outright," at his inauguration.

Frost wanted his poetry to appeal to the general book-buying public rather than to find favor in literary circles. He wanted readers to look beyond the realism of the natural environment, seeking deeper meaning and significance in his poems.

Frost's life was based in skepticism and deep thought driven by a desire to achieve success as a poet. He was born in San Francisco but moved to New England at the age of eleven. While still in high school he developed a love of poetry, a passion he shared with his future wife and fellow student, Elinor White. Frost published his first poem, "My Butterfly: An Elegy," at twenty. The next year, he and Elinor were married.

> "Poetry is a process
> Poetry is the renewal of words
> Poetry is the dawning of an idea"
>
> —Robert Frost

His Own Man True to his unconventional path to acclaim as a writer, Frost had abandoned his college studies. He once explained that organized education was "never [his] taste." Instead he worked on a farm and at a variety of blue-collar jobs. Nonetheless, he continued to pursue his literary goals and eventually returned to college, this time as a teacher. His tenacity and ambition, motivation, and hardiness provided the essential characteristics underlying his many literary accomplishments.

Cultural Connections Frost spent much of his life in New England and used its natural environment and culture as the basis for his poetry. In his poetry, Frost used ordinary language that revealed complex feelings and undercurrents of doubt and uncertainty. Although Frost used traditional rhyme schemes, meter, and verse forms, his poems contain emotions and ideas linked typically to Modernist poets.

Frost was awarded Pulitzer Prizes for four books, including his *Collected Poems*. He was poet-in-residence for Harvard University, Amherst College, and Dartmouth University. Finally, he was the poetry consultant (now referred to as "poet laureate") to the Library of Congress from 1958 to 1959.

Author Search For more about Robert Frost, go to glencoe.com and enter QuickPass code GL59794u3.

Literature and Reading Preview

Connect to the Poems
How have your thoughts shaped who you are? Write a journal entry about where you fit in the world.

Build Background
Much of Robert Frost's work focuses on the lifestyle and landscape of rural New England, where he spent many years working on farms, teaching, and writing. His poems also explore such universal issues as war, love, death, and desire, often through the use of metaphor and symbol.

Set Purposes for Reading

Big Idea Issues of Identity

As you read the poems, ask yourself, Does the identity of the speaker change from one poem to the next?

Literary Element Assonance and Consonance

Assonance is the repetition of the same or similar vowel sounds. **Consonance** is the repetition of consonant sounds, typically within or at the end of nonrhyming words and preceded by different vowel sounds. As you read, ask yourself, Where does Frost use assonance and consonance and what effect does this create in the poems?

Reading Strategy Clarify Meaning

An author's meaning is not always obvious in a literary work. When you **clarify meaning,** you better understand what you are reading. Reread any confusing or challenging lines or examine how end punctuation signals a complete thought.

Tip: Find Alternative Meanings As you read, ask yourself, What other meanings might a phrase contain? Create a chart like the following, writing the line or phrase from the poem in the first column and an alternative meaning in the second.

Complete Phrase	Alternative Meaning
"Toward heaven still"	trying unsuccessfully to climb to heaven

Learning Objectives
For pages 599–605

In studying these texts, you will focus on the following objectives:

Literary Study: Analyzing assonance and consonance.

Reading: Clarifying meaning.

Vocabulary

bough (bou) *n.* a tree branch; p. 601 *Akim broke off a bough to chop for firewood, while Roman gathered smaller twigs for kindling.*

essence (es′əns) *n.* necessary characteristics of a thing; p. 601 *The essence of a democratic republic is having elected representatives.*

hoary (hôr′ē) *adj.* white or gray with age; covered with frost; p. 601 *The old, dusty photographs had a hoary sheen.*

russet (rus′it) *adj.* a deep reddish-brown; p. 602 *The tree's russet-colored leaves were a definite sign that fall was approaching.*

Tip: Synonyms Synonyms are always the same part of speech.

Scrumping Apples. Caroline Paterson.
Watercolor on paper. Private collection.

After Apple-Picking

Robert Frost

My long two-pointed ladder's sticking through a tree
Toward heaven still,
And there's a barrel that I didn't fill
Beside it, and there may be two or three
5   Apples I didn't pick upon some **bough**.
But I am done with apple-picking now.
Essence of winter sleep is on the night,
The scent of apples: I am drowsing off.
I cannot rub the strangeness from my sight
10   I got from looking through a pane of glass
I skimmed this morning from the drinking trough
And held against the world of **hoary** grass.

Vocabulary

bough (bou) *n.* a tree branch
essence (es´əns) *n.* necessary characteristics of a thing
hoary (hôr´ē) *adj.* white or gray with age; covered with frost

It melted, and I let it fall and break.
But I was well
15 Upon my way to sleep before it fell,
And I could tell
What form my dreaming was about to take.
Magnified apples appear and disappear,
Stem end and blossom end,
20 And every fleck of russet showing clear.
My instep arch not only keeps the ache,
It keeps the pressure of a ladder-round.
I feel the ladder sway as the boughs bend.
And I keep hearing from the cellar bin
25 The rumbling sound
Of load on load of apples coming in.
For I have had too much
Of apple-picking: I am overtired
Of the great harvest I myself desired.
30 There were ten thousand thousand fruit to touch,
Cherish in hand, lift down, and not let fall.
For all
That struck the earth,
No matter if not bruised or spiked with stubble,
35 Went surely to the cider-apple heap
As of no worth.
One can see what will trouble
This sleep of mine, whatever sleep it is.
Were he not gone,
40 The woodchuck could say whether it's like his
Long sleep, as I describe its coming on,
Or just some human sleep.

Assonance and Consonance What effect does this example of assonance create for you? Explain.

Issues of Identity How might these lines help you identify the speaker's state of mind?

Clarify Meaning How does this phrase evoke a darker, hidden meaning in Frost's poem?

Vocabulary

russet (rus′it) *adj.* a deep reddish-brown

Fire and Ice

Robert Frost

Essay, Force. Frantisek Kupka (1871–1957). Museum Moderner Kunst, Vienna, Austria.

Some say the world will end in fire,
Some say in ice.
From what I've tasted of desire
I hold with those who favor fire.

But if it had to perish twice,
I think I know enough of hate
To know that for destruction ice
Is also great
And would suffice.

Issues of Identity *Poets often speak of the "human condition." To what aspect of the human condition and identity does this line refer?*

After You Read

Respond and Think Critically

Respond and Interpret

1. What emotions did "After Apple-Picking" and "Fire and Ice" stir in you? Explain.

2. (a) In "After Apple-Picking," what happens to the pane of glass that the speaker looks through? (b) What deeper meaning do you suppose Frost tries to convey with the "pane of glass" image?

3. (a) In line 15 of "After Apple-Picking," where is the speaker going? (b) What deeper meaning does the line suggest?

4. (a) According to the speaker in "Fire and Ice," what are the two ways that the world might end? (b) What human events might trigger destruction by ice?

Analyze and Evaluate

5. In the first five lines of "After Apple-Picking," how does the speaker feel about apple-picking? Explain.

6. According to many cultures, the world has been destroyed once by water. Why do you think the speaker in "Fire and Ice" sides with those who believe that the next destruction will occur by fire?

Connect

7. **Big Idea** Issues of Identity How does Frost identify the speaker in "After Apple-Picking"? Explain.

8. **Connect to the Author** How might Frost's personal experiences in war-time Europe and on a farm contribute to his poems' impact?

Primary Source Quotation

The Meaning of Poetry

Robert Frost wrote many times about what poetry meant to him and how he personally interpreted it. Read the following quotations about poetry from Robert Frost, then answer the questions that follow.

> "A poem begins in delight and ends in wisdom."
>
> "A poem begins as a lump in the throat, a sense of wrong, a homesickness, a lovesickness."
>
> "Poetry has got me indirectly or directly practically all the living I have had."
>
> —Robert Frost

1. What might Frost mean when he says that a poem begins with "delight and ends in wisdom"? Have you had any personal experiences with delight or wisdom as a result of reading poetry?

2. What might a "lump in the throat," homesickness, lovesickness, and feelings that something is wrong have in common? Why might these things motivate someone to write?

3. How can poetry "get" you life experiences? Do you agree with this statement? Explain.

4. Of these three quotations, which do you respond to the most? Explain your choice.

604 UNIT 3 POETRY

Literary Element **Assonance and Consonance**

Assonance and **consonance** are sound devices that are more readily apparent to most of us when hearing a poem read aloud rather than reading it silently. Poets use assonance and consonance to enhance both the rhythm and imagery in a poem.

1. Identify an example of assonance in "After Apple-Picking." What vowel sound is repeated?
2. Identify an example of consonance in "After Apple-Picking." What consonant sound is repeated?

Review: Alliteration

As you learned on page 469, **alliteration** is the repetition of consonant sounds at the beginning of words. Alliteration can be used to emphasize words, reinforce meaning, or create a musical effect. An example of alliteration might be the phrase "Later we located the laughing loons of Laredo."

Partner Activity Discuss alliteration in "After Apple-Picking" and "Fire and Ice" with a classmate. Create a chart as below and fill it with examples from the poems that demonstrate alliteration.

Poem	Alliteration
"After Apple-Picking"	"My long two-pointed ladder's"
"Fire and Ice"	"Some say"
"After Apple-Picking"	

After you have identified examples of alliteration in the poems, discuss with your partner the possible significance of each example.

LOG ON **Literature** Online

Selection Resources For Selection Quizzes, eFlashcards, and Reading-Writing Connection activities, go to glencoe.com and enter QuickPass code GL59794u3.

Reading Strategy **Clarify Meaning**

Poets sometimes might not include punctuation stops or might use them inconsistently. The poet assumes that the reader will determine meaning in the text by rereading the poem and imagining the punctuation stops. Review the chart you made on page 600 and answer the following questions.

1. How might Frost's meaning in "After Apple-Picking" be clarified by finding the punctuation stops?
2. To support your opinion, list three details from the selection.

Vocabulary Practice

Practice with Synonyms A synonym is a word that has the same or nearly the same meaning as another word. With a partner, match each boldfaced vocabulary word below with its synonym. Use a thesaurus or dictionary to check your answers.

1. bough   a. reddish
2. essence   b. frosty
3. hoary   c. essential
4. russet   d. core
                  e. branch
                  f. creek

Academic Vocabulary

A **potential** interpretation for the sleep at the end of "After Apple-Picking" is eternal rest.

Potential is a multiple-meaning word. Using context clues, try to figure out the meaning of *potential* in each sentence.

1. Before it falls over the dam, the water has **potential** energy.
2. Alphonso considered the career because of the **potential** earning power he associated with it.

For more on academic vocabulary, see pages 52 and 53.

Respond Through Writing

Expository Essay

Learning Objectives

In this assignment, you will focus on the following objectives:

Writing: Writing an expository essay.

Grammar: Understanding how to use comparative and superlative degrees of adverbs.

Evaluate Sound Devices "After Apple-Picking" and "Fire and Ice" are full of sound devices. Write an essay of 1,500 words in which you evaluate how well the sound devices support the meaning of each poem.

Understand the Task Sound devices are techniques writers use to emphasize particular sounds in order to underscore the meaning of certain words, enhance rhythm, or add a musical quality to the work. They include onomatopoeia, rhyme, alliteration, assonance, and consonance. When you **evaluate** something, you make judgments based on certain criteria.

Prewrite List sound devices from both poems that seem especially interesting or effective. Make a three-column chart in which you list the poem, an example of a sound device, and the function or purpose of the device. Use the ideas in column three of your chart to formulate your essay's thesis or controlling idea. Then outline an order for your body paragraphs.

Draft Each of your paragraphs should contain a topic sentence that makes an evaluative statement, evidence from the poem that supports the statement, and an explanation of how the evidence relates to your judgment. Follow this model:

Evaluative Paragraph Structure

Topic Sentence: Frost uses <sound device> such as "effectively" to ___.

Sentence 2: For example, in line ___ of <name of poem>, Frost uses <alliteration, assonance, consonance, repetition, or onomatopoeia> to show/emphasize/suggest ___.

Other Sentences: Explanation, relationship to thesis.

Revise As you revise, be sure that you have correctly used terms that name sound devices. Identify objections that the reader may present and add details and explanations to clarify and strengthen your own argument. Also consider adding a graphic organizer or another visual to display sound devices and your evaluations.

Edit and Proofread Proofread your paper, correcting any errors in spelling, grammar, and punctuation. Use the Grammar Tip in the side column to help you use comparative forms of adverbs correctly.

Grammar Tip

Comparative and Superlative Degrees of Adverbs

Use the comparative form of adverbs to compare two actions. Use the superlative form of adverbs to compare three or more actions. Most adverbs add *more* to create the comparative form and *most* to create the superlative form.

*Will the speaker sleep **more deeply** tonight than before?*

*Of all Frost's poems, does "After Apple-Picking" end **most quietly**?*

A few words can function as either adjectives or adverbs. For example, *well,* in the sense of being healthy, is an adjective. In most cases, however, *well* functions as an adverb.

*The speaker was **well** on his way to sleep.*

Before You Read

Arabic Coffee

Meet Naomi Shihab Nye
(born 1952)

Naomi Shihab Nye published her first poem at the age of seven, in *Wee Wisdom*, a children's magazine. Nye loved reading and writing from a very young age. She writes, "I liked the portable, comfortable shape of poems. . . . And especially the way they took you to a deeper, quieter place."

Quiet Observer Indeed, Nye has been called a "quiet observer of the human condition." Of her own work, Nye writes, "I have always loved the gaps, the spaces between things, as much as the things. I love staring, pondering, mulling, puttering. I love the times when someone or something is late—there's that rich possibility of noticing more, in the meantime."

Born to an American mother and a Palestinian father in St. Louis, Missouri, Nye was a perceptive child. In the introduction to her collection of poems *19 Varieties of Gazelle*, she writes, "I got into the habit of writing little things down from the very beginning—not because they were more interesting than anyone else's 'little things,' but just so I could think about them."

Professional Poet Nye attended high school in a variety of exotic locales: Ramallah, Jordan; Old City, Jerusalem; and San Antonio, Texas. She earned a bachelor's degree from Trinity University in 1974 and began working as a writer-in-residence at various universities around the country. She has authored or edited over twenty volumes of poetry, essays, and fiction.

Nye has won several prestigious awards and fellowships, including four Pushcart Prizes and, in 1997, a Guggenheim Fellowship. She was also a finalist in 2002 for a National Book Award in young people's literature.

> "We have no borders when we read."
> —Naomi Shihab Nye

No Borders In her writing, Nye explores shared experiences and differences between cultures, as well as perspectives of people from countries around the world. She also writes about the tragedy of cultural and political conflicts, such as the Palestinian-Israeli conflict, and the power of strength in the face of adversity. One consistent theme of her poetry is how people are connected, whether they are neighbors, strangers, or enemies.

Author Search For more about Naomi Shihab Nye, go to glencoe.com and enter QuickPass code GL59794u3.

Literature and Reading Preview

Connect to the Poem
When you spend time with loved ones, what actions do you use to show that you care for them? List several of these actions.

Build Background
Tasseography, or fortune-telling with tea leaves, began centuries ago in China. One interprets the pattern of tea leaves or coffee grounds left in a cup or saucer after drinking the beverage. The reader may use certain symbols to interpret the pattern or may intuitively "read" the residue for deeper meaning.

Set Purposes for Reading

Big Idea Issues of Identity

As you read, ask yourself, How does the speaker explore the significance of people gathering together?

Literary Element Symbol

A **symbol** is any person, place, object, or experience that exists on a literal level within a work but also represents something on a figurative level. As you read the poem, ask yourself, How does Nye use the preparation and serving of coffee as a symbol?

Reading Strategy Analyze Rhythm

Rhythm is the pattern of beats created by the arrangement of stressed and unstressed syllables in a line. When you **analyze rhythm** in an unrhymed poem, you pay attention to how structure, diction, and sound devices work together to create rhythm. As you read this poem, ask yourself, How does Nye create a flow and pace events and emotions?

Tip: Note Rhythm Note how the author creates rhythm using the elements listed above. Create a list of passages from the poem and explain how these passages convey rhythm.

Passage from Poem	Rhythm style
"small white cups"	Succession of using short words

Learning Objectives

For pages 607–611

In studying this text, you will focus on the following objectives:

Literary Study: Analyzing symbol.

Reading: Analyzing rhythm.

Vocabulary

grounds (grounds) *n.* the remains of the coffee beans after water has been passed through them; sediment; p. 609 *When the filter tore, the wet coffee grounds made a mess on the countertop.*

offering (ô′fər ing) *n.* something that is presented as a gift; p. 609 *An olive branch symbolizes a peace offering.*

Arabic Coffee

Naomi Shihab Nye

Creamers, 2001. Pam Ingalls.

It was never too strong for us:
make it blacker, Papa, thick in the bottom,
tell again how years will gather
in small white cups,
5 how luck lives in a spot of **grounds.**

Leaning over the stove, he let it
boil to the top,[1] and down again.
Two times. No sugar in his pot.
And the place where men and women
10 break off from one another[2]
was not present in that room.
The hundred disappointments,
fire swallowing olive-wood beads[3]
at the warehouse, and the dreams
15 tucked like pocket handkerchiefs
into each day, took their places
on the table, near the half-empty
dish of corn. And none was
more important than the others,
20 and all were guests. When
he carried the tray into the room,
high and balanced in his hands,
it was an **offering** to all of them,
stay, be seated, follow the talk
25 wherever it goes. The coffee was
the center of the flower.
Like clothes on a line saying
You will live long enough to wear me,
a motion of faith. There is this,
30 and there is more.

1. *Boil to the top* refers to the preparation of coffee. As the water begins to boil, the grounds rise to the top. The boiling stops and the grounds settle at the bottom of the pot. Some of the grounds are transferred when the coffee is poured into a cup.
2. *The place where men and women break off from one another* refers to a practice that exists in many cultures, in which men and women stay separated from one another during public and social functions.
3. *Olive-wood beads* are wooden beads made from olive trees, often used for religious or ornamental jewelry.

Issues of Identity *What does the speaker mean by this statement?*

Vocabulary

grounds (groundz) *n.* the remains of the coffee beans after water has been passed through them; sediment

offering (ô′ fər ing) *n.* something that is presented as a gift

After You Read

Respond and Think Critically

Respond and Interpret

1. Do you identify with the experience described in the poem? Explain why or why not.

2. (a) How does the speaker like coffee prepared? (b) Why do you think the speaker first tells us her personal preference before explaining how Papa prepares it for others?

3. (a) What things are said to take their place at the table? (b) Why do you think the speaker chooses these images?

4. (a) As the talk flows wherever it goes, what does the coffee become? (b) What does this suggest about the importance of the coffee for this gathering?

Analyze and Evaluate

5. (a) Why might the speaker compare dark coffee grounds in the bottom of small white cups to luck and people gathering together? (b) Is this an effective image? Explain.

6. (a) How do you interpret the following line: "You will live long enough to wear me"? (b) Why do you think Nye chose to italicize this line?

Connect

7. **Big Idea** Issues of Identity In what ways is this poem about identity? Explain.

8. **Connect to the Author** In what ways does this poem express Nye's interest in cross-cultural exploration and connections between people?

Literary Element Symbol

Nye uses symbols throughout "Arabic Coffee" to help the reader understand the meaning of the poem.

1. When the speaker explains in short sentences that her father boils the coffee two times, no sugar, and in preparation for guests, what do you think this act symbolizes? Explain.

2. How do "clothes on a line" symbolize hope and faith?

Review: Speaker

As you learned on page 472, the speaker in poetry, like the narrator in prose, is the voice that communicates with the reader. The speaker may be the poet or a fictional character created to express a particular point of view. Identifying the speaker and understanding his or her point of view can be essential to an understanding of the poem.

Partner Activity Read "Arabic Coffee" aloud to one of your classmates. Then discuss the following questions.

1. Who is the speaker in the poem? How do you know? Explain.

2. How does the speaker shift her point of view in lines 2–5? What is the purpose of this shift?

3. How does the speaker feel about her father's coffee ritual? What is its significance for her?

610 UNIT 3 POETRY

Reading Strategy **Analyze Rhythm**

"Arabic Coffee" has a **rhythm** and pace that are established by the author's choice of words (diction) and where she chooses to start and end lines. A reader should be aware of the many elements an author uses to create and maintain rhythm in poetry. Review the chart you made on page 608 and answer the following questions.

1. What effect does the author create by making the first stanza one long sentence?
2. How does Nye's diction help create rhythm?

Vocabulary Practice

Practice with Denotation and Connotation Denotation is the literal, or dictionary, meaning of a word. **Connotation** is the implied, or cultural, meaning of a word. For example, the words *grieving* and *sad* have a similar denotation, but they have different connotations.

Use a graphic organizer like the one shown.

Weaker	Stronger
sad	grieving

Work with a partner to complete a graphic organizer like the one below for each vocabulary word. Include the vocabulary word in one box and a word that has a similar denotation in another. Then explain which word has the stronger connotation.

| grounds | offering |

Vocabulary word: grieving

Similar word: sad

Explanation: Grieving has the stronger connotation. Both words refer to feeling sorrow, but grieving suggests the great sorrow one might feel at a time of tragedy, while sad can suggest lesser sorrow, such as sadness at not seeing someone as planned.

Write with Style

 Apply Symbolism

Assignment Write several lines of free verse in which an object, an animal, or an event symbolizes an abstract concept.

Get Ideas Make a list of symbols and their corresponding abstractions, such as a dove for peace and an owl for wisdom. Then think of an abstraction, such as beauty or despair, and brainstorm ideas for a symbol that might convey the concept. Alternatively, think of an object, an animal, or an event, such as a deer or an eclipse, that you might shape into a symbol. Use a thesaurus to find and list associations with the abstraction. Use an encyclopedia to find and list ideas about the object, animal, or event you will portray.

Give It Structure Write about the symbol (for example, a soccer game) but be sure the underlying abstraction (for example, life) is clear.

EXAMPLE:
After the kickoff, some players fall behind, some surge ahead,

On the field of play, there will be blocks, attempts, assists, fouls, and goals.

Look at Language Have a peer reader identify the symbol and the abstraction. Add precise words or revise for sharper, clearer language to make the focus clear or to improve your free verse.

 Literature Online

Selection Resources For Selection Quizzes, eFlashcards, and Reading-Writing Connection activities, go to glencoe.com and enter QuickPass code GL59794u3.

Learning Objectives

For pages 612–616

In studying this text, you will focus on the following objectives:

Reading:

Analyzing cultural context.
Analyzing informational text.

Set a Purpose for Reading

Read to discover Chang-rae Lee's identification with his Korean family and culture.

Preview the Article

In "We Are Family," writer Chang-rae Lee comments on the unshakable bond between his relatives in Korea and himself.

1. From the title, what do you think the author values?
2. Skim the first paragraph. What mood do you think the author is trying to establish?

Reading Strategy Analyze Cultural Context

When you analyze cultural context, you consider the customs, beliefs, values, arts, and intellectual activities of a group of people and use this knowledge to better understand the theme or message of a literary work. To understand the cultural context of this selection, consider the cultural characteristics of the author's experiences in Korea and in the United States.

TIME

We Are Family

During a visit to his native South Korea, novelist Chang-rae Lee learns that living abroad and losing his language are no barriers to belonging.

By CHANG-RAE LEE

The author with his parents in 1967, before they emigrated from South Korea to the United States.

THE LAST TIME I STOOD BEFORE MY GRANDFATHER'S grave, in the spring of 1989, it had been newly dug. My uncle had driven my father and me to Yong-In City, one hour south of Seoul, so that we could pay our respects. I remember the fog burning off to reveal the new season bursting forth in blooms of wild cherry and persimmon all around us on the hillside. And yet, there was a worn-out quality at the site. The burial ground was a three-meter-wide amphitheater carved out of the steep face of the hillside. The fresh earth was laid bare, roughly cut roots jutting out from the sheer wall of dirt. In the center of the dugout, the mound beneath which my grandfather was buried showed the first wispy strands of baby grass. There was no headstone as yet.

My father was on the verge of tears, finally seeing where his father lay. I wanted to feel the same pinch of loss, the same onrush of sadness. But I couldn't. Our family left Korea for America when I wasn't yet three, and since then I'd spent perhaps five hours total in my grandfather's presence. All I knew of him was that he'd lost his hardware business in Pyongyang to the communists on the eve of the Korean War. And when my father knelt low and bowed respectfully, the image I saw of my grandfather's face was drawn not from any memory of life but from the black-and-white picture of him that hung prominently in my childhood home.

I pictured that image once more when I visited his grave in May 2003. I was in Korea to visit my family, particularly to see my ailing maternal grandmother, and to do some research for my next novel. I had come once again with my uncle, a professor of business, but this time with his two sons as well, one of whom was just back from a year of language study in San Diego. Our mood as we climbed up the hill was expansive and lighthearted, and it seemed we were more on a picnicking hike than a dutiful visit to our ancestral dead. But as we ascended the path to the grave, the talk quieted.

Finally, at the end of a narrow deer path, there came an opening, and we emerged onto the same burial landing I had visited 14 years ago. To my surprise, there were two mounds instead of one and now a black granite headstone centered between, carved on the faces and sides with Chinese characters. I asked about the second mound and my uncle said that my grandmother and stepgrandmother had been unearthed from their resting places in Seoul and moved here some years before to join my grandfather.

"What is all the writing?" I asked. We were crouched by the black slab of rock.

"It's your grandfather's name. Your grandmothers' names are here," he said, pointing them out.

"And what about all these other characters?"

> **"IN THEIR FIRST YEARS IN AMERICA... THEY DIDN'T ALWAYS ALLOW THEMSELVES TO EXPERIENCE MANY EMOTIONS."**

"These are his children. Here's your father. Here are your other uncles, then me, and your aunt. And here are the names of our spouses. This one is your mother's."

"My mother's?"

I touched the unfamiliar language sharply carved into the stone, almost saying her name aloud. She died a few years after my grandfather did, of stomach cancer.

"I didn't know it was done this way."

"Oh yes," my uncle said. "Everyone is here."

Learning to Belong

I kept thinking back on that phrase during the rest of my stay in Seoul: Everyone is here. As uttered by my uncle, it was a simple answer to a simple question, a matter of fact and a literal record. And so it was. And yet, as I thought about the notion, it became more than just a straightforward record of my ancestors. For I realized how differently than I my uncle and his sons viewed that dark stone, how the names to them were just an ordinary fact of their lives, like the ancient arrangement of the planets. To me, raised away in the States, the listing seemed more remarkable than that, a kind of supernatural alliance, extraordinary and wonderful.

For in our immigrant family of four, we were all we ever had. In the town where we lived (a small northern suburb of New York City), we were one of a handful of nonwhite families. Every great once in a while, there would be an uncle or aunt passing through New York, and they'd stay with us a few days or a week. In the evenings, my parents would chatter at the dinner table with special enthusiasm about all the reports from Seoul. My parents were generally happy, easygoing people, but in their first years in America, I would say they didn't always allow themselves to experience many emotions, perhaps because they felt outside of and flustered by all

Informational Text

BLOOD TIES
Lee's ailing grandmother gave him a reason to journey home and reconnect with his mother's extended family.

the strangeness of their new world. And it was only when "home" made its return that they seemed to truly liven up.

In later years, my parents considered America to be their only home, and although they possessed the means to do so by the time my mother died in 1991, our family had made only four visits to Korea in 23 years. Even as a serious teen, I didn't mind the summer trips we took as a family. Korea was a lot better than, say, a car trip to family friends, not so much because of any reconnecting with the family but for the food.

Best of all, were the grand meals we'd have at our relatives' cramped apartments or houses, the dozens of dishes completely covering the low tables they'd set out for us—the men sitting at the main table, the women lodged at one nearer the kitchen.

In the fog of my jet-lagged mind, the only things that made sense to me amid the superfast talk, which I mostly couldn't understand, were all the bracing flavors, the radish kimchi and marinated raw crab and sesame-leaf pancakes. Even my father seemed somewhat over–whelmed by the rush of native language, occasionally asking people to repeat what they'd said.

And this is how I found myself on my recent trip, out with my father's side of the family at a popular barbecue restaurant, straining to understand everyone's questions about my family and work. I could say only a few words in response, my speaking ability in Korean not as developed as my aural comprehension. After the initial assurances that I could tolerate spicy food and a recounting of the names and ages of my daughters, I naturally retreated into the customary table rituals of the barbecue. I attended to grilling the meat and whole cloves of garlic, readying the bean paste and the fragrant shoots of chrysanthemum, cupping the fresh lettuce leaf to wrap all of it in. While the others ate heartily and engaged in their lively conversations, I was happy for their company and just as pleased simply to sit there and eat, gleaning what talk I could.

There was no awkwardness due to the differences of our language or the brief time we'd spent together during our lives. Somehow all was fine. They

> **"MY GRANDMOTHER WAS STARING RIGHT INTO MY EYES, GAZING, I'M SURE, AT THE REMNANTS OF HER FIRST CHILD."**

Informational Text

GENERATIONS Author Lee with daughters Annika (left) and Eva, at their Princeton, New Jersey, home.

were family. There was a certain ease in the gathering that I have rarely felt in my life. There was a level of comfort drawn, I think, from not having to explain myself in the customary ways. I wasn't defined by the cultural and personal stereotypes that are part of my "regular" existence as a teacher and writer and maybe (if there really is such a person) as an Asian American.

I kept thinking how plainly, deeply satisfying it was to be back among my cousins and aunts and uncles. With them, at least, I was not a provisional "I," not an ethnic, or outsider, or an artist or intellectual, but simply someone whose connections to others were clear and traceable and real.

Keep the Family Together

The next night, I went to my maternal aunt's house south of the Han River, where my grandmother Halmoni was staying. She was my only living grandparent, in her late 80s, and from recent reports, not doing terribly well. Her back was finally giving way, and she wasn't very mobile; my cousin told me she sometimes crawled to the bathroom rather than ask anyone for help.

I was nervous about seeing Halmoni in a bad state, not only for the sadness of such a sight but for the sake of her own pride. I almost wished I could have simply telephoned her my wishes of good health and love. When I rang the bell of my aunt's house, a young cousin greeted me and led me inside. My two aunts were busy back in the kitchen making final preparations for dinner. My cousin and I sat down in the living room. Before I could say anything, my aunts came out, both wiping their hands on their aprons. We all hugged each other, then my younger aunt asked her son where Halmoni was.

My cousin said he'd go look for our grandmother upstairs, but then Halmoni cleared her throat in the next room, effectively announcing herself. She came in, not crawling at all but walking with slowed, careful steps, her hunched back bent down almost to 90 degrees. She wrapped her arms around me, her face pressed into my chest, hardly taller now with her fallen posture than my six-year-old daughter. I could smell the faint almondy oiliness of her hair. And as much as I didn't want to think of her as frail, she most clearly was, her hold of me like the cling of someone straining to grab on more than to hug. Soon enough, we were sitting together on the sofa, her hands cupping mine, gently kneading them just as she had often done to my sister and me as children.

"It's too far for you to come," she said. "It's good you didn't try to bring your family. You yourself shouldn't have bothered."

"It's no bother."

My cousin piped in, "Halmoni, he came over to see you, you know."

"Even more reason," she said, though half-smiling. She asked earnestly, "Are you tired?"

"I'm fine."

"You must be hungry."

"Not so much."

She called out to the kitchen, telling her daughters that I needed to eat right away. My younger aunt came out and said

Informational Text

she could set the table, that we didn't have to wait for the men to arrive (which was of course possible, though an impossibility).

"Really," I told her. "I want to wait."

She nodded and went back to the kitchen. Halmoni made a raspy sound in her throat at me, a distinctive Korean mother-style scold, the sound of which contains just the pitch to make one feel at once guilty and beloved.

"Are you feeling well these days?" I asked, having practiced the phrase (in Korean) on the subway ride.

"Sometimes I have a little trouble with my back. But not today. Your father is in good health?"

"Yes."

"You visit him regularly?"

"I try to."

"You must do so always," she said, tapping my hand for emphasis. "Keep the family together." She paused. "And your stepmother, she is well, too?"

"Yes."

Halmoni nodded.

"That's good," she said. "It's how it should be."

She was staring right into my eyes, gazing, I'm sure, at the remnants of her first child, my mother, the only one, with any mercy, who would precede her to the grave. I pictured my mother's black granite headstone back in New York, and then, too, my paternal grandfather's stone, and then Halmoni's and my father's and even my own, all the written names, cast wide.

—Updated 2005, from TIME Asia, August 18/25, 2003

Respond and Think Critically

Respond and Interpret

1. Write a brief summary of the main ideas in this article before you answer the following questions. For help on writing a summary, see page 415.

2. Why do you think Lee opens his article with a description of his grandfather's gravesite?

3. (a) How did Lee react to the names of his late family members on the black granite headstone? (b) Why do you think this reaction is significant?

4. (a) What might have made Lee feel like an outsider in the town in which he was raised? (b) How do you think being an outsider influenced Lee's perspective on family?

5. What were Lee's ties to his Korean heritage?

Analyze and Evaluate

6. (a) How does Lee approach the subject of loss in the article? (b) What does he learn or gain from his losses?

7. Lee does not follow a traditional structure in his writing. It is not chronological or sequential. What techniques does he use to organize the article? Support your answer citing lines from the text.

Connect

8. Lee comments that he did not have to explain himself to his relatives "as a teacher and writer and maybe (if there really is such a person) as an Asian American." What is he saying about Asian American identity?

Comparing Literature
Across Genres

Compare Literature About Jazz

Jazz music is an essential part of American culture. The selections compared here highlight the contributions of African Americans to literature and music.

Dream Boogie by Langston Hughes.............................poem 620

Motto by Langston Hughes......................................poem 621

Dizzy Gillespie, Explorer of New Sounds
from *Giants of Jazz* by Studs Terkel...................biography 623

Playing Jazz by Wynton Marsalis ....letter 627

Learning Objectives

For pages 617–631

In studying these texts, you will focus on the following objectives:

Literary Study: Comparing across genres. Analyzing rhyme and rhyme scheme.

Reading: Making inferences about theme.

Writing: Writing an annotation.

COMPARE THE Big Idea Issues of Identity

Identity may be defined as individuality or character. It is both who we are and what we are. Identity relates to our family histories, where we come from, and where we are now. As you read, ask yourself, How is jazz an important part of each author's identity?

COMPARE Author's Purpose

An author's purpose can be described as his or her intent in creating a literary work. As you read, ask yourself, How are these writers inspired by one or more of the following goals: to persuade, to inform, to entertain, or to describe?

Jazz Singer, 1997. Gil Mayers.

COMPARE Author's Viewpoint

An author's viewpoint can be seen as his or her position or perspective in relation to the subject being discussed. These three authors share a love of jazz but each writes from a different viewpoint—Langston Hughes from that of a poet, Studs Terkel from that of a biographer and critic, and Wynton Marsalis from that of a musician and teacher. As you read, ask yourself, How does the viewpoint of each writer determine the content and style of each selection?

Author Search For more about Langston Hughes, Studs Terkel, and Wynton Marsalis, go to glencoe.com and enter QuickPass code GL59794u3.

Comparing Literature

Before You Read

Dream Boogie and *Motto*

Meet **Langston Hughes**
(1902–1967)

African American writer Langston Hughes dedicated his life to improving race relations. His works linked prejudice and poverty to feelings of heartbreak and hopelessness among African Americans.

> *"I have discovered in life that there are ways of getting almost anywhere you want to go, if you really want to go."*
>
> —Langston Hughes

Early Wanderings Hughes was born in Joplin, Missouri, to parents who soon separated. His childhood consisted of living with either one parent or the other, or with a relative. Hughes turned to books for companionship. The love of reading inspired Hughes to write. The poetry of Walt Whitman and Carl Sandburg inspired him to use free verse and common speech patterns.

During the 1920s, Hughes held a variety of odd jobs in Harlem in New York City and then became a steward on a ship bound for West Africa. While abroad, Hughes learned about other cultures by traveling to Europe, Africa, Mexico, Russia, and Japan.

Speaking His Mind In 1921 Hughes published his first poem, "The Negro Speaks of Rivers," in the journal *Crisis*, edited by the noted African American author and civil rights leader W. E. B. Du Bois. Like Du Bois, Hughes believed that African Americans could find renewal by understanding and taking pride in their cultural roots.

In 1926 Hughes published his first book of verses, *The Weary Blues*. He blended African American and white rhythms and poetic forms. He became a major force in a growing African American cultural movement called the Harlem Renaissance. When Hughes graduated from Lincoln University in 1929, he became one of the first African Americans to earn a living solely through writing. Hughes became a leader in integrating major forms of African American music—jazz, blues, and gospel—with his poetic lyrics.

Bountiful Fruits Hughes grew more prosperous through his hard work. He became involved in such literary pursuits as prose writing, playwriting, journalism, and film projects. In later life, Hughes received the Spingarn Medal from the NAACP for his many contributions to the betterment of African Americans. He was invited to join the National Institute of Arts and Letters in 1961.

Author Search For more about Langston Hughes, go to glencoe.com and enter QuickPass code GL59794u3.

Literature and Reading Preview

Connect to the Poems
How much power do published words have to bring about change in people's lives? Freewrite for a few minutes about a book or story that affected you in a profound way.

Build Background
Hughes portrayed the African American experience in the mid-1900s. During this time, many African Americans had dreams that went unrealized because of racism.

Set Purposes for Reading

Big Idea Issues of Identity

As you read, ask yourself, How does Hughes express his thoughts in a style that displays a distinctively African American musical quality, reminiscent of jazz music?

Literary Element Rhyme and Rhyme Scheme

Rhyme is the repetition of the same stressed vowel sounds and any succeeding sounds in two or more words. **Rhyme scheme** is the pattern that **end rhymes** (rhymes occurring at the ends of lines of poetry) form in a stanza or poem. As you read the poems, ask yourself, How does Hughes use rhyme and rhyme scheme to help him convey his message?

Reading Strategy Make Inferences About Theme

To **make inferences about theme** is to draw a conclusion about the meaning of a literary work based on textual evidence and your background knowledge. As you read, ask yourself, What are the main points that help the reader find the poem's theme?

> **Vocabulary**
>
> **deferred** (di furd′) *adj.* put off, postponed; p. 620 *Joan's deferred loans would not have to be paid until after graduation.*

Tip: Question Create a chart like the one below to organize your ideas through questioning as you read the poems.

Poem	Question	My Response
"Motto"	What message does this poem convey to its readers?	Your behavior toward others can affect how they treat you.
	What is your response after your initial reading of the poem?	

LANGSTON HUGHES 619

Comparing Literature

Dream Boogie

Langston Hughes

Show Time (of the Blues), 20th century. Romare Bearden.

Good morning, daddy!
Ain't you heard
The boogie-woogie rumble
Of a dream **deferred**?

5   Listen closely:
You'll hear their feet
Beating out and beating out a—

>   You think
>   It's a happy beat?

10   Listen to it closely:
Ain't you heard
something underneath
like a—

>   What did I say?

15   Sure,
I'm happy!
Take it away!

>   Hey, pop!
>   Re-bop![1]
20   Mop!
>
>   Y-e-a-h!

---

1. *Re-bop* is another term for "bebop," a style of jazz characterized by a staccato two-note phrase that was the music's trademark.

Make Inferences About Theme Why does the speaker ask if it's "a happy beat" and if "something underneath" is heard?

Issues of Identity What do you think Hughes suggests in the concluding lines beginning with "I'm happy"?

Vocabulary

deferred (di furd´) *adj.* put off, postponed

Comparing Literature

Bopping at Birdland (Stomp Time), 1979. Romare Bearden. Color lithograph on paper, 24 x 33¼ in. Smithsonian American Art Museum, Washington, DC.

Langston Hughes

I play it cool
And dig[1] all jive[2]
That's the reason
I stay alive.

5 My motto,
As I live and learn,
                    is:

*Dig And Be Dug
In Return.*

---

1. *Dig* is slang for "to like."
2. *Jive* may refer to swing music and the dancing performed to it or to the glib jargon of hipsters.

Rhyme and Rhyme Scheme What is the rhyme scheme in this stanza?

Comparing Literature

After You Read

Respond and Think Critically

Respond and Interpret

1. If you could ask Langston Hughes one question about his poetry, what would it be?

2. (a) In "Motto," how does the speaker say that he stays alive? (b) What does this suggest to you about his situation in life?

3. (a) In "Motto," what are the speaker's actual words for the motto? (b) Rephrase the motto in your own words.

Analyze and Evaluate

4. (a) In "Dream Boogie," what questions does the speaker ask the audience? (b) What is their effect on the poem? Explain.

5. In "Dream Boogie," how does Hughes convey the speaker's energy?

6. In "Dream Boogie," why does Hughes deviate from the rhyme scheme in some lines?

Connect

7. **Big Idea** **Issues of Identity** What does Hughes mean when he refers to a deferred dream? Explain.

8. **Connect to the Author** Hughes integrated forms of African American music into his poetry to communicate feelings of desperation. Where in these two poems does Hughes hint at the desperation that many African Americans felt at this time?

Literary Element **Rhyme and Rhyme Scheme**

Established poets such as Hughes adapt rhyme scheme for added meaning and innovation.

1. How do the italicized words in "Dream Boogie" contribute to the poem's rhyme scheme?

2. How do you think the rhyme schemes affect the meanings of Hughes's poems?

Reading Strategy **Make Inferences About Theme**

Looking at the words and phrases in a poem can help you **make inferences about theme** and understand implied meanings. Use your chart from page 619 to help you answer the following.

1. What theme is conveyed in these two poems?

2. In support of your opinion, list two details from the poems.

 **Literature** Online

Selection Resources For Selection Quizzes, eFlashcards, and Reading-Writing Connection activities, go to glencoe.com and enter QuickPass code GL59794u3.

Vocabulary Practice

Word Parts Your knowledge of word roots can help you understand unfamiliar words. Read the roots and definitions below. Then use your knowledge of roots, prefixes, and suffixes to pick the best definition for the vocabulary word.
Latin Root: *deferre*—"to carry away" or "to transfer"
Latin Root: *fistula*—"pipe, ulcer"

Vijay **deferred** his plans of becoming a rock star until after he finished college.
a. postponed **b.** abandoned **c.** followed

Writing

Write an Annotation Write a footnote explaining the use of the term *boogie-woogie* in line 3 of "Dream Boogie." Use a dictionary to find the basic definition of the term, but do additional research, on the Internet or in the library, to help you explain the significance of Hughes's use of the term in the context of the poem.

Comparing Literature

Build Background

Giants of Jazz, from which this Dizzy Gillespie chapter is taken, was Studs Terkel's first book. It contains biographies of thirteen jazz greats. *Giants of Jazz* was reprinted in 2002 and still sells well, fifty years after its initial publication.

Dizzy Gillespie
Explorer of New Sounds

From *Giants of Jazz* — Studs Terkel

John Birks Gillespie was a lively, impish little boy.

"John Birks! John Birks!" his harried mother called out. "Where in the world is that child?" Of her nine children, this youngest one was the most irrepressible.

From the parlor came the sound of a pounding piano. She peered into the room, chuckled softly to herself, and shook her head. The four-year-old had clambered up on the high stool and was furiously stabbing at the keyboard with his pudgy little fingers. He gloried in the making of loud sounds.

All kinds of instruments were strewn about the Gillespie household, in Cheraw, South Carolina. The father was a bricklayer by day and an amateur musician by night. As leader of the local band, he was the guardian of the other members' instruments.

The small boy quickly tired of the piano and scurried toward a clarinet that lay upon the table. He tooted into it a few times. His large, luminous eyes wandered to the nearby mandolin. Curious, he plucked at the strings. Now a huge instrument loomed up before him. It rested in a corner, against the wall. It was a bass viol.[1] He approached it cautiously. With all his might, he plucked at a thick, taut string. The vibrating sound startled him. He jumped back. Soon he was at the piano again, blithely pounding away. Here he could make the most noise with the least effort. John Birks Gillespie was acquainting himself with musical instruments. All kinds. . . .

[At the age of fourteen, John's] idol was a trumpet player. There was a radio at the Harringtons. Each week it was a ritual to listen to the broadcast from New York's Savoy Ball Room.[2] Roy Eldridge's trumpet was featured with the band of Teddy Hill. Young Gillespie listened intently to the solos of Eldridge. This man had his own

---

1. A *viol* is one of a family of stringed instruments with a flat back that is played with a curved bow.
2. The *Savoy Ball Room,* in the Harlem neighborhood of New York City, was where many big bands played.

Comparing Literature

special style; his horn had an amazingly wide range, rich colors, and a sharp bite.

"Little Jazz," as Eldridge was called, had gone beyond the New Orleans trumpet style as perfected by Louis Armstrong. He had discovered in the trumpet its own special quality. He added a new dimension to its playing. Young Gillespie sensed this and determined to simulate the style of Eldridge as closely as possible. He began to teach himself the technique of this horn with thoroughness and persistence. At times it was an ordeal for his mother in her search for peace and quiet. She was not the only one who moaned, "That noise is driving me crazy."

The members of the school band practiced wherever they could. As soon as they were kicked out of one home, they paraded into another. When the last weary mother cried, "Out, children. I can't hear myself think," they played in the open field. They blew loudly, joyously, and often off-key.

John Gillespie had a good ear. Soon he was considered the best trumpet player around. But he had one trouble. He could play in only one key: B-flat. It was his best-kept secret. That is, till the day Sonny Matthews returned to town. Sonny was Cheraw's best piano player. During his absence, Gillespie had gained his fine reputation as a trumpeter.

"Where's this John Birks I been hearin' about?" Sonny asked on his first day back. He invited Gillespie to his house for a two-man jam session.

"What do you wanna play, man?" asked the host.

"Anything. I don't care," replied the cocky young trumpeter.

"Okay, let's make it 'Nagasaki.'"

Sonny struck up a few chords on the piano. No sound came from the horn. John Birks Gillespie was mortified. Matthews was playing in the key of C!

From that moment on, an embarrassed young man with a horn vowed to learn every key. . . .

Lottie Gillespie moved her family to Philadelphia in 1935. Though it was a new world for John, he wasn't one bit afraid. He was confident and saucy. Hat cocked to one side, eyes twinkling mischievously, he was ready for any kind of prank. Here his fun-loving ways earned him the nickname of Dizzy. It stuck. . . .

In his constant quest for a new style on the trumpet, he heard a sound that intrigued him. It was 1939. He was working for Edgar Hayes at the World's Fair in New York. Hayes's clarinet player, Rudy Powell, was playing a riff, a repeated phrase, of changing chords. Dizzy rushed to the piano.

"I always go to the piano when I want to try out something new. You see, you can skip around on the piano so easily. You can pick out chords, skip notes, jump intervals. Then you transpose it for the trumpet."

He played the arrangement over and over. He was excited. An idea was taking form in his mind. "I realized there could be so much more in music than what everybody else was playing." Gillespie knew now there must be some new way of playing the trumpet.

Late in 1939, he joined the orchestra of Cab Calloway. There were some excellent musicians in the band. Among them were Chu Berry at the tenor sax, Hilton Jefferson at the alto, Cozy Cole at the drums, and Milt Hinton at the bass. During his two years with Calloway, Dizzy recorded more than fifty sides. More important, it was his period of groping for new ways to express himself. There were difficulties. Some of the band's veterans were irritated by Gillespie's unorthodoxies.

A portrait of trumpeter Dizzy Gillespie (1917–1993) in performance. He was known for his co-creation of the popular jazz bebop style.

"What's he trying to do anyway?"

"Why doesn't he stick to the arrangements?"

"The guy's a 'character.'"

Calloway himself was not too happy with Dizzy's didoes.[3] Occasionally during his musical explorations Dizzy would get lost. When he'd miss the final high note, after a long-range progression, the leader angrily muttered, "All right now! Enough of that! No more of that Chinese music!"

There were others in the band who sensed the pioneer in young Gillespie. Gently they encouraged him.

"Come here, kid," said Milt Hinton, the bass player, during an intermission. "Let's go on the roof and practice."

During the Calloway engagement at New York's Cotton Club, the two men were often on the roof, quietly working together. Hinton walked the bass, while Gillespie tried different chords and melodic patterns on his trumpet.

"I like what you're trying to do," said Hinton. "Keep it up, kid."

Dizzy did keep it up, thanks to the opening of a little nightclub in Harlem. It was called Minton's Play House. Teddy Hill managed it. He encouraged young musicians to gather here after hours, to play exactly as they felt.

Gillespie became a regular habitué, together with Thelonious Monk, a pianist, and Kenny Clarke, a drummer. Clarke was experimenting as a drummer as Dizzy was as a trumpeter. His rhythm was implied rather than emphasized. He varied his punctuation, instead of steadily pounding away at the drum at four-to-the-bar. Here, too, Charlie Christian often came, after his regular stint with Goodman.

Another young musician seeking a new avenue in jazz frequented Minton's. He was an alto-sax player in the swing band of Jay McShann, recently arrived from Kansas City. His name was Charlie Parker. Later, Dizzy and he were to really cross paths and become the two major figures in the development of the jazz known as "bop."

At Minton's, Dizzy's closest associate was Thelonious Monk.

"Monk and I would work on an idea," remembers Dizzy. "Then I'd try it out the next night with Calloway. Cab didn't like it. It was too strange for him."

The word spread quickly among musicians. Minton's was the place to visit for exciting jam sessions and new approaches. Soon the place was packed with players, many of whom had limited talents. The regulars had to find some way to keep the mediocre ones off the bandstand.

"What're we going to do about those cats who can't blow at all, but it takes

---

3. A *dido* is a mischievous prank.

them seven choruses to prove it?" asked the perplexed Gillespie. "By the time they get off, the night's shot."

"Let's practice in the afternoon," suggested Monk. "We'll work out variations so complex it'll scare 'em away."

That's how it began. Bewildered musicians of lesser talents shook their heads and walked off the stand. Gradually Dizzy and his colleagues became more and more interested in what they were doing. They explored more deeply. And a new jazz style was evolving. . . .

When Dizzy and Parker played, the music had drive and humor and warmth. Many of their imitators lacked this, because they lacked musicianship. These two artists were not seeking mimics, but colleagues. In the years that followed, numerous young musicians came into prominence. They were happily equipped with the attributes Gillespie and Bird sought—good craftsmanship, imagination, and daring. Hundreds of records were cut, originals as well as standards. Young musicians were developing new melodic lines based on chord sequences of popular jazz numbers. New recording companies came into being, scores of them.

Modern jazz was here to stay.

In Europe as in America the impact was felt. Though Gillespie's 1948 tour through Scandinavia was a financial flop, it was not due to the music. The band was mismanaged. Dizzy's later appearances in Europe were enthusiastically received.

Perhaps the highlight of Dizzy Gillespie's career was his tour of the Middle East in 1956. Under the auspices of the U.S. State Department, he led a big band into such lands as India, Iraq, Turkey, and Lebanon. These were places where most people had never heard live jazz, let alone American artists. These concerts were divided into two parts. The first half dealt with origins, ranging from the African drums and spirituals to big band classics. The second half consisted of modern jazz.

Dizzy Gillespie was a wonderful ambassador of goodwill. He and his music won over these people immediately.

"I have never seen these people let themselves go like this," observed an American official at Damascus.[4] He himself had been suspicious of jazz.

In Ankara, Dizzy refused to play at an important gathering until the little ragamuffins outside the wall were let in.

"Man, we're here to play for the people."

Dizzy called a young native trumpeter to the stage. The boy was so moved he could hardly speak. Gillespie handed him his cigarette case. Engraved on it were the words: "In token of the brotherhood of jazz."

Does it matter what label is given to jazz? Be it traditional or be it modern, if a talented man plays it with joy and love, that's all that matters.

Says Dizzy Gillespie: "I'm playing the same notes, but it comes out different. You can't teach the soul. You got to bring out your soul on those valves."

---

4. *Damascus* is the capital of Syria.

Quickwrite

Terkel chose "Explorer of New Sounds" for the title of his chapter on Dizzy Gillespie. Is this the best title for the chapter? Write a paragraph about the effectiveness of the title and whether you think, from the information in this excerpt, that Gillespie was an "explorer of new sounds."

Comparing Literature

Build Background

Wynton Marsalis, who is known for his jazz artistry, continues to inspire budding musicians today. This letter is from his book, *To a Young Musician*, a collection of letters written to a young musician who admired Marsalis's talent.

Expression of Jazz, 1993. Maurice Faulk. Acrylic on canvas board.

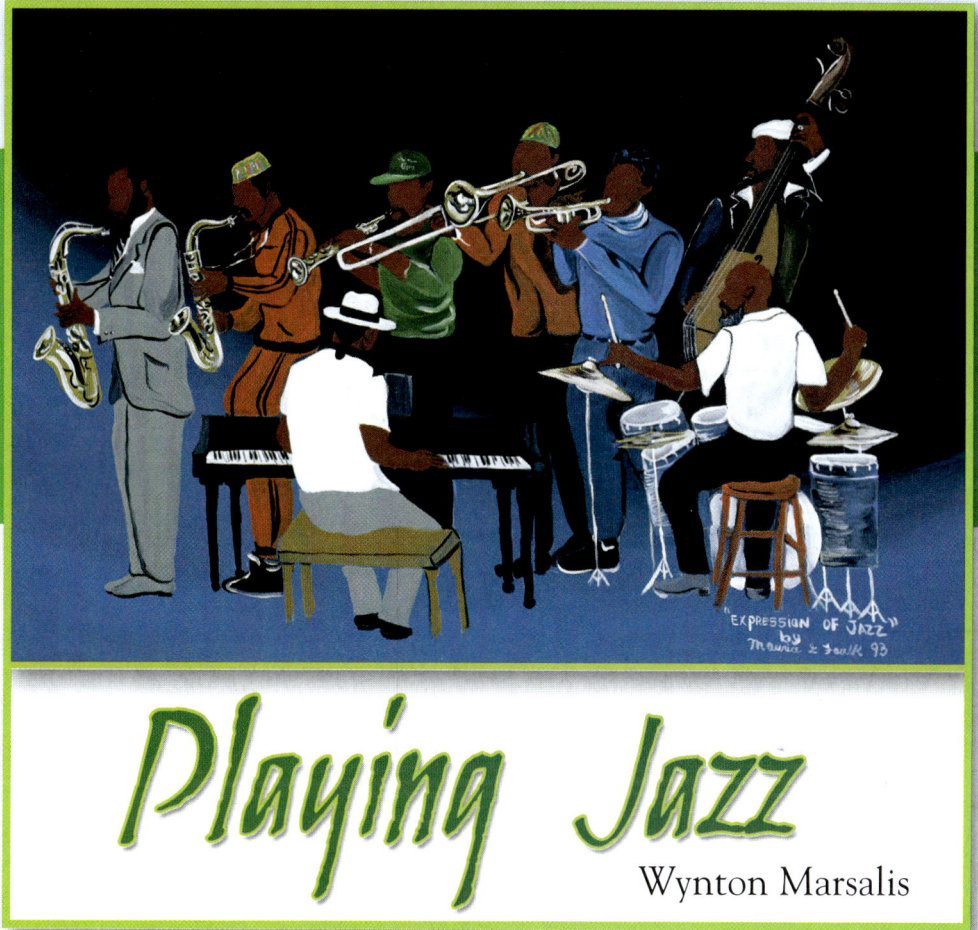

Playing Jazz

Wynton Marsalis

July 18, 2003

Dear Anthony,

How are you, man? Glad to hear you got something from my last letter. Don't just read that stuff and lock it away in your head. Figure out how to apply it.

Tours go on and on. We just out here, from one city to the next. I just head where they tell me. So excuse the distance between these notes. I try to write when I can.

Man, last night we played a small, intimate club inside a Boston hotel. Can't complain at all; gig just felt good. Small places, man. The people all around you, making all kind of noise and grooving. It just inspires the band. Folks in the audience let the sound wash all over them, especially when our drummer, Herlin,[1] gets sanctified on the tambourine in 5/4.

After the gig, someone brought us a full-course meal—black-eyed peas, corn bread, barbecued ribs, mashed potatoes,

---

1. *Herlin* is Wynton Marsalis's longtime drummer Herlin Riley.

Comparing Literature

even had the nerve to have some corn pudding. People cook for you when you sound good and have good manners. In all seriousness, though, no matter how often something like that happens, and it happens a lot, the love and generosity of spirit that we feel out here is always humbling. And it makes missing your family a bit more tolerable. But boy, if you don't like people, you'll have a lonely time out here.

I wanted to rap with you about playing. Yes, that simply, that essentially—what it takes to play jazz music. Playing covers four essential bases: the expansion of your musical vocabulary, employing charisma in your sound, locating your personal objective, and embracing swing. Let's spend some time chopping all four up.

First, the more vocabulary you know, the more you can play. It's just like talking. A person can know twenty words very well and communicate successfully. But there's gonna be a whole pile of things that he or she never talks about. You need to have vocabulary on all aspects of jazz—melodies, harmonies, rhythms, and personal effects. It's always best to start with what you should know—things from your region, then national things. In other words, if you're from Kansas City, you need to know what the Kansas City blues sounds like. Then you need to know American themes and tunes. And today you need to know more music, especially in the global sense. All over the world, styles of music have specific objectives. Learning those objectives will serve you well, allowing you to incorporate a greater breadth of material into your own vocabulary. Musicians in the Latin tradition always complain that the jazz musicians don't know any of their music. Study and learn whatever music catches your fancy from around the world with people who know it and can play it. The enhancement to your own music will be invaluable. Studying the vocabulary of music is like etymology.[2] If they're interested in romance languages, people will study Latin, from which all those languages descend. In the same manner, most groove music comes from the African 6/8 rhythm—the claves[3] in Cuban music to the shuffle of the Mississippi blues. But if you don't know your own language, your own vocabulary, forget about learning someone else's.

Second, always bring charisma to your sound. People want to *hear* some music. They don't come out to see robots toot horns. They want to be uplifted, amazed, and enlightened. Infuse your sound with charisma. What you do when playing for the public isn't much different from any stage-based performance. Imagine the actor who trots out onstage only to deliver lines in bland fashion with no regard to distinguishing his or her craft. Would that make you enthusiastic? You have to understand and locate your distinct approach to the music, and then infuse your playing with that sentiment. Whatever your approach turns out to be, deliver it with force, power, and conviction. With *fun*, man. This is *playing*.

But while you're up on that bandstand blowing with force and power, keep in mind that playing jazz is like anything else in life: When you start a thing off, you're much more enthusiastic than when you get to the middle. If you're running a race, you shoot out like Jesse Owens reborn. Playing ball? That enthusiasm might make you think you're Joe Montana.[4] Then after a couple of interceptions the thrill is gone. This happens in almost every activity in the world.

---

2. *Etymology* means the history of a word.
3. *Claves* are a two-bar syncopated pattern of music.
4. *Jesse Owens* was an Olympic gold medalist in track. *Joe Montana* is a former professional football player.

Wynton Marsalis, 1999. New York City.

So when you play, don't get carried away or burned out by the importance of your own effort. Start good. Finish good. Sound good. No more complicated than that. And when I say sound good, I mean sounding good enough to get a job. Because when you sound good, people will hire you; when you sound good, people will be calling.

Of course, sounding good also goes beyond the marketplace; it goes right to the heart of your personal objectives—our third base of playing. Although objectives vary, depending on the individual, there exists a central, common point: What do you want to give to people? Let me lay this on you.

Once I asked Sweets Edison,[5] "Why is it that you always sound good, from the first note that you play?"

"There's only one way to play, baby boy," Sweets answered. "There ain't but one way to do it."

Sweets means that you project your way with the ultimate feeling all the time, whether you're playing in a sad band, a great band, for elementary school students, at someone's birthday party at their house, or 'cause someone fixed a meal for you. When you pull your horn out, you should play as if that's the most important moment in your life. If it's not, make it be.

Remember when you were a kid and you really, really wanted something? It could have been the most trivial thing. Remember the way you begged and pleaded for it? Imagine playing with that passion, that desire, as if this was the most needed thing in your life. When we get older, we learn how to temper our wanting, our desire. Well, tap back into that childhood fervor and freedom of expression. That's what you have to have when you play. That thing you wanted the most and the way you were willing to sacrifice any speck of pride or dignity to obtain it. Remember how you wanted it; remember how you cried when you didn't get it? What about the girl who couldn't stand you? Or who liked you until Amos came around? Play with *that* passion.

Realize that the fundamentals of jazz help you develop your individuality, help you find that passion. Don't say, "I'm not going to really play blues," or "I'm not going to address swing." Don't run from you. Running carries a cost. Have you ever noticed that when you hear a contemporary Latin band play and juxtapose it with

---

5. *Sweets Edison* is the late jazz trumpeter Harry "Sweets" Edison.

Comparing Literature

a jazz band, the Latin music almost always sounds better? You wonder why that's the case? Just look at the bandstand. You'll see that the Latin musicians appear invested and involved; they believe in the integrity of their groove. Now look at the jazz band: not accepting the swing, trying to find some quasi-funk groove or, even worse, that sad jazz quasi-Latin groove. You can practically hear them muttering to themselves—"Swing is dead; let's try something else." They take detours to avoid sounding bad and run right into what they flee. The fourth and perhaps most important facet of playing jazz, *swing* and swinging.

You may hear about "quintessentially American" things. Well, what makes a thing quintessential is that it reflects the values of the thing it is supposed to be quintessentially about. In the case of an art form, it not only reflects the values, it embodies them, it ennobles them, and it emboldens them. That's why people study art forms with such intensity, because the artist channels the spirit of the nation. In the case of the swing, no one person created it; democracy is a collective experience. And swing is a democratic and *quintessentially* American concept.

Swing is supreme coordination under the duress of time. Swing is democracy made manifest; it makes you constantly adjust. At any given time, what's going to go on musically may not be to your liking. You have to know how to maintain your equilibrium and your balance, even if things are changing rapidly. Swing is designed for you to do that. Why? Each musician has a different concept of time. Sometimes I tell my students, "I want you all to stand up when a minute is over." And some people get up after twenty seconds. Some get up after a minute and a half. That shows the variance between individual concepts of time. As a player you have to, of your own volition, come to a conclusion about how you approach time.

But swing has a hierarchy, like a government. The president of the swing is the drummer. The drummer has the loudest instrument and the cymbal is in the highest register. In African music it's called the bell rhythm. It's always the high rhythm, because you can hear that rhythm. In jazz, the bell rhythm is on the cymbal. You follow the bell rhythm.

But, like a government, swing also has checks and balances, because if the drummer rushes, the bass player might bring the time back. Sometimes the president of the swing is whoever has the best time. When Charlie Parker played, his time was so good that the bell rhythm would follow him. So you have that possibility. This is also a democratic proposition. If you have a weak president, man, you might need a strong legislative branch, or a stronger judiciary—checks and balances.

Swing ties in with the heart of the American experience: You make your way; you invent your way. In jazz, that means you challenge the time, and you determine the degree of difficulty of the rhythms you choose to play. You could play quarter notes, which are difficult to play in time. Or any type of impossible, fun syncopations. Or you could just play strings of eighth notes. You try to maintain your equilibrium with style, and work within the flow. That's what the swing offers.

> **Discussion Starter**
>
> What is the author's purpose in writing what he did? Why does he discuss learning about different types of music? Why does he want the boy to understand the "democracy" of swing? Discuss your opinions in a small group.

Wrap-Up: Comparing Literature
Across Genres

- ***Dream Boogie* and *Motto*** by Langston Hughes
- from ***Giants of Jazz*** by Studs Terkel
- ***Playing Jazz*** by Wynton Marsalis

COMPARE THE Big Idea Issues of Identity

Writing Jazz may be the only major art form that truly originated in the United States. Jazz involves several forms of music—African rhythms and American band music—blended with some European influence. The best jazz music is improvised. Creating new music during a performance is what tends to separate the true jazz musician from those who can play only the notes written in a musical score. Many musicians, as well as aficionados, have found their identities in jazz. Think about the selections you have just read. Compare these writers in terms of the subjects they discuss. Are the writers alike in some ways? What makes each writer unique? How has music, specifically jazz, affected each writer?

Jump Up, 2000. Margie Livingston Campbell. Watercolor.

COMPARE Author's Purpose

Partner Activity Which of the authors and selections in this lesson had the greatest impact on you? With a partner, discuss the following questions:

1. What will you remember from the readings in this section?
2. What did these readings teach you?
3. What further questions do you have?

COMPARE Author's Viewpoints

Speaking and Listening Langston Hughes, Studs Terkel, and Wynton Marsalis each have a different viewpoint on the subject of jazz. Draw conclusions about each author's viewpoint on the following topics:

- the role of improvisation and experimentation in jazz
- the place of tradition in jazz
- the importance of creating a personal style

Present your conclusions to the class in an oral report. Be sure to support your conclusions with evidence from the selections.

Selection Resources For Selection Quizzes, eFlashcards, and Reading-Writing Connection activities, go to glencoe.com and enter QuickPass code GL59794u3.

Learning Objectives

For pages 632–639

In this workshop, you will focus on the following objectives:

Writing: Writing a reflective essay.

Grammar: Understanding how to correct unclear pronoun references.

Writing Workshop

Reflective Essay

Literature Connection In Gwendolyn Brooks's "Horses Graze," the speaker reflects on the lessons animals can teach us if we pay attention.

> "And at the crest of their brute satisfaction, / with wonderful gentleness, in affirmation, / they lift their clean calm eyes and they lie down / and love the world."

Poems often present reflections—understandings and interpretations of experiences. Essays can do the same thing in paragraph form: look back, find significance, and present it in a meaningful and interesting way to an audience. In a reflective essay, you narrate and describe an experience or observation to show its effect on you. To write a successful reflective essay, begin by reading the goals and strategies below.

Writing Process

At any stage of a writing process, you may think of new ideas. Feel free to return to earlier stages as you write.

Prewrite

Draft

Revise

Focus Lesson:
Use Sensory Details

Edit and Proofread

Focus Lesson:
Pronoun References

Present

Literature Online

Writing and Research For prewriting, drafting, and revising tools, go to glencoe.com and enter QuickPass code GL59794u3.

Checklist

Goals	Strategies
To present a meaningful personal experience	✓ Retell an experience or observation Set the experience in a specific time and place Use the first-person point of view
To present actions, events, and reactions in a logical order	✓ Present your experience as a chronological narrative with a beginning, a middle, and an end, or create flashbacks
To engage the audience	✓ Include sensory details and figurative language Show your own and others' thoughts, gestures, feelings, movements, and dialogue Use action verbs and other precise language
To express meaning and significance	✓ Establish and maintain a controlling idea of the experience Maintain a tone that is consistent with the events you narrate

632 UNIT 3 POETRY

> **Assignment: Reflect on an Observation or Experience**
>
> Write a reflection of at least 1,500 words on an observation you have made or an experience you have had. As you work, keep your audience and purpose in mind.
>
> **Audience:** classmates and peers
>
> **Purpose:** to explore the meaning and effect of a personal observation or experience

Analyze a Professional Model

As you read this reflection on Joy Harjo's life-changing experience of hearing jazz for the first time, identify the essay's narrative elements and the ways in which reflective details make the essay come alive.

"Suspended" by Joy Harjo

Once I was so small that I could barely peer over the top of the backseat of the black Cadillac my father polished and tuned daily; I wanted to see everything. It was around the time I acquired language, or even before that time, when something happened that changed my relationship to the spin of the world. My concept of language, of what was possible with music was changed by this revelatory moment. It changed even the way I looked at the sun. This suspended integer of time probably escaped ordinary notice in my parents' universe, which informed most of my vision in the ordinary world. They were still omnipresent gods. We were driving somewhere in Tulsa, the northern border of the Creek Nation. I don't know where we were going or where we had been, but I know the sun was boiling the asphalt, the car windows open for any breeze as I stood on tiptoes on the floorboard behind my father, a handsome god who smelled of Old Spice, whose slick black hair was always impeccably groomed, his clothes perfectly creased and ironed. The radio was on. I loved the radio, jukeboxes or any magic thing containing music even then.

Narration/Description

Real-World Connection

Present your essay or read it aloud to someone who shared the experience with you, to someone who might be inspired by it, or to someone who would be personally or professionally interested in the way it affected or changed you.

First-Person Point of View

Write your description from the first-person point of view. Use the pronouns *I, we, me,* and *us* and adjectives such as *my* and *our*.

Tone

Match your tone to your subject. You can also use your tone to invite your reader into the time, the place, and your experience or observation.

Narrative Elements

Include the elements you find in a story—setting, characters, and events.

Audience Engagement

Help your reader imagine seeing, hearing, smelling, tasting, or touching what you experienced.

Brass Section (Jamming at Minton's), From the Jazz Series, 1979. Romare Bearden. Color lithograph on paper, 24 x 32¾ in. Gift of Eugene Ivan Schuster. Smithsonian American Art Museum, Washington, DC.

Tone and Focus
Maintain a consistent tone and focus.

Audience Engagement
Use figurative language, precise nouns, and active verbs. Strive to show rather than just tell.

Contolling Idea
Relate all details to a single experience and its significance.

Meaning
Be sure to tell the meaning of the observation or experience

I wonder now what signaled this moment, a loop of time that on first glance could be any place in time. I became acutely aware of the line the jazz trumpeter was playing (a sound I later associated with Miles Davis). I didn't know the word *jazz* or *trumpet*, or the concepts. I don't know how to say it, with what sounds or words, but in that confluence of hot southern afternoon, in the breeze of aftershave and humidity, I followed that sound to the beginning, to the place of the birth of sound. I was suspended in whirling stars, a moon to which I'd traveled often by then. I grieved my parents' failings, my own life which I saw stretched the length of that rhapsody.

My rite of passage into the world of humanity occurred then, via jazz. The music made a startling bridge between familiar and strange lands, an appropriate vehicle, for though the music is predominantly west African in concept, with European associations, jazz was influenced by the Creek (or Muscogee) people, for we were there when jazz was born. I recognized it, that humid afternoon in my formative years, as a way to speak beyond the confines of ordinary language. I still hear it.

Reading–Writing Connection Think about the writing techniques that you have encountered and try them out in the reflective essay you write.

Prewrite

Find a Topic Make a time frame for completing the assignments. Then follow these steps. Think about different periods of your life. Record important experiences that occurred during each time frame. Be sure that you can find some meaning or significance in each event you list. Then choose the specific memory you like best.

List Details Once you have found a topic for writing, list details that seem to bring that experience or observation to life. You can use a cluster diagram. Write your topic in the center and then list the associations, including sensory details, that you have with the experience.

Make a Plan for Writing Your next step is to outline or organize your ideas for writing. First, review your audience, purpose, and controlling idea. Then, draw a chart, or divide a piece of paper into three rows, and include the following information in each section:

- ▶ **Beginning**—The beginning of your reflective essay should accomplish the same goals that the beginning of any narrative accomplishes: it may provide important details about the time and place, introduce the people who were important in the experience or observation, or start the action. It may also present a flashback.

- ▶ **Middle**—The middle of your reflective essay should tell what happened. It may present a series of events or just one event.

- ▶ **End**—The end of your reflective essay should accomplish two goals: it should bring the action or events to a close in some way, and it should also state the meaning or significance of the experience.

Talk About Your Ideas Meet with a partner. Explain what your topic is and the significance of the experience you have chosen. Then review your organizational plan with your partner. To develop your writing voice, listen to your speaking voice now as you express the meaning of the experience or its effect on you. Work with your partner to identify words and phrases that reflect your voice and then jot them down.

Narration / Description

The Writing Plan as a Test

If you have a topic but cannot develop it into a plan with a clear beginning, middle, and end, start over with a new topic. Prewriting is not a time for developing ideas only. It is also a time for finding out whether ideas for writing will work as essays.

Avoid Plagiarism

Never download a paper from the Internet. This dishonest action can have immediate and serious consequences—especially if your teacher has seen the same paper before or routinely checks the Internet to discourage cheating.

Draft

Create a Structure As you write your ideas on paper in the form of sentences and paragraphs, remember that your essay should have a clear beginning, middle, and end. In some cases, you may be able to achieve this in just three paragraphs, one for each part of this essay. It is also fine to develop two or more paragraphs for the middle of your reflective essay and to add a full paragraph of reflection after your narrative

Analyze a Workshop Model

Here is a final draft of a reflective essay. Read the essay and answer the questions in the margin. Use the answers to these questions to guide you as you write.

Writing Frames

As you read the workshop model, think about the writer's use of the following frames:

- When we were ____.
- I felt as if ____.
- I knew that/felt that/ realized that ____.

Consider using frames like these in your own reflective essay.

Narrative Elements

How does the writer show his own and another person's feelings?

First-Person Point of View

Which pronoun tells the reader that this essay is written from the first-person point of view?

Audience Engagement

How do figurative language and sensory details help you experience what the narrator experienced?

Changed by a Chimp

"Tomorrow," Mrs. Dagostino announced enthusiastically, "we'll be visiting the Center for Great Apes." She continued brightly, "This is a very special opportunity for us. Not many people are allowed to visit, you know! I've waited two years to take a class there!"

"Who cares?" I thought. I wasn't the least bit interested in looking at a bunch of old chimps. Mrs. Dagostino then explained that this was a place for "retired" chimps—chimps that had been used in entertainment and research and were now no longer useful. "A retirement home for chimps," I groaned. "How ridiculous!"

When we arrived, the guide began to drone about "special enriching environments" and "complex primates." With glazed eyes, I shifted from foot to foot and daydreamed. The thirty-foot-high domed enclosures surrounded by guava, banana, and other tropical trees were about as interesting to me as twelve extra pages of math homework.

When we were finally allowed to walk around the perim-

636 UNIT 3 POETRY

eter of the chimps' enclosure, some students stopped to do what we had been instructed to do: observe the chimps' behaviors, take notes, and discuss what we saw. I noticed a chimp that seemed to be communicating with two adult visitors. The chimp picked up a brown bag that had been left in its enclosure and tore the bag into a piece of paper about six inches by eight inches long. Then he tore an opening in one end. When he held the paper up to his face, I realized that he had created a mask. One of the visitors brought her hand to her mouth and closed her eyes. I knew that she had experienced what I had at that moment: the animal behind the fence was, in some way, speaking to us.

The chimp handed the mask through the fence to the visitors and then made a second mask. In a few minutes, the visitors and the chimp were looking at each other through these torn bags. They were also, I understood, silently communicating. I just stood there thinking what it must be like for this "complex primate" to be used for research purposes or to live its life in any enclosure—even one as nice as the one provided by the Center for Great Apes. It was a moving realization.

Three days later, Mrs. Dagostino read my report on the Center for Great Apes aloud to the class. The following summer, I enrolled in a summer program that focused on chimpanzees and orangutans. And next year, when I apply to college, I will look for a school where I can study primates. Whatever chimps may have to tell us, I plan on finding out.

Narration / Description

Narrative Structure

How does the writer organize this narrative?

Descriptive Details

Explain how the writer shows, rather than tells, parts of his experience.

Tone

How would you describe the author's tone? How has his perspective changed? How does his attitude toward the reader, or tone, remain consistent even as his attitude toward his experience changes?

Controlling Idea / Significance

What realization does the writer come to as a result of his observations and experiences? How has the entire essay led up to this controlling idea?

Revise

Peer Review When you finish your draft, have a peer reviewer read it. Ask him or her to identify narrative and descriptive elements in your writing. Then ask your reviewer to make suggestions about where to add background information, sensory details, or reflection. Use the checklist below to evaluate and strengthen each other's writing.

Traits of Strong Writing

Include these traits of strong writing to express your ideas effectively.

- Ideas
- Organization
- Voice
- Word Choice
- Sentence Fluency
- Conventions
- Presentation

Checklist

- ✓ Do you reflect, or look back, on a meaningful experience?
- ✓ Do you use the first-person point of view throughout your essay?
- ✓ Do you have a clear beginning, middle, and end?
- ✓ Do you use sensory details, action verbs, and other precise language?
- ✓ Do you make the meaning of your experience clear to your reader?
- ✓ Do you maintain a consistent tone and focus throughout the essay?

Focus Lesson

Use Sensory Details

Sensory details are words or phrases that appeal to one of the five senses. Note how well-chosen sensory details improve the passage from the Workshop Model below.

Draft:

These students were doing everything we had been told to do.

Revision:

<u>Chatting quietly,</u>[1] these students were noticing the separate daytime and nighttime areas for the chimps, as well as the <u>ropes, swings, and hammocks that had been created to simulate their natural environment.</u>[2] Some students were also listening to the various <u>hoots and calls,</u>[3] while others sketched the animals.

1: Appeals to Hearing 2: Appeals to Sight 3: Appeals to Hearing

Word Choice

This academic vocabulary word appears in the student model:

simulate (sim′ yə lāt) *v.*
1. to re-create or copy the conditions or characteristics of; 2. to re-create or give the appearance of, usually with the intent to deceive; *The areas had been created to simulate their natural environment.* Using academic vocabulary may help strengthen your writing. Try to use one or two academic vocabulary words in your reflective essay. See the complete list on pages R80–R82.

Edit and Proofread

Get It Right When you have completed the final draft of your reflective essay, proofread it for errors in grammar, usage, mechanics, and spelling. Refer to the Language Handbook, pages R40–R59, as a guide.

> **Focus Lesson**
>
> ## Correct Unclear Pronoun References
>
> A pronoun must refer to a noun or another pronoun. Often, it refers to a noun that appears earlier in the sentence.
>
> ### Problem: Unclear Pronoun Reference
>
> The pronoun *them* refers to the antecedent *the visitors and the chimp*, yet the writer intends the pronoun *them* to refer to the masks.
>
> *[He] then made a second mask. In a few minutes, the visitors and the chimp were looking at each other through them.*
>
> **Solution A:** Replace the pronoun with the noun to which it refers.
>
> *[He] then made a second mask. In a few minutes, the visitors and the chimp were looking at each other through these torn bags.*
>
> **Solution B:** Rewrite the sentence so that the pronoun clearly refers to a previous noun or pronoun.
>
> *He then made a second mask. In a few minutes, one visitor looked through it at the chimp while the chimp eyed the visitor.*
>
> ### Problem: Unclear Pronoun Reference
>
> The pronoun *They* doesn't refer to a specific person, place, or thing.
>
> *They say that chimps have a lot to tell us, so I plan on learning more about them.*
>
> **Solution C:** Rewrite the sentence to eliminate the pronoun.
>
> *Whatever chimps may have to tell us, I plan on finding out.*

Present

Check your assignment for requirements related to presentation, such as those for margins, line spacing, page numbers, and a cover sheet. If there are no presentation requirements, be sure to use one-inch margins on all sides and to double-space your work.

Narration / Description

Peer Review Tips

A classmate may ask you to read his or her reflective essay. Take your time and jot down notes as you read so you can give constructive feedback. Use the following questions to get started:

• Does the essay create and maintain a single controlling idea?

• Does the writer create interest through the use of figurative language, as well as through characterization by means of emotions, gestures, and dialogue?

Word Processing Tip

Never rely on a computer's spell-check feature to do the whole job of proofreading. A spell-checker has limited use, because it cannot distinguish certain kinds of errors, such as misused homonyms. After using the spell-checker, reread your paper to catch additional errors.

Writer's Portfolio

Place a copy of your reflective essay in your portfolio to review later.

Writing and Research For editing and publishing tools, go to glencoe.com and enter QuickPass code GL59794u3.

Speaking, Listening, and Viewing Workshop

Learning Objectives

For pages 640–641
In this workshop, you will focus on the following objective:

Speaking and Listening: Delivering a reflective essay.

Reflective Presentation

Literature Connection Poet Joy Harjo expresses herself and her Cherokee and Creek heritage through music, art, and words. She has a band called Poetic Justice; she also paints and pursues other visual arts. According to Harjo, she approaches the art of poetry as a visual artist. In fact, any written work can be delivered, changed, or enhanced with the addition of visual aids and music. In this workshop, you will present a reflection that uses visuals to help express the events and their significance.

> **Assignment** Create an oral presentation of your reflective essay and deliver it to an audience.

Plan Your Presentation

Presenting an essay orally is not the same thing as simply reading it aloud. It is a chance to use your voice, body language, and visual aids to communicate meaning to an audience.

- Read your essay aloud to yourself and think about your audience. Ask yourself which parts of your essay will be most interesting, which will be hardest to understand, and which could be interpreted visually.
- Next, make notes. For example, circle or highlight the most important details, dialogue, and description. Underline anything that can be cut or better explained. Jot down ideas for visuals in the margins.
- Revise your essay to make it a spoken script. In the script, retain all of your best details, dialogue, and descriptions. Expand and enliven them. Omit details that contribute little to an overall impression or theme. Add brief, interesting bits of explanation wherever needed.
- Finally, make note cards. After you rehearse and learn your presentation, these cards will serve as reminders or cues during your delivery.

Choosing a Tone

If you are reflecting on a serious or sad experience, you will probably choose a formal tone. For less somber reflections, however, consider a conversational tone. You can include everyday expressions with a relaxed, person-to-person tone to draw your listeners in.

—practice the gestures you will make during your presentation
—make eye contact with your audience members

Create Your Visual Media

As you create your script and note cards, concentrate on the images you want to display or project. There are many options for visual aids—drawings, collages, photographs, and video. Be sure to credit anything that is not your own work. You can also incorporate colors, shapes, and designs into your project to represent a feeling or mood. Because you are telling a story, one way to plan your visuals is by sequencing images along a plot diagram.

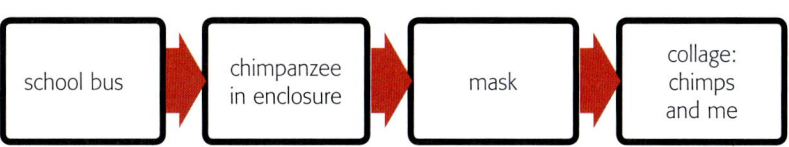

Once you have a plan, assemble your images in order and write brief prompts on your note cards that cue you to display each one at the right time.

Rehearse

Never deliver an oral presentation without rehearsing it several times.

▶ You can rehearse your presentation the first few times by yourself. Get used to using your note cards as prompts and learn your presentation thoroughly. Be sure to practice the actual gestures you will use.

▶ Next, practice in front of a classmate or a family member. Ask your listener to comment on how effectively you used each of the verbal and nonverbal techniques listed in the chart below. If possible, rehearse once more in front of the same person, incorporating his or her suggestions.

Verbal Techniques	Nonverbal Techniques
☑ **Tone** Whether your subject is light or serious, show your interest.	☑ **Visibility** Be sure that everyone can see your presentation.
☑ **Emphasis** Stress important words, details, and dialogue.	☑ **Eye Contact** Make eye contact with your audience.
☑ **Pronunciation** Make sure to pronounce each word distinctly.	☑ **Posture** Avoid leaning or slouching.
☑ **Volume** Be sure to speak loudly enough that everyone can hear you.	☑ **Gestures** Strike a balance between standing stiffly and making too many movements.

Speaking Frames
Consider using the following frames in your descriptive presentation:

- I experienced _____.
- _____ surrounded/enveloped/beckoned to me.
- Looking back on it now, _____.

Presentation Tips
Use the following checklist to evaluate your reflective presentation:

☑ Did you transform your written essay into an effective oral presentation?

☑ Were your visuals appropriate for your audience and purpose? Did they help your audience see and otherwise experience the events or observation?

☑ Did you use verbal and nonverbal techniques effectively?

Speaking, Listening, and Viewing For project ideas, templates, and presentation tips, go to glencoe.com and enter QuickPass code GL59794u3.

SPEAKING, LISTENING, AND VIEWING WORKSHOP

Independent Reading

Poetry and Novels

POETRY IS THE MOST CONCENTRATED, abbreviated genre. In relatively few words, a poet may present the same themes that a novelist explores over hundreds of pages.

As you have seen in this unit, poetry ranges from momentary glimpses of the natural world to longer, serious reflections on love and grief. For more poetry, try the two suggestions below. For novels and a play that incorporate the Big Ideas of *The Energy of the Everyday, Loves and Losses,* and *Issues of Identity,* try the titles from the Glencoe Literature Library on the next page.

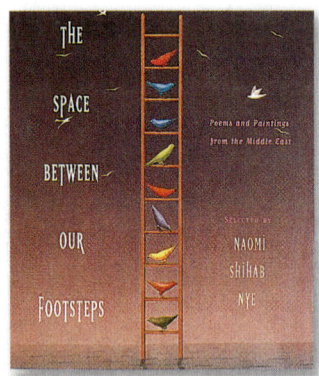

The Space Between Our Footsteps: Poems and Paintings from the Middle East

selected by Naomi Shihab Nye

This collection of works from more than one hundred poets and artists from nineteen Middle Eastern countries explores themes that include family, childhood, journeys, war, peace, and joy. Award-winning poet and anthologist Naomi Shihab Nye pairs poems with full-color art from the countries represented. Nye's respect for and appreciation of Middle Eastern culture saturates the book. Yet, the overall effect of the anthology is one that emphasizes the similarities between people.

A Haiku Menagerie: Living Creatures in Poems and Prints

Stephen Addiss with Fumiko and Akira Yamamoto

Showing how fascinating the smallest animal or insect can be, this collection of more than one hundred Japanese haiku features master poets' insights into the natural world. More than forty-eight woodblock prints illustrate the creatures described in the poems. The poems are presented both in English translations and the original Japanese.

GLENCOE LITERATURE LIBRARY

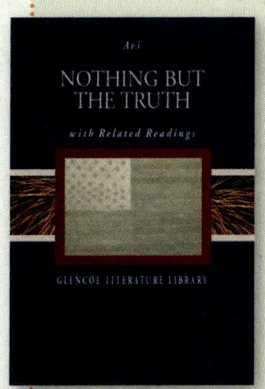

Nothing But the Truth: A Documentary Novel
Avi

A simple action gives new meaning to the energy of the everyday and leads to a national scandal.

Cyrano de Bergerac
Edmond Rostand

A poetic play about loves and losses features love, deception, and heartbreak.

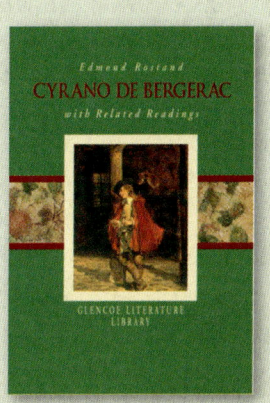

Picture Bride
Yoshiko Uchida

In this novel about issues of identity, a woman leaves Japan to marry a stranger in San Francisco.

CRITICS' CORNER

"Mary Oliver would probably never admit to anything so grandiose as an effort to connect the conscious mind and the heart (that's what she says poetry can do), but that is exactly what she accomplishes in this stunning little handbook, ostensibly written 'to empower the beginning writer. . . .' Oliver gives us tools for 'the listening mind,' tools we need to write poetry."

—Susan Salter Reynolds, the *Los Angeles Times Book Review*

A Poetry Handbook
Mary Oliver

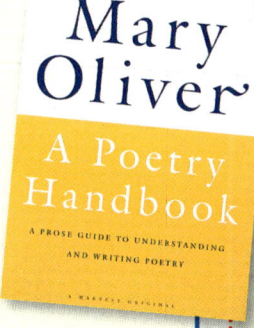

In this highly readable handbook, Oliver reminds aspiring poets about sound, line, and diction and demonstrates that "out of writing, and the rewriting, beauty is born." Citing works from other poets, such as Elizabeth Bishop, T. S. Eliot, William Carlos Williams, and Lucille Clifton, Oliver reveals that writing good poetry is a craft. She urges would-be poets to take care of the special place within them that "houses the possibility of poems."

Write a Review

Read one of the books shown and write a review of it for your classmates. Offer suggestions on how they might overcome difficulties in reading the book. Present your review to the class.

INDEPENDENT READING 643

Assessment

English–Language Arts

Reading: Poetry and Fiction

Carefully read the following two passages. Use context clues to help you define any words with which you are unfamiliar. Pay close attention to the themes, tones, and uses of literary and sound devices. Then, on a separate sheet of paper, answer the questions on page 646.

"Daybreak in Alabama" by Langston Hughes

When I get to be a composer
I'm gonna write me some music about
Daybreak in Alabama
And I'm gonna put the purtiest songs in it
5   Rising out of the ground like a swamp mist
And falling out of heaven like soft dew.
I'm gonna put some tall tall trees in it
And the scent of pine needles
And the smell of red clay after rain
10 And long red necks
And poppy colored faces
And big brown arms
And the field daisy eyes
Of black and white black white black people
15 And I'm gonna put white hands
And black hands and brown and yellow hands
And red clay earth hands in it
Touching everybody with kind fingers
And touching each other natural as dew
20 In that dawn of music when I
Get to be a composer
And write about daybreak
In Alabama.

from "Red Velvet Dress" by Naomi Shihab Nye

In the next neighborhood over from their neighborhood lived the
Collins boys and the Parker boys that Lena knew from their jobs
together working on the berry-picking farm and the Emerson girls who
spent every Saturday morning at the library like Lena did and some-
5   times they all traded favorite books and the big grandmother with the

high hair that Lena's mother stared at once in the grocery checkout line. "I should have been her," she whispered to Lena, which Lena found very strange. How could anybody be anyone else? But Lena would never go to their houses and ask to see the Africans.

Because once you knew Ricky Collins, you knew about his lizard collection and his turquoise stone that he kept in a pouch inside an egg carton with old pennies worth ten dollars each and the rusted key he dug out of the ground one day while they were plucking the berries. You knew his voice and shirts. You did not think A Group of Different People, when you were thinking of friends.

Maybe the Robitailles weren't even like any other French-Canadians at all. Maybe Annie's grandfather who snapped his suspenders and brought them a fancy cold dessert called Tiramisu which he carried on ice cubes in his green car was just himself more than An Italian. In those days not many people talked about being half-and-half, but years later Lena would know it was one of the richest kinds of milk.

So her father burned the dry leaves and a bat flew over him. Lena called out, "Bat! Daddy! Look, it's not a bird!" and he looked up. *"Ahlan wa sahlan,"* he called out, which meant "Welcome" in his own first language of Arabic, and she laughed as the bat dipped and rose in graceful arcs. He did not say, Get away. He did not say, I wish you were something else. He said "Welcome" and the bat seemed to understand by circling close above his head.

Then she took a deep breath and called out to him. "Daddy, some children came to the door. They wanted to see the Arab and I said we didn't have one. I never saw them on this street before. I never saw them at school either. But they might be from school. Are you mad at me?"

And her father came and sat beside her and took her hand in his own hand. . . .

Her father said, "The world asks us all a lot of questions, doesn't it," and stared off into a strip of pink sky. . . .

Then there was the clatter-bang muffler sound of Peter's father turning into his driveway next door.

Lena thought his feelings might be hurt. She said, "I'm sorry," and her daddy laughed so loudly he startled her. . . .

"You could have said Yes, but you were also right in saying No! All the questions have more than one good answer, don't you think? . . .

I could have put on my headdress for them! You could have pretended I didn't speak English. Maybe they'll come back and we can make them happy."

Questions 1–7 apply to "Daybreak in Alabama."

1. What literary device is used in "like a swamp mist," in line 5, and in "like soft dew," in line 6?
   A. simile
   B. personification
   C. metaphor
   D. hyperbole

2. What literary device is used in the poem's first six lines?
   A. end rhyme
   B. couplets
   C. enjambment
   D. alliteration

3. What is the overall tone of the poem?
   A. hopeful
   B. tragic
   C. comic
   D. mysterious

4. Twice the speaker says, "when I get to be a composer." From the context, which of the following do you think best expresses the meaning of this statement?
   A. The speaker wants to compose but doubts that this is possible.
   B. The speaker has means, but little hope, of achieving his goals.
   C. The speaker has an ambition to compose music as well as poetry.
   D. The speaker is an impractical dreamer.

5. What type of language is used in the poem? Consider the phrases "gonna write me," in line 2, and "purtiest songs," in line 4.
   A. formal language
   B. figurative language
   C. grammatical language
   D. dialect

6. What do the words *daybreak* and *dawn*, in Hughes's poem, evoke?
   A. harmony in life
   B. a new beginning
   C. the end of an era
   D. joyousness

7. Which of the following statements best describes the theme of the poem?
   A. The speaker dreams of a world without divisions.
   B. The landscape of Alabama stirs the speaker to write music.
   C. The speaker anticipates living in a world of music.
   D. The speaker despairs of racial unity.

Questions 8–11 apply to "Red Velvet Dress."

8. From which point of view is the selection written?
   A. first person
   B. second person
   C. third-person limited
   D. third-person omniscient

9. What is the first language of Lena's father?
   A. English
   B. Arabic
   C. French
   D. Italian

10. According to this passage, how many other members are in Lena's family?
    A. one
    B. two
    C. three
    D. four

11. What literary device is used in lines 27–28, in saying that the bat "seemed to understand"?
    A. personification
    B. metaphor
    C. simile
    D. literary comparison

Vocabulary Skills: Sentence Completion

For each item, choose the word that best completes the sentence.

1. The child soon learned that his _____ comments did not improve, but in fact worsened, his situation.
   A. embroidered
   B. meticulous
   C. querulous
   D. hoary

2. The _____ heat made it difficult for us to enjoy our summer vacation.
   A. dense
   B. hoary
   C. searing
   D. embroidered

3. Erin would no longer tolerate her employee's _____ tardiness.
   A. chronic
   B. disgruntled
   C. primal
   D. ceremonious

4. Walter could not _____ precisely when he had learned to read.
   A. marvel
   B. lag
   C. recollect
   D. tread

5. Although many in the crowd were quite _____ to the game's outcome, they cheered wildly anyway.
   A. austere
   B. melancholy
   C. indifferent
   D. serpentine

6. As the days passed into years, his memories of the farm faded into _____.
   A. conflagration
   B. oblivion
   C. essence
   D. stupor

7. The _____ on the cave wall was mysterious; its significance could not be determined.
   A. hones
   B. infirmity
   C. oblivion
   D. glyph

8. When Judy studied Chinese, she struggled with the differences in its _____ from that of English.
   A. syntax
   B. parenthesis
   C. fissure
   D. cipher

9. The house was _____ with dozens of candles, lit in celebration of the holiday.
   A. mature
   B. aglow
   C. submerged
   D. primal

10. When Aileen visited her parents, she became _____ about her childhood.
    A. ceremonious
    B. meticulous
    C. russet
    D. nostalgic

Literature Online

Assessment For additional test practice, go to glencoe.com and enter QuickPass code GL59794u3.

Grammar and Writing Skills: Paragraph Improvement

Carefully read the following draft of a student's essay. Pay close attention to sentence structure and pronoun use. Then, on a separate sheet of paper, answer the questions on pages 648–649.

(1) Walt Whitman's poem "When I Heard the Learn'd Astronomer" contrasts two distinct philosophies of life. (2) The astronomer, whom understands things by dissecting them, takes the scientific approach to life. (3) In opposition, the narrator, which represents the creative or poetic side, is a more romantic character. (4) He seem satisfied just to appreciate the world around him.

(5) As the poem begins, he describes the astronomer's lecture, in which he cites "proofs and figures" and "charts and diagrams." (6) The astronomer has gone to great lengths to understand and classify the information. (7) The narrator soon becomes bored with all the details and leaves: he "wandered off by himself" into the "night-air." (8) Once he's outside in the "mystical" night, he seems content as he looks up in "perfect silence at the stars." (9) The narrator, or poet, does not need the astronomer's charts and formulas to understand what he sees in the sky.

(10) Whitman shows us through the poem that life is mechanical and orderly just as its beautiful. (11) But as readers we learn only the narrator's point of view, so we are closer to that than to the astronomer. (12) In the end, personal experience is more to be valued than abstract and analytical theories.

1. Which of the following errors occurs in sentence 2?
   A. sentence fragment
   B. verb tense error
   C. incorrect pronoun
   D. unclear antecedent

2. Which of the following is the best way to revise sentence 2?
   A. Delete the nonessential interrupting clause.
   B. Change *whom* to *who*.
   C. Change the voice of the sentence.
   D. Make no change.

3. Which of the following is the best way to revise sentence 3?
   A. Change *which* to *whom*.
   B. Change *which* to *who*.
   C. Delete *in opposition*.
   D. Make no change.

4. Which of the following errors appears in sentence 4?
   A. lack of subject-verb agreement
   B. sentence fragment
   C. unclear antecedent
   D. incorrect verb tense

5. Which noun in the previous sentences is the antecedent for the pronouns *He* and *him* in sentence 4?
   A. poet
   B. astronomer
   C. Walt Whitman
   D. narrator

6. Which of the following errors occurs in sentence 5?
   A. lack of subject-verb agreement
   B. unclear antecedent
   C. incorrect verb tense
   D. sentence fragment

7. Which of the following is the best revision for sentence 5?
   A. As the poem begins, the narrator describes the astronomer's lecture, in which the astronomer cites "proofs and figures" and "charts and diagrams."
   B. As the poem begins, which describes the astronomer's lecture, there are "proofs and figures" and "charts and diagrams."
   C. As the poem begins, who describes the astronomer's lecture, where there are "proofs and figures" and "charts and diagrams."
   D. As the poem begins, whom describes the astronomer's lecture, where there are "proofs and figures" and "charts and diagrams."

8. Which of the following is the best revision for sentence 10?
   A. Whitman shows us through the poem that life is mechanical and orderly just as they are beautiful.
   B. Whitman shows us, through the poem that life is mechanical and orderly just as its beautiful.
   C. Whitman shows us, through the poem, that life is mechanical and orderly just as it is beautiful.
   D. Whitman shows us through the poem that life is mechanical and orderly just as beautiful.

9. Which of the following is the best revision of sentence 11?
   A. However, as readers we only get the narrator's point of view, so we are closer to his than to the astronomer.
   B. As readers, however, we learn only the narrator's point of view, so we are closer to his view than to the astronomer's.
   C. But as readers we only get the narrator's point of view, so we are closer to he than to the astronomer.
   D. But as readers we only get the narrator's point of view, so we are closer to him than to the astronomer's.

10. Which of the following is the best way to revise sentence 12 for clarification?
    A. Change the active voice to passive voice.
    B. Change *In the end* to *In the final analysis*.
    C. Rewrite the sentence to define *abstract*.
    D. Make no change.

Essay

Choose any two works from this unit and write an essay that compares or contrasts the tone in the two works. Consider how the tone contributes to the meaning of the poem or work. Explain how the tone affects the audience, or reader, of the work. As you write, keep in mind that your essay will be checked for **ideas, organization, voice, word choice, sentence fluency, conventions,** and **presentation.**

Chorus Members, also called the *Extras,* 1877. Edgar Degas. Pastel on monotype. Louvre, Paris.

View the Art Edgar Degas (dā gä´) was a French Impressionist painter who was known for his images of dancers and other figures in motion. What type of drama is probably being depicted in this painting? How can you tell?

UNIT FOUR

DRAMA

Looking Ahead

A drama, or play, is a story told mainly through the words and actions of characters. The story might unfold on a stage or on a movie or television screen. Readers of plays imagine actors speaking the dialogue and envision the setting, lighting, and actions described in the stage directions. Drama allows readers to see the story unfold before their very eyes.

Each part in Unit Four focuses on a Big Idea that can help you connect the literary works to your life.

PREVIEW	Big Ideas	Literary Focus
PART 1	Loyalty and Betrayal	Tragedy
PART 2	Portraits of Real Life	Comedy and Modern Drama

Learning Objectives

For pages 650–656

In studying this text, you will focus on the following objectives:

Literary Study:
Analyzing form and structure.
Analyzing language.
Analyzing sound devices.

Genre Focus
What do fiction and drama have in common?

Playwright August Wilson said of his purpose, "I'm trying to take culture and put it onstage, demonstrate it is capable of sustaining you. There is no idea that can't be contained by life: Asian life, European life, certainly black life. My plays are about love, honor, duty, betrayal—things humans have written about since the beginning of time." Drama contains ideas in live action. Its characters, costumes, sets, and lighting combine to communicate the message, or theme, of the work.

Tragedy

Characters

The characters to be portrayed are listed at the beginning of a play. In tragedy, the main character is sometimes a **tragic hero**. A tragic hero often has a **tragic flaw**, such as *hubris* (excessive pride), that leads to the character's downfall. The tragic flaw is sometimes called *hamartia*, ancient Greek for "error in judgment." The idea was first discussed by Aristotle and used subsequently by both ancient Greek and more recent tragedians, including Sophocles and Shakespeare. The tragic hero is usually a man of high status and qualities superior to those of his kinsmen. The tragic flaw, which can be the result of either fate or choice, causes disproportionately large problems for the tragic hero.

CHARACTERS

ANTIGONE: daughter of Oedipus
ISMENE: daughter of Oedipus
EURYDICE: wife of Creon
CREON: King of Thebes, uncle of Antigone and Ismene
HAIMON: son of Creon
TEIRESIAS: a blind prophet
A SENTRY
A MESSENGER
CHORUS: elders of Thebes
CHORAGOS: leader of the Chorus

—Sophocles, **from** *Antigone*

Tragic Plots

Tragic plots are driven by the hero's **tragic flaw**. During the rising action of the play, the audience often is aware of the flaw, which the hero cannot perceive. Tension mounts as the character takes the inevitable action that seals his or her fate. Then, in a frequently violent climax, the tragic finale plays out.

CAESAR. Nor heaven nor earth have been at peace tonight.
Thrice hath Calphurnia in her sleep cried out, "Help, ho! they murther Caesar!" Who's within?

—William Shakespeare, **from** *The Tragedy of Julius Caesar*, Act 2, Scene 2

Comedy and Modern Drama

Dialogue

Plays consist mostly of **dialogue,** or conversation, between the characters. Through dialogue, the characters reveal themselves and the plot of the play moves forward. Unlike tragedies, comedies move toward a happy ending. In the script, the name of the character comes before the dialogue he or she will speak. Dialogue is sometimes referred to as **lines.**

Two men in a park. One on the grass, reading. The other making cricket strokes with umbrella.
1. A.: (*stopping in mid-stroke*): Eh, look at that bloke, what's he got on his back, he's got a sandwich board on his back.

—Harold Pinter, **from *That's Your Trouble***

Stage Directions

Stage directions can describe the setting of a play. They may also tell actors how they should appear and actions they should take onstage. They might describe sets, props, sound effects, or lighting. Stage directions are usually set off from the dialogue by parentheses or brackets and written in italics.

SCENE: *Chubukov's mansion—the living room*
[*LOMOV enters, formally dressed in evening jacket, white gloves, top hat. He is nervous from the start.*]
CHUBUKOV. [*Rising.*] Well, look who's here!—

—Anton Chekhov, **from *A Marriage Proposal***

Acts and Scenes

Plays usually have between one and five **acts.** Acts are further divided into **scenes.** Scene changes usually indicate a change in location or the passage of time. One-act plays are usually not divided into scenes.

SCENE: *Before the palace of Creon, King of Thebes. A central double door, and two lateral doors. A platform extends the length of the façade, and from this platform three steps lead down into the "orchestra," or chorus-ground.*

Distributed By Universal Press Syndicate. Reprinted with permission. All rights reserved.

Literature Online

Literature and Reading For more selections in this genre, go to glencoe.com and enter QuickPass code GL59794u4.

LITERARY ANALYSIS MODEL
How do dramatists use literary elements?

August Wilson (1945–2005), a two-time Pulitzer prize winning dramatist, chronicled the African American experience in an epic series of ten plays. "The Janitor," one of Wilson's earlier plays, may have been informed by growing up with a mother he admired who worked as a cleaning lady.

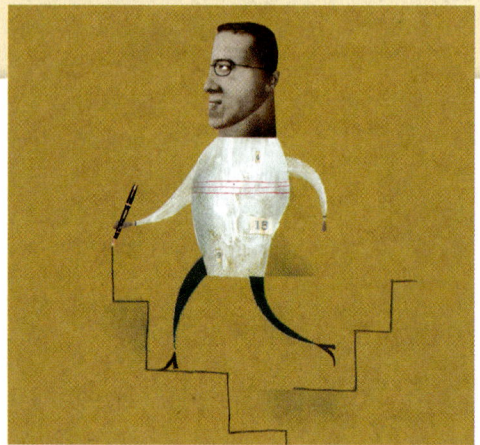

APPLYING Literary Elements

Characters
SAM and MR. COLLINS are the characters in *The Janitor*.

Setting
The story unfolds in the ballroom of a hotel.

Stage Directions
The italic text in brackets tells the actor what to do when he first comes onto the stage.

Dialogue
The words that come after the character's name are spoken by the actor on the stage. The ellipses suggest the manner in which the words should be spoken.

Monologue
A long speech by a character spoken either to others or as if alone is a monologue.

The Janitor
by August Wilson

CHARACTERS
SAM
MR. COLLINS

SETTING: A hotel ballroom

5 (*SAM enters pushing a broom near the lectern. He stops and reads the sign hanging across the ballroom.*)

SAM. National . . . Conference . . . on . . . Youth.

(*He nods his approval and continues sweeping. He gets an idea, stops, and approaches the lectern. He clears his throat and begins to speak. His*
10 *speech is delivered with the literacy of a janitor. He chooses his ideas carefully. He is a man who has approached life honestly, with both eyes open.*)

SAM. I want to thank you all for inviting me here to speak about youth. See . . . I's fifty-six years old and I knows something about youth. The first thing I knows . . . is that youth is sweet
15 before flight . . . its odor is rife with speculation and its resilience . . . that's its bounce back . . . is remarkable. But it's that sweetness that we victims of. All of us. Its sweetness . . . and its flight. One of them fellows in that Shakespeare stuff said, "I am not what I am." See. He wasn't like Popeye. This fellow
20 had a different understanding. "I am not what I am." Well, neither are you. You are just what you have been . . . whatever you are now. But what you are now ain't what you gonna become . . . even though it is with you now . . . it's inside you now this instant. Time . . . see, this how you get to this . . .

654 UNIT 4 DRAMA

25 Time ain't changed. It's just moved. Or maybe it ain't moved . . . maybe it just changed. It don't matter. We are all victims of the sweetness of youth and the time of its flight. See . . . just like you I forgot who I am. I forgot what happened
30 first. But I know the river I step into now . . . is not the same river I stepped into twenty years ago. See. I know that much. But I have forgotten the name of the river . . . I have forgotten the names of the gods . . . and like everybody else I
35 have tried to fool them with my dancing . . . and guess at their faces. It's the same with everybody. We don't have to mention no names. Ain't nobody innocent. We are all victims of ourselves. We have all had our hand in the soup . . . and
40 made the music play just so. See, now . . . this what I call wrestling with Jacob's angel. You lay down at night and that angel come to wrestle with you. When you wrestling with that angel you bargaining for you future. See. And what
45 you need to bargain with is that sweetness of youth. So . . . to the youth of the United States I says . . . don't spend that sweetness too fast! 'Cause you gonna need it. See. I's fifty-six years old and I done found that out. But it's all the same. It all comes back on you . . . just like reaping and sow-
50 ing. Down and out ain't nothing but being caught up in the balance of what you put down. If you down and out and things ain't going right for you . . . you can bet you done put a down payment on your troubles. Now you got to pay up on the balance. That's as true as I'm standing here. Sometimes
55 you can't see it like that. The last note on Gabriel's horn always gets lost when you get to realizing you done heard the first. See, it's just like. . . .

MR. COLLINS. (*Entering.*) Come on, Sam . . . let's quit wasting time and get this floor swept. There's going to be a big
60 important meeting here this afternoon.

SAM. Yessuh, Mr. Collins. Yessuh.
(*SAM goes back to sweeping as the lights go down to—*)

BLACK

Plot
The emotional height, or climax, occurs when we experience the gap between Sam's wisdom and the way Mr. Collins treats him.

Reading Check

Analyze Why might Wilson have set the play in a hotel ballroom?

INTRODUCTION 655

Wrap-Up

Guide to Reading Drama

- Like fiction, drama has plot, setting, characters, and theme.
- As you read drama, you may imagine the actors on a stage performing, or you may imagine the characters as real people.
- Preview the characters before you read.
- Read the stage directions as well as the dialogue.
- Pay special attention to what happens to the main character.

Elements of Drama

- A **tragedy** is a play in which the main character suffers a downfall.
- The main character in a tragedy is often a tragic hero.
- A **comedy** is a play that deals with its subject in a light, familiar, or satirical manner.
- The **dialogue** is what the characters say to one another.
- The **stage directions** may describe the sets, props, sound effects, lighting, and actions of the characters.
- Plays are divided into **acts** and **scenes**.

Unit Resources For additional skills practice, go to glencoe.com and enter QuickPass code GL59794u4.

Activities

Use what you have learned about reading and analyzing drama to do one of these activities.

1. Write and Evaluate Give August Wilson a grade for his use of language and grammar in "The Janitor." Base your grade on how effective his choices are in light of the character he is trying to portray. Support your grade in a written paragraph, citing examples from the play.

2. Speaking and Listening Act out some of the lines from "The Janitor" in front of the class. Then, as a class, discuss how the lines express the message of the play.

3. Take Notes Try using this study organizer to explore your personal responses to the plays you read in this unit.

FOLDABLES Study Organizer

BOUND BOOK

See page R21 for folding instructions.

PART 1

Loyalty and Betrayal

Brutus and Portia, c. 1500–1550. Michelle da Verona (attr. to). Oil on canvas. Czartoryaski Museum, Poland.

View the Art The painting depicts an encounter between Brutus and his wife Portia, who are two important characters in *Julius Caesar*. What do you think is happening in this scene? Consider the facial expressions and body language of the subjects.

BIG IDEA

It can be hard to know whom to trust. When people pursue wealth or power, they accumulate what other people are bound to desire. Even the most loyal ally can betray someone who possesses what his or her heart longs for. The selections in Part 1 deal with issues of loyalty and betrayal that have life-and-death consequences. As you read, ask yourself, What do I want most in the world, and what would I do or not do to get it?

Learning Objectives

For pages 658–659

In studying this text, you will focus on the following objective:

Literary Study: Analyzing form and structure.

LITERARY FOCUS

Tragedy

What makes a play a tragedy?

If you are interested in movie reviews, you might have noticed that comedies rarely receive more than two stars. The majority of "four star" movies are characterized as "dramas" and deal with serious themes and issues. Maybe you have asked yourself how it is possible that people enjoy being entertained by pain, loss, disappointment, and death. However, there is more to it than that. The human heart likes to be moved, and seeing how others deal with the pain and difficulties of the human experience can give a viewer insight into his or her own problems.

from *Julius Caesar,* Act 3, Scene 2

by William Shakespeare

BRUTUS. Had you rather Caesar were living, and die all slaves, than that Caesar were dead, to live all free men? As Caesar lov'd me, I weep for him; as he was fortunate, I rejoice at it; as he was valiant, I honor him; but, as he was ambitious, I slew him. There is tears for his love; joy for his fortune; honor for his valor; and death for his ambition. Who is here so base that would be a bondman? If any, speak, for him have I offended. Who is here so rude, that would not be a Roman? If any, speak, for him have I offended. Who is here so vile that will not love his country? If any, speak, for him have I offended. I pause for a reply.

The Death of Caesar. Guillaume Lethiere (1760–1832). Oil on paper. 47.5 x 71.5 cm. Private collection.

Literature and Reading For more about literary elements, go to glencoe.com and enter QuickPass code GL59794u4.

Tragedy

A **tragedy** is a play in which the main character suffers a downfall. Heroes of tragedies are often royalty. In that way, they have a lot to lose. Tragedy is about loss. Sometimes the character's downfall is the result of outside forces. Other times, the character is undone by him- or herself.

[*Enter a SERVANT.*]
SERVANT. My lord?
CAESAR. Go bid the priests do present sacrifice,
   And bring me their opinions of success.
SERVANT. I will, my lord. [*Exit.*]
[*Enter CALPHURNIA.*]
CALPHURNIA. What mean you, Caesar? Think
      you to walk forth?
You shall not stir out of your house today.
CAESAR. Caesar shall forth; the things that
      threaten'd me
Ne'er look'd but on my back; when they
      shall see
The face of Caesar, they are vanished.

—William Shakespeare, **from** *Julius Caesar,* **Act 2, Scene 2**

Hero

The **hero** is the main character of a literary work. He or she is usually someone with admirable traits or someone who performs noble deeds. The hero of a tragedy is sometimes called a **tragic hero**.

A tragic hero evokes both pity and fear in the audience. Often, the audience is aware of the hero's tragic flaw before the hero is. The audience may realize that the hero has made an irreversible mistake that will lead to a terrible fall from grace or even death.

ANTIGONE. That must be your excuse, I suppose. But as for me, I will bury the brother I love.
—Sophocles, **from** *Antigone,* **Prologue**

Tragic Flaw The tragic flaw is the part of the hero's character that leads to his or her ruin or sorrow. The art of creating a tragic character is to create a tragic flaw that does not prevent the audience from admiring the hero. The tragic flaw is not always a character defect. For example, Antigone suffers a downfall because of her staunch loyalty to the laws of the gods.

CREON. [*To ANTIGONE.*] Tell me, tell me briefly:
Had you heard my proclamation touching this matter?
ANTIGONE. It was public. Could I help hearing it?
CREON. And yet you dared defy the law.
ANTIGONE.   I dared.
It was not God's proclamation. That final Justice
That rules the world below makes no such laws.
Your edict, King, was strong,
But all your strength is weakness itself against
The immortal unrecorded laws of God.

—Sophocles, **from** *Antigone,* **Scene 2**

Quickwrite

Outline a Character Outline a character sketch for a tragic hero of your own creation. What will the character have to lose? What qualities will make him or her admirable? What is the hero's tragic flaw? What will be the hero's downfall?

> character's name:

⬇

> position or assets present at the opening that the character could lose:

⬇

> positive qualities:

⬇

> tragic flaw:

⬇

> downfall:

LITERARY FOCUS

Literary History

Classical Greek Drama

THEATER WAS FAR MORE THAN ENTERTAINMENT for the people of ancient Greece. It was part of their religion, a way of displaying loyalty to their city-state, and a method of honoring local heroes. It was also a major social event, a thrilling competition, and a place where important philosophical issues could be aired.

> *"In every dramatic hero there is the idea of the Greek people, their fate, their will, and their destiny."*
> —Arthur Miller, from "On Social Plays"

In ancient Greece, plays grew out of religion and myths. From the 6th century B.C., religious festivals featured a chorus, or group of actors, that danced and sang hymns to Dionysos, the god of wine. In about 534 B.C., the lyric poet Thespis introduced the use of a single actor separate from the chorus. The chorus voiced the attitudes of the community while the actor delivered speeches, answered the chorus, and performed the story. In the early fifth century, the great dramatist Aeschylus (525–456 B.C.) added a second actor to the stage; within a few years, his rival Sophocles (496–406 B.C.) responded by adding a third. With these changes, drama (from the Greek word for *doing,* rather than *telling*) was born, and actors today are still called thespians.

At the Theater

What would you have seen from the benches of an ancient Greek theater? Up to 15,000 spectators could watch performances in the Theater of Dionysos in Athens. Perched in the upper rows of seats, a spectator was more than 55 yards from the action below. The actors' gestures had to be exaggerated and dramatic, for no one in the back row could have interpreted slight movements.

Only men were allowed to perform. All the actors wore masks made of wool, linen, wood, or plaster. In the mid-fifth century, the time of Sophocles, masks were fairly realistic representations of human faces. In later centuries, masks grew in size and became less realistic, featuring deep eye sockets and wide, gaping mouths, making actors appear larger against the background. Typically,

Two statuettes of elderly comic actors. c. 375–350 BC., Attica.

Learning Objectives

For pages 660–661

In studying this text, you will focus on the following objective:

Literary Study: Analyzing literary periods.

tragic actors wore striking, richly decorated robes that set them apart from the audience. Chorus members wore more conventional costumes, which identified the roles they were playing: soldiers, priests, mourners, or even—in the case of comedies—frogs, birds, or wasps.

Ancient Greek theaters were open-air, so the lighting was natural. There were very few props. A hunter might carry a bow; an old man, a stick; a soldier, a sword and shield. These props served more as symbols to identify the character's role in the play than to provide an imitation of life. The violence—murder, suicide, and battles—almost always occurred offstage. Typically, a messenger would appear after the event and describe in gory detail what had just happened.

Relief in honor of Euripides. Late Hellenistic period. Height: 60 cm. Archaeological Museum, Istanbul, Turkey.

The Golden Age

During the fifth century B.C., known as the golden age of Greek drama, drama grew to be a vital part of life in Athens. The festival of Dionysos, the most important Greek religious festival, introduced a drama competition. The four greatest Greek dramatists—Aeschylus, Sophocles, Euripides (480–406 B.C.), and Aristophanes (448–385 B.C.)—presented their plays at these festivals.

These dramatists—all from Athens—wrote plays in verse, based on themes familiar to their audiences. They retold myths, rewrote history, and ridiculed politicians. Aristophanes, the sole comic writer among the four Athenian masters, boldly and uproariously satirized society, politics, and even the gods, landing himself in legal trouble for doing so. However, his three great contemporaries were all tragic poets, whose plays captured humankind's timeless struggle to find the purpose of life and to achieve self-understanding.

Central to the tragedy is the fall of a great man (or woman, though her part would have been acted by a man). According to the Greek philosopher Aristotle, who wrote the first study of tragedy, the tragic hero should be neither very good nor very bad. The hero's fate is brought about by a flaw within his or her own character. In this way, the downfall of the tragic hero would encourage audiences to examine their own lives, to define their beliefs, and to cleanse their emotions of pity and terror through compassion for the character.

 **Literature** Online

Literary History For more about classical Greek drama, go to glencoe.com and enter QuickPass code GL59794u4.

Respond and Think Critically

1. In your opinion, what is the most significant difference between ancient Greek theater and modern American theater?

2. How did the purposes of Greek comedy and tragedy differ?

3. Why do you think Aristotle argued that the tragic hero should be a person neither especially good nor especially bad?

Before You Read

Antigone, Scenes 1 and 2

World Literature
Greece

Meet **Sophocles**
(c. 496 B.C.–406 B.C.)

The year is 468 B.C. Athenians of all stripes expect the upcoming festival to be thrilling. The streets are abuzz with talk about a newcomer to the competition. This young man is going to give the old champion a run for his money, people are saying. The authorities in charge know it too. They have appointed ten well-known generals to serve on the jury that declares the winner. It turns out that the event lives up to all expectations. The winner and new champion is the twenty-eight-year-old Sophocles, whose plays—the first he has produced—are judged the best at the festival. For more than fifty years after this victory, Sophocles will be the reigning champion of Greek drama. To this day, he is revered as one of the greatest dramatists of all time.

> "The honor of life lies not in words but in deeds."
>
> —Sophocles

Born to Succeed Sophocles was born to a wealthy family from Colonus, a village near Athens. Handsome, athletic, and skilled in music, the young man was groomed for stardom. At sixteen he was chosen to lead a chorus in honor of Greece's victory at the Battle of Salamis. He studied music under Lamprus, the most acclaimed musician of his time, and tragedy, musical composition, and choreography under Aeschylus, the great writer of tragedy. Sophocles would later dethrone Aeschylus in the 468 B.C. drama competition.

This period is called the Golden Age of Greece, and Sophocles was the golden superstar of the Greek stage. He acted and played the lyre (an instrument like the harp) in dramatic productions, retiring only when his voice became too weak to fill the enormous, open theaters of the day.

A Dramatist for the Ages As a writer, Sophocles was tireless, continuing to produce plays until the very end of his ninety-year life. He brought new possibilities to drama by adding a third actor to the stage, and he is said to have introduced the art of "scene painting" to the theater. In all, he wrote 123 dramas, won twenty-four of thirty competitions, and never finished lower than second place. Only seven of his plays have survived in their entirety, but they are still studied and performed throughout the world.

Author Search For more about Sophocles, go to glencoe.com and enter QuickPass code GL59794u4.

Literature and Reading Preview

Connect to the Play
When have you had a hard time deciding to do what was right? Discuss this question with a partner.

Build Background
This play takes place in ancient Greece, in the city of Thebes, about thirty miles northwest of Athens. The Greeks of Sophocles' day believed that if a corpse was not buried or cremated according to a strict ritual, its soul would be forced to wander the earth, bringing shame upon relatives and angering the gods.

Set Purposes for Reading

Big Idea Loyalty and Betrayal

Although we assume that loyalty is a good thing, loyalty to an unworthy cause may be even worse than betrayal. As you read *Antigone*, ask yourself, What are the complexities in the relationship between loyalty and betrayal?

Literary Element Protagonist and Antagonist

The **conflict** in a work of literature is a struggle between opposing forces. The **protagonist** is the central character and the one who the reader is generally meant to sympathize with. The **antagonist** is the person or force that opposes the protagonist. As you read the play, ask yourself, Who is the antagonist, who is the protagonist, and what is their conflict?

Reading Strategy Interpret Imagery

Imagery, the "word pictures" that appeal to the senses, brings the written word to life. As you read, identify images and ask yourself, What feelings or meanings do the images suggest?

Tip: Take Notes Use a table like the one below to help you interpret imagery.

Image	Interpretation
"But his body must lie in the fields, a sweet treasure / For carrion birds to find as they search for food."	This is a disgusting image that shows how cruel Creon's edict is and how much Antigone hates it.

Learning Objectives

For pages 662–684

In studying this text, you will focus on the following objectives:

Literary Study: Analyzing protagonist and antagonist.

Reading: Interpreting imagery.

Vocabulary

repulse (ri puls′) *n.* an act of beating back or driving away, as with force; p. 665 *A day of celebration followed the repulse of the invading army.*

famished (fam′isht) *adj.* intensely hungry; ravenous; p. 669 *Exhausted and famished, the missing hikers finally struggled out of the wilderness.*

comprehensive (kom′pri hen′siv) *adj.* including nearly everything; large in scope; complete; p. 672 *A comprehensive review of our safety procedures revealed many areas that are in need of improvement.*

pious (pī′əs) *adj.* devoutly religious; p. 674 *The streets of the holy city were crowded with pious pilgrims.*

arrogance (ar′ə gəns) *n.* overbearing pride; p. 683 *Her confidence seemed like arrogance to the judge.*

Tip: Context Clues Context clues often immediately precede or follow an unfamiliar word.

ANTIGONE

Sophocles

Translated by
Dudley Fitts and
Robert Fitzgerald

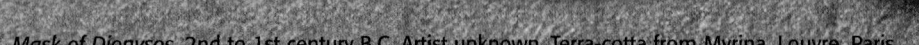
Mask of Dionysos, 2nd to 1st century B.C. Artist unknown. Terra-cotta from Myrina. Louvre, Paris.

CHARACTERS

ANTIGONE: daughter of Oedipus
ISMENE: daughter of Oedipus
EURYDICE: wife of Creon
CREON: King of Thebes, uncle of Antigone and Ismene
HAIMON: son of Creon
TEIRESIAS: a blind prophet
A SENTRY
A MESSENGER
CHORUS: elders of Thebes
CHORAGOS: leader of the Chorus

SCENE: *Before the palace of Creon, King of Thebes. A central double door, and two lateral doors. A platform extends the length of the façade, and from this platform three steps lead down into the "orchestra," or chorus-ground.* TIME: *Dawn of the day after the **repulse** of the Argive army from the assault on Thebes.*

Vocabulary
repulse (ri puls´) *n.* an act of beating back or driving away, as with force

Antigone—Chorus. Artist unknown. Collection van Branteghem, Brussels. Reproduced in *Le Theatre,* 1899.

ANTIGONE

Prologue

[ANTIGONE *and* ISMENE *enter from the central door of the Palace.*]

ANTIGONE.° Ismene,° dear sister,
You would think that we had already suffered enough
For the curse on Oedipus:°
I cannot imagine any grief
5 That you and I have not gone through. And now—
Have they told you of the new decree of our King Creon?

ISMENE. I have heard nothing: I know
That two sisters lost two brothers, a double death
In a single hour; and I know that the Argive army°
10 Fled in the night; but beyond this, nothing.

ANTIGONE. I thought so. And that is why I wanted you
To come out here with me. There is something we must do.

ISMENE. Why do you speak so strangely?

ANTIGONE. Listen, Ismene:
15 Creon buried our brother Eteocles
With military honors, gave him a soldier's funeral,
And it was right that he should; but Polyneices,
Who fought as bravely and died as miserably,—
They say that Creon has sworn
20 No one shall bury him, no one mourn for him,
But his body must lie in the fields, a sweet treasure
For carrion birds to find as they search for food.
That is what they say, and our good Creon is coming here
To announce it publicly; and the penalty—
25 Stoning to death in the public square!
　　　　　　　　　　　　　There it is,
And now you can prove what you are:
A true sister, or a traitor to your family.

ISMENE. Antigone, you are mad! What could I possibly do?

ANTIGONE. You must decide whether you will help me or not.

30 ISMENE. I do not understand you. Help you in what?

ANTIGONE. Ismene, I am going to bury him. Will you come?

ISMENE. Bury him! You have just said the new law forbids it.

ANTIGONE. He is my brother. And he is your brother, too.

ISMENE. But think of the danger! Think what Creon will do!

---

1 Antigone: (an tig′ ə nē). **Ismene:** (is mē′ nē).

3 Oedipus: (ed′ ə pəs).

8–9 two sisters . . . Argive army: After the death of Oedipus, King of Thebes (thēbz), his sons, Eteocles (ē tē′ ə klēz′) and Polyneices (pä′ lə nī′ sēz), struggled to gain the throne. Argos, a rival city-state, sent its army in support of Polyneices. Before the Argive (ar′ jīv) army was driven back, both Eteocles and Polyneices were killed in battle. Creon (krē′ on), their uncle and Oedipus's brother-in-law, became king.

Protagonist and Antagonist *From what you have read so far, what conflict do you think may develop?*

35   **ANTIGONE.** Creon is not strong enough to stand in my way.

    ISMENE. Ah sister!
      Oedipus died, everyone hating him
      For what his own search brought to light, his eyes
      Ripped out by his own hand; and Jocasta died,
40   His mother and wife at once: she twisted the cords
      That strangled her life;° and our two brothers died,
      Each killed by the other's sword. And we are left:
      But oh, Antigone,
      Think how much more terrible than these
45   Our own death would be if we should go against Creon
      And do what he has forbidden! We are only women,
      We cannot fight with men, Antigone!
      The law is strong, we must give in to the law
      In this thing, and in worse. I beg the Dead
50   To forgive me, but I am helpless: I must yield
      To those in authority. And I think it is dangerous business
      To be always meddling.

    ANTIGONE.   If that is what you think,
      I should not want you, even if you asked to come.
      You have made your choice, you can be what you
         want to be.
55   But I will bury him; and if I must die,
      I say that this crime is holy: I shall lie down
      With him in death, and I shall be as dear
      To him as he to me.
                        It is the dead,
      Not the living, who make the longest demands:
60   We die for ever . . .
                        You may do as you like,
      Since apparently the laws of the gods mean nothing to you.

    ISMENE. They mean a great deal to me; but I have no strength
      To break laws that were made for the public good.

    ANTIGONE. That must be your excuse, I suppose. But as for me,
65   I will bury the brother I love.

    ISMENE.   Antigone,
      I am so afraid for you!

    ANTIGONE.   You need not be:
      You have yourself to consider, after all.

37–41 Oedipus died . . . her life: Oedipus had killed Laïos (lī′ əs), the king of Thebes at the time, and married the queen, Jocasta (jō kas′ tə). Together, they had four children—Antigone, Ismene, and two sons. When it was revealed that Oedipus had, without realizing it, killed his own father and married his own mother, he blinded himself, was banished from Thebes, and died, and Jocasta hanged herself.

Running or fleeing maiden, 5th century B.C. Artist unknown. Greek sculpture. Archaeological Museum, Eleusis, Greece.

Loyalty and Betrayal *What is Antigone suggesting about her sister here?*

ANTIGONE

Antigone. Marie Spartali Stillman. Oil on Canvas. Simon Carter Gallery, Woodbridge, Suffolk, England.

View the Art. Marie Spartali Stillman's paintings are known for their focus on heroic women in history. What characters are portrayed here? What do the women's looks and gestures convey?

ISMENE. But no one must hear of this, you must tell no one!
  I will keep it a secret, I promise!

ANTIGONE.   Oh tell it! Tell everyone!
70   Think how they'll hate you when it all comes out
  If they learn that you knew about it all the time!

ISMENE. So fiery! You should be cold with fear.

ANTIGONE. Perhaps. But I am only doing what I must.

ISMENE. But can you do it? I say that you cannot.

75 ANTIGONE. Very well: when my strength gives out, I shall
    do no more.

ISMENE. Impossible things should not be tried at all.

ANTIGONE. Go away, Ismene:
  I shall be hating you soon, and the dead will too,
  For your words are hateful. Leave me my foolish plan:

80   I am not afraid of the danger; if it means death,
     It will not be the worst of deaths—death without honor.

   ISMENE. Go then, if you feel that you must.
     You are unwise,
     But a loyal friend indeed to those who love you.

[*Exit into the Palace.* ANTIGONE *goes off, L. Enter the* CHORUS.]

Parodos°

   CHORUS. Now the long blade of the sun, lying
     Level east to west, touches with glory
     Thebes of the Seven Gates. Open, unlidded
     Eye of golden day! O marching light
5   Across the eddy and rush of Dirce's stream,°
     Striking the white shields of the enemy
     Thrown headlong backward from the blaze of morning!

   CHORAGOS. Polyneices their commander
     Roused them with windy phrases,
10   He the wild eagle screaming
     Insults above our land,
     His wings their shields of snow,
     His crest their marshalled helms.

   CHORUS. Against our seven gates in a yawning ring
15   The **famished** spears came onward in the night;
     But before his jaws were sated with our blood,
     Or pinefire took the garland of our towers,
     He was thrown back; and as he turned, great Thebes—
     No tender victim for his noisy power—
20   Rose like a dragon behind him, shouting war.

   CHORAGOS. For God° hates utterly
     The bray of bragging tongues;
     And when he beheld their smiling,
     Their swagger of golden helms,
25   The frown of his thunder blasted
     Their first man from our walls.

   CHORUS. We heard his shout of triumph high in the air
     Turn to a scream; far out in a flaming arc

Parodos (păr′ ə dos): the first "song" of the Chorus.

5 Dirce's stream: This stream, which flows past Thebes, was named after a murdered queen.

21 God: Here, "God" refers to Zeus (zo͞os), the king of the gods, who used thunderbolts to strike down the invading Argives.

Protagonist and Antagonist *At this point, do you think Antigone is a protagonist or an antagonist? Explain.*

Interpret Imagery *What is being described in this opening stanza?*

Vocabulary

famished (făm′isht) *adj.* intensely hungry; ravenous

ANTIGONE

He fell with his windy torch, and the earth struck him.
And others storming in fury no less than his
Found shock of death in the dusty joy of battle.

CHORAGOS. Seven captains at seven gates
Yielded their clanging arms to the god
That bends the battle-line and breaks it.°
These two only, brothers in blood,
Face to face in matchless rage,
Mirroring each the other's death,
Clashed in long combat.

CHORUS. But now in the beautiful morning of victory
Let Thebes of the many chariots sing for joy!
With hearts for dancing we'll take leave of war:
Our temples shall be sweet with hymns of praise,
And the long night shall echo with our chorus.

32–34 Seven captains . . . breaks it: The Thebans offered the captains' armor (arms) as a sacrifice to Ares (ā´ rēz), the god of war.

SCENE 1

CHORAGOS. But now at last our new King is coming:
Creon of Thebes, Menoikeus'° son.
In this auspicious° dawn of his reign
What are the new complexities
That shifting Fate° has woven for him?
What is his counsel? Why has he summoned
The old men to hear him?

2 Menoikeus (me noi´ kē əs)

3 auspicious: favorable, indicating good fortune.

5 Fate: The ancient Greeks believed that three sisters, called the Fates, controlled human destiny. The first sister was said to spin the thread of human life, the second decided its length, and the third cut it.

[*Enter* CREON *from the Palace, C. He addresses the* CHORUS *from the top step.*]

CREON. Gentlemen: I have the honor to inform you that our Ship of State, which recent storms have threatened to destroy, has come safely to harbor at last,° guided by the merciful wisdom of Heaven. I have summoned you here this morning because I know that I can depend upon you: your devotion to King Laïos was absolute; you never hesitated in your duty to our late ruler Oedipus; and when Oedipus died, your loyalty was transferred to his children. Unfortunately, as you know, his two sons, the princes Eteocles and Polyneices, have killed each other in battle; and I, as the next in blood, have succeeded to the full power of the throne. I am aware, of course, that no Ruler can

8–10 Gentlemen . . . at last: The expression "Ship of State" likens a nation to a ship under sail. In reassuring the citizens of Thebes that the "storms" are over, Creon is referring to the Argive invasion and the many troubles in the house of Oedipus.

Interpret Imagery *What does this image suggest about the two brothers?*

expect complete loyalty from his subjects until he has been tested in office. Nevertheless, I say to you at the very outset that I have nothing but contempt for the kind of Governor who is afraid, for whatever reason, to follow the course that he knows is best for the State; and as for the man who sets private friendship above the public welfare,—I have no use for him, either. I call God to witness that if I saw my country headed for ruin, I should not be afraid to speak out plainly; and I need hardly remind you that I would never have any dealings with an enemy of the people. No one values friendship more highly than I; but we must remember that friends made at the risk of wrecking our Ship are not real friends at all.

These are my principles, at any rate, and that is why I have made the following decision concerning the sons of Oedipus: Eteocles, who died as a man should die, fighting for his country, is to be buried with full military honors, with all the ceremony that is usual when the greatest heroes die; but his brother Polyneices, who broke his exile to come back with fire and sword against his native city and the shrines of his fathers' gods, whose one idea was to spill the blood of his blood and sell his own people into slavery—Polyneices, I say, is to have no burial: no man is to touch him or say the least prayer for him; he shall lie on the plain, unburied; and the birds and the scavenging dogs can do with him whatever they like.

This is my command, and you can see the wisdom behind it. As long as I am King, no traitor is going to be honored with the loyal man. But whoever shows by word and deed that he is on the side of the State,—he shall have my respect while he is living, and my reverence when he is dead.

CHORAGOS. If that is your will, Creon son of Menoikeus, You have the right to enforce it: we are yours.

CREON. That is my will. Take care that you do your part.

CHORAGOS. We are old men: let the younger ones carry it out.

CREON. I do not mean that: the sentries have been appointed.

CHORAGOS. Then what is it that you would have us do?

CREON. You will give no support to whoever breaks this law.

Horseman and foot soldier fighting, 4th century B.C. Artist unknown. Relief. National Archaeological Museum, Athens.

Protagonist and Antagonist *From his speech so far, how would you characterize Creon?*

Loyalty and Betrayal *What does loyalty mean to Creon?*

ANTIGONE

CHORAGOS. Only a crazy man is in love with death!

CREON. And death it is; yet money talks, and the wisest
60 Have sometimes been known to count a few coins too many.

[*Enter* SENTRY *from L.*]

SENTRY. I'll not say that I'm out of breath from running, King, because every time I stopped to think about what I have to tell you, I felt like going back. And all the time a voice kept saying, "You fool, don't you know you're walking straight
65 into trouble?"; and then another voice: "Yes, but if you let somebody else get the news to Creon first, it will be even worse than that for you!" But good sense won out, at least I hope it was good sense, and here I am with a story that makes no sense at all; but I'll tell it anyhow, because, as
70 they say, what's going to happen's going to happen, and—

CREON. Come to the point. What have you to say?

SENTRY. I did not do it. I did not see who did it. You must not punish me for what someone else has done.

CREON. A **comprehensive** defense! More effective, perhaps,
75 If I knew its purpose. Come: what is it?

SENTRY. A dreadful thing . . . I don't know how to put it—

CREON. Out with it!

SENTRY.   Well, then;
  The dead man—
                                  Polyneices—

[*Pause. The* SENTRY *is overcome, fumbles for words.* CREON *waits impassively.*]

                    out there—
                                  someone,—

New dust on the slimy flesh!

[*Pause. No sign from* CREON.]

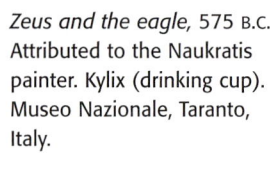

Zeus and the eagle, 575 B.C. Attributed to the Naukratis painter. Kylix (drinking cup). Museo Nazionale, Taranto, Italy.

Protagonist and Antagonist *From what you have read so far, what stand does the sentry take in the conflict? Explain.*

Vocabulary

comprehensive (kom´pri hen´siv) *adj.* including nearly everything; large in scope; complete

80 Someone has given it burial that way, and
    Gone . . .

[*Long pause.* CREON *finally speaks with deadly control.*]

CREON. And the man who dared do this?

SENTRY.   I swear I
Do not know! You must believe me!
                              Listen:
The ground was dry, not a sign of digging, no,
85 Not a wheeltrack in the dust, no trace of anyone.
    It was when they relieved us this morning: and one of them,
    The corporal, pointed to it.
                              There it was,
    The strangest—
                Look:
    The body, just mounded over with light dust: you see?
90 Not buried really, but as if they'd covered it
    Just enough for the ghost's peace. And no sign
    Of dogs or any wild animal that had been there.

    And then what a scene there was! Every man of us
    Accusing the other: we all proved the other man did it,
95 We all had proof that we could not have done it.
    We were ready to take hot iron in our hands,
    Walk through fire, swear by all the gods,
    It was not I!
    I do not know who it was, but it was not I!

[CREON's *rage has been mounting steadily, but the* SENTRY *is too intent upon his story to notice it.*]

100 And then, when this came to nothing, someone said
    A thing that silenced us and made us stare
    Down at the ground: you had to be told the news,
    And one of us had to do it! We threw the dice,
    And the bad luck fell to me.° So here I am,
105 No happier to be here than you are to have me:
    Nobody likes the man who brings bad news.

CHORAGOS. I have been wondering, King: can it be that the gods have done this?

CREON. [*Furiously.*] Stop!

103–104 We threw . . . to me: Like tossing a coin, throwing dice is a way to determine something randomly. In this case, it is who must do what no one wants to do.

Loyalty and Betrayal *What makes the sentries so willing to betray each other?*

Protagonist and Antagonist *What new role has the choragos begun to assume in this conflict?*

ANTIGONE

110   Must you doddering wrecks
      Go out of your heads entirely? "The gods!"
      Intolerable!
      The gods favor this corpse? Why? How had he served them?
      Tried to loot their temples, burn their images,
115   Yes, and the whole State, and its laws with it!
      Is it your senile opinion that the gods love to honor bad men?
      A **pious** thought!—
                            No, from the very beginning
      There have been those who have whispered together,
      Stiff-necked anarchists, putting their heads together,
120   Scheming against me in alleys.° These are the men,
      And they have bribed my own guard to do this thing.
      [*Sententiously.*] Money!
      There's nothing in the world so demoralizing as money.
      Down go your cities,
125   Homes gone, men gone, honest hearts corrupted,
      Crookedness of all kinds, and all for money!
      [*To* SENTRY.]   But you—!
      I swear by God and by the throne of God,
      The man who has done this thing shall pay for it!
      Find that man, bring him here to me, or your death
130   Will be the least of your problems: I'll string you up
      Alive, and there will be certain ways to make you
      Discover your employer before you die;
      And the process may teach you a lesson you seem to have missed:
      The dearest profit is sometimes all too dear:
135   That depends on the source. Do you understand me?
      A fortune won is often misfortune.

SENTRY.   King, may I speak?

CREON.   Your very voice distresses me.

SENTRY.   Are you sure that it is my voice, and not your conscience?

CREON.   By God, he wants to analyze me now!

117–120 A pious . . . in alleys: Anarchy is a state of disorder and confusion or lawlessness, often due to the absence of governmental authority. Anarchists believe that all forms of government are unjust and should be resisted. Here, Creon calls those who oppose him anarchists.

Loyalty and Betrayal *How does Creon ensure the loyalty of his people?*

Vocabulary

pious (pī′əs) *adj.* devoutly religious

Zeus 500 B.C. *(detail),* Attributed to the Berlin painter. Red-figure krater. Musée du Louvre, Paris.

View the Art Ancient Greeks believed that Zeus was deeply committed to morals, law, and civic justice. How do Antigone and Creon differ in their interpretations of Zeus's will?

140 SENTRY. It is not what I say, but what has been done, that
 hurts you.

CREON. You talk too much.

SENTRY. Maybe; but I've done nothing.

CREON. Sold your soul for some silver: that's all you've done.

SENTRY. How dreadful it is when the right judge judges wrong!

CREON. Your figures of speech
145 May entertain you now; but unless you bring me the man,
 You will get little profit from them in the end.

[*Exit* CREON *into the Palace.*]

SENTRY. "Bring me the man"—!
 I'd like nothing better than bringing him the man!
 But bring him or not, you have seen the last of me here.
150 At any rate, I am safe!

[*Exit* SENTRY.]

ODE° 1

Ode: a song chanted by the Chorus.

CHORUS. Numberless are the world's wonders, but none
 More wonderful than man; the stormgray sea
 Yields to his prows,° the huge crests bear him high;
 Earth, holy and inexhaustible, is graven°
5 With shining furrows where his plows have gone
 Year after year, the timeless labor of stallions.

3 prows: ships.
4 graven: formed or shaped with a chisel; sculpted.

Protagonist and Antagonist *What insight about Creon does the sentry express here?*

ANTIGONE

The lightboned birds and beasts that cling to cover,
The lithe° fish lighting their reaches of dim water,
All are taken, tamed in the net of his mind;
10   The lion on the hill, the wild horse windy-maned,
Resign to him; and his blunt yoke has broken
The sultry shoulders of the mountain bull.

Words also, and thought as rapid as air,
He fashions to his good use; statecraft is his,
15   And his the skill that deflects the arrows of snow,
The spears of winter rain: from every wind
He has made himself secure—from all but one:
In the late wind of death he cannot stand.

O clear intelligence, force beyond all measure!
20   O fate of man, working both good and evil!
When the laws are kept, how proudly his city stands!
When the laws are broken, what of his city then?
Never may the anarchic man find rest at my hearth,
Never be it said that my thoughts are his thoughts.

8 lithe: easily bent; flexible.

SCENE 2

[*Re-enter* SENTRY *leading* ANTIGONE.]

CHORAGOS. What does this mean? Surely this captive woman
   Is the Princess, Antigone? Why should she be taken?

SENTRY. Here is the one who did it! We caught her
   In the very act of burying him.—Where is Creon?

5   CHORAGOS. Just coming from the house.

[*Enter* CREON, *C.*]

CREON.   What has happened?
   Why have you come back so soon?

SENTRY. [*Expansively.*]   O King,
   A man should never be too sure of anything:
   I would have sworn
   That you'd not see me here again: your anger

Interpret Imagery Why does the author refer to snow and rain in terms of "arrows" and "spears"?

10 Frightened me so, and the things you threatened me with;
But how could I tell then
That I'd be able to solve the case so soon?

No dice-throwing this time: I was only too glad to come!

Here is this woman. She is the guilty one:
15 We found her trying to bury him.
Take her, then; question her; judge her as you will.
I am through with the whole thing now, and glad of it.

CREON. But this is Antigone! Why have you brought her here?

SENTRY. She was burying him, I tell you!

CREON. [*Severely.*]   Is this the truth?

20 SENTRY. I saw her with my own eyes. Can I say more?

CREON. The details: come, tell me quickly!

SENTRY.   It was like this:
After those terrible threats of yours, King,
We went back and brushed the dust away from the body.
The flesh was soft by now, and stinking,
25 So we sat on a hill to windward and kept guard.
No napping this time! We kept each other awake.
But nothing happened until the white round sun
Whirled in the center of the round sky over us:
Then, suddenly,
30 A storm of dust roared up from the earth, and the sky
Went out, the plain vanished with all its trees
In the stinging dark. We closed our eyes and endured it.
The whirlwind lasted a long time, but it passed;
And then we looked, and there was Antigone!
35 I have seen
A mother bird come back to a stripped nest, heard
Her crying bitterly a broken note or two
For the young ones stolen. Just so, when this girl
Found the bare corpse, and all her love's work wasted,
40 She wept, and cried on heaven to damn the hands
That had done this thing.
    And then she brought more dust
And sprinkled wine three times for her brother's ghost.

Loyalty and Betrayal Why is Creon surprised that Antigone has been arrested?

Interpret Imagery What are some of the senses to which the images in the sentry's speech appeal so far?

ANTIGONE

We ran and took her at once. She was not afraid,
Not even when we charged her with what she had done.
45 She denied nothing.
                      And this was a comfort to me,
And some uneasiness: for it is a good thing
To escape from death, but it is no great pleasure
To bring death to a friend.
                 Yet I always say
There is nothing so comfortable as your own safe skin!

50 CREON. [*Slowly, dangerously.*] And you, Antigone,
You with your head hanging,—do you confess this thing?

ANTIGONE. I do. I deny nothing.

CREON. [*To* SENTRY.]   You may go.

[*Exit* SENTRY.]

[*To* ANTIGONE.] Tell me, tell me briefly:
Had you heard my proclamation touching this matter?

55 ANTIGONE. It was public. Could I help hearing it?

CREON. And yet you dared defy the law.

ANTIGONE.   I dared.
It was not God's proclamation. That final Justice
That rules the world below makes no such laws.

Your edict,° King, was strong,
60 But all your strength is weakness itself against
The immortal unrecorded laws of God.
They are not merely now: they were, and shall be,
Operative for ever, beyond man utterly.

I knew I must die, even without your decree:
65 I am only mortal. And if I must die
Now, before it is my time to die,
Surely this is no hardship: can anyone
Living, as I live, with evil all about me,
Think Death less than a friend? This death of mine

Creon in Antigone. Artist unknown. Musée Jatta-Ruro. Reproduced in *Le Theatre*, 1899.

59 edict: an official order or decree issued by a person in authority.

Loyalty and Betrayal *Explain the sentry's philosophy about loyalty.*

Loyalty and Betrayal *What is Antigone saying about betrayal here? Who does she suggest is betraying whom?*

678 UNIT 4 DRAMA

70 Is of no importance; but if I had left my brother
Lying in death unburied, I should have suffered.
Now I do not.
            You smile at me. Ah, Creon,
Think me a fool, if you like; but it may well be
That a fool convicts me of folly.

75 CHORAGOS. Like father, like daughter: both headstrong, deaf to reason!
She has never learned to yield.

CREON.   She has much to learn.
The inflexible heart breaks first, the toughest iron
Cracks first, and the wildest horses bend their necks
At the pull of the smallest curb.
            Pride? In a slave?
80 This girl is guilty of a double insolence,
Breaking the given laws and boasting of it.
Who is the man here,
She or I, if this crime goes unpunished?
Sister's child, or more than sister's child,
85 Or closer yet in blood—she and her sister
Win bitter death for this!
[*To* SERVANTS.]   Go, some of you,
Arrest Ismene. I accuse her equally.
Bring her: you will find her sniffling in the house there.

Her mind's a traitor: crimes kept in the dark
90 Cry for light, and the guardian brain shudders;
But how much worse than this
Is brazen boasting of barefaced anarchy!

ANTIGONE. Creon, what more do you want than my death?

CREON.   Nothing.
That gives me everything.

ANTIGONE.   Then I beg you: kill me.
95 This talking is a great weariness: your words
Are distasteful to me, and I am sure that mine
Seem so to you. And yet they should not seem so:
I should have praise and honor for what I have done.
All these men here would praise me
100 Were their lips not frozen shut with fear of you.
[*Bitterly.*] Ah the good fortune of kings,

Paestan Red figured bell-krater, c. 330 BC. Python. Clay.

Protagonist and Antagonist *What other conflict does Creon suggest may exist between him and Antigone?*

ANTIGONE

    Licensed to say and do whatever they please!

CREON. You are alone here in that opinion.

ANTIGONE. No, they are with me. But they keep their tongues
  in leash.

105 CREON. Maybe. But you are guilty, and they are not.

ANTIGONE. There is no guilt in reverence for the dead.

CREON. But Eteocles—was he not your brother too?

ANTIGONE. My brother too.

CREON.   And you insult his memory?

ANTIGONE. [*Softly.*] The dead man would not say that I insult it.

110 CREON. He would: for you honor a traitor as much as him.

ANTIGONE. His own brother, traitor or not, and equal in blood.

CREON. He made war on his country. Eteocles defended it.

ANTIGONE. Nevertheless, there are honors due all the dead.

CREON. But not the same for the wicked as for the just.

115 ANTIGONE. Ah Creon, Creon,
  Which of us can say what the gods hold wicked?°

CREON. An enemy is an enemy, even dead.

ANTIGONE. It is my nature to join in love, not hate.

CREON. [*Finally, losing patience.*] Go join them, then; if you
  must have your love,
120 Find it in hell!

CHORAGOS. But see, Ismene comes:

[*Enter* ISMENE, *guarded.*]

  Those tears are sisterly, the cloud
  That shadows her eyes rains down gentle sorrow.

CREON. You too, Ismene,
125 Snake in my ordered house, sucking my blood
  Stealthily—and all the time I never knew
  That these two sisters were aiming at my throne!
            Ismene,

116 Which . . . wicked: Note Antigone's belief that people cannot understand the thinking of the gods.

Loyalty and Betrayal *What is Antigone suggesting about the loyalty of the chorus?*

Protagonist and Antagonist *How is Creon trying to strengthen his position in this debate?*

Interpret Imagery *How does Creon use imagery to make Ismene seem guilty?*

Do you confess your share in this crime, or deny it?
Answer me.

130 ISMENE. Yes, if she will let me say so. I am guilty.

ANTIGONE. [*Coldly.*] No, Ismene. You have no right to say so.
You would not help me, and I will not have you help me.

ISMENE. But now I know what you meant; and I am here
To join you, to take my share of punishment.

135 ANTIGONE. The dead man and the gods who rule the dead
Know whose act this was. Words are not friends.

ISMENE. Do you refuse me, Antigone? I want to die with you:
I too have a duty that I must discharge to the dead.

ANTIGONE. You shall not lessen my death by sharing it.

140 ISMENE. What do I care for life when you are dead?

ANTIGONE. Ask Creon. You're always hanging on his opinions.

ISMENE. You are laughing at me. Why, Antigone?

ANTIGONE. It's a joyless laughter, Ismene.

ISMENE. But can I do nothing?

ANTIGONE. Yes. Save yourself. I shall not envy you.
145   There are those who will praise you; I shall have honor, too.

ISMENE. But we are equally guilty!

ANTIGONE. No more, Ismene.
You are alive, but I belong to Death.

CREON. [*To the* CHORUS.] Gentlemen, I beg you to observe these girls:
One has just now lost her mind; the other,
150   It seems, has never had a mind at all.

ISMENE. Grief teaches the steadiest minds to waver, King.

CREON. Yours certainly did, when you assumed guilt with the guilty!

ISMENE. But how could I go on living without her?

CREON. You are.
She is already dead.

ISMENE. But your own son's bride!

Protagonist and Antagonist *The word* antagonize *has the same root as* antagonist *and means "to provoke dislike or hostility." How is Antigone antagonizing Ismene here?*

ANTIGONE

The Sisters, 2004. Chris Gollon. Mixed media on canvas, 91.4 x 61 cm. Private collection.
View the Art In what ways do the sisters in this painting reflect the sisters in Sophocles's drama?

---

155   CREON.   There are places enough for him to push his plow.
         I want no wicked women for my sons!°

   ISMENE.   O dearest Haimon, how your father wrongs you!

   CREON.   I've had enough of your childish talk of marriage!

   CHORAGOS.   Do you really intend to steal this girl from
         your son?

160   CREON.   No; Death will do that for me.

   CHORAGOS.   Then she must die?

   CREON.   [*Ironically.*] You dazzle me.
                           —But enough of this talk!
      [*To* GUARDS.] You, there, take them away and guard
         them well:
      For they are but women, and even brave men run
      When they see Death coming.

   [*Exit* ISMENE, ANTIGONE, *and* GUARDS.]

154–156 She is . . . sons: Here is a new complication: Antigone is engaged to marry Creon's son, Haimon. Thus, punishing her means punishing him, a fact that doesn't appear to bother Creon greatly.

682   UNIT 4   DRAMA

ODE 2

CHORUS. Fortunate is the man who has never tasted God's
  vengeance!
  Where once the anger of heaven has struck, that house is
    shaken
  For ever: damnation rises behind each child
  Like a wave cresting out of the black northeast,
5 When the long darkness under sea roars up
  And bursts drumming death upon the windwhipped sand.
  I have seen this gathering sorrow from time long past
  Loom upon Oedipus' children: generation from generation
  Takes the compulsive rage of the enemy god.
10 So lately this last flower of Oedipus' line
  Drank the sunlight! but now a passionate word
  And a handful of dust have closed up all its beauty.

  What mortal **arrogance**
  Transcends° the wrath of Zeus?
15 Sleep cannot lull him, nor the effortless long months
  Of the timeless gods: but he is young for ever,
  And his house is the shining day of high Olympos.°
    All that is and shall be,
    And all the past, is his.
20 No pride on earth is free of the curse of heaven.

    The straying dreams of men
    May bring them ghosts of joy:
  But as they drowse, the waking embers burn them;
  Or they walk with fixed eyes, as blind men walk.
25 But the ancient wisdom speaks for our own time:
    Fate works most for woe
    With Folly's fairest show.
  Man's little pleasure is the spring of sorrow.

14 Transcends: is greater or better than.

17 Olympos: Zeus and the other gods and goddesses were believed to live on Mount Olympus.

Zeus (detail), Greek Art. Archeological Museum, Athens.

Interpret Imagery To what does the chorus compare the rage of the gods against Oedipus's children?

Loyalty and Betrayal According to the chorus, what does Zeus consider to be the ultimate sin?

Vocabulary

arrogance (ar´ ə gəns) *n.* overbearing pride

After You Read

Respond and Think Critically

Respond and Interpret
1. What would you say to Antigone? To Creon?
2. (a) Why is Antigone brought to Creon? (b) Compare and contrast what Antigone believes to be important to what Creon values.

Analyze and Evaluate
3. (a) In what ways is the sentry different from the other characters? (b) What does he add to your appreciation of the play? Explain.
4. (a) What role does the chorus play in the drama? (b) How does their participation affect your understanding and enjoyment of the play?
5. (a) In what ways are Antigone and Creon different? How are they alike? (b) Did you think it was still possible for them to resolve their differences at any point before the end of Scene 2? Explain.

Connect
6. **Big Idea** Loyalty and Betrayal How does Sophocles demonstrate that the concepts of loyalty and betrayal are not as simple as they may seem?
7. **Connect to Today** In the ancient Greek drama *Antigone*, Sophocles puts forth an idea about the importance of making morally responsible decisions. What methods are used to communicate this message today?

Literary Element Protagonist and Antagonist

The **protagonist** in a work of literature may well be in conflict with several **antagonists**.

1. What type of internal conflict might Creon be experiencing in Scenes 1 and 2?
2. In Scene 1, line 138, what is the sentry referring to? Has he hit on the truth? Explain.

Reading Strategy Interpret Imagery

Authors use images not only to help a reader experience the world they are creating, but also to better communicate their ideas.

1. Look at *Ode 1* on page 675–676. What do the images in the second stanza have in common?
2. In line 12 of *Ode 2* on page 683, the chorus speaks of "a handful of dust." What does this image refer to?

Vocabulary Practice

Practice with Context Clues Identify the context clues that help you determine the meaning of each boldfaced vocabulary word.

1. After the **repulse**, the enemy was so badly hurt that it never attacked again.
2. If you do not eat all day, you will be **famished**.
3. Our report was **comprehensive**, unlike yours, which contained little information.
4. The **pious** woman prayed every day.
5. Hannah, known for her **arrogance**, thought she was the smartest in the room.

Writing

Write an Advice Column Imagine you are the advice columnist for the *Thebes Daily News* and that Ismene has written you, asking how she should handle her situation. Write a version of Ismene's letter, concealing the names and positions of the persons involved. Then write a response in which you explain how understanding the relationship between the protagonist and the antagonist might help Ismene find a solution to her problem.

Literature Online

Selection Resources For Selection Quizzes, eFlashcards, and Reading-Writing Connection activities, go to glencoe.com and enter QuickPass code GL59794u4.

Before You Read

Literature and Reading Preview

Connect to the Play
Have you ever been entangled in a conflict with family or friends? Write a journal entry about the situation.

Build Background
The ancient Greeks believed in the underworld, where the dead went after life. There, the unfortunate were condemned to Tartarus, sometimes described as the deepest of hells, and would be tortured by hideous women known as Furies.

Literary Element Tragic Flaw

According to the Greek philosopher Aristotle (384–322 B.C.), the hero of a tragedy is a person of great ability who comes to grief because of a **tragic flaw:** a fault within his or her character. Pride, ambition, jealousy, self-doubt, and anger are among those human weaknesses that can defeat the tragic hero. A tragic flaw can be an excess of virtue, such as the love of honor or the pursuit of duty. *Antigone*, a play that Aristotle knew well, is one of the tragedies from which he derived his definition of a tragic flaw. As you read, ask yourself, How do internal forces determine the fate of the characters?

Reading Strategy Recognize Author's Purpose

Authors usually write fiction or drama with a **purpose:** to entertain, to inform or teach a lesson, to tell a story, or to persuade readers to accept an idea. As you read the conclusion of *Antigone*, ask yourself, Why did the author choose to tell this story in this particular manner?

Tip: Record Thoughts Use a table to record your responses to events and the author's purpose for including them.

Event	My Thoughts	Author's Purpose
The choragos's opinions slowly shift during the play.	He is feeling sorry for Antigone and begins to question Creon.	Sophocles is creating sympathy for Antigone.

Learning Objectives
For pages 685–708

In studying this text, you will focus on the following objectives:

Literary Study: Analyzing tragic flaw.

Reading: Recognizing author's purpose.

Vocabulary

deference (def′ər əns) *n.* respect and honor due to another; p. 686 *My grandmother complains that kids today do not show any deference.*

perverse (pər vurs′) *adj.* determined to go against what is reasonable, expected, or desired; contrary; p. 690 *My dad tells me I am perverse when I say that I want to go winter camping.*

absolve (ab zolv′) *v.* to free from blame; p. 691 *The DNA results will absolve the suspect.*

prevail (pri vāl′) *v.* to be superior in power or influence; to succeed; p. 694 *Cunning will often prevail over brute force.*

defile (di fīl′) *v.* to spoil the purity of; to make dirty or unclean; p. 698 *His horrible crime defiled his reputation forever.*

ANTIGONE 685

ANTIGONE

SCENE 3

CHORAGOS. But here is Haimon, King, the last of all your sons.
Is it grief for Antigone that brings him here,
And bitterness at being robbed of his bride?

[*Enter* HAIMON.]

CREON. We shall soon see, and no need of diviners.°
                                                                                  —Son,
5   You have heard my final judgment on that girl:
Have you come here hating me, or have you come
With **deference** and with love, whatever I do?

HAIMON. I am your son, father. You are my guide.
You make things clear for me, and I obey you.
10 No marriage means more to me than your continuing wisdom.

CREON. Good. That is the way to behave: subordinate
Everything else, my son, to your father's will.
This is what a man prays for, that he may get
Sons attentive and dutiful in his house,
15 Each one hating his father's enemies,
Honoring his father's friends. But if his sons
Fail him, if they turn out unprofitably,
What has he fathered but trouble for himself
And amusement for the malicious?
                                                                   So you are right
20 Not to lose your head over this woman.
Your pleasure with her would soon grow cold, Haimon,
And then you'd have a hellcat in bed and elsewhere.
Let her find her husband in Hell!
Of all the people in this city, only she
25 Has had contempt for my law and broken it.

Do you want me to show myself weak before the people?
Or to break my sworn word? No, and I will not.

---

4 diviners: people who predict the future.

Recognize Author's Purpose Why do you think Sophocles makes Haimon appear so calm and reasonable?

Tragic Flaw How does Creon reveal his pride here?

Vocabulary

deference (def′ ər əns) *n.* respect and honor due to another

Aegeus, King of Athens, Consulting the Delphic Oracle, 6th–5th centuries BC. Red-Figured Kylix. Staatliche Museen zu Berlin, Germany.

The woman dies.
I suppose she'll plead "family ties." Well, let her.
30 If I permit my own family to rebel,
How shall I earn the world's obedience?
Show me the man who keeps his house in hand,
He's fit for public authority.
                        I'll have no dealings
With law-breakers, critics of the government:
35 Whoever is chosen to govern should be obeyed—
Must be obeyed, in all things, great and small,
Just and unjust! O Haimon,
The man who knows how to obey, and that man only,
Knows how to give commands when the time comes.
40 You can depend on him, no matter how fast
The spears come: he's a good soldier, he'll stick it out.

Anarchy, anarchy! Show me a greater evil!
This is why cities tumble and the great houses rain down,
This is what scatters armies!

45 No, no: good lives are made so by discipline.
We keep the laws then, and the lawmakers,
And no woman shall seduce us. If we must lose,
Let's lose to a man, at least! Is a woman stronger than we?

CHORAGOS. Unless time has rusted my wits,
50 What you say, King, is said with point and dignity.

HAIMON. [*Boyishly earnest.*] Father:
Reason is God's crowning gift to man, and you are right
To warn me against losing mine. I cannot say—
I hope that I shall never want to say!—that you
55 Have reasoned badly. Yet there are other men
Who can reason, too; and their opinions might be helpful.
You are not in a position to know everything
That people say or do, or what they feel:
Your temper terrifies them—everyone
60 Will tell you only what you like to hear.
But I, at any rate, can listen; and I have heard them
Muttering and whispering in the dark about this girl.

Loyalty and Betrayal *According to Creon, why is loyalty such an important trait?*

Antigone

The Kauffmann Head, Head of Aphrodite, copy of the Aphrodite of Cnidus by Praxiteles, c. 150 BC Marble Louvre, Paris.

    They say no woman has ever, so unreasonably,
    Died so shameful a death for a generous act:
65 "She covered her brother's body. Is this indecent?
    She kept him from dogs and vultures. Is this a crime?
    Death?—She should have all the honor that we can give her!"

    This is the way they talk out there in the city.

    You must believe me:
70 Nothing is closer to me than your happiness.
    What could be closer? Must not any son
    Value his father's fortune as his father does his?
    I beg you, do not be unchangeable:
    Do not believe that you alone can be right.
75 The man who thinks that,
    The man who maintains that only he has the power
    To reason correctly, the gift to speak, the soul—
    A man like that, when you know him, turns out empty.

Tragic Flaw *How does Haimon manage to suggest that his father is flawed without directly criticizing him?*

It is not reason never to yield to reason!

80 In flood time you can see how some trees bend,
And because they bend, even their twigs are safe,
While stubborn trees are torn up, roots and all.
And the same thing happens in sailing:
Make your sheet fast, never slacken,—and over you go,
85 Head over heels and under: and there's your voyage.
Forget you are angry! Let yourself be moved!
I know I am young; but please let me say this:
The ideal condition
Would be, I admit, that men should be right by instinct;
90 But since we are all too likely to go astray,
The reasonable thing is to learn from those who can teach.

CHORAGOS. You will do well to listen to him, King,
If what he says is sensible. And you, Haimon,
Must listen to your father.—Both speak well.

95 CREON. You consider it right for a man of my years and experience
To go to school to a boy?

HAIMON.   It is not right
If I am wrong. But if I am young, and right,
What does my age matter?

CREON. You think it right to stand up for an anarchist?

100 HAIMON. Not at all. I pay no respect to criminals.

CREON. Then she is not a criminal?

HAIMON. The City would deny it, to a man.

CREON. And the City proposes to teach me how to rule?

HAIMON. Ah. Who is it that's talking like a boy now?

105 CREON. My voice is the one voice giving orders in this City!

HAIMON. It is no City if it takes orders from one voice.

CREON. The State is the King!

HAIMON.   Yes, if the State is a desert.

[*Pause.*]

CREON. This boy, it seems, has sold out to a woman.

HAIMON. If you are a woman: my concern is only for you.

Parthenon, Porch of Caryatiids at Erechteion, Athens.

Tragic Flaw *What character fault does Haimon seem to think that his father has?*

Recognize Author's Purpose *How does this observation by the choragos affect Creon? What point does Sophocles make by including this?*

ANTIGONE

110 **CREON.** So? Your "concern"! In a public brawl with your father!

HAIMON. How about you, in a public brawl with justice?

CREON. With justice, when all that I do is within my rights?

HAIMON. You have no right to trample on God's right.

CREON. [*Completely out of control.*] Fool, adolescent fool! Taken in by a woman!

115 **HAIMON.** You'll never see me taken in by anything vile.

CREON. Every word you say is for her!

HAIMON. [*Quietly, darkly.*] And for you. And for me. And for the gods under the earth.

CREON. You'll never marry her while she lives.

HAIMON. Then she must die.—But her death will cause another.

120 **CREON.** Another? Have you lost your senses? Is this an open threat?

HAIMON. There is no threat in speaking to emptiness.

CREON. I swear you'll regret this superior tone of yours! You are the empty one!

HAIMON. If you were not my father,
125 I'd say you were **perverse.**

CREON. You girlstruck fool, don't play at words with me!

HAIMON. I am sorry. You prefer silence.

CREON. Now, by God—! I swear, by all the gods in heaven above us, You'll watch it, I swear you shall! [*To the* SERVANTS.] Bring her out!
130 Bring the woman out! Let her die before his eyes! Here, this instant, with her bridegroom beside her!

Loyalty and Betrayal *How has Haimon turned the argument to question his father's loyalty?*

Tragic Flaw *What character fault besides inflexibility does Creon exhibit in his dialogue with Haimon?*

Tragic Flaw *What new aspect of Creon's character is hinted at here?*

Vocabulary

perverse (pər vurs´) *adj.* determined to go against what is reasonable, expected, or desired; contrary

HAIMON. Not here, no; she will not die here, King.
And you will never see my face again.
Go on raving as long as you've a friend to endure you.

[*Exit* HAIMON.]

135 CHORAGOS. Gone, gone.
Creon, a young man in a rage is dangerous!

CREON. Let him do, or dream to do, more than a man can.
He shall not save these girls from death.

CHORAGOS.   These girls?
You have sentenced them both?

CREON.   No, you are right.
140   I will not kill the one whose hands are clean.

CHORAGOS. But Antigone?

CREON. [*Somberly.*]   I will carry her far away
Out there in the wilderness, and lock her
Living in a vault of stone. She shall have food,
As the custom is, to **absolve** the State of her death.
145   And there let her pray to the gods of hell:
They are her only gods:
Perhaps they will show her an escape from death,
Or she may learn,
                         though late,
That piety shown the dead is pity in vain.

[*Exit* CREON.]

ODE 3

CHORUS. Love, unconquerable
Waster of rich men, keeper
Of warm lights and all-night vigil
In the soft face of a girl:
5   Sea-wanderer, forest-visitor!
Even the pure Immortals cannot escape you,
And mortal man, in his one day's dusk,
Trembles before your glory.

Recognize Author's Purpose *What happens here for the first time? Are you surprised by this?*

Vocabulary

absolve (ab zolv´) *v.* to free from blame

ANTIGONE

      Surely you swerve upon ruin
10   The just man's consenting heart,
      As here you have made bright anger
      Strike between father and son—
      And none has conquered but Love!
      A girl's glance working the will of heaven:
15   Pleasure to her alone who mocks us,
      Merciless Aphrodite.°

16 Aphrodite (af′ rə dī′ tē): the goddess of love and beauty.

SCENE 4

CHORAGOS. [*As* ANTIGONE *enters guarded.*] But I can no longer stand in awe of this,
      Nor, seeing what I see, keep back my tears.
      Here is Antigone, passing to that chamber
      Where all find sleep at last.

5   ANTIGONE. Look upon me, friends, and pity me
      Turning back at the night's edge to say
      Good-by to the sun that shines for me no longer;
      Now sleepy Death
      Summons me down to Acheron,° that cold shore:
10 There is no bridesong there, nor any music.

   CHORUS. Yet not unpraised, not without a kind of honor,
      You walk at last into the underworld;
      Untouched by sickness, broken by no sword.
      What woman has ever found your way to death?

9 Acheron (ak′ ə ron): The Greeks believed that the souls of the dead inhabited an underworld bordered by the river Acheron.

15 ANTIGONE. How often I have heard the story of Niobe,
      Tantalos' wretched daughter, how the stone
      Clung fast about her, ivy-close: and they say
      The rain falls endlessly
      And sifting soft snow; her tears are never done.
20 I feel the loneliness of her death in mine.°

   CHORUS. But she was born of heaven, and you
      Are woman, woman-born. If her death is yours,
      A mortal woman's, is this not for you
      Glory in our world and in the world beyond?

15–20 How often . . . mine: Niobe (nī′ ō bē′), a former queen of Thebes, was punished by the gods for excessive pride. After all of her children were killed, she was turned to stone, but she continued to shed tears.

Recognize Author's Purpose What is the topic of Ode 3? Why might the author have included this theme?

Recognize Author's Purpose Why might Sophocles have opened Scene 4 with this observation by the choragos?

25 **ANTIGONE.** You laugh at me. Ah, friends, friends,
Can you not wait until I am dead? O Thebes,
O men many-charioted, in love with Fortune,
Dear springs of Dirce, sacred Theban grove,
Be witnesses for me, denied all pity,
30 Unjustly judged! and think a word of love
For her whose path turns
Under dark earth, where there are no more tears.

CHORUS. You have passed beyond human daring and come at last
Into a place of stone where Justice sits.
35 I cannot tell
What shape of your father's guilt appears in this.

ANTIGONE. You have touched it at last: that bridal bed
Unspeakable, horror of son and mother mingling:
Their crime, infection of all our family!
40 O Oedipus, father and brother!
Your marriage strikes from the grave to murder mine.

Statue of Chrysippus, the Greek philosopher, 3rd century B.C. Marble. Musée du Louvre, Paris.

View the Art Western philosophy—a field of study devoted to the pursuit of knowledge—originated in ancient Greece. What emotions does this sculpture convey? How might these emotions capture what Creon may be feeling at this point in the play?

ANTIGONE

I have been a stranger here in my own land:
All my life
The blasphemy of my birth has followed me.°

45 **CHORUS.** Reverence is a virtue, but strength
Lives in established law: that must **prevail.**
You have made your choice,
Your death is the doing of your conscious hand.

ANTIGONE. Then let me go, since all your words are bitter,
50 And the very light of the sun is cold to me.
Lead me to my vigil, where I must have
Neither love nor lamentation;° no song, but silence.

[CREON *interrupts impatiently.*]

CREON. If dirges and planned lamentations could put off death,
Men would be singing for ever.
[*To the* SERVANTS.]   Take her, go!
55 You know your orders: take her to the vault
And leave her alone there. And if she lives or dies,
That's her affair, not ours: our hands are clean.

ANTIGONE. O tomb, vaulted bride-bed in eternal rock,
Soon I shall be with my own again
60 Where Persephone° welcomes the thin ghosts underground:
And I shall see my father again, and you, mother,
And dearest Polyneices—
                    dearest indeed
To me, since it was my hand
That washed him clean and poured the ritual wine:
65 And my reward is death before my time!

And yet, as men's hearts know, I have done no wrong,
I have not sinned before God. Or if I have,
I shall know the truth in death. But if the guilt
Lies upon Creon who judged me, then, I pray,

35–44 I cannot . . . followed me: Incest, or sexual relations between siblings or between parents and children, was a sin against the gods. Oedipus and Jocasta did not know, at the time, that they were committing incest, but their marriage was cursed nonetheless, and that curse now plagues their daughter, Antigone.

52 lamentation: mournful outcry of sorrow or grief.

60 Persephone (pər sef′ ə nē): Persephone is the queen of the underworld of the dead.

Tragic Flaw Do you think this statement suggests that Antigone's flaws are inherent or beyond her control?

Loyalty and Betrayal Has the chorus changed its attitude about the struggle between Creon and Antigone? Explain.

Tragic Flaw Why does Creon say this?

Vocabulary

prevail (pri vāl′) *v.* to be superior in power or influence; to succeed

70   May his punishment equal my own.

CHORAGOS.   O passionate heart,
    Unyielding, tormented still by the same winds!

CREON. Her guards shall have good cause to regret their delaying.

ANTIGONE. Ah! That voice is like the voice of death!

CREON. I can give you no reason to think you are mistaken.

75 ANTIGONE. Thebes, and you my fathers' gods,
    And rulers of Thebes, you see me now, the last
    Unhappy daughter of a line of kings,
    Your kings, led away to death. You will remember
    What things I suffer, and at what men's hands,
80   Because I would not transgress° the laws of heaven.
    [To the GUARDS, simply.] Come: let us wait no longer.

[Exit ANTIGONE, L., guarded.]

80 transgress: break or violate.

ODE 4

CHORUS. All Danäe's beauty was locked away
    In a brazen cell where the sunlight could not come:
    A small room, still as any grave, enclosed her.
    Yet she was a princess too,
5   And Zeus in a rain of gold poured love upon her.
    O child, child,
    No power in wealth or war
    Or tough sea-blackened ships
    Can prevail against untiring Destiny!°

10   And Dryas' son also, that furious king,
    Bore the god's prisoning anger for his pride:
    Sealed up by Dionysos in deaf stone,
    His madness died among echoes.
    So at the last he learned what dreadful power
15   His tongue had mocked:
    For he had profaned the revels,
    And fired the wrath of the nine
    Implacable Sisters that love the sound of the flute.°

1–9 All Danäe's . . . Destiny: The Chorus briefly relates three Greek legends. Danäe (dan′ āē′) was imprisoned by her father when it was foretold that she would bear a child who would kill him. After Zeus visited Danäe, she gave birth to Zeus's son, who did eventually kill his grandfather.

10–18 And Dryas' . . . flute: Dionysos (dī′ ə nī′ səs) is the god of wine and fertility, and the Implacable Sisters (also called the Muses) are the goddesses of the arts and sciences. After Dryas's son (King Lycurgus) objected to the worship of Dionysos, the Sisters imprisoned him and drove him mad.

Tragic Flaw Antigone explains that she is being punished because she "would not transgress the laws of heaven." Might there be other reasons for her misfortune? Explain.

ANTIGONE

And old men tell a half-remembered tale
20 Of horror done where a dark ledge splits the sea
And a double surf beats on the gray shores:
How a king's new woman, sick
With hatred for the queen he had imprisoned,
Ripped out his two sons' eyes with her bloody hands
25 While grinning Ares watched the shuttle plunge
Four times: four blind wounds crying for revenge,

Crying, tears and blood mingled.—Piteously born,
Those sons whose mother was of heavenly birth!
Her father was the god of the North Wind
30 And she was cradled by gales,
She raced with young colts on the glittering hills
And walked untrammeled in the open light:
But in her marriage deathless Fate found means
To build a tomb like yours for all her joy.°

19–34 And old men . . . all her joy: It was King Phineus who imprisoned his first wife (the queen) and allowed his jealous new wife to blind the queen's sons. This horrible act was done under the gleeful gaze of Ares, the war god.

SCENE 5

[*Enter blind* TEIRESIAS, *led by a boy. The opening speeches of* TEIRESIAS *should be in singsong contrast to the realistic lines of* CREON.]

TEIRESIAS. This is the way the blind man comes, Princes,
Princes, Lock-step, two heads lit by the eyes of one.

CREON. What new thing have you to tell us, old Teiresias?

TEIRESIAS. I have much to tell you: listen to the prophet, Creon.

5 CREON. I am not aware that I have ever failed to listen.

TEIRESIAS. Then you have done wisely, King, and ruled well.

CREON. I admit my debt to you. But what have you to say?

TEIRESIAS. This, Creon: you stand once more on the edge of fate.°

CREON. What do you mean? Your words are a kind of dread.

10 TEIRESIAS. Listen, Creon:
I was sitting in my chair of augury, at the place
Where birds gather about me. They were all a-chatter,

Venus de Milo, detail of the back of the head, 100 B.C. Greek artist. Marble. Musée du Louvre, Paris.

1–8 This is . . . of fate: The blind prophet serves as the gods' agent, or go-between, in their dealings with people.

Recognize Author's Purpose *How do the legends in Ode 4 relate to Antigone's situation? What moral is the chorus communicating here?*

Recognize Author's Purpose *How does Sophocles prepare us for the importance of Teiresias's prediction?*

	As is their habit, when suddenly I heard
	A strange note in their jangling, a scream, a
15	Whirring fury; I knew that they were fighting,
	Tearing each other, dying
	In a whirlwind of wings clashing. And I was afraid.°
	I began the rites of burnt-offering at the altar,
	But Hephaistos failed me: instead of bright flame,
20	There was only the sputtering slime of the fat thighflesh
	Melting: the entrails dissolved in gray smoke,
	The bare bone burst from the welter. And no blaze!
	This was a sign from heaven. My boy described it,
	Seeing for me as I see for others.

11–17 I was sitting . . . afraid: Teiresias sits in his chair of augury to listen to the birds, whose sounds he interprets as messages from the gods, allowing him to foretell, or augur, the future. The birds' fighting is a very bad sign.

25 I tell you, Creon, you yourself have brought
This new calamity upon us. Our hearths and altars
Are stained with the corruption of dogs and carrion birds
That glut themselves on the corpse of Oedipus' son.
The gods are deaf when we pray to them, their fire
30 Recoils from our offering, their birds of omen
Have no cry of comfort, for they are gorged
With the thick blood of the dead.°
                              O my son,
==These are no trifles! Think: all men make mistakes,==
==But a good man yields when he knows his course is wrong,==
35 ==And repairs the evil. The only crime is pride.==

Give in to the dead man, then: do not fight with a corpse—
What glory is it to kill a man who is dead?
Think, I beg you:
It is for your own good that I speak as I do.
40 You should be able to yield for your own good.

18–32 I began . . . of the dead: Another bad sign: Hephaistos (hi fes′ təs), the god of fire, is withholding fire. Teiresias says that the gods are rejecting the Thebans' sacrificial offerings because the animals have fed on Polyneices's corpse.

CREON. It seems that prophets have made me their especial province.
All my life long
I have been a kind of butt for the dull arrows
Of doddering fortune-tellers!
                               No, Teiresias:
45 If your birds—if the great eagles of God himself
Should carry him stinking bit by bit to heaven,
I would not yield. I am not afraid of pollution:

Tragic Flaw *From what you have read so far, is Teiresias's advice likely to be followed? Explain.*

ANTIGONE

No man can **defile** the gods.
                              Do what you will,
Go into business, make money, speculate
50 In India gold or that synthetic gold from Sardis,°
Get rich otherwise than by my consent to bury him.
Teiresias, it is a sorry thing when a wise man
Sells his wisdom, lets out his words for hire!

TEIRESIAS. Ah Creon! Is there no man left in the world—

55 CREON. To do what?—Come, let's have the aphorism!°

TEIRESIAS. No man who knows that wisdom outweighs any wealth?

CREON. As surely as bribes are baser than any baseness.

TEIRESIAS. You are sick, Creon! You are deathly sick!

CREON. As you say: it is not my place to challenge a prophet.

60 TEIRESIAS. Yet you have said my prophecy is for sale.

CREON. This generation of prophets has always loved gold.

TEIRESIAS. The generation of kings has always loved brass.

CREON. You forget yourself! You are speaking to your King.

TEIRESIAS. I know it. You are a king because of me.°

65 CREON. You have a certain skill; but you have sold out.

TEIRESIAS. King, you will drive me to words that—

CREON.   Say them, say them!
Only remember: I will not pay you for them.

TEIRESIAS. No, you will find them too costly.

CREON.   No doubt. Speak:
Whatever you say, you will not change my will.

70 TEIRESIAS. Then take this, and take it to heart!
The time is not far off when you shall pay back
Corpse for corpse, flesh of your own flesh.

---

50 synthetic gold from Sardis: The people of Sardis, the capital of ancient Lydia (in modern-day Turkey), invented metallic coinage, the "synthetic gold" that Creon speaks of.

55 aphorism: a concise statement of a general truth.

64 I know . . . me: It was Teiresias who revealed the truth of Oedipus's relationship to Jocasta and thus set off the chain of events that led to Creon's becoming king.

Loyalty and Betrayal How does Creon question Teiresias's loyalty here?

Tragic Flaw What is Teiresias accusing Creon of here?

Recognize Author's Purpose Why might Sophocles have Creon say these words?

Vocabulary
defile (di fīl′) *v.* to spoil the purity of; to make dirty or unclean

Pallas Athena, or *Armoured Figure,* 1664–1665. Rembrandt Harmensz van Rijn. Oil on canvas, 118 x 81.1 cm. Museu Calouste Gulbenkian, Lisbon, Portugal.

You have thrust the child of this world into living night,
You have kept from the gods below the child that is theirs:
75 The one in a grave before her death, the other,
Dead, denied the grave. This is your crime:
And the Furies° and the dark gods of Hell
Are swift with terrible punishment for you.

Do you want to buy me now, Creon?

                                    Not many days,
80 And your house will be full of men and women weeping,
And curses will be hurled at you from far
Cities grieving for sons unburied, left to rot
Before the walls of Thebes.

These are my arrows, Creon: they are all for you.

85 [*To* BOY.] But come, child: lead me home.
Let him waste his fine anger upon younger men.
Maybe he will learn at last
To control a wiser tongue in a better head.

[*Exit* TEIRESIAS.]

CHORAGOS. The old man has gone, King, but his words
90   Remain to plague us. I am old, too,
   But I cannot remember that he was ever false.

CREON. That is true. . . . It troubles me.
   Oh it is hard to give in! but it is worse
   To risk everything for stubborn pride.

95 CHORAGOS. Creon: take my advice.

CREON.   What shall I do?

CHORAGOS. Go quickly: free Antigone from her vault
   And build a tomb for the body of Polyneices.

CREON. You would have me do this?

CHORAGOS.   Creon, yes!
   And it must be done at once: God moves
100   Swiftly to cancel the folly of stubborn men.

CREON. It is hard to deny the heart! But I
   Will do it: I will not fight with destiny.

CHORAGOS. You must go yourself, you cannot leave it to
   others.

---

77 Furies: three goddesses who avenge crimes.

Tragic Flaw *Given what you know of Creon's character, is this change of heart likely?*

ANTIGONE

CREON. I will go.
               —Bring axes, servants:
105   Come with me to the tomb. I buried her, I
Will set her free.
               Oh quickly!
My mind misgives—
The laws of the gods are mighty, and a man
  must serve them
To the last day of his life!

[*Exit* CREON.]

Paean°

CHORAGOS. God of many names
CHORUS.   O Iacchos°
                        son
of Kadmeian Semele
            O born of the Thunder!
Guardian of the West
            Regent
of Eleusis' plain
            O Prince of maenad Thebes
5   and the Dragon Field by rippling Ismenos:°
CHORAGOS. God of many names
CHORUS.   the flame of torches
flares on our hills
            the nymphs of Iacchos
dance at the spring of Castalia:

from the vine-close mountain
                come ah come in ivy:°
10   *Evohé*° *evohé*! sings through the streets of Thebes
CHORAGOS. God of many names
CHORUS.   Iacchos of Thebes
heavenly Child
            of Semele bride of the Thunderer!

Paean (pē′ən): a song of praise, joy, or thanksgiving. Here, the Chorus praises Dionysos.

3 Iacchos (yä′kəs): considered Thebes's special protector because his mother had been a Theban princess. The Chorus begs Dionysos to come to Thebes and drive out evil.

1–5 God of . . . Ismenos: The names of Dionysos refer to people and places associated with him. His mother, **Kadmeian Semele** (sem′ə lē), was the daughter of Kadmos, a king of Thebes. His father was Zeus, who controlled thunder. This plain was the site of religious ceremonies performed in honor of Dionysos, and the river **Ismenos** ran near Thebes. The **maenads** (mē′nadz) were Dionysos's devoted priestesses.

7–9 the nymphs . . . come in ivy: Dionysos was raised by **nymphs**, long-lived women who were associated with trees and other parts of nature. The **spring of Castalia** is on Parnasos, a holy mountain. The grape **vine** and **ivy** were symbols of Dionysos.

10 Evohé: "Hallelujah."

Recognize Author's Purpose *How does Sophocles build up suspense in this passage?*

Loyalty and Betrayal *How does this statement represent a significant change in Creon's attitude?*

The shadow of plague is upon us:
                                    come
  with clement° feet
                       oh come from Parnasos
15 down the long slopes
                       across the lamenting water

  CHORAGOS. Io Fire! Chorister of the throbbing stars!
    O purest among the voices of the night!
    Thou son of God, blaze for us!

  CHORUS. Come with choric rapture of circling Maenads
20 Who cry *Io Iacche!*
                       God of many names!

14 **clement:** forgiving; merciful.

Exodos°

[*Enter* MESSENGER, *L.*]

Exodos: the last part of the play.

  MESSENGER. Men of the line of Kadmos, you who live
    Near Amphion's citadel:°
                             I cannot say
    Of any condition of human life "This is fixed,
    This is clearly good, or bad." Fate raises up,
5   And Fate casts down the happy and unhappy alike:
    No man can foretell his Fate.
                                 Take the case of Creon:
    Creon was happy once, as I count happiness:
    Victorious in battle, sole governor of the land,
    Fortunate father of children nobly born.
10 And now it has all gone from him! Who can say
    That a man is still alive when his life's joy fails?
    He is a walking dead man. Grant him rich,
    Let him live like a king in his great house:
    If his pleasure is gone, I would not give
15 So much as the shadow of smoke for all he owns.

  CHORAGOS. Your words hint at sorrow: what is your news
    for us?

  MESSENGER. They are dead. The living are guilty of their death.

  CHORAGOS. Who is guilty? Who is dead? Speak!

  MESSENGER.   Haimon.
    Haimon is dead; and the hand that killed him

2 **Amphion's citadel:** the wall around Thebes, which Amphion built by charming stones into place with music.

Head of Zeus. Artist unknown. Bronze. National Archaeological Museum, Athens.

Recognize Author's Purpose What is the effect of this line and that of the Paean as a whole?

Recognize Author's Purpose What point is the Messenger making here?

ANTIGONE

20   Is his own hand.

CHORAGOS.   His father's? or his own?

MESSENGER.   His own, driven mad by the murder his father
        had done.

CHORAGOS.   Teiresias, Teiresias, how clearly you saw it all!

MESSENGER.   This is my news: you must draw what
        conclusions you can from it.

CHORAGOS.   But look: Eurydice, our Queen:
25   Has she overheard us?

[*Enter* EURYDICE *from the Palace, C.*]

EURYDICE.   I have heard something, friends:
        As I was unlocking the gate of Pallas'° shrine,
        For I needed her help today, I heard a voice
        Telling of some new sorrow. And I fainted
30   There at the temple with all my maidens about me.
        But speak again: whatever it is, I can bear it:
        Grief and I are no strangers.°

MESSENGER.   Dearest Lady,
        I will tell you plainly all that I have seen.
        I shall not try to comfort you: what is the use,
35   Since comfort could lie only in what is not true?
        The truth is always best.
                    I went with Creon
        To the outer plain where Polyneices was lying,
        No friend to pity him, his body shredded by dogs.
        We made our prayer in that place to Hecate°
40   And Pluto,° that they would be merciful. And we bathed
        The corpse with holy water, and we brought
        Fresh-broken branches to burn what was left of it,
        And upon the urn we heaped up a towering barrow
        Of the earth of his own land.
                        When we were done, we ran
45   To the vault where Antigone lay on her couch of stone.
        One of the servants had gone ahead,
        And while he was yet far off he heard a voice
        Grieving within the chamber, and he came back
        And told Creon. And as the King went closer,

27 Pallas: the goddess of wisdom; also known as Athena.

32 Grief and I . . . strangers: Eurydice (yoo rid′ i sē) is referring to the death of Megareus (me gär′ ā o͞os), her older son, who died in the battle for Thebes.

39 Hecate (hek′ ə tē): another name for Persephone, the goddess of the underworld.
40 Pluto: another name for Hades, the god of the underworld.

Recognize Author's Purpose Why might Sophocles introduce Creon's wife at this late point in the play?

Loyalty and Betrayal What does the order in which Creon and the Messenger do their business tell you about Creon's new priorities?

50   The air was full of wailing, the words lost,
      And he begged us to make all haste. "Am I a prophet?"
      He said, weeping, "And must I walk this road,
      The saddest of all that I have gone before?
      My son's voice calls me on. Oh quickly, quickly!
55   Look through the crevice there, and tell me
      If it is Haimon, or some deception of the gods!"

      We obeyed; and in the cavern's farthest corner
      We saw her lying:
      She had made a noose of her fine linen veil
60   And hanged herself. Haimon lay beside her,
      His arms about her waist, lamenting her,
      His love lost under ground, crying out
      That his father had stolen her away from him.

      When Creon saw him the tears rushed to his eyes
65   And he called to him: "What have you done, child? Speak to me.
      What are you thinking that makes your eyes so strange?
      O my son, my son, I come to you on my knees!"
      But Haimon spat in his face. He said not a word,
      Staring—
              And suddenly drew his sword
70   And lunged. Creon shrank back, the blade missed; and the boy,
      Desperate against himself, drove it half its length
      Into his own side, and fell. And as he died
      He gathered Antigone close in his arms again,
      Choking, his blood bright red on her white cheek.
75   And now he lies dead with the dead, and she is his
      At last, his bride in the houses of the dead.

[*Exit* EURYDICE *into the Palace.*]

CHORAGOS. She has left us without a word. What can this mean?

MESSENGER. It troubles me, too; yet she knows what is best,
      Her grief is too great for public lamentation,
80   And doubtless she has gone to her chamber to weep
      For her dead son, leading her maidens in his dirge.

Dionysos and his mother Semele, 6th century B.C. Artist unknown. Black-figured cup. Staatliche Antikensammlung, Munich.

Recognize Author's Purpose *Why might Sophocles have included this description?*

Recognize Author's Purpose *Do you think Sophocles expected his audience to accept the Messenger's assumption that Eurydice has left to grieve privately?*

ANTIGONE

CHORAGOS. It may be so: but I fear this deep silence

[*Pause.*]

MESSENGER. I will see what she is doing. I will go in.

[*Exit MESSENGER into the Palace.*]

[*Enter CREON with attendants, bearing HAIMON's body.*]

CHORAGOS. But here is the King himself: oh look at him,
85 Bearing his own damnation in his arms.

CREON. Nothing you say can touch me any more.
   My own blind heart has brought me
   From darkness to final darkness. Here you see
   The father murdering, the murdered son—
90 And all my civic wisdom!

   Haimon my son, so young, so young to die,
   I was the fool, not you; and you died for me.

CHORAGOS. That is the truth; but you were late in learning it.

CREON. This truth is hard to bear. Surely a god
95 Has crushed me beneath the hugest weight of heaven,
   And driven me headlong a barbaric way
   To trample out the thing I held most dear.

   The pains that men will take to come to pain!

[*Enter MESSENGER from the Palace.*]

MESSENGER. The burden you carry in your hands is heavy,
100 But it is not all: you will find more in your house.

CREON. What burden worse than this shall I find there?

MESSENGER. The Queen is dead.

CREON. O port of death, deaf world,
   Is there no pity for me? And you, Angel of evil,
105 I was dead, and your words are death again.
   Is it true, boy? Can it be true?
   Is my wife dead? Has death bred death?

MESSENGER. You can see for yourself.

[*The doors are opened, and the body of EURYDICE is disclosed within.*]

CREON. Oh pity!
110 All true, all true, and more than I can bear!
   O my wife, my son!

Funerary Mask, c. 1600 B.C. Mycenaean.

Tragic Flaw Why was Creon unable to come to this realization earlier?

MESSENGER. She stood before the altar, and her heart
　　Welcomed the knife her own hand guided,
　　And a great cry burst from her lips for Megareus dead,
115　And for Haimon dead, her sons; and her last breath
　　Was a curse for their father, the murderer of her sons.°
　　And she fell, and the dark flowed in through her closing
　　　eyes.
CREON. O God, I am sick with fear.
　　Are there no swords here? Has no one a blow for me?
120 MESSENGER. Her curse is upon you for the deaths of both.
CREON. It is right that it should be. I alone am guilty.
　　I know it, and I say it. Lead me in,
　　Quickly, friends.
　　I have neither life nor substance. Lead me in.
125 CHORAGOS. You are right, if there can be right in so much
　　　wrong.
　　The briefest way is best in a world of sorrow.
CREON. Let it come,
　　Let death come quickly, and be kind to me.
　　I would not ever see the sun again.
130 CHORAGOS. All that will come when it will; but we,
　　　meanwhile,
　　Have much to do. Leave the future to itself.
CREON. All my heart was in that prayer!
CHORAGOS. Then do not pray any more: the sky is deaf.
CREON. Lead me away. I have been rash and foolish.
135　I have killed my son and my wife.
　　I look for comfort; my comfort lies here dead.
　　Whatever my hands have touched has come to nothing.
　　Fate has brought all my pride to a thought of dust.

[*As* CREON *is being led into the house, the* CHORAGOS *advances and speaks directly to the audience.*]

CHORAGOS. There is no happiness where there is no wisdom;
140　No wisdom but in submission to the gods.
　　Big words are always punished,
　　And proud men in old age learn to be wise.

116 Was a curse . . . sons: Note that even though Haimon stabbed himself and Megareus died in battle, Eurydice blames Creon for their deaths.

Tragic Flaw *Has your attitude toward Creon changed over the course of the play? In what way?*

Recognize Author's Purpose *Why do you think Sophocles allows Creon's character to live on after those around him die?*

Loyalty and Betrayal *What is the play's final position on the issue of loyalty?*

After You Read

Respond and Think Critically

Respond and Interpret

1. Rank the main characters in order of how sympathetic you feel toward them. Explain why you rank them this way.

2. (a) Why does Haimon come to see his father? (b) How does their exchange of ideas evolve into a bitter argument?

3. (a) What does Teiresias tell Creon? (b) In your opinion, why does Creon change his mind?

4. (a) Summarize the events that occur after Teiresias leaves Creon. (b) What message, or lesson, does the audience take from these events?

Analyze and Evaluate

5. (a) Compare Antigone's demeanor in Scene 4 with her attitude in previous scenes. How has she changed? (b) Does her transformation seem believable to you?

6. (a) Explain how the house of Oedipus plays a role in *Antigone*. (b) Do these allusions affect your appreciation of the play? Explain.

Connect

7. **Big Idea** Loyalty and Betrayal Creon considers his opponents to be traitors. How loyal should citizens be to their national leaders?

8. **Connect to Today** When does criticism become disloyalty? Is it possible to remain loyal to a nation while criticizing its leader? Support your answer with a reference to modern events.

Visual Literacy

Determine Loyalty and Popularity

Much of the struggle in *Antigone* revolves around where the characters' loyalties lie. With a group, review the words and actions of the characters to determine how loyal each one is in terms of religious law, the king's law, and family bonds. Then rank each character's position on line graphs with ten meaning "very much" and zero meaning "not at all." Share your results with the the class and discuss any differences. Then answer the questions.

1. (a) Is one type of loyalty more important or valuable than the others? Explain. (b) Do you think Sophocles believed that one type of loyalty was the most noble?

2. What effect does a character's loyalty have on his or her popularity? Explain.

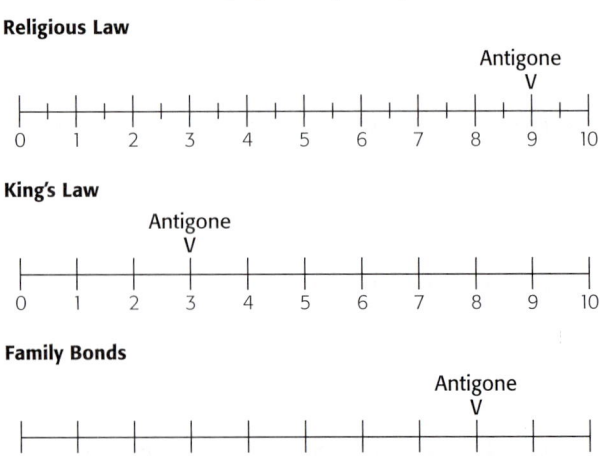

706 UNIT 4 DRAMA

Literary Element Tragic Flaw

Today we label people as heroes to acknowledge their bravery or hard work. To the writer of classical tragedies, however, a hero was a more complex character. A hero was a strong, often admirable person who failed to live up to his or her promise because of a **tragic flaw.** This might be a negative trait or a positive one that is inflexible or taken to excess.

1. Reread Teiresias's warning to Creon (Scene 5, lines 10–40). What flaw does the prophet specifically identify in the king's character? Do you believe that this weakness is sufficient to cause the tragedy that results? Explain.

2. How would you describe Antigone's personality? Does she have a trait that might qualify as a tragic flaw? Is she, too, a tragic hero, or is she an innocent victim of Creon? Explain.

Review: Characterization

As you learned on page 87, **characterization** refers to the way an author reveals the personality of a character. In drama we often learn about characters through **indirect characterization,** particularly by their words and actions.

Partner Activity Get together with a partner and create an organizer like the one below. In the left-hand boxes copy Creon's exact words. In the right-hand boxes describe things he does. Write your conclusion about Creon—based on these examples—in the bottom box. Then choose another character and create another graphic profile.

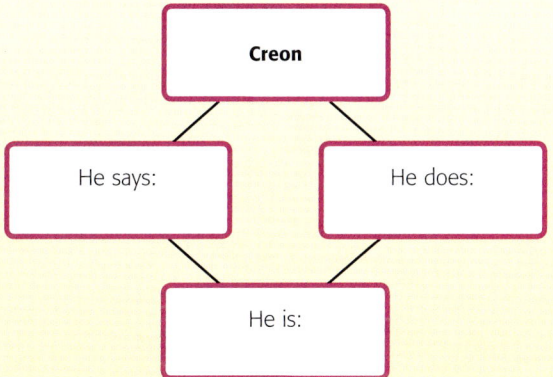

Reading Strategy Recognize Author's Purpose

SAT Skills Practice

1. Sophocles wrote *Antigone* with the primary purpose of
   (A) encouraging citizens to commit acts of civil disobedience
   (B) describing the traditional burial practices of ancient Greek culture
   (C) entertaining audiences at the Greek festivals
   (D) teaching the history of a famous family from Thebes
   (E) urging old and young to live and work together in harmony

Vocabulary Practice

Practice with Word Parts For each bold-faced word in the left column, identify the related word with a shared root in the right column. Write each word and underline the part they have in common. Use a dictionary to find the meaning of the related word. Then explain how it is related to the vocabulary word.

1. deference   conference
2. perverse   aversion
3. absolve   solvent
4. prevail   ambivalent

EXAMPLE:
bibliography, bibliophile
A bibliography is a list of books and other sources. A bibliophile is a book lover.

Selection Resources For Selection Quizzes, eFlashcards, and Reading-Writing Connection activities, go to glencoe.com and enter QuickPass code GL59794u4.

Respond Through Writing

Persuasive Essay

Argue a Position Would Antigone's fate have been different if she had been a man? Use details you have drawn from the play, as well as appeals to logic and emotion, to write a persuasive essay about this question.

Understand the Task
- An **appeal to logic** is any reference to reason, facts, or statistics to support a claim or an opinion.
- An **appeal to emotion** is any use of words or information to arouse the reader's emotions in order to persuade.

Prewrite Make a two-column chart. In the left column, list statements from the play that reveal characters' attitudes toward women and their role in Theban society. In the right column, reflect on whether these statements support the idea of gender as the determiner of Antigone's fate. Then list statements that seem to show that Antigone acts beyond the constraints of gender. When you are done, decide which side of the question you can argue most effectively, and formulate a thesis directed at an audience of your classmates and others who have read the work.

Draft As you draft, strengthen your argument through the use of persuasive techniques such as appeals to logic and emotion. Save your most persuasive reason for last. Create a clear structure by transitioning with phrases such as *more important* or *most important*.

Revise Exchange papers with a partner. Identify and evaluate each other's appeals to logic and emotion. Evaluate the use of evidence in the paper for its relevance and precision. Identify at least one way in which your partner might refute a counterclaim, using a frame like this one:

   It is true that ___, but ___.

As needed, also suggest ways for explaining that evidence and relating it to the paper's thesis by the use of frames such as these:

   Based on this evidence, it is clear that ___.
   If ___, then ___.

Revise based on your classmates' feedback.

Edit and Proofread Proofread your paper, correcting any errors in spelling, grammar, and punctuation. Use the Grammar Tip in the side column to help you with infinitives and infinitive phrases.

Learning Objectives

In this assignment, you will focus on the following objective:

Writing: Writing a persuasive essay.

Grammar Tip

Infinitives and Infinitive Phrases

An infinitive is a verb form that can be used as a noun or modifier. It usually contains the word *to*.

Antigone needs **to act.** [noun]
She is a woman **to admire.** [modifier]

Infinitives and infinitive phrases fall into a broad category called verbals. Verbals are all formed from verbs, but they act as nouns, adjectives, or adverbs in sentences. Other verbals are gerunds and participles.

Participles, which end in *-ed* or *-ing*, function as adjectives.

Determined, *Antigone acts against the law.*

Gerunds, which end in *-ing*, function as nouns.

Dying *does not frighten Antigone.*

Learning Objectives

For pages 709–712

In studying this text, you will focus on the following objective:

Reading: Distinguishing fact and opinion.

Set a Purpose for Reading

Read to learn about the history of Cleopatra VII, her legend, and how she is celebrated.

Preview the Article

1. From the title, do you think the author is biased about her subject, Cleopatra VII?
2. Read the *deck*, or the boldfaced sentence that appears underneath the title. What do you think will be the article's main focus?

Reading Strategy
Distinguish Fact and Opinion

Distinguishing fact and opinion requires you to make a distinction between statements that are true, or **facts,** and those that represent a person's beliefs, or **opinions.** As you read the article, select statements from the text, and determine whether they are fact or opinion.

TIME

EVER ALLURING

Cleopatra could draw the crowds in ancient Rome. Now she's turning on her seductive charm in London.

By MARYANN BIRD

SHE IS ONE OF THE MOST FAMOUS FIGURES OF ancient history, a name synonymous with beauty, yet no one knows what she really looked like. A Macedonian Greek, she ruled Egypt and was known for her relationships—political and romantic—with the two great Roman leaders of her time, Julius Caesar and Mark Antony. Her legend—wrapped in intrigue, conflict, and romance—lives on to this day. As Shakespeare wrote of Cleopatra in his play *Antony and Cleopatra:* "Age cannot wither her nor custom stale her infinite variety."

Although she has been dead since 30 B.C., Cleopatra VII, the last of the Ptolemaic rulers, still wields considerable power. The magic of her name drew big crowds to a 2001 exhibition called "Cleopatra of Egypt: From History to Myth" at the British Museum in London. For the show, which included new finds and interpretations, the museum attracted loans of many Cleopatra-related artifacts. Among them were sculptures, coins, paintings, ceramics, and jewelry from some 30 museums, libraries, and private collections around the world.

The Many Sides of Cleopatra

"Cleopatra's name is more evocative than any image of her," said co-curator Peter Higgs in an interview at the

Informational Text

HISTORY AND MYTH: Bronze coins.

time of the exhibition's opening. He described the show as a "biographical study" that presented many different sides of Cleopatra, all of which contributed to the legend that she began building during her lifetime. Higgs acknowledged that not all classical scholars would concur with the museum's view of Cleopatra. "We know that not everyone is going to agree with us," he said. "We're not saying we're right about everything. This is our interpretation."

On the coins on display, *Cleopatra* appeared masculine and powerful. In the sculptures, some of which portrayed her as the goddess Isis, the divine mother whose cult she followed, she looked slim and serene. The show also featured Renaissance paintings that portrayed her as a sensual and tragic figure. Modern representations of her came straight from Hollywood, embodied most famously by Elizabeth Taylor in the 1963 film *Cleopatra*. Taylor's famous off-screen affair with the film's Mark Antony, co-star Richard Burton, recalled the 14th century writer Giovanni Boccaccio's description of Cleopatra as a woman "who became an object of gossip for the whole world."

The star of the museum's exhibition, though, was a 40-inch black basalt statue on loan from the Hermitage Museum in St. Petersburg, Russia. One of the best-preserved representations of a Ptolemaic queen, it has been identified as Cleopatra VII. The striking figure holds a double horn of plenty and wears a headdress decorated with three cobras—symbols associated only with her.

A Bad Reputation

Not all the images in the exhibition were as flattering. Cleopatra's reputation in Rome declined after Octavian (later to become the emperor Augustus) defeated her and Antony at the Battle of Actium in 31 B.C. "Everything we know about Cleopatra comes from later Roman writers," explained Higgs, "and it's nearly all negative." He added that it was not surprising that "prudish and snobbish" Romans would have a low opinion of Egypt's queen, given that "she had taken away from them both Julius Caesar and Mark Antony." Still, said Higgs, even Cleopatra's critics acknowledged that she had some admirable qualities. Apart from her beauty, she is said to have been a humorous and charming conversationalist. Intelligent and savvy, she was a skilled diplomat who spoke several languages—and was clearly loved by Caesar and Antony, the fathers of her four children.

Like the pharaohs who came before her in the three centuries following Alexander the Great's conquest of Egypt in 332 B.C., Cleopatra had to appeal to both Greeks and Egyptians. She had to be seen as both a Greek monarch and an Egyptian pharaoh. She also needed to present herself as a powerful figure amid all the violence and chaos in the Mediterranean region at the time. Indeed, Cleopatra must have been ruthless in order to even gain the throne, given the bloodbaths that long characterized her family line.

Following Octavian's conquest of Egypt and Antony's death—he killed himself by falling on his sword—Cleopatra committed suicide, possibly with the help of a poisonous snake such as an asp or cobra. The new emperor then ordered that all statues of Cleopatra be

Informational Text

Love and Power

Basantite bust of Caesar

destroyed. Most of the images of her that survived depict an attractive figure with a strong face, masculine in its features, emphasizing power. Old coins bearing her image, particularly rare Greek ones, have helped to identify Cleopatra in marble and limestone sculptures. So, too, did the tiniest item displayed at the museum—a half-inch piece of etched blue glass bearing Cleopatra's profile in a more realistic Greek style.

Cleopatra's Children

On public view for the first time was a 30-inch granite head believed to represent Ptolemy XV Caesar, Cleopatra's son by Julius Caesar. Also known as Caesarion, he co-ruled Egypt with his mother from 44 B.C. to 30 B.C. The sculpture was found in the harbor at Alexandria, Cleopatra's capital, by French archaeologists in 1997. The exhibition also included rare images of Cleopatra's other children. A marble statue of Cleopatra Selene—her daughter by Mark Antony—was lent by the Archaeological Museum in Cherchel, Algeria, where it was found. (Cherchel was the capital of the ancient kingdom of Mauretania, where Cleopatra Selene lived.) The statue had never been outside Algeria before. Another marble rendering of Cleopatra Selene, found near her husband's palace, showed her as a more mature woman, with a heavier face and "snail-shell" curls around her forehead.

Also on display was a bronze statuette which historians believe depicts Cleopatra's second son, Alexander Helios, as Prince of Armenia. According to the writings of the ancient Greek historian Plutarch, Mark Antony gave his sons by Cleopatra the title of kings, as well as many lands to rule. He gave Armenia, Media, and the Parthian Empire to Alexander. He gave Phoenicia, Syria, and Cilicia to Alexander's younger brother, Ptolemy Philadelphus. After Mark Anthony and Cleopatra died, though, their children were made to live out their lives in obscurity. Their half-brother Caesarion was not so fortunate. He was executed by Octavian.

> "Everything we know about Cleopatra comes from later Roman writers, and it's nearly all negative."
>
> —Peter Higgs,
> co-curator
> British Museum in London

Informational Text

Queen of the Silver Screen

Cleopatra's amazing life and dramatic death made Egypt's exotic queen an icon—to many, the first female superstar. For several hundred years after her death, Cleopatra and all things Egyptian intrigued even those Romans who demonized her. Her influence on Roman style, customs, and culture continued for a long time. By the early Renaissance in Europe, with its revival of interest in classical traditions, Cleopatra again became a subject of art, literature, and fashion. Many of the most famous events in her life—the luxurious banquet she held for Mark Antony, his death, her grief at his tomb, and her own death—were represented in paintings and sketches at the exhibition, as well as on other objects such as watches, fans, and vases. The Renaissance portrayal of the tough and tragic seductress—as derived from the early Romans—has trickled down to the current day.

Cleopatra found her way onto the silver screen even before movies had sound. In 1917, Theda Bara starred in a silent-film version of Cleopatra. Seventeen years later, Claudette Colbert played the Egyptian queen, and Hollywood waged an all-out publicity campaign to encourage female moviegoers to adopt the "Cleopatra look." Many copied Colbert's dark bangs after hearing the speech in which she described her feelings about Mark Antony: "I've seen a god come to life. I'm no longer a queen. I'm a woman."

A woman she was, and one for all time. With so much, yet so little, known about this queen without a face, this figure of history and myth, Cleopatra lives on in the "infinite variety" cited by Shakespeare. And like so many intrigued observers through the ages, visitors to the British Museum exhibition could draw their own picture of her.

—from TIME

Cleopatra Dropping the Pearl into the Wine, c 1715. William Kent after Carlo Maratta. Red chalk drawing, 36.4 x 25.7 cm. The British Museum, London.

Respond and Think Critically

Respond

1. Write a brief summary of the main ideas in this article before you answer the following questions. For help on writing a summary, see page 415.
2. Did the article cause you to want to learn more about Cleopatra VII? Why or why not?
3. (a) Do historians know what Cleopatra looked like? (b) Why do you think there have been so many interpretations of her appearance?
4. (a) What are some of the artifacts from Cleopatra's time on exhibit at the British Museum? (b) How accurate a representation of history do you think can be derived from such artifacts?

Analyze and Evaluate

5. (a) What words does the author use to describe Cleopatra's image and character? (b) Do you think the author's conclusions are based on facts or opinions? Explain.
6. Does the author provide sufficient background information about Cleopatra? Explain.
7. The author calls Cleopatra "the first female superstar." How do you think movies have affected the legend of Cleopatra?

Connect

8. How are Antigone's and Cleopatra's characterizations similar and different?

Vocabulary Workshop

Denotation and Connotation

Literature Connection In the passage below, Sophocles uses words that have strong negative denotations and connotations—*damnation, darkness,* and *death*—to describe the vengefulness of the gods. Such **loaded words** can make speech and writing persuasive.

> "For ever: damnation rises behind each child / Like a wave cresting out of the black northeast, / When the long darkness under sea roars up / And bursts drumming death upon the windwhipped sand."
>
> —Sophocles, from *Antigone*

Here are three types of loaded words:

- **Bias**—language that expresses an author's prejudice
  Antigone bravely wants to give her brother a proper burial.

With the word *bravely,* the writer shows positive bias toward Antigone. A writer with a negative bias might have chosen *recklessly* instead.

- **Hyperbole**—exaggerated language used to make a point
  The entire world was against Antigone.

This broad overstatement by the writer expresses extreme disapproval.

- **Propaganda**—language that often includes bias and hyperbole and may distort the truth to influence the public
  Anyone who does not agree with the logic of Creon must be an anarchist.

This exaggerated and distorted statement reveals the writer's positive bias toward Creon and an attempt to influence people to think similarly.

Learning Objectives

In this workshop, you will focus on the following objective:

Vocabulary: Understanding denotation and connotation.

Loaded Words

Loaded words express strong opinions or emotions. You can read between the lines and identify a writer's opinion when you look for bias, hyperbole, and propaganda.

Tip

To identify loaded language in a reading passage, ask yourself, "Why did the writer write this? What is his or her point of view?" Then look for words or phrases that have strong denotations and connotations to support that stance.

Practice Complete each line with the loaded word or phrase that best expresses the view of a writer who sides with Antigone.

Antigone is a woman who **1.** _____ stands up for the **2.** _____ principles she believes in. Being a **3.** _____ man, Creon **4.** _____ wants his nephew unburied. The situation puts Antigone in **5.** _____ .

1. **a.** determinedly **b.** stubbornly **c.** obstinately
2. **a.** traditional **b.** simple **c.** noble
3. **a.** respectable **b.** vengeful **c.** honorable
4. **a.** strangely **b.** generously **c.** selfishly
5. **a.** a stalemate **b.** a moral dilemma **c.** a quandary

Vocabulary For more vocabulary practice, go to glencoe.com and enter QuickPass code GL59794u4.

Literary History

> **Learning Objectives**
>
> For pages 714–715
>
> In studying this text, you will focus on the following objective:
>
> **Literary Study:** Analyzing literary genres.

Shakespearean Drama

IN THE LATE 1500S, WHEN SHAKESPEARE BEGAN his career, English theater was going through major changes. For hundreds of years before this time, traveling actors, called "players," had toured the countryside, performing for audiences in towns and villages. They set up makeshift stages in public halls, marketplaces, and the courtyards of inns. Local officials, many of whom believed that "play-acting" violated biblical commandments, typically greeted acting companies with hostility.

> *"Every day at two o'clock in the afternoon in the city of London two or sometimes three comedies are performed,..."*
>
> —Thomas Platter, diary entry from 1599

Distrust of theater was so great that in 1574 the Common Council of London issued an order banishing players from London. To get around the order, actor James Burbage and his company of players built a playhouse in nearby Shorebridge. Completed in 1576, the building resembled the courtyard of an inn. Burbage's playhouse became the first public theater in England and was an immediate success, leading to the construction of other public theaters over the next few years.

The Globe Theatre, 1616. Cornelius de Visscher. Engraving. British Library, London.

Shakespeare's Globe

Shakespeare's theater company, the Lord Chamberlain's Men, performed at Burbage's theater until 1599, when they built their own playhouse, the Globe. Shakespeare referred to the Globe as "this wooden O," a term that has led historians to believe that it was a roughly circular building. The theater had three levels of galleries, covered by thatched roofs, overlooking an open courtyard. Projecting out into the yard was a platform stage about forty feet wide, with trapdoors for the entrance and exit of actors who played ghosts or other supernatural characters. At the back of the main stage was a small curtained inner stage used for indoor scenes. Above this stood a two-tiered gallery. The first tier was used to stage balcony and bedroom scenes; the second, to house musicians. Sound effects, such as the booming of thunder, were produced in a hut on top of the stage roof.

The Globe could hold about three thousand spectators. Members of the middle class and nobility typically sat in the galleries after paying a twopence admission. For sixpence (what a skilled laborer earned in a day), wealthier members of the audience could sit in the "lords' room" directly over the stage. Less well-to-do-spectators, called "groundlings," could stand and watch from the courtyard for only a penny. Their close proximity to the stage created a noisy theatrical experience. Accounts of the time suggest that the groundlings did not hesitate to shout comments to the actors onstage. As theater became more profitable, its reputation improved. Eventually, Shakespeare's company received the support of Queen Elizabeth and her successor, King James.

Elizabethan Stagecraft

Because there was no artificial lighting, all performances at the Globe took place in the afternoon. There were few props and no movable scenery. Shakespeare made up for the lack of scenery by inviting audiences to visualize the scenes based on descriptive passages spoken by the characters. For example, a character's description of a raging storm would help Elizabethan audiences picture the fury of the weather.

What the Elizabethan stage lacked in scenery, it made up for in costumes. Shakespeare's audiences considered clothing an important indication of social rank, so they demanded extravagant yet realistic costuming. An elaborate wardrobe was an Elizabethan theater company's biggest expense and most important asset.

In Shakespeare's time, audiences thought it immoral for women to appear on the stage, so boys performed the female roles. Very popular with Elizabethan theatergoers, these boy actors must have been highly skilled performers, who created convincing and moving portrayals of Shakespeare's great female roles, from Lady Macbeth and Cleopatra to Rosalind and Juliet.

Literary History For more about Elizabethan drama, go to glencoe.com and enter QuickPass code GL59794u4.

The New Globe, London, interior.

Respond and Think Critically

1. What feature of Elizabethan stagecraft do you think a modern audience would have the most difficulty accepting?

2. What effects did the social values of Shakespeare's time have on Elizabethan theater?

3. How did the Globe's lack of scenery affect Shakespeare's plays?

Before You Read

The Tragedy of Julius Caesar

World Literature: England

Meet **William Shakespeare**
(1564–1616)

When the question "Who is the greatest writer that ever lived?" is asked, nine out of ten times the response is "William Shakespeare." Shakespeare's writings are more widely read and more often quoted than any other literary work, aside from the Bible. Unfortunately, there are no biographies of Shakespeare from his own time. The information we have comes from public records and comments by his rivals and admirers, such as the playwright Ben Jonson. "He was not of an age, but for all time," proclaimed Jonson shortly after Shakespeare's death.

> "It seems to me most strange that men should fear, Seeing that death, a necessary end, Will come when it will come."
>
> —William Shakespeare, from *Julius Caesar*

The Family Man Shakespeare was born in Stratford-upon-Avon, where his father was elected bailiff (the equivalent of a mayor). William was the third of at least eight children. He was the first boy and the first child to survive past childhood. Most likely, he attended the local grammar school, where he would have studied Latin and classical literature. At age eighteen, Shakespeare married twenty-six-year-old Anne Hathaway. The couple had three children: Susanna and twins Judith and Hamnet. Hamnet, their only son, died when he was eleven.

Success in the City Shakespeare moved to London sometime between 1585 and the early 1590s and worked as an actor and a playwright. He was celebrated for his comedies and historical plays. In 1599 he and his company of players built the Globe theater. Writers at that time received no royalties and most plays were never printed, but Shakespeare grew wealthy from his share in his theater company's profits.

An Artist for All Time Shakespeare's tragic masterpieces include *Hamlet, Romeo and Juliet, Othello, Macbeth,* and *King Lear.* His comedies are also classics. Modern audiences still respond to the antics and wordplay of *A Midsummer Night's Dream, Twelfth Night,* and *Much Ado About Nothing* as Shakespeare's own audiences did four centuries ago.

Seven years after Shakespeare's death, a group of friends brought out a collection of his works known as the *First Folio.* This volume played a crucial role in preserving his plays for future generations and—very possibly—"for all time."

Author Search For more about William Shakespeare, go to glencoe.com and enter QuickPass code GL59794u4.

Literature and Reading Preview

Connect to the Play
Who is the best leader you have ever known? Discuss this question with a small group. Consider what makes a leader exceptional.

Build Background
Born in 100 B.C., Julius Caesar was an immensely gifted military leader and politician. Although he could be charming, Caesar's arrogance and ambition created enemies in the senate, and a group of conspirators assassinated him in 44 BC.

Set Purposes for Reading

Big Idea Loyalty and Betrayal

History is full of people who have turned against a cause or a person they once respected. As you read *Julius Caesar,* ask yourself, How does Shakespeare depict this change in his characters?

Literary Element Blank Verse

Much of *Julius Caesar* is written in a form of unrhymed poetry known as **blank verse.** Each line has a basic pattern of five iambic feet, or units of rhythm, with each foot made up of an unstressed syllable followed by a stressed syllable.

> He had a fever when he was in Spain . . .

As you read, ask yourself, Which characters in Act 1 speak in blank verse?

Reading Strategy Make Inferences About Characters

To **make inferences** is to use reason and knowledge of the situation in order to understand a **character's** motivation or reason for acting in a certain way. As you read, ask yourself, What can I infer about a character in order to discover what the author is not telling?

Tip: Examine the Evidence Use a chart like the one below to record details you are sure of. Then write the inferences you make based on those details.

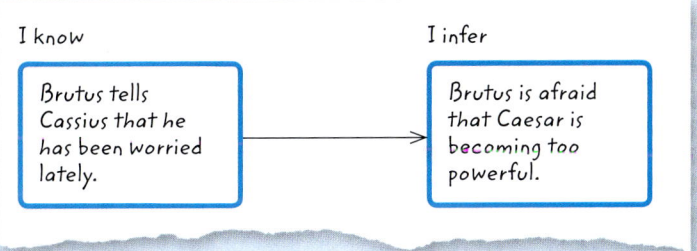

Learning Objectives

For pages 716–738

In studying this text, you will focus on the following objectives:

Literary Study: Analyzing blank verse.

Reading: Making inferences about characters.

Vocabulary

servile (sur′vil) *adj.* lacking self-respect; behaving as if other people are superior; p. 722 *The emperor's servile advisors bowed deeply in his presence.*

entreat (en trēt′) *v.* to ask earnestly; to beg; p. 727 *The charity entreated the public to help the many flood victims.*

infirmity (in fur′mə tē) *n.* a physical or mental weakness or disability; feebleness; p. 731 *After a year of therapy, she shows no signs of her former infirmity.*

enterprise (en′tər prīz′) *n.* an important project or undertaking; p. 731 *Sending human beings to Mars is an expensive and dangerous enterprise.*

incense (in sens′) *v.* to make very angry; p. 733 *Learning that three of his players had been suspended incensed the coach.*

The Tragedy of Julius Caesar

William Shakespeare

The Triumph of Julius Caesar. Paolo Uccello. Tempera on panel. Musee des Arts Decoratifs, Paris.

CHARACTERS

JULIUS CAESAR: ambitious military leader and politician; the most powerful man in Rome

CALPHURNIA: wife of Caesar

MARCUS BRUTUS: friend of Caesar, appointed by him to high office in the Roman government; a believer in the republic and member of the conspiracy against Caesar

PORTIA: wife of Brutus and daughter of a Roman patriot

CAIUS CASSIUS: brother-in-law of Brutus and member of the conspiracy against Caesar

MARK ANTONY: friend of Caesar, senator, and eloquent orator; member of the triumvirate, the three-man governing body that ruled Rome after Caesar's death

OCTAVIUS CAESAR: Caesar's great-nephew and official heir; member of the triumvirate

M. AEMILIUS LEPIDUS: military leader and member of the triumvirate

Conspirators Against Caesar

CASCA	METELLUS CIMBER	TREBONIUS
CINNA	DECIUS BRUTUS	CAIUS LIGARIUS

Senators

CICERO	PUBLIUS	POPILIUS LENA

Tribunes *(Public Officials)*

FLAVIUS	MURELLUS

Officers in the Armies of Brutus and Cassius

LUCILIUS	MESSALA	VOLUMNIUS
TITINIUS	YOUNG CATO	FLAVIUS

Servants of Brutus

LUCIUS	CLITUS	STRATO
VARRUS	CLAUDIO	DARDANIUS

Others

A SOOTHSAYER (one who predicts the future)

ARTEMIDORUS OF CNIDOS: teacher of rhetoric

CINNA: a poet

PINDARUS: servant of Cassius

ANOTHER POET

SERVANTS TO CAESAR, ANTONY, AND OCTAVIUS; CITIZENS, GUARDS, SOLDIERS

ACT 1

SCENE 1. Rome. A street.

[*Enter* FLAVIUS, MURELLUS, *and certain* COMMONERS *over the stage.*]

  FLAVIUS. Hence! Home, you idle creatures, get you home!
   Is this a holiday? What, know you not,
   Being mechanical,° you ought not walk
   Upon a laboring day without the sign
5 Of your profession? Speak, what trade art thou?°

  CARPENTER. Why, sir, a carpenter.

  MURELLUS. Where is thy leather apron and thy rule?
   What dost thou with thy best apparel on?
   You, sir, what trade are you?

10 COBBLER. Truly, sir, in respect of° a fine workman, I am but,
   as you would say, a cobbler.°

  MURELLUS. But what trade art thou? Answer me directly.

  COBBLER. A trade, sir, that, I hope, I may use° with a safe
   conscience, which is indeed, sir, a mender of bad soles.

15 FLAVIUS. What trade, thou knave? Thou naughty knave,
   what trade?

  COBBLER. Nay, I beseech you, sir, be not out° with me; yet, if
   you be out,° sir, I can mend you.

  MURELLUS. What mean'st thou by that? Mend me, thou saucy
   fellow?

20 COBBLER. Why, sir, cobble you.

  FLAVIUS. Thou art a cobbler, art thou?

  COBBLER. Truly, sir, all that I live by is with the awl;° I meddle
   with no tradesman's matters, nor women's matters; but
   withal, I am indeed, sir, a surgeon to old shoes; when they

---

2–5 Is this a . . . art thou: Flavius and Murellus, public officials, remind the laborers that they should be dressed in their work outfits rather than their best clothes.
3 mechanical: manual laborers.

10 in respect of: in comparison with.
11 cobbler: "clumsy worker" or "shoemaker." The Cobbler plays on the word's double meaning. Murellus and Flavius fail to understand his pun at first and keep pressing him to reveal a trade he has already identified.
13 use: practice.

16 out: angry.
16–17 if you be out: if your shoes are worn out.

22 awl: a tool for making holes in leather. The Cobbler puns on the words *all*, *awl*, and *withal*, which means "nevertheless."

Blank Verse *Is the Cobbler speaking in blank verse? How do you know?*

Make Inferences About Characters *What attitude do Flavius and Murellus have toward commoners, such as the Carpenter and the Cobbler?*

25   are in great danger, I recover them. As proper men as ever
        trod upon neat's leather° have gone upon my handiwork.

FLAVIUS. But wherefore art not in thy shop today?
        Why dost thou lead these men about the streets?

COBBLER. Truly, sir, to wear out their shoes, to get myself into
30   more work. But indeed, sir, we make holiday to see Caesar
        and to rejoice in his triumph.°

MURELLUS. Wherefore rejoice? What conquest brings he home?
        What tributaries° follow him to Rome,
        To grace in captive bonds° his chariot wheels?
35   You blocks, you stones, you worse than senseless things!
        O you hard hearts, you cruel men of Rome,
        Knew you not Pompey? Many a time and oft
        Have you climb'd up to walls and battlements,
        To tow'rs and windows, yea, to chimney tops,
40   Your infants in your arms, and there have sate
        The livelong day, with patient expectation,
        To see great Pompey pass the streets of Rome;
        And when you saw his chariot but° appear,
        Have you not made an universal shout,
45   That Tiber° trembled underneath her banks
        To hear the replication° of your sounds
        Made in her concave shores?
        And do you now put on your best attire?
        ==And do you now cull out a holiday?°==
50   ==And do you now strew flowers in his way,==
        ==That comes in triumph over Pompey's blood?°==
        Be gone!
        Run to your houses, fall upon your knees,
        Pray to the gods to intermit° the plague
55   That needs must light on this ingratitude.

FLAVIUS. Go, go, good countrymen, and, for this fault,
        Assemble all the poor men of your sort;
        Draw them to Tiber banks and weep your tears
        Into the channel, till the lowest stream
60   Do kiss the most exalted shores of all.°

[Exit all the COMMONERS.]

        See, whe'er their basest mettle be not mov'd;°
        They vanish tongue-tied in their guiltiness.

---

26 neat's leather: cowhide. The Cobbler claims that his shoes have been worn by as fine men as ever walked in shoes.

31 triumph: triumphal celebration. (The triumph was held to celebrate Julius Caesar's defeat of two sons of Pompey the Great, his former rival. Caesar gained control over Rome upon defeating Pompey in 48 BC.)
33 tributaries: captured enemies who pay tribute, or ransom money, for their release.
34 captive bonds: the chains of prisoners.

43 but: only.

45 Tiber: a river running through Rome.
46 replication: echo.

49 cull out a holiday: pick out this day as a holiday.

51 Pompey's blood: Pompey's sons.

54 intermit: hold back.

58–60 Draw them to . . . of all: Flavius wants the commoners to weep into the Tiber until the river's lowest water reaches its highest banks.
61 whe'er . . . mov'd: whether their humble spirits have not been touched.

Loyalty and Betrayal *Why is Murellus so angry with the commoners?*

JULIUS CAESAR

Go you down that way towards the Capitol,
This way will I. Disrobe the images,
65 If you do find them deck'd with ceremonies.°

MURELLUS. May we do so?
You know it is the feast of Lupercal.°

FLAVIUS. It is no matter, let no images
Be hung with Caesar's trophies.° I'll about,
70 And drive away the vulgar° from the streets;
So do you too, where you perceive them thick.
These growing feathers pluck'd from Caesar's wing
Will make him fly an ordinary pitch,°
Who else would soar above the view of men
75 And keep us all in **servile** fearfulness.

[*They exit.*]

SCENE 2. Rome. A public place.

[*Enter* CAESAR, ANTONY *for the course,* CALPHURNIA, PORTIA, DECIUS, CICERO, BRUTUS, CASSIUS, CASCA, CITIZENS, *and a* SOOTHSAYER; *after them* MURELLUS *and* FLAVIUS.]

CAESAR. Calphurnia!

CASCA.   Peace, ho, Caesar speaks.

[*All fall silent as* CAESAR *calls for his wife.*]

CAESAR.   Calphurnia!

CALPHURNIA. Here, my lord.

CAESAR. Stand you directly in Antonio's way
When he doth run his course. Antonio!

5 ANTONY. Caesar, my lord?

CAESAR. Forget not in your speed, Antonio,
To touch Calphurnia; for our elders say,
The barren, touched in this holy chase,
Shake off their sterile curse.°

ANTONY.   I shall remember;
10 When Caesar says, "Do this," it is perform'd.

64–65 Disrobe the images . . . ceremonies: Flavius directs Murellus to remove any decorations from the statues.

67 feast of Lupercal: religious festival for a god worshiped by shepherds as a protector of flocks

69 trophies: decorations honoring Caesar.

70 vulgar: common people.

72–73 These growing . . . pitch: Plucking feathers from a bird's wings prevents it from flying. Flavius uses this metaphor for his plan to keep Caesar's power at an ordinary **pitch**, or height.

Head of a woman, sometimes identified as Marciana, 1st quarter of the 2nd century A.D. Roman. Bronze. Louvre Museum, Paris.

View the Art Describe the woman portrayed here. How might she reflect Calphurnia's feelings at this point in the drama?

6–9 Forget not . . . curse: Caesar, who has no children, refers to a traditional belief that barren women could become fertile if they were struck by leather thongs carried by runners who passed through Rome on the feast of Lupercal.

Make Inferences About Characters *How would you describe the relationship between Caesar and Antony?*

Vocabulary

servile (sur´vil) *adj.* lacking self-respect; behaving as if other people are superior

CAESAR. Set on, and leave no ceremony out. [*Flourish.*]

SOOTHSAYER. Caesar!

CAESAR. Ha! Who calls?

CASCA. Bid every noise be still; peace yet again!

15 CAESAR. Who is it in the press° that calls on me?
I hear a tongue shriller than all the music,
Cry "Caesar!" Speak, Caesar is turn'd to hear.°

SOOTHSAYER. Beware the ides of March.°

CAESAR.   What man is that?

BRUTUS. A soothsayer bids you beware the ides of March.

20 CAESAR. Set him before me, let me see his face.

CASSIUS. Fellow, come from the throng, look upon Caesar.

CAESAR. What say'st thou to me now? Speak once again.

SOOTHSAYER. Beware the ides of March.

CAESAR. He is a dreamer, let us leave him. Pass.

[*They exit. BRUTUS and CASSIUS remain.*]

25 CASSIUS. Will you go see the order of the course?°

BRUTUS. Not I.

CASSIUS. I pray you do.

BRUTUS. I am not gamesome;° I do lack some part
Of that quick spirit that is in Antony.
30 Let me not hinder, Cassius, your desires;
I'll leave you.

CASSIUS. Brutus, I do observe you now of late;°
I have not from your eyes that gentleness
And show of love as I was wont to° have.
35 You bear too stubborn and too strange a hand
Over your friend that loves you.°

BRUTUS.   Cassius,
Be not deceiv'd: if I have veil'd my look,

---

15 press: crowd.

17 turn'd to hear: Caesar turns his good ear to the Soothsayer (he was deaf in one ear).

18 ides of March: March 15. In the Roman calendar, a day in the middle of every month was called the ides.

25 order . . . course: progress of the race.

28 gamesome: fond of games and sports.

32 of late: lately.

34 was wont to: used to.

35–36 You bear . . . loves you: Cassius uses the metaphor of a rider holding a tight rein on an unfamiliar horse to suggest Brutus's unfriendly behavior toward him.

Blank Verse *How does Shakespeare maintain the rhythm of blank verse during dialogue?*

Make Inferences About Characters *What does Caesar's behavior toward the soothsayer suggest about his character?*

Julius Caesar

I turn the trouble of my countenance
Merely upon myself.° Vexed I am
40 Of late with passions of some difference,°
Conceptions only proper to myself,
Which give some soil, perhaps, to my behaviors;°
But let not therefore my good friends be griev'd
(Among which number, Cassius, be you one),
45 Nor construe any further° my neglect,
Than that poor Brutus, with himself at war,
Forgets the shows of love to other men.

CASSIUS. Then, Brutus, I have much mistook your passion,°
By means whereof this breast of mine hath buried
50 Thoughts of great value, worthy cogitations.°
Tell me, good Brutus, can you see your face?

BRUTUS. No, Cassius; for the eye sees not itself
But by reflection, by some other things.

CASSIUS. 'Tis just,
55 And it is very much lamented, Brutus,
That you have no such mirrors as will turn
Your hidden worthiness into your eye,
That you might see your shadow.° I have heard
Where many of the best respect in Rome
60 (Except immortal Caesar), speaking of Brutus
And groaning underneath this age's yoke,
Have wish'd that noble Brutus had his eyes.°

BRUTUS. Into what dangers would you lead me, Cassius,
That you would have me seek into myself
65 For that which is not in me?

CASSIUS. Therefore, good Brutus, be prepar'd to hear;
And since you know you cannot see yourself
So well as by reflection, I, your glass
Will modestly discover to yourself
70 That of yourself which you yet know not of.°
And be not jealous on° me, gentle Brutus;
Were I a common laughter, or did use
To stale with ordinary oaths my love
To every new protester; if you know

37–39 Be not . . . upon myself: If I have seemed withdrawn, my displeased looks have been turned only on myself.
40 passions of some difference: conflicting emotions.
42 Which give . . . behaviors: Which might blemish my conduct.
45 Nor . . . further: Nor should you think any more of.

48 mistook your passion: misunderstood your feelings.

49–50 By means . . . cogitations: Because of this I have kept important thoughts to myself.

58 shadow: reflection.

58–62 I have heard . . . eyes: Cassius claims that many highly respected Roman citizens, groaning under the oppression of Caesar's rule, wished that Brutus would recognize his own worth.

68–70 I, your . . . not of: I, your mirror, will reveal without exaggeration what you do not yet know about yourself.
71 jealous on: suspicious of.

Make Inferences About Characters *What do Brutus's words suggest about his personality and inner state?*

Loyalty and Betrayal *What does Cassius reveal about his feelings here?*

75   That I do fawn on men and hug them hard,
     And after scandal them; or if you know
     That I profess myself in banqueting
     To all the rout, then hold me dangerous.°

[*Flourish and shout.*]

BRUTUS. What means this shouting? I do fear the people
80   Choose Caesar for their king.

CASSIUS.   Ay, do you fear it?
     Then must I think you would not have it so.

BRUTUS. I would not, Cassius, yet I love him well.
     But wherefore° do you hold me here so long?
     What is it that you would impart to me?
85   If it be aught toward the general good,
     Set honor in one eye and death i' th' other,
     And I will look on both indifferently;°
     For let the gods so speed° me, as I love
     The name of honor more than I fear death.

90   **CASSIUS.** I know that virtue to be in you, Brutus,
     As well as I do know your outward favor.°
     Well, honor is the subject of my story:
     I cannot tell what you and other men
     Think of this life; but for my single self,
95   I had as lief not be as live to be
     In awe of such a thing as I myself.°
     I was born free as Caesar; so were you;
     We both have fed as well, and we can both
     Endure the winter's cold as well as he;
100 For once, upon a raw and gusty day,
     The troubled Tiber chafing with her shores,°
     Caesar said to me, "Dar'st thou,° Cassius, now
     Leap in with me into this angry flood,
     And swim to yonder point?" Upon the word,
105 Accoutred° as I was, I plunged in,
     And bade him follow; so indeed he did.
     The torrent roar'd, and we did buffet it
     With lusty sinews,° throwing it aside
     And stemming it with hearts of controversy;°
110 But ere we could arrive the point propos'd,
     Caesar cried, "Help me, Cassius, or I sink!"

72–78 Were I ... dangerous: If I were a laughingstock or used to cheaply offering my affection to anyone, or if you know me to slander men after fawning on them, or if you know me to proclaim friendship to the common crowd while drinking, then consider me dangerous.

83 wherefore: why.

85–87 If it be aught ... indifferently: If it is anything that concerns the public welfare, I will face honor and death impartially.
88 speed: favor.

91 favor: appearance.

94–96 for my single ... myself: Personally, I would rather not live than live in awe of another human being.

101 chafing with her shores: dashing into the shores (as if angry with them for their restraint).
102 Dar'st thou: Do you dare?

105 Accoutred: dressed in armor.

108 sinews: muscles.
109 stemming ... controversy: making headway against the river's flow in a spirit of rivalry.

Make Inferences About Characters How would you describe Cassius's attitude toward Brutus? Why might Cassius behave in this manner?

The Flight of Aeneas from Troy. Carle van Loo. 1705–1765. Painting. Louvre, Paris.

View the Art What comparison does Cassius make between himself and Aeneas, as pictured here?

    I, as Aeneas,° our great ancestor,
    Did from the flames of Troy upon his shoulder
    The old Anchises bear, so from the waves of Tiber
115 Did I the tired Caesar. And this man
    Is now become a god, and Cassius is
    A wretched creature, and must bend his body°
    If Caesar carelessly but nod on him.
    He had a fever when he was in Spain,
120 And when the fit was on him, I did mark
    How he did shake—'tis true, this god did shake;
    His coward lips did from their color fly,
    And that same eye whose bend° doth awe the world
    Did lose his° luster; I did hear him groan;
125 Ay, and that tongue of his that bade the Romans
    Mark him, and write his speeches in their books,
    Alas, it cried, "Give me some drink, Titinius,"
    As a sick girl. Ye gods, it doth amaze me
    A man of such a feeble temper should
130 So get the start of the majestic world,
    And bear the palm alone.°

[*Shout. Flourish.*]

112 Aeneas (i nē′ əs): The legendary founder of Rome, who carried his father, Anchises, on his back as he fled the burning city of Troy after it was conquered by the Greeks.

117 bend his body: bow.

123 bend: glance, look.
124 his: its.

130–131 So get the . . . alone: get ahead of all others and carry the victor's prize himself.

Make Inferences About Characters What is Cassius's attitude toward the idea that Caesar is a god?

Blank Verse Review lines 125 to 131. How many of these lines are regular iambic pentameter, and how many vary the pattern?

BRUTUS. Another general shout?
  I do believe that these applauses are
  For some new honors that are heap'd on Caesar.

135 **CASSIUS.** Why, man, he doth bestride the narrow world
  Like a Colossus,° and we petty men
  Walk under his huge legs, and peep about
  To find ourselves dishonorable graves.
  Men at some time are masters of their fates;
140 The fault, dear Brutus, is not in our stars,°
  But in ourselves, that we are underlings.
  Brutus and Caesar; what should be in that "Caesar"?
  Why should that name be sounded more than yours?
  Write them together, yours is as fair a name;
145 Sound them,° it doth become the mouth as well;
  Weigh them, it is as heavy; conjure° with 'em,
  "Brutus" will start a spirit as soon as "Caesar."
  Now, in the names of all the gods at once,
  Upon what meat doth this our Caesar feed,
150 That he is grown so great? Age,° thou art sham'd!
  Rome, thou hast lost the breed of noble bloods!
  When went there by an age, since the great flood°
  But it was fam'd with more than with one man?°
  When could they say, till now, that talk'd of Rome,
155 That her wide walks encompass'd but one man?
  Now is it Rome indeed and room enough,°
  When there is in it but one only man.
  O! you and I have heard our fathers say
  There was a Brutus once that would have brook'd
160 Th' eternal devil to keep his state in Rome
  As easily as a king.°

BRUTUS. That you do love me, I am nothing jealous;°
  What you would work me to, I have some aim.°
  How I have thought of this, and of these times,
165 I shall recount hereafter. For this present,
  I would not (so with love I might **entreat** you)
  Be any further mov'd.° What you have said
  I will consider; what you have to say
  I will with patience hear, and find a time
170 Both meet° to hear and answer such high things.

---

136 Colossus: The Colossus of Rhodes, a gigantic statue of the Greek god Apollo in the harbor of Rhodes, was said to be so tall that ships could sail through its legs.

140 stars: fate (believed to be determined by the position of the stars and planets at someone's birth).

145 Sound them: say them.
146 conjure: call up spirits.

150 Age: the present era.

152 great flood: a time, according to Roman mythology, when a god let loose a flood that drowned all but two people.
153 But it was . . . man: That was not celebrated for more than one great man.
156 Now is it . . . enough: Cassius makes a pun on the words *Rome* and *room,* which were sometimes pronounced alike in Shakespeare's time.
159–161 There was . . . king: There once was a Brutus who would have accepted the devil ruling in Rome as easily as a king. (Cassius refers to Lucius Junius Brutus, who expelled the king and made Rome a republic in 509 BC. Brutus claimed this hero as his ancestor.)
162 am nothing jealous: have no doubt.
163 have some aim: can guess.
167 mov'd: urged.
170 meet: suitable.

Loyalty and Betrayal *What angers Cassius about Caesar's leadership?*

Vocabulary

entreat (en trēt′) *v.* to ask earnestly; to beg

Gaius Julius Caesar; Roman statesman and general—"Caesar dictates his commentaries"— Painting (detail), 1812. Pelagio Palagi. Oil on canvas. Rome Palazzo del Quirinale.

View the Art What qualities of Caesar does this painting depict? Do you think they are accurate? Why or why not?

      Till then, my noble friend, chew° upon this;
      Brutus had rather be a villager
      Than to repute himself a son of Rome
      Under these hard conditions as this time
175   Is like to lay upon us.
  CASSIUS. I am glad that my weak words
      Have struck but thus much show of fire from Brutus.

[*Enter* CAESAR *and his* TRAIN.]

  BRUTUS. The games are done, and Caesar is returning.
  CASSIUS. As they pass by, pluck Casca by the sleeve,
180   And he will (after his sour fashion) tell you
      What hath proceeded worthy note today.°
  BRUTUS. I will do so. But look you, Cassius,
      The angry spot doth glow on Caesar's brow,
      And all the rest look like a chidden train;°
185   Calphurnia's cheek is pale, and Cicero°
      Looks with such ferret° and such fiery eyes
      As we have seen him in the Capitol,
      Being cross'd in conference by some senators.
  CASSIUS. Casca will tell us what the matter is.
190 **CAESAR.** Antonio!
  ANTONY. Caesar?
  CAESAR. Let me have men about me that are fat,

171 chew: ponder.

181 What hath . . . today: What noteworthy things have occurred today.

184 chidden train: scolded band of followers.
185 Cicero: a Roman senator famous for his oratory.
186 ferret: a weasel-like animal with red eyes.

Make Inferences About Characters To what extent has Cassius succeeded in winning Brutus over to his side?

Sleek-headed men, and such as sleep a-nights.
Yond Cassius has a lean and hungry look,
195 He thinks too much; such men are dangerous.

ANTONY. Fear him not, Caesar, he's not dangerous,
He is a noble Roman, and well given.°

CAESAR. Would he were fatter! But I fear him not.
Yet if my name were liable to fear,°
200 I do not know the man I should avoid
So soon as that spare Cassius. He reads much,
He is a great observer, and he looks
Quite through the deeds of men.° He loves no plays,
As thou dost, Antony; he hears no music;
205 Seldom he smiles, and smiles in such a sort
As if he mock'd himself, and scorn'd his spirit
That could be mov'd to smile at any thing.°
Such men as he be never at heart's ease
Whiles they behold a greater than themselves,
210 And therefore are they very dangerous.
I rather tell thee what is to be fear'd
Than what I fear; for always I am Caesar.
Come on my right hand, for this ear is deaf,
And tell me truly what thou think'st of him.

[CAESAR *and his* TRAIN *exit.* CASCA *stays.*]

215 CASCA. You pull'd me by the cloak, would you speak with me?

BRUTUS. Ay, Casca; tell us what hath chanc'd° today,
That Caesar looks so sad.°

CASCA. Why, you were with him, were you not?

BRUTUS. I should not then ask Casca what had chanc'd.

220 CASCA. Why, there was a crown offer'd him; and being offer'd him, he put it by° with the back of his hand, thus, and then the people fell a-shouting.

BRUTUS. What was the second noise for?

CASCA. Why, for that too.

225 CASSIUS. They shouted thrice; what was the last cry for?

CASCA. Why, for that too.

BRUTUS. Was the crown offer'd him thrice?

---

197 well given: favorably disposed (toward Caesar).

199 if my name . . . fear: if it were possible for me to fear anyone.

202–203 looks . . . of men: sees people's true motives in their actions.

206–207 scorn'd . . . any thing: scorned anyone who ever smiles.

216 chanc'd: happened.
217 sad: serious.

221 put it by: pushed it aside.

Loyalty and Betrayal Why does Caesar think that Cassius is to be avoided?

Blank Verse What difference do you notice between Casca's way of speaking and that of Caesar in this scene?

JULIUS CAESAR

CASCA. Ay, marry, was't,° and he put it by thrice, every time gentler than other; and at every putting-by mine honest neighbors° shouted.

CASSIUS. Who offer'd him the crown?

CASCA. Why, Antony.

BRUTUS. Tell us the manner of it, gentle Casca.

CASCA. I can as well be hang'd as tell the manner of it; it was mere foolery, I did not mark° it. I saw Mark Antony offer him a crown—yet 'twas not a crown neither, 'twas one of these coronets°—and as I told you, he put it by once; but for all that, to my thinking, he would fain° have had it. Then he offer'd it to him again; then he put it by again; but to my thinking, he was very loath to lay his fingers off it. And then he offer'd it the third time; he put it the third time by; and still as he refus'd it, the rabblement hooted, and clapp'd their chopp'd° hands, and threw up their sweaty nightcaps, and utter'd such a deal of stinking breath because Caesar refus'd the crown, that it had, almost, chok'd Caesar; for he swounded,° and fell down at it; and for mine own part, I durst not laugh, for fear of opening my lips and receiving the bad air.

CASSIUS. But, soft,° I pray you; what, did Caesar swound?

CASCA. He fell down in the market place, and foam'd at mouth, and was speechless.

BRUTUS. 'Tis very like, he hath the falling sickness.°

CASSIUS. No, Caesar hath it not; but you, and I, And honest Casca, we have the falling sickness.

CASCA. I know not what you mean by that, but I am sure Caesar fell down. If the tag-rag people° did not clap him and hiss him, according as he pleas'd and displeas'd them, as they use to do the players in the theater, I am no true man.

BRUTUS. What said he when he came unto himself?

CASCA. Marry, before he fell down, when he perceiv'd the common herd was glad he refus'd the crown, he pluck'd me ope his doublet,° and offer'd them his throat to cut. And I had been a man of any occupation,° if I would not have taken him at a word,° I would I might go to hell among the rogues. And so he fell. When he came to

228 marry, was't: indeed it was.

229–230 mine honest neighbors: Casca refers ironically to his "honest neighbors," for whom he has contempt.

235 mark: pay attention to.

237 coronets: small crowns.
238 fain: rather.

243 chopp'd: chapped.

246 swounded: fainted.

249 soft: wait a minute.

252 'Tis very . . . falling sickness: It's very likely that he has epilepsy.

256 tag-rag people: ragged mob.

261–262 pluck'd . . . doublet: ripped open his short jacket.
263 And I . . . occupation: If I had been "a man of action" (or "a laborer").
264 a word: his word.

Make Inferences About Characters *Why does Caesar refuse the crown?*

himself again, he said, if he had done or said anything amiss, he desir'd their worships to think it was his **infirmity**. Three or four wenches, where I stood, cried, "Alas, good soul!" and forgave him with all their hearts.
270 But there's no heed to be taken of them; if Caesar had stabb'd their mothers, they would have done no less.

BRUTUS. And after that, he came thus sad away?

CASCA. Ay.

CASSIUS. Did Cicero say anything?

275 CASCA. Ay, he spoke Greek.

CASSIUS. To what effect?

CASCA. Nay, and I tell you that, I'll ne'er look you i' th' face again. But those that understood him smil'd at one another, and shook their heads; but for mine own part, it was Greek
280 to me.° I could tell you more news too; Murellus and Flavius, for pulling scarfs off Caesar's images, are put to silence.° Fare you well. There was more foolery yet, if I could remember it.

CASSIUS. Will you sup with me tonight, Casca?

CASCA. No, I am promis'd forth.

285 CASSIUS. Will you dine with me tomorrow?

CASCA. Ay, if I be alive, and your mind hold,° and your dinner worth the eating.

CASSIUS. Good, I will expect you.

CASCA. Do so. Farewell, both. [*Exit.*]

290 BRUTUS. What a blunt fellow is this grown to be!
He was quick mettle° when he went to school.

CASSIUS. So is he now in execution
Of any bold or noble **enterprise**,
However he puts on this tardy form.°
295 This rudeness is a sauce to his good wit,
Which gives men stomach to disgest° his words
With better appetite.

279–280 it was Greek to me: I couldn't understand a word of it.
281 put to silence: barred from speaking in public (or perhaps exiled or executed).

286 your mind hold: you don't change your mind.

291 quick mettle: lively, clever.

294 However . . . form: Although he puts on this dull manner.

296 disgest: digest.

Make Inferences About Characters *What does Casca mean by this remark? What is his attitude toward the mob?*

Loyalty and Betrayal *What does the punishment of Murellus and Flavius indicate about Caesar and his rule?*

Vocabulary

infirmity (in fur′mə tē) *n.* a physical or mental weakness or disability; feebleness
enterprise (en′tər prīz′) *n.* an important project or undertaking

 Julius Caesar

BRUTUS. And so it is. For this time I will leave you.
Tomorrow, if you please to speak with me,
300   I will come home to you, or, if you will,
Come home to me, and I will wait for you.

CASSIUS. I will do so. Till then, think of the world.°

[*Exit* BRUTUS.]

Well, Brutus, thou art noble; yet I see
Thy honorable mettle may be wrought
305   From that it is dispos'd;° therefore it is meet°
That noble minds keep ever with their likes;
For who so firm that cannot be seduc'd?
Caesar doth bear me hard,° but he loves Brutus.
If I were Brutus now and he were Cassius,
310   He should not humor° me. I will this night,
In several hands, in at his windows throw,
As if they came from several citizens,
Writings, all tending to the great opinion
That Rome holds of his name; wherein obscurely
315   Caesar's ambition shall be glanced at.°
And after this, let Caesar seat him sure,°
For we will shake him, or worse days endure. [*Exit.*]

SCENE 3. A Roman street. One month later.

[*Thunder and lightning. Enter (from opposite sides)* CASCA *(with his sword drawn) and* CICERO.]

CICERO. Good even,° Casca; brought you Caesar home?
Why are you breathless? And why stare you so?

CASCA. Are not you mov'd, when all the sway° of earth
Shakes like a thing unfirm? O Cicero,
5   I have seen tempests, when the scolding winds
Have riv'd° the knotty oaks, and I have seen
Th' ambitious ocean swell and rage and foam,
To be exalted with° the threat'ning clouds;
But never till tonight, never till now,
10   Did I go through a tempest dropping fire.
Either there is a civil strife in heaven,
Or else the world, too saucy° with the gods,

302 the world: the present state of affairs.

304–305 Thy honorable ... dispos'd: Your honorable nature can be manipulated to go against its normal inclinations.
305 meet: appropriate.
308 doth bear me hard: dislikes me.

310 humor: influence.

310–315 I will ... glanced at: Tonight I will throw letters in different handwriting, as if they came from several citizens, into Brutus's windows. The letters will relate that Brutus is highly regarded in Rome and will subtly hint at Caesar's ambition.
316 seat him sure: seat himself securely.

1 even: evening.

3 sway: realm.

6 riv'd: split.

8 exalted with: raised as high as.

12 saucy: insolent.

Make Inferences About Characters *What aspect of Cassius's character now becomes clear? What are his true feelings about Brutus?*

Blank Verse *In what way are these lines not blank verse? Why might Shakespeare have written them in this way?*

Incenses them to send destruction.

CICERO. Why, saw you any thing more wonderful?

CASCA. A common slave—you know him well by sight—
Held up his left hand, which did flame and burn
Like twenty torches join'd; and yet his hand,
Not sensible of° fire, remain'd unscorch'd.
Besides—I ha' not since put up my sword—
Against the Capitol I met a lion,
Who glaz'd° upon me and went surly by,
Without annoying me. And there were drawn
Upon a heap° a hundred ghastly women,
Transformed with their fear, who swore they saw
Men, all in fire, walk up and down the streets.
And yesterday the bird of night° did sit
Even at noonday upon the marketplace,
Hooting and shrieking. When these prodigies°
Do so conjointly meet,° let not men say,
"These are their reasons, they are natural";
For I believe they are portentous things
Unto the climate that they point upon.°

CICERO. Indeed, it is a strange-disposed time;
But men may construe things after their fashion,
Clean from the purpose of the things themselves.°
Comes Caesar to the Capitol tomorrow?

CASCA. He doth; for he did bid Antonio
Send word to you he would be there tomorrow.

CICERO. Good night then, Casca; this disturbed sky
Is not to walk in.

CASCA.   Farewell, Cicero.   [*Exit* CICERO.]

[*Enter* CASSIUS.]

CASSIUS. Who's there?

CASCA.   A Roman.

CASSIUS.   Casca, by your voice.

18 **sensible of:** sensitive to.

21 **glaz'd:** stared.

22–23 **drawn . . . heap:** huddled together.

26 **bird of night:** screech owl.

28 **prodigies:** bizarre events.
29 **conjointly meet:** coincide.

31–32 **portentous . . . point upon:** bad omens for the place where they occur.

34–35 **But men may . . . themselves:** But people may interpret things in their own way, regardless of the real meaning of the things.

Loyalty and Betrayal What connection might there be between the unnatural events described by Casca and the events of previous scenes?

Blank Verse These five syllables make up the end of a line of blank verse. Which syllables make up the beginning of the line?

Vocabulary

incense (in sens´) *v.* to make very angry

Owl, 20th century. Graham Sutherland. Oil on canvas. Private collection.

View the Art Can you infer a symbolic meaning from the presence of the "bird of night"? How does this detail affect the mood?

 JULIUS CAESAR

CASCA. Your ear is good. Cassius, what night is this!°

CASSIUS. A very pleasing night to honest men.

CASCA. Who ever knew the heavens menace so?

45 CASSIUS. Those that have known the earth so full of faults.
For my part, I have walk'd about the streets,
Submitting me° unto the perilous night;
And thus unbraced,° Casca, as you see,
Have bar'd my bosom to the thunder-stone;°
50 And when the cross blue lightning seem'd to open
The breast of heaven, I did present myself
Even in the aim° and very flash of it.

CASCA. But wherefore did you so much tempt the heavens?
It is the part of men to fear and tremble
55 When the most mighty gods by tokens° send
Such dreadful heralds to astonish° us.

CASSIUS. You are dull,° Casca; and those sparks of life
That should be in a Roman you do want,°
Or else you use not. You look pale, and gaze,
60 And put on fear, and cast yourself in wonder,
To see the strange impatience of the heavens;
But if you would consider the true cause
Why all these fires, why all these gliding ghosts,
Why birds and beasts from quality and kind,°
65 Why old men, fools, and children calculate,°
Why all these things change from their ordinance,
Their natures and preformed faculties,
To monstrous quality—why, you shall find
That heaven hath infus'd them with these spirits,
70 To make them instruments of fear and warning
Unto some monstrous state.°
Now could I, Casca, name to thee a man
Most like this dreadful night,
That thunders, lightens, opens graves, and roars
75 As doth the lion in the Capitol—
A man no mightier than thyself, or me,
In personal action, yet prodigious grown
And fearful,° as these strange eruptions are.

CASCA. 'Tis Caesar that you mean; is it not, Cassius?

---

42 what night is this: what a night this is!

47 Submitting me: exposing myself.
48 unbraced: with jacket open.
49 thunder-stone: thunderbolt.

52 in the aim: at the point where it was directed.

55 tokens: ominous signs.
56 astonish: stun with fear.

57 dull: stupid.
58 want: lack.

64 from quality and kind: act contrary to nature.
65 calculate: make prophecies.

66–71 Why all these . . . state: Cassius argues that things have changed from their normal behavior as a heavenly warning of some unnatural state of affairs.

77–78 yet prodigious . . . fearful: yet has become ominous and threatening.

Loyalty and Betrayal *Cassius has been making an argument about Roman politics. Which side of the argument does he believe nature is taking?*

CASSIUS. Let it be who it is; for Romans now
Have thews° and limbs like to their ancestors;
But, woe the while,° our fathers' minds are dead,
And we are govern'd with our mothers' spirits;
Our yoke and sufferance° show us womanish.

CASCA. Indeed, they say, the senators tomorrow
Mean to establish Caesar as a king;
And he shall wear his crown by sea and land,
In every place, save here in Italy.

CASSIUS. I know where I will wear this dagger then;
Cassius from bondage will deliver Cassius.°
Therein,° ye gods, you make the weak most strong;
Therein, ye gods, you tyrants do defeat;
Nor stony tower, nor walls of beaten brass,
Nor airless dungeon, nor strong links of iron,
Can be retentive to the strength of spirit;
But life, being weary of these worldly bars,
Never lacks power to dismiss itself.
If I know this, know all the world besides,
That part of tyranny that I do bear
I can shake off at pleasure.

[*Thunder still.*]

CASCA. So can I;
So every bondman in his own hand bears
The power to cancel his captivity.

CASSIUS. And why should Caesar be a tyrant then?
Poor man, I know he would not be a wolf,
But that he sees the Romans are but sheep;
He were no lion, were not Romans hinds.°
Those that with haste will make a mighty fire
Begin it with weak straws. What trash° is Rome?
What rubbish and what offal?° when it serves
For the base matter° to illuminate
So vile a thing as Caesar! But, O grief,
Where hast thou led me? I, perhaps, speak this
Before a willing bondman; then I know
My answer must be made.° But I am arm'd,
And dangers are to me indifferent.

CASCA. You speak to Casca, and to such a man
That is no fleering° tell-tale. Hold, my hand.

---

81 thews: muscles.
82 woe the while: alas for these times.
84 yoke and sufferance: servitude and patient submission.

89–90 I know . . . deliver Cassius: Cassius says that he would rather kill himself than submit to Caesar.
91 Therein: in that way (referring to suicide).

106 hinds: deer.

108 trash: "twigs" or "garbage."
109 offal: "chips of wood" or "garbage."
110 base matter: kindling.

112–114 I, perhaps . . . be made: Perhaps I am speaking to one who accepts his slavery; if so, I shall have to answer for my words (suggesting that Casca might inform on him).

117 fleering: sneering.

Make Inferences About Characters Why might Cassius not want to name Caesar directly?

JULIUS CAESAR

Be factious for redress of all these griefs,°
And I will set this foot of mine as far
120 As who goes farthest.
CASSIUS.   There's a bargain made.
Now know you, Casca, I have mov'd° already
Some certain of the noblest-minded Romans
To undergo with me an enterprise
Of honorable-dangerous consequence;
125 And I do know, by this they stay for me
In Pompey's Porch;° for now, this fearful night,
There is no stir or walking in the streets;
And the complexion of the element
[In] favor's like the work we have in hand,°
130 Most bloody, fiery, and most terrible.
[*Enter* CINNA.]
CASCA. Stand close awhile, for here comes one in haste.
CASSIUS. 'Tis Cinna, I do know him by his gait,
He is a friend. Cinna, where haste you so?
CINNA. To find out you. Who's that? Metellus Cimber?

118 Be factious . . . griefs: Form a group to straighten out all these problems.

121 mov'd: persuaded.

125–126 by this . . . Porch: By this time they wait for me in the entrance to the theater built by Pompey.

128–129 the complexion . . . in hand: The condition of the sky appears similar to the work we have to do.

Loyalty and Betrayal *What bargain has been made?*

Augustus and lictors, detail from the south frieze of the Ara Pacis Augustae, 13–9 BC Roman. Museum of the Ara Pacis, Rome.

View the Art One of the duties of Roman officers called *lictors* was to accompany officials like Caesar in public appearances. What does this image suggest to you about the government of Rome in Caesar's time?

135 CASSIUS. No, it is Casca, one incorporate°
To our attempts. Am I not stay'd for, Cinna?

CINNA. I am glad on't. What a fearful night is this!
There's two or three of us have seen strange sights.

CASSIUS. Am I not stay'd for? tell me.

CINNA. Yes, you are.
140 O Cassius, if you could
But win the noble Brutus to our party—

CASSIUS. Be you content. Good Cinna, take this paper,
And look you lay it in the praetor's chair,
Where Brutus may but find it; and throw this
145 In at his window; set this up with wax
Upon old Brutus' statue.° All this done,
Repair° to Pompey's Porch, where you shall find us.
Is Decius Brutus and Trebonius there?

CINNA. All but Metellus Cimber, and he's gone
150 To seek you at your house. Well, I will hie,°
And so bestow these papers as you bade me.

CASSIUS. That done, repair to Pompey's theater.

[*Exit* CINNA.]

Come, Casca, you and I will yet ere day
See Brutus at his house. Three parts of him
155 Is ours already, and the man entire
Upon the next encounter yields him ours.°

CASCA. O, he sits high in all the people's hearts;
And that which would appear offense in us,
His countenance, like richest alchemy,
160 Will change to virtue and to worthiness.°

CASSIUS. Him, and his worth, and our great need of him,
You have right well conceited.° Let us go,
For it is after midnight, and ere day
We will awake him and be sure of him.

[*They exit.*]

135 incorporate: joined.

142–146 Good Cinna . . . statue: Marcus Brutus held the office of praetor, a high-ranking judge who settled disputes brought before him. Cassius directs Cinna to leave one letter on Brutus's chair, throw a second into his window, and fasten a third onto the statue of the hero Lucius Junius Brutus.

147 Repair: go.

150 hie: hurry.

155–156 the man . . . ours: When we next meet him, he will be entirely in our hands.

159–160 His countenance . . . worthiness: Alchemy was the "science" of trying to turn base metals into gold. Casca says that Brutus's noble reputation will change the public's attitude toward their plot from condemnation to admiration.

162 conceited: understood.

Loyalty and Betrayal Why is it so important for the conspirators to have Brutus on their side?

After You Read

Respond and Think Critically

Respond and Interpret

1. Which character in Act 1 made the strongest impression on you? Why?

2. (a) After seeing the public celebrating Caesar's triumph, what do Flavius and Murellus do? (b) Why do they respond this way?

3. (a) What stories about Caesar does Cassius tell Brutus? (b) What concerns Cassius the most?

Analyze and Evaluate

4. Do you think Shakespeare's portrayal of the commoners in Act 1 is realistic? Explain.

5. What do Caesar's speech and actions tell you about his character? Explain.

Connect

6. **Big Idea** Loyalty and Betrayal From what you have read so far, would you say that the conspirators are traitors or patriots? Explain.

7. **Connect to Today** In what way does the choice facing Roman politicians between loyalty and betrayal remind you of present-day conflicts?

Literary Element Blank Verse

Because **blank verse** is intended to sound like spoken language, its meter is often not perfectly regular.

1. Find two lines with regular iambic pentameter. Indicate the stressed and unstressed syllables.

2. Find two lines with irregular iambic pentameter. Show the stressed and unstressed syllables.

Reading Strategy Make Inferences About Characters

Review the chart you made on page 717. Then read the sentences below and identify at least two reasons why the characters in question behaved as they did.

1. Cassius wants Caesar out of power.
2. Caesar refuses to accept the crown from Antony.

Vocabulary Practice

Practice with Synonyms A synonym is a word that has nearly the same meaning as another word. With a partner, brainstorm three synonyms for each boldfaced vocabulary word below. Then discuss the different shades of meaning that each synonym carries.

1. servile
2. entreat
3. infirmity
4. enterprise
5. incense

EXAMPLE:

serviceable

Synonyms: *helpful, practical, usable*

Sample explanation: *Helpful* means "giving support"; *practical* means "serving a useful purpose"; and *useful* means "able to be used."

Writing

Write an Editorial Imagine you are a journalist who has heard rumors about a plot to overthrow Caesar. Write an editorial in which you explain whether or not you think Caesar should be deposed. Use details from the play to support your opinion.

Literature Online

Selection Resources For Selection Quizzes, eFlashcards, and Reading-Writing Connection activities, go to glencoe.com and enter QuickPass code GL59794u4.

Before You Read

The Tragedy of Julius Caesar, Act 2

Connect to the Play
When you face an important decision, how do you select the best course of action? Respond to this question in your journal.

Build Background
Ancient Romans believed that observing the natural world could inform them about the future. Great storms and unusual behavior by animals were indications that not all was well.

Set Purposes for Reading

Big Idea Loyalty and Betrayal

As you read Act 2 of *Julius Caesar,* think about the motives of those who betray Caesar's trust. As you read, ask yourself, What causes their betrayal? What is the effect of their actions?

Literary Element Monologues, Soliloquies, and Asides

In a work of literature, a **monologue** is a long speech by one character. A **soliloquy** is a monologue delivered while a character is alone onstage. An **aside** is a comment that only the audience hears. As you read, ask yourself, What do you learn about the characters through these devices?

Reading Strategy Analyze Cause-and-Effect Relationships

One action often leads to another. Going to bed late may cause you to be sleepy the next day. This is an example of a **cause-and-effect relationship.** As you read, ask yourself, What cause-and-effect relationships are important in Act 2?

Tip: Create a Chain of Cause and Effect Use a graphic organizer like the one below to track cause-and-effect relationships.

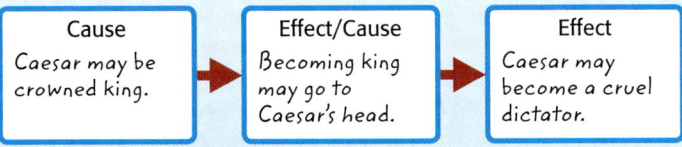

Learning Objectives

For pages 739–759

In studying this text, you will focus on the following objectives:

Literary Study: Analyzing monologues, soliloquies, and asides.

Reading: Analyzing cause-and-effect relationships.

Vocabulary

interim (in′tər im) *n.* the space of time that exists between events; p. 742 *We enjoyed the wedding and the reception, but there was nothing to do in the interim.*

commend (kə mend′) *v.* to speak highly of; to praise; p. 745 *The president commended the senator's service to the country.*

disperse (dis purs′) *v.* to break up and send in different directions; to scatter; p. 747 *It was hard for the mother dog to watch the vet disperse her litter.*

imminent (im′ə nənt) *adj.* about to occur; p. 755 *With the sky so dark and cloudy, surely a thunderstorm is imminent.*

Tip: Word Usage You should select words to suit the situation and your particular audience. For example, in a conversation you might use the word *praise;* in a formal speech, you might use the word *commend.*

JULIUS CAESAR

ACT 2

SCENE 1. BRUTUS's garden. The ides of March.

[*Enter* BRUTUS *in his orchard.*]

BRUTUS. What, Lucius, ho!
I cannot, by the progress° of the stars,
Give guess how near to day. Lucius, I say!
I would it were my fault° to sleep so soundly.
5 When, Lucius, when? Awake, I say! What, Lucius!

[*Enter* LUCIUS.]

LUCIUS. Call'd you, my lord?

BRUTUS. Get me a taper° in my study, Lucius.
When it is lighted, come and call me here.

LUCIUS. I will, my lord.

[*Exit* LUCIUS.]

10 BRUTUS. It must be by his death;° and for my part,
I know no personal cause to spurn° at him,
But for the general.° He would be crown'd:
How that might change his nature, there's the question.
It is the bright day that brings forth the adder,°
15 And that craves° wary walking. Crown him that,°
And then I grant we put a sting in him
That at his will he may do danger with.
Th' abuse of greatness is when it disjoins
Remorse from power;° and, to speak truth of Caesar,
20 I have not known when his affections° sway'd
More than his reason. But 'tis a common proof°
That lowliness° is young ambition's ladder,
Whereto the climber-upward turns his face;
But when he once attains the upmost round,°
25 He then unto the ladder turns his back,
Looks in the clouds, scorning the base degrees
By which he did ascend. So Caesar may;

2 progress: position.

4 I would . . . fault: I wish it were my weakness.

7 taper: candle.

10 his death: Caesar's death.
11 spurn: strike out.
12 the general: the public good.

14 adder: poisonous snake.
15 craves: demands. **Crown him that:** If we crown him.

18–19 Th' abuse . . . power: Greatness is misused when it separates mercy from power.
20 affections: feelings, desires.
21 a common proof: a common occurrence.
22 lowliness: humility.
24 upmost round: top rung.

Monologues, Soliloquies, and Asides *What type of speech is this? How do you know?*

Loyalty and Betrayal *What prediction is Brutus making?*

Two serpents (detail), 1st century C.E. Artist unknown. Fresco painting. Museo Archeologico Nazionale, Naples, Italy.

View the Art What qualities are generally associated with serpents? Which characters in the play display such qualities? Explain.

   Then lest he may, prevent.° And since the quarrel
   Will bear no color for the thing he is,
30 Fashion it thus: that what he is, augmented,
   Would run to these and these extremities;°
   And therefore think him as a serpent's egg,
   Which hatch'd, would as his kind grow mischievous,
   And kill him in the shell.

[*Enter* LUCIUS.]

35 LUCIUS. The taper burneth in your closet,° sir.
   Searching the window for a flint, I found
   This paper thus seal'd up, and I am sure
   It did not lie there when I went to bed.

[*Gives him the letter.*]

  BRUTUS. Get you to bed again, it is not day.
40 Is not tomorrow, boy, the [ides] of March?

  LUCIUS. I know not, sir.

  BRUTUS. Look in the calendar, and bring me word.

  LUCIUS. I will, sir. [*Exit.*]

  BRUTUS. The exhalations° whizzing in the air
45 Give so much light that I may read by them.

---

28 Then lest . . . prevent: Let us act in advance to prevent it.

28–31 since the quarrel . . . extremities: Since our complaints are not supported by Caesar's present behavior, we will have to put our case the following way: if given more power, Caesar's nature would lead him to such and such extremes.

35 closet: small private room.

44 exhalations: meteors.

Julius Caesar

[*Opens the letter and reads.*]

"Brutus, thou sleep'st; awake, and see thyself!
Shall Rome, etc. Speak, strike, redress!"°
"Brutus, thou sleep'st; awake."
Such instigations° have been often dropp'd
50   Where I have took them up.
"Shall Rome, etc." Thus must I piece it out:°
Shall Rome stand under one man's awe? What, Rome?
My ancestors did from the streets of Rome
The Tarquin° drive when he was call'd a king.
55   "Speak, strike, redress!" Am I entreated
To speak and strike? O Rome, I make thee promise,
If the redress will follow, thou receivest
Thy full petition at the hand of Brutus!°

[*Enter LUCIUS.*]

LUCIUS. Sir, March is wasted fifteen days.

[*Knock within.*]

60   BRUTUS. 'Tis good. Go to the gate, somebody knocks.

[*Exit LUCIUS.*]

Since Cassius first did whet° me against Caesar,
I have not slept.
Between the acting of a dreadful thing
And the first motion,° all the **interim** is
65   Like a phantasma,° or a hideous dream.
The Genius and the mortal instruments°
Are then in council, and the state of a man,
Like to a little kingdom, suffers then
The nature of an insurrection.°

[*Enter LUCIUS.*]

70   LUCIUS. Sir, 'tis your brother° Cassius at the door,
Who doth desire to see you.

BRUTUS.   Is he alone?

LUCIUS. No, sir, there are moe° with him.

---

47 redress: correct a wrong.

49 instigations: letters urging action.

51 piece it out: fill in the gaps in meaning.

54 Tarquin (tär′ kwin): the last king of Rome, driven out by Lucius Junius Brutus.

55–58 Speak, strike . . . Brutus: Brutus vows that Rome's petition for redress will be granted if it can be done through his words and actions.

61 whet: incite.

64 motion: prompting.
65 phantasma: nightmare.
66 Genius . . . instruments: the mental and physical powers that allow someone to take action.

67–69 the state . . . insurrection: Brutus compares his conflicted state of mind to a kingdom paralyzed by civil unrest.
70 brother: brother-in-law. (Cassius is married to Brutus's sister, Junia.)

72 moe: more.

Loyalty and Betrayal *What does the audience know about the origin of these notes?*

Analyze Cause-and-Effect Relationships *What has caused Brutus's mind to be in such turmoil?*

Vocabulary

interim (in′ tər im) *n.* the space of time that exists between events

BRUTUS. Do you know them?

LUCIUS. No, sir; their hats are pluck'd about their ears,
And half their faces buried in their cloaks,
That by no means I may discover° them
By any mark of favor.°

BRUTUS. Let 'em enter.

[*Exit* LUCIUS.]

They are the faction. O Conspiracy,
Sham'st thou° to show thy dang'rous brow by night,
When evils are most free? O then, by day
Where wilt thou find a cavern dark enough
To mask thy monstrous visage? Seek none, Conspiracy;
Hide it in smiles and affability;
For if thou path, thy native semblance° on,
Not Erebus° itself were dim enough
To hide thee from prevention.°

[*Enter the* CONSPIRATORS, CASSIUS, CASCA, DECIUS, CINNA, METELLUS, *and* TREBONIUS.]

CASSIUS. I think we are too bold upon° your rest.
Good morrow,° Brutus, do we trouble you?

BRUTUS. I have been up this hour, awake all night.
Know I these men that come along with you?

CASSIUS. Yes, every man of them; and no man here
But honors you; and every one doth wish
You had but that opinion of yourself
Which every noble Roman bears of you.
This is Trebonius.

BRUTUS. He is welcome hither.

CASSIUS. This, Decius Brutus.

BRUTUS. He is welcome too.

CASSIUS. This, Casca; this, Cinna; and this, Metellus Cimber.

BRUTUS. They are all welcome.
What watchful cares do interpose themselves
Betwixt your eyes and night?°

CASSIUS. Shall I entreat a word?

[*They whisper.*]

DECIUS. Here lies the east; doth not the day break here?

---

75 **discover:** identify.
76 **favor:** appearance.

78 **Sham'st thou:** Are you ashamed?

83 **path ... semblance:** go about undisguised.
84 **Erebus** (er′ ə bəs): in classical mythology, the dark place through which the dead pass on their way to Hades, the underworld.
85 **prevention:** discovery.
86 **too bold upon:** intruding upon.
87 **morrow:** morning.

Night. Simeon Solomon. Watercolour, ink and bodycolour on paper. Royal Albert Memorial Museum, Exeter, Devon, UK.

View the Art What mood or emotional quality is expressed by this painting?

98–99 **What watchful ... night:** What cares keep you awake?

Monologues, Soliloquies, and Asides *From this passage, what impression do you have of the role of soliloquies in Shakespearean drama?*

Julius Caesar

CASCA. No.

CINNA. O, pardon, sir, it doth; and yon gray lines
That fret° the clouds are messengers of day.

105 **CASCA.** You shall confess that you are both deceiv'd.
Here, as I point my sword, the sun arises,
Which is a great way growing on the south,
Weighing the youthful season of the year.
Some two months hence, up higher toward the north
110 He first presents his fire, and the high east
Stands, as the Capitol, directly here.°

BRUTUS. Give me your hands all over,° one by one.

CASSIUS. And let us swear our resolution.

BRUTUS. No, not an oath. If not the face of men,
115 The sufferance of our souls, the time's abuse—
If these be motives weak, break off betimes,°
And every man hence to his idle bed.
So let high-sighted° tyranny range on
Till each man drop by lottery.° But if these
120 (As I am sure they do) bear fire° enough
To kindle cowards and to steel with valor
The melting spirits of women, then, countrymen,
What need we any spur but our own cause
To prick° us to redress? What other bond
125 Than secret Romans that have spoke the word
And will not palter?° and what other oath
Than honesty to honesty engag'd
That this shall be, or we will fall for it?°
Swear priests and cowards and men cautelous,°
130 Old feeble carrions,° and such suffering souls
That welcome wrongs; unto bad causes swear
Such creatures as men doubt; but do not stain
The even virtue of our enterprise,
Nor th' insuppressive mettle of our spirits,
135 To think that or our cause or our performance

104 fret: interlace.

106–111 Here, as I . . . directly here: Casca insists that in the early spring the sun rises south of the spot pointed out by Decius and Cinna; it will rise farther north in about two months.
112 all over: all of you.

114–116 If not . . . betimes: The sadness in people's faces, the suffering of our souls, the corruption of our age—if these are weak motives, let's give up at once.
118 high-sighted: arrogant.
119 drop by lottery: die by chance (at Caesar's whim).
120 bear fire: are spirited.

124 prick: spur.

126 palter: waver; deceive.

126–128 what other oath . . . for it: What other oath is needed than that of honest men who have pledged to each other that they will prevail or die trying?
129 cautelous: wary; crafty.
130 carrions: men no better than corpses.

Analyze Cause-and-Effect Relationships Why does Shakespeare insert this bit of dialogue among Decius, Casca, and Cinna about compass directions?

Monologues, Soliloquies, and Asides What argument does Brutus make against swearing an oath?

Loyalty and Betrayal What does Brutus think is virtuous about their enterprise?

  Did need an oath;° when every drop of blood
  That every Roman bears, and nobly bears,
  Is guilty of a several bastardy,°
  If he do break the smallest particle
140 Of any promise that hath pass'd from him.°

CASSIUS. But what of Cicero? Shall we sound him?°
  I think he will stand very strong with us.

CASCA. Let us not leave him out.

CINNA.   No, by no means.

METELLUS. O, let us have him, for his silver hairs
145 Will purchase us a good opinion,
  And buy men's voices to **commend** our deeds.
  It shall be said his judgment rul'd our hands;
  Our youths and wildness shall no whit° appear,
  But all be buried in his gravity.°

150 **BRUTUS.** O, name him not! Let us not break with him,°
  For he will never follow anything
  That other men begin.

CASSIUS.   Then leave him out.

CASCA. Indeed, he is not fit.

DECIUS. Shall no man else be touch'd but only Caesar?

155 **CASSIUS.** Decius, well urg'd. I think it is not meet
  Mark Antony, so well belov'd of Caesar,
  Should outlive Caesar; we shall find of him
  A shrewd contriver; and you know, his means,°
  If he improve them,° may well stretch so far
160 As to annoy us all; which to prevent,
  Let Antony and Caesar fall together.

BRUTUS. Our course will seem too bloody, Caius Cassius,
  To cut the head off and then hack the limbs—
  Like wrath in death and envy afterwards;°
165 For Antony is but a limb of Caesar.
  Let's be sacrificers, but not butchers, Caius.
  We all stand up against the spirit of Caesar,°
  And in the spirit of men there is no blood.
  O that we then could come by° Caesar's spirit,

132–136 do not stain . . . oath: Do not insult the steadfast virtue of our undertaking or the indomitable courage of our spirits to think that either our cause or our actions require an oath.

136–140 every drop . . . from him: Brutus claims that no one of true Roman blood would break a promise.

138 Is guilty . . . bastardy: is illegitimate.

141 sound him: find out his feelings.

148 no whit: not in the least.

149 gravity: dignity.

150 break with him: reveal our plot to him.

158 means: abilities.

159 improve them: uses them fully.

164 Like wrath . . . afterwards: as if the killings were motivated by anger and malice.

167 the spirit of Caesar: what Caesar represents.

169 come by: get possession of.

Analyze Cause-and-Effect Relationships *What does Cassius think would be the effect of letting Mark Antony live?*

Vocabulary

commend (kə mend´) *v.* to speak highly of; to praise

JULIUS CAESAR

<blockquote>

170 And not dismember Caesar! But, alas,
Caesar must bleed for it. And, gentle friends,
Let's kill him boldly, but not wrathfully;
Let's carve him as a dish fit for the gods,
Not hew him as a carcass fit for hounds;
175 And let our hearts, as subtle masters do,
Stir up their servants° to an act of rage,
And after seem to chide 'em. This shall make
Our purpose necessary, and not envious;
Which so appearing to the common eyes,
180 **We shall be call'd purgers, not murderers.**
And for Mark Antony, think not of him;
For he can do no more than Caesar's arm
When Caesar's head is off.

CASSIUS.   Yet I fear him,
For in the ingrafted° love he bears to Caesar—

185 BRUTUS. Alas, good Cassius, do not think of him.
If he love Caesar, all that he can do
Is to himself—take thought and die° for Caesar.
And that were much he should,° for he is given
To sports, to wildness, and much company.

190 TREBONIUS. There is no fear in him;° let him not die,
For he will live and laugh at this hereafter.

[*Clock strikes.*]

BRUTUS. Peace, count the clock.

CASSIUS.   The clock hath stricken three.

TREBONIUS. 'Tis time to part.

CASSIUS.   But it is doubtful yet
Whether Caesar will come forth today or no;
195 For he is superstitious grown of late,
Quite from the main opinion° he held once
Of fantasy, of dreams, and ceremonies.°
It may be these apparent prodigies,
The unaccustom'd terror of this night,
200 And the persuasion of his augurers°
May hold him from the Capitol today.

DECIUS. Never fear that. If he be so resolv'd,
I can o'ersway him; for he loves to hear

</blockquote>

176 servants: hands.

184 ingrafted: deep-rooted.

187 take thought and die: die from grief.
188 that were much he should: It is unlikely that he would do such a thing.

190 no fear in him: nothing to fear from him.

196 Quite from the main opinion: contrary to the strong opinion.
197 ceremonies: omens.

200 augurers: religious officials who interpreted omens to predict future events.

Loyalty and Betrayal *What does Brutus mean in distinguishing between "purgers" and "murderers"? What do you think of this distinction?*

	That unicorns may be betray'd with trees,
205	And bears with glasses, elephants with holes,
	Lions with toils, and men with flatterers;°
	But when I tell him he hates flatterers
	He says he does, being then most flattered.
	Let me work;
210	For I can give his humor the true bent,°
	And I will bring him to the Capitol.

CASSIUS. Nay, we will all of us be there to fetch him.

BRUTUS. By the eight hour; is that the uttermost?°

CINNA. Be that the uttermost, and fail not then.

215 **METELLUS.** Caius Ligarius doth bear Caesar hard,°
Who rated° him for speaking well of Pompey.
I wonder none of you have thought of him.

BRUTUS. Now, good Metellus, go along by him.
He loves me well, and I have given him reasons;
220 Send him but hither, and I'll fashion° him.

CASSIUS. The morning comes upon 's; we'll leave you, Brutus.
And, friends, **disperse** yourselves; but all remember
What you have said, and show yourselves true Romans.

BRUTUS. Good gentlemen, look fresh and merrily;
225 Let not our looks put on our purposes,
But bear it as our Roman actors do,
With untir'd spirits and formal constancy.°
And so good morrow to you every one.

[They exit. BRUTUS remains.]

Boy! Lucius! Fast asleep? It is no matter,
230 Enjoy the honey-heavy dew of slumber.
Thou hast no figures nor no fantasies,
Which busy care draws in the brains of men;
Therefore thou sleep'st so sound.

[Enter PORTIA.]

PORTIA. Brutus, my lord!

BRUTUS. Portia! what mean you? wherefore rise you now?
235 It is not for your health thus to commit
Your weak condition to the raw cold morning.

203–206 for he loves . . . flatterers: Decius refers to legends that the mythical unicorn could be tricked into charging a tree and getting its horn stuck, and that bears can be lured by mirrors. He also refers to trapping elephants in pits and using nets to catch lions, and tricking men with flattery.
210 give his . . . bent: put him in the right mood.
213 uttermost: latest.

215 bear Caesar hard: strongly resents Caesar.
216 rated: rebuked.

220 fashion: persuade.

224–227 look fresh . . . constancy: Brutus warns the others not to let their serious expressions show their intentions; they should carry out their plot appearing at ease and dignified.

Monologues, Soliloquies, and Asides *What does this soliloquy reveal about Brutus?*

Vocabulary

disperse (dis purs´) *v.* to break up and send in different directions; to scatter

Julius Caesar

PORTIA. Nor for yours neither. Y'have ungently,° Brutus,
Stole from my bed; and yesternight at supper
You suddenly arose and walk'd about,
Musing and sighing, with your arms across;° [240]
And when I ask'd you what the matter was,
You star'd upon me with ungentle looks.
I urg'd you further; then you scratch'd your head,
And too impatiently stamp'd with your foot.
Yet I insisted, yet you answer'd not, [245]
But with an angry wafter° of your hand
Gave sign for me to leave you. So I did,
Fearing to strengthen that impatience
Which seem'd too much enkindled, and withal°
Hoping it was but an effect of humor,° [250]
Which sometimes hath his° hour with every man.
It will not let you eat, nor talk, nor sleep,
And could it work so much upon your shape
As it hath much prevail'd on your condition,
I should not know you Brutus.° Dear my lord, [255]
Make me acquainted with your cause of grief.

BRUTUS. I am not well in health, and that is all.

PORTIA. Brutus is wise and, were he not in health,
He would embrace the means to come by it.

BRUTUS. Why, so I do. Good Portia, go to bed. [260]

PORTIA. Is Brutus sick, and is it physical°
To walk unbraced and suck up the humors
Of the dank morning?° What, is Brutus sick,
And will he steal out of his wholesome bed,
To dare the vile contagion of the night, [265]
And tempt the rheumy and unpurged air°
To add unto his sickness? No, my Brutus;
You have some sick offense° within your mind,
Which by the right and virtue of my place,°
I ought to know of; and upon my knees [270]
I charm you, by my once commended beauty,
By all your vows of love, and that great vow
Which did incorporate and make us one,
That you unfold to me, yourself, your half,

237 ungently: discourteously.

240 across: folded.

246 wafter: waving.

249 withal: also.
250 but an . . . humor: only a passing mood.
251 his: its.

253–255 And could . . . Brutus: And if it could change your appearance as much as it has changed your state of mind, I would not recognize you as Brutus.

261 physical: healthy.

262–263 humors . . . morning: damp morning mist.
266 tempt the . . . air: risk the damp and impure air. (It was believed that the night air was dangerous to breathe because it wasn't purified by the sun's rays.)
268 sick offense: harmful disorder.

269 by the right . . . place: as your wife.

Loyalty and Betrayal *What effect is thinking about the conspiracy having on Brutus?*

Analyze Cause-and-Effect Relationships *What causes Portia to distrust Brutus's explanation for his odd appearance?*

Statue of Julius Caesar.
Artist unknown. Museo Laternanense, Vatican Museums, Vatican State.

View the Art What words would you use to describe Caesar in this depiction? Explain.

275 Why you are heavy, and what men tonight
Have had resort to you; for here have been
Some six or seven, who did hide their faces
Even from darkness.

BRUTUS. Kneel not, gentle Portia.

PORTIA. I should not need, if you were gentle Brutus.
280 Within the bond of marriage, tell me, Brutus,
Is it excepted I should know no secrets
That appertain to you? Am I your self
But, as it were, in sort or limitation,°
To keep with you at meals, comfort your bed,
285 And talk to you sometimes? Dwell I but in the suburbs°
Of your good pleasure? If it be no more,
Portia is Brutus' harlot, not his wife.

BRUTUS. You are my true and honorable wife,
As dear to me as are the ruddy drops
290 That visit my sad heart.

PORTIA. If this were true, then should I know this secret.
I grant I am a woman; but withal
A woman that Lord Brutus took to wife.
I grant I am a woman; but withal
295 A woman well reputed, Cato's daughter.°
Think you I am no stronger than my sex,
Being so father'd and so husbanded?
Tell me your counsels, I will not disclose 'em.
I have made strong proof of my constancy,
300 Giving myself a voluntary wound
Here, in the thigh;° can I bear that with patience,
And not my husband's secrets?

BRUTUS. O ye gods!
Render me worthy of this noble wife! [*Knock.*]

283 in sort or limitation: after a fashion or within limits.

285 suburbs: outskirts.

295 Cato's daughter: Portia's father, Marcus Porcius Cato, killed himself rather than submit to Caesar's rule after Pompey was defeated.

299–301 I have made . . . thigh: Portia reveals that she intentionally cut her thigh before approaching Brutus to show her strong determination.

Monologues, Soliloquies, and Asides To whom does Brutus make this remark?

Julius Caesar

Hark, hark, one knocks. Portia, go in a while,
And by and by thy bosom shall partake
The secrets of my heart.
All my engagements I will construe° to thee,
All the charactery of my sad brows.°
Leave me with haste.

[*Exit* PORTIA.]

Lucius, who's that knocks?

[*Enter* LUCIUS *and* CAIUS LIGARIUS.]

LUCIUS. Here is a sick man that would speak with you.

BRUTUS. Caius Ligarius, that Metellus spake of.
Boy, stand aside. [*Exit* LUCIUS.] Caius Ligarius, how?°

CAIUS. Vouchsafe° good morrow from a feeble tongue.

BRUTUS. O, what a time have you chose out, brave Caius,
To wear a kerchief!° Would you were not sick!

CAIUS. I am not sick, if Brutus have in hand
Any exploit worthy the name of honor.

BRUTUS. Such an exploit have I in hand, Ligarius,
Had you a healthful ear to hear of it.

CAIUS. By all the gods that Romans bow before,
I here discard my sickness!
                    Soul of Rome!
Brave son, deriv'd from honorable loins!
Thou, like an exorcist,° hast conjur'd up
My mortified° spirit. Now bid me run,
And I will strive with things impossible,
Yea, get the better of them. What's to do?

BRUTUS. A piece of work that will make sick men whole.

CAIUS. But are not some whole that we must make sick?

BRUTUS. That must we also. What it is, my Caius,
I shall unfold to thee, as we are going
To whom it must be done.°

CAIUS.   Set on your foot.°
And with a heart new-fir'd I follow you,
To do I know not what; but it sufficeth
That Brutus leads me on.

307 construe: explain.
308 charactery of . . . brows: what is written in my sad brows (the reasons I am sad).

312 how: how are you?
313 Vouchsafe: Please accept.

315 kerchief: a scarf (wrapped around an ill person's head to protect against drafts).

323 exorcist: one who summons up spirits.
324 mortified: deadened.

330–331 I shall . . . done: They are going to Caesar's house to escort him to the Capitol.
331 Set on your foot: Go ahead.

Analyze Cause-and-Effect Relationships *Why is Brutus persuaded to reveal the secrets of his heart to Portia?*

[*Thunder.*]

BRUTUS. Follow me, then. [*They exit.*]

SCENE 2. CAESAR's house. A few hours later.

[*Thunder and lightning. Enter* JULIUS CAESAR *in his nightgown.*]

CAESAR. Nor heaven nor° earth have been at peace tonight.
Thrice hath Calphurnia in her sleep cried out,
"Help, ho! they murther° Caesar!" Who's within?

1 Nor . . . nor: neither . . . nor.

3 murther: murder.

[*Enter a* SERVANT.]

SERVANT. My lord?

5 **CAESAR.** Go bid the priests do present sacrifice,
And bring me their opinions of success.°

5–6 Go bid . . . success: Tell the priests to make a sacrifice immediately, and bring me their interpretations of the results.

SERVANT. I will, my lord. [*Exit.*]

[*Enter* CALPHURNIA.]

CALPHURNIA. What mean you, Caesar? Think you to walk forth?
You shall not stir out of your house today.

10 **CAESAR.** Caesar shall forth; the things that threaten'd me
Ne'er look'd but on my back; when they shall see
The face of Caesar, they are vanished.

CALPHURNIA. Caesar, I never stood on ceremonies,°
Yet now they fright me. There is one within,
15 Besides the things that we have heard and seen,
Recounts most horrid sights seen by the watch.°
A lioness hath whelped° in the streets,
And graves have yawn'd,° and yielded up their dead;
Fierce fiery warriors fight upon the clouds
20 In ranks and squadrons and right form of war,°
Which drizzled blood upon the Capitol;
The noise of battle hurtled in the air;
Horses did neigh, and dying men did groan,
And ghosts did shriek and squeal about the streets.
25 O Caesar, these things are beyond all use,°
And I do fear them.

13 stood on ceremonies: believed in omens.

16 watch: night watchmen.
17 whelped: given birth.
18 yawn'd: opened.

20 right form of war: proper military formation.

25 use: normal experience.

CAESAR. What can be avoided
Whose end is purpos'd by the mighty gods?

Monologues, Soliloquies, and Asides *Why did Shakespeare include this soliloquy?*

Analyze Cause-and-Effect Relationships *Why does Calphurnia fear these strange events?*

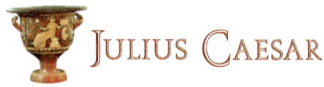

JULIUS CAESAR

        Yet Caesar shall go forth; for these predictions
        Are to the world in general as to Caesar.°

30 CALPHURNIA. When beggars die, there are no comets seen;
        The heavens themselves blaze forth the death of princes.

    CAESAR. Cowards die many times before their deaths,
        The valiant never taste of death but once.
        Of all the wonders that I yet have heard,
35   It seems to me most strange that men should fear,
        Seeing that death, a necessary end,
        Will come when it will come.

[*Enter a* SERVANT.]

                                    What say the augurers?

    SERVANT. They would not have you to stir forth today.
        Plucking the entrails of an offering forth,
40   They could not find a heart within the beast.°

    CAESAR. The gods do this in shame of° cowardice;
        Caesar should be a beast without a heart
        If he should stay at home today for fear.
        No, Caesar shall not; Danger knows full well
45   That Caesar is more dangerous than he.
        We [are] two lions litter'd in one day,°
        And I the elder and more terrible;
        And Caesar shall go forth.

    CALPHURNIA.   Alas, my lord,
        Your wisdom is consum'd in confidence.
50   Do not go forth today; call it my fear
        That keeps you in the house and not your own.
        We'll send Mark Antony to the Senate House,
        And he shall say you are not well today.
        Let me, upon my knee, prevail in this.

55 CAESAR. Mark Antony shall say I am not well,

---

29 Are to the . . . Caesar: apply to everyone as well as to me.

39–40 Plucking the . . . beast: Augurers would examine the inner organs of a sacrificed animal to predict the future. The absence of a heart would be a strange and unfavorable omen.
41 in shame of: to shame.

44–46 Danger knows . . . day: Caesar uses two figures of speech, first personifying danger and then using the metaphor that he and danger are lions born on the same day.

Analyze Cause-and-Effect Relationships *What do you think will happen because of Caesar's decision?*

Caesar and his wife Calpurnia, 1703-1767. Fabio Canal. Palazzo Mangilli-Guion, Venice.

View the Art Is this artwork effective at portraying Calphurnia's character and emotions? Explain.

Electrotype copies of two lions from Rosenborg Castle, 17th century. Elkington & Co. Electroplated copper, silvered, 98 x 165 x 64 cm and 98 x 165 x 60 cm. Victoria and Albert Museum, London.

And for thy humor,° I will stay at home.

[*Enter* DECIUS.]

Here's Decius Brutus, he shall tell them so.

DECIUS. Caesar, all hail! good morrow, worthy Caesar,
I come to fetch you to the Senate House.

60 CAESAR. And you are come in very happy time°
To bear my greeting to the senators,
And tell them that I will not come today.
Cannot, is false; and that I dare not, falser;
I will not come today. Tell them so, Decius.

65 CALPHURNIA. Say he is sick.

CAESAR. Shall Caesar send a lie?
Have I in conquest stretch'd mine arm so far
To be afeard to tell graybeards the truth?°
Decius, go tell them Caesar will not come.

DECIUS. Most mighty Caesar, let me know some cause,
70 Lest I be laugh'd at when I tell them so.

CAESAR. The cause is in my will, I will not come:
That is enough to satisfy the Senate.
But for your private satisfaction,
Because I love you, I will let you know.
75 Calphurnia here, my wife, stays° me at home:
She dreamt tonight° she saw my statue,
Which, like a fountain with an hundred spouts,

56 **humor:** whim.

60 **in very happy time:** at the right moment.

66–67 **Have I . . . truth:** Have I made such conquests to be afraid to tell old men the truth?

75 **stays:** keeps.
76 **tonight:** last night.

Loyalty and Betrayal *Does Decius seem sincere to you? Why or why not?*

Did run pure blood, and many lusty Romans
Came smiling and did bathe their hands in it.
80 And these does she apply for° warnings and portents
And evils **imminent**, and on her knee
Hath begg'd that I will stay at home today.

DECIUS. This dream is all amiss interpreted,
It was a vision fair and fortunate.
85 Your statue spouting blood in many pipes,
In which so many smiling Romans bath'd,
Signifies that from you great Rome shall suck
Reviving blood, and that great men shall press
For tinctures, stains, relics, and cognizance.°
90 This by Calphurnia's dream is signified.

CAESAR. And this way have you well expounded it.

DECIUS. I have, when you have heard what I can say;
And know it now: the Senate have concluded
To give this day a crown to mighty Caesar.
95 If you shall send them word you will not come,
Their minds may change. Besides, it were a mock
Apt to be render'd,° for someone to say,
"Break up the Senate till another time,
When Caesar's wife shall meet with better dreams."
100 If Caesar hide himself, shall they not whisper,
"Lo, Caesar is afraid"?

80 **apply for:** interpret as.

85–89 **Your statue . . . cognizance: Tinctures** are features added to a coat of arms; **relics** are the remains of saints; **cognizance** is a mark identifying one as a lord's follower. Decius interprets Calphurnia's dream as a sign of Caesar's prestige, with great men coming to him to show their political loyalty and reverence.

96–97 **it were a . . . render'd:** it would be a joke likely to be made.

Loyalty and Betrayal What does this passage suggest about how the participants will behave as the plot unfolds?

Vocabulary

imminent (im´ə nənt) *adj.* about to occur

Grave relief of an Athenian married couple, 330 A.D. Artist unknown. Marble attic relief. Antikensammlung, Staatliche Museen zu Berlin.

View the Art How would you describe the scene featured in this relief? Which characters in *Julius Caesar* would best fit in your description? Why?

 Julius Caesar

Pardon me, Caesar, for my dear dear love
To your proceeding° bids me tell you this;
And reason to my love is liable.°

105 CAESAR. How foolish do your fears seem now, Calphurnia!
I am ashamed I did yield to them.
Give me my robe, for I will go.

[*Enter* BRUTUS, LIGARIUS, METELLUS CIMBER, CASCA, TREBONIUS, CINNA, *and* PUBLIUS.]

And look where Publius is come to fetch me.

PUBLIUS. Good morrow, Caesar.

CAESAR. Welcome, Publius.
110 What, Brutus, are you stirr'd so early too?
Good morrow, Casca. Caius Ligarius,
Caesar was ne'er so much your enemy°
As that same ague° which hath made you lean.
What is't o'clock?

BRUTUS. Caesar, 'tis strucken eight.

115 CAESAR. I thank you for your pains and courtesy.

[*Enter* ANTONY.]

See, Antony, that revels long a-nights,°
Is notwithstanding up. Good morrow, Antony.

ANTONY. So to most noble Caesar.

CAESAR. Bid them prepare within;
I am to blame to be thus waited for.
120 Now, Cinna; now, Metellus; what, Trebonius,
I have an hour's talk in store for you;
Remember that you call on me today;
Be near me, that I may remember you.

TREBONIUS. Caesar, I will [*Aside.*] and so near will I be,
125 That your best friends shall wish I had been further.

CAESAR. Good friends, go in, and taste some wine with me,
And we, like friends, will straightway go together.

BRUTUS. [*Aside.*] That every like is not the same, O Caesar,
The heart of Brutus earns to think upon.°

[*They exit.*]

102–103 my dear . . . proceeding: my very deep desire for your advancement.
104 liable: subservient. Decius says that his love for Caesar forces him to say this, even though he may be overstepping himself.

112 your enemy: Caesar had recently pardoned Ligarius for his support of Pompey during the civil war.
113 ague: sickness.

116 that revels long a-nights: who carouses late into the night.

128–129 That every . . . upon: Brutus grieves to think that not everyone who appears to be a friend is a real friend.

Analyze Cause-and-Effect Relationships *What has caused Caesar to change his mind?*

Monologues, Soliloquies, and Asides *What attitude towards the plot to murder Caesar does Brutus reveal here?*

SCENE 3. A street near the Capitol. Shortly afterward.

[Enter ARTEMIDORUS (reading a paper).]

    ARTEMIDORUS. "Caesar, beware of Brutus; take heed of Cassius;
    come not near Casca; have an eye to Cinna; trust not
    Trebonius; mark well Metellus Cimber; Decius Brutus loves
    thee not; thou hast wrong'd Caius Ligarius. There is but
5   one mind in all these men, and it is bent against Caesar. If
    thou beest not immortal, look about you; security gives
    way to conspiracy.° The mighty gods defend thee!
                Thy lover,° Artemidorus."
    Here will I stand till Caesar pass along,
10 And as a suitor° will I give him this.
    My heart laments that virtue cannot live
    Out of the teeth of emulation.°
    If thou read this, O Caesar, thou mayest live;
    If not, the Fates with traitors do contrive.° *[Exit.]*

6–7 security gives . . . conspiracy: overconfidence opens the way for enemy plots.
8 lover: devoted friend.
10 suitor: person presenting a special request to a ruler.
12 Out of . . . emulation: beyond the reach of envy.
14 contrive: conspire.

SCENE 4. Another Roman street. Immediately after.

[Enter PORTIA and LUCIUS.]

    PORTIA. I prithee, boy, run to the Senate House;
    Stay not to answer me, but get thee gone.
    Why dost thou stay?

    LUCIUS.   To know my errand, madam.

    PORTIA. I would have had thee there and here again
5   Ere I can tell thee what thou shouldst do there°—
    O constancy,° be strong upon my side;
    Set a huge mountain 'tween my heart and tongue!
    I have a man's mind, but a woman's might.
    How hard it is for women to keep counsel!°—
10 Art thou here yet?

    LUCIUS.   Madam, what should I do?
    Run to the Capitol, and nothing else?
    And so return to you, and nothing else?

    PORTIA. Yes, bring me word, boy, if thy lord look well,
    For he went sickly forth; and take good note
15 What Caesar doth, what suitors press to him.
    Hark, boy, what noise is that?

    LUCIUS. I hear none, madam.

    PORTIA.   Prithee, listen well.

4–5 I would . . . do there: You could go there and return here before I could explain what you should do there.
6 constancy: firmness.
9 counsel: a secret.

Analyze Cause-and-Effect Relationships What does Artemidorus decide to do as a result of the events that have already occurred?

 JULIUS CAESAR

  I heard a bustling rumor, like a fray,°
  And the wind brings it from the Capitol.
20 LUCIUS. Sooth,° madam, I hear nothing.

[*Enter the* SOOTHSAYER.]

  PORTIA. Come hither, fellow; which way hast thou been?
  SOOTHSAYER. At mine own house, good lady.
  PORTIA. What is't a'clock?
  SOOTHSAYER.   About the ninth hour, lady.
  PORTIA. Is Caesar yet gone to the Capitol?
25 SOOTHSAYER. Madam, not yet; I go to take my stand,
  To see him pass on to the Capitol.
  PORTIA. Thou hast some suit to Caesar, hast thou not?
  SOOTHSAYER. That I have, lady, if it will please Caesar
  To be so good to Caesar as to hear me:
30 I shall beseech him to befriend himself.
  PORTIA. Why, know'st thou any harm's intended towards him?
  SOOTHSAYER. None that I know will be, much that I fear may chance.
  Good morrow to you. Here the street is narrow;
  The throng that follows Caesar at the heels,
35 Of senators, of praetors, common suitors,
  Will crowd a feeble man almost to death.
  I'll get me to a place more void,° and there
  Speak to great Caesar as he comes along.

[*Exit.*]

  PORTIA. I must go in. Ay me! How weak a thing
40 The heart of woman is! O Brutus,
  The heavens speed thee in thine enterprise!
  Sure, the boy heard me—Brutus hath a suit
  That Caesar will not grant.°—O, I grow faint.—
  Run, Lucius, and commend me to my lord,°
45 Say I am merry. Come to me again,
  And bring me word what he doth say to thee.

[*They exit separately.*]

18 bustling . . . fray: noise of some activity such as a fight.

20 Sooth: truly.

37 void: empty.
42–43 Brutus hath . . . grant: Portia makes up this excuse about Brutus's petition to explain her nervousness to Lucius.
44 commend me to my lord: send my regards to my husband.

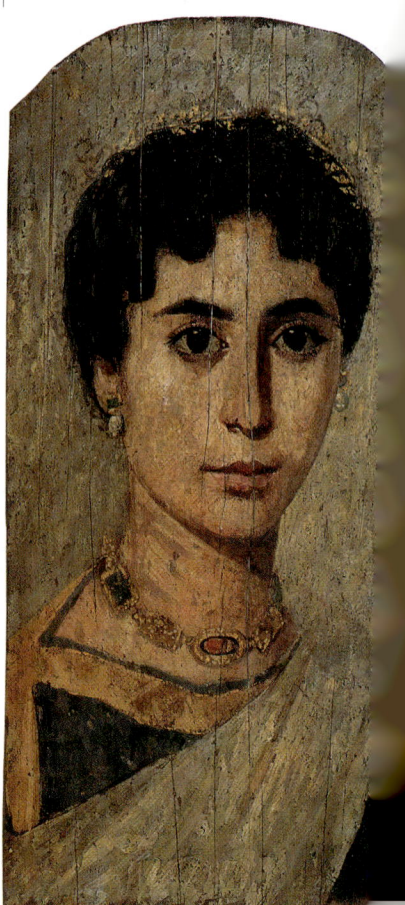

Portrait of a woman in encaustic on limewood with added gold leaf, c. 160–170 A.D., Roman period, Egypt. 44.3 x 20.4 cm. The British Museum, London.

View the Art What qualities do you think this woman possesses? Which of these qualities do you think Portia or Calphurnia shares? Explain.

After You Read

Respond and Think Critically

Respond and Interpret

1. Which character are you most sympathetic toward? Why?

2. (a) According to Brutus, why must Caesar be killed? (b) What can you infer about Cassius, Casca, and Brutus as they make their plans?

3. (a) Why does Brutus want to spare Antony's life? (b) What opinion does Brutus seem to have of Antony?

Analyze and Evaluate

4. If you were one of the conspirators, would you agree with Brutus or Cassius? Explain.

5. **Suspense** is the feeling of anticipation, even dread, which you experience as you read. What events or scenes in Act 2 contribute to its suspense? Explain.

Connect

6. **Big Idea** **Loyalty and Betrayal** (a) How do Brutus's intentions relate to the theme of loyalty and betrayal? (b) Do you accept Brutus's justification for killing Caesar? Why or why not?

7. **Connect to Today** How do Portia and Calphurnia compare with women you know or with contemporary female characters?

Literary Element: Monologues, Soliloquies, and Asides

A **monologue** is a long speech given by one character. A **soliloquy** is a monologue delivered while a character is alone onstage. An **aside** is a comment heard only by the audience, not other characters.

1. What does Brutus reveal in his soliloquy at the beginning of Act 2?

2. What does Trebonius mean in Scene 2, lines 124–125? Why are these lines written as asides?

Reading Strategy: Analyze Cause-and-Effect Relationships

In a play, one event may have an **effect** that becomes the **cause** of still another effect. Review your chart on page 740 and answer the following.

1. What causes Caesar to have misgivings about going to the Capitol?

2. What causes Portia to send a servant to the Senate House?

 **Literature** Online

Selection Resources For Selection Quizzes, eFlashcards, and Reading-Writing Connection activities, go to glencoe.com and enter QuickPass code GL59794u4.

Vocabulary Practice

Practice with Usage Respond to these statements to help you explore the meanings of vocabulary words from the selection.

1. Identify an **interim** that you have experienced.

2. Name two things for which you might **commend** a parent.

3. Tell what happens when people **disperse** after a gathering.

4. Give two examples of things that are **imminent** at dismissal time.

Writing

Write a Summary Write a summary of the plot of Act 2. Your summary should include the main events and important exchanges between the characters. Use transition words to highlight cause-and-effect relationships. For help with summarizing, see page 51.

JULIUS CAESAR **759**

Before You Read

The Tragedy of Julius Caesar, Act 3

Connect to the Play
What principles do you value? Freewrite and explain them.

Build Background
The Greek historian Plutarch recorded that Caesar attempted to defend himself against the assassins, "but when he saw Brutus with his sword drawn in his hand, then he pulled his gown over his head, and made no more resistance...."

Set Purposes for Reading

Big Idea Loyalty and Betrayal

As you read, ask yourself, Does Caesar deserve his fate? Are there wider principles that justify the betrayal by his friends?

Literary Element Plot

Plot is the sequence of events in a work. Conflicts are introduced in the **exposition**, or beginning. **Rising action** builds suspense and leads to the **climax**, or turning point. The **falling action** and **resolution** reveal the results of the climax. As you read, ask yourself, What stages of the plot can I identify?

Reading Strategy Analyze Figures of Speech

Figures of speech are a type of figurative language, language not literally true, but that expresses some truth beyond the literal level. A simile compares using *like* or *as*. A metaphor compares two unlike things. Personification gives human traits to an idea, animal, or object. Hyperbole uses exaggeration. As you read, ask yourself, What figures of speech can I identify?

Tip: Chart Memorable Language Use a chart to record striking figures of speech and your ideas about what they might mean.

Figure of Speech	Type of Figures of Speech	Meaning
"But I am constant as the northern star" p. 763	simile	Caesar is very steady and resolute.

Learning Objectives

For pages 760–782

In studying this text, you will focus on the following objectives:

Literary Study: Analyzing monologues, soliloquies, and asides.

Reading: Analyzing cause-and-effect relationships.

Vocabulary

thrive (thrīv) *v.* to be successful; to grow well; p. 761 *My sister will thrive at college.*

misgiving (mis giv′ing) *n.* a feeling of doubt; apprehension; p. 766 *My mom has misgivings about letting me go on the camping trip.*

malice (mal′is) *n.* a desire to hurt another person; p. 767 *My cousin sometimes acts with malice.*

vanquish (vang′kwish) *v.* to defeat; to overcome; p. 777 *The Greeks planned to vanquish the Trojans through a surprise attack on their city.*

orator (ôr′ə tər) *n.* a person skilled in public speaking; p. 778 *Martin Luther King Jr. was one of this country's most famous orators.*

ACT 3

SCENE 1. The Capitol in Rome. The ides of March.

[*Flourish. Enter* CAESAR, BRUTUS, CASSIUS, CASCA, DECIUS, METELLUS, TREBONIUS, CINNA, ANTONY, PUBLIUS, POPILIUS, LEPIDUS, ARTEMIDORUS, *and the* SOOTHSAYER.]

    CAESAR. The ides of March are come.

    SOOTHSAYER. Ay, Caesar, but not gone.

    ARTEMIDORUS. Hail, Caesar! Read this schedule.°   **3 schedule:** document.

    DECIUS. Trebonius doth desire you to o'er-read,
5   (At your best leisure) this his humble suit.

    ARTEMIDORUS. O Caesar, read mine first; for mine's a suit
      That touches Caesar nearer. Read it, great Caesar.

    CAESAR. <mark>What touches us ourself shall be last serv'd.</mark>

    ARTEMIDORUS. Delay not, Caesar, read it instantly.

10   CAESAR. What, is the fellow mad?

    PUBLIUS.   Sirrah,° give place.   **10 Sirrah:** an insulting form of address to an inferior.

    CASSIUS. What, urge you your petitions in the street?
      Come to the Capitol.

[CAESAR *enters the Capitol, the rest following.*]

    POPILIUS. I wish your enterprise today may **thrive**.

    CASSIUS. What enterprise, Popilius?

    POPILIUS.   Fare you well. [*Leaves
      him and joins* CAESAR.]

15   BRUTUS. What said Popilius Lena?

    CASSIUS. <mark>He wish'd today our enterprise might thrive.
      I fear our purpose is discovered.</mark>

Loyalty and Betrayal *From this remark, what do you infer about Caesar's character?*

Plot *What might happen if the plotters are discovered?*

Vocabulary

thrive (thrīv) *v.* to be successful; to grow well

JULIUS CAESAR

BRUTUS. Look how he makes° to Caesar; mark him.

CASSIUS. Casca, be sudden, for we fear prevention.°
20 Brutus, what shall be done? If this be known,
Cassius or Caesar never shall turn back,°
For I will slay myself.

BRUTUS.   Cassius, be constant;°
Popilius Lena speaks not of our purposes,
For look he smiles, and Caesar doth not change.

25 **CASSIUS.** Trebonius knows his time; for look you, Brutus,
He draws Mark Antony out of the way.

[*ANTONY and TREBONIUS exit.*]

DECIUS. Where is Metellus Cimber? Let him go
And presently prefer° his suit to Caesar.

BRUTUS. He is address'd;° press near and second him.

30 **CINNA.** Casca, you are the first that rears your hand.

CAESAR. Are we all ready? What is now amiss
That Caesar and his Senate must redress?

METELLUS. Most high, most mighty, and most puissant° Caesar,
Metellus Cimber throws before thy seat
35 An humble heart. [*Kneeling.*]

CAESAR.   I must prevent thee, Cimber.
These couchings and these lowly courtesies
Might fire the blood of ordinary men,
And turn preordinance and first decree
Into the [law] of children. Be not fond
40 To think that Caesar bears such rebel blood
That will be thaw'd from the true quality
With that which melteth fools—I mean sweet words,
Low-crooked curtsies, and base spaniel fawning.°
Thy brother by decree is banished;
45 If thou dost bend, and pray, and fawn for him,
I spurn thee like a cur° out of my way.
Know, Caesar doth not wrong, nor without cause
Will he be satisfied.°

METELLUS. Is there no voice more worthy than my own,
50 To sound more sweetly in great Caesar's ear
For the repealing of my banish'd brother?

18 **makes:** makes his way.
19 **be sudden . . . prevention:** be quick, for we fear that we will be stopped.
21 **turn back:** return alive.

22 **constant:** calm.

28 **presently prefer:** immediately present.
29 **address'd:** ready.

33 **puissant:** powerful.

36–43 **These couchings . . . fawning:** This kneeling and humble behavior might influence ordinary men and turn laws and decisions that have been firmly established into the whims of children. But don't be foolish enough to think that Caesar's emotions are so out of control that he will be swayed from the proper course with compliments, bowing, and fawning like a dog.
46 **spurn thee . . . cur:** kick you like a dog.
47–48 **Know . . . satisfied:** Caesar is not unjust, nor will he grant a pardon without good reason.

Analyze Figures of Speech What does Caesar mean when he says that Metellus's compliments are "base spaniel fawning"?

The Death of Julius Caesar, 1793. Vincenzo Camuccini. Galleria d'Arte Moderna, Rome.

View the Art What emotions do you see expressed here? Do you think the same emotions are expressed in this scene? Explain.

BRUTUS. I kiss thy hand, but not in flattery, Caesar;
Desiring thee that Publius Cimber may
Have an immediate freedom of repeal.°

55 CAESAR. What, Brutus?

CASSIUS.   Pardon, Caesar! Caesar, pardon!
As low as to thy foot doth Cassius fall,
To beg enfranchisement° for Publius Cimber.

CAESAR. I could be well mov'd, if I were as you;
If I could pray to move, prayers would move me;
60   But I am constant as the northern star,
Of whose true-fix'd and resting quality
There is no fellow in the firmament.°
The skies are painted with unnumb'red sparks,
They are all fire and every one doth shine;
65   But there's but one in all doth hold his place.
So in the world: 'tis furnish'd well with men,
And men are flesh and blood, and apprehensive;°
Yet in the number I do know but one
That unassailable holds on his rank,

54 freedom of repeal: permission to be recalled from exile.

57 enfranchisement: restoration of his rights as a citizen.

62 no fellow in the firmament: no equal in the heavens. (Because the North Star appears directly above the North Pole, it seems to be stationary; the other stars seem to change position as the earth rotates.)

67 apprehensive: capable of reason.

Loyalty and Betrayal In your opinion, why is Cassius behaving this way?

Analyze Figures of Speech What is Caesar suggesting by comparing himself to the North Star?

JULIUS CAESAR

70 Unshak'd of motion; and that I am he,
Let me a little show it, even in this—
That I was constant° Cimber should be banish'd,
And constant do remain to keep him so.

CINNA. O Caesar—

CAESAR. Hence! Wilt thou lift up Olympus?°

75 DECIUS. Great Caesar—

CAESAR. Doth not Brutus bootless° kneel?

CASCA. Speak hands for me!

[*They stab* CAESAR.]

CAESAR. Et tu, Brute?°—Then fall Caesar. [*Dies.*]

CINNA. Liberty! Freedom! Tyranny is dead!
Run hence, proclaim, cry it about the streets.

80 CASSIUS. Some to the common pulpits,° and cry out
"Liberty, freedom, and enfranchisement!"

BRUTUS. People, and senators, be not affrighted.
Fly not; stand still; ambition's debt is paid.°

CASCA. Go to the pulpit, Brutus.

DECIUS. And Cassius too.

85 BRUTUS. Where's Publius?

CINNA. Here, quite confounded with this mutiny.°

METELLUS. Stand fast together, lest some friend of Caesar's
Should chance—

BRUTUS. Talk not of standing. Publius, good cheer,
90 There is no harm intended to your person,
Nor to no Roman else. So tell them, Publius.

CASSIUS. And leave us, Publius, lest that the people,
Rushing on us should do your age some mischief.

BRUTUS. Do so; and let no man abide° this deed,
95 But we the doers.

[*All but the* CONSPIRATORS *exit. Enter* TREBONIUS.]

CASSIUS. Where is Antony?

TREBONIUS. Fled to his house amaz'd.°

---

72 constant: determined.

74 lift up Olympus: try to do the impossible. (Olympus is a mountain in Greece; in classical mythology, it was the home of the gods.)
75 bootless: in vain.

77 Et tu, Brute?: Latin for, "And you, Brutus?" (He is shocked that even Brutus would betray him.)

80 pulpits: platforms for public speaking.

83 ambition's debt is paid: Ambition received what was due to it.

86 confounded with this mutiny: confused by this uproar.

94 abide: pay the penalty for.

96 amaz'd: stunned.

Loyalty and Betrayal *What do Caesar's dying words reveal?*

Men, wives, and children stare, cry out and run,
As° it were doomsday.

BRUTUS. Fates,° we will know your pleasures.
That we shall die, we know, 'tis but the time,
And drawing days out, that men stand upon.°

CASCA. Why, he that cuts off twenty years of life
Cuts off so many years of fearing death.

BRUTUS. Grant that, and then is death a benefit.
So are we Caesar's friends, that have abridg'd
His time of fearing death. Stoop, Romans, stoop,
And let us bathe our hands in Caesar's blood
Up to the elbows, and besmear our swords.
Then walk we forth, even to the marketplace,
And waving our red weapons o'er our heads,
Let's all cry "Peace, freedom, and liberty!"

CASSIUS. Stoop then, and wash. How many ages hence
Shall this our lofty scene be acted over
In states unborn and accents yet unknown!

BRUTUS. How many times shall Caesar bleed in sport,°
That now on Pompey's basis° [lies] along
No worthier than the dust!

CASSIUS. So oft as that shall be,
So often shall the knot of us be call'd
The men that gave their country liberty.

DECIUS. What, shall we forth?

CASSIUS. Ay, every man away.
Brutus shall lead, and we will grace his heels
With the most boldest and best hearts of Rome.

[*Enter a* SERVANT.]

BRUTUS. Soft, who comes here? A friend of Antony's.

SERVANT. Thus, Brutus, did my master bid me kneel;
Thus did Mark Antony bid me fall down;
And, being prostrate, thus he bade me say;
Brutus is noble, wise, valiant, and honest;°
Caesar was mighty, bold, royal, and loving.
Say, I love Brutus, and I honor him;
Say, I fear'd Caesar, honor'd him, and lov'd him.

The Three Fates, detail from the Month of March (upper portion).
Francesco del Cossa (1435–1478). Fresco painting. Palazzo Schifanoia, Ferrara, Italy.

98 As: as if.
98 Fates: in classical mythology, three goddesses who determined human destiny.
99–100 'tis but . . . upon: It is only the time of death and prolonging of life that men care about.

114 in sport: for entertainment. (These prophecies—of reenacting Caesar's assassination in countries not yet founded and in languages not yet known—are fulfilled by the performance of Shakespeare's play.)
115 Pompey's basis: the base of Pompey's statue.

126 honest: honorable.

Plot What effect is the assassination having on Rome?

Loyalty and Betrayal What does this remark suggest about how Brutus is feeling?

JULIUS CAESAR

130   If Brutus will vouchsafe° that Antony
      May safely come to him, and be resolv'd°
      How Caesar hath deserv'd to lie in death,
      Mark Antony shall not love Caesar dead
      So well as Brutus living; but will follow
135   The fortunes and affairs of noble Brutus
      Thorough the hazards of this untrod state°
      With all true faith. So says my master Antony.

BRUTUS. Thy master is a wise and valiant Roman;
      I never thought him worse.
140   Tell him, so please him come unto this place,
      He shall be satisfied and, by my honor,
      Depart untouch'd.

SERVANT.   I'll fetch him presently.° [*Exit* SERVANT.]

BRUTUS. I know that we shall have him well to friend.°

CASSIUS. I wish we may; but yet have I a mind
145   That fears him much; and my **misgiving** still
      Falls shrewdly to the purpose.°

[*Enter* ANTONY.]

BRUTUS. But here comes Antony. Welcome, Mark Antony.

ANTONY. O mighty Caesar! dost thou lie so low?
      Are all thy conquests, glories, triumphs, spoils,
150   Shrunk to this little measure? Fare thee well.
      I know not, gentlemen, what you intend,
      Who else must be let blood,° who else is rank.°
      If I myself, there is no hour so fit
      As Caesar's death's hour, nor no instrument
155   Of half that worth as those your swords, made rich
      With the most noble blood of all this world.
      I do beseech ye, if you bear me hard,°
      Now, whilst your purpled° hands do reek and smoke,
      Fulfill your pleasure. Live a thousand years,
160   I shall not find myself so apt° to die;

130 vouchsafe: allow.
131 be resolv'd: receive a satisfactory explanation.

136 Thorough . . . state: through all the dangers of this new and uncertain state of affairs.

142 presently: immediately.
143 well to friend: as a good friend.

145–146 my misgiving . . . purpose: My suspicions always turn out to be close to the truth.

152 let blood: killed. **rank:** swollen with disease. In Antony's metaphor, political corruption is like a disease that must be treated by drawing blood from the patient.

157 bear me hard: have a grudge against me.
158 purpled: blood-stained.

160 apt: ready.

Plot *What position does Mark Antony take with regard to the killing of Caesar?*

Analyze Figures of Speech *What does Mark Antony mean when he says that the conspirators' hands "reek and smoke"? Why does he say he would not find himself so apt to die if he "lived a thousand years"?*

Vocabulary

misgiving (mis giv′ing) *n.* a feeling of doubt; apprehension

No place will please me so, no mean of death,°
As here by Caesar, and by you cut off,
The choice and master spirits of this age.

BRUTUS. O Antony! beg not your death of us.
Though now we must appear bloody and cruel,
As by our hands and this our present act
You see we do, yet see you but our hands
And this the bleeding business they have done.
Our hearts you see not, they are pitiful;°
And pity to the general wrong of Rome—
As fire drives out fire, so pity pity—
Hath done this deed on Caesar.° For your part,
To you our swords have leaden° points, Mark Antony;
Our arms in strength of **malice**,° and our hearts
Of brothers' temper, do receive you in
With all kind love, good thoughts, and reverence.

CASSIUS. Your voice shall be as strong as any man's
In the disposing of new dignities.°

BRUTUS. Only be patient till we have appeas'd
The multitude, beside themselves with fear,
And then we will deliver you the cause°
Why I, that did love Caesar when I struck him,
Have thus proceeded.

ANTONY. I doubt not of your wisdom.
Let each man render me his bloody hand.
First, Marcus Brutus, will I shake with you;
Next, Caius Cassius, do I take your hand;
Now, Decius Brutus, yours; now yours, Metellus;
Yours, Cinna; and, my valiant Casca, yours;
Though last, not least in love, yours, good Trebonius.
Gentlemen all—alas, what shall I say?
My credit° now stands on such slippery ground
That one of two bad ways you must conceit° me,
Either a coward or a flatterer.
That I did love thee, Caesar, O, 'tis true;
If then thy spirit look upon us now,
Shall it not grieve thee dearer than thy death,
To see thy Antony making his peace,

---

161 mean of death: way of dying.

169 pitiful: full of pity.
170–172 And pity . . . Caesar: Brutus says that just as one fire can extinguish another, their pity for Rome overcame their pity for Caesar.
173 leaden: blunt.
174 Our arms . . . malice: our arms seemingly full of malice (because still blood-stained).

177–178 Your voice . . . dignities: You will have equal say in deciding who will hold political office.

181 deliver you the cause: explain.

191 credit: reputation (because he was Caesar's friend).
192 conceit: judge, consider.

Loyalty and Betrayal Why is Brutus so eager to reassure Mark Antony?

Vocabulary

malice (mal´is) *n.* a desire to hurt another person

Julius Caesar

    Shaking the bloody fingers of thy foes,
    Most noble, in the presence of thy corse?°
200 Had I as many eyes as thou hast wounds,
    Weeping as fast as they stream forth thy blood,
    It would become me better than to close°
    In terms of friendship with thine enemies.
    Pardon me, Julius! Here wast thou bay'd,° brave hart,°
205 Here didst thou fall, and here thy hunters stand,
    Sign'd in thy spoil,° and crimson'd in thy lethe.°
    O world! thou wast the forest to this hart,

199 corse: corpse.

202 close: come to an agreement.

204 bay'd: cornered like a hunted animal. **hart:** male deer. Antony plays on the words *hart* and *heart* later in this speech.
206 Sign'd in thy spoil: marked with your slaughter. **lethe:** bloodstream. (In classical mythology, Lethe was a river in Hades, the underworld.)

Bedroom From the Villa of P. Fannius Sinistor (detail of west wall). 1st century BC, Roman. Fresco on lime plaster, height: (average) 8 ft. The Metropolitan Museum of Art, New York. Rogers Fund, 1903.

View the Art Do the details in this fresco reinforce or alter the images you have developed of Brutus's and Caesar's homes? Explain.

And this indeed, O world, the heart of thee.
How like a deer, strooken by many princes,
210 Dost thou here lie!

CASSIUS. Mark Antony—

ANTONY. Pardon me, Caius Cassius!
The enemies of Caesar shall say this:
Then, in a friend, it is cold modesty.°

213 **modesty:** restraint.

CASSIUS. I blame you not for praising Caesar so,
215 But what compact mean you to have with us?
Will you be prick'd° in number of our friends,
Or shall we on,° and not depend on you?

216 **prick'd:** marked down; counted.
217 **on:** proceed.

ANTONY. Therefore I took your hands, but was indeed
Sway'd from the point by looking down on Caesar.
220 Friends am I with you all, and love you all,
Upon this hope, that you shall give me reasons
Why, and wherein,° Caesar was dangerous.

222 **wherein:** in what way.

BRUTUS. Or else were this a savage spectacle.
Our reasons are so full of good regard°
225 That were you, Antony, the son of Caesar,
You should be satisfied.

224 **good regard:** sound considerations.

ANTONY. That's all I seek;
And am moreover suitor° that I may
Produce° his body to the marketplace,
And in the pulpit, as becomes a friend,
230 Speak in the order° of his funeral.

227 **am moreover suitor:** furthermore I ask.
228 **Produce:** bring forth.
230 **order:** ceremony.

BRUTUS. You shall, Mark Antony.

CASSIUS. Brutus, a word with you.
[*Aside to* BRUTUS.] You know not what you
    do. Do not consent
That Antony speak in his funeral.
Know you how much the people maybe mov'd
235 By that which he will utter?

BRUTUS. By your pardon—
I will myself into the pulpit first,
And show the reason of our Caesar's death.
What Antony shall speak, I will protest°

238 **protest:** declare.

Analyze Figures of Speech To what things does Mark Antony compare Julius Caesar? How do these comparisons help to characterize Julius Caesar's death?

Plot What is Cassius's objection to Antony's speaking at Caesar's funeral?

JULIUS CAESAR

He speaks by leave and by permission;
240 And that we are contented Caesar shall
Have all true rites and lawful ceremonies.
It shall advantage° more than do us wrong.

CASSIUS. I know not what may fall,° I like it not.

BRUTUS. Mark Antony, here, take you Caesar's body.
245 You shall not in your funeral speech blame us,
But speak all good you can devise of Caesar,
And say you do't by our permission;
Else shall you not have any hand at all
About his funeral. And you shall speak
250 In the same pulpit whereto I am going,
After my speech is ended.

ANTONY.   Be it so;
I do desire no more.

BRUTUS. Prepare the body then, and follow us.

[*They exit. ANTONY remains.*]

ANTONY. O pardon me, thou bleeding piece of earth,
255 That I am meek and gentle with these butchers!
Thou art the ruins of the noblest man
That ever lived in the tide of times.°
Woe to the hand that shed this costly blood!
Over thy wounds now do I prophesy
260 (Which like dumb mouths do ope their ruby lips
To beg the voice and utterance of my tongue)
A curse shall light° upon the limbs of men;
Domestic fury and fierce civil strife
Shall cumber° all the parts of Italy;
265 Blood and destruction shall be so in use,°
And dreadful objects so familiar,
That mothers shall but smile when they behold
Their infants quartered° with the hands of war;
All pity chok'd with custom of fell deeds;°
270 And Caesar's spirit, ranging° for revenge,
With Ate° by his side come hot from hell,
Shall in these confines with a monarch's voice
Cry "Havoc!"° and let slip the dogs of war,

Loyalty and Betrayal *What do these words reveal about Antony's true feelings regarding the conspirators?*

Analyze Figures of Speech *What figure of speech is this? What is being compared?*

The Fatal Hour: Fantastic Subject II, 19th century
Alexandre Evariste Fragonard. Oil on canvas, 56 x 45.7 cm. Private collection.

View the Art What mood is expressed by this painting? Does it correspond to the mood in the at this point? Explain.

242 **advantage:** benefit.
243 **fall:** happen.
257 **the tide of times:** all of history.

262 **light:** fall.

264 **cumber:** burden; harass.
265 **in use:** common.

268 **quartered:** cut to pieces.
269 **custom of fell deeds:** familiarity with cruel deeds.
270 **ranging:** roving (like an animal in search of prey).
271 **Ate:** goddess of vengeance and strife.
273 **Havoc:** a battle cry to kill without mercy. (Only a king could give this order.)

        That this foul deed shall smell above the earth
275   With carrion° men, groaning for burial.

[*Enter Octavius's* SERVANT.]

        You serve Octavius Caesar, do you not?

SERVANT. I do, Mark Antony.

ANTONY. Caesar did write for him to come to Rome.

SERVANT. He did receive his letters and is coming,
280   And bid me say to you by word of mouth—
        [*Seeing the body.*] O Caesar!—

ANTONY. Thy heart is big;° get thee apart and weep.
        Passion, I see, is catching, [for] mine eyes,
        Seeing those beads of sorrow stand in thine,
285   Began to water. Is thy master coming?

SERVANT. He lies tonight within seven leagues° of Rome.

ANTONY. Post° back with speed, and tell him what hath chanc'd.
        Here is a mourning Rome, a dangerous Rome,
        No Rome of safety for Octavius yet;
290   Hie hence,° and tell him so. Yet stay awhile,
        Thou shalt not back till I have borne this corse
        Into the marketplace. There shall I try,°
        In my oration, how the people take
        The cruel issue° of these bloody men,
295   According to the which thou shalt discourse
        To young Octavius of the state of things.
        Lend me your hand.

[*They exit (with* CAESAR'*s body*).]

SCENE 2. The Roman Forum, the city's great public square. A few days later.

[*Enter* BRUTUS *and* CASSIUS *with the* PLEBEIANS.]

PLEBEIANS. We will be satisfied!° Let us be satisfied!

BRUTUS. Then follow me, and give me audience, friends.
        Cassius, go you into the other street,
        And part the numbers.°
5   Those that will hear me speak, let 'em stay here;
        Those that will follow Cassius, go with him;
        And public reasons shall be rendered°
        Of Caesar's death.

---

275 carrion: dead and rotting.

282 big: swollen with grief.

286 seven leagues: twenty-one miles.
287 Post: ride back quickly.

290 Hie hence: Go quickly from here.

292 try: test.

294 cruel issue: outcome of cruelty.

1 satisfied: The common people (plebeians) demand a full explanation of the assassination.

4 part the numbers: divide the crowd.

7 rendered: presented.

Plot What are the Plebeians wanting?

Julius Caesar

FIRST PLEBEIAN. I will hear Brutus speak.

SECOND PLEBEIAN. I will hear Cassius, and compare their reasons,
10 When severally° we hear them rendered.

[*Exit* CASSIUS *with some of the* PLEBEIANS. BRUTUS *goes into the pulpit.*]

THIRD PLEBEIAN. The noble Brutus is ascended; silence!

BRUTUS. Be patient till the last.°
Romans, countrymen, and lovers,° hear me for my cause, and be silent, that you may hear. Believe me for mine
15 honor, and have respect to mine honor,° that you may believe. Censure° me in your wisdom, and awake your senses,° that you may the better judge. If there be any in this assembly, any dear friend of Caesar's, to him I say, that Brutus' love to Caesar was no less than his. If then
20 that friend demand why Brutus rose against Caesar, this is my answer; Not that I lov'd Caesar less, but that I lov'd Rome more. Had you rather Caesar were living, and die all slaves, than that Caesar were dead, to live all free men? As Caesar lov'd me, I weep for him; as he was fortunate, I
25 rejoice at it; as he was valiant, I honor him; but, as he was ambitious, I slew him. There is tears for his love; joy for his fortune; honor for his valor; and death for his ambition. Who is here so base that would be a bondman?° If any, speak, for him have I offended. ==Who is here so rude,° that
30 would not be a Roman? If any, speak, for him have I offended.== Who is here so vile that will not love his country? If any, speak, for him have I offended. I pause for a reply.

ALL. None, Brutus, none.

BRUTUS. Then none have I offended. I have done no more to
35 Caesar than you shall do to Brutus. The question of his death is enroll'd in the Capitol;° his glory not extenuated,° wherein he was worthy; nor his offenses enforc'd,° for which he suffer'd death.

[*Enter* MARK ANTONY *(and others) with* CAESAR'S *body.*]

Here comes his body, mourn'd by Mark Antony, who,
40 though he had no hand in his death, shall receive the benefit of his dying, a place in the commonwealth,° as which of you shall not? With this I depart, that, as I slew my best lover for the good of Rome, I have the same dagger for

---

10 severally: separately.

12 last: end of the speech.
13 lovers: dear friends.

15 have respect . . . honor: remember that I am honorable.
16 Censure: judge.
17 senses: reason.

28 bondman: slave.
29 rude: uncivilized.

35–36 The question . . . Capitol: The reasons for his death are recorded in the public archives of the Capitol.
37 extenuated: diminished.
38 enforc'd: exaggerated.

41 a place in the commonwealth: citizenship in a free republic.

Loyalty and Betrayal *What is Brutus implying here? Is this a valid conclusion?*

The Roman Forum, 19th century. Francis Vyvyan Jago Arundale. Watercolour on paper, 64.5 × 100 cm. Private collection.

View the Art What events in the play might this scene depict? Explain.

---

myself, when it shall please my country to need my death.

45 ALL. Live, Brutus, live, live!

FIRST PLEBEIAN. Bring him with triumph home unto his house.

SECOND PLEBEIAN. Give him a statue with his ancestors.

THIRD PLEBEIAN. Let him be Caesar.

FOURTH PLEBEIAN.   Caesar's better parts°
  Shall be crown'd in Brutus.

FIRST PLEBEIAN.   We'll bring him to his house
50 With shouts and clamors.

BRUTUS.   My countrymen—

SECOND PLEBEIAN. Peace, silence! Brutus speaks.

FIRST PLEBEIAN. Peace, ho!

BRUTUS. Good countrymen, let me depart alone,
  And, for my sake, stay here with Antony.
55 Do grace to Caesar's corpse, and grace his speech

48 parts: qualities.

Plot How do the people react to Brutus's speech? Why do they react in this way?

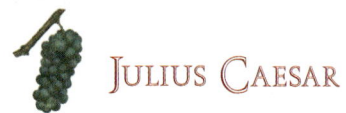

JULIUS CAESAR

Tending to Caesar's glories,° which Mark Antony
(By our permission) is allow'd to make.
I do entreat you, not a man depart,
Save I alone, till Antony have spoke.

55–56 Do grace . . . glories: Pay respect to Caesar's body and listen respectfully to Antony's speech dealing with Caesar's glories.

60 **FIRST PLEBEIAN.** Stay, ho, and let us hear Mark Antony.

THIRD PLEBEIAN. Let him go up into the public chair;°
We'll hear him. Noble Antony, go up.

61 public chair: pulpit.

ANTONY. For Brutus' sake, I am beholding° to you.

63 beholding: indebted.

[*Goes into the pulpit.*]

FOURTH PLEBEIAN. What does he say of Brutus?

THIRD PLEBEIAN.   He says, for Brutus' sake,
65   He finds himself beholding to us all.

FOURTH PLEBEIAN. 'Twere best he speak no harm of Brutus here!

FIRST PLEBEIAN. This Caesar was a tyrant.

THIRD PLEBEIAN.   Nay, that's certain.
We are blest that Rome is rid of him.

SECOND PLEBEIAN. Peace, let us hear what Antony can say.

70 **ANTONY.** You gentle Romans—

[*The noise continues.*]

ALL.   Peace, ho, let us hear him.

ANTONY. Friends, Romans, countrymen, lend me your ears!
I come to bury Caesar, not to praise him.
The evil that men do lives after them,
The good is oft interred° with their bones;
75   So let it be with Caesar. The noble Brutus
Hath told you Caesar was ambitious;
If it were so, it was a grievous fault,
And grievously hath Caesar answer'd° it.
Here, under leave° of Brutus and the rest
80   (For Brutus is an honorable man,
So are they all, all honorable men),
Come I to speak in Caesar's funeral.
He was my friend, faithful and just to me;
But Brutus says he was ambitious,
85   And Brutus is an honorable man.
He hath brought many captives home to Rome,
Whose ransoms did the general coffers° fill;

74 interred: buried.

78 answer'd: paid the penalty for.
79 leave: permission.

87 general coffers: public treasury.

Plot *What does the Plebeian mean by this remark?*

  Did this in Caesar seem ambitious?
  When that the poor have cried, Caesar hath wept;
90 Ambition should be made of sterner stuff:
  Yet Brutus says he was ambitious;
  And Brutus is an honorable man.
  You all did see that on the Lupercal°
  I thrice presented him a kingly crown,
95 Which he did thrice refuse.° Was this ambition?
  Yet Brutus says he was ambitious;
  And sure he is an honorable man.
  I speak not to disprove what Brutus spoke,
  But here I am to speak what I do know.
100 You all did love him once, not without cause;
  What cause withholds you then to mourn for him?
  O judgment, thou art fled to brutish beasts,
  And men have lost their reason. Bear with me,
  My heart is in the coffin there with Caesar,
105 And I must pause till it come back to me.

FIRST PLEBEIAN. Methinks there is much reason in his sayings.

SECOND PLEBEIAN. If thou consider rightly of the matter, Caesar has had great wrong.

THIRD PLEBEIAN.   Has he, masters?
  I fear there will a worse come in his place.

110 **FOURTH PLEBEIAN.** Mark'd ye° his words? He would not take the crown,
  Therefore, 'tis certain he was not ambitious.

FIRST PLEBEIAN. If it be found so, some will dear abide it.°

SECOND PLEBEIAN. Poor soul, his eyes are red as fire with weeping.

THIRD PLEBEIAN. There's not a nobler man in Rome than Antony.

115 **FOURTH PLEBEIAN.** Now mark him, he begins again to speak.

ANTONY. But yesterday the word of Caesar might
  Have stood against the world; now lies he there,
  And none so poor to do him reverence.°
  O masters! if I were dispos'd to stir

---

93 Lupercal: See Act 1, Scene 1, line 67.

95 Which he . . . refuse: the incident described by Casca in Act 1, Scene 2, lines 234–242.

Marcus Antonius (Mark Anthony) as Triumvirate. Artist unknown. Roman portrait bust. Vatican Museums, Vatican State.

110 Mark'd ye: Did you listen to?

112 dear abide it: pay dearly for it.

118 none . . . reverence: No one is humble enough to honor him.

Analyze Figures of Speech *What mood, or feeling, does Antony's language help to create?*

Loyalty and Betrayal *Why do the Plebeians call Antony noble?*

JULIUS CAESAR

120	Your hearts and minds to mutiny and rage,
	I should do Brutus wrong and Cassius wrong,
	Who (you all know) are honorable men.
	I will not do them wrong; I rather choose
	To wrong the dead, to wrong myself and you,
125	Than I will wrong such honorable men.
	But here's a parchment with the seal of Caesar;
	I found it in his closet, 'tis his will.
	Let but the commons° hear this testament—
	Which, pardon me, I do not mean to read—
130	And they would go and kiss dead Caesar's wounds,
	And dip their napkins° in his sacred blood;
	Yea, beg a hair of him for memory,
	And dying, mention it within their wills,
	Bequeathing it as a rich legacy
135	Unto their issue.°

128 commons: common people.

131 napkins: handkerchiefs. (Antony refers to the custom of dipping cloths in the blood of martyrs.)

135 issue: children.

FOURTH PLEBEIAN. We'll hear the will; read it, Mark Antony.

ALL. The will, the will! we will hear Caesar's will!

ANTONY. Have patience, gentle friends, I must not read it.
It is not meet° you know how Caesar lov'd you:
140 You are not wood, you are not stones, but men;
And being men, hearing the will of Caesar,
It will inflame you, it will make you mad.
'Tis good you know not that you are his heirs,
For if you should, O, what would come of it?

139 meet: proper.

145 **FOURTH PLEBEIAN.** Read the will, we'll hear it, Antony.
You shall read us the will, Caesar's will.

ANTONY. Will you be patient? Will you stay awhile?
I have o'ershot myself° to tell you of it.
I fear I wrong the honorable men
150 Whose daggers have stabb'd Caesar; I do fear it.

148 o'ershot myself: gone further than I intended.

FOURTH PLEBEIAN. They were traitors; honorable men!

ALL. The will! the testament!

SECOND PLEBEIAN. They were villains, murderers. The will, read the will!

ANTONY. You will compel me then to read the will?

Loyalty and Betrayal Why does Antony flatter the Plebeians?

Plot How would you characterize the tension in this scene? What plot complications are developing?

155 Then make a ring about the corpse of Caesar,
And let me show you him that made the will.
Shall I descend? And will you give me leave?

ALL. Come down.

SECOND PLEBEIAN. Descend.

160 THIRD PLEBEIAN. You shall have leave.

[ANTONY *comes down from the pulpit.*]

FOURTH PLEBEIAN. A ring, stand round.

FIRST PLEBEIAN. Stand from the hearse, stand from the body.

SECOND PLEBEIAN. Room for Antony, most noble Antony.

ANTONY. Nay, press not so upon me; stand far° off.

165 ALL. Stand back; room, bear back.

ANTONY. If you have tears, prepare to shed them now.
You all do know this mantle.° I remember
The first time ever Caesar put it on;
'Twas on a summer's evening, in his tent,
170 That day he overcame the Nervii.°
Look, in this place ran Cassius' dagger through;
See what a rent° the envious Casca made;
Through this the well-beloved Brutus stabb'd,
And as he pluck'd his cursed steel away,
175 Mark how the blood of Caesar followed it,
As rushing out of doors, to be resolv'd
If Brutus so unkindly knock'd or no;°
For Brutus, as you know, was Caesar's angel.°
Judge, O you gods, how dearly Caesar lov'd him!
180 This was the most unkindest cut of all;
For when the noble Caesar saw him stab,
Ingratitude, more strong than traitors' arms,
Quite **vanquish'd** him. Then burst his mighty heart,
And, in his mantle muffling up his face,
185 Even at the base of Pompey's statue
(Which all the while ran blood) great Caesar fell.
O, what a fall was there, my countrymen!
Then I, and you, and all of us fell down,

The Artemision with Artemis Ephesia. 117 A.D., Roman. Silver, diameter: 2.7 cm. Kunsthistorisches Museum, Muenzkabinett, Vienna, Austria.

164 far: farther.
167 mantle: cloak, toga.

170 Nervii: a fierce Gallic tribe defeated by Caesar in 57 BC.

172 rent: rip.

176–177 As rushing . . . no: as if rushing outside to learn for certain whether or not Brutus so cruelly and unnaturally "knocked."
178 angel: favorite.

Analyze Figures of Speech Where in these lines do you see an example of personification? Why does Antony's use of this figure of speech help to create sympathy for Caesar?

Vocabulary

vanquish (vang′kwish) *v.* to defeat; to overcome

Julius Caesar

Whilst bloody treason flourish'd° over us.
190 O now you weep, and I perceive you feel
The dint° of pity. These are gracious drops.
Kind souls, what weep you when you but behold
Our Caesar's vesture wounded? Look you here, [*Lifting
   CAESAR's mantle.*]
Here is himself, marr'd as you see with traitors.°

195 FIRST PLEBEIAN. O piteous spectacle!

SECOND PLEBEIAN. O noble Caesar!

THIRD PLEBEIAN. O woeful day!

FOURTH PLEBEIAN. O traitors, villains!

FIRST PLEBEIAN. O most bloody sight!

200 SECOND PLEBEIAN. We will be reveng'd.

ALL. Revenge! About! Seek! Burn! Fire! Kill! Slay!
Let not a traitor live!

ANTONY. Stay, countrymen.

FIRST PLEBEIAN. Peace there, hear the noble Antony.

205 SECOND PLEBEIAN. We'll hear him, we'll follow him, we'll die
   with him.

ANTONY. Good friends, sweet friends, let me not stir you up
To such a sudden flood of mutiny.
They that have done this deed are honorable.
What private griefs° they have, alas, I know not,
210 That made them do it. They are wise and honorable,
And will, no doubt, with reasons answer you.
I come not, friends, to steal away your hearts.
I am no **orator**, as Brutus is;
But (as you know me all) a plain blunt man
215 That love my friend, and that they know full well
That gave me public leave to speak of him.
For I have neither wit, nor words, nor worth,
Action, nor utterance, nor the power of speech
To stir men's blood;° I only speak right on.
220 I tell you that which you yourselves do know,

---

189 flourish'd: swaggered.

191 dint: force; blow.

192–194 Kind souls . . . traitors: In a dramatic gesture, Antony uncovers Caesar's mutilated body after remarking how much the commoners weep when they gaze merely upon Caesar's mutilated clothing.

209 private griefs: personal grievances. Antony suggests that the conspirators killed Caesar not for the public reasons Brutus has declared but rather for personal, and therefore less worthy, motives.

217–219 For I have . . . blood: Antony claims that he does not have the cleverness (**wit**), fluency (**words**), high personal standing or reputation (**worth**), gestures (**action**), and manner of speaking (**utterance**) of a skilled orator.

Loyalty and Betrayal *Antony emphasizes that he is not trying to turn the crowd against Brutus and the other plotters. Is he sincere? Explain.*

Vocabulary

orator (ôr´ə tər) *n.* a person skilled in public speaking

William Shakespeare: Julius Caesar—Forum—Stage design, 1914. Ludwig Sievert.

View the Art What feelings does this stage design stir in you? Do you think it is a good representation of the drama?

        Show you sweet Caesar's wounds, poor, poor, dumb mouths,
        And bid them speak for me. But were I Brutus,
        And Brutus Antony, there were an Antony
        Would ruffle up° your spirits, and put a tongue
225   In every wound of Caesar, that should move
        The stones of Rome to rise and mutiny.
  ALL. We'll mutiny.
  FIRST PLEBEIAN. We'll burn the house of Brutus.
  THIRD PLEBEIAN. Away then, come, seek the conspirators.
  ANTONY. Yet hear me, countrymen, yet hear me speak.
230 ALL. Peace, ho, hear Antony, most noble Antony!
  ANTONY. Why, friends, you go to do you know not what.
        Wherein hath Caesar thus deserv'd your loves?
        Alas, you know not! I must tell you then;
        You have forgot the will I told you of.
235 ALL. Most true. The will! Let's stay and hear the will.
  ANTONY. Here is the will, and under Caesar's seal:
        To every Roman citizen he gives,
        To every several° man, seventy-five drachmas.°
  SECOND PLEBEIAN. Most noble Caesar! we'll revenge his death!
240 THIRD PLEBEIAN. O royal° Caesar!
  ANTONY. Hear me with patience.

224 ruffle up: enrage.

238 several: individual. **drachmas:** silver coins.

240 royal: most generous.

Analyze Figures of Speech Why does Antony again use this comparison?

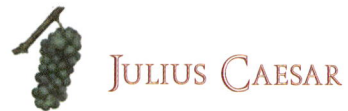

Julius Caesar

ALL. Peace, ho!

ANTONY. Moreover, he hath left you all his walks,
His private arbors and new-planted orchards,°
245 On this side Tiber; he hath left them you,
And to your heirs forever—common pleasures,°
To walk abroad and recreate yourselves.
Here was a Caesar! when comes such another?

FIRST PLEBEIAN. Never, never! Come, away, away!
250 We'll burn his body in the holy place,°
And with the brands° fire the traitors' houses.
Take up the body.

SECOND PLEBEIAN. Go fetch fire.

THIRD PLEBEIAN. Pluck down benches.

255 **FOURTH PLEBEIAN.** Pluck down forms,° windows,° anything.

[*Exit* PLEBEIANS *with the body.*]

ANTONY. Now let it work. Mischief, thou art afoot,
Take thou what course thou wilt!

[*Enter* SERVANT.]

How now, fellow?

SERVANT. Sir, Octavius is already come to Rome.

ANTONY. Where is he?

260 **SERVANT.** He and Lepidus° are at Caesar's house.

ANTONY. And thither will I straight to visit him;°
He comes upon a wish.° Fortune is merry,
And in this mood will give us anything.

SERVANT. I heard him say, Brutus and Cassius
265 Are rid° like madmen through the gates of Rome.

ANTONY. Belike° they had some notice of the people,
How I had mov'd them. Bring me to Octavius.

[*They exit.*]

244 orchards: gardens.

246 common pleasures: public recreation areas.

250 the holy place: the site of the most sacred Roman temples.
251 brands: pieces of burning wood.

255 forms: benches. **windows:** shutters.

260 Lepidus: one of Caesar's generals.

261 thither will . . . him: I will go there immediately to visit him.
262 upon a wish: just as I had wished.

265 Are rid: have ridden.

266 Belike: probably.

SCENE 3. Shortly afterward. A street near the Forum.

[*Enter* CINNA *the poet, and after him the* PLEBEIANS.]

Loyalty and Betrayal What does this remark reveal about Antony?

Analyze Figures of Speech What does Antony mean when he says fortune is "merry" and will give him anything?

Plot How would you characterize the tension at this point in the act compared to what has come before?

CINNA.° I dreamt tonight° that I did feast with Caesar,
And things unluckily charge my fantasy.°
I have no will to wander forth of doors,
Yet something leads me forth.

5 FIRST PLEBEIAN. What is your name?

SECOND PLEBEIAN. Whither are you going?

THIRD PLEBEIAN. Where do you dwell?

FOURTH PLEBEIAN. Are you a married man or a bachelor?

SECOND PLEBEIAN. Answer every man directly.

10 FIRST PLEBEIAN. Ay, and briefly.

FOURTH PLEBEIAN. Ay, and wisely.

THIRD PLEBEIAN. Ay, and truly, you were best.°

CINNA. What is my name? Whither am I going? Where do I dwell? Am I a married man or a bachelor? Then, to answer
15 every man directly and briefly, wisely and truly: wisely I say, I am a bachelor.

SECOND PLEBEIAN. That's as much as to say, they are fools that marry. You'll bear me a bang° for that, I fear. Proceed directly.

20 CINNA. Directly, I am going to Caesar's funeral.

FIRST PLEBEIAN. As a friend or an enemy?

CINNA. As a friend.

SECOND PLEBEIAN. That matter is answer'd directly.

FOURTH PLEBEIAN. For your dwelling—briefly.

25 CINNA. Briefly, I dwell by the Capitol.

THIRD PLEBEIAN. Your name, sir, truly.

CINNA. Truly, my name is Cinna.

FIRST PLEBEIAN. Tear him to pieces, he's a conspirator.

CINNA. I am Cinna the poet, I am Cinna the poet.

30 FOURTH PLEBEIAN. Tear him for his bad verses, tear him for his bad verses.

CINNA. I am not Cinna the conspirator.

FOURTH PLEBEIAN. **It is no matter, his name's Cinna. Pluck but his name out of his heart, and turn him going.**

35 THIRD PLEBEIAN. Tear him, tear him!
Come, brands, ho, firebrands! To Brutus', to Cassius'; burn all! Some to Decius' house, and some to Casca's; some to Ligarius'. Away, go!

[*All the* PLEBEIANS *exit (dragging off* CINNA*).*]

---

1 Cinna: a well-known poet, not the same Cinna who helped kill Caesar. **tonight:** last night.
2 things . . . fantasy: my imagination is burdened with bad omens.

12 you were best: you had better.

18 bear me a bang: get hit by me.

Loyalty and Betrayal How would you describe the mood of the crowd? Why are they behaving in this way?

After You Read

Respond and Think Critically

Respond and Interpret

1. What was your reaction to Caesar's murder?
2. (a) What most surprises Caesar when he is attacked? (b) What might Caesar have been thinking as he died? Explain.
3. (a) How does Antony respond to the conspirators immediately after Caesar's murder? (b) In your opinion, why does he behave this way?
4. (a) Summarize the crowd's reactions to Brutus's and Antony's funeral speeches. (b) What can you infer about the crowd from their reactions?

Analyze and Evaluate

5. How did Caesar's behavior outside the Capitol just before he died affect your reaction to his death?
6. Why might Shakespeare have chosen to include the incident of the attack on Cinna the poet?

Connect

7. **Big Idea** **Loyalty and Betrayal** As a friend to others, does Antony display loyalty, disloyalty, or both qualities? Support your answer.
8. **Connect to Today** What contemporary events might you compare to the attack on Cinna the poet? Explain.

Literary Element Plot

In Act 3, what is the point of greatest emotional intensity, known in literature as the **climax**? In fact, critics do not all agree on this matter. Several places in Act 3 could plausibly be labeled the climax.

1. Summarize Act 3's exposition and rising action; include details that contribute to the tension.
2. What, in your opinion, is the climax of Act 3? Explain.

Reading Strategy Analyze Figures of Speech

Figurative language has the power to convey experiences more vividly than literal language. Review your chart on page 761 and answer the questions.

1. (a) What figure of speech does Casca use when he stabs Caesar? (b) Explain its meaning.
2. For two other figures of speech in Act 3, identify the types and explain what you think the figure of speech was intended to convey.

LOG ON **Literature** Online

Selection Resources For Selection Quizzes, eFlashcards, and Reading-Writing Connection activities, go to glencoe.com and enter QuickPass code GL59794u4.

Vocabulary Practice

Practice with Context Clues Identify the context clues that help you determine the meaning of each boldfaced vocabulary word below.

1. The plants are **thriving** as a result of good light, fertilization, and correct watering.
2. His expression was full of **malice**; his friend also gave me a hateful look.
3. The **orator** stepped onto the podium to begin his speech.
4. Although the troops fought hard, they could not **vanquish** their determined opponents.
5. The plan appealed to the rest of the team, so Sofia did not state her **misgivings** about how it could go wrong.

Writing

Write a Memo What if the ancient Romans had been able to send messages by e-mail rather than by messenger? Reread the servant's speech (scene 1, lines 123–137) and then rewrite it as an e-mail memo from Antony to Brutus. See page R25 for the format to use for such a message.

Before You Read

The Tragedy of Julius Caesar, Act 4

Connect to the Play
Why do people quarrel? Discuss this question with a partner.

Build Background
When Antony took charge of the city, he was joined by eighteen-year-old Gaius Octavius, Caesar's great-nephew and adopted son. Octavius was intelligent, handsome, and skilled at oratory. Together with a governor named Lepidus, Octavius and Antony created a ruling group of three—a triumvirate.

Set Purposes for Reading

Big Idea Loyalty and Betrayal

As you read, ask yourself, What do the conflicts reveal about various characters' desire for loyalty and fear of betrayal?

Literary Element Foil

A **foil** is a character who provides contrast with another. A foil helps readers perceive strengths and weaknesses of another character. As you read, ask yourself, Which characters are foils?

Reading Strategy Make and Verify Predictions

When you **make predictions** as you read, you make reasoned guesses about what will happen based on clues the author provides together with your own understanding of characters and events. Then, as you continue reading, you **verify** the accuracy of the predictions and modify your thinking and continue on. As you read, ask yourself, What predictions can I make about the outcome of events in Act 4?

Tip: Chart Predictions Use a chart like the one below to make and verify predictions as you read.

Prediction	My Reason	Outcome
Brutus and Cassius are going to argue and end their alliance.	They are very different. Brutus is thoughtful and honest. Cassius is emotional and cunning.	They fight but reconcile and resolve their differences.

Learning Objectives

For pages 783–799

In studying this text, you will focus on the following objectives:

Literary Study: Analyzing plot.

Reading: Making and verifying predictions.

Vocabulary

barren (bar′ ən) *adj.* empty and dreary; without life; desolate; p. 786 *No one lives in the area surrounding the town; the land is barren.*

covert (kō′ vərt) *adj.* secret; hidden; p. 786 *The reporter discovered a covert plan to escape.*

deceitful (di sēt′ fəl) *adj.* untruthful and cunning; false; p. 787 *Some advertisements are honest; others are deceitful.*

rash (rash) *adj.* marked by haste and lack of caution or consideration; p. 792 *Meena's decision to end their friendship seemed rash to Laura.*

Tip: Denotation and Connotation
A word's **denotation** is its dictionary meaning; its **connotations** are the emotional association it evokes. To identify a word's connotations, think about the images and ideas the word brings to mind. For example, in the sentence *Meena's decision to end their friendship seemed rash to Laura,* the word *rash* has a negative connotation and suggests foolishness.

ACT 4

SCENE 1. Antony's house in Rome. A year and a half after Caesar's death.

[*Enter* ANTONY, OCTAVIUS, *and* LEPIDUS.]

ANTONY. These many then shall die, their names are prick'd.°

OCTAVIUS. Your brother too must die, consent you, Lepidus?°

LEPIDUS. I do consent—

1 **prick'd:** marked down on a list.

2 **Your brother ... Lepidus:** Lepidus's brother was a prominent politician who sided with the conspirators after Caesar's assassination.

Ancient Romans. Artist unknown. Mosaic. Currier Gallery of Art, Manchester, NH.

View the Art What impressions of people in ancient Rome do you get from this mosaic? How do those impressions relate to characters in the play?

OCTAVIUS. Prick him down, Antony.

LEPIDUS. Upon condition Publius shall not live,
Who is your sister's son, Mark Antony.

ANTONY. He shall not live; look, with a spot I damn him.
But, Lepidus, go you to Caesar's house;
Fetch the will hither, and we shall determine
How to cut off some charge in legacies.°

LEPIDUS. What? shall I find you here?

OCTAVIUS. Or here or at the Capitol.

[*Exit* LEPIDUS.]

ANTONY. This is a slight unmeritable man,
Meet° to be sent on errands; is it fit,
The threefold world° divided, he should stand
One of the three to share it?

OCTAVIUS. So you thought him,
And took his voice who should be prick'd to die
In our black sentence and proscription.°

ANTONY. Octavius, I have seen more days than you,
And though we lay these honors on this man
To ease ourselves of divers sland'rous loads,°
He shall but bear them as the ass bears gold,
To groan and sweat under the business,
Either led or driven, as we point the way;
And having brought our treasure where we will,
Then take we down his load, and turn him off
(Like to the empty ass) to shake his ears
And graze in commons.°

OCTAVIUS. You may do your will;
But he's a tried and valiant soldier.

ANTONY. So is my horse, Octavius, and for that
I do appoint him store of provender.°
It is a creature that I teach to fight,
To wind,° to stop, to run directly on,
His corporal° motion govern'd by my spirit;
And in some taste° is Lepidus but so.
He must be taught, and train'd, and bid go forth;

9 cut off . . . legacies: reduce the amount of money left to the people in Caesar's will.

13 Meet: fit.

14 threefold world: three parts of the Roman world. (In the autumn of 43 BC, Antony, Octavius Caesar, and Lepidus formed a triumvirate—a committee of three—to rule Rome. They divided up among themselves territory that the Romans had conquered.)

15–17 So you . . . proscription: Octavius wonders why Antony asked Lepidus to name people who should be sentenced to death if he had so poor an opinion of him.

20 divers sland'rous loads: the burden of accusations for our various actions.

24–27 And having . . . commons: When Lepidus has brought our treasure where we want it, we will send him off to shake his ears and graze on public land like an unburdened donkey.

30 appoint . . . provender: allot him a supply of food.

32 wind: turn.
33 corporal: bodily.
34 taste: degree.

Loyalty and Betrayal *What does Antony's statement here suggest about him?*

Foil *What does Octavius's statement indicate about the difference between Octavius and Antony?*

JULIUS CAESAR, ACT 4, SCENE 1 **785**

Julius Caesar

A **barren**-spirited fellow; one that feeds
On objects, arts, and imitations,
Which, out of use and stal'd by other men,
Begin his fashion.° Do not talk of him
40 But as a property.° And now, Octavius,
Listen great things. Brutus and Cassius
Are levying powers; we must straight make head;
Therefore let our alliance be combin'd,
Our best friends made, our means stretch'd;
45 And let us presently go sit in council,
How **covert** matters may be best disclos'd,
And open perils surest answered.°

OCTAVIUS. Let us do so; for we are at the stake,
And bay'd about with many enemies,°
50 And some that smile have in their hearts, I fear,
Millions of mischiefs. [*They exit.*]

SCENE 2. A military camp near Sardis in Asia Minor. Several months later.

[*Drum. Enter* BRUTUS, LUCILIUS, LUCIUS, *and the army.* TITINIUS *and* PINDARUS *meet them.*]

BRUTUS. Stand ho!

LUCILIUS. Give the word ho! and stand.°

BRUTUS. What now, Lucilius, is Cassius near?

LUCILIUS. He is at hand, and Pindarus is come
5 To do you salutation from his master.

BRUTUS. He greets me well. Your master, Pindarus,
In his own change, or by ill officers,
Hath given me some worthy cause to wish
Things done undone,° but if he be at hand,
10 I shall be satisfied.°

PINDARUS. I do not doubt
But that my noble master will appear
Such as he is, full of regard and honor.

36–39 A barren-spirited . . . fashion: a man with no originality, one who indulges in curiosities, tricks, and fashions, which he takes up only after they have become outmoded.
40 a property: a mere tool.

41–47 Listen great . . . answered: Listen to important matters. Brutus and Cassius are raising armies; we must press forward immediately. Therefore let us become united, choose our allies, and make the most of our resources. And let us decide at once how hidden threats may be uncovered and open dangers most safely confronted.
48–49 we are . . . enemies: Octavius's metaphor refers to bear-baiting, a popular entertainment in which bears were tied to stakes and surrounded by vicious dogs.

2 Give the . . . stand: Lucilius, one of Brutus's officers, tells his subordinates to pass on Brutus's command for the army to halt (**stand**). He has returned from Cassius's camp with Titinius, one of Cassius's officers, and Pindarus, Cassius's servant.

6–9 Your master . . . undone: Either a change in Cassius or the misconduct of his officers has given me good reason to wish I could undo what I have done. (Brutus is having some misgivings about having participated in the conspiracy because of incidents that have occurred in Cassius's army.)
10 be satisfied: receive an explanation.

> **Make and Verify Predictions** Who do you predict will emerge victorious, the conspirators or Rome's new rulers?

Vocabulary

barren (bar´ən) *adj.* empty and dreary; without life; desolate
covert (kō´vərt) *adj.* secret; hidden

BRUTUS. He is not doubted. A word, Lucilius.
How he receiv'd you; let me be resolv'd.°

15 **LUCILIUS.** With courtesy and with respect enough,
But not with such familiar instances,°
Nor with such free and friendly conference,°
As he hath us'd of old.

BRUTUS. Thou hast describ'd
A hot friend cooling. Ever note, Lucilius,
20 When love begins to sicken and decay
It useth an enforced ceremony.°
There are no tricks in plain and simple faith;
But hollow men, like horses hot at hand,
Make gallant show and promise of their mettle;

[*Low march within.*]

25 But when they should endure the bloody spur,
They fall their crests, and like **deceitful** jades
Sink in the trial.° Comes his army on?

LUCILIUS. They mean this night in Sardis to be quarter'd.
The greater part, the horse in general,°
30 Are come with Cassius.

[*Enter CASSIUS and his POWERS.*]

BRUTUS. Hark! He is arriv'd.
March gently on to meet him.

CASSIUS. Stand ho!

BRUTUS. Stand ho! Speak the word along.

FIRST SOLDIER. Stand!

35 **SECOND SOLDIER.** Stand!

THIRD SOLDIER. Stand!

CASSIUS. Most noble brother, you have done me wrong.

BRUTUS. Judge me, you gods! wrong I mine enemies?
And if not so, how should I wrong a brother.

40 **CASSIUS.** Brutus, this sober form° of yours hides wrongs,
And when you do them—

---

14 resolv'd: informed.

16 familiar instances: signs of friendship.
17 conference: conversation.

21 enforced ceremony: strained formality.
23–27 But hollow . . . trial: Brutus compares insincere men to horses that are spirited at the start but drop their proud necks as soon as they feel the spur, failing like nags (**jades**) when put to the test.
29 horse in general: main part of the cavalry.

A group of soldiers of the Praetorian guard, possibly from the Forum of Emperor Trajan, 1st–3rd century C.E. Artist unknown. Marble relief. Louvre, Paris.

40 sober form: dignified manner.

Loyalty and Betrayal *What attitude toward Cassius is Brutus expressing?*

Make and Verify Predictions *What do you predict will happen when Brutus and Cassius meet?*

Vocabulary

deceitful (di sēt´fəl) *adj.* untruthful and cunning; false

Julius Caesar

BRUTUS. Cassius, be content.
Speak your griefs softly; I do know you well.
Before the eyes of both our armies here
(Which should perceive nothing but love from us)
Let us not wrangle. Bid them move away;
Then in my tent, Cassius, enlarge your griefs,
And I will give you audience.°

CASSIUS.   Pindarus,
Bid our commanders lead their charges off
A little from this ground.

BRUTUS. Lucius, do you the like, and let no man
Come to our tent till we have done our conference.
Let Lucilius and Titinius guard our door.

[*They exit.* BRUTUS *and* CASSIUS *remain and withdraw into* BRUTUS'S *tent, while* LUCILIUS *and* TITINIUS *mount guard without.*]

SCENE 3. BRUTUS'S **tent. A few minutes later.**

CASSIUS. That you wrong'd me doth appear in this;
You have condemn'd and noted Lucius Pella
For taking bribes here of the Sardians;
Wherein my letters, praying on his side,
Because I knew the man, was slighted off.°

BRUTUS. You wrong'd yourself to write in such a case.

CASSIUS. In such a time as this it is not meet
That every nice offense should bear his comment.°

BRUTUS. Let me tell you, Cassius, you yourself
Are much condemn'd to have an itching palm,°
To sell and mart° your offices for gold
To undeservers.

CASSIUS.   I, an itching palm?
You know that you are Brutus that speaks this,
Or, by the gods, this speech were else your last.

BRUTUS. The name of Cassius honors this corruption,
And chastisement doth therefore hide his head.°

CASSIUS. Chastisement?

47–48 enlarge . . . audience: Explain your grievances, and I will listen.

1–5 That you . . . off: Cassius complains that Brutus publicly disgraced (**noted**) a man for taking bribes, ignoring Cassius's request for leniency.

7–8 not meet . . . comment: not fitting that each minor offense should be criticized.
10 condemn'd to . . . palm: blamed for being greedy.
11 mart: trade.

15–16 The name . . . head: Because you have become associated with this corruption, the bribe-takers go unpunished.

Foil What contrast between Cassius and Brutus does this passage suggest?

BRUTUS. Remember March, the ides of March remember:
Did not great Julius bleed for justice' sake?
What villain touch'd his body, that did stab
And not for justice? What? shall one of us,
That struck the foremost man of all this world
But for supporting robbers,° shall we now
Contaminate our fingers with base bribes?
And sell the mighty space of our large honors
For so much trash as may be grasped thus?
==I had rather be a dog, and bay the moon,
Than such a Roman.==

CASSIUS. Brutus, bait° not me,
I'll not endure it. You forget yourself
To hedge me in.° I am a soldier, I,
Older in practice, abler than yourself
To make conditions.°

BRUTUS. Go to; you are not, Cassius.

CASSIUS. I am.

BRUTUS. I say you are not.

CASSIUS. Urge me no more, I shall forget myself;
Have mind upon your health; tempt me no farther.

BRUTUS. Away, slight man!

CASSIUS. Is't possible?

BRUTUS. Hear me, for I will speak.
Must I give way and room to your rash choler?°
Shall I be frighted when a madman stares?

CASSIUS. O ye gods, ye gods, must I endure all this?

BRUTUS. All this? ay, more. Fret till your proud heart break.
Go show your slaves how choleric you are,
And make your bondmen tremble. Must I budge?°
Must I observe you?° Must I stand and crouch
Under your testy humor?° By the gods,
You shall digest the venom of your spleen
Though it do split you;° for, from his day forth,
I'll use you for my mirth, yea, for my laughter,
When you are waspish.

CASSIUS. Is it come to this?

---

23 supporting robbers: Brutus now suggests that one of Caesar's offenses was to protect corrupt officials.

28 bait: provoke.

30 hedge me in: limit my freedom.

32 conditions: regulations.

39 rash choler: quick temper.

44 budge: flinch.
45 observe you: defer to you.
46 testy humor: irritable mood.

47–48 digest . . . split you: swallow the poison of your own anger, even if it makes you burst. (The spleen was thought to be the source of anger.)

Loyalty and Betrayal What point does Brutus make in these lines?

JULIUS CAESAR

BRUTUS. You say you are a better soldier;
Let it appear so; make your vaunting° true,
And it shall please me well. For mine own part,
I shall be glad to learn of noble men.°

55 **CASSIUS.** You wrong me every way; you wrong me, Brutus;
I said, an elder soldier, not a better.
Did I say "better"?

BRUTUS. If you did, I care not.

CASSIUS. When Caesar liv'd, he durst° not thus have
mov'd° me.

BRUTUS. Peace, peace, you durst not so have tempted him.

60 **CASSIUS.** I durst not?

BRUTUS. No.

CASSIUS. What? durst not tempt him?

BRUTUS. For your life you
durst not.

CASSIUS. Do not presume too much upon my love,
I may do that° I shall be sorry for.

65 **BRUTUS.** You have done that you should be sorry for.
There is no terror, Cassius, in your threats;
For I am arm'd so strong in honesty
That they pass by me as the idle wind,
Which I respect not. I did send to you
70 For certain sums of gold, which you denied me;
For I can raise no money by vile means.
By heaven, I had rather coin my heart
And drop my blood for drachmas than to wring
From the hard hands of peasants their vile trash°
75 By any indirection.° I did send
To you for gold to pay my legions,
Which you denied me. Was that done like Cassius?
Should I have answer'd Caius Cassius so?
When Marcus Brutus grows so covetous
80 To lock such rascal counters° from his friends,
Be ready, gods, with all your thunderbolts,

52 **vaunting:** boasting.

54 **learn of noble men:** "learn from noble men" or "find out that you are noble."

58 **durst:** dared. **mov'd:** provoked.

64 **that:** something that.
74 **vile trash:** small sums of money.
75 **indirection:** dishonest means.
80 **rascal counters:** grubby coins.

Make and Verify Predictions What do you predict will happen next?

Foil What distinction does Brutus draw between himself and Cassius?

Jupiter Hurling a Flash of Lightning at the Titan, 17th century. Alessandro Algardi. Bronze sculpture. Louvre, Paris.

Dash him to pieces!

CASSIUS. I denied you not.

BRUTUS. You did.

CASSIUS. I did not. He was but a fool that brought
My answer back. Brutus hath riv'd° my heart.
A friend should bear his friend's infirmities;°
But Brutus makes mine greater than they are.

BRUTUS. I do not, till you practice them on me.

CASSIUS. You love me not.

BRUTUS. I do not like your faults.

CASSIUS. A friendly eye could never see such faults.

BRUTUS. A flatterer's would not, though they do appear
As huge as high Olympus.

CASSIUS. Come, Antony, and young Octavius, come,
Revenge yourselves alone on Cassius,
For Cassius is aweary of the world;
Hated by one he loves, brav'd° by his brother,
Check'd like a bondman,° all his faults observ'd,
Set in a notebook, learn'd and conn'd by rote,°
To cast into my teeth. O, I could weep
My spirit from mine eyes! There is my dagger,
And here my naked breast; within, a heart
Dearer than Pluto's mine,° richer than gold:
If that thou be'st a Roman, take it forth.
I, that denied thee gold, will give my heart:
Strike as thou didst at Caesar; for I know,
When thou didst hate him worst, thou lovedst him better
Than ever thou lovedst Cassius.

BRUTUS. Sheathe your dagger.
Be angry when you will, it shall have scope;
Do what you will, dishonor shall be humor.°
O Cassius, you are yoked° with a lamb
That carries anger as the flint bears fire,
Who, much enforced,° shows a hasty spark,
And straight° is cold again.

CASSIUS. Hath Cassius liv'd

---

85 **riv'd:** broken.
86 **bear . . . infirmities:** accept his friend's faults.

96 **brav'd:** challenged.
97 **Check'd like a bondman:** scolded like a slave.
98 **conn'd by rote:** memorized.

102 **Pluto's mine:** all the riches in the earth. (Pluto, the Roman god of the underworld, was often confused with Plutus, the god of wealth.)

108–109 **Be angry . . . humor:** Brutus says that he will give Cassius's anger free play (**scope**) and will consider his insults merely the result of a bad mood.
110 **yoked:** allied.
112 **enforced:** struck hard; irritated.
113 **straight:** immediately.

Loyalty and Betrayal What different ideas about loyalty and friendship are expressed here? With whose ideas do you agree?

Julius Caesar

                To be but mirth and laughter to his Brutus
115   When grief and blood ill-temper'd° vexeth him?

BRUTUS. When I spoke that, I was ill-temper'd too.

CASSIUS. Do you confess so much? Give me your hand.

BRUTUS. And my heart too.

CASSIUS.   O Brutus!

BRUTUS.   What's the matter?

CASSIUS. Have you not love enough to bear with me,
120   When that **rash** humor which my mother gave me
        Makes me forgetful?°

BRUTUS.   Yes, Cassius, and from henceforth,
        When you are over-earnest with your Brutus,
        He'll think your mother chides, and leave you so.°

[*Enter a* POET (*to* LUCILIUS *and* TITINIUS *as they stand on guard*).]

POET. Let me go in to see the generals;
125   There is some grudge between 'em; 'tis not meet
        They be alone.

LUCILIUS. You shall not come to them.

POET. Nothing but death shall stay me.

[BRUTUS *and* CASSIUS *step out of the tent.*]

CASSIUS. How now. What's the matter?

130 **POET.** For shame, you generals! what do you mean?
        Love, and be friends, as two such men should be,
        For I have seen more years, I'm sure, than ye.

CASSIUS. Ha, ha! how vilely doth this cynic° rhyme!

BRUTUS. Get you hence, sirrah! saucy fellow, hence!

135 **CASSIUS.** Bear with him, Brutus, 'tis his fashion.

BRUTUS. I'll know his humor when he knows his time.°
        What should the wars do with these jigging° fools?
        Companion,° hence!

Statuette of Jupiter Dolichenus (standing on a bull) detail of the god, from a shrine, BC 200–250. Bronze, height 32 cm. Kunsthistorisches Museum, Vienna, Austria.

---

115 blood ill-temper'd: moodiness.
121 forgetful: forget myself.
122–123 When you . . . so: When you are too difficult with me, I will attribute it to the quick temper you inherited from your mother, and leave it at that.

133 cynic: rude fellow.

136 I'll know . . . time: I'll accept his quirks when he learns the proper time for them.
137 jigging: rhyming.
138 Companion: fellow (used here as a term of contempt).

Make and Verify Predictions *Is this how you predicted the argument would end? What will likely happen next?*

Foil *How might the poet be said to act as a foil to Brutus and Cassius?*

Vocabulary

rash (rash) *adj.* marked by haste and lack of caution or consideration

792 UNIT 4 DRAMA

CASSIUS. Away, away, be gone! [*Exit* POET.]

BRUTUS. Lucilius and Titinius, bid the commanders
140 Prepare to lodge their companies tonight.

CASSIUS. And come yourselves, and bring Messala with you
Immediately to us.

[LUCILIUS *and* TITINIUS *exit.*]

BRUTUS. [*To* LUCIUS *within.*] Lucius, a bowl of wine!

[BRUTUS *and* CASSIUS *return into the tent.*]

CASSIUS. I did not think you could have been so angry.

BRUTUS. O Cassius, I am sick of many griefs.

145 CASSIUS. Of your philosophy you make no use,
If you give place to accidental evils.°

BRUTUS. No man bears sorrow better. Portia is dead.

CASSIUS. Ha? Portia?

BRUTUS. She is dead.

150 CASSIUS. How scap'd I killing° when I cross'd you so?
O insupportable and touching° loss!
Upon what sickness?

BRUTUS.   Impatient of° my absence,
And grief that young Octavius with Mark Antony
Have made themselves so strong—for with her death
155 That tidings came.° With this she fell distract,°
And (her attendants absent) swallow'd fire.°

CASSIUS. And died so?

BRUTUS.   Even so.

CASSIUS.   O ye immortal gods!

[*Enter Boy* (LUCIUS) *with wine and tapers.*]

BRUTUS. Speak no more of her. Give me a bowl of wine.
In this I bury all unkindness, Cassius. [*Drinks.*]

160 CASSIUS. My heart is thirsty for that noble pledge.
Fill, Lucius, till the wine o'erswell the cup;
I cannot drink too much of Brutus' love.

[*Drinks. Exit* LUCIUS.]

BRUTUS. Come in, Titinius. [*Enter* TITINIUS *and* MESSALA.]
Welcome, good Messala.
Now sit we close about this taper here,

Brutus. c. 1539–1540. Michelangelo Buonarroti. Marble, height: 29⅛ in. Museo Nazionale del Bargello, Florence, Italy.

View the Art What traits of Brutus are depicted in this statue? How do they compare with the character you have read about?

145–146 Of your . . . evils: According to the philosophy Brutus studied, people should not accept chance misfortunes.
150 How scap'd I killing: How did I escape being killed?
151 touching: painful.
152 Impatient of: unable to endure.
154–155: with her death . . . came: I received news of her death and of their strength at the same time.
155 distract: insane.
156 fire: burning coals.

Loyalty and Betrayal How would you characterize Portia's loyalty to Brutus?

JULIUS CAESAR

165   And call in question our necessities.°

CASSIUS. Portia, art thou gone?

BRUTUS.   No more, I pray you.
  Messala, I have here received letters
  That young Octavius and Mark Antony
  Come down upon us with a mighty power,°
170 Bending their expedition toward Philippi.°

MESSALA. Myself have letters of the selfsame tenure.°

BRUTUS. With what addition?

MESSALA. That by proscription° and bills of outlawry
  Octavius, Antony, and Lepidus
175 Have put to death an hundred senators.

BRUTUS. Therein our letters do not well agree;
  Mine speak of seventy senators that died
  By their proscriptions, Cicero being one.

CASSIUS. Cicero one?

MESSALA.   Cicero is dead,
180 And by that order of proscription.
  Had you your letters from your wife, my lord?

BRUTUS. No, Messala.

MESSALA. Nor nothing in your letters writ of her?

BRUTUS. Nothing, Messala.

MESSALA.   That methinks is strange.

185 BRUTUS. Why ask you? Hear you aught of her in yours?

MESSALA. No, my lord.

BRUTUS. Now as you are a Roman, tell me true.

MESSALA. Then like a Roman bear the truth I tell,
  For certain she is dead, and by strange manner.

190 BRUTUS. Why, farewell, Portia. We must die, Messala.
  With meditating that she must die once,°
  I have the patience to endure it now.

MESSALA. Even so great men great losses should endure.

CASSIUS. I have as much of this in art as you,
195 But yet my nature could not bear it so.°

BRUTUS. Well, to our work alive.° What do you think

165 call . . . necessities: discuss what we must do.

169 power: army.
170 Bending . . . Philippi: Directing their march toward Philippi (an ancient town in northern Greece).
171 tenure: basic meaning.
173 proscription: condemning to death.

191 once: at some time.
181–195 Had you your . . . bear it so: This passage contradicts lines **147–158**, where Brutus tells Cassius of Portia's death. Many scholars believe that the second passage was mistakenly printed in a revised version of the play. According to this theory, Shakespeare originally emphasized Brutus's philosophical composure, but in rewriting the play, he decided to offer a warmer view of Brutus grieving for his wife.
194–195 I have as . . . so: Cassius says that although he shares Brutus's ideal of philosophical self-control, he could not practice it as Brutus does.
196 alive: "at hand" or "of the living."

Foil In comparison to Cassius, how does Brutus react to Portia's death?

Make and Verify Predictions Considering this news, what do you predict might happen?

    Of marching to Philippi presently?

CASSIUS. I do not think it good.

BRUTUS.   Your reason?

CASSIUS.   This it is;
 'Tis better that the enemy seek us;
200 So shall he waste his means,° weary his soldiers,
 Doing himself offense,° whilst we, lying still,
 Are full of rest, defense, and nimbleness.

BRUTUS. Good reasons must of force give place to better:
 The people 'twixt Philippi and this ground
205 Do stand but in a forc'd affection;°
 For they have grudg'd us contribution.
 The enemy, marching along by them,
 By them shall make a fuller number up,
 Come on refresh'd, new-added° and encourag'd;
210 From which advantage shall we cut him off
 If at Philippi we do face him there,
 These people at our back.

CASSIUS.   Here me, good brother.

BRUTUS. Under your pardon.° You must note beside
 That we have tried the utmost of our friends,°
215 Our legions are brimful,° our cause is ripe:
 The enemy increaseth every day;
 We, at the height, are ready to decline.
 There is a tide in the affairs of men,
 Which, taken at the flood, leads on to fortune;
220 Omitted, all the voyage of their life
 Is bound in shallows and in miseries.°
 On such a full sea are we now afloat,
 And we must take the current when it serves,
 Or lose our ventures.

CASSIUS.   Then with your will° go on;
225 We'll along ourselves, and meet them at Philippi.

BRUTUS. The deep of night is crept upon our talk,
 And nature must obey necessity,
 Which we will niggard with a little rest.°
 There is no more to say?

200 waste his means: use up his supplies.
201 Doing himself offense: harming himself.

205 Do stand . . . affection: Are friendly toward us only because they have no choice.

209 new-added: reinforced.

213 Under your pardon: I beg your pardon (let me continue).
214 tried . . . friends: demanded from our allies all that they can give.
215 brimful: at full strength.

218–221 There is a . . . miseries: Brutus says that if men fail to act when the tide of fortune is flowing, they may never get another opportunity.

224 with your will: as you wish.

227–228 nature must . . . rest: Human nature has its needs, which we will grudgingly satisfy (**niggard**) by resting briefly.

Make and Verify Predictions *How are the plans proposed by Brutus and Cassius different? What is the likely outcome?*

Make and Verify Predictions *Whose ideas about strategy do you think will ultimately be proven correct, those of Cassius or those of Brutus?*

Julius Caesar

CASSIUS. No more. Good night.
230 Early tomorrow will we rise, and hence.
BRUTUS. Lucius. [*Enter* LUCIUS.] My gown. [*Exit* LUCIUS.]
Farewell, good Messala.
Good night, Titinius. Noble, noble Cassius,
Good night, and good repose.
CASSIUS. O my dear brother!
This was an ill beginning of the night.
235 Never come such division 'tween our souls!
Let it not, Brutus.

[*Enter* LUCIUS *with the gown.*]

BRUTUS. Everything is well.
CASSIUS. Good night, my lord.
BRUTUS. Good night, good brother.
TITINIUS AND MESSALA. Good night, Lord Brutus.
BRUTUS. Farewell
every one.

[*Exit (all but* BRUTUS *and* LUCIUS*).*]

Give me the gown. Where is thy instrument?
240 **LUCIUS.** Here in the tent.
BRUTUS. What, thou speak'st drowsily?
Poor knave,° I blame thee not; thou art o'erwatch'd.°
Call Claudius and some other of my men,
I'll have them sleep on cushions in my tent.
LUCIUS. Varrus and Claudio!

[*Enter* VARRUS *and* CLAUDIO.]

245 **VARRUS.** Calls my lord?
BRUTUS. I pray you, sirs, lie in my tent and sleep;
It may be I shall raise° you by and by
On business to my brother Cassius.
VARRUS. So please you, we will stand and watch your
pleasure.°
250 **BRUTUS.** I will not have it so. Lie down, good sirs,
It may be I shall otherwise bethink me.°

[VARRUS *and* CLAUDIO *lie down.*]

Look, Lucius, here's the book I sought for so;

Young Boy Singing and Playing the Lute. Michelangelo Merisi da Caravaggio, 1573–1610. Hermitage, St. Petersburg, Russia.

241 knave: lad. **o'erwatch'd:** tired from staying awake too long.

247 raise: awaken.

249 stand . . . pleasure: stay awake and be ready to serve you.

251 It may be . . . me: I might change my mind.

Loyalty and Betrayal Why does Cassius make this request? What does it tell you about Cassius's character?

I put it in the pocket of my gown.

LUCIUS. I was sure your lordship did not give it me.

255 BRUTUS. Bear with me, good boy, I am much forgetful.
Canst thou hold up thy heavy eyes awhile,
And touch thy instrument a strain or two?°

LUCIUS. Ay, my lord, an't° please you.

BRUTUS.   It does, my boy.
I trouble thee too much, but thou are willing.

260 LUCIUS. It is my duty, sir.

BRUTUS. I should not urge thy duty past thy might;
I know young bloods look for a time of rest.

LUCIUS. I have slept, my lord, already.

BRUTUS. It was well done, and thou shalt sleep again;
265 I will not hold thee long. If I do live,
I will be good to thee.

[*Music, and a song.*]

This is a sleepy tune. O murd'rous slumber!
Layest thou thy leaden mace° upon my boy,
That plays thee music? Gentle knave, good night;
270 I will not do thee so much wrong to wake thee.
If thou dost nod, thou break'st thy instrument;
I'll take it from thee; and, good boy, good night.
Let me see, let me see; is not the leaf turn'd down
Where I left reading? Here it is, I think.

[*Enter the* GHOST OF CAESAR.]

275 How ill this taper burns!° Ha! who comes here?
I think it is the weakness of mine eyes
That shapes this monstrous apparition.
It comes upon me. Art thou anything?
Art thou some god, some angel, or some devil,
280 That mak'st my blood cold, and my hair to stare?°
Speak to me what thou art.

GHOST. Thy evil spirit, Brutus.

BRUTUS.   Why com'st thou?

GHOST. To tell thee thou shalt see me at Philippi.

BRUTUS. Well; then I shall see thee again?

285 GHOST. Ay, at Philippi.

---

257 touch thy . . . two: play a song or two. (Lucius probably plays the lute, a stringed instrument.)
258 an't: if it.

267–268 O murd'rous . . . mace: Officers used to touch a rod (**mace**) to a person's shoulder as a sign of arrest. Brutus calls the mace of deathlike (**murd'rous**) sleep "leaden" because of its heaviness.
275 How ill . . . burns: It was believed that candles burn dimly when a ghost appears.
280 stare: stand on end.

Julius Caesar, Act IV, Scene III, Brutus & The Ghost, 1906. Edwin Austin Abbey. Illustration created for *Harper's Monthly.*

Loyalty and Betrayal What character traits does Brutus demonstrate in this scene?

BRUTUS. Why, I will see thee at Philippi then.

[*Exit* GHOST.]

Now I have taken heart thou vanishest.
Ill spirit, I would hold more talk with thee.
Boy! Lucius! Varrus! Claudio! Sirs, awake!
290   Claudio!

LUCIUS. The strings, my lord, are false.°

291 false: out of tune.

BRUTUS. He thinks he still is at his instrument.
Lucius, awake!

LUCIUS. My lord?

295 BRUTUS. Didst thou dream, Lucius, that thou so criedst out?

LUCIUS. My lord, I do not know that I did cry.

BRUTUS. Yes, that thou didst. Didst thou see anything?

LUCIUS. Nothing, my lord.

BRUTUS. Sleep again, Lucius. Sirrah Claudio!
300   [*To* CLAUDIO *and then* VARRUS.] Fellow thou, awake!

VARRUS. My lord?

CLAUDIO. My lord?

BRUTUS. Why did you so cry out, sirs, in your sleep?

BOTH. Did we, my lord?

BRUTUS.   Ay. Saw you anything?

305 VARRUS. No, my lord, I saw nothing.

CLAUDIO.   Nor I, my lord.

BRUTUS. Go and commend me° to my brother Cassius;
Bid him set on his pow'rs betimes before,°
And we will follow.

BOTH.   It shall be done, my lord.

[*They exit.*]

306 commend me: send my regards.

307 set on . . . before: start his troops moving early, at the lead.

Make and Verify Predictions What does the ghost's visit suggest to you? What do you think will happen at Philippi?

After You Read

Respond and Think Critically

Respond and Interpret
1. What do you think about the relationship between Brutus and Cassius?
2. Compare the political situation in Rome after Caesar's murder with that under Caesar's rule.
3. (a) What battle plan does Cassius propose? (b) Why does he agree to march to Philippi?

Analyze and Evaluate
4. (a) What is your impression of Antony in Act 4? (b) Do his actions surprise you? Explain.
5. Why, do you think, did Shakespeare include the conflict between Cassius and Brutus?
6. What is the purpose of the exchange in Brutus's tent between Brutus and Lucius as Brutus prepares to sleep (Scene 3, lines 239–244)?

Connect
7. **Big Idea** Loyalty and Betrayal What examples of loyalty do you see in this act of the play? Explain and give examples.
8. **Connect to Today** (a) What point does Shakespeare make about the effect of political power on those who hold it? (b) To which leaders in recent history might Shakespeare's point apply? Explain.

Literary Element Foil

One character's personality traits are sharper when a character with contrasting traits, a **foil**, is on stage.

1. (a) In Scene 1, which character serves as a foil to Antony? (b) What is the difference between that character and Antony?
2. What differences do you see between Cassius and Brutus? Explain.

Reading Strategy Make and Verify Predictions

In making a prediction when you read, you generally look for evidence and then make an informed guess, using your knowledge of life and human behavior. Review the chart you made on page 783 and then answer the following questions.

1. What have you predicted correctly in the play so far? What has surprised you? Explain.
2. What will happen at Philippi? Why?

Literature Online

Selection Resources For Selection Quizzes, eFlashcards, and Reading-Writing Connection activities, go to glencoe.com and enter QuickPass code GL59794u4.

Vocabulary Practice

Practice with Denotation and Connotation
Denotation is the literal, or dictionary, meaning of a word. **Connotation** is the implied, or cultural, meaning of a word. For example, the words *feeble* and *weak* have a similar denotation, "lack of strength or vigor," but they have different connotations.

Negative weak   More Negative feeble

Each of the vocabulary words is listed with a word that has a similar denotation. Choose the word that has a more negative connotation.

1. barren   empty
2. covert   secret
3. deceitful   false
4. rash   careless

Writing

Write a Journal Entry In your journal, describe a quarrel you had with a close friend. What caused the disagreement? How did you try to settle it? Were you able to remain friends afterward? Compare your conflict with that between Cassius and Brutus.

Before You Read

The Tragedy of Julius Caesar, Act 5

Connect to the Play
Can a person commit violence without being harmed by it in some way? Discuss this question with a small group.

Build Background
Julius Caesar portrays Rome's transition from a republic to an empire. The republic was governed by citizen assemblies. The defeat of the republicans who assassinated Caesar ended Rome's republican form of rule.

Set Purposes for Reading

Big Idea Loyalty and Betrayal

As you read this act, ask yourself, Which characters display their loyalty to each other?

Literary Element Tragic Hero

A tragedy is a drama that ends in the downfall of its main character, or **tragic hero**. The tragic hero is usually a high-ranking or respected person who has a fatal weakness, or tragic flaw that causes his or her downfall. This flaw may be a good quality or virtue that is carried to excess. As you read, ask yourself, Which character or characters might be the tragic hero?

Reading Strategy Evaluate Characters

When you **evaluate characters**, you make judgments about their attitudes, actions, words, and ethics. Understanding why a character behaves in a certain way can improve your understanding of the character and the work as a whole. As you read, ask yourself, What details can help me assess each character?

Tip: Track Attitudes Use a chart to track your evaluations of the characters' actions and motivations.

Character	Detail	Significance of Detail
Octavius	Says "I was not born to die on Brutus' sword."	Octavius is determined. He will be a formidable opponent.

Learning Objectives

For pages 800–815

In this assignment, you will focus on the following objective:

Literary Study: Analyzing a tragic hero.

Reading: Evaluating characters.

Vocabulary

peevish (pē′vish) *adj.* irritable; bad-tempered; p. 803 *My reply was peevish due to lack of sleep.*

peril (per′əl) *n.* exposure to harm or danger; p. 804 *A mother elephant will always protect her offspring from peril.*

disconsolate (dis kon′sə lit) *adj.* dejected; mournful; unable to be comforted; p. 807 *Maria was disconsolate after missing a penalty shot in the playoffs.*

misconstrue (mis′kən strōō′) *v.* to misinterpret; to misunderstand; p. 808 *Diplomats choose their words carefully so they are not misconstrued.*

attain (ə tān′) *v.* to accomplish; to arrive at; p. 812 *If we work hard, we will attain our goal of graduating from high school.*

Tip: Analogies To complete an analogy, decide on the relationship represented by the first pair of words. Then apply that relationship to the second pair of words.

ACT 5

SCENE 1. The Plains of Philippi in Greece. A few weeks later.

[*Enter* OCTAVIUS, ANTONY, *and their* ARMY.]

OCTAVIUS. Now, Antony, our hopes are answered.
You said the enemy would not come down,
But keep the hills and upper regions.
It proves not so: their battles° are at hand;
5   They mean to warn° us at Philippi here,
Answering before we do demand of them.°

ANTONY. Tut, I am in their bosoms,° and I know
Wherefore they do it. They could be content
To visit other places, and come down
10 With fearful° bravery, thinking by this face
To fasten in our thoughts that they have courage;°
But 'tis not so.

[*Enter a* MESSENGER.]

MESSENGER.   Prepare you, generals,
The enemy comes on in gallant show;
Their bloody sign° of battle is hung out,
15 And something to be done immediately.

ANTONY. Octavius, lead your battle softly° on
Upon the left hand of the even° field.

OCTAVIUS. Upon the right hand I, keep thou the left.

ANTONY. Why do you cross me in this exigent?°

20 **OCTAVIUS.** I do not cross you; but I will do so.° [*March.*]

[*Drum. Enter* BRUTUS, CASSIUS, *and their* ARMY; LUCIUS, TITINIUS, MESSALA, *and others.*]

BRUTUS. They stand, and would have parley.°

CASSIUS. Stand fast, Titinius; we must out and talk.

OCTAVIUS. Mark Antony, shall we give sign of battle?

ANTONY. No, Caesar, we will answer on their charge.°
25 Make forth, the generals would have some words.

4 battles: armies.
5 warn: defy.
6 Answering before . . . them: responding hostilely before we even challenge them to fight.
7 am in their bosoms: know what is in their hearts.

8–11 They could . . . courage: Antony dismisses his enemy's bravery as a false show (**face**), saying that they would really prefer to be somewhere else.
10 fearful: "frightening" or "full of fear."

14 bloody sign: A red flag was flown from a Roman general's tent to signal the start of battle.
16 softly: slowly.
17 even: level.

19 cross me in this exigent: oppose me at this moment of crisis.
20 I will do so: I will do as I said. (Octavius insists on attacking from the right, which is usually the position of the most experienced general.)
21 would have parley: request a conference.

24 answer on their charge: respond when they attack.

Evaluate Characters *In your opinion, what quality or qualities does Octavius display here?*

Julius Caesar

OCTAVIUS. Stir not until the signal.

BRUTUS. Words before blows; is it so, countrymen?

OCTAVIUS. Not that we love words better, as you do.

BRUTUS. Good words are better than bad strokes, Octavius.

30 **ANTONY.** In your bad strokes, Brutus, you give good words;
Witness the hole you made in Caesar's heart,
Crying, "Long live! hail, Caesar!"

CASSIUS.   Antony,
The posture of your blows are yet unknown;°
But for your words, they rob the Hybla° bees,
35 And leave them honeyless.

ANTONY.   Not stingless too?

BRUTUS. O, yes, and soundless too;
For you have stol'n their buzzing, Antony,
And very wisely threat before you sting.

ANTONY. Villains! you did not so, when your vile daggers
40 Hack'd one another in the sides of Caesar.
You show'd your [teeth]° like apes, and fawn'd like hounds,
And bow'd like bondmen, kissing Caesar's feet;
Whilst damned Casca, like a cur, behind
Struck Caesar on the neck, O you flatterers!

45 **CASSIUS.** Flatterers? Now, Brutus, thank yourself;
This tongue had not offended so today,
If Cassius might have rul'd.°

OCTAVIUS. Come, come, the cause.° If arguing make us sweat,
The proof of it° will turn to redder drops.
50 Look,
I draw a sword against conspirators;
When think you that the sword goes up again?°
Never, till Caesar's three and thirty wounds
Be well aveng'd; or till another Caesar
55 Have added slaughter to the sword of traitors.°

BRUTUS. Caesar, thou canst not die by traitors' hands,
Unless thou bring'st them with thee.°

OCTAVIUS.   So I hope;
I was not born to die on Brutus' sword.

---

33 The posture . . . unknown: We don't know what kind of blows you will strike.
34 Hybla: an area in Sicily noted for its honey. (Cassius is reminding Antony of his "sweet" words to the conspirators after the assassination.)

41 show'd your [teeth]: grinned.

47 If Cassius . . . rul'd: if Cassius had had his way (when he argued that Antony should be killed).
48 cause: business at hand.
49 The proof of it: deciding the argument in battle.

52 goes up again: goes back into its sheath.

54–55 till another . . . traitors: until the conspirators have killed another Caesar (that is, Octavius himself).
56–57 Caesar . . . thee: Brutus suggests that all the traitors are on the side of Octavius and Antony.

Loyalty and Betrayal *Of what flaw does Antony accuse Brutus and Cassius?*

Tragic Hero *What error on Brutus's part does Cassius allude to here?*

BRUTUS. O, if thou wert the noblest of thy strain,°
Young man, thou couldst not die more honorable.

CASSIUS. A **peevish** schoolboy,° worthless of such honor,
Join'd with a masker and a reveler!°

ANTONY. Old Cassius still!

OCTAVIUS. Come, Antony; away!
Defiance, traitors, hurl we in your teeth.
If you dare fight today, come to the field;
If not, when you have stomachs.°

[*Exit OCTAVIUS, ANTONY, and ARMY.*]

CASSIUS. Why, now blow wind, swell billow, and swim bark!
The storm is up, and all is on the hazard.°

BRUTUS. Ho, Lucilius, hark, a word with you.

[*LUCILIUS and (then) MESSALA stand forth.*]

LUCILIUS. My lord?

[*BRUTUS and LUCILIUS converse apart.*]

CASSIUS. Messala!

MESSALA. What says my general?

CASSIUS. Messala,
This is my birthday; as this very day
Was Cassius born. Give me thy hand, Messala;
Be thou my witness that against my will
(As Pompey was)° am I compell'd to set
Upon one battle all our liberties.
You know that I held Epicurus strong,°
And his opinion; now I change my mind,
And partly credit things that do presage.°
Coming from Sardis, on our former ensign°
Two mighty eagles fell, and there they perch'd,
Gorging and feeding from our soldiers' hands,
Who to Philippi here consorted° us.
This morning are they fled away and gone,
And in their steads do ravens, crows, and kites°
Fly o'er our heads, and downward look on us
As° we were sickly prey. Their shadows seem
A canopy most fatal, under which

---

59 strain: family.

61 schoolboy: Octavius was twenty-one at the time of the battle.
62 a masker and a reveler: one who indulges in lavish entertainment and drunken feasts.

66 stomachs: appetite for battle.

68 all is . . . hazard: Everything is at stake.

74 As Pompey was: Pompey was persuaded against his better judgment to fight at Pharsalus, where he was defeated by Caesar.
76 held Epicurus strong: have been a firm believer of Epicurus (a Greek philosopher whose followers did not believe in omens).
78 presage: foretell the future.
79 former ensign: foremost banner.
82 consorted: accompanied.

84 kites: hawks. (All three birds are omens of death.)

86 As: As if.

Evaluate Characters *What is Cassius's judgment of Antony? Do you agree?*

Vocabulary

peevish (pē′vish) *adj.* irritable; bad-tempered

JULIUS CAESAR

Our army lies, ready to give up the ghost.

MESSALA. Believe not so.

CASSIUS. I but believe it partly,
For I am fresh of spirit, and resolv'd
To meet all **perils** very constantly.°

BRUTUS. Even so, Lucilius.°

CASSIUS. Now, most noble Brutus,
The gods today stand friendly, that we may,
Lovers in peace, lead on our days to age!°
But since the affairs of men rests still incertain,
Let's reason with the worst that may befall.°
If we do lose this battle, then is this
The very last time we shall speak together:
What are you then determined to do?

BRUTUS. Even by the rule of that philosophy
By which I did blame Cato for the death
Which he did give himself—I know not how,
But I do find it cowardly and vile,
For fear of what might fall, so to prevent
The time of life—arming myself with patience
To stay the providence of some high powers
That govern us below.°

CASSIUS. Then, if we lose this battle,
You are contented to be led in triumph
Thorough the streets of Rome?

BRUTUS. No, Cassius, no. Think not, thou noble Roman,
That ever Brutus will go bound to Rome;
He bears too great a mind.° But this same day
Must end that work the ides of March begun.
And whether we shall meet again I know not;
Therefore our everlasting farewell take:
Forever, and forever, farewell, Cassius!
If we do meet again, why, we shall smile;
If not, why then this parting was well made.

91 constantly: resolutely.

92 Even so, Lucilius: Brutus finishes his discussion with Lucilius.

93–94 The gods . . . age: May the gods remain friendly today, so that we, dear friends in peace with each other, may live to see old age.

96 Let's reason . . . befall: Let's consider the worst that can happen.

100–107 Even by the . . . below: Brutus says that according to his beliefs, suicide is cowardly (he refers to his father-in-law, Cato, who killed himself after Caesar's defeat of Pompey). He would endure his fate rather than cut short (**prevent**) his life because of what might happen.

110–112 Think not . . . mind: Brutus is suggesting that even though he rejects suicide, his pride would force him to commit such an act rather than allow himself to be paraded through the streets of Rome.

Tragic Hero What are Brutus's beliefs concerning honor?

Evaluate Characters How would you describe Brutus and Cassius as they say good-bye to each other?

Vocabulary

peril (per′əl) *n.* exposure to harm or danger

Warrior on his death bed surrounded by mourners, 2nd century C.E. Artist unknown. Relief on a funeral stele. Museo Ostiense, Ostia, Italy.

CASSIUS. Forever, and forever, farewell, Brutus!
If we do meet again, we'll smile indeed;
If not 'tis true this parting was well made.

BRUTUS. Why then, lead on. O, that a man might know
The end of this day's business ere it come!
But it sufficeth that the day will end,
And then the end is known. Come, ho, away!

[BRUTUS, CASSIUS, and their ARMY withdraw to begin the battle.]

SCENE 2. The field of battle. Shortly afterward.

[*Alarm. Enter* BRUTUS *and* MESSALA.]

BRUTUS. Ride, ride, Messala, ride, and give these bills°
Unto the legions on the other side.°

[*Loud alarm.*]

Let them set on at once; for I perceive
But cold demeanor° in Octavio's wing,
And sudden push gives them the overthrow.
Ride, ride, Messala, let them all come down.

[*They exit.*]

1 **bills:** written orders.
2 **legions on . . . side:** other wing of troops (led by Cassius).

4 **cold demeanor:** lack of spirit.

SCENE 3. Another part of the battlefield. Several hours later.

[*Alarms. Enter* CASSIUS *and* TITINIUS.]

CASSIUS. O, look, Titinius, look, the villains° fly!
Myself have to mine own turn'd enemy.°
This ensign° here of mine was turning back;
I slew the coward, and did take it° from him.

TITINIUS. O Cassius, Brutus gave the word too early,
Who, having some advantage on Octavius,
Took it too eagerly. His soldiers fell to spoil,°
Whilst we by Antony are all enclos'd.

[*Enter* PINDARUS.]

PINDARUS. Fly further off, my lord, fly further off;
Mark Antony is in your tents,° my lord;
Fly, therefore, noble Cassius, fly far off.

CASSIUS. This hill is far enough. Look, look, Titinius!
Are those my tents where I perceive the fire?

TITINIUS. They are, my lord.

1 **villains:** Cassius's own troops (who are retreating).
2 **Myself have . . . enemy:** I have turned to fighting my own men.
3 **ensign:** standard bearer.
4 **it:** the standard, or army flag.

7 **spoil:** looting.

10 **tents:** camp.

Loyalty and Betrayal Who has betrayed Cassius's army? What has Cassius done about it?

JULIUS CAESAR

CASSIUS. Titinius, if thou lovest me,
15 Mount thou my horse, and hide° thy spurs in him
Till he have brought thee up to yonder troops.
And here again, that I may rest assur'd
Whether yond troops are friend or enemy.

TITINIUS. I will be here again, even with a thought.°

[*Exit.*]

20 **CASSIUS.** Go, Pindarus, get higher on that hill;
My sight was ever thick;° regard Titinius,
And tell me what thou not'st about the field.

[*PINDARUS goes up.*]

This day I breathed first: time is come round,
And where I did begin, there shall I end;
25 My life is run his compass.° Sirrah, what news?

PINDARUS. [*Above.*] O my lord!

CASSIUS. What news?

PINDARUS. Titinius is enclosed round about
With horsemen, that make to him on the spur,°
30 Yet he spurs on. Now they are almost on him.
Now, Titinius! Now some light.° O, he lights too!
He's ta'en!° [*Shout.*] And, hark, they shout for joy.

CASSIUS. Come down; behold no more.
O, coward that I am, to live so long,
35 To see my best friend ta'en before my face!

[*PINDARUS descends.*]

Come hither, sirrah.
In Parthia did I take thee prisoner,
And then I swore thee, saving of thy life,°
That whatsoever I did bid thee do,
40 Thou shouldst attempt it. Come now, keep thine oath;
Now be a freeman, and with this good sword,
That ran through Caesar's bowels, search° this bosom.
Stand not° to answer; here, take thou the hilts,°
And when my face is cover'd, as 'tis now,

---

15 hide: dig.

19 even with a thought: as quick as a thought.

21 My sight . . . thick: I have always been nearsighted.

25 is run his compass: has come full circle.

29 make to . . . spur: ride quickly toward him.

31 some light: some of them dismount.

32 ta'en: taken prisoner.

38 swore thee . . . life: made you swear when I saved your life.

42 search: penetrate.
43 Stand not: don't wait. **hilts:** sword handles.

Tragic Hero *From the reports of Titinius and Pindarus, what does Cassius believe is happening?*

Evaluate Characters *In your opinion, what does this remark indicate about the character of Cassius?*

45	Guide thou the sword. [*PINDARUS stabs him.*] Caesar, thou art reveng'd,
	Even with the sword that kill'd thee. [*Dies.*]
	PINDARUS. So, I am free; yet would not so have been,
	Durst I have done my will. O Cassius,
	Far from this country Pindarus shall run,
50	Where never Roman shall take note of him. [*Exit.*]

[*Enter TITINIUS and MESSALA.*]

MESSALA. It is but change,° Titinius; for Octavius
 Is overthrown by noble Brutus' power,
 As Cassius' legions are by Antony.

TITINIUS. These tidings will well comfort Cassius.

55 MESSALA. Where did you leave him?

TITINIUS.   All **disconsolate**,
 With Pindarus his bondman, on this hill.

MESSALA. Is not that he that lies upon the ground?

TITINIUS. He lies not like the living. O my heart!

MESSALA. Is not that he?

TITINIUS.   No, this was he, Messala,
60 But Cassius is no more. O setting sun,
 As in thy red rays thou dost sink tonight,
 So in his red blood Cassius' day is set!
 The sun of Rome is set. Our day is gone,
 Clouds, dews,° and dangers come; our deeds are done!
65 Mistrust of my success° hath done this deed.

MESSALA. Mistrust of good success° hath done this deed.
 O hateful error, melancholy's child,°
 Why dost thou show to the apt° thoughts of men
 The things that are not? O error, soon conceiv'd,
70 Thou never com'st unto a happy birth,
 But kill'st the mother that engend'red thee!°

TITINIUS. What, Pindarus? Where art thou, Pindarus?

MESSALA. Seek him, Titinius, whilst I go to meet
 The noble Brutus, thrusting this report

---

51 but change: only an exchange of fortune. (Pindarus was mistaken when he reported Titinius's capture—he had in fact come upon Brutus's troops.)

64 dews: Dews were considered unhealthy.
65 Mistrust of my success: Fear of my mission's outcome.
66 Mistrust of good success: Fear of how the battle would turn out.
67 O hateful . . . child: Messala suggests that Cassius's melancholy temperament caused him to misperceive events.
68 apt: ready (to be deceived).

71 the mother . . . thee: the mind that conceived the error.

Loyalty and Betrayal *What Roman ideas about loyalty and destiny are suggested by this passage?*

Vocabulary

disconsolate (dis kon′sə lit) *adj.* dejected; mournful; unable to be comforted

Julius Caesar

75 Into his ears; I may say "thrusting" it;
For piercing steel and darts° envenomed
Shall be as welcome to the ears of Brutus
As tidings of this sight.

TITINIUS. Hie you, Messala,
And I will seek for Pindarus the while.

[*Exit* MESSALA.]

76 **darts:** arrows.

80 Why didst thou send me forth, brave Cassius?
Did I not meet thy friends? and did not they
Put on my brows this wreath of victory,
And bid me give it thee? Didst thou not hear their shouts?
Alas, thou hast **misconstrued** everything.
85 But hold thee, take this garland on thy brow;
Thy Brutus bid me give it thee, and I
Will do his bidding. Brutus, come apace,°
And see how I regarded° Caius Cassius.
By your leave, gods!—this is a Roman's part;°
90 Come, Cassius' sword, and find Titinius' heart. [*Dies.*]

87 **apace:** quickly.
88 **regarded:** honored.
89 **By your . . . part:** Titinius asks the gods to pardon him because he is cutting his life short to fulfill a Roman's duty (**part**).

[*Alarm. Enter* BRUTUS, MESSALA, LUCILIUS, VOLUMNIUS, YOUNG CATO, *and* STRATO.]

BRUTUS. Where, where, Messala, doth his body lie?

MESSALA. Lo, yonder, and Titinius mourning it.

BRUTUS. Titinius' face is upward.

CATO.° He is slain.

BRUTUS. O Julius Caesar, thou art mighty yet!
95 Thy spirit walks abroad, and turns our swords
In our own proper° entrails. [*Low alarms.*]

CATO. Brave Titinius!
Look, whe'er he have not crown'd° dead Cassius!

BRUTUS. Are yet two Romans living such as these?
The last of all the Romans, fare thee well!
100 It is impossible that ever Rome
Should breed thy fellow.° Friends, I owe moe° tears

93 **Cato:** Brutus's brother-in-law, the son of Marcus Cato.

96 **our own proper:** our very own.

97 **Look . . . crown'd:** see how he has crowned.

101 **fellow:** equal. **moe:** more.

Evaluate Characters *What do you learn of Cassius's character from the reactions of Messala and Titinius to his death?*

Loyalty and Betrayal *Why does Brutus invoke the name of Julius Caesar?*

Vocabulary

misconstrue (mis′kən strōō′) *v.* to misinterpret; to misunderstand

Base of the Column of Antoninus Pius, AD 138–161, Roman. Vatican State.

View the Art In what ways does this scene add to your understanding of the battles in this play?

To this dead man than you shall see me pay.
I shall find time, Cassius; I shall find time.
Come, therefore, and to Thasos° send his body;
105 His funerals shall not be in our camp,
Lest it discomfort° us. Lucilius, come,
And come, young Cato; let us to the field.
Labio and Flavio set our battles on.
'Tis three a'clock; and, Romans, yet ere night
110 We shall try fortune in a second fight.
[*They exit.*]

104 Thasos: an island near Philippi.

106 discomfort: dishearten.

SCENE 4. Another part of the battlefield. Shortly later.

[*Alarm. Enter* BRUTUS, MESSALA, *(young)* CATO, LUCILIUS, *and* FLAVIUS.]

BRUTUS. Yet, countrymen, O, yet hold up your heads!°
 [*They exit.*]

CATO. What bastard doth not?° Who will go with me?
 I will proclaim my name about the field.
 I am the son of Marcus Cato,° ho!
5 A foe to tyrants, and my country's friend.
 I am the son of Marcus Cato, ho!

[*Enter* SOLDIERS *and fight.*]

1 Yet . . . heads: Brutus urges his troops to keep fighting.
2 What bastard doth not: Who among us was born so low that he doesn't?
4 Marcus Cato: Portia's father.

Tragic Hero What admirable qualities does Brutus display in this scene?

 JULIUS CAESAR

LUCILIUS. And I am Brutus, Marcus Brutus, I;
Brutus, my country's friend; know me for Brutus!°

[*YOUNG CATO is slain.*]

O young and noble Cato, art thou down?
10   Why, now thou diest as bravely as Titinius,
And mayst be honor'd, being Cato's son.

FIRST SOLDIER. Yield, or thou diest.

LUCILIUS.   Only I yield to die;
There is so much that thou wilt kill me straight:°
Kill Brutus, and be honor'd in his death.

15   **FIRST SOLDIER.** We must not. A noble prisoner!

[*Enter ANTONY.*]

SECOND SOLDIER. Room, ho! Tell Antony, Brutus is ta'en.

FIRST SOLDIER. I'll tell the news. Here comes the general.
Brutus is ta'en. Brutus is ta'en, my lord.

ANTONY. Where is he?

20   **LUCILIUS.** Safe, Antony, Brutus is safe enough.
I dare assure thee that no enemy
Shall ever take alive the noble Brutus;
The gods defend him from so great a shame!
When you do find him, or alive or° dead,
25   He will be found like Brutus, like himself.°

ANTONY. This is not Brutus, friend, but, I assure you,
A prize no less in worth. Keep this man safe,
Give him all kindness; I had rather have
Such men my friends than enemies. Go on,
30   And see whe'er Brutus be alive or dead,
And bring us word unto Octavius' tent
How everything is chanc'd.

[*They exit.*]

SCENE 5. Another part of the field. Late in the day.

[*Enter BRUTUS, CLITUS, DARDANIUS, VOLUMNIUS, and STRATO.*]

BRUTUS. Come, poor remains of friends, rest on this rock.

7–8 And I am . . . Brutus: Lucilius impersonates his leader to divert the enemy's attention from the real Brutus.

13 There is . . . straight: You have good reason to kill me immediately.

24 or . . . or: either . . . or.
25 like himself: behaving like his noble self.

Evaluate Characters What character traits does Shakespeare give the officers in the army of Cassius and Brutus?

Evaluate Characters What traits does Antony show in his response to Lucilius's admission that he is not actually Brutus?

CLITUS. Statilius show'd the torchlight,° but, my lord,
   He came not back. He is or ta'en or slain.
BRUTUS. Sit thee down, Clitus; slaying is the word,
   It is a deed in fashion.° Hark thee, Clitus. [*Whispering.*]
CLITUS. What, I, my lord? No, not for all the world.
BRUTUS. Peace then, no words.
CLITUS.   I'll rather kill myself.
BRUTUS. Hark thee, Dardanius. [*Whispering.*]
DARDANIUS.   Shall I do such a deed?
CLITUS. O Dardanius!
DARDANIUS. O Clitus!
CLITUS. What ill request did Brutus make to thee?
DARDANIUS. To kill him, Clitus. Look, he meditates.
CLITUS. Now is that noble vessel full of grief,
   That it runs over even at his eyes.
BRUTUS. Come hither, good Volumnius; list° a word.
VOLUMNIUS. What says my lord?
BRUTUS.   Why, this, Volumnius;
   The ghost of Caesar hath appear'd to me
   Two several° times by night; at Sardis once,
   And this last night, here in Philippi fields.
   I know my hour is come.
VOLUMNIUS.   Not so, my lord.
BRUTUS. Nay, I am sure it is, Volumnius.
   Thou seest the world, Volumnius, how it goes;°
   Our enemies have beat us to the pit.°

[*Low alarms.*]

   It is more worthy to leap in ourselves
   Than tarry till they push us. Good Volumnius,
   Thou know'st that we two went to school together;
   Even for that our love of old, I prithee
   Hold thou my sword-hilts, whilst I run on it.
VOLUMNIUS. That's not an office° for a friend, my lord.

[*Alarm still.*]

CLITUS. Fly, fly, my lord, there is no tarrying here.
BRUTUS. Farewell to you, and you, and you, Volumnius.
   Strato, thou hast been all this while asleep;

---

2 show'd the torchlight: signaled with a torch. (Statilius was sent out to see whether their camp was occupied by the enemy.)

5 It is ... fashion: So many are being killed.

15 list: hear.

18 several: separate.

22 Thou seest ... goes: You see how things are going.
23 pit: a hole into which hunted animals are driven (also, a grave).

29 office: job.

Tragic Hero What does Clitus think of Brutus?

 JULIUS CAESAR

Farewell to thee too, Strato. Countrymen,
My heart doth joy° that yet in all my life
35 I found no man but he was true to me.°
I shall have glory by this losing day
More than Octavius and Mark Antony
By this vile conquest shall **attain** unto.°
So fare you well at once, for Brutus' tongue
40 Hath almost ended his life's history.
Night hangs upon mine eyes; my bones would rest,
That have but labor'd to attain this hour.

34 **joy:** rejoice.
35 **no man . . . me:** no man to be unfaithful to me.
36–38 **I shall . . . unto:** I shall have more glory from this defeat than Octavius and Antony will achieve from their ignoble victory.

[*Alarm. Cry within, "Fly, fly, fly!"*]

CLITUS. Fly, my lord, fly!

BRUTUS. 					Hence! I will follow.

[*CLITUS, DARDANIUS, and VOLUMNIUS exit.*]

I prithee, Strato, stay thou by thy lord,
45 Thou art a fellow of a good respect;°
Thy life hath had some smatch° of honor in it.
Hold then my sword, and turn away thy face,
While I do run upon it. Wilt thou, Strato?

45 **respect:** reputation.
46 **smatch:** taste.

STRATO. Give me your hand first. Fare you well, my lord.

50 BRUTUS. Farewell, good Strato. [*Runs on his sword.*] Caesar, now be still,
I kill'd not thee with half so good a will.

[*Dies.*]

[*Alarm. Retreat. Enter* ANTONY, OCTAVIUS, MESSALA, LUCILIUS, *and the* ARMY.]

OCTAVIUS. What man is that?

MESSALA. My master's man. Strato, where is thy master?

STRATO. Free from the bondage you are in, Messala;
55 The conquerors can but make a fire of him;
For Brutus only overcame himself,°
And no man else hath honor by his death.

56 **Brutus . . . himself:** only Brutus conquered himself.

LUCILIUS. So Brutus should be found. I thank thee, Brutus,
That thou hast prov'd Lucilius' saying true.

Evaluate Characters What judgments of Brutus might you form based on his request?

Vocabulary

attain (ə tān´) *v.* to accomplish; to arrive at

Trajan's Column, AD 112–113. Roman. Marble, approximately 68 m. Rome.

View the Art What scene from the play is depicted here? Why do you think so?

60	**OCTAVIUS.** All that serv'd Brutus, I will entertain them.° Fellow, wilt thou bestow thy time with me?	**60 entertain them:** take them into my service.
	STRATO. Ay, if Messala will prefer° me to you.	**62 prefer:** recommend.
	OCTAVIUS. Do so, good Messala.	
	MESSALA. How died my master, Strato?	
65	**STRATO.** I held the sword, and he did run on it.	
	MESSALA. Octavius, then take him to follow thee, That did the latest° service to my master.	**67 latest:** last.
70	**ANTONY.** This was the noblest Roman of them all; All the conspirators, save only he, Did that they did in envy of great Caesar; He, only in a general honest thought And common good to all, made one of them.° His life was gentle,° and the elements So mix'd in him that Nature might stand up	**71–72 He, only . . . them:** He joined them only with honorable intentions for the public good. **73 gentle:** noble. **73–75 His life . . . man:** The Elizabethans believed that four elements (earth, water, air, and fire) in the body determined a person's temperament. Antony says that in Brutus the elements were perfectly balanced.
75	And say to all the world, "This was a man!"°	
	OCTAVIUS. According to his virtue let us use° him, With all respect and rites of burial. Within my tent his bones tonight shall lie, Most like a soldier, ordered honorably.°	**76 use:** treat. **79 ordered honorably:** with all due honor.
80	So call the field to rest, and let's away, To part° the glories of this happy day. [*All exit.*]	**81 part:** divide.

Tragic Hero How does Antony claim that Brutus was different from the other conspirators? Do you agree with him? Explain.

After You Read

Respond and Think Critically

Respond and Interpret

1. What went through your mind as you finished reading this play? Explain.

2. (a) What event leads to Cassius's death? (b) What influenced Cassius to accept Pindarus's report?

3. (a) What does Brutus say about Caesar's spirit at Philippi? (b) In what way does Brutus believe that Caesar is affecting the events on the battlefield? Support your answer with evidence from Act 5.

4. (a) What happens to Brutus at the end of the play? (b) What actions does Octavius take at the end of the play? (c) What message do Octavius's actions suggest about leadership?

Analyze and Evaluate

5. Compare Antony's speech at the end of the play with his remarks about Brutus at Caesar's funeral. (a) How have his views of Brutus changed? (b) Why have they changed?

6. Are Antony and Octavius motivated more by the desire for power or the wish to avenge Caesar's death? Explain and cite examples.

7. What do you consider the most significant mistake committed at Philippi? Explain.

Connect

8. **Big Idea** Loyalty and Betrayal (a) What loyalties would you say are strongest in this play? (b) What betrayals seem the most damaging?

9. **Connect to Today** How might the experiences of a modern-day audience at a performance of *Julius Caesar* differ from those of Shakespeare's original audience?

Primary Visual Artifact

Statues of Caesar

In the days before photography, how was the memory of a person's appearance kept alive? If you were a wealthy Roman, you likely commissioned an artist to paint or sculpt the face of the person you wanted to remember. Artists also created busts, or sculpted representations of the upper part of the human figure. One figure of Caesar stood in a Roman temple with the inscription, "To the undefeated god." To celebrate the circus games, Romans carried an ivory likeness of Caesar through the streets. Many antique busts of Caesar still survive.

Group Activity Discuss the following questions with your classmates.

1. What aspects of Caesar's character does this bust reveal?

2. Do you think that a piece of sculpture, such as this one, can convey certain human qualities better than a photograph can? Explain.

Contemporary bust of Gaius Julius Caesar, c. 60–44 B.C. Capitoline Palace, Rome.

Literary Element Tragic Hero

More than one character in *Julius Caesar* might be considered the **tragic hero**. Caesar is the title character, and his death is the central event in the play. However, the play focuses more on Brutus and ends with his death rather than Caesar's death.

1. (a)State Caesar's tragic flaw. (b)State Brutus's.
2. Which character's fate is more tragic? Explain.

Review: Theme

As you learned on page 3, the **theme** of a piece of literature is a central idea, or universal message about life, that the writer communicates. Works of literature can have more than one theme.

Partner Activity With a classmate, identify one important theme of *Julius Caesar*. Together create a web diagram like the one below. First, write the theme in the central oval. Next, fill in the outer ovals with evidence that supports the theme.

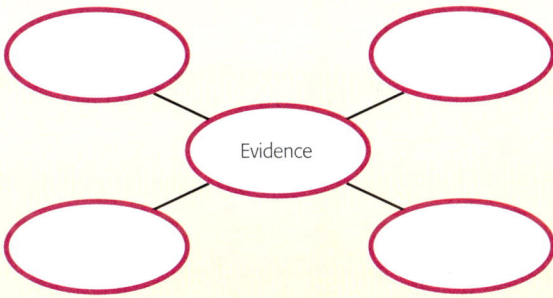

Then discuss the following questions about theme:

1. (a)Is the theme you identified **stated** (expressed directly) or **implied** (revealed gradually)? (b)Give examples from the text that support your choice and demonstrate how your theme is expressed directly or is suggested or gradually revealed.
2. Is your theme related to the Big Idea of loyalty and betrayal? Explain and give five examples.

 **Literature** Online

Selection Resources For Selection Quizzes, eFlashcards, and Reading-Writing Connection activities, go to glencoe.com and enter QuickPass code GL59794u4.

Reading Strategy Evaluate Characters

When you **evaluate a character**, you make judgments about his or her abilities and qualities.

1. (a)Which aspects of Caesar's character do you consider admirable? (b)Which aspects of his character are you critical of? Explain.
2. (a)In the first half of the play, what judgments do you form about Cassius? (b)Do these judgments change as the play progresses? Explain.
3. Do you agree with Antony that all the conspirators, except Brutus, are motivated by envy? Support your opinion with examples from the play.

Vocabulary Practice

Practice with Analogies Choose the word that best completes each analogy.

1. peevish : pleasant :: brief :
   a. sad   b. abbreviated   c. lengthy
2. danger : peril :: fear :
   a. terror   b. confidence   c. enjoyment
3. joyous : victory :: disconsolate :
   a. loss   b. sadness   c. consolation
4. bolster : undermine :: misconstrue :
   a. understand   b. confuse   c. steal
5. improve : practice :: attain :
   a. mistake   b. fail   c. strive

Academic Vocabulary

In Act I of *Julius Caesar,* Shakespeare presents the *hierarchy* of power in Rome, with Caesar at the top, the senators below him, and the commoners at the bottom.

Hierarchy is an academic word. People might refer to the **hierarchy,** or system of ranking, at the state and federal levels of government. Businesses, sports teams, and armies have a **hierarchical** structure. To explore the meaning, describe a **hierarchy** that you are familiar with.

For more on academic vocabulary, see pages 52 and 53.

Respond Through Writing

Biographical Narrative

Apply Point of View In *Julius Caesar,* Shakespeare dramatizes the events surrounding the assassination of one of ancient Rome's most powerful leaders. Think of what you learn about Julius Caesar from the details that Shakespeare provides in the play. Then write a biographical narrative of Julius Caesar, using the third-person point of view.

Understand the Task A **biographical narrative** is a story in which an author tells a sequence of events from someone else's life and reveals their significance. In **third-person point of view,** the narrator is someone outside the narrative.

Prewrite Complete a timeline like the following on which you list the key events that involve Caesar.

| Caesar tells Antony to touch Calphurnia in the race at the Saturnalia. | → | The ghost of Caesar appears to Brutus at Philippi. | → | |

Then determine your purpose and identify your audience, such as to explain Caesar's motives to your teacher and classmates. Freewrite for ten minutes to get the basic events of Caesar's life down on paper.

Draft As you draft, keep in mind the dominant impression that you want to convey to your audience. Consider whether Caesar seems to be a tyrant, hungry for power, or a good leader, devoted to the Roman people. Relate a sequence of events and communicate their significance. As you write, use concrete details (who, what, when, and where) and sensory details (sights, sounds, smells, tastes, and textures) to describe actions, events, thoughts, and feelings. These should connect to the dominant impression you reveal in your narrative. Use transitional words and phrases to connect events.

Revise After writing your narrative, reread your draft to make sure that you have used concrete and sensory details to describe the events and the setting. Then exchange essays with a classmate and evaluate each other's work. Does the narrative convey a dominant impression of Caesar? Do the events included in the narrative support that impression? Provide comments for your classmate and revise your essay according to the comments you receive.

Edit and Proofread Proofread your paper, correcting any errors in grammar, spelling, and punctuation. Use the Grammar Tip in the side column to help you with commas with appositives.

Learning Objectives

In this assignment, you will focus on the following objectives:

Writing: Writing a biographical narrative.

Grammar: Understanding how to use commas with appositives.

Grammar Tip

Commas with Appositives

An appositive is a noun or pronoun placed next to another noun or pronoun to identify it or give additional information about it. Use commas to set off an appositive if it is not essential to the meaning of a sentence.

*Caesar, a **military leader,** is the most powerful man in Rome.*

Do not set off an appositive if it gives necessary information about the noun. *Caesar is wary of the conspirator **Cassius.***

PART 2

Portraits of Real Life

Marian Anderson, Singer, 1944. Laura Wheeler Waring. Oil on canvas. National Portrait Gallery, Smithsonian Institution, Washington, DC.

View the Art Marian Anderson began her singing career in a church as a young girl. In 1955, she became the first African American to sing with the New York Metropolitan Opera. How would you describe this painting? What does it suggest about the plays you will read in this part of the unit?

BIG IDEA

When reading a comedy, sometimes it is hard to know whether to laugh or cry. People find humor in the mistakes and misfortunes that comic characters experience. Maybe we laugh because we know that, in real life, we could be in their situations. Part 2 includes plays set in realistic situations. As you read, ask yourself, What is most interesting about realistic plays? Do they mirror life as it really is?

Learning Objectives

For pages 818–819
In studying this text, you will focus on the following objective:

Literary Study: Analyzing form and structure.

LITERARY FOCUS

Comedy and Modern Drama

What are the elements of modern drama?

Modern drama often deals with everyday people. Characters in modern plays can be average people involved in personal, even petty conflicts.

Drama can be used as a synonym for *play*. Drama is traditionally separated into subcategories of comedy and tragedy. The form of a drama can include acts (large divisions) and scenes (smaller divisions within acts).

Comedy In the broadest sense, a **comedy** is a play that is humorous and often has a happy ending. Comedies typically poke fun at people's faults and limitations in order to teach something about human nature. There are different styles of comedy. **Farce** places flat characters in ridiculous situations. **Satire** exposes and ridicules vice or folly in individuals or societies. In this scene from Anton Chekhov's *A Marriage Proposal*, after fighting bitterly with Lomov, Natalia becomes hysterical upon learning that Lomov meant to propose to her.

Modern Drama While satire and farce use deliberately unrealistic situations and characters, many modern plays find their humor and sadness in everyday life. Such plays can be either comedy or tragedy, but they often do not follow the traditional elements of these forms.

In *That's Your Trouble*, for example, Harold Pinter uses everyday language to create a dialogue between two characters in a park. A conflict arises when they argue about whether a stranger will get a headache from wearing a sandwich board. Though comic on the surface, this Absurdist play suggests an underlying message about the nature of human interactions.

Dialogue

Dialogue is the conversation characters have in a play. In the example below, Lomov and Natalia are the names of the characters who are speaking. The name of the character is followed by what the character is to say.

NATALIA. He's a monster! First he tries to steal our land, and then he has the nerve to yell at you.
CHUBUKOV. Yes, and that turnip, that stupid rooster, has the gall to make a proposal. Some proposal!
NATALIA. What proposal?
CHUBUKOV. Why, he came to propose to you.
NATALIA. To propose? To me? Why didn't you tell me before?
CHUBUKOV. So he gets all dressed up in his formal clothes. That stuffed sausage, that dried up cabbage!
NATALIA. To propose to me? Ohhhh! [*Falls into a chair and starts wailing.*] Bring him back! Back! Go get him! Bring him back! Ohhhh!

NATALIA. I hate to interrupt you, my dear Ivan Vassilevitch, but you said: "my Oxen Meadows." Do you really think they're yours?
LOMOV. Why of course they're mine.
NATALIA. What do you mean? The Oxen Meadows are ours, not yours!
LOMOV. Oh, no, my dear Natalia Stepanovna, they're mine.

—Anton Chekhov, **from** *A Marriage Proposal*

Stage Directions

Stage directions are indications to the director, to the actors, and to the reader that describe the appearance of characters as well as details such as sets, props, costumes, sound effects, and lighting. Stage directions also act as a guide to specific actions, such as entrances and exits of the characters, as well as to the delivery of lines—which characters are being addressed and how.

Notice the references to actions and props in the stage directions below. The stage directions appear in italics within brackets.

MARICA. [*Trying to hide the bottle behind her.*] Raquel! What are you doing here?
RAQUEL. What did you have hidden behind the books, Marica?
MARICA. [*Attempting a forced laugh.*] I? Nothing. Why do you think I have anything?
RAQUEL. [*Taking a step toward her.*] Give it to me.
MARICA. [*Backing away from her.*] No. No, I won't.

—Josephina Niggli, from *The Ring of General Macías*

Props

Short for the word *properties,* **props** are the objects and elements of a stage play or movie set. Props are often mentioned in stage directions.

RAQUEL. Good night, little one.
[*MARICA goes out through the house door Left, taking her candle with her. RAQUEL stares down at the bottle of poison in her hand, then puts it away in one of the small drawers of the desk.*]

—Josephina Niggli, from *The Ring of General Macías*

Quickwrite

Write Dialogue Use the explanations and examples on this page as you compose dialogue. Create a graphic organizer like the one below and briefly sketch characters. Identify a conflict between them. Write what they would say to each other.

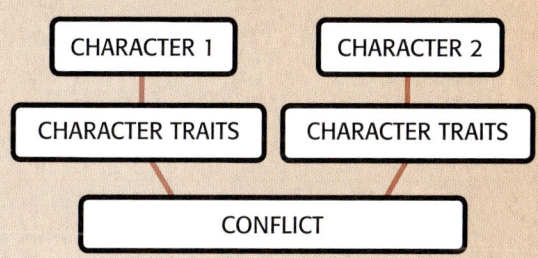

Literature and Reading For more about literary elements, go to glencoe.com and enter QuickPass code GL59794u4.

Before You Read

A Marriage Proposal

World Literature
Russia

Meet Anton Chekhov
(1860–1904)

Anton Chekhov was an unlikely genius. Who would suspect that a provincial Russian doctor and the son of a grocer would revolutionize literature? As a doctor, Chekhov was trained to observe and analyze without judging his patients; in his writing, he applied the same principles to his characters. Chekhov's stories and plays focused on everyday life, illuminating the human flaws and the failures all people experience. His new approach helped popularize the Realist school of writing.

Humble Beginnings At age sixteen, Chekhov lived alone and supported himself. His father had gone bankrupt and rushed the rest of the family to Moscow to avoid debtor's prison. Chekhov remained at home to complete his studies while supporting himself as a tutor. Three years later, in 1879, Chekhov joined his family to study medicine on scholarship at the University of Moscow. He was deeply affected by his family's financial failure, and he would frequently turn to similar themes and situations in his plays and short stories.

> "The dramatist is not meant to be a judge of his characters and what they say; his only job is to be an impartial witness."
>
> —Anton Chekhov

While he was studying medicine, Chekhov began selling anecdotes and articles to comic magazines as a way of supporting his family. In these humorous pieces, critics see the revolutionary techniques that flourished in his later works.

A "Real" Writer By 1885 Chekhov had begun submitting his stories to more serious literary journals and magazines. In 1888 he won Russia's coveted Pushkin Prize for his short story collection *In the Twilight*.

In 1895 Chekhov decided to focus on playwriting. Following the successful second run of the *Seagull* in 1898, Chekhov continued to write plays for the Moscow Art Theatre. He described his plays, including *Uncle Vanya*, *Three Sisters*, and *The Cherry Orchard*, as light social comedies. He was annoyed by productions that staged the plays as melodramas.

Just as he began to experience great success on the stage, Chekhov's career was cut short. Untreated tuberculosis had weakened his heart. He died of a heart attack at the age of forty-four. His style of narrative realism would later influence nearly every major playwright of the twentieth century, including George Bernard Shaw, Samuel Beckett, Eugene O'Neill, and Tom Stoppard.

 **Literature** Online

Author Search For more about Anton Chekhov, go to glencoe.com and enter QuickPass code GL59794u4.

Literature and Reading Preview

Connect to the Play
Have you ever made plans that someone or something later interfered with? Write a journal entry describing this experience.

Build Background
In the late 1800s, Russian serfs had been freed, yet aristocratic farmers still depended on servants to work on their estates. Chekhov's plays give a sense that the "old" Russia was dying.

Set Purposes for Reading

Big Idea Portraits of Real Life

As you read this play, ask yourself, How do Chekhov's characters' speech and actions mimic those in real life?

Literary Element Farce

A **farce** is a type of comedy with stereotyped characters in ridiculous situations. In a farce, an author uses physical action, exaggeration, improbable events, and surprises to make the audience laugh. Farce is one way to make fun of human traits and social customs. As you read, ask yourself, Which traits and customs is Chekhov highlighting?

Reading Strategy Recognize Author's Purpose

Authors often write for a particular purpose: to entertain, to inform or teach a lesson, to tell a story, to try to persuade readers to accept an idea, or for a variety of other purposes. As you read, ask yourself, What is Chekhov's purpose?

Tip: Note Details Use a graphic organizer like the one below to help you track details and draw conclusions about them.

Details	Conclusions
Chubukov repeats the phrase "and so forth" often.	Chekhov uses this character trait to show how Chubukov speaks without purpose, repeating these words that really have no meaning.

Learning Objectives

For pages 820–835

In studying this text, you will focus on the following objectives:

Literary Study: Analyzing farce.

Reading: Recognizing author's purpose.

Vocabulary

impudence (im′ pyə dəns) *n.* speech or behavior that is aggressively forward or rude; p. 826
Arnie showed his impudence when he cut in front of those who had been standing in the lunch line.

oblivious (ə bliv′ ē əs) *adj.* unmindful or unaware; not noticing; p. 833
Ana and Maria were oblivious to their teacher's desire to start class.

ANTON CHEKHOV **821**

A Marriage Proposal

Anton Chekhov
Translated by Theodore Hoffman

Return from the Fair, 1883. Illarion Mikhailovich Pryanishnikov. Oil on canvas, 48.5 x 71.5 cm. State Russian Museum, St. Petersburg.

View the Art Nineteenth century rural life in Russia was hard for the peasant class. How do the details in this image affect your understanding of the play?

CHARACTERS

STEPAN STEPANOVITCH CHUBUKOV
(ste pän′ ste pä′nô vich choo boo′ kôf):
a landowner; elderly, pompous but affable

IVAN VASSILEVITCH LOMOV
(i vän′ vä sil′ē yich lô′môf):
a landowner and Chubukov's neighbor; healthy, but a hypochondriac; nervous, suspicious

NATALIA STEPANOVNA (nä täl′yə ste pä nôv′ nə):
Chubukov's daughter; twenty-five but still unmarried

SCENE: Chubukov's mansion—the living room

[*LOMOV enters, formally dressed in evening jacket, white gloves, top hat. He is nervous from the start.*]

CHUBUKOV. [*Rising.*] Well, look who's here! Ivan Vassilevitch! [*Shakes his hand warmly.*] What a surprise, old man! How are you?

LOMOV. Oh, not too bad. And you?

CHUBUKOV. Oh, we manage, we manage. Do sit down, please. You know, you've been neglecting your neighbors, my dear fellow. It's been ages. Say, why the formal dress? Tails, gloves, and so forth. Where's the funeral, my boy? Where are you headed?

LOMOV. Oh, nowhere. I mean, here; just to see you, my dear Stepan Stepanovitch.

CHUBUKOV. Then why the full dress, old boy? It's not New Year's, and so forth.

LOMOV. Well, you see, it's like this. I have come here, my dear Stepan Stepanovitch, to bother you with a request. More than once, or twice, or more than that, it has been my privilege to apply to you for assistance in things, and you've always, well, responded. I mean, well, you have. Yes. Excuse me, I'm getting all mixed up. May I have a glass of water, my dear Stepan Stepanovitch? [*Drinks.*]

CHUBUKOV. [*Aside.*] Wants to borrow some money. Not a chance! [*Aloud.*] What can I do for you my dear friend?

LOMOV. Well, you see, my dear Stepanitch. . . . Excuse me, I mean Stepan my Dearovitch. . . . No, I mean, I get all confused, as you can see. To make a long story short, you're the only one who can help me. Of course, I don't deserve it, and there's no reason why I should expect you to, and all that.

CHUBUKOV. Stop beating around the bush! Out with it!

LOMOV. In just a minute. I mean, now, right now. The truth is, I have come to ask the hand. . . . I mean, your daughter, Natalia Stepanovna, I, I want to marry her!

CHUBUKOV. [*Overjoyed.*] Great heavens! Ivan Vassilevitch! Say it again!

LOMOV. I have come humbly to ask for the hand. . . .

CHUBUKOV. [*Interrupting.*] You're a prince! I'm overwhelmed, delighted, and so forth. Yes, indeed, and all that! [*Hugs and kisses LOMOV.*] This is just what I've been hoping for. It's my fondest dream come true. [*Sheds a tear.*] And, you know, I've always looked upon you, my boy, as if you were my own son. May God grant to both of you His Mercy and His Love, and so forth. Oh, I have been wishing for this. . . . But

---

Portraits of Real Life How would you describe Lomov's manner here?

Recognize Author's Purpose Why does Chekhov have Chubukov respond in this way?

ANTON CHEKHOV

why am I being so idiotic? It's just that I'm off my rocker with joy, my boy! Completely off my rocker! Oh, with all my soul I'm.... I'll go get Natalia, and so forth.

LOMOV. [*Deeply moved.*] Dear Stepan Stepanovitch, do you think she'll agree?

CHUBUKOV. Why, of course, old friend. Great heavens! As if she wouldn't! Why she's crazy for you! Good God! Like a love-sick cat, and so forth. Be right back. [*Leaves.*]

LUMOV. It's cold. I'm gooseflesh all over, as if I had to take a test. But the main thing is, to make up my mind, and keep it that way. I mean, if I take time out to think, or if I hesitate, or talk about it, or have ideals, or wait for real love, well, I'll just never get married! Brrrr, it's cold! Natalia Stepanovna is an excellent housekeeper. She's not too bad looking. She's had a good education. What more could I ask? Nothing. I'm so nervous, my ears are buzzing. [*Drinks.*] Besides, I've just got to get married. I'm thirty-five already. It's sort of a critical age. I've got to settle down and lead a regular life. I mean, I'm always getting palpitations,[1] and I'm nervous, and I get upset so easy. Look, my lips are quivering, and my eyebrow's twitching. The worst thing is the night. Sleeping. I get into bed, doze off, and, suddenly, something inside me jumps. First my head snaps, and then my shoulder blade, and I roll out of bed like a lunatic and try to walk it off. Then I try to go back to sleep, but, as soon as I do, something jumps again! Twenty times a night, sometimes....

---

1. If Lomov does in fact get *palpitations*, he experiences rapid, irregular heartbeats, which are often caused by stress or nervousness.

Farce What makes Chubukov's reaction to Lomov's request an example of farce?

Recognize Author's Purpose How do you think Chekhov wants the audience to feel about Lomov?

[*NATALIA STEPANOVNA enters.*]

NATALIA. Oh, it's only you. All Papa said was: "Go inside, there's a merchant come to collect his goods." How do you do, Ivan Vassilevitch?

LOMOV. How do you do, dear Natalia Stepanovna?

NATALIA. Excuse my apron, and not being dressed. We're shelling peas. You haven't been around lately. Oh, do sit down. [*They do.*] Would you like some lunch?

LOMOV. No thanks, I had some.

NATALIA. Well, then smoke if you want. [*He doesn't.*] The weather's nice today ... but yesterday, it was so wet the workmen couldn't get a thing done. Have you got much hay in? I felt so greedy I had a whole field done, but now I'm not sure I was right. With the rain it could rot, couldn't it? I should have waited. But why are you so dressed up? Is there a dance or something? Of course, I must say you look splendid, but.... Well, tell me, why are you so dressed up?

LOMOV. [*Excited.*] Well, you see, my dear Natalia Stepanovna, the truth is, I made up my mind to ask you to ... well, to, listen to me. Of course, it'll probably surprise you and even maybe make you angry, but.... [*Aside.*] It's so cold in here!

NATALIA. Why, what do you mean? [*A pause.*] Well?

LOMOV. I'll try to get it over with. I mean, you know, my dear Natalia Stepanovna that I've known, since childhood, even, known, and had the privilege of knowing, your family. My late aunt, and her husband, who, as you know, left me my estate, they always had the greatest respect for your father, and your late mother. The Lomovs and the Chubukovs have always been very friendly,

Portraits of Real Life Why do you suppose it is taking so long for Lomov to ask Natalia his question?

you might even say affectionate. And, of course, you know, our land borders on each other's. My Oxen Meadows touch your birch grove. . . .

NATALIA. I hate to interrupt you, my dear Ivan Vassilevitch, but you said: "my Oxen Meadows." Do you really think they're yours?

LOMOV. Why of course they're mine.

NATALIA. What do you mean? The Oxen Meadows are ours, not yours!

LOMOV. Oh, no, my dear Natalia Stepanovna, they're mine.

NATALIA. Well, this is the first I've heard about it! Where did you get that idea?

LOMOV. Where? Why, I mean the Oxen Meadows that are wedged between your birches and the marsh.

NATALIA. Yes, of course, they're ours.

LOMOV. Oh, no, you're wrong, my dear Natalia Stepanovna, they're mine.

NATALIA. Now, come, Ivan Vassilevitch! How long have they been yours?

LOMOV. How long! Why, as long as I can remember!

NATALIA. Well, really, you can't expect me to believe that!

LOMOV. But, you can see for yourself in the deed, my dear Natalia Stepanovna. Of course, there was once a dispute about them, but everyone knows they're mine now. There's nothing to argue about. There was a time when my aunt's grandmother let your father's grandfather's peasants use the land, but they were supposed to bake bricks for her in return. Naturally, after a few years they began to act as if they owned it, but the real truth is. . . .

NATALIA. That has nothing to do with the case! Both my grandfather and my great-grandfather said that their land went as far as the marsh, which means that the Meadows are ours! There's nothing whatever to argue about. It's foolish.

LOMOV. But I can show you the deed, Natalia Stepanovna.

NATALIA. You're just making fun of me. . . . Great Heavens! Here we have the land for hundreds of years, and suddenly you try to tell us it isn't ours. What's wrong with you, Ivan Vassilevitch? Those meadows aren't even fifteen acres, and they're not worth three hundred rubles, but I just can't stand unfairness! I just can't stand unfairness!

LOMOV. But, you must listen to me. Your father's grandfather's peasants, as I've already tried to tell you, they were supposed to bake bricks for my aunt's grandmother. And my aunt's grandmother, why, she wanted to be nice to them. . . .

NATALIA. It's just nonsense, this whole business about aunts and grandfathers and grandmothers. The Meadows are ours! That's all there is to it!

LOMOV. They're mine!

NATALIA. Ours! You can go on talking for two days, and you can put on fifteen evening coats and twenty pairs of gloves, but I tell you they're ours, ours, ours!

LOMOV. Natalia Stepanovna, I don't want the Meadows! I'm just acting on principle. If you want, I'll give them to you.

NATALIA. I'll give them to *you!* Because they're ours! And that's all there is to it! And if I may say so, your behavior, my dear Ivan Vassilevitch, is very strange. Until now, we've always considered you a

---

Portraits of Real Life What does Natalia and Lomov's conversation tell you about the life of the Russian aristocracy in the nineteenth century?

good neighbor, even a friend. After all, last year we lent you our threshing machine, even though it meant putting off our own threshing until November. And here you are treating us like a pack of gypsies. Giving me my own land, indeed! Really! Why that's not being a good neighbor. It's sheer **impudence**, that's what it is. . . .

LOMOV. Oh, so you think I'm just a land-grabber? My dear lady, I've never grabbed anybody's land in my whole life, and no one's going to accuse me of doing it now! [*Quickly walks over to the pitcher and drinks some more water.*] The Oxen Meadows are mine!

NATALIA. That's a lie. They're ours!

LOMOV. Mine!

NATALIA. A lie! I'll prove it. I'll send my mowers out there today!

LOMOV. What?

NATALIA. My mowers will mow it today!

LOMOV. I'll kick them out!

NATALIA. You just dare!

LOMOV. [*Clutching his heart.*] The Oxen Meadows are mine! Do you understand? Mine!

NATALIA. Please don't shout! You can shout all you want in your own house, but here I must ask you to control yourself.

LOMOV. If my heart wasn't palpitating the way it is, if my insides weren't jumping like mad, I wouldn't talk to you so calmly. [*Yelling.*] The Oxen Meadows are mine!

NATALIA. Ours!

LOMOV. Mine!

Farce How does Chekhov make Lomov's behavior farcical here?

Vocabulary

impudence (im′pyə dəns) *n.* speech or behavior that is aggressively forward or rude

NATALIA. Ours!

LOMOV. Mine!

[*Enter* CHUBUKOV.]

CHUBUKOV. What's going on? Why all the shouting?

NATALIA. Papa, will you please inform this gentleman who owns the Oxen Meadows, he or we?

CHUBUKOV. [*To* LOMOV.] Why, they're ours, old fellow.

LOMOV. But how can they be yours, my dear Stepan Stepanovitch? Be fair. Perhaps my aunt's grandmother did let your grandfather's peasants work the land, and maybe they did get so used to it that they acted as if it was their own, but. . . .

CHUBUKOV. Oh, no, no . . . my dear boy. You forget something. The reason the peasants didn't pay your aunt's grandmother, and so forth, was that the land was disputed, even then. Since then it's been settled. Why, everyone knows it's ours.

LOMOV. I can prove it's mine.

CHUBUKOV. You can't prove a thing, old boy.

LOMOV. Yes, I can!

CHUBUKOV. My dear lad, why yell like that? Yelling doesn't prove a thing. Look, I'm not after anything of yours, just as I don't intend to give up anything of mine. Why should I? Besides, if you're going to keep arguing about it, I'd just as soon give the land to the peasants, so there!

LOMOV. There nothing! Where do you get the right to give away someone else's property?

CHUBUKOV. I certainly ought to know if I have the right or not. And you had better

---

Farce What makes Chubukov's statement here ridiculous?

Agnus. Peter Harrap. Oil on canvas. Private collection.

realize it, because, my dear young man, I am not used to being spoken to in that tone of voice, and so forth. Besides which, my dear young man, I am twice as old as you are, and I ask you to speak to me without getting yourself into such a tizzy, and so forth!

LOMOV. Do you think I'm a fool? First you call my property yours, and then you expect me to keep calm and polite! Good neighbors don't act like that, my dear Stepan Stepanovitch. You're no neighbor, you're a land grabber!

CHUBUKOV. What was that? What did you say?

NATALIA. Papa, send the mowers out to the meadows at once!

CHUBUKOV. What did you say, sir?

NATALIA. The Oxen Meadows are ours, and we'll never give them up, never, never, never, never!

LOMOV. We'll see about that. I'll go to court. I'll show you!

CHUBUKOV. Go to court? Well, go to court, and so forth! I know you, just waiting for a chance to go to court, and so forth. You pettifogging[2] cheater, you! All of your family is like that. The whole bunch of them!

LOMOV. You leave my family out of this! The Lomovs have always been honorable, upstanding people, and not a one of them was ever tried for embezzlement,[3] like your grandfather was.

CHUBUKOV. The Lomovs are a pack of lunatics, the whole bunch of them!

NATALIA. The whole bunch!

CHUBUKOV. Your grandfather was a drunkard, and what about your other aunt, the one who ran away with the architect? And so forth.

NATALIA. And so forth!

LOMOV. Your mother limped! [*Clutches at his heart.*] Oh, I've got a stitch in my side.... My head's whirling.... Help! Water!

CHUBUKOV. Your father was a gambler.

NATALIA. And your aunt was queen of the scandalmongers![4]

LOMOV. My left foot's paralyzed. You're a plotter.... Oh, my heart. It's an open secret that in the last elections you brib.... I'm seeing stars! Where's my hat?

NATALIA. It's a low-mean, spiteful....

CHUBUKOV. And you're a two-faced, malicious schemer!

LOMOV. Here's my hat.... Oh, my heart.... Where's the door? How do I get out of here?... Oh, I think I'm going to die.... My foot's numb. [*Goes.*]

CHUBUKOV. [*Following him.*] And don't you ever set foot in my house again!

NATALIA. Go to court, indeed! We'll see about that!

[LOMOV *staggers out.*]

CHUBUKOV. The devil with him! [*Gets a drink, walks back and forth excited.*]

NATALIA. What a rascal! How can you trust your neighbors after an incident like that?

CHUBUKOV. The villain! The scarecrow!

NATALIA. He's a monster! First he tries to steal our land, and then he has the nerve to yell at you.

---

2. A *pettifogging* person squabbles over unimportant matters or uses mean, tricky methods.
3. *Embezzlement* is the act of stealing money entrusted to one's care; a bank official, for example, might embezzle funds from customers' accounts.

Recognize Author's Purpose What do you think is Chekhov's purpose in including this detail?

---

4. People who spread vicious gossip are *scandalmongers*.

Farce How does Lomov's hypochondria contribute to the farcical aspects of the play?

CHUBUKOV. Yes, and that turnip, that stupid rooster, has the gall[5] to make a proposal. Some proposal!

NATALIA. What proposal?

CHUBUKOV. Why, he came to propose to you.

NATALIA. To propose? To me? Why didn't you tell me before?

CHUBUKOV. So he gets all dressed up in his formal clothes. That stuffed sausage, that dried up cabbage!

NATALIA. To propose to me? Ohhhh! [*Falls into a chair and starts wailing.*] Bring him back! Back! Go get him! Bring him back! Ohhhh!

CHUBUKOV. Bring who back?

NATALIA. Hurry up, hurry up! I'm sick. Get him! [*Complete hysterics.*]

CHUBUKOV. What for? [*To her.*] What's the matter with you? [*Clutches his head.*] Oh, what a fool I am! I'll shoot myself! I'll hang myself! I ruined her chances!

NATALIA. I'm dying. Get him!

CHUBUKOV. All right, all right, right away! Only don't yell!

[*He runs out.*]

NATALIA. What are they doing to me? Get him! Bring him back! Bring him back!

[*A pause.* CHUBUKOV *runs in.*]

CHUBUKOV. He's coming, and so forth, the snake. Oof! You talk to him. I'm not in the mood.

NATALIA. [*Wailing.*] Bring him back! Bring him back!

---

5. *Gall*, a synonym for impudence, means "shocking boldness; scornful disrespect."

Farce *What makes Natalia's reaction here farcical?*

CHUBUKOV. [*Yelling.*] I told you, he's coming! What agony to be the father of a grown-up daughter. I'll cut my throat some day, I swear I will. [*To her.*] We cursed him, we insulted him, abused him, kicked him out, and now . . . because you, you. . . .

NATALIA. Me? It was all your fault!

CHUBUKOV. My fault? What do you mean my fau . . . ? [LOMOV *appears in the doorway.*] Talk to him yourself! [*Goes out.* LOMOV *enters, exhausted.*]

LOMOV. What palpitations! My heart! And my foot's absolutely asleep. Something keeps giving me a stitch in the side. . . .

NATALIA. You must forgive us, Ivan Vassilevitch. We all got too excited. I remember now. The Oxen Meadows are yours.

LOMOV. My heart's beating something awful. My Meadows. My eyebrows, they're both twitching!

NATALIA. Yes, the Meadows are all yours, yes, yours. Do sit down. [*They sit.*] We were wrong, of course.

LOMOV. I argued on principle. My land isn't worth so much to me, but the principle. . . .

NATALIA. Oh, yes, of course, the principle, that's what counts. But let's change the subject.

LOMOV. Besides, I have evidence. You see, my aunt's grandmother let your father's grandfather's peasants use the land. . . .

NATALIA. Yes, yes, yes, but forget all that. [*Aside.*] I wish I knew how to get him going. [*Aloud.*] Are you going to start hunting soon?

Recognize Author's Purpose *What is the author saying here about his characters' convictions?*

> *To propose to me? Ohhhhhhh!*

LOMOV. After the harvest I'll try for grouse.[6] But oh, my dear Natalia Stepanovna, have you heard about the bad luck I've had? You know my dog, Guess? He's gone lame.

NATALIA. What a pity. Why?

LOMOV. I don't know. He must have twisted his leg, or got in a fight, or something. [*Sighs.*] My best dog, to say nothing of the cost. I paid Mironov 125 rubles for him.

NATALIA. That was too high, Ivan Vassilevitch.

LOMOV. I think it was quite cheap. He's a first class dog.

NATALIA. Why Papa only paid 85 rubles for Squeezer, and he's much better than Guess.

LOMOV. Squeezer better than Guess! What an idea! [*Laughs.*] Squeezer better than Guess!

NATALIA. Of course he's better. He may still be too young but on points[7] and pedigree,[8] he's a better dog even than any Volchanetsky owns.

LOMOV. Excuse me, Natalia Stepanovna, but you're forgetting he's overshot, and overshot dogs are bad hunters.

NATALIA. Oh, so he's overshot, is he? Well, this is the first time I've heard about it.

LOMOV. Believe me, his lower jaw is shorter than his upper.

NATALIA. You've measured them?

LOMOV. Yes. He's all right for pointing, but if you want him to retrieve. . . .

---

6. A fowl-like bird, the *grouse* is often hunted for game or food.
7. Natalia is referring to her dog's physical characteristics and ancestry. In dog shows today, a dog is judged on specific characteristics, or *points*. Each breed has point standards that cover everything from skull shape and tail length to eye color and hair texture.
8. A dog's ancestry, or *pedigree*, is proof that a dog is purebred.

NATALIA. In the first place, our Squeezer is a thoroughbred, the son of Harness and Chisel, while your mutt doesn't even have a pedigree. He's as old and worn out as a peddler's horse.

LOMOV. He may be old, but I wouldn't take five Squeezers for him. How can you argue? Guess is a dog, Squeezer's a laugh. Anyone you can name has a dog like Squeezer hanging around somewhere. They're under every bush. If he only cost twenty-five rubles you got cheated.

NATALIA. The devil is in you today, Ivan Vassilevitch! You want to contradict everything. First you pretend the Oxen Meadows are yours, and now you say Guess is better than Squeezer. People should say what they really mean, and you know Squeezer is a hundred times better than Guess. Why say he isn't?

LOMOV. So, you think I'm a fool or a blind man, Natalia Stepanovna! Once and for all, Squeezer is overshot!

NATALIA. He is not!

LOMOV. He is so!

NATALIA. He is not!

LOMOV. Why shout, my dear lady?

NATALIA. Why talk such nonsense? It's terrible. Your Guess is old enough to be buried, and you compare him with Squeezer!

LOMOV. I'm sorry, I can't go on. My heart . . . it's palpitating!

NATALIA. I've always noticed that the hunters who argue most don't know a thing.

LOMOV. Please! Be quiet a moment. My heart's falling apart. . . . [*Shouts.*] Shut up!

Farce How does the argument over the dogs increase the farcical element of the play?

Golden Autumn in the Village, 1889. Isaak Ilyich Levitan. Oil on canvas, 43 x 67.2 cm. State Russian Museum, St. Petersburg.

NATALIA. I'm not going to shut up until you admit that Squeezer's a hundred times better than Guess.

LOMOV. A hundred times worse! His head. . . . My eyes . . . shoulder . . .

NATALIA. Guess is half-dead already!

LOMOV. [*Weeping.*] Shut up! My heart's exploding!

NATALIA. I won't shut up!

[*CHUBUKOV comes in.*]

CHUBUKOV. What's the trouble now?

NATALIA. Papa, will you please tell us which is the better dog, his Guess or our Squeezer?

LOMOV. Stepan Stepanovitch, I implore you to tell me just one thing: Is your Squeezer overshot or not? Yes or no?

CHUBUKOV. Well what if he is? He's still the best dog in the neighborhood, and so forth.

LOMOV. Oh, but isn't my dog, Guess, better? Really?

CHUBUKOV. Don't get yourself so fraught up,[9] old man. Of course, your dog has his

---

9. The expression *fraught up* means "excited; charged up."

good points—thoroughbred, firm on his feet, well sprung ribs, and so forth. But, my dear fellow, you've got to admit he has two defects; he's old and he's short in the muzzle.

LOMOV. Short in the muzzle? Oh, my heart! Let's look at the facts! On the Marusinsky hunt my dog ran neck and neck with the Count's, while Squeezer was a mile behind them. . . .

CHUBUKOV. That's because the Count's groom hit him with a whip.

LOMOV. And he was right, too! We were fox hunting; what was your dog chasing sheep for?

CHUBUKOV. That's a lie! Look, I'm going to lose my temper . . . [*Controlling himself.*] my dear friend, so let's stop arguing, for that reason alone. You're only arguing because we're all jealous of somebody else's dog. Who can help it? As soon as you realize some dog is better than yours, in this case our dog, you start in with this and that, and the next thing you know—pure jealousy! I remember the whole business.

LOMOV. I remember too!

> *Ha! You only go hunting to get in good with the count, and to plot, and intrigue, and scheme. . . .*

Farce How does Chekhov make Chubukov's insight here seem humorous?

CHUBUKOV. [*Mimicking.*] "I remember too!" What do you remember?

LOMOV. My heart . . . my foot's asleep . . . I can't . . .

NATALIA. [*Mimicking.*] "My heart . . . my foot's asleep." What kind of a hunter are you? You should be hunting cockroaches in the kitchen, not foxes. "My heart!"

CHUBUKOV. Yes, what kind of a hunter are you anyway? You should be sitting at home with your palpitations, not tracking down animals. You don't hunt anyhow. You just go out to argue with people and interfere with their dogs, and so forth. For God's sake, let's change the subject before I lose my temper. Anyway, you're just not a hunter.

LOMOV. But you, you're a hunter? Ha! You only go hunting to get in good with the count, and to plot, and intrigue, and scheme. . . . Oh, my heart! You're a schemer, that's what!

CHUBUKOV. What's that? Me a schemer? [*Shouting.*] Shut up!

LOMOV. A schemer!

CHUBUKOV. You infant! You puppy!

LOMOV. You old rat!

CHUBUKOV. You shut up, or I'll shoot you down like a partridge! You fool!

LOMOV. Everyone knows that—oh, my heart—that your wife used to beat you. . . . Oh, my feet . . . my head . . . I'm seeing stars . . . I'm going to faint! [*He drops into an armchair.*] Quick, a doctor! [*Faints.*]

CHUBUKOV. [*Going on, **oblivious**.*] Baby! Weakling! Fool! I'm getting sick. [*Drinks water.*] Me! I'm sick!

NATALIA. What kind of a hunter are you? You can't even sit on a horse! [*To her father.*] Papa, what's the matter with him? Look, papa! [*Screaming.*] Ivan Vassilevitch! He's dead.

CHUBUKOV. I'm choking, I can't breathe. . . . Give me air.

NATALIA. He's dead! [*Pulling LOMOV's sleeve.*] Ivan Vassilevitch! Ivan Vassilevitch! What have you done to me? He's dead! [*She falls into an armchair. Screaming hysterically.*] A doctor! A doctor! A doctor!

CHUBUKOV. Ohhhh. . . . What's the matter? What happened?

NATALIA. [*Wailing.*] He's dead! He's dead!

CHUBUKOV. Who's dead? [*Looks at LOMOV.*] My God, he is! Quick! Water! A doctor! [*Puts glass to LOMOV's lips.*] Here, drink this! Can't drink it—he must be dead, and so forth. . . . Oh what a miserable life! Why don't I shoot myself! I should have cut my throat long ago! What am I waiting for? Give me a knife! Give me a pistol! [*LOMOV stirs.*] Look, he's coming to. Here, drink some water. That's it.

Portraits of Real Life What do you think audiences in Russia when this play was first produced would have thought of this recent argument?

Farce Do you think Lomov is actually dead? Why or why not?

Vocabulary

oblivious (ə bliv´ē əs) *adj.* unmindful or unaware; not noticing

LOMOV. I'm seeing stars . . . misty . . . Where am I?

CHUBUKOV. Just you hurry up and get married, and then the devil with you! She accepts. [*Puts LOMOV's hand in NATALIA's.*] She accepts and so forth! I give you my blessing, and so forth! Only leave me in peace!

LOMOV. [*Getting up.*] Huh? What? Who?

CHUBUKOV. She accepts! Well? Kiss her!

NATALIA. He's alive! Yes, yes, I accept.

CHUBUKOV. Kiss each other!

LOMOV. Huh? Kiss? Kiss who? [*They kiss.*] That's nice. I mean, excuse me, what happened? Oh, now I get it . . . my heart . . . those stars . . . I'm very happy, Natalia Stepanovna. [*Kisses her hand.*] My foot's asleep.

NATALIA. I . . . I'm happy too.

CHUBUKOV. What a load off my shoulders! Whew!

NATALIA. Well, now maybe you'll admit that Squeezer is better than Guess?

LOMOV. Worse!

NATALIA. Better!

CHUBUKOV. What a way to enter matrimonial bliss! Let's have some champagne!

LOMOV. He's worse!

NATALIA. Better! Better, better, better, better!

CHUBUKOV. [*Trying to shout her down.*] Champagne! Bring some champagne! Champagne! Champagne!

CURTAIN

Farce What makes this dialogue humorous?

After You Read

Respond and Think Critically

Respond and Interpret

1. Did you like the ending of the play? Explain why or why not.

2. (a) Why has Lomov come to Chubukov's house? (b) What does his behavior tell you about his personality?

3. (a) What is the cause of both arguments? (b) Why, in your opinion, do the arguments start so easily?

Analyze and Evaluate

4. Compare and contrast the bickering between characters in the play with similar interactions you have witnessed between people in real life. How is it similar? How is it different?

5. (a) In your opinion, are Lomov and Natalia a good match for each other? Explain. (b) Do you think they should marry? Why or why not?

6. Does the **dialogue**, or speech, in Chekhov's play seem realistic to you? Why or why not?

Connect

7. **Big Idea** Portraits of Real Life Chekhov's aristocratic characters seem to be in their own little world; they have no interaction with people outside the Russian provinces. Do you think this detail is realistic for Chekhov's time and place? For yours?

8. **Connect to Today** Even though they argue constantly, Lomov and Natalia marry because they feel like they are running out of time. Why do people today get married?

Literary Element Farce

Many authors use **farce** to ridicule societal norms and make their audiences laugh. In *A Marriage Proposal*, Chekhov has Lomov continually complain about physical ailments in order to mock him.

1. List three examples of statements made by the characters that made you laugh. Tell what you think Chekhov is mocking in each example.

2. Identify three points in this play that you found particularly funny. Why are they humorous? What techniques of farce does Chekhov use to create each situation?

Review: Irony

As you learned on page 158, **irony** is a contrast between expectation and reality. In **situational irony,** the outcome of a situation is the opposite of what is expected. In **dramatic irony,** the audience knows something that the characters do not know.

Partner Activity Find one example of situational irony and one example of dramatic irony in the play and record them in a chart as below. With a partner, discuss your examples and how audiences—teenagers, single adults, couples, socialites, homeowners—may react to them. Share your findings with your class.

Example	Type of Irony	Audience & Reaction
When Natalia enters on p. 824, she does not know that Lomov intends to propose.	Dramatic irony—the audience knows Lomov's intent.	

 **Literature** Online

Selection Resources For Selection Quizzes, eFlashcards, and Reading-Writing Connection activities, go to glencoe.com and enter QuickPass code GL59794u4.

Reading Strategy: Recognize Author's Purpose

SAT Skills Practice

1. One of Chekhov's reasons for writing *A Marriage Proposal* was probably to

   (A) mock the landowning class
   (B) satirize a society in which land ownership evoked more passion than marriage
   (C) point out how foolish it is to want to be married at any cost
   (D) suggest that most squabbles arise over property rights
   (E) make fun of hypochondriacs

Vocabulary Practice

Practice with Word Origins Studying the etymology, or origin and history, of a word helps you understand and explore its meaning. Create a word map, like the one below, for each of these vocabulary words from the play.

impudence   oblivious

EXAMPLE:

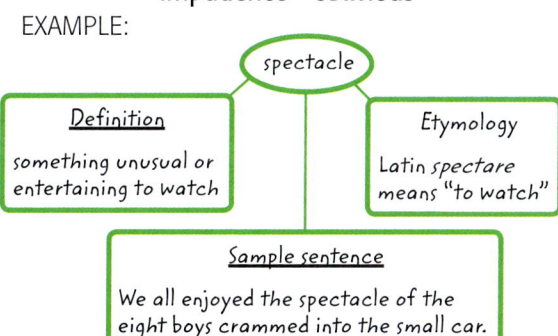

Academic Vocabulary

A reader can only wonder what married life will be like for the **couple** in *A Marriage Proposal*.

Couple is a multiple-meaning word. In casual conversation, a person might mention a **couple** of days. Using context clues, figure out the meaning of the word in the sentence about the play above. Check your guess in a dictionary.

For more on academic vocabulary, see pages 52–53.

Write with Style

Apply Irony

Assignment A twist ending, also known as a surprise ending, is a type of situational irony. Write a narrative of at least 750 words that includes a twist ending.

Get Ideas Look through newspapers, magazines, or blogs for accounts of events with unexpected outcomes. Choose an event and recount the story in your own words. Feel free to change or add to the story. Be sure to focus on the twist ending.

Give It Structure Make two timelines to list major story events. On the first, record the events that lead to an expected outcome. On the second, plot the events in your story that lead to the twist ending. As you write, draw on the first timeline for story structure and background information, but use the second timeline to create rising action and deliver the surprise ending.

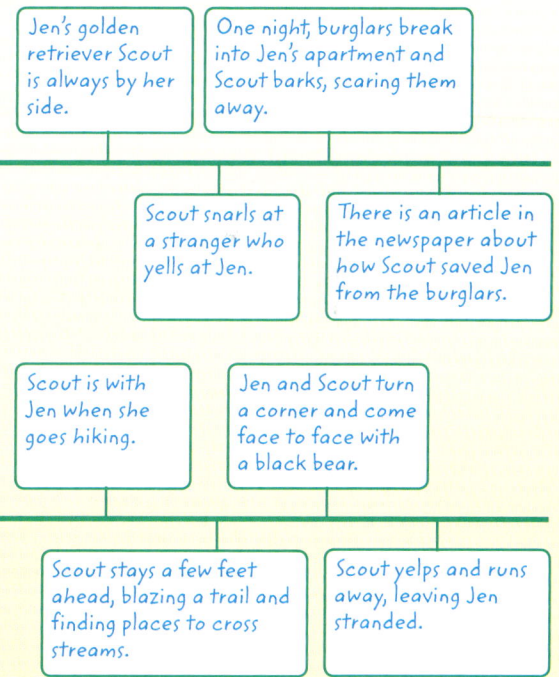

Look at Language Consider creating a completely detached tone that will keep the reader guessing. You may want to deliberately mislead the reader by emphasizing the wrong events or characteristics. As you revise, try to ensure that your twist ending is truly a surprise.

Learning Objectives

Grammar: Understand how to use commas with interjections and parenthetical expressions.

Grammar Workshop

Commas with Interjections and Parenthetical Expressions

Literature Connection In the quotation below, Chekhov introduces the sentences with the expressions *of course* and *well*.

> "Of course, I must say you look splendid, but . . . Well, tell me, why are you so dressed up?"
>
> — Anton Chekhov, from "A Marriage Proposal"

Of course is a **parenthetical expression,** which adds explanatory information to the sentence. Other common parenthetical expressions include *in fact, on the other hand, for example, by the way,* and *nevertheless.* The word *well* is an **interjection,** a word that expresses emotion. *Alas, good grief, oh, uh-oh, sorry,* and *wow* are other common interjections. Because interjections and parenthetical expressions have no grammatical connection to the rest of the sentence, they should be set off with commas.

Interjections These usually occur at the beginning of a sentence. Interjections that express strong emotion may be followed by an exclamation point.

> Sorry, we weren't expecting you.
> Good heavens, he was wearing a suit and top hat!

Parenthetical expressions These may appear at the beginning, at the end, or in the middle of a sentence and are set off by one or two commas.

> In fact, Lomov had come to Natalia with the intention of proposing.
> Lomov had come to Natalia, in fact, with the intention of proposing.
> Lomov had come to Natalia, with the intention of proposing, in fact.

Interjections and Parenthetical Expressions

Interjections and **parenthetical expressions** act as interrupters—to express emotion or add explanatory information. They have no grammatical connection to the rest of the sentence, however, so should be set off with commas.

Test-Taking Tip

Overuse of interjections and parenthetical expressions can make writing appear over-casual and informal, so use them sparingly when writing for a test.

Language Handbook

For more about interjections and parenthetical expressions, see the Language Handbook, pp. R40–R59.

Revise Rewrite these sentences to correct any comma mistakes.

1. Well if you check the background information, you can see that the story was written in the year 1888.
2. Oh I see that Chekhov had earned a degree in medicine.
3. Chekhov unfortunately was poor and had to support himself by writing hundreds of articles for comic magazines.
4. These writings on the other hand showed the revolutionary literary style and promise of the masterpieces he was soon to create.
5. One masterpiece is of course the one-act play "A Marriage Proposal."

Grammar For more grammar practice, go to glencoe.com and enter QuickPass code GL59794u4.

Before You Read

That's Your Trouble

World Literature: **England**

Meet **Harold Pinter**
(1930–2008)

After a performance of his play *The Collection*, Harold Pinter gave an unusual bit of feedback to one of the actors. "Michael, I wrote dot, dot, dot," Pinter told the actor, "and you're giving me dot, dot."

The comment was more than just critical nit-picking. As one of the twentieth century's top playwrights, Pinter reinvented the language of drama. Using small talk and long silences, he suggests deeper layers of meaning and conflict beneath the surface of daily life. In a style that has often been called "the comedy of menace," Pinter dramatizes tense, antagonistic relationships that break down into brutal power struggles. As a tribute to his unique style, critics have added a word to the *New Shorter Oxford English Dictionary*: "Pinteresque."

> *"There are no hard distinctions between what is real and what is unreal."*
>
> —Harold Pinter

Art and Danger As a child, Pinter experienced both beauty and violence. Pinter's father was a working-class tailor, but his family loved art and culture. In contrast, Pinter's mother came from a hard-scrabble family whose behavior, including that of her bare-knuckle boxer brother, sometimes verged on criminal.

The young Pinter also faced the terrors of World War II. Threatened by Nazi bombings, Pinter was twice evacuated from the city with other London children.

Stage and Screen In 1956 Pinter began writing his own plays. Influenced by Samuel Beckett, he also wrote Absurdist plays. One of his early plays, *The Birthday Party*, initially flopped, but it later won acclaim. Later successes included *The Caretaker* (1960) and *The Homecoming* (1965).

In *Betrayal* (1978), Pinter used material inspired by his life and wrote dialogue that was less stylized than in his earlier plays. But the play was still revolutionary: Pinter shows how a marriage falls apart, but he presents the scenes in reverse chronological order.

Pinter continued to act and direct, both in his own plays and in those by other playwrights. He also had a career as a screenwriter. Some of his screenplays include *The French Lieutenant's Woman* (1981), *The Handmaid's Tale* (1990), and *Sleuth* (2007).

In 2005 Pinter was awarded the Nobel Prize in Literature. The Nobel presenter described Pinter as "the foremost representative of British drama in the second half of the twentieth century."

Author Search For more about Harold Pinter, go to glencoe.com and enter QuickPass code GL59794u4.

Literature and Reading Preview

Connect to the Dramatic Sketch
In what way can everyday language mask or hide how a person really feels about something? Write a list of words or phrases you use regularly that might hide your true feelings.

Build Background
Theater of the Absurd refers to dramas that contain no plot but instead present a series of scenes in which the characters speak in meaningless conversations or perform actions with little or no purpose. Absurdist plays are comic on the surface but can express underlying feelings, such as dread or uncertainty.

Set Purposes for Reading

Big Idea Portraits of Real Life

As you read, ask yourself, How do the characters communicate, or miscommunicate, with each other?

Literary Element Conflict

The **conflict** is the central struggle between two opposing forces in a story or drama. As you read, ask yourself, What is the conflict in Pinter's dramatic sketch?

Reading Strategy Analyze Mood

When you **analyze mood,** you examine the emotional quality or atmosphere of a literary work. A writer's choice of language, subject matter, setting, and tone, as well as sound devices such as repetition, rhyme, and rhythm, contribute to mood. As you read, ask yourself, How do the setting and stage directions of the play contribute to the overall mood?

Tip: Ask Questions When trying to determine mood, ask yourself questions and record these questions and your answers as you read. Use a chart to organize your questions and answers.

Question	Answer
At what point does a character dramatically change the mood?	In line 24, B responds "ferociously."

Learning Objectives

For pages 837–841

In studying this text, you will focus on the following objectives:

Literary Study: Analyzing conflict.

Reading: Analyzing mood.

Vocabulary

ferociously (fə rō′shəs lē) *adv.* cruelly; savagely; p. 840 *The beast ferociously bared his teeth at the hunter.*

ignorant (ig′nər ənt) *adj.* lacking knowledge or experience; uninformed; p. 840 *He was ignorant in thinking that the earth was flat.*

Tip: Connotation and Denotation As you read, keep in mind that a word's definition in a dictionary may tell only a fraction of the meaning that the word can convey. *Ignorant,* for example, often carries a negative connotation.

That's Your Trouble

Harold Pinter

Sandwich Man in Trafalgar Square, 1898. William Nicholson. Stapleton Collection, London.

Two men in a park. One on the grass, reading. The other making cricket[1] strokes with umbrella.

1. A.: *(stopping in mid-stroke)*: Eh, look at that bloke[2], what's he got on his back, he's got a sandwich board[3] on his back.
2. B.: What about it?
3. A.: He wants to take it off, he'll get a headache.
4. B.: Rubbish.[4]
5. A.: What do you mean?
6. B.: He won't get a headache.
7. A.: I bet he will.
8. B.: The neck! It affects his neck! He'll get a neckache.
9. A.: The strain goes up.
10. B.: Have you ever carried a sandwich board?
11. A.: Never.
12. B.: Then how do you know which way the strain *goes*? *(Pause.)*

1. *Cricket* is a game played with a ball and bat.
2. *Bloke* is British slang for "man" or "guy."
3. A *sandwich board* consists of two hinged boards that hang front and back from the shoulders of a person. It typically is used as a display advertisement.
4. *Rubbish* is a British term for "garbage," "lies," or "nonsense."

Analyze Mood *Describe the mood that this setting creates.*

Conflict *How and where does the conflict between these two men begin?*

It goes down! The strain goes down, it starts with the neck and it goes down. He'll get a neckache and a backache.

13. A.: He'll get a headache in the end.
14. B.: There's no end.
15. A.: That's where the brain is.
16. B.: That's where the *what* is?
17. A.: The brain.
18. B.: It's nothing to do with the brain.
19. A.: Oh, isn't it?
20. B.: It won't go anywhere *near* his brain.
21. A.: That's where you're wrong.
22. B.: I'm not wrong. I'm right. *(Pause.)* You happen to be talking to a man who knows what he's talking about. *(Pause.)* His brain doesn't come into it. If you've got a strain, it goes down. It's not like heat.
23. A.: What do you mean?
24. B.: (*ferociously*): If you've got a strain it goes down! Heat goes up! (Pause.)
25. A.: You mean sound.
26. B.: I what?
27. A.: Sound goes up.
28. B.: Sound goes anywhere it likes! It all depends where you happen to be standing, it's a matter of physics, that's something you're just completely **ignorant** of, but you just try carrying a sandwich board and you'll find out soon enough. First the neck, then the shoulders, then the back, then it worms[5] into the buttocks, that's where it worms. The buttocks. Either the right or the left, it depends how you carry your weight. Then right down the thighs–a straight drop to his feet and he'll collapse.
29. A.: He hasn't collapsed yet.
30. B.: He will. Give him a chance. A headache! How can he get a headache? He hasn't got anything on his head! I'm the one who's got the headache. *(Pause.)* You just don't know how to listen to what other people tell you, that's your trouble.
31. A.: I know what my trouble is.
32. B.: You don't know what your trouble is, my friend. That's your trouble.

5. Here, *worms* means "to move down into; make its way."

Portraits of Real Life *What does B mean by the word "trouble" here?*

Vocabulary

ferociously (fə rō′shəs lē) *adv.* cruelly; savagely
ignorant (ig′nər ənt) *adj.* lacking knowledge or experience; uninformed

After You Read

Respond and Think Critically

Respond and Interpret

1. (a) What was your first reaction to this dramatic sketch? (b) What is your opinion of the dialogue in *That's Your Trouble*?

2. (a) After reading the dialogue, what does the conflict appear to be about? (b) What is the underlying conflict between these two men?

Analyze and Evaluate

3. (a) What is ironic about B's accusation that his companion is ignorant? (b) What purpose does irony serve in this dialogue?

4. (a) Do you think that the two men are friends? (b) How do these characters change or complicate your definition of friendship?

Connect

5. **Big Idea** **Portraits of Real Life** What larger comments about human interaction does Pinter's sketch make through his characters? Explain.

6. **Connect to the Author** How might Pinter's childhood experiences in war-time England have affected his opinions about certainty, reality, and order?

Literary Element | Conflict

An **external conflict** exists when a character struggles against some outside force, such as another person, nature, society, or fate. An **internal conflict** is a struggle that takes place within the mind of a character.

1. What is the external conflict in the dialogue?
2. What are the internal conflicts of these characters?

Reading Strategy | Analyze Mood

Mood is the emotional quality of a literary work. Refer to your chart on page 838 and then answer the following questions

1. What is the overall mood of this dramatic sketch?
2. How does the mood contribute to the playwright's tone?

Vocabulary Practice

Practice with Denotation and Connotation
Denotation is the literal, or dictionary, meaning of a word. **Connotation** is the implied, or cultural, meaning of a word. For example, the words *incapable* and *helpless* have a similar denotation, "unable to act or accomplish something," but they have different connotations.

Negative	More Negative
incapable	helpless

Each of the vocabulary words is listed with a word that has a similar denotation. Choose the word that has a more negative connotation.

ferociously	cruelly
ignorant	uninformed

Writing

Write a List Harold Pinter is noted for his use of pauses in dialogue to signal conflicts within and between characters. Reread the play, keeping a lookout for the stage direction "Pause." Make a list in which you explain, in one sentence for each entry, why you think Pinter has his character pause at that particular moment.

LOG ON **Literature** Online

Selection Resources For Selection Quizzes, eFlashcards, and Reading-Writing Connection activities, go to glencoe.com and enter QuickPass code GL59794u4.

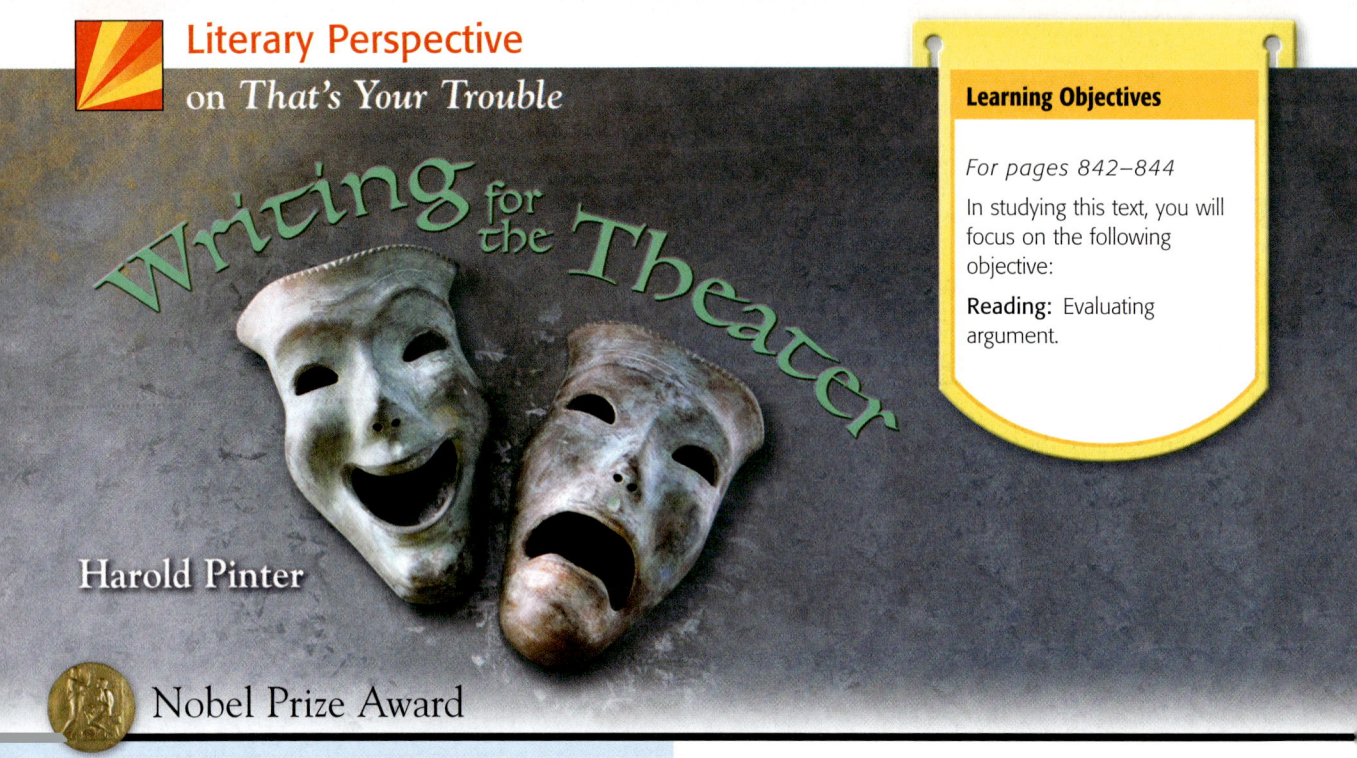

Literary Perspective
on *That's Your Trouble*

Writing for the Theater

Harold Pinter

Nobel Prize Award

Learning Objectives

For pages 842–844

In studying this text, you will focus on the following objective:

Reading: Evaluating argument.

Set a Purpose for Reading
Read to discover the author's opinion and how he supports it.

Build Background
Harold Pinter, a British playwright, was the recipient of the Nobel Prize in Literature in 2005. In "Writing for the Theater," Pinter discusses how he creates roles and chooses the language he uses in plays.

Reading Strategy
Evaluate Argument
Evaluating an argument requires that you make a judgment or form an opinion about what you have read. Consider if the author clearly states his or her position and supports it with reasons and examples. Also, decide if you agree with the author's opinion. As you read, use a chart to determine Pinter's opinions and how he supports them. Then, consider an opposing viewpoint for each opinion.

Pinter's Opinion	Support	Opposing Viewpoint
What he writes only has obligations to itself.	Responsibility is to the play, not the audience.	Playwrights need to consider their audiences.

The theater is a large, energetic, public activity. Writing is, for me, a completely private activity, a poem or a play, no difference. These facts are not easy to reconcile. The professional theater, whatever the virtues it undoubtedly possesses, is a world of false climaxes, calculated tensions, some hysteria, and a good deal of inefficiency. And the alarms of this world which I suppose I work in become steadily more widespread and intrusive. But basically my position has remained the same. What I write has no obligation to anything other than to itself. My responsibility is not to audiences, critics, producers, directors, actors or to my fellow men in general, but to the play in hand, simply. I warned you about definitive statements but it looks as though I've just made one.

I have usually begun a play in quite a simple manner; found a couple of characters in a particular context, thrown them together and listened to what they said, keeping my nose to the ground. The context has always been, for me, concrete and particular, and the characters concrete also. I've never started a play from any kind of abstract idea or theory

842 UNIT 4 DRAMA

... Apart from any other consideration, we are faced with the immense difficulty, if not the impossibility, of verifying the past. I don't mean merely years ago, but yesterday, this morning. What took place, what was the nature of what took place, what happened? If one can speak of the difficulty of knowing what in fact took place yesterday, one can I think treat the present in the same way. What's happening now? We won't know until tomorrow or in six months' time, and we won't know then, we'll have forgotten, or our imagination will have attributed quite false characteristics to today. A moment is sucked away and distorted, often even at the time of its birth. We will all interpret a common experience quite differently, though we prefer to subscribe to the view that there's a shared common ground, a known ground. I think there's a shared common ground all right, but that it's more like a quicksand. Because "reality" is quite a strong firm word we tend to think, or to hope, that the state to which it refers is equally firm, settled and unequivocal.[1] It doesn't seem to be, and in my opinion, it's no worse or better for that.

. . . There is a considerable body of people just now who are asking for some kind of clear and sensible engagement to be evidently disclosed in contemporary plays. They want the playwright to be a prophet. There is certainly a good deal of prophecy indulged in by playwrights these days, in their plays and out of them. Warnings, sermons, admonitions,[2] ideological exhortations,[3] moral judgments, defined problems with built-in solutions; all can camp under the banner of prophecy. The attitude behind this sort of thing might be summed up in one phrase: "*I'm* telling *you!*"

It takes all sorts of playwrights to make a world, and as far as I'm concerned "X" can follow any course he chooses without my acting as his censor. To propagate[4] a phoney war between hypothetical schools of playwrights doesn't seem to me a very productive pastime and it certainly isn't my intention. But I can't but feel that we have a marked tendency to stress, so glibly, our empty preferences. The preference for *Life* with a capital *L,* which is held up to be very different to life with a small *l,* I mean the life we in fact live. The preference for goodwill, for charity, for benevolence, how facile they've become, these deliverances.

If I were to state any moral precept[5] it might be: beware of the writer who puts forward his concern for you to embrace, who leaves you in no doubt of his worthiness, his usefulness, his altruism,[6] who declares that his heart is in the right place, and ensures that it can be seen in full view, a pulsating mass where his characters ought to be. What is presented, so much of the time, as a body of active and positive thought is in fact a body lost in a prison of empty definition and cliché.

This kind of writer clearly trusts words absolutely. I have mixed feelings about words myself. Moving among them, sorting them out, watching them appear on the page, from this I derive a considerable pleasure. But at the same time I have another strong feeling about words which amounts to nothing less than nausea. Such a weight of words confronts us day in, day out, words spoken in a context such as this, words written by me and by others, the bulk of it a stale dead terminology; ideas endlessly repeated and permutated,[7] become platitudinous,[8] trite, meaningless. Given this nausea, it's very easy to be overcome by it and step back into paralysis. I

---

1. *Unequivocal* means "clear" or "without doubt."
2. *Admonitions* are "cautionary advice."
3. *Exhortations* are "appeals" or "arguments."
4. Here, *propagate* means "publicize."
5. *Precept* means "standard."
6. *Altruism* means "unselfish behavior" or "attention to the welfare of others."
7. *Permutated* means "transformed entirely."
8. *Platitudinous* means "unoriginal" or "banal."

Informational Text

imagine most writers know something of this kind of paralysis. But if it is possible to confront this nausea, to follow it to its hilt, to move through it and out of it, then it is possible to say that something has occurred, that something has even been achieved.

Language, under these conditions, is a highly ambiguous business. So often, below the word spoken, is the thing known and unspoken. My characters tell me so much and no more, with reference to their experience, their aspirations, their motives, their history. Between my lack of biographical data about them and the ambiguity of what they say lies a territory which is not only worthy of exploration but which it is compulsory to explore. You and I, the characters which grow on a page, most of the time we're inexpressive, giving little away, unreliable, elusive,[9] evasive,[10] obstructive, unwilling. But it's out of these attributes that a language arises. A language, I repeat, where under what is said, another thing is being said.

Musee Grevin Poster, 1900. Jules Cheret.

---

9. *Elusive* means "not able to be defined or described."
10. *Evasive* means "intentionally vague."

Respond and Think Critically

Respond and Interpret

1. Write a brief summary of the main ideas in this article before you answer the following questions. For help on writing a summary, see page 415.

2. (a) Does Pinter write plays to convey a certain ideology or make a moral judgment? Explain. (b) What does this say about how readers and audiences interpret theatrical works?

3. (a) What does Pinter say language offers other than the actual "words spoken"? (b) What do you think conveying the meaning of Pinter's language requires of actors who perform in his plays?

Analyze and Evaluate

4. (a) What is Pinter's opinion about the responsibility of the playwright? (b) Does this support the idea of theater being a collaborative art form? Why or why not?

5. Konstantin Stanislavsky was a Russian actor and theorist who developed an acting technique known as The Method. He asked students to consider "the subtext" of characters, or the meaning that underlies the written text. Does Pinter's writing serve Stanislavsky's approach to acting? Why or why not?

Connect

6. How do Pinter's ideas about characterization apply to *That's Your Trouble?*

Comparing Literature
Across Genres

Learning Objectives

For pages 845–873

In studying these texts, you will focus on the following objectives:

Literary Study: Comparing across genres.

Reading: Analyzing plot and setting

Writing: Writing an interior monologue.

Compare Literature About Loyalty

Expectations for women have varied tremendously across countries, cultures, and time periods. In most places today, women can expect to have choices when it comes to education, employment, and marriage. A century or more ago, expectations for women were very different. The three works compared here—by Josephina Niggli, Carmen Tafolla, and Isak Dinesen—explore cultural expectations, especially those relating to women, and how the characters in their works face the challenges that result from those expectations.

The Ring of General Macías
by Josephina Niggli .... drama 846

Marked by Carmen Tafolla .... poem 866

The Ring by Isak Dinesen .... short story 867

COMPARE THE **Big Idea** Portraits of Real Life

Capturing life in literature is a task that requires an author to incorporate realistic characters, events, and details into a literary work. Josephina Niggli, Carmen Tafolla, and Isak Dinesen attempt to portray real life with their writing. As you read, ask yourself, While each author focuses on a different time and place, how do they develop their characters in such a way that allows the reader to form a personal connection with them?

COMPARE Theme

The **theme** is the central message of a work of literature. The theme provides some insight or lesson with which readers can connect. As you read, ask yourself, How do Niggli, Tafolla, and Dinesen each explore the theme of loyalty and its impact on the lives of women?

COMPARE Cultures

Culture is an important consideration for the authors of the following selections. All of the authors draw heavily on their surroundings and heritages for the inspiration and content of their works. As you read, ask yourself, How do the writers use their cultural backgrounds to draw the reader into their literary worlds?

In the Trenches (En la trinchea). Diego Rivera. Banco de Mexico Trust. Mural, 2.03 x 3.98 m. Secretaria de Educacion Publica, Mexico City, Mexico.

Author Search For more about the authors, go to glencoe.com and enter QuickPass code GL59794u4.

Comparing Literature

Before You Read

The Ring of General Macías

Meet Josephina Niggli
(1910–1983)

Although Josephina Niggli was the child of European American parents, she most strongly identified with the Mexican culture into which she was born and raised. Her willingness to tackle subjects such as the oppression of women in Mexican culture and the Mexican revolution inspired a new generation of Mexican American authors.

Between Borders Niggli came of age during the Mexican Revolution. In 1913, the assassination of President Francisco Madero led the Niggli family to flee Mexico, which had descended into political turmoil. The family lived in various places in the Southwestern United States but never settled down. During the revolution of 1925, Niggli was sent away to school in San Antonio, Texas. Niggli's talent was first recognized and encouraged by a teacher—a nun who locked Niggli in her room until she emerged with a finished short story to enter in a magazine competition. Her entry won second place.

> "Once you have experienced the emotion of having a play produced, you are forever lost to the ordinary world."
>
> —Josephina Niggli, from *Pointers on Playwriting*

After college, Niggli moved to North Carolina, where she joined the Carolina Playmakers, a graduate program at the University of North Carolina at Chapel Hill. She wrote several plays during this time that focused on the Mexican Revolution.

Critical Acclaim Her first novel, *Mexican Village*, portrays the experiences of an obstinate Mexican American who gradually learns to appreciate Mexican village culture and traditions. According to one critic, the novel was ahead of its time; as Raymond Paredes says, "*Mexican Village* . . . pointed forward to an emerging school of realism, confronting such issues as racism, the oppression of women, and the failure of the Mexican Revolution." The novel remains her most famous work. Like much of Niggli's writing, *Mexican Village* reflects both alienation from and loyalty to the two cultures in which she was raised.

Niggli eventually returned to North Carolina, where she taught playwriting at Western Carolina University for many years.

 **Literature** Online

Author Search For more about Josephina Niggli, go to glencoe.com and enter QuickPass code GL59794u4.

846 UNIT 4 DRAMA

Comparing Literature

Literature and Reading Preview

Connect to the Play
What qualities or things are you proud of? List several things you are proud of and explain their significance in your life.

Build Background
The Mexican Revolution had its roots in the dictatorship of President Porfirio Díaz, under whose rule the majority of citizens suffered hardship and repression. In 1910 armed resistance to Díaz's rule began. The revolutionary struggle helped define Mexican identity.

Set Purposes for Reading

Big Idea Portraits of Real Life
Notice how Niggli describes the women in the play. As you read, ask yourself, How do these women accurately represent those in real life?

Literary Element Characterization
Characterization is the method(s) a writer uses to reveal a character's personality to the reader. A character's personality might be revealed through the character's own words, thoughts, or actions or through what other characters think and say about the character. As you read, ask yourself, How does understanding characterization help me comprehend the author's message?

Reading Strategy Analyze Plot and Setting
The **plot**, or series of events that occur in a literary work, reveals the conflicts that keep the story moving forward. The **setting** tells the reader when and where the work takes place. By **analyzing the plot and the setting** of a play or another literary work, you can learn a lot about the author's intended purpose for the work. As you read, ask yourself, What is the significance of the sequence of events and the setting in the play?

Tip: Sequence of Events Use a graphic organizer as below to record the sequence of the events that form the plot.

Sequence of Events

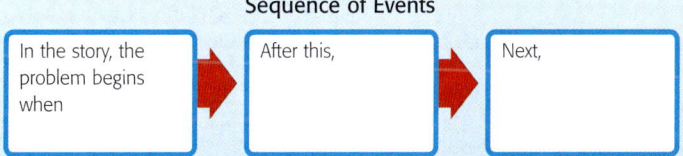

Vocabulary

regally (rē′gəl lē) *adv.* in a grand, dignified manner befitting a king or a queen; p. 853 *The homecoming queen waved regally at the crowd.*

ostentatiously (os′tən tā′shəs lē) *adv.* in a way intended to attract attention or impress others; p. 853 *Their home was decorated ostentatiously.*

notorious (nō tôr′ē əs) *adj.* widely and unfavorably known; p. 858 *The students' antics were notorious among the substitute teachers.*

repressed (ri prest′) *adj.* held back or kept under control; restrained; p. 859 *The two normally exuberant boys repressed their behavior.*

impertinent (im purt′ən ənt) *adj.* inappropriately bold or forward; p. 861 *The girl's brash behavior toward her teacher was impertinent.*

Tip: Word Parts Word meanings are changed by adding suffixes, prefixes, or both to root words.

JOSEPHINA NIGGLI

Comparing Literature

THE RING OF
General Macias

Josephina Niggli

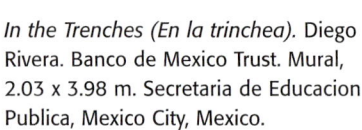

In the Trenches (En la trinchea). Diego Rivera. Banco de Mexico Trust. Mural, 2.03 x 3.98 m. Secretaria de Educacion Publica, Mexico City, Mexico.

CHARACTERS

MARICA (mär ē′kə): the sister of General Macías

RAQUEL (rə kel′): the wife of General Macías

ANDRÉS DE LA O (än′dräs dā lə ō): a captain in the Revolutionary Army

CLETO (klā′tō): a private in the Revolutionary Army

BASILIO FLORES (bə sēl′yō flô′räs): a captain in the Federal Army

PLACE: *Just outside Mexico City.*

TIME: *A night in April 1912.*

[*The living room of General Macías's[1] home is luxuriously furnished in the gold and ornate style of Louis XVI.[2] In the Right wall are French windows leading into the patio. Flanking these windows are low bookcases. In the Back wall is, Right, a closet door; and, Center, a table holding a wine decanter[3] and glasses. The Left wall has a door Upstage, and Downstage a writing desk with a straight chair in front of it. Near the desk is an armchair. Down Right is a small sofa with a table holding a lamp at the Upstage end of it. There are pictures on the walls. The room looks rather stuffy and unlived in.*

When the curtains part, the stage is in darkness save for the moonlight that comes through the French windows. Then the house door opens and a young girl in negligee enters stealthily. She is carrying a lighted candle. She stands at the door a moment listening for possible pursuit, then moves quickly across to the bookcase Down Right. She puts the candle on top of the bookcase and begins searching behind the books. She finally finds what she wants: a small bottle. While she is searching, the house door opens silently and a woman, also in negligee, enters. (These negligees are in the latest Parisian style.) She moves silently across the room to the table by the sofa, and as the girl turns with the bottle, the woman switches on the light. The girl gives a half-scream and draws back, frightened. The light reveals her to be quite young—no more than twenty—a timid, dovelike creature. The woman has a queenly air, and whether she is actually beautiful or not, people think she is. She is about thirty-two.]

MARICA. [*Trying to hide the bottle behind her.*] Raquel! What are you doing here?

RAQUEL. What did you have hidden behind the books, Marica?

MARICA. [*Attempting a forced laugh.*] I? Nothing. Why do you think I have anything?

RAQUEL. [*Taking a step toward her.*] Give it to me.

MARICA. [*Backing away from her.*] No. No, I won't.

RAQUEL. [*Stretching out her hand.*] I demand that you give it to me.

MARICA. You have no right to order me about. I'm a married woman. I . . . I . . . [*She begins to sob and flings herself down on the sofa.*]

RAQUEL. [*Much gentler.*] You shouldn't be up. The doctor told you to stay in bed. [*She bends over* MARICA *and gently takes the bottle out of the girl's hand.*] It was poison. I thought so.

---

1. Macías (mä sē′əs)
2. France's King *Louis XVI* lived a life of luxury and elegance until he was beheaded in 1793 during the French Revolution.
3. A *decanter* is a decorative bottle with a stopper.

Analyze Plot and Setting What might you infer from this description of the setting?

Characterization What can you infer about Raquel from this description?

Comparing Literature

Self-Portrait, 1930. Frida Kahlo. Oil on canvas, 25½ x 21⅛ in. Museum of Fine Arts, Boston. Anonymous loan.

View the Art Frida Kahlo, a Mexican painter, is known for her vibrant and dramatic self-portraits. Is the woman portrayed here closer to the image you have developed of Marica or of Raquel? Explain.

MARICA. [*Frightened.*] You won't tell the priest, will you?

RAQUEL. Suicide is a sin, Marica. A sin against God.

MARICA. I know. I . . . [*She catches* RAQUEL'S *hand.*] Oh, Raquel, why do we have to have wars? Why do men have to go to war and be killed?

RAQUEL. Men must fight for what they believe is right. It is an honorable thing to die for your country as a soldier.

MARICA. How can you say that with Domingo[4] out there fighting, too? And fighting what? Men who aren't even men. Peasants. Ranch slaves. Men who shouldn't be allowed to fight.

RAQUEL. Peasants are men, Marica. Not animals.

MARICA. Men. It's always men. But how about the women? What becomes of us?

RAQUEL. We can pray.

MARICA. [*Bitterly.*] Yes, we can pray. And then comes the terrible news, and it's no use praying any more. All the reason for our praying is dead. Why should I go on living with Tomás[5] dead?

RAQUEL. Living is a duty.

MARICA. How can you be so cold, so hard? You are a cold and hard woman, Raquel. My brother worships you. He has never even looked at another woman since the first day he saw you. Does he know how cold and hard you are?

RAQUEL. Domingo is my—honored husband.

MARICA. You've been married for ten years. And I've been married for three months. If Domingo is killed, it won't be the same for you. You've had ten years. [*She is crying wildly.*] I haven't anything . . . anything at all.

RAQUEL. You've had three months—three months of laughter. And now you have tears. How lucky you are. You have tears. Perhaps five months of tears. Not more. You're only twenty. And in five months Tomás will become just a lovely memory.

MARICA. I'll remember Tomás all my life.

RAQUEL. Of course. But he'll be distant and far away. But you're young . . . and the young need laughter. The young can't live on tears. And one day in Paris, or Rome, or even Mexico City, you'll meet another man. You'll marry again. There will be children in your house. How lucky you are.

MARICA. I'll never marry again.

RAQUEL. You're only twenty. You'll think differently when you're twenty-eight, or nine, or thirty.

MARICA. What will you do if Domingo is killed?

RAQUEL. I shall be very proud that he died in all his courage . . . in all the greatness of a hero.

MARICA. But you'd not weep, would you? Not you! I don't think there are any tears in you.

RAQUEL. No, I'd not weep. I'd sit here in this empty house and wait.

MARICA. Wait for what?

RAQUEL. For the jingle of his spurs as he walks across the tiled hall. For the sound of his laughter in the patio. For the echo of

---

4. Domingo (də ming′gō)
5. Tomás (tō mäs′)

Analyze Plot and Setting What do these lines tell you about the culture in which the play takes place?

Characterization How does Niggli characterize Marica here?

JOSEPHINA NIGGLI

Comparing Literature

his voice as he shouts to the groom to put away his horse. For the feel of his hand . . .

MARICA. [*Screams.*] Stop it!

RAQUEL. I'm sorry.

MARICA. You do love him, don't you?

RAQUEL. I don't think even he knows how much.

MARICA. I thought that after ten years people slid away from love. But you and Domingo—why, you're all he thinks about. When he's away from you he talks about you all the time. I heard him say once that when you were out of his sight he was like a man without eyes or ears or hands.

RAQUEL. I know. I, too, know that feeling.

MARICA. Then how could you let him go to war? Perhaps to be killed? How could you?

RAQUEL. [*Sharply.*] Marica, you are of the family Macías. Your family is a family of great warriors. A Macías man was with Ferdinand when the Moors were driven out of Spain. A Macías man was with Cortés when the Aztecans surrendered. Your grandfather fought in the War of Independence. Your own father was executed not twenty miles from this house by the French.[6] Shall his son be any less brave because he loves a woman?

MARICA. But Domingo loved you enough to forget that. If you had asked him, he wouldn't have gone to war. He would have stayed here with you.

RAQUEL. No, he would not have stayed. Your brother is a man of honor, not a whining, creeping coward.

MARICA. [*Beginning to cry again.*] I begged Tomás not to go. I begged him.

RAQUEL. Would you have loved him if he had stayed?

MARICA. I don't know. I don't know.

RAQUEL. There is your answer. You'd have despised him. Loved and despised him. Now come, Marica, it's time for you to go to bed.

MARICA. You won't tell the priest—about the poison, I mean?

RAQUEL. No. I won't tell him.

MARICA. Thank you, Raquel. How good you are. How kind and good.

RAQUEL. A moment ago I was hard and cruel. What a baby you are. Now, off to bed with you.

MARICA. Aren't you coming upstairs, too?

RAQUEL. No . . . I haven't been sleeping very well lately. I think I'll read for a little while.

MARICA. Good night, Raquel. And thank you.

RAQUEL. Good night, little one.

[*MARICA goes out through the house door Left, taking her candle with her. RAQUEL stares down at the bottle of poison in her hand, then puts it away in one of the small drawers of the desk. She next selects a book from the Downstage case and sits on the sofa to read it, but feeling chilly, she rises and goes to the closet, Back Right, and takes out an afghan.[7] Coming back to the sofa, she makes herself comfortable, with the afghan across her knees. Suddenly she hears a noise in the patio. She listens, then convinced it is*

---

6. In 1492 *Ferdinand* of Aragon defeated the *Moors*, a Muslim people from northwest Africa who had controlled most of Spain since the 700s. Through the *War of Independence*, Mexico won freedom from Spain in 1821. The *French* invaded and occupied Mexico City in 1863.

Characterization What do these lines tell you about Raquel's attitude toward men going to war?

7. An *afghan* is a knitted or crocheted wool blanket.

nothing, returns to her reading. But she hears the noise again. She goes to the patio door and peers out.]

RAQUEL. [*Calling softly.*] Who's there? Who's out there? Oh! [*She gasps and backs into the room. Two men—or rather a man and a young boy—dressed in the white pajama suits of the Mexican peasants, with their sombreros tipped low over their faces, come into the room.* RAQUEL *draws herself up* **regally***. Her voice is cold and commanding.*] Who are you, and what do you want here?

ANDRÉS. We are hunting for the wife of General Macías.

RAQUEL. I am Raquel Rivera de Macías.

ANDRÉS. Cleto, stand guard in the patio. If you hear any suspicious noise, warn me at once.

CLETO. Yes, my captain. [*The boy returns to the patio.*]

[*The man, hooking his thumbs in his belt, strolls around the room, looking it over. When he reaches the table at the back he sees the wine. With a small bow to* RAQUEL *he pours himself a glass of wine and drains it. He wipes his mouth with the back of his hand.*]

RAQUEL. How very interesting.

ANDRÉS. [*Startled.*] What?

RAQUEL. To be able to drink wine with that hat on.

ANDRÉS. The hat? Oh, forgive me, señora. [*He flicks the brim with his fingers so that it drops off his head and dangles down his back from the neck cord.*] In a military camp one forgets one's polite manners. Would you care to join me in another glass?

RAQUEL. [*Sitting on the sofa.*] Why not? It's my wine.

ANDRÉS. And very excellent wine. [*He pours two glasses and gives her one while he is talking.*] I would say Amontillado[8] of the vintage of '87.

RAQUEL. Did you learn that in a military camp?

ANDRÉS. I used to sell wines . . . among other things.

RAQUEL. [**Ostentatiously** *hiding a yawn.*] I am devastated.

ANDRÉS. [*Pulls over the armchair and makes himself comfortable in it.*] You don't mind, do you?

RAQUEL. Would it make any difference if I did?

ANDRÉS. No. The Federals are searching the streets for us, and we have to stay somewhere. But women of your class seem to expect that senseless sort of question.

RAQUEL. Of course I suppose I could scream.

ANDRÉS. Naturally.

RAQUEL. My sister-in-law is upstairs asleep. And there are several servants in the back of the house. Mostly men servants. Very big men.

ANDRÉS. Very interesting. [*He is drinking the wine in small sips with much enjoyment.*]

RAQUEL. What would you do if I screamed?

Characterization What do the remarks that Raquel makes to Andrés reveal about her?

8. *Amontillado* (ə mŏn′til ä dō) is a kind of sherry, which is a strong wine.

Vocabulary

regally (rē′gəl lē) *adv.* in a grand, dignified manner befitting a king or a queen

Vocabulary

ostentatiously (os′tən tā′shəs lē) *adv.* in a way intended to attract attention or impress others

JOSEPHINA NIGGLI

> **Comparing Literature**

ANDRÉS. [*Considering the request as though it were another glass of wine.*] Nothing.

RAQUEL. I am afraid you are lying to me.

ANDRÉS. Women of your class seem to expect polite little lies.

RAQUEL. Stop calling me "woman of your class."

ANDRÉS. Forgive me.

RAQUEL. You are one of the fighting peasants, aren't you?

ANDRÉS. I am a captain in the Revolutionary Army.

RAQUEL. This house is completely loyal to the Federal government.

ANDRÉS. I know. That's why I'm here.

RAQUEL. And now that you are here, just what do you expect me to do?

ANDRÉS. I expect you to offer sanctuary to myself and to Cleto.

RAQUEL. Cleto? [*She looks toward the patio and adds sarcastically.*] Oh, your army.

CLETO. [*Appearing in the doorway.*] I'm sorry, my captain. I just heard a noise. [*RAQUEL stands. ANDRÉS moves quickly to her and puts his hands on her arms from the back. CLETO has turned and is peering into the patio. Then the boy relaxes.*] We are still safe, my captain. It was only a rabbit. [*He goes back into the patio. RAQUEL pulls away from ANDRÉS and goes to the desk.*]

RAQUEL. What a magnificent army you have. So clever. I'm sure you must win many victories.

ANDRÉS. We do. And we will win the greatest victory, remember that.

RAQUEL. This farce has gone on long enough. Will you please take your army and climb over the patio wall with it?

ANDRÉS. I told you that we came here so that you could give us sanctuary.

RAQUEL. My dear captain—captain without a name . . .

ANDRÉS. Andrés de la O, your servant. [*He makes a bow.*]

RAQUEL. [*Startled.*] Andrés de la O!

ANDRÉS. I am flattered. You have heard of me.

RAQUEL. Naturally. Everyone in the city has heard of you. You have a reputation for politeness—especially to women.

ANDRÉS. I see that the tales about me have lost nothing in the telling.

RAQUEL. I can't say. I'm not interested in gossip about your type of soldier.

ANDRÉS. Then let me give you something to heighten your interest. [*He suddenly takes her in his arms and kisses her. She stiffens for a moment, then remains perfectly still. He steps away from her.*]

RAQUEL. [*Rage forcing her to whisper.*] Get out of here—at once!

ANDRÉS. [*Staring at her in admiration.*] I can understand why Macías loves you. I couldn't before, but now I can understand it.

RAQUEL. Get out of my house.

ANDRÉS. [*Sits on the sofa and pulls a small leather pouch out of his shirt. He pours its contents into his hand.*] So cruel, señora, and I with a present for you? Here is a holy medal. My mother gave me this medal. She died when I was ten. She was a street beg-

---

Analyze Plot and Setting What does Andrés's comment imply about wealthy women at the time the play is set?

Portraits of Real Life Is Raquel's abrupt change in behavior toward Andrés realistic? Explain.

gar. She died of starvation. But I wasn't there. I was in jail. I had been sentenced to five years in prison for stealing five oranges. The judge thought it a great joke. One year for each orange. He laughed. He had a very loud laugh. [*Pause.*] I killed him two months ago. I hanged him to the telephone pole in front of his house. And I laughed. [*Pause.*] I also have a very loud laugh. [RAQUEL *abruptly turns her back on him.*] I told that story to a girl the other night and she thought it very funny. But of course she was a peasant girl—a girl who could neither read nor write. She hadn't been born in a great house in Tabasco.⁹ She didn't have an English governess.¹⁰ She didn't go to school to the nuns in Paris. She didn't marry one of the richest young men in the Republic. But she thought my story very funny. Of course she could understand it. Her brother had been whipped to death because he had run away from the plantation that owned him. [*He pauses and looks at her. She does not move.*] Are you still angry with me? Even though I have brought you a present? [*He holds out his hand.*] A very nice present—from your husband.

RAQUEL. [*Turns and stares at him in amazement.*] A present! From Domingo?

ANDRÉS. I don't know him that well. I call him the General Macías.

RAQUEL. [*Excitedly.*] Is he well? How does he look? [*With horrified comprehension.*] He's a prisoner . . . your prisoner!

---

9. On the southern coast of the Gulf of Mexico, *Tabasco* is one of Mexico's thirty-five states.
10. A *governess* is a woman employed to teach children in a private household.

Characterization Why do you think Andrés describes what the young woman did not have or do?

ANDRÉS. Naturally. That's why I know so much about you. He talks about you constantly.

RAQUEL. You know nothing about him. You're lying to me.

[CLETO *comes to the window.*]

ANDRÉS. I assure you, señora . . .

CLETO. [*Interrupting.*] My captain . . .

ANDRÉS. What is it, Cleto? Another rabbit?

CLETO. No, my captain. There are soldiers at the end of the street. They are searching all the houses. They will be here soon.

ANDRÉS. Don't worry. We are quite safe here. Stay in the patio until I call you.

CLETO. Yes, my captain. [*He returns to the patio.*]

RAQUEL. You are not safe here. When those soldiers come I shall turn you over to them.

ANDRÉS. I think not.

RAQUEL. You can't escape from them. And they are not kind to you peasant prisoners. They have good reason not to be.

ANDRÉS. Look at this ring. [*He holds his hand out, with the ring on his palm.*]

RAQUEL. Why, it's—a wedding ring.

ANDRÉS. Read the inscription inside of it. [*As she hesitates, he adds sharply.*] Read it!

RAQUEL. [*Slowly takes the ring. While she is reading her voice fades to a whisper.*] "D. M.—R. R.—June 2, 1902." Where did you get this?

ANDRÉS. General Macías gave it to me.

RAQUEL. [*Firmly and clearly.*] Not this ring. He'd never give you this ring. [*With dawning horror.*] He's dead. You stole it from his dead finger. He's dead.

JOSEPHINA NIGGLI 855

> **Comparing Literature**

ANDRÉS. Not yet. But he will be dead if I don't return to camp safely by sunset tomorrow.

RAQUEL. I don't believe you. I don't believe you. You're lying to me.

ANDRÉS. This house is famous for its loyalty to the Federal government. You will hide me until those soldiers get out of this district. When it is safe enough Cleto and I will leave. But if you betray me to them, your husband will be shot tomorrow evening at sunset. Do you understand? [*He shakes her arm.* RAQUEL *looks dazedly at him.* CLETO *comes to the window.*]

CLETO. The soldiers are coming closer, my captain. They are at the next house.

ANDRÉS. [*To* RAQUEL.] Where shall we hide? [*Raquel is still dazed. He gives her another little shake.*] Think, woman! If you love your husband at all—think!

RAQUEL. I don't know. Marica upstairs—the servants in the rest of the house—I don't know.

ANDRÉS. The General has bragged to us about you. He says you are braver than most men. He says you are very clever. This is a time to be both brave and clever.

CLETO. [*Pointing to the closet.*] What door is that?

RAQUEL. It's a closet . . . a storage closet.

ANDRÉS. We'll hide in there.

RAQUEL. It's very small. It's not big enough for both of you.

Analyze Plot and Setting How does this situation contribute to the development of the plot?

Characterization Is the General's description of his wife consistent with the characterization of her thus far? Explain.

ANDRÉS. Cleto, hide yourself in there.

CLETO. But, my captain . . .

ANDRÉS. That's an order! Hide yourself.

CLETO. Yes, Sir. [*He steps inside the closet.*]

ANDRÉS. And now, señora, where are you going to hide me?

RAQUEL. How did you persuade my husband to give you his ring?

ANDRÉS. That's a very long story, señora, for which we have no time just now. [*He puts the ring and medal back in the pouch and thrusts it inside his shirt.*] Later I will be glad to give you all the details. But at present it is only necessary for you to remember that his life depends upon mine.

RAQUEL. Yes—yes, of course. [*She loses her dazed expression and seems to grow more queenly as she takes command of the situation.*] Give me your hat. [ANDRÉS *shrugs and passes it over to her. She takes it to the closet and hands it to* CLETO.] There is a smoking jacket hanging up in there. Hand it to me. [CLETO *hands her a man's velvet smoking jacket. She brings it to* ANDRÉS.] Put this on.

ANDRÉS. [*Puts it on and looks down at himself.*] Such a pity my shoes are not comfortable slippers.

RAQUEL. Sit in that chair. [*She points to the armchair.*]

ANDRÉS. My dear lady . . .

RAQUEL. If I must save your life, allow me to do it in my own way. Sit down. [ANDRÉS *sits. She picks up the afghan from the couch and throws it over his feet and legs, carefully tucking it in so that his body is covered to the waist.*] If anyone speaks to you, don't answer. Don't turn your head. As far as you are concerned, there is no one in this room—not even me. Just look straight ahead of you and . . .

ANDRÉS. [*As she pauses.*] And what?

856 UNIT 4 DRAMA

Comparing Literature

Triumph of the Revolution—Distribution of Food (Trionfo de la revolucion, reparto de los alimentos), 1926-27. Diego Rivera. Banco de Mexico Trust. Fresco, 3.54 x 3.67 m. Chapel, Universidad Autonoma, Chapingo, Mexico.

View the Art Diego Rivera, a world famous Mexican muralist, believed art should have a political message. The heroes in his paintings are ordinary hard-working Mexicans. What insight does this scene give you about social conditions in Mexico at the time of this play?

JOSEPHINA NIGGLI

Comparing Literature

RAQUEL. I started to say "and pray," but since you're a member of the Revolutionary Army I don't suppose you believe in God and prayer.

ANDRÉS. My mother left me a holy medal.

RAQUEL. Oh, yes, I remember. A very amusing story. [*There is the sound of men's voices in the patio.*] The Federal soldiers are here. If you can pray, ask God to keep Marica upstairs. She is very young and very stupid. She'll betray you before I can shut her mouth.

ANDRÉS. I'll . . .

RAQUEL. Silence! Stare straight ahead of you and pray. [*She goes to the French window and speaks loudly to the soldiers.*] Really! What is the meaning of this uproar?

FLORES. [*Off.*] Do not alarm yourself, señora. [*He comes into the room. He wears the uniform of a Federal officer.*] I am Captain Basilio Flores, at your service, señora.

RAQUEL. What do you mean, invading my house and making so much noise at this hour of the night?

FLORES. We are hunting for two spies. One of them is the **notorious** Andrés de la O. You may have heard of him, señora.

RAQUEL. [*Looking at ANDRÉS.*] Considering what he did to my cousin—yes, I've heard of him.

FLORES. Your cousin, señora?

RAQUEL. [*Comes to ANDRÉS and puts her hand on his shoulder. He stares woodenly in front of him.*] Felipe[11] was his prisoner before the poor boy managed to escape.

FLORES. Is it possible? [*He crosses to ANDRÉS.*] Captain Basilio Flores, at your service. [*He salutes.*]

RAQUEL. Felipe doesn't hear you. He doesn't even know you are in the room.

FLORES. Eh, it is a sad thing.

RAQUEL. Must your men make so much noise?

FLORES. The hunt must be thorough, señora. And now if some of my men can go through here to the rest of the house . . .

RAQUEL. Why?

FLORES. But I told you, señora. We are hunting for two spies . . .

RAQUEL. [*Speaking quickly from controlled nervousness.*] And do you think I have them hidden someplace, and I the wife of General Macías?

FLORES. General Macías! But I didn't know . . .

RAQUEL. Now that you do know, I suggest you remove your men and their noise at once.

FLORES. But, señora, I regret—I still have to search this house.

RAQUEL. I can assure you, captain, that I have been sitting here all evening, and no peasant spy has passed me and gone into the rest of the house.

FLORES. Several rooms open off the patio, señora. They needn't have come through here.

RAQUEL. So . . . you do think I conceal spies in this house. Then search it by all means. Look under the sofa . . . under the table. In the drawers of the desk. And don't miss

---

11. *Felipe* (fə lē pā)

Vocabulary

notorious (nō tôr´ē əs) *adj.* widely and unfavorably known

Characterization What do these lines tell you about Raquel?

that closet, captain. Inside that closet is hidden a very fierce and wicked spy.

FLORES. Please, señora . . .

RAQUEL. [*Goes to the closet door.*] Or do you prefer me to open it for you?

FLORES. I am only doing my duty, señora. You are making it very difficult.

RAQUEL. [*Relaxing against the door.*] I'm sorry. My sister-in-law is upstairs. She has just received word that her husband has been killed. They were married three months ago. She's only twenty. I didn't want . . .

MARICA. [*Calling off.*] Raquel, what is all that noise downstairs?

RAQUEL. [*Goes to the house door and calls.*] It is nothing. Go back to bed.

MARICA. But I can hear men's voices in the patio.

RAQUEL. It is only some Federal soldiers hunting for two peasant spies. [*She turns and speaks rapidly to FLORES.*] If she comes down here, she must not see my cousin. Felipe escaped, but her husband was killed. The doctor thinks the sight of my poor cousin might affect her mind. You understand?

FLORES. Certainly, señora. What a sad thing.

MARICA. [*Still off.*] Raquel, I'm afraid! [*She tries to push past RAQUEL into the room. RAQUEL and FLORES stand between her and ANDRÉS.*] Spies! In this house. Oh, Raquel!

RAQUEL. The doctor will be very angry if you don't return to bed at once.

MARICA. But those terrible men will kill us. What is the matter with you two? Why are you standing there like that? [*She tries to see past them, but they both move so that she can't see ANDRÉS.*]

FLORES. It is better that you go back to your room, señora.

MARICA. But why? Upstairs I am alone. Those terrible men will kill me. I know they will.

FLORES. Don't be afraid, señora. There are no spies in this house.

MARICA. Are you sure?

RAQUEL. Captain Flores means that no spy would dare to take refuge in the house of General Macías. Isn't that right, captain?

FLORES. [*Laughing.*] Of course. All the world knows of the brave General Macías.

RAQUEL. Now go back to bed, Marica. Please, for my sake.

MARICA. You are both acting very strangely. I think you have something hidden in this room you don't want me to see.

RAQUEL. [*Sharply.*] You are quite right. Captain Flores has captured one of the spies. He is sitting in the chair behind me. He is dead. Now will you please go upstairs!

MARICA. [*Gives a stifled sob.*] Oh! That such a terrible thing could happen in this house. [*She runs out of the room, still sobbing.*]

FLORES. [*Worried.*] Was it wise to tell her such a story, señora?

RAQUEL. [*Tense with repressed relief.*] Better that than the truth. Good night, captain, and thank you.

Portraits of Real Life *How is Raquel handling the search?*

Vocabulary

repressed (ri prest´) *adj.* held back or kept under control; restrained

JOSEPHINA NIGGLI 859

Comparing Literature

Wall with a Door and Tree (Muro con puerta y arbol). Pablo Burchard.

View the Art This painting draws the viewer's eye to the brightness visible just beyond the partially opened door. What is the mood of this painting? How does it compare with the mood in the play?

FLORES. Good night, señora. And don't worry. Those spies won't bother you. If they were anywhere in this district, my men would have found them.

RAQUEL. I'm sure of it.

[*The Captain salutes her, looks toward* ANDRÉS *and salutes him, then goes into the patio. He can be heard calling his men. Neither* ANDRÉS *nor* RAQUEL *moves until the voices outside die away. Then Raquel staggers and nearly falls, but Andrés catches her in time.*]

ANDRÉS. [*Calling softly.*] They've gone, Cleto. [ANDRÉS *carries Raquel to the sofa as Cleto comes out of the closet.*] Bring a glass of wine. Quickly.

CLETO. [*As he gets the wine.*] What happened?

ANDRÉS. It's nothing. Just a faint. [*He holds the wine to her lips.*]

CLETO. She's a great lady, that one. When she wanted to open the closet door my knees were trembling, I can tell you.

ANDRÉS. My own bones were playing a pretty tune.

CLETO. Why do you think she married Macías?

ANDRÉS. Love is a peculiar thing, Cleto.

CLETO. I don't understand it.

RAQUEL. [*Moans and sits up.*] Are they—are they gone?

ANDRÉS. Yes, they're gone. [*He kisses her hand.*] I've never known a braver lady.

RAQUEL. [*Pulling her hand away.*] Will you go now, please?

ANDRÉS. We'll have to wait until the district is free of them—but if you'd like to write a letter to your husband while we're waiting . . .

RAQUEL. [*Surprised at his kindness.*] You'd take it to him? You'd really give it to him?

ANDRÉS. Of course.

RAQUEL. Thank you. [*She goes to the writing desk and sits down.*]

ANDRÉS. [*To* CLETO, *who has been staring steadily at* RAQUEL *all the while.*] You stay here with the señora. I'm going to find out how much of the district has been cleared.

CLETO. [*Still staring at* RAQUEL.] Yes, my captain.

[ANDRÉS *leaves by the French windows.* CLETO *keeps on staring at* RAQUEL *as she starts to write. After a moment she turns to him.*]

RAQUEL. [*Irritated.*] Why do you keep staring at me?

CLETO. Why did you marry a man like that one, señora?

RAQUEL. You're very **impertinent**.

CLETO. [*Shyly.*] I'm sorry, señora.

RAQUEL. [*After a brief pause.*] What do you mean: "a man like that one"?

CLETO. Well, you're very brave, señora.

RAQUEL. [*Lightly.*] And don't you think the general is very brave?

CLETO. No, señora. Not very.

RAQUEL. [*Staring at him with bewilderment.*] What are you trying to tell me?

CLETO. Nothing, señora. It is none of my affair.

RAQUEL. Come here. [*He comes slowly up to her.*] Tell me what is in your mind.

Portraits of Real Life If this were a true story, would you expect this behavior from a revolutionary toward his enemy? Why or why not?

Vocabulary

impertinent (im purt´ ən ənt) *adj.* inappropriately bold or forward

JOSEPHINA NIGGLI

Comparing Literature

CLETO. I don't know, señora. I don't understand it. The captain says love is a peculiar thing, but I don't understand it.

RAQUEL. Cleto, did the general willingly give that ring to your captain?

CLETO. Yes, señora.

RAQUEL. Why?

CLETO. The general wanted to save his own life. He said he loved you and he wanted to save his life.

RAQUEL. How would giving that ring to your captain save the general's life?

CLETO. The general's supposed to be shot tomorrow afternoon. But he's talked about you a lot, and when my captain knew we had to come into the city, he thought perhaps we might take refuge here if the Federals got on our trail. So he went to the general and said that if he fixed it so we'd be safe here, my captain would save him from the firing squad.

RAQUEL. Was your trip to the city very important—to your cause, I mean?

CLETO. Indeed yes, señora. The captain got a lot of fine information. It means we'll win the next big battle. My captain is a very clever man, señora.

RAQUEL. Did the general know about this information when he gave his ring to your captain?

CLETO. I don't see how he could help knowing it, señora. He heard us talking about it enough.

RAQUEL. Who knows about that bargain to save the general's life beside you and your captain?

CLETO. No one, señora. The captain isn't one to talk, and I didn't have time to.

RAQUEL. [*While the boy has been talking, the life seems to have drained completely out of her.*] How old are you, Cleto?

CLETO. I don't know, señora. I think I'm twenty, but I don't know.

RAQUEL. [*Speaking more to herself than to him.*] Tomás was twenty.

CLETO. Who is Tomás?

RAQUEL. He was married to my sister-in-law. Cleto, you think my husband is a coward, don't you?

CLETO. [*With embarrassment.*] Yes, señora.

RAQUEL. You don't think any woman is worth it, do you? Worth the price of a great battle, I mean?

CLETO. No, señora. But as the captain says, love is a very peculiar thing.

RAQUEL. If your captain loved a woman as much as the general loves me, would he have given an enemy his ring?

CLETO. Ah, but the captain is a great man, señora.

RAQUEL. And so is my husband a great man. He is of the family Macías. All of that family have been great men. All of them—brave and honorable men. They have always held their honor to be greater than their lives. That is a tradition of their family.

CLETO. Perhaps none of them loved a woman like you, señora.

RAQUEL. How strange you are. I saved you from the Federals because I want to save my husband's life. You call me brave, and yet you call him a coward.

Analyze Plot and Setting *How might this information provided by Cleto affect the plot?*

There is no difference in what we have done.

CLETO. But you are a woman, señora.

RAQUEL. Has a woman less honor than a man, then?

CLETO. No, señora. Please, I don't know how to say it. The general is a soldier. He has a duty to his own cause. You are a woman. You have a duty to your husband. It is right that you should try to save him. It is not right that he should try to save himself.

RAQUEL. [*Dully.*] Yes, of course. It is right that I should save him. [*Becoming practical again.*] Your captain has been gone some time, Cleto. You'd better find out if he is still safe.

CLETO. Yes, señora. [*As he reaches the French windows she stops him.*]

RAQUEL. Wait, Cleto. Have you a mother—or a wife, perhaps?

CLETO. Oh, no, señora. I haven't anyone but the captain.

RAQUEL. But the captain is a soldier. What would you do if he should be killed?

CLETO. It is very simple, señora. I should be killed, too.

RAQUEL. You speak about death so calmly. Aren't you afraid of it, Cleto?

CLETO. No, señora. It's like the captain says . . . dying for what you believe in—that's the finest death of all.

RAQUEL. And you believe in the Revolutionary cause?

CLETO. Yes, señora. I am a poor peasant, that's true. But still I have a right to live like a man, with my own ground, and my own family, and my own future. [*He stops speaking abruptly.*] I'm sorry, señora. You are a fine lady. You don't understand these things. I must go and find my captain. [*He goes out.*]

RAQUEL. [*Rests her face against her hand.*] He's so young. But Tomás was no older. And he's not afraid. He said so. Oh, Domingo—Domingo! [*She straightens abruptly, takes the bottle of poison from the desk drawer and stares at it. Then she crosses to the decanter and laces the wine with the poison. She hurries back to the desk and is busy writing when* ANDRÉS *and* CLETO *return.*]

ANDRÉS. You'll have to hurry that letter. The district is clear now.

RAQUEL. I'll be through in just a moment. You might as well finish the wine while you're waiting.

ANDRÉS. Thank you. A most excellent idea. [*He pours himself a glass of wine. As he lifts it to his lips she speaks.*]

RAQUEL. Why don't you give some to—Cleto?

ANDRÉS. This is too fine a wine to waste on that boy.

RAQUEL. He'll probably never have another chance to taste such wine.

ANDRÉS. Very well. Pour yourself a glass, Cleto.

CLETO. Thank you. [*He pours it.*] Your health, my captain.

RAQUEL. [*Quickly.*] Drink it outside, Cleto. I want to speak to your captain. [*The boy looks at Andrés, who jerks his head toward the patio.* CLETO *nods and goes out.*] I want you to give my husband a message for me. I

Portraits of Real Life *What does Cleto's statement tell you about the culture in which he lives?*

Characterization *How does Raquel feel about Cleto?*

Comparing Literature

can't write it. You'll have to remember it. But first, give me a glass of wine, too.

ANDRÉS. [*Pouring the wine.*] It might be easier for him if you wrote it.

RAQUEL. I think not. [*She takes the glass.*] I want you to tell him that I never knew how much I loved him until tonight.

ANDRÉS. Is that all?

RAQUEL. Yes. Tell me, captain, do you think it possible to love a person too much?

ANDRÉS. Yes, señora. I do.

RAQUEL. So do I. Let us drink a toast, captain—to honor. To bright and shining honor.

ANDRÉS. [*Raises his glass.*] To honor. [*He drains his glass. She lifts hers almost to her lips and then puts it down. From the patio comes a faint cry.*]

CLETO. [*Calling faintly in a cry that fades into silence.*] Captain. Captain.

[ANDRÉS *sways, his hand trying to brush across his face as though trying to brush sense into his head. When he hears* CLETO *he tries to stagger toward the window but stumbles and can't quite make it. Hanging on to the table by the sofa he looks accusingly at her. She shrinks back against her chair.*]

ANDRÉS. [*His voice weak from the poison.*] Why?

RAQUEL. Because I love him. Can you understand that?

ANDRÉS. We'll win. The Revolution will win. You can't stop that.

RAQUEL. Yes, you'll win. I know that now.

ANDRÉS. That girl—she thought my story was funny—about the hanging. But you didn't . . .

RAQUEL. I'm glad you hanged him. I'm glad.

[ANDRÉS *looks at her and tries to smile. He manages to pull the pouch from his shirt and extend it to her. But it drops from his hand.*]

RAQUEL. [*Runs to French window and calls.*] Cleto. Cleto! [*She buries her face in her hands for a moment, then comes back to* ANDRÉS. *She kneels beside him and picks up the leather pouch. She opens it and, taking the ring, puts it on her finger. Then she sees the medal. She rises and, pulling out the chain from her own throat, she slides the medal on to the chain. Then she walks to the sofa and sinks down on it.*]

MARICA. [*Calling off.*] Raquel! Raquel! [RAQUEL *snaps off the lamp, leaving the room in darkness.* MARICA *opens the house door. She is carrying a candle which she shades with her hand. The light is too dim to reveal the dead* ANDRÉS.] What are you doing down here in the dark? Why don't you come to bed?

RAQUEL. [*Making an effort to speak.*] I'll come in just a moment.

MARICA. But what are you doing, Raquel?

RAQUEL. Nothing. Just listening . . . listening to an empty house.

QUICK CURTAIN

Portraits of Real Life Why do you think Raquel says this?

After You Read

Respond and Think Critically

Respond and Interpret
1. What aspect of the play did you find most surprising?
2. What are the political differences between the intruders and General Macías and his wife?

Analyze and Evaluate
3. In your opinion, is Raquel a hero? Explain.
4. In what ways does this play help an audience understand the Mexican Revolution?
5. (a)What do the ring of General Macías and the medal of Andrés symbolize to their owners? (b)What do they represent to Raquel?

Connect
6. **Big Idea** **Portraits of Real Life** (a)Explain how this play speaks to both loyalty and betrayal. (b)What connections can you make between loyalty and betrayal in the play and loyalty and betrayal in real life?
7. **Connect to the Author** Niggli's works show a concern for social issues, particularly those related to women. How does this selection demonstrate Raquel's oppression as well as her strength?

Literary Element Characterization

Characterization might be revealed to the reader through the character's own words. Sometimes authors will have characters present a long speech, or **monologue**, that tells the reader something about the character's personality.

1. Which character in the play delivers a monologue?
2. What does the reader learn about the characters as a result of this monologue?

Reading Strategy Analyze Plot and Setting

A reader needs to understand the basic chain of events that make up the story (**plot**) and the time and place in which the story takes place (**setting**).

1. How does the description of the setting help you understand the characters and their actions?
2. What is the climax, or highest emotional point, in *The Ring of General Macías*? Explain.

Literature Online

Selection Resources For Selection Quizzes, eFlashcards, and Reading-Writing Connection activities, go to glencoe.com and enter QuickPass code GL59794u4.

Vocabulary Practice

Tip: **Word Parts** You can find the meanings of common suffixes, such as *-ate, -ish, -ism, -ite,* and *-ly,* by looking them up in a dictionary.

Practice with Word Parts Use a dictionary to find the meaning of each vocabulary word's root. Look for definitions of any prefixes or suffixes in the word. Then use the word correctly in a sentence.

EXAMPLE: Prefix: *dis-*, apart, away, reversal; Root: *dignare*, to deign; Suffix: *-ful*, "full of" Sentence: Disdainful of the simple food, Rick refused to touch it

regally   ostentatiously   notorious
     repressed   impertinent

Writing

Write an Interior Monologue What is going through Raquel's mind as she sits "listening to an empty house" at the end of the play? Write an interior monologue—an account of her thoughts, as if she were speaking them to herself—that conveys her situation, feelings, and outlook on the future.

Comparing Literature

Build Background

Carmen Tafolla uses the word *m'ija* (mˈhə), a contraction of the Spanish words *mi* ("my") and *hija* ("daughter"). By calling the reader "m'ija," Tafolla follows the Mexican American tradition of addressing readers as if they were her own children and makes the poem a message to them..

Marked

Carmen Tafolla

Collage Series II, No. 3, 1993. Katherine S. Nemanich. Oil pastel on paper and board, 12 x 9 in. Private collection.

Never write with pencil,
m'ija
It is for those
who would
5   erase.
Make your mark proud
       and open,
Brave,
         beauty folded into
10   its imperfection,
Like a piece of turquoise
         marked.

Never write
with pencil,
15 m'ija.
Write with ink
      or mud,
or berries grown in
gardens never owned,
20   or, sometimes,
         if necessary,
            blood.

💬 Discussion Starter

How is Carmen Tafolla's advice about making a mark in the world useful? With a small group, discuss the question. Refer to the poem's words and discuss situations where her advice might be most beneficial.

Comparing Literature

Build Background
"The Ring" is about a life-changing encounter in the Danish countryside around 1800. At that time, most people in Denmark lived on farms.

The Ring

Isak Dinesen

On a summer morning a hundred and fifty years ago a young Danish squire and his wife went out for a walk on their land. They had been married a week. It had not been easy for them to get married, for the wife's family was higher in rank and wealthier than the husband's. But the two young people, now twenty-four and nineteen years old, had been set on their purpose for ten years; and in the end her haughty parents had had to give in to them.

They were wonderfully happy. The stolen meetings and secret, tearful love letters were now things of the past. To God and man they were one; they could walk arm in arm in broad daylight and drive in the same carriage, and they would walk and drive so till the end of their days. Their distant paradise had descended to earth and had proved, surprisingly, to be filled with the things of everyday life: with jesting and railleries,[1] with breakfasts and suppers, with dogs, haymaking and sheep. Sigismund, the young husband, had promised himself that from now there should be no stone in his bride's path, nor should any shadow fall across it. Lovisa, the wife, felt that now, every day and for the first time in her young life, she moved and breathed in perfect freedom because she could never have any secret from her husband.

To Lovisa—whom her husband called Lise—the rustic atmosphere of her new life was a matter of wonder and delight. Her husband's fear that the existence he could offer her might not be good enough for her filled her heart with laughter. It was not a long time since she had played with dolls; as now she dressed her own hair, looked over her linen press and arranged her flowers she again lived through an enchanting and cherished experience: one was doing everything gravely and solicitously, and all the time one knew one was playing.

It was a lovely July morning. Little woolly clouds drifted high up in the sky, the air was

---

1. *Railleries* are instances of good-natured ridicule or teasing.

Comparing Literature

full of sweet scents. Lise had on a white muslin frock and a large Italian straw hat. She and her husband took a path through the park; it wound on across the meadows, between small groves and groups of trees, to the sheep field. Sigismund was going to show his wife his sheep. For this reason she had not brought her small white dog, Bijou, with her, for he would yap at the lambs and frighten them, or he would annoy the sheep dogs. Sigismund prided himself on his sheep; he had studied sheep-breeding in Mecklenburg[2] and England, and had brought back with him Cotswold rams by which to improve his Danish stock. While they walked he explained to Lise the great possibilities and difficulties of the plan.

She thought: "How clever he is, what a lot of things he knows!" and at the same time: "What an absurd person he is, with his sheep! What a baby he is! I am a hundred years older than he."

But when they arrived at the sheepfold the old sheepmaster Mathias met them with the sad news that one of the English lambs was dead and two were sick. Lise saw that her

Visual Vocabulary
Cotswold is a breed of sheep with long, coarse hair, originally bred in the Cotswold Hills of southwestern England.

---

2. *Mecklenburg* is a farming region in northeastern Germany.

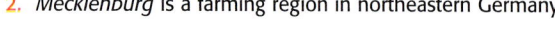

Gentle Spring, 1889. Edward Wilkins Waite. Oil on canvas, 51 x 76 cm. Private collection.

View the Art This painting depicts a landscape with animals. What is the mood of this painting? At what point in "The Ring" does the story reflect this mood?

husband was grieved by the tidings; while he questioned Mathias on the matter she kept silent and only gently pressed his arm. A couple of boys were sent off to fetch the sick lambs, while the master and servant went into the details of the case. It took some time.

Lise began to gaze about her and to think of other things. Twice her own thoughts made her blush deeply and happily, like a red rose, then slowly her blush died away, and the two men were still talking about sheep. A little while after their conversation caught her attention. It had turned to a sheep thief.

This thief during the last months had broken into the sheepfolds of the neighborhood like a wolf, had killed and dragged away his prey like a wolf and like a wolf had left no trace after him. Three nights ago the shepherd and his son on an estate ten miles away had caught him in the act. The thief had killed the man and knocked the boy senseless, and had managed to escape. There were men sent out to all sides to catch him, but nobody had seen him.

Lise wanted to hear more about the horrible event, and for her benefit old Mathias went through it once more. There had been a long fight in the sheep house, in many places the earthen floor was soaked with blood. In the fight the thief's left arm was broken; all the same, he had climbed a tall fence with a lamb on his back. Mathias added that he would like to string up the murderer with these two hands of his, and Lise nodded her head at him gravely in approval. She remembered Red Ridinghood's wolf, and felt a pleasant little thrill running down her spine.

Sigismund had his own lambs in his mind, but he was too happy in himself to wish anything in the universe ill. After a minute he said: "Poor devil."

Lise said: "How can you pity such a terrible man? Indeed Grandmamma was right when she said that you were a revolutionary and a danger to society!" The thought of Grandmamma, and of the tears of past days, again turned her mind away from the gruesome tale she had just heard.

The boys brought the sick lambs and the men began to examine them carefully, lifting them up and trying to set them on their legs; they squeezed them here and there and made the little creatures whimper. Lise shrank from the show and her husband noticed her distress.

"You go home, my darling," he said, "this will take some time. But just walk ahead slowly, and I shall catch up with you."

So she was turned away by an impatient husband to whom his sheep meant more than his wife. If any experience could be sweeter than to be dragged out by him to look at those same sheep, it would be this. She dropped her large summer hat with its blue ribbons on the grass and told him to carry it back for her, for she wanted to feel the summer air on her forehead and in her hair. She walked on very slowly, as he had told her to do, for she wished to obey him in everything. As she walked she felt a great new happiness in being altogether alone, even without Bijou. She could not remember that she had ever before in all her life been altogether alone. The landscape around her was still, as if full of promise, and it was hers. Even the swallows cruising in the air were hers, for they belonged to him, and he was hers.

She followed the curving edge of the grove and after a minute or two found that she was out of sight to the men by the sheep house. What could now, she wondered, be sweeter than to walk along the path in the

Comparing Literature

long flowering meadow grass, slowly, slowly, and to let her husband overtake her there? It would be sweeter still, she reflected, to steal into the grove and to be gone, to have vanished from the surface of the earth from him when, tired of the sheep and longing for her company, he should turn the bend of the path to catch up with her.

An idea struck her; she stood still to think it over.

A few days ago her husband had gone for a ride and she had not wanted to go with him, but had strolled about with Bijou in order to explore her domain. Bijou then, gamboling, had led her straight into the grove. As she had followed him, gently forcing her way into the shrubbery, she had suddenly come upon a glade in the midst of it, a narrow space like a small alcove with hangings of thick green and golden brocade, big enough to hold two or three people in it. She had felt at that moment that she had come into the very heart of her new home. If today she could find the spot again she would stand perfectly still there, hidden from all the world. Sigismund would look for her in all directions; he would be unable to understand what had become of her and for a minute, for a short minute—or, perhaps, if she was firm and cruel enough, for five—he would realize what a void, what an unendurably sad and horrible place the universe would be when she was no longer in it. She gravely scrutinized the grove to find the right entrance to her hiding-place, then went in.

She took great care to make no noise at all, therefore advanced exceedingly slowly. When a twig caught the flounces of her ample skirt she loosened it softly from the muslin, so as not to crack it. Once a branch took hold of one of her long golden curls; she stood still, with her arms lifted, to free it. A little way into the grove the soil became moist; her light steps no longer made any sound upon it. With one hand she held her small handkerchief to her lips, as if to emphasize the secretness of her course. She found the spot she sought and bent down to divide the foliage and make a door to her sylvan[3] closet. At this the hem of her dress caught her foot and she stopped to loosen it. As she rose she looked into the face of a man who was already in the shelter.

He stood up erect, two steps off. He must have watched her as she made her way straight toward him.

She took him in in one single glance. His face was bruised and scratched, his hands and wrists stained with dark filth. He was dressed in rags, barefooted, with tatters wound round his naked ankles. His arms hung down to his sides, his right hand clasped the hilt of a knife. He was about her own age. The man and the woman looked at each other.

This meeting in the wood from beginning to end passed without a word; what happened could only be rendered by pantomime. To the two actors in the pantomime it was timeless; according to a clock it lasted four minutes.

She had never in her life been exposed to danger. It did not occur to her to sum up her position, or to work out the length of time it would take to call her husband or Mathias, whom at this moment she could hear shouting to his dogs. She beheld the man before her as she would have beheld a forest ghost: the apparition itself, not the sequels[4] of it, changes the world to the human who faces it.

Although she did not take her eyes off the face before her she sensed that the alcove

---

3. *Sylvan* means "in or among woods" or "formed by trees."
4. Here, *sequels* means "results or consequences."

Weary but Watchful, late 19th Century. John Sargent Noble.

View the Art In the story, the husband and wife have very different feelings about Sigismund's flock of sheep. How might each react to this image?

had been turned into a covert.[5] On the ground a couple of sacks formed a couch; there were some gnawed bones by it. A fire must have been made here in the night, for there were cinders strewn on the forest floor.

After a while she realized that he was observing her just as she was observing him. He was no longer just run to earth and crouching for a spring, but he was wondering, trying to know. At that she seemed to see herself with the eyes of the wild animal at bay[6] in his dark hiding-place; her silently approaching white figure, which might mean death.

He moved his right arm till it hung down straight before him between his legs. Without lifting the hand he bent the wrist and slowly raised the point of the knife till it pointed at her throat. The gesture was mad, unbelievable. He did not smile as he made it, but his nostrils distended,[7] the corners of his mouth quivered a little. Then slowly he put the knife back in the sheath by his belt.

She had no object of value about her, only the wedding ring which her husband had set on her finger in church, a week ago. She drew it off, and in this movement dropped her handkerchief. She reached out her hand with the ring toward him. She did not bargain for her life. She was fearless by nature, and the horror with which he inspired her was not fear of what he might do to her. She commanded him, she besought[8] him to vanish as he had come, to take a dreadful figure out of her life, so that it should never have been there. In the dumb[9] movement her young form had the grave authoritativeness of a priestess conjuring down some monstrous being by a sacred sign.

He slowly reached out his hand to hers, his finger touched hers, and her hand was steady at the touch. But he did not take the ring. As she let it go it dropped to the ground as her handkerchief had done.

For a second the eyes of both followed it. It rolled a few inches toward him and stopped before his bare foot. In a hardly perceivable movement he kicked it away and again looked into her face. They remained like that, she knew not how long, but she felt that during that time something happened, things were changed.

He bent down and picked up her handkerchief. All the time gazing at her, he again

---

5. As a noun, *covert* means "a hiding place." More often, you will see the word used as an adjective to mean "secret, hidden, or concealed."
6. *At bay* refers to the position of a cornered animal that is forced to turn and confront its pursuers.
7. *Distended* means "enlarged or expanded."
8. *Besought* is the past tense of *beseech* and means "begged or asked earnestly."
9. Here, *dumb* means "silent" and "without words."

> Comparing Literature

drew his knife and wrapped the tiny bit of cambric[10] round the blade. This was difficult for him to do because his left arm was broken. While he did it his face under the dirt and sun-tan slowly grew whiter till it was almost phosphorescent.[11] Fumbling with both hands, he once more stuck the knife into the sheath. Either the sheath was too big and had never fitted the knife, or the blade was much worn—it went in. For two or three more seconds his gaze rested on her face; then he lifted his own face a little, the strange radiance still upon it, and closed his eyes.

The movement was definitive and unconditional. In this one motion he did what she had begged him to do: he vanished and was gone. She was free.

She took a step backward, the immovable, blind face before her, then bent as she had done to enter the hiding-place, and glided away as noiselessly as she had come. Once outside the grove she stood still and looked round for the meadow path, found it, and began to walk home.

Her husband had not yet rounded the edge of the grove. Now he saw her and helloed to her gaily; he came up quickly and joined her.

The path here was so narrow that he kept half behind her and did not touch her. He began to explain to her what had been the matter with the lambs. She walked a step before him and thought: All is over.

After a while he noticed her silence, came up beside her to look at her face and asked, "What is the matter?"

She searched her mind for something to say, and at last said: "I have lost my ring."

"What ring?" he asked her.

She answered, "My wedding ring."

As she heard her own voice pronounce the words she conceived their meaning.

Her wedding ring. "With this ring"—dropped by one and kicked away by another—"with this ring I thee wed." With this lost ring she had wedded herself to something. To what? To poverty, persecution, total loneliness. To the sorrows and the sinfulness of this earth. "And what therefore God has joined together let man not put asunder."[12]

"I will find you another ring," her husband said. "You and I are the same as we were on our wedding day; it will do as well. We are husband and wife today too, as much as yesterday, I suppose."

Her face was so still that he did not know if she had heard what he said. It touched him that she should take the loss of his ring so to heart. He took her hand and kissed it. It was cold, not quite the same hand as he had last kissed. He stopped to make her stop with him.

"Do you remember where you had the ring on last?" he asked.

"No," she answered.

"Have you any idea," he asked, "where you may have lost it?"

"No," she answered. "I have no idea at all."

---

10. *Cambric* is the soft, lightweight linen of which Lise's handkerchief is made.
11. Here, *phosphorescent* (fos´fə res´ənt) means "glowing."
12. *Asunder* (ə sun´dər) means "in separate parts." This biblical quotation (Matthew 19:6) is often repeated at the end of a traditional Christian marriage ceremony.

Quickwrite

Reread the story to identify passages that reveal the personalities of Sigismund, Lise, and the thief. Then refer to these passages and write an analysis of how Dinesen uses characterization to reveal the characters' personalities. Write at least one paragraph for each character.

Wrap-Up: Comparing Literature
Across Genres

- *The Ring of General Macías* by Josephina Niggli
- *Marked* by Carmen Tafolla
- *The Ring* by Isak Dinesen

COMPARE THE Big Idea Portraits of Real Life

Writing Activity These texts portray female characters facing particular conflicts and challenges. Are the concerns portrayed in these works still relevant to all women or only to certain groups of women? Might these concerns apply to men as well? Consider contemporary issues and how they affect the lives of women today. Then write a brief essay in which you discuss your thoughts about these issues in relation to the texts.

COMPARE Theme

Group Activity A **genre** is a category, or type, of literature. Each of the selections compared here represents different genres—drama, poetry, and short story—while conveying a theme, or message, about loyalty. With a small group, discuss the following questions:

1. To whom or what do the main characters in these selections believe they owe their loyalty? Explain.
2. In what ways do these selections show that girls and women are capable of acting bravely or of fulfilling roles once reserved for men?

COMPARE Cultures

Speaking and Listening Josephina Niggli and Carmen Tafolla both weave Latino culture into their literary works. Niggli was raised in Mexico by Anglo parents, while Tafolla was raised in the United States by Mexican American parents. Do the different time periods and childhood circumstances have an effect on the writers' attitudes and beliefs? Make inferences about each author's beliefs regarding the following:

1. the role of women and girls in society
2. the importance of culture in people's lives
3. the effect of history—especially family history—upon future generations

Support your inferences with details from the texts. Then share your insights by presenting an oral report to the class.

Collage Series II, No. 3, 1993. Katherine S. Nemanich. Oil pastel on paper and board, 12 x 9 in. Private collection.

Selection Resources For Selection Quizzes, eFlashcards, and Reading-Writing Connection activities, go to glencoe.com and enter QuickPass code GL59794u4.

Learning Objectives

For pages 874–881

In this workshop, you will focus on the following objective:

Writing: Writing a persuasive speech.

Writing Workshop

Persuasive Speech

Literature Connection After Brutus kills Caesar, he must convince his audience that his reasons for killing Caesar were both noble and just. In this workshop, you will write a speech that uses appeals and other persuasive techniques to convince an audience. Study the rubric below to learn the goals and strategies for writing a successful persuasive speech.

> If [you] demand why Brutus rose against Caesar, this is my answer: Not that I lov'd Caesar less, but that I lov'd Rome more. Had you rather Caesar were living, and die all slaves, than that Caesar were dead, to live all free men? As Caesar lov'd me, I weep for him; as he was fortunate, I rejoice at it; as he was valiant, I honor him; but, as he was ambitious, I slew him."
>
> —William Shakespeare, from *The Tragedy of Julius Caesar*

Writing Process

At any stage of a writing process, you may think of new ideas. Feel free to return to earlier stages as you write.

Prewrite

Draft

Revise

Focus Lesson:
Use Evidence

Edit and Proofread

Focus Lesson: Parallel Construction

Present

Checklist

Goals	Strategies
To present a clearly stated position or claim to a target audience	✓ Maintain a clear focus on your claim throughout your essay
To support your position or claim	✓ Support your thesis or claim with emotional appeals, specific evidence, and reasoning
	✓ Organize ideas logically and for greatest effect on your audience
	✓ Use persuasive techniques such as appeals to authority, hyperbole, repetition, and word choice
To anticipate and address audience concerns	✓ Refute opposing arguments

Writing and Research For prewriting, drafting, and revising tools, go to glencoe.com and enter QuickPass code GL59794u4.

Persuasion

> **Assignment**
>
> ## Write a Persuasive Speech
>
> Write a persuasive speech of about 1,500 words. As you work, keep your audience and purpose in mind.
>
> ---
>
> **Audience:** members of a high school assembly, including classmates, teachers, and the principal
>
> **Purpose:** to persuade through logical and emotional appeals; precise, relevant evidence; and other techniques.

Real-World Connection

If your speech addresses an issue in your community, submit it to your local newspaper for publication. If it addresses an issue in your school, submit it to your school newspaper.

Analyze a Professional Model

In the short speech that follows, former senator Everett Dirksen explains why the marigold should be the national flower. As you read the speech, note how Dirksen presents a clear opinion, uses logical reasoning, and addresses counterarguments. Pay close attention to the comments in the margin. They point out features to include in your own speech.

Why Marigolds Should Be the National Flower
by Senator Everett Dirksen, Republican, Illinois

Mr. President: On January 8, 1965, I introduced Senate Joint Resolution 19, to designate the American marigold—*Tagetes erecta*—as the national floral emblem of the United States. Today I am introducing the same resolution with the suggestion that it again be referred to the Committee on the Judiciary.

The American flag is not a mere assembly of colors, stripes and stars but, in fact, symbolizes our origin, development, and growth.

The American eagle, king of the skies, is so truly representative of our might and power.

A national floral emblem should represent the virtues of our land and be national in character.

The marigold is a native of North America and can in truth and in fact be called an American flower.

It is national in character, for it grows and thrives in

Opinion/Thesis Statement

Be sure to state your opinion clearly and forcefully at or near the beginning of your speech.

Emotional Appeals and Analogy

The emotional appeal to national symbols and the analogy "king of the skies" arouse feelings of pride. Appeal to your listeners' emotions as well as to their logic.

Clarify Your Position

Present facts and opinions that make your position stronger or easier to understand.

Logical Reasoning

Use logical reasoning to support your opinion.

Support

Present facts and examples both to keep your audience engaged and to back up your argument.

Counterarguments

Others may suggest different national flowers. Make your case stronger by addressing opposing opinions or viewpoints.

Logical Order

Dirksen presents his points in order of importance. Present your argument in a logical order.

Conclusion

Forcefully restate your thesis. Also write a "clincher" statement, make a final emotional or logical appeal, or end in another memorable way.

---

every one of the fifty states of this nation. It conquers the extremes of temperature. It well withstands the summer sun and the evening chill.

Its robustness reflects the hardihood and character of the generations who pioneered and built this land into a great nation. It is not temperamental about fertility. It resists its natural enemies, the insects. It is self-reliant and requires little attention. Its spectacular colors—lemon and orange, rich brown and deep mahogany—befit the imaginative qualities of this nation.

It is as sprightly as the daffodil, as colorful as the rose, as resolute as the zinnia, as delicate as the carnation, as haughty as the chrysanthemum, as aggressive as the petunia, as ubiquitous as the violet, and as stately as the snapdragon.

It beguiles the senses and ennobles the spirit of man. It is the delight of the amateur gardener and a constant challenge to the professional.

Since it is native to America and nowhere else in the world, and common to every state in the Union, I present the American marigold for designation as the national floral emblem of our country.

The Right Topic

Remember that a speech is ultimately intended for listeners, not readers, so choose a topic that will interest your audience from the very beginning. Also, choose a topic that you can support without long explanations, densely embedded facts, or statistics that will be hard for listeners to follow.

Reading-Writing Connection Think about the writing techniques that you have just encountered and try them out in the persuasive speech you write.

Prewrite

Choose an Issue Choose an issue that you truly care about. Keep your audience in mind: Your readers and listeners will be more interested if you select a topic that they truly care about too.

Gather Ideas Your next step is to test your issue by making sure that it has two sides. At the same time, you can begin to develop ideas for writing by making a pro-and-con chart.

State Your Opinion Study your graphic organizer. Decide what you want to say about the issue. Sum up your opinion in a single sentence. This is your opinion statement, or thesis. You can revise it during the drafting or revising stages to make it sharper, clearer, or more accurate.

Talk About Your Ideas Meet with a partner. Read your opinion statement out loud. Briefly discuss your reasons for holding the opinion. As you do so, listen to your voice. How do you sound as you discuss this topic? What makes you most excited or personally involved as you explain your ideas? What specific words and what kinds of sentences do you use to convey your opinion and feelings? To develop your writing voice, listen to your speaking voice now so that you can remember and re-create it as you write later.

Make an Organizational Plan Outline your persuasive speech by planning the main points you will make, jotting down supporting details, listing counterarguments you will address, and making notes on how you will conclude.

▶ Create a focus for your listeners by stating your opinion in the first sentence or near the beginning of your speech.

▶ Win the reader over by sounding as reasonable and as logical as possible. Address and nullify counterarguments, while building support for your opinion.

▶ Present reasons, facts, examples, short stories or anecdotes, case studies, or analogies to support your opinion. Then conclude forcefully.

▶ Use one of these methods of organization or create a similar order that includes the elements shown below.

Persuasion

Use Persuasive Techniques

Try out these persuasive techniques in your speech:

Repetition: Emphasize your point by repeating your thesis. You can also repeat words with especially positive or negative connotations to move or sway your audience.

Testimonials: Incorporate the supporting opinions of authorities to bolster your position or evidence.

Avoid Plagiarism

Remember that using another person's words—even just one short, memorable phrase—without crediting those words is dishonest. It is also against the law.

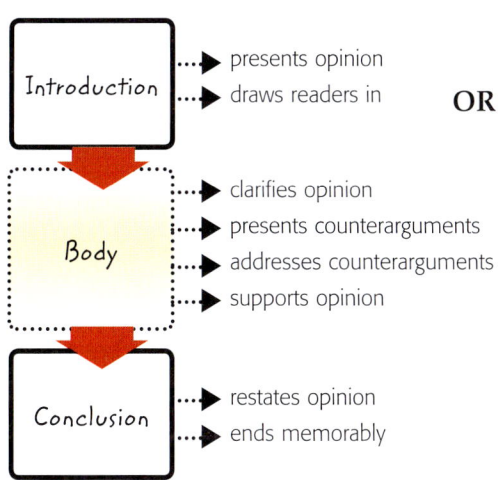

OR

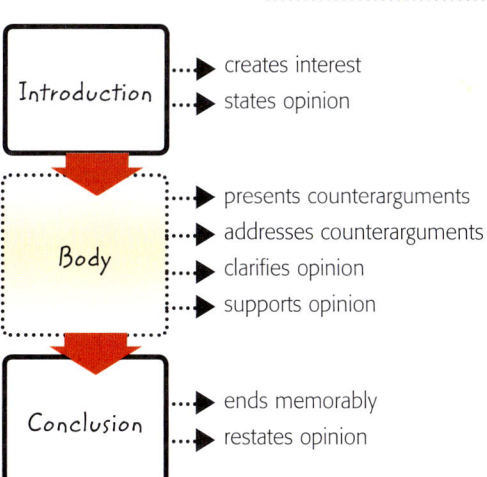

Writing Frames

As you read the workshop model, think about the writer's use of the following frames:

- We must not let _____.
- There is another practical reason for opposing the _____.
- It is admirable for _____. However, _____.

Consider using frames like these in your own persuasive essay.

Introduction
How does the writer create interest and draw in the target audience?

Opinion/Thesis Statement
What is the writer's opinion? Where is it stated?

Counterarguments
How does the writer anticipate audience concerns and address the opposing point of view?

Draft

Use Transitions As you get your ideas down on paper, remember to link them with appropriate transitions. In persuasive writing, you can help your audience distinguish your most important reasons and points by introducing them with words such as *first, second,* and *last*. Other transition expressions that are similarly useful include *more important, most important,* and *finally*. Remember to link your ideas between paragraphs as well as within them.

Analyze a Workshop Model

Here is a final draft of a persuasive speech. Read the speech and answer the questions in the margin. Use the answers to these questions to guide you as you write.

Down with Worn-Out Dress Codes!

Imagine never again being permitted to wear a pair of sneakers, blue jeans, or a sports cap to school. Imagine having to set aside most kinds of jewelry or almost anything metal. Imagine having to wear your hair the way the principal thinks it should look. If the school board has its way, that is what will happen at Wilkerson School. We must not let this outdated, unrealistic, and impractical dress code become reality.

The school board has published several reasons for instituting the new dress code. First, members say that the new dress code will help prepare students for the real world. They explain that well-dressed students will behave more like adults at a job. As a result, they say, students will get down to the business of learning: They will work harder and receive higher grades. Second, according to the school board, the dress code will build students' self-respect as they take pride in their appearance. This, in turn, will be carried into greater respect for teachers and other students, who will be less likely to fight or disrupt classes.

These arguments are simplistic for several reasons. First, there is no proof that the clothing a student wears will change the stu-

878 UNIT 4 DRAMA

dent or that it will cause a student to focus more on learning. Also, the idea that a student's grades can be improved by wearing certain clothes is entirely illogical. I am sure that if I used that reasoning in one of my papers, Mrs. LeBlanc would circle it and write *This is faulty logic.* Finally, students' self-respect is not based on the kinds of clothes they wear. Self-respect results from accomplishments and inner growth, not from putting on specific kind of footwear or removing jewelry. In fact, requiring students to conform to a dress code shows disrespect for students' ability to choose clothes that they think are acceptable for school.

Every aspect of the new dress-code policy is unacceptable, especially the ban on blue jeans and sneakers. Jeans are practical, do not wear out quickly, and are machine-washable. Sneakers are practical because they are sturdier than dress shoes and provide better support for the feet. In addition, sneakers are safer because they have rubber soles that prevent students from slipping on the slick tile floors and stairways.

There is another practical reason for opposing the dress code. Many families in our community live on a limited budget with little money for wardrobes for their school-aged children. Dress pants and shoes often cost more, and wear out faster, than jeans and sneakers. It is not practical to require students to have two sets of clothing. This expense is especially unfair to parents on fixed income.

In today's business world, clothing is often more casual than it was a few decades ago. In fact, many offices have at least one "casual dress" day, typically Friday, and many workers can do their work from their homes. These people can work in jeans, sweat suits, or pajamas if they want to.

It is admirable for the school board to want to make Wilkerson School a better place and to improve the prospects of its students. However, the first thing the school board should do to help achieve this goal is to withdraw its proposal for a new dress code.

Persuasion

Logical Order
Identify the organization of the speech so far. Is it logical? Explain.

Emotional Appeal/Word Choices
How does the writer appeal to emotions? Which words have special force?

Logical Appeal
How does the writer appeal to logic?

Emotional Appeal
How does the writer appeal to emotions?

Conclusion
How does the writer conclude? What makes the final paragraph effective?

Revise

Traits of Strong Writing

Include these traits of strong writing to express your ideas effectively.

Ideas

Organization

Voice

Word Choice

Sentence Fluency

Conventions

Presentation

For more information on using the Traits of Strong Writing, see pages R28–R30.

Peer Review When you finish your draft, ask a classmate to read it. Have your classmate identify your opinion statement or thesis, your use of facts and examples, and your counterarguments. If your reviewer cannot identify any of these major elements, revise your speech to create them or make them clear. Then ask your reviewer to consider how well your work reflects the traits of strong writing. Again, revise as needed. Use the checklist below to help you evaluate and stengthen each other's writing.

Checklist

- ✓ Do you present a clear position or claim in your introduction?
- ✓ Do you maintain a clear focus on your claim throughout your essay?
- ✓ Do you support your thesis with specific evidence, reasoning, and emotional appeals?
- ✓ Do you organize ideas logically and for greatest effect on your audience?
- ✓ Do you use persuasive techniques such as word choice, repetition, testimonials, hyperbole, or irony?
- ✓ Do you answer opposing arguments effectively?

Word Choice

This academic vocabulary word appears in the student model:

institute (in´stə tüt) *v.* 1. to begin, cause to be established, or set into motion; 2. to organize. *The school board has published several reasons for instituting the new dress code.* Using academic vocabulary may help strengthen your writing. Try to use one or two academic vocabulary words in your persuasive speech. See the complete list on pages R80–R82

> **Focus Lesson**
>
> ## Elaborate on Ideas with Evidence
>
> To make a point or counterargument convincing, you need to explain it fully or elaborate upon it. You can elaborate through clarification, restatement, and the addition of evidence or support: facts, examples, and other details that develop your main ideas. Here is a sentence from the Workshop Model followed by a revision that elaborates on the ideas.
>
> **Draft:**
>
> Many families in our community live on a limited budget.
>
> **Revision:**
>
> Many families in our community live on a limited budget with little money for wardrobes for their school-aged children.[1] Dress pants and shoes often cost more, and wear out faster, than jeans and sneakers.[2]
>
> **1:** Elaboration with Fact   **2:** Elaboration with Fact and Examples

Writing and Research For editing and publishing tools, go to glencoe.com and enter QuickPass code GL59794u4.

Edit and Proofread

Get It Right When you have completed the final draft of your speech, proofread it for errors in grammar, usage, mechanics, and spelling. Refer to the Language Handbook, pages R40–R59, as a guide.

Focus Lesson

Parallel Construction

Parts of a sentence joined by *and* or another coordinating conjunction must be parallel. This means that these parts must all be nouns, verbs, or the same type of phrases or clauses.

Problem:

These people can work in jeans, wearing sweats, or in pajamas if they want to.

Three items—*jeans, wearing sweat suits,* and *in pajamas*—joined by a coordinating conjunction are not parallel: *jeans* is a noun, *wearing sweats* is a participial phrase, and *in pajamas* is a prepositional phrase.

Solution A: Make all of the items noun objects of prepositions.

These people can work in jeans, sweat suits, or pajamas if they want to.

Solution B: Make all of the items participial phrases.

These people can work dressed in jeans, clothed in sweat suits, or clad in pajamas if they want to.

Solution C: Make all of the items prepositional phrases.

These people can work in jeans, in sweat suits, or in pajamas if they want to.

Present

Make It Legible If you are writing your essay by hand, use blue or black ink and perfectly neat, legible handwriting. If you have torn the pages from a spiral-bound notebook, trim them neatly with scissors. If you are word-processing, double-check your teacher's manuscript or format guidelines.

Persuasion

Peer Review Tips

A classmate may ask you to read his or her persuasive essay. Take your time and jot down notes as you read so you can give constructive feedback. Use the following questions to get started:

- Does the writer present convincing, well-supported reasons for the position or claim?
- Does the writer persuade through the effective use of appeals, word choice, and other persuasive techniques?

Word-Processing Tip

Your teacher may require a title sheet or cover page. If your teacher does not specify different requirements for a cover sheet, include these elements in the upper right-hand corner of the first page:

- your name
- the course name
- your teacher's name
- the date

Center your title in the middle of the page. Do not include a page number.

Writer's Portfolio

Place a copy of your speech in your portfolio to review later.

Speaking, Listening, and Viewing Workshop

Persuasive Speech

Learning Objectives

For pages 882–883

In this workshop, you will focus on the following objective:

Listening and Speaking: Delivering a persuasive speech.

Literature Connection When Brutus presented his speech after Caesar's assassination, persuading his audience was a matter of life or death. Brutus could not afford to mumble, speak too softly, shuffle his feet, or forget an important point. Instead, he had to master all of his rhetorical skills to make his message convincing. In this workshop, you will learn how to deliver an effective, powerful, and persuasive speech to a real audience.

> **Assignment** Deliver a persuasive speech to an audience.

Plan Your Delivery

A speech *may* be read aloud. It is far more effective, however, when the written word, which readers can study and review, is transformed into the spoken word, which listeners must understand as it is delivered. Follow these steps to turn your persuasive writing into persuasive speaking:

- Start by reading your speech aloud to a partner. Find out what your listener notices immediately and what he or she misses. Most important, ask your partner whether he or she can identify your opinion statement. Then ask to what extent your speech was persuasive.
- Use your partner's comments to help you make your opinion statement clearer or more definite. Also brainstorm with your partner to devise ways to make your speech more dramatic, forceful, interesting, and persuasive.
- Make note cards that list the main ideas and details of your speech. Number the cards and refer to them only if needed.

Sound Devices

Do you remember the sound devices you learned in the poetry unit? Some of those work well in speeches. Repetition, for example, can often be effective. (Think of the many times that Martin Luther King Jr. said, "I have a dream.") Alliteration, too, can be powerfully persuasive.

School Board's Position
Dress codes prepare students for the professional world
Increase effort to improve learning and grades...

Rehearse

Practice your speech several times before you deliver it in class. Set a goal of learning your speech so well that you need no more than a glance at your note cards. Rehearse by yourself in front of a mirror. Try different gestures and tones of voice. Then, when you are confident that you are almost ready, ask a classmate or family member to listen. Work with that person to iron out any remaining wrinkles in your delivery.

Evaluate a Speech

Use these techniques to evaluate the content of your own speech or a partner's speech.

- Identify the opinion and the main ideas that support it.
- Analyze the types of arguments the speaker uses, such as appeals to emotion, logic, or authority, or the use of an analogy, anecdotes, or a case study.
- Study how well the speech anticipates and answers the listener's counterarguments.

Use the list below to help you evaluate the delivery of your own speech or a partner's speech.

Techniques for Delivering a Persuasive Speech

Verbal Techniques	Nonverbal Techniques
☑ **Enunciation** Speak as clearly as you can. Do not alter your voice drastically—even for emphasis—but do not mumble either.	☑ **Audience Feedback** Watch the audience's faces for hints that you are speaking too fast, too slowly, too loudly, or too softly.
☑ **Pitch** Eliminate the highs and lows in your voice as you make your points.	☑ **Eye Contact** Look directly at your audience except to refer briefly to note cards.
☑ **Tone** Be sure that your tone of voice suits the seriousness of your subject. Remember that you can also use your tone to emphasize key words and ideas.	☑ **Body Language** Show interest by standing tall and comfortably, not slouching or folding your arms.
☑ **Rate** Never race through your speech. Speak at a normal rate of speed.	☑ **Facial Expressions** Make sure that your facial expressions suit the content of your speech.

Watch a Public Speaker

Watch a performance of an accomplished public speaker, recorded or online. Note how the speaker uses gestures, voice, and posture to persuade the audience.

Speaking Frames

Consider using the following frames in your speech:

- My own view is that ____ because ____.
- Of course, some may disagree with my claim and say that ____.
- For these reasons, ____ should be ____.

Presentation Tips

Use the following checklist to evaluate your speech.

- ☑ Did you organize your ideas effectively?
- ☑ Did you use appropriate listening strategies, such as identifying the opinion and main ideas that support it?
- ☑ Did you use effective verbal and nonverbal techniques?

Speaking, Listening, and Viewing For project ideas, templates, and presentation tips, go to glencoe.com and enter QuickPass code GL59794u4.

Independent Reading

Drama and Novels

DRAMA RELIES ALMOST ENTIRELY ON TWO THINGS: dialogue and stage direction. Most dramas tell a story, present a theme, and move, shock, or entertain their viewers by means of conversations between characters as well as movements on a stage. Readers who wish to get the most out of a play have to hear those conversations and visualize those movements. For more drama on a range of themes, try the two suggestions below. For novels that incorporate the Big Ideas of *Loyalty and Betrayal*, as well as *Portraits of Real Life*, try the titles from the Glencoe Literature Library on the next page.

Seven Against Thebes
Aeschylus

A prophecy was made about the two sons of Oedipus, Eteocles and Polyneices: they would divide their inheritance with a sword in order to obtain equal shares. As *Seven Against Thebes* opens, Thebes is under siege by an Argive army led by Polyneices, the son of Oedipus and brother of Eteocles. Eteocles pledges to save Thebes and fiercely defend its seven gates against the Argive army's seven armored chiefs and their warriors. Trying to avoid disaster, the Theban women warn Eteocles to stay away from the seventh gate. A battle ensues, and the prophecy proves true.

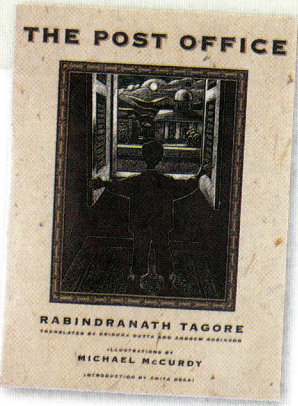

The Post Office
Rabindranath Tagore

In this short, two-act play, an adopted child named Amal is confined to his home as the result of an illness. His only entertainment is watching the neighborhood as he sits at his open window. As Amal engages in conversations with the townspeople who stroll by, he forms relationships and expresses keen insight into life. He also becomes drawn to the post office, which he can see from his window. After a watchman identifies the post office as the King's office, Amal becomes hopeful that the King will send him a letter.

884 UNIT 4 DRAMA

GLENCOE LITERATURE LIBRARY

Wuthering Heights
Emily Brontë

This brooding romance tells of Loyalty and Betrayal through the story of the thwarted relationship between a privileged woman and the penniless servant who loves her.

A House for Mr Biswas
V. S. Naipaul

In this Portrait of Real Life in Trinidad in 1961, a man struggles to break the bonds of dependence on the domineering family he married into as he tries to buy a house of his own.

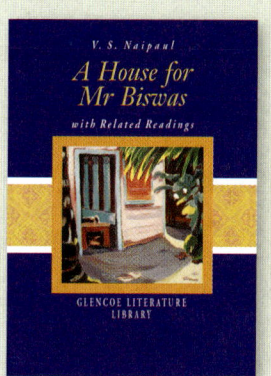

CRITICS' CORNER

"[Antony and Cleopatra] may be world leaders but they are also, after all, only human beings—flawed and aging ones at that. We as human beings share their mortality; many of us recognize their strong feelings of jealousy, love, shame, and insecurity. Despite their historical grandeur and thanks to Shakespeare's sensitive portrayal of them, Antony and Cleoptara are no more—and no less—extraordinary than we are."

—Kathy D. Darrow and Ira Mark Milne, *Shakespeare for Students Review*

Antony and Cleopatra
William Shakespeare

The married Roman leader Mark Antony, who is living in Alexandria, Egypt, falls in love with Cleopatra, the Queen of Egypt. In this thrilling tale, both Antony and Cleopatra face the harsh reality of their ill-fated love.

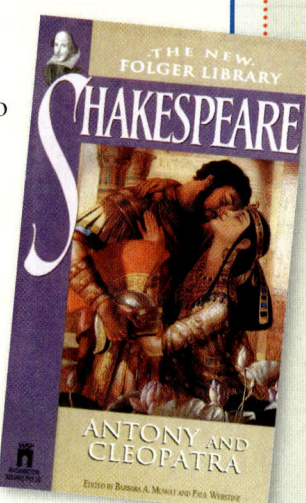

Write a Review

Read one of the books listed on this page and write a review of it for your classmates. Be sure to explain why other students might enjoy the book, or offer suggestions on how they might overcome difficulties in reading the book. Present your review to the class.

INDEPENDENT READING

Assessment

English–Language Arts

Reading: Drama

Carefully read the following passage. Use context clues to help you define any words with which you are unfamiliar. Pay close attention to the mood, theme, and characters. Then, on a separate sheet of paper, answer the questions on page 888.

from *Oedipus the King* by Sophocles

TIME AND SCENE: *The royal house of Thebes. Many years have passed since Oedipus ascended the throne of Thebes, and now a plague has struck the city. A Chorus, the citizens of Thebes, along with Oedipus and Jocasta, are on stage.*

Chorus. My king
I've said it once, I'll say it time and again—
I'd be insane, you know it,
senseless, ever to turn my back on you.
5 You who set our beloved land—storm-tossed, shattered—
straight on course. Now again, good helmsman,
steer us through the storm!
[*The* Chorus *draws away, leaving* Oedipus *and* Jocasta *side by side.*]
Jocasta. For the love of god,
Oedipus, tell me too, what is it?
Why this rage? You're so unbending.
10 **Oedipus.** I will tell you. I respect you, Jocasta,
much more than these men here . . . [*Glancing at the Chorus.*]
Creon's to blame. Creon schemes against me.
Jocasta. Tell me clearly, how did the quarrel start?
Oedipus. He says I murdered Laius—I am guilty.
15 **Jocasta.** How does he know? Some secret knowledge
or simply hearsay?
Oedipus. Oh, he sent his prophet in
to do his dirty work. You know Creon,
Creon keeps his own lips clean.
Jocasta. A prophet?
Well then, free yourself of every charge!
20 Listen to me and learn some peace of mind:
no skill in the world,
nothing human can penetrate the future.
Here is proof, quick and to the point.
An oracle came to Laius one fine day

(I won't say from Apollo himself
but his underlings, his priests) and it said
that doom would strike him down at the hands of a son,
our son, to be born of our own flesh and blood. But Laius,
so the report goes at least, was killed by strangers,
thieves, at a place where three roads meet . . . my son—
he wasn't three days old and the boy's father
fastened his ankles, had a henchman fling him away
on a barren, trackless mountain. There, you see?
Apollo brought neither thing to pass. My baby
no more murdered his father than Laius suffered—
his wildest fear—death at his own son's hands.
That's how the seers and their revelations
mapped out the future. Brush them from your mind.
Whatever the god needs and seeks
he'll bring to light himself, with ease.

Oedipus.   Strange,
hearing you just now . . . my mind wandered,
my thoughts racing back and forth.
Jocasta. What do you mean? Why so anxious, startled?
Oedipus. I thought I heard you say that Laius
was cut down at a place where three roads meet.
Jocasta. That was the story. It hasn't died out yet.
Oedipus. Where did this thing happen? Be precise.
Jocasta. A place called Phocis, where two branching roads,
one from Daulia, one from Delphi,
come together—a crossroads.
Oedipus. When? How long ago?
Jocasta. The heralds no sooner reported Laius dead
than you appeared and they hailed you king of Thebes.
Oedipus. My god, my god—what have you planned to do to me?
Jocasta. What, Oedipus? What haunts you so?
Oedipus.   Not yet.
Laius—how did he look? Describe him.
Had he reached his prime?
Jocasta.   He was swarthy,
and the gray had just begun to streak his temples,
and his build . . . wasn't far from yours.
Oedipus.   Oh no no,
I think I've just called down a dreadful curse
upon myself—I simply didn't know!

1. Who was the king of Thebes before Oedipus?
   A. Apollo
   B. Laius
   C. Creon
   D. Delphi

2. What does the Chorus represent?
   A. the aristocracy
   B. the citizenry
   C. rebels
   D. prophets

3. What literary device is used in lines 6 and 7, where the Chorus compares Oedipus to a helmsman?
   A. simile
   B. irony
   C. allusion
   D. metaphor

4. Why is Oedipus in a rage at the beginning of the selection?
   A. The Chorus has insulted him.
   B. He does not trust Jocasta.
   C. He suspects Creon of being in a plot.
   D. A plague has infected Thebes.

5. From the context of this passage, what can you conclude about the way in which Oedipus has ruled Thebes until now?
   A. He is given to fits of rage and intolerance.
   B. He is an admired and effective ruler.
   C. He is the most admired ruler in history.
   D. He is a cursed and doomed man.

6. From the context, what do you think that the word *hearsay*, in line 16, means?
   A. rumor
   B. report
   C. fact
   D. prophecy

7. What does Oedipus mean by saying, in line 18, "Creon keeps his own lips clean"?
   A. Creon is no more than a scoundrel.
   B. Creon is notorious for telling lies.
   C. Creon uses others to spread rumors.
   D. Creon speaks carefully so as not to offend.

8. From the context, what do you think that the word *charge*, in line 19, means?
   A. accusation
   B. complaint
   C. misdeed
   D. judgment

9. What is Jocasta's attitude toward prophecies?
   A. They should be heeded.
   B. They should be considered.
   C. They should be ignored.
   D. They should be excused.

10. From this selection, who do you think that this play's protagonist is?
    A. Oedipus
    B. Jocasta
    C. Creon
    D. Laius

11. What can be inferred from Oedipus's reaction at the end of the selection?
    A. Oedipus will remain the king.
    B. The gods have cursed Creon.
    C. Oedipus is now angry with Jocasta.
    D. Oedipus grasps his role in Laius's death.

12. Which of the following best describes the theme of the selection?
    A. Destiny can be changed.
    B. Life is a game of chance.
    C. One cannot avoid his or her fate.
    D. The gods are fickle creatures.

13. What is the overall mood of the selection?
    A. calm
    B. troubled
    C. humorous
    D. serene

Vocabulary Skills: Sentence Completion

For each item, choose the word that best completes the sentence.

1. Shakespeare's tragic figures are often undone by their _____ and pride.
   A. rash
   B. deceit
   C. arrogance
   D. ignorance

2. The old woman's illness had left her with a/an _____ that required extended care.
   A. enterprise
   B. infirmity
   C. peril
   D. orator

3. Many athletes _____ in a competitive atmosphere.
   A. thrive
   B. vanquish
   C. commend
   D. disperse

4. The _____ prince was quick to smile and make small talk with any villager.
   A. affable
   B. ostentatious
   C. impudent
   D. arrogant

5. The hermit lived high in the mountains, _____ to what was happening in the world below.
   A. notorious
   B. oblivious
   C. peevish
   D. imminent

6. The gang of bandits was _____ in the territory.
   A. pompous
   B. notorious
   C. impertinent
   D. repressed

7. She worked for many years to _____ success.
   A. disperse
   B. commend
   C. thrive
   D. attain

8. Her _____ decision to quit school limited her job opportunities.
   A. rash
   B. imminent
   C. servile
   D. affable

9. His missions into enemy territory involved _____ actions.
   A. pious
   B. disconsolate
   C. covert
   D. barren

Literature Online

Assessment For additional test practice, go to glencoe.com and enter QuickPass code GL59794u4.

Grammar and Writing Skills: Paragraph Improvement

Read carefully through the following passage from the first draft of a student's essay. Pay close attention to the writer's use of commas and parallelism. Then answer the questions on pages 890–891.

(1) *Sophocles based* Oedipus the King *on a popular folk tale of his time.* (2) *To be sure Athenian audiences were familiar with the tale, a fact that made the play an ideal medium for questioning some of the popular beliefs of his time.* (3) *Sophocles questions in particular the idea of predestination.* (4) *The belief that people have no real choices in life, that destiny is inalterable.* (5) *Oedipus's tale is tragic but the story is told with multiple levels of irony that, at times, make his inalterable fate seem ridiculous.*

(6) *Sophocles goes out of his way to present Oedipus as a capable and compassionate leader.* (7) *For example the city of Thebes prospers under Oedipus after he solves the sphinx's riddle.* (8) *Never once is it suggested that Oedipus has brought his destiny on himself by any* hubris, *which is excessive pride, or* hamartia, *which implies bad judgment or a flaw in character.* (9) *The gods rather have made the prophecies that lead Oedipus into disaster.* (10) *Apollo's oracle simply says "Find the killer," which leads to the cruel ironies of the play.* (11) *In other words, Sophocles is saying that Oedipus's tragic misfortune is the intentional work of "the gods."*

(12) *The Golden Age of Athens was a time for thinkers, scientists, and inventors, a time for people to share ideas freely, a place where all philosophers were welcomed.* (13) *The Greeks were impressed with the power of reason and the overall human potential.* (14) *Surely they must have been asking whether they still believed in their gods.* (15) *Hence the audience's sympathy for the tragic figure becomes something more complex.*

1. Which of the following is the best way to revise sentence 2?
   A. Insert an exclamation point after *To be sure.*
   B. Change *audiences were* to *audience was.*
   C. Insert a comma after *To be sure.*
   D. Change *that* to *which.*

2. Which of the following is the best way to revise sentence 3?
   A. Transpose *questions* and *in particular.*
   B. Insert commas around *in particular.*
   C. Change *questions* to *wonder about.*
   D. Make no change.

3. Which of the following errors appears in sentence 4?
   A. comma splice
   B. lack of parallelism
   C. sentence fragment
   D. subject-verb disagreement

4. Which of the following is the best way to revise sentence 5?
   A. Insert a semicolon after *tragic.*
   B. Delete the commas around *at times.*
   C. Insert a comma after *tragic.*
   D. Make no change.

5. Which of the following is the best revision for sentence 7?
   A. For example, the city of Thebes prospers under Oedipus after he solves the sphinx's riddle.
   B. For example, the city of Thebes, prospers under Oedipus after he solves the sphinx's riddle.
   C. The city of Thebes for example prospers under Oedipus after he solves the sphinx's riddle.
   D. Make no change.

6. Which of the following is the best revision for sentence 9?
   A. The gods would rather make prophecies that lead to disaster.
   B. The gods have made the prophecies that rather lead Oedipus into disaster.
   C. On the contrary, it is the gods who have made the prophecies that lead Oedipus into disaster.
   D. Make no change.

7. Which of the following is the best revision for sentence 10?
   A. Apollo's oracle simply says "Find the killer!" which leads to the cruel ironies of the play.
   B. Apollo's oracle simply says, "Find the killer," which leads to the cruel ironies of the play.
   C. Apollo's oracle simply says, "Find the killer" who leads to the cruel ironies of the play.
   D. Make no change.

8. Which of the following is the best revision of sentence 12?
   A. The Golden Age of Athens was a time for thinkers, scientists, and inventors to share ideas, all philosophers were welcome.
   B. The Golden Age of Athens welcomed all thinkers, scientists, philosophers, and inventors to share their ideas freely.
   C. The Golden Age of Athens was a time for philosophers, scientists, and inventors to share ideas freely in a place where all thinkers were welcomed.
   D. Make no change.

9. Which of the following is the best way to revise sentence 15?
   A. Insert a comma after *Hence*.
   B. Insert a colon after *Hence*.
   C. Insert a dash after *Hence*.
   D. Insert commas around *the tragic figure*.

10. Which of the following would be the best title for this essay?
    A. "Irony and Fate in *Oedipus the King*"
    B. "Greek Comedy, Greek Tragedy"
    C. "A Greek Perspective of Modern Drama"
    D. "The Use of Irony in Greek Farce"

Essay

Throughout history, theater has been valued in cultures all over the world. In your opinion, is drama as important in the modern world? How does it influence our culture? Write a short persuasive essay supporting your opinion with evidence from texts as well as personal experience. As you write, keep in mind that your essay will be checked for **ideas, organization, voice, word choice, sentence fluency, conventions,** and **presentation.**

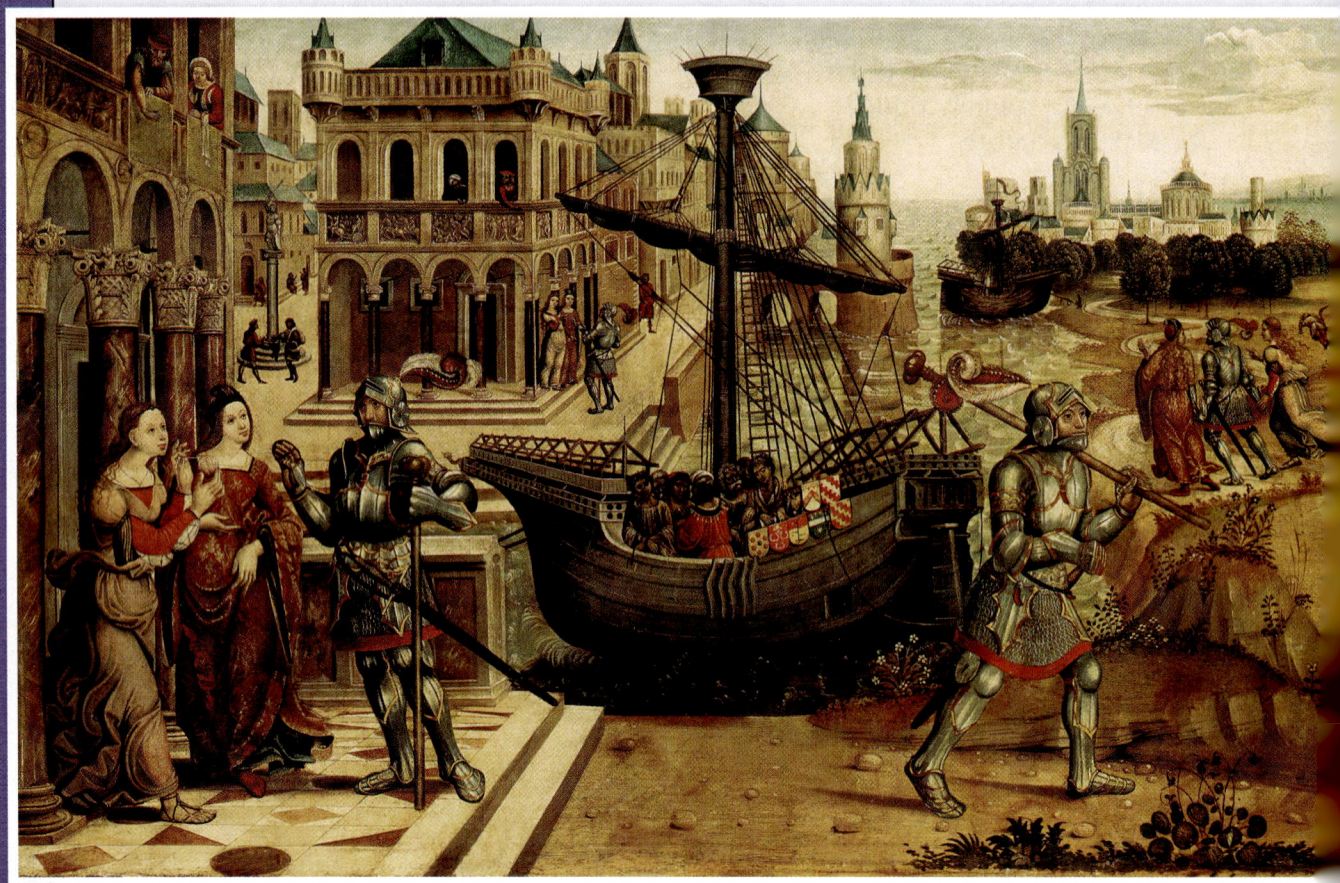

Theseus and the Minotaur, from the Story of Theseus (detail), c. 1510. Master of the Campana Cassoni. Oil on panel, Musée du Petit Palais, Avignon, France.

View the Art According to legend, Theseus, a great Greek hero, conquered the minotaur, a fearsome creature that lived in a labyrinth and was half man and half bull. Based on the depiction of Theseus in this painting, what are some of the characteristics of heroes in legends and myths?

UNIT FIVE

Legends and Myths

Looking Ahead

Legends and myths are stories that usually have long histories. Often, they have been written and rewritten, or told and retold, for countless generations. Both legends and myths come from **oral tradition**—that is, literature passed by word of mouth from generation to generation. Legends are usually based on historical figures such as saints or kings, and they generally involve less of the supernatural than myths do. Myths may reflect the values, beliefs, and deepest truths of the cultures they spring from.

Each part in Unit Five focuses on a Big Idea that can help you connect the texts to your life.

PREVIEW	Big Ideas	Literary Focus
PART 1	Acts of Courage	The Legendary Hero
PART 2	Rescuing and Conquering	Myth and the Oral Tradition

Learning Objectives

For pages 892–898

In studying this text, you will focus on the following objectives:

Literary Study:
Analyzing the legendary hero.
Analyzing myth and the oral tradition.

Genre Focus
What can readers gain from Legends and Myths?

The role models, beliefs, and values of a culture are often preserved in their legends and myths. According to Thomas Bulfinch, one of America's first collectors of world myths and legends, ". . . if that which tends to make us happier and better can be called useful, then we claim that epithet for our subject. For Mythology is the handmaid of literature; and literature is one of the best allies of virtue and promoters of happiness." Here, happiness and the deepest truths go hand in hand.

The Legendary Hero

Legend

Legends are traditional stories handed down from generation to generation. Legends are usually based on actual events that have been exaggerated over time. Many legends describe the deeds of kings and noble heroes, especially those who lived at a time when stories were more likely to be told orally.

> Sir Launcelot took another spear, and unhorsed sixteen more of the King of North Galys' knights, and with his next, unhorsed another twelve; and in each case with such violence that none of the knights ever fully recovered. The King of North Galys was forced to admit defeat, and the prize was awarded to King Bagdemagus.
>
> —Sir Thomas Malory, **from** *Le Morte d'Arthur*

Hero

A **hero** is the main character in a literary work. The term can refer to either a female or a male. Legendary heroes are idealized figures, sometimes based on real people, who embody qualities admired by the cultural group to which they belong. These characters serve to inspire readers to emulate the qualities that their culture values.

> In order to defeat Soumaoro it was necessary first of all to destroy his magical power. At Sibi, Sundiata decided to consult the soothsayers, of whom the most famous in Mali were there.
>
> —D. T. Niane, **from** *Sundiata*

 **Literature** Online

Literature and Reading For more selections in the genre, go to glencoe.com and enter QuickPass code GL59794u5.

Myth and Oral Tradition

Myths

Myths are ancient stories whose authors are unknown, or **anonymous**. Myths tell of gods and goddesses, their interventions in the lives of heroes, and supernatural events. Many myths attempt to account for a belief, a custom, or a force of nature. Across cultures, mythic themes show many similarities. For example, virtually every culture has a myth that explains the creation of the world.

The Minotaur was a monster, half bull, half human, the offspring of Minos' wife Pasiphaë and a wonderfully beautiful bull. Poseidon had given this bull to Minos in order that he should sacrifice it to him, but Minos could not bear to slay it and kept it for himself. To punish him, Poseidon had made Pasiphaë fall madly in love with it.

—Edith Hamilton, **from Theseus**

Oral Tradition

A culture's **oral tradition** includes its myths and legends, and it also includes its folklore and folktales. **Folklore** is the broader term that includes traditional beliefs, customs, stories, songs, and dances. **Folktales** are the stories within the culture's folklore. As a story is told by each generation, it may gradually change, sounding a little different over time. Most folklore takes as its subject the concerns of common people.

When I hear the old men
Telling of heroes,
Telling of great deeds
Of ancient days,
When I hear that telling
Then I think within me
I, too, am one of these.

—Chippewa Traditional Song, *from* **A Song of Greatness**

Gilgamesh, the Sumerian King of Uruk, Slays the Bull of Ishtar Helped by Ea-bani, ca. 20th century. E. Wallcousins.

INTRODUCTION **895**

Literary Analysis Model
How is *The Journey of Gilgamesh* an epic?

Gilgamesh may be the oldest known story to ever have been written down. It is based on a historical Babylonian king.

**APPLYING
Literary Elements**

from *The Journey of Gilgamesh*
(Sumerian epic)

retold by Joan C. Verniero and Robin Fitzsimmons

Epic Hero

Gilgamesh has admirable qualities typical of an **epic hero.**

Epic Hero

Gilgamesh demonstrates strength and courage, two heroic traits.

"Gilgamesh, although you come from the gods, part of you is still mortal. You cannot know and experience everything. One day you will die, as all mortals die."

When Gilgamesh heard what his mother had told him, he
5 flew into a rage.

"I do not wish to die!" he exclaimed angrily. "My great friend Enkidu died. I miss him terribly, and I do not wish to follow him into the land of the dead. I will learn the secret of living forever."

Gilgamesh's mother tried to comfort her son.
10 "I only know of one person who has managed to escape death. His name is Uta-Napishtim, or Uta-Napishtim, the Remote. He survived a mighty ordeal and was granted everlasting life. He lives beyond Mount Mashu, which is very far away."

Gilgamesh made up his mind to find Uta-Napishtim, the
15 Remote. He traveled toward Mount Mashu. It was a long journey filled with many perils. He was pursued by the fierce lions of the forest. The Scorpion Men, who hid behind the boulders of the mountains, jumped out at him and tried to frighten him.

Gilgamesh continued on his way. Sometimes it was so dark
20 he could barely see in front of himself. Finally, in the distance, Gilgamesh saw a great, glowing light. He had reached the home of Uta-Napishtim.

The old man greeted Gilgamesh and asked him why he had come so far from his home.
25 "Tell me how you have earned the right to live forever, Uta-Napishtim," Gilgamesh asked him. "This is what I wish to learn."

Uta-Napishtim invited Gilgamesh to sit beside him on the ground.

"Here is my story. I lived in Shurippak, the city of the sun.
30 One day the god Ea came to me and told me that the gods were

displeased with humans and wished to destroy the earth. They were going to send a great flood to cover the world.

"Ea instructed me to build a very large ship and to prepare for the deluge. Then he told me to bring my family into the ship, as well as many animals, and to wait for the rains to fall. I did this. A great storm came and the skies were filled with black clouds. Thunder shook the ground and bolts of lightning raced through the heavens with hot, white light. For many days it rained and rained without stopping. We almost forgot what it was like to see the sun or to walk on dry land.

"We were very afraid, but I trusted that Ea had told me the truth, and that I would be saved. After a long while, the rains stopped falling and I sent a bird out from my ship to seek land. The bird returned to me, exhausted after failing to find a place to land. In time I sent another bird, a raven, to fly from the ship. I was overjoyed when the raven did not return to me, for it had found a dry patch of earth on which to live. This was a very good sign.

"Eventually the great flood waters receded and our ship rested upon a cliff. We left the ship with all of the creatures we had carried with us, and gave thanks to Ea and Ishtar, the goddess of heaven."

"But how did you come to be immortal?" Gilgamesh asked.

"The gods saw that I obeyed Ea, and as a reward they granted me immortality."

Gilgamesh jumped to his feet. "That does not help me, Uta-Napishtim, for I have not been tested as you have. Is there no way I can live forever?"

"Everything in this world lives and dies, Gilgamesh," Uta-Napishtim told him. "Yet, there may be a way for you to get your wish. Here is a special plant. Take this plant with you, back to your home. When you are there, you may eat it, and perhaps it will give you eternal youth."

Gilgamesh did as he was told and began the long journey home again. On the way he stopped to rest near a clear pool of water. He was so thirsty that he put the magic plant on the ground, and stepped into the pool to drink from it. Gilgamesh did not notice the snake that crawled in the grass, not far from the water. The snake saw the plant and ate it.

Gilgamesh had lost his chance for immortality. Finally he realized that even though he was a rich and powerful man, he could not escape death.

Legend tells us that the snake, after eating the plant intended for Gilgamesh, was able to shed his skin and regain his youth. Therefore, all snakes have kept this unique ability to this very day.

Epic

Notice the universal theme of Earth being wiped clean by a flood.

Humbaba, demon genie and guardian of the cedar forests of the Lebanon-range. Period of the Amorite dynasties. In the Gilgamesh epic, Gilgamesh and his friend Enkidu cut off the demon's head, ca. 20th-16th BC. Terracotta. Iraq Museum, Baghdad, Iraq.

Epic

The story encourages its audience to learn along with Gilgamesh to accept their mortality.

Epic

This story explains an aspect of the natural world.

Reading Check

Analyze How is this epic similar to and different from myths, legends, and folktales? Explain.

Wrap-Up

Guide to Reading Legends and Myths

- Read to enjoy.
- Consider the purpose of the work. Was it written to inspire, instruct, or motivate?
- Be aware of the cultural origin of the story.
- If you are reading a legend, be aware of historical elements in the text.
- If you are reading a myth, look for hints about the values of the culture that created it.

Elements of Legends and Myths

- **Legends** are ancient stories with elements of history and elements of fantasy.
- **Legendary heroes** are admirable and noble. They perform great deeds, often with the help of gods.
- **Myths** tell stories of gods, heroes, and supernatural interventions.
- **Folklore** includes the folktales, dances, songs, beliefs and customs of a culture.
- **Folktales** tell stories of common people.
- **Oral tradition** is the myths, legends, folklore, and folktales of a culture that are passed orally from generation to generation.

Unit Resources For additional skills practice, go to glencoe.com and enter QuickPass code GL59794u5.

Activities Use what you have learned about reading and analyzing legends, myths, and folktales.

1. Speaking and Listening You may be surprised to find that myths and folktales are relatively easy to remember and retell. Set aside class time for retelling some of the myths, legends, and folktales from this unit. You will enjoy hearing the personal touches each person gives the story and experience firsthand the tradition of storytelling.

2. Visual Literacy Create a promotion for reading legends and myths to be mounted in your library. Aim your promotion at your peers.

3. Take Notes Try using this study organizer to practice identifying elements of legends and myths. For each selection, write clues you used to identify the element.

FOLDABLES Study Organizer

THREE-TAB BOOK

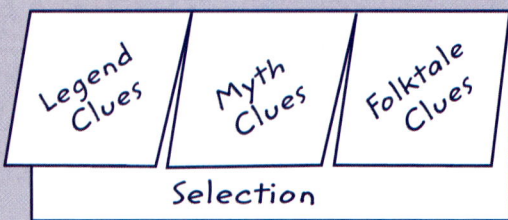

See page R20 for folding instructions.

PART 1

Acts of Courage

A Joust Between Two Knights, late 15th century. Artist unknown. The British Library, London.

View the Art Jousting, which is depicted in this painting, was a popular form of entertainment in the Middle Ages. Two knights wearing heavy armor would gallop toward each other and with their lances attempt to knock their opponent off his horse. What qualities do the jousters display? What does this painting suggest about legendary heroes?

Courage comes in many forms. An audition, a first date, a speech, even everyday life can require acts of courage. The legends in Part 1 tell of acts of courage that made people heroes to entire cultures. As you read the selections, ask yourself, Who are some modern heroes? What makes them heroic?

LITERARY FOCUS

Learning Objectives

For pages 900–901

In studying this text, you will focus on the following objective:

Literary Study: Analyzing the legendary hero.

LITERARY FOCUS

The Legendary Hero

The word *legend* originates from the Latin word *legenda*, an adjective that means "for reading" or "to be read." Initially, *legenda* was used only when referring to written stories, not the stories that made up the oral tradition. In the fourteenth century, the English word *legend* was used similarly: it only referred to written accounts of saints' lives. Beginning in the fifteenth century, *legend* began to be used to refer to traditional stories as well. Legends communicated the heroic acts of knights and the greatness of kings and queens, and such stories became more widespread after the invention of the printing press. Eventually the term *legend* acquired its current meaning—a person or an act worthy of inspiring a story.

The secret of Arthur's birth was known only to a few of the nobles surviving from the days of King Uther. The Archbishop urged them to make Arthur's cause their own; but their support proved ineffective. The tournament was repeated at Candlemas and at Easter, and with the same outcome as before.

Finally at Pentecost, when once more Arthur alone had been able to remove the sword, the commoners arose with a tumultuous cry and demanded that Arthur should at once be made king. The nobles, knowing in their hearts that the commoners were right, all knelt before Arthur and begged forgiveness for having delayed his succession for so long. Arthur forgave them, and then, offering his sword at the high altar, was dubbed first knight of the realm. The coronation took place a few days later, when Arthur swore to rule justly, and the nobles swore him their allegiance.

—Thomas Malory, *from Le Morte d'Arthur*

An illustration from *A History of the Development and Customs of Chivalry* by Dr. Franz Kottenkamp, published in 1842. Friedrich Martin von Reibisch.

Legend

A **legend** is a traditional story handed down from one generation to the next, originally by word of mouth. Legends are believed to be based on true events and a historical hero. In the following passage, King Arthur becomes king of Britain by pulling a sword from a stone. Over the years, legends have gained elements of fantasy and magic. Because legends are the stories of the people, they often express the values or character of a nation.

"Why," said Arthur, "do you both kneel before me?" "My lord," Sir Ector replied, "there is only one man living who can draw the sword from the stone, and he is the true-born King of Britain."

—Thomas Malory, *from Le Morte d'Arthur*

Epic

A long poem that tells the story of a hero and his or her adventures is called an **epic**. Like legends, epics have extraordinary heroes. One of the supernatural elements that often appears in epics is the intervention of gods and goddesses in the lives of humans. Such supernatural happenings are less common in legends.

Hero

The **hero** is the main character, generally one the reader admires, in a literary work. His or her good deeds and noble character allow the hero to defeat all enemies. The hero often sets out on a journey or quest to save his or her nation or family. A test or a series of tests during the quest reveals the hero's true worth.

A hero may be male or female. One well-known example of a modern female hero is Dorothy from *The Wizard of Oz*. She receives some guidance from superhuman forces—the good witch—and shows unusual courage, intelligence, independence, and leadership.

The heroes of literature face great difficulties but reap great rewards. Some authors have speculated what it might be like for an ordinary person to try to live a hero's life. A famous example of this sort of tale is *Don Quixote*, in which Don Quixote has some trouble finding monsters to slay.

At that moment they caught sight of some thirty or forty windmills, which stand on that plain, and as soon as Don Quixote saw them he said to his squire: "Fortune is guiding our affairs better than we could have wished. Look over there, friend Sancho Panza, where more than thirty monstrous giants appear. I intend to do battle with them and take all their lives."

—Miguel de Cervantes, *from Don Quixote*

Shield of the duchy of Krain, 1463. Gilded and painted wood. Wien Museum Karlsplatz, Vienna, Austria.

Quickwrite

Write Descriptive Phrases These days, we use the word *legend* more loosely than it was used in the fourteenth century. We speak of music legends and sports legends; anyone whose fame is likely to last might be called a legend. Choose a modern legend from the list below or think of your own. Write four exaggerated phrases to describe your hero.

Rosa Parks
Tiger Woods
Eleanor Roosevelt
Abraham Lincoln
Martin Luther King Jr.

Before You Read

from *Le Morte d'Arthur*

World Literature
England

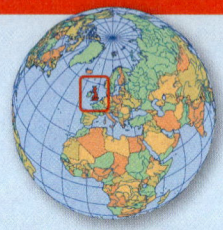

Meet **Sir Thomas Malory**
(c. 1405–1471)

Who wrote one of the most famous works in literary history, *Le Morte d'Arthur*? For years, scholars have argued about the answer to this question. Considered by some to be the first novel and largely based on French poems of Arthurian legends, *Le Morte d'Arthur* is said to exist in two versions. One is the printed version that William Caxton published in 1485, of which one complete, original copy exists. The other is a mysterious manuscript discovered at Winchester College in 1934. Known as the Winchester text, its relationship to the Caxton manuscript is not clear.

> *"There is only one man living who can draw the sword from the stone…."*
>
> —Sir Thomas Malory,
> from *Le Morte d'Arthur*

The Knight Prisoner Because a "syr Thomas Maleore knight" is named in the colophon, or inscription, of the 1485 version, Sir Thomas Malory is often identified as the author. Malory spent the first part of his life as a soldier and then as a country gentleman. He inherited estates from his father, married, fathered a son, and in 1445 became a member of Parliament. Thereafter, however, his life seemed to spiral out of control. Malory was cited in a multitude of lawsuits from the time period; he was charged with murder, robbery, and an attack on a religious institution, the Abbey of Coombe. In one incident, he was accused of stealing seven cows, two calves, 335 sheep, and a farmer's cart. During the last twenty years of his life, Malory served at least four prison sentences for his crimes. In fact, he likely completed *Le Morte d'Arthur* while in prison during 1469 and 1470. At the end of his retelling of the epic tale, Malory describes himself as a "knight prisoner" and urges his readers to pray for his safe release.

A Lasting Work of Art Malory's version of the legend has had the most influence and longevity; the book has remained in print since its first publication, more than five hundred years ago. According to scholar Edmund Reiss, "Many writers had worked on the French Arthurian prose romances between the thirteenth and fifteenth centuries; there had been adaptations of it in Spain and Germany. All this is now dead and buried, and Malory alone stands as a rock, defying all changes of taste and style and morals; not as a grand paradox of nature, but as a lasting work of art."

Literature Online

Author Search For more about Sir Thomas Malory, go to glencoe.com and enter QuickPass code GL59794u5.

Literature and Reading Preview

Connect to the Story
Who is your hero? What makes that person a hero to you? Freewrite for a few minutes about how the person you selected embodies the qualities of heroism.

Build Background
In late medieval Europe (the twelfth to fifteenth centuries), knights and noblemen tried to behave according to a strict code of chivalry. Chivalry is derived from the French word *chevalier*, meaning "horseman." A chivalrous knight, however, was more than a skilled rider. He also strove to be generous to the weak and courteous to women.

Set Purposes for Reading

Big Idea Acts of Courage

As you read this selection, ask yourself, How does Malory's legend provide evidence that Arthur is a courageous hero?

Literary Element Dialogue

Dialogue is conversation between characters in a literary work. Dialogue can contribute to characterization, create mood, advance the plot, and develop theme. As you read, ask yourself, How is dialogue used in this legend?

Reading Strategy Analyze Plot

When you **analyze plot**, you critically examine the sequence of events in a narrative work. Most plots develop around a conflict, or a struggle between opposing forces. A legend's plot may consist of a series of random conflicts. As you read, ask yourself, How do the conflicts in this legend help to shape the plot?

Tip: Take Notes Compare and contrast the plot of *Le Morte d'Arthur* with the plot of a short story you have read.

Learning Objectives
For pages 902–923

In studying this text, you will focus on the following objectives:

Literary Study: Analyzing dialogue.

Reading: Analyzing plot.

Vocabulary

abashed (ə basht′) *adj.* self-conscious; embarrassed or ashamed; p. 906 *Mike was abashed about his too-short haircut.*

inscribe (in skrīb′) *v.* to write, carve, or mark on a surface; p. 908 *The wedding band was inscribed with the couple's initials.*

ignoble (ig nō′ bəl) *adj.* of low birth or position; without honor or worth; p. 909 *They were shocked to discover that the charming young man had such ignoble beginnings.*

tumultuous (too mul′ choō əs) *adj.* wildly excited, confused, or agitated; p. 909 *The horse galloped away, taking the girl on a tumultuous ride.*

prowess (prou′ is) *n.* great ability or skill; p. 910 *Her prowess on the violin was evident as she played the solo.*

LEGENDS AND MYTHS

King Arthur and Sir Lancelot, 1862. William Morris. Stained glass. Bradford Art Galleries and Museums, West Yorkshire, UK.

from Le Morte d'Arthur
The Tale of King Arthur

Sir Thomas Malory
retold by Keith Baines

King Uther[1] Pendragon,[2] ruler of all Britain, had been at war for many years with the Duke of Tintagil in Cornwall when he was told of the beauty of Lady Igraine,[3] the duke's wife. Thereupon he called a truce and invited the duke and Igraine to his court, where he prepared a feast for them, and where, as soon as they arrived, he was formally reconciled to the duke through the good offices of his courtiers.

In the course of the feast, King Uther grew passionately desirous of Igraine and, when it was over, begged her to become his paramour.[4] Igraine, however, being as naturally loyal as she was beautiful, refused him.

"I suppose," said Igraine to her husband, the duke, when this had happened, "that the king arranged this truce only because he wanted to make me his mistress. I suggest that we leave at once, without warning, and ride overnight to our castle." The duke agreed with her, and they left the court secretly.

The king was enraged by Igraine's flight and summoned his privy council.[5] They advised him to command the fugitives' return under threat of renewing the war; but when this was done, the duke and Igraine defied his summons. He then warned them that they could expect to be dragged from their castle within six weeks.

The duke manned and provisioned[6] his two strongest castles: Tintagil for Igraine, and Terrabyl, which was useful for its many sally ports, for himself. Soon King Uther arrived with a huge army and laid siege to Terrabyl; but despite the ferocity of the fighting, and the numerous casualties suffered by both sides, neither was able to gain a decisive victory.

Still enraged, and now despairing, King Uther fell sick. His friend Sir Ulfius came to him and asked what the trouble was. "Igraine has broken my heart," the king

Merlin the Magician, c.1352 Ms. Add. Meladius, 12228, fol. 202v. British Library, London.

View the Art Merlin was a wise and trusted advisor to the king and could perform powerful acts of magic. How does this image suggest Merlin's power?

Visual Vocabulary
Sally ports are gates or openings in castle walls through which a ruler's troops could make sudden attacks.

---

1. *Uther* (o͞o′ thər)
2. In ancient Britain, *Pendragon,* meaning "supreme leader," was a title attached after a ruler's name.
3. *Igraine* (ē grān′)
4. A man's lover or mistress is his *paramour.*
5. A *privy council* is a group of a ruler's closest advisors.
6. The duke supplied (*provisioned*) the castles with food and goods.

Dialogue How does this dialogue help characterize Igraine?

SIR THOMAS MALORY 905

replied, "and unless I can win her, I shall never recover."

"Sire," said Sir Ulfius, "surely Merlin the Prophet could find some means to help you? I will go in search of him."

Sir Ulfius had not ridden far when he was accosted by a hideous beggar. "For whom are you searching?" asked the beggar; but Sir Ulfius ignored him.

"Very well," said the beggar, "I will tell you: You are searching for Merlin, and you need look no further, for I am he. Now go to King Uther and tell him that I will make Igraine his if he will reward me as I ask; and even that will be more to his benefit than to mine."

"I am sure," said Sir Ulfius, "that the king will refuse you nothing reasonable."

"Then go, and I shall follow you," said Merlin.

Well pleased, Sir Ulfius galloped back to the king and delivered Merlin's message, which he had hardly completed when Merlin himself appeared at the entrance to the pavilion. The king bade him welcome.

"Sire," said Merlin, "I know that you are in love with Igraine; will you swear, as an anointed[7] king, to give into my care the child that she bears you, if I make her yours?"

The king swore on the gospel that he would do so, and Merlin continued: "Tonight you shall appear before Igraine at Tintagil in the likeness of her husband, the duke. Sir Ulfius and I will appear as two of the duke's knights: Sir Brastius and Sir Jordanus. Do not question either Igraine or her men, but say that you are sick and retire to bed. I will fetch you early in the morning, and do not rise until I come; fortunately Tintagil is only ten miles from here."

The plan succeeded: Igraine was completely deceived by the king's impersonation of the duke, and gave herself to him, and conceived Arthur. The king left her at dawn as soon as Merlin appeared, after giving her a farewell kiss. But the duke had seen King Uther ride out from the siege on the previous night and, in the course of making a surprise attack on the king's army, had been killed. When Igraine realized that the duke had died three hours before he had appeared to her, she was greatly disturbed in mind; however, she confided in no one.

Once it was known that the duke was dead, the king's nobles urged him to be reconciled to Igraine, and this task the king gladly entrusted to Sir Ulfius, by whose eloquence[8] it was soon accomplished. "And now," said Sir Ulfius to his fellow nobles, "why should not the king marry the beautiful Igraine? Surely it would be as well for us all."

The marriage of King Uther and Igraine was celebrated joyously thirteen days later; and then, at the king's request, Igraine's sisters were also married: Margawse, who later bore Sir Gawain, to King Lot of Lowthean and Orkney; Elayne, to King Nentres of Garlot. Igraine's daughter, Morgan le Fay, was put to school in a nunnery; in after years she was to become a witch, and to be married to King Uryens of Gore, and give birth to Sir Uwayne of the Fair Hands.

A few months later it was seen that Igraine was with child, and one night, as she lay in bed with King Uther, he asked her who the father might be. Igraine was greatly **abashed.**

---

7. An *anointed* king was believed to have been chosen by God to be king.

Analyze Plot How do you think this event will advance the plot?

8. Here, *eloquence* is speech or writing that is expressive, stirring, and effective.

Vocabulary

abashed (ə basht′) *adj.* self-conscious; embarrassed or ashamed

"Do not look so dismayed," said the king, "but tell me the truth and I swear I shall love you the better for it."

"The truth is," said Igraine, "that the night the duke died, about three hours after his death, a man appeared in my castle—the exact image of the duke. With him came two others who appeared to be Sir Brastius and Sir Jordanus. Naturally I gave myself to this man as I would have to the duke, and that night, I swear, this child was conceived."

"Well spoken," said the king; "it was I who impersonated the duke, so the child is mine." He then told Igraine the story of how Merlin had arranged it, and Igraine was overjoyed to discover that the father of her child was now her husband.

Sometime later, Merlin appeared before the king. "Sire," he said, "you know that you must provide for the upbringing of your child?"

"I will do as you advise," the king replied.

"That is good," said Merlin, "because it is my reward for having arranged your impersonation of the duke. Your child is destined for glory, and I want him brought to me for his baptism. I shall then give him into the care of foster parents who can be trusted not to reveal his identity before the proper time. Sir Ector would be suitable: he is extremely loyal, owns good estates, and his wife has just borne him a child. She could give her child into the care of another woman, and herself look after yours."

Sir Ector was summoned, and gladly agreed to the king's request, who then rewarded him handsomely. When the child was born he was at once wrapped in a gold cloth and taken by two knights and two ladies to Merlin, who stood waiting at the rear entrance to the castle in his beg-

Acts of Courage *Read to the end of the next paragraph. What is so remarkable about the king's statement?*

Lancelot witnessed by King Arthur draws the sword out of the rock, 1470. French illumination.

View the Art What does the king's expression seem to suggest? Why do you think so?

gar's disguise. Merlin took the child to a priest, who baptized him with the name of Arthur, and thence to Sir Ector, whose wife fed him at her breast.

Two years later King Uther fell sick, and his enemies once more overran his kingdom, inflicting heavy losses on him as they advanced. Merlin prophesied that they could be checked only by the presence of the king himself on the battlefield, and suggested that he should be conveyed there on a horse litter.[9] King Uther's army met the invader on the plain at St. Albans, and the king duly appeared on the horse litter. Inspired by his presence, and by the lively leadership of Sir Brastius and Sir Jordanus, his army quickly defeated the enemy and

---

9. The king was to be carried *(conveyed)* on a stretcher *(litter)* pulled by a horse.

the battle finished in a rout.[10] The king returned to London to celebrate the victory.

But his sickness grew worse, and after he had lain speechless for three days and three nights Merlin summoned the nobles to attend the king in his chamber on the following morning. "By the grace of God," he said, "I hope to make him speak."

In the morning, when all the nobles were assembled, Merlin addressed the king: "Sire, is it your will that Arthur shall succeed to the throne, together with all its prerogatives?"[11]

The king stirred in his bed, and then spoke so that all could hear: "I bestow on Arthur God's blessing and my own, and Arthur shall succeed to the throne on pain of forfeiting my blessing."[12] Then King Uther gave up the ghost. He was buried and mourned the next day, as befitted his rank, by Igraine and the nobility of Britain.

During the years that followed the death of King Uther, while Arthur was still a child, the ambitious barons fought one another for the throne, and the whole of Britain stood in jeopardy. Finally the day came when the Archbishop of Canterbury, on the advice of Merlin, summoned the nobility to London for Christmas morning. In his message the Archbishop promised that the true succession to the British throne would be miraculously revealed. Many of the nobles purified themselves during their journey, in the hope that it would be to them that the succession would fall.

---

10. A *rout* (rout) is an overwhelming defeat.
11. *Prerogatives* (pri rog′ ə tivz) are the rights and privileges belonging solely to a particular person (such as a king) or group.
12. *Forfeiting my blessing* means that Uther is withholding his blessing if Arthur does not eventually become king.

Analyze Plot What purpose have the events in this story served up until this point?

The Archbishop held his service in the city's greatest church (St. Paul's), and when matins[13] were done the congregation filed out to the yard. They were confronted by a marble block into which had been thrust a beautiful sword. The block was four feet square, and the sword passed through a steel anvil which had been struck in the stone, and which projected a foot from it. The anvil had been **inscribed** with letters of gold:

> **WHOSO PULLETH OUTE THIS SWERD OF THIS STONE AND ANVLYD IS RIGHTWYS KYNGE BORNE OF ALL BRYTAYGNE**

The congregation was awed by this miraculous sight, but the Archbishop forbade anyone to touch the sword before mass had been heard. After mass, many of the nobles tried to pull the sword out of the stone, but none was able to, so a watch of ten knights was set over the sword, and a tournament proclaimed for New Year's Day, to provide men of noble blood with the opportunity of proving their right to the succession.

Sir Ector, who had been living on an estate near London, rode to the tournament with Arthur and his own son Sir Kay, who had been recently knighted. When they arrived at the tournament, Sir Kay found to his annoyance that his sword was missing from its sheath, so he begged Arthur to ride back and fetch it from their lodging.

Arthur found the door of the lodging locked and bolted, the landlord and his wife having left for the tournament. In order not to disappoint his brother, he rode on to St. Paul's, determined to get for him the sword which was lodged in the stone. The yard was empty, the guard also having slipped

---

13. *Matins* (mat′inz) are morning prayers.

Vocabulary

inscribe (in skrīb′) *v.* to write, carve, or mark on a surface

off to see the tournament, so Arthur strode up to the sword, and, without troubling to read the inscription, tugged it free. He then rode straight back to Sir Kay and presented him with it.

Sir Kay recognized the sword, and taking it to Sir Ector, said, "Father, the succession falls to me, for I have here the sword that was lodged in the stone." But Sir Ector insisted that they should all ride to the churchyard, and once there bound Sir Kay by oath to tell how he had come by the sword. Sir Kay then admitted that Arthur had given it to him. Sir Ector turned to Arthur and said, "Was the sword not guarded?"

"It was not," Arthur replied.

"Would you please thrust it into the stone again?" said Sir Ector. Arthur did so, and first Sir Ector and then Sir Kay tried to remove it, but both were unable to. Then Arthur, for the second time, pulled it out. Sir Ector and Sir Kay both knelt before him.

"Why," said Arthur, "do you both kneel before me?"

"My lord," Sir Ector replied, "there is only one man living who can draw the sword from the stone, and he is the true-born King of Britain." Sir Ector then told Arthur the story of his birth and upbringing.

"My dear father," said Arthur, "for so I shall always think of you—if, as you say, I am to be king, please know that any request you have to make is already granted."

Sir Ector asked that Sir Kay should be made Royal Seneschal,[14] and Arthur declared that while they both lived it should be so. Then the three of them visited the Archbishop and told him what had taken place.

All those dukes and barons with ambitions to rule were present at the tournament on New Year's Day. But when all of them had failed, and Arthur alone had succeeded in drawing the sword from the stone, they protested against one so young, and of **ignoble** blood, succeeding to the throne.

The secret of Arthur's birth was known only to a few of the nobles surviving from the days of King Uther. The Archbishop urged them to make Arthur's cause their own; but their support proved ineffective. The tournament was repeated at Candlemas and at Easter,[15] and with the same outcome as before.

Finally at Pentecost,[16] when once more Arthur alone had been able to remove the sword, the commoners arose with a **tumultuous** cry and demanded that Arthur should at once be made king. The nobles, knowing in their hearts that the commoners were right, all knelt before Arthur and begged forgiveness for having delayed his succession for so long. Arthur forgave them, and then, offering his sword at the high altar, was dubbed first knight of the realm. The coronation took place a few days later, when Arthur swore to rule justly, and the nobles swore him their allegiance.

---

14. In medieval times, the *Royal Seneschal* (sen′ ə shəl) managed the king's estate, ran his household, and sometimes also had official state duties or a military command.

Analyze Plot What conflict is being revealed here?

Dialogue What does this response reveal about Arthur?

15. *Candlemas* and *Easter* are Christian festivals; *Candlemas* is celebrated on February 2 and *Easter* in early spring.
16. *Pentecost* is a Christian feast observed on the seventh Sunday after Easter.

Vocabulary

ignoble (ig nō′ bəl) *adj.* of low birth or position; without honor or worth

tumultuous (too mul′ choo əs) *adj.* wildly excited, confused, or agitated

The Tale of Sir Launcelot du Lake

When King Arthur returned from Rome he settled his court at Camelot, and there gathered about him his knights of the Round Table, who diverted[17] themselves with jousting and tournaments. Of all his knights one was supreme, both in **prowess** at arms and in nobility of bearing, and this was Sir Launcelot, who was also the favorite of Queen Gwynevere, to whom he had sworn oaths of fidelity.[18]

One day Sir Launcelot, feeling weary of his life at the court, and of only playing at arms, decided to set forth in search of adventure. He asked his nephew Sir Lyonel to accompany him, and when both were suitably armed and mounted, they rode off together through the forest.

Head of King Arthur, from the *Beautiful Fountain,* 14th century. Artist unknown. Statue. Germanisches Nationalmuseum, Nuremberg, Germany.

At noon they started across a plain, but the intensity of the sun made Sir Launcelot feel sleepy, so Sir Lyonel suggested that they should rest beneath the shade of an apple tree that grew by a hedge not far from the road. They dismounted, tethered their horses, and settled down.

"Not for seven years have I felt so sleepy," said Sir Launcelot, and with that fell fast asleep, while Sir Lyonel watched over him.

Soon three knights came galloping past, and Sir Lyonel noticed that they were being pursued by a fourth knight, who was one of the most powerful he had yet seen. The pursuing knight overtook each of the others in turn, and as he did so, knocked each off his horse with a thrust of his spear. When all three lay stunned he dismounted, bound them securely to their horses with the reins, and led them away.

Without waking Sir Launcelot, Sir Lyonel mounted his horse and rode after

---

17. Here, *diverted* means "amused" or "entertained."
18. Launcelot swore his loyalty and devotion *(fidelity)* to Gwynevere.

Vocabulary

prowess (prou′ is) *n.* great ability or skill

Analyze Plot What does this action reveal about Sir Lyonel?

the knight, and as soon as he had drawn close enough, shouted his challenge. The knight turned about and they charged at each other, with the result that Sir Lyonel was likewise flung from his horse, bound, and led away a prisoner.

The victorious knight, whose name was Sir Tarquine, led his prisoners to his castle, and there threw them on the ground, stripped them naked, and beat them with thorn twigs. After that he locked them in a dungeon where many other prisoners, who had received like treatment, were complaining dismally.

Meanwhile, Sir Ector de Marys, who liked to accompany Sir Launcelot on his adventures, and finding him gone, decided to ride after him. Before long he came upon a forester.

"My good fellow, if you know the forest hereabouts, could you tell me in which direction I am most likely to meet with adventure?"

"Sir, I can tell you: Less than a mile from here stands a well-moated castle. On the left of the entrance you will find a ford where you can water your horse, and across from the ford a large tree from which hang the shields of many famous knights. Below the shields hangs a caldron, of copper and brass: strike it three times with your spear, and then surely you will meet with adventure—such, indeed, that if you survive it, you will prove yourself the foremost knight in these parts for many years."

"May God reward you!" Sir Ector replied.

The castle was exactly as the forester had described it, and among the shields Sir Ector recognized several as belonging to knights of the Round Table. After watering his horse, he knocked on the caldron and Sir Tarquine, whose castle it was, appeared.

They jousted, and at the first encounter Sir Ector sent his opponent's horse spinning twice about before he could recover.

"That was a fine stroke; now let us try again," said Sir Tarquine.

This time Sir Tarquine caught Sir Ector just below the right arm and, having impaled him on his spear, lifted him clean out of the saddle, and rode with him into the castle, where he threw him on the ground.

"Sir," said Sir Tarquine, "you have fought better than any knight I have encountered in the last twelve years; therefore, if you wish, I will demand no more of you than your parole[19] as my prisoner."

"Sir, that I will never give."

"Then I am sorry for you," said Sir Tarquine, and with that he stripped and beat him and locked him in the dungeon with the other prisoners. There Sir Ector saw Sir Lyonel.

"Alas, Sir Lyonel, we are in a sorry plight. But tell me, what has happened to Sir Launcelot? for he surely is the one knight who could save us."

"I left him sleeping beneath an apple tree, and what has befallen him since I do not know," Sir Lyonel replied; and then all the unhappy prisoners once more bewailed their lot.

While Sir Launcelot still slept beneath the apple tree, four queens started across the plain. They were riding white mules and accompanied by four knights who held above them, at the tips of their spears, a green silk canopy, to protect them from the sun. The party was startled by the neighing of Sir Launcelot's horse and, changing direction, rode up to the apple tree, where they discovered the sleeping knight. And as each of the queens gazed at the handsome Sir Launcelot, so each wanted him for her own.

---

19. A knight's *parole* was his pledge to fulfill certain conditions in exchange for full or partial freedom.

Analyze Plot What does this action reveal about Sir Lyonel?

King Arthur and Queen Guinevere, 14th century. Artist unknown. British Library, London.

"Let us not quarrel," said Morgan le Fay. "Instead, I will cast a spell over him so that he remains asleep while we take him to my castle and make him our prisoner. We can then oblige him to choose one of us for his paramour."

Sir Launcelot was laid on his shield and borne by two of the knights to the Castle Charyot, which was Morgan le Fay's stronghold. He awoke to find himself in a cold cell, where a young noblewoman was serving him supper.

"What cheer?"[20] she asked.

---

20. *What cheer?* meant the same as asking "How are you?"

"My lady, I hardly know, except that I must have been brought here by means of an enchantment."

"Sir, if you are the knight you appear to be, you will learn your fate at dawn tomorrow." And with that the young noblewoman left him. Sir Launcelot spent an uncomfortable night but at dawn the four queens presented themselves and Morgan le Fay spoke to him:

"Sir Launcelot, I know that Queen Gwynevere loves you, and you her. But now you are my prisoner, and you will have to choose: either to take one of us for your paramour, or to die miserably in this cell—just as you please. Now I will tell you who we are: I am Morgan le Fay, Queen of Gore; my companions are the Queens of North Galys, of Estelonde, and of the Outer Isles. So make your choice."

"A hard choice! Understand that I choose none of you, lewd sorceresses[21] that you are; rather will I die in this cell. But were I free, I would take pleasure in proving it against any who would champion[22] you that Queen Gwynevere is the finest lady of this land."

"So, you refuse us?" asked Morgan le Fay.

"On my life, I do," Sir Launcelot said finally, and so the queens departed.

Sometime later, the young noblewoman who had served Sir Launcelot's supper reappeared.

"What news?" she asked.

"It is the end," Sir Launcelot replied.

"Sir Launcelot, I know that you have refused the four queens, and that they wish to kill you out of spite. But if you will be ruled by me, I can save you. I ask that you

---

21. Launcelot accuses the women of being unchaste *(lewd)* witches *(sorceresses)*.
22. As a verb, *champion* means "to defend a person or cause."

Acts of Courage *From this statement, what do you think Sir Launcelot values?*

will champion my father at a tournament next Tuesday, when he has to combat the King of North Galys, and three knights of the Round Table, who last Tuesday defeated him ignominiously."[23]

"My lady, pray tell me, what is your father's name?"

"King Bagdemagus."[24]

"Excellent, my lady, I know him for a good king and a true knight, so I shall be happy to serve him."

"May God reward you! And tomorrow at dawn I will release you, and direct you to an abbey which is ten miles from here, and where the good monks will care for you while I fetch my father."

"I am at your service, my lady."

As promised, the young noblewoman released Sir Launcelot at dawn. When she had led him through the twelve doors to the castle entrance, she gave him his horse and armor, and directions for finding the abbey.

"God bless you, my lady; and when the time comes I promise I shall not fail you."

Sir Launcelot rode through the forest in search of the abbey, but at dusk had still failed to find it, and coming upon a red silk pavilion, apparently unoccupied, decided to rest there overnight, and continue his search in the morning. . . .

As soon as it was daylight, Sir Launcelot armed, mounted, and rode away in search of the abbey, which he found in less than two hours. King Bagdemagus' daughter was waiting for him, and as soon as she heard his horse's footsteps in the yard, ran to the window, and, seeing that it was Sir Launcelot, herself ordered the servants to stable his horse. She then led him to her chamber, disarmed him, and gave him a long gown to wear, welcoming him warmly as she did so.

King Bagdemagus' castle was twelve miles away, and his daughter sent for him as soon as she had settled Sir Launcelot. The king arrived with his retinue[25] and embraced Sir Launcelot, who then described his recent enchantment, and the great obligation he was under to his daughter for releasing him.

"Sir, you will fight for me on Tuesday next?"

"Sire, I shall not fail you; but please tell me the names of the three Round Table knights whom I shall be fighting."

"Sir Modred, Sir Madore de la Porte, and Sir Gahalantyne. I must admit that last Tuesday they defeated me and my knights completely."

"Sire, I hear that the tournament is to be fought within three miles of the abbey. Could you send me three of your most trustworthy knights, clad in plain armor, and with no device,[26] and a fourth suit of armor which I myself shall wear? We will take up our position just outside the tournament field and watch while you and the King of North Galys enter into combat with your followers; and then, as soon as you are in difficulties, we will come to your rescue, and show your opponents what kind of knights you command."

This was arranged on Sunday, and on the following Tuesday Sir Launcelot and the three knights of King Bagdemagus waited in a copse,[27] not far from the pavilion which had been erected for the lords

---

23. The woman's father was defeated shamefully or dishonorably (ignominiously).
24. Bagdemagus (bag´ də mag´ əs)

Dialogue *What does this dialogue reveal about Sir Launcelot?*

25. The king's *retinue* is the group of people who accompany and serve him.
26. Armor with no *device* has no ornamental design.
27. A *copse* is a thicket of trees.

Analyze Plot *Why do you think Sir Launcelot makes these requests?*

and ladies who were to judge the tournament and award the prizes.

The King of North Galys was the first on the field, with a company of ninescore knights; he was followed by King Bagdemagus with fourscore[28] knights, and then by the three knights of the Round Table, who remained apart from both companies. At the first encounter King Bagdemagus lost twelve knights, all killed, and the King of North Galys six.

With that, Sir Launcelot galloped on to the field, and with his first spear unhorsed five of the King of North Galys' knights, breaking the backs of four of them. With his next spear he charged the king, and wounded him deeply in the thigh.

"That was a shrewd blow," commented Sir Madore, and galloped onto the field to challenge Sir Launcelot. But he too was tumbled from his horse, and with such violence that his shoulder was broken.

Sir Modred was the next to challenge Sir Launcelot, and he was sent spinning over his horse's tail. He landed head first, his helmet became buried in the soil, and he nearly broke his neck, and for a long time lay stunned.

Finally Sir Gahalantyne tried; at the first encounter both he and Sir Launcelot broke their spears, so both drew their swords and hacked vehemently at each other. But Sir Launcelot, with mounting wrath, soon struck his opponent a blow on the helmet which brought the blood streaming from eyes, ears, and mouth. Sir Gahalantyne slumped forward in the saddle, his horse panicked, and he was thrown to the ground, useless for further combat.

Sir Launcelot took another spear, and unhorsed sixteen more of the King of North Galys' knights, and with his next, unhorsed another twelve; and in each case with such violence that none of the knights ever fully recovered. The King of North Galys was forced to admit defeat, and the prize was awarded to King Bagdemagus.

That night Sir Launcelot was entertained as the guest of honor by King Bagdemagus and his daughter at their castle, and before leaving was loaded with gifts.

"My lady, please, if ever again you should need my services, remember that I shall not fail you."

The next day Sir Launcelot rode once more through the forest, and by chance came to the apple tree where he had previously slept. This time he met a young noblewoman riding a white palfrey.

"My lady, I am riding in search of adventure; pray tell me if you know of any I might find hereabouts."

Visual Vocabulary
A *palfrey* is a gentle saddle horse, especially one trained for a woman rider.

"Sir, there are adventures hereabouts if you believe that you are equal to them; but please tell me, what is your name?"

"Sir Launcelot du Lake."

"Very well, Sir Launcelot, you appear to be a sturdy enough knight, so I will tell you. Not far away stands the castle of Sir Tarquine, a knight who in fair combat has overcome more than sixty opponents whom he now holds prisoner. Many are from the court of King Arthur, and if you can rescue them, I will then ask you to deliver me and my companions from a knight who distresses us daily, either by robbery or by other kinds of outrage."

"My lady, please first lead me to Sir Tarquine, then I will most happily challenge this miscreant[29] knight of yours."

---

28. One *score* is twenty, so more than 260 knights have gathered.

29. A *miscreant* knight is an evil, villainous one.

Miniature Painting Depicting the Knights of the Round Table, 15th century. Artist unknown. Archivo Iconográfico, S.A.

View the Art During the Middle Ages, most tables were rectangular or square, and round tables were highly unusual. Why do Arthur and his knights sit at a round table? What might a round table symbolize?

When they arrived at the castle, Sir Launcelot watered his horse at the ford, and then beat the caldron until the bottom fell out. However, none came to answer the challenge, so they waited by the castle gate for half an hour or so. Then Sir Tarquine appeared, riding toward the castle with a wounded prisoner slung over his horse, whom Sir Launcelot recognized as Sir Gaheris, Sir Gawain's brother and a knight of the Round Table.

"Good knight," said Sir Launcelot, "it is known to me that you have put to shame many of the knights of the Round Table. Pray allow your prisoner, who I see is wounded, to recover, while I vindicate[30] the honor of the knights whom you have defeated."

"I defy you, and all your fellowship of the Round Table," Sir Tarquine replied.

"You boast!" said Sir Launcelot.

At the first charge the backs of the horses were broken and both knights stunned. But they soon recovered and set to with their swords, and both struck so lustily that neither shield nor armor could resist, and within two hours they were cutting each other's flesh, from which the blood flowed liberally. Finally they paused for a moment, resting on their shields.

"Worthy knight," said Sir Tarquine, "pray hold your hand for a while, and if you will, answer my question."

"Sir, speak on."

"You are the most powerful knight I have fought yet, but I fear you may be the one whom in the whole world I most hate. If you are not, for the love of you I will release all my prisoners and swear eternal friendship."

---

30. Launcelot wishes to defend against opposition, or *vindicate*, the honor of Tarquine's prisoners.

Roman de Tristan: Scenes from the Legend of King Arthur, 15th century. Artist unknown. Archivo Iconográfico, S.A.

tell you: **I am Sir Launcelot du Lake, son of King Ban of Benwick, of Arthur's court, and a knight of the Round Table. So defend yourself!"**

"Ah! this is most welcome."

Now the two knights hurled themselves at each other like two wild bulls; swords and shields clashed together, and often their swords drove into the flesh. Then sometimes one, sometimes the other, would stagger and fall, only to recover immediately and resume the contest. At last, however, Sir Tarquine grew faint, and unwittingly lowered his shield. Sir Launcelot was swift to follow up his advantage, and dragging the other down to his knees, unlaced his helmet and beheaded him.

Sir Launcelot then strode over to the young noblewoman: "My lady, now I am at your service, but first I must find a horse."

"What is the name of the knight you hate above all others?"

"Sir Launcelot du Lake; for it was he who slew my brother, Sir Carados of the Dolorous Tower, and it is because of him that I have killed a hundred knights, and maimed[31] as many more, apart from the sixty-four I still hold prisoner. And so, if you are Sir Launcelot, speak up, for we must then fight to the death."

"Sir, I see now that I might go in peace and good fellowship, or otherwise fight to the death; but being the knight I am, I must

Then the wounded Sir Gaheris spoke up: "Sir, please take my horse. Today you have overcome the most formidable knight, excepting only yourself, and by so doing have saved us all. But before leaving, please tell me your name."

"Sir Launcelot du Lake. Today I have fought to vindicate the honor of the knights of the Round Table, and I know that among Sir Tarquine's prisoners are two of my brethren, Sir Lyonel and Sir Ector, also your own brother, Sir Gawain. According to the

---

Acts of Courage Why do you think Launcelot reveals himself, exposing himself to further danger?

---

31. To *maim* is to injure seriously or horribly.

shields there are also: Sir Brandiles, Sir Galyhuddis, Sir Kay, Sir Alydukis, Sir Marhaus, and many others. Please release the prisoners and ask them to help themselves to the castle treasure. Give them all my greetings and say I will see them at the next Pentecost. And please request Sir Ector and Sir Lyonel to go straight to the court and await me there."

When Sir Launcelot had ridden away with the young noblewoman, Sir Gaheris entered the castle, and finding the porter in the hall, threw him on the ground and took the castle keys. He then released the prisoners, who, seeing his wounds, thanked him for their deliverance.

"Do not thank me for this work, but Sir Launcelot. He sends his greetings to you all, and asks you to help yourselves to the castle treasure. He has ridden away on another quest, but said that he will see you at the next Pentecost. Meanwhile, he requests Sir Lyonel and Sir Ector to return to the court and await him there."

==Certainly we shall not ride back to the court, but rather we shall follow Sir Launcelot wherever he goes,==" said Sir Ector.

"And I too shall follow him," said Sir Kay.

The prisoners searched the castle for their armor and horses and the castle treasure; and then a forester arrived with supplies of venison, so they feasted merrily and settled down for the night in the castle chambers—all but Sir Ector, Sir Lyonel, and Sir Kay, who set off immediately after supper in search of Sir Launcelot.

Sir Launcelot and the young noblewoman were riding down a broad highway when the young noblewoman said they were within sight of the spot where the knight generally attacked her.

"For shame that a knight should so degrade his high calling," Sir Launcelot replied. "Certainly we will teach him a much-needed lesson. Now, my lady, I suggest that you ride on ahead, and as soon as he molests you, I will come to the rescue."

Sir Launcelot halted and the young noblewoman rode gently forward. Soon the knight appeared with his page, and seized the young noblewoman from her horse; she cried out at once, and Sir Launcelot galloped up to them.

"Scoundrel! What sort of knight do you think you are, to attack defenseless women?"

In answer the other knight drew his sword. Sir Launcelot did likewise, and they rushed together. With his first stroke Sir Launcelot split open the knight's head, down to the throat.

"Let that be your payment, though long overdue," said Sir Launcelot.

"Even so; he certainly deserved to die. His name was Sir Percy of the Forest Sauvage."

"My lady, do you require anything more of me?"

"No, good Sir Launcelot; and may the sweet Lord Jesu[32] protect you, ==for certainly you are the bravest and gentlest knight I have known.== But pray tell me one thing: why is it you do not take to yourself a wife? Many good ladies, both high born and low born, grieve that so fine a knight as yourself should remain single. It is whispered, of course, that Queen Gwynevere has cast a spell over you so that you shall love no other."

"As for that, people must believe what they will about Queen Gwynevere and me. But married I will not be, for then I should

---

32. *Jesu* (jē′ zōō) is a form of *Jesus*.

Dialogue How do the other characters' responses to Launcelot help characterize them?

Acts of Courage The noblewoman tells Launcelot that he is the "bravest and gentlest" knight she has known. What is the significance of these two adjectives?

Sir Launcelot then took his leave of the young noblewoman, and for two days wandered alone through the forest, resting at night at the most meager of lodgings. On the third day, as he was crossing a bridge, he was accosted by a churlish porter,[34] who, after striking his horse on the nose so that it turned about, demanded to know by what right Sir Launcelot was riding that way.

"And what right do I need to cross this bridge? Surely, I cannot ride beside it," said Sir Launcelot.

"That is not for you to decide," said the porter, and with that he lashed at Sir Launcelot with his club. Sir Launcelot drew his sword, and after deflecting the blow, struck the porter on the head and split it open.

At the end of the bridge was a prosperous-looking village, overtopped by a fine castle. As Sir Launcelot advanced he heard someone cry: "Good knight, beware! You have done yourself no good by killing the chief porter of the castle."

Sir Launcelot rode on regardless, through the village and into the castle court, which was richly grassed. Thinking to himself that this would be a good place for combat, Sir Launcelot tied his horse to a

Knight with Armor, Artist unknown. Archivo Iconografico, S. A.

have to attend my lady instead of entering for tournaments and wars, or riding in search of adventure. And I will not take a paramour, both for the fear of God and in the belief that those who do so are always unfortunate when they meet a knight who is purer of heart; for whether they are defeated or victorious in such an encounter, either result must be equally distressing and shameful. I believe that a true knight is neither adulterous nor lecherous."[33]

---

33. A true knight is pure. He does not commit adultery (*adulterous*), nor is he preoccupied with indecent thoughts and desires (*lecherous*).

34. Here, the gatekeeper (*porter*) is bad-tempered and very rude (*churlish*).

ring in the wall and started across the lawn. Meanwhile people were peering at him from every door and window, and again he heard the warning: "Good knight, you come here at your peril!"

Before long two giants appeared, fully armed except for their heads, and brandishing huge clubs. Together they rushed at Sir Launcelot, who raised his shield to defend himself, and then struck at one of the giants and beheaded him. Thereupon the second giant roared with dismay and fled into the forest, where Sir Launcelot pursued him. In a few minutes, Sir Launcelot drew abreast of the giant and struck him on the shoulder with a blow that carried through to the navel, and the giant dropped dead.

When Sir Launcelot returned to the castle, he was greeted by threescore ladies, who all knelt before him.

"Brave knight! we thank you for delivering us. Many of us have been prisoners for seven years now, and although we are all high born, we have had to work like servants for our keep, doing silk embroidery. Pray tell us your name, so that our friends can know who has saved us."

"My ladies, I am called Sir Launcelot du Lake."

"Welcome, Sir Launcelot! It was you alone whom the giants feared, and you alone who could have overcome them. How often have we prayed for your coming!"

"My ladies, please greet your friends for me; and when I pass through this country again, grant me what hospitality you may feel is my due. Please recompense[35] yourselves from the castle treasure, and then insure that the castle is restored to the rightful owner."

"Sir Launcelot, this is the castle of Tintagil, and belonged formerly to the duke of that name. But after his death, Igraine, who had been his wife, was made queen by King Uther Pendragon, to whom she bore Arthur, our present king."

"And so, after all, I know the owner of this castle. My ladies, I bless you, and farewell."

Always in quest of adventure, Sir Launcelot rode through many different countries, through wild valleys and forests, and across strange rivers; and at night he slept where he could, often in the roughest of lodgings. Then one day he came to a well-kept house where the lady offered him the best of hospitality. After supper he was taken to his chamber, which overlooked the front door, and there Sir Launcelot disarmed and fell comfortably asleep.

He was awakened a short time later by a tremendous knocking at the door below, and looking through the window recognized Sir Kay in the moonlight, and three knights galloping toward him with drawn swords. The moment they got to the house, they dismounted and set upon Sir Kay, who turned about and drew his sword to defend himself. Sir Launcelot hastily armed, saying to himself: "If they kill Sir Kay I shall be a party to his death, for three against one is unjust."

He let himself down from the window by means of his sheet, and then challenged the three attackers, whispering to Sir Kay to stand by while he dealt with them. Sir Kay did as he was advised, and then Sir Launcelot, with seven tremendous blows, brought all three knights to their knees and begging for mercy.

"Your lives will be spared if you yield to Sir Kay," said Sir Launcelot.

"Sir, it is surely you to whom we should yield, since we could easily have overcome Sir Kay."

---

35. Launcelot invites the ladies to *recompense* themselves, or divide the treasure among themselves, as a way to make up for their treatment by the giants.

Analyze Plot Why do you think Malory returns Sir Launcelot to Tintagil?

"If you wish to be spared, you will go as prisoners of Sir Kay, and yield to Queen Gwynevere."

Each of the knights then swore on his sword to abide by the conditions of his surrender, and Sir Launcelot knocked once more at the door of the house.

"Why, I thought you were safely in bed," said the landlady, recognizing Sir Launcelot as she opened the door.

"Madam, I was, but then I had to jump out of the window and rescue this comrade of mine."

As they came into the light, Sir Kay recognized Sir Launcelot and thanked him humbly for twice saving his life.

"It was no more than I should have done, but come up to my chamber; you must be tired and hungry."

When Sir Kay had eaten, he lay on Sir Launcelot's bed, and they slept together until dawn. Sir Launcelot woke first, and rising quietly, clad himself in Sir Kay's armor, and then, mounting Sir Kay's horse, rode away from the house.

When Sir Kay awoke, he was astonished to find that Sir Launcelot had exchanged armor with him, but then he realized he had done it so that he should ride home unmolested, while Sir Launcelot encountered his opponents. And when Sir Kay had taken his leave of the landlady he rode back to the court without further incident.

For several days Sir Launcelot rode through the forest, and then he came to a countryside of low meadows and broad streams. At the foot of a bridge he saw three pavilions, and a knight standing at the entrance to each, with a white shield hanging above, and a spear thrust into the ground at one side. Sir Launcelot recognized the three knights, who were from Arthur's court, as Sir Gawtere, Sir Raynolde, and Sir Gylmere. However, he rode straight past them, looking neither to right nor to left, and without saluting them.

"Why, there rides Sir Kay, the most overbearing[36] knight of all, in spite of his many defeats. I think I will challenge him and see if I cannot shake his pride a little," said Sir Gawtere.

He then galloped up to Sir Launcelot and challenged him. They jousted, and Sir Gawtere was flung violently from the saddle.

"That is certainly not Sir Kay," said Sir Raynolde. "For one thing, he is very much bigger."

"Probably it is some knight who has killed Sir Kay and is riding in his armor," Sir Gylmere replied.

"Well, since he has overcome our brother we shall have to challenge him. But I think it must be either Sir Launcelot, Sir Tristram, or Sir Pelleas; and we may not come well out of this."

Sir Gylmere challenged Sir Launcelot next, and was also overthrown. Then Sir Raynolde rode up to him.

"Sir, I would prefer not to challenge a knight so powerful as you, but since you have probably killed my brothers, I am obliged to; so defend yourself!"

They jousted; both broke their spears and they continued the combat with swords. Sir Gawtere and Sir Gylmere recovered, and attempted to rescue their brother, but Sir Launcelot saw them in time, and using more strength than hitherto, struck each off his horse again. At this, Sir Raynolde, badly wounded as he was, and with blood streaming from his

---

36. An *overbearing* person is excessively proud and superior in attitude and behavior.

Dialogue What does this statement reveal about the fraternity of knights?

head, picked himself up and once more rushed at Sir Launcelot.

"Sir, I should let things be," said Sir Launcelot. "I was not far away when you were knighted, and I know you to be worthy: therefore do not oblige me to kill you."

"May God reward you!" Sir Raynolde replied. "But speaking both for myself and my brothers, I would prefer to know your name before yielding to you, because we know very well that you are not Sir Kay, whom any one of us could have overcome."

"That is as may be; but I still require that you yield to Queen Gwynevere at the next Pentecost, and say that Sir Kay sent you."

The three brothers took their oath, and Sir Launcelot left them. He had not ridden much further when, coming to a glade, he found four more knights of the Round Table: Sir Gawain, Sir Ector, Sir Uwayne, and Sir Sagramour le Desyrus.

"Look!" said Sir Sagramour, "there rides Sir Kay. I will challenge him."

Sir Sagramour first, then each of the other knights in turn, challenged Sir Launcelot, and was flung from his horse. Sir Launcelot left them gasping on the ground, and said to himself as he rode away: "Blessed be the maker of this spear; with it I have tumbled four knights off their horses." Meanwhile the four knights were picking themselves up and consoling each other.

"To the devil with him! He is indeed powerful," said one.

"I believe that it must be Sir Launcelot," said another.

"Anyhow, let him go now; we shall discover when we return to Camelot," said a third, and so on. . . .

Sir Launcelot returned to Camelot two days before the feast of Pentecost, and at the court was acclaimed[37] by many of the knights he had met on his adventures.

Sir Gawain, Sir Uwayne, Sir Ector, and Sir Sagramour all laughed when they saw him in Sir Kay's armor, but without the helmet, and readily forgave his joke at their expense.

Sir Gaheris described to the court the terrible battle Sir Launcelot had fought with Sir Tarquine, and how sixty-four prisoners had been freed as a result of his victory.

Sir Kay related how Sir Launcelot had twice saved his life, and then exchanged armor with him, so that he should ride unchallenged.

Sir Gawtere, Sir Gylmere, and Sir Raynolde described how he had defeated them at the bridge, and forced them to yield as prisoners of Sir Kay; and they were overjoyed to discover that it had been Sir Launcelot nevertheless.

Sir Modred, Sir Mador, and Sir Gahalantyne described his tremendous feats in the battle against the King of North Galys; and Sir Launcelot himself described his enchantment by the four queens, and his rescue at the hands of the daughter of King Bagdemagus. . . .

And thus it was, at this time, that Sir Launcelot became the most famous knight at King Arthur's court.

---

37. Launcelot was *acclaimed*, or greeted with loud, enthusiastic praise.

Acts of Courage Why does Sir Launcelot refrain from describing his acts of courage?

After You Read

Respond and Think Critically

Respond and Interpret

1. What is your reaction to the world of King Arthur and his knights? If you could be transported there for a day, would you go? Why or why not?

2. (a) What events lead Arthur to pull the sword from the stone? (b) What does Arthur's behavior immediately after pulling the sword free tell you about him?

3. (a) Why is Sir Tarquine so determined to kill Sir Launcelot? (b) Why do you think Sir Launcelot reveals his identity, knowing that the ensuing fight will lead to death?

Analyze and Evaluate

4. Do the characters of King Uther Pendragon and Igraine seem realistic? Why or why not?

5. If you were one of the nobles, would you have proclaimed the young Arthur to be king as described in "The Tale of King Arthur"? Explain.

6. What do you learn about Sir Kay's character in "The Tale of King Arthur" that foreshadows what his fellow knights think of him in "The Tale of Sir Launcelot du Lake"?

Connect

7. **Big Idea** **Acts of Courage** Why would Sir Launcelot be described as courageous? Is he a hero? Explain.

8. **Connect to Today** In "The Tale of Sir Launcelot du Lake," Sir Launcelot repeatedly risks his own life to protect and defend others. Who are the people who take those risks in the modern world? What might be their motivation?

Literary Element Dialogue

Le Morte d'Arthur uses **dialogue**, the written conversation between characters. Dialogue gives readers a sense of a character's personality and feelings. For example, the reader realizes the importance of King Uther's feelings when Uther says "Igraine has broken my heart, and unless I can win her, I shall never recover."

1. Reread the scene on page 909 in which Sir Ector realizes that Arthur has removed the sword from the stone. Why do you think the author chose to use dialogue here?

2. Which passage of dialogue in the selection do you find particularly effective or striking? Why?

Review: Hero

As you learned on page 653, a **hero** is the main character in a literary work and typically has qualities that arouse the admiration of the reader.

Partner Activity Critic Jeffrey Helterman observes that "Arthur institutes a code of behavior which stresses always succoring [aiding] ladies . . . and never taking up battles for a wrongful cause." With a partner, find examples from "The Tale of Sir Launcelot du Lake" of knights following this code of behavior. Use a chart like the one below. What can you infer from the code about the values held by this society?

Example	Inference
When a knight attacks a noblewoman, Sir Launcelot fights and defeats him.	Protecting women and their honor is valued in his society.
Sir Launcelot refuses Morgan le Fay.	

Reading Strategy: Analyze Plot

Determining the author's purpose in **plotting** certain episodes can help readers understand the theme of a legend. Review your plot diagram from page 903 and answer the following questions.

1. Why do you think Malory included Launcelot's refusal to choose a paramour from among Morgan le Fay and her companions?
2. Why might Malory have included Launcelot's killing of Sir Tarquine within the plot?

Vocabulary Practice

Practice with Word Origins Studying the etymology, or origin and history, of a word can help you better understand and explore its meaning. Create a word map, like the one below, for each of these vocabulary words from the selection.

abashed   inscribe   ignoble   tumultuous   prowess

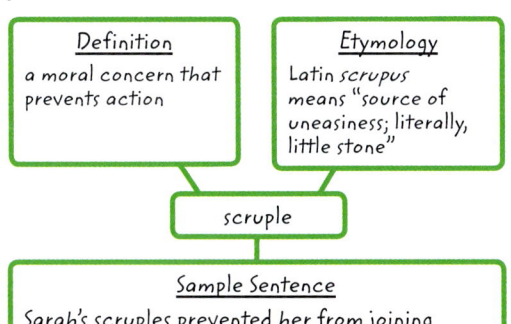

Academic Vocabulary

*Malory's story had an enormous **impact** on subsequent retellings of the Arthur legend.*

Impact is an academic word. A more familiar word that is similar in meaning is *effect.* Answer this question in one or more complete sentences: Which event or person has had the greatest **impact** on how you spend your free time or after-school time? Why?

For more on academic vocabulary, see pages 52 and 53.

Write with Style

 Apply Dialogue

Assignment Write a short dialogue that reveals the personality traits of two characters of your own invention.

Get Ideas How a writer uses dialogue reveals part of his or her personal style. Recall how the dialogue in *Le Morte d'Arthur* and in the Literary Analysis Model "The Journey of Gilgamesh" on pages 896–897 helps reveal the characters. Then think of two contrasting traits, such as aggressiveness and reluctance, confidence and uncertainty, or cruelty and sympathy. List words and phrases that might be spoken by characters with those traits.

Responsible	Irresponsible
I'll do it.	Who says I have to do that?
This is my job, and I won't let you down.	It's not my job!
No matter what it takes, I'm going to come through for you.	If you care so much about it, do it yourself!

Give It Structure Think of an issue that might pit two characters with contrasting personality traits against one another. Then write a dialogue in which the issue comes to light. Use speaker tags to convey the tone of what each character says. Embrace your personal style and make your dialogue realistic by using everyday speech and by allowing characters to interrupt each other or trail off.

Look at Language Use a thesaurus to replace weak verbs, such as *said,* in your speaker tags with more vivid verbs, such as *insisted, demanded,* or *jested.*

 Literature Online

Selection Resources For Selection Quizzes, eFlashcards, and Reading-Writing Connection activities, go to glencoe.com and enter QuickPass code GL59794u5.

Learning Objectives

In this workshop, you will focus on the following objective:

Grammar: Understanding how to use phrases and clauses.

Grammar Workshop

Main and Subordinate Clauses

Literature Connection In *Le Morte d'Arthur*, Keith Baines uses sentences that include both main (or independent) and subordinate (or dependent) clauses.

> "In the course of the feast, King Uther grew passionately desirous of Igraine and, when it was over, begged her to become his paramour."
>
> —Keith Baines, from Sir Thomas Malory's *Le Morte d'Arthur*

Both main and subordinate clauses contain subjects and predicates. A **main clause**, however, expresses a complete thought, so it can stand alone as a sentence. A **subordinate clause** is dependent for its meaning on the main clause. In the quotation above, the main clause is *In the course of the feast, King Uther grew passionately desirous of Igraine and begged her to become his paramour*. The subordinate clause, *when it was over*, cannot stand alone.

Here is how to identify main and subordinate clauses and turn subordinate clauses into complete sentences.

Main clause *The story was written by Malory and retold by Baines*

Explanation Because the clause has a subject (*story*) and a predicate (*was written*) and expresses a complete thought, it can stand alone as a complete sentence.

Solution To create a sentence, add a period to the main clause.

The story was written by Malory and retold by Baines.

Subordinate clause *Because the story was interesting*

Explanation The clause has a subject (*story*) and a predicate (*was*) but does not express a complete thought.

Solution To create a sentence, combine subordinate and main clauses.

Because the story was interesting, <u>I wanted to read more of it</u>.

Clauses

A **main clause** has a subject and a predicate, expresses a complete thought, and can stand alone as a sentence. A **subordinate clause** has a subject and a predicate, does not express a complete thought, and cannot stand alone as a sentence.

Tip

If a clause begins with one of the following—*if, which, when, where, who, that, if,* and similar words—what follows is a subordinate clause, dependent on the main clause for its meaning.

Language Handbook

For more on main and subordinate clauses, see the Language Handbook, pp. R40–R59.

Revise Rewrite the subordinate clauses to make complete sentences. Write "correct" if the clause is a sentence.

1. Since the boy was able to pull the sword out easily, unlike the others who tried.
2. While it was clear that he was the new king.
3. Sir Ector and the other men were amazed by the feat.
4. After Wart pulled the sword.

Grammar For more grammar practice, go to glencoe.com and enter QuickPass code GL59794u5.

Before You Read

from Don Quixote

Meet Miguel de Cervantes
(1547–1616)

Little is known about Miguel de Cervantes Saavedra's early years and education except that he was the son of a doctor and he worked for a cardinal. By 1570 he enlisted in the Spanish army regiment stationed in Rome, and the following year, he fought against the Turks in the Lepanto naval battle. Though feverish and seriously wounded, Cervantes fought bravely. While returning to Spain in 1576, Barbary pirates captured his ship, and Cervantes and his brother were sold into slavery in Algiers. Even as a slave, Cervantes gained a reputation for courage and leadership and mounted several attempts to escape. In 1580 Cervantes's family finally managed to buy his freedom, but the price ruined his family's finances.

Struggles to Find Work Once back in Spain, Cervantes struggled to write and support his family; he finally obtained a short-lived position as royal messenger to Algeria in 1581. During this time, Cervantes's only child, Isabel de Saavedra, was born.

In 1585 Cervantes published his first work, *La Galatea*, a pastoral romance written in both prose and verse. Cervantes claimed to have written more than twenty plays during this time (1582–1587), although only two survive: *La Numancia* (a historical tragedy) and *El trato de Argel (The Traffic of Algiers)*. He once noted that these plays were received by audiences without booing or pelting the actors with vegetables. When Cervantes's literary career languished, he looked for more consistent work.

Cervantes was hired as a purchasing agent for the Spanish Armada. However, accounting errors landed him in trouble with his superiors, municipal authorities, and the church, which excommunicated him several times. Cervantes started writing short stories, but his earlier accounting troubles caught up with him, and he was jailed until April 1598.

> "It can be said that all prose fiction is a variation on the theme of Don Quixote."
>
> —Lionel Trilling

Publishing Success In 1605 Cervantes published Part I of *Don Quixote*, whose main character, an idealistic gentleman devoted to reading chivalric romances, sets off in search of adventure. Readers responded enthusiastically, and Cervantes achieved literary success.

Over the next decade or so, Cervantes wrote other works of fiction. But none surpassed the creation of Don Quixote, one of the world's most beloved and enduring literary figures.

Author Search For more about Miguel de Cervantes, go to glencoe.com and enter QuickPass code GL59794u5.

Literature and Reading Preview

Connect to the Story

Can you remember a time when you or someone else defied the odds? Write a journal entry about being an underdog, or someone who is not expected to succeed.

Build Background

Don Quixote presents two different perspectives of the world: idealism (envisioning things in an ideal form) and realism (envisioning things as they actually are). The work can be appreciated as a satire of idealism in an imperfect world.

Set Purposes for Reading

Big Idea Acts of Courage

As you read, ask yourself, Is Don Quixote a hero or not?

Literary Element Parody

A **parody** is a humorous imitation of a literary work that aims to illustrate the work's shortcomings. A parody may imitate the plot, characters, or style of another work but usually exaggerates those characteristics. As you read, ask yourself, How is this work a parody of chivalry and stories about knights?

Reading Strategy Evaluate Characters

When you **evaluate characters**, you make judgments or form opinions about them by paying close attention to their actions, statements, thoughts, and feelings. As you read, ask yourself, How does Cervantes provide details about the characters' personalities, physical attributes, and ways, particularly knightly life?

Tip: Look for Clues Think about clues the author gives about each character's personality. Some clues will be subtle, while others will be directly stated. As you read, use a diagram like this to write down clues about each character.

Learning Objectives

For pages 925–936

In studying this text, you will focus on the following objectives:

Literary Study: Analyzing parody.

Reading: Evaluating characters.

Vocabulary

interminable (in tur′ mi nə bəl) *adj.* having or seeming to have no end; p. 928 *The students found the exam to be interminable.*

renown (ri noun′) *n.* a state of being widely acclaimed; p. 929 *In the 1920s my aunt was a singer of worldwide renown.*

redress (ri dres′) *v.* to correct or compensate for wrong or loss; p. 929 *The man felt there was no way to redress the tragic loss of his dog.*

discourteous (dis kur′ tē əs) *adj.* impolite; p. 932 *The angry pedestrian was discourteous to the driver of the car that hit him.*

enmity (en′ mə tē) *n.* hatred or ill will; p. 934 *The organization has enmity toward anyone who abuses animals.*

Don Quixote Armed as a Knight. Cristobal Valero. Museo del Prado, Madrid, Spain.

from DON QUIXOTE

Which treats of the quality and way of life of the famous knight Don Quixote de la Mancha.[1]

In a certain village in La Mancha, which I do not wish to name, there lived not long ago a gentleman—one of those who have always a lance in the rack, an ancient shield, a lean hack[2] and a greyhound for coursing. His habitual diet consisted of a stew, more beef than mutton, of hash most nights, boiled bones on Saturdays, lentils on Fridays, and a young pigeon as a Sunday treat; and on this he

---

1. *La Mancha* is a region in south-central Spain.
2. Unlike a warhorse or show horse, a *hack* is a horse used for transportation.

Visual Vocabulary
A *doublet* is a close-fitting jacket worn by men in Europe especially during the Renaissance.

spent three-quarters of his income. The rest of it went on a fine cloth doublet,³ velvet breeches and slippers for holidays, and a homespun suit of the best in which he decked himself on weekdays. His household consisted of a housekeeper of rather more than forty, a niece not yet twenty, and a lad for the field and market, who saddled his horse and wielded the pruning hook.

Our gentleman was verging on fifty, of tough constitution, lean-bodied, thin-faced, a great early riser and a lover of hunting. They say that his surname was Quixada or Quesada—for there is some difference of opinion amongst authors on this point. However, by very reasonable conjecture we may take it that he was called Quexana. But this does not much concern our story; enough that we do not depart by so much as an inch from the truth in the telling of it.

The reader must know, then, that this gentleman, in the times when he had nothing to do—as was the case for most of the year—gave himself up to the reading of books of knight-errantry;⁴ which he loved and enjoyed so much that he almost entirely forgot his hunting, and even the care of his estate. So odd and foolish, indeed, did he grow on this subject that he sold many acres of cornland to buy these books of chivalry⁵ to read, and in this way brought home every one he could get. And of them all he considered none so good as the works of the famous Feliciano de Silva. For his brilliant style and those complicated sentences seemed to him very pearls, especially when he came upon those love passages and challenges frequently written in the manner of: "The reason for the unreason with which you treat my reason, so weakens my reason that with reason I complain of your beauty"; and also when he read: "The high heavens that with their stars divinely fortify you in your divinity and make you deserving of the desert that your greatness deserves."

These writings drove the poor knight out of his wits; and he passed sleepless nights trying to understand them and disentangle their meaning, though Aristotle⁶ himself would never have unraveled or understood them, even if he had been resurrected for that sole purpose. He did not much like the wounds that Sir Belianis gave and received, for he imagined that his face and his whole body must have been covered with scars and marks, however skillful the surgeons who tended him. But, for all that, he admired the author for ending his book with the promise to continue with that **interminable** adventure, and often the desire seized him to take up the pen himself, and write the promised sequel for him. No doubt he would have done so, and perhaps successfully, if other greater and more persistent preoccupations had not prevented him.

In short, he so buried himself in his books that he spent the nights reading from twilight till daybreak and the days from dawn till dark; and so from little sleep and much

---

3. A *doublet* is a close-fitting jacket worn by men of this time.
4. *Knights-errant* traveled about in search of adventure.
5. Medieval knights lived by a code of honorable behavior known as *chivalry*.

Evaluate Characters Do you think Don Quixote is behaving like a typical knight? Explain.

6. The Greek philosopher *Aristotle* (384–322 BC) was considered to possess one of the greatest minds of the ancient world.

Vocabulary

interminable (in tur′ mi nə bəl) *adj.* having or seeming to have no end

Don Quixote in his Study. George Cattermole. Victoria & Albert Museum, London.

reading, his brain dried up and he lost his wits. He filled his mind with all that he read in them, with enchantments, quarrels, battles, challenges, wounds, wooings, loves, torments and other impossible nonsense; and so deeply did he steep his imagination in the belief that all the fanciful stuff he read was true, that to his mind no history in the world was more authentic. . . .

In fact, now that he had utterly wrecked his reason he fell into the strangest fancy that ever a madman had in the whole world. He thought it fit and proper, both in order to increase his **renown** and to serve the state, to turn knight-errant and travel through the world with horse and armor in search of adventures, following in every way the practice of the knights-errant he had read of, **redressing** all manner of wrongs, and exposing himself to chances and dangers, by the overcoming of which he might win eternal honor and renown. Already the poor man fancied himself crowned by the valor of his arm, at least with the empire of Trebizond; and so, carried away by the strange pleasure he derived from these agreeable thoughts, he hastened to translate his desires into action.

The first thing that he did was to clean some armor which had belonged to his ancestors, and had lain for ages forgotten in a corner, eaten with rust and covered with mold. But when he had cleaned and repaired it as best he could, he found that there was one great defect: the helmet was a simple headpiece without a visor. So he ingeniously made good this deficiency by fashioning out of pieces of pasteboard a kind of half-visor which, fitted to the helmet, gave the appearance of a complete headpiece. However, to see if it was strong enough to stand up to the risk of a sword cut, he took out his sword and gave it two strokes, the first of which demolished in a moment what had taken him a week to make. He was not too pleased at the ease with which he had destroyed it, and to safeguard himself against this danger, reconstructed the visor, putting some strips of iron inside, in such a way as to satisfy himself of his protection; and, not caring to make another trial of it, he accepted it as a fine jointed headpiece and put it into commission.

Next he went to inspect his hack, but though, through leanness, he had more quarters than there are pence in a groat,[7] and more blemishes than Gonella's[8]

Parody What is Cervantes implying about Don Quixote?

Acts of Courage Do you think Don Quixote is ready to perform acts of courage? Explain.

Vocabulary

renown (ri noun´) *n.* a state of being widely acclaimed

redress (ri dres´) *v.* to correct or compensate for wrong or loss

---

7. The *groat*, an old coin, was worth four pence (four pennies). Don Quixote's horse was so bony that it appeared to have more than four quarters (the part of an animal's body that includes a leg).
8. Pietro *Gonella* was a famous court jester. He had a horse that was equally famous for being skinny.

Parody How is Cervantes parodying typical knight behavior with Don Quixote's behavior?

horse, which was nothing but skin and bone, he appeared to our knight more than the equal of Alexander's Bucephalus and the Cid's Babieca.[9] He spent four days pondering what name to give him; for, he reflected, it would be wrong for the horse of so famous a knight, a horse so good in himself, to be without a famous name. Therefore he tried to fit him with one that would signify what he had been before his master turned knight-errant, and what he now was; for it was only right that as his master changed his profession, the horse should change his name for a sublime and high-sounding one, befitting the new order and the new calling he professed. So, after many names invented, struck out and rejected, amended, canceled and remade in his fanciful mind, he finally decided to call him Rocinante,[10] a name which seemed to him grand and sonorous, and to express the common horse he had been before arriving at his present state: the first and foremost of all hacks in the world.

Having found so pleasing a name for his horse, he next decided to do the same for himself, and spent another eight days thinking about it. Finally he resolved to call himself Don Quixote. And that is no doubt why the authors of this true history, as we have said, assumed that his name must have been Quixada and not Quesada, as other authorities would have it. Yet he remembered that the valorous Amadis had not been content with his bare name, but had added the name of his kingdom and native country in order to make it famous, and styled himself Amadís[11] of Gaul. So, like a good knight, he decided to add the name of his country to his own and call himself Don Quixote de la Mancha. Thus, he thought, he very clearly proclaimed his parentage and native land and honored it by taking his surname from it.

Sancho Panza, 1839. Charles Robert Leslie. Oil on panel, 12 x 9 in. Victoria & Albert Museum, London.

---

9. *Bucephalus* was the favorite horse of Alexander the Great (356–323 BC). *Babieca* was the horse of El Cid (Rodrigo Díaz de Vivar, 1040–1099), Spain's national hero.
10. *Rocinante* is a combination of two Spanish words: *rocín,* meaning "nag or old horse," and *ante,* meaning "before or first." Rocinante could be translated into English with several meanings: as "the first old horse," "premiere (and therefore best) old horse," or "former old horse."
11. *Amadís* was the protagonist of the romance *Amadís de Gaula (Amadis of Gaul). Amadís de Gaula* was the foremost chivalric romance, written in the late thirteenth century. The character Amadís was widely considered the ideal knight: the most handsome and courageous of all. *Amadís de Gaula* was the object of parody for much of *Don Quixote.*

Now that his armor was clean, his helmet made into a complete headpiece, a name found for his horse, and he confirmed in his new title, it struck him that there was only one more thing to do: to find a lady to be enamored of. For a knight-errant without a lady is like a tree without leaves or fruit and a body without a soul. He said to himself again and again: "If I for my sins or by good luck were to meet with some giant hereabouts, as generally happens to knights-errant, and if I were to overthrow him in the encounter, or cut him down the middle or, in short, conquer him and make him surrender, would it not be well to have someone to whom I could send him as a present, so that he could enter and kneel down before my sweet lady and say in tones of humble submission: 'Lady, I am the giant Caraculiambro, lord of the island of Malindrania, whom the never-sufficiently-to-be-praised knight, Don Quixote de la Mancha, conquered in single combat and ordered to appear before your Grace, so that your Highness might dispose of me according to your will'?" Oh, how pleased our knight was when he had made up this speech, and even gladder when he found someone whom he could call his lady. It happened, it is believed, in this way: in a village near his there was a very good-looking farm girl, whom he had been taken with at one time, although she is supposed not to have known it or had proof of it. Her name was Aldonza Lorenzo, and she it was he thought fit to call the lady of his fancies; and, casting around for a name which should not be too far away from her own, yet suggest and imply a princess and great lady, he resolved to call her Dulcinea del Toboso—for she was a native of El Toboso—a name which seemed to him as musical, strange and significant as those others that he had devised for himself and his possessions.

In spite of the arguments of his family and friends, Don Quixote is determined to live out his dream. Most knights-errant in books were accompanied by a squire—a young man of noble birth aspiring to knighthood. Don Quixote's squire is slightly different. . . .

from Chapter VII

Of the Second Expedition of our good knight Don Quixote de la Mancha.

All this while Don Quixote was plying a laborer, a neighbor of his and an honest man—if a poor man may be called honest—but without much salt in his brainpan. In the end, he talked to him so much, persuaded him so hard and gave him such promises that the poor yokel[12] made up his mind to go out with him and serve him as squire. Don Quixote told him, amongst other things, that he ought to feel well disposed to come with him, for some time or another an adventure might occur that would win him in the twinkling of an eye some isle, of which he would leave him governor. These promises and others like them made Sancho Panza—for this was the laborer's name—leave his wife and children and take service as his neighbor's squire. Then Don Quixote set about raising money, and by selling one thing, pawning another, and making a bad bargain each time, he raised a reasonable sum. He also fixed himself up with a shield, which he borrowed from a friend, and patching up his broken helmet as best he could, he gave his squire Sancho notice of the day and the hour on which he proposed to set out, so that he

---

12. *Yokel* describes a naïve or gullible inhabitant of a rural area or small town.

Acts of Courage What kind of person does Don Quixote choose as a squire? Is he a suitable choice? Why or why not?

Don Quixote and Sancho, 19th century. Alexandre Gabriel Decamps. Oil on canvas.

should provide himself with all that was most needful; and he particularly told his squire to bring saddlebags. Sancho said that he would, and that he was also thinking of bringing a very fine donkey he had, for he was not too good at much traveling on foot. At the mention of the donkey Don Quixote hesitated a little, racking his brains to remember whether any knight-errant ever had a squire mounted on donkey back; but no case came to his memory. But, for all that, he decided to let him take it, intending to provide him with a more proper mount at the earliest opportunity by unhorsing the first **discourteous** knight he should meet. He provided himself also with shirts and everything else he could, following the advice which the innkeeper had given him. And when all this was arranged and done, without Panza saying good-bye to his wife and children, or Don Quixote taking leave of his housekeeper and niece, they departed from the village one evening, quite unobserved, and rode so far that night that at daybreak they thought they were safe, and that even if anyone came out to search for them they would not be found.

Sancho Panza rode on his donkey like a patriarch,[13] with his saddlebags and his leather bottle, and a great desire to see himself governor of the isle his master had promised him. It chanced that Don Quixote

---

13. A *patriarch* is the oldest and most respected male member of a family.

Evaluate Characters What do Panza's and Don Quixote's actions here tell you about them?

Vocabulary

discourteous (dis kur′ tē əs) *adj.* impolite

took the same route and struck the same track across the plain of Montiel as on his first expedition; but he traveled with less discomfort than before, as it was the hour of dawn, and the sun's rays, striking them obliquely, did not annoy them. . . .

from Chapter VIII

Of the valorous Don Quixote's success in the dreadful and never before imagined Adventure of the Windmills, with other events worthy of happy record.

At that moment they caught sight of some thirty or forty windmills, which stand on that plain, and as soon as Don Quixote saw them he said to his squire: "Fortune is guiding our affairs better than we could have wished. Look over there, friend Sancho Panza, where more than thirty monstrous giants appear. I intend to do battle with them and take all their lives. With their spoils we will begin to get rich, for this is a fair war, and it is a great service to God to wipe such a wicked brood from the face of the earth."

"What giants?" asked Sancho Panza.

"Those you see there," replied his master, "with their long arms. Some giants have them about six miles long."

"Take care, your worship," said Sancho; "those things over there are not giants but windmills, and what seem to be their arms are the sails, which are whirled round in the wind and make the millstone turn."

"It is quite clear," replied Don Quixote, "that you are not experienced in this matter of adventures. They are giants, and if you are afraid, go away and say your prayers, while I advance and engage them in fierce and unequal battle."

As he spoke, he dug his spurs into his steed Rocinante, paying not attention to his squire's shouted warning that beyond all doubt they were windmills and no giants he was advancing to attack. But he went on, so positive that they were giants that he neither listened to Sancho's cries nor noticed what they were, even when he got near them. Instead he went on shouting in a loud voice: "Do not fly, cowards, vile creatures, for it is one knight alone who assails you."

At that moment a slight wind arose, and the great sails began to move. At the sight of which Don Quixote shouted: "Though you wield more arms than the giant Briareus, you shall pay for it!" Saying this, he commended himself with all his soul to his Lady Dulcinea, beseeching her aid in his great peril. Then, covering himself with his shield and putting his lance in the rest, he urged Rocinante forward at a full gallop and attacked the nearest windmill, thrusting his lance into the sail. But the wind turned it with such violence that it shivered his weapon in pieces, dragging the horse and his rider with it, and sent the knight rolling badly injured across the plain. Sancho Panza rushed to his assistance as fast as his donkey could trot, but when he came up he found that the knight could not stir. Such a shock had Rocinante given him in their fall.

"O my goodness!" cried Sancho. "Didn't I tell your worship to look what you were doing, for they were only windmills? Nobody could mistake them, unless he had windmills on the brain."

"Silence, friend Sancho," replied Don Quixote. "Matters of war are more subject than most to continual change. What is more, I think—and that is the truth—that the same sage Friston who robbed me of

---

Acts of Courage Do you think Don Quixote is behaving courageously or foolishly? Explain.

Parody How does this scene parody traditional tales of knighthood?

my room and my books has turned those giants into windmills, to cheat me of the glory of conquering them. Such is the **enmity** he bears me; but in the very end his black arts shall avail him little against the goodness of my sword."

"God send it as He will," replied Sancho Panza, helping the knight to get up and remount Rocinante, whose shoulders were half dislocated.

As they discussed this last adventure they followed the road to the pass of Lapice where, Don Quixote said, they could not fail to find many and various adventures, as many travelers passed that way. He was much concerned, however, at the loss of his lance, and, speaking of it to his squire, remarked: "I remember reading that a certain Spanish knight called Diego Perez de Vargas, having broken his sword in battle, tore a great bough or limb from an oak, and performed such deeds with it that day, and pounded so many Moors, that he earned the surname of the Pounder, and thus he and his descendants from that day onwards have been called Vargas y Machuca.[14] I mention this because I propose to tear down just such a limb from the first oak we meet, as big and as good as his; and I intend to do such deeds with it that you may consider yourself most fortunate to have won the right to see them. For you will witness things which will scarcely be credited."

"With God's help," replied Sancho, "and I believe it all as your worship says. But sit a bit more upright, sir, for you seem to be riding lopsided. It must be from the bruises you got when you fell."

"That is the truth," replied Don Quixote. "And if I do not complain of the pain, it is because a knight-errant is not allowed to complain of any wounds, even though his entrails[15] may be dropping out through them."

"If that's so, I have nothing more to say," said Sancho, "but God knows I should be glad if your worship would complain if anything hurt you. I must say, for my part, that I have to cry out at the slightest twinge, unless this business of not complaining extends to knights-errants' squires as well."

Don Quixote could not help smiling at his squire's simplicity,[16] and told him that he could certainly complain how and when he pleased, whether he had any cause or no, for up to that time he had never read anything to the contrary in the law of chivalry.

Sancho reminded him that it was time for dinner, but his master replied that he had need of none, but that his squire might eat whenever he pleased. With this permission Sancho settled himself as comfortably as he could on his donkey and, taking out what he had put into the saddlebags, jogged very leisurely along behind his master, eating all the while; and from time to time he raised the bottle with such relish that the best-fed publican[17] in Malaga might have envied him. Now, as he went along like this, taking repeated gulps, he entirely forgot the promise his master had made him, and reckoned that going in search of adventures, however dangerous, was more like pleasure than hard work. . . . ∾

---

14. The name *Machuca* comes from the Spanish verb *machucar*, "to crush."

Vocabulary

enmity (en′mə tē) *n.* hatred or ill will

15. *Entrails* are internal organs, especially the intestines.
16. Here, *simplicity* means "innocence" or "silliness."
17. *Publican* is another term for innkeeper.

Evaluate Characters What character traits does Don Quixote reveal?

After You Read

Respond and Think Critically

Respond and Interpret

1. (a) How did you react to the character of Don Quixote? (b) Is he someone you would consider heroic? Explain.

2. (a) How does Don Quixote persuade Sancho Panza to become his squire? (b) How would you describe Sancho Panza's philosophy of life?

3. (a) What is Don Quixote's purpose in becoming a knight errant? (b) Satire holds up something or someone to ridicule or critique. What is the target of Cervantes's satire when the narrator describes Don Quixote's lofty goals?

4. (a) How do Don Quixote and Sancho Panza each view the windmills? (b) What might the windmills symbolize? Explain.

Analyze and Evaluate

5. Cervantes's depiction of his hero is the source of the English word *quixotic,* which describes a person caught up in the romantic pursuit of unreachable goals without regard for practicality. (a) What do you think are the dangers of seeing the world in this way? (b) Are there any advantages? Explain.

Connect

6. **Big Idea** Acts of Courage Do you agree that Don Quixote is a courageous yet sympathetic character, or do you think that he is merely a buffoon? Explain your opinion.

7. **Connect to the Author** How do you think Cervantes's experiences in battle might have influenced his creation of Don Quixote?

Literary Element Parody

A **parody** seeks to poke fun at or critique some aspect of society. Cervantes uses parody in *Don Quixote* to offer his critique of a life and time dominated by greed and violence, as well as to poke fun at popular novels about chivalry, such as *Amadís de Gaula.*

1. How does Cervantes use Don Quixote's madness to help him parody aspects of life?

2. What are some particular incidents in this selection that use humor to show that Don Quixote is not an ideal knight like those in Arthurian legends or others in chivalric romances?

3. How do the names used throughout *Don Quixote* contribute to its humor and its use of parody?

Review: Foil

As you learned on page 783, every character in literature has certain personality traits or qualities that are revealed to us in the course of a literary work. Sometimes a writer creates characters who are **foils** for one another—those who have opposite personality traits and are best understood in contrast with each other. By showing us the two figures side by side in the same situations, the author stresses their differences and highlights their individual qualities.

Partner Activity Pair up with a classmate and discuss the following questions about the use of foils in *Don Quixote:*

1. How do Don Quixote's traits compare with those of Sancho Panza?

2. In the code of medieval chivalry, a squire served as an apprentice or knight-in-training. How does the portrayal of Sancho Panza by Cervantes mock the role of the squire in medieval courtly romances?

Reading Strategy Evaluate Characters

Most people in Don Quixote's time thought of the ideal knight as being strong, capable, and honorable. Don Quixote is weak and somewhat delusional. His squire, Sancho Panza, is poor and concerned about the welfare of his own family. The **characters** in *Don Quixote* highlight qualities that traditional knights did not aspire to possess.

1. How might the story be different if Don Quixote or Sancho Panza were ideal types?
2. Why do you think Don Quixote chose Sancho Panza as his squire instead of a more suitable candidate?

Vocabulary Practice

Practice with Synonyms A synonym is a word that has the same or nearly the same meaning as another word. With a partner, match each boldfaced vocabulary word below with its synonym. You will not use all the answer choices. Use a thesaurus or dictionary to check your answers.

1. interminable
2. renown
3. redress
4. discourteous
5. enmity

a. endless
b. renew
c. outfit
d. hatred
e. rude
f. remedy
g. fame

Speaking and Listening

Interview

Assignment With two partners, prepare and present an interview with Don Quixote that reflects your understanding of the selection.

Prepare Write a list of relevant questions phrased in mature, sensitive, respectful language. Then prepare responses that accurately reflect the personality and concerns of Don Quixote. When you are satisfied with your questions and answers, mark them up with performance cues, such as places for eye contact, a humorous or serious tone, and appropriate body language such as leaning forward or back.

Interview Have one person act as interviewer, one as Don Quixote, and one as stage manager. The host should follow these guidelines:

- Allow your subject to respond completely; don't interrupt.
- Take notes, and, when necessary, ask further questions to clarify information.
- Review your subject's statements as a final check.
- Thank your subject for his or her cooperation.

Both the host and Don Quixote should follow these guidelines:

- Make frequent eye contact.
- Adjust your tone of voice or body language in response to the questions and answers.

The stage manager should keep all the guidelines in mind and give nonverbal cues as reminders to the host and Don Quixote when they need them during the interview.

Report Summarize the interview information in a written report that comments on how well the interview reflected an understanding of the selection and character. Use quotations from the interview to support your judgments.

Evaluate Write an evaluation of the interview based on how clearly, accurately, and effectively it communicated information about the selection and the character. Use the rubric on page 267 to help in your evaluation.

 Literature Online

Selection Resources For Selection Quizzes, eFlashcards, and Reading-Writing Connection activities, go to glencoe.com and enter QuickPass code GL59794u5.

Learning Objectives

For pages 937–941

In studying this text, you will focus on the following objectives:

Reading: Analyzing informational text.

Reading: Clarifying meaning.

Set a Purpose for Reading

Read to discover contrasting ideas about heroes.

Preview the Article

1. What answers can you give to the question in the article's title?
2. Skim the first paragraph. Make a prediction about the content of the article.

Reading Strategy — Clarify Meaning

When you **clarify the meaning** of a text, you unlock the meaning of each section or paragraph. To clarify meaning, answer the following:

- What does this section mean? Why might the writer have chosen to include this?
- How does this information relate to the main idea and other ideas in the text?

Create your own list of questions as you read and answer them to help you clarify meaning.

TIME

What Makes A HERO?

Some heroes act boldly on the world stage. Others make a difference outside the public eye by identifying problems, finding solutions, and inspiring the rest of us.

By AMANDA RIPLEY

WAR BREEDS HEROES—AND A DEEP NEED TO ANOINT them. The soldier who sacrifices himself for his comrades, the civilian who walks more than six miles to get help for a wounded prisoner of war, the medic who makes no distinction between a bleeding ally and a bleeding enemy, the aid worker who passes through a combat zone to bring water to a crippled city—all are called heroes, and all deserve to be. But the word *hero* is also used as a way to excuse senseless deaths, a way to support the fiction that courage and bravery will be enough to carry men and women through the valley of death. The truth is more complicated and sad. Sometimes heroic virtue means the difference between life and death and sometimes it does not. Sometimes a hero is not born until the moment he or she recognizes that heroism may not solve anything—and yet behaves heroically anyway.

In the 1980s, Xavier Emmanuelli, cofounder of the medical humanitarian organization Doctors Without Borders, was working on the border between Cambodia and Thailand. With bombs falling uncomfortably nearby, Emmanuelli and another doctor attended to wounded refugees. The first victim was a young woman. She was alive but critically wounded, her body nearly sliced in

Informational Text

two by a bomb fragment. Emmanuelli made a quick diagnosis. "I thought there was nothing to be done and went on to another victim," he remembers.

But when he looked back, the other doctor, a young man named Daniel Pavard, had not moved on. He was cradling the woman's head and caressing her hair. "He was helping her die," says Emmanuelli. "He did it very naturally. There was no public, no cameras, no one looking. The bombing continued, and he did this as if he was all alone in his humanity."

In his 35-year career, Emmanuelli has witnessed most of the tragedies of our era, from Saigon to Sierra Leone, locations where warfare has resulted in thousands of deaths—places where heroes are made if ever there are heroes. But he has never found heroes in the obvious spots—behind podiums, say, or on armored personnel carriers. Sometimes he has not even recognized them until later, reflecting on what he has seen them do. "It is in gestures," he says, "that you know a person's true nature—gestures that almost escape detection."

Today, the newspapers are full of hero nominees, some more convincing than others. The British papers gushed over Lieut. Colonel Tim Collins, who became a national hero in England for giving a speech to his troops before they marched into war in Iraq: "We go to liberate, not to conquer,"

WARMTH AMID WAR
In a village south of Basra, a British army medic cares for an Iraqi newborn.

he said. "If you are ferocious in battle, remember to be magnanimous [noble and fair-minded] in victory."

News reporters have been called heroic for doing their jobs, and bombing victims have been called courageous for surviving. There have been grainy black-and-white portraits of U.S. General Tommy Franks and sad images of France's President Jacques Chirac, the "white knight of peace," as the French newspaper *Le Figaro* called him. Still, many people find it hard to believe in any of the major leaders for more than half an hour. A hero, by most definitions, must be both brave and generous, a rare combination.

American and European Heroes

For some, the very idea of a "European hero" is problematic. It is Americans, after all—whom the Irish-born writer Oscar Wilde mockingly called "hero worshippers"—who put all their faith in a romantic notion of the individual. Europeans like to put their faith in the group; they believe that they know better than to overestimate the lone actor. Is it not unrealistic to think that a single, flawed human can change the world? Have we not learned by now that history is a mix of complicated circumstances, not a totem pole of individual men—heroic as they may be?

"In the U.S., it is more likely that the rugged individualist will be admired more," says Oxford University philosopher Roger Crisp. "It's kind of old-fashioned. There's a sense [in Europe] that we've already been through that." Billionaire businessmen are not embraced as society's saviors. That is what the state is for. When TIME asked Italian novelist Umberto Eco who his hero was, he responded with a quotation from German playwright Bertolt Brecht: "Unhappy the land that needs heroes."

And yet, for all of Europe's worldly skepticism, there is no doubt that heroes live there—and not all of them went to the war zone. People still crave heroes, still rely on individuals—if not to solve problems single-handedly, then at least to identify them, to point the way toward a solution and, not least, to inspire the rest of us.

"People do need heroes in Europe," insists Sister Emmanuelle, the Belgian-born nun who spent 22 years living among the garbage pickers of Cairo, Egypt, forcing the rest of the world to acknowledge their existence. "Currently there is a real search for grandness, in a different way than wealth. I can see how people need this when they cry as I tell them about the love and deep commonality that saves people. That touches them deep in their hearts," says Emmanuelle. She is living proof that for the European hero, the good of the group and individual accomplishment can exist together.

LIBERATION
Lech Walesa, founder of Poland's Solidarity movement (top), and Charles de Gaulle. Both helped to free their nations from tyrannical rule.

Heroes Past and Present

In ancient Greece, heroes inhabited a space between gods and men. "Their heroes were very often flawed," says Crisp. "[The ancient Greek warrior] Achilles was sulky and arrogant, but admired because he was big and tough." The same might be said of some European heroes today. In a 2003 survey of six European nations, people were asked to name a famous figure from European history with whom they would like to pass an hour. The study, sponsored by three European associations, was meant to identify the "great men" who inhabit an overall European memory.

In the end, despite the fact that they have spent decades throwing politicians out of office, people chose their country's current leaders. The Germans wanted an hour with Foreign Minister Joschka Fischer. The British picked their prime minister, Tony Blair. The Spanish, President José María Aznar. The French . . . well, the French picked Charles de Gaulle, of course. The greatly admired general and statesman became the symbol of France during its battle against Nazi occupation and later as its president. But the second most popular choice in France was the current president, Chirac.

Even as we disparage our leaders, we still want to believe in them. In late 2002, the BBC

Informational Text

television channel caused hours of dinner-table bickering when it invited the public to vote for the greatest Briton of all time. Beatle John Lennon and Princess Diana made the short list. But the winner was Winston Churchill, who led the country through the dark and difficult days of the Second World War.

Everyday Heroes

If you asked a thousand people for a definition of heroism, you would get a thousand different answers. The French celebrity philosopher Bernard-Henri Levy defines a hero narrowly, as someone who tells the truth when it means risking his or her life. Others are so uncomfortable with the word that they prefer to use different, subtle labels like "role model" or "uncommon man."

Many people take a broader view and define heroes as people who have stood without flinching in the face of very bad odds. Some say people who put themselves in mortal danger are heroes. Others define heroes as activists, in the old-fashioned sense, stubbornly beating a drum to remind us of problems we would prefer to ignore. Some believe that heroes are able to turn grief that would have destroyed most of us into defiant hope. Still others say that heroes live comfortably while inspiring millions to hope for better things.

Most heroes are walking contradictions. A hero has to be, on the one hand, a dreamer—to believe against overwhelming odds that something can change. But a hero is also a realist who does something useful; giving up is not an option.

And so in France, a businessman has begun collecting résumés in the decaying housing projects of the Parisian suburbs so he can help young immigrants find jobs. In Iceland, a former engineer convinced people to save the whales not because they are pretty, but because the whale-watching industry could make more

BORN LEADER
Nelson Mandela, the one-man dynamo in the fight to end South Africa's apartheid.

Informational Text

money than the whale-killing industry. And in the West Bank, a Palestinian surgeon endures a six-hour round-trip commute through armed checkpoints to save lives—both Arab and Jewish—in the operating room of an Israeli hospital. After decades of assuming the state would look after the collective good, Europeans—and Americans—have been forced to acknowledge that the government cannot manage the job alone. Individuals must fill the gaps.

True heroes, adds Emmanuelli, never know that they are heroes. They just find themselves in a situation for which they have been preparing, unwittingly, all their lives. Then they do the right thing. "A hero understands that he is a tool," he says.

In every case, if heroism requires courage and generosity, the last ingredient is circumstance. Novelist Jean-Christophe Rufin, winner of France's top literary award, and president of *Action Contre la Faim* (Action Against Hunger), a private humanitarian organization, says his model of a hero was his grandfather. Until he was sent to a Nazi prison camp for hiding people in his garage, he raised Rufin himself. "Physically, he was absolutely not a hero. He was short, thin and weak, though he resisted many things that would have killed me 10 times," Rufin says. "All the choices he made were kind of obvious things. It was the circumstances that made him a hero."

—from TIME

Respond and Think Critically

Respond and Interpret

1. Write a brief summary of the main ideas in this article before you answer the following questions. For help on writing a summary, see page 415.

2. (a) Why did Xavier Emmanuelli, cofounder of Doctors Without Borders, think that his colleague, Daniel Pavard, was a hero? (b) How does this challenge the traditional definition of a hero?

3. (a) According to Oxford University philospher Roger Crisp, how do people in the United States define heroes? (b) Do you agree with him? Why or why not?

4. (a) According to the writer, what are two qualities that a hero must have? (b) What do you think some other qualities of a hero might be?

Analyze and Evaluate

5. The article cites German playwright Bertolt Brecht, who once said, "Unhappy the land that needs heroes." What do you think this means? Do you agree? Explain.

6. (a) How does the writer conclude the article? (b) Do you think it is an effective conclusion? Why or why not?

7. What do you think is the main idea of the article? Support your ideas with evidence from the article.

Connect

8. Compare and contrast the heroes of Sir Thomas Malory's *Le Morte d'Arthur* and of Cervantes's *Don Quixote* and those described in this TIME article.

Before You Read

from Sundiata

World Literature
Africa

Meet **D. T. Niane and the Storytellers**

The *Sundiata* (sōōn dyä′tə) is the national epic of the Mandingo people, who live in present-day Mali and parts of the coastal region of West Africa. It celebrates the founding of the ancient Mali empire, which occurred around 1235. A king named Sundiata played an important role in establishing Mali as a powerful state. Stories and legends about Sundiata are told to this day.

The Griot or Jali All over the world, storytellers have helped to pass down history and tradition from generation to generation in times and places where literacy was not widespread. In Africa one name for the storyteller—a name which may come from French or Portuguese—is *griot* (grē′o). A Mende, or native African, word for griot is *jali* (or *jeli* or *djali*). Griots or jalis are steeped in oral tradition from childhood onward.

During Sundiata's time, griots were employed by kings and other leaders to recite their country's legendary history. In African society prior to colonization, griots held a high place in social status hierarchies. They were valued for recording the history and traditions of their societies. Since they did not work from a written text, they could alter their stories to suit occasions and their audiences. This process led to the development of many different versions of the *Sundiata*. The episode you will read comes from a version told by storyteller Mamadou Kouyaté (ma′mä dōō kōō yä′ tā) to historian and professor D. T. Niane, who adapted it into prose.

> "We are repositories which harbor secrets centuries old. . . ."
>
> —Mamadou Kouyaté

From the Storytellers to Us Today, the *Sundiata* is recited by Mandingo griots. Their performances, which can last several hours, are enlivened by musical accompaniment, dramatic gestures, and frequent interjections from the audience, suggesting agreement and enthusiasm.

When D. T. Niane, a specialist in the Mande world, met griots in Mali, he felt that his eyes had "been opened [to the] mysteries of eternal Africa." In his introduction to the *Sundiata*, he wrote, "May this book open the eyes of more than one African and induce him to come and sit humbly beside the ancients and hear the words of the griots who teach wisdom and history."

 Literature Online

Author Search For more about D. T. Niane and the storytellers, go to glencoe.com and enter QuickPass code GL59794u5.

Literature and Reading Preview

Connect to the Epic
Why do people enjoy listening to stories about heroes? Discuss this question with a partner.

Build Background
Sundiata (soon dyä′tə) came to power around 1235, when he freed Mali from the control of a neighboring kingdom. Mali was known as a safe and orderly place. "Neither traveler nor inhabitant in it has anything to fear from robbers or men of violence," wrote an early Arab visitor.

Set Purposes for Reading

Big Idea Acts of Courage

As you read, ask yourself, How do the characters in *Sundiata* display their courage?

Literary Element Dialogue

Dialogue is the written conversation between characters in a literary work. Through dialogue, an author reveals the feelings, thoughts, and intentions of characters, develops conflicts, and moves the plot forward. As you read, ask yourself, How does the dialogue reveal characters and advance the plot?

Reading Strategy Identify Genre

Genre is a category of literary work characterized by a particular form or style. One genre is the **epic**, a long narrative poem about a larger than life hero who embodies the values of his or her people. As you read, ask yourself, What elements of this story indicate that it is an epic?

Tip: Focus on Details: Record details of the *Sundiata* that help you identify its genre.

Sundiata	
Details that reveal Mandingo customs, beliefs, and values	Sundiata has great charm and the strength of ten men. Charm and strength are valued.
fantastic or exaggerated details	

Learning Objectives

For pages 942–950

In studying this text, you will focus on the following objectives:

Literary Study: Analyzing dialogue.

Reading: Identifying genre.

Vocabulary

scrupulous (skroo′pyə ləs) *adj.* thoroughly attentive to even the smallest details; precise; p. 945 *Ana's knitting was scrupulous.*

elude (i lood′) *v.* to avoid or escape, especially through cleverness or quickness; p. 945 *As one child gave chase, the other child tried to elude her.*

confidante (kon′ fə dant′) *n.* a person who is entrusted with secrets or private affairs; p. 946 *Only Eric's confidante knew about his secret plans.*

perpetuate (pər pech′oo āt′) *v.* to cause to continue to be remembered; p. 947 *Gossip can perpetuate hurtful and untrue rumors.*

D. T. NIANE AND THE STORYTELLERS

Sahelian Landscape, Mali, 1991. Tilly Willis. Oil on canvas. Private collection.

from SUNDIATA

Recorded by D. T. Niane
Translated by G. D. Pickett

Even before he was born, Sundiata was destined for greatness. Acting on the instructions of a soothsayer,[1] his father, the king of Mali, had married a hideous, hunchbacked woman named Sogolon. As foretold, the couple had a son. It seemed, however, that the boy was unlikely to become a great leader as had been predicted. The young Sundiata could not even walk. He and his ugly mother became the object of cruel jokes and jealous abuse by the old king's first wife. At the age of seven, Sundiata suddenly reacted to an insult by standing up and tearing a tree from the ground. He instantly became the center of attention, a boy with great charm and the strength of ten men. Among his constant companions were the princes Fran Kamara and Kamandjan.[2] Even more important to him was his griot, Balla Fasséké,[3] who taught

---

1. A soothsayer is someone who claims to be able to foretell the future.
2. *Kamara* (kä′mä rä), *Kamandjan* (kä′män jän)
3. *Balla Fasséké* (bä′lä fä sā′kā)

him the history of his people and of the world beyond.

Still fearing persecution from the jealous queen, Sogolon escaped with Sundiata to neighboring Ghana. There the amazing boy grew up. In his absence, Mali was taken over by the king of Sosso, a cruel sorcerer named Soumaoro,[4] whose secret chamber was tapestried with human skins and adorned with the skulls of his enemies. Soumaoro captured Balla Fasséké and Sundiata's half-sister, Nana Triban.[5] Enraged by Soumaoro's barbarism, Sundiata raised an army and prepared to restore his country to its rightful people. Although he succeeded in defeating Soumaoro in a great battle, he could not capture or kill the man himself, for the magician had the power to appear and disappear at will. While Sundiata rested in the town of Sibi,[6] Soumaoro once again raised a powerful army.
The two prepared to meet in a final battle.

Sundiata and his mighty army stopped at Sibi for a few days. The road into Mali lay open, but Soumaoro was not yet vanquished. The king of Sosso had mustered a powerful army and his sofas were numbered by the thousand. He had raised contingents[7] in all the lands over which he held sway and got ready to pounce again on Mali.

With **scrupulous** care, Sundiata had made his preparations at Sibi. Now he had sufficient sofas to meet Soumaoro in the open field, but it was not a question of having a lot of troops. In order to defeat Soumaoro it was necessary first of all to destroy his magical power. At Sibi, Sundiata decided to consult the soothsayers, of whom the most famous in Mali were there.

On their advice Djata[8] had to sacrifice a hundred white bulls, a hundred white rams and a hundred white cocks. It was in the middle of this slaughter that it was announced to Sundiata that his sister Nana Triban and Balla Fasséké, having been able to escape from Sosso, had now arrived. Then Sundiata said to Tabon Wana, "If my sister and Balla have been able to escape from Sosso, Soumaoro has lost the battle."

Leaving the site of the sacrifices, Sundiata returned to Sibi and met his sister and his griot.

"Hail, my brother," said Nana Triban.

"Greetings, sister."

"Hail Sundiata," said Balla Fasséké.

"Greetings, my griot."

After numerous salutations, Sundiata asked the fugitives to relate how they had been able to **elude** the vigilance of a king such as Soumaoro. But Triban was weeping for joy. Since the time of their childhood she had shown much sympathy towards the crippled child that Sundiata had been. Never had she shared the hate of her mother, Sassouma Bérété.

"You know, Djata," she said, weeping, "for my part I did not want you to leave the country. It was my mother who did all that. Now Niani is destroyed, its inhabitants scattered, and there are many whom Soumaoro has carried off into captivity in Sosso."

---

4. *Soumaoro* (sōō ́ mər ō)
5. *Nana Triban* (nä ́ na tri ́ ban)
6. *Sibi* (si ́ bē)
7. The *sofas* are soldiers or warriors, and *contingents* are additional troops.

Identify Genre Which items in this summary indicate that the epic will include exaggerated elements?

Vocabulary

scrupulous (skrōō ́ pyə ləs) *adj.* thoroughly attentive to even the smallest details; precise

---

8. *Djata* (dynä ́ tə) is a shortened form of Sundiata.

Dialogue What does Nana Triban wish to convey to her half-brother?

Vocabulary

elude (i lōōd ́) *v.* to avoid or escape, especially through cleverness or quickness

She cried worse than ever. Djata was sympathetic to all this, but he was in a hurry to know something about Sosso. Balla Fasséké understood and said, "Triban, wipe away your tears and tell your story, speak to your brother. You know that he has never thought ill of you, and besides, all that was in his destiny."

Nana Triban wiped her tears away and spoke.

"When you left Mali, my brother sent me by force to Sosso to be the wife of Soumaoro, whom he greatly feared. I wept a great deal at the beginning but when I saw that perhaps all was not lost I resigned[9] myself for the time being. I was nice to Soumaoro and was the chosen one among his numerous wives. I had my chamber in the great tower where he himself lived. I knew how to flatter him and make him jealous. Soon I became his **confidante** and I pretended to hate you, to share the hate which my mother bore you. It was said that you would come back one day, but I swore to him that you would never have the presumption[10] to claim a kingdom you had never possessed, and that you had left never to see Mali again. However, I was in constant touch with Balla Fasséké, each of us wanting to pierce the mystery of Soumaoro's magic power. One night I took the bull by the horns and said to Soumaoro: 'Tell me, oh you whom kings mention with trembling, tell me Soumaoro, are you a man like others or are you the same as the jinn[11] who protects

---

9. When Nana *resigned* herself, she gave in without resistance or complaint.
10. Here, *presumption* means "excessive boldness."
11. In Arab folklore, a *jinn*, or genie, was an angel-like spirit that had magical powers and could take on other forms.

Archer Figure. Inland Delta Region, Mali. Ceramic. Height 61.9 cm. National Museum of African Art, Smithsonian Institution.

Vocabulary

confidante (kon′ fə dant′) *n.* a person who is entrusted with secrets or private affairs

humans? No one can bear the glare of your eyes, your arm has the strength of ten arms. Tell me, king of kings, tell me what jinn protects you so that I can worship him also.' These words filled him with pride and he himself boasted to me of the might of his Tana. That very night he took me into his magic chamber and told me all.

"Then I redoubled my zeal to show myself faithful to his cause, I seemed more overwhelmed than him. It was even he who went to the extent of telling me to take courage, that nothing was yet lost. During all this time, in complicity[12] with Balla Fasséké, I was preparing for the inevitable flight. Nobody watched over me any more in the royal enclosure, of which I knew the smallest twists and turns. And one night when Soumaoro was away, I left that fearsome tower. Balla Fasséké was waiting for me at the gate to which I had the key. It was thus, brother, that we left Sosso."

Balla Fasséké took up the story.

"We hastened to you. The news of the victory of Tabon made me realize that the lion had burst his chains. Oh son of Sogolon, I am the word and you are the deed, now your destiny begins."

Sundiata was very happy to recover his sister and his griot. He now had the singer who would **perpetuate** his memory by his words. There would not be any heroes if deeds were condemned to man's forgetfulness, for we ply our trade to excite the admiration of the living, and to evoke the veneration[13] of those who are to come.

Djata was informed that Soumaoro was advancing along the river and was trying to block his route to Mali. The preparations were complete, but before leaving Sibi, Sundiata arranged a great military review in the camp so that Balla Fasséké, by his words, should strengthen the hearts of his sofas. In the middle of a great circle formed by the sofas, Balla Fasséké extolled[14] the heroes of Mali. To the king of Tabon he said: "You whose iron arm can split ten skulls at a time, you, Tabon Wana, king of the Sinikimbon and the Djallonké,[15] can you show me what you are capable of before the great battle is joined?"

The griot's words made Fran Kamara leap up. Sword in hand and mounted on his swift steed he came and stood before Sundiata and said, "Maghan Sundiata, I renew my oath to you in the sight of all the Mandingoes gathered together. I pledge myself to conquer or to die by your side. Mali will be free or the smiths[16] of Tabon will be dead."

The tribes of Tabon shouted their approval, brandishing their weapons, and Fran Kamara, stirred by the shouts of the sofas, spurred his charger and charged forward. The warriors opened their ranks and he bore down on a great mahogany tree. With one stroke of his sword he split the giant tree just as one splits a paw-paw.[17] The flabbergasted army shouted, "Wassa Wassa . . . Ayé . . ."

Then, coming back to Sundiata, his sword held aloft, the king of Tabon said, "Thus on

---

12. People acting in *complicity* are involved together, as accomplices in a crime or, as here, in secret activities.

Acts of Courage What risks does Nana Triban take while staying with Soumaoro? What does the epic imply about how one should act in times of danger?

Dialogue What do you think Balla Fasséké means by this remark?

Vocabulary

perpetuate (pər pech′ o͞o āt′) *v.* to cause to continue to be remembered

---

13. To *evoke veneration* is to call up feelings of deep respect.
14. Balla highly praised (*extolled*) the heroes.
15. *Sinikimbon* (si′ nē kim′ bōn), *Djallonké* (jä lôn′ kā)
16. The *Mandingoes* were various peoples who inhabited the upper and middle Niger River valley. *Smiths* make or repair metal objects, such as swords, but Fran Kamara is speaking figuratively, referring to his sword-bearing troops.
17. *Paw-paw* is a banana-like fruit.

Seated Figure, 13th century. Terracotta, height: 10 in. Purchase, Buckeye Trust and Mr. and Mrs. Milton Rosenthal Gifts, Joseph Pulitzer Bequest and Harris Brisbane Dick and Rogers Funds, 1981. The Metropolitan Museum of Art, New York, NY.

the Niger plain will the smiths of Tabon cleave those of Sosso in twain."[18] And the hero came and fell in beside Sundiata.

Turning towards Kamandjan, the king of Sibi and cousin of the king of Tabon, Balla Fasséké said, "Where are you, Kamandjan, where is Fama Djan? Where is the king of the Dalikimbon Kamaras? Kamandjan of Sibi, I salute you. But what will I have to relate of you to future generations?"

Before Balla had finished speaking, the king of Sibi, shouting his war cry, started his fiery charger off at full gallop. The sofas, stupefied, watched the extraordinary horseman head for the mountain that dominates[19] Sibi. . . . Suddenly a tremendous din filled the sky, the earth trembled under the feet of the sofas and a cloud of red dust covered the mountain. Was this the end of the world? . . . But slowly the dust cleared and the sofas saw Kamandjan coming back holding a fragment of a sword. The mountain of Sibi, pierced through and through, disclosed a wide tunnel!

Admiration was at its highest pitch. The army stood speechless and the king of Sibi, without saying a word, came and fell in beside Sundiata.

Balla Fasséké mentioned all the chiefs by name and they all performed great feats; then the army, confident in its leadership, left Sibi.

---

18. To *cleave in twain* is to split in two.
19. The mountain *dominates* Sibi because it towers over it.

Dialogue Why does Balla Fasséké ask this question?

Identify Genre What characteristic of epics is found in this passage?

After You Read

Respond and Think Critically

Respond and Interpret

1. What do you think might happen next in this story? Share your predictions with your classmates.

2. (a) What does Sundiata first plan to do in order to defeat Soumaoro? (b) Later, what does he do before leaving Sibi? What do his methods suggest about him as a leader?

3. (a) What astonishing deeds do Fran Kamara and Kamandjan perform at the urging of Balla Fasséké? (b) Why do Balla Fasséké's words cause the warriors to react as they do?

Analyze and Evaluate

4. Why do you think Sundiata has such a strong desire to be remembered by future generations?

5. What knowledge of human nature does Balla Fasséké reveal through his speeches?

Connect

6. **Big Idea** Acts of Courage At one point, the story says, "There would not be any heroes if deeds were condemned to man's forgetfulness." How would you interpret this statement?

7. **Connect to Today** Does our society today have any methods comparable to Balla Fasséké's for making people famous? Explain.

Literary Element Dialogue

In this epic, **dialogue** helps to advance the plot and to develop the characters. Dialogue brings characters to life by showing what they are thinking and feeling as they react to other characters.

1. (a) Why do you think Nana Triban mentions that she "knew how to flatter [Soumaoro] and make him jealous"? (b) From her words, what impressions do you have of Nana Triban? Explain.

2. What does the king of Tabon mean when he says, "Thus on the Niger plain will the smiths of Tabon cleave those of Sosso in twain"? Explain.

Review: Epic

As you learned on page 894, **epics** have extraordinary heroes. Epics blend myths, legends, and history, reflecting the values of the societies in which they originate. Although a king named Sundiata played an important role in establishing Mali as a powerful state, the *Sundiata* is not a historical account of his rule. Instead, Sundiata functions as the epic hero, someone of high social standing whose fate affects the destiny of his people. Epic plots typically involve supernatural events, long periods of time, distant journeys, and life-and-death struggles between good and evil. Works such as the *Sundiata* are called **folk epics** because they have uncertain authorship and arise, usually through oral storytelling, from the collective experiences of a people.

Partner Activity Work with a partner to answer the following questions. Share your discussion results with your class.

1. What is extraordinary about Sundiata?

2. Why do you think epics are important in many different cultures?

Reading Strategy: Identify Genre

Historically, kings and other leaders in Mali employed griots, or oral poets, to recite the *Sundiata,* their nation's **epic.** Review the chart you made on page 943 and answer the following.

1. Identify three exaggerated or fantastic details in this epic. Which detail did you consider most entertaining or inspiring? Explain.

2. From this epic, what traits or qualities would you say the Mandingo people valued in a person?

Vocabulary Practice

Practice with Denotation and Connotation
A word's **denotation** is its dictionary meaning; its **connotations** are the emotional associations it evokes. For example, the words *delighted* and *euphoric* have a similar denotation, "a positive emotional feeling," but different connotations.

Weaker	Stronger
delighted	euphoric

Work with a partner to complete a graphic organizer like the one below for each vocabulary word. Include the vocabulary word in one box and a word that has a similar denotation in another. Then explain which of the two words has the stronger connotations.

scrupulous   elude   confidante   perpetuate

EXAMPLE:

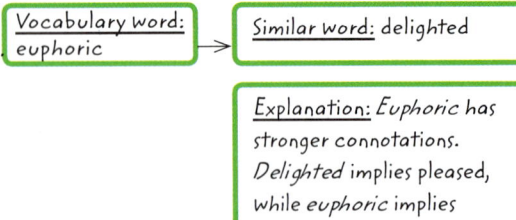

 **Literature** Online

Selection Resources For Selection Quizzes, eFlashcards, and Reading-Writing Connection activities, go to glencoe.com and enter QuickPass code GL59794u5.

Speaking and Listening

 Debate

Assignment The *Sundiata* tells the story of an epic hero and his larger-than-life deeds. Do you think that Sundiata as a leader of the people is more heroic than leaders from the recent past or the present day, such as Dr. Martin Luther King Jr. or Nelson Mandela? Divide into two teams to conduct a debate on this question. Use evidence from the text and real life examples to support your argument.

Prepare Work with your group to create a list of arguments that support your side of the issue. Evidence—and how you use it—is key to a successful debate. Organize your arguments and evidence in a chart like the one shown to make sure you include all the important points.

Argument	Evidence
Sundiata inspires his warriors to perform superhuman feats.	Fran Kamara splits a giant tree; Kamandjan carves out a tunnel through a mountain.

Try to anticipate your opponents' possible arguments and plan ways to counter them.

Debate During the debate, listen carefully to your team members' points so you can build on them when it is your turn to speak. Also listen to the opposing team's arguments so you can challenge them with counter-arguments and evidence. When you do speak, use effective and interesting language and appropriate eye contact, body movements, and vocal tones.

Evaluate Write one paragraph evaluating your team's performance and that of your opponents. Consider the preparation and delivery of the arguments. Conclude with a few statements about where you succeeded, what you learned, and what you might do differently next time.

Visual Perspective on *Sundiata*

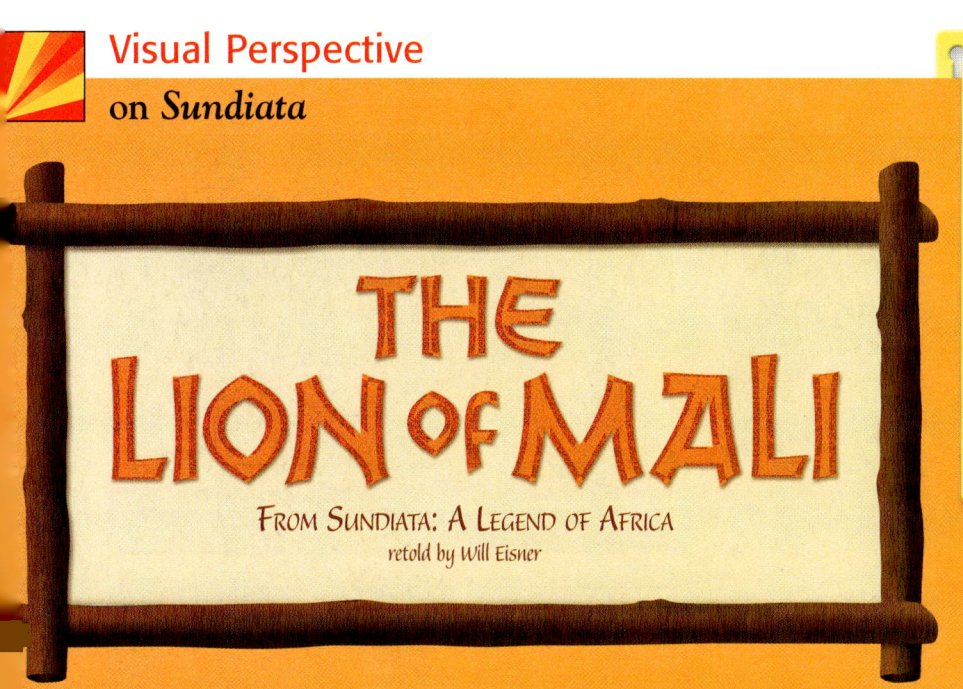

THE LION OF MALI

FROM SUNDIATA: A LEGEND OF AFRICA
retold by Will Eisner

Learning Objectives

For pages 951–954

In studying this text, you will focus on the following objectives:

Reading: Comparing and contrasting versions of a story.

Reading: Making connections across literature.

National Book Award Winner

Set a Purpose for Reading

Read to discover similarities and differences between the graphic-novel and text versions of the tale of Sundiata.

Build Background

The tale of Sundiata is based on the real person Sundiata, a monarch who established the Sudanese empire of Mali. According to oral tradition, he had eleven brothers. Sumanguru, ruler of the adjacent land of Kaniaga, killed all of Sundiata's brothers. Sundiata, who was already ill and weak, was spared. Will Eisner, an acclaimed graphic-novel artist most famous for the character the Spirit, depicts the beginning of this tale in this graphic-novel version of "The Lion of Mali."

Reading Strategy

Compare and Contrast Versions of a Story

There are many different versions of the tale of Sundiata. When you **compare and contrast versions,** you identify similarities and differences between them. This graphic-novel excerpt and the prose excerpt by Niane cover different portions of Sundiata's story, but there are still many points of comparison between them. As you read, think about how plot, setting, and characters are conveyed in each excerpt. Take notes to help you keep track of the similarities and differences.

Similarities	Differences

WILL EISNER **951**

Informational Text

Informational Text

Respond and Think Critically

Respond and Interpret

1. Write a brief summary of the story told in this graphic novel before you answer the following questions. For help on writing a summary, see page 51.

2. Does the graphic-novel version of the tale of Sundiata enhance your understanding of the text version? Why or why not?

3. What are two examples of simile in this graphic novel? (b) How does Eisner illustrate the similes?

Analyze and Evaluate

4. Do you think Eisner's illustrations tell the tale of "The Lion of Mali" in an effective way? Explain.

5. What comment about Sumanguru's powers is Eisner making in the last three panels?

Connect

6. What characteristics of legends are demonstrated in the graphic-novel retelling of the tale of Sundiata?

PART 2

Rescuing and Conquering

The Life Line, 1884. Homer, Winslow. Oil on canvas, 28.62 x 44.75 in. Philadelphia Museum of Art, PA.

View the Art Some of Homer's paintings depict scenes from the English Sea fishing village of Cullercoats on the North Sea. He created images of the sea and humans' attempts to deal with the uncontrollable elements of nature. What does Homer's painting suggest about rescuing and conquering?

BIG IDEA

Leaders and warriors may use their strength to rescue allies and conquer enemies. But often strength is not enough. The tales in Part 2 tell of heroes who use their brains and bravery in rescues and conquests—and sometimes outwit themselves. As you read these myths and folktales, ask yourself, How do the hero's intelligence and other personal qualities contribute to these rescues and conquests?

Learning Objectives

For pages 956–957

In studying this text, you will focus on the following objective:

Literary Study: Analyzing myth and the oral tradition.

LITERARY FOCUS

Myth and the Oral Tradition

What are the elements of myth and folktales?

Joseph Campbell devoted his career to the study and teaching of world myths and oral traditions. He once said: "Read myths. They teach you that you can turn inward, and you begin to get the message of the symbols." In the passage from a myth below, the king of the giants has stolen Thor's hammer, which is Thor's protector. The Norse gods meet in council to plan how to get the hammer back.

Such a serious situation had to be made known to Odin. At once, he called a council meeting of all the Æsir and without delay they sat in deliberation upon their judgement stools. "Who's the first with any ideas?" asked Odin.

Tyr suggested an armed invasion of Jotunheim. Niord agreed, saying it should be an attack by sea and land and air with the Valkyries on their flying horses spear-heading the aerial battalions.

Loki said, "I can tell you this: a direct attack will be useless. Let me remind you of the magic spells employed by the giant king to frustrate Thor in the past. Even if an attack was successful, the hammer would still lie hidden. There is only one way to get it back and that is to trick King Loki of Outgard into producing it."

—Brian Branston, *from "The Stealing of Thor's Hammer"*

Thor's Fight with the Giants, 1872. Martin Eskel Winge. Oil on canvas, 484 x 333 cm. National Museum, Stockholm, Sweden.

 Literature Online

Literature and Reading For more about literary elements, go to glencoe.com and enter QuickPass code GL59794u5.

Myth

Myths are traditional stories that deal with gods, heroes and supernatural forces. They may offer role models, try to explain the natural world, or suggest the beliefs, customs, or ideals of a society.

> He [Theseus] steadfastly refused, therefore, the ship his mother and grandfather urged on him, telling them that to sail on it would be a contemptible flight from danger, and he set forth to go to Athens by land. The journey was long and very hazardous because of the bandits that beset the road. He killed them all, however; he left not one alive to trouble future travelers. His idea of dealing justice was simple, but effective: what each had done to others, Theseus did to him.
>
> —Edith Hamilton, *from "Theseus"*

Oral Tradition

A culture's **oral tradition** includes stories and other oral transmissions that preserve the culture's history, ancestry, and literature. Although writing allows a story to be remembered unchanged, oral transmission allows a story to evolve for the benefit of each generation of listeners. Many well-loved stories were preserved orally before they were written down. Some oral wisdom has not been written down to this very day.

> "If a man held an important position among the Cheyenne, such as the keeper of the Sacred Arrows, then his wife, too, would have to be of the highest moral character, for she shared the weight of his responsibility."
>
> —Joseph Bruchac and Gayle Ross, *from "Where the Girl Rescued Her Brother"*

Oral tradition includes folklore, folktales, and tall tales.

Folklore The traditional beliefs, practices, stories, songs, and dances of a culture make up its **folklore.** It is based on the concerns of the common people, as in the selection below about John Henry. In this selection, John Henry is a man defined by his work on the railroad.

> John Henry told his Captain,
> Man ain't nothing but a man,
> And 'fore I'll let that steam drill beat me down
> I'll die with this hammer in my hand,
> Die with this hammer in my hand.
>
> —Zora Neale Hurston, *from "John Henry"*

Folktale Animal stories, trickster stories, fairy tales, myths, legends and tall tales are all included in the larger category of folktales. A **folktale** is a traditional story that has been passed down orally long before being written down.

Tall Tale A **tall tale** is a kind of folktale. In a tall tale, the fantastic adventures and amazing feats of folk heroes are wildly exaggerated, but the realistic local settings and tone suggest that the exaggerations are true.

Quickwrite

Analyze Examples In a few sentences, explain how each of the quoted text examples on this page illustrates an element of myth or oral tradition. Use the following sentence frame to help you present your evaluation.

> The quote from <title> illustrates _____ _____ ; it shows how <character> is an example of _____ by saying _____.

LITERARY FOCUS **957**

Before You Read

World Literature
Scandinavia

The Stealing of Thor's Hammer

Meet Brian Branston
(born 1914)

How many writers do you know who have visited the most remote, inaccessible corners of the world, including Iceland, Greenland, and the Great Barrier Reef? How many writers have ridden the Great Rapids of the Orinoco River in South America—in a hovercraft? British writer Brian Branston, author of "The Stealing of Thor's Hammer," has done these things and more, including traveling in a dugout canoe in search of the Yanamamo Indians in Brazil. Branston, working in the Travel and Exploration unit for the British Broadcasting Corporation (BBC), traveled to remote locations all over the world to capture them on film.

For twenty-five years, Branston also wrote books on the occult and mythology. In *Gods & Heroes from Viking Mythology* (1978), he brings Viking myths to life with vivid descriptions.

> "Our forefathers of fifteen hundred years ago…were not creatures apart, different from the birds, plants, or animals."
>
> —Brian Branston

Seafaring Warriors Viking mythology (also called Norse or Scandinavian mythology) encompasses stories from four countries: Iceland, Norway, Sweden, and Denmark. The Vikings are most familiar to modern readers as seafaring warriors.

The Vikings were not merely fearsome, unimaginative brutes, however. The long, dark Scandinavian winters were conducive to storytelling. Viking storytellers tried to make sense of their world with its dark forests and forbidding mountains. Their mythology makes use of natural elements familiar in that northern landscape, such as volcanoes and bears.

Viking mythology is based on several gods: Odin (the One-Eyed Allfather, also known as Woden or Wotan), Thor (god of thunder), Tyr (god of war and treaties), and Frey and Freya (god and goddess of fertility). On a plain called Ida, these gods built the city of Asgard, which had twelve realms, the highest being Valhalla, where the heroic went after dying.

Influences of Mythology Traces of Viking mythology are still found in the English language, music, and literature today. For example, the Viking gods gave their names to the days of the week: Tuesday (Tyr), Wednesday (Woden), Thursday (Thor), and Friday (Frey). J. R. R. Tolkien drew heavily from these stories to create his *Lord of the Rings* trilogy. Composer Richard Wagner used the myths in his "Rings of the Nibelung" opera cycle. The archetypal plots and characters of these stories give them lasting appeal.

Literature Online

Author Search For more about Brian Branston, go to glencoe.com and enter QuickPass code GL59794u5.

Literature and Reading Preview

Connect to the Myth
Is physical strength or cunning more important in resolving a conflict? In a small group, discuss the pros and cons of mental and physical strength.

Build Background
In Viking mythology, the Norse god Thor is known as the strongest of the gods but not the smartest. Armed with the hammer Mjollnir, he defends the gods against their enemies. When Thor throws his hammer, it creates lightning.

Set Purposes for Reading

Big Idea Rescuing and Conquering

As you read, ask yourself, Why is it so important for the characters to retrieve Thor's hammer?

Literary Element Plot Pattern Archetypes

Plot pattern archetypes are story elements and themes common to a wide variety of cultures and stories. An example of a plot pattern archetype is characters fooling dangerous and powerful enemies. As you read, ask yourself, What are some possible plot pattern archetypes in the story?

Reading Strategy Make Inferences About Characters

When you **make inferences about characters,** you make assumptions about characters based on how they act and are described. As you read, ask yourself, How does the author use description, narration, and dialogue to show character?

Tip: Create a Web Use a web like the one below to record the inferences you draw about one of the main characters in this myth.

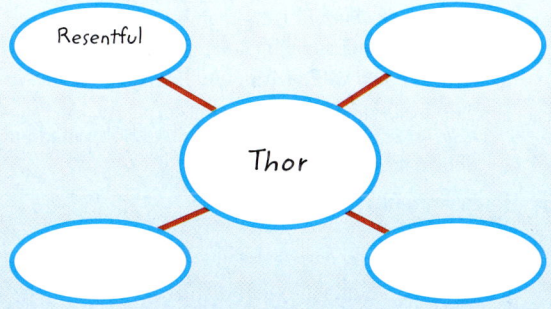

Learning Objectives

For pages 958–966

In studying this text, you will focus on the following objectives:

Literary Study: Analyzing plot pattern archetype.

Reading: Making inferences about characters.

Vocabulary

disdainful (dis dān′fəl) *adj.* scornful; mocking; p. 960 *The senator held a disdainful view of the opposing candidate.*

aggrieved (ə grēvd′) *adj.* disturbed; upset; p. 960 *The aggrieved customer got a refund.*

guile (gīl) *n.* cunning; p. 961 *The spy used guile to outsmart the guards.*

deliberation (di lib′ə rā′shən) *n.* an official meeting or consultation; p. 963 *The town leaders decided that deliberation was necessary.*

jubilantly (jōō′bə lənt lē) *adv.* joyfully or happily; p. 964 *The bride and groom walked jubilantly down the aisle together.*

Tip: Word Usage Always select words carefully, keeping their specific usage in mind. For example, don't use the word *jubilantly* if you are merely pleased.

BRIAN BRANSTON

The Stealing of Thor's Hammer

Brian Branston

THOR, 1911. Arthur Rackham. In Wagner's 'The Rhinegold & the Valkrie.'

The god Thor always resented the **disdainful** way he had been treated by King Loki of Outgard.[1] He was quite determined that one day he would get his own back. Then a dreadful thing happened which made him fear that revenge might prove impossible: his hammer was stolen!

One evening he had retired as usual after a hearty supper in his palace of Bilskirnir and in an unusually tidy mood he placed his shoes together neatly, folded his clothes and laid his hammer on the table next to his pillow before getting into bed beside Sif.[2]

Daylight was squeezing through the gaps in the shutters and the dawn chorus of birdsong was pealing in from the countryside when Thor awoke from a disturbing dream. He fancied in his sleep that a thief had crept into the bedroom and had stolen the one sure protection the gods had against the giants—his hammer. Half awake, he fumbled a hand out of the sheets and felt along the top of the bedside table. It was empty.

He sat up in bed with such a jolt that his wife Sif was shot out onto the floor. Before she could open her mouth to protest, Thor was yelling, "My hammer! My hammer's been stolen! Æsir![3] Elves! Quick! Wait! No! Yes! Who's stolen my hammer? LOKI! LOKEE … !" and his red hair and beard tossed about in all directions as he wrathfully dragged on his clothes. He absent-mindedly picked the **aggrieved**

---

1. *King Loki* (lō′kē) is the king of the giants in Norse mythology. *Outgard* is the name of his home. *King Loki* is not to be confused with *Loki*, the fire god.
2. *Sif* (sif) is the wife of Thor and the Norse goddess of fertility and crops.
3. *Æsir* (a′zir) is another name for the group made up of the principal Norse gods.

Vocabulary

disdainful (dis dān′fəl) *adj.* scornful; mocking
aggrieved (ə grēvd′) *adj.* disturbed; upset

Sif off the floor and put her back into bed, by which time Loki[4] had come running up panting.

"You had anything to do with this, Loki?" bellowed Thor.

"What, what ... ?" gasped Loki as Thor gripped him by the scruff.

"My hammer—have you stolen it?"

"No, no, no," stammered Loki. "Only one lot dare do that, and you don't need me to tell you who they are. The giants!"

"Come on then!" cried Thor, "My chariot—you are coming with me to Jotunheim[5] to get it back!" and he started to drag Loki downstairs to the stables.

"Stop!" shouted Loki. "Do have the sense to stop! Can't you see that's just what the giants want? Without your hammer you'd be killed. We need stealth here. We need **guile**."

"Well, you're the one for that," replied Thor, simmering down, "What do you suggest?"

The upshot was that Loki volunteered to borrow Freya's[6] feather coat and fly as a hawk into Jotunheim to find out if possible what had happened to Thor's hammer. He winged his way swiftly over the ocean to the shores of Jotunheim and across the tops of the towering forest trees towards the mountains and the stronghold of King Loki.

From a distance he saw the king sitting on the gravemound of his ancestors just outside the city walls. There was a rune-carved stone commemorating the dead giants who were sitting upright in their high seats below in the mound waiting for the Ragnarok.[7] Loki flew to the top of the tall stone and perched there. King Loki of Outgard was amusing himself plaiting[8] gold leashes for his hunting dogs and trimming the manes of his horses. He glanced up.

"It's Loki, isn't it?" he asked.

"Yes," replied the hawk, "you are quite right, of course."

"How goes it with the Æsir, and how with the elves? Very well, I trust?"

"The elves are upset and the Æsir worse. Someone has stolen Thor's hammer."

"And who's the culprit?" asked King Loki of Outgard.

"You are, your gigantic majesty," answered the Mischief Maker at which the giant let out such an exploding guffaw of cruel laughter that his horses shied in fear and his hounds cringed in terror.

"There's no use pretending with a clever fellow like you," he said. "You are quite right. I *have* stolen Thor's hammer; and the Thundering Nuisance will only get it back on conditions."

"What conditions?"

"Don't think the hammer can be regained by force. It can't. I have buried it deep in the earth, seven leagues[9] down. Only one thing will redeem it. You must bring me the goddess Freya to be my wife!"

---

4. Here, *Loki* refers to the god of fire and mischief, not to be confused with King Loki.
5. *Jotunheim* (yō′toon ham′) is one of the nine worlds in Norse mythology and the realm of the giants. *Jotun* is another word for *giant*.
6. *Freya* (frā′ə) is the Norse goddess of fertility and love.

Make Inferences About Characters *From what you have read so far, what can you infer about Thor's personality?*

Vocabulary

guile (gīl) n. cunning

---

7. *Ragnarok* is the climactic final battle between the gods in Norse mythology.
8. *Plaiting* (plāt′ing) means "braiding."
9. One *league* (lēg) is equal to about three miles, or five kilometers.

Making Inferences About Characters *What qualities does King Loki possess? How can he be tricked?*

BRIAN BRANSTON

Thor was dragging him to Freya's palace, bursting into it without any politeness or ceremony.

"Here's your feather coat, dear Freya," said Thor, "thanks for the loan of it. Now hurry up please and find yourself a bride's veil."

"A bride's veil?" asked Freya, surprised.

"Who's getting married?"

"You are," said Thor.

"I?" exclaimed Freya beginning to get angry, "to whom, pray? Or is it a secret?"

"It's no secret," said the simple Thor, "to Loki of Outgard, of course."

Freya's lovely breasts rose with such fury that her famous necklace Brisingamen snapped apart and the precious jewels scattered across the marble floor. She picked up the nearest weapon to hand, a distaff,[11] and started to belabor[12] Loki, shouting, "I shan't, I shan't, I shan't!" It was no use trying to reason with her. She flatly refused to marry any giant even though he was a king.

Such a serious situation had to be made known to Odin.[13] At once, he called a council meeting of all the Æsir and without

Donar-Thor, School wall Chart. Colour print after a painting by Max Koch. No. 4 of Series, 1905. Sagenbilder, Leipzig.

View the Art This print shows a powerful Thor brandishing his hammer while riding in a chariot. How does this image compare with Branston's description of Thor?

Loki made no reply but flew straight back to Asgard[10] and before he could alight Thor was asking him for news.

"Tell me at once, before you perch," he cried, "have you found out where my hammer is?"

The Mischief Maker explained precisely all he knew and told the terms necessary for retrieving the hammer. He had scarcely taken off the feather coat when

---

10. *Asgard* (as′gärd′) is another of the nine worlds and the realm where the gods live.

11. A *distaff* (dis′taf) is a pole used to hold wool for spinning.
12. To *belabor* (bi la′bər) is to strike or hit.
13. *Odin* is a Norse god of war. He is also the god of poets.

Plot Pattern Archetypes What plot elements do you recognize so far in this story?

delay they sat in **deliberation** upon their judgement stools. "Who's first with any ideas?" asked Odin.

Tyr suggested an armed invasion of Jotunheim. Niord[14] agreed, saying it should be an attack by sea and land and air with the Valkyries[15] on their flying horses spear-heading the aerial battalions.

Loki said, "I can tell you this: a direct attack will be useless. Let me remind you of the magic spells employed by the giant king to frustrate Thor in the past. Even if an attack was successful, the hammer would still lie hidden. There is only one way to get it back and that is to trick King Loki of Outgard into producing it."

Heimdall,[16] the whitest and sometimes the wisest of the gods, said he had an idea.

"If we were to dress Thor himself up as a bride and send Loki disguised as a handmaid to do the talking, then once the hammer is brought out Thor can snatch it up and—hey presto!—heads will roll!"

"Jumping Jormungander!"[17] shouted Thor, foaming at the mouth. "Vexatious Vergelmir![18] Nobody dresses me up as a woman!"

But it was no use Thor's continuing to protest. Heimdall's suggestion was voted best in the end and the Thunderer had to submit to being clothed in petticoats to hide his hairy legs and a long-sleeved blouse stuffed out a bit in the appropriate places, topped by an embroidered tunic. Brooches were pinned onto his false bust and a set of housewife's keys was set to dangle from his girdle.[19] To show he really was 'Freya', he had to wear the goddess's famous necklace, now repaired, Brisingamen. And to complete the disguise he was draped to the waist in a white bride's veil. Loki in turn was dressed up as a woman, a rather saucy[20] lady's maid.

Thor's goats[21] were led from the stable and harnessed to the chariot. "Come on there, Toothgnasher! Gee up, Toothgrinder!" he shouted and cracked his whip while the smile vanished from Loki's lips as he nearly slipped out of the back. In a flash of lightning they were halfway across the sky.

In Jotunheim King Loki of Outgard heard the thunder of the chariot wheels and he called out to his servants to strew the carved wooden settles with cushions and goat skins to make them comfortable, to broach the sparkling, foamy ale, to set up the trestle tables and prepare the wedding feast for him and his new bride the lovely, the delectable, the incomparable Freya. He rubbed his gigantic hands with satisfaction as he thought of all his possessions, of the gold-horned oxen with jet black hides thronging his paddocks, of his horses and hounds, his hunting hawks, of the gold and jewels in his iron-bound

---

14. *Niord* is the Norse god of the sea.
15. *Valkyries* (val kēr´ ēs) are Odin's twelve handmaidens, who ride onto the battlefield on winged horses to take souls of the brave to Valhalla, one of the nine realms.
16. *Heimdall* (hīm dəl) is the watchman of the gods; he possesses keen eyesight and hearing, as well as the ability to see the future.
17. The *Jormungander* is Loki's son, a mighty serpent that encircles the Earth.
18. *Vexatious* (vek sā´shēs) means "troublesome." *Vergelmir* is a spring in Norse mythology that was instrumental in forming the first giants.

Rescuing and Conquering Why might the gods decide against attacking King Loki directly?

Vocabulary

deliberation (di lib´ə rā´shən) *n.* an official meeting or consultation

19. Thor's female costume includes *petticoats* (pet´ē kōts´), which are decorative feminine undergarments; a *tunic* (tōō´nik), which is a long, loose shirt; and a *girdle* (gurd´əl), which here means "a wide belt." He is also wearing a set of *housewife's keys*. Women in Scandinavian cultures ruled the household and, therefore, held the keys to the house.
20. *Saucy* (sô´sē) means "spirited."
21. Thor drove a chariot pulled by two *goats*.

coffers;[22] he seemed to need only one thing to complete his happiness—the goddess Freya.

By the time the 'bride' and her 'lady's maid' had arrived it was early evening and the banquet was ready.

The bride was placed on King Loki's right hand and the maid on his left. The giant was very surprised when, during the feasting, the bride had no difficulty in despatching a whole ox, eight fine salmon and all the dainties intended for the lady giants. He was even more astonished to see this mountain of food washed down with three firkins of mead—and a firkin holds nine gallons! "I don't think I ever saw a giant maiden with such a thirst or such an appetite," he said. "It *is* unusual," said the cunning lady's maid, "but you have to remember that when Freya knew she was going to marry you … " and here Loki was forced to gulp as he thought of the thumping lie he was about to tell, "she was so excited, your majesty, that she couldn't eat for a week. Not a morsel passed her lovely lips. When we arrived here she was ravenous."[23]

"You can say that again," muttered King Loki. He was getting impatient and wanted to steal a kiss from the bride so he lifted a corner of her veil.

> And the giant king's hair almost stood on end at the sight of the flashing eyes he saw there in the lacy shadows.

Loki was petrified. And the giant king's hair almost stood on end at the sight of the flashing eyes he saw there in the lacy shadows. Handmaid Loki hastened to tell him not to worry, Freya's eyes were rather red because she had not been able to sleep for a week before coming to Outgard.

At last King Loki of Outgard called for the marriage to be solemnized[24] in the traditional way by the bride and groom swearing their vows on Thor's hammer. The hammer was fetched from its hiding-place and laid on the bride's lap while the happy pair placed their hands on it and swore to be true to each other.

Thor's hand was underneath and when he felt Mullicrusher[25] within his grasp once more all his confidence returned. He did not bother to throw off his veil. With one great lunge he felled his old enemy the giant king.

Then the pair of imposters strode out of the hall, mounted the chariot and rattled **jubilantly** back to Asgard again.

---

22. *Settles* (set′əls) are large wooden benches or seats. Here, to *broach* (brōch) means "to open." *Paddocks* (pad′əks) are fields where horses graze, and *coffers* (kô′fərs) are chests or boxes used to store valuables.
23. *Ravenous* (rav′ ə nəs) means "very hungry."

Plot Pattern Archetypes Based on stories you have read or heard before, what might happen next between the fake bride and the eager groom?

24. When a marriage is *solemnized* (sol′ əm nīzd′), it is formally established.
25. *Mullicrusher* (mə lē′ crə shər) is the nickname the author uses for Thor's hammer.

Rescuing and Conquering Why do you think Thor's confidence returns when he grasps his hammer?

Vocabulary

jubilantly (jōō′bə lənt lē) *adv.* joyfully or happily

After You Read

Respond and Think Critically

Respond and Interpret

1. (a) What is your view of Norse heroes and villains after reading this myth? (b) How did the events of the story influence your view?

2. (a) Who does Thor initially suspect of stealing his hammer? (b) What does this suspicion indicate about their relationship?

3. (a) What course of action do Tyr and Niord suggest? (b) If their suggestions had been followed, how would this story have changed?

Analyze and Evaluate

4. (a) How would you summarize the role of females in this story? (b) How does this role pertain to Thor dressing up as a bride?

5. (a) Explain Loki's role in this story. (b) What does the prominence of such a character in a heroic myth suggest?

6. Why do you think King Loki would risk war or invasion over Thor's hammer?

Connect

7. **Big Idea** **Rescuing and Conquering** (a) Thor went to extreme measures to retrieve his hammer. Why does this myth cast the thunder god in such a role? (b) What does Thor's story suggest about the gods and about the importance placed on recovering stolen items?

8. **Connect to Today** What do you think is the appeal of Norse myths, such as this one, to people today? Support your response.

Literary Element **Plot Pattern Archetype**

The plot of a story that seems familiar may incorporate **plot pattern archetypes.**

The archetype of a stolen item being recovered through trickery is central to "The Stealing of Thor's Hammer."

1. List the major plot points from this myth.

2. What other stories have a similar plot pattern?

3. Why do you think the idea of stolen artifacts being recovered is an archetype that is used so often?

Review: Myth

As you learned on page 895, a **myth** is a traditional story that uses gods and supernatural forces to explain a belief, a custom, a force of nature, or some aspect of human behavior. The gods in myths have established roles and use emblems or tools that help them perform their symbolic duties.

Partner Activity Pair up with a classmate and discuss the mythic ideas and characters in this story. Working with your partner, create a chart like the one below showing how the characteristics of "The Stealing of Thor's Hammer" define it as myth.

Characteristics of Myth	Examples
Explains a force of nature	Thor's hammer creates lightning.

BRIAN BRANSTON

Reading Strategy: Make Inferences About Characters

ACT Skills Practice

1. A reader can infer that Thor has an impulsive and vengeful nature when he:

   I. discovers that his hammer is missing.

   II. masquerades as Freya at the wedding feast.

   III. asks for Loki's advice on how to get his hammer back.

   A. I and II only
   B. I and III only
   C. II and III only
   D. I, II, and III

Vocabulary Practice

Practice with Usage Respond to these statements to help you explore the meanings of vocabulary words from the selection.

1. Name something you are **disdainful** of and tell why.
2. Describe an action or a situation that might cause you to feel **aggrieved**.
3. Identify a circumstance in which the use of **guile** might be a good idea.
4. Name two decisions that would require **deliberation** on your part.
5. Identify two things that you might say or shout **jubilantly**.

Academic Vocabulary

It is impossible to **assess** the power of mythical beings over the imagination.

Assess is a multiple-meaning word. A tax collector might **assess** the worth of a home or car, and a referee might **assess** a player with a foul. Using context clues, try to figure out the meaning of the word in the sentence above about the power of mythical beings. Check your guess in a dictionary.

For more on academic vocabulary, see pages 52 and 53.

Speaking and Listening

 Performance

Assignment With a group of classmates, plan and present a performance of the scene in which the Æsir sit in council to decide how to recover Thor's hammer.

Prepare Together, assign a character to each group member. Then plan how to present the scene. Discuss staging (how and where actors move on the stage), any necessary props, how to best convey the humor of the scene, and additional dialogue beyond that supplied by the text. Then write the dialogue for your assigned character. Rehearse your performance, making eye contact and using appropriate body language and tone.

Perform Present your performance to your class. Be sure that your chosen body language and tone of voice match your character, contribute to the comic effect, and grab the attention of your audience.

Evaluate After the performance, get together with your group and discuss how successful your performance was and how it might have been better. Use a chart like the one below to record your group's ideas. (Check your evaluation using the rubric on page 1127.)

What worked well	What needed improvement
We got the humor across. (Audience laughed.)	At times actors were playing to the audience rather than staying "in the scene."

 Literature Online

Selection Resources For Selection Quizzes, eFlashcards, and Reading-Writing Connection activities, go to glencoe.com and enter QuickPass code GL59794u5.

Vocabulary Workshop

Word Origins

Norse Mythology

Literature Connection The angry, noisy Thor was the Norse god of thunder. The English word *Thursday* ("Thor's day") comes from his name.

> "*The god Thor always resented the disdainful way he had been treated by King Liki of Outgard.*"
>
> —Brian Branston, from "The Stealing of Thor's Hammer"

Tracing the **word origins,** or etymology, of this word explains how this Norse name entered our language. Modern English has its roots in the language of the Anglo-Saxons who lived in England in the early Middle Ages. Viking peoples from Denmark and other Scandinavian countries later invaded and settled in England. Terms from the Vikings' Old Norse language and mythology, like *Thor*, were assimilated into English.

"The Stealing of Thor's Hammer" offers other examples of terms from Norse myths that have entered the English language. In the attempt to retrieve his hammer, Thor disguises himself as the beautiful goddess Freya. What day of the week takes its name from hers?

This chart shows the Old Norse origins of some English words.

English Word	Old Norse Word
geyser *n.* a spring that produces jets of water	**geysa** *v.* to gush; to rush forward
score *n.* twenty; a group of twenty items; a record mark	**skor** *n.* notch; twenty
snub *v.* to rebuke; to neglect or treat rudely	**snubba** *v.* to curse

Learning Objectives

In this workshop, you will focus on the following objective:

Vocabulary: Examining words from Norse myth.

Word Origins

Word origins, or etymology, is the history and development of words.

Tip

To determine the meaning of an unfamiliar word in a reading passage, break the word into its parts—root, prefix, and suffix. If you recognize the root, you can probably figure out what the word means.

Practice Match the English words below with the meanings of the words from their Norse origins. Use a dictionary if you need help.

1. Wednesday
2. berserk
3. husband
4. window

a. wind eye
b. Odin's day
c. householder
d. bear shirt

Vocabulary For more vocabulary practice, go to glencoe.com and enter QuickPass code GL59794u5.

Before You Read

from Theseus

Meet Edith Hamilton
(1867–1963)

Throughout her life, Edith Hamilton was committed to education. As headmistress at Bryn Mawr School in Baltimore (a preparatory school for girls), she touched the lives of hundreds of students. Later in life, Hamilton brought the ancient world to life for a new generation of readers by providing the modern world with engaging editions of Greek and Roman literature.

Early Education Hamilton was born in Dresden, Germany, to an intellectual family. For most of her childhood, she was educated at her home in Fort Wayne, Indiana. From an early age, Hamilton was fascinated with Greek and Roman literature, and she began studying Latin with her father when she was only seven years old. She also studied French, German, and Greek.

> *"To be able to be caught up into the world of thought—that is educated."*
>
> —Edith Hamilton

Scholar and Teacher Hamilton left home to attend a girls' finishing school at age sixteen. She next attended Bryn Mawr College and received her master's degree in classics in 1894. After graduation, Hamilton and her younger sister, Alice, studied in Germany. Together, they were the first women to attend courses at the university in Munich.

After returning to the United States, Hamilton accepted an offer to serve as the first headmistress of Bryn Mawr School. Hamilton was a success as a teacher and an administrator. Students enjoyed her classes (especially her senior class on Virgil) and admired her high standards.

A Second Career Hamilton retired from Bryn Mawr in 1922 with the intention of writing about the classics. Her friends, enthusiastic about her teachings of Greek tragedies, encouraged her to publish her works. Hamilton wrote various articles about Greek drama, which were so successful that she was encouraged to rework them as a book. As a result, she published *The Greek Way* in 1930. Hamilton went on to write numerous books and translations, including *The Roman Way* (1932), *Mythology* (1943), and *Echo of Greece* (1957).

Hamilton almost single-handedly popularized the study of the ancient world. When Hamilton died at age ninety-five, she left behind fans worldwide who treasured the teacher and writer who "[talked] about Aeschylus exactly as though he were her eldest son."

Author Search For more about Edith Hamilton, go to glencoe.com and enter QuickPass code GL59794u5.

Literature and Reading Preview

Connect to the Story
How do you handle difficult choices? Write a journal entry in which you describe how you deal with challenging decisions.

Build Background
The body of stories that tell of the gods, heroes, and ceremonies of the ancient Greeks is known as Greek mythology. This mythology is a source of inspiration for contemporary writers.

Set Purposes for Reading

Big Idea Rescuing and Conquering
As you read, ask yourself, How do the opposing themes of rescuing and conquering emerge, often side by side?

Literary Element Image Archetype
Image archetypes, images that recur throughout literature across cultures, are believed to have universal meaning. The stone in Greek mythology, for example, is symbolic of an obstacle in life. A cup is symbolic of one's fate or destiny. As you read, ask yourself, What archetypical images can I find?

Reading Strategy Identify Sequence
Identifying sequence in a story means recognizing the logical order of events or ideas. Events in fiction usually occur in chronological order, or the order in which they happen in time. As you read, ask yourself, Where are signal words such as *first*, *there*, *following*, *during*, and *before*?

Tip: Annotate When you read, annotate (or take note of) time and place sequences. Watch for transitional and signal words. Write critical notes that comment on the sequences.

Signal Word	Type of Sequence	Annotation
"Aegeus went back to Athens <u>before</u> the child was born, but <u>first</u> he placed in a hollow a sword...."	Time and place.	The words "before" and "first" signal time sequences linking key events.

Learning Objectives
For pages 968–977

In studying this text, you will focus on the following objectives:

Literary Study: Analyzing image archetype.

Reading: Identifying sequence.

Vocabulary

contemptible (kən temp′ tə bəl) *adj.* worthy of contempt; loathsome; p. 971 *The bank robbery was a contemptible act that endangered lives.*

endear (en dēr′) *v.* to cause to adore or admire; p. 972 *Writing a letter to show gratitude would endear the child to his parents' friend.*

confinement (kən fīn′ mənt) *n.* the state of being restricted or confined; p. 972 *Confinement was the most dreaded punishment for the teenager.*

Tip: Word Parts You can find the meanings of common roots online. Choose sites with reputable print versions or sites sponsored by respected institutions.

EDITH HAMILTON **969**

The Passions of Pasiphae, wife of King Minos of Crete, from the Story of Theseus, c.1510. Master of the Campana Cassoni. Oil on panel, 69 x 182 cm. Musée du Petit Palais, Avignon, France.

From THESEUS

Retold by Edith Hamilton

The great Athenian hero was Theseus. He had so many adventures and took part in so many great enterprises[1] that there grew up a saying in Athens, "Nothing without Theseus."

He was the son of the Athenian King, Aegeus. He spent his youth, however, in his mother's home, a city in southern Greece. Aegeus went back to Athens before the child was born, but first he placed in a hollow a sword and a pair of shoes and covered them with a great stone. He did this with the knowledge of his wife and told her that whenever the boy—if it was a boy—grew strong enough to roll away the stone and get the things beneath it, she could send him to Athens to claim him as his father. The child was a boy and he grew up strong far beyond others, so that when his mother finally took him to the stone he lifted it with no trouble at all. She told him then that the time had come for him to seek his father, and a ship was placed at his disposal[2] by his grandfather. But Theseus refused to go by water, because the voyage was safe and easy. His idea was to become a great hero as quickly as possible, and easy safety was certainly not the way to do that. Hercules, who was the most magnificent of all the heroes of Greece, was always in his mind, and the determination to be just as magnificent himself. This was quite natural since the two were cousins.

---

1. Here, *enterprises* are undertakings or projects of great difficulty, risk, or complication.

2. Here, *disposal* means "to use as one chooses."

Image Archetype What might lifting a great stone typically represent?

Theseus Discovering His Father's Sword. Reynaud Levieux. Oil on canvas. The Cummerland Museum of Art and Gardens, Jacksonville, FL.

View the Art Theseus easily moved the large stone to discover his father's sword and shoes. Is this how you pictured the scene that Hamilton describes? Why or why not?

He steadfastly refused, therefore, the ship his mother and grandfather urged on him, telling them that to sail on it would be a **contemptible** flight from danger, and he set forth to go to Athens by land. The journey was long and very hazardous because of the bandits that beset[3] the road. He killed them all, however; he left not one alive to trouble future travelers. His idea of dealing justice was simple, but effective: what each had done to others, Theseus did to him. Sciron, for instance, who had made those he captured kneel to wash his feet and then kicked them down into the sea, Theseus hurled over a precipice.[4] Sinis, who killed people by fastening them to two pine trees bent down to the ground and letting the trees go, died in that way himself. Procrustes was placed upon the iron bed which he used for his victims, tying them to it and then making them the right length for it by stretching

---

3. *Beset* means "to trouble or badger."

Vocabulary

contemptible (kən temp′ tə bəl) *adj.* worthy of contempt; loathsome

---

4. A *precipice* is an extremely steep place.

Rescuing and Conquering How does this method of justice exhibit the ideas of rescuing and conquering?

EDITH HAMILTON

those who were too short and cutting off as much as was necessary from those who were too long. The story does not say which of the two methods was used in his case, but there was not much to choose between them and in one way or the other Procrustes' career ended.

It can be imagined how Greece rang with the praises of the young man who had cleared the land of these banes[5] to travelers. When he reached Athens he was an acknowledged hero and he was invited to a banquet by the King, who of course was unaware that Theseus was his son. In fact he was afraid of the young man's great popularity, thinking that he might win the people over to make him king, and he invited him with the idea of poisoning him. The plan was not his, but Medea's, the heroine of the Quest of the Golden Fleece[6] who knew through her sorcery who Theseus was. She had fled to Athens when she left Corinth in her winged car, and she had acquired great influence over Aegeus, which she did not want disturbed by the appearance of a son. But as she handed him the poisoned cup Theseus, wishing to make himself known at once to his father, drew his sword. The King instantly recognized it and dashed the cup to the ground. Medea escaped as she always did and got safely away to Asia.

Aegeus then proclaimed to the country that Theseus was his son and heir. The new heir apparent soon had an opportunity to **endear** himself to the Athenians.

Years before his arrival in Athens, a terrible misfortune had happened to the city. Minos, the powerful ruler of Crete, had lost his only son, Androgeus, while the young man was visiting the Athenian King. King Aegeus had done what no host should do, he had sent his guest on an expedition full of peril—to kill a dangerous bull. Instead, the bull had killed the youth. Minos invaded the country, captured Athens and declared that he would raze it to the ground unless every nine years the people sent him a tribute of seven maidens and seven youths. A horrible fate awaited these young creatures. When they reached Crete they were given to the Minotaur to devour.

The Minotaur was a monster, half bull, half human, the offspring of Minos' wife Pasiphaë and a wonderfully beautiful bull. Poseidon had given this bull to Minos in order that he should sacrifice it to him, but Minos could not bear to slay it and kept it for himself. To punish him, Poseidon had made Pasiphaë fall madly in love with it.

When the minotaur was born Minos did not kill him. He had Daedalus, a great architect and inventor, construct a place of **confinement** for him from which escape was impossible. Daedalus built the Labyrinth, famous throughout the world. Once inside, one would go endlessly along its twisting paths without ever finding the exit. To this place the young Athenians were each time taken and left to the Minotaur. There was no possible way to escape. In whatever direction they ran they might be running straight to the monster; if

---

5. *Banes* refers to harmful or poisonous things.
6. In Greek mythology, Jason and the Argonauts went on the *Quest of the Golden Fleece* to secure Theseus the throne.

Image Archetype *A sword in Greek mythology often represents legacy. Why is it important that Theseus establishes his legacy at this point in the story?*

Identify Sequence *What does the signal word "then" indicate?*

Vocabulary

endear (en dēr′) *v.* to cause to adore or admire
confinement (kən fīn′mənt) *n.* the state of being restricted or confined

Theseus Fighting the Minotaur. Antoine-Louis Barye, 1795–1875. Bronze Sculpture. Mohammed Khalil Museum, Cairo.

View the Art This sculpture depicts Theseus dominating the Minotaur. Why might the sculptor have chosen to depict the battle in this way? Explain.

told his father, however, and promised him that if he succeeded, he would have the black sail which the ship with its cargo of misery always carried changed to a white one, so that Aegeus could know long before it came to land that his son was safe.

When the young victims arrived in Crete they were paraded before the inhabitants on their way to the Labyrinth. Minos' daughter Ariadne was among the spectators and she fell in love with Theseus at first sight as he marched past her. She sent for Daedalus and told him he must show her a way to get out of the Labyrinth, and she sent for Theseus and told him she would bring about his escape if he would promise to take her back to Athens and marry her. As may be imagined, he made no difficulty about that, and she gave him the clue she had got from Daedalus, a ball of thread which he was to fasten at one end to the inside of the door and unwind as he went on. This he did and, certain that he could retrace his steps whenever he chose, he walked boldly into the maze looking for the Minotaur. He came upon him asleep and fell upon him, pinning him to the ground; and with his fists—he had no other weapon—he battered the monster to death.

they stood still he might at any moment emerge from the maze. Such was the doom which awaited fourteen youths and maidens a few days after Theseus reached Athens. The time had come for the next installment of the tribute.

At once Theseus came forward and offered to be one of the victims. All loved him for his goodness and admired him for his nobility, but they had no idea that he intended to try to kill the Minotaur. He

Rescuing and Conquering *How does the ball of thread reflect the idea of rescuing and conquering?*

EDITH HAMILTON

Theseus with Ariadne and Phaedra, the Daughters of Minos, 1702. Benedetto Gennari.

View the Art Hamilton claims that women often fell in love with Theseus at first sight. What artistic choices did Gennari make that allowed him to successfully depict Theseus's allure?

As an oak tree falls on the hillside
Crushing all that lies beneath,
So Theseus. He presses out the life,
The brute's savage life,
and now it lies dead.
Only the head sways
slowly, but the horns are
useless now.

When Theseus lifted himself up from that terrific struggle, the ball of thread lay where he had dropped it. With it in his hands, the way out was clear. The others followed and taking Ariadne with them they fled to the ship and over the sea toward Athens.

On the way there they put in at the island of Naxos and what happened then is differently reported. One story says that Theseus deserted Ariadne. She was asleep and he sailed away without her, but Dionysus found her and comforted her. The other story is much more favorable to Theseus. She was extremely seasick, and he set her ashore to recover while he returned to the ship to do some necessary work. A violent wind carried him out to sea and kept him there a long time. On his return he found that Ariadne had died, and he was deeply afflicted.

Both stories agree that when they drew near to Athens he forgot to hoist the white sail. Either his joy at the success of his voyage put every other thought out of his head, or his grief for Ariadne. The black sail was seen by his father, King Aegeus, from the Acropolis, where for days he had watched the sea with straining eyes. It was to him the sign of his son's death and he threw himself down from a rocky height into the sea, and was killed. The sea into which he fell was called the Aegean ever after.

So Theseus became King of Athens, a most wise and disinterested king. He declared to the people that he did not wish to rule over them; he wanted a people's government where all would be equal. He resigned his royal power and organized a commonwealth,[7] building a

---

7. A *commonwealth* is a political unit that gives supreme power to the common man.

Identify Sequence How does this sentence help you understand the sequence of events?

Theseus's Arrival in Crete, 1990. Peter Connolly. Watercolor.

council hall where the citizens should gather and vote. The only office he kept for himself was that of Commander in Chief. Thus Athens became, of all earth's cities, the happiest and most prosperous, the only true home of liberty, the one place in the world where the people governed themselves. It was for this reason that in the great War of the Seven against Thebes, when the victorious Thebans refused burial to those of the enemy who had died, the vanquished[8] turned to Theseus and Athens for help, believing that free men under such a leader would never consent to having the helpless dead wronged. They did not turn in vain. Theseus led his army against Thebes, conquered her and forced her to allow them to be buried. But when he was victor he did not return evil to the Thebans for the evil they had done. He showed himself the perfect knight. He refused to let his army enter and loot the city. He had come not to harm Thebes, but to bury the Argive dead, and that duty done he led his soldiers back to Athens.

In many other stories he shows the same qualities. He received the aged Oedipus whom everyone else had cast out. He was with him when he died, sustaining and comforting him. He protected his two helpless daughters and sent them safely home after their father's death. When Hercules in his madness killed his wife and children and upon his return to sanity determined to kill himself, Theseus alone stood by him. Hercules' other friends fled, fearing to be polluted by the presence of one who had done so horrible a deed, but Theseus gave him his hand, roused his courage, told him to die would be a coward's act, and took him to Athens.

---

8. Here, *vanquished* is used as a noun and means those overcome through battle.

Rescuing and Conquering Explain how Theseus's actions employ both ideas of rescuing and conquering.

EDITH HAMILTON

After You Read

Respond and Think Critically

Respond and Interpret

1. From this retelling, what are your impressions of Theseus's character?

2. (a) Why does Theseus refuse to seek his father by water? (b) How does this decision affect the myth's plot?

3. (a) How does Aegeus intend to kill Theseus? (b) What image archetype does this represent?

Analyze and Evaluate

4. (a) How does the author reveal a lack of certainty in the myth's legacy? (b) Does this uncertainty diminish the myth's credibility? Explain.

5. (a) How has Theseus changed by the story's conclusion? (b) What events have led to this change, and why are they significant?

Connect

6. **Big Idea** Rescuing and Conquering Greek mythology encompasses many acts of rescuing and conquering. Which do you think is more prevalent in "Theseus"—rescuing or conquering? Support your opinion.

7. **Connect to Today** Which of Theseus's traits would be welcome in the leaders of today? Explain.

Daily Life & Culture

Pleasing the Gods

Greeks, in their daily lives, had to consider the happiness of countless gods. Pleasing the gods through daily rituals was more important than knowing exactly how many gods there were. In fact, some special altars were created specifically for worshipping potential unknown gods. The contentment of the gods was assured not through correct beliefs, but through proper action. Greek people worshipped their gods diligently and made appropriate sacrifices to them to lessen the chances of retribution.

Group Activity Discuss the following questions with your classmates.

1. The ancient Greeks were expected to keep the gods happy. How might everyday activities be affected by this responsibility? Explain.

2. In Greek mythology, what action might take place if a human displeased a god?

Jupiter. Benvenuto Cellini (1500–1571). Bronze Sculpture. Museo Nazionale del Bargello, Florence.

Literary Element Image Archetype

The use of **image archetypes** in works of mythology can help an author communicate with his or her readers. Since the meanings and importance of a work's images have already been established, the author does not have to work to make readers understand the significance of the images.

1. Which image archetypes stand out the most in "Theseus"? Select one that you think is true to life. Explain your choice.

2. Can a reader who is unfamiliar with the image archetypes of Greek literature understand and enjoy "Theseus"? Explain.

3. How does the use of image archetypes in "Theseus" strengthen or weaken the plot?

Review: Plot Pattern Archetype

As you learned on page 959, **plot pattern archetype** is a recurring plot arrangement found across cultures in literary works.

Partner Activity Meet with a classmate to discuss the plot pattern archetypes of "Theseus." Work with your partner to create a two-column chart like the one below. Fill in the left-hand column with examples of plot pattern archetypes. Use the right-hand column to list examples of each archetype from "Theseus."

Plot Pattern Archetype	Example from Text
secret birth	Theseus is born and lives his childhood without any knowledge of who his father is.
series of impossible tasks involving monsters or evildoers and formidable situations	
revelation as favored heir	

Reading Strategy Identify Sequence

ACT Skills Practice

1. Minos's son, Androgeus, is killed by a bull:
   A. a few days before Theseus first arrives in Athens.
   B. a few days after fourteen young people go to meet their doom.
   C. at about the time Theseus lifts the stone and discovers his father's sword.
   D. long before Theseus meets his father.

Vocabulary Practice

Practice with Word Parts For each boldfaced vocabulary word, use a dictionary to find the meaning of the word's root. Also look for definitions of any prefixes or suffixes in the word. List the meanings in a diagram like the one shown. Then use the word correctly in a sentence.

contemptible   endear   confinement

EXAMPLE:

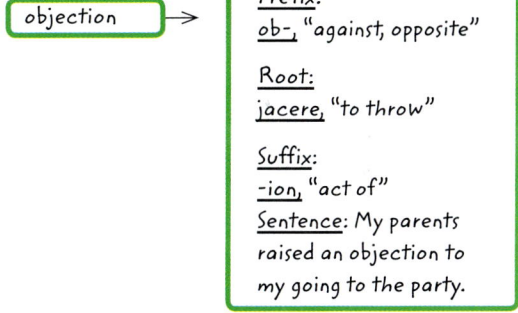

Literature Online

Selection Resources For Selection Quizzes, eFlashcards, and Reading-Writing Connection activities, go to glencoe.com and enter QuickPass code GL59794u5.

Respond Through Writing

Expository Essay

Analyze Cause and Effect Hamilton retells a series of heroic episodes from the life of Theseus in a unified narrative. Choose one critical point in the life of Theseus and analyze the causes, or the causal chain of events, that lead up to it. Also explain how the effects of those events stretch beyond the life of the hero.

Prewrite Review the sequence chart you made as you read. Jot down two or more events that interest you. Then develop a cause-and-effect chain like the one below for one of those events, adding as many boxes as you need to explain the event and its results.

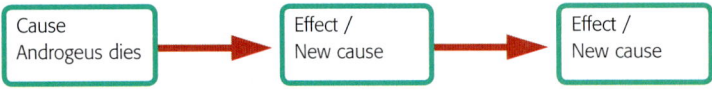

Discuss your ideas with a partner before you begin to draft.

Draft Use your introduction to spark the reader's interest about Theseus. Present a thesis that provides an overview of the cause-and-effect relationships you will analyze. In your body paragraphs, discuss the causal chain of events in chronological order, drawing the best evidence from the text to support your claims about causes, a critical or crisis point, and effects.

Revise Trade papers with a partner. Ask your partner to underline your evidence and to assess its clarity and validity. Revise by substituting stronger evidence or by making clearer connections between your claims and evidence and between your causes and their effects. In your conclusion, use a graphic to summarize your essay or include a summary statement based on this sentence frame:

> Hamilton shows how a chain of events beginning with _____ eventually led to _____.

Edit and Proofread Proofread your paper, correcting any errors in grammar, spelling, and punctuation. Use the Grammar Tip in the side column to help you with transitional expressions.

Learning Objectives

In this assignment, you will focus on the following objectives:

Writing: Writing an expository essay.

Grammar: Understanding transitional expressions.

Grammar Tip

Transitional Expressions

Make your writing clearer and more coherent by using cause-and-effect transitional words and phrases.

Because Theseus failed to change the sail, Aegeus leapt into the sea. Therefore, the bull killed the youth, and Minos invaded the country.

Other transitional words and phrases that show cause-and-effect relationships include:

as a result	consequently
and so	then
led to	since
for	so that

Sentence Frames

You might use the following sentence frames in your essay.

- As a result, _____.
- Hamilton shows how a chain of events beginning with _____ eventually led to _____.

Vocabulary Workshop

Word Origins

Greek and Roman Mythology

Literature Connection In the passage below, Hamilton mentions the Labyrinth built by Daedalus, the famed mythological architect and sculptor.

> "Daedalus built the Labyrinth, famous throughout the world. Once inside, one would go endlessly along its twisting paths without ever finding the exit."
>
> —Edith Hamilton, from *Theseus*

The term *labyrinth* initially referred only to Daedalus's creation, which was used to house the Minotaur, a fearsome creature that was part man and part bull. However, over time the term's meaning has come to refer to any kind of maze, or a complex structure or idea. The etymology, or history, of this word is not an anomaly; in fact, Greek and Roman mythology is the source of many words that are currently used in English.

Becoming familiar with word origins, or the sources of words from other languages or older forms of English, can increase your vocabulary.

This chart shows the Greek and Roman origins of some English words.

English Word	Greek or Roman Word
herculean (hur´kyə lē´ən) *adj.* of tremendous power or difficulty	**Hercules** (hur´kyə lēz´) *n.* Greek hero renowned for his strength
Olympian (o lim´pē ən) *adj.* godlike, lofty, or extraordinary	**Olympus** (ō lim´pəs) *n.* mountain and home of the Greek gods
mercurial (mər kyoor´ē əl) *adj.* eloquent or ingenious; unpredictable or inconstant	**Mercury** (mur´kyər ē) *n.* fleet-footed Roman messenger god

Practice For each item below, choose the English word from the chart above that best completes the sentence.

1. Crushing boulders for the new road would have been a _____ task without the help of machinery.
2. The actor's _____ temper made him difficult to work with.
3. A roar from the fans cheered the _____ track star on.

Learning Objectives

In this workshop, you will focus on the following objective:

Vocabulary: Examining words from Greek and Roman myth.

Word Origins

Word origins are the histories of words. Word origins generally include the other languages or earlier forms of English that words came from.

Tip

Learning to recognize Greek and Latin word roots, such as those in the chart, can help you determine the meanings of unfamiliar words on a test.

Literature Online

Vocabulary For more vocabulary practice, go to glencoe.com and enter QuickPass code GL59794u5.

Comparing Literature
Across Time and Place

Compare Literature About Heroism

Heroes come in many forms and show up in the most unexpected places. In times of war, some heroes fall and new heroes rise. Faced with the possibility of becoming obsolete, heroes will fight to prove themselves. And, with history to inspire and guide them, heroism is born in the hearts and minds of children. The three works compared here explore timeless themes of heroism: self-sacrifice, courage, and the strength of the human spirit.

Where the Girl Rescued Her Brother
by Joseph Bruchac and Gayle Ross.............................legend..............981

John Henry
by Zora Neale Hurston..tall tale..............988

A Song of Greatness
....Chippewa song...............990

Learning Objectives

For pages 980–991

In studying these texts, you will focus on the following objectives:

Literary Study: Comparing across genres. Analyzing suspense.

Reading: Synthesizing.

COMPARE THE Big Idea Rescuing and Conquering

Every culture tells heroic stories of rescue and victory. The Native American and African American cultures depicted in these literary works experienced the horror of conquest at the hands of white settlers. As you read, ask yourself, How do these works turn the bleak history of conquest into a celebration of the strength of the human spirit?

COMPARE Oral Tradition

An **oral tradition** transmits literature by word of mouth from one generation to the next. Oral literature is a way of recording the past, glorifying leaders, and teaching morals and traditions to young people. These literary works began in the oral tradition but are now recorded in print, making them available to a wider audience. As you read, ask yourself, How would you react differently to these stories if you could hear them recited by a storyteller?

COMPARE Cultural Beliefs

Although these literary works were born of different cultures—Cheyenne, African American, and Chippewa—they all center on the theme of the individual's power to change the world. As you read, ask yourself, How does this unusual theme reveal the common humanity inherent in all cultures?

Dress. 19th century, Southern Cheyenne. Buckskin, elk teeth, glass beads, tin cones, and yellow and red pigments, length: 48 in., width: 35 in. Smithsonian Institution, Washington, DC.

Author Search For more about the authors, go to glencoe.com and enter QuickPass code GL59794u5.

Before You Read

Where the Girl Rescued Her Brother

Meet Joseph Bruchac
(born 1942)

Meet Gayle Ross
(born 1951)

Joseph Bruchac and Gayle Ross share a common interest—they both draw from their Native American heritage for their literary inspiration. Bruchac is a writer of Abenaki descent who has published books of poetry, essays, and novels that weave together Native American history and myth. Ross is a direct descendant of John Ross, Principal Chief of the Cherokee during the Trail of Tears. As a child, she learned traditional Cherokee stories and songs from her grandmother.

Native American Mythology Native American mythology is a rich collection of legends and folklore. Different tribal groups each developed their own stories about the creation of the world and why things are the way they are. These stories have been passed down by word of mouth. Many traditional myths are sacred and are narrated through movement, song, and dance using symbols and imagination. They begin and end in a certain way each time they are told. According to Ross, she and Bruchac have been taught "that stories are living spirits and that the role of the storyteller is to care for the tales in [his or her] keeping."

Native American myths consist of hero stories, trickster stories, stories that impart a moral lesson or give warnings to children, and stories that celebrate family and community. For example, the myth of Apotamkin, a hairy human figure with long fangs, was used to instill fear into children to prevent them from wandering away from parental supervision.

> "In a sense, you could say the stories know more than we do, and so we have a great responsibility to tell them well."
>
> —Joseph Bruchac

Native American mythology often draws upon living things or natural objects regarded as sacred representations of their beliefs and values. In many tribal creation stories, animals are considered equals of humans and the creators of the universe. In some myths, animals have the ability to speak, think, and behave like humans.

Native Americans do not share a unified body of mythology. Hundreds of different tribes have their own languages, as well as a variety of unique rituals and traditions. By studying their myths, we can learn how Native Americans view themselves and the world and discover similarities between the different tribes that lived many years ago and those that thrive today.

Author Search For more about Joseph Bruchac and Gayle Ross, go to glencoe.com and enter QuickPass code GL59794u5.

Comparing Literature

Literature and Reading Preview

Connect to the Story
Have you heard about a person who responded heroically in a crisis? Freewrite about what made this person a hero.

Build Background
After a series of unprovoked attacks on his people, Sitting Bull summoned the Sioux, Cheyenne, and Arapaho to Montana. Soon after, this confederation surprised General George Crook's troops at Rosebud Creek in southern Montana, and a battle soon took place there on June 17, 1876.

Set Purposes for Reading

Big Idea Rescuing and Conquering

As you read this story, ask yourself, How do Bruchac and Ross explore women's roles in rescuing and conquering in the story?

Literary Element Suspense

Suspense is a feeling of curiosity, uncertainty, or even dread about what is going to happen next in a story. Suspense can heighten your interest in a story's outcome. As you read, ask yourself, How do Bruchac and Ross create and build suspense?

Reading Strategy Synthesize

To **synthesize** is to build an understanding of a literary work by combining your knowledge of different subjects and applying it to your reading. As you read, ask yourself, How does my knowledge of legend, Native American culture, gender roles, and U.S. history help me to synthesize my understanding of the text's depiction of heroism?

Tip: Heroic Act Checklist What elements are common to acts of heroism? Create a checklist that can be used to identify heroic acts. As you read, fill in the checklist with heroic elements and examples of these elements from the text.

Heroic Elements	Examples
courage	Head of the Society of Quilters approaches the grizzly bear

Vocabulary

confront (kən frunt′) v. to come face-to-face with; to oppose; p. 984 *James had to confront his fear of flying when his employer made him travel to New York.*

vault (vôlt) v. to jump; to spring; p. 985 *Maria vaulted over the puddle to keep her shoes dry.*

strategic (strə tē′ jik) adj. highly important to an intended goal; p. 986 *The president knew the most strategic way to advertise the product.*

Tip: Synonyms Some dictionary entries list synonyms. Look for them at the end of the entry.

Where the Girl Rescued Her Brother

A Cheyenne Brave, 1901. Frederic Remington. Color lithograph. Private collection.

Joseph Bruchac and Gayle Ross

It was the moon when the chokecherries were ripe. A young woman rode out of a Cheyenne camp with her husband and her brother. The young woman's name was Buffalo Calf Road Woman. Her husband, Black Coyote, was one of the chiefs of the Cheyenne, the people of the plains who call themselves Tsis-tsis-tas, meaning simply "The People." Buffalo Calf Road Woman's brother, Comes-in-Sight, was also one of the Cheyenne chiefs, and it was well-known how close he was to his sister.

Like many of the other young women of the Cheyenne, Buffalo Calf Road Woman was respected for her honorable nature. Although it was the men who most often went to war to defend the people—as they were doing on this day—women would accompany their husbands when they went to battle. If a man held an important position among the Cheyenne, such as the keeper of the Sacred Arrows, then his wife, too, would have to be of the highest moral character, for she shared the weight of his responsibility.

Buffalo Calf Road Woman was well aware of this, and as she rode by her husband she did so with pride. She knew that today they were on their way to meet their old allies, the Lakota.[1] They were going out to try to drive back the *veho*, the spider people who were trying to claim all the lands of the Native peoples.

The Cheyenne had been worried about the *veho*, the white people, for a long time. They had given them that name because, like the black widow spider, they were

---

1. The *Lakota* were the largest group of the Sioux (sōō) people. Their traditional hunting grounds were in the western Dakotas and Nebraska.

very beautiful but it was dangerous to get close to them. And unlike the Cheyenne, they seemed to follow a practice of making promises and not keeping them. Although their soldier chief Custer had promised to be friendly with the Cheyenne, now he and the others had come into their lands to make war upon them.

Buffalo Calf Road Woman wore a robe embroidered with porcupine quills. The clothing of her brother and her husband, Black Coyote, was also beautifully decorated with those quills, which had been flattened, dyed in different colors, folded, and sewed on in patterns. Buffalo Calf Road Woman was proud that she belonged to the Society of Quilters. As with the men's societies, only a few women—those of the best character—could join. Like the men, the women had to be strong, honorable, and brave. Buffalo Calf Road Woman had grown up hearing stories of how Cheyenne women would defend their families when the men were away. The women of the Cheyenne were brave, and those in the Society of Quilters were the bravest of all.

Buffalo Calf Road Woman smiled as she remembered one day when the women of the Society of Quilters showed such bravery. It was during the Moon of Falling Leaves. A big hunt had been planned. The men who acted as scouts had gone out and located the great buffalo herd. They had seen, too, that there were no human enemies anywhere near their camp. So almost none of the men remained behind.

On that day, when all the men were away, a great grizzly bear came into the camp. Such things seldom happened, but this bear was one that had been wounded in the leg by a white fur-trapper's bullet. It could no longer hunt as it had before, and hunger brought it to the Cheyenne camp, where it smelled food cooking.

When the huge bear came walking into the camp, almost everyone scattered. Some women grabbed their little children. Old people shut the door flaps of their tepees, and the boys ran to find their bows and arrows. Only a group of seven women who had been working on the embroidery of an elk-skin robe did not run. They were members of the Society of Quilters, and Buffalo Calf Road Woman was among them. The seven women put down their work, picked up the weapons they had close to hand, and stood to face the grizzly bear.

Now of all of the animals of the plains, the only one fierce enough and powerful enough to attack a human was the grizzly. But **confronted** by that determined group of women, the grizzly bear stopped in its tracks. It had come to steal food, not fight. The head of the Society of Quilters stepped forward a pace and spoke to the bear.

"Grandfather," she said, her voice low and firm, "we do not wish to harm you, but we will protect our camp. Go back to your own home."

The grizzly shook its head and then turned and walked out of the camp. The women stood and watched it as it went down through the cottonwoods and was lost from sight along the bend of the stream.

Buffalo Calf Road Woman turned her mind away from her memories. They were

---

Synthesize From your previous knowledge of U.S. history, Native American history, and war in general, is Custer's shift expected or surprising? Explain.

Rescuing and Conquering How is the grizzly bear similar to and different from other threats confronting the Cheyenne?

Vocabulary

confront (kən frunt′) *v.* to come face-to-face with; to oppose

close to Rosebud Creek. The scouts had told them that a great number of the *veho* soldiers would be there and that the Gray Fox, General George Crook, was in command. The Cheyenne had joined up now with the Oglala,[2] led by Crazy Horse. The Lakota people were always friends to the Cheyenne, but this man, Crazy Horse, was the best friend of all. Some even said that he was one of their chiefs, too, as well as being a war leader of his Oglala.

There were Crow and Shoshone[3] scouts with Crook, and the *veho* had many cannons. The Lakota and the Cheyenne were outnumbered by the two thousand men in Crook's command. But they were prepared to fight. They had put on their finest clothes, for no man should risk his life without being dressed well enough so that if he died, the enemy would know a great warrior had fallen. Some of the men raised their headdresses three times, calling out their names and the deeds they had done. Those headdresses of eagle feathers were thought to give magical protection to a warrior. Other men busied themselves painting designs on their war ponies.

Now they could hear Crook's army approaching. The rumble of the horses' hooves echoed down the valley, and

Cheyenne war shirt.

View the Art Cheyenne warriors earned the right to wear decorated garments like the one above through acts of bravery in battle. What types of status symbols do people from your own or other societies receive when they show great bravery?

there was the sound of trumpets. War ponies reared up and stomped their feet. Many of the Cheyenne men found it hard to put on the last of their paint as their hands shook from the excitement of the coming battle.

Crazy Horse **vaulted** onto his horse and held up one arm. *"Hoka Hey,"* he cried. "It is a good day to die."

Buffalo Calf Road Woman watched from a hill as the two lines of men—the blue soldiers to one side, and the Lakota and Cheyenne to the other—raced toward each other. The battle began. It was not a quick fight or an easy one. There were brave men on both sides. Two Moons, Little Hawk, Yellow Eagle, Sitting Bull, and Crazy Horse

---

Suspense *To which senses do the images in this paragraph appeal in order to create suspense?*

Vocabulary

vault (vôlt) *v.* to jump; to spring

---

2. Also a Sioux people, the *Oglala* (ōglä′lə) lived in what is now South Dakota.
3. The *Crow* and *Shoshone* (shə shō′nē) peoples lived primarily in the Rocky Mountains.

were only a few of the great warriors who fought for the Cheyenne and the Lakota. And Crook, the Gray Fox general of the whites, was known to be a tough fighter and a worthy enemy.

Buffalo Calf Road Woman's husband, Black Coyote, and her brother, Comes-in-Sight, were in the thick of the fight. The odds in the battle were almost even. Although the whites had more soldiers and guns, the Lakota and the Cheyenne were better shots and better horsemen. Had it not been for the Crow and Shoshone scouts helping Crook, the white soldiers might have broken quickly from the ferocity of the attack.

From one side to the other, groups of men attacked and retreated as the guns cracked, cannons boomed, and smoke filled the air. The war shouts of the Lakota and the Cheyenne were almost as loud as the rumble of the guns. The sun moved across the sky as the fight went on, hour after hour, while the confusion of battle swirled below.

Then Buffalo Calf Road Woman saw something that horrified her. Her brother had been drawn off to one side, surrounded by Crow scouts. He tried to ride free of them, but his pony went down, struck by a rifle bullet and killed. Now he was on foot, still fighting. The Crow warriors were trying to get close, to count coup[4] on him. It was more of an honor to touch a living enemy, so they were not firing their rifles at him. And he was able to keep them away with his bow and arrows. But it was clear that soon he would be out of ammunition and would fall to the enemy.

Buffalo Calf Road Woman waited no longer. She dug her heels into her pony's sides and galloped down the hill. Her head low, her braids streaming behind her, she rode into the heart of the fight. Some men moved aside as they saw her coming, for there was a determined look in her eyes. She made the long howling cry that Cheyenne women used to urge on the warriors. This time, however, she was the one going into the fight. Her voice was as strong as an eagle's. Her horse scattered the ponies of the Crow scouts who were closing in on her brother, Comes-in-Sight. She held out a hand; her brother grabbed it and vaulted onto the pony behind her. Then she wheeled, ducking the arrows of the Crow scouts, and heading back up the hill.

That was when it happened. For a moment, it seemed as if all the shooting stopped. The Cheyenne and the Lakota, and even the *veho* soldiers, lowered their guns to watch this act of great bravery. A shout went up, not from one side but from both, as Buffalo Calf Road Woman reached the safety of the hilltop again, her brother safe behind her on her horse. White men and Indians cheered her.

So it was that Buffalo Calf Road Woman performed the act for which the people would always remember her Inspired by her courage, the Cheyenne and Lakota drove back the Gray Fox—Crook made a **strategic** withdrawal.

"Even the *veho* general was impressed," said the Cheyenne people. "He saw that if our women were that brave, he would stand no chance against us in battle."

So it is that to this day, the Cheyenne and the Lakota people do not refer to the fight as the Battle of the Rosebud. Instead, they honor Buffalo Calf Road Woman by calling the fight Where the Girl Rescued Her Brother.

---

4. Among some Native Americans, to *count coup* (ko͞o) was to touch a living enemy and get away safely—an act requiring both skill and courage.

> **Vocabulary**
>
> **strategic** (strə tē′ jik) *adj*. highly important to an intended goal

After You Read

Respond and Think Critically

Respond and Interpret

1. Were you surprised by the response of those who witnessed Buffalo Calf Road Woman's bravery at Rosebud Creek? Explain.

2. (a) Describe the meeting at the beginning of the story. (b) How will this meeting help the Cheyenne people?

3. What special meaning does Buffalo Calf Road Woman's clothing have?

Analyze and Evaluate

4. (a) How do the Cheyenne people seem to view the role of women in their society? (b) Do you think their views are typical for other people in the United States during that time period? Explain.

5. Why might the authors have included the bear story in their tale?

Connect

6. **Big Idea** **Rescuing and Conquering** If you were a close friend of Buffalo Calf Road Woman and realized what she was about to do, would you have tried to stop her? Why or why not?

7. **Connect to the Authors** Bruchac and Ross are from different Native American groups. Why do you think they collaborated to write this story?

Literary Element **Suspense**

Writers build **suspense** through characters' actions and words, by providing sensory details, and by targeting readers' prior knowledge.

1. What sensory details in the battle scene describe the ferocity of the battle?

2. How do these sensory details, combined with your prior knowledge, build suspense?

Reading Strategy **Synthesize**

Synthesizing what you already know can help you better understand the text. Review your list from page 981 and answer the following.

1. How do the authors portray the role of women in Cheyenne society? Give details from the story.

2. At what points in the story does legend become more important than history? Explain.

Vocabulary Practice

Practice with Synonyms A synonym is a word that has the same or nearly the same meaning as another word. With a partner, match each boldfaced vocabulary word below with its synonym. You will not use all the answer choices. Use a thesaurus or dictionary to check your answers.

1. confront
2. vault
3. strategic

a. oppose
b. crucial
c. languish
d. jump
e. diminish

Writing

Write a Blurb If you worked in the marketing department of a publishing company, how would you describe this story on its book jacket in a way that would make a reader want to buy the book? Write a brief account of the story that builds interest and suspense without giving away the ending.

Literature Online

Selection Resources For Selection Quizzes, eFlashcards, and Reading-Writing Connection activities, go to glencoe.com and enter QuickPass code GL59794u5.

Comparing Literature

Build Background

"John Henry" is a **tall tale**, a type of folktale associated with the U.S. frontier. Zora Neale Hurston retells the tall tale of John Henry, a worker who died during his successful, superhuman attempt to out-hammer a steam drill. The story is told in the form of a **ballad**, a narrative song or poem.

Zora Neale Hurston

Resting, 1944. Claude Clark.
Smithsonian American Art Museum, Washington, DC.

1. John Henry driving on the right hand side,
   Steam drill[1] driving on the left,
   Says, 'fore I'll let your steam drill beat me down
   I'll hammer my fool self to death,
   Hammer my fool self to death.

2. John Henry told his Captain,[2]
   When you go to town
   Please bring me back a nine pound hammer
   And I'll drive your steel on down,
   And I'll drive your steel on down.

3. John Henry told his Captain,
   Man ain't nothing but a man,
   And 'fore I'll let that steam drill beat me down
   I'll die with this hammer in my hand,
   Die with this hammer in my hand.

4. Captain ast John Henry,
   What is that storm I hear?
   He says Cap'n that ain't no storm,
   'Tain't nothing but my hammer in the air,
   Nothing but my hammer in the air.

5. John Henry told his Captain,
   Bury me under the sills of the floor,
   So when they get to playing good old Georgy skin,[3]
   Bet 'em fifty to a dollar more,
   Fifty to a dollar more.

6. John Henry had a little woman,
   The dress she wore was red,
   Says I'm going down the track,
   And she never looked back.
   I'm going where John Henry fell dead,
   Going where John Henry fell dead.

7. Who's going to shoe your pretty li'l' feet?
   And who's going to glove your hand?
   Who's going to kiss your dimpled cheek?
   And who's going to be your man?
   Who's going to be your man?

8. My father's going to shoe my pretty li'l' feet;
   My brother's going to glove my hand;
   My sister's going to kiss my dimpled cheek;
   John Henry's going to be my man,
   John Henry's going to be my man.

9. Where did you get your pretty li'l' dress?
   The shoes you wear so fine?
   I got my shoes from a railroad man,
   My dress from a man in the mine,
   My dress from a man in the mine.

---

1. A *steam drill* is a steam-powered machine used to drill through rock. The human workers hammer the rock by hand.
2. Here, the *Captain* is the boss of the railroad workers.
3. *Georgy skin* is slang for Georgia Skin, a card game.

Quickwrite

Write a two- or three-paragraph response to the following questions: Why do you think Henry competes with the steam drill? What heroic traits does Henry possess? What flaw(s) does Henry possess? Why do you think "John Henry" is considered an important tall tale?

Comparing Literature

Build Background

The Chippewa (chip′ə wä′), or Ojibwa (ō jib′wä′), is a Native American group that lives in Canada and on reservations in the northern United States. From the seventeenth until the nineteenth centuries, the Chippewa were involved in a number of conflicts. After the War of 1812, they enacted a treaty with the United States.

A Song of Greatness

Chippewa

Fireside. Eanger Irving Couse (1866–1936).

When I hear the old men
Telling of heroes,
Telling of great deeds
Of ancient days—
5   When I hear that telling,
Then I think within me
I, too, am one of these.

When I hear the people
Praising great ones,
10 Then I know that I too—
Shall be esteemed;
I, too, when my time comes
Shall do mightily.

💬 Discussion Starter

Meet with a small group to discuss the roles of history and heritage in the life of a hero. How old is the speaker in the poem? Why does the speaker believe he/she will "do mightily"? How is the oral tradition important to this poem? Summarize your discussion for the rest of the class.

Wrap-Up: Comparing Literature
Across Genres

- ***Where the Girl Rescued Her Brother*** by Joseph Bruchac and Gayle Ross
- ***John Henry*** by Zora Neale Hurston
- ***A Song of Greatness*** —Chippewa Traditional

COMPARE THE Big Idea Rescuing and Conquering

Write "Where the Girl Rescued Her Brother," "John Henry," and "A Song of Greatness" offer explorations of the heroic ideas of rescuing and conquering. Are the concepts of rescue and of conquest the focus in each work? Are the ideas stated directly or implied? Which stages of the hero's life are depicted? Think about these questions, then write a brief essay discussing how the ideas of rescuing and conquering are conveyed in the texts.

COMPARE Oral Tradition

Partner Activity Though the texts compared here come from different genres—short story, tall tale, and poem—each originated in the oral tradition of its respective culture. Work with a partner, and each of you think of a story about an event that to your knowledge has not been written down, but that someone told. Then each of you choose a form—short story, tall tale, or poem—and write down the story you heard. Add details or exaggerations if you wish. Exchange and read aloud your finished compositions. Then consider these questions:

1. Do your stories communicate best on paper or when read aloud?
2. Do you find one genre more effective than the other? Why or why not?
3. How did the genres you chose affect how you each told your story?

Great Plains Indian hunting buffalo with bow and arrow. c.1890–c.1927.

COMPARE Cultural Beliefs

Speaking and Listening Each of these texts communicates beliefs of its culture. "Where the Girl Rescued Her Brother" comes from the Cheyenne people, "John Henry" from the African American culture, and "A Song of Greatness" from the Chippewa tradition. How do these cultures differ? How are they similar? Make inferences about each culture's beliefs, the role of women in society, and the importance of history, heritage, and courage.

Support your inferences with details from the selections. Then share your insights by presenting an oral report to the class.

Selection Resources For Selection Quizzes, eFlashcards, and Reading-Writing Connection activities, go to glencoe.com and enter QuickPass code GL59794u5.

Learning Objectives

For pages 992–1001

In this workshop, you will focus on the following objectives:

Writing: Writing a research paper. Developing coherent paragraphs.

Grammar: Understanding how to use nonessential transition words.

Writing Process

At any stage of a writing process, you may think of new ideas. Feel free to return to earlier stages as you write.

Prewrite

Draft

Revise

Focus Lesson: **Coherent Paragraphs**

Edit and Proofread

Focus Lesson: **Commas**

Present

Writing Workshop

Research Report

Literature Connection In *Le Morte d'Arthur*, Sir Thomas Malory presents a fiction that is often confused with fact.

> "Whoso pulleth oute this swerd of this stone and anvyld is rightwys kynge borne of all brytaygne"

Legends do, however, contain hints of events that may have happened. In a research report, a writer may explore the possibility of historical truth in such events as well as other questions related to the work. To find out how to write a research report on any topic, begin by reading the goals and strategies below.

Checklist

Goals	Strategies
To present an insightful thesis with a clear perspective on a topic	✓ Draw a valid, central conclusion from your research and state it clearly
To explain and support the thesis	✓ Read and take notes from a variety of reliable, valid primary and secondary sources ✓ Synthesize information from multiple sources and perspectives ✓ Support main ideas with substantial, relevant evidence ✓ Explain why some evidence is more valuable, convincing, or significant
To anticipate and answer your reader's questions and concerns	✓ Introduce, explain, and draw conclusions based on evidence ✓ Define technical or other terms, or address other gaps in the reader's knowledge ✓ Use precise language and the active voice
To use sources correctly and honestly	✓ Correctly and accurately quote, paraphrase, and summarize sources ✓ Correctly use a standardized method of documentation

Exposition

> **Assignment: Write a Research Report**
>
> Write a research report of at least 1,500 words in which you present a thesis that is based on your reading of several sources. As you move through the stages of the writing process, keep your audience and purpose in mind.
>
> **Audience:** classmates and teacher
>
> **Purpose:** to research a topic and present your conclusions supported by evidence

Real-World Connection

In careers that range from public health to investment banking, you will be required to research and analyze a variety of sources and also to draw conclusions from your findings and present them in a coherent, focused fashion.

Prewrite

Make a Time Frame Create a schedule for completing each stage of your research and writing process.

Find and Narrow a Topic Make a list of topics that interest you. Gather information about each topic by reading an encyclopedia article.

▶ **Ask Questions** Write out questions you have about your topic. Focus on what interests you and what you want to know more about.

▶ **Narrow Your Topic** Think about the length of the paper you have been assigned to write. Match that length with a question you have asked.

Audience and Purpose

Most research reports are formal writing exercises. Remember that your purpose is to inform and not to entertain. Usually teachers will ask you to use the third person and to avoid using *I*. Maintain a serious tone and avoid slang and contractions.

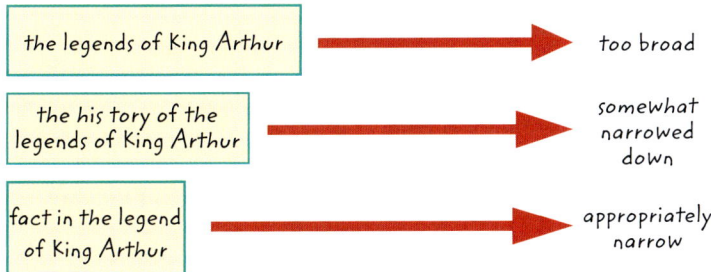

Read Specific Sources Once you decide on your research question, consult specialized sources. Use reliable, valid sources such as library databases. For sources on the Internet, use these criteria:

▶ Who is the author? Is he or she an unbiased expert in the field?

▶ Is there documentation? Are the sources used to create the site listed on the site? Are there footnotes or a bibliography?

▶ What is the purpose of the site? Personal Web pages or Web pages created to sell merchandise may not be reliable. However, you can trust Web pages created by reputable public institutions.

Writing and Research For prewriting, drafting, and revising tools, go to glencoe.com and enter QuickPass code GL59794u5.

Avoid Plagiarism

Plagiarism is using other people's exact words or their ideas as if they are one's own. One good way to avoid plagiarism is to use several sources. Doing this will help you develop a broader view of your topic. What is common knowledge—that is, what almost all the sources say—will become clear, and so will what is unique and must therefore be acknowledged in your paper.

Develop a Thesis

Writing a thesis for a research paper is a process. Your thesis should begin to "come to you" as you read and take notes. It is a good idea to start out with a working thesis statement and refine it as you go along to make it clearer, more precise, and more reflective of the actual body of your paper.

Take Notes Even though your report will be based on other people's ideas, it must be your own work, and you must identify your sources. One way to ensure that you do your own work—and avoid plagiarism—is to prewrite by taking notes. Once you begin your draft, you should be working from your own notes—all of your sources should be set aside.

Make four kinds of note cards.

▶ **Bibliography note cards** Write on a separate card the full publishing information for each source you use.

▶ **Summary note cards** Label each of these cards *summary*. Start with the author's last name or the title of the source. Then write down the main ideas of what you read. A good way to do this is to start with a key point and then to make a brief bulleted list of details. Record the page number(s) on which you found this information.

▶ **Paraphrase note cards** Label each of these cards *paraphrase*. Write down the author's last name or the title of the source. Then paraphrase, or retell in your own words, the information you found. Record the page number(s) on which you found this information.

▶ **Quotation note cards** Label each of these cards *quotation*. Start with the author's last name or the title of the source. Then quote, or copy exactly, the information. Record the page number(s) on which you found the quotation.

Find Your Main Ideas One good reason to use note cards is that you can organize them easily into groups of related ideas. This organization can help you develop a sense of the paragraphs that you will write to support your thesis. Group the cards into possible topics for paragraphs. Clip together each group of cards. Then try arranging the cards in each clipped group in the order in which you will present them in your paper.

Make a Plan One final prewriting step before drafting is to develop an outline or another organizational plan. One purpose of this step is to be sure that your main ideas truly relate to and support your thesis. If they do not, revise your thesis. A second purpose is to establish the order of main ideas in your draft.

Working Thesis: The legend of King Arthur is all fiction.

- **Main Idea:** Stories exist about a historical figure named Artorius, but he was not a king.
- **Main Idea:** The person named Artorius did not live and fight where Arthur is supposed to have lived and fought.
- **Main Idea:** There is much doubt about the "body" of King Arthur and the site of his tomb.
- **Main Idea:** The "Round Table" found at Winchester is a fake.

Draft

Support Your Thesis The success of a research paper depends in large part on the thesis. Be sure that you state your thesis in the introduction of your draft. As you develop the body, be sure that each paragraph relates to and supports the thesis. If you wish, you can write the body of your paper first and then draw your thesis from it.

Analyze a Workshop Model

Here is a final draft of a research report. As you read it, answer the questions in the margin. Use your answers to these questions to guide you as you write your own research report.

Exposition

Writing Frames

As you read the workshop model, think about the writer's use of the following frames:

- This quotation explains why _____.
- It is important to note that _____.
- As _____ notes in/on _____.
- Even though the facts _____ ...

Consider using frames like these in your own research report.

The Legend of King Arthur: The Facts of the Matter

Did Merlin exist? Was there once a place called Camelot? Did Sirs Lancelot, Gawain, Galahad, and other knights ever sit around a round table? The answer to all of these questions is no. The legend of King Arthur is powerful, enduring, and important to many people, but it is not true. There is nothing about the legend of King Arthur that is definitely based on fact.

Thesis Statement

Be sure that your introduction includes a thesis statement. What do you expect every body paragraph in this paper to be about?

The Faithful Knight in Equal Field Subdues his Faithless Foe. Frederick and Pickford Marriot.

Visual Aids

Include visual aids to convey information. How does the writer integrate and credit this source? How was technology used to insert and size the image?

Main Ideas

Each paragraph should develop one main idea related to the thesis. What is the main idea of this paragraph? What are the specific, relevant supporting details?

Audience Concerns

Your reader may not be familiar with your topic or your terms. What background information appears here?

Paraphrase

Most information in your paper should be summarized or paraphrased. Why is a direct quotation not needed here?

　　Nevertheless, there most certainly were knights like the ones named above, and people want to believe in a factual basis for the King Arthur legend. Their most important argument is that there really was a man named Arthur who has come down in legend as King Arthur. Some think that they find Arthur in an actual historical figure called Artorius, which may be a Roman name for Arthur. Others cite a hero called Arth Fawr, a Welsh term meaning "great bear," which sounds very much like Arthur (Barber 37). If the existing records can be believed, Artorius or Arth Fawr lived in the late fifth and early sixth centuries AD (Lacey 18). This was a terrible time in the history of Great Britain, which had been part of the Roman Empire since the first century AD. As the Roman Empire declined and fell in the fourth and fifth centuries, killing, looting, and burning began. Fierce fighters came from the west and the east (Day 11). Many Britons (people living on the island that now forms part of Great Britain) were killed, and many lived in terrible fear. After about AD 450, the whole eastern part of the land fell to two groups of invaders: the Angles and the Saxons. The "West Country" remained free (Day 29).

　　Battles raged on in the West Country. About the year 500, a man appeared who won a series of twelve battles against the invaders (Byrd). A sixth-century document, *The Ruin and Conquest of Britain* by Gildas describes these battles, including the final battle known as the Battle of Badon Hill. This was the decisive battle that brought peace to the people of the West Country for perhaps forty years. This account also includes an unidentified fierce fighter whose name may—or may not—have been some form of Arthur (Alexander). It is important to note that the fighter's name is never mentioned in this account, but people have still just assumed the warrior has to be Arthur. An early ninth-century source by Nennius is the first text that mentions Arthur's name.

Nennius's account also associates Arthur (or in this case, Artorius) with the Battle of Badon and eleven other victories. It does not refer to Artorius as king, however. Instead, it records Arthur's title as *Dux Bellorum,* or "leader of battles" (Echard). Neither source proves that the leader is Arthur.

Once a hero story is started, it is easy to see how it can be carried along. In our own time, people communicate ideas on the Internet that are not true but are believed to be, especially as more and more people repeat them. It is easy to imagine this happening in the early Middle Ages when storytelling was probably the main form of entertainment. If Artorius really was a fierce and fantastic fighter, the stories about him probably kept getting bigger. In *The Search for King Arthur,* David Day comments on Arthur's growing fame.

> The deeds of the Dux Bellorum [who brought peace after so much war] were forever remembered by proud Britons. Arthur was not only the saviour of a people on the brink of extinction, but he gave them the glory of a dozen victories. The deeds of other heroes . . . soon became associated with his name (15).

This quotation explains why Arthur—or Arth Fawr, or Artorius—became so famous. It does not, however, prove that the stories about this figure were true.

There are also geographical problems with the story of Arthur and his great battles. One proposed site of Arthur's supposed last great battle is Badon Hill, which is thought to be located in southwest England (Echard). The historical *Dux Bellorum* did not live there, however. Instead, Day says, "[T]here is little doubt" that he lived and fought north of where the English border is today, in an area we now call southern Scotland (18). The Welsh, for whom Arthur was a "national hero" (Lupack), offer other sources of the story in their poetry and other writing. Some of these sources call Arthur's final battle the Battle of Camlann, where he was

---

Exposition

Multiple Sources

Merge and relate a variety of sources, noting the discrepancies, if any, between them. How do the sources in this paragraph vary by type and by the information they provide?

Audience Concerns

In addition to supporting a thesis, a research paper should address the reader's biases and expectations. How does the author do that here?

Long Quotations

Begin a new line and indent quotations more than four lines long. If you have to leave something out, use an ellipsis. If you have to add something, put it in brackets. Why do you think a long quotation was used here?

Multiple Sources and Perspectives

Sources may conflict with or complement one another. How does this paragraph make distinctions between the relative value of varying ideas?

killed fighting Medraut or Mordred. Camlann may be in the north of England near Hadrian's Wall, or it may be in the south of England at Slaughter's Bridge (Lacey 69). Wherever it was, it is unlikely that Arthur lived and fought in two places that were so far away from each other.

In about 1124, the medieval historian William of Malmesbury called the stories of Arthur "deceitful fables." Historian William of Newburgh, who wrote between 1196 and 1198, said that Geoffrey of Monmouth "weaves the most ridiculous figments of imagination." He also said that Geoffrey "cloaked" his fables about Arthur with the "honorable name of history" (Echard). In so many words, then, real historians called these early stories about Arthur lies.

A twelfth-century French poet named Chrétien de Troyes added much of the romance of the legend, including the great adventures (in both battle and love) of the knights of the Round Table (Alexander). Sir Thomas Malory, who is credited with first bringing together in English the many related tales (including stories about Lancelot, Guinevere, and the Holy Grail), combined all of the stories into one very long work called *Le Morte d'Arthur (Glencoe Literature)*. By the time he was finished, the tales already had had a long history of imagination and invention.

Even though the facts of invention are so clear and so well-known, no one seems to stop looking for proof that Arthur existed. In 1191 monks claimed to have "discovered" the tomb of Arthur and Guinevere at Glastonbury in southern England, a place that had long been called Avalon by some (and which many people continue to call Avalon today). As Caroline Alexander notes, however, the monks certainly had their motives. The abbey had burned to the ground in 1184, but the "discovery" brought a rich tourist industry that helped the monks rebuild their home. Also, no one could really disprove or prove the claim. After all, there

---

Interest and Precision

Remember to use precise language, the active voice, and a variety of sentence structures. How are these choices consistent with audience and purpose?

Correct Documentation

Use a style manual for correct parenthetical references. Why is there no page number in this citation?

Support

Be sure that your support is convincing. How do these sources help the writer prove the thesis?

was no DNA testing then, and the tomb conveniently disappeared in 1589, so there is no DNA testing now, either. The article on Glastonbury in *The New Arthurian Encyclopedia* notes that many historians "dismissed the grave as a fabrication and a publicity stunt" (200). Nevertheless, to this day, a sign proudly marks the spot as "Site of King Arthur's Tomb," and tourists remain eager to visit—and to believe.

The truest thing that can be said is that there is a history of trying to turn the legend of King Arthur into fact. If a great battle leader named Arthur existed, he was not a king, and he could not have lived in both the North and the Southwest at once. Those who love the story of King Arthur may want desperately to believe that some part of the legend really took place, but that seems as likely as pulling a sword from a stone.

Works Cited

Alexander, Caroline. "A Pilgrim's Search for Relics of the Once and Future King." Smithsonian (Feb. 1996). 25 Mar. 2008 <http://www.galegroup.net>.

Barber, Chris, and David Pykitt. Journey to Avalon: The Final Discovery of King Arthur. York Beach: Weiser, 1997.

Byrd, Laura. "A Place of Legends." World and I 16.11(2001). 3 Oct. 2008 <http://www.galegroup.net>.

Day, David. The Search for King Arthur. New York: Facts on File, 1995.

Echard, Siân. "King Arthur in History: Texts." <http://faculty.arts.ubc.ca/sechard/344art.htm>.

Glencoe Literature. Chicago: McGraw-Hill, 2009.

Lacey, Norris J., ed. The New Arthurian Encyclopedia. New York: Garland, 1996.

Lupack, Alan, and Barbara Tepa Lupack. "The Tomb of King Arthur." The Camelot Project at the University of Rochester. 4 Oct. 2008. <http://www.lib.rochester.edu/camelot/gerald.htm>.

Exposition

Direct Quotations
Use direct quotations sparingly. Why are these words quoted directly? How does the writer integrate source material while maintaining the flow of ideas?

Focus
Stay with your focus throughout your paper. How does the writer draw logical conclusions based on all the evidence?

Conclusion
Conclude with a brief summary and a final insight. How does this author summarize without repeating?

Variety of Sources
Use a variety of sources. What different kinds of sources are shown here?

Reliable Sources
Your sources should be reliable. What would you check to be sure that this source is reliable?

Encyclopedia Sources
Encyclopedia articles can provide excellent overviews. How is this encyclopedia different from a general encyclopedia?

Revise

Use the rubric below to help you evaluate your writing.

Checklist

- ☑ Do you clearly state your thesis in your introduction?
- ☑ Do you anticipate and address your reader's questions?
- ☑ Do you include and fully explain supporting details from a range of sources and perspectives, including primary and secondary sources?
- ☑ Do you correctly cite all your sources, including visual aids, and present a complete, accurate Works Cited list?
- ☑ Do you explain why some evidence is more valuable, convincing, or significant than other evidence?
- ☑ Do you create interest and precision through language choices that are consistent with your purpose and audience?

Traits of Strong Writing

Include these traits of strong writing to express your ideas effectively.

- Ideas
- Organization
- Voice
- Word Choice
- Sentence Fluency
- Conventions
- Presentation

For more information on using the traits of strong writing, see pages R28–R30.

Word Choice

This academic vocabulary word appears in the student model:

document (dok′ yə mənt) *n.* 1. a printed record; 2. an original paper or record considered as proof; *v.* to credit one's sources. Using academic vocabulary may help strengthen your writing. Try to use one or two academic vocabulary words in your research report. See the complete list on pages R80–R82.

Focus Lesson

Develop Coherent Paragraphs

To make paragraphs coherent, change the order of ideas, add transitions, and take out words or sentences that do not belong.

Draft: Incoherent Paragraph

Another attempt to confirm that the legend is "fact" occurred when the so-called Round Table was produced. The real home of Camelot appeared to be known once and for all. A huge solid-oak table painted to show the place where each of Arthur's knights sat was "found" at Winchester Castle in Wessex. One can just imagine the knights gathered around it.

Revision:

Another attempt to confirm that the legend is "fact" occurred when the so-called Round Table was produced. <u>A huge solid-oak table painted to show the place where each of Arthur's knights sat was "found" at Winchester Castle in Wessex.</u>[1] One can just imagine the knights gathered around it.[2] Suddenly,[3] the real home of Camelot appeared to be known once and for all.

1. **Improve the order of ideas**
2. **Delete unrelated ideas**
3. **Link ideas with transitions**

1000 UNIT 5 LEGENDS AND MYTHS

Edit and Proofread

Get It Right When you have completed the final draft of your research report, proofread it for errors in grammar, usage, mechanics, and spelling. Refer to the Language Handbook, pages R40–R59, as a guide.

> **Focus Lesson**
>
> ## Use Commas with Nonessential Transitions
>
> In general, commas should be used to set off transition words and phrases—such as *first, as a result, consequently,* and *on the other hand*—whether they are introductory expressions (at the beginning of a sentence) or interrupters (in the middle of a sentence).
>
> **Original:** In this sentence, *nevertheless* is an introductory transition word.
>
> *Nevertheless people want to believe in a factual basis for the King Arthur legend.*
>
> **Improved:** Add a comma after the introductory transition word.
>
> *Nevertheless, people want to believe in a factual basis for the King Arthur legend.*
>
> **Original:** In this sentence, the transitional word *however* interrupts the sentence.
>
> *That does not prove however that the stories were true.*
>
> **Improved:** Use commas before and after the transition.
>
> *That does not prove, however, that the stories were true.*

Exposition

Peer Review Tips

A classmate may ask you to read his or her research report. Take your time and jot down notes as you read so you can give constructive feedback. Use the following questions to get started:

- Does all of the writer's support clearly relate to, develop, and explain the writer's thesis?
- Do others' ideas appear to be honestly, carefully, and correctly documented?

Word-Processing Tips

Be sure you have included beginning and end quotation marks for all quoted material and followed each quotation, paraphrase, or summary with the correct form of citation. If you must cite a book title, italicize it.

Writer's Portfolio

Place a copy of your research report in your portfolio to review later.

Present/Publish

Follow Style Guidelines Before you hand in your final copy, be sure that all paragraphs and long quotations are indented correctly and that all sources are cited correctly. Be sure that your paper has a complete Works Cited list. Follow any other guidelines your teacher may require for a cover sheet, page numbers, margins, and other presentation details.

Writing and Research For editing and publishing tools, go to glencoe.com and enter QuickPass code GL59794u5.

Learning Objectives

For pages 1002–1005

In this workshop, you will focus on the following objective.

Speaking and Listening: Delivering a multimedia presentation.

Workshop Model

In this workshop, note the examples used from a multimedia presentation titled "King Arthur: The Facts of the Matter." You might try out some of the techniques shown in the multimedia presentation that you create.

Real-World Connection

History museums often present multimedia exhibits. Before delivering your presentation, visit a gallery for inspiration and ideas. If you cannot visit a museum, use the Internet to find multimedia images

Speaking, Listening, and Viewing Workshop

Multimedia Presentation

Literature Connection When Malory—or another writer—wrote *Le Morte d'Arthur,* he or she probably had many sounds and images in mind. Options for presenting them, however, were limited by the technology of the time. Today the story of Arthur can be told in many ways, ranging from stage and film productions to Web sites and Web casts. In this workshop, you will learn how to transform your historical investigation report into a multimedia presentation.

Assignment

Plan and deliver a multimedia presentation of your historical investigation report. As you develop your presentation, keep your audience and purpose in mind.
Audience: classmates and teacher
Purpose: to inform and describe; to engage

Plan Your Presentation

A multimedia presentation combines text, sound, and images (art, photos, video clips, animation, and print). Multimedia presentations include narrated slide or transparency presentations, Web sites, and Web casts.

Begin by thinking about the type of multimedia presentation that you will create. Consider your access to equipment. Check with your school media or IT (information technology) person to find out which of the following resources might be available for your use:

- digital cameras
- sound and video recording equipment
- projection equipment
- software programs, including photo, graphics, animation, and multimedia authorship programs

Keep in mind that a librarian or media specialist can also point out available databases or free programs for downloadable audio and video clips. The chart on the next page shows some options for a multimedia presentation:

Ways to Create a Multimedia Presentation

	Equipment	Application
Low-tech ↓ **High-tech**	Camera, slide or overhead projector, and tape recorder	Use 35-mm slides or overhead transparencies for the visuals—images or text, or images with text
	Computer with speakers, monitor, and microphone	Use presentation software to create a computer-based slide show combining text, graphics, images, and sound
	Computer with speakers, monitor, a microphone plus a digital camera, video camera, and scanner	Use a hypertext program to combine text, graphics, images, and sounds to create a series of "cards" containing hyperlinks that make different sequences possible

Choose Your Media

After you have decided on a type of presentation, examine your historical investigation report for ideas you might portray using sound and images. Notice how the writer has annotated this sentence outline with ideas for sounds and images.

1. Introduction
   Thesis: The legend of King Arthur is pure fiction.
   Images: Show different images of Camelot, Arthur, Guinevere, Lancelot
   Sound: Soundtrack from the movie King Arthur or Camelot?
   Sound: Dramatic reading of introduction to my report
2. Stories of a historical Artorious, but he was not a king.
   Image: map of West Country?
   Image: page/text from Ruin and Conquest of Great Britain?
   Image: Write out/ explain term/find or create image of Dux Bellorum
   Sound: Dramatic reading of quotation from David Day
3. Artorius did not live or fight where Arthur is supposed to have lived and fought.
   Image: map of Wales, northern and southern England today
4. The "body" of the King and his tomb are highly questionable
   Image: Glastonbury
   Image: sign
5. The "Round Table" found at Winchester is a fake.
   Image: Winchester Castle
   Image: fake Round Table
6. Conclusion
   Sound: Return to soundtrack from the movie King Arthur or Camelot?
   Image: Fine art image of Arthur or the sword in the stone

Use a search engine and databases to find sounds and images, or locate recordings using your school and public library.

Select Appropriate Media

When you wrote your historical investigation report, you made sure that your sources were objective, reliable, and valid. Before you select media, evaluate them too. Identify the author or sponsoring institution of any site or source from which you draw. Ask yourself whether the writer or sponsor is an authority, why the work was created, and how the work might have been checked or edited before publication or release.

Edit the Media

Select only parts of the media you find, being sure that what you choose either explains or supports your thesis or proposition—or engages your audience. Use your narration to help your audience understand what the images and sounds convey and to make meaningful links between the different parts of your presentation.

Develop Your Presentation

Avoid Plagiarism
Correctly credit each image, video clip, and sound, along with all your print sources, in your Works Cited list. (See pages R31–R37 for standardized citation styles.)

- *Focus on your purpose.* Your main purpose is to inform. Above all, be accurate and clear as you explain and present ideas. Consider displaying title pages or print examples of information on the topic, so that your listeners can focus on the information as you explain how your sources treated different ideas. To do so, scan in, photocopy, and enlarge or otherwise re-create pages and ideas from your primary or secondary sources.
- *Remember the audience and occasion.* Your main proposition, claim, or thesis is the most important idea you will present. Your audience could miss it if you only read it once, so take care to display and repeat it. Think about other potential problems your audience might have in understanding or following your presentation. Be sure to explain any unfamiliar or technical terms; to use maps, graphs, or charts to display unfamiliar concepts; and to address biases your audience may have, such as the belief that the Arthur legend is partially true. Keep in mind that you can use various software programs, as well as drawing tools within some word-processing programs, to create precise and professional looking charts, spreadsheets, graphs, and other visual displays.
- *Add narration.* Carefully consider what you need to explain and how and where you will convey information from your sources to complement and link the sounds and images.

Organize Your Presentation

Create a storyboard like the one below. Make a frame for each slide, card, or transparency you will use. Begin with a title and author frame. End with a Works Cited frame for listing, in standardized form, all your research sources, as well as all your visual and sound sources. In all the remaining frames of your storyboard, note which images, sounds, and text you will use.

• title • drawing of Camelot • "Camelot" music	• thesis • bring music down • read my introduction	• map—West Country • explain Dux Bellorum • read source quotation	• source title page • explain how sources vary
• map—England today • recall thesis • point out different places	• photo—Glastonbury • text—varying beliefs • monks chanting (low volume)	• photo—Winchester • photo—Round Table • sound effect: clash of armor • narration	• thesis • Works Cited • "Camelot" music

Note these two examples of slides based on ideas mapped out in the model storyboard.

Rehearse and Deliver Your Presentation

Practice the entire presentation until you have the timing down. Then rehearse the presentation in front of a small audience of classmates or family members. Ask them to explain which ideas, sounds, and images are clearest. You may need to adjust your pace, volume, images, and narration.

As you rehearse and deliver your presentation, keep the presentation techniques below in mind. When you are an audience member, keep the listening and viewing techniques in mind.

Evaluation Checklist
- ☑ Is the thesis clear?
- ☑ Do the text, images, and sounds clearly support the thesis and main ideas?
- ☑ Does the presentation flow smoothly from beginning to end?
- ☑ How well do you inform?
- ☑ How well do you also engage the audience?

Techniques for a Multimedia Presentation

Presentation Techniques	Listening and Viewing Techniques
☑ **Pace** Give your audience enough time to view and hear each segment.	☑ **Body Language** Show respect for the presenter by sitting upright.
☑ **Volume** Make your words and sounds loud enough so that your entire audience can hear them, but do not blast them.	☑ **Movement and Facial Expression** Show that you are listening and understanding. Nod occasionally. Keep an interested look on your face.
☑ **Eye Contact** Look at your images as you direct audience attention to them.	☑ **Focus** Look only at the presenter or the images.

Speaking, Listening, and Viewing For project ideas, templates, and presentation tips, go to glencoe.com and enter QuickPass code GL59794u5.

Independent Reading

Legends and Myths

LEGENDS, MYTHS, AND FOLKTALES are all traditional stories that vary in their forms and content. Legends generally glorify historical figures, giving them fictional traits and describing them in a sentimental tone. Folktales often focus on justice and may have a serious, humorous, or sentimental tone. Myths can explain natural phenomena or human relationships; their tone tends to be dignified. For more legends, myths, and folktales on a range of themes, try the first three suggestions below. For a novel and an epic poem that incorporate the Big Ideas of *Acts of Courage* and *Rescuing and Conquering,* try the titles from the Glencoe Literature Library on the next page.

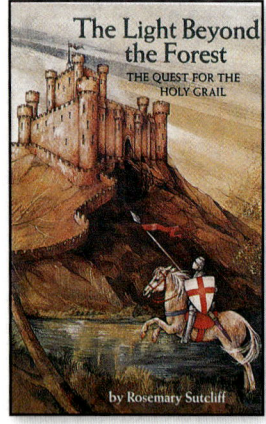

The Light Beyond The Forest
Rosemary Sutcliff

In this retelling of part of the legend of King Arthur, the Knights of the Round Table set out in search of a relic known as the Holy Grail. This is a tale of heroism and adventure, but it also has tender, human moments, such as when the brave Lancelot first meets up with his son Galahad. Sir Lancelot, Sir Galahad, Sir Bors, and Sir Percival encounter many adventures but always triumph over the forces of evil that threaten them physically and spiritually. This book is the second in a trilogy.

Cut from the Same Cloth: American Women of Myth, Legend, and Tall Tale
Robert D. San Souci

Discover the United States' unheralded heroines who are as strong-willed and clever as their male counterparts. San Souci retells fifteen folktales, ballads, and stories about legendary women, presenting three tales from each of five regions of the United States: the Northeast, South, Midwest, Southwest, and West. The heroines, who range from Molly Cottontail to Pale-Faced Lightning, represent African Americans, Anglo Americans, Native Americans (including the Eskimo and Hawaiians), and Mexican Americans.

The Red Badge of Courage
Stephen Crane

Facing his own fears, Henry Fleming performs acts of courage and returns to fight in the Civil War.

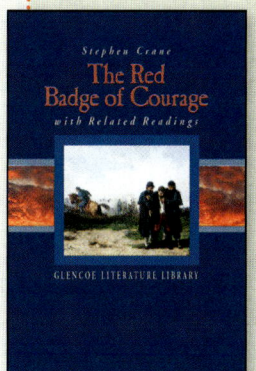

Beowulf
translated by Burton Raffel

A great warrior leads his people and slays a dragon in this tale of adventure and rescuing and conquering.

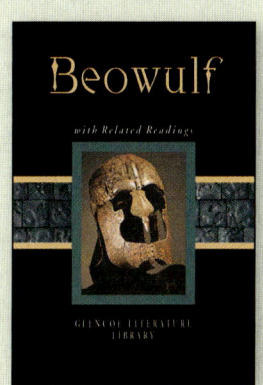

CRITICS' CORNER

"[The] quick, plainly told fables [in The Girl Who Married a Lion and Other Tales from Africa] feature places where people and animals live in close proximity and somebody has to walk miles to a river everyday just to collect water. The personalities of Africa's animals—the wiliness of the hare, the gullibility of the lion, the laziness of the baboon—take shape as the book proceeds. And there are clear moral lessons here. . . ."

—Maggie Galehouse, the *New York Times Book Review*

The Girl Who Married a Lion and Other Tales from Africa
Alexander McCall Smith

The values and traditions of Zimbabwe and Botswana come alive in this collection of short tales collected and edited for an international audience by fiction writer Alexander McCall Smith. Like other tales from around the world, these stories have themes of ambition, jealousy, and love; they value community; they show greed being punished and loyalty rewarded; and they reflect a sense of humor.

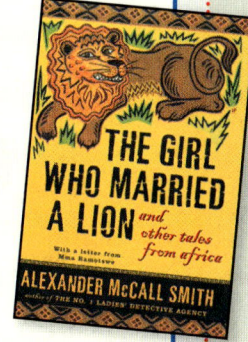

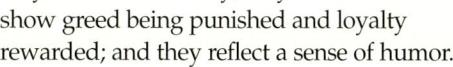

Write a Review

Read one of the books listed on this page and write a review of it for your classmates. Be sure to explain the typical characteristics of the book's fictional genre and discuss how the author uses that genre to convey the book's theme. Present your review to the class.

Assessment

English–Language Arts

Reading: Epic and Myth

Carefully read the following passage. Use context clues to help you define any words with which you are unfamiliar. Pay close attention to rhetorical devices and character development. Then, on a separate sheet of paper, answer questions 1–9, on page 1010.

from "King Arthur" by Donna Rosenberg

based on *History of the Kings of Britain* by Geoffrey of Monmouth

line

The horrible appearance of the fiend was matched only by the terrible nature of his deeds. His face was darkly splotched like the skin of a frog. His eyebrows hung low over his eyes, which burned with fire. His ears were enormous, and his nose was hooked like a hawk's beak. His mouth was as flat as a flounder's, and his fat, loose, fleshy lips spread apart to display his swollen
5 gums. His bristly black beard fell over his chest, concealing part of his fat body. He had the broad neck and shoulders of a bull. His arms and legs stretched out like the limbs of a mighty oak tree. From the top of his head to the tip of his shovel-shaped feet, he was thirty feet tall.

The giant wore a tunic made from human hair, fringed with the beards of men. He carried the corpses of twelve peasants tied together on his back. In his hand, he carried a club so mighty
10 that the two strongest farmers in the land could not have lifted it off the ground.

The giant dropped the corpses by the fire and approached Arthur with broad strides. As Arthur fingered Excalibur, he saw that the giant's mouth was still smeared with the clotted blood and scraps of flesh from his last meal. Even his beard and his hair were strewn with gore.

Arthur said to him, "May great God in heaven, who rules the world, give you a short life and
15 a shameful death! Surely you are the most foul fiend that was ever formed! Guard yourself, you dog, and prepare to die, for this day my hands will kill you!"

The giant responded by raising his fearsome club. He grinned like a ferocious boar, confident of its menacing tusks. Then he growled, and foam spilled from his gaping mouth.

King Arthur raised his shield and prayed to God that it would protect him against the fiend's
20 mighty club. The giant's first blow fell upon Arthur's shield, making the cliffs clang like an anvil and shattering his source of protection. The shock of the impact almost knocked Arthur to the ground, but he quickly recovered.

The blow ignited King Arthur's rage, and he furiously struck the giant on the forehead with his sword. Blood gushed into the giant's eyes and down his cheeks, blinding him.
25 Just as an enraged boar, its flesh torn from the attacks of hunting hounds, turns and charges upon a hunter, so the giant, maddened with the pain of his wound, rushed with a roar upon King Arthur. Groping blindly with his hands, the giant grabbed the king by the shoulders and clasped him to his chest, trying to crush Arthur's ribs and burst his heart. King Arthur summoned all of his strength and twisted his body out from under the giant's grasp.

30   "Peace to you, my lord!" the giant exclaimed. "Who are you that fights so skillfully with me? Only Arthur, the most noble of all kings, could defeat me in combat!"

"I am that Arthur of whom you speak," the king replied. Then, quick as lightning, Arthur struck the giant repeatedly with his sword.

Informational Reading Carefully read the following data, paying close attention to details and specific instructions. Then answer questions 10–12 on page 1010.

FANTASCOPE
Now Showing: King Arthur Festival
100 hours of continuous viewing—October 13 to October 19
The *BEST* and *WORST* of cinematographic treatments of the LEGEND
Program for October 13

5   *King Arthur,* directed by Antoine Fuqua
Writing credit: David Franzoni
Cast: Clive Owen, Ioan Gruffudd, Keira Knightley
Saturn Award nominee, 2005
10   Review: *Chicago Sun-Times* ROGER EBERT—*** "Considerable production values," "Charisma"
Show times: 8 A.M., 6 P.M., 4 A.M.

Monty Python and the Holy Grail, directed by Terry Gilliam and Terry Jones
Writing credits: Graham Chapman, John Cleese
Cast: Graham Chapman, John Cleese, Eric Idle, Terry Gilliam, Terry Jones, Michael Palin
15   Winner of the 1976 **Hugo Award** for Best Dramatic Presentation
Review: GEORGE PERRY—"a classic comedy"
Show times: 8 A.M., 6 P.M., 4 A.M.

The Spaceman and King Arthur, directed by Russ Mayberry
Writing credits: Don Tait, Mark Twain (novel)
20   Cast: Dennis Dugan, Jim Dale, Ron Moody, Kenneth More, John Le Mesurier
Review: *Cold Fusion Video Review*—"overcontrived," "clueless," "lackluster," "Twain's *A Connecticut Yankee in King Arthur's Court* . . . inexplicably tempts movie producers to make variations on it."
Show times: 10 A.M., 8 P.M.

25   *Camelot,* directed by Josh Logan
Writing credits: T. H. White (novel), Alan Jay Lerner
Cast: Richard Harris, Vanessa Redgrave
Winner of three **Oscars** and three **Golden Globe Awards**
Review: *Shadows on the Wall*—"So corny you've got to love it."
Show times: noon, 10 P.M.

Items 1–9 apply to "from 'King Arthur.'"

1. From the context, what do you think that the word *fiend,* in line 1, means?
   A. animal
   B. cohort
   C. felon
   D. villian

2. Which of the following literary elements is used in the phrase *his nose was hooked like a hawk's beak,* in line 3?
   A. simile
   B. irony
   C. allusion
   D. metaphor

3. What is the giant's tunic made from?
   A. a mighty oak
   B. boars' hair
   C. human hair
   D. scraps of flesh

4. Which of the following sound devices appears in the phrase *bristly black beard,* in line 5?
   A. consonance
   B. alliteration
   C. assonance
   D. allusion

5. Which of the following words best describes Arthur's role in the passage?
   A. protagonist
   B. antagonist
   C. rival
   D. narrator

6. From the context, what do you think that the word *summoned,* in line 28, means?
   A. appeared
   B. found
   C. sent for
   D. called forth

7. Which of the following literary elements is used in the words *quick as lightning Arthur struck* in line 32?
   A. simile
   B. irony
   C. allusion
   D. metaphor

8. From the context, what might qualify Arthur as a mythic hero?
   A. He possesses magical powers.
   B. He defeats an evil monster.
   C. He risks his fortune.
   D. He is a nobleman.

9. Which of the following plot-pattern archetypes appears in this passage?
   A. secret birth
   B. overcoming a formidable task
   C. honorable death as ruler
   D. revelation as favored heir

Items 10–12 apply to "Fantascope."

10. Which film did Twain's novel inspire?
    A. *Monty Python and the Holy Grail*
    B. *The Spaceman and King Arthur*
    C. *Camelot*
    D. *A Connecticut Yankee in King Arthur's Court*

11. Which film is described as a comedy?
    A. *Monty Python and the Holy Grail*
    B. *The Spaceman and King Arthur*
    C. *Camelot*
    D. *King Arthur*

12. Which component of the movie billings offers a critical opinion of each film's merit?
    A. review excerpts
    B. directing credits
    C. writing credits
    D. awards and nominations

Vocabulary Skills: Sentence Completion

For each item, choose the word that best completes the sentence.

1. Each soldier trained for long hours to engage a(n) _____ in battle.
   A. confidante
   B. enmity
   C. combatant
   D. bane

2. The country club members considered an average person too _____ for their exclusive society.
   A. vulgar
   B. scrupulous
   C. interminable
   D. tumultuous

3. The brawny hero demonstrated great physical _____ when engaged in mortal combat.
   A. bane
   B. prowess
   C. guile
   D. renown

4. The jury spent hours in _____ before reaching a decision.
   A. guile
   B. jubilance
   C. prowess
   D. deliberation

5. His _____ birth doomed him to remain always a peon, excluded from the rights of landowners.
   A. ignoble
   B. aggrieved
   C. disdainful
   D. discourteous

6. The _____ banquet pleased the king, though his taste was usually for simpler fare.
   A. strategic
   B. interminable
   C. vulgar
   D. sumptuous

7. The escaped criminal crept through back alleys in an effort to _____ his pursuers.
   A. perpetuate
   B. vault
   C. confront
   D. elude

8. Skilled chess players may sacrifice a game piece in order to make a(n) _____ move.
   A. petulant
   B. strategic
   C. contemptible
   D. aggrieved

9. The only way to restore their friendship was to _____ the wrong she had done.
   A. redress
   B. elude
   C. beset
   D. perpetuate

10. Disease-carrying insects are the _____ of explorers in the tropics.
    A. deliberation
    B. renown
    C. bane
    D. guile

Literature Online

Assessment For additional test practice, go to glencoe.com and enter QuickPass code GL59794u5.

Grammar and Writing Skills: Paragraph Improvement

In the following excerpt from a student's first draft of a persuasive essay, numbers appear beneath underlined parts. The numbers correspond to items below that provide options for replacing, or ask questions about, the underlined parts. On a separate sheet of paper, record the letter of the best option in each item. If you think that the original should not be changed, choose "NO CHANGE."

Numbers that appear in boxes refer to questions about specific paragraphs or about the essay as a whole. If one of these questions is about the sentence order in a paragraph, sentence numbers within that paragraph correspond to question numbers, not to the sequence of sentences or paragraphs.

Read the passage through once before you begin to answer the questions. As you read, pay close attention to the writer's use of main and subordinate clauses, commas, and organization.

[1]

(1) While central to England's Age of Chivalry the legend of King Arthur extends to the whole of Western civilization. The legends of Arthur may have originated with an actual chieftain in Wales, and most historical novels place Arthur in the sixth century. (2) Even so, the mythology surrounding Camelot and King Arthur have been told and retold in countless versions over time. (3) Movies. Novels. Poems. Parodies. The legend developed from a popular myth to become something far more universal.

[2]

[4] (5) He probably bore little resemblance to the legendary hero scholars assume that an actual person inspired the myth. But in his earliest literary form, Arthur appears almost entirely mythical. (6) Although he does have some human characteristics Arthur and his companions often demonstrate superhuman strength and consort with mythological creatures. (7) By the time of the 13th century however Arthur becomes more like a typical king and less of a hero, no longer the powerful warrior of the early tradition.

[3]

(8) The debate about Arthur's actual existence, will continue because there is no conclusive evidence. (9) Whether lived or invented, however, the story of Arthur has had an undeniable influence on literature, art, music, and all Western society. Maybe it is the appeal to a lost ideal that attracts so many of us to this legendary figure.

1. A. NO CHANGE
   B. Lowercase *Chivalry*.
   C. Insert a semicolon after *Chivalry*.
   D. Insert a comma after *Chivalry*.

2. A. NO CHANGE
   B. Change *have* to *has*.
   C. Change *Even so* to *Although*.
   D. Change *Even so* to *In fact*.

3. A. NO CHANGE
   B. Examples include movies, novels, poems, and parodies written from many perspectives and in different languages.
   C. Examples include; movies, novels, poems, and parodies written from many perspectives and in different languages.
   D. Examples including movies, novels, poems, and parodies written from many perspectives and in different languages.

4. Which sentence, if inserted here, would provide the most effective transition into this paragraph?
   A. The existence of Arthur is unimportant.
   B. No question about it—Arthur did exist.
   C. There is still debate about whether Arthur was an actual historical figure.
   D. Few care whether Arthur actually lived or not.

5. A. NO CHANGE
   B. Insert a comma after the word *hero*.
   C. Insert a comma and the word *but* after *hero*.
   D. Insert commas around *to the legendary hero*.

6. A. NO CHANGE
   B. Insert semicolons after *characteristics* and after *strength*.
   C. Insert a comma after the word *characteristics*.
   D. Change the verb *consort* to *consorts*.

7. A. NO CHANGE
   B. By the time of the thirteenth century; however,
   C. By the time of the thirteenth century, however;
   D. By the time of the thirteenth century, however,

8. A. NO CHANGE
   B. The debate about Arthur's actual existence will continue because: there is no conclusive evidence.
   C. The debate about Arthur's actual existence will continue, because there is no conclusive evidence.
   D. Because no conclusive evidence exists the debate about Arthur's actual existence will continue.

9. A. NO CHANGE
   B. While
   C. Although
   D. Once

Essay

The hero has long been part of literature and society. Write an essay in which you discuss the importance of that role. First, define some qualities that characterize a hero. Next, with examples from one or more of the readings in this unit, show how these larger-than-life figures function in literature and what you think they mean to society and the average person. As you write, keep in mind that your essay will be checked for **ideas, organization, voice, word choice, sentence fluency, conventions,** and **presentation.**

The Homecoming, 1996. Peter Szumowski. Oil on canvas, 91.4 x 152.4 cm. Private collection.

View the Art This painting depicts a scene that might come from a science fiction story. How does this image relate to the Big Idea of The Extraordinary and Fantastic in Unit 6?

UNIT SIX

Genre Fiction

Looking Ahead

Genre fiction is a term used to group works of fiction that have similar characters, plots, or settings. Bookstores and libraries often shelve some of their fiction by genre categories—for example, romance, mystery, science fiction, and fantasy. Different from myths and folktales, genre fiction does not emerge from the oral traditions of cultures, nor is it usually rooted in history. Mysteries are often set in the present, fantasies in an indeterminate past or a distorted present, and science fiction in a distant future. This unit includes genres that reveal the unlimited potential of the human imagination.

Each literary work in Unit 6 focuses on a Big Idea that can help you make connections to your life.

PREVIEW	Big Ideas	Literary Focus
	The Extraordinary and Fantastic	Description and Style

Learning Objectives

For pages 1014–1020

In studying this text, you will focus on the following objectives:

Literary Study:
Analyzing description.
Analyzing style and tone.

Genre Focus

What are science fiction, modern fables, and mystery?

This unit includes four kinds of genre fiction: science fiction, fantasy, modern fable, and mystery. Writers of these kinds of fiction use all of the techniques of good storytelling. The writers create unusual settings and characters, develop intriguing plot patterns, and use vivid descriptions to draw readers into imagined worlds or investigations. Writers of science fiction, fantasy, and mystery often create characters who appear in subsequent works, where the story develops further. In this way, genre fiction writers create series.

Types of Genre Fiction

Science Fiction

Science fiction is fiction that deals with the impact of science and technology—real or imagined—on society and individuals. Sometimes occurring in the future, science fiction commonly portrays space travel, exploration of the planets, future societies, and scientific and technological advances.

> The sign on the wall seemed to quaver under a film of sliding warm water. Eckels felt his eyelids blink over his stare, and the sign burned in this momentary darkness:
>   TIME SAFARI, INC.
>   SAFARIS TO ANY YEAR IN THE PAST.
>   YOU NAME THE ANIMAL.
>   WE TAKE YOU THERE.
>   YOU SHOOT IT.
>
> —Ray Bradbury, **from "A Sound of Thunder"**

Fantasy

Fantasy is a highly imaginative type of fiction, usually set in an unfamiliar world or a distant, heroic past. Fantasy stories may include people, but they often include gnomes, elves, or other fantastical beings or supernatural forces. The use of magic is common in fantasy stories.

> I turned around and looked ahead of me again. A deep hole had opened up before me. I looked in. The hole was deep and dark and I couldn't see the bottom. I thought, What's down there?, so on purpose I fell in. I fell and I fell, over and over, as if I were an old suitcase.
>
> —Jamaica Kincaid, **from "What I Have Been Doing Lately"**

Fable

A **fable** is a brief, usually simple story intended to teach a lesson about human behavior or to give advice about how to behave. Themes in fables are often stated directly. Modern fables also focus on themes relating to human behavior, with little development of individual characters.

"Here's what you must do. Look for a happy man, a man who's happy through and through, and exchange your son's shirt for his."

—Italo Calvino, **from "The Happy Man's Shirt"**

Mystery

The genre of **mystery** includes a variety of types, all of which follow a standard plot pattern. Spy stories are often mysteries, as are tales of danger or adventure. A **detective story** usually follows a standard plot pattern—a crime is committed and a detective searches for clues that lead him or her to the criminal. Any story that relies on the unknown or the terrifying can be considered a mystery.

"Who, then, in your opinion, murdered Miss French?"

"Why, a burglar, of course, as was thought at first. The window was forced, you remember. She was killed with a heavy blow from a crowbar, and the crowbar was found lying on the floor beside the body."

—Agatha Christie, **from "The Witness for the Prosecution"**

Style and Tone

Style, Voice, and Diction

The expressive qualities that distinguish an author's work, including word choice, sentence structure, and figures of speech, contribute to **style**. **Voice,** an author's distinctive use of language to convey the author's or narrator's personality to the reader, is determined by elements of style. **Diction,** the writer's choice of words, is an important element in the writer's voice or style.

Mr. Mayherne adjusted his pince-nez and cleared his throat with a little dry-as-dust cough that was wholly typical of him. Then he looked again at the man opposite him, the man charged with willful murder.

—Agatha Christie, **from "The Witness for the Prosecution"**

Attitude

Tone is the writer's attitude toward his or her subject. Tone is conveyed through elements such as word choice, punctuation, sentence structure, and figures of speech. A writer's tone may be sympathetic, objective, serious, ironic, sad, bitter, or humorous.

Literature and Reading For more selections in this genre, go to glencoe.com and enter QuickPass code GL59794u6.

Literary Analysis Model
How do readers analyze style and tone?

Italo Calvino (1923–1985) is one of the most important Italian fiction writers of the twentieth century. "The Happy Man's Shirt" is Calvino's retelling of a traditional Italian fable, one of two hundred he collected for his 1956 book, *Italian Folktales*.

The Happy Man's Shirt

retold by Italo Calvino
translated by George Martin

APPLYING Literary Elements

Tone
The narrator's tone is objective, which makes him sound reliable. When he says the prince is unhappy, we believe him.

Style
Paragraph length is a stylistic choice. This paragraph is just one sentence long.

Imagery
The "word picture" Calvino creates of the prince's face causes the reader to feel pity for the prince.

A king had an only son that he thought the world of. But this prince was always unhappy. He would spend days on end at his window staring into space.

"What on earth do you lack?" asked the king. "What's wrong with you?"

"I don't even know myself, Father."

"Are you in love? If there's a particular girl you fancy, tell me, and I'll arrange for you to marry her, no matter whether she's the daughter of the most powerful king on earth or the poorest peasant girl alive!"

"No, Father, I'm not in love."

The king tried in every way imaginable to cheer him up, but theaters, balls, concerts, and singing were all useless, and day by day the rosy hue drained from the prince's face.

The king issued a decree, and from every corner of the earth came the most learned philosophers, doctors, and professors. The king showed them the prince and asked for their advice. The wise men withdrew to think, then returned to the king. "Majesty, we have given the matter close thought and we have studied the stars. Here's what you must do. Look for a happy man, a man who's happy through and through, and exchange your son's shirt for his."

That same day the king sent ambassadors to all parts of the world in search of the happy man.

A priest was taken to the king. "Are you happy?" asked the king.

"Yes, indeed, Majesty."

"Fine. How would you like to be my bishop?"

1018   UNIT 6   GENRE FICTION

"Oh, Majesty, if only it were so!"

30 "Away with you! Get out of my sight! I'm seeking a man who's happy just as he is, not one who's trying to better his lot."

Thus the search resumed, and before long the king was told about a neighboring king, who everybody said was a truly happy man. He had a wife as good as she was beautiful and a
35 whole slew of children. He had conquered all his enemies, and his country was at peace. Again hopeful, the king immediately sent ambassadors to him to ask for his shirt.

The neighboring king received the ambassadors and said, "Yes, indeed, I have everything anybody could possibly want.
40 But at the same time I worry because I'll have to die one day and leave it all. I can't sleep at night for worrying about that!" The ambassadors thought it wiser to go home without this man's shirt.

At his wit's end, the king went hunting. He fired at a hare
45 but only wounded it, and the hare scampered away on three legs. The king pursued it, leaving the hunting party far behind him. Out in the open field he heard a man singing a refrain. The king stopped in his tracks. "Whoever sings like that is bound to be happy!" The song led him into a vineyard, where
50 he found a young man singing and pruning the vines.

"Good day, Majesty," said the youth. "So early and already out in the country?"

"Bless you! Would you like me to take you to the capital? You will be my friend."

55 "Much obliged, Majesty, but I wouldn't even consider it. I wouldn't even change places with the Pope."

"Why not? Such a fine young man like you . . ."

"No, no, I tell you. I'm content with just what I have and want nothing more."

60 "A happy man at last!" thought the king. "Listen, young man. Do me a favor."

"With all my heart, Majesty, if I can."

"Wait just a minute," said the king, who, unable to contain his joy any longer, ran to get his retinue. "Come with me! My
65 son is saved! My son is saved!" And he took them to the young man. "My dear lad," he began, "I'll give you whatever you want! But give me. . . give me . . ."

"What, Majesty?"

"My son is dying! Only you can save him. Come here!"
70 The king grabbed him and started unbuttoning the youth's jacket. All of a sudden he stopped, and his arms fell to his sides.

The happy man wore no shirt.

Diction
The choice of the word "slew" is informal.

Voice
Medium-length sentences contribute to the narrator's straightforward reporter-like voice.

Sensory Details
The vivid physical description appeals to the sense of touch.

Reading Check

Evaluate Would you say that Calvino's stylistic choices were successful in "The Happy Man's Shirt"? Explain your answer.

Wrap-Up

Guide to Reading Genre Fiction
- Identify the genre category.
- Evaluate your enjoyment as you read.
- Pay attention to characters, settings, plot development, and themes, as you do with other genres of fiction.
- Evaluate the consistency with which the author creates the imaginary world.
- Notice elements of the author's style.

Elements of Genre Fiction
- **Imagery** paints "word pictures" in the reader's imagination.
- **Sensory** details appeal to the reader's five senses.
- **Voice** tells the reader about the author's or narrator's personality.
- **Tone** communicates the author's or narrator's attitude toward the audience or the subject matter.
- **Diction** refers to the words the author chooses.
- **Style** refers to all the choices the author makes and includes voice, diction, and tone.

 **Literature** Online

Unit Resources For additional skills practice, go to glencoe.com and enter QuickPass code GL59794u6.

Activities

Use what you have learned about reading and analyzing mysteries, fantasy, and science fiction to do one of these activities.

1. Visual Literacy Create an illustration for some part of the story "The Happy Man's Shirt," and share it with your class. Discuss which details of the story support the illustration and how the illustration complements the text.

2. Speaking and Listening "The Happy Man's Shirt" was translated from Italian. In a small group, discuss the likely effects of translation on style, diction, tone, and voice. Prepare a statement summing up the writing techniques that help make a translation good.

3. Take Notes You might try using this study organizer to keep track of the literary elements in this unit. As you read, record examples that you feel exemplify the author's style, voice, tone, or diction within each work. Write notes explaining your examples.

  **BOUND BOOK**

See pages R20–R21 for folding instructions.

The Extraordinary and Fantastic

Classic Domed Disk with Windows and Four-Piece Landing Gear Hovers over Country Home near Helena, Montana, USA, ca. 20th century. Artist Unknown.

View the Art This painting appears to depict the moments just before the residents of the home encounter the UFO. Based on your knowledge of the science fiction genre in literature and movies, what would you expect to happen if this scene were to play out?

BIG IDEA

Imagine a world where extraordinary things happen. Imagine traveling to distant galaxies or living in a world where dreams become real. The fantasy, science fiction, and mystery stories in Unit 6 will expand your imagination. As you read these tales, ask yourself, What makes these stories so appealing?

Learning Objectives

For pages 1022–1023

In studying this text, you will focus on the following objective:

Literary Study: Analyzing description and style.

LITERARY FOCUS

Description and Style

How do writers of genre fiction use description and style?

Description is a detailed account of a person, an object, or an event. **Style** is the distinctive way that a writer uses language. The writer might use imagery to create "word pictures" that evoke an emotional response. Or the writer might use sensory details or evocative words or phrases that appeal to your senses of sight, sound, touch, and smell. In the following description of a time travel advertisement, notice the specific images and vivid words that characterize Ray Bradbury's style.

Figurative Language

Figurative language contains expressions that are not literally true but express truths that go beyond the literal level of meaning. Three types of figurative language are simile, metaphor, and personification.

Simile and **metaphor** are figures of speech that compare two seemingly unlike things in order to suggest their underlying similarities. A simile uses *like* or *as*, whereas a metaphor makes a direct comparison. Notice how the following metaphor conveys the direction of time travel in Bradbury's story.

Eckels glanced across the vast office at a mass and tangle, a snaking and humming of wires and steel boxes, at an aurora that flickered now orange, now silver, now blue. There was a sound like a gigantic bonfire burning all of Time, all the years and all the parchment calendars, all the hours piled high and set aflame.

—Ray Bradbury, from "A Sound of Thunder"

Time was a film run backward.

—Ray Bradbury, from "A Sound of Thunder"

1022 UNIT 6 GENRE FICTION

Personification

Personification is a figure of speech that attributes human qualities to an animal, an object, a force of nature, or an idea. Notice how the personification of the fluorescent light in Levertov's poem creates a vivid visual image.

> The fluorescent light flickers sullenly, a / pause. But you command. It grabs / each face and holds it up / by the hair for you, mask after mask.
>
> —Denise Levertov, from "People at Night"

Imagery

Good descriptive writing uses **imagery**—language that appeals to one or more of the five senses: sight, hearing, touch, taste, and smell. Imagery helps to create an emotional response in the reader.

> But the giant squid is real, growing up to lengths of at least 60 feet, with eyes the size of dinner plates and a tangle of tentacles lined with long rows of sucker pads.
>
> —William J. Broad, from "One Legend Found, Many Still to Go"

Diction

An important element of an author's style or voice is **diction,** a writer's choice of words. Good writers choose their words carefully to convey a particular meaning or feeling. Notice how Stephen Vincent Benét's word choice and short sentences create **suspense,** or a feeling of curiosity, uncertainty, or dread, in the passage below.

> I was in darkness—I found stairs and climbed. There were many stairs, turning around till my head was dizzy. At the top was another door—I found the knob and opened it. I was in a long small chamber—on one side of it was a bronze door that could not be opened, for it had no handle.
>
> —Stephen Vincent Benét, from "By the Waters of Babylon"

Tone

Tone is a writer's or speaker's attitude toward the subject matter. In this passage, the narrator uses a cold, impersonal tone.

> Imagine a prison. There is something you know that you have not yet told. Those in control of the prison know that you know.
>
> —Margaret Atwood, from "Bread"

Quickwrite

Describe a Person Write a journal entry in which you use specific details to describe your favorite teacher. Use diction, imagery, and other elements of style to create a specific tone and mood.

Literature and Reading For more about literary elements, go to glencoe.com and enter QuickPass code GL59794u6.

LITERARY FOCUS

Before You Read

A Sound of Thunder

Meet Ray Bradbury
(born 1920)

Picture a twelve-year-old boy sitting spellbound on Christmas Day, typing words on a toy typewriter, composing a story about life on Mars. Ray Bradbury's dream of becoming a writer was just over the horizon.

Bradbury, born in Waukegan, Illinois, learned to read at age four. He loved fairy tales and other stories containing fantasy plots or magic, such as *The Wizard of Oz* and *Tarzan*. Bradbury was a fan of the *Buck Rogers* comic strip, one of the first series in a genre people were calling "science fiction."

In 1933 when Bradbury visited the World's Fair in Chicago, he was fascinated by a roaring mechanical dinosaur. Bradbury said, "You pose the question, what if I had given up on dinosaurs? I wouldn't have had my career."

The Sky's the Limit At age fourteen Bradbury moved to Los Angeles with his family. He loved "Tinseltown" and wanted to become part of its culture by writing, directing, and acting. Following his high school graduation in 1938, he bought a real typewriter, rented an office, and began his career as a writer.

Although he never went to college, Bradbury continued his education by observing, listening, and visiting public libraries. He learned about the media world in Hollywood and introduced himself to the important people around town. He published his first science fiction stories in pulp magazines. Later his stories appeared in the *New Yorker* and the *Saturday Evening Post*. The publication of his short story collection *The Martian Chronicles* in 1950 was a major breakthrough in his career.

When television became popular in American homes during the 1950s, Bradbury wrote teleplays, including Rod Serling's *The Twilight Zone*. His novel *Fahrenheit 451* (1953) became a Hollywood film.

> "The ability to fantasize is the ability to survive."
>
> —Ray Bradbury

Basking in the Limelight Since the 1940s, Bradbury has published more than five hundred works. In 2002 he received a star on the Hollywood Walk of Fame for his accomplishments in the film industry. Film producer and director Steven Spielberg is one of Bradbury's many admirers. In 2004 President and Mrs. Bush presented him with the National Medal of Arts. Today Bradbury is considered one of the most popular and widely read short story writers in the world.

 **Literature** Online

Author Search For more about Ray Bradbury, go to glencoe.com and enter QuickPass code GL59794u6.

Literature and Reading Preview

Connect to the Story
How might your actions during your lifetime affect someone living one hundred years in the future? Write a journal entry about ways your actions today could affect the distant future.

Build Background
Sometimes the technology in science fiction is real; sometimes it is entirely imagined. Sometimes what a science fiction author imagines is later brought to reality by scientists.

Set Purposes for Reading

Big Idea | The Extraordinary and Fantastic
As you read "A Sound of Thunder," ask yourself, How does Bradbury use a fantastic idea to imagine a setting no human has actually seen before?

Literary Element | Foreshadowing
Foreshadowing is the author's use of clues to hint at events that will occur later in the story. As you read, ask yourself, Are there clues in the story that indicate how the story will end?

Reading Strategy | Identify Genre
A **genre** is a category or type of literature, such as fiction or poetry. Each genre can be subdivided into more specific categories that can be identified by subject matter, content, or style. As you read, ask yourself, How does identifying the genre of this text help me establish what I should expect from it?

Tip: Analyze Clues Readers can understand the genre of a literary work by analyzing its characteristics. Use a chart as below to record characteristics of "A Sound of Thunder." Then analyze your clues to determine common elements in science fiction.

Characteristic	Description
Setting:	The story occurs in an unknown place in 2055.
Conflict:	
Theme:	

Learning Objectives
For pages 1024–1038

In studying this text, you will focus on the following objectives:

Literary Study: Analyzing foreshadowing.

Reading: Identifying genre.

Vocabulary

expendable (iks pen′də bəl) *adj.* not strictly necessary; capable of being sacrificed; p. 1029 *Mother said our vacation was expendable.*

correlate (kôr′ə lāt) *v.* to bring (one thing) into relation (with another thing); calculate; p. 1030 *The old data correlated with the new results.*

paradox (par′ə doks′) *n.* something that seems illogical, contradictory, or absurd, but that in fact may be true; p. 1030 *It was a paradox, but she found that she both liked and disliked him.*

resilient (ri zil′yənt) *adj.* capable of springing back into shape or position after being bent, stretched, or compressed; p. 1031 *The rubber ball is so resilient that it still bounces after being frozen.*

primeval (prī mē′vəl) *adj.* of or having to do with the first or earliest age; primitive; p. 1034 *The will to live is a primeval instinct.*

RAY BRADBURY

A Sound of Thunder

Ray Bradbury

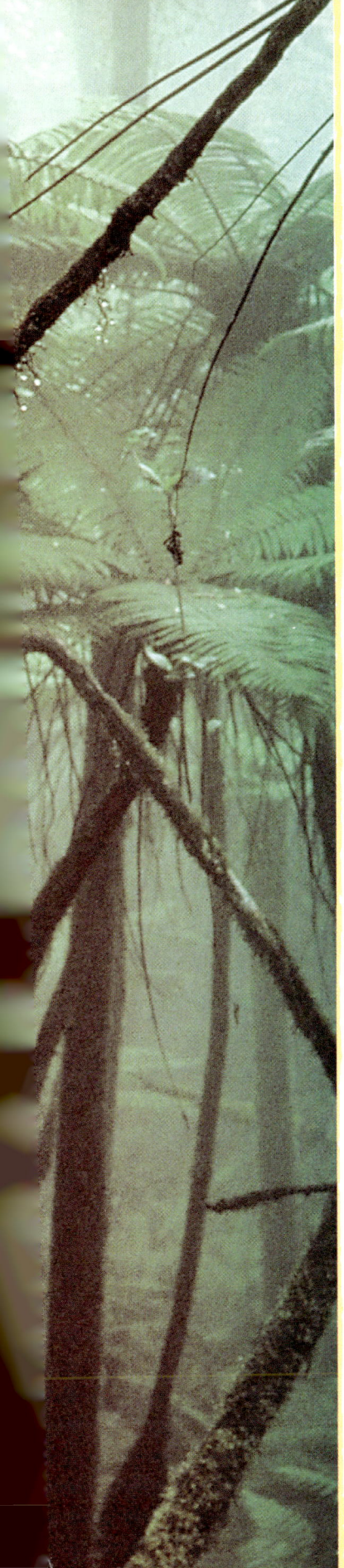

The sign on the wall seemed to quaver under a film of sliding warm water. Eckels felt his eyelids blink over his stare, and the sign burned in this momentary darkness:

> TIME SAFARI, INC.
> SAFARIS TO ANY YEAR IN THE PAST.
> YOU NAME THE ANIMAL.
> WE TAKE YOU THERE.
> YOU SHOOT IT.

A warm phlegm gathered in Eckels' throat; he swallowed and pushed it down. The muscles around his mouth formed a smile as he put his hand slowly out upon the air, and in that hand waved a check for ten thousand dollars to the man behind the desk.

"Does this safari guarantee I come back alive?"

"We guarantee nothing," said the official, "except the dinosaurs." He turned. "This is Mr. Travis, your Safari Guide in the Past. He'll tell you what and where to shoot. If he says no shooting, no shooting. If you disobey instructions, there's a stiff penalty of another ten thousand dollars, plus possible government action, on your return."

Eckels glanced across the vast office at a mass and tangle, a snaking and humming of wires and steel boxes, at an aurora[1] that flickered now orange, now silver, now blue. There was a sound like a gigantic bonfire burning all of Time, all the years and all the parchment calendars, all the hours piled high and set aflame.

A touch of the hand and this burning would, on the instant, beautifully reverse itself. Eckels remembered the wording in the advertisements to the letter. Out of chars and ashes, out of dust and coals, like golden salamanders, the old years, the green years, might leap; roses sweeten the air, white hair turn Irish-black, wrinkles vanish; all, everything fly back to seed, flee death, rush down to their beginnings, suns rise in western skies and set in glorious easts, moons eat themselves opposite to the custom, all and everything cupping one in another like Chinese boxes, rabbits into hats, all and

---

1. Here, *aurora* refers to the shimmering lights that come off of the time machine.

Identify Genre *How might the sign on the wall indicate the genre of the selection?*

Foreshadowing *What future events might this passage foreshadow?*

RAY BRADBURY

everything returning to the fresh death, the seed death, the green death, to the time before the beginning. A touch of a hand might do it, the merest touch of a hand.

"Unbelievable." Eckels breathed, the light of the Machine on his thin face. "A real Time Machine." He shook his head. "Makes you think. If the election had gone badly yesterday, I might be here now running away from the results. Thank God Keith won. He'll make a fine President of the United States."

"Yes," said the man behind the desk. "We're lucky. If Deutscher had gotten in, we'd have the worst kind of dictatorship. There's an anti-everything man for you, a militarist, anti-Christ, anti-human, anti-intellectual. People called us up, you know, joking but not joking. Said if Deutscher became President they wanted to go live in 1492. Of course it's not our business to conduct Escapes, but to form Safaris. Anyway, Keith's President now. All you got to worry about is—"

"Shooting my dinosaur," Eckels finished it for him.

"A *Tyrannosaurus rex*. The Tyrant Lizard, the most incredible monster in history. Sign this release. Anything happens to you, we're not responsible. Those dinosaurs are hungry."

Eckels flushed angrily. "Trying to scare me!"

"Frankly, yes. We don't want anyone going who'll panic at the first shot. Six Safari leaders were killed last year, and a dozen hunters. We're here to give you the severest thrill a *real* hunter ever asked for. Traveling you back sixty million years to bag the biggest game in all of Time. Your personal check's still there. Tear it up."

Mr. Eckels looked at the check for a long time. His fingers twitched.

"Good luck," said the man behind the desk. "Mr. Travis, he's all yours."

They moved silently across the room, taking their guns with them, toward the Machine, toward the silver metal and the roaring light. First a day and then a night and then a day and then a night, then it was day-night-day-night-day. A week, a month, a year, a decade! A.D. 2055. A.D. 2019. 1999! 1957! Gone! The Machine roared.

They put on their oxygen helmets and tested the intercoms.

Eckels swayed on the padded seat, his face pale, his jaw stiff. He felt the trembling in his arms and he looked down and found his hands tight on the new rifle. There were four other men in the Machine. Travis, the Safari Leader, his assistant, Lesperance, and two other hunters, Billings and Kramer. They sat looking at each other, and the years blazed around them.

"Can these guns get a dinosaur cold?" Eckels felt his mouth saying.

"If you hit them right," said Travis on the helmet radio. "Some dinosaurs have two brains, one in the head, another far down the spinal column. We stay away from those. That's stretching luck. Put your first two shots into the eyes, if you can, blind them, and go back into the brain."

The Machine howled. Time was a film run backward. Suns fled and ten million moons fled after them. "Think," said Eckels. "Every hunter that ever lived would envy us today. This makes Africa seem like Illinois."

The Machine slowed; its scream fell to a murmur. The Machine stopped.

Foreshadowing *Why might Bradbury have included a reference to an election and who won it in a story about hunting dinosaurs?*

Identify Genre *Do you believe that time travel might really be possible by the year 2055 when this story occurs? Why or why not?*

The sun stopped in the sky.

The fog that had enveloped the Machine blew away and they were in an old time, a very old time indeed, three hunters and two Safari Heads with their blue metal guns across their knees.

"Christ isn't born yet," said Travis. "Moses has not gone to the mountain to talk with God. The Pyramids are still in the earth, waiting to be cut out and put up. *Remember* that. Alexander, Caesar, Napoleon, Hitler—none of them exists."

The men nodded.

"That"—Mr. Travis pointed—"is the jungle of sixty million two thousand and fifty-five years before President Keith."

He indicated a metal path that struck off into green wilderness, over steaming swamp, among giant ferns and palms.

"And that," he said, "is the Path, laid by Time Safari for your use. It floats six inches above the earth. Doesn't touch so much as one grass blade, flower, or tree. It's an anti-gravity metal. Its purpose is to keep you from touching this world of the past in any way. Stay on the Path. Don't go off it. I repeat. *Don't go off.* For *any* reason! If you fall off, there's a penalty. And don't shoot any animal we don't okay."

"Why?" asked Eckels.

> *"With a stamp of your foot, you annihilate first one, then a dozen, then a thousand, a million, a* billion *possible mice!"*

They sat in the ancient wilderness. Far birds' cries blew on a wind, and the smell of tar and an old salt sea, moist grasses, and flowers the color of blood.

The Extraordinary and Fantastic What makes this paragraph so fantastic?

"We don't want to change the Future. We don't belong here in the Past. The government doesn't *like* us here. We have to pay big graft to keep our franchise.[2] A Time Machine is finicky business. Not knowing it, we might kill an important animal, a small bird, a roach, a flower even, thus destroying an important link in a growing species."

"That's not clear," said Eckels.

"All right," Travis continued, "say we accidentally kill one mouse here. That means all the future families of this one particular mouse are destroyed, right?"

"Right."

"And all the families of the families of the families of that one mouse! With a stamp of your foot, you annihilate first one, then a dozen, then a thousand, a million, a *billion* possible mice!"

"So they're dead," said Eckels. "So what?"

"So what?" Travis snorted quietly. "Well, what about the foxes that'll need those mice to survive? For want of ten mice, a fox dies. For want of ten foxes, a lion starves. For want of a lion, all manner of insects, vultures, infinite billions of life forms are thrown into chaos and destruction. Eventually it all boils down to this: fifty-nine million years later, a cave man, one of a dozen on the *entire world*, goes hunting wild boar or saber-tooth tiger for food. But you, friend, have *stepped* on all the tigers in that region. By stepping on one single mouse. So the cave man starves. And the cave man, please note, is not just *any* **expendable** man, no! He is an *entire future nation*. From his loins would have sprung ten sons. From their loins one hundred sons, and thus onward to a civilization. Destroy this

---

2. Time Safari, Inc., pays money as bribes to government officials in return for continued permission to run its business.

Vocabulary

expendable (iks pen′də bəl) *adj.* not strictly necessary; capable of being sacrificed

RAY BRADBURY

one man, and you destroy a race, a people, an entire history of life. It is comparable to slaying some of Adam's grandchildren. The stomp of your foot, on one mouse, could start an earthquake, the effects of which could shake our earth and destinies down through Time, to their very foundations. With the death of that one cave man, a billion others yet unborn are throttled in the womb. Perhaps Rome never rises on its seven hills. Perhaps Europe is forever a dark forest, and only Asia waxes healthy and teeming. "Step on a mouse and you crush the Pyramids. Step on a mouse and you leave your print, like a Grand Canyon, across Eternity." Queen Elizabeth might never be born. Washington might not cross the Delaware, there might never be a United States at all. So be careful. Stay on the Path. *Never* step off!"

"I see," said Eckels. "Then it wouldn't pay for us even to touch the *grass*?"

"Correct. Crushing certain plants could add up infinitesimally.³ A little error here would multiply in sixty million years, all out of proportion. Of course maybe our theory is wrong. Maybe Time *can't* be changed by us. Or maybe it can be changed only in little subtle ways. A dead mouse here makes an insect imbalance there, a population disproportion later, a bad harvest further on, a depression, mass starvation, and, finally, a change in *social* temperament in far-flung countries. Something much more subtle, like that. Perhaps only a soft breath, a whisper, a hair, pollen on the air, such a slight, slight change that unless you looked close you wouldn't see it. Who knows? Who really can say he knows? We don't know. We're guessing. But until we do know for certain whether our messing around in Time *can* make a big roar or a little rustle in history, we're being careful. This Machine, this Path, your clothing and bodies, were sterilized, as you know, before the journey. We wear these oxygen helmets so we can't introduce our bacteria into an ancient atmosphere."

"How do we know which animals to shoot?"

"They're marked with red paint," said Travis. "Today, before our journey, we sent Lesperance here back with the Machine. He came to this particular era and followed certain animals."

"Studying them?"

"Right," said Lesperance. "I track them through their entire existence, noting which of them lives longest. Very few. How many times they mate. Not often. Life's short. When I find one that's going to die when a tree falls on him, or one that drowns in a tar pit, I note the exact hour, minute, and second. I shoot a paint bomb. It leaves a red patch on his hide. We can't miss it. Then I **correlate** our arrival in the Past so that we meet the Monster not more than two minutes before he would have died anyway. This way, we kill only animals with no future, that are never going to mate again. You see how *careful* we are?"

"But if you came back this morning in Time," said Eckels eagerly, "you must've bumped into *us*, our Safari! How did it turn out? Was it successful? Did all of us get through—alive?"

Travis and Lesperance gave each other a look.

"That'd be a **paradox**," said the latter. "Time doesn't permit that sort of mess—

---

3. Infinitesimally (in′fi nə tes′ə məl le) describes something being done "in a way that is too small to be measured."

The Extraordinary and Fantastic *In your own words, explain the extraordinary consequences of killing a single prehistoric mouse.*

Identify Genre *How might this warning help you to determine the genre of this selection?*

> **Vocabulary**
> **correlate** (kôr′ə lāt) *v.* to bring (one thing) into relation (with another thing); calculate
> **paradox** (par′ə doks′) *n.* something that seems illogical, but that in fact may be true

a man meeting himself. When such occasions threaten, Time steps aside. Like an airplane hitting an air pocket. You felt the Machine jump just before we stopped? That was us passing ourselves on the way back to the Future. We saw nothing. There's no way of telling *if* this expedition was a success, *if we* got our monster, or whether all of us—meaning *you,* Mr. Eckels—got out alive."

Eckels smiled palely.

"Cut that," said Travis sharply. "Everyone on his feet!"

They were ready to leave the Machine. The jungle was high and the jungle was broad and the jungle was the entire world forever and forever. Sounds like music and sounds like flying tents filled the sky, and those were pterodactyls soaring with cavernous gray wings, gigantic bats of delirium and night fever. Eckels, balanced on the narrow Path, aimed his rifle playfully.

Visual Vocabulary
Pterodactyls (ter′ə dak′tilz) are extinct flying reptiles with wingspans of up to forty feet.

"Stop that!" said Travis. "Don't even aim for fun, blast you! If your gun should go off—"

Eckels flushed. "Where's our *Tyrannosaurus?*"

Lesperance checked his wristwatch. "Up ahead. We'll bisect his trail in sixty seconds. Look for the red paint! Don't shoot till we give the word. Stay on the Path. *Stay on the Path!*"

Foreshadowing What do you think Travis was going to say? What sort of ending to the story might Travis's warning foreshadow?

They moved forward in the wind of morning.

"Strange," murmured Eckels. "Up ahead, sixty million years, Election Day over. Keith made President. Everyone celebrating. And here we are, a million years lost, and they don't exist. The things we worried about for months, a lifetime, not even born or thought about yet."

"Safety catches off, everyone!" ordered Travis. "You, first shot, Eckels. Second, Billings. Third, Kramer."

"I've hunted tiger, wild boar, buffalo, elephant, but now, this is *it,*" said Eckels. "I'm shaking like a kid."

"Ah," said Travis.

Everyone stopped.

Travis raised his hand. "Ahead," he whispered. "In the mist. There he is. There's His Royal Majesty now."

The jungle was wide and full of twitterings, rustlings, murmurs, and sighs.

Suddenly it all ceased, as if someone had shut a door.

Silence.

A sound of thunder.

Out of the mist, one hundred yards away, came *Tyrannosaurus rex.*

"It," whispered Eckels. "It . . ."

"Sh!"

It came on great oiled, **resilient**, striding legs. It towered thirty feet above half of the trees, a great evil god, folding its delicate watchmaker's claws close to its oily reptilian[4] chest. Each lower leg was a piston, a thousand pounds of white bone, sunk in thick ropes of muscle, sheathed over in a gleam of pebbled skin like the

---

4. *Reptilian* (rep til′ē ən) means "of or like a reptile."

Vocabulary

resilient (ri zil′ yənt) *adj.* capable of springing back into shape or position after being bent, stretched, or compressed

RAY BRADBURY

Visual Vocabulary
Mail is a flexible body armor made of small, overlapping or interlinked metal plates or rings.

mail of a terrible warrior. Each thigh was a ton of meat, ivory, and steel mesh. And from the great breathing cage of the upper body those two delicate arms dangled out front, arms with hands which might pick up and examine men like toys, while the snake neck coiled. And the head itself, a ton of sculptured stone, lifted easily upon the sky. Its mouth gaped, exposing a fence of teeth like daggers. Its eyes rolled, ostrich eggs, empty of all expression save hunger. It closed its mouth in a death grin. It ran, its pelvic bones crushing aside trees and bushes, its taloned feet clawing damp earth, leaving prints six inches deep wherever it settled its weight. It ran with a gliding ballet step, far too poised and balanced for its ten tons. It moved into a sunlit arena warily, its beautifully reptilian hands feeling the air.

"Why, why," Eckels twitched his mouth. "It could reach up and grab the moon."

"Sh!" Travis jerked angrily. "He hasn't seen us yet."

"It can't be killed." Eckels pronounced this verdict quietly, as if there could be no argument. He had weighed the evidence and this was his considered opinion. The rifle in his hands seemed a cap gun. "We were fools to come. This is impossible."

"Shut up!" hissed Travis.

"Nightmare."

"Turn around," commanded Travis. "Walk quietly to the Machine. We'll remit one half your fee."

The Extraordinary and Fantastic What has Eckels just realized?

"I didn't realize it would be this *big*," said Eckels. "I miscalculated, that's all. And now I want out."

"It *sees* us!"

"There's the red paint on its chest!"

The Tyrant Lizard raised itself. Its armored flesh glittered like a thousand green coins. The coins, crusted with slime, steamed. In the slime, tiny insects wriggled, so that the entire body seemed to twitch and undulate,[5] even while the monster itself did not move. It exhaled. The stink of raw flesh blew down the wilderness.

"Get me out of here," said Eckels. "It was never like this before. I was always sure I'd come through alive. I had good guides, good safaris, and safety. This time, I figured wrong. I've met my match and admit it. This is too much for me to get hold of."

"Don't run," said Lesperance. "Turn around. Hide in the Machine."

"Yes." Eckels seemed to be numb. He looked at his feet as if trying to make them move. He gave a grunt of helplessness.

"Eckels!"

He took a few steps, blinking, shuffling.

"Not *that* way!"

The Monster, at the first motion, lunged forward with a terrible scream. It covered one hundred yards in four seconds. The rifles jerked up and blazed fire. A windstorm from the beast's mouth engulfed them in the stench of slime and old blood. The Monster roared, teeth glittering with sun.

Eckels, not looking back, walked blindly to the edge of the Path, his gun limp in his arms, stepped off the Path, and walked, not knowing it, in the jungle. His feet sank into green moss. His legs moved him, and he felt alone and remote from the events behind.

---

5. *Undulate* (un´jə lāt´) means "to move like a wave."

Foreshadowing Which of Eckels's earlier questions foreshadows his action here?

The rifles cracked again. Their sound was lost in shriek and lizard thunder. The great level of the reptile's tail swung up, lashed sideways. Trees exploded in clouds of leaf and branch. The Monster twitched its jeweler's hands down to fondle at the men, to twist them in half, to crush them like berries, to cram them into its teeth and its screaming throat. Its boulder-stone eyes leveled with the men. They saw themselves mirrored. They fired at the metallic eyelids and the blazing black iris.

Like a stone idol, like a mountain avalanche, *Tyrannosaurus* fell. Thundering, it clutched trees, pulled them with it. It wrenched and tore the metal Path. The men flung themselves back and away. The body hit, ten tons of cold flesh and stone. The guns fired. The Monster lashed its armored tail, twitched its snake jaws, and lay still. A fount of blood spurted from its throat. Somewhere inside, a sac of fluids burst. Sickening gushes drenched the hunters. They stood, red and glistening.

The thunder faded.

The jungle was silent. After the avalanche, a green peace. After the nightmare, morning.

Billings and Kramer sat on the pathway and threw up. Travis and Lesperance stood with smoking rifles, cursing steadily.

In the Time Machine, on his face, Eckels lay shivering. He had found his way back to the Path, climbed into the Machine.

Travis came walking, glanced at Eckels, took cotton gauze from a metal box, and returned to the others, who were sitting on the Path.

"Clean up."

They wiped the blood from their helmets. They began to curse too. The Monster lay, a hill of solid flesh. Within, you could hear the sighs and murmurs as the furthest chambers of it died, the organs malfunctioning, liquids running a final instant from pocket to sac to spleen, everything shutting off, closing up forever. It was like standing by a wrecked locomotive or a steam shovel at quitting time, all valves being released or levered tight. Bones cracked; the tonnage of its own

Brachiosaurus. English School, 20th century. Oil on canvas. Natural History Museum, London.

View the Art Unlike the tyrannosaurus, the brachiosaurus was an herbivore and ate only plants. Do you think Eckels would have had a different reaction if he had encountered a brachiosaurus? Why or why not?

flesh, off balance, dead weight, snapped the delicate forearms, caught underneath. The meat settled, quivering.

Another cracking sound. Overhead, a gigantic tree branch broke from its heavy mooring, fell. It crashed upon the dead beast with finality.

"There." Lesperance checked his watch. "Right on time. That's the giant tree that was scheduled to fall and kill this animal originally." He glanced at the two hunters. "You want the trophy picture?"

"What?"

"We can't take a trophy back to the Future. The body has to stay right here where it would have died originally, so the insects, birds, and bacteria can get at it, as they were intended to. Everything in balance. The body stays. But we *can* take a picture of you standing near it."

The two men tried to think, but gave up, shaking their heads.

They let themselves be led along the metal Path. They sank wearily into the Machine cushions. They gazed back at the ruined Monster, the stagnating mound, where already strange reptilian birds and golden insects were busy at the steaming armor.

A sound on the floor of the Time Machine stiffened them. Eckels sat there, shivering.

"I'm sorry," he said at last.

"Get up!" cried Travis.

Eckels got up.

"Go out on that Path alone," said Travis. He had his rifle pointed. "You're not coming back in the Machine. We're leaving you here!"

Lesperance seized Travis' arm. "Wait—"

"Stay out of this!" Travis shook his hand away. "This fool nearly killed us. But it isn't *that* so much, no. It's his *shoes*! Look at them! He ran off the Path. That *ruins* us! We'll forfeit! Thousands of dollars of insurance! We guarantee no one leaves the Path. He left it. Oh, the fool! I'll have to report to the government. They might revoke[6] our license to travel. Who knows what he's done to Time, to History!"

"Take it easy, all he did was kick up some dirt."

"How do we *know*?" cried Travis. "We don't know anything! It's all a mystery! Get out there, Eckels!"

Eckels fumbled his shirt. "I'll pay anything. A hundred thousand dollars!"

Travis glared at Eckels' checkbook and spat. "Go out there. The Monster's next to the Path. Stick your arms up to your elbows in his mouth. Then you can come back with us."

"That's unreasonable!"

"The Monster's dead, you idiot. The bullets! The bullets can't be left behind. They don't belong in the Past; they might change anything. Here's my knife. Dig them out!"

The jungle was alive again, full of the old tremorings and bird cries. Eckels turned slowly to regard the **primeval** garbage dump, that hill of nightmares and terror. After a long time, like a sleepwalker, he shuffled out along the Path.

He returned, shuddering, five minutes later, his arms soaked and red to the elbows. He held out his hands. Each held a number of steel bullets. Then he fell. He lay where he fell, not moving.

"You didn't have to make him do that," said Lesperance.

"Didn't I? It's too early to tell."

Travis nudged the still body. "He'll live. Next

---

6. *Revoke* means "to cancel or withdraw."

Identify Genre What conflict is described here? How does it define a characteristic of this genre?

Vocabulary

primeval (prī mē´ vəl) *adj.* of or having to do with the first or earliest age; primitive

Brachiosaurus. Zdenek Burian (1905–1981).

time he won't go hunting game like this. Okay." He jerked his thumb wearily at Lesperance. "Switch on. Let's go home."

1492. 1776. 1812.

They cleaned their hands and faces. They changed their caking shirts and pants. Eckels was up and around again, not speaking. Travis glared at him for a full ten minutes.

"Don't look at me," cried Eckels. "I haven't done anything."

"Who can tell?"

Foreshadowing What might this statement foreshadow?

"Just ran off the Path, that's all, a little mud on my shoes—what do you want me to do—get down and pray?"

"We might need it. I'm warning you, Eckels, I might kill you yet. I've got my gun ready."

"I'm innocent. I've done nothing."

1999. 2000. 2055.

The Machine stopped.

"Get out," said Travis.

The room was there as they had left it. But not the same as they had left it. The same man sat behind the same desk. But the same man did not quite sit behind the same desk.

Travis looked around swiftly. "Everything okay here?" he snapped.

"Fine. Welcome home!"

Travis did not relax. He seemed to be looking at the very atoms of the air itself, at the way the sun poured through the one high window.

"Okay, Eckels, get out. Don't ever come back."

Eckels could not move. "You heard me," said Travis. "What're you *staring* at?"

Eckels stood smelling of the air, and there was a thing to the air, a chemical taint[7] so subtle, so slight, that only a faint cry of his subliminal[8] senses warned him it was there. The colors, white, gray, blue, orange, in the wall, in the furniture, in the sky beyond the window, were . . . were . . . And there was a *feel*. His flesh twitched. His hands twitched. He stood drinking the oddness with the pores of his body. Somewhere, someone must have been screaming one of those whistles that only a dog can hear. His body screamed silence in return. Beyond this room, beyond this wall, beyond this man who was not quite the same man seated at this desk that was not quite the same desk . . . lay an entire world of streets and people. What sort of world it was now, there was no telling. He could feel them moving there, beyond the walls, almost, like so many chess pieces blown in a dry wind. . .

But the immediate thing was the sign painted on the office wall, the same sign he had read earlier today on first entering.

Somehow, the sign had changed:

---

7. A *taint* is a trace of something that harms or spoils.
8. *Subliminal* (sub lim′ ə nəl) means "existing below the limits of sensation or consciousness; subconscious."

The Extraordinary and Fantastic *In what ways are the details in this passage extraordinary or fantastic?*

TYME SEFARI INC.
SEFARIS TU ANY YEER EN THE PAST.
YU NAIM THE ANIMALL.
WEE TAEKYUTHAIR.
YU SHOOT ITT.

Eckels felt himself fall into a chair. He fumbled crazily at the thick slime on his boots. He held up a clod of dirt, trembling, "No, it *can't* be. Not a *little* thing like that. No!"

Embedded in the mud, glistening green and gold and black, was a butterfly, very beautiful and very dead.

"Not a little thing like *that*! Not a butterfly!" cried Eckels.

It fell to the floor, an exquisite thing, a small thing that could upset balances and knock down a line of small dominoes and then big dominoes and then gigantic dominoes, all down the years across Time. Eckels' mind whirled. It *couldn't* change things. Killing one butterfly couldn't be *that* important! Could it?

His face was cold. His mouth trembled, asking: "Who— Who won the presidential election yesterday?"

The man behind the desk laughed. "You joking? You know very well. Deutscher, of course! Who else? Not that fool weakling Keith. We got an iron man now, a man with guts!" The official stopped. "What's wrong?"

Eckels moaned. He dropped to his knees. He scrabbled at the golden butterfly with shaking fingers. "Can't we," he pleaded to the world, to himself, to the officials, to the Machine, "can't we take it *back*, can't we *make* it alive again? Can't we start over? Can't we—"

He did not move. Eyes shut, he waited, shivering. He heard Travis breathe loud in the room; he heard Travis shift his rifle, click the safety catch, and raise the weapon.

There was a sound of thunder.

Foreshadowing *Why does Bradbury allow the reader to infer what happens at the end of the story?*

After You Read

Respond and Think Critically

Respond and Interpret

1. What was your reaction to the story's outcome?

2. What feelings does Eckels experience during his first journey in the Machine? Explain.

3. (a) What do the men discover when they return from their trip? (b) Why do you think Eckels and Travis are so dismayed by the changes?

Analyze and Evaluate

4. Within the fictional world that Bradbury has created, do events seem to occur in a logical, predictable way? Cite examples from the story.

5. Identify at least three metaphors the author uses to describe the *Tyrannosaurus rex*. What two things are being compared in each metaphor?

Connect

6. **Big Idea** **The Extraordinary and Fantastic** Consider the repercussions of a very small change in prehistoric time, as described in the story. What might be the repercussions of that change?

7. **Connect to Today** If it were possible to travel to the past in order to change an event that could affect today's world, what might you want to change? Why?

Primary Source Quotation

The Butterfly Effect

This excerpt from a newspaper editorial describes the possible influence of Ray Bradbury's story on the expression *butterfly effect*.

> A conjecture made to the New York Academy of Sciences in 1963 by meteorologist Edward Lorenz eventually spawned the popular term "butterfly effect." Lorenz suggested that the atmospheric disturbance caused by flapping wings could eventually amplify into a catastrophic event worthy of a Weather Channel special. . . . Chaos theory says that any system, simple or complex, has an elemental order that will react in unpredictable ways when subjected to simple events. . . . Ray Bradbury published the sci-fi story "A Sound of Thunder," in which a man named Eckels travels back to the Jurassic period. . . .
>
> Upon returning to his future, Eckels finds that everything has changed. He's horrified when he examines primordial goo on his boots: 'Embedded in the mud . . . was a butterfly, very beautiful and very dead. . . .' Ray Bradbury published his story 11 years before Lorenz's [example] flapped into existence.
>
> —Bob Saar, The Hawkeye, from "The Butterfly Effect"

1. Explain the butterfly effect in your own words.

2. Why might the story "A Sound of Thunder" have had such a lasting effect on our culture?

RAY BRADBURY **1037**

Literary Element Foreshadowing

Bradbury uses **foreshadowing** throughout "A Sound of Thunder" to prepare the reader for the eventual outcome of the story. Foreshadowing helps to build suspense in the reader by hinting at events to come.

1. What clues help prepare you for the way Eckels behaves in a crisis?

2. Reread the last section of the story beginning with the words "1492. 1776. 1812" (page 1035). Identify two clues that foreshadow the outcome of the story.

Review: Description

As you learned on pages 1022–1023, **description** is a detailed portrayal of a person, a place, an object, or an action.

Partner Activity With a classmate, discuss Bradbury's use of description. Working together, choose a particularly vivid character, object, or scene from the story and depict it in a poster, collage, or painting. You may want to brainstorm details about your subject before you begin creating your depiction. Use a web like the one below to keep track of descriptive details.

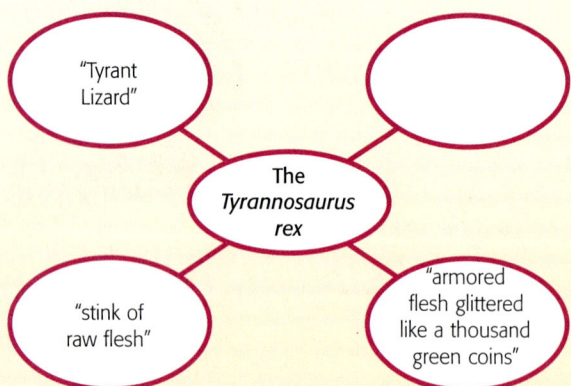

Reading Strategy Identify Genre

Different **genres**—or types of literature—are created for different purposes. Properly categorizing a work can help you develop conclusions about the meaning of the work and the author's message.

1. What is the overall purpose or message of "A Sound of Thunder"? Explain.

2. How does this message help you categorize the story?

3. What other characteristics helped you to categorize the story? Explain your answer.

Vocabulary Practice

Practice with Analogies Choose the word that best completes each analogy.

1. dependable : reliable :: expendable :
   a. unnecessary b. needful
   c. imperceptible

2. monitor : symptom :: correlate :
   a. interaction b. illness c. data

3. paradigm : model :: paradox :
   a. reason b. opinion c. contradiction

4. permanent : sustain :: resilient :
   a. recover b. retract c. rely

5. contemporary : computer :: primeval :
   a. information age b. stone tool
   c. prime number

 **Literature** Online

Selection Resources For Selection Quizzes, eFlashcards, and Reading-Writing Connection activities, go to glencoe.com and enter QuickPass code GL59794u6.

Respond Through Writing

Review

Convince an Audience Imagine you are a science fiction buff telling other science fiction fans about "A Sound of Thunder." How would you rate the story? How well do you think it conveys the paradoxes of time travel? Write a review of the story that you might post on a Web site for fans of classic science fiction.

Prewrite Review the characteristics of science fiction on page 1016. Then create a three-column chart in which you outline characteristics, examples of them from the story, and your evaluation of how well they are realized in the story. Use your chart to help you plan your essay.

I. Introduction	II. Body Paragraphs	III. Conclusion
A. Audience: grab audience's attention by _____	A. Characteristic of classic sci-fi in the story: _____	A. Purpose: my recommendation: _____
B. Purpose: present thesis stating my overall evaluation/controlling idea: _____	B. Evidence/example from story: _____	B. Audience: a memorable final thought: _____
	C. My evaluation: _____	

Draft As you draft, remember that you are trying to convince an audience. Use persuasive techniques such as appeals to logic and emotion, rhetorical questions, hyperbole, and repetition. Entice and convince your audience with well-chosen quotations from the story. Also, anticipate the audience's potential disagreements with your argument by refuting counterclaims and fully explaining your own viewpoints.

Revise As you revise, focus on the logical structure of your ideas. Be sure your evaluation of each science fiction characteristic follows logically from the evidence you have provided, and that your overall evaluation reflects the content of your body paragraphs. Use the checklist on page 874 to assess and revise other aspects of your essay.

Edit and Proofread Proofread your paper, correcting any errors in grammar, spelling, and punctuation. Use the Grammar Tip in the side column to help you with the use of italics (or underlining).

Learning Objectives

In this assignment, you will focus on the following objectives:

Writing: Writing a review.

Grammar: Understanding how to use comparative adverbs.

Grammar Tip

Italics

You should italicize (or underline if you are not using a computer) words you refer to as words. If a sentence is already in italics, then remove the italics from the word. For more about using italics, see page R55.

The word *clairvoyant* comes to mind when discussing Ray Bradbury.

Also italicize (or underline) scientific or species names.

Was Tyrannosaurus rex *the most fearsome dinosaur to ever live?*

Before You Read

By the Waters of Babylon

Meet Stephen Vincent Benét
(1898–1943)

Themes of history and war march through the works of Stephen Vincent Benét, who was born in Bethlehem, Pennsylvania, into a military family.

Benét spent his childhood on army posts in California and attended school at a military academy. Benét's first book of poems, *Five Men and Pompey*, was published in 1915 when he was just seventeen years old and a student at Yale University. His studies were interrupted by a year of government service during World War I, when he worked in the same department as writer James Thurber. For his master's degree thesis, Benét submitted a volume of poems entitled *Heavens and Earth* (1920).

> "Books are not men and yet they stay alive."
> —Stephen Vincent Benét

A Literary Career Benét then turned to fiction, publishing the autobiographical novel *The Beginning of Wisdom* in 1921. He moved to France to continue his studies at the Sorbonne, where he met his wife, writer Rosemary Carr.

While living in France, Benét wrote the epic Civil War poem *John Brown's Body* (1928). The poem achieved immediate critical and popular acclaim, and Benét won the Pulitzer Prize for the book in 1929. That same year, he was elected to the National Institute of Arts and Letters.

Benét also was interested in horror, mystery, and science fiction. In 1937 he published a one-act play entitled *The Headless Horseman*, based on the Washington Irving story "The Legend of Sleepy Hollow." That same year, Benét published the short story collection *Thirteen O'Clock*, which included his famous story "The Devil and Daniel Webster." Based on the German legend of Faust, it features a man who sells his soul to the devil. It was adapted as a play, an opera, and two movies.

During the 1940s, Benét worked in radio and as a screenwriter in Hollywood. Throughout his life, he suffered from poor vision and other illnesses but continued to publish and earn honors as a writer, receiving the O. Henry Story Prize and the Roosevelt Medal. Benét was awarded a second Pulitzer Prize posthumously for his epic poem *Western Star*.

 **Literature** Online

Author Search For more about Stephen Vincent Benét, go to glencoe.com and enter QuickPass code GL59794u6.

Literature and Reading Preview

Connect to the Story
How do you know when you become an adult? Discuss this question with a partner.

Build Background
Many readers and critics have interpreted this story as an allegory about the aftermath of a nuclear holocaust. Although this story was written in 1937, years before the first atomic weapons were developed, our knowledge of the devastation caused by nuclear bombings makes the scenes depicted in Benét's tale all the more affecting.

Set Purposes for Reading

Big Idea   The Extraordinary and Fantastic
As you read, ask yourself, How is Benét's main character awed and amazed by the places he visits?

Literary Element   Moral
A **moral** is a practical lesson about right and wrong. Some modern stories, especially science fiction stories, use these straightforward messages. As you read, ask yourself, What is the moral of this story?

Reading Strategy   Visualize
Visualizing means using an author's words to form a mental picture of what is being described. Visualizing allows you to enter a story's world and better understand the action taking place. As you read, ask yourself, What do I see in each scene?

Tip: Note Descriptive Words   Practice visualizing by paying careful attention to the descriptive words the author uses. Use a chart like the one below to record what you visualize in each paragraph.

Paragraph	Visualization
"Yet, after a while, my eyes were opened and I saw."	I picture the ruins of road bridges crossing over a river.
"It felt like ground underfoot; it did not burn me."	The narrator is describing the ruins of a big city.

Learning Objectives
For pages 1040–1056

In studying this text, you will focus on the following objectives:

Literary Study: Analyzing moral.

Reading: Visualizing.

Vocabulary

bade (bād) *v.* past tense of bid, to command, order, or ask; p. 1043 *The babysitter bade the two naughty children to stop running in the house.*

anteroom (an′ tē room′) *n.* a small room serving as a waiting area or an entrance to a larger main room; p. 1049 *My grandmother always greeted her guests in the anteroom.*

perplexed (pər plekst′) *adj.* troubled with doubt or uncertainty; puzzled; p. 1052 *I felt perplexed by the complicated math formula.*

Tip: Word Usage   Reserve formal usage, such as the word *bade*, for formal occasions, such as a speech or paper; reserve informal usage, such as *asked*, for conversation or friendly e-mail.

A Pyramid of Skulls, 1898–1900. Paul Cézanne. Oil on canvas. Private collection.

By the Waters of Babylon

Stephen Vincent Benét

The north and the west and the south are good hunting ground, but it is forbidden to go east. It is forbidden to go to any of the Dead Places except to search for metal and then he who touches the metal must be a priest or the son of a priest. Afterwards, both the man and the metal must be purified.[1] These are the rules and the laws; they are well made. It is forbidden to cross the great river and look upon the place that was the Place of the Gods—this is most strictly forbidden. We do not even say its name though we know its name. It is there that spirits live, and demons—it is there that there are the ashes of the Great Burning. These things are forbidden—they have been forbidden since the beginning of time.

My father is a priest; I am the son of a priest. I have been in the Dead Places near us, with my father—at first, I was afraid.

---

1. *Purification* refers to the process of cleansing one's body to rid it of impurities. Here, the word has the additional meaning of detoxifying or removing any harmful contaminants from the metal.

Moral *What does this opening paragraph suggest about the morals of the people who live in this unidentified place?*

When my father went into the house to search for the metal, I stood by the door and my heart felt small and weak. It was a dead man's house, a spirit house. It did not have the smell of man, though there were old bones in a corner. But it is not fitting that a priest's son should show fear. I looked at the bones in the shadow and kept my voice still.

Then my father came out with the metal—a good, strong piece. He looked at me with both eyes but I had not run away. He gave me the metal to hold—I took it and did not die. So he knew that I was truly his son and would be a priest in my time. That was when I was very young—nevertheless, my brothers would not have done it, though they are good hunters. After that, they gave me the good piece of meat and the warm corner by the fire. My father watched over me—he was glad that I should be a priest. But when I boasted or wept without a reason, he punished me more strictly than my brothers. That was right.

After a time, I myself was allowed to go into the dead houses and search for metal. So I learned the ways of those houses—and if I saw bones, I was no longer afraid. The bones are light and old—sometimes they will fall into dust if you touch them. But that is a great sin.

I was taught the chants and the spells—I was taught how to stop the running of blood from a wound and many secrets. A priest must know many secrets—that was what my father said. If the hunters think we do all things by chants and spells, they may believe so—it does not hurt them. I was taught how to read in the old books and how to make the old writings—that was hard and took a long time. My knowledge made me happy—it was like a fire in my heart. Most of all, I liked to hear of the Old Days and the stories of the gods. I asked myself many questions that I could not answer, but it was good to ask them. At night, I would lie awake and listen to the wind—it seemed to me that it was the voice of the gods as they flew through the air.

We are not ignorant like the Forest People—our women spin wool on the wheel, our priests wear a white robe. We do not eat grubs from the tree, we have not forgotten the old writings, although they are hard to understand. Nevertheless, my knowledge and my lack of knowledge burned in me—I wished to know more. When I was a man at last, I came to my father and said, "It is time for me to go on my journey. Give me your leave."

Visual Vocabulary
A *grub* is the soft, wormlike larva of an insect, especially of a beetle.

He looked at me for a long time, stroking his beard, then he said at last, "Yes. It is time." That night, in the house of the priesthood, I asked for and received purification. My body hurt but my spirit was a cool stone. It was my father himself who questioned me about my dreams.

He **bade** me look into the smoke of the fire and see—I saw and told what I saw. It was what I have always seen—a river, and, beyond it, a great Dead Place and in it the gods walking. I have always thought about that. His eyes were stern when I told him—he was no longer my father but a priest. He said, "This is a strong dream."

"It is mine," I said, while the smoke waved and my head felt light. They were

---

Visualize What image of the narrator does this metaphor communicate?

Vocabulary

bade (bād) *v.* past tense of bid, to command, order, or ask

Where Eagles Dare! James Noel Smith.

singing the Star song in the outer chamber and it was like the buzzing of bees in my head.

He asked me how the gods were dressed and I told him how they were dressed. We know how they were dressed from the book, but I saw them as if they were before me. When I had finished, he threw the sticks three times and studied them as they fell.

"This is a very strong dream," he said. "It may eat you up."

"I am not afraid," I said and looked at him with both eyes. My voice sounded thin in my ears but that was because of the smoke.

He touched me on the breast and the forehead. He gave me the bow and the three arrows.

"Take them," he said. "It is forbidden to travel east. It is forbidden to cross the river. It is forbidden to go to the Place of the Gods. All these things are forbidden."

"All these things are forbidden," I said, but it was my voice that spoke and not my spirit. He looked at me again.

"My son," he said. "Once I had young dreams. If your dreams do not eat you up, you may be a great priest. If they eat

The Extraordinary and Fantastic What does John's father imply by this statement?

Moral What moral might be contained in these words?

you, you are still my son. Now go on your journey."

I went fasting,[2] as is the law. My body hurt but not my heart. When the dawn came, I was out of sight of the village. I prayed and purified myself, waiting for a sign. The sign was an eagle. It flew east.

Sometimes signs are sent by bad spirits. I waited again on the flat rock, fasting, taking no food. I was very still—I could feel the sky above me and the earth beneath. I waited till the sun was beginning to sink. Then three deer passed in the valley, going east—they did not wind me or see me. There was a white fawn with them—a very great sign.

I followed them, at a distance, waiting for what would happen. My heart was troubled about going east, yet I knew that I must go. My head hummed with my fasting—I did not even see the panther spring upon the white fawn. But, before I knew it, the bow was in my hand. I shouted and the panther lifted his head from the fawn. It is not easy to kill a panther with one arrow but the arrow went through his eye and into his brain. He died as he tried to spring—he rolled over, tearing at the ground. Then I knew I was meant to go east—I knew that was my journey. When the night came, I made my fire and roasted meat.

It is eight suns' journey to the east and a man passes by many Dead Places. The Forest People are afraid of them but I am not. Once I made my fire on the edge of a Dead Place at night and, next morning, in the dead house, I found a good knife, little rusted. That was small to what came afterward but it made my heart feel big. Always when I looked for game, it was in front of my arrow, and twice I passed hunting parties of the Forest People without their knowing. So I knew my magic was strong and my journey clean, in spite of the law.

Toward the setting of the eighth sun, I came to the banks of the great river. It was half-a-day's journey after I had left the god-road—we do not use the god-roads now for they are falling apart into great blocks of stone, and the forest is safer going. A long way off, I had seen the water through trees but the trees were thick. At last, I came out upon an open place at the top of a cliff. There was the great river below, like a giant in the sun. It is very long, very wide. It could eat all the streams we know and still be thirsty. Its name is Ou-dis-sun, the Sacred, the Long. No man of my tribe had seen it, not even my father, the priest. It was magic and I prayed.

Then I raised my eyes and looked south. It was there, the Place of the Gods.

How can I tell what it was like—you do not know. It was there, in the red light, and they were too big to be houses. It was there with the red light upon it, mighty and ruined. I knew that in another moment the gods would see me. I covered my eyes with my hands and crept back into the forest.

Surely, that was enough to do, and live. Surely it was enough to spend the night upon the cliff. The Forest People themselves do not come near. Yet, all through the night, I knew that I should have to cross the river and walk in the places of the gods, although the gods ate me up. My magic did not help me at all and yet there was a fire in my bowels, a fire in my mind. When the sun rose, I thought, "My journey has been clean. Now I will go home from my journey." But, even as I thought so, I knew I could not. If I went to the Place of

---

2. *Fasting* is the process of not eating, often in preparation for a religious ritual.

The Extraordinary and Fantastic What elements of the fantastic are in this passage?

the Gods, I would surely die, but, if I did not go, I could never be at peace with my spirit again. It is better to lose one's life than one's spirit, if one is a priest and the son of a priest.

Nevertheless, as I made the raft, the tears ran out of my eyes. The Forest People could have killed me without fight, if they had come upon me then, but they did not come. When the raft was made, I said the sayings for the dead and painted myself for death. My heart was cold as a frog and my knees like water, but the burning in my mind would not let me have peace. As I pushed the raft from the shore, I began my death song—I had the right. It was a fine song.

> "I am John, son of John," I sang. "My people are the Hill People. They are the men.
> I go into the Dead Places but I am not slain. I take the metal from the Dead Places but I am not blasted.
> I travel upon the god-roads and am not afraid. E-yah! I have killed the panther, I have killed the fawn!
> E-yah! I have come to the great river. No man has come there before.
> It is forbidden to go east, but I have gone, forbidden to go on the great river, but I am there.
> Open your hearts, you spirits, and hear my song.
> Now I go to the Place of the Gods, I shall not return.
> My body is painted for death and my limbs weak, but my heart is big as I go to the Place of the Gods!"

All the same, when I came to the Place of the Gods, I was afraid, afraid. The current of the great river is very strong—it gripped my raft with its hands. That was magic, for the river itself is wide and calm. I could feel evil spirits about me, in the bright morning; I could feel their breath on my neck as I was swept down the stream. Never have I been so much alone—I tried to think of my knowledge, but it was a squirrel's heap of winter nuts. There was no strength in my knowledge any more, and I felt small and naked as a new-hatched bird—alone upon the great river, the servant of the gods.

Yet, after a while, my eyes were opened and I saw. I saw both banks of the river—I saw that once there had been god-roads across it, though now they were broken and fallen like broken vines. Very great they were, and wonderful and broken—broken in the time of the Great Burning when the fire fell out of the sky. And always the current took me nearer to the Place of the Gods, and the huge ruins rose before my eyes.

I do not know the customs of rivers—we are the People of the Hills. I tried to guide my raft with the pole but it spun around. I thought the river meant to take me past the Place of the Gods and out into the Bitter Water of the legends. I grew angry then—my heart felt strong. I said aloud, "I am a priest and the son of a priest!" The gods heard me—they showed me how to paddle with the pole on one side of the raft. The current changed itself—I drew near to the Place of the Gods.

When I was very near, my raft struck and turned over. I can swim in our

---

Moral What moral does this statement communicate? Do you agree with it? Explain.

Visualize Explain in your own words what John describes.

lakes—I swam to the shore. There was a great spike of rusted metal sticking out into the river—I hauled myself up upon it and sat there, panting. I had saved my bow and two arrows and the knife I found in the Dead Place but that was all. My raft went whirling downstream toward the Bitter Water. I looked after it, and thought if it had trod me under, at least I would be safely dead. Nevertheless, when I had dried my bowstring and restrung it, I walked forward to the Place of the Gods.

It felt like ground underfoot; it did not burn me. It is not true what some of the tales say, that the ground there burns forever, for I have been there. Here and there were the marks and stains of the Great Burning, on the ruins, that is true. But they were old marks and old stains. It is not true either, what some of our priests say, that it is an island covered with fogs and enchantments. It is not. It is a great Dead Place—greater than any Dead Place we know. Everywhere in it there are god-roads, though most are cracked and broken. Everywhere there are the ruins of the high towers of the gods.

How shall I tell what I saw? I went carefully, my strung bow in my hand, my skin ready for danger. There should have been the wailings of spirits and the shrieks of demons, but there were not. It was very silent and sunny where I had landed—the wind and the rain and the birds that drop seeds had done their work—the grass grew in the cracks of the broken stone. It is a fair island—no wonder the gods built there. If I had come there, a god, I also would have built.

"I felt small and naked as a new-hatched bird--"

How shall I tell what I saw? The towers are not all broken—here and there one still stands, like a great tree in a forest, and the birds nest high. But the towers themselves look blind, for the gods are gone. I saw a fish hawk, catching fish in the river. I saw a little dance of white butterflies over a great heap of broken stones and columns. I went there and looked about me—there was a carved stone with cut-letters, broken in half. I can read letters but I could not understand these. They said UBTREAS. There was also the shattered image of a man or a god. It had been made of white stone and he wore his hair tied back like a woman's. His name was ASHING, as I read on the cracked half of a stone. I thought it wise to pray to ASHING, though I do not know that god.

How shall I tell what I saw? There was no smell of man left, on stone or metal. Nor were there many trees in that wilderness of stone. There are many pigeons, nesting and dropping in the towers—the gods must have loved them, or, perhaps, they used them for sacrifices. There are wild cats that roam the god-roads, green-eyed, unafraid of man. At night they wail like demons but they are not demons. The wild dogs are more dangerous, for they hunt in a pack, but them I did not meet till later. Everywhere there

---

The Extraordinary and Fantastic *What does John think is extraordinary about this place? What do you think is extraordinary?*

Visualize *Images are descriptions that appeal to one or more of the five senses. Visualize the animals in the Dead Place. To which senses do these images appeal?*

Abismo. David Alfaro Siqueiros. Piroxyline on Masonite, 23⅝ x 27½ in. © Estate of David Alfaro Siqueiros/SOMAAP Mexico/Licensed by VAGA, NY.

View the Art What elements in this painting remind you of the setting of the story?

are the carved stones, carved with magical numbers or words.

I went north—I did not try to hide myself. When a god or a demon saw me, then I would die, but meanwhile I was no longer afraid. My hunger for knowledge burned in me—there was so much that I could not understand. After a while, I knew that my belly was hungry. I could have hunted for my meat, but I did not hunt. It is known that the gods did not hunt as we do—they got their food from enchanted boxes and jars. Sometimes these are still found in the Dead Places— once, when I was a child and foolish, I opened such a jar and tasted it and found the food sweet. But my father found out and punished me for it strictly, for, often, that food is death. Now, though, I had long gone past what was forbidden, and I

1048 UNIT 6 GENRE FICTION

entered the likeliest towers, looking for the food of the gods.

I found it at last in the ruins of a great temple in the mid-city. A mighty temple it must have been, for the roof was painted like the sky at night with its stars—that much I could see, though the colors were faint and dim. It went down into great caves and tunnels—perhaps they kept their slaves there. But when I started to climb down, I heard the squeaking of rats, so I did not go—rats are unclean, and there must have been many tribes of them, from the squeaking. But near there, I found food, in the heart of a ruin, behind a door that still opened. I ate only the fruits from the jars—they had a very sweet taste. There was drink, too, in bottles of glass—the drink of the gods was strong and made my head swim. After I had eaten and drunk, I slept on the top of a stone, my bow at my side.

When I woke, the sun was low. Looking down from where I lay, I saw a dog sitting on his haunches. His tongue was hanging out of his mouth; he looked as if he were laughing. He was a big dog, with a gray-brown coat, as big as a wolf. I sprang up and shouted at him but he did not move—he just sat there as if he were laughing. I did not like that. When I reached for a stone to throw, he moved swiftly out of the way of the stone. He was not afraid of me; he looked at me as if I were meat. No doubt I could have killed him with an arrow, but I did not know if there were others. Moreover, night was falling.

I looked about me—not far away there was a great, broken god-road, leading north. The towers were high enough, but not so high, and while many of the dead-houses were wrecked, there were some that stood. I went toward this god-road, keeping to the heights of the ruins, while the dog followed. When I had reached the god-road, I saw that there were others behind him. If I had slept later, they would have come upon me asleep and torn out my throat. As it was, they were sure enough of me; they did not hurry. When I went into the dead-house, they kept watch at the entrance—doubtless they thought they would have a fine hunt. But a dog cannot open a door and I knew, from the books, that the gods did not like to live on the ground but on high.

I had just found a door I could open when the dogs decided to rush. Ha! They were surprised when I shut the door in their faces—it was a good door, of strong metal. I could hear their foolish baying beyond it but I did not stop to answer them. I was in darkness—I found stairs and climbed. There were many stairs, turning around till my head was dizzy. At the top was another door—I found the knob and opened it. I was in a long small chamber—on one side of it was a bronze door that could not be opened, for it had no handle. Perhaps there was a magic word to open it but I did not have the word. I turned to the door in the opposite side of the wall. The lock of it was broken and I opened it and went in.

Within, there was a place of great riches. The god who lived there must have been a powerful god. The first room was a small **anteroom**—I waited there for some time, telling the spirits of the place that I came in peace and not as a robber. When it seemed to me that they had had time to hear me, I went on. Ah, what riches! Few, even, of the

---

The Extraordinary and Fantastic What type of building do you think John has entered? Why does he believe it was so important to the gods?

Vocabulary

anteroom (an′ tē room′) *n.* a small room serving as a waiting area or an entrance to a larger, main room

STEPHEN VINCENT BENÉT

August, 1982. Avigdor Arikha. Oil on canvas, 31¾ x 39¼ in. Marlborough Gallery, NY. Licensed by VAGA, NY.

View the Art Compare the view in this picture with what John imagined he saw when he looked out the window.

windows had been broken—it was all as it had been. The great windows that looked over the city had not been broken at all though they were dusty and streaked with many years. There were coverings on the floors, the colors not greatly faded, and the chairs were soft and deep. There were pictures upon the walls, very strange, very wonderful—I remember one of a bunch of flowers in a jar—if you came close to it, you could see nothing but bits of color, but if you stood away from it, the flowers might have been picked yesterday. It made my heart feel strange to look at this picture—and to look at the figure of a bird, in some hard clay, on a table and see it so like our birds. Everywhere there were books and writings, many in tongues that I could not read. The god who lived there must have been a wise god and full of knowledge. I felt I had right there, as I sought knowledge also.

Visualize What do you see when you visualize the pictures that John describes?

Nevertheless, it was strange. There was a washing-place but no water—perhaps the gods washed in air. There was a cooking-place but no wood, and though there was a machine to cook food, there was no place to put fire in it. Nor were there candles or lamps—there were things that looked like lamps but they had neither oil nor wick. All these things were magic, but I touched them and lived—the magic had gone out of them. Let me tell one thing to show. In the washing-place, a thing said "Hot" but it was not hot to the touch—another thing said "Cold" but it was not cold. This must have been a strong magic but the magic was gone. I do not understand—they had ways—I wish that I knew.

It was close and dry and dusty in their house of the gods. I have said the magic was gone but that is not true—it had gone from the magic things but it had not gone from the place. I felt the spirits about me, weighing upon me. Nor had I ever slept in a Dead Place before—and yet, tonight, I must sleep there. When I thought of it, my tongue felt dry in my throat, in spite of my wish for knowledge. Almost I would have gone down again and faced the dogs, but I did not.

I had not gone through all the rooms when the darkness fell. When it fell, I went back to the big room looking over the city and made fire. There was a place to make fire and a box with wood in it, though I do not think they cooked there. I wrapped myself in a floor-covering and slept in front of the fire—I was very tired.

Now I tell what is very strong magic. I woke in the midst of the night. When I woke, the fire had gone out and I was cold. It seemed to me that all around me there were whisperings and voices. I closed my eyes to shut them out. Some will say that I slept again, but I do not think that I slept. I could feel the spirits drawing my spirit out of my body as a fish is drawn on a line.

Why should I lie about it? I am a priest and the son of a priest. If there are spirits, as they say, in the small Dead Places near us, what spirits must there not be in that great Place of the Gods? And would not they wish to speak? After such long years? I know that I felt myself drawn as a fish is drawn on a line. I had stepped out of my body—I could see my body asleep in front of the cold fire, but it was not I. I was drawn to look out upon the city of the gods.

It should have been dark, for it was night, but it was not dark. Everywhere there were lights—lines of light—circles and blurs of light—ten thousand torches would not have been the same. The sky itself was alight—you could barely see the stars for the glow in the sky. I thought to myself "This is strong magic" and trembled. There was a roaring in my ears like the rushing of rivers. Then my eyes grew used to the light and my ears to the sound. I knew that I was seeing the city as it had been when the gods were alive.

That was a sight indeed—yes, that was a sight: I could not have seen it in the body—my body would have died. Everywhere went the gods, on foot and in chariots—there were gods beyond number and counting and their chariots blocked the streets. They had turned night to day for their pleasure—they did not sleep with the sun. The noise of their coming and going was the noise of many waters. It was magic what they could do—it was magic what they did.

I looked out of another window—the great vines of their bridges were mended

---

Visualize *What object does John observe?*

and the god-roads went east and west. Restless, restless, were the gods and always in motion! They burrowed tunnels under rivers—they flew in the air. With unbelievable tools they did giant works—no part of the earth was safe from them, for, if they wished for a thing, they summoned it from the other side of the world. And always, as they labored and rested, as they feasted and made love, there was a drum in their ears—the pulse of the giant city, beating and beating like a man's heart.

Were they happy? What is happiness to the gods? They were great, they were mighty, they were wonderful and terrible.

As I looked upon them and their magic, I felt like a child—but a little more, it seemed to me, and they would pull down the moon from the sky. I saw them with wisdom beyond wisdom and knowledge beyond knowledge. And yet not all they did was well done—even I could see that—and yet their wisdom could not but grow until all was peace.

Then I saw their fate come upon them and that was terrible past speech. It came upon them as they walked the streets of their city. I have been in the fights with the Forest People—I have seen men die. But this was not like that. When gods war with gods, they use weapons we do not know. It was fire falling out of the sky and a mist that poisoned. It was the time of the Great Burning and the Destruction. They ran about like ants in the streets of their city—poor gods, poor gods! Then the towers began to fall. A few escaped—yes, a few. The legends tell it. But, even after the city had become a Dead Place, for many years the poison was still in the ground. I saw it happen, I saw the last of them die. It was darkness over the broken city and I wept.

All this, I saw. I saw it as I have told it, though not in the body. When I woke in the morning, I was hungry, but I did not think first of my hunger for my heart was **perplexed** and confused. I knew the reason for the Dead Places but I did not see why it had happened. It seemed to me it should not have happened, with all the magic they had. I went through the house looking for an answer. There was so much in the house I could not understand—and yet I am a priest and the son of a priest. It was like being on one side of the great river, at night, with no light to show the way.

Then I saw the dead god. He was sitting in his chair, by the window, in a room I had not entered before and, for the first moment, I thought that he was alive. Then I saw the skin on the back of his hand—it was like dry leather. The room was shut, hot and dry—no doubt that had kept him as he was. At first I was afraid to approach him—then the fear left me. He was sitting looking out over the city—he was dressed in the clothes of the gods. His age was neither young nor old—I could not tell his age. But there was wisdom in his face and great sadness. You could see that he would have not run away. He had sat at his window, watching his city die—then he himself had died. But it is better to lose one's life than one's spirit—and you could see

---

The Extraordinary and Fantastic What is extraordinary about John's vision?

Moral What does this description of the gods tell you about the story's moral?

The Extraordinary and Fantastic What happened to the city and its people?

Vocabulary

perplexed (pər plekst′) adj. troubled with doubt or uncertainty; puzzled

from the face that his spirit had not been lost. I knew, that, if I touched him, he would fall into dust—and yet, there was something unconquered in the face.

That is all of my story, for then I knew he was a man—I knew then that they had been men, neither gods nor demons. It is a great knowledge, hard to tell and believe. They were men—they went a dark road, but they were men. I had no fear after that—I had no fear going home, though twice I fought off the dogs and once I was hunted for two days by the Forest People. When I saw my father again, I prayed and was purified. He touched my lips and my breast, he said,

"You went away a boy. You come back a man and a priest." I said, "Father, they were men! I have been in the Place of the Gods and seen it! Now slay me, if it is the law—but still I know they were men."

He looked at me out of both eyes. He said, "The law is not always the same shape—you have done what you have done. I could not have done it in my time, but you come after me. Tell!"

I told and he listened. After that, I wished to tell all the people but he showed me otherwise. He said, "Truth is a hard deer to hunt. If you eat too much truth at once, you may die of the truth. It was not idly that our fathers

---

Moral How does John's characterization of the man he finds help make the story's moral clear?

Moral What moral is John's father preaching in this statement? Do you agree with him? Explain

STEPHEN VINCENT BENÉT

Clytie, c. 1890–92. Frederic Leighton. Oil on canvas, 85.1 x 137.8 cm. Fitzwilliam Museum, University of Cambridge, UK.

View the Art What mood does this scene evoke? Is it similar to the mood evoked by this story? Explain.

forbade the Dead Places." He was right—it is better the truth should come little by little. I have learned that, being a priest. Perhaps, in the old days, they ate knowledge too fast.

Nevertheless, we make a beginning. It is not for the metal alone we go to the Dead Places now—there are the books and the writings. They are hard to learn. And the magic tools are broken—but we can look at them and wonder. At least, we make a beginning. And, when I am chief priest we shall go beyond the great river. We shall go to the Place of the Gods—the place newyork—not one man but a company. We shall look for the images of the gods and find the god ASHING and the others—the gods Lincoln and Biltmore[3] and Moses.[4] But they were men who built the city, not gods or demons. They were men. I remember the dead man's face. They were men who were here before us. We must build again.

---

3. The *Biltmore* is a famous hotel in New York City.
4. Robert *Moses* (1888–1981) was a New York state public official whose name appears on many bridges and other structures built during his administration.

After You Read

Respond and Think Critically

Respond and Interpret

1. Which line or passage in the story had the greatest impact on you? Why?

2. (a) Which event determines that John will one day be a priest? (b) In your opinion, does John consider his priestly calling a privilege or a burden? Explain.

3. (a) Where does John decide to travel? Why? (b) What internal conflict must John overcome before choosing a direction for his journey? Explain.

Analyze and Evaluate

4. (a) How does John's journey change him? (b) In your opinion, what long-term impact will his journey have on John's people?

5. Do you believe that John is being disrespectful by ignoring his father's advice and the law? Explain.

Connect

6. **Big Idea** **The Extraordinary and Fantastic** While in the Place of the Gods, John has an extraordinary vision of what it was once like, followed by a vision of its destruction. Do you think the author was making a cautionary statement about modern society through this story? Explain.

7. **Connect to the Author** How do you think Benét's military experiences might have affected his view of war, weapons, and destruction

---

Literary Element Moral

Although **morals** are usually found in fables or parables, modern stories—science fiction in particular—often present morals that warn of future catastrophic events.

1. Explain the moral of "By the Waters of Babylon."

2. In your opinion, what does the story reveal about the author's convictions about right and wrong and about his views of the conflicts between good and evil in the world?

Review: Archetypes

As you learned on pages 959 and 969, an **archetype** is an original model upon which other versions are based. An archetypal theme, plot, or character represents a universal element that applies to people across time and place. The archetypes found in "By the Waters of Babylon" would have been just as recognizable to the ancient Greeks as they are to modern readers.

The holocaust or post-apocalypse **theme archetype** found in "By the Waters of Babylon" involves superstition and ignorance about the past. The **plot pattern archetype** involves a young person experiencing a rite of passage. The **character archetype** is that of a naïve young hero who breaks the rules of his culture for the sake of knowledge. Benét's protagonist is a similar character archetype to J. K. Rowling's popular character Harry Potter.

Partner Activity With a classmate, discuss the archetypes described above. Make a list of stories, books, movies, legends, and other sources that contain similar themes, plots, and character archetypes. Discuss how the items on your list compare with the theme, plot, and character archetypes found in "By the Waters of Babylon."

Selection Resources For Selection Quizzes, eFlashcards, and Reading-Writing Connection Activities, go to glencoe.com and enter QuickPass code GL59794u6.

Reading Strategy: Visualize

When we read or listen, we form mental images of what the speaker or writer is describing. We create pictures in our minds automatically, even when we have never actually seen what is being described. This mental process is called **visualizing**. Benét uses many descriptive words and phrases that encourage readers to form mental images of the setting in his story, even though we have never actually seen it with our own eyes.

1. Read the following sentence from "By the Waters of Babylon," then close your eyes and imagine the scene: "I saw a little dance of white butterflies over a great heap of stone." After forming your mental image, write a few sentences describing how you imagine the scene.

2. Find another descriptive passage of your choice, form a mental image, and describe it.

Vocabulary Practice

Practice with Usage Respond to these statements to help you explore the meanings of vocabulary words from the selection.

1. Identify a possible who, what, where, when, and why for **bade**.
2. Name two actions you might perform in an **anteroom**.
3. Describe the look on the face of someone who is **perplexed**.

Academic Vocabulary

*John's motivation for his journey is **intrinsic**: an inner drive compels him to go forward.*

Intrinsic is an academic word. A more familiar synonym for *intrinsic* is *built-in*. What is an endeavor in which you have an intrinsic motivation? Name it and explain it in one or more complete sentences.

For more on academic vocabulary, see pages 52 and 53.

Speaking and Listening

Speech

Assignment Adopt the persona of John and make a speech in which you rebut your father's argument that truth is dangerous.

Prepare Reread and analyze John's inner thoughts, as well as his song, for rhetorical devices that characterize his style and voice. List examples and the devices they embody:

Example	Rhetorical Device
p. 1043, paragraph 4	• repetition ("I was taught") • dashes (used for dramatic pauses, for examples, and for amplification) • figure of speech (a fire in my heart helps make the idea memorable) • simple, concrete diction (*stop, know, hunters, hurt, books*)

Develop an engaging introduction, which might incorporate Thomas Henry Huxley's rhetorical question, "If a little knowledge is dangerous, where is the man who has so much as to be out of danger?" Use your body paragraphs to rebut John's father's argument. Use your conclusion to present your most persuasive reason or a final, memorable thought. Link your ideas with transitions.

Deliver Speak in John's confident voice and serious tone. Maintain good posture and make frequent eye contact to reflect his confidence.

Evaluate Evaluate your speech by writing examples of and rating how well you adopted John's persona, employed his characteristic rhetorical devices, organized your speech, and reflected his confidence through delivery techniques such as eye contact and posture. Use the checklist on page 1127 for help.

Grammar Workshop

Dangling Participles

Learning Objectives

In this workshop, you will focus on the following objective:

Grammar: Understanding how to avoid dangling participles.

Literature Connection In the quotation below, Stephen Vincent Benét uses a **participial phrase,** a phrase that contains a participle, to add a descriptive detail. The detail helps readers visualize the scene.

> "He looked at me for a long time, stroking his beard. . . ."
>
> —Stephen Vincent Benét, from "By the Waters of Babylon"

The phrase *stroking his beard* modifies the subject *he* in this sentence.

A participial phrase that has no **referent**—that modifies nothing—is a **dangling participle.** If a participial phrase is misplaced or dangling, it can create confusion and misunderstanding. For clear writing, you want to avoid these errors. Below are some solutions to correcting dangling participles. Often you have to add other words to complete the meaning of the sentence.

Dangling participle

Stooping down, the piece of metal was picked up.

Solution A Position the modifier next to a referent.

Stooping down, the boy picked up the piece of metal.

Solution B Change the dangling participle to a main or subordinate clause.

As he stooped down, the boy picked up the piece of metal.
The boy stooped down to pick up the piece of metal.

Participial Phrases

A **participial phrase** is a phrase that contains a verb participle. It is usually used to modify a word or a phrase in a sentence. A phrase that has no **referent,** the word to which the phrase refers, is called a **dangling participle.**

Tip

In a test, think about the meaning of the sentence. Then, make sure that any modifiers are located as close as possible to the word or words they describe.

Language Handbook

For more on participles, see the Language Handbook, page R43 and page R51.

Revise Rewrite the following sentences to correct four dangling participles.

1. Finding U.S. history intriguing, stories were written about it by Benét.
2. Sounding like the title, readers are reminded of a story in the Bible.
3. Reading on the bus, "By the Waters of Babylon" was fascinating.
4. Taking a necessary journey, the main character is confused and alone.
5. Writing, Benét's epic poem *Western Star* won the Pulitzer Prize.

Grammar For more grammar practice, go to **glencoe.com** and enter QuickPass code GL59794u6.

Comparing Literature
Across Genres

Compare Literature About Dreams and Reality

Our dreams often reflect experiences in our daily lives. Our daily experiences can be as haunting as our dreams. These three selections, which include a dream narrative, a poem about identity in the crowded darkness, and a poem about a dream, reveal fragments of both the inner and outer worlds of the narrator and speakers.

What I Have Been Doing Lately
by Jamaica Kincaid..short story 1059

People at Night by Denise Levertov..........................poem 1065

A Dream by Anna Akhmatova...poem 1067

Learning Objectives

For pages 1058–1069

In studying these texts, you will focus on the following objectives:

Literary Study: Analyzing stream of consciousness. Comparing literature across genres.

Reading: Interpreting imagery.

Writing: Writing a stream-of-consciousness essay.

COMPARE THE Big Idea The Extraordinary and Fantastic

The relationship between the real world and the dream world is both extraordinary and fantastic. The writers featured here all explore this divide and the ways in which the two worlds are related. Jamaica Kincaid's short story integrates both the real world and two distinct dreams to show the relationship between all three. Denise Levertov's poem uses the contrasts between night and day and the individual and society to describe what is unknown and imagined. Anna Akhmatova's poem relates "unearthly dreams" and questions whether they can foretell future events. As you read, ask yourself, How does each writer use imagery to evoke the extraordinary and fantastic?

COMPARE Description

A **description** is a detailed portrayal of a person, a place, an object, or an event. Each writer uses rich sensory details to re-create experiences and impressions. As you read, ask yourself, How do these details help you picture settings, events, and characters?

COMPARE Author's Culture

Each work is rooted in its author's culture: Kincaid infuses her dream setting with elements from her native island, Antigua; Levertov evokes the hectic culture of the city at night; and Akhmatova provides a glimpse into the culture of fear and loss that she once inhabited. As you read, ask yourself, What do these cultures have in common, and how are they different?

 **Literature** Online

Author Search For more about the authors, go to glencoe.com and enter QuickPass code GL59794u6.

1058 COMPARING LITERATURE

Comparing Literature

Before You Read

What I Have Been Doing Lately

World Literature
Antigua

Meet Jamaica Kincaid
(born 1949)

Troublemaker is how teachers used to describe Elaine Potter Richardson. Growing up on the tiny island of Antigua in the Caribbean was not easy. Richardson would later adopt the pen name *Jamaica Kincaid* and become famous for her poetic language, but at a young age her way with words often landed her in hot water. Precocious and rebellious, Kincaid had a rocky relationship with her mother, and she often escaped the confines of her life by stealing away to read books.

A Need to Escape As a child, Kincaid felt trapped. The sea that surrounded Antigua formed a geographic jail. Racism and conventional ways of thinking stifled her dreams. As she later commented, "In the place I'm from you don't have much room." At the age of seventeen, Kincaid left her island home to become an *au pair*, or nanny, in the United States. Within ten years of her departure, Kincaid managed to publish a few nonfiction articles in magazines. She changed her surname because her family disapproved of her writing. She later explained that she adopted the name *Jamaica*, subconsciously, as a way of re-creating a part of her past. Kincaid's work quickly drew the attention of William Shawn, a former editor of the *New Yorker*. She wrote an article for him, and soon she was a regular contributor, which ensured that her work would reach a wide audience.

Books About Home and Family Kincaid's first book was a short story collection called *At the Bottom of the River*. It includes "What I Have Been Doing Lately" and nine other stories.

Critics immediately recognized the author's fresh, new, and compelling voice in fiction. They admired Kincaid's style, which created poetry through repetition; her use of rich details; and her narrators' suspensions between dreams and reality.

> "For me, writing isn't a way of being public or private; it's just a way of being."
>
> —Jamaica Kincaid

A Writing Life Kincaid's second work of fiction, the novel *Annie John*, brought her wide popularity and ensured her literary reputation. In this work and in her second novel, *Lucy*, Kincaid explores the theme of family, especially a daughter's relationship to her mother.

 **Literature** Online

Author Search For more about Jamaica Kincaid, go to glencoe.com and enter QuickPass code GL59794u6.

Comparing Literature

Literature and Reading Preview

Connect to the Story
Have you ever had a dream that you felt contained a message or lesson? Write a journal entry that describes a meaningful dream.

Build Background
The setting of this story is a bizarre dreamland, but it does contain some realistic elements, such as cloudless skies, monkeys, and flowering trees, that are similar to those on the island of Antigua, where the author grew up.

Set Purposes for Reading

Big Idea The Extraordinary and Fantastic

As you read, ask yourself, What are some of the extraordinary and fantastic places people can experience in dreams?

Literary Element Stream of Consciousness

Stream of consciousness is the literary representation of a character's free-flowing thoughts, feelings, and memories. Emotions, impressions, images, and ideas—both rational and irrational—unfold on the page as they occur in the character's mind. As you read "What I Have Been Doing Lately," ask yourself, What are the free associations that identify the narrator's thoughts as stream of consciousness?

Reading Strategy Interpret Imagery

Interpreting imagery means looking carefully at sensory details, such as those that describe things the narrator sees and hears, and determining their importance in the story. As you read, ask yourself, What is the importance of the imagery in this story?

Tip: List Images As you read, list the images and interpret what they tell you about the setting, the events, or the narrator.

Image	Interpretation
p. 1061 "Either it was drizzling or there was a lot of dust in the air and the dust was damp."	• This is a world of sensation. • The narrator feels dampness but is confused about her surroundings.

Vocabulary

verandah (və ran′ də) *n.* a long porch, usually with a roof, that extends along a house; p. 1062 *The man sat on the verandah and watched the rain.*

horizon (hə rī′ zən) *n.* the place where the earth and sky appear to meet; p. 1062 *From the meadow, we could see the clouds on the horizon.*

dutiful (dōō′ ti fəl) *adj.* acting out of a sense of obligation or a sense of what is required; p. 1062 *The dutiful worker always did every task carefully.*

interlaced (in′ tər lāst′) *adj.* connected by or woven together; p. 1063 *The fabric was interlaced gold threads.*

1060 UNIT 6 GENRE FICTION

Eight Huts in Haiti. D. Roosevelt (b. 1952). Oil on canvas. Private collection.

What I Have Been Doing Lately

Jamaica Kincaid

What I have been doing lately: I was lying in bed and the doorbell rang. I ran downstairs. Quick. I opened the door. There was no one there. I stepped outside. Either it was drizzling or there was a lot of dust in the air and the dust was damp. I stuck out my tongue and the drizzle or the damp dust tasted like government school ink. I looked north. I looked south. I decided to start walking north. While walking north, I noticed that I was barefoot. While walking north, I looked up and saw the planet Venus. I said, "It must be almost morning." I saw a monkey in a tree. The tree had no leaves. I said, "Ah, a monkey. Just look at that. A monkey." I

Comparing Literature

walked for I don't know how long before I came up to a big body of water. I wanted to get across it but I couldn't swim. I wanted to get across it but it would take me years to build a boat. I wanted to get across it but it would take me I didn't know how long to build a bridge. Years passed and then one day, feeling like it, I got into my boat and rowed across. When I got to the other side, it was noon and my shadow was small and fell beneath me. I set out on a path that stretched out straight ahead. I passed a house, and a dog was sitting on the <u>verandah</u> but it looked the other way when it saw me coming. I passed a boy tossing a ball in the air but the boy looked the other way when he saw me coming. I walked and I walked but I couldn't tell if I walked a long time because my feet didn't feel as if they would drop off. I turned around to see what I had left behind me but nothing was familiar. Instead of the straight path, I saw hills. Instead of the boy with his ball, I saw tall flowering trees. I looked up and the sky was without clouds and seemed near, as if it were the ceiling in my house and, if I stood on a chair, I could touch it with the tips of my fingers. I turned around and looked ahead of me again. A deep hole had opened up before me. I looked in. The hole was deep and dark and I couldn't see the bottom. I thought, What's down there?, so on purpose I fell in. I fell and I fell, over and over, as if I were an old suitcase. On the sides of the deep hole I could see things written, but perhaps it was in a foreign language because I couldn't read

them. Still I fell, for I don't know how long. As I fell I began to see that I didn't like the way falling made me feel. Falling made me feel sick and I missed all the people I had loved. I said, I don't want to fall anymore, and I reversed myself. I was standing again on the edge of the deep hole. I looked at the deep hole and I said, You can close up now, and it did. I walked some more without knowing distance. I only knew that I passed through days and nights, I only knew that I passed through rain and shine, light and darkness. I was never thirsty and I felt no pain. Looking at the <u>horizon</u>, I made a joke for myself: I said, "The earth has thin lips," and I laughed.

Looking at the horizon again, I saw a lone figure coming toward me, but I wasn't frightened because I was sure it was my mother. As I got closer to the figure, I could see that it wasn't my mother, but still I wasn't frightened because I could see that it was a woman.

When this woman got closer to me, she looked at me hard and then she threw up her hands. She must have seen me somewhere before because she said, "It's you. Just look at that. It's you. And just what have you been doing lately?"

I could have said, "I have been praying not to grow any taller."

I could have said, "I have been listening carefully to my mother's words, so as to make a good imitation of a <u>dutiful</u> daughter."

I could have said, "A pack of dogs, tired from chasing each other all over town, slept in the moonlight."

Stream of Consciousness *What is irrational or illogical about this statement?*

Vocabulary

verandah (və ran′də) *n.* a long porch, usually with a roof, that extends along a house

Vocabulary

horizon (hə rī′zən) *n.* the place where the earth and sky appear to meet

dutiful (do͞o′ti fəl) *adj.* acting out of a sense of obligation or a sense of what is required

Instead, I said, What I have been doing lately: I was lying in bed on my back, my hands drawn up, my fingers **interlaced** lightly at the nape of my neck.[1] Someone rang the doorbell. I went downstairs and opened the door but there was no one there. I stepped outside. Either it was drizzling or there was a lot of dust in the air and the dust was damp. I stuck out my tongue and the drizzle or the damp dust tasted like government school ink. I looked north and I looked south. I started walking north. While walking north, I wanted to move fast, so I removed the shoes from my feet. While walking north, I looked up and saw the planet Venus and I said, "If the sun went out, it would be eight minutes before I would know it." I saw a monkey sitting in a tree that had no leaves and I said, "A monkey. Just look at that. A monkey." I picked up a stone and I threw it at the monkey. The monkey, seeing the stone, quickly moved out of its way. Three times I threw a stone at the monkey and three times it moved away. The fourth time I threw the stone, the monkey caught it and threw it back at me. The stone struck me on my forehead over my right eye, making a deep gash. The gash healed immediately but now the skin on my forehead felt false to me. I walked for I don't know how long before I came to a big body of water. I wanted to get across, so when the boat came I paid my fare. When I got to the other side, I saw a lot of people sitting on the beach and they were having a picnic. They were the most beautiful people I had ever seen. Everything about them was black and shiny. Their skin was black and shiny. Their shoes were black and shiny. Their hair was black and shiny. The clothes they wore were black and shiny. I could hear them laughing and chatting and I said, I would like to be with these people, so I started to walk toward them, but when I got up close to them I saw that they weren't at a picnic and they weren't beautiful and they weren't chatting and laughing. All around me was black mud and the people all looked as if they had been made up out of the black mud. I looked up and saw that the sky seemed far away and nothing I could stand on would make me able to touch it with my fingertips. I thought, If only I could get out of this, so I started to walk. I must have walked for a long time because my feet hurt and felt as if they would drop off. I thought, If only just around the bend I would see my house and inside my house I would find my bed, freshly made at that, and in the kitchen I would find my mother or anyone else that I loved making me a custard. I thought, If only it was a Sunday and I was sitting in a church and I had just heard someone sing a psalm. I felt very sad so I sat down. I felt so sad that I rested my head on my own knees and smoothed my own head. I felt so sad I couldn't imagine feeling any other way again. I said, I don't like this. I don't want to do this anymore. And I went back to lying in bed, just before the doorbell rang.

---

1. The *nape of my neck* refers to the back of the neck.

Vocabulary

interlaced (in´tər lāst´) *adj.* connected by or woven together

Comparing Literature

Interpret Imagery How would you describe the mood that the images in this sentence and the previous sentence evoke?

The Extraordinary and Fantastic In what way is this an extraordinary and fantastic journey?

JAMAICA KINCAID

Comparing Literature

After You Read

Respond and Think Critically

Respond and Interpret

1. How might you feel if you awoke from the dream described by the narrator? Explain.

2. (a) Who is the narrator of this story? (b) What can you infer about the narrator's age and family relationships? Support your inferences with details.

3. (a) Describe the picnic scene in the second part of the story. (b) How does the change in the picnic scene affect the narrator? Explain.

Analyze and Evaluate

4. How does Kincaid's use of dialogue expand the portrayal of the subconscious mind?

5. Evaluate Kincaid's use of stream-of-consciousness narration and first-person point of view.

6. (a) Why does the narrator go back to bed at the end of the story? (b) What might be the cause of the narrator's sadness and anxiety in the dream?

Connect

7. **Big Idea** **The Extraordinary and Fantastic** In what ways might the extraordinary and fantastic images of the dream world give the reader insight into the narrator's waking life?

8. **Connect to the Author** According to Kincaid, people "live for dreaming" in the Caribbean world. In what way is the narrator of this story suspended between dreams and reality?

Literary Element **Stream of Consciousness**

Stream of consciousness is characterized by random association of ideas, repetition, and disregard for conventional punctuation and sentence structure.

1. Which characteristics does the story feature?

2. Why do you think the author chose to write this story using the stream-of-consciousness technique?

Reading Strategy **Interpret Imagery**

Imagery is the use of word pictures to evoke vivid sensory details. In a dream, these details often have symbolic meaning.

1. The narrator encounters obstacles: a body of water and a deep hole. What might these obstacles symbolize?

2. Name another image in the story that has a symbolic meaning. Discuss what it might represent.

 **Literature** Online

Selection Resources For Selection Quizzes, eFlashcards, and Reading-Writing Connection activities, go to glencoe.com and enter QuickPass code GL59794u6.

Vocabulary Practice

Practice with Analogies Choose the word that best completes each analogy.

1. porch : verandah :: house :
   a. car   b. mansion   c. sculptor

2. dutiful : disobedient :: plentiful :
   a. cautious   b. beneficial   c. scarce

3. sky : horizon :: color :
   a. earth   b. boundary   c. rainbow

4. interlaced : entwined :: distinct :
   a. enrobed   b. separate   c. mixed

Writing

Write an Essay Write a stream-of-consciousness essay about a day when you engaged in different activities. Include your thoughts, feelings, memories, and a few fantastical details. Capture your impressions of time passing by experimenting with sentence length, diction, imagery, and rhetorical devices.

Build Background

Denise Levertov (1923–1977) noted that "People at Night" is derived from the work of German poet Rainer Maria Rilke. Levertov's poem, like many of Rilke's poems and letters, deals with the isolation of the individual.

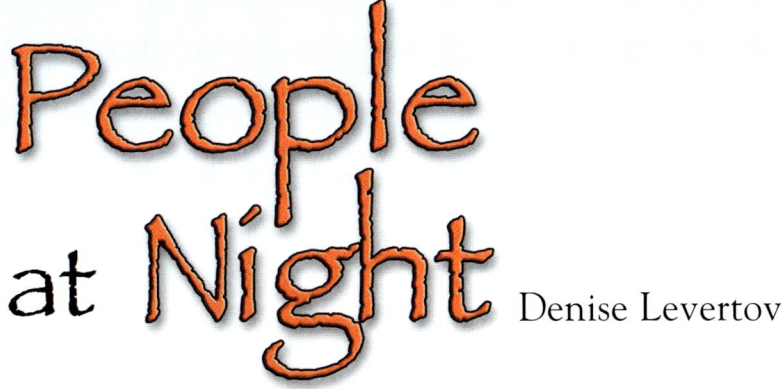

People at Night
Denise Levertov

Melancholy Woman.
Jose Ortega.

View the Art Ortega, originally from Ecuador, is known for his vivid murals. What mood does Ortega convey here? How does the mood suit the mood of the poem?

Comparing Literature

(Derived from Rilke)
    A night that cuts between you and you
and you   and you   and you
and me : jostles us apart, a man elbowing
through a crowd.   We won't
       look for each other, either—
wander off, each alone, not looking
in the slow crowd. Among sideshows
      under movie signs,
      pictures made of a million lights,
      giants that move and again move
      again, above a cloud of thick smells,
      franks, roasted nutmeats—

Or going up to some apartment, yours
        or yours, finding
someone sitting in the dark:
who is it, really? So you switch the
light on to see: you know the name but
who is it?
    But you won't see.
The fluorescent light flickers sullenly, a
pause. But you command. It grabs
each face and holds it up
by the hair for you, mask after mask.
      You and you and you and I repeat
      gestures that make do when speech
      has failed   and talk
      and talk, laughing, saying
        'I', and 'I',
meaning 'Anybody'.
                No one.

 Discussion Starter

In this poem, the speaker re-creates two scenes at night: one on the street and one in an apartment. In a small group, compare and contrast the speaker's experience in these two places. Begin by identifying the images and symbols in each setting, and then retell what happens in each place.

Comparing Literature

Build Background

In "A Dream," the speaker refers to August as "a terrible anniversary." For Akhmatova, it truly was: Her husband died in August 1921; Russia entered World War I in August 1914; and in August 1941, Akhmatova's friend and fellow poet Marina Tsvetaeva died.

Starry Night, 1889. Vincent van Gogh. Oil on canvas. Museum of Modern Art, New York.

View the Art Van Gogh's art is known for its intensity, both in color and in conveying impressions and emotion. How would you describe the night sky that Van Gogh depicts here? What dream-like quality does the painting convey to you?

Comparing Literature

A Dream

Anna Akhmatova
translated by Judith Hemschemeyer

Isn't it sweet to have unearthly dreams?
A. Blok[1]

This dream was prophetic or not prophetic . . .
Mars shone among the heavenly stars,
Becoming crimson, sparkling, sinister—
And that same night I dreamed of your arrival.

It was in everything . . . in the Bach Chaconne,[2]
And in the roses, which bloomed in vain,
And in the ringing of the village bells
Over the blackness of ploughed fields.

And in the autumn, which came close
And suddenly, reconsidering, concealed itself.
Oh my August, how could you give me such news
As a terrible anniversary?

How can I repay this royal gift?
Where do I go and with whom do I celebrate?
And now I am writing, as before, no crossing out,
My poems in the burnt notebook.[3]

August 14, 1956
Near Kolomna

1. *A. Blok* is Alexander Blok, one of Russia's most important poets before the Communist era. Akhmatova greatly admired him.

2. A *chaconne* is a musical form in 3/4 time in which a set of variations is played over a bass line.

3. The *burnt notebook* refers to the work Akhmatova had to burn during the Stalinist era for fear of imprisonment or death. By 1956 this era had ended when Nikita Khrushchev (premier of the Soviet Union from 1958 to 1964) denounced Stalin's police.

Quickwrite

In this poem, the speaker refers to "your arrival." How do you know this unidentified arrival is important to the speaker? What do you think is the "news" or "royal gift" to which the speaker refers? How does the speaker react to this news or gift? Write a paragraph in which you address these questions.

Wrap-Up: Comparing Literature
Across Genres

- *What I Have Been Doing Lately* by Jamaica Kincaid
- *People at Night* by Denise Levertov
- *A Dream* by Anna Akhmatova

COMPARE THE Big Idea The Extraordinary and Fantastic

Writing Write a brief essay in which you focus on how the three selections are alike in their portrayal of other-worldly, fantastic, or strange people, places, or events. Cite evidence from the selections to support your main ideas.

COMPARE Description

Group Activity Each writer uses description to transport the reader to an inner world or a dream state. With a small group, discuss the following questions. Cite evidence from the selection to support your answers.

1. How does each author use description to give the reader a sense of place?
2. How does each author use description to create atmosphere or set the mood?
3. Provide examples of imagistic or symbolic description that help you understand the work's message. Explain the examples you selected.

Man Sleeping Beneath A Nighttime Sky. Steve Kropp.

COMPARE Author's Culture

Make a Chart Each author reflects her own time and place. Kincaid uses elements of her island world; Levertov re-creates a city at night; and Akhmatova takes us to the repressive environment of the Soviet Union. Create a chart in which you compare these cultures.

Kincaid	Levertov	Akhmatova
p. 1062		
houses with verandahs		
tall flowering trees		

Selection Resources For Selection Quizzes, eFlashcards, and Reading-Writing Connection activities, go to glencoe.com and enter QuickPass code GL59794u6.

Scientific Perspective
on "The Extraordinary and Fantastic"

One Legend Found, Many Still to Go

by William J. Broad

Learning Objectives

For pages 1070–1073
In studying this text, you will focus on the following objectives:

Literary Study: Comparing and contrasting events and ideas.

Reading: Analyzing informational text.

Science debunks fabulous creatures, but sometimes they turn out to be more than just imaginary.

Set a Purpose for Reading
Read to discover opposing ideas and events within the article "One Legend Found, Many Still to Go."

Build Background
Often ridiculed for not being an actual science, cryptozoology is the study of animals that may or may not exist. In this article, William J. Broad discusses the field of cryptozoology.

Reading Strategy

Compare and Contrast Events and Ideas
When you compare and contrast events and ideas, you find similarities and differences between them and consider what they mean. As you read, take notes on the similarities and differences between the defining moments for mainstream scientists and those of cryptozoologists. Use a Venn diagram like the one below as a guide.

Science
- shatters myths with facts

Both
- discovered the coelacanth

Cryptozoology
- "embroider" upon natural phenomena

The human instinct to observe nature has always been mixed with a tendency to embroider upon it. So it is that, over the ages, societies have lived alongside not only real animals, but a shadow bestiary[1] of fantastic ones—mermaids, griffins,[2] unicorns and the like. None loomed larger than the giant squid, the kraken,[3] a great, malevolent devil of the deep. "One of these Sea-Monsters," Olaus Magnus[4] wrote in 1555, "will drown easily many great ships."

Science, of course, is in the business of shattering myths with facts, which it did again, last week when Japanese scientists reported that they hooked a giant squid, a relatively small one estimated at 26 feet long—some 3,000 feet down and photographed it before it tore off a tentacle to

---

1. Here, *bestiary* means a medieval collection of symbolic tales about the traits of animals.
2. *Griffins* are mythological creatures with the body of a lion and the head of a bird.
3. *Krakens* are fabled sea monsters, based on sightings of giant squids.
4. *Olaus Magnus* (1490–1557) was a Catholic priest and author of Scandinavian history.

Ideas and Trends

escape. It was the first peek humanity has ever had of such animals in their native habitat. Almost inevitably, the creature seemed far less terrifying than its ancient image.

Scientists celebrated the find not as an end, but as the beginning of a new chapter in understanding the shy creature. "There're always more questions, more parts to the mystery than we'll ever be able to solve," said Clyde F. E. Roper, a squid expert at the National Museum of Natural History of the Smithsonian Institution.

Monster lovers take heart. Scientists argue that so much of the planet remains unexplored that new surprises are sure to show up; if not legendary beasts like the Loch Ness monster[5] or the dinosaur-like reptile said to inhabit Lake Champlain, then animals that in their own way may be even stranger.

A forthcoming book by the noted naturalist Richard Ellis, *Singing Whales, Flying Squid and Swimming Cucumbers* (Lyon Press, 2006), reinforces that notion by cataloguing recent discoveries of previously unknown whales, dolphins and other creatures, some of which are quite bizarre.

"The sea being so deep and so large, I'm sure other mysteries lurk out there, unseen and unsolved," said Mr. Ellis, also the author of *Monsters of the Sea* (Knopf, 1994). Explorers, he said, recently stumbled on an odd squid more than 20 feet long with fins like elephant ears and very skinny arms and tentacles, all of which can bend at right angles, like human elbows. "We know nothing about it," Mr. Ellis said. "But we've seen it."

Historically, many unknown creatures have come to light purely by accident. In 1938, for example, a fisherman pulled up an odd, ancient-looking fish with stubby, limblike fins. It turned out to be a coelacanth, a beast thought to have gone extinct 70 million years ago. Since then, other examples of the species have occasionally been hauled out of the sea.

Land, too, occasionally gives up a secret. About 1900, acting on tips from the local population, Sir Harry H. Johnston, an English explorer, hunted through the forests of Zaire (then the Belgian Congo) and found a giraffe-like animal known as the okapi. It was hailed as a living fossil.

In 1982, a group of animal enthusiasts founded the International Society of Cryptozoology (literally, the study of hidden creatures) and adopted the okapi as its symbol. Today, self-described cryptozoologists range from amateur unicorn hunters to distinguished scientists.

At the Web site for the group, www.internationalsocietyofcryptozoology. org, there is a list of 15 classes[6] of unresolved claims about unusual beasts, including big cats, giant crocodiles, huge snakes, large octopuses, mammoths, biped primates like the yeti in the Himalayas and long-necked creatures resembling the gigantic dinosaurs called sauropods.

Lake Champlain, on the border between Vermont and New York, is notorious as the alleged home of Champ, a beast said to be similar to a plesiosaur, an extinct marine reptile with a small head, long neck and four paddle-shaped flippers.

There, as at Loch Ness and elsewhere, myth busters and believers do constant battle. "Not only is there not a single piece of convincing evidence for Champ's existence, but there are many reasons against it," Joe Nickel, a researcher who investigates claims of paranormal[7] phenomena, argued in *Skeptical*

---

5. The *Loch Ness monster* is a fabled lake monster said to reside in Scotland's Loch Ness.

6. *Classes* are a biological classification of organism that is below the rank of phylum, above that of order.

7. *Paranormal* means a phenomenon or an experience that is unable to be explained scientifically.

Ideas and Trends

Inquirer, a monthly magazine that rebuts what it considers to be scientific hokum.[8]

Then there are the blobs. For more than a century, scientists and laymen imagined that the mysterious gooey masses—some as large as a school bus—that wash ashore on beaches around the world came from great creatures with tentacles long enough to sink cruise ships. Warnings were issued. Perhaps, cryptozoologists speculated, the blobs were the remains of recently deceased living fossils more fearsome than the dinosaurs, or perhaps an entirely new sea creature unknown to science.

Then last year, a team of biologists based at the University of South Florida applied DNA analysis to the mystery. It turned out they were nothing more than old whale blubber. "To our disappointment," the scientists wrote, "we have not found any evidence that any of the blobs are the remains of gigantic octopods, or sea monsters of unknown species."

Psychologists say raw nature is simply a blank slate for the expression of our subconscious fears and insecurities, a Rorschach test[9] that reveals more about the viewer than the viewed.

But the giant squid is real, growing up to lengths of at least 60 feet, with eyes the size of dinner plates and a tangle of tentacles lined with long rows of sucker pads. Scientists, their appetites whetted[10] by the first observations of the creature in the wild, are now gearing up to discover its remaining secrets.

"Wouldn't it be fabulous to see a giant squid capturing its prey?" asked Dr. Roper of the Smithsonian. "Or a battle between a sperm whale and a giant? Or mating? Can you imagine that?"

"We've cracked the ice on this," he said "but there's a lot more to do."

---

8. *Hokum* means nonsense.

9. A *Rorschach* test is a psychological examination that evaluates personality based on interpretation of ten abstract designs.
10. Here, *whetted* means stimulated.

Respond and Think Critically

Respond and Interpret

1. Write a brief summary of the main ideas in this article before you answer the following questions. For help on writing a summary, see page 415.

2. Do you believe that there is any truth to creatures such as the Loch Ness monster or "Champ," the creature in Lake Champlain? Explain.

3. (a) What is a cryptozoologist? (b) Do you think that they do important work? Why or why not?

4. (a) What are the "blobs" that interest scientists? (b) Why do you think people like to speculate about where the blobs originated?

Analyze and Evaluate

5. Do you think that the author supports the belief in imaginary creatures? Explain.

6. (a) The author writes that "psychologists say raw nature is simply a blank slate for the expression of our subconscious fears and insecurities." What do you think this means? (b) What ideas in the selection oppose this one about psychology? Explain.

Connect

7. Naturalist Richard Ellis explains, "The sea being so deep and so large, I'm sure other mysteries lurk out there, unseen and unsolved." What relationship does this article suggest exists between science and the extraordinary and fantastic? In what ways do the two complement each other?

Before You Read

Robot Dreams

Meet **Isaac Asimov**
(1920–1992)

The grandfather of present-day science fiction, Isaac Asimov exhibited a vivid imagination and dogged persistence that readied the world for the study of robotics—both fictional and real.

Born in the Soviet Union, Asimov's parents brought him to New York in 1923. A precocious youth, the four-year-old Asimov taught himself to read using Brooklyn's street signs. He skipped several grades, graduating from high school at fifteen.

Early Success Asimov earned a bachelor's degree from Columbia University in 1939 and a master's degree in 1941. That same year, Asimov's short story "Nightfall," a tale of a planet where nightfall descends once every thousand years, was published. In 1969 the Science Fiction Writers of America voted "Nightfall" the best science-fiction short story written.

Asimov returned to Columbia University for a PhD in chemistry, which he earned in 1948. In 1949 he accepted a position at Boston University's School of Medicine. "By 1951 I was writing a textbook on biochemistry, and I finally realized the only thing I really wanted to be was a writer," he said in 1969.

And write Asimov did, authoring mystery novels, short stories, limericks, guides to Shakespeare and the Bible, personal memoirs, letters, autobiographies, children's books, and textbooks. Asimov is credited with writing nearly five hundred books at a prolific speed of ten books per year. "Writing is more fun than ever," Asimov said in a 1984 interview. "The longer I write, the easier it gets."

> *"Knowledge has its dangers, yes, but is the response to be a retreat from knowledge?"*
>
> —Isaac Asimov

The Three Laws of Robotics In 1940 Asimov formulated "The Three Laws of Robotics," rules that provide for human control over artificial intelligences. Asimov subjected all of the robots in his stories to these laws.

The influence of the Three Laws of Robotics can be seen today, from movie adaptations (*I, Robot* in 2004) to the work of real-life scientists. Joseph F. Engelberger, the pioneering engineer who built the first industrial robot in 1958 and founded the world's first robotics company in 1961, attributed his fascination with robots to his reading of *I, Robot* as a teenager. At Engelberger's request, Asimov later wrote the foreword to his robotics manual.

Author Search For more about Isaac Asimov, go to glencoe.com and enter QuickPass code GL59794u6.

Literature and Reading Preview

Connect to the Story
Are there any technologies that frighten you? Write a journal entry about technologies that you think might have the potential to be abused or to get out of control.

Build Background
The protagonist of "Robot Dreams," Dr. Susan Calvin, appears in a number of Asimov's other robot stories. She is one of Asimov's robot experts who take an active role in enhancing and advancing robotic intelligence and whose lives span the evolution of robots from fairly mindless automatons to complex, emotional beings.

Set Purposes for Reading

Big Idea The Extraordinary and Fantastic

As you read, ask yourself, How does Asimov explore the conflict between humanity and technology?

Literary Element Analogy

An **analogy** is a comparison that shows similarities between two things that are otherwise dissimilar. Recognizing an author's use of analogies can help you better discern the meaning of or intention behind a particular comparison. As you read, ask yourself, How does Asimov use analogies?

Reading Strategy Activate Prior Knowledge

From *Star Trek* to *Star Wars,* machines and robots have long figured prominently in literature and film. Activating your prior knowledge about a topic can enrich your understanding of a particular text. As you read, ask yourself, What do I already know about technology?

....

Tip: Use Prior Knowledge Use a chart like the one below to record what you know about robots and computers, how you know it, and what you learn from the story.

What I Know About Robots	How I Know It	What I Learn from the Story
Some robots can be programmed to react with anger, happiness, or fear when they are touched in different ways.	I read about a robot called Feelix in a nonfiction book.	Elvex, the robot in the story, can dream.

Learning Objectives

For pages 1073–1082

In studying this text, you will focus on the following objectives:

Literary Study: Analyzing analogy.

Reading: Activating prior knowledge.

Vocabulary

gnarled (närld) *adj.* roughened and coarse from age or work; full of knots, as in a tree; p. 1076 *Susan found it difficult to climb the old gnarled tree.*

dismantle (dis mant′əl) *v.* to take apart; p. 1077 *The workers dismantled the broken scoreboard in the gym so they could put in a new one.*

accord (ə kôrd′) *n.* agreement; conformity; p. 1078 *The candidate acted in accord with federal law when he turned down a contribution that was too large.*

precedence (pres′ə dəns) *n.* order of importance or preference; priority; p. 1079 *Repairing the broken window takes precedence over buying baseballs.*

inert (i nurt′) *adj.* not able to move; p. 1079 *The detective examined the inert body lying on the floor.*

Robot Dreams

Isaac Asimov

"Last night I dreamed," said LVX-1, calmly. Susan Calvin said nothing, but her lined face, old with wisdom and experience, seemed to undergo a microscopic twitch.

"Did you hear that?" said Linda Rash, nervously. "It's as I told you." She was small, dark-haired, and young. Her right hand opened and closed, over and over.

Calvin nodded. She said, quietly, "Elvex, you will not move nor speak nor hear us, until I say your name again."

There was no answer. The robot sat as though it were cast out of one piece of metal, and it would stay so until it heard its name again.

Calvin said, "What is your computer entry code, Dr. Rash? Or enter it yourself if that will make you more comfortable. I want to inspect the positronic[1] brain pattern."

Linda's hands fumbled, for a moment, at the keys. She broke the process and started again. The fine pattern appeared on the screen.

Calvin said, "Your permission, please, to manipulate your computer."

Permission was granted with a speechless nod. Of course! What could Linda, a new and unproven robopsychologist, do against the Living Legend?

Slowly, Susan Calvin studied the screen, moving it across and down, then up, then suddenly throwing in a key-combination so rapidly that Linda didn't see what had been done, but the pattern displayed a new portion of itself altogether and had been enlarged. Back and forth she went, her **gnarled** fingers tripping over the keys.

---

1. *Positronic* is a fictional word often used in science fiction to refer to robotic brains. A positron is a subatomic particle equal in mass to an electron but which holds a positive charge.

Vocabulary

gnarled (närld) *adj.* roughened and coarse from age or work; full of knots, as in a tree

No change came over the old face. As though vast calculations were going through her head, she watched all the pattern shifts.

Linda wondered. It was impossible to analyze a pattern without at least a handheld computer, yet the Old Woman simply stared. Did she have a computer implanted in her skull? Or was it her brain which, for decades, had done nothing but devise, study, and analyze the positronic brain patterns? Did she grasp such a pattern the way Mozart grasped the notation of a symphony?

Finally Calvin said, "What is it you have done, Rash?"

Linda said, a little abashed, "I made use of fractal geometry."[2]

"I gathered that. But why?"

"It had never been done. I thought it would produce a brain pattern with added complexity, possibly closer to that of the human."

"Was anyone consulted? Was this all on your own?"

"I did not consult. It was on my own."

Calvin's faded eyes looked long at the young woman. "You had no right. Rash your name; rash your nature. Who are you not to ask? I myself, I, Susan Calvin, would have discussed this."

"I was afraid I would be stopped."

"You certainly would have been."

"*Am* I," her voice caught, even as she strove to hold it firm, "going to be fired?"

"Quite possibly," said Calvin. "Or you might be promoted. It depends on what I think when I am through."

"Are you going to **dismantle** El—" She had almost said the name, which would have reactivated the robot and been one more mistake. She could not afford another mistake, if it wasn't already too late to afford anything at all. "Are you going to dismantle the robot?"

She was suddenly aware, with some shock, that the Old Woman had an electron gun in the pocket of her smock. Dr. Calvin had come prepared for just that.

"We'll see," said Calvin. "The robot may prove too valuable to dismantle."

"But how can it dream?"

"You've made a positronic brain pattern remarkably like that of a human brain. Human brains must dream to reorganize, to get rid, periodically, of knots and snarls. Perhaps so must this robot, and for the same reason. Have you asked him what he has dreamed?"

"No, I sent for you as soon as he said he had dreamed. I would deal with this matter no further on my own, after that."

"Ah!" A very small smile passed over Calvin's face. "There are limits beyond which your folly will not carry you. I am glad of that. In fact, I am relieved. And now let us together see what we can find out."

She said, sharply, "Elvex."

The robot's head turned toward her smoothly. "Yes, Dr. Calvin?"

"How do you know you have dreamed?"

"It is at night, when it is dark, Dr. Calvin," said Elvex, "and there is suddenly light, although I can see no cause for the appearance of light. I see things that have no connection with what I conceive of as reality. I hear things. I react oddly. In searching my vocabulary for words to express what was happening, I came across the word 'dream.' Studying its meaning I finally came to the conclusion I was dreaming."

---

2. *Fractal geometry* is a type of mathematics that deals with irregular objects and forms.

Analogy What does this analogy say about Susan Calvin's skill in robot science?

Vocabulary

dismantle (dis mant′ əl) *v.* to take apart

The Extraordinary and Fantastic Why might such a humanlike robot be especially valuable?

"How did you come to have 'dream' in your vocabulary, I wonder."

Linda said, quickly, waving the robot silent, "I gave him a human-style vocabulary. I thought—"

"You really thought," said Calvin. "I'm amazed."

"I thought he would need the verb. You know, 'I never dreamed that—' Something like that."

Calvin said, "How often have you dreamed, Elvex?"

"Every night, Dr. Calvin, since I have become aware of my existence."

"Ten nights," interposed Linda, anxiously, "but Elvex only told me of it this morning."

"Why only this morning, Elvex?"

"It was not until this morning, Dr. Calvin, that I was convinced that I was dreaming. Till then, I had thought there was a flaw in my positronic brain pattern, but I could not find one. Finally, I decided it was a dream."

"And what do you dream?"

"I dream always very much the same dream, Dr. Calvin. Little details are different but always it seems to me that I see a large panorama in which robots are working."

"Robots, Elvex? And human beings, also?"

"I see no human beings in the dream, Dr. Calvin. Not at first. Only robots."

"What are they doing, Elvex?"

"They are working, Dr. Calvin. I see some mining in the depths of the earth, and some laboring in heat and radiation. I see some in factories and some undersea."

Calvin turned to Linda. "Elvex is only ten station. How does he know of robots in such detail?"

Linda looked in the direction of a chair as though she longed to sit down, but the Old Woman was standing and that meant Linda had to stand also. She said, faintly, "It seemed to me important that he know about robotics and its place in the world. It was my thought that he would be particularly adapted to play the part of overseer[3] with his—his new brain."

"His fractal brain?"

"Yes."

Calvin nodded and turned back to the robot. "You saw all this—undersea, and underground, and aboveground—and space, too, I imagine."

"I also saw robots working in space," said Elvex. "It was that I saw all this, with the details forever changing as I glanced from place to place, that made me realize that what I saw was not in **accord** with reality and led me to the conclusion, finally, that I was dreaming."

"What else did you see, Elvex?"

"I saw that all the robots were bowed down with toil and affliction, that all were weary of responsibility and care, and I wished them to rest."

Calvin said, "But the robots are not bowed down, they are not weary, they need no rest."

"So it is in reality, Dr. Calvin. I speak of my dream, however. In my dream, it seemed to me that robots must protect their own existence."

Calvin said, "Are you quoting the Third Law of Robotics?"

"I am, Dr. Calvin."

"But you quote it in incomplete fashion. The Third Law is 'A robot must protect its own existence as long as such protection does not conflict with the First or Second Law.'"

"Yes, Dr. Calvin. That is the Third Law in reality, but in my dream, the Law ended with the word 'existence.' There was no mention of the First or Second Law."

Activate Prior Knowledge *How does your knowledge about robotic self-awareness as portrayed in other media influence your reading of Elvex's statement?*

---

3. An *overseer* is a person who supervises or oversees.

Vocabulary

accord (ə kôrd′) *n.* agreement; conformity

Tin God, 2003. P.J. Crook. Acrylic on canvas and wood. Private collection.

"Yet both exist, Elvex. The Second Law, which takes **precedence** over the Third is 'A robot must obey the orders given it by human beings except where such orders would conflict with the First Law.' Because of this, robots obey orders. They do the work you see them do, and they do it readily and without trouble. They are not bowed down; they are not weary."

"So it is in reality, Dr. Calvin. I speak of my dream."

"And the First Law, Elvex, which is the most important of all, is 'A robot may not injure a human being, or, through inaction, allow a human being to come to harm.'"

"Yes, Dr. Calvin. In reality. In my dream, however, it seemed to me there was neither First nor Second Law, but only the Third, and the Third law was 'A robot must protect its own existence.' That was the whole of the Law."

"In your dream, Elvex?"

"In my dream."

Calvin said, "Elvex, you will not move nor speak nor hear us until I say your name again." And again the robot became, to all appearances, a single **inert** piece of metal.

Calvin turned to Linda Rash and said, "Well, what do you think, Dr. Rash?"

Linda's eyes were wide, and she could feel her heart beating madly. She said, "Dr. Calvin, I am appalled. I had no idea. It would never have occurred to me that such a thing was possible."

"No," said Calvin, calmly. "Nor would it have occurred to me, not to anyone. You have created a robot brain capable of dreaming and by this device you have revealed a layer of thought in robotic brains that might have remained undetected, otherwise, until the danger became acute."

"But that's impossible," said Linda. "You can't mean that other robots think the same."

"As we would say of a human being, not consciously. But who would have thought there was an unconscious layer beneath the obvious positronic brain paths, a layer that was not necessarily under the control of the Three Laws? What might this have

Vocabulary
precedence (pres′ ə dəns) *n.* order of importance or preference; priority

The Extraordinary and Fantastic Why might this dream be dangerous for humanity?

Vocabulary
inert (i nurt′) *adj.* not able to move

brought about as robotic brains grew more and more complex—had we not been warned?"

"You mean by Elvex?"

"By *you*, Dr. Rash. You have behaved improperly, but, by doing so, you have helped us to an overwhelmingly important understanding. We shall be working with fractal brains from now on, forming them in carefully controlled fashion. You will play your part in that. You will not be penalized for what you have done, but you will henceforth work in collaboration with others. Do you understand?"

"Yes, Dr. Calvin. But what of Elvex?"

"I'm still not certain."

Calvin removed the electron gun from her pocket and Linda stared at it with fascination. One burst of its electrons at a robotic cranium and the positronic brain paths would be neutralized and enough energy would be released to fuse the robot-brain into an inert ingot.

Visual Vocabulary
An *ingot* is a hunk of metal.

Linda said, "But surely Elvex is important to our research. He must not be destroyed."

"*Must* not, Dr. Rash? That will be my decision, I think. It depends entirely on how dangerous Elvex is."

She straightened up, as though determined that her own aged body was not to bow under *its* weight of responsibility. She said, "Elvex, do you hear me?"

"Yes, Dr. Calvin," said the robot.

"Did your dream continue? You said earlier that human beings did not appear *at first*. Does that mean they appeared afterward?"

Activate Prior Knowledge What usually happens in stories and movies when robots and computers are not controlled?

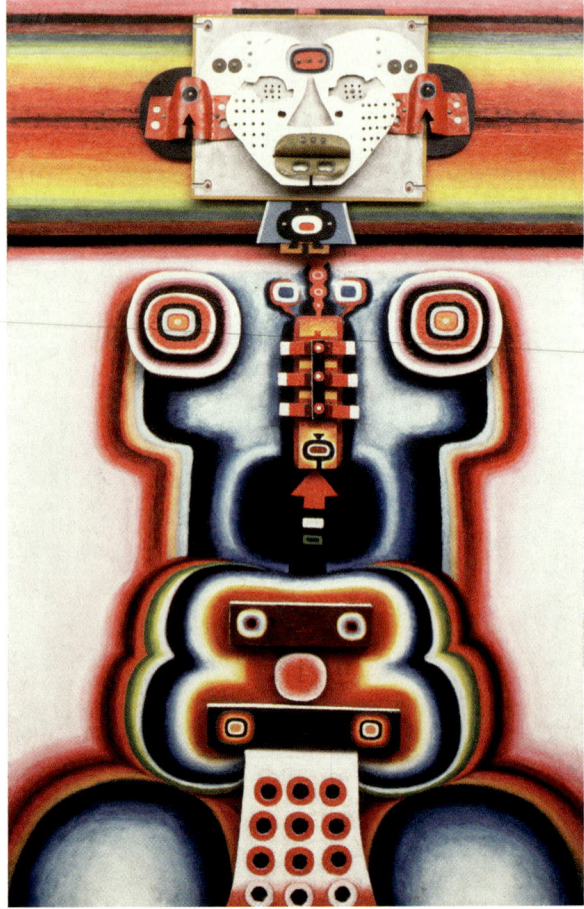

Torso, 1965. Vladimir Yankilevski. Oil, metal and wood. Private collection.

"Yes, Dr. Calvin. It seemed to me, in my dream, that eventually one man appeared."

"One man? Not a robot?"

"Yes, Dr. Calvin. And the man said, 'Let my people go!'"

"The *man* said that?"

"Yes, Dr. Calvin."

"And when he said 'Let my people go,' then by the words 'my people' he meant the robots?"

"Yes, Dr. Calvin. So it was in my dream."

"And did you know who the man was—in your dream?"

"Yes, Dr. Calvin. I knew the man."

"Who was he?"

And Elvex said, "I was the man."

And Susan Calvin at once raised her electron gun and fired, and Elvex was no more.

After You Read

Respond and Think Critically

Respond and Interpret

1. (a) What was your first reaction to Elvex? Explain. (b) Did you feel sympathy for Elvex at the end of the story? Why or why not?

2. (a) What is Elvex's real name? (b) Why do you think Asimov chose to have the characters call him Elvex?

3. (a) How did Elvex learn the word *dream*? (b) Why do robots normally not know this word?

4. (a) Who is the man in Elvex's dream? (b) Why does a man appear instead of a robot?

Analyze and Evaluate

5. How does Asimov show Linda's anxiety at the beginning of the story?

6. How does Asimov convey Calvin's immense experience in robotic science?

Connect

7. **Big Idea** The Extraordinary and Fantastic Why do you think Susan Calvin decides to destroy Elvex.

8. **Connect to the Author** How do you think Asimov's scientific background might have contributed to his science fiction stories?

Literary Element Analogy

Writers often use an **analogy** to explain something unfamiliar by comparing it to something familiar. For example, Asimov compared brain patterns to Mozart symphonies to show that both are complex. That analogy also shows the similar process that Asimov suggests both humans and robots use for comprehension. Asimov uses other analogies to show similarities between robots and humans throughout the story.

1. What other analogies does Asimov use to show how these robots are similar to humans? Make a Venn diagram to show the similarities and differences between robots and humans.

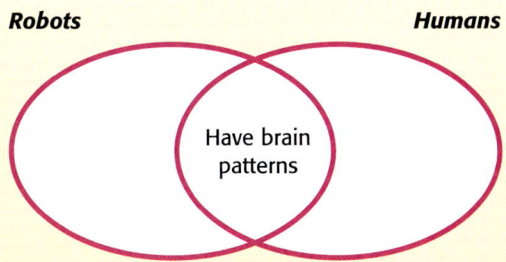

2. How can these similarities be both beneficial and harmful to humankind?

Review: Theme Archetype

As you learned on page 3, a **theme** in a literary work is a central understanding about life. An **archetype** is a model or pattern that recurs throughout literature and history. One of the primary themes in "Robot Dreams" is the archetype of *person versus machine*.

Partner Activity With a classmate, discuss the archetype of *person versus machine* as expressed in "Robot Dreams." Make a list of details from the text that exemplify the *person versus machine* archetype. Use a chart like the one below to record details:

Detail	How it supports the theme archetype
"In my dream, it seemed to me that robots must protect their own existence."	Elvex implies that robots have to protect their existence from humans.

ISAAC ASIMOV 1081

Reading Strategy: Activate Prior Knowledge

Applying what you already know to your reading of a literary work can help you to put the work in perspective. Review the chart you made on page 1075 and answer the following questions.

1. Think of a book or movie that portrays an unfriendly relationship between robots or computers and humans. Why was the relationship unfriendly?
2. How is this relationship similar to or different from the robot-human relationship portrayed in "Robot Dreams"?

Vocabulary Practice

Practice with Context Clues Identify the context clues in the following sentences that help you determine the meaning of each boldfaced vocabulary word.

1. The old woman's **gnarled** hands had performed decades of work in the fields.
2. The television set lay in pieces on the living room floor: Jamie had completely **dismantled** it.
3. We were in perfect **accord**: I accepted Lee's decision, and he agreed to pay me for the damage.
4. The repair to the roof takes **precedence** over the repair to the window: it's more important for us to be dry than warm!
5. Because the dog was completely **inert**, Mark thought, at first, that it was asleep.

Speaking and Listening

Oral Report

Assignment Present an oral report in which you respond to Asimov's three laws of robotics and outline a similar set of laws for humans. Include a visual aid.

Prepare Consider whether Asimov's three laws are logical, beneficial for both humans and robots, and likely to promote civility and equality. Chart your judgments and the evidence for them:

My Judgment	Evidence/Support
laws are logically constructed—yes	the laws are hierarchical; the second law cannot contradict the first
laws benefit humans	
laws promote civility and equality	

Write your report. Then cue it for your delivery by highlighting words and statements you will emphasize, places where you will pause and make eye contact, and places where you might add gestures or incorporate movements.

Report As you report, be sure to make frequent eye contact and to use your voice and movements to call attention to key points. Include a visual in your presentation to help command your audience's attention and to help clarify your own laws or Asimov's laws.

Evaluate Write a paragraph evaluating your oral report for its content, especially its use of evidence and visual aids, as well as for aspects of your delivery, including your diction, movement, and eye contact. Use the checklist on page 1127 to help you evaluate.

Selection Resources For Selection Quizzes, eFlashcards, and Reading-Writing Connection activities, go to glencoe.com and enter QuickPass code GL59794u6.

Learning Objectives

For pages 1083–1087

In studying this text, you will focus on the following objectives:

Reading:
Analyzing informational text. Connecting to contemporary issues.

Set a Purpose for Reading

Read to learn about robots with human-like qualities and why they were invented.

Preview the Article

1. Judging from the title, what do you think this article is about?
2. Skim the article, including the subheadings. What topics do you think it discusses?

Reading Strategy: Connect to Contemporary Issues

When you **connect to contemporary issues,** you link what you have read to modern-day events or issues. As you read, take notes on how the article connects to current issues you are familiar with. Use a web like the one below as a guide.

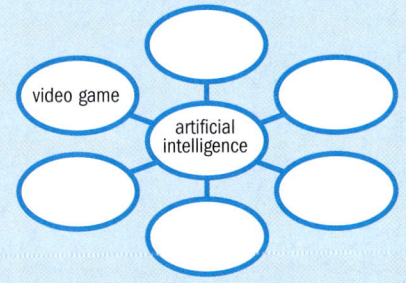

TIME

The Machine Nurturer

Kismet has a winning personality that draws people in. That's just what Cynthia Breazeal intended when she built her very sociable robot.

By ADAM COHEN

WALK INTO ROOM 922 OF THE ARTIFICIAL intelligence lab at the Massachusetts Institute of Technology (M.I.T.), and you may notice a robot in the corner trying desperately to get your attention. When Kismet is lonely and spots a human, it cranes its head forward. It flaps its pink paper ears and excitedly makes babylike noises. Kismet's creators call this an "attention-getting display." You would have to have a heart of stone to ignore this cute little aluminum . . . thing.

From a physical standpoint, Kismet isn't much of a robot. It can't walk and grab things, as many robots today can. It doesn't even have arms, legs, or a body. What sets Kismet apart is that it has been built with drives and equipped to interact with people. In social terms, big-eyed, babbling Kismet may be the most human robot ever built. And it may be the closest we have yet come to building the kind of robots that appear in science fiction and interact with humans in a natural way, like C-3PO from *Star Wars*.

Kismet is the creation of Cynthia Breazeal, an advanced student in the Humanoid Robotics Group at M.I.T. Breazeal has studied for years under Rodney Brooks, perhaps the leading figure in the world of robotics. Breazeal got the idea for Kismet when she was working with Cog, another robot in Brooks' lab that was built to have the physical

Informational Text

capacities of a human infant. Cog has a head, arms, and an upper body, and it can engage in simple tasks like turning a crank or playing with a slinky. Cog is physically gifted but completely lacking in social skills.

That lack was driven home to Breazeal one day when she was interacting with Cog. Breazeal put an eraser down in front of Cog, and Cog used its arm to pick up the eraser. When the robot put the eraser down, Breazeal picked it up. Breazeal and Cog continued taking turns picking up the eraser and putting it down. To an outside observer, it might have looked like the robot was intentionally playing with Breazeal, but Cog's mind just didn't work that way. It was while taking part in this interaction that Breazeal decided to try to build a new kind of robot—one that could play the eraser game with her and mean it.

A Child of Science

Breazeal was uniquely suited to the task of building this new robot. She grew up near the technology-rich area that would become Silicon Valley. Her father was a mathematician and her mother a computer scientist, and they raised her, she says, to be "pro-technology." Breazeal became captivated by robots at age 8 when she saw Star Wars for the first time. "I just fell in love with the Droids," she says, especially R2–D2. "But I was old enough to realize those kinds of robots didn't exist." Growing up, she considered becoming a doctor and an astronaut. But she never gave up her interest in robots. When she studied astronomy, she was particularly intrigued by lunar rovers, which are really just a specialized form of robot. After graduating from the University of California at Santa Barbara, Breazeal went to M.I.T. in the early 1990s to become part of one of the world's most innovative robotics labs.

At the time, Rodney Brooks was working on smaller, insect-like robots. Breazeal helped out and ended up with a small role in *Fast, Cheap, and Out of Control,* a documentary in which filmmaker Errol Morris profiles four people—including Brooks—who were pursuing unusual passions. When Brooks moved on to larger robots, Breazeal became the chief architect on Cog.

Breazeal played an active role in building Kismet. Drawing on her experience helping build two prior complex robots, she worked on everything from the mechanized design for Kismet's facial features to tinkering with its body parts in the shop. Breazeal took great care with the robot's facial features, which she considered important to making it an appealing social actor. She found a special-effects expert to make human-like eyes and personally glued on false eyelashes purchased in a beauty-supply store. And she put bright red lips on its metal mouth, using surgical tubing colored in with a red pen.

Informational Text

Body Parts

Kismet has an array of built-in features that help it act in a human-like way. It has four color cameras that allow it to "see," and its computers are programmed to help it recognize objects and measure distances. Kismet actively seeks out colorful toys and faces. It recognizes faces by looking for flesh tones and eyes. Kismet can hear, but only when humans speak into its microphone. And Kismet has motor capabilities that allow it to shift its eyes and crane its head toward particular sights and sounds. One of the robot's best features is its ability to register expressions that correspond to its emotional state. When it is surprised, it can raise its eyebrows. When it is sad, it can frown. Kismet can also vocalize, in a sing-song babble of meaningless sounds.

Kismet was designed with motivational drives, drawn from developmental psychology. A computer attached to the robot displays bar graphs that reflect its three drives—social, stimulation, and fatigue. Kismet's desire to satisfy these drives leads it to engage in a variety of purposeful behaviors, much as a human baby would. When its social drive is high, indicating that it is lonely, the robot actively seeks out human interaction. When its stimulation drive is high, it is drawn to other forms of interaction, including playing with colorful toys. Since it has no arms, it can't pick up a toy itself. But if it stares plaintively at a toy, a nearby human will usually pick it up and bring it over. When Kismet has had enough stimulation, its fatigue drive kicks in.

Kismet is able to engage in the kind of purposeful human interactions that cousin Cog could not. Kismet calls people toward it. And when they get too close for its cameras to see them well, it protects its personal space and pulls away. When an object suddenly appears in front of it, Kismet quickly withdraws and flashes a look of bewilderment. Most winningly, the robot is able to engage in a babbling "conversation" with humans in its midst. When it "talks," it takes turns with the person with whom it is speaking; the result resembles a conversation between an adult and an infant.

By one measure, Kismet is a clear success: people love it. When visitors arrive in the lab, they are drawn to the robot. When Kismet engages them, they are invariably charmed. "It's human nature," says Breazeal. "They are very concerned about keeping it happy." Proof of its winning personality: a box of toys given to it by human friends, including a yellow teddy bear sent from Japan.

The Urge to Invent

Breazeal is attracted to inventing because it is hands-on and real-world. "I would much rather build something and interact with it than philosophize about it," she says. "Or philosophize about someone else doing it." But at the same time, she has used robotics to explore some complex intellectual issues. At M.I.T., Breazeal has studied brains and cognitive science, and her work with Kismet raises important questions about how humans think and learn.

In designing Kismet, Breazeal made a critical decision about how she wanted it to develop. There are two rival schools about ways to build robots. One holds that robotmakers should decide in advance what knowledge and skills they want their robots to have and then program them accordingly. Breazeal has a different view. She thinks robots should be designed to learn from experience and from their environment. This socially situated learning, as it is called, allows Kismet to learn much like a human baby would.

The problem is that robots have fewer opportunities than babies to learn from their environment. Humans spend a great deal of time talking to and nurturing young people. Robots do not get that kind of attention and outside stimulation. "We don't learn in impoverished educational environments, but that's what we expect the robot to do," she says. Breazeal has tried to provide Kismet with the tools to engage in this kind of socially situated learning.

Despite all the help from Breazeal, Kismet still has a lot to learn. Breazeal is working on helping the computer with some simple skills that human babies are hardwired for. She wants Kismet to be able to use the information it learns. One day, she hopes, when Kismet is told the name of a toy, it will later be able to ask for it by name. "Through more interactions, Kismet could learn, 'When I'm in this state, I can take this action that leads to a person's taking this behavior

Informational Text

MOOD SWINGS Kismet can use its expressive face to reflect a variety of humanlike emotions. When Kismet is startled, its expression changes from calm, left, to a widemouthed look of surprise, right.

and getting my needs satiated,'" Breazeal says. She also wants Kismet to be able to remember the people it meets, so it can distinguish old friends from people it is meeting for the first time.

Who's Teaching Whom?

Kismet's educational journey prompts an obvious question: Why? What is the purpose of building humanoid robots and then programming and training them to act like us? One view of robotics holds that being able to build a machine that acts like a human is itself a worthy goal. "There's certainly a great challenge in creating something as sophisticated as what humans do," says Breazeal. It doesn't necessarily mean engaging in the Frankensteinian mission of trying to create a human being, she says. "Of course, we're never going to do that, but we can look for a commonality," she says. "Even though your dog is not human, it doesn't mean you can't communicate with it in a human-like way."

But Breazeal is at least as interested in using the robot to better understand humans. Thinking about how robots learn turns out to be a good way to think about human development. A case in point: In helping Kismet learn, researchers have observed that one of the hardest parts of the learning process is figuring out what to pay attention to. And watching Kismet interact with people provides insight into human social dynamics. At some point, Breazeal wants to build a second Kismet to see how the two robots interact. "A lot of times kids compete for attention," she says. "It would be interesting to program the robot to get attention."

As a woman robotmaker, Breazeal is in a distinct minority. A major reason, she says, is that girls do not get enough support in pursuing careers in science. "Girls aren't discouraged," she says, "but they aren't encouraged either." And they don't have enough positive role models. When she was growing up, Breazeal says, she did not see many women scientists, and the ones she did encounter were mainly "difficult people" she did not want to emulate. What made the difference for her is that her mother was a scientist and encouraged her to pursue a career in the sciences.

Informational Text

Breazeal thinks more girls would be attracted to the hard sciences (including physics, chemistry, and biology) if they realized how creative they can be. Contrary to popular conceptions of hard science as dry and rigid, she sees it as a rich field for self-expression. "Technology is flexible enough that you can make it what you want," she says. And Breazeal is certainly doing just that. By emphasizing the social aspect of robotics, she is taking the field in a bold new direction. "I'm trying to challenge the stereotypes," she says, "[by] putting a human face on them."

It's impossible to spend time with Kismet without seeing that face. It is a long way from being a human. But it has enough human qualities that its interactions are, in some way, clearly social. And it forms bonds with people that may fall short of human bonds but are far different from the ones people form with most inanimate objects. Breazeal freely acknowledges that her little creation tugs at her own heartstrings. "I definitely have an attachment to it," she says, admitting that she missed it while on a recent trip to Australia. So what will happen if she ever has to part with Kismet? "I really don't know," she says. "The legal system doesn't have parental rights for robots."

—from TIME

Editor's note: After the publication of this article, Breazeal went on to become an associate professor at M.I.T., as well as director of the school's Robotic Life Group. She published her first book, Designing Sociable Robots, *in 2002 and continues to create robots like Kismet that work and learn in partnership with people.*

> **"Technology is flexible enough that you can make it what you want."**

Respond and Think Critically

Respond and Interpret

1. Write a brief summary of the main ideas in this article before you answer the following questions. For help on writing a summary, see page 415.

2. (a) What is the difference between Kismet and Cog? (b) What can their interactions reveal about human interactions?

3. What are the "two rival schools" of thought on how to build robots?

Analyze and Evaluate

4. (a) How does the author describe the characteristics of the robots and their interactions? (b) Do the descriptions enable you to visualize the robots well? Why or why not? (c) Review your diagram from page 1082. Do these characteristics connect to other technologies today?

5. How does the author use the subject of Cynthia Breazeal to make a point about women in science?

Connect

6. After reading about Kismet, do you think there is any aspect of reality in Isaac Asimov's "Robot Dreams"? Explain.

THE MACHINE NURTURER

Before You Read

World Literature: Canada

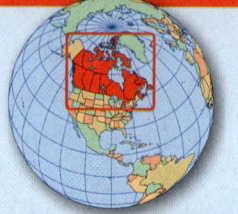

Bread

Meet Margaret Atwood
(born 1939)

Margaret Atwood has become one of Canada's most respected and most popular writers, producing award-winning poems, novels, children's books, short stories, and essays. "I became a poet at the age of sixteen. I did not intend to do it. It was not my fault," Atwood has said.

Growing Up Atwood was born in Ottawa, Ontario, Canada, but her childhood was divided between a variety of Canadian cities and the forests of northwestern Quebec, where her father, a scientist, conducted research about insects. Both her parents were avid readers and encouraged her love of words.

Atwood earned a bachelor's degree from the University of Toronto in 1961 and a graduate degree from Radcliffe College a year later. For the next several years, she combined jobs waiting tables, working at a market research company, and teaching grammar, with off-and-on studies at Harvard University.

> "I began as a profoundly apolitical writer, but then I began to do what all novelists and some poets do; I began to describe the world around me."
>
> —Margaret Atwood

A Focus on Humanity In 1966 Atwood won her first major literary prize, Canada's Governor General's Award, for her second book of poems, *The Circle Game*. The publication of her first novel, *The Edible Woman*, in 1969 coincided with the growing feminist movement and helped put Atwood on the literary map. While much of her writing focuses on women, Atwood is also known for writing that explores human behavior in general.

Though critics have noted the political nature of much of Atwood's writing, Atwood says that she begins new works without a political agenda in mind. "One works by simple observation, looking into things. . . . As an artist your first loyalty is to your art. Unless this is the case, you're going to be a second-rate artist." Pressed by an interviewer to name her "discrete truth," Atwood mentioned her belief that "money should not be the measure of all things."

In recent years, Atwood has become so famous in Canada that people follow her around on the streets and in stores. She is a frequent guest on Canadian television and radio. Atwood has remarked, "I'm a serious writer and I never expected to become a popular one."

Literature Online

Author Search For more about Margaret Atwood, go to glencoe.com and enter QuickPass code GL59794u6.

Literature and Reading Preview

Connect to the Story
What do you think of when you hear the word *bread*? What do you associate with bread, and why do you make these associations? Respond to these questions in your journal.

Build Background
In the twentieth century, an estimated 70 million people died from famine, which is still a problem in some third world countries. Most famines are caused by climate, crop failure, disease, war, and misguided economic policies. Political imprisonment is also widespread, especially in countries ruled by dictators.

Set Purposes for Reading

Big Idea The Extraordinary and Fantastic
In this story, Atwood includes both realistic and fantastic details. As you read, ask yourself, What message do these details suggest about human nature?

Literary Element Point of View
Point of view refers to the vantage point from which a story is told. In the second-person point of view, the word "you" establishes the reader's view of the action. As you read "Bread," ask yourself, How does Atwood's use of the second-person point of view force readers into a personal confrontation with stark realities?

Reading Strategy Recognize Author's Purpose
The **author's purpose** is the author's intent in writing a work. Authors usually write for one or more of the following purposes: to persuade, to inform, to explain, to entertain, or to describe a process. As you read, consider what Atwood describes. Ask yourself, What does her inclusion of these details tell you about her purpose for writing?

Tip: Analyze Scenes "Bread" evokes five different scenes, or contexts. As you read, record your thoughts about why Atwood included each scene.

Scene	Author's Purpose
Cutting yourself a slice of bread and eating it with honey and peanut butter	To show how many people eat bread or take it for granted

---

Learning Objectives

For pages 1088–1092

In studying this text, you will focus on the following objectives:

Literary Study: Analyzing point of view.

Reading: Recognizing author's purpose.

Vocabulary

bloated (blō′tid) *adj.* puffed up; swollen; p. 1090 *After eating too much, Rick felt bloated.*

scavenger (skav′in jər) *n.* one who searches through discarded materials for something useful; p. 1091 *A scavenger found the bicycle at the dump and began riding it.*

subversive (səb vur′ siv) *adj.* intended to destroy or undermine; p. 1091 *He authored a subversive article revealing the councilwoman had broken the law.*

treacherous (trech′ ər əs) *adj.* likely to betray a trust, disloyal; p. 1091 *Her actions toward me were treacherous; I suffered as a result of them.*

dupe (doop) *v.* to fool; to trick; p. 1091 *The salesperson duped me into buying something I did not need.*

MARGARET ATWOOD

BREAD

Still Life. Francisco de Zurbarán (1598–1664). Private collection.

Margaret Atwood

Imagine a piece of bread. You don't have to imagine it, it's right here in the kitchen, on the breadboard, in its plastic bag, lying beside the bread knife. The bread knife is an old one you picked up at an auction; it has the word BREAD carved into the wooden handle. You open the bag, pull back the wrapper, cut yourself a slice. You put butter on it, then peanut butter, then honey, and you fold it over. Some of the honey runs out onto your fingers and you lick it off. It takes you about a minute to eat the bread. This bread happens to be brown, but there is also white bread, in the refrigerator, and a heel of rye you got last week, round as a full stomach then, now going moldy. Occasionally you make bread. You think of it as something relaxing to do with your hands.

Imagine a famine. Now imagine a piece of bread. Both of these things are real but you happen to be in the same room with only one of them. Put yourself into a different room, that's what the mind is for. You are now lying on a thin mattress in a hot room. The walls are made of dried earth, and your sister, who is younger than you, is in the room with you. She is starving, her belly is **bloated**, flies land on her eyes; you brush them off with your hand. You have cloth too, filthy but damp, and you press it to her lips and forehead. The piece of bread is the bread you've been saving, for days it seems. You are as hungry as she is, but not yet as weak. How long does this take? When will someone come with more bread? You think of going out to see if you might find something that could be eaten, but outside the streets are infested with

Point of View In this first scene, what type of situation is the point of view used to evoke?

Vocabulary
bloated (blō′tid) *adj.* puffed up; swollen

1090   UNIT 6   GENRE FICTION

scavengers and the stink of corpses is everywhere.

Should you share the bread or give the whole piece to your sister? Should you eat the piece of bread yourself? After all, you have a better chance of living, you're stronger. How long does it take to decide?

Imagine a prison. There is something you know that you have not yet told. Those in control of the prison know that you know. So do those not in control. If you tell, thirty or forty or a hundred of your friends, your comrades, will be caught and will die. If you refuse to tell, tonight will be like last night. They always choose the night. You don't think about the night, however, but about the piece of bread they offered you. How long does it take? This piece of bread was brown and fresh and reminded you of sunlight falling across a wooden floor. It reminded you of a bowl, a yellow bowl that was once in your home. It held apples and pears; it stood on a table you can also remember. It's not the hunger or the pain that is killing you but the absence of the yellow bowl. If you could only hold the bowl in your hands, right here, you could withstand anything, you tell yourself. The bread they offered you is **subversive**, it's **treacherous**, it does not mean life.

Recognize Author's Purpose *What do these questions suggest about the author's purpose?*

Point of View *According to the story, you, as the prisoner, feel that the offered bread is "subversive" and "treacherous." Why might a prisoner feel this way?*

Vocabulary

scavenger (skav′ in jər) *n.* one who searches through discarded materials for something useful

subversive (səb vur′ siv) *adj.* intended to destroy or undermine

treacherous (trech′ ər əs) *adj.* likely to betray a trust; disloyal

---

There were once two sisters. One was rich and had no children, the other had five children and was a widow, so poor that she no longer had any food left. She went to her sister and asked her for a mouthful of bread. "My children are dying," she said. The rich sister said, "I do not have enough for myself," and drove her away from the door. Then the husband of the rich sister came home and wanted to cut himself a piece of bread; but when he made the first cut, out flowed red blood.

Everyone knew what that meant.

This a traditional German fairy tale.

The loaf of bread I have conjured[1] for you floats about a foot above your kitchen table. The table is normal, there are no trap doors in it. A blue tea towel[2] floats beneath the bread, and there are no strings attaching the cloth to the bread or the bread to the ceiling or the table to the cloth, you've proved it by passing your hand above and below. You didn't touch the bread though. What stopped you? You don't want to know whether the bread is real or whether it's just a hallucination I've somehow **duped** you into seeing. There's no doubt that you can see the bread, you can even smell it, it smells like yeast, and it looks old enough, solid as your own arm. But can you trust it? Can you eat it? You don't want to know, imagine that. ∽

---

1. *Conjured* means "caused to appear, as by magic."
2. A *tea towel* is a towel used for drying dishes.

The Extraordinary and Fantastic *What might the story be suggesting about the reader's desire to confront reality?*

Vocabulary

dupe (do͞op) *v.* to fool; to trick

After You Read

Respond and Think Critically

Respond and Interpret
1. Which scene affected you most strongly? Why?
2. (a) What does the narrator describe in the first paragraph? (b) What attitude toward bread does the description convey?
3. How does the message of the traditional German fairy tale relate to the other situations in the story?

Analyze and Evaluate
4. (a) What do you think happens to the prisoner in the night? (b) What does the yellow bowl symbolize for the prisoner?
5. How does reading the first paragraph affect your perception of the next three scenes? Explain.

Connect
6. **Big Idea** The Extraordinary and Fantastic How does the story upend common ideas about what is ordinary in life and what is extraordinary? Explain.
7. **Connect to Today** What scenes in the story help create empathy for prisoners and starving people in today's world?

Literary Element Point of View
Point of view is the vantage point from which a story is told.

1. How did the use of second-person point of view affect your reaction to the story?
2. (a) How would this story be different if it had been told from the first-person point of view? (b) Would it have been as effective? Explain.

Reading Strategy Recognize Author's Purpose
The **author's purpose** is the author's intent in writing a literary work. Review the chart you made on page 1087 and answer the following questions.

1. Early on, the story says, "Put yourself into a different room, that's what the mind is for." What does this command suggest about the purpose of the story?
2. In your opinion, what were Atwood's goals?

Vocabulary Practice

Practice with Denotation and Connotation
Denotation is the literal, or dictionary, meaning of a word. **Connotation** is the implied, or cultural, meaning. For example, the words *stubborn* and *intractable* have a similar denotation, "unwilling to cooperate," but have different connotations. While *stubborn* has a negative connotation, *intractable* has a more negative connotation.

Each vocabulary word is paired with another word. For each pair, choose the word that has a more negative connotation. Explain your answer.

1. bloated — swollen
2. scavenger — searcher
3. subversive — illegal
4. treacherous — disloyal
5. dupe — mislead

Writing
Write a Story Write a short fantasy story, similar to "Bread," in which you describe an object with symbolic meaning. Try using the second-person point of view as Atwood does. Begin by freewriting about images and ideas you associate with the object.

Literature Online
Selection Resources For Selection Quizzes, eFlashcards, and Reading-Writing Connection activities, go to glencoe.com and enter QuickPass code GL59794u6.

Before You Read

The Witness for the Prosecution

Meet Agatha Christie
(1890–1976)

After a lifetime of writing, Agatha Christie was an expert at inventing—and solving—murder mysteries with complex plots, ingenious twists and turns, and satisfying solutions. In story after story, Christie, who was sometimes called the "Queen of Crime" and the "Duchess of Death," subtly directs the reader's attention away from the most crucial clues.

> "There's nothing like boredom to make you write."
>
> —Agatha Christie

Bored to Death? How did this author of approximately seventy novels, more than one hundred short stories, and over one dozen plays get started? In an interview, Christie revealed that she began imagining stories as a child to combat boredom. At the age of eighteen, she was recovering from influenza when her mother suggested that she write a story. Christie's very first attempt, entitled "The House of Beauty," was published in a magazine.

By the age of twenty-six, Christie had written her first novel, *The Mysterious Affair at Styles*, and had begun to establish her reputation.

The Christie Detectives Christie created a number of fictional detectives. Hercule Poirot is the private eye in what may be Christie's most famous work, *Murder on the Orient Express*. Jane Marple is an amateur sleuth in her seventies with a knack for solving mysteries, who first appears in *The Murder at the Vicarage*. Novels featuring Poirot and Marple established Christie as the most popular mystery writer of all time.

Many Faithful Readers Only surpassed by sales of the Bible and the works of William Shakespeare, Christie's books have sold a spectacular two billion copies. Ironically, Christie once claimed, "I don't enjoy writing detective stories. I enjoy thinking of a detective story, planning it, but when the time comes to write it, it is like going to work everyday, like having a job." Among the many honors she received was the New York Drama Critics Circle Award for best foreign play, *The Witness for the Prosecution*. Christie continued writing until the last year of her life, publishing her eightieth book at the age of eighty.

Author Search For more about Agatha Christie, go to glencoe.com and enter QuickPass code GL59794u6.

Literature and Reading Preview

Connect to the Story
Do people notice habits that are performed unconsciously, such as foot tapping or nail biting? What might these habits reveal? Discuss these questions with a partner.

Build Background
"The Witness for the Prosecution" is about a man in England who is accused of "willful murder," meaning premeditated, or planned, murder. In a British court of law, the solicitor prepares the case for the defense but does not argue it at the trial. That is the job of the counsel for the defense, referred to in this story as the K.C., or King's Counsel.

Set Purposes for Reading

Big Idea The Extraordinary and Fantastic

As you read, ask yourself, What seems convincing and real, and what seems suspicious or mysterious, about the accused man, his story, and the woman who testifies against him?

Literary Element Motivation

Motivation is the stated or implied reason or cause for a character's actions. As you read, ask yourself, Which motivations do characters attribute to themselves? Which motivations do characters suggest as belonging to another?

Reading Strategy Make Inferences About Characters

When you **make inferences about characters,** you use your reason and experience to figure out what an author is not saying directly about a character. As you read, ask yourself, What can I infer about these characters?

Tip: Take Notes Use a chart to record details about the characters and your inferences.

Detail	+ My Reason or Experience	= My Inference

Learning Objectives

For pages 1093–1115

In studying this text, you will focus on the following objectives:

Literary Study: Analyzing motivation.

Reading: Make inferences about characters.

Vocabulary

cultivate (kul′tə vāt′) v. to encourage or further the development of; p. 1097 *Lauren cultivated Rachel's friendship by calling her every night.*

pretext (prē′tekst) n. a reason or motive offered in order to disguise real intentions; p. 1098 *Jill wanted to stay home, so she told her mother she was sick, but that was just a pretext.*

amicable (am′ə kə bəl) adj. friendly; p. 1101 *George and Tameka, who had an amicable relationship, talked to each other every day.*

recoil (ri koil′) v. to shrink back physically or emotionally; p. 1104 *Zach recoils at the thought of telling on his best friend.*

animosity (an′ə mos′ə tē) n. ill will or resentment; active strong dislike or hostility; p. 1110 *Jorge's animosity toward Greg showed itself in his tense posture and scowl.*

The Witness for the Prosecution

Agatha Christie

The Barrister. Thomas Davidson (1863–1908). Oil on canvas. Roy Miles Fine Paintings, London.

Visual Vocabulary
Pince-nez (pans′ nā′) are eyeglasses that are clipped to the nose rather than held on by pieces that bend around the ears.

Mr. Mayherne adjusted his pince-nez and cleared his throat with a little dry-as-dust cough that was wholly typical of him. Then he looked again at the man opposite him, the man charged with willful murder.

Mr. Mayherne was a small man, precise in manner, neatly, not to say foppishly[1] dressed, with a pair of very shrewd and piercing gray eyes, by no means a fool. Indeed, as a solicitor, Mr. Mayherne's reputation stood very high. His voice, when he spoke to his client, was dry but not unsympathetic.

"I must impress upon you again that you are in very grave danger, and that the utmost frankness is necessary."

Leonard Vole, who had been staring in a dazed fashion at the blank wall in front of him, transferred his glance to the solicitor.

"I know," he said hopelessly. "You keep telling me so. But I can't seem to realize yet that I'm charged with murder—*murder.* And such a dastardly[2] crime too."

Mr. Mayherne was practical, not emotional. He coughed again, took off his pince-nez, polished them carefully, and replaced them on his nose. Then he said:

---

1. *Foppishly* means "fashionable in a silly or vain way."
2. *Dastardly* means "mean."

Make Inferences About Characters What inferences can you make about Mayherne based on the details so far?

"Yes, yes, yes. Now, my dear Mr. Vole, we're going to make a determined effort to get you off—and we shall succeed—we shall succeed. But I must have all the facts. I must know just how damaging the case against you is likely to be. Then we can fix upon the best line of defense."

Still the young man looked at him in the same dazed, hopeless fashion. To Mr. Mayherne the case had seemed black enough, and the guilt of the prisoner assured. Now, for the first time, he felt a doubt.

"You think I'm guilty," said Leonard Vole, in a low voice. "But, by God, I swear I'm not! It looks pretty black against me; I know that. I'm like a man caught in a net—the meshes of it all round me, entangling me whichever way I turn. But I didn't do it, Mr. Mayherne; I didn't do it!"

In such a position a man was bound to protest his innocence.[3] Mr. Mayherne knew that. Yet, in spite of himself, he was impressed. It might be, after all, that Leonard Vole was innocent.

"You are right, Mr. Vole," he said gravely. "The case does look very black against you. Nevertheless, I accept your assurance. Now, let us get to facts. I want you to tell me in your own words exactly how you came to make the acquaintance of Miss Emily French."

"It was one day in Oxford Street. I saw an elderly lady crossing the road. She was carrying a lot of parcels. In the middle of the street she dropped them, tried to recover them, found a bus was almost on top of her and just managed to reach the curb safely, dazed and bewildered by people having shouted at her. I recovered her parcels, wiped the mud off them as best I could, retied the string of one, and returned them to her."

"There was no question of your having saved her life?"

"Oh, dear me, no! All I did was to perform a common act of courtesy. She was extremely grateful, thanked me warmly, and said something about my manners not being those of most of the younger generation—I can't remember the exact words. Then I lifted my hat and went on. I never expected to see her again. But life is full of coincidences. That very evening I came across her at a party at a friend's house. She recognized me at once and asked that I should be introduced to her. I then found out that she was a Miss Emily French and that she lived at Cricklewood. I talked to her for some time. She was, I imagine, an old lady who took sudden and violent fancies to people. She took one to me on the strength of a perfectly simple action which anyone might have performed. On leaving, she shook me warmly by the hand, and asked me to come and see her. I replied, of course, that I should be very pleased to do so, and she then urged me to name a day. I did not want particularly to go, but it would have seemed churlish[4] to refuse, so I fixed on the following Saturday. After she had gone, I learned something about her from my friends. That she was rich, eccentric, lived alone with one maid and owned no less than eight cats."

"I see," said Mr. Mayherne. "The question of her being well off came up as early as that?"

"If you mean that I inquired—" began Leonard Vole hotly, but Mr. Mayherne stilled him with a gesture.

"I have to look at the case as it will be presented by the other side. An ordinary

---

3. To *protest* one's *innocence* is to steadfastly declare it.

Motivation What is Mayherne's motivation for preparing the best possible defense?

---

4. Here, *churlish* means "rude" or "ill-bred."

Motivation Why do you think Vole includes these details?

Make Inferences About Characters What might Mayherne infer from Vole's anger?

Caricature of Émile Zola, 1880. Artist unknown.

View the Art The subject of this painting, French novelist Émile Zola, wears pince-nez eyeglasses, like Mr. Mayherne in the story. What other similarities can you find between the man in the painting and the solicitor in Christie's story?

"My friend, George Harvey, at whose house the party took place."

"Is he likely to remember having done so?"

"I really don't know. Of course it is some time ago now."

"Quite so, Mr. Vole. You see, the first aim of the prosecution will be to establish that you were in low water financially—that is true, is it not?"

Leonard Vole flushed.

"Yes," he said, in a low voice. "I'd been having a run of infernal[5] bad luck just then."

"Quite so," said Mr. Mayherne again. "That being, as I say, in low water financially, you met this rich old lady and **cultivated** her acquaintance assiduously.[6] Now if we are in a position to say that you had no idea she was well off, and that you visited her out of pure kindness of heart—"

"Which is the case."

"I daresay. I am not disputing the point. I am looking at it from the outside point of view. A great deal depends on the memory of Mr. Harvey. Is he likely to remember that conversation, or is he not? Could he be confused by counsel into believing that it took place later?"

Leonard Vole reflected for some minutes. Then he said steadily enough, but with a rather paler face:

"I do not think that that line would be successful, Mr. Mayherne. Several of those present heard his remark, and one or two observer would not have supposed Miss French to be a lady of means. She lived poorly, almost humbly. Unless you had been told the contrary, you would in all probability have considered her to be in poor circumstances—at any rate to begin with. Who was it exactly who told you that she was well off?"

---

5. *Infernal* means "hellish."
6. Here, *assiduously* means "with a great deal of effort and determination."

Vocabulary

cultivate (kul′tə vāt′) *v.* to encourage or further the development of

of them chaffed[7] me about my conquest of a rich old lady."

The solicitor endeavored to hide his disappointment with a wave of the hand.

"Unfortunate," he said. "But I congratulate you upon your plain speaking, Mr. Vole. It is to you I look to guide me. Your judgment is quite right. To persist in the line I spoke of would have been disastrous. We must leave that point. You made the acquaintance of Miss French; you called upon her; the acquaintanceship progressed. We want a clear reason for all this. Why did you, a young man of thirty-three, good-looking, fond of sport, popular with your friends, devote so much of your time to an elderly woman with whom you could hardly have anything in common?"

Leonard Vole flung out his hands in a nervous gesture.

"I can't tell you—I really can't tell you. After the first visit, she pressed me to come again, spoke of being lonely and unhappy. She made it difficult for me to refuse. She showed so plainly her fondness and affection for me that I was placed in an awkward position. You see, Mr. Mayherne, I've got a weak nature—I drift—I'm one of those people who can't say 'No.' And believe me or not, as you like, after the third or fourth visit I paid her I found myself getting genuinely fond of the old thing. My mother died when I was young, an aunt brought me up, and she too died before I was fifteen. If I told you that I genuinely enjoyed being mothered and pampered, I daresay you'd only laugh."

Mr. Mayherne did not laugh. Instead he took off his pince-nez again and polished them, a sign with him that he was thinking deeply.

"I accept your explanation, Mr. Vole," he said at last. "I believe it to be psychologically probable. Whether a jury would take that view of it is another matter. Please continue your narrative. When was it that Miss French first asked you to look into her business affairs?"

"After my third or fourth visit to her. She understood very little of money matters and was worried about some investments."

Mr. Mayherne looked up sharply.

"Be careful, Mr. Vole. The maid, Janet Mackenzie, declares that her mistress was a good woman of business and transacted all her own affairs, and this is borne out[8] by the testimony of her bankers."

"I can't help that," said Vole earnestly. "That's what she said to me."

Mr. Mayherne looked at him for a moment or two in silence. Though he had no intention of saying so, his belief in Leonard Vole's innocence was at that moment strengthened. He knew something of the mentality of elderly ladies. He saw Miss French, infatuated with the good-looking young man, hunting about for **pretexts** that would bring him to the house. What more likely than that she should plead ignorance of business and beg him to help her with her money affairs? She was enough of a woman of the world to realize that any man is slightly flattered by such an admission of his superiority. Leonard Vole had been flattered. Perhaps, too, she had not been averse[9] to letting this young man know that she was wealthy. Emily French had been a strong-willed old woman, willing to pay her price for what she wanted. All this passed rap-

---

7. *Chaffed* means "teased in a playful way."
8. *Borne out* means "verified by facts, testimony, or events."
9. Here, *averse* means "against" or "disinclined."

The Uncanny and Mysterious *So far, what is mysterious to you about Vole's relationship with Miss French?*

Vocabulary

pretext (prē′tekst) *n.* a reason or motive offered in order to disguise real intentions

idly through Mr. Mayherne's mind, but he gave no indication of it and asked instead a further question.

"And you did handle her affairs for her at her request?"

"I did."

"Mr. Vole," said the solicitor, "I am going to ask you a very serious question, and one to which it is vital I should have a truthful answer. You were in low water financially. You had the handling of an old lady's affairs—an old lady who, according to her own statement, knew little or nothing of business. Did you at any time, or in any manner, convert to your own use the securities which you handled? Did you engage in any transaction for your own pecuniary[10] advantage which will not bear the light of day?" He quelled[11] the other's response. "Wait a minute before you answer. There are two courses open to us. Either we can make a feature of your probity[12] and honesty in conducting her affairs whilst pointing out how unlikely it is that you would commit murder to obtain money which you might have obtained by such infinitely easier means. If, on the other hand, there is anything in your dealings which the prosecution will get hold of—if, to put it baldly, it can be proved that you swindled the old lady in any way—we must take the line that you had no motive for the murder, since she was already a profitable source of income to you. You perceive the distinction. Now, I beg of you, take your time before you reply."

But Leonard Vole took no time at all.

"My dealings with Miss French's affairs were all perfectly fair and aboveboard. I acted for her interests to the very best of my ability, as anyone will find who looks into the matter."

"Thank you," said Mr. Mayherne. "You relieve my mind very much. I pay you the compliment of believing that you are far too clever to lie to me over such an important matter."

"Surely," said Vole eagerly, "the strongest point in my favor is the lack of motive. Granted that I cultivated the acquaintanceship of a rich old lady in the hopes of getting money out of her—that, I gather, is the substance of what you have been saying—surely her death frustrates all my hopes?"

The solicitor looked at him steadily. Then, very deliberately, he repeated his unconscious trick with his pince-nez. It was not until they were firmly replaced on his nose that he spoke.

"Are you not aware, Mr. Vole, that Miss French left a will under which you are the principal beneficiary?"[13]

"What?" The prisoner sprang to his feet. His dismay was obvious and unforced. "My God! What are you saying? She left her money to me?"

Mr. Mayherne nodded slowly. Vole sank down again, his head in his hands.

"You pretend you know nothing of this will?"

"Pretend? There's no pretense about it. I knew nothing about it."

"What would you say if I told you that the maid, Janet Mackenzie, swears that you *did* know? That her mistress told her distinctly that she had consulted you in the matter and told you of her intentions?"

"Say? That she's lying! No, I go too fast. Janet is an elderly woman. She was a faithful watchdog to her mistress, and she didn't like me. She was jealous and suspicious. I should say that Miss French confided her intentions to Janet, and that Janet either mistook something she said or else was convinced in her own mind that I

---

10. *Pecuniary* means "relating to money" or "monetary."
11. *Quelled* means "crushed" or "quieted."
12. *Probity* is moral uprightness.
13. *A beneficiary* is a person who receives money from a will.

AGATHA CHRISTIE

Bond Street, 1999. Peter Miller. Oil on canvas, 35.6 x 40.6 cm. Private collection.

View the Art Bond Street is an upscale, exclusive shopping street in London. What role does the exchange of money play in this story?

---

had persuaded the old lady into doing it. I daresay that she herself believes now that Miss French actually told her so."

"You don't think she dislikes you enough to lie deliberately about the matter?"

Leonard Vole looked shocked and startled.

"No, indeed! Why should she?"

"I don't know," said Mr. Mayherne thoughtfully. "But she's very bitter against you."

The wretched young man groaned again.

"I'm beginning to see," he muttered. "It's frightful. I made up to her, that's what they'll say, I got her to make a will leaving her money to me, and then I go there that night, and there's nobody in the house—they find her the next day—oh! my God, it's awful!"

"You are wrong about there being nobody in the house," said Mr. Mayherne. "Janet, as you remember, was to go out for the evening. She went, but about half past nine she returned to fetch the pattern of a blouse sleeve which she had promised to a friend. She let herself in by the back door, went upstairs and fetched it, and went out again. She heard voices in the sitting room, though she could not distinguish what they said, but she will swear that one of them was Miss French's and one was a man's."

"At half past nine," said Leonard Vole. "At half past nine . . ." He sprang to his feet. "But then I'm saved—saved—"

Motivation What does Vole say motivates Mackenzie? What else might motivate her?

"What do you mean, saved?" cried Mr. Mayherne, astonished.

"By half past nine I was at home again! My wife can prove that. I left Miss French about five minutes to nine. I arrived home about twenty past nine. My wife was there waiting for me. Oh, thank God—thank God! And bless Janet Mackenzie's sleeve pattern."

In his exuberance,[14] he hardly noticed that the grave expression on the solicitor's face had not altered. But the latter's words brought him down to earth with a bump.

"Who, then, in your opinion, murdered Miss French?"

"Why, a burglar, of course, as was thought at first. The window was forced, you remember. She was killed with a heavy blow from a crowbar, and the crowbar was found lying on the floor beside the body. And several articles were missing. But for Janet's absurd suspicions and dislike of me, the police would never have swerved from the right track."

"That will hardly do, Mr. Vole," said the solicitor. "The things that were missing were mere trifles of no value, taken as a blind.[15] And the marks on the window were not at all conclusive. Besides, think for yourself. You say you were no longer in the house by half past nine. Who, then, was the man Janet heard talking to Miss French in the sitting room? She would hardly be having an **amicable** conversation with a burglar!"

"No," said Vole. "No—" He looked puzzled and discouraged. "But, anyway," he added with reviving spirit, "it lets me out. I've got an alibi. You must see Romaine—my wife—at once."

"Certainly," acquiesced[16] the lawyer. "I should already have seen Mrs. Vole but for her being absent when you were arrested. I wired to Scotland at once, and I understand that she arrives back tonight. I am going to call upon her immediately I leave here."

Vole nodded, a great expression of satisfaction settling down over his face.

"Yes, Romaine will tell you. My God! it's a lucky chance that."

"Excuse me, Mr. Vole, but you are very fond of your wife?"

"Of course."

"And she of you?"

"Romaine is devoted to me. She'd do anything in the world for me."

He spoke enthusiastically, but the solicitor's heart sank a little lower. The testimony of a devoted wife—would it gain credence?[17]

"Was there anyone else who saw you return at nine-twenty? A maid, for instance?"

"We have no maid."

"Did you meet anyone in the street on the way back?"

"Nobody I knew. I rode part of the way in a bus. The conductor might remember."

Mr. Mayherne shook his head doubtfully.

"There is no one, then, who can confirm your wife's testimony?"

"No. But it isn't necessary, surely?"

"I daresay not. I daresay not," said Mr. Mayherne hastily. "Now there's just one thing more. Did Miss French know that you were a married man?"

"Oh, yes."

"Yet you never took your wife to see her. Why was that?"

---

14. *Exuberance* means "excited enthusiasm."
15. Here, a *blind* refers to an action undertaken to throw an investigator off the track.

Make Inferences About Characters Which details here might lead you to infer that Vole is telling the truth?

Vocabulary

amicable (am′ ə kə bəl) *adj.* friendly

16. *Acquiesced* means "agreed."
17. *Credence* is acceptance that something is true.

The Tea Party. Henry Lamb (1885–1960). Oil on board. The Arts Club, London.

View the Art Tea parties are a long-standing British tradition and often feature displays of hospitality and polite conversation. How do different settings, influence the behavior of the characters in this story?

For the first time, Leonard Vole's answer came halting and uncertain.

"Well—I don't know."

"Are you aware that Janet Mackenzie says her mistress believed you to be single and contemplated marrying you in the future?"

Vole laughed.

"Absurd! There was forty years' difference in age between us."

"It has been done," said the solicitor dryly. "The fact remains. Your wife never met Miss French?"

"No—" Again the constraint.[18]

"You will permit me to say," said the lawyer, "that I hardly understand your attitude in the matter."

Vole flushed, hesitated, and then spoke.

"I'll make a clean breast of it. I was hard up, as you know. I hoped that Miss French might lend me some money. She was fond of me, but she wasn't at all interested in the struggles of a young couple. Early on, I found that she had taken it for granted that my wife and I didn't get on—were living apart. Mr. Mayherne—I wanted the money—for Romaine's sake. I said nothing, and allowed

Motivation How does this information suggest a motivation for murder?

18. *Constraint* refers to "the act of holding something back."

the old lady to think what she chose. She spoke of my being an adopted son to her. There was never any question of marriage—that must be just Janet's imagination."

"And that is all?"

"Yes—that is all."

Was there just a shade of hesitation in the words? The lawyer fancied so. He rose and held out his hand.

"Good-bye, Mr. Vole." He looked into the haggard young face and spoke with an unusual impulse. "I believe in your innocence in spite of the multitude of facts arrayed against you.[19] I hope to prove it and vindicate[20] you completely."

Vole smiled back at him.

"You'll find the alibi is all right," he said cheerfully.

Again he hardly noticed that the other did not respond.

"The whole thing hinges a good deal on the testimony of Janet Mackenzie," said Mr. Mayherne. "She hates you. That much is clear."

"She can hardly hate me," protested the young man.

The solicitor shook his head as he went out.

"Now for Mrs. Vole," he said to himself.

He was seriously disturbed by the way the thing was shaping.

The Voles lived in a small shabby house near Paddington Green. It was to this house that Mr. Mayherne went.

In answer to his ring, a big slatternly[21] woman, obviously a charwoman,[22] answered the door.

"Mrs. Vole? Has she returned yet?"

---

19. The *multitude of facts arrayed against you* refers to the many facts that suggest Vole's guilt.
20. To *vindicate* is to free from blame or suspicion.
21. Here, *slatternly* means "disorderly in personal appearance."
22. A *charwoman* is a woman hired to clean.

Motivation Vole just said he and his wife had no maid. What motivation might he have for not mentioning this charwoman?

"Got back an hour ago. But I dunno if you can see her."

"If you will take my card to her," said Mr. Mayherne quietly, "I am quite sure that she will do so."

The woman looked at him doubtfully, wiped her hand on her apron and took the card. Then she closed the door in his face and left him on the step outside.

In a few minutes, however, she returned with a slightly altered manner.

"Come inside, please."

She ushered him into a tiny drawing room. Mr. Mayherne, examining a drawing on the wall, started up suddenly to face a tall, pale woman who had entered so quietly that he had not heard her.

"Mr. Mayherne? You are my husband's solicitor, are you not? You have come from him? Will you please sit down?"

Until she spoke, he had not realized that she was not English. Now, observing her more closely, he noticed the high cheekbones, the dense blue-black of the hair, and an occasional very slight movement of the hands that was distinctly foreign. A strange woman, very quiet. So quiet as to make one uneasy. From the very first Mr. Mayherne was conscious that he was up against something that he did not understand.

"Now, my dear Mrs. Vole," he began, "you must not give way—"[23]

He stopped. It was so very obvious that Romaine Vole had not the slightest intention of giving way. She was perfectly calm and composed.

"Will you please tell me about it?" she said. "I must know everything. Do not think to spare me. I want to know the worst." She hesitated, then repeated in a lower tone, with

---

23. *Give way* suggests breaking down emotionally.

The Extraordinary and Fantastic What is so mysterious to Mayherne about this woman?

a curious emphasis which the lawyer did not understand: "I want to know the worst."

Mr. Mayherne went over his interview with Leonard Vole. She listened attentively, nodding her head now and then.

"I see," she said, when he had finished. "He wants me to say that he came in at twenty minutes past nine that night?"

"He did come in at that time?" said Mr. Mayherne sharply.

"That is not the point," she said coldly. "Will my saying so acquit him? Will they believe me?"

Mr. Mayherne was taken aback. She had gone so quickly to the core of the matter.

"That is what I want to know," she said. "Will it be enough? Is there anyone else who can support my evidence?"

There was a suppressed[24] eagerness in her manner that made him vaguely uneasy.

"So far there is no one else," he said reluctantly.

"I see," said Romaine Vole.

She sat for a minute or two perfectly still. A little smile played over her lips.

The lawyer's feeling of alarm grew stronger and stronger.

"Mrs. Vole—" he began. "I know what you must feel—"

"Do you?" she asked. "I wonder."

"In the circumstances—"

"In the circumstances—I intend to play a lone hand."

He looked at her in dismay.

"But, my dear Mrs. Vole—you are overwrought.[25] Being so devoted to your husband—"

"I beg your pardon?"

The sharpness of her voice made him start. He repeated in a hesitating manner:

"Being so devoted to your husband—"

Romaine Vole nodded slowly, the same strange smile on her lips.

"Did he tell you that I was devoted to him?" she asked softly. "Ah! yes, I can see he did. How stupid men are! Stupid—stupid—stupid—"

She rose suddenly to her feet. All the intense emotion that the lawyer had been conscious of in the atmosphere was now concentrated in her tone.

"I hate him, I tell you! I hate him. I hate him. I hate him! I would like to see him hanged by the neck till he is dead."

The lawyer **recoiled** before her and the smoldering passion in her eyes.

She advanced a step nearer and continued vehemently:

"Perhaps I shall see it. Supposing I tell you that he did not come in that night at twenty past nine, but at twenty past ten? You say that he tells you he knew nothing about the money coming to him. Supposing I tell you he knew all about it, and counted on it, and committed murder to get it? Supposing I tell you that he admitted to me that night when he came in what he had done? That there was blood on his coat? What then? Supposing that I stand up in court and say all these things?"

Her eyes seemed to challenge him. With an effort, he concealed his growing dismay, and endeavored to speak in a rational tone.

"You cannot be asked to give evidence against your husband—"

"He is not my husband!" The words came out so quickly that he fancied he had misunderstood her.

"I beg your pardon? I—"

Motivation *What is the woman's motivation for making this statement?*

Vocabulary

recoil (ri koil´) *v.* to shrink back physically or emotionally

---

24. Here, *suppressed* means "restrained."
25. Someone who is *overwrought* is upset or agitated.

Make Inferences About Characters *What is Mayherne most likely to infer from these questions?*

Still Life With Book, Papers, and Inkwell, 1876. François Bonvin. National Gallery, London.

View the Art The objects depicted in still life paintings in the nineteenth century often served an allegorical, or symbolic, purpose. What might the objects in this painting symbolize in relation to the story?

"He is not my husband." The silence was so intense that you could have heard a pin drop.

"I was an actress in Vienna. My husband is alive but in a madhouse. So we could not marry. I am glad now."

She nodded defiantly.

"I should like you to tell me one thing," said Mr. Mayherne. He contrived[26] to appear as cool and unemotional as ever. "Why are you so bitter against Leonard Vole?"

She shook her head, smiling a little.

"Yes, you would like to know. But I shall not tell you. I will keep my secret. . . ."

Mr. Mayherne gave his dry little cough and rose.

"There seems no point in prolonging this interview," he remarked. "You will hear from me again after I have communicated with my client."

She came closer to him, looking into his eyes with her own wonderful dark ones.

"Tell me," she said, "did you believe—honestly—that he was innocent when you came here today?"

"I did," said Mr. Mayherne.

"You poor little man," she laughed.

"And I believe so still," finished the lawyer. "Good evening, madam."

He went out of the room, taking with him the memory of her startled face.

"This is going to be the devil of a business," said Mr. Mayherne to himself as he strode along the street.

Extraordinary, the whole thing. An extraordinary woman. A very dangerous woman. Women were the devil when they got their knife into you.

What was to be done? That wretched young man hadn't a leg to stand upon. Of course, possibly he did commit the crime. . . .

"No," said Mr. Mayherne to himself. "No—there's almost too much evidence against him. I don't believe this woman. She was trumping up[27] the whole story. But she'll never bring it into court."

He wished he felt more conviction[28] on the point.

---

26. Here, *contrived* means "made a great effort."
27. To *trump up* is to make up or concoct.
28. Here, *conviction* means "certainty."

Make Inferences About Characters *What inferences can you draw about Mayherne's character based on this comment?*

The police court proceedings[29] were brief and dramatic. The principal witnesses for the prosecution were Janet Mackenzie, maid to the dead woman, and Romaine Heilger, Austrian subject, the mistress of the prisoner.

Mr. Mayherne sat in court and listened to the damning story that the latter told. It was on the lines she had indicated to him in their interview.

The prisoner reserved his defense and was committed for trial.

Mr. Mayherne was at his wits' end. The case against Leonard Vole was black beyond words. Even the famous K.C.[30] who was engaged for the defense held out little hope.

"If we can shake that Austrian woman's testimony, we might do something," he said dubiously.[31] "But it's a bad business."

Mr. Mayherne had concentrated his energies on one single point. Assuming Leonard Vole to be speaking the truth, and to have left the murdered woman's house at nine o'clock, who was the man Janet heard talking to Miss French at half past nine?

The only ray of light was in the shape of a scapegrace[32] nephew who had in bygone days cajoled[33] and threatened his aunt out of various sums of money. Janet Mackenzie, the solicitor learned, had always been attached to this young man and had never ceased urging his claims upon her mistress. It certainly seemed possible that it was this nephew who had been with Miss French after Leonard Vole left, especially as he was not to be found in any of his old haunts.

In all other directions, the lawyer's researches had been negative in their result. No one had seen Leonard Vole entering his own house, or leaving that of Miss French. No one had seen any

Mrs. Seymour Fort, 1778. John Singleton Copley.

View the Art Painter John Singleton Copley is considered one of the most highly acclaimed portrait artists of the colonial United States. How do you imagine the personality of the woman in the painting? Which character in the story might she reflect, and why?

---

29. *Police court proceedings* are similar to proceedings that result in an indictment in the United States: on the basis of testimony given in court, Vole is "committed for trial," or required to stand trial.
30. *K.C.* is the King's Counsel, who is referred to later in this story as Sir Charles.
31. *Dubiously* means "doubtfully."
32. A *scapegrace* is a rascal.
33. *Cajoled* means "urged in a flattering way in order to achieve one's own ends."

Motivation What motivation does Mackenzie have for pinning the crime on Vole?

other man enter or leave the house in Cricklewood. All inquiries drew blank.[34]

It was the eve of the trial when Mr. Mayherne received the letter which was to lead his thoughts in an entirely new direction.

It came by the six o'clock post. An illiterate scrawl, written on common paper and enclosed in a dirty envelope with the stamp stuck on crooked.

Mr. Mayherne read it through once or twice before he grasped its meaning.

> "Dear Mister:
> "You're the lawyer chap wot acts for the young feller. If you want that painted foreign hussy showd up for wot she is an her pack of lies you come to 16 Shaw's Rents Stepney tonight It ull cawst you 2 hundred quid Arsk for Misses Mogson."[35]

The solicitor read and reread this strange epistle. It might, of course, be a hoax,[36] but when he thought it over, he became increasingly convinced that it was genuine, and also convinced that it was the one hope for the prisoner. The evidence of Romaine Heilger damned him completely, and the line the defense meant to pursue, the line that the evidence of a woman who had admittedly lived an immoral life was not to be trusted, was at best a weak one.

Mr. Mayherne's mind was made up. It was his duty to save his client at all costs. He must go to Shaw's Rents.

He had some difficulty in finding the place, a ramshackle building in an evil-smelling slum, but at last he did so, and on inquiry for Mrs. Mogson was sent up to a room on the third floor. On this door he knocked and, getting no answer, knocked again.

At this second knock, he heard a shuffling sound inside, and presently the door was opened cautiously half an inch, and a bent figure peered out.

Suddenly the woman, for it was a woman, gave a chuckle and opened the door wider.

"So it's you, dearie," she said, in a wheezy voice. "Nobody with you, is there? No playing tricks? That's right. You can come in—you can come in."

With some reluctance the lawyer stepped across the threshold into the small dirty room, with its flickering gas jet. There was an untidy unmade bed in a corner, a plain deal table[37] and two rickety chairs. For the first time Mr. Mayherne had a full view of the tenant of this unsavory apartment. She was a woman of middle age, bent in figure, with a mass of untidy gray hair and a scarf wound tightly round her face. She saw him looking at this and laughed again, the same curious, toneless chuckle.

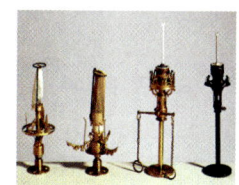

Visual Vocabulary
A *gas jet* is used to turn on light created by gas rather than by electricity.

"Wondering why I hide my beauty, dear? He, he, he. Afraid it may tempt you, eh? But you shall see—you shall see."

She drew aside the scarf, and the lawyer recoiled involuntarily before the almost formless blur of scarlet. She replaced the scarf again.

---

34. *Drew blank* means "were left unanswered."
35. This note is written to suggest the speech of lower-class people in London. *Wot* means "who" in the first line and "what" in the third line; *ull cawst* means "will cost"; and 200 *quid* is 200 pounds, a huge sum at the time.
36. A *hoax* is an act intended to deceive or trick.
37. A *deal table* is a simple table made of fir or pine boards, which the British call "deal."

Make Inferences About Characters *What inference might you make about this woman, based on her appearance?*

The Trial of Mr Pickwick. Cecil Charles Windsor Aldin (1870–1935). Color lithograph. Dickens House Museum, London.

View the Art This lithograph depicts a British courtroom during a trial. Could this scene be an accurate representation of the trial of Leonard Vole? Why or Why not?

"So you're not wanting to kiss me, dear-ie? He, he, I don't wonder. And yet I was a pretty girl once—not so long ago as you'd think, either. Vitriol,[38] dearie, vitriol—that's what did that. Ah! but I'll be even with 'em—"

She burst into a hideous torrent of profanity which Mr. Mayherne tried vainly to quell. She fell silent at last, her hands clenching and unclenching themselves nervously.

"Enough of that," said the lawyer sternly. "I've come here because I have reason to believe you can give me information which will clear my client, Leonard Vole. Is that the case?"

Her eyes leered at him cunningly.

"What about the money, dearie?" she wheezed. "Two hundred quid, you remember."

"It is your duty to give evidence, and you can be called upon to do so."

"That won't do, dearie. I'm an old woman, and I know nothing. But you give me two hundred quid, and perhaps I can give you a hint or two. See?"

"What kind of hint?"

"What should you say to a letter? A letter from *her*. Never mind how I got hold of it. That's my business. It'll do the trick. But I want my two hundred quid."

Mr. Mayherne looked at her coldly and made up his mind.

"I'll give you ten pounds, nothing more. And only that if this letter is what you say it is."

"Ten pounds?" She screamed and raved at him.

"Twenty," said Mr. Mayherne, "and that's my last word."

---

38. *Vitriol* is a chemical substance that can burn the skin.

He rose as if to go. Then, watching her closely, he drew out a pocketbook and counted out twenty one-pound notes.

"You see," he said. "That is all I have with me. You can take it or leave it."

But already he knew that the sight of the money was too much for her. She cursed and raved impotently,[39] but at last she gave in. Going over to the bed, she drew something out from beneath the tattered mattress.

"Here you are, damn you!" she snarled. "It's the top one you want."

It was a bundle of letters that she threw to him, and Mr. Mayherne untied them and scanned them in his usual cool, methodical manner. The woman, watching him eagerly, could gain no clue from his impassive face.

He read each letter through, then returned again to the top one and read it a second time. Then he tied the whole bundle up again carefully.

They were love letters, written by Romaine Heilger, and the man they were written to was not Leonard Vole. The top letter was dated the day of the latter's arrest.

"I spoke true, dearie, didn't I?" whined the woman. "It'll do for her, that letter?"

Mr. Mayherne put the letters in his pocket, then he asked a question.

"How did you get hold of this correspondence?"

"That's telling," she said with a leer. "But I know something more. I heard in court what that hussy said. Find out where she was at twenty past ten, the time she says she was at home. Ask at the Lion Road Cinema. They'll remember—a fine upstanding girl like that—curse her!"

"Who is the man?" asked Mr. Mayherne. "There's only a Christian name here."

The other's voice grew thick and hoarse, her hands clenched and unclenched. Finally she lifted one to her face.

"He's the man that did this to me. Many years ago now. She took him away from me—a chit[40] of a girl she was then. And when I went after him—and went for him too—he threw the cursed stuff at me! And she laughed—damn her! I've had it in for her for years. Followed her, I have, spied upon her. And now I've got her! She'll suffer for this, won't she, Mr. Lawyer? She'll suffer?"

"She will probably be sentenced to a term of imprisonment for perjury,"[41] said Mr. Mayherne quietly.

"Shut away—that's what I want. You're going, are you? Where's my money? Where's that good money?"

Without a word, Mr. Mayherne put down the notes on the table. Then, drawing a deep breath, he turned and left the squalid room. Looking back, he saw the old woman crooning over the money.

He wasted no time. He found the cinema in Lion Road easily enough, and, shown a photograph of Romaine Heilger, the commissionaire[42] recognized her at once. She had arrived at the cinema with a man some time after ten o'clock on the evening in question. He had not noticed her escort particularly, but he remembered the lady who had spoken to him about the picture that was showing. They stayed until the end, about an hour later.

Mr. Mayherne was satisfied. Romaine Heilger's evidence was a tissue of lies from beginning to end. She had evolved it out of her passionate hatred. The lawyer wondered whether he would ever know what lay

---

39. Here, *impotently* means "helplessly" or "powerlessly."

The Uncanny and Mysterious What is mysterious about this woman, the circumstances, and the letters?

---

40. Here, *chit* refers to a rude young person.
41. *Perjury* is the act of lying under oath in a court of law.
42. *Commissionaire* is a British term for a theater attendant.

behind that hatred. What had Leonard Vole done to her? He had seemed dumbfounded when the solicitor had reported her attitude to him. He had declared earnestly that such a thing was incredible—yet it had seemed to Mr. Mayherne that after the first astonishment his protests had lacked sincerity.

He did know. Mr. Mayherne was convinced of it. He knew, but he had no intention of revealing the fact. The secret between those two remained a secret. Mr. Mayherne wondered if someday he should come to learn what it was.

The solicitor glanced at his watch. It was late, but time was everything. He hailed a taxi and gave an address.

"Sir Charles must know of this at once," he murmured to himself as he got in.

The trial of Leonard Vole for the murder of Emily French aroused widespread interest. In the first place the prisoner was young and good-looking, then he was accused of a particularly dastardly crime, and there was the further interest of Romaine Heilger, the principal witness for the prosecution. There had been pictures of her in many papers, and several fictitious stories as to her origin and history.

The proceedings opened quietly enough. Various technical evidence came first. Then Janet Mackenzie was called. She told substantially the same story as before. In cross-examination counsel for the defense succeeded in getting her to contradict herself once or twice over her account of Vole's association with Miss French; he emphasized the fact that though she had heard a man's voice in the sitting room that night, there was nothing to show that it was Vole who was there, and he managed to drive home a feeling that jealousy and dislike of the prisoner were at the bottom of a good deal of her evidence.

Then the next witness was called.

"Your name is Romaine Heilger?"

"Yes."

"You are an Austrian subject?"

"Yes."

"For the last three years you have lived with the prisoner and passed yourself off as his wife?"

Just for a moment Romaine Heilger's eyes met those of the man in the dock. Her expression held something curious and unfathomable.[43]

"Yes."

The questions went on. Word by word the damning facts came out. On the night in question the prisoner had taken out a crowbar with him. He had returned at twenty minutes past ten and had confessed to having killed the old lady. His cuffs had been stained with blood, and he had burned them in the kitchen stove. He had terrorized her into silence by means of threats.

As the story proceeded, the feeling of the court which had, to begin with, been slightly favorable to the prisoner, now set dead against him. He himself sat with downcast head and moody air, as though he knew he were doomed.

Yet it might have been noted that her own counsel sought to restrain Romaine's **animosity**. He would have preferred her to be more unbiased.

---

43. *Unfathomable* means "impossible to understand."

Motivation Why would Heilger's lawyer have preferred a more unbiased testimony?

Vocabulary

animosity (an′ ə mos′ə tē) *n.* ill will or resentment; active strong dislike or hostility

---

The Extraordinary and Fantastic What remains a mystery to Mayherne?

Formidable and ponderous,[44] counsel for the defense arose.

He put it to her that her story was a malicious fabrication[45] from start to finish, that she had not even been in her own house at the time in question, that she was in love with another man and was deliberately seeking to send Vole to his death for a crime he did not commit.

Romaine denied these allegations with superb insolence.[46]

Then came the surprising denouement,[47] the production of the letter. It was read aloud in court in the midst of a breathless stillness.

Bishop Street, Coventry, 1929. Joan Murphy. Oil on canvas. Herbert Art Gallery & Museum, Coventry, UK.

"Max, beloved, the Fates have delivered him into our hands! He has been arrested for murder—but, yes, the murder of an old lady! Leonard, who would not hurt a fly! At last I shall have my revenge. The poor chicken! I shall say that he came in that night with blood upon him—that he confessed to me. I shall hang him, Max—and when he hangs he will know and realize that it was Romaine who sent him to his death. And then—happiness, Beloved! Happiness at last!"

---

44. The phrase *formidable and ponderous* is meant to suggest the mental and emotional strength and weight of the counsel for the defense.
45. The phrase *malicious fabrication* suggests a story that has been elaborately made up for evil purposes.
46. *Insolence* is a display of an obviously contrary attitude.
47. A *denouement* (dā´ noō mäṅ´) is an action that follows a climax, or high point, of a story.

There were experts present ready to swear that the handwriting was that of Romaine Heilger, but they were not needed. Confronted with the letter, Romaine broke down utterly and confessed everything. Leonard Vole had returned to the house at the time he said, twenty past nine. She had invented the whole story to ruin him.

With the collapse of Romaine Heilger, the case for the Crown collapsed also. Sir Charles called his few witnesses; the prisoner himself went into the box and told his story in a manly straightforward manner, unshaken by cross-examination.

The prosecution endeavored to rally, but without great success. The judge's summing up was not wholly favorable to the prisoner, but a reaction had set in, and the jury needed little time to consider their verdict.

"We find the prisoner not guilty."

Leonard Vole was free!

Little Mr. Mayherne hurried from his seat. He must congratulate his client.

He found himself polishing his pince-nez vigorously and checked himself. His wife had told him only the night before that he was getting a habit of it. Curious things, habits. People themselves never knew they had them.

An interesting case—a very interesting case. That woman, now, Romaine Heilger.

The case was dominated for him still by the exotic figure of Romaine Heilger. She had seemed a pale, quiet woman in the house at Paddington, but in court she had flamed out against the sober background, flaunting herself like a tropical flower.

If he closed his eyes, he could see her now, tall and vehement, her exquisite body bent forward a little, her right hand clenching and unclenching itself unconsciously all the time.

Curious things, habits. That gesture of hers with the hand was her habit, he supposed. Yet he had seen someone else do it quite lately. Who was it now? Quite lately—

He drew in his breath with a gasp as it came back to him. The woman in Shaw's Rents . . .

He stood still, his head whirling. It was impossible—impossible— Yet, Romaine Heilger was an actress.

The K.C. came up behind him and clapped him on the shoulder.

"Congratulated our man yet? He's had a narrow shave, you know. Come along and see him."

But the little lawyer shook off the other's hand.

He wanted one thing only—to see Romaine Heilger face to face.

He did not see her until some time later, and the place of their meeting is not relevant.

"So you guessed," she said, when he had told her all that was in his mind. "The face? Oh! that was easy enough, and the light of that gas jet was too bad for you to see the makeup."

"But why—why—"

"Why did I play a lone hand?" She smiled a little, remembering the last time she had used the words.

"Such an elaborate comedy!"

"My friend—I had to save him. The evidence of a woman devoted to him would not have been enough—you hinted as much yourself. But I know something of the psychology of crowds. Let my evidence be wrung from me, as an admission, damning me in the eyes of the law, and a reaction in favor of the prisoner would immediately set in."

"And the bundle of letters?"

"One alone, the vital one, might have seemed like a—what do you call it?—put-up job."

"Then the man called Max?"

"Never existed, my friend."

"I still think," said little Mr. Mayherne, in an aggrieved manner, "that we could have got him off by the—er—normal procedure."

"I dared not risk it. You see, you thought he was innocent—"

"And you knew it? I see," said little Mr. Mayherne.

"My dear Mr. Mayherne," said Romaine, "you do not see at all. I knew—he was guilty!"

Make Inferences About Characters *What inferences did Heilger make about both the jury and Mayherne?*

After You Read

Respond and Think Critically

Respond and Interpret

1. Were you surprised by the ending? Explain.

2. (a) What crime is Leonard Vole accused of? (b) How does Vole convince Mr. Mayherne that he did not commit the crime?

3. (a) Who is Romaine Heilger? (b) Why does Mayherne's first meeting with her startle him?

4. (a) What happens when Heilger testifies at the trial? (b) How does the jury respond to Vole during the trial? Explain.

Analyze and Evaluate

5. From beginning to end, the facts are against Vole, and yet Christie convinces most readers to think of him as innocent. How does she do this?

6. (a) Why does Christie cast Vole's companion as an actress? (b) How well does Heilger "perform" as a witness for the prosecution?

7. Who, in your opinion, had a better knowledge of the legal system and English court proceedings: Mayherne or Heilger? Explain.

Connect

8. **Big Idea** The Extraordinary and Fantastic What mysteries remain unanswered at the end of the story? Explain.

9. **Connect to the Author** From reading this story, do you think Christie deserves to be called the "Queen of Crime"? Explain.

Visual Literacy

Acting on a Set

Here is a still photo from the 1957 movie version of "Witness for the Prosecution." Directed by Billy Wilder, the film features Tyrone Power as Leonard Vole and Marlene Dietrich as the witness for the prosecution. Here, Marlene Dietrich is shown in the witness box.

Group Activity Work with classmates to discuss and answer the following questions.

1. (a) How does the woman in this picture look the same as or different from the way Christie presents Romaine Heilger in the story?

   (b) How do you expect the woman pictured here to talk? to act? Explain why.

2. What emotions do you see in this photograph? How do they match or contradict the emotions conveyed in the parallel scene in the story?

Still from the movie *"Witness for the Prosecution,"* 1957

After You Read

Literary Element Motivation

In a mystery, the author or characters make or imply suggestions about other characters' **motivations**. Every character in this story typically has at least one transparent or implied motive.

1. (a) What is Heilger's "lone hand"? (b) What is her motivation for playing it? (c) Is this motivation stated or implied? (d) How does Heilger's real motivation differ from motivations that other characters state, suggest, or infer?

2. (a) What motivates the jury to acquit Vole? (b) What motivates Mayherne to visit Heilger after the acquittal?

Review: Style

As you learned on page 185, **style** is composed of the expressive qualities that distinguish an author's work, including word choice. In "The Witness for the Prosecution," **diction**, or word choice, reflects the author's culture, a primarily upper-middle-class British world.

Partner Activity With a partner, find several examples of Vole's polite, sophisticated speech. Write alternative, more plain-speaking, or working-class ways in which Vole might have expressed the same thoughts. Then discuss what effect Vole's diction has on Mayherne.

Example	Alternative
"I'd been having a run of infernal bad luck just then."	"I couldn't catch a break."

 **Literature** Online

Selection Resources For Selection Quizzes, eFlashcards, and Reading-Writing Connection activities, go to glencoe.com and enter QuickPass code GL59794u6.

Reading Strategy Make Inferences About Characters

ACT Skills Practice

1. At the end of the trial, members of the jury (and most readers) infer that Romaine Heilger is:

   I. devoted to Leonard Vole.
   II. intent on incriminating her "husband."
   III. a brilliantly successful actress.

   A. I only
   B. II only
   C. I and II only
   D. II and III only

Vocabulary Practice

Practice with Word Origins Studying the etymology, or origin and history, of a word can help you better understand and explore its meaning. Create a word map, like the one below, for each of these vocabulary words from the selection.

cultivate   pretext   amicable
recoil   animosity

Definition	Etymology
to captivate one's interest or curiosity	Latin *intricare* means "entangle"

intrigue

Sample sentence
Christie intrigues her reader with conflicting clues.

Academic Vocabulary

The great **incentive** for reading Christie's mysteries is to discover all the clever ways in which she disguises both the perpetrator and the motive.

Incentive is an academic word. More familiar words that are similar in meaning are *reason* and *motive*. Complete this sentence: My **incentives** for turning work in on time are ____.

1114   UNIT 6   GENRE FICTION

Respond Through Writing

Expository Essay

Learning Objectives

In this assignment, you will focus on the following objectives:

Writing: Analyzing cause and effect.

Grammar: Understanding how to use colons.

Analyze Cause and Effect To hide the murderer in plain sight, Christie invents an ingenious chain of causes and effects. Together with both concealed and obvious motives, these causes and effects create the suspense and rising action of an entertaining plot. Analyze the cause-and-effect relationships that finally reveal the killer's identity and explain how they create suspense.

Prewrite Go back and scan the story for events that lead to the revelation of the killer. Sketch a cause-and-effect chain or flowchart showing the causal relationship between the events. Study your plan to help you generate a thesis, a statement that provides an overview of the causes and effects and explains how they create suspense.

Draft After you create interest in your topic and present your thesis, use your body paragraphs to discuss the causal chain of events in chronological order and to present the best possible evidence from the story to support your statements of cause and effect. Use this paragraph frame as a guide to structuring your body paragraphs:

Sentence 1:	Statement of event or cause.
Sentence 2:	As Christie writes, [quoted evidence].
Sentence 3:	Eventually, this leads to ____.
Other Sentences:	Explanation/analysis of effects; how causes and effects create suspense.

Conclude your essay by presenting a graphic aid that shows how causes and effects drive the plot and create suspense.

Revise Ask a classmate to identify your evidence and tell how well it supports your main points and how well it explains how the author creates suspense. Decide whether to replace some or all of your evidence and how to make the connections between your claims and your evidence clearer or more effective.

Edit and Proofread Proofread your paper, correcting any errors in grammar, spelling, and punctuation. Use the Grammar Tip in the side column to help you with colons.

Grammar Tip

Colons

Sometimes, a colon can act like a megaphone, amplifying or calling attention to what follows it:

Mayherne wants to view Vole as a gentleman, not as a murderer: in short, Mayherne is a gullible fool.

Learning Objectives

In this workshop, you will focus on the following objective:

Grammar: Understanding how to use semicolons.

Grammar Workshop

Semicolons as Connectors

Literature Connection In this quotation from "The Witness for the Prosecution," Christie uses a **semicolon** (a punctuation mark that links related ideas).

> In cross-examination counsel for the defense succeeded in getting her to contradict herself once or twice over her account of Vole's association with Miss French; he emphasized the fact that though she had heard a man's voice in the sitting room that night, there was nothing to show that it was Vole who was there.
>
> —Agatha Christie, from "The Witness for the Prosecution"

A semicolon may link closely related main (or independent) clauses. For example, a semicolon could connect *At first she raged against the idea* and *then at last she agreed with their plan,* to create *At first she raged against the idea; then at last she agreed with their plan.*

Semicolons can also connect compound sentences that contain a **conjunction** (a word that connects words or groups of words of equal weight) or a **conjunctive adverb** (a word that creates a transition between main clauses).

Situation To replace a comma and a coordinating conjunction and accentuate a close relationship between two clauses

> They were love letters, and the man they were written to was not Vole.
> They were love letters; the man they were written to was not Vole.

Situation To use a semicolon before a conjunctive adverb to join two sentences

> His wife was to testify against him. Therefore, the trial might be doomed.
> His wife was to testify against him; therefore, the trial might be doomed.

Revise Rewrite the following sentences, using a semicolon.

1. Agatha Christie wrote many exciting stories and her writing was full of suspense.
2. Her story "Witness for the Prosecution" was incredibly popular—Therefore, it was made into a movie.
3. The story describes the criminal trial of Leonard Vole. He is charged with murder.

Connectors

A **semicolon** is a punctuation mark that, among other things, can link main clauses. A **coordinating conjunction**—such as *and, but, or,* and *yet*—connects words or groups of words of equal weight. A **conjunctive adverb** is a word that creates a transition between main clauses.

Tip

When deciding whether or not to use a semicolon between main clauses, first determine whether the ideas are closely related.

Language Handbook

For more on semicolons, see the Language Handbook pp. R40–R59.

 **Literature** Online

Grammar For more grammar practice, go to glencoe.com and enter QuickPass code GL59794u6.

Vocabulary Workshop

Thesaurus Use

Learning Objectives

In this workshop, you will focus on the following objective:

Vocabulary: Understanding how to use a thesaurus.

Literature Connection In the quotation below, Asimov uses words that have synonyms, words with similar but not usually identical meanings, to describe both the Old Woman and her typing.

> "Back and forth she went, her gnarled fingers tripping over the keys."
> —Isaac Asimov, from "Robot Dreams"

Asimov might have described the *gnarled* fingers as *lumpy* or *twisted*, but neither term would have conveyed a sense of age. Instead of *tripping*, he might have used *stumbling* or *skipping* to convey the action.

When searching for a word, you can consult a **thesaurus**, a source of synonyms and antonyms. Thesauri (or thesauruses) are available in CD-ROM, Internet, software, and print formats, organized in two ways.

Traditional Style This style organizes words by general concept. To find a synonym for the adjective *fast*, for example, look in the alphabetical index for entries such as *speedy* and *hasty*, with page references. On those pages, you would find related synonyms—*velocity* and *haste*. Probably the best-known traditional thesaurus is *Roget's Thesaurus*.

Dictionary Style This type of thesaurus presents words in alphabetical order. Each word is followed by several synonyms, which are listed by part of speech and direct the reader to related entries. In this type of thesaurus, you must look up a specific word to find its synonyms. J. I. Rodale's *The Synonym Finder* is an example of a dictionary-style thesaurus.

Here is a sample entry for the word *gnarled*.

gnarled *adj.* The swing hung from the gnarled branches of an old and twisted tree: knotted, contorted, knobby, crooked, distorted, bent, twisted, warped, misshapen, leathery, rugged.
Ant. straight, smooth, even, flat, sleek.

— part of speech
← example sentence
← list of synonyms with the most common ones first
← list of antonyms

Thesaurus Terms

A **thesaurus** is a specialized dictionary that lists synonyms and antonyms.

Tip

To skim through a dictionary or thesaurus quickly, use the guide words located at the top of each page. These list the first and last entry on a page.

Practice

1. Using a thesaurus, find two synonyms for each word listed below. Then find the precise meaning for each one in a dictionary.
   a. grief **b.** honor **c.** strange **d.** hesitate **e.** shining
2. Use each word and the synonyms you have found in a sentence. Be sure your sentences reflect the slight differences in meanings.

Vocabulary For more vocabulary practice, go to glencoe.com and enter QuickPass code GL59794u6.

Learning Objectives

For pages 1118–1125

In this workshop, you will focus on the following objective:

Writing: Writing a short story.

Grammar: Understanding how to use dialogue. Understanding how to correct shifts in point of view.

Writing Process

At any stage of a writing process, you may think of new ideas. Feel free to return to earlier stages as you write.

Prewrite

Draft

Revise

Focus Lesson: Dialogue

Edit and Proofread

Focus Lesson: Shifts in Point of View

Present

Writing Workshop

Short Story

Literature Connection To entertain the reader of "A Sound of Thunder," Ray Bradbury crafts an exciting plot and uses a wide range of effective narrative techniques including dialogue.

> The Machine howled. Time was a film run backward. Suns fled and ten million moons fled after them. "Think," said Eckles. "Every hunter that ever lived would envy us today. This makes Africa seem like Illinois."
>
> The Machine slowed; its scream fell to a murmur. The Machine stopped.
>
> The sun stopped in the sky.

This type of writing is called science fiction, but it has all the elements of any great story. Study the rubric below to learn the goals and strategies for writing a successful short story.

Checklist

Goals	Strategies
To create an engaging plot	✓ Present a focused sequence of at least three events
	✓ Include a conflict and a satisfying resolution
To engage the reader from beginning to end	✓ Locate scenes and incidents in specific places
	✓ Create an interesting problem or conflict
	✓ Pace the narrative to show changes in time or mood
	✓ Use the active voice, action verbs, and other precise word choice
	✓ Choose and maintain an appropriate point of view and tone
To introduce believable or interesting characters	✓ Use concrete, sensory details to show appearances, movements, gestures, feelings
	✓ Write convincing dialogue and/or interior monologue

1118 UNIT 6 GENRE FICTION

Narration / Description

> **Assignment: Write a Short Story**
>
> Write a story of at least 1,500 words that contains dialogue. As you work, keep your audience and purpose in mind.
>
> **Audience:** classmates and peers
>
> **Purpose:** to entertain by including all of the elements of a good short story, including setting, characters, events, exposition, conflict, rising action, resolution, falling action, and dialogue

Real-World Connection

When you write letters, recommendations, or performance reviews, you may need to relate a brief story or document a series of events in order to make a point about a person's abilities or potential.

Analyze a Professional Model

In the short story that follows, Isaac Asimov presents a not-so-future world in which computers are used to create conditions for, and to fight, wars. As you read the story, identify story elements and pay close attention to the comments in the margin. They point out features to include in your own story.

from *"Frustration"* by Isaac Asimov

Herman Gelb turned his head to watch the departing figure. Then he said, "Wasn't that the Secretary?"

"Yes, that was the Secretary of Foreign Affairs. Old man Hargrove. Are you ready for lunch?"

"Of course. What was he doing here?"

Peter Jonsbeck didn't answer immediately. He merely stood up, and beckoned Gelb to follow. They walked down the corridor and into a room that had the steamy smell of spicy food.

"Here you are," said Jonsbeck. "The whole meal has been prepared by computer. Completely automated. Untouched by human hands. And my own programming. I promised you a treat, and here you are."

It *was* good. Gelb could not deny it and didn't want to. Over dessert, he said, "But what was Hargrove doing here?"

Jonsbeck smiled. "Consulting me on programming. What else am I good for?"

"But why? Or is it something you can't talk about?"

"It's something I suppose I *shouldn't* talk about, but it's a

Locate Scenes and Incidents
Introduce details that show time and place.

Dialogue
Write convincing dialogue to show characters and tell the story.

 **Literature** Online

Writing and Research For prewriting, drafting, and revising tools, go to glencoe.com and enter QuickPass code GL59794u6.

WRITING WORKSHOP   **1119**

Conflict

Be sure that the story contains a problem or conflict.

fairly open secret. There isn't a computer man in the capital who doesn't know what the poor frustrated simp is up to."

"What is he up to then?"

"He's fighting wars."

Gelb's eyes opened wide. "With whom?"

"With nobody, really. He fights them by computer analysis. He's been doing it for I don't know how long."

"But why?"

"He wants the world to be the way we are—noble, honest, decent, full of respect for human rights and so on."

"So do I. So do we all. We have to keep up the pressure on the bad guys, that's all."

"And they're keeping the pressure on us, too. They don't think we're perfect."

"I suppose we're not, but we're better than they are. You know that."

Characterization

Use movements and gestures, as well as appearances and dialogue, to show characters.

Jonsbeck shrugged. "A difference in point of view. It doesn't matter. We've got a world to run, space to develop, computerization to extend. Cooperation puts a premium on continued cooperation and there is slow improvement. We'll get along. It's just that Hargrove doesn't want to wait. He hankers for quick improvement—by force. You know, *make the bums shape up*. We're strong enough to do it."

"By force? By war, you mean. We don't fight wars any more."

"That's because it's gotten too complicated. Too much danger. We're all too powerful. You know what I mean? Except that Hargrove thinks he can find a way. You punch certain starting conditions into the computer and let it fight the war mathematically and yield the results."

"How do you make equations for war?"

"Well, you try, old man. Men. Weapons. Surprise. Counterattack. Ships. Space stations. Computers. We mustn't forget computers. There are a hundred factors and thousands of intensities and millions of combinations. Hargrove thinks it is possible to find *some* combination of starting conditions and courses of development that will result in clear victory for us and not too much damage to the world, and he labors under constant frustration."

"But what if he gets what he wants?"

"Well, if he can find the combination—if the computer says, 'This is it,' then I suppose he thinks he can argue our government into fighting exactly the war the computer has worked out so that, barring random events that upset the indicated course, we'd have what we want."

"There'd be casualties."

"Yes, of course. But the computer will presumably compare the casualties and other damage—to the economy and ecology, for instance—to the benefits that would derive from our control of the world, and if it decides the benefits will outweigh the casualties, then it will give the go-ahead for a 'just war.' After all, it may be that even the losing nations would benefit from being directed by us, with our stronger economy and stronger moral sense."

Gelb stared his disbelief and said, "I never knew we were sitting at the lip of a volcanic crater like that. What about the 'random events' you mentioned?"

"The computer program tries to allow for the unexpected, but you never can, of course. So I don't think the go-ahead will come.... And because it lacks what is most needed, the computers will always give Hargrove, and all others who hanker for war, nothing but frustration."

"What is it that a computer doesn't have, then?"

"Why, Gelb. It totally lacks a sense of self-righteousness."

Narration / Description

Plot
Build up narrative tension or suspense.

Time Order
Tell events in time order or use a flashback. The story at this point is told by means of a conversation in time order.

Point of View/Tone
Choose and maintain an appropriate point of view and tone.

Engage the Reader
Raise the conflict to a high point of tension, or climax. Pace the narrative to show changes in time and mood.

Resolution
Provide an interesting or satisfying resolution or ending.

Reading-Writing Connection Think about the writing techniques that you have just encountered and try them out in the short story you write.

Prewrite

Brainstorm Setting, Characters, Events, and Focus Before writing your story, think through many ideas and then choose the best.

▶ Begin by thinking about where and when your story will take place. Make a list of possible settings.

▶ Think about who will appear in your story. List your characters.

▶ Decide what will happen to your characters. List possible events.

Make a Story Map A story must have a conflict or a problem to solve and be told in a logical order. Make a story map to help ensure that you have ideas for all the story elements before you begin writing. The map will help you put your ideas, especially the events, in order.

Setting:	time—3005; place—in space
Characters:	star traveler and his wife, Laura
Problem or Conflict:	The star traveler wants to visit other planets and galaxies, but his wife wants him home on Earth.
Events:	1. Husband decides on life of travel. 2. Husband goes into space. 3. Husband has a crisis—is torn between star traveling and wife. 4. Husband decides on space.
Ending:	the beauty and joy of star traveling

Talk About Your Ideas With a partner, use your story map and summarize your story ideas. Ask your partner for suggestions about what to add, take out, or do differently. To develop your writing voice, listen to your own speaking voice as you retell parts of your story. Together, identify and write down words and phrases to include that reflect your voice.

Develop Dialogue Look at your events. Decide what the characters will be thinking or saying at important moments. Make notes about how the characters' words and thoughts can help move the plot along.

Draft

Create Paragraphs Whenever the time or place changes, or when you write dialogue, be sure to create a new paragraph. Also state your ending or resolution in a separate paragraph.

What If Questions

One way to think of story ideas is to ask questions that begin with *What if*, such as *What if an alien landed on the roof of my apartment building?* or *What if a child in 1858 discovered her neighbor's house was a stop on the Underground Railroad?*

Avoid Plagiarism

If you are tempted to reuse an older student's work, think twice! Not only will you lose a chance to develop your own narrative skills, but you will also be cheating.

Analyze a Workshop Model

Read the following final draft of a science fiction story. Answer the questions in the margin. Use the answers to guide you as you write.

"Star Traveler"

I am unwrapping my recycled Stardust Fries when my transmitter beeps. "Please come home," flashes across the screen from my wife Laura. I think of her back on Earth, just getting home from work. My thoughts are disrupted when the captain's face appears on my transmitter. He announces, "We are within sight of Paradiscus. All officers are invited on deck."

I toss my food, uneaten, into the Stardust snack-recycling bin. I remember how upset Laura was when I told her of my plan to join the crew of the *Zodiac*, a space explorer.

"You'll be gone so much. I may not see you again!" she cried.

"Come with me," I pleaded. "and work on the *Zodiac*."

She just kept shaking her head and saying, "Earth's my home." But I think, it's 3005, and the atmosphere is so toxic there. A person couldn't last thirty seconds without a suit.

After Laura had cried herself to sleep, I put on an atmosphere suit. I knew that the wide-open universe was calling me. I packed my things. In the morning, in tears, I left.

When I reach the deck, Paradiscus lies straight ahead—a marblelike mixture of blue and green in the black void of space—how Earth must have looked a thousand years ago.

"Tonight," the captain says, breaking into my meditation, "we enter the gravitational field of Anterpodia galaxy. No further communication with the Milky Way will be possible for several years." Within hours Laura will be totally out of range.

It is not too late for me to reverse my decision. The transport room is still operative; my cozy living room is waiting for me. But then I look out at the stars and I know that I have made the right decision. What drives us star travelers?

Narration / Description

Locate Scenes and Incidents
How does this opening show time and place?

Interior Monologue / Dialogue
How does the writer reveal the conflict?

Time Order
Are the events told in time order? Explain.

Characterization
How do details about actions and appearances reveal characters?

Plot and Pacing
How does the writer engage the reader?

Resolution
How does the story end? How are point of view and tone consistent from start to finish?

Revise

Peer Review When you finish your draft, ask a classmate to read it and identify characters, the problem or conflict, events, and the resolution or ending. Ask your reviewer to make suggestions about where to change background information, dialogue, or details about the conflict and how it builds up. Together review the traits of strong writing; then apply them to your work. Use the checklist below to help you evaluate.

Checklist: Writing an Effective Reflective Essay

- ☑ Do you show time and place?
- ☑ Do you use dialogue, interior monologue, appearance, gestures, and actions to show characters?
- ☑ Do you include a conflict or problem to solve?
- ☑ Do you pace your story effectively?
- ☑ Do you solve the problem or conflict and include a satisfying ending?

Focus Lesson

Use Dialogue

Dialogue in a story helps bring characters to life. It can show their motives, thoughts, and values and reveal their relationships to other characters and to the conflict. Revise your narrative. Look for places where you can add dialogue or replace flat statements with dialogue. Note how dialogue improves the passage from the model below.

Draft:

> As I make my way to the bridge, I remember Laura was upset when I told her of my plan to join the crew of the *Zodiac*. She didn't want me to be away. I said I'd get her a job on the *Zodiac*.

Revision:

> As I make my way to the bridge, I remember how upset Laura was when I told her of my plan to join the crew of the *Zodiac*, a space explorer.
>
> "You'll be gone so much. I may not see you again!" she cried.[1]
>
> "Come with me," I pleaded. "I can get you a job on the *Zodiac*, too."[2]

1: shows character's feelings   **2: shows character's values**

Traits of Strong Writing

Include these traits of strong writing to express your ideas effectively.

Ideas

Organization

Voice

Word Choice

Sentence Fluency

Conventions

Presentation

For more information on using the traits of strong writing, see pages R28–R30.

Word Choice

Find this academic vocabulary word in the student model:

reverse (ri vurs´) *v.* to turn completely around in direction, position, or thoughts. *It is not, in fact, too late for me to reverse my decision.* Using academic vocabulary may help strengthen your writing. Try to use one or two academic vocabulary words in your short story. See the complete list on pages R82–R83.

Edit and Proofread

Get It Right When you have completed the final draft of your story, proofread it for errors in grammar, usage, mechanics, and spelling. Refer to the Language Handbook, pages R40–R59, as a guide.

> **Focus Lesson**
>
> ## Correct Shifts in Point of View
>
> When stories are told from the third-person point of view, the narrator uses pronouns such as *he, she,* and *they* to tell the story. When stories are told from the first-person point of view, a character in the story uses the pronoun *I* to tell what is happening. Tell your story in third person or first person, not both. Avoid shifting to the second person. Below are examples of shifts in point of view.

Problem: The narrative shifts from the first person to the third.

I knew that the wide-open universe was calling me. He packed his things. In the morning, in tears, he left.

Solution: Make all personal pronouns first-person pronouns.

I knew that the wide-open universe was calling me. I packed my things. In the morning, in tears, I left.

Problem: The narrative shifts inappropriately to the second person (you).

The atmosphere is so toxic there that you couldn't last thirty seconds without a suit.

Solution: Use a noun or another pronoun that makes sense in the context of the sentence.

The atmosphere is so toxic there that a person couldn't last thirty seconds without a suit.

Narration / Description

Peer Review

When asked to read a classmate's short story, read carefully and write notes as you read. Give constructive feedback. Use the following questions to get started:

Do you get a good sense of time, place, and characters?

Is there a series of events, a climax, and a resolution?

Is there sensory language and other precise language?

Word-Processing Tips

Story format uses standard paragraphing: five-space indents for the first line; no additional spaces between lines. Start a new paragraph when a speaker in dialogue changes. Double-space; use one-inch margins, all sides.

Writer's Portfolio

Place a copy of your story in your portfolio to review later.

Present

Manuscript Requirements Be sure to follow your teacher's guidelines for a cover sheet, page numbers, margins, or other requirements. Remember to use extremely neat handwriting or to select a highly readable, conservative font in a 12-point type size.

Literature Online

Writing and Research For editing and publishing tools, go to glencoe.com and enter QuickPass code GL59794u6.

Learning Objectives

For pages 1126–1127

In this workshop, you will focus on the following objective:

Speaking and Listening: Delivering an oral interpretation of a story.

Speaking, Listening, and Viewing Workshop

Oral Interpretation of a Story

Literature Connection "Witness for the Prosecution" was not just a great short story. It was also very successfully adapted for both the stage and the screen. In this workshop, you will work with others to re-create your original short story or a short story from this unit as a dramatic performance.

> **Assignment** Recreate a short story as a dramatic performance.

Plan Your Presentation

Follow these steps to get started:

Choose a type of performance. For example, you might present a dramatic reading of the entire story. You might act out just one scene. You might use moving images or a computer slide presentation to show all or part of the story. You might also present a radio show, a web cast, or even a puppet show.

Consider audience and occasion. After you choose a type of performance, think about your audience and performance space. For example, consider the size of the room and the technology you may or may not have available. Consider how people might be seated and what kind of screen, stage, or other presentation size you will require for everyone to be able to see and hear easily. Think about the occasion, too. Will this be just the usual classroom scene? Or will you perform for parents or other guests?

Focus on your purpose. Your goal is to state one central message about the story through the events or scenes you portray. Your central message may be about any one or more of the following:

- the time and place
- the theme
- the characters
- the conflict and/or the resolution

Develop Your Presentation

Whatever kind of performance you present, you will want to engage your audience from beginning to end. Follow these guidelines:

- Begin boldly. Surprise, tension, conflict, and an arresting sound effect are all options. Capture your audience's attention from moment one.
- Create visual interest. If you are using computer screens, make them bold and colorful but easy to follow. For a dramatic reading or staging a scene, make a backdrop, or bring in props for visual interest. For a radio broadcast, consider projecting a series of images.
- Use language to its fullest effect. If you are presenting a story or scene from a story, use many of the author's exact words. If you are presenting your own story, add vivid language, including action verbs, and use sensory details and figurative language.
- End memorably. Think about your final words, pose, or image. Do not say, "The end." Convey the end through sound effects, well-chosen words, a fitting closing image, or another closing device.

Rehearse

Practice your dramatic presentation by performing it aloud as a group and then performing it for a small group. As you rehearse, elicit feedback from your listeners, listen to others practice their dramatic presentation, and consider the following techniques.

Techniques for Dramatic Presentations

Speaking Techniques	Listening Techniques
✓ **Use Audience Feedback** Watch the looks on your listeners' faces for clues about how to adjust your performance.	✓ **Focus** Look directly at the performers and images and concentrate on what they convey.
✓ **Volume** Adjust your volume to the size of your audience and for dramatic effect.	✓ **Respond** Show interest. If you are surprised, taken aback, amused, or momentarily startled, show it.
✓ **Entertain** Let go of the everyday you to slip into the role of performer.	✓ **Evaluate** Identify the most successful parts or aspects of the presentation.

Presentation Tips

Use the following checklist to evaluate your dramatic presentation:

Did you entertain your audience? Where did the audience respond best?

Did you achieve your purpose of re-creating one central idea from the story?

Did you correctly tailor your presentation to the occasion and your performance space?

Listening Tips

Use the following checklist to evaluate your listening and viewing skills:

Did you focus directly on the performance, showing both respect and interest?

Did you respond appropriately?

Did you correctly interpret the purpose of the performance?

Did you identify weaknesses and strengths of the performance?

Speaking, Listening, and Viewing For project ideas, templates, and presentation tips, go to glencoe.com and enter QuickPass code GL59794u6.

Independent Reading

Genre Fiction

SOME TYPES OF FICTION FOLLOW SUCH DISTINCT PATTERNS that they have their own classification, or genre. Among these types of genre fiction are mysteries (in which characters use clues to solve a problem) and science fiction (which presents imagined events related to science or technology). Fantasy stories with invented characters, settings, and other elements are another subset of fiction. Modern fables, or stories that are usually based on a single event and use stock characters, also follow a distinct pattern. For more genre fiction on a range of themes, try the two suggestions below. For novels that incorporate the Big Idea of *The Extraordinary and Fantastic,* try the titles from the Glencoe Literature Library on the next page.

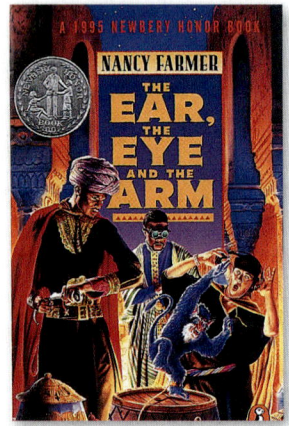

The Ear, the Eye, and the Arm
Nancy Farmer

The place is Zimbabwe. The year is 2194. After sneaking into a dangerous city, three children are kidnapped and forced into a life of hard labor in a plastics mine. Many fast-paced adventures follow. The children's parents hire a trio of mutant detectives to find them, but the sensitive yet absurd rescuers are constantly just one step behind the children. This novel combines elements of science fiction, humor, and traditional African culture. Notes and a glossary help readers with the traditional African tribal language and lore.

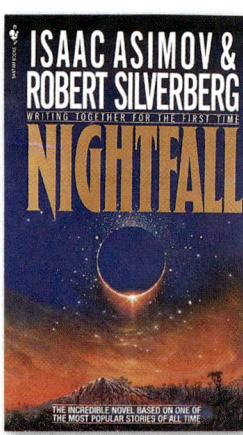

Nightfall
Isaac Asimov and Robert Silverberg

Two of the greatest science-fiction writers of the twentieth century collaborated on this suspenseful tale, based on a 1941 short story by Asimov. *Nightfall* explores what happens when darkness slowly falls in a world that has seen nothing but sunlight for the last two thousand years. Readers experience the event through the eyes of a newspaperman, an astronomer, a psychologist, an archaeologist, and a religious person. As a terrified society verges on chaos, only a few citizens are prepared to face a truth.

GLENCOE LITERATURE LIBRARY

The Strange Case of Dr. Jekyll and Mr. Hyde

By Robert Louis Stevenson

Good reigns by day and evil by night in this extraordinary and fantastic divided self.

Frankenstein

By Mary Shelley

Dr. Frankenstein is obsessed with giving his creation life—but the results will shock him and the readers of this uncanny and mysterious gothic novel.

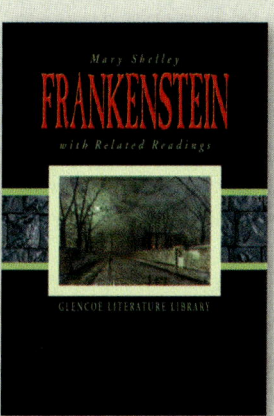

CRITICS' CORNER

"The pretense, disguise, play-acting, and outward show that are essential to the mystery genre are given a special intensity in Christie's work by her constant emphasis on and reference to the "theatricality" of her characters' actions. A well-known example is Murder on the Orient Express *(1934), in which Hercule Poirot comes to realize that he has been an audience of one for a careful series of performances."*

—Nicholas Birns and Margaret Boe Birns, from *The Cunning Craft: Original Essays on Detective Fiction and Contemporary Literary Theory*

Murder on the Orient Express

Agatha Christie

In this novel, the most well known of Agatha Christie's many mysteries, the extraordinary murder of an American gentleman occurs on the Orient Express, a luxury train traveling from Istanbul to Paris. The man is found dead in his train compartment with the door locked from the inside.

 Write a Review

Read one of the books listed on these pages and write a review of it for your classmates. Be sure to explain its strengths and why you recommend it. Present your review to the class.

Assessment

English–Language Arts

Reading: Genre Fiction

Carefully read the following passage. Pay close attention to the author's main idea and use of literary devices. Also note the other qualities of the story, such as character development, setting, plot, and mood—all of which contribute to the author's style. Use context clues to help you define any words with which you are unfamiliar. Then, on a separate sheet of paper, answer the questions on pages 1131–1132.

from "The Metamorphosis" by Franz Kafka
translated by David Wyllie

One morning, when Gregor Samsa woke from troubled dreams, he found himself transformed in his bed into a horrible vermin. He lay on his armor-like back, and if he lifted his head a little he could see his brown belly, slightly domed and divided by arches into stiff sections.
5 The bedding was hardly able to cover it and seemed ready to slide off any moment. His many legs, pitifully thin compared with the size of the rest of him, waved about helplessly as he looked.
   "What's happened to me?" he thought. It wasn't a dream. His room, a proper human room although a little too small, lay peacefully
10 between its four familiar walls. A collection of textile samples lay spread out on the table—Samsa was a traveling salesman—and above it there hung a picture that he had recently cut out of an illustrated magazine and housed in a nice, gilded frame. It showed a lady fitted out with a fur hat and fur boa who sat upright, raising a heavy fur muff that
15 covered the whole of her lower arm towards the viewer.
   Gregor then turned to look out the window at the dull weather. Drops of rain could be heard hitting the pane, which made him feel quite sad. "How about if I sleep a little bit longer and forget all this nonsense," he thought, but that was something he was unable to do
20 because he was used to sleeping on his right, and in his present state couldn't get into that position. However hard he threw himself onto his right, he always rolled back to where he was. He must have tried it a hundred times, shut his eyes so that he wouldn't have to look at the floundering legs, and only stopped when he began to feel a mild, dull
25 pain there that he had never felt before.
   "Oh, God," he thought, "what a strenuous career it is that I've chosen! Traveling day in and day out. Doing business like this takes much more

effort than doing your own business at home, and on top of that there's the curse of traveling, worries about making train connections, bad and
30 irregular food, contact with different people all the time so that you can never get to know anyone or become friendly with them. It can all go to Hell!" He felt a slight itch up on his belly; pushed himself slowly up on his back towards the headboard so that he could lift his head better; found where the itch was, and saw that it was covered with lots of little white
35 spots which he didn't know what to make of; and when he tried to feel the place with one of his legs he drew it quickly back because as soon as he touched it he was overcome by a cold shudder.

He slid back into his former position. "Getting up early all the time," he thought, "it makes you stupid. You've got to get enough sleep. . . ."

1. What is the setting of the passage?
   A. Gregor's dream
   B. Gregor's office
   C. Gregor's bed
   D. Gregor's room

2. From what point of view is the passage written?
   A. first person
   B. second person
   C. third-person limited
   D. third-person omniscient

3. What does the word *housed*, in line 13, mean?
   A. contained
   B. dwelled
   C. limited
   D. addressed

4. Which of the following is a synonym for the word *state*, in line 20?
   A. dilemma
   B. condition
   C. location
   D. declare

5. According to the context, which of the following best describes Gregor's transformation?
   A. gradual
   B. ongoing
   C. sudden
   D. transitional

6. What is Gregor's initial reaction to his transformation into an insect?
   A. He is frantic.
   B. He is worried.
   C. He is incredulous.
   D. He is unconcerned.

7. To what element of the story does the second paragraph most contribute?
   A. characters
   B. setting
   C. conflict
   D. mood

8. To what element of the story does the fourth paragraph mainly contribute?
   A. character
   B. setting
   C. conflict
   D. plot

ASSESSMENT 1131

9. Which of the following adjectives best describes Gregor's attitude toward his transformation?
   A. terrified
   B. resigned
   C. angry
   D. indifferent

10. What is Gregor most distressed about in the passage?
    A. his career
    B. his body
    C. his family
    D. his possessions

11. From the context, what do you think the word *irregular*, in line 30, means?
    A. various
    B. unusual
    C. occasional
    D. unhealthy

12. How is Gregor's personality revealed in the third and fourth paragraphs?
    A. through metaphor
    B. through symbol
    C. through direct characterization
    D. through indirect characterization

13. What can Gregor's transformation into a "horrible vermin" be considered?
    A. an allegory
    B. extended metaphor
    C. epic
    D. myth

14. From the passage, what can you conclude about Gregor's life before his transformation?
    A. His job was challenging but rewarding.
    B. His chronic illness made his life miserable.
    C. His home life was unfulfilling.
    D. His job was exhausting and unsatisfying.

Literature Online

Assessment For additional test practice, go to glencoe.com and enter QuickPass code GL59794u6

Vocabulary Skills: Sentence Completion

For each item, choose the word that best completes the sentence.

1. Because he had worked with his hands all his life, his fingers were badly _____ in his old age.
   A. sonorous
   B. gnarled
   C. amicable
   D. erroneous

2. He has known nothing but _____ since he suffered that tragic loss.
   A. precedence
   B. pretext
   C. anguish
   D. paradox

3. For our camping trip, we left all _____ items at home and took only the essentials.
   A. expendable
   B. dutiful
   C. exclusive
   D. invaluable

4. Emergency-care workers need a _____ state of mind to cope on a daily basis.
   A. treacherous
   B. resilient
   C. primeval
   D. guttural

5. The professor did his best to explain string theory, but the concept _____ more of the audience than it illuminated.
   A. dismantled
   B. cultivated
   C. perplexed
   D. accosted

6. On their arrival, guests were kept waiting on the _____ until the host could greet them.
   A. verandah
   B. horizon
   C. psalm
   D. retribution

7. Thoughts are like the fiber strands of a blanket, _____ to form a unified whole.
   A. interlaced
   B. bloated
   C. livid
   D. inert

8. The true measure of a great magician is the ability to _____ the audience before they know that they have been tricked.
   A. recoil
   B. bade
   C. dupe
   D. accost

9. Scientists do not know whether the *Tyrannosaurus rex* was a hunter or a/an _____ that ate others' leftovers.
   A. retribution
   B. animosity
   C. impediment
   D. scavenger

10. He spent the afternoon _____ editing his report to ensure that it was free of errors.
    A. unobtrusively
    B. assiduously
    C. resiliently
    D. erroneously

Grammar and Writing Skills: Paragraph Improvement

Read carefully through the following paragraphs from the first draft of a student's reflective essay. Pay close attention to the writer's use of grammar and the location and appropriateness of modifiers. Then answer the questions on pages 1134–1135.

(1) *Franz Kafka's "The Metamorphosis" is the story of Gregor Samsa, a young man who wakes up one morning transformed into an insect-like creature.* (2) *Gregor is strangely indifferent to his plight, indeed his manner seems almost too odd.* (3) *Likewise, he worries about the daily obligations that have drained him.*

(4) *Attempting to satisfy the demands of his family and employer, Gregor's maddening life falls into tragedy.* (5) *The horrible insect becomes a metaphor, signifying Gregor's fading identity and inability to function in society.*

(6) *Gregor's world changes drastically; and his physical abilities are the first to go.* (7) *Unable to work, Gregor can no longer support his family.* (8) *Not all of his changes come from his altered body, in fact some changes are caused by the world's reaction to him.* (9) *His family's rejection brings on emotional deterioration just as severe as his physical decline.* (10) *Even his sister becomes indifferent to him at last, who at first showed him compassion and pity.*

(11) *The cruelest irony, however, is in the positive changes that occur in the Samsa family as Gregor descends into insignificance.* (12) *As Gregor becomes more isolated and worthless; but, his family becomes more self-reliant.* (13) *Gregor becomes a sacrifice, given up so that the others can prosper.*

1. Which of the following is the best revision of sentence 2?
   A. Gregor is, strangely, indifferent to his plight, indeed, his manner seems almost too odd.
   B. Gregor is strangely indifferent to his plight: indeed, his manner seems almost too odd.
   C. Gregor is strangely indifferent to his plight, indeed, his manner seems almost too odd.
   D. Gregor is strangely indifferent to his plight; indeed, his manner seems almost too odd.

2. Which of the following words is the best substitute for *likewise* in sentence 3?
   A. finally
   B. also
   C. instead
   D. thus

3. Which of the following errors appears in sentence 4?
   A. run-on sentence
   B. incorrect parallelism
   C. sentence fragment
   D. dangling modifier

4. Which of the following is the best revision of sentence 8?
   A. Not all of his changes come from his altered body; in fact some changes are caused by the world's reaction to him.
   B. Not all of his changes come from his altered body; in fact, some changes are caused by the world's reaction to him.
   C. In fact, not all of his changes come from his altered body some changes are caused by the world's reaction, to him.
   D. Not all of his changes come from his altered body, in fact, some changes are caused by the world's reaction to him.

5. Which of the following errors appears in sentence 10?
   A. run-on sentence
   B. misplaced modifier
   C. sentence fragment
   D. lack of subject-verb agreement

6. What addition to the third paragraph would show the severity of Gregor's emotional trauma?
   A. a description of Gregor's reaction to his sister
   B. more details about Gregor's physical changes
   C. elaboration on Gregor's family life
   D. an illustration of how limited Gregor's movements are

7. What could the writer add to the concluding paragraph in order to develop the point made there?
   A. examples
   B. quotations
   C. objections
   D. dates

8. Which of the following is the best revision of sentence 12?
   A. As Gregor becomes more isolated and worthless, but his family becomes more, self-reliant.
   B. Gregor becomes more isolated and worthless, but, his family becomes more self-reliant.
   C. As Gregor becomes more isolated and worthless, his family becomes more self-reliant.
   D. Gregor becomes more isolated; and worthless but his family becomes more self-reliant.

9. Which of the following does the writer include in the concluding paragraph?
   A. the introduction of opposing viewpoints
   B. ideas not included in previous paragraphs
   C. a summary of the key points
   D. information not related to the writer's literary analysis

Essay

Choose one of the readings from this unit and write an essay that discusses how the author's use of imagery contributes to the theme or purpose of the text. What do the main character or characters learn, about themselves or the world in general, from being in a foreign or strange setting? Use specific examples from the readings. Be sure to organize your ideas and write in complete sentences. Proofread your work and correct any grammatical errors. As you write, keep in mind that your essay will be checked for **ideas, organization, voice, word choice, sentence fluency, conventions,** and **presentation.**

UNIT SEVEN

CONSUMER AND WORKPLACE DOCUMENTS

LESSON 1	E-mail, Application, Cover Letter
LESSON 2	Professional Article, Warranty, Software Product Information, Installation Guide
LESSON 3	Announcement Memo, Train Schedule and Itinerary, Meeting Itinerary, Written Directions, Meeting Agenda
LESSON 4	Pamphlet, Contract, Web Site

Learning Objectives

For pages 1138–1139

In studying this text, you will focus on the following objectives:

Reading:
Analyzing functional documents.
Thinking about credibility.

FOCUS ON FUNCTIONAL DOCUMENTS

Why Read Functional Documents

You probably depend on functional documents every single day. Functional documents do not all look the same, but they all share the same basic **purpose**: to successfully communicate information. Here are some examples of funtional documents.

Examples of Functional Documents		
product information	menus	flyers
instructions	e-mails	written directions
cover letters	maps	memos
schedules	rules or handbooks	labels
applications	meeting agendas	warranties

Evaluating Functional Documents

What's the Plan?

Writers try to use a logical plan—or **text structure**—to organize their work. By figuring out what text structure a writer uses, you can better find, follow, and understand the information you need. Here are some text structures that you'll frequently find in functional documents.

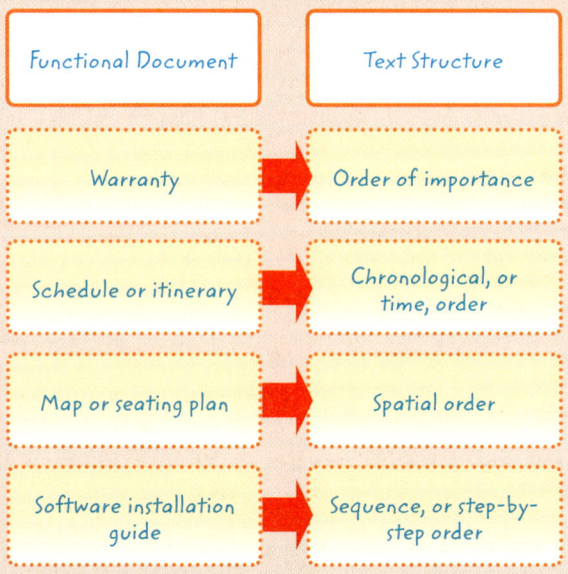

Functional Document	Text Structure
Warranty	Order of importance
Schedule or itinerary	Chronological, or time, order
Map or seating plan	Spatial order
Software installation guide	Sequence, or step-by-step order

1138   UNIT 7   FUNCTIONAL DOCUMENTS

Evaluate the Credibility

Would you take a flyer for a new diet pill seriously if it claimed that the pill could cause immediate and drastic weight loss? Would you believe a promotional poster for a new CD if it stated that the CD only contained musical gems? When you read functional documents, it is important to determine the credibility of an argument or claim. Below are a few tips for evaluating credibility:

- **Examine the statements the writer makes.** Do they seem plausible based on your experiences? If, for instance, the writer of a software information document states that a certain program will allow you to create comic-book masterpieces, you might not believe him. If, on the other hand, the writer states that the program will expand your creative horizons, you might accept this statement as true.

- **Consider the evidence the writer uses to support statements.** Are there sufficient facts? Are there testimonials from users or product testers?

- **Look at the possible motivation of the writer.** Is a writer, for instance, trying to sell a product? If so, you might conclude that he is slanting the facts so that the product sounds more appealing or more effective than it might really be.

Using Functional Documents

Publishing a Graphic Novel

In this chapter, you will encounter different functional documents while you follow the progress of Devin Gregory, who is attempting to publish his graphic novel *Kosmo Fantastic Versus Mr. Meriadeck*. You will pick up on Devin's publishing adventure at the point when he is ready to enter his finished manuscript in a graphic novel contest.

As you accompany Devin through the publishing process, you will gain knowledge of a variety of functional documents. You will also learn about some of the stages involved in transforming a manuscript into a bound book.

As you read the functional documents in this unit, be sure to

- Examine text structures to understand how information is organized and to unlock meaning. For more about text structure, see the Reading Handbook, pages R38–R39.

- Form opinions and make judgments about what you are reading. Use the tips above to guide you in this process.

Before You Read

Build Background

After completing what he felt was a great manuscript, Devin wanted to submit his graphic novel to a writing contest. He visited the website of the journal *Golden Gate Comics*. He then sent an **e-mail** to the journal's editor about the guidelines. Devin downloaded the **application form** that appears on page 1142 and carefully reviewed it. Next, he filled out the form as neatly as possible and checked it for grammatical, punctuation, and spelling errors. Finally, Devin composed a **cover letter** in which he demonstrated his familiarity with the journal and highlighted his qualifications that related to the contest.

Cover letters, e-mails, and **application forms** are all functional documents. The ability to understand such documents is a skill that will be helpful to you throughout your life.

Learning Objectives

For pages 1140–1144

Reading:
Making generalizations.
Distinguishing fact and opinion.

Writing:
Writing a business letter.

Reading Preview

Make Generalizations One way to help you understand what you read is to **make generalizations.** When you form a generalization, you look at specific details or facts and try to identify patterns or trends within them. As you read each document, identify, organize, and analyze its key details and facts. Then use your analysis to make general statements about a particular topic or type of document.

Distinguish Fact and Opinion The documents in this lesson contain both **facts**—statements that can be proved—and **opinions**—statements that express personal views, attitudes, or interpretations. To help differentiate the two, use the tips below.

- Look at the author's wording. Phrases such as *I think,* and *I believe* indicate opinions, as do *view, feeling,* and *always.*

- Examine the evidence. Does the author supply enough evidence and facts to support a statement?

Workplace Vocabulary

E-mail: A message or messages sent and received electronically over a computer network

Application: A written form to be completed by an applicant

Cover letter: A letter sent along with other documents to give additional information

1140 UNIT 7 FUNCTIONAL DOCUMENTS

Lesson 1

Read an E-mail

Let's take a look at the e-mail Devin sent to learn more about the submission process.

To: mjones@goldengatecomics.net ❶
From: DGregory@dkvworld.net
Date: September 7, 2007
Subject: Dragon Fire Graphic Novel Contest ❷

Dear Mr. Jones:

❸ I am the author of a graphic novel, and I would like to ask you a few questions regarding the submission process for the graphic novel contest. The first question I have is, Can I submit my novel either via e-mail or via regular snail mail? I couldn't find information concerning your submissions preferences on your website and want to follow your guidelines correctly. My second question is, Are you open to simultaneous submissions, or do you prefer that writers submit their works to only one publication at a time? To improve my chances of being published, I would like to submit my novel simultaneously to several publishers, but I can limit myself to your contest should you disallow simultaneous submissions. ❹

Thank you in advance for your prompt response to my questions. ❺

Devin Gregory

---

❶ The heading identifies the recipient of the e-mail, the sender, the date, and the subject.

❷ The subject line tells the reader what the e-mail is about.

❸ The purpose of the e-mail is stated in the first sentence.

❹ The e-mail requests additional information specifically related to the submission process.

❺ The writer expresses his thanks.

Reading Check

Distinguish Fact and Opinion Name a fact that appears in the first sentence of the e-mail.

Make Generalizations How is the structure of this e-mail similar to other e-mails you have seen?

Paraphrase What kinds of information is Devin asking for in the e-mail?

Read an Application

Devin downloaded this form from the Golden Gate Comics Web site.

Dragon Fire Graphic Novel Contest
Official Entry Form

Name of writer: ____Devin Gregory_____
Name of artist: ____Devin Gregory_____
Address: ____3777 N. Halsted Street, Chicago, Illinois, 60613____
Home phone: __(773) 555-1234____ Work phone: ___none____
Cell phone: __none__ ❶ E-mail: DGregory@dkvworld.net_____
Title of novel: __Kosmo Fantastic Versus Mr. Meriadeck____ ❷
Story genre: ____Adventure, science fiction_____
Number of pages: 112 pages   Hand drawn? xx yes __ no.
Story Synopsis: Orphaned teenager Kosmo Fantastic must defeat the evil Mr. Meriadeck before his planet, Bork Bersi, comes to an end. Kosmo Fantastic uses his powers to defeat Meriadeck.

Have you ever had a graphic novel published? ❸ __yes xx no. If so, title of work/publisher:_____
Published in a literary magazine/journal? xx yes __ no. If so, give example: "Stymir the Stouthearted," published in Manga Madness (Fall 2008) Other accomplishments? accomplished musician and poet; active naturalist. **Send entry form; check for $10; 6 pages of sequential art; com-pleted script; and a self-addressed stamped envelope to** ❹

Dragon Fire Graphic Novel Contest, Golden Gate Comics, 3100 Geary Blvd., San Francisco, CA 94118

---

❶ Contact information appears at the top of the application.

❷ The application requests information related to the book.

❸ The application is designed so that it is easy to fill out.

❹ Specific instructions are given at the bottom of the application.

Reading Check

Make Generalizations How is the text in application forms typically structured?

Distinguish Fact and Opinion In which section of the application can you find opinions about the writer's experiences?

Analyze Think about the kinds of information the application is requesting. Based on this information, what do you think is the main purpose of the application?

Read a Cover Letter

Here is the letter Devin sent to inspire interest in his graphic novel.

3777 N. Halsted Street
Chicago, IL 60613
September 15, 2007

Mr. Mark Jones
Editor
Dragon Fire Graphic Novel Contest
Golden Gate Comics
4440 Sunset Boulevard
San Francisco, CA 90027

Dear Mr. Jones,

❶ Enclosed is my manuscript, *Kosmo Fantastic Versus Mr. Meriadeck,* for consideration in your Dragon Fire Graphic Novel Contest. I read *Golden Gate Comics* and am a fan of your imaginative comics. **❷**

Kosmo Fantastic Versus Mr. Meriadeck is my first novel. However, my comics were published in literary journals, including *Manga Madness* and *American Saga: A Comic Magazine.* My comic strip *Stanley and Livingston* appeared in a local newspaper during June of 2006. **❸**

Enclosed are six sample pages from my novel, a full script of the novel, a completed application form, a check for $10, and a stamped, self-addressed envelope. If you have any questions, please contact me by phone (773-555-1234) or e-mail (DGregory@dkvworld.net). **❹**

I look forward to hearing from you in the near future. **❺**

Sincerely, **❻**

Devin Gregory

❶ The main purpose of the letter is stated clearly in the first sentence.

❷ The writer demonstrates familiarity with the content of the journal.

❸ The writer mentions publishing credits that specifically relate to the contest.

❹ The writer provides contact information.

❺ The writer uses a block format. With this type of format, the text is justified left, and one line of space separates each paragraph.

❻ The writer inserts four lines of space to leave adequate room for his signature.

Reading Check

Make Generalizations Why do you think the block format is the most popular format for business letters?

Distinguish Fact and Opinion Reread the second paragraph. Which sentence there is most difficult to verify? Why?

Evaluate Do you think the author demonstrates that he has the necessary experience to write a strong graphic novel?

After You Read

Respond and Think Critically

Directions: Read the questions about documents below and select the best answer.

1. What is the purpose of the **e-mail**?
   A. to highlight Devin's publishing credits
   B. to request additional information about the submissions process
   C. to improve Devin's chances of having his novel accepted
   D. to make the editor aware of Devin's graphic novel

2. In which section of the **application form** would you find the most information about the content of the graphic novel?
   A. story synopsis
   B. estimated number of pages
   C. story genre
   D. name of writer

3. Conventional **cover letters** have all of the following parts EXCEPT
   A. a salutation
   B. the recipient's inside address
   C. a closing
   D. the recipient's e-mail address

4. Which of the following is NOT discussed in the **cover letter**?
   A. why the writer chose the Dragon Fire Graphic Novel Contest
   B. which documents the writer has enclosed
   C. who will enjoy reading the novel
   D. what qualifications the writer has

Write a Business Letter

Assignment Think of a situation in which writing a business letter might help you achieve a long-held goal. Perhaps you want to be chosen for an internship or receive funding for a community project. A business letter can help you in these efforts.

Once you are clear about what you want to achieve, begin drafting. Clearly state your purpose for writing and convincingly describe your qualifications in the body of the letter. Use business letter format.

Get Ideas First impressions matter. Strive for clear, lively writing and correct spelling, punctuation, and grammar. Awkward sentences leave a negative impression. To write an effective letter

- Include the standard **parts** of a business letter: a return address, the date, an inside address, a salutation, the text of the letter, a complimentary close, a signature, and a printed name.
- Use either the **block format** or the **modified block format**. In the modified block style, the date and closing are centered on the page; other parts are aligned on the left.
- Use only one **font** and make sure it is easy to read. Avoid fancy unreadable fonts.
- Use vocabulary and grammar that you think your **audience** would employ.
- Keep to the **main points** and cut out all information that is irrelevant to these points.
- Arrange the information in the letter into the best **order** for getting the results you want.

Give It Structure Before you begin writing, consider your audience. Who will read your letter? What does this person need to know? Then choose a style that your audience will find appealing and easy to understand. Try to strike a balance between too formal and impersonal and too casual and personal. This means using standard punctuation, spelling, and grammar and steering away from slang, jargon, or buzzwords.

Before You Read

Build Background

When Devin received an e-mail from the editor of *Golden Gate Comics* instructing him to submit his novel electronically, he found an online **professional article** to guide him. Devin's first step was to scan his hand-drawn cartoons into his computer.

Before purchasing a scanner, Devin reviewed its **warranty** to find out what its manufacturer would cover. He then purchased software, reviewing its **product information description,** which appears on page 1148. Finally, Devin consulted the software **installation guide** to install the program smoothly.

Warranties, product information descriptions, and installation guides are types of **consumer documents.** They explain consumer products. Here are strategies to help you read these documents.

Reading Preview

Identify Sequence As you read, try to determine the order, or **sequence** that organizes a document. An effective sequence arranges information so readers understand how information is related. Here are three common types of logical sequences:

- **Chronological, or time, order** (See article on page 1146.)
- **Order of importance** (See warranty on page 1147.)
- **Sequence, or step-by-step order** (See guide, page 1149.)

To identify the type of sequence in a document, look carefully at its features. Does the document contain numbered lists? Have words that indicate time order? Have headings that signal sequence? All of these features can provide clues about the type of order the writer uses to structure a document.

Summarize While reading, **summarize,** or briefly state, the main ideas of a passage in a logical sequence and in your own words. Ask yourself who, what, where, why, how, and when questions about the information provided.

Learning Objectives

For pages 1145–1150

In studying this text, you will focus on the following objectives:

Reading:
Identifying sequence.
Summarizing.

Writing:
Writing a list of tips.

Workplace Vocabulary

Installation guide: a manual that explains how to install or operate a product

Warranty: an agreement that describes a customer's rights and a company's obligations if a product is defective

LESSON 2   **1145**

Read a Professional Article

Here is the professional article Devin found while surfing the Internet.

Ten Tips for Creating Visually Satisfying Graphic Novels
By Maya Hering

In this article, I explain how to create a professional looking comic from your hand-drawn art. ❶

1. Use pencil and 8 x 12 sheets of paper to create each panel. Include one action per panel; 4 to 6 panels per page. ❷
2. Trace over your pencil lines with a black gel pen, which does not bleed.
3. Once the ink is dry, gently erase all pencil lines using a soft eraser. A scanner will capture all of the stray marks on a piece of paper.
4. Create a new folder on your computer. Name it appropriately.
5. Scan your panels into your computer. Save them in your new folder.
6. Using a comic-book software program, create a layout for each page. Create your own layouts or choose from layout templates. ❸
7. Import your scanned drawings into the computer program; drag them into place in the layouts. Then use the Image Crop option in your program to get rid of areas of drawings that you don't want to keep.
8. Next you can edit your drawings. To get rid of bumpy lines, apply the Smoothing and Straightening options in your software program.
9. Now add color to help convey your characters' personalities. Select the blank areas inside your drawings where you want to add color and use the Color tools in your program to fill in these areas. ❹
10. Once you've finished editing, insert captions and word balloons (i.e., the bubbles that convey characters' thoughts and spoken words) in all of the panels. First, draw ovals for the balloons and place them in the appropriate positions, and then fill the balloons with text.

Sidebar notes:

❶ The purpose of the article is stated clearly and concisely.

❷ The writer makes the tips easier to follow by organizing them into a list.

❸ The writer describes when, how, and why to carry out each tip in the list.

❹ The text in each tip is brief and direct in its tone.

Reading Check

Identify Sequence In what kind of **order** does the writer list the tips?

Summarize In your own words, summarize the tips the article offers.

Draw Conclusions Based on your reading of this article, what do you think are the most important things you can do to give hand-drawn artwork a professional look?

Read a Warranty

Here is the warranty that came with the scanner Devin purchased.

Kambara Super Scanner

Full One Year Warranty ❶

Congratulations! You have purchased a Kambara Super Scanner. It should meet all of your scanning needs for many years to come and with minimal care. Please read the following information and save these instructions.

Activation: This warranty will become active after you fill out the enclosed card and mail it to the address below. ❷

Period of Coverage: This warranty covers defects in workmanship/material under normal use for a period of one year from the date of purchase. ❸

Claims: If your scanner has any mechanical defects during the warranty period, pack the scanner carefully and ship to the address below. Include proof of purchase, your name and address, and a description of the problem. ❹

Kambara Corp. Repair, 550 S. State Street, Easton, NY 11030 ❺

Our trained technicians will inspect the scanner and repair or replace it free of charge. However, if they discover product defects resulted from improper use or storage, you will be billed for the repair or replacement.

Exceptions: This warranty does not cover Kambara products purchased outside of the United States.

Additional Information: This warranty gives you specific legal rights; you may have other rights, which vary from state to state. Contact your state attorney general's office for further information. ❻

❶ In the title, the writer specifies the period of coverage and the type of coverage (i.e., full or limited).

❷ One line space is placed between each section so that the document is easy to read.

❸ The writer spells out the types of problems the warranty covers.

❹ The writer describes the steps customers should take if a problem arises.

❺ The contact information is set off so that it can be easily located.

❻ The final section tells customers how to find out about other rights they may have.

Reading Check

Summarize In your own words, state the main ideas contained under the heading "Claims."

Identify sequence The information in the warranty is arranged in which type of logical sequence?

Question What is the only way for a customer to activate the warranty?

Read Software Product Information

Here is the description for Devin's Comic Universe software program.

Comic Universe

For drawing comics from scratch or manipulating scanned artwork, Comic Universe lets you create personalized comic masterpiece in no time. **❶**

Program Features

- **Layouts** Offers you more than 300 distinctive layout templates for you to turn your ideas into a professional-looking book. **❷**
- **Original and Scanned Art** Allows you to draw original art or to enhance the appearance of scanned artwork.
- **Imported Art** Allows you to import photos/artwork from your own collection or from the application's extensive library of clipart.
- **Inking** Makes it possible for you to ink your drawings digitally. With the pen tool, you can trace and boldly outline drawings. **❸**
- **Graphics** Includes an abundance of action-word graphics that you can position within the layout templates.
- **Text Balloons** Provides a wealth of caption boxes and text balloons or lets you easily create your own customized balloons.
- **Compatible Formats** Works with JPEG, BMP, GIF, and PNG. **❹**
- **Online Sharing** Permits you to save the finished comic as a PDF or HTML file so that you can share it online with family and friends.
- **Coloring** Combines paint and erase tools so that you can create visually exciting images.

"We highly recommend this product for budding and established comic artists. It can turn their creative ideas into high-quality comics."

—*Comics Galore*

---

❶ The description provides a brief introduction to the software program.

❷ The writer uses headings that can help customers find the information they're looking for easily.

❸ The clear, simple design makes the content easy to read.

❹ The writer gives information that is important for readers to know.

Reading Check

Identify Sequence Where in the document should the section "Coloring" be moved so that information is presented in a logical order?

Summarize In your own words, summarize the information under the heading "Imported Art."

Paraphrase Using your own words, describe the highlights of the Comic Universe software program.

Read an Installation Guide

Here is the installation guide that Devin used to install his new comic-book computer program.

Comic Universe Installation Guide ❶
1. Insert the Comic Universe installation disc into your computer's DVD-ROM drive.
2. Double-click the Comic Universe icon and follow the on-screen prompts.
3. Read the License Agreement. Click Continue. Click Agree. ❷
4. Enter your name, organization (optional), and your registration number, where appropriate. Your registration number is located inside the front cover of your user's manual. ❸ *Please note that you must register your software in order to obtain technical support and important product updates. ❹
5. Click Register.
6. Click Install to perform the installation. If the installation doesn't proceed smoothly, refer to page 9 of the user's manual for troubleshooting information
7. Once you have completed the installation process, click Exit.

❶ The title indicates the specific procedure to be explained.

❷ The writer gives direct and simple commands.

❸ The writer places one line space between each step so that the steps are easy to follow.

❹ Additional information related to the registration process is provided.

Reading Check

Identify Sequence The information in this "Installation Guide" is arranged in which type of logical sequence?

Summarize What is the benefit of registering the software?

Analyze Why must readers perform the steps in the order in which they are presented?

After You Read

Respond and Think Critically

Directions: Read the questions about workplace and consumer documents below and select the best answer.

1. Under which heading in the **warranty** would you find information about getting service?
   A. Activation
   B. Claims
   C. Exceptions
   D. Additional Information

2. The **professional article** provides the LEAST information about
   A. preparing hand-drawn art for the scanner
   B. scanning the art
   C. enhancing the lines in the art
   D. adding color to the art

3. The **Product Information** description suggests that customers should purchase Comic Universe because it is
   A. unique
   B. fun to use
   C. inexpensive
   D. easy to use

4. According to the information in the **Installation Guide,** customers must register their software in order
   A. to obtain a refund for the cost of the software
   B. to legally use the software
   C. to receive updates to their program
   D. to show their acceptance of the license agreement

Write a List of Tips

Assignment Write a set of tips that explains to other students how to transform information from a nondigital to a digital format. To get yourself started, think about occasions when having a digital version of something might have made your life easier or helped you achieve a goal. For example, have you ever missed an important event because you misplaced your calendar or lost track of a friend because you mislaid your phone book? A digital version of the item might have been very helpful.

Once you have determined the content for your set of tips, log on to the Internet and search for sites related to your topic. Gather any information geared specifically toward that topic. Then use what you have learned to write a clear, concise, and accurate set of tips.

Get Ideas Write your tips to make them as useful as possible. Use the guidelines below to help you.

- **Know your audience.** When prewriting, determine your reader's level of familiarity with your topic and with the technical terms you plan to include. Then use what you have learned to come up with easy-to-understand vocabulary and definitions for the technical terms.

- **Arrange your tips in the right order.** Remember you can cause impatience, and even confusion, if you put your tips in the wrong order.

- **Use the conventional format, or style, of a set of tips.** In the majority of these documents, information is presented in the form of a bulleted or numbered list, and bold type is used to emphasize key words and ideas.

Give It Structure When you are trying to explain a procedure to people, it is vital that you present information in a logical order. For example, for the creation of an online portfolio, if you told your readers to clean up and then select their best art work, they would be thoroughly confused. If, on the other hand, you told them to choose and then clean up their best artwork, they would understand your instructions. To get the right order, try following your tips yourself. Can you easily understand them, or do you find yourself confused in certain places? Based on what you have learned, arrange the tips in the order that makes the most sense.

Before You Read

Build Background

Devin won the Dragon Fire Graphic Novel Contest and received a memo requesting he visit the publisher in San Francisco. He also received an envelope with **travel documents:** bus, train, and airplane **schedules** listing departure and arrival times; an **itinerary** specifying the activities that would occur; **a map** showing how to get from the airport, bus station, or train station to the publisher's office; and detailed **driving instructions.** Devin also received a **written agenda** for each meeting.

In this lesson, you will learn how to read and interpret **travel documents** and **workplace documents,** such as these. You will also learn how to write **driving directions.** Here are strategies to help you with such documents.

Learning Objectives

For pages 1151–1157

In studying this text, you will focus on the following objectives:

Reading:
Reviewing.
Visualizing.

Writing:
Writing directions to a location.
Writing meeting minutes.

Reading Preview

Review While reading, pause and summarize main points in a passage or steps in a procedure. If you want to go back and find a piece of information, **scan** the text. Look for key words or phrases and for section headings or terms in **boldfaced** type.

Visualize As you read, try to form a mental picture of what the author is describing. Turning an author's descriptions into mental images can help you better understand complex instructions, such as an involved set of driving directions or a complicated set of assembly instructions. In order to visualize, pay careful attention to the concrete nouns and active verbs the author uses. According to these details and your own imagination, how does one step relate to the next one in a set of instructions?

Workplace Vocabulary

Memo: a short, informal note that conveys important information

Transportation schedule: a list of days and times of regular departures and arrivals

Itinerary: a detailed plan for a journey or event

Directions: instructions about how to get from one place to another

Map: a flat representation of an area

Meeting agenda: a list of things to be accomplished in a meeting

Lesson 3

Read an Announcement Memo

Here is the letter Devin received informing him that he won the contest.

❶ There is no salutation in a memo. One line space is placed between the headings and the message.

❷ All essential information is provided in the first paragraph.

❸ The second paragraph provides additional details.

❹ The contact information is succinctly summarized here.

TO: Devin Gregory
FROM: Mark Jones
SUBJECT: Meetings
DATE: October 2, 2009 ❶

Once again, I would like to send our heartfelt congratulations to you for winning the Dragon Fire Graphic Novel Contest! ❷ We are excited to be bringing your novel into print, and we look forward to meeting with you to discuss details. We have tentatively scheduled meetings for Thursday, November 5, between 2:00 and 5:30 P.M., and Friday, November 6, between 9:00 and 11:45 A.M. During the meetings, representatives from the publicity, production, and editorial departments will be on hand to discuss the schedule for the production and marketing of your novel, and to offer their advice and guidance. Our publicists will go over events related to the book's launching.

If you are unable to attend the meetings, please contact us immediately, so that we can find a date that is convenient for everyone. ❸ Next week, I will send you travel information, an itinerary, and agendas for the several meetings that will be held. If you have any questions in the meantime, you can contact me at (415) 555-1313 or send an e-mail to mjones@goldengatecomics.net. ❹

Reading Check

Review Go back over the first paragraph. What is the most important piece of information provided in this passage?

Make Inferences From the clues given in the first paragraph, what inference can you draw about the publisher's plans for celebrating the release of the book?

Read a Train Schedule and an Itinerary

Once Devin confirmed his availability, Mark Jones sent him a variety of travel documents to help him plan his trip to San Francisco. Let's take a look at two of the documents he mailed—a train schedule and an itinerary.

Chicago–San Francisco Service ❶

Train Name	California Quail	California Redwood
Train Number ❷	10	20
Days of Operation	Daily	Daily
	miles	
Chicago, IL	0	2:00p[1]	6:00p[1] ❸
Des Moines, IA	308	8:30p[1]	12:30a[1]
Omaha, NE	431	11:00p[1]	3:00a[1]
Denver, CO	918	8:15a[2]	12:15p[2]
Clifton, CO	1108	4:30p[2]	8:30p[2]
Salt Lake City, UT	1322	12:15a[2]	4:15a[2]
Sparks, NV	1744	9:15a[3] ❹	-
Sacramento, CA	1950	2:30p[3]	6:30p[3]
San Francisco, CA	2030	6:00p[3]	10:00p[3]

1. **Chicago**, Des Moines, and Omaha times are Central Time.
2. Denver, Clifton, and Salt Lake City times are Mountain Time.
3. Sparks, Sacramento, and San Francisco times are Pacific Time.

❶ The title indicates the train's point of departure and final destination.

❷ Both the name and number of each train are provided.

❸ The information is organized in rows and columns.

❹ The schedule uses hyphens to indicate stations where a train doesn't stop.

Reading Check

Review Scan the document to determine when each train leaves Chicago and arrives in San Francisco. How long does the trip between the two cities take?

Visualize Where will the California Quail be at midnight of the first day of the journey from Chicago to San Francisco?

Identify Sequence In what **sequence**, or order, is the information in this schedule presented?

LESSON 3

Read a Meeting Itinerary

Here is Devin's itinerary from Golden Gate Comics.

- **1** The date is set off in a separate line.
- **2** The writer provides the timetable for each event.
- **3** A brief description of each event is included.
- **4** The writer gives the location for each event.

Thursday, November 5 **1**

2:00–2:30 P.M.	Meet with Mark Jones, the contest judge and acquisitions editor at Golden Gate Comics—Suite 200
2:30–4:30 P.M.	Create a production schedule with production editor Sally Smith—Suite 200
4:30–5:00 P.M. **2**	Meet with copyeditor James Reinhart to discuss the editing style for the book—Suite 200
5:00–5:30 P.M.	Go over cover samples with designer Laura Albrecht—Suite 420
6:00 P.M.	Dinner at the Yellow Rose Café

Friday, November 6

9:00–9:30 A.M.	Pose for a series of author photos—Building Lobby **3**
9:30–10:15 A.M.	Review the marketing schedule with publicity director Francis Adams—Suite 300
10:15–11:00 A.M.	Discuss details of book tours with publicist John Griffith—Suite 300
11:00–11:45 A.M.	Discuss details of book-release party with publicist Lisa Wrobel—Suite 300 **4**
12:00–1:00 P.M.	Lunch with staff members—Company Cafeteria

Reading Check

Review Glance quickly over the timetables for the different activities. Has a sufficient amount of time been allotted for each activity?

Visualize Who will Devin be meeting with at 10:30 Friday morning?

Identify Logical Sequence Why does the writer list the timetable for each activity before he or she lists its location?

Read Written Directions

Let's take a look at the driving instructions that Devin received.

Directions to Golden Gate Comics by Car ❶

From the airport:

Upon exiting the airport, merge onto US 101 North toward San Francisco. Take exit 434A onto Mission St./US-101 North. Take a slight left onto S. Van Ness Avenue. Turn left onto Geary Boulevard. After going 1 ½ miles, look for the building marked 3100 Geary Boulevard. Garage parking is available in the neighborhood. ❷

From the train station: ❸

Upon exiting the train station, head toward King Street. Turn left onto King Street. Turn left onto 3rd Street. Continue on Kearny Street. Turn left onto Geary Street. Continue onto Geary Boulevard. After going 1 ½ miles, look for the building marked 3100 Geary Boulevard. Garage parking is available in the neighborhood.

From the bus station:

Upon exiting the bus station, head north on Mission Street toward 23rd Street. Continue on Mission Street. Take a slight left onto S. Van Ness Avenue. Turn left onto Geary Boulevard. After going 1 ½ miles, look for the building marked 3100 Geary Boulevard. Garage parking is available in the neighborhood.

Parking:

Since we provide discounted parking for our visitors at all of the local garages, be sure to give your parking ticket to the receptionist so that it can be validated. ❹

❶ The purpose of the directions is stated clearly in the title.

❷ The information is presented in a step-by-step order.

❸ The writer uses informative headings to make it easy for readers to find the directions they need.

❹ Useful information is presented in the final section.

Reading Check

Visualize Use the nouns and verbs the writer gives to help you visualize each step and how it relates to the next step.

Review How are the three sets of directions similar?

Evaluate How could the writer have changed the structure of the driving directions to make them more helpful to readers?

Read a Meeting Agenda

Here is one of the meeting agendas that Mark Jones mailed to Devin.

❶ The purpose of the meeting is clearly stated in the title.

❷ The date, time, and place of the meeting follow the title.

❸ The items are listed in the order in which they will be discussed.

❹ A timetable is provided for each of the topics to be discussed.

Creating a production schedule for *Kosmo Fantastic versus Mr. Meriadeck* ❶

Thursday, November 1, 2009 ❷
2:30 P.M.–4:30 P.M.
Golden Gate Comics, 3100 Geary Blvd., Suite 200

❸

Overview of the stages of book production by Sally Smith.......... 2:30 P.M.

Discussion: Establishing dates for editing steps .... 3:00 P.M.

Coffee/tea break .... 3:30 P.M.

Discussion: Establishing dates for design steps........................... 3:45 P.M. ❹

Discussion: Creating timetable for proofreading[1], indexing, and author book review... 4:00 P.M.

Wrap-up..4:15 P.M.

---

1. **proofreading:** reading printed materials for the purpose of identifying and correcting mistakes

Reading Check

Review Go back over the agenda. Then state, in your own words, the topics that will be covered during the meeting.

Visualize How much time does the agenda allow for a coffee/tea break?

Determine Main Idea Look carefully at the items in this agenda. Based on these items, what do you think is the main purpose of the meeting?

After You Read

Respond and Think Critically

Directions: Read the questions about workplace and consumer documents below and select the best answer.

1. Which of the following BEST describes the purpose of the **memo**?
   A. to provide information about the production schedule for the book
   B. to summarize the company's marketing plans for the book
   C. to indicate when and where important meetings will occur
   D. to congratulate the author on winning the graphic novel contest

2. Which of the following is NOT covered within the **train schedule**?
   A. the trains' point of departure
   B. the trains' names and numbers
   C. the mileage for the trip
   D. the fares for different classes

3. Which addition to the **written directions** would make them more helpful to readers?
   A. the distance in miles from one place to another
   B. a detailed description of the city's major highways
   C. the inclusion of shorter and more simple commands
   D. a detailed description of the city's major landmarks

4. Which of the following is NOT one of the purposes served by the **meeting agenda**?
   A. to help participants prepare for the meeting
   B. to inform participants how much time is scheduled for each part of the meeting
   C. to provide an overview of the goals of the meeting
   D. to report on activities related to the meeting

Write Travel Directions

Assignment Imagine that a group of your friends is meeting at an unfamiliar location to plan an upcoming event, and you have been asked to write directions on how to get there from your school. To get started, locate your school and the meeting place on a map of your hometown and trace the path from one place to the other. Then write a clear set of directions that your friends could follow to get to the location from your school. Be sure to include street, route, and highway names in your directions, as well as distances between places.

Get Ideas To be effective, directions must meet the following criteria:

- The directions must contain accurate and detailed instructions. If you tell your readers, for example, to turn left when you mean right, they might not end up in the right location.

- The directions can include comprehension aids, such as graphic elements and alternate scenarios. Arrows, and U-turn, start, and finish signs, for instance, can help readers follow your directions. Providing an alternative route in the event a certain highway or road is closed is also important.

Give It Structure Graphic elements can contribute to good directions, since they can help clarify the actions readers need to take. The inclusion of arrows, for example, in a set of directions can help readers quickly and easily determine when and where they need to make a turn. Before inserting a graphic element in your directions, however, make sure that it directly relates to nearby text. Use universal signs and graphics to be sure your intended audience can easily understand them. Unfamiliar graphics can confuse readers.

Before You Read

Build Background

During his visit to San Francisco, Devin signed his contract and met with publicists at Golden Gate Comics to develop a marketing plan. They decided that a great way to generate publicity for the novel was to produce a **pamphlet** that would convince readers that the book was fresh and exciting.

Devin resolved to create a **Web site** for other emerging graphic artists that would provide them with information on imagining, creating, and publishing graphic novels. On his site, he included appropriate, appealing graphics and easy-to-read text.

Reading Preview

Here are effective strategies for reading and understanding documents such as Contracts, pamphlets, and websites.

Determine Main Idea To increase your comprehension, identify the **main idea** of individual paragraphs and passages. First look at the major points the writer is making. Which one seems to be the most important? The main idea of a paragraph is the basic point the writer is making in that paragraph.

Some writers directly state the main idea in a topic sentence. When writers imply a main idea, readers need to put examples and clues together to identify the main idea. Once you determine the main idea, you can use the **supporting details** to learn additional information about it.

Analyze Cause-and-Effect Relationships A cause-and-effect relationship exists when one event causes another to happen. If you can answer *why* something happened, you know its cause. If you can answer *what happened as a result of* something, you know the effect. Words and phrases such as *because, as a result,* and *consequently* often signal cause-and-effect relationships.

Learning Objectives

For pages 1158–1163

In studying this text, you will focus on the following objectives:

Reading: Determining main idea. Analyzing cause-and-effect relationships.

Writing: Writing a Web site links list.

Workplace Vocabulary

Pamphlet: A short printed publication that is usually stitched or stapled together

Contract: An agreement between two or more parties to do or not to do something

Web site: A group of interrelated web pages devoted to one or more topics

Read a Pamphlet

Lesson 4

Here is the pamphlet from Golden Gate Comics.

New and Notable Graphic Novels

At Golden Gate Comics, we publish graphic novels with striking illustrations and themes that are meaningful to readers of all ages. Here are three upcoming graphic novels that we believe fit this bill. **❶**

❷ Paris: City of Light by Emma Lyons
When Peter Jones accepts a professional opportunity in Paris, his thirteen-year-old son Jack and fourteen-year-old daughter Helen must go with him. The move from northern Michigan to the city of light disrupts everything that is important to Jack. But when he meets fifteen-year-old Jean in the Jardin du Luxembourg, this budding friendship helps Jack appreciate his new home. **❸**

Kosmo Fantastic Versus Mr. Meriadeck by Devin Gregory
Orphaned teenager Kosmo Fantastic must defeat the evil Mr. Meriadeck before his planet, Bork Bersi, comes to an end. In Kosmo Fantastic's most difficult hour, he is joined by the powerful and cunning Lady in Red. **❹**

The Girl Who Went Back by Ty Mooney
Award-winning cartoonist Ty Mooney tells the story of high-school student Melissa Johnson, who lives with her grandparents on the South Side of Chicago in the 1970s. Melissa discovers that her parents met after their arrest during the Montgomery Bus Boycott in 1956. As she learns more about the story of the civil rights movement in the Deep South and the courage of its participants, she develops a deep pride in the parents she never knew.

❶ The topic of the pamphlet is stated clearly in the introduction.

❷ The pamphlet uses bold type to draw the reader's attention to the titles of the novels.

❸ All text is flush left.

❹ The pamphlet provides a succinct and engaging summary of each novel.

Reading Check

Determine Main Idea In the description of *Paris: City of Light*, what sentence contains the main idea?

Analyze Cause-and-Effect Relationships In the description of Kosmo Fantastic Versus Mr. Meriadeck, what causes Kosmo to fight Mr. Meriadeck?

Compare and Contrast Look carefully at the descriptions of the three novels. How are the styles of the descriptions similar and different?

Read a Contract

❶ A space is provided for the date of the signing, and for the name of the author.

❷ Under the heading "Grant," the contract indicates that Golden Gate Comics will be the ONLY publisher putting out the book.

❸ The contract clearly states what percentage of the sales the author will receive.

1. **Libel:** Any false or malicious words or pictures that damage a person's reputation
2. **Indemnify:** To compensate for expense brought on by oneself
3. **Royalty:** Share of the sales from a work

PUBLISHING CONTRACT

THIS AGREEMENT, made and entered into this ___5th___ day of ___November___, 20_09_, by and between ___Devin Gregory___, hereinafter referred to as the Author, and Golden Gate Comics, hereinafter referred to as the Publisher. ❶

Grant The Author hereby grants to the Publisher the exclusive English-language rights to publish throughout the world ___Kosmo Fantastic Versus Mr. Meriadeck,___ hereinafter referred to as the Work. ❷

Author Warranties and Representations The Author affirms that he is the sole owner of the Work, and that it is entirely original. The Author warrants that the Work does not violate any copyright or other intellectual property right or any personal right of any person or entity, and that the Work does not contain any libel[1] or obscenity. The Author agrees to indemnify[2] and hold the Publisher harmless from any liability, damage, cost, and expense in connection with any claim, action, or proceeding inconsistent with Author's warranties.

Publication and Selling Price

The Publisher shall publish the Work no later than 14 months after this contract is signed. The Publisher agrees to assign to the Work a retail price that is comparable to like other works of a similar length and format.

Copyright The Author shall exclusively own the copyright of the Work. In each copy of the Work, the Publisher shall include a notice recognizing the Author as the copyright owner, per U.S. Copyright Act.

Royalty Payments The Publisher shall pay to the Author the following royalty[3] commissions. For electronic copies of the work, the Publisher shall pay the author 50% of net profits. For printed copies of the work, the Publisher shall pay the author 25% of net profits. ❸ The Publisher shall send the Author quarterly royalty statements on the following dates: September 1, December 1, March 1, and June 1. Royalties collected for the quarter shall accompany the statement. ❹

Termination

Either the Author or Publisher may terminate this contract with a ninety (90) day written notice, to be sent by a traceable mail service. At the time of the termination, all rights granted to the Publisher shall return to the Author and final royalty payments shall be made.

Signatures The two parties have read this contract and agree to the terms laid out herein. _____
Author

_____Publisher

❹ The contract clearly indicates when the author will receive his share of the net profits.

❺ Lines are provided for the signatures of the two parties.

Girl drawing manga art.

Reading Check

Determine Main Idea What is the main idea that the "Termination" section conveys?

Analyze Cause-and-Effect Relationships What might happen if the author submitted a work that was not entirely original?

Clarify Restate the information in "Author Warranties and Representations."

Read a Web Site

Devin reviewed these Web sites for other emerging comic artists.

> **How to Write a Graphic Novel** This Web site will introduce you to other Web sites that contain information on imagining, creating, and publishing graphic novels.
>
> ## Annotated Links
>
> **Adobe Photoshop Elements 2.0 President's Day Project**
> http://www.adobe.com/education/pdf/pse_tutorials/presidents_day.pdf ❶ This site takes readers through the process of creating a comic book using original hand-drawn art. It teaches how to add color to original art and how to create layout pages using Adobe Photoshop Elements.
>
> **Creating Comics** ❷ http://members.shaw.ca/creatingcomics/
> Creating Comics provides writers and artists with various resources related to making and publishing comic books. Here you'll find links to sites that can help you with writing, illustrating, lettering, submitting, self-publishing, and publicizing.
>
> **Time Magazine** http://www.time.com/time/2005/100books/0,24459,graphic_novels,00.html A brief, engaging description for the ten best graphic novels ever written is provided on this Web site. Reading these descriptions can help you determine what makes a graphic novel exciting. ❸
>
> **wisegeek/What are Different Types of Comic Books?** http://www.wisegeek.com/what-are-different-types-of-comic-books.htm
> This site provides definitions for some of the most popular comic-book genres, including: superhero, alternative/esoteric, horror, humor, fantasy, action/adventure, science fiction, and manga. Look through the site to expand your ideas about suitable topics and themes for graphic novels.

❶ The writer accurately reproduces the URL (uniform resource locator) for each Web site. For more information about citing Web resources, go to page R32.

❷ The title of each Web site is included.

❸ The writer provides a concise description of each site and conveys its value or relevance.

Reading Check

Analyze Cause and Effect According to the description of the Time Magazine site, what can be an effect of reading its descriptions of great graphic novels?

Determine Main Idea What is the main idea of the description of the Wisegeek site?

Summarize In your own words, state the main ideas conveyed in the introductory paragraph.

After You Read

Respond and Think Critically

Directions: Read the questions about workplace and consumer documents below and select the best answer.

1. What is the main purpose of the **pamphlet**?
   - **A.** to inform readers of new titles
   - **B.** to describe the themes of new titles
   - **C.** to specify the price of new titles
   - **D.** to provide the publication dates for new titles

2. The **contract** provides the LEAST information on
   - **A.** ownership of the copyright of the novel
   - **B.** ownership of characters
   - **C.** the publication and selling price of the novel
   - **D.** the dates for royalty payments

3. Which of the following would make the **contract** easier to understand?
   - **A.** an explanation of the publisher's marketing strategy
   - **B.** the inclusion of a specific price for the novel
   - **C.** the inclusion of sample pages from the novel
   - **D.** an explanation of legal terms

4. Devin correctly reproduced the Internet addresses listed on his **Web site** so that readers could
   - **A.** learn how to cite sources
   - **B.** e-mail these addresses to friends
   - **C.** easily remember the addresses
   - **D.** quickly find the corresponding sites

Write Annotations

Assignment Think about a topic that fascinates you and that will be of wide interest to other students. Then create a list of annotated links to websites that are related to your given topic. For each link, write a brief note summarizing the content of the site and explaining its value or significance. Refer to examples of annotated bibliographies for guidance on what exactly you should include. After writing, check to make sure that all of your links are relevant to your topic and are free of spelling, punctuation, and grammatical errors.

Get Ideas Below are a few guidelines for writing links that will help browsers find the information they're looking for easily and quickly.

- Keep your language simple and concise. Convoluted writing or complex words will confuse browsers, causing them to move on.

- Use language that conveys the central ideas, or organizing thoughts, of the site.

- Write text that is appropriate for your intended audience.

- List the links in a logical order. You may, for instance, wish to follow the style of an annotated bibliography by arranging links alphabetically.

Give It Structure When writing an explanatory note for a site, it is important to summarize the central topics that are covered. Begin by carefully reading the text on a site and writing down your findings and impressions. What is the purpose of the site? What are the most important ideas? Use your answers to these questions to write a brief summary.

After completing your summary, add a sentence explaining how the site was useful to you. You may also wish to briefly describe the site's strengths and weaknesses.

Reference Section

Literary Terms Handbook R1

Foldables R20

Functional Documents R22

Writing Handbook R28
Using the Traits of Strong Writing R28
Research Paper Writing R31

Reading Handbook R38

Language Handbook R40
Grammar Glossary R40
Troubleshooter R47
Mechanics R53
Spelling R57

Logic and Persuasion Handbook R60

Glossary/Glosario R64

Academic Word List R80
Index of Skills R83
Index of Authors and Titles R95
Acknowledgments R98

Literary Terms Handbook

A

Abstract language Language that expresses an idea or intangible reality, as opposed to a specific object, occurrence, or a concrete reality. "On Women's Right to Vote," page 394, includes abstract language such as *liberty, power, blessings,* and *posterity.*

See also CONCRETE LANGUAGE.

Absurd, Theater of the See THEATER OF THE ABSURD.

Act A major unit of a drama, or play. Modern dramas generally have one, two, or three acts. Older dramas often have five acts. Although Shakespeare did not separate his plays into acts, each play was later divided into five acts. Acts may be divided into one or more scenes.

See page 653.

See also DRAMA, SCENE.

Allegory A literary work in which all or most of the characters, settings, and events stand for ideas, qualities, or figures beyond themselves. The overall purpose of an allegory is to teach a moral lesson.

See page 74.

See also SYMBOL.

Alliteration The repetition of consonant sounds, generally at the beginnings of words. Alliteration can be used to emphasize words, reinforce meaning, or create a musical effect. Note the repeated *s* sounds in the opening of Jean Toomer's "Reapers":

> Black reapers with the sound of steel on stones / Are sharpening scythes.

See pages 592-593, 595.
See also SOUND DEVICES.

Allusion A reference to a well-known character, place, or situation from history, music, art, or another work of literature. Discovering the meaning of an allusion can often be essential to understanding a work. For example, in "Farewell to Manzanar," Jeanne Wakatsuki Houston refers to the residents of the camp as "a band of Charlie Chaplins." This allusion is to Charlie Chaplin, a famous film comedian.

See page 402.

Ambiguity The state of having more than one meaning. The richness of literary language lies in its ability to evoke multiple layers of meaning. The title of E. E. Cummings's poem "since feeling is first," is intentionally ambiguous.

Analogy A comparison that shows similarities between two things that are otherwise dissimilar. A writer may use an analogy to explain something unfamiliar by comparing it to something familiar.

See page 1075.

See also METAPHOR, RHETORICAL DEVICES, SIMILE.

Anecdote A short written or oral account of an event from a person's life. Essayists often use anecdotes to support their opinions, clarify their ideas, grab the reader's attention, or entertain.

See page 357.

Antagonist A person or a force in society or nature that opposes the *protagonist,* or central character, in a story or drama. The reader is generally not meant to sympathize with the antagonist. Mark Antony is Brutus's antagonist in Shakespeare's *Julius Caesar.*

See page 663.

See also CHARACTER, CONFLICT, PROTAGONIST.

Anthropomorphism The assignment of human characteristics to gods, animals, or inanimate objects. It is a key element in fables and folktales, where the main characters are often animals.

See also FABLE.

Antithesis The technique of putting opposite ideas side-by-side in order to point out their differences or to draw attention to the superiority of one. Antithesis is often used in logical argument.

See also ARGUMENT, PERSUASION.

LITERARY TERMS HANDBOOK **R1**

Aphorism A short, pointed statement that expresses a wise or clever observation about human experience.

Apostrophe A literary device in which a speaker addresses an inanimate object, an idea, or an absent person.

See also PERSONIFICATION.

Archetype Ideas, characters, stories, or images that are common to human experience across cultures and throughout the world. In their purest form, archetypes occur in oral tradition, but they also appear in written works of literature. They can be divided into the following categories:

Character archetype: Includes familiar individuals such as the wise leader, the rebel, the damsel in distress, and the traitor. Coyote, the trickster of Native American folklore, is a character archetype.

Image archetype: Objects or places that have a universal symbolism. For example, a lily can be a symbol of purity.

Plot pattern archetype: Stories that occur in many cultures. Making the long journey home, completing the "impossible" task, or outwitting the formidable enemy are all archetypal plots.

Theme archetype: Ideas that occur wherever people tell stories. The idea that good can overcome evil, that people can redeem themselves, or that an underworld exists are all archetypal themes.

See pages 959, 969.

See also FOLKLORE, MYTH, ORAL TRADITION, STOCK CHARACTER, SYMBOL.

Argument A type of persuasive writing in which logic and reason are used to try to influence a reader's ideas or actions.

See pages 392-393.

See also PERSUASION.

Aside In a play, a comment that a character makes to the audience, which other characters onstage do not hear. The speaker turns to one side—or "aside"—away from the action onstage. Asides, which are rare in modern drama, reveal what a character is thinking or feeling. For example, Act 2, Scene 2, of Shakespeare's *Julius Caesar* includes the following exchange:

> CAESAR. Be near me, that I may remember you.
>
> TREBONIUS. Caesar, I will [*Aside.*] and so near will I be, That your best friends shall wish I had been further.

See page 739.

See also SOLILOQUY.

Assonance The repetition of same or similar vowel sounds in words that are close together. For example, the short *i* sound is repeated in this line from Shakespeare's "Shall I Compare Thee to a Summer's Day?":

> So long lives this, and this gives life to thee.

See pages 592-593, 600.

See also SOUND DEVICES.

Atmosphere The dominant emotional feeling of a literary work that contributes to the mood. Authors create atmosphere primarily through details of setting, such as time, place, and weather. The description of the rooms at the ball in Edgar Allan Poe's "The Masque of the Red Death" builds an atmosphere of suspense and foreboding.

See also *MOOD*.

Author's purpose An author's intent in writing a literary work. For example, the author may want to persuade, inform, describe a process, entertain, or express an opinion.

See pages 329, 443.

See also DICTION, STYLE, THEME.

Autobiography A person's account of his or her life. The author typically focuses on the most significant events in his or her life. Autobiographies give insights into the author's view of himself or herself and of the society in which he or she lived. For example, *Farewell to Manzanar* is Jeanne Wakatsuki Houston's autobiography.

See pages 278, 284-285.

See also BIOGRAPHY, MEMOIR, NONFICTION.

B

Ballad A musical narrative song or poem that recounts an exciting or dramatic episode. Folk ballads were passed down by word of mouth for generations before being written down. A typical ballad consists of *ballad stanzas.* Literary ballads, such as "Ballad of Birmingham," are written in imitation of folk ballads and have a known author. Many ballads include the elements of plot, such as exposition, conflict, climax, and resolution.

See also BALLAD STANZA, FOLKLORE, NARRATIVE POETRY, ORAL TRADITION, PLOT.

Ballad Stanza A quatrain, or four-line stanza, in which the first and third lines have four stressed syllables, and the second and fourth lines have three stressed syllables. Only the second and fourth lines rhyme. Although the basic foot in this stanza is the iamb (˘ ′), there tend to be many irregularities.

See also METER, QUATRAIN, STANZA.

Bias An inclination toward a certain opinion or position on a topic, possibly stemming from prejudice.

See also NONFICTION.

Biography A nonfiction account of a person's life written by another person. Biographies can vary in length, from brief encyclopedia entries to works that span several volumes.

See pages 278, 284-285.
See also AUTOBIOGRAPHY, JOURNAL, MEMOIR.

Blank verse Unrhymed poetry or dramatic verse written in a meter known as *iambic pentameter.* Each line of iambic pentameter has five units, or feet; each foot is made up of an unstressed syllable followed by a stressed syllable. Much of Shakespeare's work is written in blank verse. The following line, spoken by Mark Antony in Act 3, Scene 1, of Shakespeare's *Julius Caesar*, is an example of blank verse:

˘ ′ ˘ ′ ˘ ′ ˘ ′
O par / don me / thou bleed / ing piece /
˘ ′
of earth . . .

See page 717.
See also FOOT, IAMB, METER, RHYTHM

C

Cadence The rhythmic rise and fall of language when it is spoken or read aloud.

See also FREE VERSE, METER

Catalog The listing of images, details, people, or events in a literary work.

Character An individual in a literary work. *Main characters* are central to the story and are typically fully developed. *Minor characters* display few personality traits and are used to help develop the story. A character who shows varied and sometimes contradictory traits, such as the daughter in Amy Tan's "Two Kinds," is a *round character.* A character who reveals only one personality trait is called a *flat character.* A *stock character* is a flat character of a familiar and often-repeated type. A *dynamic character*, such as Luis in Judith Ortiz Cofer's "Catch the Moon," changes during the story. A *static character,* such as Luis's father, remains the same throughout the story.

See pages 86-87, 652.

See also ANTAGONIST, CHARACTERIZATION, FOIL, STEREOTYPE, STOCK CHARACTER, PROTAGONIST.

Character archetype See ARCHETYPE.

Characterization The methods a writer uses to reveal the personality of a character. In *direct characterization,* the writer makes explicit statements about a character. In *indirect characterization,* the writer reveals a character's personality through that individual's words, thoughts, and actions and through what other characters think and say about that character.

See pages 145, 847.

See also CHARACTER.

Climax The point of greatest emotional intensity, interest, or suspense in the plot of a literary work. Also called the turning point, the climax usually comes near the end of a story or drama. For example, in Doris Lessing's "Through the Tunnel," the climax occurs when Jerry finally swims through the tunnel.

See also CONFLICT, PLOT.

Comedy A type of drama that is humorous and typically has a happy ending. Comedy can be divided into two categories: high and low. *High comedy* makes fun of human behavior in a witty, sophisticated manner. *Low comedy* involves physical humor and simple, often vulgar, wordplay.

See pages 818–819.

See also DRAMA, FARCE, HUMOR, PARODY, SATIRE.

Comic relief A humorous scene, an event, or a speech in an otherwise serious work. It provides relief from emotional intensity, while at the same time highlighting the seriousness of the story. The sentry's lines in *Antigone* often provide comic relief.

Concrete language Specific language about actual things or occurrences. Words like *dog* and *sky* are concrete, while words like *truth* and *evil* are abstract.

See also ABSTRACT LANGUAGE.

Conflict The struggle between opposing forces in a story or drama. An *external conflict* exists when a character struggles against some outside force, such as another person, nature, society, or fate. In Doris Lessing's "Through the Tunnel," for example, when Jerry tries to swim through the tunnel, he is involved in an external conflict with nature. An *internal conflict* is a struggle that takes place within the mind of a character who is torn between opposing feelings or goals. Jerry wrestles with an internal conflict when he tries to overcome his own fear in order to swim through the tunnel.

See pages 34, 838.

See also ANTAGONIST, PLOT, PROTAGONIST.

Connotation The suggested or implied meanings associated with a word beyond its dictionary definition, or *denotation.* A word can have a positive or negative connotation, or neutral connotation.

See also DENOTATION, FIGURATIVE LANGUAGE.

Consonance The repetition of consonant sounds, typically within or at the end of words that do not rhyme and preceded by different vowel sounds, as in the following line from Lucille Clifton's "Miss Rosie":

> sitting, waiting for your mind.

See pages 592–593, 600.

See also SOUND DEVICES.

Couplet Two consecutive lines of rhymed verse that work together as a unit to make a point or to express an idea. The last two lines of Shakespeare's "Shall I Compare Thee to a Summer's Day?" are a couplet.

See also RHYME, SONNET, STANZA.

D

Denotation The literal, or dictionary, meaning of a word.

See also CONNOTATION.

Denouement The resolution of a story. Denouement is a French word meaning "unknotting." The denouement comes after the climax and often ties in with the falling action.

See also FALLING ACTION, RESOLUTION.

Literary Terms Handbook

Description A detailed portrayal of a person, a place, an object, or an event. Good descriptive writing helps readers to see, hear, smell, taste, or feel the subject.

See also FIGURATIVE LANGUAGE, IMAGERY.

Descriptive essay See ESSAY.

Dialect A variation of a language spoken by a group of people, often within a particular region. Dialects may differ from the standard form of a language in vocabulary, pronunciation, or grammatical form. "Civil Peace" contains examples of dialect.

See page 65.

Dialogue Written conversation between characters in a literary work. Dialogue brings characters to life by revealing their personalities and by showing what they are thinking and feeling as they react to other characters. Dialogue can also create mood, advance the plot, and develop theme. Plays are composed almost completely of dialogue.

See pages 104, 653, 818–819, 903, 943.

See also MONOLOGUE.

Diction A writer's choice of words; an important element in the writer's voice or style. Skilled writers choose their words carefully to convey a particular meaning or feeling. These lines from "A Child's Christmas in Wales" give an example of Dylan Thomas's diction:

> All the Christmases roll down toward the two-tongued sea, like a cold and headlong moon bundling down the sky that was our street. . . .

See page 573.

See also AUTHOR'S PURPOSE, CONNOTATION, STYLE, TONE, VOICE.

Drama A story written to be performed by actors before an audience. The script of a dramatic work, or play, often includes the author's instructions to the actors and the director, known as *stage directions*. A drama may be divided into *acts*, which may also be broken up into *scenes*, indicating changes in location or the passage of time.

See also ACT, COMEDY, DIALOGUE, SCENE, STAGE DIRECTIONS, TRAGEDY.

Dramatic irony See IRONY.

Dramatic monologue A form of dramatic poetry in which a speaker, describing a crucial moment in his or her life, addresses a silent listener.

See also MONOLOGUE.

Dynamic character See CHARACTER.

E

Elegy A serious poem mourning a death or a great loss.

End rhyme The rhyming of words at the ends of lines.

End-stopped line A line of poetry that ends in a punctuation mark. An end-stopped line usually contains a complete thought or image. The following example from Edna St. Vincent Millay's "Well, I Have Lost You; and I Lost You Fairly," contains an end-stopped line:

> Should I outlive this anguish—and men do—
> I shall have only good to say of you.

See also ENJAMBMENT.

Enjambment The continuation of a sentence or phrase from one line of a poem to the next, without a pause between the lines. The following lines from Robert Hayden's "Those Winter Sundays" are an example of enjambment:

> What did I know, what did I know
> of love's austere and lonely offices.

See page 482.

See also END-STOPPED LINE.

Epic A long narrative poem that recounts, in formal language, the exploits of a larger-than-life hero. This *epic hero* is usually a person of high social status who embodies the ideals of his or her people. He or she is often of historical or legendary importance. Epic plots typically involve supernatural events, long time periods, distant journeys, and life-and-death struggles between good and evil. Folk epics have no known author and usually arise through storytelling and collective experiences. Literary epics are written by known authors. Sometimes print translations are in prose form.

See pages 900-901.

See also FOLKLORE, HERO, LEGEND, MYTH, NARRATIVE POETRY, ORAL TRADITION.

Epic hero See EPIC, HERO.

Epic simile See SIMILE.

Essay A short work of nonfiction on a single topic. *Descriptive essays* describe a person, place, or thing. *Narrative essays* relate true stories. *Persuasive essays* promote an opinion. *Reflective essays* reveal an author's observations on a subject. Essays fall into two categories, according to their style. A *formal essay* is serious and impersonal, often with the purpose of instructing or persuading. Typically, the author strikes a serious tone and develops a main idea, or *thesis*, in a logical, highly organized way. An *informal*, or *personal essay*, entertains while it informs, usually in light, conversational style.

See pages 278, 366-367.

See also NONFICTION.

Exaggeration See HYPERBOLE.

Exposition An author's introduction of the characters, setting, and conflict at the beginning of a story, novel, or play.

See also PLOT.

Extended metaphor A metaphor that compares two unlike things in various ways throughout a paragraph, stanza, or an entire selection. William Shakespeare uses an extended metaphor in the poem "Shall I Compare Thee to a Summer's Day?"

See also METAPHOR.

F

Fable A short, usually simple tale that teaches a moral and sometimes uses animal characters. Themes in fables are often stated directly. Italo Calvino's "The Happy Man's Shirt" is a modern fable.

See also LEGEND, MORAL, PARABLE, THEME.

Falling action The action that follows the climax in a play or a story. The falling action may show the results of the climax. It may also include the *denouement*, a French word meaning "unknotting." The denouement, or *resolution*, explains the plot or unravels the mystery.

See also CLIMAX, DENOUEMENT, PLOT.

Fantasy A highly imaginative genre of fiction, usually set in an unfamiliar world or a distant, heroic past. Fantasy stories commonly take place in imaginary worlds and may include gnomes, elves, or other fantastical or supernatural beings and forces. The use of some type of magic is common in fantasy stories.

See page 1016.

See also SCIENCE FICTION.

Farce A type of comedy with stereotyped characters in ridiculous situations. Anton Chekhov's *A Marriage Proposal* is an example of a farce.

See page 821.

See also COMEDY, HUMOR, PARODY, SATIRE.

Fiction Literature in which situations and characters are invented by the writer. Fiction includes both short stories, such as Edgar Allan Poe's "The Masque of the Red Death," and novels, such as T. H. White's *The Once and Future King*. Aspects of a fictional work may be based on fact or experience.

See also DRAMA, NONFICTION, NOVEL, SHORT STORY.

Figurative language Language that uses *figures of speech*, or expressions that are not literally true, but express some truth beyond the literal level. Types of figurative language include hyperbole, metaphor, personification, simile, and understatement.

See pages 532-533, 1022-1023.

See also HYPERBOLE, IMAGERY, METAPHOR, OXYMORON, PERSONSIFICATION, SIMILE, SYMBOL, UNDERSTATEMENT.

Figures of speech See *FIGURATIVE LANGUAGE*.

Flashback An interruption in the chronological order of a narrative to describe an event that happened earlier. A flashback gives readers information that may help explain the main events of the story. For example, in Leslie Marmon Silko's "Lullaby," the narrator includes a flashback to the day Ayah and Chato found out that Jimmie had died.
See page 11.

Flat character See *CHARACTER*.

Foil A character who provides a strong contrast to another character, usually a main character. By using a foil, a writer calls attention to the strengths or weaknesses of a character. For example, the self-controlled Octavius is a foil to the excitable Mark Antony in Shakespeare's *Julius Caesar*.
See page 783.
See also *CHARACTER*.

Folklore The traditional beliefs, customs, stories, songs, and dances of a culture. Folklore is based in the concerns of ordinary people and is passed down through oral tradition.
See also *BALLAD, EPIC, FOLKTALE, LEGEND, MYTH, ORAL TRADITION, TALL TALE*.

Folktale An anonymous traditional story passed down orally long before being written down. Folktales include animal stories, trickster stories, fairy tales, myths, legends, and tall tales.
See also *EPIC, FOLKLORE, LEGEND, MYTH, ORAL TRADITION, TALL TALE*.

Foot The basic unit in the measurement of rhythm in poetry. A foot usually contains one stressed syllable (´) and one or more unstressed syllables (˘).
See also *METER, RHYTHM, SCANSION*.

Foreshadowing An author's use of clues or hints to prepare readers for events that will happen later in a story.
See pages 18, 1025.
See also *PLOT, RISING ACTION, SUSPENSE*.

Form The structure of a poem. Many modern writers use loosely structured poetic forms instead of following traditional or formal patterns. These poets vary the lengths of lines and stanzas, relying on emphasis, rhythm, pattern, and the placement of words and phrases to convey meaning.
See pages 468, 474-475.

Formal essay See *ESSAY*.

Formal speech A speech of which the main purpose is to persuade, although it may also inform and entertain. Anthony's "On Women's Right to Vote," page 396, is a formal speech to persuade. The four main types of formal speech are legal, political, ceremonial, and religious.

Frame story A plot structure that includes the telling of a story within a story. The frame is the outer story, which usually precedes and follows the inner, more important story. Some literary works have frames that bind together many different stories.

Free verse Poetry that has no fixed pattern of meter, rhyme, line length, or stanza arrangement. Gwendolyn Brooks's "Horses Graze" is a poem composed in free verse.
See page 497.
See also *POETRY, RHYTHM*.

G

Genre A category or type of literature. Examples of genres are poetry, drama, fiction, nonfiction, essay, and epic. The term also refers to subcategories of literary work. For example, fantasy, magical realism, mystery, romance, and science fiction are genres of fiction. Ray Bradbury's "A Sound of Thunder" belongs to both the short story and science fiction genres.

Gothic literature A novel or short story that has a gloomy, foreboding mood and contains strong elements of horror, mystery, and the supernatural.

H

Haiku A traditional Japanese form of poetry that has three lines and seventeen syllables. The first and third lines have five syllables each; the second line has seven syllables. The purpose of traditional Haiku is to capture a flash of insight that occurs during an observation of nature.

See page 517.

See also *TANKA*.

Hero The main character in a literary work, typically one whose admirable qualities or noble deeds arouse admiration. In contemporary usage, the term can refer to either a female or male. For example, Buffalo Calf Road Woman is the hero of "Where the Girl Rescued Her Brother" by Joseph Bruchac and Gayle Ross.

See pages 658-659, 894, 900-901.

See also *EPIC, MYTH, PROTAGONIST, TRAGEDY*.

Hexameter A line of verse consisting of six feet.
See also *FOOT, METER*.

High comedy See *COMEDY*.

Historical fiction Fiction that sets characters against a backdrop of actual events. Some works of historical fiction include actual historical people along with fictitious characters.

See also *FICTION*.

Historical narrative A work of nonfiction that tells the story of important historical events or developments. *Farewell to Manzanar* by Jeanne Wakatsuki Houston and James D. Houston is a historical narrative.

See page 287.

Humor The quality of a literary work that makes the characters and their situations seem funny, amusing, or ludicrous. Humor often points out human failings and the irony found in many situations. Humorous language includes sarcasm, exaggeration, and verbal irony. Humorous writing can be equally effective in fiction and nonfiction.

See also *COMEDY, FARCE, PARODY, PUN, SATIRE*.

Hyperbole A figure of speech that uses exaggeration to express strong emotion, make a point, or evoke humor. "You've asked me a million times" is an example of hyperbole.

See also *FIGURATIVE LANGUAGE, UNDERSTATEMENT*.

I

Iamb (ī´amb) A two-syllable metrical foot consisting of one unaccented syllable (˘) followed by one accented syllable (´), as in the word *divide*.

Iambic pentameter A specific poetic meter in which each line has five metric units, or feet, and each foot consists of an unstressed syllable (˘) followed by a stressed syllable (´). The rhythm of a line of iambic pentameter would be indicated as shown in this example from Shakespeare's "Shall I Compare Thee to a Summer's Day?":

> Rough winds do shake the darling buds of May,

See also *BLANK VERSE, METER, SCANSION*.

Idiom An expression whose meaning is different from its literal meaning. Idioms are readily understood by native speakers but are often puzzling to non-native speakers. Phrases such as "catch his eye," "turn the tables," "over the hill," and "keep tabs on" are idiomatic expressions in English. Idioms can add realism to dialogue in a story and contribute to characterization.

See also *DIALECT*.

Image archetype See *ARCHETYPE*.

Imagery Descriptive language that appeals to one or more of the five senses: sight, hearing, touch, taste, and smell. This use of sensory detail helps create an emotional response in the reader. For example, the following lines from Doris Lessing's "Through the Tunnel" use imagery to make an underwater scene vivid:

> A few inches above them the water sparkled as if sequins were dropping through it . . . it was like swimming in flaked silver.

See pages 532-533, 569, 1023.
See also *FIGURATIVE LANGUAGE*.

Informal essay See *ESSAY*.

Interior monologue A technique that records a character's emotions, memories, and opinions. Interior monologue contributes to the stream-of-consciousness

effect. Joyce's "Araby" contains interior monologue.
See also STREAM OF CONSCIOUSNESS.

Internal conflict. See CONFLICT.

Internal rhyme Rhyme that occurs within a single line of poetry. Poets use internal rhyme to convey meaning, to evoke mood, or to create a musical effect. Randall uses internal rhyme in his poem "The Ballad of Birmingham":

"<u>No</u>, baby, <u>no</u>, you may not <u>go</u>,"

See also RHYME.

Inversion The reversal of the usual word order in a prose sentence or a line of poetry. Writers use inversion to maintain *rhyme scheme* or *meter* or to emphasize certain words or phrases. An example of inversion occurs in the final line of Shakespeare's sonnet "Shall I Compare Thee to a Summer's Day?":

So long <u>lives this</u>, and this gives life to thee.

Irony A contrast or discrepancy between expectation and reality, or between what is expected and what actually happens.

In *situational irony*, the actual outcome of a situation is the opposite of what is expected. In Shakespeare's *Julius Caesar*, for example, the suitors spare Mark Antony's life because they believe he is harmless. Instead, he turns out to be a vengeful, deadly enemy.

In *verbal irony*, a person says one thing and means another. For example, in *Julius Caesar*, Mark Antony uses verbal irony when he praises Brutus and the conspirators to the crowd at Julius Caesar's funeral, while actually trying to turn the people against them.

In *dramatic irony*, the audience or reader knows information that the characters do not know. For example, in *Julius Caesar*, Caesar's wife warns him not to go to the Senate. The audience knows of the murder plot, although Caesar and his wife do not.

See page 158.

See also PARADOX.

J

Journal. A daily record of events kept by a participant in those events or a witness to them. A journal is usually less intimate than a diary and emphasizes events rather than emotions.

See also DIARY, NONFICTION.

Juxtaposition The placement of two or more distinct things side by side in order to contrast or compare them. It is commonly used to evoke an emotional response in the reader.

See page 560.

L

Language. See DICTION, FIGURATIVE LANGUAGE, IMAGERY, SENSORY DETAILS.

Legend A traditional story handed down from past generations and believed to be based on actual people and events. Legends usually celebrate the heroic qualities of a national or cultural leader. Because legends are the stories of the people, they are often expressions of the values or character of a nation. For example, "Where the Girl Rescued Her Brother," retold by Joseph Bruchac and Gayle Ross, is a legend.

See pages 894, 900-901.

See also EPIC, FABLE, FOLKLORE, HERO, MYTH, ORAL TRADITION.

Legendary heroes Idealized figures, sometimes based on real people, who embody qualities admired by the cultural group to which they belong. The adventures and accomplishments of these heroes are preserved in legends or tales that are handed down from generation to generation. In the Sumerian epic "The Journey of Gilgamesh" as told by Joan C. Verniero and Robin Fitzsimmons, Gilgamesh is a legendary hero.

See also FOLKTALE.

Line The basic unit of poetry. A line consists of a word or a row of words. In metered poems, lines are measured by the number of feet they contain.

See page 477.

See also FOOT, STANZA.

Literal language Language that is simple, straightforward, and free of embellishment. It is the opposite of figurative language, which conveys ideas indirectly.

See also DENOTATION.

Local color The use of specific details to re-create the language, the customs, the geography, and the habits of a particular area. In "The Californian's Tale," for example, Mark Twain recreates the mining country of California by describing the speech, dress, and habits of his characters.

See also DIALECT.

Lyric poetry Poetry that expresses a speaker's personal thoughts and feelings. Lyric poems are usually short and musical. While the subject of a lyric poem might be an object, a person, or an event, the emphasis of the poem is on the experience of emotion. Among the lyric poems in this book are Robert Hayden's "Those Winter Sundays" and Shakespeare's "Shall I Compare Thee to a Summer's Day?"

See page 548.

See also POETRY.

M

Magical realism Fiction that combines fantasy and realism. Magical realism inserts fantastic, sometimes humorous, events and details into a believable reality.

See also GENRE.

Memoir A type of narrative nonfiction that presents an author's personal experience of an event or period. A memoir is usually written from the first-person point of view. It often emphasizes the writer's thoughts and feelings, his or her relationships with other people, or the impact of significant historical events on his or her life. Maya Angelou's "Living Well. Living Good." is an example of a memoir.

See page 322.

See also AUTOBIOGRAPHY.

Metaphor A figure of speech that makes a comparison between two seemingly unlike things. Unlike a *simile*, a metaphor implies an underlying similarity between the two and does not use of the words *like* or *as*. The following lines from Jimmy Santiago Baca's "I Am Offering This Poem" feature a metaphor:

> [love] is a pot full of yellow corn
> to warm your belly in winter

See page 555.

See also ANALOGY, FIGURATIVE LANGUAGE, SIMILE.

Meter A regular pattern of stressed and unstressed syllables that gives a line of poetry a predictable rhythm. The unit of meter within the line is the *foot*. Each type of foot has a unique pattern of stressed (´) and unstressed (˘) syllables:

iamb (˘´) as in *complete*

trochee (´˘) as in *trouble*

anapest (˘˘´) as in *intervene*

dactyl (´˘˘) as in *majesty*

spondee (´´) as in *blue-green*

A particular meter is named for the type of foot and the number of feet per line. For example, *trimeter* has three feet, *tetrameter* has four feet, *pentameter* has five feet, and *hexameter* has six feet. The most common meter in English poetry is *iambic pentameter*, as in this line from Shakespeare's *Julius Caesar*:

> O par / don me / thou bleed / ing pie ce / of earth

See page 487.

See also FOOT, IAMBIC PENTAMETER, RHYTHM, SCANSION.

Monologue A long speech or written expression of thoughts by a character in a literary work. The burial speeches of Brutus and Antony in Act 3, Scene 2, in Shakespeare's *Julius Caesar* are monologues.

See page 739.

See also DIALOGUE, SOLILOQUY.

R10 LITERARY TERMS HANDBOOK

Mood The emotional quality of a literary work. A writer's choice of language, subject matter, setting, diction, and tone, as well as sound devices such as rhyme, rhythm, and meter can help create mood.

See pages 55, 542.

See also ATMOSPHERE, SETTING, TONE.

Moral A practical lesson about right and wrong conduct. Morals are typically found in fables. Some science fiction, such as Stephen Vincent Bénet's short story "By the Waters of Babylon," presents a moral.

See also FABLE, THEME.

See page 1041.

Motif A significant word, phrase, image, description, idea, or other element that is repeated throughout a literary work and is related to the theme. For example, in "A Swimming Lesson," Jewelle L. Gomez repeats the word *rhythm* to convey a message about life.

Motivation The stated or implied reason a character acts, thinks, or feels a certain way. Motivation may be an external circumstance, an internal moral, or an emotional impulse.

See pages 89, 1094.

Mystery A genre of fiction that follows a standard plot pattern: a crime is committed and a detective searches for clues that lead him or her to the criminal. Any story that relies on the unknown or the terrifying can be considered a mystery.

See page 1017.

See also FICTION, GENRE.

Myth A traditional story that deals with goddesses, gods, heroes, and supernatural forces. A myth may explain a belief, a custom, or a force of nature. Sophocles' *Antigone* draws on traditional elements of ancient Greek mythology.

See pages 895, 956-957.

See also EPIC, FOLKLORE, LEGEND, ORAL TRADITION.

Literary Terms Handbook

N

Narrative Writing or speech that tells a story. Driven by a *conflict* or problem, a narrative unfolds event by event and leads to a *resolution*. The story is narrated, or told, by a *narrator* and can take the form of a novel, an essay, a poem, or a short story.

See also NARRATIVE POETRY, NARRATOR, PLOT.

Narrative essay See ESSAY.

Narrative poetry Verse that tells a story. Narrative poems are usually contrasted with lyric poems. *Ballads, epics,* and *romances* are all types of narrative poetry. For example, Dudley Randall's "Ballad of Birmingham" is a narrative poem.

See page 577.

See also BALLAD, EPIC, LYRIC POETRY, NARRATIVE.

Narrator The person who tells a story. The narrator may be a character in the story, as in Amy Tan's "Two Kinds," or outside the story, as in Judith Ortiz Cofer's "Catch the Moon." Narrators are not always truthful. A narrator in a work of literature may be *reliable* or *unreliable.* Some unreliable narrators intentionally mislead readers. Others fail to understand the true meaning of the events they describe. Most stories with unreliable narrators are written in the first person.

See page 187.

See also NARRATIVE, POINT OF VIEW, SPEAKER.

Nonfiction Literature about real people, places, and events. Among the categories of nonfiction are biographies, autobiographies, and essays. For example, Maya Angelou's "Living Well. Living Good." is nonfiction.

See also AUTOBIOGRAPHY, BIOGRAPHY, ESSAY, FICTION, MEMOIR.

Novel A book-length fictional prose narrative. Because of its length, the novel has greater potential to develop plot, character, setting, and theme than does a short story.

See also FICTION, PLOT, SHORT STORY.

LITERARY TERMS HANDBOOK **R11**

O

Octave An eight-line stanza. The term is used mainly to describe the first eight lines of a *Petrarchan,* or *Italian,* sonnet.

See also SONNET.

Ode A long, serious lyric poem that is elevated in tone and style. Some odes celebrate a person, an event, or even a power; others are more private meditations. Odes are traditionally written in three stanzas and include rhyme.

See also LYRIC POETRY.

Onomatopoeia The use of a word or phrase that imitates or suggests the sound of what it describes. Some examples are *mew, hiss, crack, swish, murmur,* and *buzz.*

See pages 592-593.

See also SOUND DEVICES.

Oral tradition Literature that passes by word of mouth from one generation to the next. Oral literature is a way of recording the past, glorifying leaders, and teaching morals and traditions to young people. Stories of the legendary African hero Sundiata are passed on in this manner.

See pages 895, 956-957.

See also BALLAD, EPIC, FOLKLORE, FOLKTALE, LEGEND, MYTH.

Oxymoron A figure of speech in which opposite ideas are combined. Examples are "bright darkness," "wise fool," and "hateful love."

See also FIGURATIVE LANGUAGE, PARADOX.

P

Paradox A situation or a statement that appears to be contradictory but is actually true, either in fact or in a figurative sense.

See also OXYMORON.

Parallelism The use of a series of words, phrases, or sentences that have similar grammatical form. Parallelism shows the relationship between ideas and helps emphasize thoughts.

See also REPETITION.

Parody A humorous imitation of a literary work that aims to point out the work's shortcomings. A parody may imitate the plot, characters, or style of another work, usually through exaggeration. Miguel de Cervantes's *Don Quixote* is a parody of chivalry and novels about knight-errantry.

See page 926.

See also COMEDY, FARCE, HUMOR, SATIRE.

Persona The person created by the author to tell a story. Even if a story is told from a first-person point of view, as in Isabel Allende's story "And of Clay Are We Created," the narrator is not the author. The attitudes and beliefs of the persona may not be the same as those of the author.

See page 231.

See also NARRATOR, POINT OF VIEW.

Personification A figure of speech in which an animal, object, force of nature, or idea is given human characteristics. William Shakespeare personifies death in this line from "Shall I Compare Thee to a Summer's Day?":

> Nor shall Death brag thou wand'rest in his shade

See page 535.

See also APOSTROPHE, FIGURATIVE LANGUAGE.

Persuasion A type of writing, usually nonfiction, that attempts to convince readers to think or act in a particular way. Writers of persuasive works use appeals to logic, emotion, morality, and authority to sway their readers.

See pages 392-393.

See also ARGUMENT.

Persuasive Essay See ESSAY.

R12 LITERARY TERMS HANDBOOK

Literary Terms Handbook

Play A literary work of any length intended for performance on stage with actors assuming the roles of the characters and speaking the lines from a playwright's script.

See also DRAMA.

Plot The sequence of events in a narrative work. The plot begins with the *exposition,* which introduces the *characters, setting,* and *conflict.* Conflicts are introduced in the *exposition,* the first stage of the plot. As the work progresses, *rising action* builds suspense and adds complications, which lead to the *climax,* or turning point. After the climax, which is the moment of highest emotional pitch or greatest suspense, comes the *falling action* and the *resolution,* sometimes called the *denouement,* which reveal the logical results of the climax.

See pages 8-9, 760.

See also CLIMAX, CONFLICT, DENOUEMENT, EXPOSITION, FALLING ACTION, FORESHADOWING, RESOLUTION, RISING ACTION.

Plot pattern archetype. See ARCHETYPE.

Poetic license The freedom given to poets to ignore standard rules of grammar or proper diction in order to create a desired artistic effect.

Poetry A form of literary expression that differs from prose in emphasizing the line, rather than the sentence, as the unit of composition. Many other traditional characteristics of poetry apply to some poems but not to others. Some of these characteristics are emotional, imaginative language; use of figures of speech; division into stanzas; and the use of rhyme and regular meter.

See also FIGURATIVE LANGUAGE, METER, PROSE, RHYME, STANZA.

Point of view The perspective from which a story is told. In a story with *first-person* point of view, the narrator is a character in the story, referred to as "I." The reader sees everything through that character's eyes. Amy Tan's "Two Kinds" is told from first-person point of view. In a story with *third-person limited* point of view, the narrator reveals the thoughts, feelings, and observations of only one character, referring to that character as "he" or "she." Judith Ortiz Cofer's short story "Catch the Moon" uses third-person limited point of view. In a story with *third-person omniscient,* or all-knowing, point of view, the narrator is not a character in the story, but rather someone who stands outside the story and comments on the action. A third-person omniscient narrator, such as the one in Doris Lessing's "Through the Tunnel," knows everything about the characters and events and may reveal details that the characters themselves could not reveal. Occasionally an author uses *second-person* point of view, addressing the reader or one of the characters as "you." Margaret Atwood uses the second-person point of view in "Bread."

See pages 184-185, 200, 219, 1089.

See also NARRATOR, SPEAKER.

Prologue An introductory section of a play, speech, or other literary work. Sophocles' play *Antigone* contains a prologue, which sets the scene and provides background information for the drama.

Propaganda Written or spoken material designed to bring about a change or damage a cause through the use of emotionally charged words, name-calling, or other techniques.

Props A theater term (a shortened form of *properties*) for the objects and elements of the scenery used in a stage play, movie, or television show.

See also STAGE DIRECTIONS.

Prose Literature that is written in sentences and paragraphs (as distinguished from poetry, which is arranged in lines and stanzas). Essays, short stories, magazine articles, and most plays are examples of prose. Shakespeare alternates between prose and poetry in the dialogue of *Julius Caesar.*

See also POETRY.

Prose poem Short prose composition that uses rhythm, imagery, and other poetic devices to express an idea or emotion. Prose poetry does not have line breaks; instead, the sentences appear in standard paragraph form.

See page 505.

See also POETRY, PROSE.

Protagonist The central character in a literary work around whom the main conflict revolves. During the course of the literary work, the protagonist undergoes a conflict that is crucial to the plot. Generally, the reader or audience is meant to sympathize with the protagonist. Prince Prospero is the protagonist in Edgar Allan Poe's story "The Masque of the Red Death."

See page 663.

See also ANTAGONIST, CHARACTER, CONFLICT, HERO.

Pun A humorous play on words. Puns usually involve words that are similar in sound (*merry* and *marry*) or a word that has several meanings. In Shakespeare's *Julius Caesar*, for example, a shoemaker identifies himself by saying "all that I live by is with the *awl*," making a pun on *all* and *awl*, a tool for punching holes in leather.

See also HUMOR.

Q

Quatrain A four-line stanza. The quatrain is the most common stanza form in English poetry. It may be unrhymed or have a variety of rhyme schemes.

See also COUPLET, OCTAVE, SONNET, STANZA.

Quotation A passage by another author, used word-for-word in a literary work. A quotation is enclosed in quotation marks, or otherwise set apart, to indicate that it is not written by the person in whose work it appears. Quotations can serve to illustrate ideas and to show that other people share the author's opinions.

See page 432.

R

Reflective essay See ESSAY.

Refrain A line or lines repeated at regular intervals in a poem or song, usually at the end of a stanza.

See also REPETITION.

Reliable narrator See NARRATOR.

Repetition The recurrence of sounds, words, phrases, lines, or stanzas in a poem, speech, or other piece of writing. Writers use repetition to emphasize an important point, to expand upon an idea, to help create rhythm, and to increase the feeling of unity in a work.

See page 564.

See also PARALLELISM, RHETORICAL DEVICES, RHYME.

Resolution Also called the *denouement,* a French word meaning "unknotting," the resolution is the part of a plot that concludes the falling action by revealing or suggesting the outcome of the conflict.

See also CONFLICT, DENOUEMENT, FALLING ACTION, PLOT.

Rhetorical devices Persuasive techniques used by public speakers and writers of literary works, especially those written to persuade. Rhetorical devices include repetition, parallelism, analogy, logic, and the skillful use of connotation and anecdote. Effective rhetoric often appeals to logic, emotion, morality, or authority.

See pages 395, 418.

See also ANALOGY, ANECDOTE, ARGUMENT, CONNOTATION, PARALLELISM, PERSUASION, REPETITION.

Rhyme The repetition of the same stressed vowel sounds and any succeeding sounds in two or more words. *End rhyme* occurs at the ends of lines of poetry. *Internal rhyme* occurs within a single line. *Slant rhyme* occurs when words include sounds that are similar but not identical (*jackal* and *buckle*). Slant rhyme typically involves some variation of *consonance* (the repetition of similar consonant sounds) or *assonance* (the repetition of similar vowel sounds).

See pages 493, 592-593, 619.

See also ASSONANCE, CONSONANCE, RHYME SCHEME, SOUND DEVICES.

Rhyme scheme The pattern that end rhymes form in a stanza or a poem. Rhyme scheme is designated by the assignment of a different letter of the alphabet to each new rhyme. The rhyme scheme of Edna St. Vincent Millay's "Well I Have Lost You; and I Lost You Fairly" begins as follows:

> Well, I have lost you; and I lost you fairly; a
> In my own way, and with my full consent.   b
> Say what you will, kings in a tumbrel rarely a
> Went to their deaths more proud than this
> one went.   b

See pages 493, 619.

See also RHYME.

Rhythm The pattern of beats created by the arrangement of stressed and unstressed syllables, especially in poetry. Rhythm gives a poem a musical quality. It can also emphasize certain words or ideas to help convey meaning. Rhythm can be *regular*, with a predictable pattern or meter, or *irregular*.

See page 487.

See also BLANK VERSE, FOOT, IAMBIC PENTAMETER, METER, SCANSION.

Rising action The part of a plot where complications to the conflict develop and increase the reader's interest.

See PLOT.

Round character. See CHARACTER.

Run-on line The continuation of a sentence from one line of a poem the next.

> To him who in the love of Nature holds
> Communion with her visible forms, she speaks
> A various language;
>   Bryant, "Thanatopsis"

Run-on lines enable poets to create a conversational tone, breaking lines at a point where people would normally pause in conversation, yet still maintaining the unit of thought.

See also END-STOPPED LINE.

S

Sarcasm The use of bitter or caustic language to point out shortcomings or flaws.

See also IRONY, SATIRE.

Satire Writing that uses humor or wit to ridicule the vices or follies of people or societies to bring about improvement. Satire uses devices such as *exaggeration, understatement,* and *irony*. Luisa Valenzuela's short story "The Censors" is a satire of repressive government.

See page 173.

See also COMEDY, FARCE, HUMOR, PARODY, SARCASM, WIT.

Scansion The analysis of the meter of a line of verse. To scan a line of poetry means to note the stressed(´) and unstressed syllables (˘) and to divide the line into its *feet,* or rhythmical units.

See also FOOT, METER, RHYTHM.

Scene A subdivision of an act in a play. Each scene usually takes place in a specific setting and time.

See page 652.

See also ACT, DRAMA.

Science fiction Fiction that deals with the impact of science and technology—real or imagined—on society and on individuals. Sometimes occurring in the future, science fiction commonly portrays space travel, exploration of other planets, and future societies. Ray Bradbury's "A Sound of Thunder" is an example of science fiction.

See page 1016.

See also FANTASY, GENRE.

Sensory details Evocative words or phrases that convey sensory experiences—seeing, hearing, tasting, touching, and smelling. Sensory details make writing come alive by helping readers imagine what is being described.

See also IMAGERY.

Septet A seven-line poem or stanza.

Literary Terms Handbook

Sestet A six-line poem or stanza.
See also SONNET.

Setting The time and place in which the events of a literary work occur. Setting includes not only the physical surroundings, but also the ideas, customs, values, and beliefs of a particular time and place. Setting often helps create an atmosphere or mood. For example, the setting of Dylan Thomas's "A Child's Christmas in Wales" is a Welsh seaside town in the early twentieth century.
See pages 8-9.
See also ATMOSPHERE, MOOD.

Shakespearean sonnet See SONNET.

Short story A brief fictional narrative in prose. A short story usually focuses on a single event and has only a few characters. Elements of the short story include *setting, characters, plot, point of view,* and *theme.*
See also FICTION, NOVEL, PLOT.

Simile A figure of speech that uses the word *like* or *as* to compare two seemingly unlike things. For example, this simile appears in Amy Tan's story "Two Kinds":

> And she also did a fancy sweep of a curtsy, so that the fluffy skirt of her white dress cascaded to the floor like the petals of a large carnation.

An *epic simile* is a long, elaborate comparison that continues for several lines. It is a feature of epic poems, but is found in other poems as well.
See page 555.
See also ANALOGY, FIGURATIVE LANGUAGE, METAPHOR.

Situational irony See IRONY.

Slant rhyme See RHYME.

Soliloquy A dramatic device in which a character, alone on stage (or while under the impression of being alone), reveals his or her private thoughts and feelings as if thinking aloud. For example, Antony vows his revenge of Caesar's murder in a soliloquy in Act 3, Scene 1, of Shakespeare's *Julius Caesar.*
See page 739.
See also ASIDE, MONOLOGUE.

Sonnet A lyric poem of fourteen lines, typically written in *iambic pentameter* and usually following strict patterns of stanza division and rhyme.

> The *Shakespearean sonnet,* also called the *English sonnet,* consists of three *quatrains,* or four-line stanzas, followed by a *couplet,* or pair of rhyming lines. The rhyme scheme is typically *abab cdcd efef gg.* The rhyming couplet often presents a conclusion to the issues or questions presented in the three quatrains.

> In the *Petrarchan sonnet,* also called the *Italian sonnet,* fourteen lines are divided into two stanzas, the eight-line *octave* and the six-line *sestet.* The sestet usually responds to a question or situation posed by the octave. The rhyme scheme is typically *abbaabba cdecde* or *abbaabba cdcdcd.*

See also COUPLET, LYRIC POETRY, RHYME SCHEME, STANZA.

Sound devices Techniques used to emphasize particular sounds in writing. Writers use sound devices such as *alliteration* and *assonance* to underscore the meaning of certain words, to enhance rhythm, and to add a musical quality to the work.
See page 469.
See also ALLITERATION, ASSONANCE, CONSONANCE, ONOMATOPOEIA, RHYME, RHYTHM.

Speaker The voice that communicates with the reader of a poem, similar to the narrator in a work of prose. Sometimes the speaker's voice is that of the poet, sometimes that of a fictional person or even a thing. For example, the speaker in Robert Hayden's poem "Those Winter Sundays" is a man thinking back to his poor childhood and remembering the sacrifices his father made while raising him.
See page 511.
See also NARRATOR, TONE.

Spondee A metrical foot of two accented syllables.
See also FOOT, METER.

Stage directions Instructions written by a playwright that describe the appearance and actions of characters, as well as the sets, props, costumes, sound effects, and lighting for a play.

See pages 653, 819.

See also DRAMA, PROPS.

Stanza A group of lines forming a unit in a poem or song. A stanza in a poem is similar to a paragraph in prose. Typically, stanzas in a poem are separated by a line of space.

See page 477.

See also COUPLET, OCTAVE, QUATRAIN, SONNET.

Stereotype A generalization about a group of people that is made without regard for individual differences. In literature, this term is often used to describe a conventional or flat character who conforms to an expected, fixed pattern of behavior. Stereotypes are used to make or reflect broad generalizations about a group of people. The nervous, hypochondriac Lomov in Anton Chekhov's "A Marriage Proposal" is a stereotype.

See also STOCK CHARACTER.

Stock character A character who represents a type that is recognizable as belonging to a particular genre. For example, a cruel stepmother or charming prince is often found in fairy tales. Valiant knights and heroes are found in legends and myths. The hard-boiled detective is found in detective stories. Stock characters have conventional traits and mannerisms shared by all members of their type.

See also ARCHETYPE, CHARACTER, STEREOTYPE.

Stream of consciousness The literary representation of an author's or character's free-flowing thoughts, feelings, and memories. Stream-of-consciousness writing does not always employ conventional sentence structure or other rules of grammar and usage.

See page 1060.

Structure The particular order or pattern a writer uses to present ideas. For example, narratives sometimes follow a chronological order. Listing detailed information, comparing and contrasting, analyzing cause-and-effect relationships, or describing a problem and then offering a solution are some other ways a writer can structure a text. Poetic structure—more commonly known as *form*—refers to the organization of words, lines, and images as well as of ideas.

See pages 376, 468, 474-475.

See also FORM.

Style The expressive qualities that distinguish an author's work, including word choice, sentence structure, and figures of speech.

See pages 184-185, 246, 1017. See also AUTHOR'S PURPOSE, DICTION, IMAGERY, TONE, VOICE.

Subject The topic of a literary work.

Surprise ending A plot twist at the end of a story that is unexpected because the author provides misleading clues or withholds important information.

Suspense A feeling of curiosity, uncertainty, or even dread about what is going to happen next in a story. To build suspense, an author may create a threat to the central character or use *foreshadowing*. Suspense is especially important in the plot of an adventure or mystery story. In Doris Lessing's "Through the Tunnel," for example, suspense builds as the reader wonders whether Jerry will be able to succeed in the physical and mental challenge he has set for himself.

See page 982.

See also FORESHADOWING, MOOD.

Symbol Any person, animal, place, object, or event that exists on a literal level within a work but also represents something on a figurative level. Swimming through the tunnel, for example, is a symbolic achievement for Jerry in Doris Lessing's "Through the Tunnel." The act means that he is growing up.

See page 608.

See also ALLEGORY, FIGURATIVE LANGUAGE.

T

Tall tale A wildly imaginative story, usually passed down orally, about the fantastic adventures or amazing feats of folk heroes in realistic local settings. The ballad "John Henry" as told by Zora Neale Hurston is an example of a tall tale.

See also *FOLKLORE*.

Tanka Unrhymed Japanese verse form consisting of five lines. The first and third lines have five syllables each; the other lines have seven syllables each.

See page 522.

See also *HAIKU*.

Teleplay The script of a drama written for television, which, in addition to dialogue and stage directions, usually contains detailed instructions about camera shots and angles.

See also *STAGE DIRECTIONS*.

Theater of the Absurd Drama, primarily of the 1950s and 1960s, that does not contain a plot but instead presents a series of scenes in which the characters speak in meaningless conversations or perform actions with little purpose. The central concern of this drama is to show that people are helpless or confused in an alienating world.

See also *DRAMA*.

Theme The main idea or message of a story, a poem, a novel, or a play, sometimes expressed as a general statement about life. Some works have a *stated theme*, which is expressed directly. Other works have an *implied theme*, which is revealed gradually through other elements such as plot, character, setting, point of view, and symbol. A literary work may have more than one theme. Themes and subjects are different. The subject of a work might be love; the theme would be what the writer says about love—for example, love is cruel; love is wonderful; or love is fleeting.

See pages 86-87, 113, 124, 305.

See also *AUTHOR'S PURPOSE, FABLE, MORAL*.

Theme archetype See *ARCHETYPE*.

Thesis The main idea of an essay or other work of nonfiction. The thesis may be implied but is commonly stated directly.

See page 383.

See also *ESSAY, NONFICTION*.

Title The name given to a literary work. The title can help explain setting, provide insight into the theme, or describe the action that will take place in the work.

Tone An author's attitude toward his or her subject matter. Tone is conveyed through elements such as word choice, punctuation, sentence structure, and figures of speech. A writer's tone may convey a variety of attitudes, such as sympathy, seriousness, irony, sadness, bitterness, or humor. For example, James Thurber's amused and affectionate tone in "The Car We Had to Push" contrasts with Isabel Allende's solemn tone in "And of Clay Are We Created."

See page 1017.

See also *ATMOSPHERE, AUTHOR'S PURPOSE, DICTION, MOOD, NARRATOR, SPEAKER, STYLE, VOICE*.

Tragedy A play in which the main character, or *tragic hero,* suffers a downfall as a result of a fatal character flaw, errors in judgment, or forces beyond human control, such as fate. Traditionally, the tragic hero is a person of high rank who, out of *hubris* (an exaggerated sense of power and pride) violates a human, a natural, or a divine law. By breaking the law, the hero poses a threat to society and causes the suffering or death of family members, friends, and associates. In the last act of a traditional tragedy, these wrongs are set right when the tragic hero is punished or dies and order is restored. For example, *Antigone* by Sophocles is a tragedy which describes the downfall of Creon, a king whose pride is his *tragic flaw* and leads to his destruction.

See pages 652, 658-659, 685, 800.

See also *DRAMA, HERO*.

Tragic hero See *TRAGEDY*.

U

Understatement Language that makes something seem less important than it really is. Understatement may be used to add humor or to focus the reader's attention on something the author wants to emphasize.

See also HYPERBOLE.

Unreliable narrator. See NARRATOR.

V

Verbal irony. See IRONY.

Verse paragraph A group of lines in a poem that form a unit. Unlike a stanza, a verse paragraph does not have a fixed number of lines. While poems written before the twentieth century usually contain stanzas, many contemporary poems are made up of verse paragraphs. Verse paragraphs help to organize a poem into thoughts, as paragraphs help to organize prose.

See page 526.

See also FREE VERSE, STANZA.

Voice The distinctive use of language that conveys the author's or narrator's personality to the reader. Voice is determined by elements of style such as word choice and tone.

See pages 184-185, 342.

See also DICTION, NARRATOR, STYLE, TONE.

W

Wit An exhibition of cleverness and humor. The works of Dorothy Parker and Mark Twain are known for their wit.

See also COMEDY, HUMOR, SARCASM, SATIRE.

Word choice. See DICTION.

 # Reading and Thinking with Foldables®

by Dinah Zike, M.Ed., Creator of Foldables®

Using Foldables® Makes Learning Easy and Enjoyable

Anyone who has paper, scissors, and maybe a stapler or some glue can use Foldables in the classroom. Just follow the illustrated step-by-step directions. Check out the following sample:

 **Reading Objective:** to understand how one character's actions affect other characters in a short story

Use this Foldable to keep track of what the main character does and how his or her actions affect the other characters.

 **Step 1** Place a sheet of paper in front of you so that the short side is at the top. Fold the paper in half from top to bottom.

 **Step 2** Fold in half again, from side to side, to divide the paper into two columns. Unfold the paper so that the two columns show.

 **Step 3** Draw a line along the column crease. Then, through the top layer of paper, cut along the line you drew, forming two tabs.

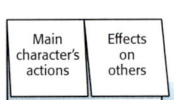 **Step 4** Label the tabs *Main character's actions* and *Effects on others.*

Step 5 As you read, record the main character's actions under the first tab. Record how each of those actions affects other characters under the second tab.

 ## Short Story

Reading Objective: to analyze a short story on the basis of its literary elements

As you read, use the following Foldable to keep track of five literary elements in the short story.

 Step 1 Stack three sheets of paper with their top edges about a half-inch apart. Be sure to keep the side edges straight.

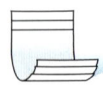 **Step 2** Fold up the bottom edges of the paper to form six tabs, five of which will be the same size.

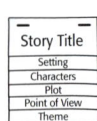 **Step 3** Crease the paper to hold the tabs in place and staple the sheets together along the crease.

Step 4 Turn the sheets so that the stapled side is at the top. Write the title of the story on the top tab. Label the five remaining tabs *Setting, Characters, Plot, Point of View,* and *Theme.*

Step 5 Use your Foldable as you read the short story. Under each labeled tab, jot down notes about the story in terms of that element.

You may adapt this simple Foldable in several ways.
- Use it with dramas, longer works of fiction, and some narrative poems—wherever five literary elements are present in the story.
- Change the labels to focus on something different. For example, if a story or a play has several settings, characters, acts, or scenes, you could devote a tab to each one.

Foldables

Drama

Reading Objective: to understand conflict and plot in a drama

As you read the drama, use the following Foldable to keep track of conflicts that arise and ways that those conflicts are resolved.

Step 1 Place a sheet of paper in front of you so that the short side is at the top. Fold the paper in half from side to side.

Step 2 Fold the paper again, one inch from the top as shown here.

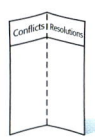

Step 3 Unfold the paper and draw lines along all of the folds. This will be your chart.

Step 4 At the top, label the left column *Conflicts* and the right column *Resolutions*.

Step 5 As you read, record in the left column the various conflicts that arise in the drama. In the right column, explain how each conflict is resolved by the end of the drama.

You may adapt this simple Foldable in several ways.
- Use it with short stories, longer works of fiction, and many poems—wherever conflicts and their resolutions are important.
- Change the labels to focus on something different. For example, you could record the actions of two characters, or you could record the thoughts and feelings of a character before and after the story's climax.

Lyric Poem

Reading Objective: to interpret the poet's message by understanding the speaker's thoughts and feelings

As you read the poem, use the following Foldable to help you distinguish between what the speaker *says* and what the poet *means*.

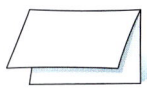

Step 1 Place a sheet of paper in front of you so that the short side is at the top. Fold the paper in half from top to bottom.

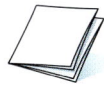

Step 2 Fold the paper in half again from left to right.

Step 3 Unfold and cut through the top layer of paper along the fold line. This will make two tabs.

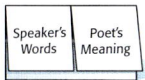

Step 4 Label the left tab *Speaker's Words*. Label the right tab *Poet's Meaning*.

Step 5 Use your Foldable to jot down notes on as you read the poem. Under the left tab, write down key things the speaker says. Under the right tab, write down what you think the poet means by having the speaker say those things.

You may adapt this simple Foldable in several ways.
- Use it to help you visualize the images in a poem. Just replace *Speaker's Words* with *Imagery* and replace *Poet's Meaning* with *What I See*.
- Replace the label *Speaker's Words* with *Speaker's Tone* and under the tab write adjectives that describe the tone of the speaker's words.
- If the poem you are reading has two stanzas, you might devote each tab to notes about one stanza.

Functional Documents

Functional documents are specialized forms of expository writing that serve specifc purposes. Functional documents are an every day part of business, school, and even home life. They must be clear, concise, accurate, and correct in style and usage.

Letter of Application

A letter of application is a form of business writing. It can be used when applying for a job, an internship, or a scholarship. In most cases, the letter is intended to accompany a résumé or an application. Because detailed information is usually included in the accompanying form, a letter of application should provide a general overview of your qualifications and the reasons you are submitting an application. A letter of application should be concise. You should clearly state which position you are applying for and then explain why you are interested and what makes you qualified. The accompanying material should speak for itself.

---

32 South Street
Austin, Texas 78746
May 6, 2009

Melissa Reyes
City Life magazine
2301 Davis Avenue
Austin, Texas 78764

❶ Re: Internship

❷ Dear Ms. Reyes:

❸ I am a junior at City High School and editor of the City High Herald. I am writing to apply for your summer internship at City Life magazine. As a journalism student and a longtime fan of your magazine, I feel that an internship with your magazine would provide me with valuable experience in the field of journalism. I believe that my role with the City High Herald has **❹** given me the skills necessary to be a useful contributor to your magazine this summer. In addition, my enclosed application shows that I am also a **❺** diligent worker.

I thank you for considering my application for your summer internship, and I hope to be working with you in the coming months.

Sincerely,
Anne Moris
Anne Moris

---

❶ The optional subject line indicates the topic of the letter.

❷ In a business letter, the greeting is followed by a colon.

❸ The writer states her purpose directly and immediately.

❹ The writer comments briefly on her qualifications.

❺ The writer makes reference to the accompanying material.

Activity

Choose a local business where you might like to work. Write a letter of application for an internship at that business. Assume that you will be submitting this letter along with a résumé or an internship application that details your experience and qualifications.

Functional Documents

Résumé

The purpose of a résumé is to provide the employer with a comprehensive record of your background information, related experience, and qualifications. Although a résumé is intended to provide a great deal of information, the format is designed to provide this information in the most efficient way possible.

---

❶ Jane Wiley
909 West Main Street, Apt. #1
Urbana, Illinois 61802
(217) 555-0489 • jane@internet.edu

Goal
Seeking position in television news production

❷ Education
Junior standing in the College of Communications at the University of Illinois, Urbana-Champaign
2005 Graduate of City High School

Honors
Member of National Honor Society

Activities
❸ Member, Asian American Association: 2005–Present
Environmental Committee Chairperson, Asian American Association: August 2006–May 2007

Work Experience
❹ Radio Reporter, WPGU, 107.1 FM, Champaign, Illinois: May 2007–Present
❺ • Rewrote and read stories for afternoon newscasts
 • Served as field reporter for general assignments

Cashier, Del's Restaurant, Champaign, Illinois: May 2006–August 2006
 • Responsible for taking phone orders
 • Cashier for pickup orders

Assistant Secretary, Office of Dr. George Wright, Woodstock, Illinois: May 2005–August 2005
 • Answered phones
 • Made appointments

---

❶ Header includes all important contact information.
❷ All important education background is included.
❸ Related dates are included for all listed activities.
❹ Job title is included along with the place of employment.
❺ Job responsibilities are briefly listed, with a parallel structure used in each bulleted item.

Activity

Create an outline that lists the information that you would want to include in a résumé. Use a word processor to help format your outline.

Functional Documents

Job Application

When applying for a job, you usually need to fill out a job application. When you fill out the application, read the instructions carefully. Examine the entire form before beginning to fill it out. If you fill out the form by hand, make sure that your handwriting is neat and legible. Fill out the form completely, providing all information directly and honestly. If a question does not apply to you, indicate that by writing *n/a,* short for "not applicable." Keep in mind that you will have the opportunity to provide additional information in your résumé, in your letter of application, or during the interview process.

---

❶ Please type or print neatly in blue or black ink.

❷ Name: _____ **Today's date:** _____
Address: _____
Phone #: _____ **Birth date:** _____ **Sex:** ___ **Soc. Sec. #:** ___

* *

❸ Job History (List each job held, starting with the most recent job.)

1. Employer: _____ Phone #: _____
   Dates of employment: _____
   Position held: _____
❹ Duties: _____

2. Employer: _____ Phone #: _____
   Dates of employment: _____
   Position held: _____
   Duties: _____

* *

Education (List the most recent level of education completed.)
_____

* *

Personal References:

1. Name: _____ Phone #: _____
   Relationship: _____
2. Name: _____ Phone #: _____
   Relationship: _____

---

❶ The application provides specific instructions.

❷ All of the information requested should be provided in its entirety.

❸ The information should be provided legibly and succinctly.

❹ Experience should be stated accurately and without embellishment.

Activity
Pick up a job application from a local business or use the sample application shown. Complete the application thoroughly. Fill out the application as if you were actually applying for the job. Be sure to pay close attention to the guidelines mentioned above.

Functional Documents

Memos

A memorandum (memo) conveys precise information to another person or a group of people. A memo begins with a leading block. It is followed by the text of the message. A memo does not have a formal closing.

TO: All Employees
FROM: Jordan Tyne, Human Resources Manager
❶ SUBJECT: New Human Resources Assistant Director
DATE: November 3, 2009

❷ Please join me in congratulating Daphne Rudy on her appointment as assistant director in the Human Resources Department. Daphne comes to our company with five years of experience in the field. Daphne begins
❸ work on Monday, November 10. All future general human resource inquiries should be directed to Daphne.

Please welcome Daphne when she arrives next week.

❶ The topic of the memo is stated clearly in the subject line.
❷ The announcement is made in the first sentence.
❸ All of the important information is included briefly in the memo.

Business E-mail

E-mail is quickly becoming the most common form of business communication. While e-mail may be the least formal and most conversational method of business writing, it shouldn't be written carelessly or too casually. The conventions of business writing—clarity, attention to your audience, proper grammar, and the inclusion of relevant information—apply to e-mail.

An accurate subject line should state your purpose briefly and directly. Use concise language and avoid rambling sentences.

To: LiamS@internet.com
From: LisaB@internet.com
CC: EricC@internet.com
Date: January 7, 8:13 a.m.
❶ Subject: New Product Conference Call

Liam,

❷ I just wanted to make sure that arrangements have been made for next week's conference call to discuss our new product. The East Coast sales team has already scheduled three sales meetings at the end of the month with potential buyers, so it's important that our sales team is prepared to talk about the product. Please schedule the call when the manufacturing director
❸ is available, since he will have important information for the sales team.

Lisa

❶ Subject line clearly states the topic.
❷ The purpose is stated immediately and in a conversational tone.
❸ Important details are included in a brief, direct fashion.

Activity

Write an e-mail to your coworkers. Inform them of a change in company procedure that will affect them.

FUNCTIONAL DOCUMENTS **R25**

Functional Documents

Travel Directions

When planning an event or a social occasion, it is often necessary to provide people with detailed directions to the location. These directions must be clear enough that anyone who is unfamiliar with the surrounding area can easily find their way. Creating a map that shows the route with clearly labeled streets can also be a great help.

Directions to Darien High School's Graduation Ceremony

From I-95 North, take Exit 11. ❶

Turn Left onto Post Road (Route 1).

At the first light, turn Left onto Samuel Avenue. Travel 2.5 miles. ❷

Turn Right onto Cherry Hill Road.

Turn Left onto High School Lane. ❸

Follow signs to Visitor Parking.

❶ Begins at a point from which most people will be coming

❷ Offers travel distances to help travelers locate streets

❸ Gives the name of each street along the route

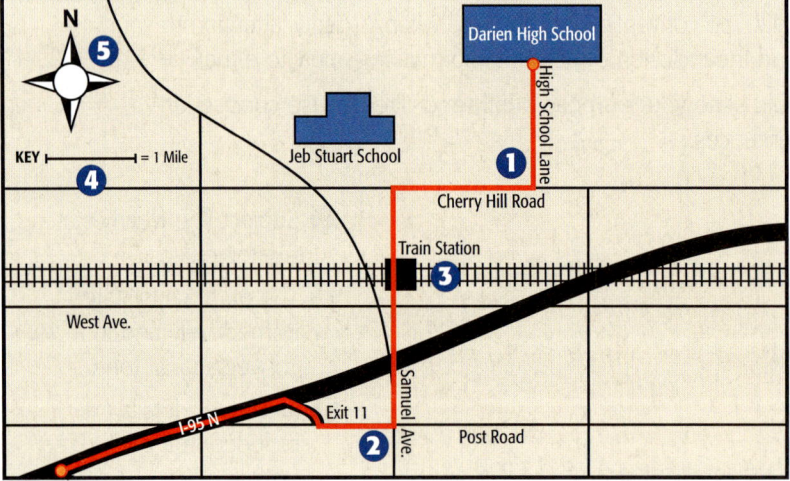

❶ Clearly labels all streets to be traveled

❷ Labels major cross streets so the traveler can keep better track of his or her progress

❸ Includes landmarks to help identify the area

❹ Includes legend to show scale

❺ Includes compass rose to help orientate the traveler

Activity

Write directions and draw an accompanying map to a location in your town. Be sure to include enough details and give enough clear directions so that even someone who is unfamiliar with the area could find the destination.

Functional Documents

Technical Writing

Technical writing involves the use of very specific vocabulary and a special attention to detail. The purpose of technical writing is to describe a process clearly enough so that the reader can perform the steps and reach the intended goal, such as installing software, connecting a piece of equipment, or programming a device.

Instructions for Connecting DVD Player to HDTV

❶ Your DVD player can be connected to an HDTV using RCA cables or, for best picture quality, an HDMI cable.

Connecting with RCA Cables:

❷ Step 1: Insert the ends of the red, white, and yellow cables into the jacks labeled "AUDIO/VIDEO OUT." Be sure to match the colors of the cable with the color of the jack.

Step 2: Insert the other ends of the RCA cables into the jacks labeled "AUDIO/VIDEO IN" on your HDTV. These are usually located on the side or the back of the television. Again, be sure to match the colors of the cables with the colors of the jacks.

Connecting with HDMI Cable:

Step 1: Insert one end of the HDMI cable into the HDMI port located on the back of the DVD player.

Step 2: Insert the other end of the HDMI cable into the HDMI port on your HDTV.

❸ Note: Your HDTV may have more than one HDMI port. If so, be sure that you set your HDTV to the correct input when viewing.

---

❶ Uses specific language to clearly describe the process

❷ Lists each step individually

❸ Directs attention to possible variations the reader may encounter

Activity

Choose a device that you own or have access to, such as an mp3 player or a cell phone. Write brief step-by-step directions on how to perform a specific function on the device, so that someone else can follow your instructions and perform the function successfully.

Writing Handbook

Using the Traits of Strong Writing

What are some basic terms you can use to discuss your writing with your teacher or classmates? What should you focus on as you revise and edit your compositions? Check out the following terms, or traits, that describe the qualities of strong writing. Learn the meaning of each trait and find out how using the traits can improve your writing.

Ideas

The message or the theme and the details that develop it

Writing is clear when readers can grasp the meaning of your ideas right away. Check to see whether you're getting your message across.

- ☑ Does the title suggest the theme of the composition?
- ☑ Does the composition focus on a single narrow topic?
- ☑ Is the thesis—the main point or central idea—clearly stated?
- ☑ Do well-chosen details elaborate your main point?

Organization

The arrangement of main ideas and supporting details

An effective plan of organization points your readers in the right direction and guides them easily through your composition from start to finish. Find a structure, or order, that best suits your topic and writing purpose. Check to see whether you've ordered your key ideas and details in a way that keeps your readers on track.

- ☑ Are the beginning, middle, and end clearly linked?
- ☑ Is the internal order of ideas easy to follow?
- ☑ Does the introduction capture your readers' attention?
- ☑ Do sentences and paragraphs flow from one to the next in a way that makes sense?
- ☑ Does the conclusion wrap up the composition?

Writing Handbook

Voice

A writer's unique way of using tone and style

Your writing voice comes through when your readers sense that a real person is communicating with them. Readers will respond to the **tone** (or attitude) that you express toward a topic and to the **style** (the way that you use language and shape your sentences). Read your work aloud to see whether your writing voice comes through.

- ☑ Does your writing sound interesting?
- ☑ Does your writing reveal your attitude toward your topic?
- ☑ Does your writing sound like you—or does it sound like you're imitating someone else?

Sentence Fluency

The smooth rhythm and flow of sentences that vary in length and style

The best writing is made up of sentences that flow smoothly from one sentence to the next. Writing that is graceful also sounds musical—rhythmical rather than choppy. Check for sentence fluency by reading your writing aloud.

- ☑ Do your sentences vary in length and structure?
- ☑ Do transition words and phrases show connections between ideas and sentences?
- ☑ Does parallelism help balance and unify related ideas?

Word Choice

The vocabulary a writer uses to convey meaning

Words work hard. They carry the weight of your meaning, so make sure you choose them carefully. Check to see whether the words you choose are doing their jobs well.

- ☑ Do you use lively verbs to show action?
- ☑ Do you use vivid words to create word pictures in your readers' minds?
- ☑ Do you use precise words to explain your ideas simply and clearly?

Conventions

Correct spelling, grammar, usage, and mechanics

A composition free of errors makes a good impression on your readers. Mistakes can be distracting, and they can blur your message. Try working with a partner to spot errors and correct them. Use this checklist to help you.

- ☑ Are all words spelled correctly?
- ☑ Are all proper nouns—as well as the first word of every sentence—capitalized?
- ☑ Is your composition free of sentence fragments?
- ☑ Is your composition free of run-on sentences?
- ☑ Are punctuation marks—such as apostrophes, commas, and end marks—inserted in the right places?

Presenting and Publishing

The formatting of writing for various purposes

For many writers, the writing process is not complete until they present their work to an audience. This can mean submitting your writing for publication in a school paper or a national magazine, or it can simply mean preparing your writing in a neat and presentable format. For readers to fully appreciate your writing, it is very important that you present it neatly, effectively, and according to professional standards.

Format

- The standard typeface setting for most writing submissions is Courier 12 point.
- Double-space your work so that it is easy to read.
- Leave one-inch margins on all sides of every page.
- Italicize titles or when using terms from other languages. You may also italicize words to add emphasis, but do this only when it is necessary to make your point clear. (If you are submitting your writing to a professional publication, underline words that should appear in italics.)
- Most word processing programs make it easy to set the page number to appear in the upper right-hand corner of each page. Include your last name before each page number after the first page.
- If you are including charts, graphs, maps, or other visual aids, consider setting them on their own page. This will allow you to show the graphic at a full size that is easy to read.

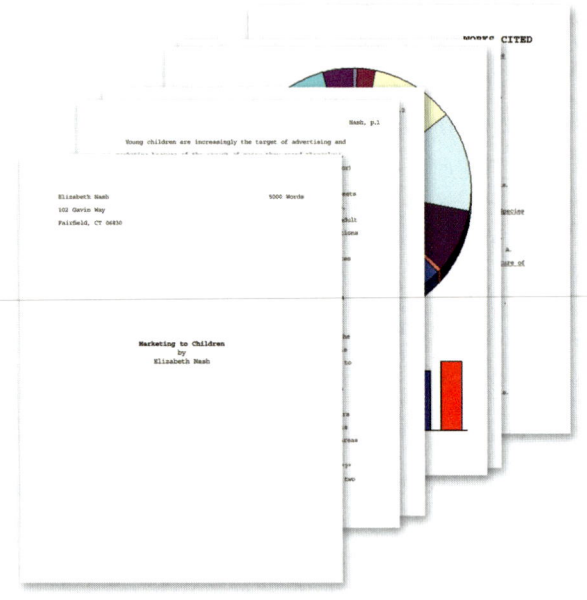

Organization

- On a separate sheet of paper, center your name under the title of your work. If you are submitting your writing for publication, include the total number of words in the upper right-hand corner, and your name and address in the upper left-hand corner.
- The body of your work follows immediately.
- End your presentation with you list of works cited.

Research Paper Writing

More than any other type of paper, research papers are the product of a search—a search for data, for facts, for informed opinions, for insights, and for new information.

Selecting a topic
- If a specific topic is not assigned, choose a topic. Begin with the assigned subject or a subject that interests you. Read general sources of information about that subject and narrow your focus to some aspect of it that interests you. Good places to start are encyclopedia articles and the tables of contents of books on the subject. A computerized library catalog will also display many subheads related to general topics. Find out if sufficient information about your topic is available.
- As you read about the topic, develop your paper's central idea, which is the purpose of your research. Even though this idea might change as you do more research, it can begin to guide your efforts. For example, if you were assigned the subject of the Civil War, you might find that you're interested in women's roles during that war. As you read, you might narrow your topic down to women who went to war, women who served as nurses for the Union, or women who took over farms and plantations in the South.

Conducting a broad search for information
- Generate a series of researchable questions about your chosen topic. Then research to find answers to your questions.
- Among the many sources you might use are the card catalog, the computer catalog, the *Reader's Guide to Periodical Literature* (or an electronic equivalent), newspaper indexes, and specialized references such as biographical encyclopedias.
- If possible, use primary sources as well as secondary sources. A **primary source** is a firsthand account of an event—for example, the diary of a woman who served in the army in the Civil War is a primary source. **Secondary sources** are sources written by people who did not experience or influence the event. Locate specific information efficiently by using the table of contents, indexes, chapter headings, and graphic aids.

Developing a working bibliography
If a work seems useful, write a **bibliography card** for it. On an index card, write down the author, title, city of publication, publisher, date of publication, and any other information you will need to identify the source. Number your cards in the upper right-hand corner so you can keep them in order.

Following are model bibliography, or source, cards.

Book

❶ Settle, Mary Lee   ❷ 6
  ❸ *All the Brave Promises.*
  ❹ Columbia: University of
     South Carolina
  ❺ Press, 1995.

  ❻ Evanston Public Library   D810.W754

❶ Author   ❺ Date of publication
❷ Source number   ❻ Location of source
❸ Title   ❼ Library call number
❹ City of publication/
   Publisher

Periodicals

> ❶ Chelminski. R. ❷ 2
> ❸ "The Maginot Line"
> ❹ *Smithsonian*, June 1997: 90–99

❶ Author
❷ Source number
❸ Title
❹ Title of magazine/date/page number(s)

Online Source

> ❶ "Job Hunting Resources" ❷ 6
> ❸ The Career Building Network
> ❹ CareerBuilder
> ❺ 14 Feb. 2002
> ❻ http://www.careerbuilder.com

❶ Title ❹ Sponsoring organization
❷ Source number ❺ Date of access
❸ Title of database ❻ URL

Evaluating your sources

Your sources should be **a**uthoritative, **r**eliable, **t**imely, and **s**uitable **(arts)**.

- The source should be **authoritative**. The author should be well-known in the field. An author who has written several books or articles about a subject or who is frequently quoted may be considered an authority. You might also consult *Book Review Index* and *Book Review Digest* to find out how other experts in the field have evaluated a book or an article.
- The source should be **reliable**. If possible, avoid material from popular magazines in favor of that from more scholarly journals. Be especially careful to evaluate material from online sources. For example, the Web site of a well-known university is more reliable than that of an individual. (You might also consult a librarian or your instructor for guidance in selecting reliable online sources.)
- The source should be **timely**. Use the most recent material available, particularly for subjects of current importance. Check the publication date of books as well as the month and year of periodicals.
- The source should be **suitable**, or **appropriate**. Consider only material that is relevant to the purpose of your paper. Do not waste time on books or articles that have little bearing on your topic. If you are writing on a controversial topic, you should include material that represents more than one point of view.

Compiling and organizing note cards

Careful notes will help you to organize the material for your paper.

- As you reread and study sources, write useful information on index cards. Be sure that each note card identifies the source (use the number of the bibliography card that corresponds to each source).
- In the lower right-hand corner of the card, write the page number on which you found the information. If one card contains several notes, write the page number in parentheses after the relevant material.
- Three helpful ways to take notes are paraphrasing, summarizing, and quoting directly.
  1. **Paraphrase** important details that you want to remember; that is, use your own words to restate specific information.
  2. **Summarize** main ideas that an author presents. When you summarize several pages, be sure to note the page on which the material begins and the page on which it ends—for example, 213–221.
  3. **Quote** the exact words of an author only when the actual wording is important. Be careful about placing the author's words in quotation marks.
- Identify the subject of each note card with a short phrase written in the upper left.

Writing Handbook

See the sample note card below, which includes information about careers and goals from three pages.

> Careers and goals　　　　　　　　12
> Many people "crave work that will spark...excitement and energy." (5) Sher recognizes that a career does not necessarily satisfy a person's aim in life. (24) She also offers advice on how to overcome obstacles that people experience in defining their goals. (101)

- Organize your note cards to develop a **working outline.** Begin by sorting them into piles of related cards. Try putting the piles together in different ways that suggest an organizational pattern. (If, at this point, you discover that you do not have enough information, go back and do further research.) Many methods of organization are possible. You might also combine methods of organization.

Developing a thesis statement

A thesis statement tells what your topic is and what you intend to say about it—for example, "World War II changed the lives of African Americans and contributed to the rise of the civil rights movement."

- Start by examining your central idea.
- Refine it to reflect the information that you gathered in your research.
- Next, consider your approach to the topic. What is the purpose of your research? Are you proving or disproving something? illustrating a cause-and-effect relationship? offering a solution to a problem? examining one aspect of the topic thoroughly? predicting an outcome?
- Revise your central idea to reflect your approach.
- Be prepared to revise your thesis statement if necessary.

Drafting your paper

Consult your working outline and your notes as you start to draft your paper.

- Concentrate on getting your ideas down in a complete and logical order.
- Write an introduction and a conclusion. An effective introduction creates interest, perhaps by beginning with a question or a controversial quotation; it should also contain your thesis statement. An effective conclusion will summarize main points, restate your thesis, explain how the research points to important new questions to explore, and bring closure to the paper.

Avoiding Plagiarism

Plagiarism is the act of presenting an author's words or ideas as if they were your own. This is not only illegal, it is also unethical. You must credit the source not only for material directly quoted but also for any facts or ideas obtained from the source.

Consider this example:

From the original SparkNotes study guide by Melissa and Stephanie Martin

> Throughout the novel, Twain depicts the society that surrounds Huck as little more than a collection of degraded rules and precepts that defy logic. This faulty logic appears early in the novel, when the new judge in town allows Pap to keep custody of Huck.

Plagiarized usage

> Twain's depiction of society is as a collection of illogical rules and principles. A good example of this is when Pap is awarded custody of Huck.

Simply rewording the original passage is not enough. In order to legally and ethically use the words or ideas of another writer you must credit the writer of the original or rework the original into your own new idea.

Using Material Without Plagiarizing

1. **Quote the original directly and credit the author.**
   As Melissa and Stephanie Martin note in their SparkNotes study guide, Huck lives in a society that is "little more than a collection of degraded rules and precepts that defy logic." They offer the example of Pap being awarded custody of Huck.

2. **Paraphrase the original and credit the author.**
   In their SparkNotes study guide, Melissa and Stephanie Martin note that Twain's depiction of society is as a collection of illogical rules and principles. A good example of this is when Pap is awarded custody of Huck.

3. **Use the information in the original to create your own idea.**
   It is hard to blame Huck for wanting to escape from a world where he is forced to follow arbitrary rules, and where he is forced to live with an abusive father.

Crediting your source is not only fair to the writer of the original source, it is also the law. Plagiarism is a serious offence and can result in failing grades, expulsion, and even legal action.

- In addition to citing books and periodicals from which you take information, cite song lyrics, letters, and excerpts from literature.
- Also credit original ideas that are expressed graphically in tables, charts, and diagrams, as well as the sources of any visual aids you may include, such as photographs.
- You do not need to cite the source of any information that is common knowledge, such as "John F. Kennedy was assassinated in 1963 in Dallas, Texas."

In-text citations The most common method of crediting sources is with parenthetical documentation within the text. Generally a reference to the source and page number is included in parentheses at the end of each quotation, paraphrase, or summary of information borrowed from a source. An in-text citation points readers to a corresponding entry in your **works-cited list**—a list of all your sources, complete with publication information, that will appear as the final page of your paper. The Modern Language Association (MLA) recommends the following guidelines for crediting sources in text. You may wish to refer to the *MLA Handbook for Writers of Research Papers* by Joseph Gibaldi for more information and examples.

- Put in parentheses the author's last name and the page number where you found the information. An art historian has noted, "In Wood's idyllic farmscapes, man lives in complete harmony with Nature; he is the earth's caretaker" (Corn 90).
- If the author's name is mentioned in the sentence, put only the page number in parentheses. Art historian Wanda Corn has noted, "In Wood's idyllic farmscapes, man lives in complete harmony with Nature; he is the earth's caretaker" (90).
- If no author is listed, put the title or a shortened version of the title in parentheses. Include a page number if you have one. Some critics believe that Grant Wood's famous painting *American Gothic* pokes fun at small-town life and traditional American values ("Gothic").

Compiling a list of works cited

At the end of your text, provide an alphabetized list of published works or other sources cited.

- Include complete publishing information for each source.
- For magazine and newspaper articles, include the page numbers. If an article is continued on a different page, use + after the first page number.
- For online sources, include the date accessed.
- Cite only those sources from which you actually use information.
- Arrange entries in alphabetical order according to the author's last name. Write the last name first. If no author is given, alphabetize by title.
- For long entries, indent five spaces every line after the first.

Writing Handbook

How to cite sources
On the next three pages, you'll find sample style sheets that can help you prepare your list of sources—the final page of the research paper. Use the one your teacher prefers.

MLA Style
MLA style is most often used in English and social studies classes. Center the title *Works Cited* at the top of your list.

Source	Style
Book with one author	Isaacson, Walter. *Einstein: His Life and Universe.* New York: Simon, 2007.
Book with two or three authors	Mortenson, Greg, and David Oliver Relin. *Three Cups of Tea: One Man's Mission to Promote Peace … One School at a Time.* New York: Penguin, 2006. [If a book has more than three authors, name only the first author and then write "et al." (Latin abbreviation for "and others")]
Book with editor(s)	Lehman, David and Heather McHugh, eds. *The Best American Poetry 2007.* New York: Scribner's, 2007.
Book with an organization or a group as author or editor	Adobe Creative Team. *Adobe Photoshop CS3 Classroom in a Book.* Berkeley: Adobe, 2007.
Work from an anthology	Kilmer, Joyce. "Trees." *The Poetry Anthology, 1912–2002.* Ed. Joseph Parisi. Chicago: Dee, 2004. 7.
Introduction in a published book	Jackson, Peter. Introduction. *The Making of Star Wars: The Definitive Story Behind the Original Film.* By J. W. Rinzler. New York: Del Rey, 2007. iii.
Encyclopedia article	"Jazz." *The New Encyclopaedia Britannica: Micropaedia.* 15th ed. 1998.
Weekly magazine article	Sacks, Oliver. "A Bolt from the Blue." *New Yorker* 23 July 2007: 38–42.
Monthly magazine article	Plotnikoff, David. "Hungry Man." *Saveur* July 2007: 35–36.
Newspaper article	Long, Ray, and Jeffrey Meitrodt. "Some Budget Progress Made." *Chicago Tribune* 26 July 2007: B3. [If no author is named, begin the entry with the title of the article.]
Internet	Onion, Amanda. "Americans Embracing 'Green' Cleaning." *ABC News.* 30 Jan. 2006. ABC News Internet Ventures. 1 Aug. 2007 <http://abcnews.go.com/Technology/Business/story?id=1544322>.
Online magazine article	Parks, Bob. "Robot Buses Pull In to San Diego's Fastest Lane." *Wired Magazine* July 2007. 25 Oct. 2007 <http://www.wired.com/cars/futuretransport/magazine/15-08/st_robot>.
Radio or TV program	"Jungles." *Planet Earth.* Dir. Alastair Fothergill. Discovery Channel. 19 Nov. 2006.
Videotape or DVD	Guggenheim, Davis, dir. *An Inconvenient Truth.* 2006. DVD. Paramount, 2006. [For a videotape (VHS) version, replace "DVD" with "Videocassette."]
Interview	Campeche, Tanya. E-mail interview. 25 Feb. 2004. [If an interview takes place in person, replace "E-mail" with "Personal"; if it takes place on the telephone, use "Telephone."]

CMS Style

CMS style was created by the University of Chicago Press to meet its publishing needs. This style, which is detailed in *The Chicago Manual of Style* (CMS), is used in a number of subject areas. Center the title *Bibliography* at the top of your list.

Source	Style
Book with one author	Isaacson, Walter. *Einstein: His Life and Universe.* New York: Simon & Schuster, 2007.
Book with two to ten authors	Mortenson, Greg, and David Oliver Relin. *Three Cups of Tea: One Man's Mission to Promote Peace … One School at a Time.* New York: Penguin Books, 2006. [If a book has more than ten authors, name only the first seven and then write "et al." (Latin abbreviation for "and others")].
Book with editor(s)	Lehman, David, and Heather McHugh, eds. *The Best American Poetry 2007.* New York: Scribner's, 2007.
Book with an organization or a group as author or editor	Adobe Creative Team. *Adobe Photoshop CS3 Classroom in a Book.* Berkeley: Adobe Press, 2007.
Work from an anthology	Kilmer, Joyce. "Trees." In *The "Poetry" Anthology, 1912–2002.* Ed. Joseph Parisi. Chicago: Ivan R. Dee, 2004.
Introduction in a published book	Jackson, Peter. Introd. to *The Making of "Star Wars": The Definitive Story behind the Original Film,* by J. W. Rinzler. New York: Del Rey, 2007.
Encyclopedia article	[Credit for encyclopedia articles goes in your text, not in your bibliography.]
Weekly magazine article	Sacks, Oliver. "A Bolt from the Blue." *The New Yorker,* July 23, 2007.
Monthly magazine article	Plotnikoff, David. "Hungry Man." *Saveur,* July 2007.
Newspaper article	Long, Ray, and Jeffrey Meitrodt. "Some Budget Progress Made." *Chicago Tribune,* sec. B. July 26, 2007. [Credit for unsigned newspaper articles goes in your text, not in your bibliography.]
Internet	Onion, Amanda. "Americans Embracing 'Green' Cleaning." *ABC News,* January 30, 2006. http://abcnews.go.com/Technology/Business/story?id=1544322.
Online magazine article	Parks, Bob. "Robot Buses Pull In to San Diego's Fastest Lane." *Wired Magazine,* July 2007. http://www.wired.com/cars/futuretransport/magazine/15-08/st_robot.
Radio or TV program	[Credit for radio and TV programs goes in your text, not in your bibliography.]
Videotape or DVD	Guggenheim, Davis, dir. *An Inconvenient Truth.* DVD. Hollywood, CA: Paramount Home Video, 2006. [For a videotape (VHS) version, replace "DVD" with "VHS."]
Interview	[Credit for interviews goes in your text, not in your bibliography.]

APA Style

The American Psychological Association (APA) style is commonly used in the sciences. Center the title *References* at the top of your list.

Source	Style
Book with one author	Isaacson, W. (2007). *Einstein: His life and universe.* New York: Simon & Schuster.
Book with two or three authors	Mortenson, G., & Relin, D. O. *Three cups of tea: One man's mission to promote peace … one school at a time.* New York: Penguin, 2006. [If a book has more than six authors, name only the first six and then write "et al." (Latin abbreviation for "and others")].
Book with editor(s)	Lehman, D., & McHugh, H. (Eds.). (2007). *The best American poetry 2007.* New York: Scribner's.
Book with an organization or a group as author or editor	Adobe Creative Team. (2007). *Adobe Photoshop CS3 classroom in a book.* Berkeley, CA: Adobe Press.
Work from an anthology	Kilmer, J. (2004) Trees. In J. Parisi (Ed.), *The Poetry anthology, 1912–2002* (p. 7). Chicago, Ivan R. Dee. (Reprinted from *Poetry*, August 1913, p. 25.)
Introduction in a published book	[Credit for introductions goes in your text, not in your references.]
Encyclopedia article	Jazz. (1998). In *The new encyclopaedia britannica.* (Vol. 6, pp. 519–520). Chicago: Encyclopaedia Britannica.
Weekly magazine article	Sacks, O. (2007, July 23). A bolt from the blue. *The New Yorker, 83,* 38–42.
Monthly magazine article	Plotnikoff, D. (2007, July). Hungry man. *Saveur, 103,* 35–36.
Newspaper article	Long, R., & Meitrodt, J. (2007, July 26). Some budget progress made. *Chicago Tribune,* p. B3. [If no author is named, begin the entry with the title of the article.]
Internet	Onion, A. (2006, January 30). Americans embracing 'green' cleaning." *ABC News.* Retrieved August 1, 2007, from http://abcnews.go.com/Technology/Business/story?id=1544322
Online magazine article	Parks, B. (2007, July). Robot buses pull in to San Diego's fastest lane. *Wired Magazine, 15.08.* Retrieved July 25, 2007, from http://www.wired.com/cars/futuretransport/magazine/15-08/st_robot
Radio or TV program	Fothergill. A. (Director). (2006, November 19). Jungles [Television series episode]. In S. Malone (Producer), *Planet Earth.* Silver Spring, MD: Discovery Channel.
Videotape or DVD	Bender, L. (Producer), & Guggenheim, D. (Director). (2006). *An inconvenient truth* [Motion picture]. United States: Paramount Home Video. 2006.
Interview	[Credit for interviews goes in your text, not in your references.]

Reading Handbook

Reading Handbook

Being an active reader is a crucial part of being a lifelong learner. It is also an ongoing task. Good reading skills are recursive; that is, they build on each other, providing the tools you'll need to understand text, to interpret ideas and themes, and to read critically.

Understanding Text Structure

To follow the logic and message of a selection and to remember it, analyze the **text structure,** or organization of ideas, within a writer's work. Recognizing the pattern of organization can help you discover the writer's purpose and will focus your attention on important ideas in the selection. **Look for signal words** to point you to the structure.

- **Spatial sequence** uses words or phrases such as *nearby, to the left, above,* and *behind* to show the physical arrangement of people and objects in an area.
- **Order of importance** will use words such as *most important* and *least necessary* to compare the importance of things or ideas.
- **Chronological order** often uses such words as *first, then, after, later,* and *finally* to show a sequence of events in time.
- **Cause-and-effect order** discusses chains of events using words or phrases such as *therefore, because, subsequently,* or *as a result.*
- **Comparison-contrast order** may use words or phrases such as *similarly, in contrast, likewise,* or *on the other hand.*
- **Problem-solution order** presents a problem and then offers one or more solutions. A problem-solution structure may incorporate other structures such as order of importance, chronological order, or comparison-contrast order.

Comprehension Strategies

Because understanding is the most critical reading task, lifelong learners use a wide variety of reading strategies before, during, and after reading to ensure their comprehension.

Determining the Main Idea

The **main idea** of a selection is the writer's purpose in writing the selection. As you read, it will be helpful to determine the main idea not only of the entire piece, but also of each paragraph. After identifying the important details in each paragraph, pause and ask yourself

- What is the main point of this selection?
- What do these details add up to?
- What is the writer trying to communicate?

Summarizing

A summary is a short restatement of the main ideas and important details of a selection. Summarizing what you have read is an excellent tool for understanding and remembering a passage. To summarize a selection:

- Identify the **main ideas.**
- Determine the essential **supporting details.**
- Relate all the main ideas and essential details in a **logical sequence.**
- **Paraphrase**—that is, restate the selection in your own words.
- Answer **who, what, where, when,** and **why** questions.

The best summaries can easily be understood by someone who has not read the selection. If you're not sure whether an idea is a main idea or a supporting detail, try taking it out of your summary. Does your summary still sound complete?

Reading Handbook

Distinguishing between fact and opinion
It is always important to be able to tell whether the ideas in a selection are facts or the writer's opinions.

- **Facts** can be proven or measured; you can verify them in reference materials. Sometimes you can observe or test them yourself.

  Example: Chicago is about 800 miles from New York City.

- **Opinions** are often open to interpretation and contain phrases such as "I believe" or "from my point of view."

  Example: Chicago to New York is too far to drive.

As you read a selection, evaluate any facts as well as any opinions you find. Ask yourself:

- Are the facts relevant? Are they actually true?
- Are the opinions well informed and based on verifiable facts? Are they persuasive?

Drawing inferences and supporting them
An **inference** involves using your reason and experience to come up with an idea based on what a writer implies or suggests but does not directly state.

- **Drawing a conclusion** is making a general statement you can explain with reason or with supporting details from the text.
- **Making a generalization** is generating a statement that can apply to more than one item or group.

What is most important when inferring is to be sure that you have accurately based your thoughts on supporting details from the text as well as on your own knowledge.

Making a prediction
A **prediction** is an educated guess about what a text will be about based on initial clues a writer provides. You can also make predictions about what will happen next in a story as you read.

- Take breaks during your reading and **ask yourself questions** about what will happen next, such as, "How will this character react to this news?"
- **Answer these questions for yourself,** supporting your answers with evidence from the text. For example, "Sam will be jealous when he hears the news, because he is in love with Antonia."
- As you continue reading, **verify** your predictions.

Reading silently for sustained periods
When you read for long periods of time, your task is to avoid distractions. Check your comprehension regularly by summarizing what you've read so far. Using study guides or graphic organizers can help you get through difficult passages. Take regular breaks when you need them and vary your reading rate with the demands of the task.

Keep in mind:
Whichever strategies you choose to use while reading, it will always be helpful to:

- Read slowly and carefully.
- Reread difficult passages.
- Take careful notes.

Also, when reading more difficult material, consider these steps to modify or change your reading strategies when you don't understand what you've read.

- Reread the passage.
- Consult other sources, including text resources, teachers, and other students.
- Write comments or questions on another piece of paper for later review or discussion.

Language Handbook

Grammar Glossary

This glossary will help you quickly locate information on parts of speech and sentence structure.

A

Absolute phrase. *See* Phrase.

Abstract noun. *See* Noun chart.

Action verb. *See* Verb.

Active voice. *See* Voice.

Adjective A word that modifies a noun or pronoun by limiting its meaning. Adjectives appear in various positions in a sentence. (The *gray* cat purred. The cat is *gray*.)

Many adjectives have different forms to indicate degree of comparison. (short, shorter, shortest)

The positive degree is the simple form of the adjective. (easy, interesting, good)

The comparative degree compares two persons, places, things, or ideas. (easier, more interesting, better)

The superlative degree compares more than two persons, places, things, or ideas. (easiest, most interesting, best)

A predicate adjective follows a linking verb and further identifies or describes the subject. (The child is happy.)

A proper adjective is formed from a proper noun and begins with a capital letter. Many proper adjectives are created by adding these suffixes: *-an, -ian, -n, -ese,* and *-ish.* (Chinese, African)

Adjective clause. *See* Clause chart.

Adverb A word that modifies a verb, an adjective, or another adverb by making its meaning more specific. When modifying a verb, an adverb may appear in various positions in a sentence. (Cats *generally* eat less than dogs. *Generally,* cats eat less than dogs.) When modifying an adjective or another adverb, an adverb appears directly before the modified word. (I was *quite* pleased that they got along so well.) The word *not* and the contraction *-n't* are adverbs. (Mike *wasn't* ready for the test today.) Certain adverbs of time, place, and degree also have a negative meaning. (He's *never* ready.)

Some adverbs have different forms to indicate degree of comparison. (soon, sooner, soonest)

The comparative degree compares two actions. (better, more quickly)

The superlative degree compares three or more actions. (fastest, most patiently, least rapidly)

Adverb clause. *See* Clause chart.

Antecedent. *See* Pronoun.

Appositive A noun or a pronoun that further identifies another noun or pronoun. (My friend *Julie* lives next door.)

Appositive phrase. *See* Phrase.

Article The adjective *a, an,* or *the.*

Indefinite articles (*a* and *an*) refer to one of a general group of persons, places, or things. (I eat *an* apple *a* day.)

The definite article (*the*) indicates that the noun is a specific person, place, or thing. (*The* alarm woke me up.)

Auxiliary verb. *See* Verb.

B

Base form. *See* Verb tense.

C

Clause A group of words that has a subject and a predicate and that is used as part of a sentence. Clauses fall into two categories: *main clauses,* which are also called *independent clauses,* and *subordinate clauses,* which are also called *dependent clauses.*

A main clause can stand alone as a sentence.

Language Handbook

Types of Subordinate Clauses

Clause	Function	Example	Begins with . . .
Adjective clause	Modifies a noun or a pronoun	Songs *that have a strong beat* make me want to dance.	A relative pronoun such as *which, who, whom, whose,* or *that*
Adverb clause	Modifies a verb, an adjective, or an adverb	*Whenever Al calls me,* he asks to borrow my bike.	A subordinating conjunction such as *after, although, because, if, since, when,* or *where*
Noun clause	Serves as a subject, an object, or a predicate nominative	*What Philip did* surprised us.	Words such as *how, that, what, whatever, when, where, which, who, whom, whoever, whose,* or *why*

There must be at least one main clause in every sentence. (**The rooster crowed,** and **the dog barked.**)

A subordinate clause cannot stand alone as a sentence. A subordinate clause needs a main clause to complete its meaning. Many subordinate clauses begin with subordinating conjunctions or relative pronouns. (**When Geri sang her solo,** the audience became quiet.) The chart on the next page shows the main types of subordinate clauses.

Collective noun. See Noun chart.

Common noun. See Noun chart.

Comparative degree. See Adjective; Adverb.

Complement A word or phrase that completes the meaning of a verb. The four basic kinds of complements are *direct objects, indirect objects, object complements,* and *subject complements.*

A direct object answers the question *What?* or *Whom?* after an action verb. (Kari found a *dollar.* Larry saw *Denise.*)

An indirect object answers the question *To whom? For whom? To what?* or *For what?* after an action verb. (Do *me* a favor. She gave the *child* a toy.)

An object complement answers the question *What?* after a direct object. An object complement is a noun, a pronoun, or an adjective that completes the meaning of a direct object by identifying or describing it. (The director made me the *understudy* for the role. The little girl called the puppy *hers.*)

A subject complement follows a subject and a linking verb. It identifies or describes a subject. The two kinds of subject complements are *predicate nominatives* and *predicate adjectives.*

A predicate nominative is a noun or pronoun that follows a linking verb and tells more about the subject. (The author of "The Raven" is *Poe.*)

A predicate adjective is an adjective that follows a linking verb and gives more information about the subject. (Ian became *angry* at the bully.)

Complex sentence. See Sentence.

Compound preposition. See Preposition.

Compound sentence. See Sentence.

Compound-complex sentence. See Sentence.

Conjunction A word that joins single words or groups of words.

A coordinating conjunction (*and, but, or, nor, for, yet, so*) joins words or groups of words that are equal in grammatical importance. (David *and* Ruth are twins. I was bored, *so* I left.)

Correlative conjunctions (*both . . . and, just as . . . so, not only . . . but also, either . . . or, neither . . . nor, whether . . . or*) work in pairs to join words and groups of words of equal importance.

(Choose *either* the muffin *or* the bagel.)

A subordinating conjunction *(after, although, as if, because, before, if, since, so that, than, though, until, when, while)* joins a dependent idea or clause to a main clause. **(Beth acted *as if* she felt ill.)**

Conjunctive adverb An adverb used to clarify the relationship between clauses of equal weight in a sentence. Conjunctive adverbs are used to replace *and (also, besides, furthermore, moreover)*; to replace *but (however, nevertheless, still)*; to state a result *(consequently, therefore, so, thus)*; or to state equality *(equally, likewise, similarly)*. **(Ana was determined to get an A; *therefore*, she studied often.)**

Coordinating conjunction. See Conjunction.
Correlative conjunction. See Conjunction.

D

Declarative sentence. See Sentence.
Definite article. See Article.
Demonstrative pronoun. See Pronoun.
Direct object. See Complement.

E

Emphatic form. See Verb tense.

F

Future tense. See Verb tense.

G

Gerund A verb form that ends in *-ing* and is used as a noun. A gerund may function as a subject, the object of a verb, or the object of a preposition. **(*Smiling* uses fewer muscles than *frowning*. Marie enjoys *walking*.)**

Gerund phrase. See Phrase.

I

Imperative mood. See Mood of verb.
Imperative sentence. See Sentence chart.
Indicative mood. See Mood of verb.

Indirect object. See Complement.

Infinitive A verb form that begins with the word *to* and functions as a noun, an adjective, or an adverb. **(No one wanted *to answer*.)** Note: When *to* precedes a verb, it is not a preposition but instead signals an infinitive.

Infinitive phrase. See Phrase.
Intensive pronoun. See Pronoun.

Interjection A word or phrase that expresses emotion or exclamation. An interjection has no grammatical connection to other words. Commas follow mild ones; exclamation points follow stronger ones. **(*Well*, have a good day. *Wow!*)**

Interrogative pronoun. See Pronoun.
Intransitive verb. See Verb.

Inverted order In a sentence written in *inverted order*, the predicate comes before the subject. Some sentences are written in inverted order for variety or special emphasis. **(Up the beanstalk *scampered Jack*.)** The subject also generally follows the predicate in a sentence that begins with *here* or *there*. **(*Here* was the solution to his problem.)** Questions, or interrogative sentences, are generally written in inverted order. In many questions, an auxiliary verb precedes the subject, and the main verb follows it. **(*Has* anyone *seen* Susan?)** Questions that begin with *who* or *what* follow normal word order.

Irregular verb. See Verb tense.

L

Linking verb. See Verb.

M

Main clause. See Clause.

Mood of verb A verb expresses one of three moods: indicative, imperative, or subjunctive.

> The indicative mood is the most common. It makes a statement or asks a question. **(We *are* out of bread. *Will* you *buy* it?)**

> The imperative mood expresses a command or makes a request. **(*Stop* acting like a child! Please *return* my sweater.)**

Language Handbook

Types of Nouns

Noun	Function	Examples
Abstract noun	Names an idea, a quality, or a characteristic	capitalism, terror
Collective noun	Names a group of things or persons	herd, troop
Common noun	Names a general type of person, place, thing, or idea	city, building
Compound noun	Is made up of two or more words	checkerboard, globe-trotter
Noun of direct addrress	Identifies the person or persons being spoken to	*Maria,* please stand.
Possessive noun	Shows possession, ownership, or the relationship between two nouns	my *sister's* room
Proper noun	Names a particular person, place, thing, or idea	Cleopatra, Italy, Christianity

The subjunctive mood is used to express, indirectly, a demand, suggestion, or statement of necessity (I demand that he *stop* acting like a child. It's necessary that she *buy* more bread.) The subjunctive is also used to state a condition or wish that is contrary to fact. This use of the subjunctive requires the past tense. (If you *were* a nice person, you *would return* my sweater.)

N

Nominative pronoun. *See* Pronoun.

Noun A word that names a person, a place, a thing, or an idea. The chart on this page shows the main types of nouns.

Noun clause. *See* Clause chart.

Noun of direct address. *See* Noun chart.

Number A noun, pronoun, or verb is *singular* in number if it refers to one; *plural* if it refers to more than one.

O

Object. *See* Complement.

P

Participle A verb form that can function as an adjective. Present participles always end in *-ing*. (The woman comforted the *crying* child.) Many past participles end in *-ed*. (We bought the beautifully *painted* chair.) However, irregular verbs form their past participles in some other way. (Cato was Caesar's *sworn* enemy.)

Passive voice. *See* Voice.

Past tense. *See* Verb tense.

Perfect tense. *See* Verb tense.

Personal pronoun. *See* Pronoun, Pronoun chart.

Phrase A group of words that acts in a sentence as a single part of speech.

An absolute phrase consists of a noun or pronoun that is modified by a participle or participial phrase but has no grammatical relation to the complete subject or predicate. (*The vegetables being done,* we finally sat down to eat dinner.)

An appositive phrase is an appositive along with any modifiers. If not essential to the meaning of the sentence, an appositive phrase is set off by commas. (Jack plans to go to the jazz concert, *an important musical event.*)

A gerund phrase includes a gerund plus its complements and modifiers. (*Playing the flute* is her hobby.)

An infinitive phrase contains the infinitive plus its complements and modifiers. (It is time *to leave for school.*)

A **participial phrase** contains a participle and any modifiers necessary to complete its meaning. **(The woman *sitting over there* is my grandmother.)**

A **prepositional phrase** consists of a preposition, its object, and any modifiers of the object. A prepositional phrase can function as an adjective, modifying a noun or a pronoun. **(The dog *in the yard* is very gentle.)** A prepositional phrase may also function as an adverb when it modifies a verb, an adverb, or an adjective. **(The baby slept *on my lap*.)**

A **verb phrase** consists of one or more auxiliary verbs followed by a main verb. **(The job *will have been completed* by noon tomorrow.)**

Positive degree. See Adjective.

Possessive noun. See Noun chart.

Predicate The verb or verb phrase and any objects, complements, or modifiers that express the essential thought about the subject of a sentence.

A **simple predicate** is a verb or verb phrase that tells something about the subject. **(We *ran*.)**

A **complete predicate** includes the simple predicate and any words that modify or complete it. **(We *solved the problem in a short time*.)**

A **compound predicate** has two or more verbs or verb phrases that are joined by a conjunction and share the same subject. **(We *ran to the park and began to play baseball*.)**

Predicate adjective. See Adjective; Complement.

Predicate nominative. See Complement.

Preposition A word that shows the relationship of a noun or pronoun to some other word in the sentence. Prepositions include *about, above, across, among, as, behind, below, beyond, but, by, down, during, except, for, from, into, like, near, of, on, outside, over, since, through, to, under, until, with*. **(I usually eat breakfast *before* school.)**

A **compound preposition** is made up of more than one word. *(according to, ahead of, as to, because of, by means of, in addition to, in spite of, on account of)* **(We played the game *in spite of* the snow.)**

Prepositional phrase. See Phrase.

Present tense. See Verb tense.

Progressive form. See Verb tense.

Pronoun A word that takes the place of a noun, a group of words acting as a noun, or another pronoun. The word or group of words that a pronoun refers to is called its **antecedent**. **(In the following sentence, *Mari* is the antecedent of *she*. *Mari* likes Mexican food, but *she* doesn't like Italian food.)**

A **demonstrative pronoun** points out specific persons, places, things, or ideas. *(this, that, these, those)*

An **indefinite pronoun** refers to persons, places, or things in a more general way than a noun does. *(all, another, any, both, each, either, enough, everything, few, many, most, much, neither, nobody, none, one, other, others, plenty, several, some)*

An **intensive pronoun** adds emphasis to another noun or pronoun. If an intensive pronoun is omitted, the meaning of the sentence will be the same. **(Rebecca *herself* decided to look for a part-time job.)**

An **interrogative pronoun** is used to form questions. *(who? whom? whose? what? which?)*

A **personal pronoun** refers to a specific person or thing. Personal pronouns have three cases: nominative, possessive, and objective. The case depends upon the function of the pronoun in a sentence. The first chart on this page shows the case forms of personal pronouns.

A **reflexive pronoun** reflects back to a noun or pronoun used earlier in the sentence, indicating that the same person or thing is involved. **(We told *ourselves* to be patient.)**

A **relative pronoun** is used to begin a subordinate clause. *(who, whose, that, what, whom, whoever, whomever, whichever, whatever)*

Proper adjective. See Adjective.

Proper noun. See Noun chart.

R

Reflexive pronoun. See Pronoun.

Relative pronoun. See Pronoun.

Language Handbook

S

Sentence A group of words expressing a complete thought. Every sentence has a subject and a predicate. Sentences can be classified by function or by structure. The second chart on this page shows the categories by function; the following subentries describe the categories by structure. *See also* Subject; Predicate; Clause.

A simple sentence has only one main clause and no subordinate clauses. *(Alan found an old violin.)* A simple sentence may contain a compound subject or a compound predicate or both. *(Alan and Teri found an old violin. Alan found an old violin and tried to play it. Alan and Teri found an old violin and tried to play it.)* The subject and the predicate can be expanded with adjectives, adverbs, prepositional phrases, appositives, and verbal phrases. As long as the sentence has only one main clause, however, it remains a simple sentence. *(Alan, rummaging in the attic, found an old violin.)*

A compound sentence has two or more main clauses. Each main clause has its own subject and predicate, and these main clauses are usually joined by a comma and a coordinating conjunction. *(Cats meow, and dogs bark, but ducks quack.)* Semicolons may also be used to join the main clauses in a compound sentence. *(The helicopter landed; the pilot had saved four passengers.)*

A complex sentence has one main clause and one or more subordinate clauses. *(Since the movie starts at eight, we should leave here by seven-thirty.)*

A compound-complex sentence has two or more main clauses and at least one subordinate clause. *(If we leave any later, we may miss the previews, and I want to see them.)*

Simple predicate. *See* Predicate.

Simple subject. *See* Subject.

Subject The part of a sentence that tells what the sentence is about.

A simple subject is the main noun or pronoun in the subject. *(**Babies** crawl.)*

A complete subject includes the simple subject and any words that modify it. *(**The man from New Jersey** won the race.)* In some sentences, the simple subject and the complete subject are the same. *(**Birds** fly.)*

Personal Pronouns			
Clause	Singular Pronouns	Plural Pronouns	Function in Sentence
Nominative	I, you, she, he, it	we, you, they	subject or predicate nominative
Objective	me, you, her, him, it	us, you, them	direct object, indirect object, or object of a preposition

Types of Sentences			
Sentence Type	Function	Ends with . . .	Examples
Declarative sentence	Makes a statement	A period	I did not enjoy the movie.
Exclamatory sentence	Expresses strong emotion	An exclamation point	What a good writer Consuela is!
Imperative sentence	Makes a request or gives a command	A period or an exclamation point	Please come to the party. Stop!
Interrogative sentence	Asks a question	A question mark	Is the composition due?

A compound subject has two or more simple subjects joined by a conjunction. The subjects share the same verb. *(Firefighters and police officers protect the community.)*

Subjunctive mood. *See* Mood of verb.

Subordinate clause. *See* Clause.

Subordinating conjunction. *See* Conjunction.

Superlative degree. *See* Adjective; Adverb.

T

Tense. *See* Verb tense.

Transitive verb. *See* Verb.

V

Verb A word that expresses action or a state of being. *(cooks, seem, laughed)*

An action verb tells what someone or something does. Action verbs can express either physical or mental action. *(Crystal decided to change the tire herself.)*

A transitive verb is an action verb that is followed by a word or words that answer the question *What?* or *Whom?* *(I held the baby.)*

An intransitive verb is an action verb that is not followed by a word that answers the question *What?* or *Whom?* *(The baby laughed.)*

A linking verb expresses a state of being by linking the subject of a sentence with a word or an expression that identifies or describes the subject. *(The lemonade tastes sweet. He is our new principal.)* The most commonly used linking verb is be in all its forms *(am, is, are, was, were, will be, been, being).* Other linking verbs include *appear, become, feel, grow, look, remain, seem, sound, smell, stay, taste.*

An auxiliary verb, or helping verb, is a verb that accompanies the main verb to form a verb phrase. *(I have been swimming.)* The forms of *be* and *have* are the most common auxiliary verbs: *(am, is, are, was, were, being, been; has, have, had, having).* Other auxiliaries include *can, could, do, does, did, may, might, must, shall, should, will, would.*

Verbal A verb form that functions in a sentence as a noun, an adjective, or an adverb. The three kinds of verbals are gerunds, infinitives, and participles. *See* Gerund; Infinitive; Participle.

Verb tense The tense of a verb indicates when the action or state of being occurs. All the verb tenses are formed from the four principal parts of a verb: a base form *(talk)*, a present participle *(talking)*, a simple past form *(talked)*, and a past participle *(talked)*. A regular verb forms its simple past and past participle by adding *-ed* to the base form. *(climb, climbed)* An irregular verb forms its past and past participle in some other way. *(get, got, gotten)*

In addition to present, past, and future tenses, there are three perfect tenses.

The present perfect tense expresses an action or a condition that occurred at some indefinite time in the past. This tense also shows an action or a condition that began in the past and continues into the present. *(She has played the piano for four years.)*

The past perfect tense indicates that one past action or condition began *and* ended before another past action started. *(Andy had finished his homework before I even began mine.)*

The future perfect tense indicates that one future action or condition will begin *and* end before another future event starts. Use *will have* or *shall have* with the past participle of a verb. *(By tomorrow, I will have finished my homework, too.)*

The progressive form of a verb expresses a continuing action with any of the six tenses. To make the progressive forms, use the appropriate tense of the verb *be* with the present participle of the main verb. *(She is swimming. She has been swimming.)*

The emphatic form adds special force, or emphasis, to the present and past tense of a verb. For the emphatic form, use *do, does,* or *did* with the base form. *(Toshi did want that camera.)*

Voice The voice of a verb shows whether the subject performs the action or receives the action of the verb.

A verb is in the active voice if the subject of the sentence performs the action. *(The referee blew the whistle.)*

A verb is in the passive voice if the subject of the sentence receives the action of the verb. *(The whistle was blown by the referee.)*

Troubleshooter

The Troubleshooter will help you recognize and correct errors that you might make in your writing.

Sentence Fragment

Problem: A fragment that lacks a subject
The grass is wet. Can't be mowed now.

Solution: Add a subject to the fragment to make it a complete sentence.
The grass is wet. It can't be mowed now.

Problem: A fragment that lacks a complete verb
We enjoyed our dinner. Beans, rice, and salad.
The storm was fierce. The wind blowing hard.

Solution A: Add either a complete verb or a helping verb to make the sentence complete.
We enjoyed our dinner. Beans, rice, and salad make a good meal.
The storm was fierce. The wind was blowing hard.

Solution B: Combine the fragment with another sentence.
We enjoyed our dinner of beans, rice, and salad.
The storm was fierce with the wind blowing hard.

Problem: A fragment that is a subordinate clause
We went to the park. Where we had often gone before.
Jan won the swimming medal. Which she gave to her parents.

Solution A: Combine the fragment with another sentence.
We went to the park, where we had often gone before.
Jan won the swimming medal, which she gave to her parents.

Solution B: Rewrite the fragment as a complete sentence, eliminating the subordinating conjunction or the relative pronoun and adding a subject or other words necessary to make a complete thought.
We went to the park. We had often gone there before.
Jan won the swimming medal. She gave it to her parents.

Problem: A fragment that lacks both a subject and a verb
The birds woke us with their songs. At six in the morning.

Solution: Combine the fragment with another sentence.
The birds woke us with their songs at six in the morning.

Rule of Thumb: Sentence fragments can make your writing hard to understand. Make sure every sentence has a subject and a verb.

Note: In almost all of the writing you do, especially for school, you should avoid sentence fragments. However, sentence fragments can be used to create special effects, such as adding emphasis or conveying realistic dialogue.
"Not again!" she cried.
The pizza was gone. All of it.

Run-On Sentence

Problem: Comma splice—two main clauses separated only by a comma
The sky is pitch black, there is no moon.

Solution A: Replace the comma with an end mark of punctuation, such as a period or a question mark, and begin the new sentence with a capital letter.
The sky is pitch black. There is no moon.

Solution B: Place a semicolon between the two main clauses.
The sky is pitch black; there is no moon.

Solution C: Add a coordinating conjunction after the comma.
The sky is pitch black, and there is no moon.

Problem: Two main clauses with no punctuation between them.
We picked the apples then we made pies.

Solution A: Separate the main clauses with an end mark of punctuation, such as a period or question mark, and begin the second sentence with a capital letter.
We picked the apples. Then we made pies.

Solution B: Separate the main clauses with a semicolon.
We picked the apples; then we made pies.

Solution C: Add a comma and a coordinating conjunction between the main clauses.
We picked the apples, and then we made pies.

LANGUAGE HANDBOOK **R47**

Problem: The main clauses with no comma before the coordinating conjunction
Elephants still live in the wild but they are endangered.

Solution: Add a comma before the coordinating conjunction to separate the two main clauses.
Elephants still live in the wild, but they are endangered.

Rule of Thumb: It often helps to have someone else read your longer sentences to see if they are clear. Since you know what the sentences are supposed to mean, you might miss the need for punctuation.

Lack of Subject-Verb Agreement

Problem: A subject that is separated from the verb by an intervening prepositional phrase
Ten pieces of the puzzle is on the floor.
The shoe department in each of our stores are closing.

Solution: Make the verb agree with the subject, which is never the object of a preposition.
Ten pieces of the puzzle are on the floor.
The shoe department in each of our stores is closing.

Problem: A predicate nominative that differs in number from the subject
Hamburgers is tonight's dinner.
Tonight's dinner are hamburgers.

Solution: Ignore the predicate nominative, and make the verb agree with the subject of the sentence.
Hamburgers are tonight's dinner.
Tonight's dinner is hamburgers.

Problem: A subject that follows the verb
On my desk is two letters from my dad.
Here is my answers to them both.

Solution: In an inverted sentence look for the subject after the verb. Then make sure the verb agrees with the subject.
On my desk are two letters from my dad.
Here are my answers to them both.

Rule of Thumb: Reversing the order of an inverted sentence may help you decide on the verb form to use: "My answers to them both are here."

Problem: A collective noun as the subject
The cross country team are in first place.
The team gathers at the captain's house after each meet.

Solution A: If the collective noun refers to a group as a whole, use a singular verb.
The cross country team is in first place.

Solution B: If the collective noun refers to each member of a group individually, use a plural verb.
The team gather at the captain's house after each meet.

Problem: A noun of amount as the subject
Five bushels are a great many tomatoes.
Three marbles is in my pocket.

Solution: Determine whether the noun of amount refers to one unit and is therefore singular or whether it refers to a number of individual unites and is therefore plural.
Five bushels is a great many tomatoes.
Three marbles are in my pocket.

Problem: A compound subject that is joined by *and*
The hill and the lake makes a lovely setting for a picnic.
Spaghetti and meatballs are her favorite dinner.

Solution A: If the parts of the compound subject do not belong to one unit or if they refer to different people of things, use a plural verb.
The hill and the lake make a lovely setting for a picnic.

Solution B: If the parts of the compound subject belong to one unit or if both parts refer to the same person or thing, use a singular verb.
Spaghetti and meatballs is her favorite dinner.

Problem: A compound subject that is joined by *or* or *nor*
Neither those trees nor that shrub are healthy.

Solution: Make the verb agree with the subject that is closer to it.
Neither those trees nor that shrub is healthy.

Language Handbook

Problem: A compound subject that is preceded by *many a, every,* or *each*
Many a dog and cat end up in an animal shelter or a pound.

Solution: When *many a, every,* or *each* precedes a compound subject, the subject is considered singular. Use a singular verb.
Many a dog and cat ends up in an animal shelter or a pound.

Problem: A subject that is separated from the verb by an intervening expression
That issue, as well as several others, are bothering me.

Solution: Certain expressions, such as these beginning with *as well as, in addition to,* and *together with,* do not change the number of the subject. Ignore an intervening expression between a subject and its verb, and make the verb agree with the subject.
That issue, along with several others, is bothering me.

Problem: An indefinite pronoun as the subject
Neither of the boys are on time.

Solution: Determine whether the indefinite pronoun is singular or plural, and make the verb agree. Some indefinite pronouns are singular—*another, anyone, everyone, one, each, either, neither, anything, everything, something,* and *somebody.* Some are plural—*both, many, few, several,* and *others.* Some can be singular or plural—*some, all, any, more, most,* and *none.* In these cases, find the noun to which the pronoun refers to determine which verb form to use.
Neither of the boys is on time.

Lack of Pronoun-Antecedent Agreement

Problem: A singular antecedent that can be either male or female.
A climber must check his equipment carefully.

Solution A: Traditionally, a masculine pronoun has been used to refer to an antecedent that may be either male or female. This usage ignores or excludes females. Reword the sentence to use *he or she, him or her,* and so on.
A climber must check his or her equipment carefully.

Solution B: Reword the sentence so that both the antecedent and the pronoun are plural.
Climbers must check their equipment carefully.

Solution C: Reword the sentence to eliminate the pronoun.
A climber must check the equipment carefully.

Rule of Thumb: Although you may see the masculine forms used exclusively in older literature, they are not acceptable in contemporary writing.

Problem: A second-person pronoun that refers to a third-person antecedent
Juan likes sitcoms that make you think as well as laugh.

Solution A: Use the appropriate third-person pronoun.
Juan likes sitcoms that make him think as well as laugh.

Solution B: Use an appropriate noun instead of a pronoun.
Juan likes sitcoms that make people think as well as laugh.

Problem: A singular indefinite pronoun as an antecedent
Each of the volumes has their own index.

Solution: *Each, every, either, neither,* and *one* are singular and therefore require singular personal pronouns even when followed by a prepositional phrase that contains a plural noun.
Each of the volumes has its own index.

Rule of Thumb: To help you remember that *each, either,* and *neither* are singular, think *each one, either one,* and *neither one.*

Lack of Clear Pronoun Reference [Unclear Antecedent]

Problem: A pronoun reference that is weak or vague
We spent several weeks at the farm this summer, and it was exciting.
The label says to shake it before pouring a serving.

Solution A: Rewrite the sentence, adding a clear antecedent for the pronoun.
We spent our vacation at the farm this summer, and it was exciting.

Solution B: Rewrite the sentence, substituting a noun for the pronoun.
The label says to shake the bottle of salad dressing before pouring a serving.

Problem: A pronoun that could refer to more than one antecedent
Lauren and Abby wrote six songs, and she recorded them all.
Don't buy a car from that dealership: it will let you down.

Solution A: Rewrite the sentence, substituting a noun for the pronoun.
Lauren and Abby wrote six songs, and Abby recorded them all.

Solution B: Rewrite the sentence, making the antecedent of the pronoun clear.
A car from that dealership will let you down; don't buy one there.

Problem: The indefinite use of *you* or *they*
You just have to laugh at that scene in the movie.
They say the weather will be clear tomorrow.

Solution A: Rewrite the sentence, substituting a noun for the pronoun.
The audience just has to laugh at that scene in the movie.

Solution B: Rewrite the sentence, eliminating the pronoun entirely.
According to the forecast, the weather will be clear tomorrow.

Shift in Pronoun

Problem: An incorrect shift in person between two pronouns
Lynn likes the front seat, where you are most comfortable.
The Chins planted a maple on the south side of the house, where you need shade the most.

Solution A: Replace the incorrect pronoun with a pronoun that agrees with its a antecedent.
Lynn likes the front seat, where she is most comfortable.

Solution B: Replace the incorrect pronoun with an appropriate noun.
The Chins plants a maple on the south side of the house, where the house needs shade the most.

Shift in Verb Tense

Problem: An unnecessary shift in tense.
The children will give their mother flowers, and they kiss her.
After the party ended, we go home.

Solution: When two or more events occur at the same time, be sure to use the same verb tense to describe each event.
The children will give their mother flowers, and they will kiss her.
After the party ended, we went home.

Problem: A lack of correct shift in tenses to show that one event precedes or follows another
By the time the concert ended, we sat for four hours.

Solution: When two past events being described have occurred at different times, shift from the past tense to the past perfect tense to indicate that one action began and ended before another past action began. Use the past perfect tense for the earlier of the two actions.
By the time the concert ended, we had sat for four hours.

Rule of Thumb: When you need to use several verb tenses in your writing, it may help to first jot down the sequence of events you're writing about. Be clear in your mind what happened first, next, last.

Incorrect Verb Tense or Form

Problem: An incorrect or missing verb ending
When I began taking lessons, I learn about quarter, half, and whole notes.
I had start the lessons two months ago.

Solution: Add –ed to a regular verb to form the past tense and the past participle.
When I began taking lessons, I learned about quarter, half, and whole notes.
I had started the lessons two months ago.

Problem: An improperly formed irregular verb
James brung the book back to the library.
Catherine has writed six pages on that topic.

Solution: Irregular verbs form their past and past participles in some way other than by adding –ed. Memorize these forms, or look them up.
James brought the book back to the library.
Catherine has written six pages on that topic.

Language Handbook

Problem: Confusion between the past form and the past participle
We have ate too many apples.
She had swam the Chesapeake last July.

Solution: Use the past participle form of an irregular verb, not the past form, when you use the auxiliary verb *have*.
We have eaten too many apples.
She had swum the Chesapeake last July.

Problem: Improper use of the past participle
The catcher thrown several runners out.
The DiCaprios done a fine job rearing those children.

Solution A: The past participle of an irregular verb cannot stand alone as a verb. Add a form of the auxiliary verb *have* to the past participle to form a complete verb.
The catcher had thrown several runners out.
The DiCaprios have done a fine job rearing those children.

Solution B: Replace the past participle with the past form of the verb.
The catcher threw several runners out.
The DiCaprios did a fine job rearing those children.

Misplaced or Dangling Modifier

Problem: A misplaced modifier
The children were swimming in the photograph.
Swooping down on a fish, I spotted the gull.
I saw a man at the movies eating popcorn.

Solution: Modifiers that modify the wrong word or seem to modify more than one word in a sentence are called misplaced modifiers. Move the misplaced phrase as close as possible to the word or words it modifies.
The children in the photograph were swimming.
I spotted the gull swooping down on a fish.
I saw a man eating popcorn at the movies.

Problem: Incorrect placement of the adverb *only*
Tricia only has enough money to buy a pencil.

Solution: Place the adverb *only* immediately before the word or group of words it modifies.
Only Tricia has enough money to buy a pencil.
Tricia has enough money to buy only a pencil.
Tricia has only enough money to buy a pencil.

Rule of Thumb: Note that each time *only* is moved, the meaning of the sentence changes. Check to be sure your sentence says what you mean.

Problem: A dangling modifier
Croaking loudly, I listened to the sounds of the frogs in the bog.
Stealing home, the game was won for the Pirates.

Solution: Dangling modifiers do not seem to logically modify any word in the sentence. Rewrite the sentence, adding a noun to which the dangling phrase clearly refers. Often you will have to add other words too.
I listened to the sounds of the frogs croaking loudly in the bog.
Stealing home, Layla won the game for the Pirates.

Missing or Misplaced Possessive Apostrophe

Problem: Singular nouns
The womans child loved the circus trapeze artists.

Solution: Use an apostrophe and –s to form the possessive of a singular noun, even one that ends in *s*.
The woman's child loved the circus's trapeze artist.

Problem: Plural nouns ending in – s
The hikers cars were parked at the base of the trail.

Solution: Use an apostrophe alone to form the possessive of a plural noun that ends in –s.
The hikers' cars were parked at the base of the trail.

Problem: Plural nouns not ending in –s
Did Brian join the mens group?

Solution: Use an apostrophe and –s to form the possessive of a plural noun that does not end in –s.
Did Brian join the men's group?

Problem: Pronouns
Everyones contribution helps.
These pencils are your's, and those pencils are their's.

Solution A: Use an apostrophe and –s to form the possessive of a singular indefinite pronoun.
Everyone's contribution helps.

Solution B: Do not use an apostrophe with any of the possessive personal pronouns.
These pencils are yours, and those pencils are theirs.

Problem: Confusion between *its* and *it's*
Will you tell me when its ten o'clock?
The cat licked it's fur.

Solution: Do not use an apostrophe to form the possessive of *it*. Use an apostrophe to form the contraction of *it is*.
Will you tell me when it's ten o'clock?
The cat licked its fur.

Missing Commas with Nonessential Element

Problem: Missing commas with nonessential participles, infinitives, and their phrases
Pounding hard on the roof the rain awakened me.
The whole set of cups chipped from many years of use was discarded.
To answer your question this software package is worth the price.

Solution: Determine whether the participle, infinitive, or phrase is essential to the meaning of the sentence. If it is not essential, set off the phrase with commas.
Pounding hard on the roof, the rain awakened me.
The whole set of cups, chipped from many years of use, was discarded.
To answer your question, this software package is worth the price.

Problem: Missing commas with nonessential adjective clauses
My mother who is a very generous woman gave us investment tips.

Solution: Determine whether the clause is essential to the meaning of the sentence. If it is not essential, set off the clause with commas.
My mother, who is a very generous woman, gave us investment tips.

Problem: Missing commas with nonessential appositives
John the lead-off batter singles on a line drive

Solution: Determine whether the appositive is essential to the meaning of the sentence. If it is not essential, set off the appositive with commas.
John, the lead-off batter, singled on a line drive.

Rule of Thumb: To determine whether a word or phrase is essential, try reading the sentence without it.

Problem: Missing commas with interjections and parenthetical expressions
Wow what a great cat that is
On Saturdays as a rule we sleep late.

Solution: Set off the interjection or parenthetical expression with commas.
Wow, what a great cat that is!
On Saturdays, as a rule, we sleep late.

Missing Commas in a Series

Problem: Missing commas in a series of words, phrases, or clauses
Alicia Nirupam and Matt made the honor roll.
Mark made the dough kneaded it and left it to rise
The firefighter carries the child out of the apartment down the stairs and into the arms of her mother.
Joe pitched the tent Meg gathered firewood and Bud unloaded the truck.

Solution: When there are three or more elements in a series, use a comma after each element that precedes the conjunction
Alicia, Nirupam, and Matt made the honor roll.
Mark made the dough, kneaded it, and left it to rise.
The firefighter carries the child out of the apartment, down the stairs, and into the arms of her mother.
Joe pitched the tent, Meg gathered firewood, and Bud unloaded the truck.

Rule of Thumb: When you're having difficulty with a rule of usage, try rewriting the rule in your own words. Then check with your teacher to be sure you have grasped the concept.

Mechanics

This section will help you use correct capitalization, punctuation, and abbreviations in your writing.

Capitalization

This section will help you recognize and use correct capitalization in sentences.

Rule: Capitalize the first word in any sentence, including direct quotations and sentences in parentheses unless they are included in another sentence.

Example: *She said, "Come back soon."*

Example: *Emily Dickinson became famous only after her death. (She published only six poems during her lifetime.)*

Rule: Always capitalize the pronoun *I* no matter where it appears in the sentence.

Example: *Some of my relatives think that I should become a doctor.*

Rule: Capitalize proper nouns, including

a. names of individuals and titles used in direct address preceding a name or describing a relationship.
Example: *George Washington; Dr. Morgan; Aunt Margaret*

b. names of ethnic groups, national groups, political parties and their members, and languages.
Example: *Italian Americans; Aztec; the Republican Party; a Democrat; Spanish*

c. names of organizations, institutions, firms, monuments, bridges, buildings, and other structures.
Example: *Red Cross; Stanford University; General Electric; Lincoln Memorial; Tappan Zee Bridge; Chrysler Building; Museum of Natural History*

d. trade names and names of documents, awards, and laws.
Example: *Microsoft; Declaration of Independence; Pulitzer Prize; Sixteenth Amendment*

e. geographical terms and regions or localities.
Example: *Hudson River; Pennsylvania Avenue; Grand Canyon; Texas; the Midwest*

f. names of planets and other heavenly bodies.
Example: *Venus; Earth; the Milky Way*

g. names of ships, planes, trains, and spacecraft.
Example: *USS Constitution; Spirit of St. Louis; Apollo 11*

h. names of most historical events, eras, calendar items, and religious names and items.
Example: *World War II; Age of Enlightenment; June; Christianity; Buddhists; Bible; Easter; God*

i. titles of literary works, works of art, and musical compositions.
Example: *"Why I Live at the P.O."; The Starry Night; Rhapsody in Blue*

j. names of specific school courses.
Example: *Advanced Physics; American History*

Rule: Capitalize proper adjectives (adjectives formed from proper nouns).

Example: *Christmas tree; Hanukkah candles; Freudian psychology; American flag*

Punctuation

This section will help you use these elements of punctuation correctly.

Rule: Use a period at the end of a declarative sentence or a polite command.

Example: *I'm thirsty.*
Example: *Please bring me a glass of water.*

Rule: Use an exclamation point to show strong feeling or after a forceful command.

Example: *I can't believe my eyes!*
Example: *Watch your step!*

Rule: Use a question mark to indicate a direct question.

Example: *Who is in charge here?*

Rule: Use a colon

a. to introduce a list (especially after words such as *these, the following,* or *as follows*) and to introduce material that explains, restates, or illustrates previous material.

Example: *The following states voted for the amendment: Texas, California, Georgia, and Florida.*
Example: *The sunset was colorful: purple, orange, and red lit up the sky.*

b. to introduce a long or formal quotation.
Example: *It was Mark Twain who stated the following proverb: "Man is the only animal that blushes. Or needs to."*

c. in precise time measurements, biblical chapter and verse references, and business letter salutations.
Example: 3:35 P.M.   7:50 A.M.
              Gen. 1:10–11   Matt. 2:23
              Dear Ms. Samuels: Dear Sir:

Rule: Use a semicolon

a. to separate main clauses that are not joined by a coordinating conjunction.
Example: *There were two speakers at Gettysburg that day; only Lincoln's speech is remembered.*

b. to separate main clauses joined by a conjunctive adverb or by *for example* or *that is*.
Example: *Because of the ice storm, most students could not get to school; consequently, the principal canceled all classes for the day.*

c. to separate the items in a series when these items contain commas.
Example: *The students at the rally came from Senn High School, in Chicago, Illinois; Niles Township High School, in Skokie, Illinois; and Evanston Township High School, in Evanston, Illinois.*

d. to separate two main clauses joined by a coordinating conjunction when such clauses already contain several commas.
Example: *The designer combined the blue silk, brown linen, and beige cotton into a suit; but she decided to use the yellow chiffon, yellow silk, and white lace for an evening gown.*

Rule: Use a comma

a. between the main clauses of a compound sentence.
Example: *Ryan was late getting to study hall, and his footsteps echoed in the empty corridor.*

b. to separate three or more words, phrases, or clauses in a series.
Example: *Mel bought carrots, beans, pears, and onions.*

c. between coordinate modifiers.
Example: *That is a lyrical, moving poem.*

d. to set off parenthetical expressions, interjections, and conjunctive adverbs.
Example: *Well, we missed the bus again.*
Example: *The weather is beautiful today; however, it is supposed to rain this weekend.*

e. to set off nonessential words, clauses, and phrases, such as:

—adverbial clauses

Example: *Since Ellen is so tall, the coach assumed she would be a good basketball player.*

—adjective clauses

Example: *Scott, who had been sleeping, finally woke up.*

—participles and participial phrases

Example: *Having found what he was looking for, he left.*

—prepositional phrases

Example: *On Saturdays during the fall, I rake leaves.*

—infinitive phrases

Example: *To be honest, I'd like to stay awhile longer.*

—appositives and appositive phrases

Example: *Ms. Kwan, a soft-spoken woman, ran into the street to hail a cab.*

f. to set off direct quotations.
Example: *"My concert," Molly replied, "is tonight."*

g. to set off an antithetical phrase.
Example: *Unlike Tom, Rob enjoys skiing.*

h. to set off a title after a person's name.
Example: *Margaret Thomas, Ph.D., was the guest speaker.*

i. to separate the various parts of an address, a geographical term, or a date.
Example: *My new address is 324 Indian School Road, Albuquerque, New Mexico 85350.*
        I moved on March 13, 1998.

j. after the salutation of an informal letter and after the closing of all letters.
Example: *Dear Helen,   Sincerely,*

k. to set off parts of a reference that direct the reader to the exact source.
Example: *You can find the article in the* Washington Post, *April 4, 1997, pages 33–34.*

Language Handbook

l. to set off words or names used in direct address and in tag questions.
Example: *Yuri, will you bring me my calculator?*
Lottie became a lawyer, didn't she?

Rule: Use a dash to signal a change in thought or to emphasize parenthetical material.
Example: *During the play, Maureen—and she'd be the first to admit it—forgot her lines.*
Example: *There are only two juniors attending—Mike Ramos and Ron Kim.*

Rule: Use parentheses to set off supplemental material. Punctuate within the parentheses only if the punctuation is part of the parenthetical expression.
Example: *If you like jazz (and I assume you do), you will like this CD. (The soloist is Miles Davis.)*
Example: *The upper Midwest (which states does that include?) was hit by terrible floods last year.*

Rule: Use brackets to enclose information that you insert into a quotation for clarity or to enclose a parenthetical phrase that already appears within parentheses.
Example: *"He serves his [political] party best who serves the country best."—Rutherford B. Hayes*
Example: *The staircase (which was designed by a famous architect [Frank Lloyd Wright]) was inlaid with ceramic tile.*

Rule: Use ellipsis points to indicate the omission of material from a quotation.
Example: *". . . Neither an individual nor a nation can commit the least act of injustice against the obscurest individual. . . ." —Henry David Thoreau*

Rule: Use quotation marks
a. to enclose a direct quotation, as follows:
Example: *"Hurry up!" shouted Lisa.*

When a quotation is interrupted, use two sets of quotation marks.
Example: *"A cynic," wrote Oscar Wilde, "is someone who knows the price of everything and the value of nothing."*

Use single quotation marks for a quotation within a quotation.
Example: *"Did you say 'turn left' or 'turn right'?" asked Leon.*

In writing dialogue, begin a new paragraph and use a new set of quotation marks every time the speaker changes.
Example: *"Do you really think the spaceship can take off?" asked the first officer.*
"Our engineer assures me that we have enough power," the captain replied.

b. to enclose titles of short works, such as stories, poems, essays, articles, chapters, and songs.
Example: *"The Lottery" [short story]*
"Provide, Provide" [poem]
"Civil Disobedience" [essay]

c. to enclose unfamiliar slang terms and unusual expressions.
Example: *The man called his grandson a "rapscallion."*

d. to enclose a definition that is stated directly.
Example: *Gauche is a French word meaning "left."*

Rule: Use italics
a. for titles of books, lengthy poems, plays, films, television series, paintings and sculptures, long musical compositions, court cases, names of newspapers and magazines, ships, trains, airplanes, and spacecraft. Italicize and capitalize articles *(a, an, the)* at the beginning of a title only when they are part of the title.
Example: *E.T. [film];* The Piano Lesson *[play]*
The Starry Night [painting]
the New Yorker *[magazine]*
Challenger [spacecraft]
The Great Gatsby [book]
the Chicago Tribune *[newspaper]*

b. for foreign words and expressions that are not used frequently in English.
Example: *Luciano waved good-bye, saying, "Arrivederci."*

c. for words, letters, and numerals used to represent themselves.
Example: *There is no Q on the telephone keypad.*
Example: *Number your paper from 1 through 10.*

Rule: Use an apostrophe

a. for a possessive form, as follows:

Add an apostrophe and *s* to all singular nouns, plural nouns not ending in *s*, singular indefinite pronouns, and compound nouns. Add only an apostrophe to a plural noun that ends in *s*.

Example: *the tree's leaves*
the man's belt
the bus's tires
the children's pets
everyone's favorite
my mother-in-law's job
the attorney general's decision
the baseball player's error
the cats' bowls

If two or more persons possess something jointly, use the possessive form for the last person named. If they possess it individually, use the possessive form for each one's name.

Example: *Ted and Harriet's family*
Ted's and Harriet's bosses
Lewis and Clark's expedition
Lewis's and Clark's clothes

b. to express amounts of money or time that modify a noun.

Example: *two cents' worth*

Example: *three days' drive* (You can use a hyphenated adjective instead: *a three-day drive.*)

c. in place of omitted letters or numerals.

Example: *haven't [have not]   the winter of '95*

d. to form the plural of letters, numerals, symbols, and words used to represent themselves. Use an apostrophe and *s*.

Example: *You wrote two 5's instead of one.*
Example: *How many s's are there in Mississippi?*
Example: *Why did he use three !'s at the end of the sentence?*

Rule: Use a hyphen

a. after any prefix joined to a proper noun or proper adjective.

Example: *all-American   pre-Columbian*

b. after the prefixes *all-, ex-,* and *self-* joined to any noun or adjective, after the prefix *anti-* when it joins a word beginning with *i,* after the prefix *vice-* (except in some instances such as *vice president*), and to avoid confusion between words that begin with *re-* and look like another word.

Example: *ex-president*
self-important
anti-inflammatory
vice-principal
re-creation of the event
recreation time
re-pair the socks
repair the computer

c. in a compound adjective that precedes a noun.
Example: *a bitter-tasting liquid*

d. in any spelled-out cardinal or ordinal numbers up to *ninety-nine* or *ninety-ninth,* and with a fraction used as an adjective.

Example: *twenty-three   eighty-fifth*
one-half cup

e. to divide a word at the end of a line between syllables.

Example: *air-port   scis-sors*
fill-ing   fin-est

Abbreviations

Abbreviations are shortened forms of words.

Rule: Use only one period if an abbreviation occurs at the end of a sentence. If the sentence ends with a question mark or an exclamation point, use the period and the second mark of punctuation.

Example: *We didn't get home until 3:30 A.M.*
Example: *Did you get home before 4:00 A.M.?*
Example: *I can't believe you didn't get home until 3:30 A.M.!*

Rule: Capitalize abbreviations of proper nouns and abbreviations related to historical dates.

Example: *John Kennedy Jr.   P.O. Box 333*
800 B.C.   A.D. 456   1066 C.E.

Use all capital letters and no periods for most abbreviations of organizations and government agencies.

Example: *CBS   CIA   PIN*
CPA   IBM   NFL
MADD   GE   FBI

Spelling

The following basic rules, examples, and exceptions will help you master the spellings of many words.

Forming plurals

English words form plurals in many ways. Most nouns simply add *s*. The following chart shows other ways of forming plural nouns and some common exceptions to the pattern.

General Rules for Forming Plurals		
if the word ends in	**Rule**	**Example**
ch, s, sh, x, z	add *es*	glass, glasses
a consonant + *y*	change *y* to *i* and add *es*	caddy, caddies
a vowel + *y* or *o*	add only *s*	cameo, cameos monkey, monkeys
a consonant + *o* common exceptions	generally add *es* but sometimes add only *s*	potato, potatoes cello, cellos
f or *ff* common exceptions	add *s* change *f* to *v* and add *es*	cliff, cliffs hoof, hooves
lf	change *f* to *v* and add *es*	half, halves

A few plurals are exceptions to the rules in the previous chart, but they are easy to remember. The following chart lists these plurals and some examples.

Special Rules for Forming Plurals	
Rule	**Example**
To form the plural of most proper names and one-word compound nouns, follow the general rules for plurals.	Cruz, Cruzes Mancuso, Mancusos crossroad, crossroads
To form the plural of hyphenated compound nouns or compound nouns of more than one word, make the most important word plural.	sister-in-law, sisters-in-law motion picture, motion pictures
Some nouns have unusual plural forms.	goose, geese child, children
Some nouns have the same singular and plural forms.	moose scissors pants

LANGUAGE HANDBOOK R57

Adding prefixes

When adding a prefix to a word, keep the original spelling of the word. Use a hyphen only when the original word is capitalized or with prefixes such as *all-*, *ex-*, and *self-* joined to a noun or adjective.

   co + operative = cooperative
   inter + change = interchange
   pro + African = pro-African
   ex + partner = ex-partner

Suffixes and the silent *e*

Many English words end in a silent letter *e*. Sometimes the *e* is dropped when a suffix is added. When adding a suffix that begins with a consonant to a word that ends in silent *e*, keep the *e*.

   like + ness = likeness   sure + ly = surely
   COMMON EXCEPTIONS awe + ful = awful;
   judge + ment = judgment

When adding a suffix that begins with a vowel to a word that ends in silent *e*, usually drop the *e*.

   believe + able = believable
   expense + ive = expensive
   COMMON EXCEPTION mile + age = mileage

When adding a suffix that begins with *a* or *o* to a word that ends in *ce* or *ge*, keep the *e* so the word will retain the soft *c* or *g* sound.

   notice + able = noticeable
   courage + ous = courageous

When adding a suffix that begins with a vowel to a word that ends in *ee* or *oe*, keep the final *e*.

   see + ing = seeing   toe + ing = toeing

Drop the final silent *e* after the letters *u* or *w*.

   argue + ment = argument
   owe + ing = owing

Keep the final silent *e* before the suffix *-ing* when necessary to avoid ambiguity.

   singe + ing = singeing

Suffixes and the final *y*

When adding a suffix to a word that ends in a consonant + *y*, change the *y* to *i* unless the suffix begins with *i*. Keep the *y* in a word that ends in a vowel + *y*.

   try + ed = tried   fry + ed = fried
   stay + ing = staying   display + ed = displayed
   copy + ing = copying joy + ous = joyous

Adding *ly* and *ness*

When adding *ly* to a word that ends in a single *l*, keep the *l*, but when the word ends in a double *l*, drop one *l*. When the word ends in a consonant + *le*, drop the *le*. When adding *-ness* to a word that ends in *n*, keep the *n*.

   casual + ly = casually
   practical + ly = practically
   dull + ly = dully
   probable + ly = probably
   open + ness = openness
   mean + ness = meanness

Doubling the final consonant

Double the final consonant in words that end in a consonant preceded by a single vowel if the word is one syllable, if it has an accent on the last syllable that remains there even after the suffix is added, or if it is a word made up of a prefix and a one-syllable word.

   stop + ing = stopping
   admit + ed = admitted
   replan + ed = replanned

Do not double the final consonant if the accent is not on the last syllable, or if the accent shifts when the suffix is added. Also do not double the final consonant if the final consonant is *x* or *w*. If the word ends in a consonant and the suffix begins with a consonant, do not double the final consonant.

   benefit + ed = benefited
   similar + ly = similarly
   raw + er = rawer
   box + like = boxlike
   friend + less = friendless
   rest + ful = restful

Forming Compound Words

When joining a word that ends in a consonant to a word that begins with a consonant, keep both consonants.

> out + line = outline
> after + noon = afternoon
> post + card = postcard
> pepper + mint = peppermint

ie and *ei*

Learning this rhyme can save you many misspellings: "Write *i* before *e* except after *c,* or when sounded like *a* as in *neighbor* and *weigh.*" There are many exceptions to this rule, including *seize, seizure, leisure, weird, height, either, neither, forfeit.*

-cede, -ceed, and *-sede*

Because of the relatively few words with *sēd* sounds, these words are worth memorizing.

> These words use *-cede:* **accede, precede, secede.**
> One word uses *-sede:* **supersede.**
> Three words use *-ceed:* **exceed, proceed, succeed.**

Logic and Persuasion Handbook

Persuasion

Propositions
One of the main reasons people write and talk is to persuade each other. Persuasive writing and speaking attempts to convince someone of the truth of a **proposition,** that is, a statement or claim. There are four basic types of proposition:

- A proposition of **fact** is a claim that certain information is correct.
  Candidate Wilkins comes from Illinois.
- A proposition of **value** is a statement that a feeling or judgment is valid.
  Candidate Wilkins is a friendly woman.
- A proposition about a **problem** combines fact and judgment.
  Candidate Wilkins is not qualified to run.
- A proposition of **policy** is a claim that someone should do something.
  Everyone should vote for candidate Wilkins.

A proposition may be **true** or **false.** In evaluating persuasive speaking and writing, you need to know which type of proposition is being made so that you can decide whether it is true or false.

Evidence and Arguments
Persuasive writing and speaking usually includes **evidence,** that is, reasons why someone should accept a proposition. Together, a proposition and a reason for accepting it make up an **argument.**

Everyone should vote for candidate Wilkins, because she is the most qualified.

An argument may be **valid** or **invalid,** that is, reasonable or unreasonable.

Appeals
Arguments are meant to appeal to certain beliefs, values, or feelings belonging to the reader or listener. Most reasons given in support of a proposition make at least one of four types of **appeal:**

- An **appeal to logic** is a claim based on fact and reason.
  Wilkins is unqualified, because she does not meet the age requirement.
- An **appeal to ethics or values** is a claim based on shared values or judgments.
  Wilkins is best, because she is the most honest and caring.
- An **appeal to authority** is a claim based on sources believed to be reliable.
  Wilkins is best, because the Metropolitan Bar Association supports her.
- An **appeal to emotion** is a claim based on shared feelings.
  Wilkins is best, because she has overcome hardship.

In evaluating arguments, you need to know which type of appeal is being made so that you can decide whether it is valid or invalid. Note that an argument may involve more than one type of appeal.

Exercise: Analyzing an Argument
Read the following statements. For each statement, identify the type of proposition made and the type of appeal used to support it..

1. If we want clean beaches, then we need to provide trash cans and arrange for garbage removal in the summer.
2. It is our responsibility as human beings to keep ocean ecosystems healthy by polluting them as little as possible or not at all.
3. According to eminent marine biologists, we have a lot to learn about the animals that live in the ocean depths.
4. Restricting owners of beachfront property from building wherever they want to on their property is highly unfair.

Statement	Proposition	Appeal
1	about a problem	
2		
3		
4		to ethics or values

Logic

Inductive Reasoning

Inductive reasoning involves putting facts together to come up with a generalized statement as a conclusion.

Specific facts:

Fact 1. *Star Wars* is the second-biggest money maker of all time.

Fact 2. The number one movie at the box office in 2004 was *Shrek 2*.

Fact 3. *Spider-man* broke many box office records in 2002.

Generalization: Science fiction and fantasy films do very well at the box office.

Errors In Inductive Reasoning

To avoid errors in inductive reasoning, be sure you use a large enough sample of specific facts, and of course, make sure your facts are accurate. Assuming you have a large enough sample of accurate facts, make sure that your generalization is logical.

For example, it would be illogical to conclude from the facts above that movies whose titles begin with the letter *S* do well at the box office.

Deductive Reasoning

Deductive reasoning is essentially the opposite of inductive reasoning. With deductive reasoning you start with a generalization to come to a conclusion about a specific case.

Generalization: Paul can only eat vegetarian food.
Specific fact: The Glory Diner offers vegetarian food.
Conclusion: Paul can eat at the Glory Diner.

Syllogisms

A syllogism is a formal statement of a deductive argument. It consists of a **major premise,** or general statement; a **minor premise,** or related fact; and a **conclusion** based on the two.

Major premise: People who travel between countries need a passport.
Minor premise: Jody is flying from the United States to Spain.
Conclusion: Jody needs a passport.

Errors In Deductive Reasoning

Errors in deductive reasoning result from faulty construction of the argument. Make sure the major premise is a universal statement, that both premises are true, and that the conclusion follows logically from the premises.

Note: A syllogism is *valid* if it follows the rules of deductive reasoning. A syllogism is *true* if the statements are factually accurate. Therefore, a perfectly valid syllogism can be untrue. For example:

Major premise: All voters are good citizens. [There is more to good citizenship than voting.]
Minor premise: My parents are voters.
Conclusion: Therefore, my parents are good citizens.

This conclusion is valid according to the premises; however, it isn't necessarily true because the major premise is flawed.

Exercise: Analyzing Logical Reasoning

For each argument below, identify whether inductive or deductive reasoning is used. Evaluate whether the conclusion is valid or invalid and explain your evaluation.

1. An epic poem is a serious, long narrative poem centered on the life of a cultural or national hero or heroine. *El Cid* is an epic poem. In more than 30,000 lines, it celebrates the life and accomplishments of a Spanish military and political leader who lived in the eleventh century.

2. If a computer can play compact discs, the computer must have been built before 1985. This computer can play CDs. This computer must have been built before 1985.

3. Many humorists use puns. Mark Twain used puns in his writing and his speeches. Ogden Nash used puns in his poems. Woody Allen uses puns in his movies.

Exercise: Using Logical Reasoning

Write a short essay arguing a proposition. In your argument, use at least two examples each of valid inductive and deductive reasoning.

Logical Fallacies

A **logical fallacy** is a particular type of faulty reasoning. Fallacies often seem reasonable at face value, so they are often used, both intentionally and unintentionally. Some fallacies are so common that they have names.

To identify fallacies in the writing and speaking of others and to avoid it in your own persuasive communication, you need to be able to identify fallacies and to understand why they are illogical.

- **Ad Hominem**

  Don't listen to what Smyth says about the election; he spent time in prison.

  An ad hominem argument (literally, an argument "against the person") implies that a defect in a person's character or behavior is evidence that what he says is unreliable. Note that the ad hominem fallacy contains a hidden premise: *People who have spent time in prison cannot have valid opinions.* Because this premise is untrue, the argument about Smyth is untrue also.

- **Non Sequitur or False Causality**

  This shirt is unlucky: every time I wear it, something bad happens.

  Non sequitur literally means "it doesn't follow." Just because two events occur together, it doesn't follow logically that one caused the other.

- **Glittering Generalities**

  If you love freedom, vote for Jack.

  Glittering generalities are words with overwhelmingly positive connotations, used to make it seem impossible to disagree with an idea. How can you argue against the idea of freedom? A listener's initial reaction to this statement might be, "Freedom is a good thing, so I must vote for Jack."

- **Overgeneralization and Stereotype**

  Tall people make excellent basketball players.

  An overgeneralization is any conclusion that may be accurate about a small group, but is inaccurate when applied to a much larger group. An overgeneralization about a group of people is called a stereotype.

- **Argument from Authority and Celebrity Endorsement**

  Four out of five doctors recommend Pumpidox for most heart conditions.

  Argument from authority is the quoting of an alleged expert on a certain topic. As a logical fallacy, arguments from authority rely solely on the mention of the word "expert," and give no clear facts from the expert. Companies often hire celebrities to appear in commercials for their products in the hope that audiences will respond to the likability of the famous person, even if that person has no real expert knowledge about the product.

- **The Bandwagon Effect**

  Choose America's favorite toothpaste!

  The term "jumping on the bandwagon" means doing or thinking something because everyone else is doing it or thinking it. This type of reasoning provides no evidence to support a decision or viewpoint.

- **Card Stacking**

  Senator Porter voted against childcare laws and recycling programs. It's time for new leadership!

  Card stacking involves piling on evidence that supports one side of an argument while ignoring or suppressing valid evidence supporting the other side. Saying that a politician voted against positive-sounding programs does not mean that he or she didn't have good reason to, or that the opposition has a better record.

Logic and Persuasion Handbook

Ethical Reasoning and Propaganda

Propaganda
Propaganda is the process of persuading by deliberately misleading or confusing an audience. Through the use of combinations of logical fallacies, propaganda can appeal to ethics or values, authority, or emotion, but they do so in a way that is unsupported or inappropriate.

Political propaganda
A vote for Marmelard is a vote for the enemy!
America: You're with us or against us!

Advertising
Be the best parent you can be: Serve your kids Super Goody cereal.
The most successful people shop at Blorland's Department Store.

Ethical Reasoning
Reasoning that persuades by helping its intended audience make informed decisions is called **ethical reasoning.** As a writer or speaker, you have the responsibility to use ethical reasoning and avoid propaganda. This means that you must gather complete information about a topic, check your facts for accuracy, and make sure that your reasoning includes no errors in logic or false conclusions. You should address opposing evidence with clear and accurate argumentation. Using ethical reasoning in your persuasive writing or speeches will strengthen your positions as your audience sees that you have logically addressed all sides of an idea.

Identifying Unethical Persuasive Techniques
The following essay contains several examples of faulty reasoning. Read through the entire text once, then go back and look for logical fallacies, invalid arguments, and manipulative appeals. For each example you find, make an entry in a chart like the one shown. Then write a paragraph evaluating the essay's argument.

Passage	Type(s) of Appeals	Why Invalid
"Principal Spaly"	Appeal to logic	Card stacking

Don't Take Away Our Freedom
The school board recently announced plans to remove all vending machines from our schools' cafeterias. They say that candy, snacks, and cola are bad for students. But is starvation good for students? Is taking away freedom to choose good for students?

Every expert on nutrition agrees that it is not healthy for kids to go for hours between meals without some sort of snack in between to tide them over. If the school board has its way, students will be passing out at their desks from hunger and dehydration. Principal Spaly claims that students are more likely to pass out from a "sugar crash." This is the same Principal Spaly who recently showed what he thought of students when he denied sophomores the right to park at the high school.

We are taught in these very schools that America is a land of democracy, freedom, and liberty. It is clear that the school board has forgotten this. Any student who loves his or her school will write to the school board and let them know how we feel.

Glossary/Glosario

This glossary lists the vocabulary words found in the selections in this book. The definition given is for the word as it is used in the selection; you may wish to consult a dictionary for other meanings of these words. The key below is a guide to the pronunciation symbols used in each entry.

Pronunciation Key

a	**a**t	ō	h**o**pe	ng	si**ng**	
ā	**a**pe	ô	f**o**rk, **a**ll	th	**th**in	
ä	f**a**ther	oo	w**oo**d, p**u**t	<u>th</u>	**th**is	
e	**e**nd	o͞o	f**oo**l	zh	trea**s**ure	
ē	m**e**	oi	**oi**l	ə	**a**go, tak**e**n, penc**i**l,
i	**i**t	ou	**ou**t		lem**o**n, circ**u**s
ī	**i**ce	u	**u**p	´	indicates primary stress
o	h**o**t	ū	**u**se	ˌ	indicates secondary

English

A

abashed (ə basht´) *adj.* self-conscious; embarrassed or ashamed **p. 906**

absolve (ab zolv´) *v.* to free from blame **p. 691**

abstraction (ab strak´ shən) *n.* theoretical concept isolated from real application **p. 445**

accord (ə kôrd´) *n.* agreement; conformity **p. 1078**

admonish (ad mon´ish) *v.* to warn, as against a specific action **p. 309**

advocate (ad´ və kāt´) *v.* to publicly support **p. 360**

affirmation (af ər mā´ shən) *n.* positive agreement or judgment **p. 566**

agenda (ə jen´ də) *n.* an outline of tasks to be accomplished **p. 408**

aggrieved (ə grēvd´) *adj.* disturbed; upset **p. 960**

aglow (ə glō´) *adj.* glowing **p. 570**

Español

A

abashed/avergonzado *adj.* vergonzoso; abochornado o que siente vergüenza **p. 906**

absolve/absolver *v.* liberar de culpa **p. 691**

abstraction/abstracción *s.* concepto teórico a aislado de la aplicación real **p. 445**

accord/acuerdo *s.* convenio; conformidad **p. 1078**

admonish/amonestar *v.* advertir, en oposición a una acción específica **p. 309**

advocate/abogar *v.* apoyar públicamente **p. 360**

affirmation/afirmación *s.* expresión u opinión positiva **p. 566**

agenda/agenda *s.* un esquema general de las actividades que se han de realizar **p. 408**

aggrieved/agraviado *adj.* alterado; disgustado **p. 960**

aglow/radiante *adj.* resplandeciente **p. 570**

albeit (ôl bē′ it) *conj.* although; even if p. 175

alleviate (ə lē′vē āt′) *v.* to make easier to bear; relieve; lessen p. 294

amenable (ə mē′ nə bəl) *adj.* responsive; able to be controlled p. 66

amicable (am′ə kə bəl) *adj.* friendly p. 1101

animosity (an′ə mos′ə tē) *n.* ill will or resentment; active strong dislike or hostility p. 1110

anteroom (an′tē rōōm) *n.* a small room serving as a waiting area or an entrance to a larger, main room p. 1049

aristocracy (ar′is tok′rə sē) *n.* a type of government in which a minority of upper-class individuals rule p. 397

arrogance (ar′ ə gəns) *n.* overbearing pride p. 683

arrogant (ar′ ə gənt) *adj.* full of self-importance; haughty p. 150

arroyo (ə roi′ ō) *n.* a dry gully or stream bed p. 248

artisan (är′ tə zən) *n.* a skilled craftsman p. 332

ascertaining (as′ər tan′ ing) *v.* finding out definitely p. 125

attain (ə tān′) *v.* to accomplish; to arrive at p. 812

attribute (at′rə būt′) *n.* a quality or characteristic of a person or thing p. 379

austere (ôs tēr′) *adj.* without ornament, very simple p. 127

austere (ôs tēr′) *adj.* stern; severe in appearance p. 478

B

bade (bād) *v.* past tense of bid, to command, order, or ask p. 1043

barren (bar′ən) *adj.* empty and dreary; without life; desolate p. 786

belie (bi lī′) *v.* to misrepresent; to give a false impression of p. 334

benevolence (bə nev′ ə ləns) *n.* kindness; generosity p. 371

---

albeit/aunque *conj.* si bien, aun cuando p. 175

alleviate/aliviar *v.* hacer más fácil de soportar; atenuar; aminorar p. 294

amenable/dócil *adj.* receptivo; que se puede controlar p. 66

amicable/amigable *adj.* amistoso p. 1101

animosity/animosidad *s.* malevolencia o resentimiento; aversión potente u hostilidad p. 1110

anteroom/antesala *s.* sala pequeña que sirve de lugar de espera o entrada a una sala principal más grande p. 1049

aristocracy/aristocracia *s.* tipo de gobierno en el que gobierna una minoría de individuos de clase alta p. 397

arrogance/arrogancia *s.* orgullo dominante p. 683

arrogant/arrogante *adj.* engreído; altanero p. 150

arroyo/arroyo *s.* lecho de agua u hondonada con poco caudal p. 248

artisan/artesano *s.* trabajador manual habilidoso p. 332

ascertaining/constatar *v.* averiguar en forma definitiva p. 125

attain/alcanzar *v.* lograr; llegar a p. 812

attribute/atributo *s.* calidad o característica de alguien o algo p. 379

austere/austero *adj.* sin decoración, muy sencillo p. 127

austere/austero *adj.* riguroso; severo en apariencia p. 478

B

bade/pidió *v.* tiempo pasado de pedir; ordenar, requerir o solicitar p. 1043

barren/yermo *adj.* vacío y lúgubre; sin vida; desolado p. 786

belie/distorsionar *v.* tergiversar; dar una impresión falsa p. 334

benevolence/benevolencia *s.* amabilidad; generosidad p. 371

beseeching (bi sēch′ ing) *adj.* begging; asking earnestly **p. 206**

blasphemous (blas′ fə məs) *adj.* showing disrespect or scorn for God or anything sacred **p. 80**

bloated (blō′ tid) *adj.* puffed up; swollen **p. 1090**

boding (bōd′ ing) *n.* a warning or indication, especially of evil **p. 24**

bough (bou) *n.* a tree branch **p. 601**

bureau (byoor′ ō) *n.* a chest of drawers for the bedroom **p. 483**

C

ceremonious (ser′ ə mō′ nē əs) *adj.* carefully observant of the formal acts required by ritual, custom, or etiquette **p. 536**

chaos (kā′ os) *n.* a state of disorder and confusion **p. 507**

china (chī′ nə) *n.* fine, glossy pottery used for tableware **p. 570**

chronic (kron′ ik) *adj.* persistent; ongoing, especially of sickness or pain **p. 478**

cipher (sī′ fər) *n.* a signifying figure; a number or symbol **p. 512**

commandeer (kom′ ən dēr′) *v.* to seize for use by the military or government **p. 66**

commend (kə mend′) *v.* to speak highly of; to praise **p. 745**

commodious (kə mō′ dē əs) *adj.* having or containing ample room; spacious **p. 324**

compassionate (kəm pash′ ə nit) *adj.* having or showing sympathy for another's misfortune, combined with a desire to help **p. 409**

comprehensive (kom′ pri hen′ siv) *adj.* including nearly everything; large in scope; complete **p. 672**

confidante (kon′ fə dant′) *n.* a person who is entrusted with secrets or private affairs **p. 946**

---

beseeching/suplicante *adj.* que ruega o pide seriamente **p. 206**

blasphemous/blasfemo *adj.* que muestra una falta de respeto o desdén por Dios o algo sagrado **p. 80**

bloated/abotagado *adj.* inflamado; hinchado **p. 1090**

boding/presagio *n.* aviso o indicación, especialmente de algo malo **p. 24**

bough/rama *s.* cada una de las partes que nacen del tronco del árbol **p. 601**

bureau/cómoda *s.* mueble con cajones que se usa en el dormitorio **p. 483**

C

ceremonious/ceremonioso *adj.* que observa atentamente las formalidades requeridas por un ritual, una costumbre o el protocolo **p. 536**

chaos/caos *s.* estado de confusión y desorden **p. 507**

china/vajilla *s.* conjunto de platos, tazas y otros recipientes finos y relucientes utilizados para el servicio de mesa **p. 570**

chronic/crónico *adj.* persistente; continuo, especialmente una enfermedad o un dolor **p. 478**

cipher/cifra *s.* un guarismo significativo; un número o símbolo **p. 512**

commandeer/usurpar *v.* tomar para uso por el ejército o el gobierno **p. 66**

commend/elogiar *v.* hablar muy bien de alguien o algo; alabar **p. 745**

commodious/cómodo *adj.* que tiene espacio amplio; espacioso **p. 324**

compassionate/compasivo *adj.* que tiene o muestra compasión por el infortunio ajeno, combinado con un deseo de ayudar **p. 409**

comprehensive/exhaustivo *adj.* que incluye casi todo; amplio en alcance; completo **p. 672**

confidante/confidente *s.* persona a la que se le confían secretos o asuntos personales **p. 946**

confinement (kən fīn´mənt) *n.* the state of being constricted or confined **p. 972**

conflagration (kon´flə grā´shən) *n.* a huge fire **p. 513**

confront (kən frunt´) *v.* to come face-to-face with; to oppose **p. 984**

conscientiously (kon´ shē en´ shəs lē) *adv.* thoughtfully and carefully **p. 201**

contemptible (kən temp´ tə bəl) *adj.* worthy of contempt; loathsome; **p. 971**

contend (kən tend´) *v.* to declare or maintain as a fact; argue **p. 108**

contrition (kən trish´ ən) *n.* sorrow for one's sin or wrongdoing; repentance **p. 201**

convivial (kən viv´ē əl) *adj.* fond of merriment and parties with good company; sociable **p. 325**

convoluted (kon´və lōō´ tid) *adj.* turned in or wound up upon itself; coiled; twisted **p. 37**

correlate (kôr´ə lāt) *v.* to bring (one thing) into relation (with another thing); calculate **p. 1030**

coterie (ko´tə rē) *n.* a small group of people who share a particular interest and often meet socially **p. 309**

countenance (koun´ tə nəns) *n.* the face **p. 77**

covert (kō´vərt) *adj.* secret; hidden **p. 786**

credence (krēd´əns) *n.* trustworthiness, especially in the reports or statements of others **p. 313**

crest (krest) *n.* a peak, high point, or climax **p. 566**

crevice (krev´ is) *n.* a narrow crack into or through something **p. 251**

cultivate (kul´ tə vāt´) *v.* to encourage or further the development of **p. 1097**

D

debasement (di bās´mənt) *n.* the state of being lowered in quality, value, or character; degradation **p. 379**

decapitate (di kap´ə tāt´) *v.* to cut off the head of **p. 223**

confinement/confinamiento *s.* el estado de estar restringido o confinado **p. 972**

conflagration/conflagración *s.* un gran incendio **p. 513**

confront/confrontar *v.* enfrentar cara a cara; oponerse **p. 984**

conscientiously/concienzudamente *adv.* cuidadosamente y reflexivamente **p. 201**

contemptible/despreciable *adj.* digno de desprecio; aborrecible **p. 971**

contend/contender *v.* declarar o mantener como un hecho; discutir **p. 108**

contrition/contrición *s.* pena por los pecados o las malas acciones propias; arrepentimiento **p. 201**

convivial/convival *adj.* que le gusta la alegría y las fiestas con buena compañía; sociable **p. 325**

convoluted/retorcido *adj.* trenzado; arrollado, en espiral; enroscado **p. 37**

correlate/correlacionar *v.* poner algo en relación con otra cosa; calcular **p. 1030**

coterie/camarilla *s.* grupo pequeño de personas que comparten un interés particular y a menudo se reúnen socialmente **p. 309**

countenance/semblante *s.* el rostro **p. 77**

covert/encubierto *adj.* secreto; oculto **p. 786**

credence/crédito *s.* fiabilidad, especialmente en informes o declaraciones de otros **p. 313**

crest/cresta *s.* pico, punto elevado o clímax **p. 566**

crevice/hendedura *s.* una grieta angosta en o a través algo **p. 251**

cultivate/cultivar *v.* auspiciar o fomentar el desarrollo **p. 1097**

D

debasement/degradación *s.* estado de ser disminuido en calidad, valor, o carácter **p. 379**

decapitate/decapitar *v.* cortar la cabeza **p. 223**

deceitful (di sēt′fəl) *adj.* untruthful and cunning; false p. 787

decrepit (di krep′ it) *adj.* broken down by long use or old age p. 149

deference (def′ər əns) *n.* respect and honor due to another p. 686

deferred (di furd′) *adj.* put off, postponed p. 620

defile (di fīl′) *v.* to spoil the purity of; to make dirty or unclean p. 698

deflect (di flekt′) *v.* to cause to turn aside; to bend or deviate p. 445

deliberation (di lib′ə rā′shən) *n.* an official meeting or consultation p. 963

dense (dens) *adj.* thick p. 556

designation (dez′ig nā′shən) *n.* a distinguishing name or mark p. 292

dilution (di lōō′ shən) *n.* something weakened by the presence of another element p. 422

disconsolate (dis kon′sə lit) *adj.* dejected; mournful; unable to be comforted p. 807

discordant (dis kôrd′ənt) *adj.* not in agreement or harmony p. 94

disdainful (dis dān′fəl) *adj.* scornful; mocking p. 960

disgruntled (dis grun′tld) *adj.* in a state of sulky dissatisfaction p. 527

dismantle (dis mant′əl) *v.* to take apart p. 1077

disperse (dis purs′) *v.* to break up and send in different directions; to scatter p. 747

dissension (di sen′shən) *n.* disagreement within a group p. 397

distortion (dis tôr′ shən) *n.* an appearance of being twisted or bent out of shape p. 255

doctrine (dok′ trin) *n.* a particular principle or position that is taught or supported, as of a religion p. 193

domestic (də mes′ tik) *adj.* relating to one's own country p. 396

dominion (də min′ yən) *n.* control or the exercise of control p. 444

duly (dōō′ lē) *adv.* rightfully; suitably p. 12

deceitful/engañoso *adj.* falso y astuto; falaz p. 787

decrepit/decrépito *adj.* arruinado por el uso prolongado o la edad p. 149

deference/deferencia *s.* respeto y honor hacia alguien p. 686

deferred/diferido *adj.* aplazado; pospuesto p. 620

defile/manchar *v.* estropear la pureza; ensuciar p. 698

deflect/desviar *v.* apartar; doblar p. 445

deliberation/deliberación *s.* una reunión o consulta oficial p. 963

dense/denso *adj.* espeso p. 556

designation/designación *s.* denominación p. 292

dilution/dilución *s.* algo debilitado por la presencia de otro elemento p. 422

disconsolate/desconsolado *adj.* afligido; acongojado; que no tiene consuelo p. 807

discordant/discordante *adj.* que no tiene concordancia o no está en armonía p. 94

disdainful/desdeñoso *adj.* despreciativo; burlón p. 960

disgruntled/descontento *adj.* en estado de insatisfacción p. 527

dismantle/desmantelar *v.* desarmar p. 1077

disperse/dispersar *v.* separar y repartir en distintas direcciones; desperdigar p. 747

dissension/disensión *s.* desacuerdo dentro de un grupo p. 397

distortion/distorsión *s.* apariencia de estar torcido o con otra forma p. 255

doctrine/doctrina *s.* un principio o una posición particular que es enseñada o mantenida, como la de una religión p. 193

domestic/doméstico *adj.* relacionado al país propio p. 396

dominion/dominio *s.* control o ejercicio del control p. 444

duly/debidamente *adv.* justamente; apropiadamente p. 12

Glossary/Glosario

dupe (dōōp) *v.* to fool; to trick **p. 1091**

dutiful (dōō′ ti fəl) *adj.* acting out of a sense of obligation or a sense of what is required **p. 1062**

E

edifice (ed′ ə fis) *n.* a building, especially a large, important-looking one **p. 67**

elation (i lā′shən) *n.* a feeling of great joy; ecstasy **p. 377**

elude (i lōōd′) *v.* to avoid or escape, especially through cleverness or quickness **p. 945**

emanate (em′ə nāt′) *v.* to come or set forth, as from a source **p. 445**

emancipation (i man′sə pā′shən) *n.* the process of becoming free from control or the power of another **p. 434**

embroidered (em broi′dərd) *adj.* decorated with needlework **p. 550**

endear (en dēr′) *v.* to cause to adore or admire **p. 972**

enhance (en hans′) *v.* to make greater, as in beauty or value **p. 56**

enterprise (en′ tər prīz′) *n.* an important project or undertaking **p. 731**

entreat (en trēt′) *v.* to ask earnestly; to beg **p. 727**

equanimity (ēk′ wə nim′ ə tē) *n.* the ability to remain calm and assured **p. 233**

eradicate (i rad′ə kāt′) *v.* to do away with completely **p. 164**

eschew (es chōō′) *v.* to keep apart from something disliked or harmful; avoid **p. 359**

essence (es′əns) *n.* necessary characteristics of a thing **p. 601**

exhortation (eg′zôr tā′ shən) *n.* a strong appeal or warning **p. 106**

expendable (iks pen′də bəl) *adj.* not strictly necessary; capable of being sacrificed **p. 1029**

exultation (eg′ zul tā′ shən) *n.* joy; jubilation **p. 378**

dupe/engañar *v.* embaucar; timar **p. 1091**

dutiful/cumplidor *adj.* que actúa motivado por un sentido de obligación o de lo que es necesario **p. 1062**

E

edifice/edificio *s.* una construcción, especialmente una grande o que parece importante **p. 67**

elation/elación *s.* un sentimiento de gran alegría **p. 377**

elude/eludir *v.* evitar o escapar, especialmente a través de habilidad o rapidez **p. 945**

emanate/emanar *v.* despedir o salir, como de una fuente **p. 445**

emancipation/emancipación *s.* el proceso de liberarse del control o el poder de otro **p. 434**

embroidered/bordado *adj.* adornado con costura o bordadura **p. 550**

endear/encariñar *v.* despertar cariño o admiración **p. 972**

enhance/intensificar *v.* hacer más grande, como en la belleza o el valor **p. 56**

enterprise/empresa *s.* proyecto o emprendimiento importante **p. 731**

entreat/suplicar *v.* pedir fervientemente; rogar **p. 727**

equanimity/ecuanimidad *s.* habilidad de permanecer calmo y protegido **p. 233**

eradicate/erradicar *v.* eliminar por completo **p. 164**

eschew/evitar *v.* separarse de algo dañoso o detestado; prevenir **p. 359**

essence/esencia *s.* lo característico de algo; lo necesario **p. 601**

exhortation/exhortación *s.* una apelación o advertencia fuerte **p. 106**

expendable/prescindible *adj.* no estrictamente necesario; capaz de ser sacrificado **p. 1029**

exultation/exultación *s.* alegría; júbilo **p. 378**

F

famished (fam´isht) *adj.* intensely hungry; ravenous p. 669

ferociously (fə rō´shəs lē) *adv.* cruelly; savagely p. 840

fetish (fet´ish) *n.* abnormally obsessive preoccupation or attachment; a fixation p. 444

fiasco (fē as´kō) *n.* a complete or humiliating failure p. 97

fissure (fish´ər) *n.* a narrow crack p. 484

flecking (flek´ing) *v.* leaving spots or streaks p. 528

formidable (fôr´mi də bəl) *adj.* causing fear, dread, or awe by reason of size, strength, or power p. 148

fortitude (fôr´ tə tōōd´) *n.* firm courage or strength of mind in the face of pain or danger p. 233

fortnight (fôrt´ nīt´) *n.* two weeks p. 67

furtive (fur´ tiv) *adj.* secret; shifty; sly p. 190

G

glyph (glif) *n.* an engraved, symbolic figure p. 512

gnarled (närld) *adj.* roughened and coarse from age or work; full of knots, as in a tree p. 1076

gorge (gôrj) *n.* the passageway between two higher land areas, such as a narrow valley p. 507

grapple (grap´ əl) *v.* to struggle, as though wrestling; to come to terms with p. 404

grimace (gri mās´) *v.* to make a face expressing disgust, disapproval, or pain p. 484

guile (gīl) *n.* cunning p. 961

H

hapless (hap´ lis) *adj.* unlucky or unfortunate p. 544

harass (hə ras´) *v.* to bother or annoy repeatedly p. 221

hoary (hôr´ē) *adj.* white or gray with age; covered with frost p. 601

F

famished/famélico *adj.* intensamente hambriento; voraz p. 669

ferociously/ferozmente *adv.* cruelmente; salvajemente p. 840

fetish/fetiche *s.* afecto o preocupación anormalmente obsesivo; una fijación p. 444

fiasco/fiasco *s.* un fracaso completo o humillante p. 97

fissure/fisura *s.* hendidura poco profunda p. 484

flecking/salpicando *v.* manchando con gotas p. 528

formidable/formidable *adj.* que causa miedo, temor o pavor a causa del tamaño, fuerza o poder p. 148

fortitude/fortaleza *s.* valor sólido o fuerza de la mente al enfrentar dolor o peligro p. 233

fortnight/quincena *s.* dos semanas p. 67

furtive/furtivo *adj.* secreto; disimulado; mañoso p. 190

G

glyph/glifo *s.* figura simbólica grabada p. 512

gnarled/nudoso *adj.* áspero y grueso por la edad o el trabajo; lleno de nudos, como un árbol p. 1076

gorge/desfiladero *s.* pasillo entre dos zonas de tierra más altas, como un valle angosto p. 507

grapple/forcejear *v.* luchar, como si fuese lucha libre; enfrentarse p. 404

grimace/mueca *v.* hacer gestos para expresar disgusto, desaprobación o dolor p. 484

guile/astucia *s.* sagacidad p. 961

H

hapless/desventurado *adj.* desdichado o desafortunado p. 544

harass/atormentar *v.* molestar repetidamente p. 230

hoary/canoso *adj.* blanco o gris con la edad; cubierto de escarcha p. 601

hones (hōnz) *n.* whetstones or similar tools used to sharpen knives and other types of blades p. 494

horizon (hə rī′ zən) *n.* the place where the earth and sky appear to meet p. 1062

hurtle (hurt′ əl) *v.* to move rapidly, especially with much force or noise p. 150

hones/piedras de afilar *n.* herramienta que se usan para sacarle filo a cuchillos y otros tipo de hojas p. 494

horizon/horizonte *s.* lugar donde parecen juntarse el cielo y la tierra p. 1062

hurtle/lanzar *v.* moverse rápidamente, especialmente con mucha fuerza o ruido p. 150

I

ignoble (ig nō′ bəl) *adj.* of low birth or position; without honor or worth p. 909

ignorant (ig′ nər ənt) *adj.* lacking knowledge or experience; uninformed p. 840

immense (i mens′) *adj.* immeasurable; vast; huge p. 499

imminent (im′ ə nənt) *adj.* about to occur p. 755

impeccably (im pek′ ə blē) *adv.* without error or flaw p. 128

imperative (im per′ ə tiv) *adj.* expressing a command or an order p. 434

imperceptible (im′ pər sep′ tə bəl) *adj.* slight, barely capable of being seen or sensed p. 129

impertinent (im purt′ ən ənt) *adj.* inappropriately bold or forward p. 861

impetuous (im pech′ oō əs) *adj.* rushing headlong into things; rash p. 57

imploring (im plôr′ ing) *adj.* asking earnestly; begging p. 24

improvised (im′ prə vīzd′) *adj.* invented, composed, or done without preparation p. 38

impudence (im′ pyə dəns) *n.* speech or behavior that is aggressively forward or rude p. 826

incantation (in′ kan tā′ shən) *n.* words spoken in casting a spell p. 58

incense (in sens′) *v.* to make very angry p. 733

incredulous (in krej′ ə ləs) *adj.* unwilling or unable to believe p. 208

ignoble/innoble *adj.* de posición social baja; sin honor ni valor p. 909

ignorant/ignorante *adj.* que carece conocimiento o experiencia; sin información p. 840

immense/inmenso *adj.* inconmensurable; vasto; enorme p. 499

imminent/inminente *adj.* que está a punto de ocurrir p. 755

impeccably/impecablemente *adv.* sin defecto ni imperfección p. 128

imperative/imperativo *adj.* que expresa una orden o un comando p. 434

imperceptible/imperceptible *adj.* leve, apenas capaz de ser visto o sentido p. 129

impertinent/impertinente *adj.* atrevido o descarado de manera inapropiada p. 861

impetuous/impetuoso *adj.* precipitado; imprudente p. 57

imploring/implorante *adj.* que pide seriamente; suplicante p. 24

improvised/improvisado *adj.* inventado, compuesto o hecho sin preparación de antemano p. 38

impudence/impudencia *s.* lenguaje o conducta que es agresivamente descarado o grosero p. 826

incantation/encantación *s.* palabras dichas para encantar o hechizar p. 58

incense/indignar *v.* enfadar mucho p. 733

incredulous/incrédulo *adj.* reacio o incapaz de creer p. 208

indifferently/lucid

indifferently (in dif′ər ənt lē) *adv.* not concerned about someone or something; without a preference p. 478

induce (in do͞os′) *v.* to lead or move by persuasion; to bring about p. 345

inert (i nurt′) *adj.* not able to move p. 1079

infirmity (in fur′mə tē) *n.* a weakness or an ailment pp. 513, 731

inhibit (in hib′ it) *v.* to hold back one's natural impulses; to restrain p. 325

inscribe (in skrīb′) *v.* to write, carve, or mark on a surface p. 908

inscrutable (in skro͞o′ tə bəl) *adj.* mysterious p. 118

intact (in takt′) *adj.* entire; untouched, uninjured, and having all parts p. 378

interim (in′tər im) *n.* the space of time that exists between events p. 742

interject (in′ tər jekt′) *v.* to cut into with a comment p. 160

interlaced (in′ tər lāst′) *adj.* connected by or woven together p. 1063

interminable (in tur′ mi nə bəl) *adj.* lasting, or seeming to last, forever; endless p. 114

intimidation (in tim′ ə dā shən) *n.* act of making one feel afraid or discouraged p. 134

intuitively (in to͞o′ə tiv lē) *adv.* knowing, sensing, understanding; instinctively p. 385

invaluable (in val′ ū ə bəl) *adj.* very great in value p. 371

irreproachable (ir′ i prō chə bəl) *adj.* free from blame or criticism; faultless p. 174

J

jubilantly (jo͞o′ bə lənt lē) *adv.* joyfully or happily p. 964

L

lag (lag) *v.* to fall behind p. 537

lucid (lo͞o′ sid) *adj.* clear-headed; mentally alert p. 109

indifferently/indiferentemente *adv.* sin preocuparse por algo o alguien; sin una preferencia p. 478

induce/inducir *v.* guiar o moverse por persuasión; provocar p. 345

inert/inerte *adj.* que no se puede mover p. 1079

infirmity/padecimiento *s.* una debilidad o dolencia pp. 513, 731

inhibit/inhibir *v.* contener los impulsos naturales; refrenar p. 325

inscribe/inscribir *v.* escribir, labrar o señalar un superficie p. 908

inscrutable/inescrutable *adj.* misterioso p. 118

intact/intacto *adj.* entero; sin tocar, indemne y que tiene todas las partes p. 378

interim/ínterin *s.* intervalo de tiempo que existe entre dos hechos p. 742

interject/interponer *v.* interrumpir con un comentario p. 160

interlaced/entrelazado *adj.* conectado por o entretejido p. 1063

interminable/interminable *adj.* duradero o que parece durar para siempre; infinito p. 114

intimidation/intimidación *s.* acto de provocar miedo o desaliento p. 134

intuitively/intuitivamente *adv.* con conocimiento, sensación o comprensión; instintivamente p. 385

invaluable/invaluable *adj.* inestimable p. 371

irreproachable/irreprochable *adj.* libre de culpa o crítica; sin defecto p. 174

J

jubilantly/alborozadamente *adv.* con gran regocijo y alegría p. 964

L

lag/rezagarse *v.* quedarse atrás p. 537

lucid/lúcido *adj.* con la mente despejada; mentalmente alerta p. 109

M

mainstream (mān′ strēm′) *adj.* representing the most widespread attitudes and values of a society or group **p. 371**

makeshift (māk′ shift′) *adj.* suitable as a temporary substitute for the proper or desired thing **p. 222**

malice (mal′is) *n.* a desire to hurt another person **p. 767**

malicious (mə lish′ əs) *adj.* having or showing a desire to harm another **p. 154**

marvel (mär′vəl) *v.* to become filled with wonder or astonishment **p. 574**

mature (mə choor′) *adj.* having reached a desired state **p. 556**

melancholy (mel′ən kol′ē) *adj.* depressed; dejected **p. 484**

mesmerize (mez′ mə rīz′) *v.* to hypnotize **p. 163**

meticulous (mi tik′yə ləs) *adj.* precise; careful; worried about details **p. 512**

minuscule (min′ əs kūl′) *adj.* very, very small **p. 543**

misconstrue (mis′ kən stroo′) *v.* to misinterpret; to misunderstand **p. 808**

misgiving (mis giv′ing) *n.* a feeling of doubt; apprehension **p. 766**

N

nostalgic (nos tal′jik) *adj.* longing for persons, things, or situations from the past **p. 574**

notorious (nō tôr′ē əs) *adj.* widely and unfavorably known **p. 858**

O

obligatory (ə blig′ə tôr′ē) *adj.* required or necessary **p. 331**

oblivion (ə bliv′ē ən) *n.* a lack of awareness or memory **p. 565**

oblivious (ə bliv′ē əs) *adj.* unmindful or unaware; not noticing **p. 833**

odious (ō′dē əs) *adj.* disgusting or offensive **p. 397**

M

mainstream/predominante *adj.* que representa las actitudes y los valores más comunes de una sociedad o grupo **p. 371**

makeshift/provisional *adj.* apto como sustituto temporal de aquello adecuado o deseado **p. 222**

malice/malicia *s.* deseo de dañar a otra persona **p. 767**

malicious/malicioso *adj.* que muestra o que tiene un deseo de dañar a otro **p. 154**

marvel/maravillar *v.* lleno de admiración o asombro **p. 574**

mature/maduro *adj.* que ha alcanzado un estado deseado **p. 556**

melancholy/melancólico *adj.* deprimido; desanimado **p. 484**

mesmerize/fascinar *v.* hipnotizar **p. 163**

meticulous/meticuloso *adj.* preciso; cuidadoso; preocupado por los detalles **p. 512**

minuscule/minúsculo *adj.* extremadamente pequeño **p. 543**

misconstrue/malinterpretar *v.* interpretar incorrectamente; entender mal **p. 808**

misgiving/recelo *s.* un sentimiento de duda; aprensión **p. 766**

N

nostalgic/nostálgico *adj.* que anhela a personas, cosas o situaciones del pasado **p. 574**

notorious/notorio *adj.* conocido extensa y desfavorablemente **p. 858**

O

obligatory/obligatorio *adj.* exigido o necesario **p. 331**

oblivion/inconsciencia *s.* falta de conciencia o memoria **p. 565**

oblivious/abstraído *adj.* descuidado o desprevenido; que no nota algo **p. 833**

odious/odioso *adj.* repugnante o ofensivo **p. 397**

oppress/piqued

oppress (ə pres´) *v.* to control or govern by the cruel and unjust use of force or authority p. 192

orator (ôr´ə tər) *n.* a person skilled in public speaking p. 778

ordain (ôr dān´) *v.* to order or establish; to appoint p. 396

ostentatiously (os´tən tā´shəs lē) *adv.* in a way intended to attract attention or impress others p. 853

P

pandemonium (pan´ də mō´ nē əm) *n.* wild disorder and uproar p. 235

paradox (par´ə doks´) *n.* something that seems illogical, but that in fact may be true p. 1030

paraphernalia (par´ ə fər nāl´ yə) *n.* things used in a particular activity; equipment p. 58

parenthesis (pə ren´thə sis) *n.* digression or afterthought; disruption in continuity p. 561

patriarch (pā´trē ärk´) *n.* the male head of a family or group p. 291

peevish (pē´vish) *adj.* irritable; bad-tempered p. 803

pent-up (pent´ up) *adj.* not expressed or released; held in p. 42

peril (per´əl) *n.* exposure to harm or danger p. 804

perpetuate (pər pech´ oo āt´) *v.* to cause to continue to be remembered p. 947

perplexed (pər plekst´) *adj.* troubled with doubt or uncertainty; puzzled p. 1052

peruse (pə rooz´) *v.* to read through or examine carefully p. 311

perverse (pər vurs´) *adj.* determined to go against what is reasonable, expected, or desired; contrary p. 690

pious (pī´əs) *adj.* devoutly religious p. 674

piqued (pēkt) *adj.* aroused in anger or resentment; offended p. 58

---

oppress/oprimir *v.* controlar o gobernar mediante el uso cruel o injusto de la fuerza o la autoridad p. 192

orator/orador *s.* persona especialista en hablar en público p. 778

ordain/decretar *v.* ordenar o establecer; designar p. 396

ostentatiously/ostentosamente *adv.* en una manera que intenta atraer la atención o impresionar a otros p. 853

P

pandemonium/pandemónium *s.* gran desorden y alboroto p. 235

paradox/paradoja *s.* algo que parece ilógico pero que aun puede ser cierto p. 1030

paraphernalia/parafernalia *s.* cosas usadas en una actividad particular; equipo p. 58

parenthesis/paréntesis *s.* digresión o ocurrencia tardía; interrupción en la continuidad p. 561

patriarch/patriarca *s.* el jefe de una familia o un grupo p. 291

peevish/displicente *adj.* irritable; malhumorado p. 803

pent-up/contenido *adj.* que no se expresa o libera; reprimido p. 42

peril/riesgo *s.* exposición a daño o peligro p. 804

perpetuate/perpetuar *v.* hacer que siga siendo recordado p. 947

perplexed/perplejo *adj.* confundido; inseguro p. 1052

peruse/repasar *v.* leer o examinar con cuidado p. 311

perverse/obstinado *adj.* determinado a oponerse a lo que es razonable, previsto o deseado; contrario p. 690

pious/pío *adj.* devotamente religioso p. 674

piqued/resentido *adj.* irritado o con resentimiento; ofendido p. 58

potent (pot´ənt) *adj.* having strength or authority; powerful **p. 345**

precedence (pres´ə dəns) *n.* order of importance or preference; priority **p. 1079**

predecessor (pred´ ə ses´ ər) *n.* one who comes, or has come before in another time **p. 19**

presentiment (pri zen´ tə mənt) *n.* a feeling that something is about to happen **p. 233**

pretext (pre´ tekst) *n.* a reason or motive offered in order to disguise real intentions **p. 1098**

prevail (pri vāl´) *v.* to be superior in power or influence; to succeed **p. 694**

primal (prī´məl) *adj.* a basic, original state of being **p. 507**

primeval (prī mē´ vəl) *adj.* of or having to do with the first or earliest age; primitive **p. 1034**

prodigy (prod´ə jē) *n.* an extraordinarily gifted or talented person, especially a child **p. 90**

profuse (prə fūs´) *adj.* great in amount, plentiful **p. 75**

prowess (prou´ is) *n.* great ability or skill **p. 910**

Q

querulous (kwer´ə ləs) *adj.* argumentative; uncooperative **p. 527**

R

rapier (rā´peē ər) *n.* a narrow, long-bladed, two-edged sword **p. 347**

rash (rash) *adj.* marked by haste and lack of caution or consideration **p. 792**

reapers (rē´pərs) *n.* machines or people that cut grain for harvesting **p. 494**

recoil (ri koil´) *v.* to shrink back physically or emotionally **p. 1104**

recollect (rek´ə lekt´) *v.* to remember **p. 536**

regally (rē´gəl lē) *adv.* in a grand, dignified manner befitting a king or a queen **p. 852**

potent/potente *adj.* que tiene fuerza o autoridad; poderoso **p. 345**

precedence/precedencia *s.* orden de importancia o preferencia; prioridad **p. 1079**

predecessor/predecesor *s.* alguien que viene o que ha venido antes en otro tiempo **p. 19**

presentiment/presentimiento *s.* una sensación de que algo va a ocurrir **p. 233**

pretext/pretexto *s.* razón o motivo ofrecido para encubrir intenciones reales **p. 1098**

prevail/prevalecer *v.* ser superior en poder o influencia; tener éxito **p. 694**

primal/primitivo *adj.* estado de ser original y básico **p. 507**

primeval/primigenio *adj.* perteneciente o relacionado con la primera época o la era más temprana; primitivo **p. 1034**

prodigy/prodigio *s.* una persona extraordinariamente dotada o talentosa, especialmente un niño **p. 90**

profuse/profuso *adj.* grande en cantidad; abundante **p. 75**

prowess/proeza *s.* habilidad o capacidad grande **p. 910**

Q

querulous/quejumbroso *adj.* discutidor; poco dispuesto a colaborar **p. 527**

R

rapier/estoque *s.* espada de hoja larga y estrecha, de doble filo **p. 347**

rash/impulsivo *adj.* marcado por la prisa y la falta de cautela o consideración **p. 792**

reapers/cosechadoras *s.* personas o máquinas que sirven para cortar granos **p. 494**

recoil/retroceder *v.* encogerse física o emocionalmente **p. 1104**

recollect/recordar *v.* traer a la memoria **p. 536**

regally/regiamente *adv.* en forma majestuosa y señorial como corresponde a un rey o reina **p. 852**

relevant (rel′ ə vənt) *adj.* related to the issue at hand **p. 407**

relic (rel′ik) *n.* an object that has survived decay, destruction, or the passage of time and is valued for its historic interest **p. 225**

remorse (ri môrs′) *n.* distress stemming from the guilt of past wrongs **p. 500**

renaissance (ren′ə säns′) *n.* rebirth or comeback **p. 428**

repercussion (rē′ pər kush′ ən) *n.* an effect or result of some action **p. 105**

repressed (ri prest′) *adj.* held back or kept under control; restrained **p. 859**

reproach (ri prōch′) *n.* blame, disgrace, discredit **p. 91**

repulse (ri puls′) *n.* an act of beating back or driving away, as with force **p. 665**

resilient (ri zil′yənt) *adj.* capable of springing back into shape or position after being bent, stretched, or compressed **p. 1031**

retail (rē′tāl) *v.* to sell directly to the consumer **p. 67**

reveling (rev′ əl ing) *adj.* taking great pleasure **p. 42**

reverie (rev′ər ē) *n.* fanciful thinking, daydream **p. 94**

russet (rus′it) *adj.* a deep reddish-brown **p. 602**

S

sacred (sā′ krid) *adj.* worthy of reverence **p. 500**

scavenger (skav′ in jər) *n.* one who searches through discarded materials for something useful **p. 1091**

scenario (si när′ ē ō′) *n.* an outline or model of an expected or imagined series of events **p. 325**

scrupulous (skrōō′ pyə ləs) *adj.* thoroughly attentive to even the smallest details; precise **p. 945**

scrutinize (skrōōt′ ən īz′) *v.* to look at closely; to inspect carefully **p. 117**

relevant/pertinente *adj.* relacionado con el tema en cuestión **p. 407**

relic/reliquia *n.* un objeto valorado por su interés histórico **p. 225**

remorse/remordimiento *s.* angustia que surge de la culpa de errores pasados **p. 500**

renaissance/renacimiento *s.* renovación; rehabilitación **p. 428**

repercussion/repercusión *s.* el efecto o resultado de una acción **p. 105**

repressed/reprimido *adj.* contenido o mantenido bajo control; comedido **p. 859**

reproach/oprobio *n.* culpa, deshonra, descrédito **p. 91**

repulse/rechazo *n.* el acto de ahuyentar o alejar, con fuerza **p. 665**

resilient/elástico *adj.* capaz de recuperar la forma o posición después de ser doblado, estirado o comprimido **p. 1031**

retail/vender al por menor *v.* vender directamente al consumidor **p. 67**

reveling/deleitarse *adj.* producir gran placer **p. 42**

reverie/ensueño *s.* pensamientos imaginativos; fantasías **p. 94**

russet/bermejo *adj.* marrón rojizo intenso **p. 602**

S

sacred/sagrado *adj.* digno de veneración **p. 500**

scavenger/hurgador *s.* persona que busca algo útil en los materiales de desecho **p. 1091**

scenario/escenario *s.* descripción general o modelo de una serie de sucesos esperados o imaginados **p. 325**

scrupulous/escrupuloso *adj.* completamente atento hasta al más mínimo detalle; preciso **p. 945**

scrutinize/escudriñar *v.* examinar cuidadosamente; inspeccionar detenidamente **p. 117**

scythes (sīths) *n.* cutting implements made of a long, curved single-edged blade **p. 494**

searing (sēr´ing) *adj.* extremely hot or bright **p. 507**

sedate (si dāt´) *adj.* quiet and restrained in style or manner; calm **p. 23**

self-possessed (self´ pə zest´) *adj.* in control of oneself; composed **p. 12**

serenity (sə ren´ ə tē) *n.* calmness; peacefulness **p. 115**

serpentine (sur´pən tēn´) *adj.* snake-like, twisting, winding **p. 507**

servile (sur´vil) *adj.* lacking self-respect; behaving as if other people are superior **p. 722**

sidle (sīd´əl) *v.* to move sideways **p. 189**

skeptical (skep´ ti kəl´) *adj.* having or showing doubt or suspicion; questioning; disbelieving **p. 118**

solace (sol´ is) *n.* relief from sorrow or disappointment; comfort **p. 20**

sparse (spärs) *adj.* thinly spread or distributed **p. 254**

spectral (spek´ trəl) *adj.* ghostlike **p. 80**

stolid (stol´ id) *adj.* showing little or no emotion **p. 361**

strategic (strə tē´ jik) *adj.* highly important to an intended goal **p. 986**

stupor (stoo´pər) *n.* a state of extreme lethargy **p. 536**

submerged (səb murjd´) *adj.* hard to see; sunken **p. 483**

subordinate (sə bôr´də nāt´) *v.* to cause to be, or treat as, secondary, inferior, or less important **p. 300**

subversive (səb vur´ siv) *adj.* seeking to weaken, destroy, or overthrow **p. 176**

superfluous (soo pur´ floo əs) *adj.* not needed; unnecessary **p. 371**

scythes/guadañas *s.* implementos cortantes formados por una cuchilla curva y puntiaguda, de un solo filo **p. 494**

searing/abrasador *adj.* extremadamente caliente o brillante **p. 507**

sedate/sereno *adj.* callado y comedido en estilo o manera; calmo **p. 23**

self-possessed/sosegado *adj.* en control de sí mismo; sereno **p. 12**

serenity/serenidad *s.* tranquilidad; calma **p. 115**

serpentine/serpentino *adj.* similar a una serpiente; serpenteante, zigzagueante **p. 507**

servile/servil *adj.* que carece de autoestima; que se comporta como si las otras personas fuesen superiores **p. 722**

sidle/andar de lado *v.* moverse hacia un lado **p. 189**

skeptical/escéptico *adj.* que tiene o muestra duda o sospecha; inquisitivo; incrédulo **p. 118**

solace/solaz *s.* alivio del dolor o desilusión; consuelo **p. 20**

sparse/ralo *adj.* apenas distribuido o esparcido **p. 254**

spectral/espectral *adj.* fantasmal **p. 80**

stolid/impasible *adj.* que muestra poca o ninguna emoción **p. 361**

strategic/estratégico *adj.* de gran importancia para una meta planeada **p. 986**

stupor/estupor *s.* un estado de letargo extremo **p. 536**

submerged/sumergido *adj.* difícil de ver; hundido **p. 483**

subordinate/subordinar *v.* hacer que esté o tratar como si fuera secundario, inferior o menos importante **p. 300**

subversive/subversivo *adj.* que intenta debilitar, destruir o derrocar **p. 176**

superfluous/superfluo *adj.* que no es necesario; innecesario **p. 371**

supplication/vanquish

supplication (sup′lə kā shən) *n.* an earnest and humble request **p. 203**

syntax (sin′taks) *n.* ordered structure or systematic arrangement; the rules of language **p. 561**

T

taboo (ta boo′) *n.* a cultural or social rule forbidding something **p. 385**

taut (tôt) *adj.* tense; tight **p. 39**

temperate (tem′pər it) *adj.* calm and free from extremes of temperature **p. 488**

testament (tes′ tə mənt) *n.* proof of or tribute to **p. 165**

thrive (thrīv) *v.* to be successful; to grow well **p. 761**

torrential (tô ren′chəl) *adj.* flowing rapidly and abundantly **p. 334**

translucent (trans loo′sənt) *adj.* allowing light to pass through; almost clear, see-through **p. 528**

treacherous (trech′ ər əs) *adj.* likely to betray a trust; disloyal **p. 1091**

tread (tred) *v.* to step or walk on **p. 550**

tremulously (trem′ yə ləs lē) *adv.* in a trembling or vibrating way **p. 359**

tribulation (trib′ yə lā′ shən) *n.* great misery or distress; suffering **p. 239**

tumultuous (too mul′ choo əs) *adj.* wildly excited, confused, or agitated **p. 909**

turbulent (tur′byə lənt) *adj.* causing unrest, violent action, or disturbance **p. 434**

U

ulterior (ul tēr′ ē ər) *adj.* intentionally withheld or concealed **p. 175**

V

valor (val′ər) *n.* courageous spirit, personal bravery **p. 435**

vanquish (vang′kwish) *v.* to defeat; to overcome **p. 777**

supplication/súplica *s.* un ruego serio y humilde **p. 203**

syntax/sintaxis *s.* estructura ordenada u ordenación sistemática; las reglas de una idioma **p. 561**

T

taboo/tabú *s.* regla cultural o social que prohíbe algo **p. 385**

taut/tirante *adj.* tenso; ajustado **p. 39**

temperate/templado *adj.* tranquilo y sin extremos de temperatura **p. 488**

testament/testamento *s.* prueba de o tributo a **p. 165**

thrive/prosperar *v.* tener éxito; salir adelante **p. 761**

torrential/torrencial *adj.* que fluye rápida y abundantemente **p. 334**

translucent/translúcido *adj.* que permite que pase la luz; casi transparente **p. 528**

treacherous/traicionero *adj.* propenso a traicionar la confianza; desleal **p. 1091**

tread/pisar *v.* poner los pies sobre el suelo o andar **p. 550**

tremulously/trémulamente *adv.* en una manera temblorosa o vibrante **p. 359**

tribulation/tribulación *s.* gran miseria o dolor; sufrimiento **p. 239**

tumultuous/tumultuoso *adj.* excitado, confundido o agitado ferozmente **p. 909**

turbulent/turbulento *adj.* que causa inquietud, acción violenta o perturbación **p. 434**

U

ulterior/ulterior *adj.* intencionalmente retenido o disimulado **p. 175**

V

valor/valor *s.* espíritu valeroso, bravura personal **p. 435**

vanquish/subyugar *v.* derrotar o vencer **p. 777**

vault/wanton

vault (vôlt) *v.* to jump; spring **p. 985**

vehemently (vē′ə mənt lē) *adv.* strongly; intensely; passionately **p. 315**

verandah (və ran′ də) *n.* a long porch, usually with a roof, that extends along a house **p. 1062**

vintage (vin′ tij) *adj.* characterized by enduring appeal; classic **p. 222**

vulnerability (vul′ nər ə bil′ ə tē) *n.* state of being open to harm, damage, or illness **p. 164**

vulnerable vulnerable (vul′ nər ə bəl) *adj.* easily damaged or hurt **p. 371**

W

wanton (wont′ ən) *adj.* shamelessly unrestrained; immoral **p. 78**

Glossary/Glosario

vault/brincar *v.* saltar; rebotar **p. 985**

vehemently/vehementemente *adv.* fuertemente; intensamente; obstinadamente **p. 315**

verandah/veranda *s.* una terraza en la parte de afuera de un edificio como una casa **p. 1062**

vintage/reliquia *adj.* caracterizado por un atractivo que perdura en el tiempo; clásico **p. 222**

vulnerability/vulnerabilidad *s.* condición de quedar expuesto a daños o enfermedades **p. 164**

vulnerable/vulnerable *adj.* que se daña o lastima con facilidad **p. 371**

W

wanton/despiadado *adj.* descaradamente desmedido; inmoral **p. 78**

Academic Word List

To succeed academically in high school and prepare for college, it is important to know academic vocabulary—special terms used in classroom discussion, assignments, and tests. These words are also used in the workplace and among friends to share information, exchange ideas, make decisions, and build relationships. Research has shown that the words listed below, compiled by Averil Coxhead in 2000, are the ones most commonly used in these ways. You will encounter many of them in the Glencoe Language Arts program. You will also focus on specific terms in connection with particular reading selections.

Note: The lists are ordered by frequency of use from most frequent to least frequent.

List One

- analysis
- approach
- area
- assessment
- assume
- authority
- available
- benefit
- concept
- consistent
- constitutional
- context
- contract
- create
- data
- definition
- derived
- distribution
- economic
- environment
- established
- estimate
- evidence
- export
- factors
- financial
- formula
- function
- identified
- income
- indicate
- individual
- interpretation
- involved
- issues
- labor
- legal
- legislation
- major
- method
- occur
- percent
- period
- policy
- principle
- procedure
- process
- required
- research
- response
- role
- section
- sector
- significant
- similar
- source
- specific
- structure
- theory
- variables

List Two

- achieve
- acquisition
- administration
- affect
- appropriate
- aspects
- assistance
- categories
- chapter
- commission
- community
- complex
- computer
- conclusion
- conduct
- consequences
- construction
- consumer
- credit
- cultural
- design
- distinction
- elements
- equation
- evaluation
- features
- final
- focus
- impact
- injury
- institute
- investment
- items
- journal
- maintenance
- normal
- obtained
- participation
- perceived
- positive
- potential
- previous
- primary
- purchase
- range
- region
- regulations
- relevant
- resident
- resources
- restricted
- security
- select
- site
- sought
- strategies
- survey
- text
- traditional
- transfer

List Three

- alternative
- circumstances
- comments
- compensation
- components
- consent
- considerable
- constant
- constraints
- contribution
- convention
- coordination
- core
- corporate
- corresponding
- criteria
- deduction
- demonstrate
- document
- dominant
- emphasis
- ensure
- excluded
- framework
- funds
- illustrated
- immigration
- implies
- initial

instance
interaction
justification
layer
link
location
maximum
minorities
negative
outcomes
partnership
philosophy
physical
proportion
published
reaction
registered
reliance
removed
scheme
sequence
sex
shift
specified
sufficient
task
technical
techniques
technology
validity
volume

List Four
access
adequate
annual
apparent
approximated
attitudes
attributed
civil
code
commitment
communication

concentration
conference
contrast
cycle
debate
despite
dimensions
domestic
emerged
error
ethnic
goals
granted
hence
hypothesis
implementation
implications
imposed
integration
internal
investigation
job
label
mechanism
obvious
occupational
option
output
overall
parallel
parameters
phase
predicted
principal
prior
professional
project
promote
regime
resolution
retained
series
statistics
status

stress
subsequent
sum
summary
undertaken

List Five
academic
adjustment
alter
amendment
aware
capacity
challenge
clause
compounds
conflict
consultation
contact
decline
discretion
draft
enable
energy
enforcement
entities
equivalent
evolution
expansion
exposure
external
facilitate
fundamental
generated
generation
image
liberal
license
logic
marginal
medical
mental
modified
monitoring

network
notion
objective
orientation
perspective
precise
prime
psychology
pursue
ratio
rejected
revenue
stability
styles
substitution
sustainable
symbolic
target
transition
trend
version
welfare
whereas

List Six
abstract
accurate
acknowledged
aggregate
allocation
assigned
attached
author
bond
brief
capable
cited
cooperative
discrimination
display
diversity
domain
edition
enhanced

estate
exceed
expert
explicit
federal
fees
flexibility
furthermore
gender
ignored
incentive
incidence
incorporated
index
inhibition
initiatives
input
instructions
intelligence
interval
lecture
migration
minimum
ministry
motivation
neutral
nevertheless
overseas
preceding
presumption
rational
recovery
revealed
scope
subsidiary
tapes
trace
transformation
transport
underlying
utility

List Seven
adaptation
adults
advocate
aid
channel
chemical
classical
comprehensive
comprise
confirmed
contrary
converted
couple
decades
definite
deny
differentiation
disposal
dynamic
eliminate
empirical
equipment
extract
file
finite
foundation
global
grade
guarantee
hierarchical
identical
ideology
inferred
innovation
insert
intervention
isolated
media
mode
paradigm
phenomenon
priority
prohibited
publication
quotation
release
reverse
simulation
solely
somewhat
submitted
successive
survive
thesis
topic
transmission
ultimately
unique
visible
voluntary

List Eight
abandon
accompanied
accumulation
ambiguous
appendix
appreciation
arbitrary
automatically
bias
chart
clarity
conformity
commodity
complement
contemporary
contradiction
crucial
currency
denote
detected
deviation
displacement
dramatic
eventually
exhibit
exploitation
fluctuations
guidelines
highlighted
implicit
induced
inevitably
infrastructure
inspection
intensity
manipulation
minimized
nuclear
offset
paragraph
plus
practitioners
predominantly
prospect
radical
random
reinforced
restore
revision
schedule
tension
termination
theme
thereby
uniform
vehicle
via
virtually
visual
widespread

List Nine
accommodation
analogous
anticipated
assurance
attained
behalf
bulk
ceases
coherence
coincide
commenced
concurrent
confined
controversy
conversely
device
devoted
diminished
distorted
duration
erosion
ethical
format
founded
incompatible
inherent
insights
integral
intermediate
manual
mature
mediation
medium
military
minimal
mutual
norms
overlap
passive
portion
preliminary
protocol
qualitative
refine
relaxed
restraints
revolution
rigid
route
scenario
sphere
subordinate
supplementary
suspended
team
temporary
trigger
unified
violation
vision

List Ten
adjacent
albeit
assembly
collapse
colleagues
compiled
conceived
convinced
depression
encountered
enormous
forthcoming
inclination
integrity
intrinsic
invoked
levy
likewise
nonetheless
notwithstanding
odd
ongoing
panel
persistent
posed
reluctant
so-called
straightforward
undergo
whereby

Index of Skills

> References beginning with **R** refer to handbook pages.

Literary Concepts

Act 653
Allegory 49, 74, 79
Alliteration 469, 470, 593, 595, 597, 605
Allusion 402, 413
Ambiguity 244
Analogy 429, 446, 1075, 1081
Anecdote 357, 364, 373
Antagonist 3, 663, 684
Appeal
  emotional 708, 879
  logical 708, 879
  persuasive 416, 417, 430
Archetype 1055, 1081
Argument 279, 367, 393, 398, 417, 842
Aside 739, 759
Assonance 469, 593, 600, 605
Author's purpose 87, 329, 338, 352, 388, 443, 446, 617, 631, 685, 707, 821, 1089, 1092
Author's viewpoint 416, 430, 617, 631
Autobiographical narrative 171
Autobiography 278, 282, 285, 301
Bias 395, 399, 713
Biography 278, 281, 282, 285, 338
Blank verse 717, 738
Cause and effect structure 380
Character 4, 6, 87, 120, 124, 246, 257, 652, 654, 717
  antagonist 3, 663, 684
  dynamic 87
  flat 87, 120
  foil 783, 799
  protagonist 3, 663, 684
  round 87, 120
  static 87
  tragic hero 652, 656
Characterization 87, 145, 156, 707, 847, 865
  direct 87, 145, 156
  indirect 87, 145, 156, 707
Comedy 656, 818
Comparison/contrast
  structure 380
Conflict 9, 34, 50, 170, 663, 838, 841
  external 9, 34, 50, 170, 841
  internal 9, 34, 50, 170, 841
Connotation 32, 65, 71, 329, 339, 438, 542, 546, 555, 558, 581, 595, 611, 713, 783, 838, 841, 950, 1089, 1092
Consonance 469, 593, 600, 605
Couplet 474
Cultural context 55, 62, 217, 873, 980, 1058
Denotation 32, 65, 71, 329, 339, 438, 542, 546, 555, 558, 581, 595, 611, 713, 783, 838, 841, 950, 1089, 1092
Description 62, 1022, 1038, 1058
Dialect 65, 71, 110
Dialogue 104, 110, 653, 654, 656, 818, 903, 922, 943, 949
Diction 185, 540, 542, 546, 573, 575, 1017, 1019, 1020
Drama
  act 653, 656
  aside 739, 759
  classical Greek 660
  comedy 656
  dialogue 653, 654, 656
  elements of 656
  lines 653
  modern 818
  monologue 654, 739, 759
  scene 653, 656
  setting 654
  Shakespearean 714
  soliloquy 739, 759
  stage directions 653, 654, 656
  tragedy 656, 658
  tragic hero 652, 656, 659, 800, 815
End rhyme 469, 592, 619
Enjambment 482, 485, 529
Epic 896, 897, 901, 949
Epic hero 896
Essay 279, 282, 367
  expository 367
  formal 279, 282
  informal 279, 282
  narrative 369
  personal 279, 282, 367
  persuasive 279, 282, 367
  reflective 390
Evidence 588
Exposition 367
Expository essay 367
Extended metaphor 533, 558
Fable 1017
Fact 432, 709
Fallacy
  deductive 417
  inductive 417
  logical 583
Fantasy 49, 1016
Farce 821, 834
Figurative language 471, 472, 533, 782
Figure of speech 468, 760, 782
Flashback 11, 15, 61
Foil 783, 799, 935
Folklore 895, 898, 957
Folktale 957
Foreshadowing 9, 18, 26, 50, 1025, 1038
Formal essay 279
Free verse 475, 497, 501
Functional documents 1137–1163
Greek drama, classical 660
Hero 901, 922
  epic 896
  legendary 894, 898, 900
  tragic 652, 656, 659, 800, 815

Historical context 65, 71
Historical influences 28
Historical narrative 287, 301
Hyperbole 533, 713
Iambic pentameter 490, 717, 738
Image archetype 969, 977
Imagery 469, 470, 472, 533, 569, 571, 1018, 1020, 1023
Implied theme 113, 120
Informal essay 279
Interior monologue 111
Internal rhyme 469, 593
Irony 158, 170, 834, 877
    dramatic 158, 834
    situational 158, 170, 834
Jargon 340
Juxtaposition 560, 562
Legend 894, 898, 901
Legendary hero 894, 898, 900
Line (in poetry) 472, 474, 479, 517, 519
Literary criticism 16, 258
Literary history 660, 714
Loaded words 713
Logical fallacy 583
Lyric poetry 475, 548, 552, 557
Memoir 278, 282, 285, 322, 326, 350
Metaphor 468, 533, 555, 557, 558
    extended 533, 558
Meter 469, 474, 487, 490, 493
    hexameter 475
    iamb 475
    iambic pentameter 490
    pentameter 475
    tetrameter 475
    trimeter 475
Modern drama 818
    dialogue 818
    props 819
    stage directions 819
Monologue 654, 739, 759
Mood 55, 61, 110, 171, 542, 545, 551
Moral 1041, 1055
Motivation 89, 101, 139, 1094, 1114

Multiple-meaning words 122
Mystery 1017
Myth 895, 898, 957, 965
Narrative
    autobiographical 171
    historical 287, 301
Narrative essay 369, 373
Narrative nonfiction 278
Narrative poetry 577, 580
Narrator 3, 4, 6, 187, 197, 198, 217, 256
    reliable 187, 197
    unreliable 187, 197
Nonfiction 280
Nuance 244
Octave 474
Onomatopoeia 469, 592, 593
Opinion 432, 709
Oral tradition 895, 898, 957, 980
Parody 926, 935
Persona 231, 243
Personal essay 279, 367
Personification 468, 490, 533, 535
Persuasion 393, 438
Persuasive appeal 416, 417, 430
Persuasive essay 279, 367, 393
Plot 2, 5, 6, 15, 26, 158, 655, 760, 782
    climax 2, 655, 760, 782
    conflict 9
    exposition 2, 760
    falling action 2, 760
    resolution 2, 760
    rising action 2, 760
    tragic 652
Plot pattern archetype 959, 965, 977, 1055
Poetry
    blank verse 717, 738
    couplet 474
    end rhyme 469, 592, 619
    foot 469, 475, 487
    form 474, 487
    free verse 475, 497, 501
    hexameter 475
    iamb 475

iambic pentameter 490, 717, 738
internal rhyme 469, 593
line 472, 474, 479, 517
lyric 475, 548, 552, 557
meter 469, 474, 475, 479, 493
narrative poetry 577, 580
pentameter 475
prose poetry 505, 508, 514
octave 474
quatrain 474
repetition 470, 548
rhyme 469, 472, 493, 495, 539, 548, 580, 592, 619, 622
rhyme scheme 469, 474, 493, 495, 580, 619, 622
rhythm 469, 471, 472, 474, 475, 493, 539, 610, 717
sestet 474
slant rhyme 593
stanza 470, 472, 474, 477, 479, 487, 517
structure 474
tetrameter 475
trimeter 475
Point of view 3, 184, 198, 200, 211, 217, 219, 1089, 1092
    first-person 3, 184, 217
    second-person 1089
    third-person 3
    third-person limited 184, 217, 219
    third-person omniscient 184, 200, 211, 217
Problem/solution structure 380
Propaganda 713
Prose poetry 505, 508, 514
Protagonist 3, 663, 684
Quatrain 474
Quotation 432, 438
Reasoning
    deductive 417
    inductive 417
Reflective essay 390
Repetition 470, 548, 552, 562, 567, 877

Rhetorical devices 395, 398, 418, 429, 447
Rhyme 469, 472, 493, 495, 539, 548, 552, 580, 592, 619, 622
　end 469, 592, 619
　internal 469, 593
　slant 593
Rhyme scheme 469, 474, 493, 495, 580, 619, 622
Rhythm 469, 471, 472, 474, 475, 487, 493, 539, 610, 717
Satire 173, 177
Scansion 475
Scene 653, 656
Science fiction 1016
Sensory details 231, 243, 595, 1020, 1058
Sestet 474
Setting 2, 4, 6, 8, 79, 654
Shakespearean drama 714
Simile 468, 533, 538, 545, 555, 557, 558
Slant rhyme 593
Soliloquy 739, 759
Sonnet 490
Sound devices 606
Speaker 470, 472, 511, 514, 552, 611
Stage directions 653, 656
Stanza 470, 472, 474, 477, 479, 487, 517, 519
　octave 474
　quatrain 474
　sestet 474
Stream of consciousness 111, 1060, 1064
Structure 376, 380, 383, 389, 443, 447, 502
　cause and effect 380
　comparison/contrast 380
　problem/solution 380
Style 185, 246, 256, 1017, 1018, 1020, 1022, 1114
Suspense 982, 987
Symbol 74, 80, 608, 611
Tall tale 957, 988
Tanka 522, 524
Text structure *see* Structure

Theme 3, 5, 6, 86, 101, 120, 124, 139, 305, 319, 326, 390, 545, 553, 619, 815, 845, 873
　archetype 1081
　implied 86, 113, 120, 124, 139, 319, 815
　stated 86, 124, 139, 319, 815
Thesis 383, 388, 553, 878
Tone 185, 327, 413, 477, 479, 535, 1018, 1020
Tragedy 656, 658
Tragic flaw 652, 659, 685, 707
Tragic hero 652, 656, 659, 800, 815
Tragic plot 652
Verse, blank 717, 738
Verse paragraph 526, 529, 545
Voice 3, 5, 6, 185, 242, 319, 342, 350, 380, 1017, 1019, 1020

Reading and Critical Thinking

Activating prior knowledge 1075, 1082
See also Connecting, to personal experience
Ambiguities, identifying 418, 429
Analyzing 15, 31, 49, 61, 71, 78, 101, 110, 120, 139, 156, 169, 177, 182, 197, 211, 242, 256, 301, 318, 326, 338, 342, 355, 364, 373, 380, 388, 398, 413, 429, 437, 441, 446, 479, 485, 489, 495, 501, 508, 514, 519, 524, 529, 538, 545, 551, 557, 562, 567, 571, 575, 580, 590, 597, 604, 610, 616, 622, 684, 706, 712, 738, 759, 782, 799, 814, 834, 841, 844, 865, 922, 935, 941, 949, 954, 965, 976, 987, 1037, 1055, 1064, 1073, 1081, 1087, 1092, 1113

　cause-and-effect relationships 18, 27, 173, 177, 305, 739, 759, 978, 1115, 1158
　cultural context 55, 62, 612, 980
　diction 542, 546
　figures of speech 760, 782
　form 490
　historical context 65, 71
　imagery 244
　meter 493, 495
　mood 838, 841
　plot 158, 170, 847, 865, 903, 923
　poetic structure 482
　repetition 548, 552
　rhyme 548, 552
　rhythm 493, 495, 608, 610
　sensory details 231, 243, 595, 598
　setting 847, 865
　style 342, 540
　symbolism 80
　text structure 383, 389, 443, 447
　theme 553
　visual image 439
Applying
　background knowledge 511, 515, 577, 581
　characterization 141
　description 62
　imagery 520
　interior monologue 111
　irony 171
　point of view 816
　repetition 447
Arguing a position 400, 708
Argument, evaluating 842
Assumptions, identifying 418, 429
Audience, convincing an 1039
Author's purpose
　comparing and contrasting 617, 631
　recognizing 352, 685, 707, 821, 1089, 1092

Authors' cultures, comparing and contrasting 198, 217, 1058, 1069
Background knowledge, applying 511, 515, 577, 581
Bias, recognizing 395, 399
Big Idea
  Acts of Courage 899
  Encountering the Unexpected 7
  Energy of the Everyday, The 473
  Extraordinary and Fantastic, The 1021
  Issues of Identity 591
  Keeping Freedom Alive 391
  Life Transitions 183
  Loves and Losses 517
  Loyalty and Betrayal 657
  Making Choices 85
  Portraits of Real Life 817
  Power of Memory, The 283
  Rescuing and Conquering 892
  Quests and Encounters 365
Building background 11, 18, 28, 34, 55, 65, 74, 89, 104, 113, 124, 145, 158, 173, 187, 200, 212, 215, 219, 231, 246, 287, 305, 322, 329, 342, 352, 357, 369, 376, 383, 395, 402, 418, 419, 422, 426, 432, 443, 477, 482, 487, 493, 497, 505, 511, 517, 522, 526, 535, 542, 548, 555, 560, 564, 569, 573, 577, 584, 586, 588, 595, 600, 608, 619, 623, 627, 663, 685, 717, 739, 760, 783, 800, 821, 838, 842, 847, 866, 867, 903, 926, 943, 951, 959, 969, 982, 988, 990, 1025, 1041, 1060, 1065, 1067, 1070, 1075, 1089, 1094
Cause-and-effect relationships, analyzing 18, 27, 173, 177, 305, 739, 759, 978, 1115, 1158
Characterization, applying 141

Characters
  comparing and contrasting 124, 140
  evaluating 246, 257, 800, 815, 926
  making generalizations about 104, 111
  making inferences about 145, 156, 717, 738, 959, 966, 1094, 1114
  responding to 34
Clarifying meaning 600, 605, 937
Comparing and contrasting
  authors' cultures 198, 217, 1058, 1069
  author's purpose 617, 631
  author's viewpoint 416, 430, 617, 631
  Big Idea treatments 198, 217, 416, 430, 617, 631, 845, 873, 980, 991, 1058, 1069
  characters 124, 140
  cultures 845, 873, 980, 991
  description 1069
  events and ideas 1070
  genres 661, 715
  imagery 524
  media genres 582–587
  narrators 198, 217
  oral tradition 980, 991
  persuasive appeals 416, 430
  theme 845, 873
  tone 535, 539
  versions of a story 951
Comparison, developing 491
Comprehension, monitoring 497, 502
Conclusions, drawing 322, 376, 381, 564, 567
Connecting
  to contemporary issues 1083
  to personal experience 89, 102, 357, 374
  to reading selections 11, 18, 31, 34, 55, 65, 74, 89, 104, 113, 124, 145, 158, 173, 177, 187, 200, 211, 219, 231, 246, 287, 305, 322, 329, 342, 355, 357, 369, 376, 383, 395, 402, 418, 432, 441, 443, 477, 482, 487, 493, 497, 505, 511, 517, 522, 524, 526, 529, 535, 542, 548, 555, 557, 560, 564, 569, 573, 577, 590, 595, 600, 608, 616, 619, 663, 685, 712, 717, 739, 760, 783, 800, 821, 838, 844, 847, 903, 926, 941, 943, 954, 959, 969, 982, 1025, 1041, 1060, 1073, 1075, 1087, 1089, 1094
  to the Big Idea 15, 26, 49, 61, 71, 78, 101, 110, 120, 139, 156, 169, 197, 242, 256, 301, 318, 326, 338, 342, 364, 373, 380, 388, 398, 413, 429, 437, 446, 479, 485, 489, 495, 501, 508, 514, 519, 524, 538, 545, 551, 562, 567, 571, 575, 580, 597, 604, 610, 622, 684, 706, 738, 759, 782, 799, 814, 834, 841, 865, 922, 935, 949, 965, 976, 987, 1037, 1055, 1064, 1081, 1092, 1113
Contemporary issues, connecting to 1083
Convincing an audience 1039
Cultural context, analyzing 55, 62, 612, 980
Cultures, comparing and contrasting 845, 873, 980, 991
Description
  applying 62
  comparing and contrasting 1069
Determining
  main idea 178, 1158
  supporting details 178
Developing a comparison 491
Diction, analyzing 542, 546

Distinguishing fact and opinion 432, 438, 709
Drawing conclusions
  about author's beliefs 322
  about meaning 376, 381, 564, 567
Evaluating 15, 26, 31, 49, 61, 71, 78, 101, 110, 120, 139, 156, 169, 177, 182, 197, 211, 242, 256, 301, 318, 326, 338, 342, 355, 364, 373, 380, 388, 398, 413, 429, 437, 441, 446, 479, 485, 489, 495, 501, 508, 514, 519, 524, 529, 538, 545, 551, 557, 562, 567, 571, 575, 580, 590, 597, 604, 610, 616, 622, 684, 706, 712, 738, 759, 782, 799, 814, 834, 841, 844, 865, 922, 935, 941, 949, 954, 965, 976, 987, 1037, 1055, 1064, 1073, 1081, 1087, 1092, 1113
  argument 842
  characters 246, 257, 800, 815, 926
  credibility 1139
  evidence 588
  historical influences 28
  literary criticism 16
  sound devices 606
Events
  comparing and contrasting 1070
  making generalizations about 329
  reporting 415
Evidence, evaluating 588
Exploring theme 390
Fact and opinion, distinguishing 432, 438, 709, 1140
Figures of speech, analyzing 760, 782
Form, analyzing 490
Generalizations, making 104, 111, 329, 1140
Genre
  comparing and contrasting 661, 715
  identifying 943, 950, 1025, 1038
Graphic organizer
  alliteration chart 605
  alternative meanings chart 600
  background knowledge chart 577
  cause-and-effect diagram 18, 173, 305, 739
  character chart 120, 124, 707, 800
  characteristics chart 1025
  chart 74, 83, 89, 102, 187, 246, 257, 319, 338, 342, 350, 357, 373, 380, 395, 398, 438, 487, 490, 514, 529, 542, 555, 842, 951, 977, 1075, 1089
  compare cultures chart 1069
  conflict chart 170
  description web 1038
  details chart 287, 301, 564, 821, 1081, 1094
  fact and opinion chart 432, 588
  flow chart 26, 573
  Foldables 6, 472, 656, 898, 1020
  foreshadowing diagram 50
  generalization chart 104, 329
  heroic act checklist 982
  image list 1060
  implied theme diagram 113
  important words chart 560
  inferences chart 145, 418, 717
  interpret imagery chart 219, 663
  memorable language chart 760
  narrator chart 256
  paraphrasing chart 497
  plot diagram 15
  predictions chart 783
  problem and solution chart 402
  question and answer chart 376, 383, 535, 619, 838
  record thoughts chart 685
  rhyme scheme chart 539, 580
  rhythm chart 608
  sensory description chart 200
  sensory details chart 231, 595
  sequence chart 11, 847
  speaker chart 552
  stanza chart 557, 569
  structure chart 502
  thesis chart 16
  timeline 28, 242
  understand perspective chart 511
  Venn diagram 158, 369, 903, 1070, 1081
  verse paragraph chart 545
  visualization chart 493, 517, 1041
  web diagram 65, 101, 243, 326, 413, 443, 815, 959, 1083
  word clues chart 526
Historical context, analyzing 65, 71
Historical influences, evaluating 28
Ideas, comparing and contrasting 1070
Identifying
  assumptions and ambiguities 418, 429
  genre 943, 950, 1025, 1038
  problem and solution 402, 414
  sensory descriptions 200
  sequence 11, 969, 977, 1145
Imagery
  analyzing 244
  applying 520
  comparing and contrasting 524

INDEX OF SKILLS **R87**

interpreting 74, 219, 517, 519, 569, 571, 684, 1060, 1064
Implied meanings, understanding 622
Independent reading 268–269, 458–459, 642–643, 884–885, 1006–1007, 1128–1129
Inferences, making 113, 121, 145, 156, 526, 530, 619, 622, 717, 738, 783, 799, 959, 966
Interior monologue, applying 111
Interpreting 15, 26, 31, 49, 61, 71, 78, 101, 110, 120, 139, 156, 169, 177, 182, 197, 211, 242, 256, 301, 318, 326, 338, 349, 355, 364, 373, 380, 388, 398, 413, 429, 437, 441, 446, 479, 485, 489, 495, 501, 508, 514, 519, 524, 538, 545, 551, 557, 562, 567, 571, 575, 580, 590, 597, 604, 610, 616, 622, 684, 706, 738, 759, 782, 799, 814, 834, 841, 844, 865, 922, 935, 941, 949, 954, 965, 976, 987, 1037, 1055, 1064, 1073, 1081, 1087, 1092, 1113
  imagery 74, 219, 517, 519, 569, 571, 684, 1060, 1064
Investigating poetry 503
Irony, applying 171
Literary criticism, evaluating 16
Main idea
  determining 178, 1158
  reporting 415
Making generalizations 1140
  about characters, 104, 111
  about events 329
Making inferences
  about characters 145, 156, 717, 738, 959, 966, 1094, 1114
  about the speaker 526, 530
  about theme 113, 121, 619, 622
Making predictions 783, 799
Meaning
  clarifying 600, 605, 937

drawing conclusions
  about 376, 381, 564, 567
  understanding implied 622
Media genres, comparing 582–587
Meter and rhythm, analyzing 493, 495
Monitoring comprehension 497, 502
Mood, analyzing 838, 841
Narrators, comparing and contrasting 198, 217
Offering a solution 351
Oral tradition, comparing and contrasting 980, 991
Paraphrasing 560, 562
Personal experience, connecting to 89, 102, 357, 374
Persuasive appeals, comparing and contrasting 416, 430
Plot, analyzing 158, 170, 847, 865, 903, 923
Poetic structure, analyzing 482
Poetry, investigating 503
Point of view, applying 816
Position, arguing a 400, 708
Predictions, making and verifying 783, 799
Previewing 178, 439, 555, 558, 612, 709, 937, 1083
Primary sources 349, 604, 1037
Problem and solution, identifying 402, 414
Questioning 187, 197
Reading Check 5, 281, 471, 655, 897, 1019
Recognizing
  author's purpose 352, 685, 707, 821, 1089, 1092
  bias 395, 399
Repetition
  analyzing 548
  applying 447
Reporting main ideas or events 415
Responding 15, 26, 31, 49, 61, 71, 78, 101, 110, 120, 139,

156, 169, 177, 182, 197, 211, 242, 256, 301, 318, 326, 338, 349, 355, 364, 373, 380, 388, 398, 413, 429, 437, 441, 446, 479, 485, 489, 495, 501, 508, 514, 519, 524, 529, 538, 545, 551, 557, 562, 567, 571, 575, 580, 590, 597, 604, 610, 616, 622, 684, 706, 712, 738, 759, 782, 799, 814, 834, 841, 844, 865, 922, 935, 941, 949, 954, 965, 976, 987, 1037, 1055, 1064, 1073, 1081, 1087, 1092, 1113
  to characters 34
Reviewing 555, 558, 1151
Rhyme, analyzing 548, 552
Rhythm, analyzing 493, 495, 608, 610
Sensory descriptions, identifying 200
Sensory details, analyzing 231, 243, 595, 598
Sequence, identifying 11, 969, 977, 1145
Setting, analyzing 847, 865
Setting purpose for reading 11, 18, 28, 34, 55, 65, 74, 104, 113, 124, 145, 158, 173, 178, 187, 200, 219, 231, 246, 287, 305, 322, 329, 342, 352, 369, 376, 383, 395, 402, 418, 432, 439, 443, 477, 482, 487, 493, 497, 505, 511, 517, 522, 526, 535, 542, 548, 555, 560, 562, 569, 573, 577, 588, 595, 600, 608, 612, 619, 663, 709, 717, 739, 760, 783, 800, 821, 838, 842, 847, 903, 926, 937, 943, 951, 959, 969, 982, 1025, 1041, 1060, 1070, 1075, 1083, 1089, 1094
Solution, offering a 351
Sound devices, evaluating 606
Speaker, making inferences about 526, 530
Style, analyzing 342, 540

Summarizing 51, 287, 302, 415, 1145
Supporting details, determining 178
Symbolism, analyzing 80
Synthesizing 982, 987
Text structure, analyzing 383, 389, 443, 447
Theme
  analyzing 553
  comparing and contrasting 845, 873
  exploring 390
  making inferences about 113, 121, 619, 622
Tone, comparing and contrasting 535, 539
Understanding implied meanings 622
Verifying predictions 783, 799
Versions of a story, comparing and contrasting 951
Visual image, analyzing 439
Visualizing 200, 211, 493, 505, 508, 517, 573, 575, 1041, 1056, 1151

Vocabulary

Academic vocabulary 16, 27, 50, 52, 62, 79, 102, 111, 121, 140, 170, 243, 257, 302, 319, 327, 339, 350, 381, 389, 399, 414, 447, 490, 502, 515, 519, 524, 530, 539, 546, 552, 577, 598, 605, 707, 815, 835, 923, 936, 950, 966, 977, 1038, 1056, 1082, 1114
Analogies 34, 50, 74, 79, 243, 327, 383, 389, 487, 490, 505, 508, 562, 800, 815, 1038, 1064
Antonyms 200, 211, 381, 539, 1117
Bias 713
Connotation 32, 65, 71, 329, 339, 438, 542, 546, 555, 558, 581, 595, 611, 713, 783, 838, 841, 950, 1089, 1092

Context clues 16, 140, 319, 369, 374, 447, 479, 552, 569, 571, 663, 684, 782, 1082
Denotation 32, 65, 71, 329, 339, 438, 542, 546, 555, 558, 581, 595, 611, 713, 783, 838, 841, 950, 1089, 1092
Dictionary entries 72
Etymology 967, 1094, 1114
  See also Word origins
Graphic organizer
  connotation/denotation chart 558, 611
  jargon chart 340
  semantic chart 32
  web diagram 243, 539
  word map 111, 923, 1114
Homographs 72, 480
Homonyms 480
Homophones 480
Hyperbole 713
Jargon 340
Language resources 72
Loaded words 713
Multiple-meaning words 122
Propaganda 713
Roots
  Latin 622
  shared 27, 121, 622, 977
Synonyms 364, 414, 497, 502, 600, 605, 926, 936, 982, 987, 1117
Thesaurus use 1117
Word origins 55, 62, 104, 111, 257, 342, 350, 495, 515, 573, 575, 835, 923, 967, 979, 1094, 1114
Word parts 27, 121, 287, 302, 357, 395, 399, 526, 530, 622, 707, 847, 865, 969, 977
  prefix 121, 622, 977
  root 121, 622, 977
  suffix 121, 622, 977
Word usage 89, 102, 158, 170, 187, 197, 418, 429, 482, 564, 567, 739, 759, 959, 966, 1041, 1056

Writing

Action verbs, using 454
Analysis
  personal 999
Analyzing
  cause-and-effect relationships 978, 1115
  cultural context 217, 873, 991
  imagery 244
  plot 6
  professional writing model 259, 449, 633, 875, 1119
  style 540
  symbolism 80
  theme 553
  workshop model 452, 636, 878, 995
Anecdote 364
Annotations 1163
Appeal
  emotional 708, 879
  logical 708, 879
Applying
  characterization 141
  description 62
  dialogue 923
  figurative language 558
  imagery 520
  interior monologue 111
  irony 171, 835
  point of view 816
  repetition 447
  tone 327
Arguing a position 400, 708
Audience 451, 633, 634, 637, 993, 996, 997, 1039
Autobiographical narrative 171
Biographical narrative 448–455, 816
Business letter 1144
Cause-and-effect relationships, analyzing 978
Character sketch 197, 327, 479
Characterization, applying 141, 1120, 1123
Choosing a topic 876
Coherence, paragraph 1000

Comparison, developing 491
Conflict 1120
Controlling impression 452
Convincing an audience 1039
Counterargument 876, 878, 880
Cultural context, analyzing 217, 873, 991
Creative writing
    advice column 684
    dialogue 257
    editorial 351
    journal entry 177
    letter, 211, 429
    letter to the editor, 447
    magazine blurbs 438
    movie scene 495
    travel brochure 121
Description
    applying 62
    writing 571
Details 261, 635, 637, 638, 1119
Developing a comparison 491
Dialogue 156, 575, 923, 1119, 1122, 1123, 1124
Documenting sources 339, 530, 998
Drafting 51, 84, 141, 171, 244, 262, 320, 351, 390, 400, 452, 491, 503, 540, 553, 606, 636, 708, 816, 878, 978, 1039, 1115, 1123
Editing 51, 84, 141, 171, 244, 265, 320, 390, 455, 491, 540, 553, 606, 639, 816, 881, 978, 1001, 1039, 1115, 1125
Editorial 351
Elaborating on ideas 880
Essay 562
    expository 259–265, 448–455, 992–1001
    persuasive 400, 708
    reflective 390, 632–639
    stream-of-consciousness 1064
Evaluating
    literary criticism 16
    paragraph structure 606

sound devices 606
sources 121, 530, 993
Exploring theme 390
Expository essay 259–265, 448–455, 992–1001
Figurative language, applying 558
Finding a topic 993
Focus 259, 260, 263, 634
    historical 263
Graphic organizer for prewriting
    chart 217, 302, 339, 540, 553, 819, 1039
    cluster diagram 520
    concept web 87, 593
    story map 1122
    timeline 816, 835
Historical focus 263
Imagery
    analyzing 244
    applying 520
Impression, controlling 452
Interior monologue 111, 485, 865
Investigating poetry 503
Irony, applying 171, 835
Journal entry 177
Letter 211, 429
Letter to the editor 447
List 71, 1150
Literary criticism 258, 259–265
    biographical 261
    evaluating 16
    historical approach 261
Literature groups 102
Magazine blurbs 438
Main idea 261, 263, 994, 996
Making a time frame 993
Manuscript guidelines 265, 455, 639, 1001
Meaning 634
Monologue 1123
Movie scene 495
Multimedia presentation 339
Narrative
    autobiographical 171
    biographical 448–455, 816
    elements 633, 636
    structure 637

techniques 452, 453
Narrowing a topic 993
Note cards 994
Note taking 121, 994
Offering a solution 351
Organizational plan 259, 261, 263, 451, 553, 633, 877, 994
Outline
    developing 121
    formal 451
    informal 451
Paragraph coherence 1000
Paragraph structure, evaluating 606
Parallel construction 881
Paraphrasing 121, 994, 996
Personal analysis 999
Persuasive essay 400
Persuasive speech 874–881
Persuasive techniques 877
Plagiarism 261, 451, 635, 994, 1004, 1122
Plot
    analyzing 6
    building 1121
Poem 524
Poetry, investigating 503
Point of view
    applying 816
    choosing 1121
    correcting shifts in 1125
    first-person 633, 636
    third-person 816
Position, arguing 400, 708
Presentation, multimedia 339
Presenting 265, 455, 639, 1001
Prewriting 51, 84, 141, 171, 244, 261, 320, 351, 390, 400, 415, 451, 491, 503, 540, 553, 606, 635, 708, 816, 876, 978, 993, 1039, 1115, 1122
Professional writing model, analyzing 259, 449, 633, 875, 1119
Proofreading 51, 84, 141, 171, 244, 265, 320, 390, 455, 491, 540, 553, 606, 639, 816, 881, 978, 1001, 1039, 1115, 1125

Prose poem 508
Publishing 265, 639
Purpose 259, 263, 451, 993
Quickwrite 9, 87, 185, 216, 285, 367, 393, 428, 475, 533, 593, 626, 659, 819, 872, 901, 957, 989, 1067
Quotations 997, 999
Quoting sources 994, 997, 999
Readability 455
Reflective essay 390, 632–639
Repetition, applying 447
Reporting main ideas or events 415
Research report 27, 302, 320, 339, 438, 503, 530, 992–1001
Revising 51, 80, 141, 171, 244, 264, 320, 351, 390, 400, 454, 491, 503, 540, 553, 606, 638, 708, 816, 880, 978, 999, 1039, 1115, 1124
Rubrics 258, 264, 448, 454, 503, 632, 638, 874, 880, 992, 1000, 1118, 1124
Scenes and incidents 453
Sensory details 638
Sentence openers, varying 264
Sequence of events, creating 452
Short story 1118–1125
Sound devices, evaluating 606
Sources
    documenting 339, 530, 998
    evaluating 121, 530, 993
    multiple 997
    paraphrasing 994, 996
    primary 320
    quoting 994, 997, 999
    secondary 320
    summarizing 994
Speech, persuasive 874–881, 1056
Story map, making 1122
Structure, creating 636
Style
    analyzing 540
    conventional 265
Subject, choosing 451

Summarizing 51, 121, 415
    sources 994
Summary 567
Supporting details 260, 262, 876, 998
Symbolism, analyzing 80
Theme
    analyzing 553
    exploring 390
Thesaurus, using a 1117
Thesis 260, 261, 262, 383, 388, 553, 875, 878, 994, 995
Time frame, making 993
Time order 1121, 1123
Tone 259, 262, 263, 327, 633, 634, 637, 1121
Topic
    choosing 876
    finding 993
    narrowing 993
Transitions 878
Travel brochure 121
Travel directions 1157
Using action verbs 454
Varying sentence openers 264
Word choice 454
Workshop model,
    analyzing 452, 636, 878, 995
Writing about literature 51, 80, 141, 244, 351

Grammar

Absolute phrases 351
Absolutes 351
Active voice 400
Adjective clause 143
Adjectives
    comparative 491
    superlative 491
Adverbs
    comparative 606
    conjunctive 1116
    superlative 606
Agreement
    pronoun-antecedent 509
    subject-verb 303
Apostrophes 63
Appositive 142, 816

Clauses
    adjective 143
    main 924
    subordinate 924
Colons 80, 1115
Commas 553, 816, 836, 1001
Comparative adjectives 491
Comparative adverbs 606
Conjunction
    coordinating 143, 1116
    subordinating 143
Coordinating conjunction 143
Dangling participle 1057
Dashes 390
Ellipses 503
Fragments 171, 229, 415
Gerunds 708
Hyphens 320
Infinitive phrases 708
Infinitives 708
Interjections 836
Introductory phrases 553
Italics 1039
Main clause 924
Nouns
    possessive 63
Paragraphing 244
Parentheses 1057
Parenthetical expressions 836
Participial phrase 143, 1057
Participles, dangling 1057
Parts of speech
    adjectives 491
    adverbs 606
    clauses 143, 924
    conjunctions 143
    nouns 63
    pronouns 63, 509, 639
    verbs 303, 708
Passive voice 400
Phrases
    absolute 351
    appositive 142
    infinitive 708
    introductory 553
    participial 143, 1057
    prepositional 142
    transitional 553, 978
Possessives 63

INDEX OF SKILLS **R91**

Prepositional phrase 142
Pronoun reference 509
Pronouns
  possessive 63
  pronoun-antecedent
    agreement 509
  pronoun reference 509, 639
Punctuation
  apostrophes 63
  colons 80, 1115
  commas 553, 816, 836
  dashes 390
  ellipses 503
  hyphens 320
  parentheses 1057
  semicolons 540, 1116
Quotations 141
Run-on sentences 265
Semicolons 540, 1116
Sentence
  combining 142
  fragments 171, 229, 415
  run-on 265
Subject-verb agreement 303
Subjects 303
  compound 303
Subordinate clause 924
Subordinating conjunction 143
Superlative adjectives 491
Superlative adverbs 606
Transitional phrases 553, 978, 1001
Verbals 708
Verb tenses 51, 455
Verbs 303
  infinitives 708
  plural 303
  singular 303
Voice 400
  active 400
  passive 400

Speaking, Listening, and Viewing

Analyzing media
  messages 582–587
Choosing media 1003
Coordinating words and
  images 457
Critical viewing 242, 415, 489, 706, 814, 1113
Debate 381, 950
Discussion starter 214, 425, 630, 866, 990, 1065
Editing media 1003
Expository presentation 266, 456, 640, 882, 1002, 1126
Graphic organizer 217, 381, 430, 515, 546, 581, 583, 598, 950, 966, 1056, 1082
Group discussion 214, 425, 585, 587, 630, 866, 898, 990, 1020
Interview 936
Listening techniques 1005, 1127
Literary criticism 49, 169, 389, 501, 551
Literature groups 102, 374
Media 1002
  analyzing messages 582–587
  choosing 1003
  documentary 586
  editing 1003
  electronic 582
  equipment 1003
  print 582
  radio transcript 584
Multimedia
  presentation 1002–1005
Multimedia research
  report 339
Nonverbal techniques 267, 457, 515, 641, 883, 1127
Oral interpretation 515, 546
Oral presentation
  dramatic performance 1126
  interpretation of a story 1126
  literary criticism 266
  multimedia 1002–1005
  narrative 456, 457
  organizing an 1004
  poetry 472, 546
  reflective 640
  research report 530
  speech 581, 882
Oral report 16, 27, 102, 217, 339, 374, 430, 438, 530, 598, 631, 873, 991, 1082
Organizing a
  presentation 1004
Performing
  dialogue 257, 656, 966
  poetry 515, 546
  short story recreation 1126
Presentation techniques 1005, 1127
Reflective presentation 640
Rehearsing 267, 546, 641, 883, 1005, 1127
Speech, delivering 581, 882, 1056
Storyboard 1004
Verbal techniques 267, 457, 515, 641, 883, 1127
Viewing techniques 1005
Visual aids, in
  presentations 27, 267, 339, 456, 472, 641, 995
  biopic 456
  montage 456
  time line 456

Research, Test-Taking, and Study Skills

Evaluating sources 121, 993
Grammar tests 274, 890, 1012, 1134
Graphic organizer
  alliteration chart 605
  alternative meanings
    chart 600
  background knowledge
    chart 577
  cause-and-effect diagram
    18, 173, 305, 739
  character chart 120, 124, 707, 800
  characteristics chart 1025
  chart 62, 74, 83, 89, 102, 187, 217, 246, 257, 302, 319, 338, 339, 342, 350, 357, 373, 380, 381, 395, 398, 438, 487, 490, 514, 529, 540, 542, 546, 553, 555, 581, 598, 819, 842, 950, 951, 966, 977, 1039, 1056, 1075, 1082, 1089

cluster diagram 520
compare cultures chart 1069
concept web 87, 593
conflict chart 170
connotation/denotation chart 558, 611
description web 1038
details chart 178, 287, 301, 430, 564, 821, 1081, 1094
fact and opinion chart 432, 588
flowchart 26, 27, 573
Foldables 6, 472, 656, 898, 1020
foreshadowing diagram 50
generalization chart 104, 329
heroic act checklist 982
image list 1060
implied theme diagram 113
important words chart 560
inferences chart 145, 418, 717
interpret imagery chart 219, 663
jargon chart 340
memorable language chart 760
narrator chart 256
paraphrasing chart 497
plot diagram 15
predictions chart 783
problem and solution chart 402
question and answer chart 376, 383, 535, 619, 838
record thoughts chart 685
rhyme scheme chart 539, 580
rhythm chart 608
semantic chart 32
sensory description chart 200
sensory details chart 231, 595
sequence chart 11, 847
speaker chart 552
stanza chart 557, 569
story map 1122
structure chart 502
study organizer 282
thesis chart 16
timeline 28, 242, 816, 835
understand perspective chart 511
Venn diagram 158, 369, 903, 1070, 1081
verbal/nonverbal techniques chart 515
verse paragraph chart 545
visual image chart 439
visualization chart 493, 517, 1041
web diagram 65, 101, 243, 326, 352, 413, 414, 443, 815, 959, 1083
word clues chart 526
word map 111, 923, 1114
Internet research 27, 121, 302
Multimedia report 339
Note cards 994
Note taking 6, 11, 15, 16, 18, 26, 27, 28, 32, 34, 50, 62, 65, 74, 83, 89, 101, 102, 104, 111, 113, 120, 124, 145, 158, 170, 173, 178, 187, 200, 217, 219, 231, 242, 243, 246, 256, 257, 265, 282, 287, 301, 302, 305, 319, 326, 329, 338, 339, 340, 342, 350, 352, 357, 369, 373, 376, 380, 381, 383, 395, 398, 402, 413, 414, 418, 430, 432, 438, 439, 443, 451, 472, 487, 490, 493, 497, 502, 511, 514, 515, 517, 520, 526, 529, 535, 539, 540, 542, 545, 546, 552, 553, 555, 557, 558, 560, 564, 569, 573, 577, 580, 581, 593, 595, 598, 600, 605, 608, 611, 619, 656, 663, 685, 707, 717, 739, 760, 783, 800, 815, 816, 819, 821, 835, 838, 842, 847, 898, 903, 923, 950, 951, 959, 966, 977, 982, 994, 1020, 1025, 1038, 1039, 1056, 1060, 1069, 1070, 1075, 1081, 1082, 1083, 1089, 1094, 1114, 1122
Paraphrasing sources 994, 996
Peer review 264, 265, 455, 638, 639, 881, 1001, 1124, 1125
Plagiarism 261, 451, 635, 877, 994, 1004, 1122
Quotations
  direct 994
  long 997
Quoting sources 994
Reading tests 270, 886, 1008, 1130
Research reports 121, 302, 320, 339, 992–1001
  oral 16, 438, 530
  oral, with visual aids 27, 339
Sources
  evaluating 121, 993
  multiple 997
  paraphrasing 994, 996
  quoting 994
  summarizing 994
Subject, choosing 451
Summarizing sources 994
Test practice
  grammar 274, 890, 1012, 1134
  reading 270, 886, 1008, 1130
  vocabulary 273, 889, 1011, 1133
  writing 275, 891, 1013, 1135
Test-taking tip 32, 52, 53, 63, 143, 229, 340, 509, 713, 836, 924, 967, 979, 1057
Thesis 260, 261, 262, 553, 875, 878, 994, 995
Topic
  choosing 451, 876
  finding 993
  narrowing 993
Vocabulary tests 273, 889, 1011, 1133
Writing tests 275, 891, 1013, 1135

INDEX OF SKILLS R93

Interdisciplinary Activities

Daily life and culture 139, 318, 538, 976
Geology 27
Science 27, 1070
Social studies 530

Index of Authors and Titles

A
Achebe, Chinua 64
Address on the Anniversary of Lincoln's Birth 431
After Apple Picking 599
After great pain, a formal feeling comes 534
Akhmatova, Anna 1067
Alexie, Sherman 572
Allende, Isabel 230
American Childhood, An, from 356
And of Clay Are We Created 230
Angelou, Maya 321, 460
Angela's Ashes, from 341
Anthony, Susan B. 394
Antigone 662
Arabic Coffee 607
Arnold, Andrew 426
Asimov, Isaac 1074, 1119
Astrologer's Day, An 54
Atwood, Margaret 1088

B
Baca, Jimmy Santiago 554
Ballad of Birmingham 576
Bashō, Matsuo 516
Baughn, Alice Jackson 449
Benét, Stephen Vincent 1040
Bird, Maryann 709
Book of the Dead, The 151
Bradbury, Ray 1026
Branston, Brian 958
Bread 1088
Broad, William J. 1070
Brooks, Gwendolyn 563
Brown, Chester 417
Bruchac, Joseph 981
By the Waters of Babylon 1040

C
Californian's Tale, The 17
Calvino, Italo 1018
Car We Had to Push, The 103
Catch the Moon 218
Censors, The 172
Cervantes, Miguel de 925
Chekhov, Anton 820
Christie, Agatha 1093
Cinderella's Stepsisters 442
Cisneros, Sandra 382
Civil Peace 64
Clifton, Lucille 594
Cofer, Judith Ortiz 218
Cohen, Adam 1083
Collins, Billy 481
Contents of the Dead Man's Pocket 33
Creatures 481
Cry of the Ancient Mariner 178
Cummings, E. E. 559

D
Danticat, Edwidge 151
Dear Pie 215
Dickinson, Emily 534
Dillard, Annie 356
Dinesen, Isak 867
Dirksen, Everett 875
Divakaruni, Chitra Banerjee 525
Don Quixote, from 925
Dove, Rita 568
Down by the Salley Gardens 547
Dream, The 1067
Dream Boogie 618

E
Ebert, Roger 588
Eisner, Will 951
Eudora Welty: 1909–2001, from 449
Ever Alluring 709
Everyday Use 186

F
Farewell to Manzanar, from 286
Finney, Jack 33
Fire and Ice 603
First Impressions, from *De Kooning, An American Master* 328
Fitzgerald, F. Scott 215
Fitzsimmons, Robin 896
4 Little Girls 588
Frost, Robert 599
Frustration 1119

G
Giants of Jazz, from 623
Gomez, Jewelle L. 368
Graphic Novel Silver Anniversary, The 426

H
Hamilton, Edith 968
"Hamlet" Too Hard? Try a Comic Book 422
Happy Man's Shirt, The 1018
Harjo, Joy 633
Hayden, Robert 476
He Wishes for the Cloths of Heaven 550
Heart! We will forget him! 537
Hemenway, Robert E. 280
Horses Graze 563

Houston, James D. 286
Houston, Jeanne Wakatsuki 286
Hughes, Carolyn T. 352
Hughes, Langston 618
Hurston, Zora Neale 988

I

I Am Offering This Poem 554
Ise, Lady 521
I've Been to the Mountaintop 401

J

Janitor, The 654
John Henry 988
Journey of Gilgamesh, The 896
Julius Caesar, The Tragedy of 716

K

Kaffir Boy, from 304
Kafka, Franz 1130
Kincaid, Jamaica 1059
King Arthur, from 1008
King, Martin Luther Jr. 401

L

Lahiri, Jhumpa 123
Lame Deer 212
Le Morte d'Arthur, from 902
Lee, Chang-Rae 612
Lessing, Doris 199
Levertov, Denise 1065
Lion of Mali, The 951
Living Well. Living Good. 321
Looking Forward to the Past, from 352
Lullaby 245

M

Machine Nurturer, The 1083
Malory, Sir Thomas 902
Marked 866
Márquez, Gabriel García 112
Marriage Proposal, A 820
Marsalis, Wynton 627
Marshall, Paule 144, 259
Masque of the Red Death, The 73
Mathabane, Mark 304
McCourt, Frank 341, 352
McGrath, Charles 470
Meadow Mouse, The 541
Méndez, Teresa 422
Metamorphosis, from 1130
miss rosie 594
Momaday, N. Scott 510
Morrison, Toni 442
Motto 621

N

Narayan, R. K. 54
Neruda, Pablo 496
Niane, D. T. 942
Niggli, Josephina 846
Not Just Comic Books 417
Nye, Naomi Shihab 607, 645

O

O Captain! My Captain! 470
Oates, Joyce Carol 28
Obama, Barack 439
Ode to My Socks 496
Oedipus the King, from 886
On Women's Right to Vote 394
One Legend Found, Many Still to Go 1070
Open Window, The 10

P

Parlor 568
People at Night 1065
Pinter, Harold 837, 842
Playing Jazz 627
Poe, Edgar Allan 73
Print of the Paw, The 510

R

Randall, Dudley 576
Real-Life Story Behind "To Da-duh, In Memoriam" 259
Reapers 492
Red Velvet Dress, from 645
Ring, The 867
Ring of General Macías, The 846
Ripley, Amanda 937
Robot Dreams 1074
Roethke, Theodore 541
Rosenberg, Donna 1008
Ross, Gayle 981

S

Safina, Carl 178
Saki (H. H. Munro) 10
Sandburg, Carl 431
Secondhand Grief 572
Shakespeare, William 486, 716
Shall I Compare Thee to a Summer's Day 486
Silko, Leslie Marmon 245
since feeling is first 559
Solzhenitsyn, Aleksandr 504
Song of Greatness, A 990
Sonnet 18 (Morice) 602
Sophocles 662, 886
Sound of Thunder, A 1026
Storytelling Is As Old As Mankind 28
Stealing of Thor's Hammer, The 958

Storm in the Mountains, A 504
Straw into Gold: The Metamorphosis of the Everyday 382
Sundiata (Niane), from 942
Sundiata: A Legend of Africa, from (Eisner) 951
Suspended 633
Swan, Annalyn 328
Swimming Lesson, A 368

T

Tafolla, Carmen 866
Tan, Amy 88
Terkel, Studs 623
Terwilliger Bunts One, from *An American Childhood* 356
That's Your Trouble 837
Theseus, from 968
Thomas, Lewis 375
Those Winter Sundays 476
Three Haiku 516
Through the Tunnel 199
Thurber, James 103, 271
To An Aged Bear 513
To Da-duh, In Memoriam 144
Toomer, Jean 492

Tragedy of Julius Caesar, The 716
Tucson Zoo, The 375
Tuesday Siesta 112
Twain, Mark 17, 270
Two Kinds 88
Two Tanka 521
Typhoid Fever, from *Angela's Ashes* 341

U

Unicorn in the Garden, The 271

V

Valenzuela, Luisa 172
Verniero, Joan C. 896
Vision Quest, The 212

W

Walker, Alice 186
We Are Family 612
What I Have Been Doing Lately 1059
What I See in Lincoln's Eyes 439
What Makes a Hero? 937

When Mr. Pirzada Came to Dine 123
When the Buffalo Climbed a Tree, from 270
Where the Girl Rescued Her Brother 981
Whitman, Walt 470
Why Marigolds Should Be the National Flower 875
Wilson, August 654
Witness for the Prosecution, The 1093
Woman with Kite 525
Wouldn't Take Nothing for My Journey Now, from 460
Writing for the Theater 842

Y

Yeats, William Butler 547

Z

Zora Neale Hurston, from 280

Acknowledgments

Unit 1

"Old Man at the Bridge," reprinted with permission of Scribner, an imprint of Simon & Schuster Adult Publishing Group, from *The Short Stories of Ernest Hemingway*. Copyright 1938 by Ernest Hemingway. Copyright renewed © 1966 by Mary Hemingway.

From "Introduction" from *The Oxford Book of American Short Stories,* edited by Joyce Carol Oates. Copyright © 1992 by The Ontario Review, Inc. Reprinted by permission of The Ontario Review, Inc.

"The Book of the Dead" by Edwidge Danticat. First published in *The New Yorker* and reprinted by permission of Edwidge Danticat and Aragi Inc.

"An Astrologer's Day" from *The Grandmother's Tale and Selected Stories* by R. K. Narayan. Copyright © 1994 by R. K. Narayan. Reprinted by permission of the Wallace Literary Agency, Inc.

"Civil Peace" from *Girls at War and Other Stories* by Chinua Achebe, copyright © 1972, 1973 by Chinua Achebe. Used by permission of Doubleday, a division of Random House, Inc. and the Emma Sweeney Agency.

"Two Kinds" by Amy Tan, copyright © 1989 by Amy Tan. First appeared in *The Joy Luck Club*. Reprinted by permission of the author and the Sandra Dijkstra Literary Agency

"The Car We Had to Push" from *My Life and Hard Times* by James Thurber. Copyright © 1933 by James Thurber. Copyright © renewed 1961 by Helen Thurber and Rosemary A. Thurber. Reprinted by arrangement with the Barbara Hogenson Agency.

"Tuesday Siesta" from *No One Writes to the Colonel and Other Stories* by Gabriel García Márquez and translated by J. S. Bernstein. Copyright © 1968 in the English translation by Harper & Row Publishers, Inc. Reprinted by permission of HarperCollins Publishers.

"When Mr. Pirzada Came to Dine" from *Interpreter of Maladies* by Jhumpa Lahiri. Copyright © 1999 by Jhumpa Lahiri. Reprinted by permission of Houghton Mifflin Company. All rights reserved.

Paule Marshall, Introduction and "To Da-duh, In Memoriam" from *Reena and Other Stories.* Copyright © 1983 by The Feminist Press. Reprinted with the permission of The Feminist Press at the City University of New York, www.feministpress.org.

"Contents of the Dead Man's Pocket" by Jack Finney. Reprinted by permission of Don Congdon Associates. Copyright © 1956 by the Crowell Collier Publishing Company, renewed 1984 by Jack Finney.

Anderson Literary Management, LLC: "The Censors," copyright © 1988 by Luisa Valenzuela, from *Open Door: Stories* (North Point Press), copyright © 1998 by Luisa Valenzuela

"Everyday Use" from *In Love & Trouble: Stories of Black Women,* copyright © 1973 by Alice Walker, reprinted by permission of Harcourt, Inc. and The Wendy Weil Agency.

"Through the Tunnel" from *The Habit of Loving* by Doris Lessing. Copyright © 1955 by Doris Lessing. Originally appeared in *The New Yorker.* Reprinted by permission of HarperCollins Publishers

"The Vision Quest" from *American Indian Myths and Legends* by Richard Erdoes and Alfonso Ortiz, copyright © 1984 by Richard Erdoes and Alfonso Ortiz. Used by permission of Pantheon Books, a division of Random House, Inc.

"Catch the Moon" from *An Island Like You: Stories of the Barrio* by Judith Ortiz Cofer. Published by Scholastic Inc./Orchard Books. Copyright © 1995 by Judith Ortiz Cofer. All rights reserved. Used by permission.

"And of Clay Are We Created" reprinted with the permission of Scribner, an imprint of Simon & Schuster Adult Publishing Group, from *The Stories of Eva Luna* by Isabel Allende. Copyright © 1989 by Isabel Allende. English translation copyright © 1991 by Macmillan Publishing Company.

"Lullaby," copyright © 1981 by Leslie Marmon Silko. Reprinted from *Storyteller* by Leslie Marmon Silko, published by Seaver Books, New York, New York.

"The Unicorn in the Garden" from *Fables for Our Time* by James Thurber. Copyright © 1939, 1940 by James Thurber. Reprinted by arrangement with the Barbara Hogenson Agency

Unit 2

From *Zora Neale Hurston: A Literary Biography* by Robert E. Hemenway. Copyright © 1997 by the Board of Trustees of the University of Illinois. Reprinted by permission.

Chapters 2–4 from *Farewell to Manzanar* by James D. and Jeanne Wakatsuki Houston. Copyright © 1973 by James D. Houston. Reprinted by permission of Houghton Mifflin Co. All rights reserved.

Reprinted with the permission of Scribner, an imprint of Simon & Schuster Adult Publishing Group, from *Kaffir Boy* by Mark Mathabane. Copyright © 1986 by Mark Mathabane

From *Wouldn't Take Nothing For My Journey Now* by Maya Angelou, copyright © 1993 by Maya Angelou. Used by permission of Random House, Inc.

"First Impressions" from *De Kooning: An American Master* by Mark Stevens and Annalyn Swan. Copyright © 2004 by Mark Stevens and Annalyn Swan. Used by permission of Alfred A. Knopf, a division of Random House, Inc.

"Typhoid Fever" reprinted with the permission of Scribner, an imprint of Simon & Schuster Adult Publishing Group, from *Angela's Ashes* by Frank McCourt. Copyright © 1996 by Frank McCourt.

Carolyn T. Hughes, "Looking Forward to the Past: A Profile of Frank McCourt," *Poets & Writers Magazine*, September/October 1999. Reprinted by permission of the publishers, Poets & Writers, Inc., 72 Spring Street, New York, NY 10012. www.pw.org.

Excerpt from *An American Childhood* by Annie Dillard. Copyright © 1987 by Annie Dillard. Reprinted by permission of HarperCollins Publishers, Inc.

"A Swimming Lesson" from *Forty-Three Septembers*, copyright © 1993 by Jewelle Gomez. Reprinted by permission of Firebrand Books.

"The Tucson Zoo," copyright © 1977 by Lewis Thomas, from *The Medusa and the Snail* by Lewis Thomas. Used by permission of Viking Penguin, a division of Penguin Group (USA) Inc.

"Straw Into Gold," copyright © 1987 by Sandra Cisneros. First published in *The Texas Observer*, September 1987. Reprinted by permission of Susan Bergholz Literary Services, New York. All rights reserved.

"I've Been to the Mountaintop" reprinted by arrangement with the Estate of Martin Luther King Jr., c/o Writers House as agent for the proprietor New York, NY. Copyright 1968 Martin Luther King Jr., copyright renewed 1966 Coretta Scott King.

"'Hamlet' too hard? Try a comic book" by Teresa Méndez. *Christian Science Monitor*, October 12, 2004. Reprinted by permission of the Copyright Clearance Center.

"Cinderella's Stepsisters" by Toni Morrison. Reprinted by permission of International Creative Management, Inc. Copyright © 1979 by Toni Morrison.

"Getups" from *Wouldn't Take Nothing For My Journey Now* by Maya Angelou, copyright © 1993 by Maya Angelou. Used by permission of Random House, Inc.

Unit 3

"Those Winter Sundays" Copyright © 1966 by Robert Hayden, from *Collected Poems of Robert Hayden* by Robert Hayden, edited by Frederick Glaysher. Used by permission of Liveright Publishing Corporation.

"Creatures," copyright © 2002 by Billy Collins, from *Nine Horses* by Billy Collins. Used by permission of Random House, Inc..

"Ode to My Socks" from *Neruda and Vallejo: Selected Poems*, translated by Robert Bly and James Wright, Boston, Beacon Press 1976. © 1972 by Robert Bly. Reprinted by permission.

From *In the Bear's House* by N. Scott Momaday. Copyright © 1999 by the author and reprinted by permission of St. Martin's Press, LLC.

Three haiku by Bashō from *The Essential Haiku: Versions of Bashō, Buson & Issa*, edited and with an introduction by Robert Haas. Introduction and selection copyright © 1994 by Robert Haas. Unless otherwise noted, all translations copyright © 1994 by Robert Haas. Reprinted by permission of HarperCollins Publishers.

Two tanka by Lady Ise, from *A Book of Women Poets from Antiquity to Now* by Willis Barnstone and Aliki Barnstone, copyright © 1980 by Schocken Books, a division of Random House, Inc. Used by permission of Schocken Books, a division of Random House, Inc.

"Woman with Kite" from *Leaving Yuba City* by Chitra Banerjee Divakaruni, copyright © 1997 by Chitra Banerjee Divakaruni. Used by permission of Doubleday, a division of Random House, Inc.

"Heart we will forget him" and "After great pain, a formal feeling comes" reprinted by permission of the publishers and the Trustees of Amherst College from *The Poems of Emily Dickinson*, Thomas H. Johnson, ed., Cambridge, Mass: The Belknap Press of Harvard University Press, Copyright © 1951, 1955, 1979, 1983 by the President and Fellows of Harvard College.

"The Meadow Mouse" copyright © 1963 by Beatrice Roethke, Administratrix of the Estate of Theodore Roethke, from *Collected Poems of Theodore Roethke*, by Theodore Roethke. Used by permission of Doubleday, a division of Random House, Inc.

"since feeling is first" Copyright 1926, 1954 © 1991 by the Trustees for the E.E. Cummings Trust. Copyright © 1985 by George James Firmage, from *Complete Poems: 1904-1962* by E.E. Cummings, edited by George J. Firmage. Used by permission of Liveright Publishing Corporation.

"Horses Graze" by Gwendolyn Brooks. Reprinted by consent of Brooks Permissions.

"Parlor" from *On the Bus with Rosa Parks,* W. W. Norton & Co., New York. Copyright © 1999 by Rita Dove. Used by permission of the author.

"Secondhand Grief" by Sherman Alexie, from *One Stick Song,* copyright © 2000 by Sherman Alexie. Reprinted by permission of Hanging Loose Press.

"4 Little Girls" by Roger Ebert (October 24, 1997) Copyright © the Ebert Company. Reprinted by permission.

"miss rosie" copyright © 1987 by Lucille Clifton. Reprinted from *Good Woman: Poems and a Memoir: 1969–1980* with permission from The Permissions Company on behalf of BOA editions, Rochester, NY

"After Apple-Picking" and "Fire and Ice" from *The Poetry of Robert Frost,* edited by Edward Connery Lathem. 1923, 1930, 1939, 1969 by Henry Holt and Company, copyright 1951, 1958 by Robert Frost © 1967 by Lesley Frost Ballantine. Reprinted by permission of Henry Holt and Company LLC.

"Arabic Coffee" from *19 Varieties of Gazelle: Poems of the Middle East.* Copyright © 1994, 1995, 1998, 2002 by Naomi Shihab Nye. Reprinted by permission of the author.

"Dizzy Gillespie" from *Giants of Jazz* by Studs Terkel. Reprinted by permission of Donadio & Olsen, Inc. Copyright © 1957, 1975 by Studs Terkel.

From *To A Young Jazz Musician* by Wynton Marsalis and Selwyn Seyfu Hinds, copyright © 2004 by Wynton Marsalis Enterprises. Used by permission of Random House, Inc.

"Suspended" by Joy Harjo. Reprinted by permission of the author.

"Daybreak in Alabama" from *The Collected Poems of Langston Hughes* by Langston Hughes, copyright © 1994 by The Estate of Langston Hughes. Used by permission of Alfred A. Knopf, a division of Random House, Inc.

Excerpt from "Red Velvet Dress" by Naomi Shihab Nye. Reprinted by permission of the author.

Unit 4

"The Janitor" by August Wilson. Copyright © 1985 by August Wilson. Reprinted by permission of the Estate of August Wilson.

The Antigone of Sophocles, an English Version by Dudley Fitts and Robert Fitzgerald, copyright 1939 by Harcourt, Inc., and renewed 1967 by Dudley Fitts and Robert Fitzgerald, reprinted by permission of the publisher. CAUTION: All rights, including professional, amateur, motion picture, recitation, lecturing, performance, public reading, radio broadcasting, and television are strictly reserved. Inquiries on all rights should be addressed to Harcourt, Inc., Permissions Department, Orlando, FL 32887-6777.

"A Marriage Proposal" from *The Brute and Other Farces* by Anton Chekhov, English version by Theodore Hoffman, edited by Eric Bentley. Copyright © 1958 by Eric Bentley. International Copyright Secured. All Rights Reserved.

"That's Your Trouble" from *Complete Works: Three* by Harold Pinter. Copyright © 1966 by H. Pinter Ltd. Used by permission of Grove/Atlantic, Inc.

"Writing for the Theater" from *Complete Works: One* by Harold Pinter. Copyright © 1962, 1964 by H. Pinter Ltd. Used by permission of Grove/Atlantic, Inc.

"The Ring" copyright © 1958 by Isak Dinesen, from *Anecdotes of Destiny* by Isak Dinesen. Used by permission of Random House, Inc.

"Marked" by Carmen Tafolla. Reprinted by permission of the author.

Excerpt from "Oedipus the King" from *Three Theban Plays* by Sophocles, translated by Robert Fagles, copyright © 1982 by Robert Fagles. Used by permission of Viking Penguin, a division of Penguin Group (USA) Inc.

Unit 5

"The Journey of Gilgamesh" by Joan C. Verniero and Robin Fitzsimmons, from *One-Hundred-and-One Read-Aloud Myths,* copyright © 1999, Black Dog & Leventhal Publishers. Reprinted by permission of Black Dog & Leventhal Publishers.

From *Le Morte d'Arthur* by Sir Thomas Malory, translated by Keith Baines, copyright © 1967 by Keith Baines. Used by permission of Clarkson Potter Publishers, a division of Random House, Inc.

From *The Adventures of Don Quixote* by Miguel de Cervantes Saavedra, translated by J. M. Cohen (Penguin Classics, 1950). Translation copyright © 1950 by J. M. Cohen. Reprinted by permission of Penguin Group (UK).

From *Sundiata: An Epic of Old Mali* by D. T. Niane. Copyright © 1965 by Longmans, Green & Co. Reprinted by permission of Pearson Education.

"Theseus" from *Mythology* by Edith Hamilton. Copyright © 1942 by Edith Hamilton. Copyright © renewed 1969 by Dorian Fielding Reid and Doris Fielding Reid. By permission of Little, Brown and Co., Inc.

"Where the Girl Rescued Her Brother," from *The Girl Who Married the Moon,* copyright © 1994 by Joseph Bruchac and Gayle Ross. Reprinted by permission of Barbara S. Kouts.

"John Henry" verse as taken from *Mules and Men* by Zora Neale Hurston. Copyright 1935 by Zora Neale Hurston; renewed © 1963 by John C. Hurston and Joel Hurston. Reprinted by permission of HarperCollins Publishers.

"A Song of Greatness" from *The Children Sing in the Far West* by Mary Austin. Copyright 1928 by Mary Austin, © renewed 1956 by Kenneth M. Chapman and Mary C. Wheelwright. Reprinted by permission of Houghton Mifflin Company. All rights reserved.

Unit 6

"The Happy Man's Shirt" from *Italian Folktales: Selected and Retold* by Italo Calvino, copyright © 1956 by Giulio Einaudi editore, s.p.p., English translation by George Martin copyright © 1980 by Harcourt, Inc., reprinted by permission of Harcourt, Inc.

"A Sound of Thunder" by Ray Bradbury. Reprinted by permission of Don Congdon Associates, Inc. Copyright © 1952 by the Crowell Collier Publishing Company, renewed 1980 by Ray Bradbury.

"By the Waters of Babylon" by Stephen Vincent Benet. Copyright © 1937 by Stephen Vincent Benet. Copyright renewed © 1965 by Thomas C. Benet, Stephanie Mahin and Rachel B. Lewis. Reprinted by permission of Brandt & Hochman Literary Agents, Inc.

"What I Have Been Doing Lately" from *At the Bottom of the River* by Jamaica Kincaid. Copyright © 1983 by Jamaica Kincaid. Reprinted by permission of Farrar, Straus & Giroux, Inc.

"People at Night" by Denise Levertov, from *Collected Earlier Poems 1940–1960,* copyright © 1957, 1958, 1959, 1960, 1961, 1979 by Denise Levertov. Reprinted by permission of New Directions Publishing Corp.

"A Dream" from *The Complete Poems of Anna Akhmatova,* translated by Judith Hemschemeyer, edited and introduced by Roberta Reeder. Copyright © 1989, 1992, 1997 by Judith Hemschemeyer. Reprinted by permission of Zephyr Press.

"One Legend Found, Many Still To Go," by William J. Broad, *The New York Times,* October 2, 2005. Copyright © 2005 by The New York Times Co. Reprinted with permission.

"Robot Dreams" by Isaac Asimov, published by permission of the Estate of Isaac Asimov c/o Ralph M. Vicinanza, Ltd.

"Bread" from *Good Bones and Simple Murders* by Margaret Atwood, copyright © 1983, 1992, 1994 by O. W. Toad Ltd. A Nan Talese Book. Used by permission of Doubleday, a division of Random House, Inc.

"Witness for the Prosecution" from *Witness for the Prosecution and Other Stories* by Agatha Christie, copyright 1924, 1926, 1929, 1943, 1947, 1948, renewed 1952, 1954 © 1957, 1971, 1975 by Agatha Christie Mallowan. Copyright 1932 by The Curtis Publishing Co. Used by permission of G.P. Putnam's Sons, a division of Penguin Group (USA) Inc.

"Frustration" by Isaac Asimov. Published by permission of The Estate of Isaac Asimov c/o Ralph M. Vicinanza, Ltd.

Reference Section

Content from The Academic Word List, developed at the School of Linguistics and Applied Language Studies at Victoria University of Wellington, New Zealand, is reprinted by permission of Averil Coxhead.
http://language.massey.ac.nz/staff/awl/index.shtml.

Maps

Mapping Specialists, Inc.

Image Credits

COVER (inset)The Gallery Collection/CORBIS, (bkgd)MaryBeth Thielhelm/Getty Images; **ix** Getty Images; **vi** Malcah Zeldis/Art Resource, NY; **vii** Schalkwijk/Art Resource, NY; **xi** Bridgeman Art Library; **xiv** SuperStock; **xviii** Paolo Uccello/Bridgeman Art Library/Getty Images; **xx** HIP/Art Resource, NY; **xxii** SuperStock; **xxv** Pam Ingalls/CORBIS; **xxvii** akg-images/Jean-Louis Nou; **xxx** Getty Images; **xxxvii** Digital Vision/Getty Images; **0** Kunstmuseum, Basel, Switzerland/Bridgeman Art Library; **4** The Art Archive/Culver Pictures; **7** Getty Images; **8** Steve Smith/Getty Images; **10** E. O. Hoppe/Mansell/Time Life Pictures/Getty Images; **12** Alan Klehr/Veer; **14** Gift of Mrs. Henry Worlf, Austin M. Wolf, and Hamilton A. Wolf/Brooklyn Museum of Art/CORBIS; **17** The Art Archive/Culver Pictures; **19** Grant Wood/Cedar Rapids Museum of Art; **20** Judith Miller/Dorling Kindersley/Clevedon Salerooms; **21** Getty Images; **22** Tim Ridley/DK Images; **23** Private Collection, Avant-Demain/Bridgeman Art Library; **25** Bettmann/CORBIS; **28** Cathy McKinty/Acclaim Images; **29** SuperStock; **30** Getty Images; **31** Lauros/Giraudon/Bridgeman Art Library; **33** Time Life Pictures/Getty Images; **35** F.M. Hall Collection/Sheldon Memorial Art Gallery, University of Nebraska-Lincoln; **36** Jeremy Annett/Bridgeman Art LIbrary; **40** Purestock/SuperStock; **44** Richard Haas/Licensed by VAGA, NY; **48** Stock Illustration Source/Todd Davidson; **49** Allied Artists/The Kobal Collection; **49** Getty Images; **54** THE HINDU/AFP/Getty Images; **56** The Image Works; **59** IMAGEZOO/SuperStock; **64** AP Images; **66** Jason Hosking/Getty Images; **67** Keren Su/CORBIS; **68** Peter

Turnley/CORBIS; **69** The Butler Institute of American Art, Youngstown, Ohio/©Estate of Robert Gwathmey/Licensed by VAGA, NY; **70** Per Karlsson - BKWine.com/Alamy Images; **73** Bettmann/CORBIS; **75** Mary Evans Picture Library; **76** Manuel Bellver/CORBIS; **77** MPI/Getty Images; **78** Erich Lessing/Art Resource, NY; **79** Getty Images; **81** Thomas Hartwell/CORBIS; **82** (b)Hulton Archive/Getty Images, (tc l)Getty Images; **85** Bridgeman Art Library; **88** Getty Images; **90** Bettmann/CORBIS; **90** Royalty-Free/CORBIS; **92** ©Sylvie Allouche/The Bridgeman Art Library; **93** Bridgeman Art Library/Getty Images; **94** (r)Stock Montage/SuperStock, (l)Calvin and Hobbes ©1986 Watterson. Dist. By Universal Press Syndicate. Reprinted with permission. All rights reserved; **95** Mark Burnett; **96** Philadelphia Museum of Art/CORBIS; **96** The Granger Collection, NY; **98** Louis K. Meisel Gallery, Inc./CORBIS; **99** Christie's Images/CORBIS; **103** ©Denyse B. Smith; **105 106** James Thurber; **107** Burke/Triolo/Brand X Pictures/Jupiter Images; **108** James Thurber; **109** Pixtal/age Fotostock; **112** Albert Gea/Reuters /CORBIS; **115** Roger Wood/CORBIS; **116** ©1999 Artists Rights Society, NY/ADAGP, Paris/Christie's Images; **119** ©1999 Artists Rights Society, NY/ADAGP, Paris/Kactus Foto, Santiago, Chile/SuperStock; **123** Scott Gries/Getty Images; **125** Christies Images/CORBIS; **126** Image Source/PunchStock; **127** Authors Image/Alamy Images; **128** Victoria & Albert Museum, London/Art Resource, NY; **129** Getty Images; **131** Gerry Charm/SuperStock; **134** Shanti Panchal/Private Collection/Bridgeman Art Library; **137** SuperStock; **144** AP Images; **146** Bridgeman Art Library; **148** Mary Iverson/CORBIS; **149** Car Culture/Getty Images; **152** Time & Life Pictures/Getty Images; **155** Christie's Image/Bridgeman Art Library; **157** Pascal Le Segretain/Getty Images; **159** Tony Arruza/CORBIS; **161** Pam Ingalls/CORBIS; **162** Punchstock; **165** Patti Mollica/SuperStock; **166** (l)PictureQuest, (tr)SAS/Alamy; **167** Francis G. Mayer/CORBIS; **169** Getty Images; **172** Miriam Berkley; **174** Natalie Racioppa/Getty Images; **179** Joe Oliver/Odyssey Chicago; **180** Kevin Schafer/TIME; **183** Bridgeman Art Library; **183** Images.com/CORBIS; **184** Musee des Beaux-Arts, Lille, France, Lauros/Giraudon/Bridgeman Art Library; **186** Anthony Barboza/Black Images; **188** William Manning/CORBIS; **189** Carson Entertainment; **191** Smithsonian American Art Museum, Washington, DC/Art Resource, NY; **192** SuperStock; **193** The Barnes Foundation, Merion Station, Pennsylvania/CORBIS; **194** JupiterImages/Comstock Images/Alamy Images; **195** Anna Belle Lee Washington/SuperStock; **196** Boltin Picture Library/Bridgeman Art Library; **198** Kari Van Tine/Veer; **199** Nancy Crampton/Writer Pictures; **201** Getty Images; **202** Richard J. Green/Photo Researchers; **203** Kari Van Tine/Veer; **204-205** John Bunker/SuperStock; **207** CORBIS; **209** Edward Hopper/Whitney Museum of American Art; **210** Fred Whitehead/Animals Animals-Earth Scenes; **210** Roy Miles Fine Paintings/Bridgeman Art Library; **212** Images.com/CORBIS; **213** (b)Jan Butchofsky-Houser/CORBIS; **213** (t)Library of Congress; **215** Minnesota Historical Society/CORBIS; **216** Bettmann/CORBIS; **218** Miriam Berkley; **220** Henry Diltz/CORBIS; **223** The Minneapolis Institute of Arts, Gift of Marguerite and Russell Cowles in memory of his Uncle Russell Cowles ©1999 C. Herscovici, Brrussels/Artists Rights Society, NY; **224** Bridgeman Art Library; **225** David Young-Wolff/PhotoEdit; **230** Riccardo De Luca/Writer Pictures; **232** Bridgeman Art Library; **234** Albright-Knox Art Gallery/CORBIS; **240** Scala/Art Resource, NY; **242** Getty Images; **245** Christopher Felver/CORBIS; **247** Images.com/CORBIS; **248** Paul Conklin/Imagestate; **250** USDA/Natural Resource Conservation Service; **251** Robert McIntosh/CORBIS; **252** Andrew J. Martinez/Photo Researchers, Inc.; **253** John Newcomb/Superstock; **255** Courtesy of NASA; **260** Victor Collector/Private Collection/Bridgeman Art Library; **276** Malcah Zeldis/Art Resource, NY; **278** Calvin and Hobbes ©1989 Watterson. Dist. By Universal Press Syndicate. Reprinted with permission. All rights reserved; **279** Flip Schulke/CORBIS; **281** CORBIS; **283** Bridgeman Art Library; **284** Erich Lessing/Art Resource, NY; **285** Gift of the Harmon Foundation/Smithsonian American Art Museum, Washington, DC/Art Resource, NY; **286** Robert Scheer; **288** Dorothea Lange/CORBIS; **289** DEA/A. DAGLI ORTI/Getty Images; **290** image100/SuperStock; **291** Dorothea Lange/CORBIS; **293** Aaron Haupt Photography; **295** Dorothea Lange/National Archives/Time & Life Pictures/Getty Images; **297** Dorothea Lange/CORBIS; **298** (b)Radius/PunchStock, (t)Dorothea Lange/Wra/National Archives/Time Life Pictures/Getty Images; **299** Hulton-Deutsch Collection/CORBIS; **304** William F. Campbell/Time Life Pictures/Getty Images; **306** David Turnley/CORBIS; **308** (b)Seeing eye/Den Reader/Alamy Images, (t)Louise Gubb/The Image Works; **310** Paul Almasy/CORBIS; **313** JUDA NGWENYA/Reuters/CORBIS; **315** Lauren Goodsmith/The Image Works; **316** Louise Gubb/The Image Works; **318** (c l)Getty Images; **318** JUDA NGWENYA/Reuters/CORBIS; **321** Jim Stratford/Black Star; **323** Erich Lessing/Art Resource, NY; **325** Bridgeman Art Library; **328** Tina Fineberg/AP Images; **330** Christie's Images/CORBIS; **333** Tony Vaccaro/akg-images; **335** Bridgeman Art Library; **336** Geoffrey Clements/CORBIS; **341** Francine Fleischer/CORBIS; **343** Giraudon/Bridgeman Art Library; **345** Mary Evans Picture Library; **346** Erich Lessing/Art Resource, NY; **347** Michael Nicholson/CORBIS; **349** (b)Bill Kaye/Paramount/Universal/The Kobal Collection, (t)Getty Images; **352** (b)Mark Lennihan/AP Images, (t)Francine Fleischer/CORBIS; **354** Tore Bergsaker/Sygma/CORBIS; **356** Rollie McKenna; **358** The Andy Warhol Foundation for the Visual Arts/CORBIS; **359** Stockbyte/Punchstock; **360** Reprinted with permission of King Features Syndicate, Inc.; **362** Art Resource, NY; **365** Israel Museum, Jerusalem/Bridgeman Art Library; **366** DigitalVision/PunchStock; **368** Diane Sabin; **372** Private Collection/Bridgeman Art Library; **375** Bettmann/CORBIS; **377** BRAUD, DOMINIQUE/Animals Animals; **378** Wayne Lankinen/DRK Photo; **379** Photodisc/PunchStock; **382** AP Images; **384** The Art Archive/Ministry of Public Information Mexico/Dagli Orti; **386** Franklin McMahon/CORBIS; **388** (t)Getty Images; **391** Smithsonian American Art Museum, Washington, DC/Art Resource, NY; **392** Bettmann/CORBIS; **394** Frances Benjamin Johnston/CORBIS; **396 397** Bettmann/CORBIS; **398** (tc tl)Getty Images; **398** Lake County Museum/CORBIS; **401** Flip Schulke/CORBIS; **403** (b)Adam Crowley/Getty Images, (t)Bettmann/CORBIS; **404** National Museum/akg-images; **405 408** Flip Schulke/CORBIS; **410 411** Bettmann/CORBIS; **413** (t)Getty Images; **416** Steve & Ghy Sampson/Getty Images; **419 420 421** Chester Brown; **422** Robert Dale/Getty Images; **424** Christian

Pierre/SuperStock; **425** Getty Images; **426** Steve & Ghy Sampson/Getty Images; **428** Andy Warhol Foundation/CORBIS; **430** Chester Brown; **431** Time & Life Pictures/Getty Images; **433** North Wind/North Wind Picture Archives; **435** Chicago Historical Society, Chicago/Bridgeman Art Library; **436** Bettmann/CORBIS; **440** (b)Spencer Platt/Getty Images, (t)Collection of Keya Morgan/Keya Gallery; **442** Danny Hoffman/CORBIS SYGMA; **444** Erich Lessing/Art Resource, NY; **450** Hulton Archive/Getty Images; **452** Walter Geiersperger/CORBIS; **453** Phil Schermeister/CORBIS; **456** (bcl)Richard Hamilton Smith/CORBIS, (bcr)age fotostock/SuperStock, (bl)Raul Touzon/Getty Images, (br)Raymond Gehman/Getty Images; **459** (2 3 4)Aaron Haupt Photography; **466** Scala/Art Resource, NY; **470** Bettmann/CORBIS; **471** (b)CORBIS, (bkgd)Bettmann/CORBIS; **473** Archivo Iconografico, S.A./CORBIS; **474** Calvin and Hobbes ©1989 Watterson. Dist. By Universal Press Syndicate. Reprinted with permission. All rights reserved.; **476** Pach/CORBIS; **478** Private Collection/Bridgeman Art Library; **481** Christopher Felver/CORBIS; **483** The Art Archive/Private Collection/Joseph Martin; **486** Bettmann/CORBIS; **488** Charles Neal/SuperStock; **489** (tc tl)Getty Images, (b)Archivo Iconografico, S.A./CORBIS; **492** Bettmann/CORBIS; **494** Ciurlionis State Art Museum, Kaunas, Lithuania/Bridgeman Art Library; **496** Getty Images; **498** SuperStock; **501** (t)Getty Images, Kactus Foto, Santiago, Chile/SuperStock; **504** Vyto Starinskas/Rutland Herald/CORBIS SYGMA; **506** Brenda Chrystie/CORBIS; **510** Giulio Marcocchi/Getty Images; **512** akg-images; **513** Smithsonian American Art Museum, Washington, DC/Art Resource, NY; **516** Snark/Art Resource, NY; **517** American Museum of Natural History, New York, Photo ©Boltin Picture Library/ Bridgeman Art Library; **518** Private Collection, Boltin Picture Library/Bridgeman Art Library; **519** Werner Forman/Art Resource, NY; **521** The Art Archive/The Picture Desk; **522** Mori Sushin Tessan/British Library, London/Bridgeman Art Library.; **523** Christie's Images/CORBIS; **525** Neela Banerjee; **527** akg-images/Jean-Louis Nou; **531** Daniel Nevins/SuperStock; **532** Francis G. Mayer/CORBIS; **534** Bettmann/CORBIS; **536** Charles Neal/SuperStock; **537** akg-images/Electa; **538** (c l)Getty Images; **538 541** Bettmann/CORBIS; **545** Ditz/Bridgeman Art Library/Getty Images; **547** Hulton Archive/Getty Images; **549** Archivo Iconografico, S.A./CORBIS; **550** Scala/Art Resource, NY; **551** (b)BlueMoon Stock/Alamy Images, (t)Getty Images; **554** Larry Ford/CORBIS Outline; **556** Smithsonian American Art Museum, Washington, DC/Art Resource, NY; **559** The Art Archive/Culver Pictures; **559** The Granger Collection; **561** Bridgeman-Giraudon/Art Resource, NY; **563** Bettmann/CORBIS; **565** Boltin Picture Library; **566** The Art Archive/Musée Guimet Paris/Gianni Dagli Orti; **568** Christopher Felver/CORBIS; **570** Images.com/CORBIS; **572** Christopher Felver/CORBIS; **574** Banque d'Images, ADAGP/Art Resource, NY; **576** Reprinted by Permission of the Dudley Randall Literary Estate; **577** Julian Cifuentes/Getty Images; **579** Ben Watson III/SuperStock; **585** Raymond Gehman/CORBIS; **586-587** AP Photos; **588** Mark Lennihan/AP Images; **589** Iyler Mallory/AP Images; **590** Andy Warhol Foundation/CORBIS; **591** Jerzy Kolacz/Getty Images; **592** Calvin and Hobbes ©1987 Watterson. Dist. By Universal Press Syndicate. Reprinted with permission. All rights reserved.; **594** Gerardo Somoza/CORBIS Outline; **596** Courtesy of the Bill Hodges Gallery; **601** Bourne Gallery, Reigate, Surrey, UK/Bridgeman Art Library; **603** Erich Lessing/Art Resource, NY; **604** (t)Getty Images; **607** Gerardo Somoza/CORBIS Outline; **609** Pam Ingalls/CORBIS; **612** Courtesy of Chang-Rae Lee; **614** Tara Sasrowardoyo/TIME; **615** Scott Jones/TIME; **617** Gilbert Mayers/SuperStock; **618** CORBIS; **620** Christie's Images/CORBIS; **621** Smithsonian American Art Museum, Washington, DC/Art Resource, NY; **625** Bettmann/CORBIS; **627** Maurice Faulk/SuperStock; **629** Arnold Newman/Getty Images; **631** Margie Livingston Campbell/SuperStock; **637** image100/PunchStock; **640** McGraw-Hill Companies; **642** (bl)Gerardo Somoza/CORBIS Outline, (r)Aaron Haupt Photography, (tl)Book provided by Little Professor Book Company. Photo by Aaron Haupt.; **643** (l)Book provided by Little Professor Book Company. Photo by Aaron Haupt.; Aaron Haupt Photography; **650** Reunion des Musees Nationaux/Art Resource, NY; **653** Calvin and Hobbes © 1986 Watterson. Dist. By Universal Press Syndicate. Reprinted with permission. All rights reserved.; **657** Michelle da Verona/Czartoryski Museum, Cracow, Poland/The Bridgeman Art Library; **658** Bridgeman Art Library; **660** Ashmolean Museum, Oxford/Bridgeman Art Library; **661** Erich Lessing/Art Resource, NY; **662** Museo Archeologico Nazionale, Naples, Italy/Bridgeman Art Library; **664** Réunion des Musées Nationaux /Art Resource, NY; **665** Mary Evans Picture Library; **667** Scala/Art Resource, NY; **668** Simon Carter Gallery/Bridgeman Art Library; **671** The Art Archive/National Archaeological Museum Athens/Dagli Orti; **672** The Art Archive/Museo Nazionale Tarant/Dagli Orti; **675** The Art Archive/Musée du Louvre Paris/Dagli Orti; **678** Mary Evans Picture Library; **679** Bridgeman Art Library/Getty Images; **682** Private Collection, Courtesy of IAP Fine Art/Bridgeman Art Library; **683** Spiros Tselentis/SuperStock; **686** The Gallery Collection/CORBIS; **688** The Bridgeman Art Library/Getty Images; **689** Grant Faint/Getty Images; **693** Bridgeman-Giraudon/Art Resource, NY; **696** Louvre, Paris, Peter Willi/Bridgeman Art Library; **698** Museu Calouste Gulbenkian, Lisbon, Portugal, Giraudon/Bridgeman Art Library; **699** The Art Archive/National Archaeological Museum Athens/Dagli Orti; **703** Erich Lessing/Art Resource, NY; **704** Photo by Studio Kontos; **706** Getty Images; **710 711 712** The British Museum; **714** British Library, London, Great Britain/Art Resource, NY; **715** Nigel Hawkins/Collections Picture Library; **716** The Art Archive/Musée du Château de Versailles/Dagli Orti; **718** Paolo Uccello/Bridgeman Art Library/Getty Images; **720 722** Chase Manhattan Bank Archive; **722** Louvre, Paris/Bridgeman Art Library; **724** Chase Manhattan Bank Archive; **726** Scala/Art Resource, NY; **728** akg-images/Pirozzi; **730 732** Chase Manhattan Bank Archive; **733** Private Collection/Bridgeman Art Library; **734 736** Chase Manhattan Bank Archive; **736** Scala/Art Resource, NY; **740** Smithsonian Institution; **741** Erich Lessing/Art Resource, NY; **742** Smithsonian Institution; **743** Royal Albert Memorial Museum, Exeter, Devon, UK/Bridgeman Art Library; **744 746 748** Smithsonian Institution; **749** Alinari/Art Resource, NY; **750 752** Smithsonian Institution; **753** Cameraphoto Arte, Venice/Art Resource, NY; **754** Victoria & Albert Museum, London/Art Resource, NY; **755** Bildarchiv Preussischer

Kulturbesitz/Art Resource, NY; **756** Smithsonian Institution; **758** Smithsonian Institution, The Image Works; **763** The Art Archive/Galleria d'Arte Moderna Rome/Dagli Orti; **765** Erich Lessing/Art Resource, NY; **768** The Metropolitan Museum of Art, Rogers Fund, 1903 (03.14.13a-g) Photograph ©1986 The Metropolitan Museum of Art; **770** Private Collection, Stair Sainty Matthiesen Gallery, New York/Bridgeman Art Library; **773** Private Collection, Christopher Wood Gallery, London/Bridgeman Art Library; **775** Alinari/Art Resource, NY; **777** Erich Lessing/Art Resource, NY; **779** akg-images; **784** David Forbert/SuperStock; **787 790** Erich Lessing/Art Resource, NY; **792** Kunsthistorisches Museum, Vienna, Austria, Ali Meyer/Bridgeman Art Library; **793** Museo Nazionale del Bargello/Bridgeman Art Library; **796** Scala/Art Resource, NY; **797** Mary Evans Picture Library; **804** Erich Lessing/Art Resource, NY; **809** Scala/Art Resource, NY; **813** Canterbury, Kent/CM Dixon/Photo Resources; **814** (tc tl)Getty Images; **814** Archive/Photo Researchers; **817** National Portrait Gallery, Smithsonian Institution/Art Resource, NY; **819** Siri Stafford/Getty Images; **820** Bettmann/CORBIS; **822 824** State Russian Museum/Bridgeman Art Library; **829** Private Collection/Bridgeman Art Library; **837** Getty Images; **839** Stapleton Collection/CORBIS; **842** (b)AP Images, (t)CORBIS; **844** Swim Ink 2, LLC/CORBIS; **845** (t)Schalkwijk/Art Resource, NY; **846** Courtesy of Western Carolina University; **847** Schalkwijk/Art Resource, NY; **850** Frida Kahlo/Museum of Fine Arts, Boston; **856** Schalkwijk/Art Resource, NY; **860** Kactus Foto/SuperStock; **868** Edward Wilkins Waite/Private Collection/Bridgeman Art Library; **869** Kelmscott Farms; **871** Christie's Images/CORBIS; **875** Getty Images; **882** McGraw-Hill Companies; **884** (br)Bettmann/CORBIS, (l tr)Aaron Haupt Photography; **892** Master of the Campana Casson/Musee du Petit Palais, Avignon, France/Bridgeman Art Library; **895** Mary Evans Picture Library; **897** (b t)Erich Lessing/Art Resource, NY; **899** The British Library/Topham-HIP/The Image Works; **900** Stapleton Collection/CORBIS; **901** Erich Lessing/Art Resource, NY; **902** Lambeth Palace Library/Bridgeman Art Library; **904** Bradford Art Galleries and Museums, West Yorkshire, UK/Bridgeman Art Library; **905** (t)British Library, LondonArt Resource, NY; **906** (b)Roy Stedall-Humphryes/Collections Picture Library; **907** akg-images; **910** Scala/Art Resource, NY; **912** (t)HIP/Art Resource, NY; **915** (b)Brian Shuel/Collections Picture Library; **915 916** Archivo Iconografico, S.A./CORBIS; **916** Bridgeman Art Library/Getty Images; **918** Archivo Iconografico, S.A./CORBIS; **925** Hulton Archive/Getty Images; **927** Bridgeman-Giraudon/Art Resource, NY; **927** The Gallery Collection/CORBIS; **929** Victoria & Albert Museum, London/Bridgeman Art Library; **930** Victoria & Albert Museum, London/Art Resource, NY; **932** Musee des Beaux-Arts, Rouen, France, Peter Willi/The Bridgeman Art Library; **946** Archer figure; Inland Niger Delta Style, Mali; 13th -15th century; ceramic; H x W x D: 61.9 x 16.5 x 16.5 cm Museum purchase; 86-12-1; Photograph by Franko Khoury; National Museum of African Art, Smithsonian Institution; **947** The Metropolitan Museum of Art/Art Resource, NY; **951** Mark Lennihan/AP Images; **952-954** Excerpt from Sundiata, A Legend of Africa © 2002 Will Eisner, published by permission from NBM Publishing; **955** The Philadelphia Museum of Art/Art Resource, NY; **956** Nationalmuseum, Stockholm, Sweden/Bridgeman Art Library; **958** National Museum of Iceland, Reykjavik/Bridgeman Art Library; **960** MARY EVANS/ARTHUR RACKHAM; **962** akg-images; **965** Werner Forman/CORBIS; **968** Time & Life Pictures/Getty Images; **970** Musee du Petit Palais, Avignon, France, Peter Willi/Bridgeman Art Library; **971** Reynaud Levieux/Cummer Museum of Art & Gardens/SuperStock; **973** The Art Archive/Mohammed Khalil Museum Cairo/Dagli Orti; **974** Ali Meyer/CORBIS; **975** akg-images/Peter Connolly; **976** (b)Scala/Art Resource, NY, (c l)Getty Images; **980** Catalogue No. 153048, Department of Anthropology, Smithsonian Institution.; **981** (l)Martin Benjamin/Black Star, (r)Courtesy of Gayle Ross; **983** Private Collection, Peter Newark Western Americana/Bridgeman Art Library; **985** The Art Archive/Bill Manns; **988** Smithsonian American Art Museum, Washington, DC/Art Resource, NY; **990** SuperStock; **991** Art Media/Heritage-Images/The Image Works; **995** Sotheby's Picture Library; **1005** (t)HIP/Art Resource, NY; **1006** (l)Aaron Haupt Photography, (r)Book provided by Little Professor Book Company/Aaron Haupt Photography; **1007** (cr)Aaron Haupt Photography; **1014** Peter Szumowski/Private Collection/Bridgeman Art Library; **1018** Sophie Bassouls/CORBIS SYGMA; **1021** Mary Evans Picture Library; **1022** Bauer Photography; **1023** Calvin and Hobbes ©1987 Watterson. Dist. By Universal Press Syndicate. Reprinted with permission. All rights reserved.; **1024** Vince Bucci/Getty Images; **1026** Bauer Photography; **1031** Martin Dohrn/Photo Researchers; **1032** ©By kind permission of the Trustees of the Wallace Collection, London; **1032** Natural History Museum, London/Bridgeman Art Library; **1035** SuperStock; **1037** (b t)Getty Images; **1040** Herbert Gehr/Time & Life Pictures/Getty Images; **1042** CORBIS SYGMA; **1043** David M. Schleser/Photo Researchers; **1044** James Noel Smith/Illustration Works/Getty Images; **1048** David Siqueiros/Christie's Images; **1050** ©Avigdor Arikha, courtesy, Marlborough Gallery, New York/Licensed by VAGA; **1053** Getty Images; **1054** Freddric Leighton/Fitzwilliam Museum, University of Cambridge, UK/Bridgeman Art Library; **1058** Alberto Ruggieri/Stock Illustration Source/Getty Images; **1059** Jeremy Bembaron/CORBIS SYGMA; **1061** Van Hoorick/SuperStock; **1065 1066** Images.com/CORBIS; **1067** Museum of Modern Art, New York/Bridgeman Art Library; **1069** Images.com/CORBIS; **1070** age fotostock/SuperStock; **1071** Stefano Bianchetti/CORBIS; **1074** Deborah Feingold Photography; **1076** Illustration Works; **1079** Private Collection/Bridgeman Art Library; **1080** Private Collection, ©DACS/Bridgeman Art Library; **1084** Jason Grow/SABA for TIME; **1086** (l r)Jason Grow/SABA for TIME; **1088** Time Life Pictures/Getty Images; **1090** Scala/Art Resource, NY; **1093** Getty Images; **1095** Roy Miles Fine Paintings/Bridgeman Art Library; **1097** Bettmann/CORBIS; **1100** Private Collection/Bridgeman Art Library; **1102** The Arts Club, London/Bridgeman Art Library; **1105** Fine Art Photographic Library/CORBIS; **1106** Francis G. Mayer/CORBIS; **1111** National Gallery Collection; By kind permission of the Trustees of the National Gallery, London/CORBIS; **1113** Dickens House Museum, London/Bridgeman Art Library; **1119** Getty Images; **1122** Digital Vision/PunchStock; **1128** (l r)Aaron Haupt